A SHORT HISTORY OF
WESTERN CIVILIZATION

A SHORT HISTORY OF
WESTERN
CIVILIZATION

by

John B. Harrison and Richard E. Sullivan

MICHIGAN STATE UNIVERSITY

ALFRED·A·KNOPF   NEW YORK   1960

L. C. Catalog card number: 59–8682

© *John B. Harrison and Richard E. Sullivan, 1960*

THIS IS A BORZOI BOOK,

PUBLISHED BY ALFRED A. KNOPF, INC.

FIRST EDITION

to Mary and Vivian

Bibliographical Note

IN COMPILING the bibliographies the authors have made no attempt to supply an exhaustive list of the latest titles. Books have been selected chiefly for their readability. Brief descriptions have been supplied for each title to guide the reader. A special effort was made to utilize to the fullest the numerous inexpensive books now available. All books published in paperback or inexpensive hardback editions have been designated by an asterisk (*) placed before the title. The series in which each volume has been published (Meridian, Penguin, etc.) has also been noted.

Preface

THIS book is designed primarily as a college or university textbook for a survey course in the history of Western civilization. We hope, however, that the serious general reader will also find it profitable and interesting.

Next to accuracy, the qualities we have concentrated upon most are clarity and brevity. During our many years of teaching college and university students we have discovered that there is no substitute for clarity. Any serious account of the story of Western civilization is involved and complicated at best; and since most of the students in such a survey course are not history majors, they need all the help they can get in making this long and complex story manageable and clear. We have, therefore, steadfastly refrained from turning the clever or sophisticated phrase or displaying any specialized erudition that we may have acquired, in order that we might make the narrative and analysis as direct as possible.

Of all our objectives none has been more difficult to achieve than brevity. It would have been twice as easy to write a history twice as long. Again, however, our experience in teaching survey courses in the history of Western civilization indicates that many textbooks are much too long, presenting more material than can be covered in one academic year and leaving little or no room either for the instructor's personal contribution or for additional readings.

In planning this text we have tried to take into account the practical realities of the academic year. In most American colleges and universities there are approximately ninety class meetings of a course during the year, the typical class meeting three times a week. We have broken our story into sixty chapters, each designed as a single day's assignment. In this way two of the three weekly class meetings may be devoted to textbook material, and the third to additional readings, discussions, and (or) quizzes. We have limited our chapters to ten or at most twelve pages since we believe that this amount of compactly written textbook material is all that the average student is likely to absorb in one day's assignment. We have also kept our bibliographies brief, listing only those readings that will be useful to freshmen, sophomores, and the general reader. We hope the brief descriptions of selected readings will be helpful and encouraging.

Still a third quality we have attempted to give this book is specificity. We believe that it is futile to generalize and philosophize about history until the student has the basic facts in mind. To be specific and yet brief requires careful selection of facts, which in itself represents, of course, the authors' basic interpretation.

We are quite aware of the importance of civilizations other than our own and have tried to show their impact upon the West. However, space simply does not allow for anything approaching equal treatment of all the major civilizations.

Finally, we wish to acknowledge the help that we have received. It would be suicidal for any two persons to attempt writing a history of Western civilization from primary sources alone. We have been aided by scores of specialized researchers, synthesizers, teachers, colleagues, and friends. To all of these we acknowledge our indebtedness. We are especially indebted to Professor John F. A. Taylor of Michigan State University for sharing with us his broad knowledge of art history. Mr. Harrison would like to express his personal gratitude to Professor C. P. Higby of the University of Wisconsin and to Professor Carlton J. H. Hayes of Columbia University for their professional assistance, their inspiration, and, above all, their friendship. Mr. Sullivan would like to acknowledge the debt he owes to President Charles E. Odegaard of the University of Washington, to Professor Joseph Ward Swain of the University of Illinois, and to Professor Edgar N. Johnson of Brandeis University.

J.B.H.
R.E.S.

Contents

Illustrations

Maps

By Theodore R. Miller

SECTION I

The Ancient Near East,

4000 – 300 B.C.

Our account of the history of Western civilization will be prefaced by a study of the cultures that emerged in the great river valleys of the Near East about 6000 years ago. But first a few introductory remarks must be made about the long era of human history that preceded the birth of the higher civilizations of the Near East.

The origin of man is still shrouded in mystery. Skeletons, perhaps 600,000 years old, bearing a remarkable physical resemblance to modern man have been found. Other skeletons from more recent dates show increasing development and suggest that man was the product of a long process of biological evolution, although it was probably not until about 30,000 years ago that the human species assumed its present physical form. However, even the earliest specimen of man-like creatures possessed a combination of physical qualities that distinguished them from the other animals. Among their assets were an upright posture, superior eyesight, a digestive system capable of utilizing nearly any kind of food, a voice mechanism capable of producing a wide variety of sounds, and a complex brain allowing them to remember and to co-ordinate their bodies better than other creatures. These were the physical powers that permitted primitive man to survive and to flourish.

Even the most primitive manlike creatures of 500,000 or 600,000 years ago were beginning to develop patterns of living or cultures. These early cultures, traces of which are scattered all over the earth, were all essentially the same and have been given the common name Paleolithic, which means Old Stone Age. The distinctive feature of Paleolithic culture was the fact that man lived as a hunter and food gatherer. The greatest accomplishment of the Paleolithic era was man's acquisition of the knowledge and skills to create weapons from stone and wood that made him an effective killer. Primitive hunters lived in small groups, their whole existence being involved in pursuing the animals off which they lived. We know very little about the thinking of Paleolithic man. There are scanty bits of evidence to suggest that he had developed religious concepts centering around the belief that spirits existed in all things and that survival depended on getting along with these spirits. In all probability these concepts represent the first attempt at organizing the knowledge man had acquired about the world around him.

If we date the dawn of human history from the time when tools began to be *made by hunting societies, then the Paleolithic phase of history stretches over nine tenths of all human history. Not until about 10,000 B.C. did hunting culture begin to disappear in a few parts of the world; and some remnants of it persist even today in Australia, the Pacific islands, and Alaska. The revolutionary changes that brought hunting cultures to an end were the development of agriculture and the domestication of animals. These two developments ushered into existence the Neolithic, or New Stone Age, culture. How, when, and where this change first occurred is a hotly disputed subject. The best evidence suggests that agricultural activity first appeared in Southwest Asia about 10,000 or 11,000 years ago. During the next few thousand years the new way of life appeared over nearly all of the rest of the world.*

The domestication of plants and animals revolutionized man's living habits. He ceased wandering and settled permanently in villages. He produced new tools and techniques such as houses, hoes, sickles, pottery, and weaving to meet his new needs. With a little foresight he could accumulate enough wealth for better dwellings, clothing, and luxuries. Systematic farming yielded sufficient surplus to permit the specialization of labor, with a resultant increase in skill and efficiency and the broadening of the economic base of society. Village communities presented new social problems, again placing demands on human ingenuity. Neolithic man met these problems by creating tribal governments with authority vested in the hands of one or a few men to direct the activities of the whole community. The family developed into an institution capable of disciplining and directing the activities of all its members. Neolithic man undoubtedly had to stretch his mind to embrace new concepts. His religion, which increasingly centered around worship of the forces of nature that made a lifeless seed spring from the earth and that added new animals to his precious flocks, challenged him with ideas that were not quite as tangible as the animal spirits Paleolithic man grappled with daily. Neolithic man's answer to this challenge was to place more trust in religious experts—his priests—and to dedicate more energy and wealth to the worship of the great spirits that nourished his crops and protected his village.

About 4000 B.C. a few groups of Neolithic men, living in the two great river valleys in the Near East, the Nile and the Tigris-Euphrates, developed a pattern of life still more complicated and more productive than that of the Neolithic agricultural villages. These higher civilizations of the Near Eastern river valleys

TIME CHART OF WESTERN CIVILIZATION

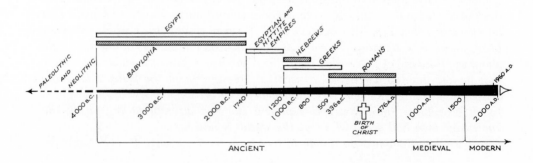

mark the proper beginning of the history of civilization. Yet they would have been impossible without the slow but steady perfection of agriculture, government, social institutions, and religion by Paleolithic and Neolithic societies.

The civilizations that developed in Egypt and Babylonia spread outward from the river valleys in the centuries following 4000 B.C., eventually covering a large area in Northeast Africa and Southwest Asia. Numerous other peoples absorbed ideas and institutions from Egypt and Babylonia and in the course of time made their own contributions. Until at least 500 B.C. the Near East stood at the head of the civilized world, rivaled only by the civilizations that had formed in China and India almost as early as those of the Near East.

CHAPTER I

Egyptian Civilization, 4000–1750 B.C.

ONE of the earliest areas in which a highly developed civilization emerged was the Nile Valley in Northeast Africa. About 6000 years ago peoples living near that valley began to learn how to take advantage of its resources. As a result they developed highly organized government, accumulated vast wealth, and produced an impressive art and literature.

1. The Nile Valley

During the period centering around 5000 B.C. the numerous Neolithic farming communities of North Africa began to feel relentless pressure from nature. The amount of rainfall in North Africa was steadily declining as the rain belt, which had once extended across the whole area, moved northward, while the glacial cap of the North Pole receded. Faced with the advancing desert, the residents of North Africa sought new means of survival. Some fled south into the jungles; others moved across the Mediterranean into the peninsulas jutting out from Europe. A few bold groups turned from the emerging desert to the Nile Valley.

The Nile Valley—a narrow ribbon of land, ranging from ten to thirty miles wide —is in startling contrast with the surrounding desert. The Nile River draws its water supply from Central Africa, beyond the desert. It flows the year round, providing a water supply in a land almost completely lacking in rainfall. Even more important, the Nile floods annually, inundating the whole valley, soaking the soil, and depositing a layer of silt that restores the fertility of the soil. The flood waters soon evaporate under Egypt's burning sun unless they are stored. However, if the water can be saved and distributed over the rich soil during the growing season, the valley has a tremendous productive capacity.

The Nile Valley possesses another distinctive feature of importance to the early history of Egypt: it is shielded from invaders by forbidding natural barriers. The deserts on the east and west, the rapids (cataracts) that block the river for navigation about seven hundred miles from its mouth, and the Mediterranean Sea isolate the valley from outsiders. The only readily accessible entry into the valley is a narrow and easily defensible belt of land connecting the delta region with Asia.

In spite of the regular water supply, the rich soil, the beneficial climate, and the safety from outsiders, the Nile Valley is not a paradise. Ruinous floods, tropical growths, snakes, insects, and wild animals prevail unless the river can be controlled. Unless water can be provided artificially, the scorching sun quickly ruins the vegetation that springs from the rich soil. Tremendous effort has always been required to make the valley inhabitable, and for a long time primitive men hovered on the fringes of the valley, unable to utilize the full po-

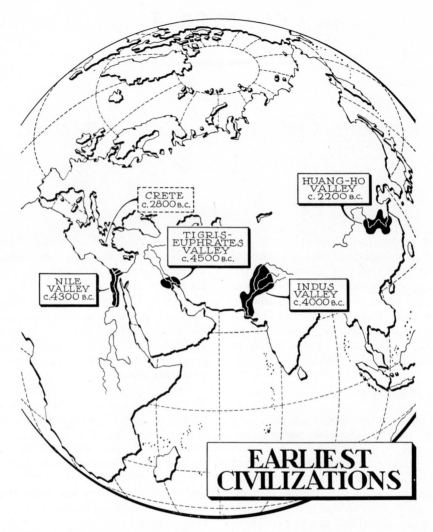

HUANG-HO
VALLEY
c. 2200 B.C.

CRETE
c. 2800 B.C.

TIGRIS-
EUPHRATES
VALLEY
c. 4500 B.C.

NILE
VALLEY
c. 4300 B.C.

INDUS
VALLEY
c. 4000 B.C.

EARLIEST CIVILIZATIONS

tential of the river. Between 5000 and 4000 B.C.,[1] however, some Neolithic farmers, spurred by the increasing pressure of the desert, began to conquer the river. To succeed, they were forced to make so many changes in their primitive pattern of life that they created a new civilization.

2. Egyptian Government, 4000–1750 B.C.

At first glance it might seem that Neolithic men needed only to develop an irriga-

[1] Dates for the early history of the Near East are approximate, since records are scanty.

tion system in order to master the Nile. However, a mere technical advance was not sufficient to harness the floods to human use. More vital was the problem of combining the labor and skills of many men into a great co-operative effort. That co-operation could be gained only through the perfection of government. The history of the Egyptians must begin with a description of the amazing progress they made in the arts of government.

The development of highly organized government began between 5000 and 4000 B.C. In about 5000 B.C. many Neolithic villages were scattered along the fringes of the valley. By 4000 B.C. a fundamental change had occurred. A number of new governmental units had been created. Each unit consisted of the people living within a well-defined geographical area and organized under a king. The king had established himself in a city which served as a center of all the activity for the surrounding territory. His chief task was to direct the labors of his subjects toward controlling the river. He managed canal and reservoir construction, assigned specific jobs to his subjects during the flood and the planting and the harvest seasons, and supervised the division of the harvest. No one can be certain how this transition occurred, since the records are extremely scanty. However, it marked a tremendous advance over older Neolithic forms of government by creating larger groups and supplying each with more effective leaders who had the ability and the power to plan co-operative effort and to compel their people to perform their tasks.

The era of the formation of city-states in Egypt, called the Predynastic Age, saw another important development. As city-states developed in the narrow confines of the Nile Valley, struggles for the precious land and water arose. These wars ended in the conquest of one city-state by another and the consolidation of the two under the conquering king. Slowly Egypt moved toward political unity. By about 3200 B.C. the number of states had been reduced to two —Upper Egypt and Lower Egypt. As consolidation took place, the powers of kings increased and the means of exercising power became more complex.

By that time Egypt was ripe for the final step—the unification of the Nile Valley into a single state. Egyptian tradition gave credit for unification to Menes, the ruler of Upper Egypt, who conquered Lower Egypt and founded the first dynasty of pharaohs, a dynasty being a royal family whose members succeeded one another for several generations. Menes's unification of Egypt ushered in the Old Kingdom, the first great age in Egyptian history. For nearly a thousand years (3200–2200 B.C.) Egypt was ruled by an orderly succession of pharaohs, six dynasties in all, who held sway over the whole valley and succeeded in achieving close co-operation among several million subjects. The last traces of division disappeared. Peace, order, and prosperity characterized almost the whole period. As monuments of the wealth and the high degree of co-operation achieved during the Old Kingdom, there still stand in Egypt the three pyramids at Gizeh.

During the Old Kingdom the Egyptian government assumed its fundamental form. The pharaoh was the absolute ruler and owner of the state. So great were his powers that the Egyptians accepted him as a god. His mere word was the law of the land. He was able to command the wealth and the services of all his subjects. In actual practice most of the pharaohs of the first six dynasties were active statesmen, taking a leading role in administering their state. They kept informed on the condition of the irrigation system, directed building programs, took special care to render justice to all their subjects, and sponsored trading projects to acquire needed materials from abroad. In spite of their being treated as gods they kept close to Egypt's problems and served as the fountainhead from which came the direction and planning necessary to maintain control over the Nile.

The Egyptian government of the Old Kingdom evolved a set of institutions through which the pharaoh exercised his vast powers. At his royal palace in Memphis the pharaoh gathered a group of trusted friends and delegated to them certain jobs to be carried out under his supervision. Among the high officials prominent in the records of the Old Kingdom were a vizier, a treasurer, a chief of irrigation, a chief justice, record keepers, and high priests. Most important was the vizier, who served as chief assistant to the pharaoh. Each of these major officials was assisted by numerous lesser state servants.

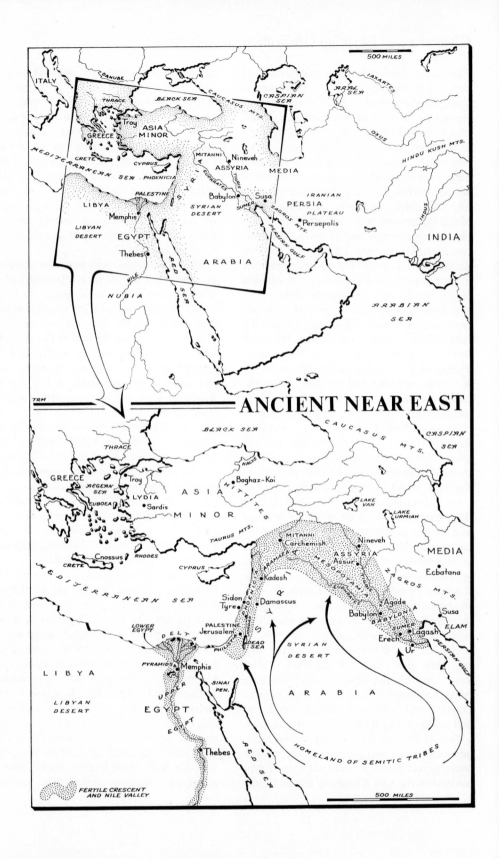

ANCIENT NEAR EAST

The pharaoh's officials were also spread over Egypt to enforce royal orders. Egypt was divided into forty-two governmental units, called nomes, each controlled by royal officials. Every nome was divided into villages, where the mass of the people lived and where officials appeared from time to time to enforce the pharaoh's orders and collect taxes.

After a thousand years, however, the Old Kingdom collapsed. Its downfall and the resultant period of confusion, called the Feudal Age (2200–2050 B.C.), demonstrated the necessity of a strong central authority. During the Feudal Age the pharaohs lost most of their powers to the officials who had previously served them. The cause of this loss of power is not entirely clear. Perhaps the pharaohs grew lax in ruling Egypt, tending to place too much trust in their officials. Perhaps they discredited themselves by imposing too great a burden upon their subjects for such costly efforts as pyramid building. Whatever the reason, their former officials carved out states for themselves and became the independent rulers of these petty states. There continued to be pharaohs who claimed authority over Egypt, but they exercised little power. For a century and a half local princes did as they pleased, and Egypt suffered from internal wars, lawlessness, injustice, and depression.

Eventually someone was bound to attempt to reunite Egypt and to bring back the "good old days." About 2050 B.C. the princes of Thebes began such a campaign. By force they restored unity and established the Middle Kingdom (2050–1750 B.C.). The pharaohs of the Middle Kingdom revived most of the institutions that had served so well during the Old Kingdom. Certain important changes, however, were initiated. The new pharaohs made notable efforts to provide the lower classes with a definite status in society and to assure them a greater measure of justice and security. In their efforts to supply the masses with a new status the rulers sought to decrease the power of the nobles who

had exercised such great influence in the Old Kingdom. To achieve this end, the rulers of the Middle Kingdom developed a new class of civil servants, drawn from all classes on the basis of ability. These officials, called scribes, devoted all their efforts to specific governmental duties and probably increased the efficiency of the government.

After nearly three hundred years of orderly government and prosperity the Middle Kingdom also began to decline. Its end was hastened by the emergence of a threat for which the Egyptians were not prepared. About 1750 B.C. a warlike, barbarian horde, called the Hyksos, swept out of Asia and seized control of the Nile Valley. The government quickly fell into chaos. Lawlessness and violence replaced orderly government. Eventually Egypt recovered from this catastrophe, but that story represents a completely new chapter in the history of the Near East and must be reserved for later.

3. Economic and Social Life

Organized under a strong government, Egyptian society produced tremendous wealth. The chief source of that wealth was agriculture. Huge yields of wheat, barley, vegetables, and fruit were gathered each harvest. Herds of cattle, sheep, pigs, and goats pastured in the valley. The bulk of the Egyptian population devoted itself to farming. The peasants, crowded together in small villages, supplied the farm labor. Their mud huts, scanty clothing, and simple furniture certainly do not suggest a high standard of living. Life from one generation to the next consisted of constant labor to keep the irrigation system under control and to cultivate the crops. Most of the labor was done by hand. The peasants were never permitted to keep much of the product of their labors. After the owners of the land, the state, and the priests claimed their shares, the peasant had only a bare subsistence. In spite of his hard lot and his lack of freedom the Egyptian peasant certainly benefitted from the social and political order that his labor supported. Working on his own and without the knowledge and skill of the ruling class, he never would have been able to exploit the resources of the river or secure justice for himself.

Although Egyptian civilization rested chiefly on agriculture, a considerable number of artisans and merchants produced wealth by their handicraft work and their trading ventures. This group produced primarily luxury goods to satisfy the needs of the pharaoh, his court, and the nobility. Most of the artisans and merchants worked directly for the pharaoh or for rich nobles. Their status in society was often much like that of the peasants. They too received little more than subsistence in return for their labor.

Egyptian economy and society were dominated by a relatively small aristocracy. At the peak of society stood the pharaoh, whose power permitted him to indulge his every whim. All elements of society and the total wealth of the state were at his command. The rest of the aristocracy consisted of those to whom the pharaoh chose to give high status and to reward with wealth. The priestly class enjoyed an especially high rank. The non-priestly aristocrats, who served the pharaoh as government officials, played a leading role in organizing the labor of peasants and artisans and enjoyed large incomes derived from land. This wealth was used to provide them with every comfort—fine homes, costly food and clothing, expensive furniture, and a variety of other luxuries.

The Egyptian economic and social order was marked by certain significant departures from that of Neolithic societies. Wealth was produced by extensive division of labor and specialization. Different groups plowed and reaped, built things with their hands, traded, ruled, and prayed, to mention only the broadest divisions of labor. The combination of all these specialties, each as necessary as any other, permitted millions of people to exploit successfully a small but rich geographical area.

The efforts of these many "specialists" were rigidly directed from the top down, creating a regimented society. Thus Egyptian civilization was built upon the leadership of a few people whose intelligence, vigor, and foresight supplied the needed guidance for the labors of the rest of the society. Aristocratic leadership over society was to remain a keynote of civilized people for long ages after Egypt had declined.

4. Religion

Egyptian life was dominated by religious ideas that penetrated every institution and controlled nearly every action of all Egyptians. The Egyptians believed that everything that happened was caused by otherworldly spirits. Their religion was highly polytheistic, the gods worshipped at various times numbering into the thousands. The Egyptians conceived of their gods as existing in the form of animals or human beings. They firmly believed that the gods circulated freely on earth and in heaven and were apt to be around at any moment to control human affairs.

One of the major developments of Egyptian religion was the effort made to create order among this horde of gods, and especially to decide which were more important. An elaborate body of mythology developed during the centuries prior to the end of the Middle Kingdom. Certain gods emerged as the chief ones in the minds of the Egyptians, with the rest of the gods assuming a subordinate position. During the Predynastic and Old Kingdom periods there was a tendency for the gods of those city-states which were victorious in wars to become supreme. For instance, when Menes unified all of Egypt, the falcon god Horus, formerly the god of Upper Egypt, became the supreme god of all Egypt. Myths then developed, telling how Horus came to be chief of the gods and made the other gods his servants. However, political changes were not always the cause of the ascendancy of a god. By the end of the Old Kingdom the sun god Ra was accepted as a god demanding reverence from all Egyptians and as the supreme figure in the heavens. The growing popularity of sun-god worship was undoubtedly due to the importance of the sun in the life of every Egyptian. Especially significant was the emergence of the god Osiris, who was believed to possess the power of granting men a happy life after death. By the end of the Middle Kingdom the Egyptians had evolved a much more organized set of beliefs than they had held at the beginning of their history. A few gods, especially Ra and Osiris, were recognized as most powerful. Most of the other gods had been subordinated to these major ones, although few had been eliminated. The important thing to remember is that several million Egyptians accepted a few great gods as being most powerful, knew a common set of stories about these powerful figures, and joined together in worshipping them. These common religious beliefs, supplying a unified guide for the conduct of large numbers of people, were a powerful force holding Egyptian society together.

Since everything from the Nile floods to the smallest household incident was a consequence of the will of some god, Egyptian religion placed a heavy emphasis on man's need to do things that would please the gods. Man's religious obligations became fixed early in Egyptian history. The gods required living quarters. Therefore, the Egyptians built temples and shrines, ranging all the way from the great temples built by the pharaohs in honor of the chief gods to tiny chapels in villages and homes. The gods enjoyed finery, and the Egyptians lovingly decorated the temples with their best artistic efforts. The gods required offerings of food, and elaborate religious festivals were arranged in honor of the great gods to make these offerings in a fitting fashion. Prayers and songs were a regular part of religious worship and were composed in great numbers to fit any request that men had to make of the gods. The necessity of pleasing the gods was so great that Egypt maintained a vast number of priests who specialized in this job. Probably most Egyptians felt that their efforts to please the gods were fully repaid. The abundant harvests, the peaceful condition of the kingdom, and the security with which a man could live his life made it seem that the gods were satisfied with the Egyptians.

Besides earthly benefits the gods held another precious gift for deserving Egyptians —a happy life after death. From early times the Egyptians believed that every man had a *ka*, which was a double for his body and which lived on after death in some kind of close association with the divine spirits. The struggle to assure happy existence for the ka was one of the chief concerns of most Egyptians. In early Egyptian history there was apparently a belief that life after death was reserved for those whose earthly bodies were preserved and cared for after death. This led to the construction of elaborate tombs equipped with those material goods the dead had used in life, to the mummification of the body, and to the endowment of certain priests with income necessary to care for the dead man's needs in the hereafter. This was expensive, and only the pharaohs could well afford all that was required to gain the hereafter. The pharaohs apparently hoped to enjoy after death the companionship of their earthly friends, since on some occasions they paid for the proper burial of some members of the nobility.

Gradually, however, the hope of gaining immortality was extended to the whole Egyptian population through the worship of Osiris. A famous myth told how Osiris had been murdered by his wicked brother, Seth, who dismembered the god's body and scattered the parts over the face of the earth. However, Osiris's wife, Isis, patiently gathered the members of her beloved's body. When her task was finished Osiris returned to life. Thereafter, he had the power to raise everyone from death to life, no matter what a man's social status was. When any Egyptian died, he appeared before Osiris in the other world. Osiris placed the dead man's heart on the pan of

EGYPTIAN FUNERARY PAPYRUS. This papyrus, dating from about 1000 B.C., was intended to be buried with a deceased princess. The god Anubis is shown weighing a princess's heart while the god Osiris watches. If the heart were stained with evil, and therefore depressed its side of the balance, the princess would be deprived of eternal sojourn in the presence of Osiris. The smaller scenes at the top of the picture depict the princess in other steps involved in the transition from life on earth to the hereafter. (*Courtesy of the Metropolitan Museum of Art*)

a balance. On the other pan was a feather. If the heart was weighted with evil, then the dead man was not fit for eternal happiness and was tossed to a ferocious beast. If his heart was buoyant with goodness, then he was allowed to live forever in a heavenly place that was very much like the earthly Nile Valley. The rise of Osiris worship, which was fully developed by the period of the Middle Kingdom, introduced a new concept into Egyptian religion. Moral values and good conduct began to count in evaluating a man's worth. No longer did wealth and high social position alone dignify the individual. The followers of Osiris thought long and hard about what virtues would please Osiris at that dramatic moment when men had to be judged. By the end of the Middle Kingdom they had established codes of good conduct that undoubtedly refined Egyptian society.

Religion was the paramount force in Egyptian society. It sanctioned absolute obedience to the pharaohs because they were gods. It made notable inroads upon the economy, owing to the fact that the population dedicated a vast part of its products to the honor of the gods. Egyptian art and literature were religiously inspired. All the activities of daily life unfolded in terms of what the gods liked men to do. Egypt's religious development was destined to play a significant role in later history, contributing religious ideas that affected people beyond the valley of the Nile. Especially important were the concepts of gods ruling over a large number of people, ideas about immortality, the idea that moral uprightness impressed the gods with man's excellence, and the numerous forms of worship that the Egyptians developed in order to honor their gods.

5. Egyptian Science, Literature, and the Arts

Perhaps the chief glory of Egypt's history down to about 1750 B.C. was her intellectual and artistic achievement. Remembering that Egyptian culture flowered as a result of political stability, prosperity, and the inspiration of Egyptian religion, we may turn to a consideration of some of its most notable characteristics.

One of Egypt's achievements was her system of hieroglyphic writing, which began to develop about the time the Old Kingdom came into existence (about 3200 B.C.). Egyptian writing began as picture writing, an object being represented by a picture of it. Gradually various pictures began to be accepted as representations of sound values. By putting several of these symbols together words could be formed. The Egyptians never developed a complete alphabet, since symbols representing sounds existed only for consonants. Writing probably developed as a practical tool, useful in government. Once it was perfected, however, it allowed the Egyptians to set down their ideas in a clear and artistic fashion.

Most of the Egyptian literature consisted of religious writings. On the internal walls of the pyramids were carved numerous hymns, prayers, myths, and magical phrases intended to influence the gods, all supplying precious information about religious feelings. In addition the pyramids contained hieroglyphic writings praising the rulers for their good government, their justice, their concern for the welfare of the people, their temple building, and their defense of Egypt. In spite of a tendency toward exaggeration this kind of writing was one of the earliest human attempts to write history. Not all Egyptian literature was religious. Especially during the Middle King-

dom there was a great deal of writing devoted to worldly matters. Some of it dealt with scientific problems. The Egyptians were always interested in guides to worldly success, and produced numerous collections of maxims and wise sayings, intended for the instruction of young men who desired to succeed in this world. Sometimes this kind of writing contained severe criticisms of Egyptian society and its evils. Apparently the Egyptians loved a good story, since some traces of pure fiction have survived.

Egyptian art tells us a great deal more about the vigor of Egyptian thought than does literature. The arts demonstrate in a spectacular way the technical skill of the Egyptians. Architecture was the queen of all the arts in Egypt, most of the other forms serving to adorn architectural monuments. The Egyptian architects worked in many materials, including mud, reeds, brick, and wood; but the most monumental work was done in stone. The first flowering of stonework came about in tomb building, which reached its perfection in the construction of the pyramids. The pyramid of Khufu (built about 2600 B.C.) stands as one of the great construction feats of all time. This structure measures 767 feet on each side at the base, which was intended to be square. It fell short of a geometrically perfect square by about eight inches of difference between the north and south sides, and by less than a half inch of difference between the east and west sides. The pyramid is 480 feet high, containing over two million blocks of stone weighing on an average two and one half tons each. Some of the stones used to roof the internal chambers weigh as much as thirty tons. The outside of the pyramid was covered with polished stone. Most of the stone was precut, probably with copper saws and wedges, in quarries many miles away and floated down the Nile to the pyramid site, a procedure that must have entailed tremendous planning. The huge blocks were probably elevated into position up dirt ramps built alongside the pyramid. The labor was performed by hand with almost no mechanical aid. The masons who fitted the stones together did a remarkably accurate job. The internal passages and rooms that honeycomb the pyramid were skillfully vaulted, again demonstrating the technical progress of Egyptian builders. Seldom have stoneworkers produced a more enduring or a more imposing structure than Khufu's pyr-

Egyptian sculptors matched the skill of the architects. At a very early date art styles became highly conventionalized and changed little down to the end of the Middle Kingdom. The pharaohs and their families and companions were a common subject for sculptors. The representations of human forms were usually massive, stiff, and unemotional. The faces were sometimes presented with striking accuracy, but

EGYPTIAN PYRAMIDS. Built about twenty-six centuries before the birth of Christ, these three great pyramids at Gizeh seem a fitting symbol of eternity. Deep within each pyramid is the burial chamber of the pharaoh for whom it was built. The pyramid in the foreground, the largest of all, is that of Khufu (Cheops); the center was built in honor of Kephren; and the smallest one was built for Menkuare. Around each pyramid there developed a vast complex of temples where appropriate worship of the pharaoh was carried on after his death. (*Courtesy, Museum of Fine Arts, Boston*)

amid. These same talents led to the construction of splendid temples and luxurious palaces in which advanced technical skills and brilliant decorative skills were employed. Whatever the Egyptians built was characterized by massiveness and solidity, qualities that probably resulted from a lack of the technical skills and knowledge needed to construct lighter structures.

other parts of the body were distorted. A study of a few of these statues will clearly demonstrate that the sculptor was not interested in a realistic representation of his subject. Rather he sought to portray the majesty that marked a great ruler. The Egyptian sculptors were also skilled at relief work. Inside the tombs and on the pillars and walls of temples they carved end-

AN EGYPTIAN PHARAOH AND HIS QUEEN. This statue of Menkure, an important pharaoh of the fourth dynasty, and his queen is typical of the portrait sculpture that flourished in Egypt throughout most of its history. The artist has succeeded in portraying the dignity, majesty, and power attributed to a god–king. The rather rigid posture of the bodies, the stylized clothing, the position of the feet, and the headdress are typical features of the treatment of rulers in Egyptian sculpture. This treatment persisted for centuries, giving the impression that art styles changed little in Egypt. (*Courtesy, Museum of Fine Arts, Boston*)

distorted, the feet and faces usually being shown in profile while the main trunk of the body faces the viewer. Many of the statues and the reliefs were painted to heighten the effect.

Viewed as a whole, Egyptian art suggests certain generalizations about Egyptian thought. The artistic legacy of Egypt shows how completely thought was dominated by religion. The Egyptian artist almost always created for eternity, emphasizing massiveness, solid construction, and stability. He thereby displayed great confidence in his work and the civilization he was representing. Egyptian artists were not experimenters; once they had found a way of expressing an idea, they kept it for ages. This might be interpreted as a demonstration of the Egyptian artist's sense of the permanence of his society, as well as his satisfac-

AN EGYPTIAN SCRIBE. This limestone statue illustrates the dignity and forcefulness achieved by Egyptian sculptors. The hand poised over the papyrus sheet, the straight posture, the intent eyes, the sense of eagerness all combine to suggest to the viewer the faithful service for which Egyptian scribes were famous. During the period of the Middle Kingdom these specially trained civil servants replaced the nobles as the chief agents of government. (*Archives Photographiques, Paris*)

less series of scenes from Egyptian daily life, telling us more about the way Egyptians lived and worked than does all Egyptian writing. Again the sculptor seldom tried to be realistic. He let the space he had determine the size and shape of his figures; and he often used conventional designs to represent objects. The human shapes were

tion with the existing order. Egyptian art demonstrates pride in Egypt. The emphasis on size in building and sculpture was in part motivated by the desire to show what tremendous things this people could do. The art as a whole portrays a stable, unemotional, proud people, impressed by what they had achieved and eager to maintain it.

The Egyptians made remarkable advances in technology and science. They compiled a substantial body of knowledge about the movement of the stars, and in connection with this devised at an early date an accurate system of reckoning time, based on the annual appearance of the star Sirius. Their calendar consisted of twelve months of thirty days each plus five days added at the end of the year. They perfected a system of numbers by which they could perform the basic mathematical operations, although they did not use zero and had great difficulty working with fractions. They could perform some of the basic operations of geometry, including the computation of the areas of triangles, rectangles, and hexagons, and the volumes of pyramids and cylinders. The inquiry of Egyptian scientists was not restricted to those fields involving the use of mathematics, however. They also accumulated considerable knowledge about metals and their properties. Certainly the Egyptians knew a tremendous amount about plant and animal life. In medicine they developed surgical techniques and learned to use a wide range of drugs, indicating a rather considerable knowledge of human anatomy.

However, in spite of all this body of knowledge, pure science held little interest for the Egyptians. They seldom sought new scientific knowledge after the fashion of modern scientists. Most of their scientific knowledge was the result of practical experience and was gained by pragmatic methods. Once they had found a workable solution for a problem of engineering or medicine or metallurgy, they sought no further information. In spite of this lack of interest in pure science credit must be given the Egyptians for accumulating considerable information that not only solved their own problems adequately but also served people of later civilizations with a solid base from which to proceed toward more fully developed scientific knowledge.

Egypt's history was not yet finished when the Hyksos invaded the Nile Valley about 1750 B.C. But her long isolation had ended. Her future role was to be played in a much larger frame of reference than the Nile Valley, and, to a study of this expanded role, we shall return in a later chapter. However, the achievements we have just described were to remain the fundamental bases of Egyptian society in the future. The Egyptians had made their creative contributions to the world by the end of the Middle Kingdom; thereafter Egypt's role would be that of a model for other peoples.

SUGGESTED READING

Ralph E. Turner, *The Great Cultural Traditions: The Foundations of Civilization*, 2 vols. (1941). A good general introduction to the history of the ancient world, containing useful material on the topics covered in the early chapters of the text. The book is especially helpful in understanding preliterate cultures.
J. H. Breasted, *Ancient Times*, 2nd ed., rev. (1935). An interesting and reliable survey of the whole field of ancient history down to the fall of the Roman Empire. It supplies in brief form an over-all view of Egypt's place in early history, and can be read with profit for several succeeding chapters of this text.

* Graham Clark, *From Savagery to Civilization* (Abelard-Schuman paperback). A brief description of the main steps by which man advanced from his most primitive condition to higher civilization.
William White Howells, *Back of History: The Story of Our Own Origins* (1954). A spirited, amusing description of prehistoric society.
* V. Gordon Childe, *Man Makes Himself* (Mentor). A brief account of the stages through

which man passed in his advance from Paleolithic savagery to the higher civilizations that developed in the Near East.

J. H. Breasted, A *History of Egypt from the Earliest Times to the Persian Conquest*, 2nd ed. (1912). A pioneering work in Egyptian history, now out of date in some respects but still useful for its detailed treatment of all phases of Egyptian history.

* John A. Wilson, *The Culture of Ancient Egypt* (Phoenix). Published earlier in a hardback edition under the title *The Burden of Egypt* (1951). A brilliant book that claims to be only an interpretation of Egyptian history but that provides a sound survey of the total span of ancient Egyptian history. It is especially good in analyzing the nature of Egyptian political life and institutions.

G. Steindorff and K. C. Seele, *When Egypt Ruled the East* (1942). A relatively brief survey of Egyptian history down to the sixth century B.C. The book does a good job describing Egyptian institutions. It is especially useful because of its splendid illustrations and its many quotations from Egyptian sources.

* H. Frankfort, H. A. Frankfort, John A. Wilson, and Thorkild Jacobsen, *Before Philosophy* (Penguin). Published earlier in a hardback edition under the title *The Intellectual Adventure of Ancient Man* (1946). A difficult but highly rewarding book that discusses the intellectual outlook of the ancient Egyptians and Babylonians and contrasts that outlook with modern views.

* I. E. S. Edwards, *The Pyramids of Egypt* (Penguin). A thorough treatment of the complicated but always fascinating question of how the pyramids were built.

Jaroslav Černý, *Ancient Egyptian Religion* (1952). A brief description of the basic religious ideas and practices of the Egyptians, written for laymen and with a minimum of difficult terminology.

Josephine Mayer and Tom Prideaux, *Never to Die: The Egyptians in Their Own Words* (1938). An excellent collection of writings from ancient Egyptian sources illustrating the nature of Egyptian thought and expression.

CHAPTER 2

Babylonian Civilization, 4000–1750 B.C.

A<small>T ALMOST</small> exactly the same time that the civilization of Egypt was developing, another new and independent civilization emerged a few hundred miles to the east in the Tigris-Euphrates Valley. Although similar in many ways to Egyptian civilization, that of Mesopotamia was unique.

1. The Tigris-Euphrates Valley

Babylonian civilization had its origins in a setting similar to that of Egypt.[1] The progressive drying up of Southwest Asia forced primitive farming groups to turn toward the valley formed by the Tigris and the Euphrates rivers, which begin in the Caucasus Mountains and follow roughly parallel paths southward across a semi-arid plateau into the Persian Gulf. The plateau ends about three hundred miles above the mouths of the rivers, where the rivers come close together. For the rest of their course

[1] The term "Babylonian" will henceforth be used to refer to the whole cultural tradition extending in time from the first appearance of the Sumerians in the Tigris-Euphrates Valley (about 4000 B.C.) to the time of the Amorite Empire of Hammurabi (about 1750 B.C.). This cultural tradition represents a unity in which the Sumerians created the basic elements, while the Semitic peoples (such as the Amorites) carried on and developed the tradition. The cultural tradition reached its peak at the time when Hammurabi was master of the river valleys. The name of his capital, Babylon, is used to designate a way of life that had begun to develop 2000 years earlier.

the distance between them varies from twenty to forty-five miles, creating a flat valley considerably wider than that of the Nile. The two rivers, especially the Euphrates, meander across this lower valley rather freely, changing their courses repeatedly. By the time they reach the point where they come close together, they have slowed down and broadened out considerably. The area immediately surrounding these two rivers in their lower reaches is called Mesopotamia.

The Tigris and Euphrates rivers, like the Nile, flood annually, supplying the lower valley with an adequate amount of water and constantly refertilizing the land by depositing a heavy layer of silt. Because of the heat and the lack of rainfall, agriculture in Mesopotamia is entirely dependent on the flood waters.

The valley of the Tigris-Euphrates differed from the Nile Valley in one important way. The surrounding geographical features invited invasion instead of isolating the valley. The Persian Gulf gave easy access from the south. On the east lay the Zagros Mountains, catching enough rainfall to permit herds to thrive. The mountaineers who lived there in antiquity were always ready to prey on the richer valley only a short distance away. To the north, stretching across the two valleys, lay a plateau region that in ancient times sustained primitive yet hardy farmers who likewise found no barrier against moving southward.

West of Mesopotamia is the Arabian Desert, which in the north was capable of supporting nomads who also found no obstacles barring them from Mesopotamia. The lack of natural barriers shielding the lower valley of the Tigris-Euphrates encouraged a constant movement of men, producing an important effect on Babylonian civilization, quite in contrast with Egypt, whose peace was hardly disturbed by outsiders for more than two thousand years.

Like the Nile Valley, the Tigris-Euphrates Valley for a long time defied the people who lived in the area. Again it was the terror of the flood that held Neolithic men at a distance. Only the pressure of the growing desert was able to produce a bold effort to control the mighty floods.

2. Babylonian Political History

Babylonian history began with a transformation of Neolithic villages into city-states, thereby creating larger and more complex political groupings. This transformation began about 4000 B.C. at roughly the same time a similar development was occuring in Egypt. In Mesopotamia the change was made by a group of invaders called Sumerians, who probably moved into the river valley area from the east and settled in the region of the valley nearest the Persian Gulf. They quickly established irrigation systems to control the rivers and built new cities as the centers of their new states. These well-governed city-states soon were producing tremendous wealth, which in turn served as the base for a complicated civilization. By 3000 B.C. a considerable number of flourishing cities dotted the southern part of Mesopotamia just north of the Persian Gulf in the territory sometimes called Sumer. Each of these cities was independent and controlled a definite area of land. Furthermore, each maintained that strong control over its citizens which alone made it possible to use the flood waters.

The Sumerians did not have the Tigris-Euphrates Valley to themselves. In northern Mesopotamia, still within the area where the rivers flow close together, another group of outsiders, the Semites, learned enough from the Sumerians to enable them to master the rivers. The Semites wandered into the valley from the Arabian Desert. As a result of their borrowings from the Sumerians, they also created several thriving city-states, some of which matched those of the Sumerians in splendor and wealth.

Once the Tigris-Euphrates Valley was dotted with well-organized city-states, we might expect a process of consolidation to have begun, as in Egypt. But it did not. The city-states, Sumerian and Semitic alike, waged war on one another constantly. Occasionally one city conquered and ruled over several others for a short period of time. During the period from 3000 to 2400 B.C. some of the Sumerian city-states, like Ur, Erech, and Lagash, even managed to conquer the entire valley. Later tradition tried to assign to this period a series of dynasties, each credited with ruling the whole valley, but in fact political unity was never permanently established in the Tigris-Euphrates Valley during this era. Any Sumerian city that succeeded in conquering others was soon defeated by the resistance of the conquered cities. Thus, long after Egypt had been unified by Menes, the Tigris-Euphrates Valley was still torn by violent competition among many cities.

Perhaps the failure of the Sumerians to achieve unification can be explained by the fierce local patriotism which resulted from the kind of government that developed in their cities. Each Sumerian city was a theocracy, that is, a state ruled by priests. The chief priest in each state was called a *patesi*. He was assisted by a corps of other priests who performed a variety of political functions. The patesi and his fellow priests were believed to be the agents of a patron god who in the dim past had founded the city and who now owned it and possessed all its residents as his slaves. The priestly groups were managers of the estates of the god. The god's temple was the capitol of the city-state. Annually the residents of the city-state "offered" part of their income to the god through the priests. The god gave orders, that is, laws, through the priests. The labor required to maintain the dikes and canals of the irrigation system was performed as a service to the gods. In short, each Sumerian city-state was a community in which all the residents worked together in the belief that they were serving a god who was usually absent from the city because of his involvement in heavenly affairs, but who revealed his will and his commands to a chosen few, the priests. This political system gave birth to a fierce patriotism that was difficult to extinguish. Conquest by an outsider usually provoked in a city a strong desire, fed by religious convictions, to regain independence. The Sumerians seemed to lack the ability to develop political institutions and techniques that would overcome strong local patriotism. As long as they remained the leaders in Mesopotamia, true political unity was not achieved.

The Semites, although they long imitated the Sumerians, took the lead in overcoming this localism. About 2400 B.C. there appeared among the Semites a leader who demonstrated that on occasion the Semites were able to do what the Sumerians could not do, that is, unify the valley. This leader was Sargon I, the ruler of the city of Akkad. He used the sword to force the Sumerian city-states to accept his overlordship. Sargon not only conquered the city-states located in the valley, but he also led his armies into the Zagros Mountains on the east and to the Mediterranean on the west. His conquests outside the valley were especially important because they were accompanied by a spread of the valley's civilization into surrounding territories. Sargon's empire was carried on by his successors for nearly two centuries (2400–2200 B.C.). We know nothing of how it was governed, although we may guess that military power was a fundamental factor in holding it together.

The Akkadian Empire finally fell because it was too large. Outsiders from the Arabian Desert and the Zagros mountain region began to make inroads into the empire. The Sumerian cities, always restless under a foreign master, rose in revolt. As the Akkadian power declined, the chief beneficiaries were the old Sumerian cities, which once again entered an age of independence and glory. From 2200 to 2000 B.C. such cities as Ur, Erech, and Lagash were the chief centers of power. Again, however, the Sumerians made no progress toward unity.

By 2000 B.C. a new group of Semitic empire builders, the Amorites, appeared on the scene. They had only recently migrated from the Arabian Desert and made the city of Babylon their capital. Then the Amorites turned to conquest. Their greatest leader, Hammurabi (reigned about 1800 B.C.), repeated the conquests of Sargon I, creating an empire that had its heart in the Tigris-Euphrates Valley and extended from the Mediterranean to the Zagros (see map, p. 10). Babylon became a great city, the seat of a government that maintained peace and unity over a broad expanse of territory. The Amorite rulers absorbed the high culture of the conquered Sumerians and aided in its spread. Under Amorite rule Babylonian civilization reached its culmination.

In spite of the brilliance of Hammurabi and his successors the Amorite Empire began suffering from outside assaults. By about 1750 B.C. foreign peoples like the Hittites and the Kassites began to push in from the north. These new peoples were a part of the same disturbance that had resulted in the Hyksos conquest of Egypt. Eventually the Kassites seized control of the Tigris-Euphrates Valley. The old Sumerian cities did not have the strength to rise against them. Amorite rule had apparently succeeded in crushing local patriotism. Therefore, about 1750 B.C. the Tigris-Euphrates Valley sank into a state of political decline that lasted for several centuries. Never again would the people of the valley itself create a strong political power, although Babylonia was destined to serve as a base upon which future conquerors would build great empires.

As we have noted, the history of Mesopotamia was dominated after 2400 B.C. by Semitic empire builders like Sargon I and Hammurabi. These rulers instituted several new ideas and practices of government that must be carefully noted. The Sumerians clung to their theocracies and continued to be ruled by priests who claimed to be enacting the will of the patron god of the city. These governments were not fitted for ruling large empires that contained a variety of peoples. The great political challenge facing a "king of kings," as Hammurabi called himself, was to overcome the difference that divided the peoples over whom he ruled. Hammurabi was especially successful in this venture.

One of Hammurabi's achievements was to break the monopoly of power previously held by the priests. He created a new concept in which the king himself was judge, lawgiver, and general in his own right. This powerful figure at the head of the state served as a symbolic center around which his subjects could rally, thus undercutting the utter dependence upon priests who ruled over small areas that a god was believed to have made sacred. Hammurabi did not neglect to develop institutions that made it possible to exercise the powers he claimed as king. He was always backed by a well-organized army, ready to curb those who threatened the peace in his empire. He established at his capital in Babylon a centralized bureaucracy where men of his choice headed specialized departments of finance, public works, justice, and defense. He subdivided his empire into local units and sent out more royal servants to collect taxes, raise troops, suppress uprisings, and judge disputes. Hammurabi used religion to bind his subjects together, promoting the worship of the god of Babylon, Marduk, throughout his empire.

Probably the most spectacular of all of Hammurabi's measures was the institution of his famous law code. Prior to the time of

Hammurabi the people had been judged under differing legal systems, depending upon the area in which they lived. It is apparent that this great degree of diversity in the administration of justice constituted an obstacle to the unity Hammurabi sought. By establishing uniform rules dealing with such matters as property, wages, family re-

HAMMURABI'S CODE. Skillfully executed, this relief carved on the top of a stone cylinder shows Hammurabi receiving his code of laws from a god. The stiff, rather formalized style employed by the artist typifies a good deal of Babylonian art. By erecting this column in a public place the ruler "published" his code, which is inscribed in cuneiform symbols on the cylinder. (*Archives Photographiques, Paris*)

lationships, and crime, he hoped to bolster the political and religious unity he was creating. Since the code represented a more enlightened system of justice than many people had enjoyed under their old systems of law, it was to their advantage to accept Hammurabi's legislation and to acknowledge his overlordship. Moreover, the institution of a written code undoubtedly limited the power of those who administered the law. They were obligated to treat people according to the law and not simply as they chose at the moment. In searching for means of ruling people of different origins Hammurabi's law code proved to be not only an effective tool for his own purposes but also a political institution of great significance for the future.

3. Babylonian Social and Economic System

The Babylonians prospered economically in spite of their recurrent political troubles. Like that of Egypt, Babylonian civilization was based on agriculture. Skillful farmers exploited the rich soil and the water supply of the Tigris-Euphrates to the fullest. Society was organized to serve this purpose. The mass of the people were required to serve as agricultural laborers, seldom owning land of their own. Rather, landownership was confined chiefly to a small upper class. During the early period in Babylonian history this class was peopled largely by priests. However, by the time of Hammurabi, non-priestly nobles, especially soldiers, had possession of large portions of land. Farming was conducted under the careful supervision of landowners or their agents. The individual peasant did little thinking about his job; his task was that of laboring. His reward, as in the case of the Egyptian peasant, was a bare subsistence for himself and his family. The surplus wealth was used to build the magnificent cities of Babylonia and to permit the nobility to live in luxury.

Babylonian economy was enriched by a flourishing trade and industry, in which the Babylonians probably excelled the Egyptians. Many cities maintained well-developed industries, devoted to making textiles, pottery, jewelry, metal goods, and especially clay bricks for building. The temples played an important role in promoting industry. The priests used the vast religious offerings as capital to hire labor and procure raw ma-

terial for industrial production. However, the priests did not have a monopoly on manufacturing; great rulers like Hammurabi likewise sponsored industrial operations. By Hammurabi's time there even existed craftsmen who were able to engage in industrial production on their own.

Lack of many raw materials, especially stone and metals, and constant contact with outsiders encouraged the Babylonians to become active traders. Every city maintained a class of people who spent their lives in trading ventures, either with neighboring cities or in the uncivilized areas surrounding the river valley. The Code of Hammurabi makes it clear that highly developed business methods had evolved to aid in trading. The commercial class employed complicated contracts, standard weights and measures, credit buying, lending for interest, deeds, promissory notes, and many of the devices that are used today to carry on trade. Traders gave every indication of a truly capitalistic spirit, seeking to increase their wealth by wise investment and to exploit any trading situation for as great a profit as possible.

Babylonian society was dominated by a small aristocracy of priests and nobles. As we have seen, the priests were especially powerful in early Babylonian cities, but the lay aristocracy had become more prominent by the time of Hammurabi. Regardless of who constituted this class, however, it was this aristocracy that benefitted most from Babylon's wealth and that created a glittering life for itself in every city in Mesopotamia. By twentieth-century standards much of this wealth was ill-gotten, resulting from the exploitation of the masses. Nonetheless, the aristocracy performed an important function in society, directing the efforts of hundreds of thousands of individuals, each of whom possessed a different talent, toward a common end. Without such a guiding force the high degree of co-operation needed to control the rivers would have been impossible. In a very real sense the aristocrats earned their rewards. Perhaps their wealth was not too deeply resented by the rest of society; at least we hear nothing of attempts to overthrow the ruling priests and nobles. It seems likely that many Babylonian nobles possessed a highly developed sense of obligation toward the rest of society. At any rate, the principle embodied in Hammurabi's code, according to which nobles should be punished more severely for certain crimes than other members of society, is presumed to reflect the conviction that nobles were expected to conduct themselves better than those with inferior status.

Even though Babylonian society was dominated by a small aristocracy, care was taken to define and protect the status of other classes. Hammurabi's code was careful to state the rights and duties of slaves, peasants, merchants, and artisans. The Babylonians were class-conscious indeed, but it was understood that each social class had a role in society, a role that all other classes must respect.

4. Babylonian Religion

Like the Egyptians, the Babylonians were powerfully influenced by religion. Most of their beliefs were extremely ancient, making it difficult to describe the origins of their religion. By the time a record of civilized life in Babylonia began to be kept, it is quite clear that Sumerian religious ideas and practices predominated in the river valley. The Semitic groups, such as the Akkadians and Amorites, subsequently adopted the Sumerian religion, but added very little to it.

The Sumerians were polytheistic, believing that every event was the work of one of the numerous divine spirits that inhabited the universe. However, at an early date certain gods had already emerged as the chief gods. Especially prominent among the Sumerian city-states were those gods who controlled the great forces of nature: Anu, the sky god; Enlil, the wind god; Ea, the earth and water god; Sen, the moon god; and Utu (or Shamash), the sun god. These nature gods usually were accepted as the patrons of the various city-states, their fate thus becoming bound with the fate of a particular city. They were represented as human beings, possessing terrible powers and capable of doing great damage to anyone who displeased them. In addition to the city gods each Babylonian family worshipped household gods in great numbers. Likewise, every Babylonian believed that the world was filled with demons, capable of bringing no end of discomfort to human beings. Perhaps almost everyone in the Tigris-Euphrates Valley worshipped one deity in common from an early date. This was a mother goddess, who was responsible for the renewal of life in all forms at the beginning of each year. This goddess, called Inanna by the Sumerians and Ishtar by the Semites, was by far the most popular deity among all members of society.

With the passing of centuries Babylonian religious leaders tended to clarify the nature and power of these many gods, creating a considerable body of mythology. The numerous political changes outlined in a previous section played an important role in this process. Since the Babylonians believed that each city-state was the property of a god, some explanation had to be given when one city-state conquered another. Usually the wars between city-states resulted in myths about similar wars between the gods, one conquering the other. Once they realized the impossibility of further resistance, the people of the conquered city usually accepted the conquering god as their chief god, their old god being reduced to a subordinate rank. At one time or another most of the great gods of nature mentioned above were accepted by large numbers of people as a result of one city conquering several others. Thus there was a tendency for national gods to emerge in Babylonia. This development culminated in the time of Hammurabi, when the god of the city of Babylon, Marduk, was universally worshipped in Hammurabi's empire. There likewise developed a body of mythology, recounting how Marduk had subdued other evil gods at the beginning of time, created new ones to serve him, made the world and all within it, and ruled over all the gods and all the world since. Some gods and goddesses became powerful by means other than conquest. For instance, by the time of Hammurabi, the goddess Ishtar and her lover, Tammuz, were the objects of an elaborate myth explaining the revival of nature that occurred each spring. Babylonian mythology became a great storehouse from which numerous religious ideas were lifted by later peoples.

Babylonian religion was a great deal gloomier and more terror-filled than Egyptian religion. The gods were vengeful, angry forces that might heap disaster on mankind at any moment and for any reason. Therefore, the Babylonians were especially careful to please their gods. Magnificent temples were built as dwellings for the great gods, and countless shrines were maintained in every home to placate the lesser spirits. Sacrifices were constantly offered to supply every need that the gods might demand. Large numbers of priests manned every temple. No great project was ever undertaken without magnificent ceremonies, first to ask the gods to look with favor on the project before it was initiated and later to thank them for its success.

As one might expect from a society whose members lived in constant fear of the gods, the Babylonians were especially anxious to find out in advance what the gods might be planning. They developed a whole battery of techniques to achieve this end. Dreams were carefully interpreted in the hope that the gods would reveal themselves to sleepers. The entrails of animals, especially the liver, were studied to find signs of the future. Also, the movement of the stars was carefully observed, the astrologer being a powerful figure in Babylonian society. By adding these many facts together it is perhaps safe to say that the Babylonians explored nearly every mode of external worship conceivable, creating a set of ritual practices that long remained a model for imitation by later peoples.

Babylonian religion quite clearly emphasized the outward aspects of religious life.

The Babylonians had no god who placed heavy ethical demands on his believers. They believed that, if they dutifully performed the prescribed rites of worship and made liberal sacrifices, then the gods would be happy and would reciprocate with bountiful material rewards. Seldom did the Babylonians give much thought to the problem of moral standards; certainly this question was probed much more deeply in Egypt in connection with Osiris worship. Perhaps this lack of concern with morality and ethics was connected with the absence of any deep feeling about immortality among the Babylonians. They believed that there was an afterlife, but it was hardly worth working for. The dead passed on to a place that was dreary and cold, lacking completely in those things that made life worth while. Very little attention was paid to expensive burial or to the care for the dead, in striking contrast with Egyptian practice. Babylonian religion was concerned chiefly with the living.

5. Babylonian Literature, Art, and Science

The achievements of the Babylonians in the arts, literature, and science have always seemed less significant than those of the Egyptians, probably because Egyptian cultural monuments have survived so much better. Probably it would be wrong to judge the Babylonians inferior. What has remained of their culture suggests a great deal of creative power and notable advance over peoples who lived in the area prior to them. By and large the Sumerians were the original artistic creators in Mesopotamia. The Semites sometimes modified and developed Sumerian cultural accomplishments, but more often they merely imitated them.

The Sumerians developed a writing system as early as the Egyptians. Their original method of writing employed pictographs, but gradually a system of symbols representing sounds was developed. Eventually several hundred such symbols were accepted, permitting writers to combine signs to express almost any idea. After the time of Sargon I the Sumerian written language began to be replaced by Semitic writing, which was little more than an imitation of Sumerian writing. Both Sumerians and Semites wrote on clay tablets, pressing the symbols into soft clay with a wedge-shaped reed stylus and then baking the tablets. This writing style has been called "cuneiform," a term derived from the Latin word meaning "wedge."

Writing in the early Sumerian cities probably developed for record-keeping purposes. Once a usable system was perfected, it was employed to preserve an extensive body of literature, usually religious. The most impressive writings were the magnificent religious epics, of which the *Creation Epic* and the *Epic of Gilgamesh* are the best examples. The *Creation Epic* consists of a series of stirring episodes describing how Marduk won supremacy over the spirit world and created the earth and man. The *Epic of Gilgamesh* recounts the doings of a legendary hero named Gilgamesh, ruler of the city of Erech. The story leads Gilgamesh through numerous encounters with angry gods and with the forces they create to destroy him. Woven into these adventures are such themes as war, love, death, natural catastrophes, and almost any other subject that makes for excitement. These epics contained the essence of Babylonian mythology, therefore serving as religious works as well as adventure stories. The Babylonians also wrote impressive hymns addressed to the gods but containing countless references to worldly affairs. Several pieces of "wisdom" literature, embodying advice on how to get along in this world, have survived. There were attempts at historical writing in the form of chronicles in which the deeds of famous rulers were recounted. The Babylonians were prolific letter writers, especially toward the end of the period. Unquestionably these literary works were read by a small circle, since literacy was not general. Nonetheless, Babylonian literature clearly indicates a lively cultural atmosphere.

From the beginning of their civilization the Babylonians were skilled and creative artists. However, lack of evidence makes it difficult to form a complete appraisal of their talent. Their art did not survive so well as Egyptian art, owing chiefly to the shortage of stone and the consequent employment of more perishable materials. As architects their main concern was with temple building. From earliest times every Sumerian city had an impressive temple, or ziggurat, at its center. These were rebuilt again and again through the centuries, usually becoming larger each time. The ziggurats were constructed of clay bricks. Often these structures reached tremendous size. Around the ziggurats there usually stood numerous dwellings, offices, and lesser shrines for the use of the priests of the temples. In many of the cities brick palaces and private dwellings were built on a luxurious scale. Babylonian architects perfected the dome, the arch, and the vault, and employed them constantly in building temples and dwellings.

The Babylonians were also skillful sculptors. They carved animal and human forms, usually for temple decorations. Some of the best carving was done to represent some historic event, such as a victory of a great king. For such occasions the sculptors did work in low relief on stone. Some of these "steles" portray action very skillfully. Equally great skill is reflected in the cylinder seals, which were carved to make impressions on clay tablets. These seals give especially vivid portrayals of animals and religious themes. The same skill is also illustrated in the jewelry, metalwork, and decorated pottery that were created in great abundance. All of this work reflects not only a great deal of technical skill but also a strong sense of beauty.

The Babylonians, like the Egyptians, produced a body of knowledge that can be called science. They had a system of time reckoning in which the length of the year was based on the sun's movement and that of the months on the moon's cycles. They also used a seven-day week. Their system required constant juggling since the cycles

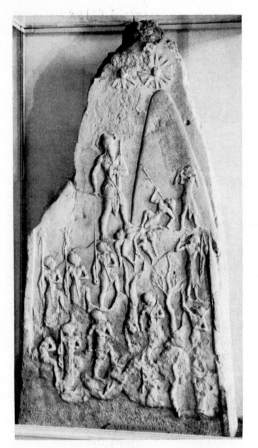

able to add, subtract, multiply, and divide. Also they were able to perform simple geometrical operations, such as finding the area of a plane surface or the volume of a cylinder. Most of their mathematics was practical, intended only to serve the needs of surveyors, architects, and engineers. Babylonian medicine mixed intelligent observations about the causes and cures of disease with a tremendous amount of superstition. There existed a rather extensive knowledge of geography among the Babylonians, as a result of their wide travels. Since the stars played such a large part in their religious beliefs, the Babylonians ac-

BABYLONIAN VICTORY STELE. This excellent relief commemorates a victory of the Akkadian ruler Naram Sin (reigned about 2300 B.C.), grandson of Sargon the Great, over enemies who appear to have been mountain dwellers. The great king, whose rank is indicated by his size, advances against the crushed enemy while his troops follow in an orderly fashion. This manner of commemorating historical events flourished for many centuries in the ancient Near East, and it is possible that rulers erected slabs of stone bearing such scenes (steles) for propaganda purposes. (*Archives Photographiques, Paris*)

of the sun and moon did not coincide. Extra days were added periodically to keep the two systems together. They also developed a standard of weights and measures, used almost universally by the end of Hammurabi's dynasty. Their number system was based on both a decimal system and units of sixty, a system we still use, for instance, in our divisions of the hour. They were

A BABYLONIAN RULER. This statue of about 2000 B.C., which portrays Gudea, a great ruler of the important Sumerian city Lagash, is a typical example of early Babylonian portrait sculpture. The sculptor's chief purpose was to symbolize the religious functions of the ruler, rather than to create a realistic portrayal. This statue offers some interesting contrasts with that of the Egyptian pharaoh Menkure (see p. 17). (*Archives Photographiques, Paris*) cumulated a large body of accurate information about the movements of the stars, thus laying the basis for astronomy. Their attitude toward this information was typical. Their knowledge of the stars did not lead them to consider the nature of the heavenly bodies. Astronomy merely served as a means of foretelling the future. And so it was with all Babylonian scientific knowledge. They had no interest in discovering knowledge of the natural world for its own sake. What they knew was retained only because it served a practical purpose.

When the semi-barbarian Kassites began to occupy the lower Tigris-Euphrates Valley about 1750 B.C., the first phase of Babylonian civilization had ended. For 2000 years the Sumerians and their Semitic imitators had struggled successfully to create an orderly society and a highly developed culture. After 1750 B.C., Babylonian civilization began to exert a powerful influence over a much wider area. Hardly a single people was to emerge in the later history of the Near East who did not borrow heavily from Babylonia. Thus Babylonian influences lived on long after the Babylonians ceased to be politically strong in the Near East.

SUGGESTED READING

* Henri Frankfort, *The Birth of Civilization in the Near East* (Anchor). Also published in 1951 in a hardback edition under the same title. An excellent, although sometimes difficult, discussion of the knotty problem of the emergence of highly civilized life in the Near Eastern river valleys.

Maurice Jastrow, *The Civilization of Babylonia and Assyria* (1915). This book provides an excellent view of nearly every aspect of Babylonian civilization. Its only fault is its age; much new information has become available since its writing, especially as a result of archaeological discoveries.

L. Delaporte, *Mesopotamia: The Babylonian and Assyrian Civilization*, tr. by V. Gordon Childe (1925), pp. 11–236. The first part of this book provides a good description of Babylonian political and social institutions, economic activities, religious life, and artistic and literary achievements.

C. Leonard Woolley, *The Sumerians* (1929). A well-written account by an expert archaeologist of the achievements of the people who founded Babylonian civilization.

* Edward Chiera, *They Wrote on Clay* (Phoenix). Also published in a hardback edition under the title *They Wrote on Clay: The Babylonian Tablets Speak Today* (1938). A discussion, written for laymen, of the highly technical subject of ancient Babylonian writing.

C. Leonard Woolley, *Ur of the Chaldees*, 2nd ed. (1950). A description of the findings of the archaeologists who excavated the ancient Sumerian city of Ur. Especially valuable because it shows how most of the information used to reconstruct ancient Near Eastern history has been obtained.

S. H. Hooke, *Babylonian and Assyrian Religion* (1953). A brief but thorough description of the religion of the peoples of the Tigris-Euphrates Valley, emphasizing Babylonian ideas about the gods, methods of worship, and the relationship of religion to other aspects of Babylonian life.

James B. Pritchard, ed., *Ancient Near Eastern Texts Relating to the Old Testament*, 2nd ed. (1955). This extensive collection of literary texts contains materials relating to nearly every important people in Near Eastern history: Egyptians, Babylonians, Assyrians, Persians, Hittites, and others. It will therefore be useful in connection with the first four chapters of the text. Included in the sections dealing with Babylonian sources are the texts of Hammurabi's code and of the *Gilgamesh Epic*.

CHAPTER 3

The Diffusion of Near Eastern Civilization

ABOUT 1800 B.C. the whole Near Eastern political scene was rocked to its foundations by a series of barbarian invasions from outside the Near East. In the wake of these invasions new peoples emerged to positions of leadership, and old inhabitants of the area were forced to conduct themselves in new ways. The river-valley peoples no longer monopolized the history of the Near East, although their civilizations served as models for the newcomers to imitate. For several centuries after 1800 B.C. the history of the Near East centered around the mixing of peoples and cultures, a process that resulted in a further elaboration and an extensive spread of the basic elements of Egyptian and Babylonian civilizations.

1. The Indo-European Invasions of the Near East

A people called the Indo-Europeans, heretofore unknown in the Near East, began the vast disturbances that opened the new era. The Indo-Europeans represented a new racial group in the Near East; they were large men with fair skins and blond hair, in contrast to the small, dark peoples who predominated in ancient Egypt and Babylonia. Their language was also different, being related to Latin, Greek, and most modern European languages. Their invasion of the Near East originated in the steppe land of southern Russia. Here they had

practiced a primitive herding economy and had lived under a strong clan system as early as 3000 B.C. During the next thousand years they slowly adopted a settled agricultural life, but they were still barbarians by Near Eastern standards when they began to move southward about 2000 B.C. They crossed the mountain barrier between Europe and the Near East by several routes —across the straits connecting the Black Sea and the Aegean Sea into Asia Minor; across the Caucasian Mountains into the area stretching across the upper reaches of the Tigris and Euphrates; across the mountains east of the Caspian Sea into the vast Iranian plateau. As happens so often when barbarians invade more highly civilized areas, the Indo-Europeans, probably because of their superior iron weapons and horse-drawn chariots, were able to establish political dominance over the natives.

No sooner did the invaders appear than new political groupings, usually ruled by Indo-Europeans, were formed. In Asia Minor the Hittites rose to dominance and began to push eastward and southward, especially into the territory that had been a part of Hammurabi's Babylonian Empire. Farther to the east groups called the Mitanni and the Kassites formed and drove southward. The Kassites were especially successful, managing to destroy the Babylonian Empire of Hammurabi's successors and to occupy the Tigris-Euphrates Valley. Still other Indo-Europeans sifted into the Syria-

Palestine region, where they were joined by Semitic marauders from the Arabian Desert to form the Hyksos, who soon invaded Egypt and brought the magnificent Middle Kingdom to an end. Important groups settled in Iran, to emerge later as the Medes and the Persians. The Indo-Europeans achieved more than political dominance. They soon began to adopt the ways of the more highly civilized peoples they conquered, quickly losing the barbaric traits that had characterized them when they arrived in the Near East.

2. The Egyptian Empire, 1600–1200 B.C.

The assault of the barbarian-led hordes on Babylonia provoked little resistance from the residents of the Tigris-Euphrates Valley. The Kassites established political control over these peoples and maintained it for several centuries after their initial invasion about 1750 B.C. Kassite rule resulted in a gradual deterioration of Babylonian political influence in the Near East.

Proud Egypt endured foreign rule for nearly two centuries (about 1750–1580 B.C.), but never willingly. The regime of the Hyksos was eventually challenged by a revolt beginning at Thebes. This revolt was quickly transformed into a war of liberation in which most of Egypt joined. Flying the banner of the god Amon-Ra, Egyptian armies led by the Theban prince, Ahmose I, smashed the Hyksos in Egypt and pursued the remnants into Syria-Palestine, where the destruction of the Hyksos was completed. Capitalizing on the spirit of unity surging through Egypt, Ahmose was able to establish a new dynasty, the eighteenth, ruling over all Egypt. The first rulers of this dynasty quickly repaired the ravages caused by the Hyksos. The centralized administration, the agricultural system, the old religion, and the ancient social order were revived. This New Kingdom was outwardly a continuation of the Old and the Middle kingdoms.

However, a new spirit welled up in the revived Egypt. She was haunted by a fear that more outsiders would attack her, thus making it impossible for her leaders to restrict their attentions to the Nile Valley. Moreover, Egypt's defensive raids abroad had demonstrated that the exploitation of foreigners could be profitable. An urge to expand mounted slowly in Egypt. Conservative elements fought this trend, but they failed. With the accession of Thutmose III (1484–1447 B.C.) to the throne, Egypt cast her lot for conquest and imperialism.

Thutmose III, often called "the Napoleon of Egypt," established the bases of the Egyptian Empire by a series of brilliant campaigns into Syria-Palestine, Nubia, and Libya. He created an invincible army and began the process of regimenting Egyptian society to serve military ends. His immediate successors continued his program. Within a century after Thutmose III's accession Egypt was absolute ruler over a territory stretching from the fourth cataract of the Nile to the Euphrates River in north Syria. Heavy tribute was extracted from the numerous victims of Egypt's might. Important powers like the Hittites, Mitanni, and Kassites showed their respect for Egypt by seeking desperately to remain at peace with her.

Successful imperialism brought to Egypt one of her most magnificent periods. Her government reached peak efficiency in exercising absolute control over the population. Agriculture and trade, coupled with the tribute extracted from foreign subjects, produced unprecedented prosperity. Artistic and intellectual life blossomed again, inspired by pride in Egypt's power and supported by her great wealth. The greatest landmarks of Egyptian artistic vigor were the magnificent temples built at Luxor and Karnak in honor of Amon-Ra, the chief god in Egypt at this time. Like the pyramids built about 1200 years previously, these giant pillared structures, brilliantly decorated with carvings and paint, illustrate the Egyptian genius for building structures that seem destined to last forever. The artistic outburst of the New Kingdom was not marked by originality or creativity. The artists looked back to earlier times for models,

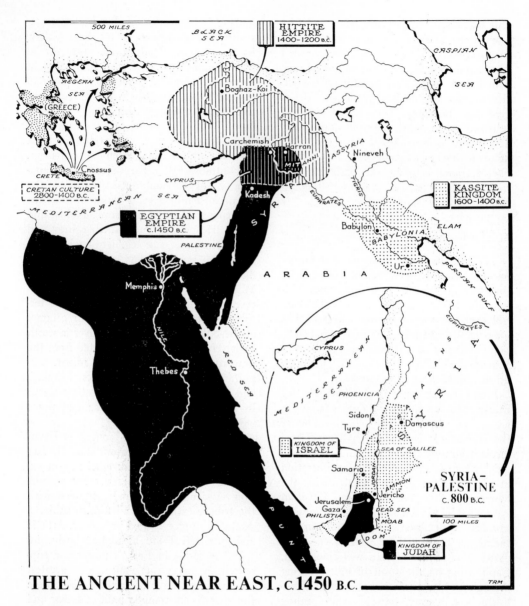

THE ANCIENT NEAR EAST, c. 1450 B.C.

thereby maintaining the static quality in Egyptian art. Nevertheless, Egypt's activity established her as the cultural leader of the Near East and kept alive a cultural tradition in the face of advancing barbarism.

The Egypt of the New Kingdom, though, was not quite the Egypt of old. Successful imperialism presented serious problems that the Egyptians were ill equipped to handle. One new problem was that of dealing with conquered peoples. Egypt adopted a system of permitting conquered subjects to keep their own rulers, who were compelled to sign treaties with Egypt pledging friendship and payment of tribute. Egypt sought to hold this intricate alliance system together by establishing garrisons abroad and by sending diplomats abroad to keep account of semi-independent powers. As long as the armies and diplomats were vigilant the system worked, but each independent prince always remained a potential source of rebellion.

A second problem facing Egypt was the fear and hostility her expansion aroused among peoples outside her borders. The Egyptians discovered that expansion did not necessarily safeguard a nation from outside attack, but instead increased the possibility of such attacks. The Hittites proved to be Egypt's most dangerous foe. After the establishment of the Hittites in Asia Minor about 1800 B.C. they slowly increased their power. By 1400 B.C. they were able to begin attacking the northern fringes of Egypt's empire. As they advanced they successfully encouraged rebellion among the princes ruling the numerous petty states within Egypt's empire.

A third problem was the tension caused in Egypt's internal structure. The demands of war enlarged the army and the bureaucracy, requiring ever-increasing expenditures. This resulted in increasing exploitation of the Egyptian population by the state. Foreign problems monopolized the attention of the pharaohs so completely that they neglected internal affairs, turning such matters over to bureaucrats. Special groups within Egypt schemed to seize control of state policy in hopes of grabbing a greater share of the wealth. The priests were especially guilty, even attempting to demote the pharaoh to the rank of a mere man and claiming that they had the power to stand between the gods and the pharaoh as interpreters of divine will. Other elements, especially the army, disputed such claims.

MODEL OF AN EGYPTIAN TEMPLE. This model of the great hypostyle hall of the Temple of Karnak in Egypt, which was built during the great days of the Empire, illustrates the architectural style employed in most Egyptian temples. Note the capitals of the great center columns (about 80 feet tall), which are stylized imitations of the papyrus plant. Shorter side columns allow windows to be built high in the walls, and heavy beams support the roof and walls. The decoration is elaborate, with painted reliefs on every available surface inside the temple. The basic architectural style represented here played a highly significant role in later architectural development. Its influence on the Roman basilica and early Christian churches is especially obvious (see p. 170). (*Courtesy of the Metropolitan Museum of Art*)

Excessive wealth tended to soften the high officials of state and to distract them from their responsibilities. Egypt's power and wealth were not unmixed blessings. They bred exploitation, dissension, and corruption—a situation far from desirable for a nation faced with the problem of ruling an extensive empire.

The troubled society of the New Kingdom was finally brought face to face with its problems by the actions of Akhenaton (about 1375–1358 B.C.). In complete contrast with his active, vigorous predecessors, Akhenaton turned his back on problems of imperialism. He dedicated his career to religious reform, creating a new religion and trying to compel his subjects to accept it. Akhenaton proclaimed that his subjects must worship a new god, Aton. The temples of the old gods were to be destroyed and their priests demoted. The pharaoh personally helped develop a new theology explaining the nature and powers of Aton. A new set of rituals was perfected and a new style of art developed to give honor to the one god of all Egypt.

Akhenaton's reforms provoked a storm of protest in Egypt and gripped the population in a struggle that consumed everyone's energy. The opposition to Akhenaton was led by the priests of Amon-Ra, the god who had leaped to prominence in Egypt during the period of successful expansion. The priests found adequate support elsewhere in society. Akhenaton's reforms were bound to disturb his subjects because religion lay at the very foundations of Egyptian civilization. Although no one can now be sure of his motives, it seems that his program offered Egyptian civilization a supreme challenge. Would it continue to progress or would it remain conservative and backward-looking? Akhenaton was trying to hasten his people along a path leading to the worship of one almighty god who demanded moral goodness of his worshippers. This was Akhenaton's substitute for a religious system based on adherence to a welter of gods who asked material offerings. He was seeking to reduce the power of the priests who had been using religion as a means of gaining power and prestige at the expense of the pharaoh. He was trying to guide Egypt's intellectuals and artists into new channels, to divert them from their increasing tendency to worship the past. In

AKHENATON WORSHIPPING ATON. This relief illustrates a ceremony of the new religion inaugurated by the pharaoh Akhenaton. The ruler and his wife are shown making offerings to the sun god Aton, symbolized by the disk with rays reaching down to earth. This representation of the supreme deity, which Akhenaton ordered all the Egyptians to worship in place of their old gods, is more abstract than in the older religions, which represented gods as animals, birds, reptiles, or men. Note, however, that at the ends of the rays emanating from the sun god are hands dropping gifts to earthly worshippers, indicating that the new religion still expressed religious ideas in easily recognizable forms. The art style used to portray the pharaoh contrasts sharply with the more majestic, monumental style of earlier periods (see p. 17). (*Photograph by Egyptian Expedition, The Metropolitan Museum of Art*)

short, he was trying to find in a new religion a means of arousing the Egyptians to take the lead in exploiting the new currents that were running strong in Near Eastern society in this era of the mixing and mingling of cultures. His efforts were fruitless. By the time of his death his foes had already forced him to abandon his reforms. The last members of his dynasty devoted their energy to a restoration of the pre-Akhenaton order in religion, art, and politics.

Akhenaton's reform movement was fatal to Egypt's power in the Near East. While her energies were absorbed in internal struggles, her empire in Syria-Palestine melted away. Rebellion, abetted by the Hittites, spread everywhere. The first rulers of the nineteenth dynasty (about 1320–1200 B.C.), especially Seti I and Rameses II, made valiant attempts to restore Egyptian control abroad. Their military campaigns, although sometimes successful, involved Egypt in an almost constant war with the Hittites and with rebellious subject princes, especially in Syria and Palestine. Incessant warfare impoverished Egypt and led to increasing oppression of her people. Both Egypt and the Hittites finally paid a high price for their struggle. The Hittites were attacked about 1200 B.C. by new waves of Indo-European invaders and disappeared from history as a separate state. Egypt's fate was not so sudden. By 1200 B.C. she too was under attack from Nubia, Libya, and the Aegean Sea area. These attacks forced her back into her old boundaries and from time to time put foreigners on her exalted throne. Under these circumstances Egypt fell into a state of torpor, imitating and worshiping her past greatness without any marked creative innovations. After 1200 B.C. she never again stood out as a leader in civilization.

3. The Era of Small Nations, 1200–800 B.C.: Phoenicians and Aramaeans

The collapse of the Hittite and Egyptian empires around 1200 B.C. left the Near East without a strong political power. This in no way checked the diffusion of culture that had accompanied Egypt's expansion. Numerous small groups, some old and some new, seized the opportunity to establish their political independence. For the next four centuries these small nations dominated the history of the Near East. As they struggled to establish and maintain their independence, they tried to utilize the ideas of their predecessors as the basis for their new life. Their efforts resulted in a continued spread over most of the Near East of ideas and institutions that had originated in the great river valleys. A few of the smaller groups did more than borrow; as a result of their unique experiences, they were able to add new elements to the existing cultural life, thereby enriching the Near Eastern tradition as well as spreading it.

Two small nations stand out especially as borrowers and disseminators of the older civilizations—the Phoenicians and the Aramaeans. Both of these groups were Semitic in origin, migrating from the Arabian Desert into modern Syria prior to 2000 B.C. The Phoenicians settled in the narrow band of territory lying between the Mediterranean Sea and the mountains of Lebanon. The Aramaeans were located east of these mountains between the northern end of the Arabian Desert and the Euphrates River. Both groups were repeatedly conquered by the Babylonians, Egyptians, and Hittites, and were strongly influenced by all of their conquerors. Consequently, by 1200 B.C., they were already highly civilized peoples, and when Egypt and the Hittites declined in power both groups were able to establish their political independence. Ultimately a number of independent city-states emerged in Phoenicia, the chief of which were Tyre and Sidon. Meanwhile the Aramaeans organized themselves into a number of small kingdoms, centering around cities like Damascus, Kadesh, and Palmyra. For about four centuries these principalities were among the chief states in the Near East. Their independence was finally crushed, however, by the rising power of the Assyrians in the eighth century B.C.

During the four centuries of their independent existence the Phoenicians and the Aramaeans were spreaders of Near Eastern civilization. Both groups were active traders, most of their wealth being derived from trading ventures. The Phoenicians took to the seas, establishing a virtual monopoly on trade in the Mediterranean. Phoenician merchants touched nearly every important point around the Mediterranean, carrying manufactured goods from the whole Near East to the backward peoples of Greece, Italy, North Africa, Spain, and southern France, and bringing the raw materials of these areas back to the Near East. From these merchants many barbarians around the Mediterranean got their first taste of higher civilization. The Phoenicians, not content to trade, also established colonies abroad. The chief Phoenician colony was the North African city of Carthage, which became one of the leading centers of civilization in the Western Mediterranean after 800 B.C. The Aramaeans were land traders, exploiting the trade routes that linked Egypt, Babylonia, Asia Minor, and points beyond. Both Phoenicians and Aramaeans reaped a rich reward from their trading ventures. This wealth was in part devoted to patronizing the arts and learning. Their cities were active cultural centers. The Phoenicians and Aramaeans were not particularly creative, depending upon Egyptian and especially Babylonian models in their art, literature, and religion. The Phoenicians did perfect an alphabet that later served as a model for the written languages of the Mediterranean world.

4. The Era of Small Nations, 1200–800 B.C.: The Hebrews

The most influential of the small nations during the period following the decline of the Egyptian Empire was that of the Hebrews, Semitic nomads who migrated from the Arabian Desert in search of a new home. The Hebrew tradition preserved in the Old Testament speaks of wandering Hebrews first settling in Ur on the Euphrates and then being led farther up the river to Haran by Abraham. About 1800 B.C. the search for a new home led the Hebrew tribes toward the Syria-Palestine area. There was still no unified Hebrew nation. Tribe after tribe moved into Syria-Palestine over several centuries, each seeking its own place to live.

In Palestine the newcomers encountered the well-established and highly civilized Canaanites, whose culture was heavily affected by Egyptian and Babylonian influences. While some Hebrews quickly adopted Canaanite civilization, others, forced to settle in semi-arid parts of Palestine, retained their ancient desert way of life. A few of the more restless moved on to Egypt, probably hoping to escape Palestine's famines by settling in the fertile Nile Valley. Once in Egypt, the Hebrews were permitted to stay, and were assigned land in the delta region (the Biblical land of Goshen). They carried on their lives pretty much in their accustomed way, and some of them rose to high positions in Egypt, as the Old Testament story of Joseph suggests. Eventually, however, life in Egypt became intolerable, probably chiefly because the Hebrews became victims of the increasing oppression of the pharaohs of the nineteenth dynasty, who were fighting costly wars to save Egypt's foreign empire. This oppression set the stage for the first great turning point in Hebrew history—the Exodus from Egypt, which occurred shortly before 1200 B.C.

The familiar story of the Exodus and of Moses's inspired leadership of those Hebrews who fled Egypt need not be recounted here. During forty trying years spent wandering about the Sinai Peninsula a dramatic transformation occurred among Moses's followers. They underwent a religious experience that laid the basis for a Hebrew nation. The Hebrews had not had a common religion up to this time. At the time they began to invade Palestine, each tribe probably had its own deities. Some of the newcomers accepted Canaanite religious practices and forgot their old desert religion.

But other Hebrew groups clung to their ancient gods, one of whom was Yahweh. Yahweh had at one time been a purely local god, but one who had made a powerful impression on some tribes and who was worshipped by these tribes even after they came to Palestine. Yahweh was a powerful nature god, capable of caring for the material needs of his adherents. But to the early Hebrews he was simply one god among many. Even Moses's followers had no common religion, since religious dissension arose among them during their sojourn in the Sinai Peninsula.

During their stay in the desert, however, the followers of Moses pledged themselves to the worship of Yahweh and accepted certain ideas about that god and their relationship to him. These basic formulations became the basis for all later religious development among the Hebrews. Prompted by the inspired leadership of Moses, the Hebrews of the Exodus entered into a covenant, or contract, with Yahweh. They pledged themselves to worship only Yahweh. In return their god promised that he would care for them under any circumstances in the future, just as he had done during the escape from Egypt. The Hebrews also accepted from Yahweh a set of laws that were to govern the manner in which each follower of Yahweh conducted himself toward Yahweh and toward his fellow men. Yahweh's wrath would fall on those who violated these commands. By the acceptance of these ideas Moses's "mixed multitude" became a "nation," bound together by the exclusive worship of one god who promised to support them and who told them how to live with one another. These religious ideas, when fully developed by the Hebrews, served as the basis for their own religion and for other great religions that eventually dominated a large part of the world.

The first task that the newly inspired Hebrews of the Exodus turned to was the discovery of the Promised Land. Armed with their portable "temple," the Ark of the Covenant, which they carried with them as a mark of their allegiance to Yahweh, this impoverished band set themselves against the Canaanites and the other Hebrew tribes in Palestine. Shortly after 1200 B.C. they crossed the Jordan to strike at the Canaanite city of Jericho. The next hundred and fifty years were monopolized by the wars of the Hebrews to establish their dominion over Palestine. Usually the Hebrews were successful, although their own disunity made their task difficult. Only in periods of great crisis were they able to overcome their tribal jealousies for a united effort. As their control over Palestine widened, the Hebrews enjoyed increasing prosperity. The primitive culture of desert dwellers was replaced by the higher culture of settled farmers, which the Hebrews borrowed from the conquered Canaanites. The worship of Yahweh gained new adherents during the period of conquest, probably because Yahweh seemed to be fulfilling his promise to watch over the interests of those who worshipped him. The Hebrew system of law, still closely allied to the worship of Yahweh, continued to expand and to serve as a common tie among many Hebrew tribes. However, Yahweh worship was still not accepted by all the Hebrews. Repeatedly during the period of conquest there arose leaders who tried to rally backsliding Hebrews to return to the worship of Yahweh. These leaders, called "judges" in the Old Testament and represented by figures like Gideon, Samson, and Samuel, sought to convince the Hebrews that their many military setbacks were punishment for their failure to serve Yahweh and for their tendency to fall under the spell of the Canaanite gods.

Although they succeeded in overpowering the Canaanites, the Hebrews eventually met a foe they could not handle so easily. Shortly after 1100 B.C. the Hebrews began to clash with the Philistines, a people probably from Asia Minor who had recently settled in southern Palestine along the Mediterranean shore after having been rebuffed in an attempt to seize Egypt. By 1050 B.C. most of the Hebrews had been conquered by the Philistines. This disaster eventually proved to be a blessing for the Hebrews because it forced upon them the necessity for political union. As a step toward ending Philistine overlordship, several Hebrew tribes agreed to accept a king, selecting Saul for that honor.

The reigns of Saul and his successors, David and Solomon, covering the years about 1020 to 930 B.C., mark the high point in Hebrew political history. These kings smashed the Philistine power and subdued many other enemies around Syria-Palestine, making the Hebrew nation the leading power in that area. A centralized government was established at Jerusalem, giving the king the means to exercise control over all the Hebrews. Active diplomatic relations were established between the kings of the Hebrews and rulers in most other nations of the Near East. Hebrew traders entered into Near Eastern commerce with great vigor and success, bringing prosperous times to the new kingdom. The royal court at Jerusalem patronized the arts and letters. Occasionally there were elements within the Hebrew nation who caused trouble. Often this dissidence arose in protest to personal conduct of the kings; Saul's jealousy of the youthful David, David's passion for other men's wives, and Solomon's heavy expenditures to satisfy his own tastes outraged the feelings of some Hebrews. However, in the long run, the kings were able to curb the dissatisfied elements and to maintain a unified kingdom enjoying power and prestige.

The reigns of Saul, David, and Solomon represented a significant chapter in the history of Jewish religion. These kings were all active champions of Yahweh, claiming that they were his agents and that they had been anointed to lead the Hebrews to the victory promised in the Covenant. Nearly all the Hebrews now accepted the worship of Yahweh. David and Solomon created a center for Yahweh worship by building the temple at Jerusalem. To ensure the proper worship of Yahweh, they provided priests, under whose leadership the ritual practices dedicated to Yahweh became much more elaborate. A body of religious writings, much of

it later to be incorporated in the final form of the Old Testament, was set down at this time. Yahweh worship was becoming a full-fledged religious system, fitted for a prosperous, powerful, civilized people.

Even while Solomon reigned in all his glory, however, deep-seated economic, political, and religious dissension threatened the Hebrew nation, and many Hebrews, remembering their tribal freedom, hated the autocratic methods used by the kings to hold the kingdom together. The old social equality characteristic of tribal life had disappeared as the Hebrews became more civilized, and a definite aristocracy emerged and sought to subdue the mass of the Hebrews. This social and economic inequality was detestable to many Hebrews. As for their religion, despite the fact that Yahweh was championed by their kings, many Hebrews were dissatisfied. They resented the non-Hebrew ideas and practices that had slipped into the religion practiced at the great temple in Jerusalem. Furthermore, they deplored Solomon's tolerance of the foreign religions of his many non-Jewish wives, all such forbearance of the alien appearing to be a compromise with Yahweh worship. Immediately after Solomon's death this discontent found expression, and the northern part of the kingdom refused to recognize his son as king and formed a new kingdom called Israel. The southern Hebrews formed a second kingdom called Judah, under kings descended from David.

The kingdoms of Israel and Judah proceeded rapidly toward destruction, both becoming the victims of internal disturbances and of misrule, which sapped their will to resist foreign attack. In 722 B.C. Israel was destroyed by the Assyrians. Judah survived until 586 B.C., when the Chaldeans (see p. 46) captured Jerusalem and carried off large numbers of Jews into captivity in Babylonia. Thus ended the independent political history of the Hebrews. The Persians did free some of the captives in 538 B.C., allowing them to return to Jerusalem and to re-establish the Hebrew religion, but this did not mean political independence; it simply meant that Hebrew priests were given permission by the Persians to exercise a great deal of influence in Palestine, but always under Persian supervision.

As the Hebrew political glory faded in the centuries after 900 B.C., Hebrew religious life took on new depth. The period of the divided kingdoms and foreign conquest was characterized by a searching examination and a new expression of Hebrew religious ideas. This development was the work of some of the world's greatest religious leaders: the prophets, including especially Elijah (ninth century), Amos and Isaiah (eighth century), Jeremiah (seventh century), Ezekiel and the second Isaiah (sixth century), and Nehemiah (fifth century). The stinging attacks these men leveled against Hebrew life and the new concepts and practices that they developed can be read in the Old Testament. The prophets did not fight in vain, for out of their efforts came a series of religious ideas that became the essence of Hebrew religion, ideas that represented a departure from conventional religious thought in the Near East.

First of all, the prophets proclaimed a true monotheism. They made Yahweh the only god and denied that any other gods existed. Before the time of the prophets the Hebrews had believed that Yahweh was the only god they should worship, but they had never denied the existence of other gods. The prophets repudiated this idea by claiming that only Yahweh existed and that those who did not worship him were idolators.

Second, the prophets proclaimed a whole new concept of the nature of Yahweh. He was a god outside nature, not existing in any natural object; he was a god of justice, acting according to a definite law instead of his own fancy; he was omnipotent, controlling the whole universe and causing everything in the past, present, and future to happen; he was a god with a plan for the world; his will would be worked out in the history of the world. He was a god of righteousness, pleased by those who did

good, vengeful toward those who did evil. This was truly the most exalted concept of deity yet expressed in the Near East.

Third, the prophets defined a new basis for human conduct. Just as Yahweh treated men with righteousness and justice, so also must each individual treat his fellow men according to those same principles. Yahweh had handed down to man a code of law (called the Torah) that must serve as the basis for earthly society. Transgression of the law would invite the wrath of Yahweh and bring down his punishment on the offender. Decent treatment of other men became a major obligation of each Hebrew. Goodness would not be reckoned by Yahweh in terms of wealth or the size of offering made to him; instead a man would be judged in terms of his treatment of others. The religion of the prophets emphasized ethical concepts far above ritual practices.

Finally, the prophets proclaimed that the Hebrews were the people chosen to carry out Yahweh's will on earth. No matter what disasters had befallen them at the moment, they would eventually emerge victorious over the other peoples of the earth, and through them the one god would eventually be worshipped by all. Yahweh would aid in this venture, since it was his plan for the world, and eventually he would send a Messiah to lead the Hebrews to their victory. While awaiting their final victory the Hebrews must retain their ties with one another. If they could not all live in an independent kingdom, they could retain their common religious beliefs as a binding tie. The Hebrew "nation" would live on as a religious community, awaiting its victory over the non-Hebrews.

By the fourth century B.C., when the ancient Near East was conquered by Alexander the Great and its civilization submitted to heavy Greek influences, the Hebrews had made no progress toward winning the world to a worship of their god. Near Eastern peoples were too accustomed to the worship of a multitude of nature gods, to their elaborate mythology, and to the ingrained habits of winning the favor of these gods by elaborate sacrifices, to listen to Hebrew concepts of a single almighty god living outside nature and expecting men to live by a law requiring high moral standards. Although no one then paid attention to these ideas, they had tremendous impact on later civilizations, serving as the base upon which Christianity and Mohammedanism would be built. Certainly the Hebrews stand as a monument to the fact that power and wealth are not the only bases for greatness on the historical scene.

SUGGESTED READING

Several of the books referred to in the suggested reading list for Chapter 1 contain material dealing with the history of Egypt in the period of imperial expansion. Especially useful will be the appropriate chapters in Breasted, *A History of Egypt*, and Wilson, *The Culture of Ancient Egypt*.

Old Testament. Perhaps the best way for a student of history to begin a study of Hebrew history is by reading the Old Testament. Most readers are familiar with the King James version of the Old Testament. In spite of its splendid language this version can sometimes be misleading to a student of history. It might be advisable to turn to a more recent translation in which an attempt has been made to express the sense of the Old Testament text in modern language. Especially recommended are J. M. P. Smith and E. J. Goodspeed, ed., *The Complete Bible: An American Translation* (1939), which is a Protestant version; or the Ronald Knox translation of the Vulgate, which is a Roman Catholic version. A student interested in reading the Old Testament as a source for the history of the Hebrews might find it useful to employ a good biblical commentary. Two convenient commentaries are *The Abingdon Bible Commentary* (1929) and *A Catholic Commentary on Holy Scripture* (1953).

* Harry M. Orlinsky, *Ancient Israel* (Cornell). A brief but well-balanced survey of Hebrew history.

T. H. Robinson and W. O. E. Oesterley, *A History of Israel*, 2 vols. 2nd ed. (1937). A full, well-organized history of the Hebrews to A.D. 135, Especially thorough in its treatment of Hebrew religious development, although some authorities would take issue with the interpretation given. The book is a "must" for any student interested in a thorough knowledge of Hebrew history.

Giuseppe Ricciotti, *The History of Israel*, tr. by Clement della Penta and Richard T. A. Murphy, 2 vols. (1955). A more recent study by a Roman Catholic author covering the same ground as the Robinson and Oesterly book.

* W. Robertson-Smith, *The Religion of the Semites* (Meridian). A brief study that will serve as an introduction to the religious ideas of the Hebrews.

* W. F. Albright, *The Archaeology of Palestine*, rev. ed. (Penguin). A summary of what archaeology tells about the history of Palestine. A student will find it fascinating to measure this information alongside the account of Hebrew history presented in the Old Testament and to discover how extensively archaeology corroborates the biblical account.

A. T. Olmstead, *History of Syria and Palestine to the Macedonian Conquest* (1931). Contains excellent material on the history of the less-well-known people of Syria and Palestine, especially the Phoenicians and Aramaeans, as well as on the history of the Hebrews. Olmstead's book is marred by his extremely harsh treatment of the Old Testament as a reliable historical source.

* O. R. Guerney, *The Hittites* (Penguin). A brief survey of the history of the Hittites based on the best evidence available today. Especially strong on cultural history.

CHAPTER 4

The Great Empires: Assyria and Persia, 800–300 B.C.

DURING the ninth century B.C. the rising might of Assyria heralded a new era in Near Eastern history. After nearly a thousand years, during which the Near East had progressed toward a common culture and during which the barriers that separated people disintegrated, it was inevitable that someone would try to unite the Near East under a single political control. Such attempts became the dominant theme of Near Eastern history after 800 B.C. The Assyrians and the Persians were the most successful "empire builders" between about 800 and 300 B.C.

1. The Assyrian Empire

The Assyrians were a people of Semitic origin, migrating out of the Arabian Desert as early as 3000 B.C. and settling on either side of the upper Tigris Valley. They eventually spread out toward the Zagros Mountains and into the plateau area between the Tigris and Euphrates rivers. This was a highland area, contrasting with the rich river valley to the south. Assyria was a land suited for farming and herding, but incapable of producing such great wealth as the region to the south.

For centuries after 3000 B.C. the main lines of Assyrian history are extremely vague. Perhaps the chief development was the powerful influence exercised by Babylonian civilization over the Assyrians, who never demonstrated any ability to create a pattern of life of their own. Babylonian art styles, writing techniques, religious ideas, and political and economic institutions were copied to such an extent that Assyria can be called a cultural offspring of Babylonia. A few Babylonian conquerors, like Hammurabi, even managed to establish political control over Assyria. However, Assyria never lost her identity completely to Babylonia, and when the Babylonians began to decline after 1750 B.C., Assyria continued as an independent nation.

The era from 1750 to 1000 B.C. was the testing period for Assyria. In an age of general confusion she was subjected to great pressure from beyond her borders, her location making her a constant target for the invading Indo-European hordes sweeping into the Near East. Kassites, Hittites, and Mitanni all assaulted Assyria at one time or another, and new hordes of Semites from the Arabian Desert likewise attacked Assyria. The hardy farmers of Assyria met this challenge by subordinating all other interests to a defense of their homeland, and they became one of the best military forces in the Near East, especially after they adopted the new iron weapons introduced there. As early as 1200 B.C. the Assyrians demonstrated their military abilities by successfully raiding a wide area stretching west of Assyria. Only a serious threat of invasion from the north checked a wider expansion of Assyria at this time.

In the ninth century B.C. the Assyrians returned to their program of expansion, for the pressure from the north had abated. No great powers existed in this era of small nations. Assyria was blessed after 800 B.C. with excellent rulers who capitalized on the warlike sentiments of the tough Assyrian farmers to launch new raids on surrounding nations. During the next two centuries these armies marched victoriously over most of the Near East, building the largest state that had yet existed there.

At first Assyria's expansion took the form of tribute-collecting raids against her neighbors, and the barbarian peoples of the north, the Hebrews, the Phoenicians, the Aramaeans, and the Babylonians were all victims. No one offered serious resistance to the Assyrian armies, well armed with iron weapons, excellent siege engines, and strong cavalry units. The Assyrians added to their military efficiency by pursuing a deliberate policy of cruelty, using slaughter and torture as means of terrorizing their victims. So awesome did their reputation become that many peoples refused to resist, preferring to pay any price to avoid the scourge of the Assyrian army. However, the Assyrian policy of raiding in quest of tribute was not completely effective. Rebellion and refusal to pay tribute occurred as soon as Assyrian armies departed from any conquered land, requiring repeated expeditions to restore respect for Assyria.

After 750 B.C. the Assyrians turned from simple raiding expeditions to building an empire in which Assyrian authority could be exercised more consistently. King Tiglath-pileser III (reigned 746–727 B.C.) inaugurated a policy of building the Assyrian Empire on sounder foundations. His greatest successors, Sargon II (722–705 B.C.), Sennacherib (705–681 B.C.), Esarhaddon (681–669 B.C.), and Ashurbanipal III (669–625 B.C.) followed his footsteps. After 750

B.C. the Assyrians began to destroy the ruling dynasties of conquered states, replacing them with Assyrian governors. Large numbers of the upper classes in conquered kingdoms were deported to spots far from their native homes, thus destroying the potential leadership of revolts, and within a relatively short time Assyria had established her dominion solidly over Syria-Palestine and northern Babylonia, creating an extensive state where peace and order reigned. To protect her rule in this territory, Assyria was compelled to extend her gaze over a wider area of the Near East. Peoples beyond her empire insisted on interfering with her rule over conquered subjects; Assyria's answer was to send her armies to deal with the troublemakers. After a trying struggle all of Babylonia was eventually conquered, Egypt was attacked for causing trouble in Syria-Palestine and was forced to accept Assyrian overlordship, and Assyrian influence was extended deep into Asia Minor, although her armies conquered very little territory there. Several semi-barbaric states north and east of Assyria were subdued. Semitic tribes in Arabia were beaten into submission. The mountain peoples in the Zagros region accepted Assyrian rule. By 650 B.C. the whole civilized Near East accepted a single master, the great king of Assyria, whose unbeatable armies had not yet met a rival strong enough to check Assyrian expansion.

The Assyrian state was not so strong as its size indicated. Assyrian terrorism had aroused a fierce, irreconcilable hatred among subject peoples. Constant warfare caused a fatal depletion of Assyrian manpower and a consequent crippling of the Assyrian armies. Eventually the Assyrians had to rely on levies from conquered subjects to replace Assyrian soldiers; the non-Assyrians were much less efficient than native Assyrians. Some of the later Assyrian rulers were more inclined to enjoy the fruits of victory than to exercise the active leadership needed to hold their empire together. Worst of all, Assyria encountered the plague of all empire builders—enemies beyond the

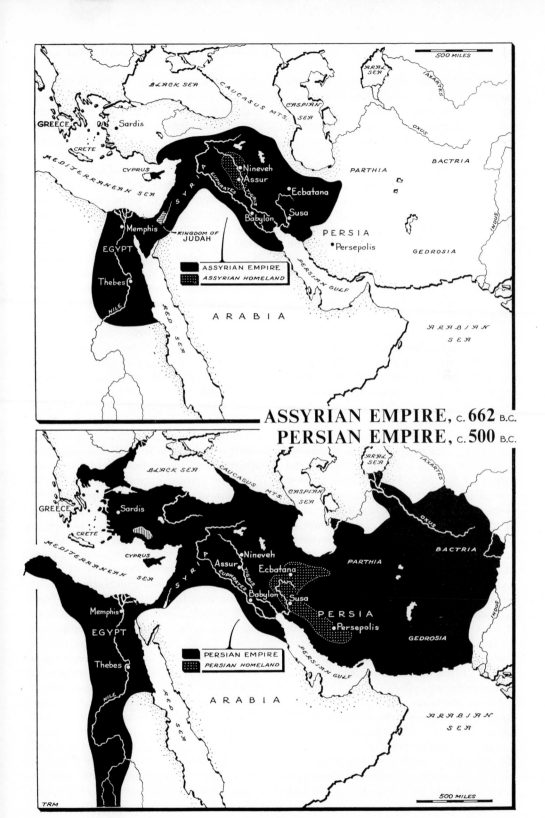

ASSYRIAN EMPIRE, c. 662 B.C.
PERSIAN EMPIRE, c. 500 B.C.

frontier, aroused by the threat of absorption. Assyria's enemies included the Medes, living east of the Zagros Mountains, Semitic tribes pushing into Babylonia, and barbarians pouring into the territory north of Assyria.

Destruction began to rain on Assyria during the time of Ashurbanipal and mounted in fury after his death in 625 B.C. The Egyptians successfully revolted and caused discontent among the Assyrian subjects in Syria and Palestine. A Semitic group, the Chaldeans, raised the standard of revolt in Babylonia. Assyria committed most of her strength to checking this particular liberation movement, weakening herself beyond repair as a result. Then the Medes, who had learned a great deal by imitating Assyrian military techniques, struck out of the east. In 612 B.C. the forces of the Medes and the Chaldeans destroyed the Assyrian capital at Nineveh. Assyrian power vanished immediately, leaving her empire at the mercy of her many foes.

The Near East did not lament the passing of Assyria. However, her bad reputation should not conceal her contributions to the history of the Near East. She broke new ground in trying to solve the complicated problem of creating a single state composed of many different peoples. Her attempt to create a centralized monarchy, centering around a single ruler, as the common factor in the lives of different people was destined to be imitated by others. Assyria had wiped out many artificial political boundaries that kept small groups at sword's point. She had at least briefly imposed a beneficial peace on the Near East, protecting it for several centuries against barbarians who might have destroyed its civilization had they succeeded in seizing control.

Economically the Assyrian regime had significant results. The Assyrians themselves added very little to Near Eastern economy, remaining simple farmers and warriors. Their own prosperity depended largely on plunder. However, the Assyrians encouraged their subjects to trade and assisted them by breaking down barriers against the movement of goods. People like the Aramaeans and the Babylonians seized this opportunity gladly, and through their efforts goods flowed freely across the Near East, and technical skills associated with the production of goods for trade spread widely among peoples still technologically backward.

In cultural activities the Assyrians also made a notable contribution. Their efforts were not creative, since they were usually content to imitate the work of others, especially the Babylonians, but their imitations resulted in the continuation of cultural activity. This can be seen best in the fields of architecture and sculpture. Assyrian kings were avid builders, constructing the great cities of Nineveh, Sargonsburg, and Ashur as monuments of their power and glory. In these cities Babylonian architectural styles were followed closely and thus kept alive. The temples and palaces were decorated with massive sculptured pieces and with excellent stone reliefs. Again traditions from the past were vigorously applied, assuring the Near East of a new period of artistic glory. In the field of literature the Assyrians devoted a great deal of effort to the task of collecting and copying Babylonian works. One of Assyria's kings, Ashurbanipal, built a huge library at Nineveh as a repository for thousands of cuneiform tablets copied from Babylonian sources. Most of the present knowledge of Babylonian literature was gained through the copying done by Assyrians. They were especially skilled at compiling annals recounting their innumerable military campaigns, thereby making an important contribution to the art of history writing. Their religion was likewise strongly colored by borrowings from Babylonia. The great state god of Assyria, Ashur, was very similar to the Babylonian Marduk. Assyrian rituals, prayers, and priesthoods are almost indistinguishable from those of the Babylonians. In all these ways the Assyrians kept alive some of the most precious cultural traditions in the Near East, and their conquests helped to

ASSYRIAN RELIEFS. These casts of reliefs now in the British Museum portray typical activities of the Assyrian armies. In the top panel an Assyrian king and his soldiers are shown attacking a city; below, the king receives prisoners of war. The reliefs illustrate the skill of Assyrian artists in portraying the details of everyday life and have proved invaluable to historians studying Assyrian society. (*Courtesy of The Metropolitan Museum of Art*)

spread those traditions throughout the region.

2. Successors of Assyria, 612–550 B.C.

Assyria's sudden collapse opened a brief but spirited era of competition for the spoils of her empire, and this struggle ended when it produced another empire builder, Persia, who crushed the other contenders for Assyrian power.

Egypt was one power that seemed destined to benefit by the fall of Assyria. Foreign rule had again had the effect of uniting Egypt under a single pharaoh, Psammetichus (also known as Psamtik; reigned, 663–609 B.C.), who founded the twenty-sixth dynasty. Internal order, prosperity, and international prestige briefly characterized Egypt's situation. However, Egypt was incapable of meeting the needs of the new era. Her pharaohs had to rely on foreign mercenaries (chiefly Greeks) to man the armies. These troops caused trouble within Egypt, being thoroughly hated by the antiforeign Egyptians. Egyptian artists and writers, too intent on worshipping the past to detect and reflect newer trends in Near Eastern society, failed to produce anything new that would establish Egyptian reputation abroad. The priests were even more reactionary, using religion as a means of resisting necessary changes. Old age had gripped Egypt, making her incapable of facing new problems. She failed to capitalize on Assyria's destruction and was unable to check the rise of Persia, falling to Persian armies with almost no struggle in 526 B.C.

In Asia Minor the small kingdom of Lydia, which first emerged after the fall of the Hittites, was the chief beneficiary of Assyria's fall, and Lydia quickly established control over nearly all of Asia Minor. The rapid rise of Lydia was especially significant in Greek history, since Lydia lay as a link between the Near East and Greece. During the reign of Croesus (560–546 B.C.), the greatest Lydian king, many Greeks living in Asia Minor were ruled by the Lydians.

However, Lydian power was shaky, succumbing in 546 B.C. to one blow by Persia.

Still another contender for the Assyrian power was Media. The Medes, living east of the Zagros Mountains, had long been restless dependents of Assyria. When Assyria began to weaken, the Medes furnished most of the armed might to destroy Assyria. Once Assyria was defeated, the Medes seized control of a large part of the northern areas of the empire and built up a vast state in the Iranian plateau area. However, the state was poorly organized. One of the Median vassal princes, Cyrus of Persia, succeeded in deposing the Median king and laying successful claim to old Median territory.

The most spectacular of all the successor states of Assyria was the Chaldean Empire. The Chaldeans were a Semitic people who had entered Babylonia while it was under Assyrian rule. When Assyria began to decline, the Chaldean princes led a revolt, representing themselves as champions of ancient Babylonian civilization. Once Assyria was destroyed, the Chaldean princes seized some of the most valuable parts of the conquered territory. Under the one great Chaldean ruler, Nebuchadnezzar II (reigned 604–562 B.C.), all of Syria-Palestine was joined with the Tigris-Euphrates Valley in a single empire. Among the victims of Nebuchadnezzar's conquests was the Hebrew kingdom of Judah, which had managed to keep its independence in the great days of Assyria by paying tribute. Jerusalem was destroyed in 586 B.C. and many of its citizens were carried off to Babylonia as captives.

Nebuchadnezzar not only prided himself as a conqueror, but also acted as a champion of culture. He rebuilt the city of Babylon as his capital, making it one of the most spectacular cities of the ancient world, highlighted by its great palace and its hanging gardens; the old Babylonian religious practices were restored; and attempts were made to arouse interest in literature and the arts. Nonetheless, Nebuchadnezzar's empire was not strong. It was guilty of worshipping the past, and its military resources were limited.

Nebuchadnezzar's heirs were weak and little interested in political problems, and when the Persians captured Babylon in 539 B.C., the Chaldean state collapsed immediately.

3. The Persian Empire, 550–323 B.C.

The final victory in the competition to succeed Assyria fell to a people who hardly seemed in the running—the Persians. The Persians were of Indo-European origin, their ancestors having migrated to the Near East about 2000 B.C. from north of the Black Sea. The original Persians settled in the barren plateau of Iran, becoming simple farmers and herders. For many centuries they maintained their own political independence, although they eventually recognized the overlordship of the Medes, who were closely akin to them in language and culture. In 550 B.C. the Persians suddenly reversed this situation. Their king, Cyrus, overthrew the Median king and began to call himself "king of the Medes and the Persians." This event launched the Persians on their spectacular career as masters of the Near East.

Cyrus's accession to power resulted immediately in a rapid extension of Persia's boundaries. Cyrus (550–529 B.C.) and his successors, Cambyses (529–522 B.C.) and Darius (521–486 B.C.), succeeded in destroying all other powers in the Near East. Cyrus was the most successful conqueror. His first victory was over Lydia, the key to control of all Asia Minor. He then conquered the Chaldean Empire, which made him master of the Tigris-Euphrates Valley and of Syria and Palestine. During his last years he subdued various nations in eastern Iran, pushing Persian power to the borders of India. Cambyses conquered Egypt. Darius pushed Persian power into Europe by conquering a territory west of the Black Sea. However, his expansion into Europe was checked by the Greeks in 490 B.C. in a war we shall describe later. When Darius died in 486 B.C., the Persian Empire stretched from the Aegean and Mediterranean seas to India and from the mountains bounding the Near East on the north to far south in

the Nile Valley. This was one of the largest empires ever created.

The first Persian rulers were intelligent statesmen as well as conquerors. Their statesmanship laid the basis for sound government of their huge empire. Cyrus established a good reputation for Persian rule by practicing a policy of tolerance toward defeated peoples. He avoided slaughtering captured kings. He always showed a deep respect for the religions of his victims and earned himself a hero's role by allowing the Hebrew exiles to return to Jerusalem to rebuild the temple of Yahweh. These actions convinced most peoples in the Near East that the Persians did not intend to continue the terrorism and brutality of the Assyrians.

Darius was the most constructive of the Persian statesmen. Borrowing from old ideas and practices in government and adapting them to the new situation, he laid the basis for one of the great political systems of all history. He established himself as absolute ruler, taking the title "king of kings." In this capacity he claimed full authority to make laws, to judge, and to command the services of his subjects. At his court in the capital cities of Ecbatana, Susa, and Persepolis he created a magnificent court etiquette intended to impress upon everyone that he was lord of the earth. He surrounded his position with powerful religious sanctions, claiming that he was the representative of the great Persian god, Ahura-Mazda, selected to rule all men. Darius gathered around him numerous officials and servants, assigning to each a specific task. These servants, usually of Median or Persian origin, became a kind of aristocracy fanatically devoted to the maintenance of Persian power.

Darius's greatest political innovation lay in the techniques he devised for ruling his widely scattered possessions inhabited by so many different peoples. He divided his empire into twenty large districts, called satrapies. Over each he appointed a governor, usually a Persian and often a member of the royal family, who was given power sufficient to make him a king in his own right. The governors, called satraps, were removable at the will of the great king and were held strictly accountable for the administration of their districts. Darius and his successors made it their main business to supervise carefully the conduct of the satraps. An excellent road system was developed binding the satrapies to the capital, and a constant stream of correspondence flowed to and from the royal court, carried by a royal postal system. Periodically Darius sent out inspectors to investigate the administration and report to the king. Spies in the pay of the king swarmed through the empire to keep him informed. Contingents of the royal army under trusted commanders were garrisoned in strategic spots, ready to strike down a rebellious governor. Careful records of taxation were kept at the capital as a means of accounting for each governor's administration. By these methods Darius managed to create twenty semi-independent governments and still keep an eye on each in a fashion that co-ordinated and unified policy over the whole empire.

In the final analysis the armed forces of Darius were the key to his power. The Persian army was built around a corps of professional soldiers recruited from the Persians and the Medes. These elite soldiers, sometimes called the Immortals, were given special treatment and were usually fanatically devoted to the king. The army was rounded out by contingents supplied by the conquered peoples as part of their obligations to their king. The quality of these levies left much to be desired; often they deserted at the height of a battle. But they could be recruited in such vast numbers that they made the Persian armies awe-inspiring. The Persians also commanded excellent naval forces, composed largely of hired Phoenician, Egyptian, and Greek ships and crews. In view of this armed might very few peoples were willing to challenge the Persian king. In a real sense peace reigned within his boundaries.

Darius's imperial system endured about 150 years. The history of Persia after his death contains very few events worthy of our attention. There were wars with outsiders. The Persians seldom won these wars; consequently, their empire did not increase. On the other hand they did not lose much territory. Rebellions occurred within the empire, only to be smashed eventually by the superior power of the king. Perhaps the most significant aspect of this period was a slow rotting of Persian royal power. The Persian royal family declined in vigor and political intelligence. This was a fatal blow because the empire depended so greatly on the ability of one man. The court became corrupt, torn by conspiracy and intrigue among the friends and officials of the king. Several later Persian kings spent more time trying to survive the plots of their many wives and children and their ambitious servants than administering their empire. The satraps could not resist the temptation to overthrow the king. Often they raised a rebellion by putting themselves forward as champions of subject peoples within the empire or by promising great rewards to anyone who would follow them against the king.[1] The only protection against these rebellions was a rigid control over the satraps, which the Persian kings were unable to maintain. With the passage of time the Persian army declined in power, still another fatal weakness. By the middle of the fourth century B.C. all that was needed to destroy Persian power was a strong attack from the outside. This attack was soon forthcoming, led by a Macedonian king, Alexander the Great, whose sledge-hammer blows gave him possession of the whole Persian Empire before his untimely death in 323 B.C.

The Persians, emerging suddenly to mastery of the Near East and confronted constantly with the problem of holding their empire together, devoted most of their talents to administrative and military affairs. As a consequence, their contributions to the cultural development in the Near East

[1] A good example of this is recounted in the Greek historian Xenophon's *Anabasis*, where the harrowing adventures of ten thousand Greeks who joined a Persian satrap, Xerxes, to march from Asia Minor to Ecbatana are described.

were not spectacular. In general they played a role similar to that of the Assyrians, borrowing from the cultural treasure that already existed in the Near East. They utilized already-existent written languages, especially Aramaean, for administrative purposes. The Persian kings were lavish in their patronage of the arts, the results showing chiefly in the royal palaces built at Susa, Persepolis, and Ecbatana. The kings continued the Assyrian practice of commissioning artists to render in stone pictorial records of their military exploits. The Persians welcomed in their cities men who were schooled in the literary and scientific traditions of the past, and thereby helped to keep alive the ancient traditions of the Near East. One of the most admirable characteristics of Persian rule was the tolerant attitude held by the Persians toward the many different cultural elements in their empire.

The Persians avoided any attempts to smother local differences, and even lent their aid to the support of local institutions as long as their subjects refrained from political revolt. Under Persian rule the Near East remained culturally alive. This condition was especially important in the history of Western civilization because the Persian world was the world that the Greeks encountered and from whence many Near Eastern ideas and institutions were carried westward.

In spite of their lack of brilliance in cultural affairs the Persians did make one outstanding contribution to Near Eastern history. They created a new religion, Zoroastrianism, and aided in the spread of some of its ideas. The origins of Zoroastrianism are difficult to discern, since the religion developed over a long period of time. Its beginnings seem certainly to have rested on

RUINS OF THE PERSIAN ROYAL AUDIENCE HALL. These ruins at Persepolis represent what was once the governmental seat of some of the most powerful rulers that ever lived, the great Persian kings. The magnificent stairway in the foreground led into a great hall where the kings received subjects from all over their vast empire and where majestic rites in honor of the "king of kings" occurred regularly. The height of the pillars indicates the size of the audience hall. Note the numerous reliefs used to decorate every available stone surface. (*Courtesy, The Oriental Institute, The University of Chicago*)

the original religion held by the Persians before they became the rulers of the Near East. Early Persian religion centered around the worship of several gods who represented forces of nature, including especially a god of the sky and a god of fire. Along with the chief gods the ancient Persians believed in innumerable lesser spirits who were capable of doing both good and evil. A complicated ritual, including sacrifices, magic, and prayer, had developed as a means of winning the favor of the gods and the spirits. A group of priests, called Magi, had developed and played a prominent role in the early religious life of the Persians.

One man, Zoroaster, was responsible for a radical change in this religion. Although most of the facts about his career have become so clouded with legend that it is nearly impossible to speak with certainty, it seems likely that Zoroaster lived in the seventh or sixth century before Christ. According to tradition he spent the early part of his life in contemplation in the desert, finally receiving a revelation from one of the gods the Persians had worshipped for a long time, Ahura-Mazda, the god of the sky. Zoroaster then began a career as a preacher, trying to win converts to his new ideas. At first he had no success, but toward the end of his life he won the support of at least one Persian king and of numerous disciples. The new religion had been launched on a long and significant career.

Zoroaster's exact teachings have also been blurred with the passing of centuries, new ideas being added constantly. The basic teachings of his religion are contained in a sacred work called the Zend-Avesta, a book compiled over many centuries. In some parts it reflects Zoroaster's own teachings, but most of its material was added much later. In spite of this it seems clear that Zoroaster himself preached the basic ideas associated with his religion. He repudiated the worship of many gods, and in place of polytheism he insisted that his followers worship Ahura-Mazda, whom he portrayed as the creator of all things and the embodiment of the perfect good. Zoroaster, a monotheist,

was comparable to some of the Hebrew prophets who at about the same time were propounding similar ideas about Yahweh. Zoroaster taught that, opposed to the good deity, there was a diabolical force of evil called Ahriman. Ahura-Mazda and Ahriman were engaged in a struggle for the universe. Eventually, at a final day of judgment, Ahura-Mazda would win. In the meantime the war between the good and the evil forces would rage. The conflict extended into the soul of each man, demanding of him that he choose to fight for good or evil. On the day of judgment, when Ahura-Mazda won over Ahriman, men would be judged on the basis of their choice; the good would be rewarded with eternal happiness, while the evil would suffer untold misery.

By emphasizing the goodness of Ahura-Mazda and the evil of Ahriman, Zoroaster made man's religious duty clear. He insisted that man could win favor in the eyes of Ahura-Mazda only by being good. Exhorting his followers to cease their ancient sacrifices and magical practices, Zoroaster imposed on them a vigorous moral code: men must tell the truth, keep their vows, obey their rulers, help their fellow men, and perform their daily labor as well as possible. He set forth a clear-cut concept of sin, spelled out in specific terms. Certainly none of the religions within the empire the Persians were soon to rule, with the exception of Judaism, asked so much of an ethical nature of its followers. Zoroaster's insistence on the worship of one almighty, all-good god, and on high moral standards, was a radical departure from the usual religions in the Near East.

Zoroastrianism took firm hold among the Persians and the Medes after the prophet's death. Especially significant was the acceptance of the new religion by the Persian kings from the reign of Darius onward. The Persian government made no attempt to force its subjects to accept Zoroastrianism, but the new creed received a strong boost because it was the official state religion. Its success perhaps had a bad effect upon the purity of some of the ideas of Zoroaster. The Magi were early converts to the new religion. Under their influence a great deal of ritualism that Zoroaster had condemned was revived, a ritualism that sometimes obscured the moral precepts of Zoroaster. Many of the old gods reappeared in the official religion, definitely compromising the monotheism of the prophet, and a growing emphasis came to be placed upon associating all things of this world with evil, only the spiritual things being good. This movement tended to belittle the practice of virtue in the everyday world and to emphasize withdrawal into some form of secluded life. Increasing hosts of angels and devils were placed in the camps of Ahura-Mazda and Ahriman to assist in the incessant war for souls, a development that encouraged superstition.

The conquest of the Persians by Alexander and his Greeks represented a setback for Zoroastrianism. In spite of this and later defeats the religion has survived until today, when it has adherents, called Parsees, in India and Iran. During the twenty-five centuries of its existence it has not only satisfied its adherents, but it has powerfully affected other religions, including Judaism, Christianity, and Mohammedanism. Especially influential has been the teaching about the struggle between good and evil, which has become imbedded in most of the major religions of the world.

The collapse of the Persian Empire under the blows of Alexander the Great rang down the curtain on a brilliant episode in the history of the ancient Near East. Alexander's victory represented the greater vitality of a new way of life that had arisen from the barren soil of the Greek Peninsula and the seas surrounding Greece. However, the peoples of the Near East had supplied an important heritage to fertilize the minds and guide the actions of the new peoples emerging to take over the cultural leadership of the Mediterranean world. They had perfected techniques of government, developed technical skills in agriculture, trade, and industry, created styles in art and literature, and probed the mysteries of the universe in religion.

SUGGESTED READING

A. T. Olmstead, *History of Assyria* (1923). A standard work, long and full of colorful details about the Assyrians. The book tends to glorify the Assyrians a little too much, but it is still the only complete history of their empire.

Georges Contenau, *Everyday Life in Babylonia and Assyria*, tr. by K. R. and A. R. Maxwell-Hyslop (1954). A well-written, well-illustrated description of daily life among all classes of people in Assyria-Babylonia in about the eighth century B.C. The book is full of details about matters that often do not find their way into history books.

L. Delaporte, *Mesopotamia: The Babylonian and Assyrian Civilization*, tr. by V. Gordon Childe (1925), pp. 239–359. The last part of this book supplies a good view of Assyrian institutions, customs, and arts, as well as a brief summary of Assyrian history.

* A. T. Olmstead, *History of the Persian Empire* (Phoenix). Published in a hardback edition in 1948. An extensive, brilliantly written account of Persian history. The book requires careful reading but will provide a sound basis for judging the importance of the Persians in world history.

Clément Huart, *Ancient Persia and Iranian Civilization*, tr. by M. R. Dobie (1927). A scholarly description of the chief features of Persian civilization. Presents an especially clear picture of the Persian system of government in the various stages of its development.

Maneckji Nusservanji Dhalla, *History of Zoroastrianism* (1938). A full treatment of Zoroastrianism from its origin to the present by a high priest of the Parsees, who are modern Zoroastrians living in India. The book is especially good in discussing Zoroastrian doctrines.

SECTION 2

———◆———

Graeco-Roman Civilization,

1200 B.C.—A.D. *200*

While the civilizations of the Near East were reaching maturity under the political sway of the Assyrians and the Persians, a new civilization was emerging in the lands around the Aegean Sea, especially in the Greek Peninsula. The new civilization began to emerge about 1200 B.C. and reached its most creative phase in the fifth century B.C., when the city-states of Greece produced literary, artistic, philosophical, and scientific works that departed radically from those of Near Eastern culture. The great intellectual and artistic outburst of fifth-century Greece was nourished in a political and social order that was likewise revolutionary.

From its Aegean center the new civilization exerted a powerful influence over non-Greek peoples. In the latter part of the fourth century the Greeks, led by Alexander the Great and his Macedonian soldiers, conquered the old centers of civilization in the Near East and pushed onward to India. All across this vast stretch Greek ideas made a powerful impression, and in the territory bordering on the eastern end of the Mediterranean Greek ideas became supreme. In the third century Greek ideas began to penetrate the Western Mediterranean world, where Rome was emerging as a world power. The Greeks were eventually absorbed politically in the Roman state, but Greek civilization influenced almost every corner of the Roman Empire. From about 200 B.C. until A.D. 200 Greek ideas, propagated and enlarged upon by Romans, penetrated wide areas in Western Europe and North Africa while retaining their predominance around the eastern end of the Mediterranean. Not until the third century after Christ did the ideals shaped in Greece centuries earlier finally begin to lose their force and suffer from competing ideals.

CHAPTER 5

The Origins and Development of the
Greek City-State Polity

G RAECO-ROMAN civilization originated in a group of small, independent communities around the Aegean Sea. No one can understand that civilization until he understands the nature of these communities, which spurred their inhabitants to creative activities radically different from anything preceding. However, none of the city-states sprang full-grown from nothing. Each was a product of long experimentation.

1. Physical Environment

Certain geographical features of Greece had a strong influence on Greek life. Greece is predominantly a land of mountains, peninsulas, and bays. These features divide Greece into many small pockets and corners of tillable land, creating barriers against political unity and encouraging the development of isolated communities. The mountainous terrain provided poor soil, sentencing the Greeks to poverty unless they could discover other sources of wealth. Theirs was not to be a life tied to the eternal cycle of a flooding river and rich harvests. Only the use of wits and the development of new talents would permit an escape from the poor soil. But an opportunity was offered by the seas that surrounded Greece and blended into the land in a thousand bays and gulfs. These seas, especially the

Aegean, the Black, and the Mediterranean, were blessed with excellent climate and convenient ports, making navigation easy even for primitive sailors. The exploitation of the seas was the making of the Greeks, giving them access to wealth and putting them in touch with other centers of civilization from which they could get new ideas.

2. The Origins of the City-States

The foundations of the Greek city-states were laid during the long period from 2000 to 800 B.C. These beginnings were the result of a meeting of three different influences. Long before 2000 B.C. the Greek Peninsula and the Aegean Islands were populated by a native people who had advanced to a Neolithic stage of culture. Beginning about 2000 B.C. and continuing until nearly 1000 B.C. Indo-Europeans swept into this area from the north and imposed their rule on the older population. The invaders established small kingdoms, ruled by tribal chiefs and a few heads of families. About the time when the Indo-Europeans began to occupy Greece, powerful cultural influences entered the area from the island of Crete. A brilliant civilization had emerged there about 2500 B.C., centering around thriving trading centers. Cretan art, technical skills, religion, and social customs were far superior to those existing on the Greek mainland. The primitive Greeks, especially the new Indo-Europeans, were eager to imitate them.

At first it seemed that the barbarian Greeks would make a rapid transition to a higher civilization. By 1500 B.C. several communities in the Greek Peninsula had imitated Cretan civilization so well that they had become important centers of culture. However, the Greeks were not capable of sustaining their borrowed finery. Mycenaean civilization, as historians have named the version of Cretan civilization that developed in the Greek Peninsula and the Aegean Islands, slowly declined, especially after 1400 B.C., when marauders from the Greek Peninsula attacked Crete and destroyed the source of the borrowed civilization. The final blow came when the last great wave of Indo-Europeans swept into Greece about 1200 B.C. This invasion was followed by a dark age that lasted until about 800 B.C.

We know almost nothing about events in Greece from 1200 to 800 B.C. Yet fundamental developments certainly occurred. The Indo-European leaders of society gave up their attempt to imitate a foreign civilization. A new way of life emerged, one based on a combination of ancient Indo-European institutions and of ideas borrowed from Cretan civilization and from Asia Minor, where influences from the great civilizations of the Near East were strong. By 800 B.C. the new way of life had taken deep roots. Its chief features can best be seen in two magnificent epic poems, the *Iliad* and the *Odyssey*, composed by Homer about 800 B.C.

Homer's poems describe a simple agricultural society dominated by an aristocracy of warriors. The aristocrats owed their dominance to their ownership of most of the land and to their position as heads of large families. The aristocrats with their followings grouped themselves together in petty kingdoms, each ruled by a king who was respected chiefly for his ability as a warrior and who conducted the simple affairs of government with the advice of the nobles. In this society the lower classes had a definite status as freemen and citizens of the community. Sometimes they were even called upon to voice their opinion when decisions of great importance to the community had to be faced.

Life in each small kingdom was dominated by agricultural, military, and family interests. However, already there was emerging a center that served as the focus of political, social, and economic life in each community. That center was a town within the boundaries of each kingdom. These towns served as fortresses, residences for the kings and their warriors, market places, and temple sites, and every citizen, rich or poor, found something in the town that served his interests. Thus the citizens of each tiny kingdom began drawing together around the city, which served as a center of common life. Such groupings were small enough so that citizens could know problems at first hand and could become acquainted with most of their fellow citizens. This intimacy gave each citizen a sense of concern for other citizens and a feeling of belonging. It bred in all a pride of community that spurred them to try to better it. Slowly the fundamental bases of the Greek city-states were being laid by 800 B.C. The history of each of these city-states after 800 B.C. is a story of the increasing identification of each citizen with a city.

3. The Expansion of the Greeks and the Economic Revolution, 800–500 B.C.

Until 800 B.C. most Greek communities faced no graver problem than attacks by other Greek kingdoms or competition for power among the nobles. After that date a heavier burden began to trouble most communities. Poverty, inflicted on the Greeks by their barren soil, began to cause social tension. The advantage in the competition for limited wealth naturally lay with the ruling aristocrats. Increasingly they turned to oppression of the lower classes and to an abuse of political power. Greek society

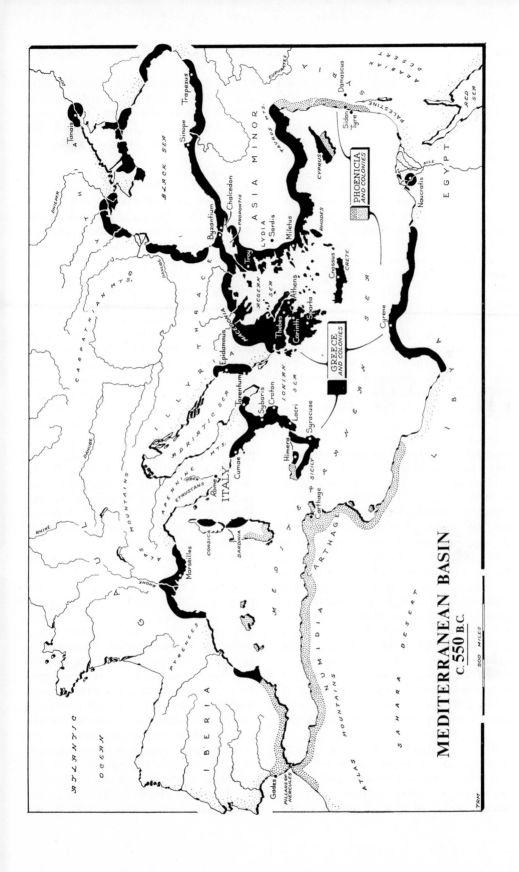

MEDITERRANEAN BASIN
c. 550 B.C.

seemed headed for the kind of order usual in the Near East—the few exploiting the many.

The pressure of poverty and land shortage evoked from the Greeks a saving burst of energy. Bold leaders and willing followers began to migrate from Greece in search of new homes. For three centuries after 800 B.C. Greek settlers established new communities almost everywhere around the shores of the Aegean, Black, and Mediterranean seas. New city-states, modeled after those the settlers left behind in Greece, sprang up everywhere, marking the first important extension of the Greek pattern of life beyond Greece.

Overseas colonization had a revolutionary effect on Greek society, especially on its economy. Although they originally ventured abroad in search of new farmland, the Greeks soon saw opportunities for acquiring wealth other than by farming. Many began to trade, reaping a fortune such as the Greek soil would never produce, and by 500 B.C. Greek traders were the most active merchants in the Mediterranean. Trading, in turn, created a demand for products to exchange, causing other Greeks to turn to manufacturing, thus transforming some cities into teeming productive centers. Here was still another way to escape grinding poverty. Even the old agricultural system could not survive. Many Greeks realized that it was unprofitable to try to produce food supplies on Greece's rocky soil when grains could be brought into Greece from areas better suited to grain raising. These enterprising individuals turned to crops promising greater profits, especially grapes and olives. Large estates began to appear devoted to farming for profit instead of for simple subsistence. Slowly the center of Greek economic life shifted to the market place, signifying that to nearly every Greek the city was more vital than ever.

The social structure of Greece changed rapidly under the impact of the economic revolution. The landowning nobles were challenged as leaders of Greek society by wealthy traders. Many small farmers, ruined

by the new capitalistic farming, were forced either to accept a role as day laborers on the large estates or to move to the cities. This change dissolved ancient family ties and raised new problems of controlling and protecting those torn loose. The colonies offered an escape for the discontented, making them harder to control. Slavery became more prevalent since it proved profitable on large estates. The economic revolution thus raised social questions affecting every element in Greek society.

The Greeks met these new problems by a vigorous outburst of political activity, bringing about radical changes in most cities. In essence these innovations meant that new and more powerful bonds were created, binding the total life of each citizen to the community. These changes increased in each citizen's mind a sense of dependence on, responsibility for, and pride in the city-state. By 500 B.C. most Greeks would have felt that life was not worth living unless they could be members of a city-state, look to it for defense of their interests, and participate in its activities.

Every city-state went its own way in solving its problems, each ending with its own peculiar political system and social order. However, all passed through certain general steps. It will serve our purposes best first to describe these steps in general terms and then to study a few representative Greek city-states.

As we have noted previously, in 800 B.C. most cities were ruled by kings sharing power with a small group of wealthy, highborn nobles. After 800 B.C. this conservative, aristocratic element fought desperately to protect its monopoly of power against the new classes produced by the economic revolution. Only under the most severe pressure would the aristocrats make any concessions to non-noble citizens, concessions that were seldom sufficient to meet the social and economic needs resulting from colonization and the growth of trade and industry.

Usually revolutions were necessary to unseat the nobles and to remodel the governments. Revolutionary leaders, called tyrants, spearheaded the revolts against the nobles, using force to seize control of the city governments. Tyrants were often men of noble origin, and many of them had acquired great wealth as traders and were impatient with the agricultural outlook of the ruling class. The real secret of their success, however, lay in their willingness to promote a program designed to satisfy the poor, socially oppressed citizens. This concern for the lower classes and willingness to advance their cause, contrasting so completely with the viewpoint of Egyptian and Babylonian leaders, was a unique feature of Greek political life. Probably it is explained by the fact that patriotic leaders, genuinely concerned about the fate of their cities, realized that steps must be taken to retain the allegiance and the services of valuable artisans, sailors, and shopkeepers who might otherwise flee to where they could enjoy better treatment. As the economic revolution progressed, it became obvious that Greek cities could not flourish without an active commercial and industrial class, free to exploit trading opportunities wherever they existed and willing to contribute to the enrichment of each city. Opportunities in the Greek colonies, where new citizens were always in demand, offered a temptation to the oppressed to leave their old cities. The trading "frontier" was thus a vital force advancing the cause of equality and democracy in most Greek cities.

Once in power, tyrants struck at the wealthy and tried to create new opportunities for the poor. Nobles were taxed heavily, deprived of part of their land, and sometimes driven into exile. Huge sums of money were spent beautifying cities, thereby increasing the people's pride in the city and furnishing jobs for the poor. The tyrants exerted every effort to increase trade and industry, and, although they sometimes used brutal methods, they performed an invaluable service. They broke the power monopoly of the nobles and increased the allegiance of the common citizen toward the city by making him realize that his economic position was dependent on it.

Rule by tyrants was brief in most cities, chiefly because tyrants seized power illegally and were incapable of making their hold permanent. Usually the aristocrats took the lead in ousting them. However, the constructive work of the tyrants was seldom undone. In some cases the aristocrats retained power but recognized the reforms made by tyrants. In the most progressive city-states the end of tyranny was accompanied by radical changes in the government that allowed the citizens to take control of the city-state. With all citizens entitled to participate in the government the last knot binding them to the city-state was tied. Their whole existence was now bound up in civic life.

4. Athens

The history of Athens will serve as an example of the long process whereby a collection of people was transformed into a city-state. At an early date Attica was inhabited by Indo-European invaders who settled down in many small villages, a single clan perhaps in each village, with the head of the clan exercising a powerful influence in his own village. Eventually the many villages coalesced into a single unit centering around the city of Athens, and a monarch emerged as the head of all the peoples. This king was assisted by an advisory council called the Areopagus, made up of the heads of the clans. The population was divided into four tribes, each consisting of a number of clans lumped together for military and religious purposes. This primitive central government, however, played only a small part in the lives of the Athenians, most matters still being handled by the clans.

About 750 B.C. the nobles in the Areopagus began an assault on the power of the king of Athens, and within a century they had abolished monarchy. In the process they inaugurated changes of great importance for the future of Athens. Elective officials, including *archons* (for civil affairs) and *polemarchs* (for military leadership), chosen to serve for one year, replaced the king.

Although at first the nobles monopolized both the right to vote and the right to hold office, an important principle had been established. The heads of state were responsible to others. The nobles also opened the ranks of the army to a much larger number of citizens. Since techniques of warfare were changing from the use of chariots to that of infantry, it was necessary to find more troops. To meet this need, all citizens were classified according to wealth derived from land. The richest classes served as knights, those of medium property as foot soldiers, and the poor (called *thetes*) performed menial tasks in war. Only the rich knights had full political rights. Nevertheless, at least in a military sense, the lower classes now had a more significant place in the community.

Despite their important contributions the aristocrats were increasingly guilty of intolerable abuses of their power. They monopolized landownership, they forced many citizens into slavery for non-payment of debts, and, as the seventh century B.C. drew to an end, Athenian citizenship was rapidly coming to mean misery and oppression. This situation was corrected by the wisdom of a few aristocratic leaders who seemed to sense that Athens could not flourish when a privileged few ruled many slaves. Probably the growing dependence of Athens on overseas expansion in this age of colonization and trade forced the aristocrats to recognize the importance of merchants and artisans. Their solution was a gradual governmental reform designed to safeguard all citizens and to create new opportunities for them, especially in trading and industrial pursuits.

The first notable reformer was Draco, archon in 621 B.C. He codified the laws of Athens, thereby making it more difficult for aristocratic judges to oppress the citizens in the courts. Previously law had been customary, giving judges a chance to "remember" it in a way that benefited the aristocrats.

A much more significant reformer was Solon, archon in 594 B.C. Although an aristocrat by birth, Solon, as a result of his experience as a trader, had a much broader vision than most of his fellow aristocrats. He was convinced that Athens would fail unless political steps were taken to curb the exploitation of the lower classes and to discover new sources of wealth. Consequently he undertook to enact legislation that would protect the interests of the lower classes and give them the power to curb the activities of the ruling nobility.

As a lawgiver Solon made it illegal to enslave any citizen for debt and freed many who were already enslaved. He carried through important legislation reducing the power the family had over an individual, thereby allowing many citizens a larger degree of freedom. Steps were taken to promote the growth of trade and industry, and an increasing number of Athenians found ways of earning a livelihood outside of agriculture. This was a real boon to those who had been ruined by the poor soil of Attica or the greed of noble landowners.

In reorganizing the government Solon made no effort to end the rule of the nobles, but he did try to give all the citizens means of checking the conduct of noble rulers. As the chief policy-making body he instituted a Council of 400, made up of citizens chosen from the noble class and from the citizens with enough property to qualify for infantry service in the army. This new body replaced the old Areopagus in most important activities. To stop the abuses in the courts, Solon established a new court, the *Heliaea*, which acted as a tribunal of appeals for all cases decided in the regular courts. This court consisted of a large jury of citizens drawn from all classes, including the thetes. By a majority vote the jurors drawn from all ranks of the citizenry could override decisions made in the regular courts, usually dominated by aristocrats. Such a veto ended the monopoly of power long exercised by the nobles and forced them to show greater concern for the interests of other citizens.

Important as they were, Solon's reforms quieted Athens only temporarily. Now that the nobles had to listen to the citizens, they sought to manipulate them by forming parties that tried to gain control of the state and then to pursue party aims at the expense of other groups. Party strife encouraged skillful leaders to think of establishing their power on a permanent basis. Thus Athens proceeded toward tyranny. Her first tyrant was a nobleman, Pisistratus, who won the support of the impoverished farmers of Attica and the commercial interests of the city. This latter group had grown steadily in numbers and wealth since Solon's time. Increasingly the prosperity of Athens depended upon its success in developing new markets and in producing manufactured goods for sale abroad. Using a combination of force and rabble-rousing, Pisistratus seized power in 546 B.C. After his death in 527 B.C. his regime was carried on by his sons until 510 B.C. Pisistratus made no attempt to change the form of government established by Solon. His importance lay in the economic changes he introduced to aid those elements of the population who had found it difficult to exercise their rights because of poverty. He forced many great landowners to surrender part of their land, which was then divided among the small farmers, giving them economic independence. He encouraged the commercial development of Athens by building a strong navy and by sending out colonizing parties. Public works projects, aimed at beautifying Athens, supplied employment for the poor of the city. To many citizens the activities of the city-state, especially in trade and colonization, now had a direct bearing on their struggles to earn a livelihood.

Tyrannical rule, so beneficial to the poor and to the commercial interests, was eventually overthrown, chiefly through the efforts of its aristocratic foes. However, the aristocrats never had an opportunity to reassert their control. Another reformer, Cleisthenes (archon in 508 B.C.), took the initiative in completing what Solon and Pisistratus had foreshadowed. He instituted changes that gave final political power to the whole citizen body.

Cleisthenes's most important reform consisted of eliminating the family as a controlling factor in political life. Up to his time all political activity on the part of an Athenian citizen had been based on his membership in one of the four ancient tribes, which were made up of clans and dominated by heads of families. Cleisthenes abolished the political functions of the old tribes. As a substitute he divided all Attica into approximately one hundred territorial units called *demes*. All freemen living in each deme were registered as citizens, family connections making no difference. The demes were then combined into ten new units called tribes. Each tribe was composed of demes from various parts of Attica, so that each tribe contained a cross-section of the population—farmers and traders, rich and poor, lumped together in voting units that would serve as the basis for political life.

Cleisthenes then rearranged the main organs of government to fit the new tribal organization. The Council of 400 was replaced by a Council of 500, fifty citizens of each tribe being selected by lot to serve annual terms in this body. No one could sit on this council more than twice in a lifetime, which meant that over the years a large number of citizens had a chance to serve on the guiding body of the city-state, supervising all activities of the government. Even the lowliest citizen might have his chance to participate in the formulation of foreign policy, the making of laws, and the disposal of state money. The Council of 500, however, did not have the final authority. Cleisthenes entrusted that power to the popular assembly, made up of all male citizens voting by tribes. This body, called together at least once a month, decided upon every law or policy presented by the Council of 500. Thus the citizen body, consisting of perhaps 30,000 or 40,000 males, had the ultimate power in the state. The assembly elected the archons, who were the administrative heads of the state but were powerless to act without popular approval. The citizens of the state were further entitled to participate in governing the state through the Heliaea, which remained as Solon had constituted it. Finally Cleisthenes assured popular control over the government by introducing the practice of ostracism. Each year the popular assembly was permitted to cast a vote to decide whether any citizen was dangerous to the state. If a majority of the assembly so decided, that citizen was forced to leave Athens for ten years.

Cleisthenes's system of government was not much changed in later years. It did require some time to accustom the citizens to using their power to stop aristocratic conservatives and aspiring tyrants from trying to overthrow the democratic constitution; not until the middle of the fifth century B.C. did Athenian democracy reach its full bloom. The guiding spirit of this later era was Pericles, the chief political figure in Athens from 461 to 429 B.C. Pericles's only important change in the constitution was to introduce pay for service in the Council of 500, the Heliaea, and the elective magistracies. This step gave the poor a chance to engage in political life without sacrificing their livelihood. Pericles's real importance lay in the encouragement he gave to citizens to participate in political life. Although aristocratic by birth and the companion of the leading intellectuals and artists of his day, he felt no fear in trusting the political destiny of Athens to the common citizens. He encouraged them to discuss issues and to make decisions. His own exemplary conduct as a leader convinced nearly all citizens that public life was a dignified, responsible, and rewarding activity.

Nor did Pericles ever forget the intimate relationship between Athenian democracy and Athenian commercial and industrial expansion. As we shall see in the next chapter, Athens under his leadership pursued a policy of naval and commercial aggression that made her the richest city-state in Greece. All citizens shared in this prosperity, and many of them depended entirely on foreign trade for their livelihood. Economic prosperity was unquestionably a major force in stimulating their patriotism.

The Greek historian Thucydides credits Pericles with saying this about Athens: "We alone regard a man who takes no interest in public affairs, not as harmless, but as a useless character." In this statement Pericles revealed the very essence of Athenian life. The citizen had the right and the obligation to participate in the government because his participation was believed to make him a more complete man. Unless he informed himself on public affairs and expressed his judgment in the conduct of public affairs, he was not worthy to be considered a fully developed man. The city-state was his making, his world. Without it he was nothing; as a member of it he had the opportunity to do things worthy of human beings.

In discussing the nature of fifth-century Athenian democracy, one important reservation must be made. Participation in political life was confined to those who were citizens. The right to be a citizen was severely limited in Periclean Athens. Only those whose ancestors had been citizens could qualify for that precious right. Large numbers of foreigners (called metics) and slaves, who were not citizens, took no part in the political life of the community. Since metics and slaves actually outnumbered those who were citizens, a minority of the population actually governed the city.

5. Sparta

Other cities followed a pattern of development similar to that of Athens, ending with a system that encouraged participation in civic affairs by all citizens. However, still other cities evolved toward different ends, as the history of Sparta illustrates.

Sparta was founded by Indo-European invaders who overran Peloponnesus shortly before 1000 B.C. The invaders first settled in many small villages, which eventually joined into a single city-state. By the seventh century B.C., Sparta was well along toward this unification. Up to that time her development had been very similar to that of Athens and most other Greek cities. In time she began to feel the sharp edge of poverty arising from land shortage, and at this point the Spartans made the decision that determined their future as a city-state. Instead of seeking new wealth through trade and industry Sparta turned to the conquest of neighboring cities, enslaving her victims and forcing them to labor for her benefit. This policy posed a serious problem. Could Sparta keep her "slaves" under control? The Spartan answer was affirmative: Sparta could continue to live at the expense of her subjects if the Spartan citizens were made into a permanent army to stand guard over the subjects.

The reorganization of Spartan society on a military basis was attributed to a great lawgiver, Lycurgus. The new constitution was probably evolved over several decades in the late seventh and early sixth centuries B.C. Its most fundamental feature was the division of the population into three classes, each with rigidly defined responsibilities. First there were the *Spartans,* consisting of about 5 per cent of the population. This class served as professional soldiers, each member dedicating his life to ruling the rest of the population. No Spartan was allowed any other occupation. Next were the *perioeci,* a class charged with conducting whatever trading and manufacturing were necessary. Finally there were the *helots,* who were state slaves who served as laborers on the land or as personal servants. Membership in each class was hereditary and passed from parents to children. There was little movement from one class to another.

The Lycurgan reforms prescribed a regimen that had to be followed by each Spartan to prepare him for his life's service as a soldier. At birth each child of a Spartan citizen was inspected by state officials for physical fitness. If the child was defective, the state ordered death by exposure. If allowed to live, the child was given over to his mother until he reached the age of seven. Then the males were sent to live in barracks, where military training continued until the age of twenty. The training was extremely severe, with an emphasis on physical toughness, bravery, obedience, and other soldierly virtues. The program allowed almost no intellectual pursuits in order that the

Spartans would never be "softened" by excessive devotion to the arts, literature, or philosophy. Spartan girls were likewise rigorously trained to become the mothers and wives of future soldiers.

When he was twenty, the Spartan youth became a regular soldier. He and a group of others—usually fifteen—formed a mess group, eating, living, and fighting together as a unit. Each soldier contributed to the support of the mess, deriving his income from a piece of land that the state assigned to him along with enough helots to farm it. A man could marry after he was twenty, although he was not permitted to live with his wife until he was thirty. After he was thirty, the citizen was permitted to take part in political life and maintain his own home. He was probably so accustomed to barrack life by this time that he continued to find the focus of his life there, leaving it to his wife to rear his children and to supervise his helots. At sixty a Spartan could retire from military service, assuming that he had survived the regimen described above.

The helots and perioeci escaped this regime, but they too were carefully disciplined. Every year the state formally declared war on the helots so that any troublemaker could be killed on the spot. The perioeci had greater freedom, even being allowed to govern themselves in some cases, but they were rigidly excluded from decisions affecting the policy of Sparta and therefore never had a chance to push their commercial interests abroad in a way that would have allowed them to command a leading position in Spartan society.

Finally, the Lycurgan reforms provided a government for Sparta. Sparta always remained a monarchy, having two kings as the formal heads of the state. Actually the power of the kings was very slight. The real power in the state was held by a council of elders, consisting of the two kings and twenty-eight other men over sixty years old elected to serve for life. This body formulated all legislation, judged the most important cases that arose, and acted as an advisory body to the administration of the state. All decisions taken in Sparta had to be presented to an assembly made up of all male Spartans over thirty. Theoretically the assembly had the power to repudiate any policy, but one can well imagine that this assembly of citizen soldiers, peopled by men taught from childhood to obey orders and to let their superiors do the thinking, was seldom able to render an independent decision. The actual execution of laws was entrusted to a board of five *ephors* elected annually by the assembly. This small group conducted foreign affairs, supervised military training, policed the helots, and handled all matters of military preparation. Throughout most of Spartan history the ephors exercised virtually dictatorial powers, especially if, as was usually the case, they agreed with the thirty members of the council of elders. Sparta was thus ruled by a narrow oligarchy of military commanders.

Once the Lycurgan constitution was finished, it proved effective. The iron discipline of the citizen body resulted in Sparta's possessing the best army in Greece, and by 500 B.C. she had forced most of the city-states in Peloponnesus to join the Peloponnesian League. The member cities were allowed to keep their independence but were forced to follow Spartan leadership in foreign affairs, thereby assuring Sparta of predominance in Peloponnesus and enhancing her power in all of Greece. The Spartan system also held the helots in check. This class constantly threatened to revolt but never succeeded.

Although her government was dictatorial and her social organization lacking in freedom, Sparta illustrates the fundamental nature of the Greek city-state as well as Athens. In shaping her social and political system Sparta made the city-state into an institution that served as the center of life for her citizens. It also provided the means for her citizens to become the best soldiers in the Greek world—brave, obedient, trustworthy, and dedicated to their city. To a Spartan this was an achievement to be proud of.

By the fifth century B.C. the Greek world had reached its fullest political and social development. It was divided into several hundred city-states, each having its own form of government, each being economically self-sufficient, and each fiercely proud of its independence. Within each city a social and political system had been hammered out to serve the interests of those who were citizens. In each case citizenship was a precious possession, making each man proud of his membership in an exclusive community, inspiring him to a deep devotion for his community, and encouraging him to perform amazing feats in its service.

SUGGESTED READING

M. Rostovtzeff, *A History of the Ancient World,* Vol. I: *The Orient and Greece,* 2nd ed. (1930). A stimulating survey of all Greek history, useful for this and the following chapters on the Greeks. Excellent illustrations add to the value of the book.

* C. E. Robinson, *Hellas: A Short History of Ancient Greece* (Beacon). A very brief but balanced outline of Greek history.

* H. D. F. Kitto, *The Greeks* (Penguin). A brief, sympathetic interpretation of Greek history that seeks to discover what the Greeks were like as a people and how they viewed the world. Not everyone would agree with all of Kitto's conclusions, but everyone will find them stimulating. The book is especially useful after the reader has some idea of the main outlines of Greek history.

* Alfred E. Zimmern, *The Greek Commonwealth; Politics and Economics in Fifth-Century Athens* (Modern Library). Published in a hardback edition, 5th ed. (1931). An excellent analysis of the origin and nature of the Greek city-states.

* N. M. Fustel de Coulanges, *The Ancient City; A Study on the Religion, Laws, and Institutions of Greece and Rome* (Anchor). Also available in several different hardback editions. A classic on the subject of the nature of the city-state, stressing especially its religious origins. The author does not confine himself wholly to Greek city-states.

Gustave Glotz, *The Greek City and Its Institutions,* tr. by N. Mallinson (1929). Still another excellent discussion of the Greek city-state, especially good for its accurate descriptions of political institutions.

* Aristotle, *On the Constitution of Athens* (many editions; a convenient one is the paperback edition published by the Hafner Publishing Co.). This brief discussion of the Athenian government by Aristotle supplies most of our information about the Athenian constitution.

Xenophon, *Constitution of the Lacedaemonians* (several editions; the one in the Loeb Classical Library is especially recommended). A primary source by a fourth-century-B.C. Greek writer, upon which most of our knowledge about the Spartan government is based. This brief work will permit a student to acquaint himself better with the nature of the Spartan government. It will also introduce him to one of the most remarkable collections of literature in the English language, namely, the Loeb Classical Library. This collection, begun in 1912, contains most of the works of the classical authors of Greece and Rome. Each work is printed with the original Greek or Latin text on one page and the English translation on the facing page. Thus these volumes provide easy access to the classical authors in either the ancient languages or in modern English.

* Plutarch, *Lives* (many editions; a good one in the Modern Library series). This work contains short biographical sketches of Lycurgus, Solon, Themistocles, Pericles, and Alcibiades, written by a second-century-A.D. Greek author. It will help to bring alive Athenian and Spartan history. Plutarch was interested in these men primarily because he thought that their lives illustrated some great moral lesson and therefore selected his materials instead of filling in all details. Nevertheless, the biographies are lively and interesting.

Jules Toutain, *The Economic Life of the Ancient World,* tr. by M. R. Dobie (1930). A thorough treatment of all aspects of Greek economic life. Since it also includes material on other peoples besides the Greeks, this volume might serve as a useful guide to economic life throughout antiquity.

Gustave Glotz, *Ancient Greece at Work,* tr. by M. R. Dobie (1926). A thorough description of the Greek economy by one of the great French students of classical Greece. This book demands careful reading but will reward its readers with a full picture of the economic basis of Greek life.

J. P. Mahaffy, *Social Life in Greece from Homer to Menander,* 7th ed. (1925). A highly readable social history emphasizing domestic and personal life among the Greeks.

Charles Burton Gulick, *The Life of the Ancient Greeks* (1902). Much like the Mahaffy book cited above, this book concentrates on social history.

CHAPTER 6

The Failure of the Greek City-State Polity

THE INTERNAL structure of the Greek city-state was a marvelous institution for bringing out the best talents of its citizens. But another aspect of Greek city-state life must now be considered: the relationships among the many city-states crowded together within the confines of Greece and along the western coast of Asia Minor. Perhaps enough has already been said to make it clear that the fiercely patriotic residents of each city could feel only hostility toward other cities. Only a great crisis, like the threat of a foreign enemy, could overcome the ill feeling each city felt for the others. Eventually intercity hatred vented itself in a series of wars among the Greek city-states that left them an easy prey to outsiders.

1. The Persian Wars, 490–479 B.C.

Throughout the early period of Greek history there were wars between Greeks, but most Greek energy was devoted to internal development, and until approximately 500 B.C. strong forces acted to unite them. Most Greeks worshiped the same gods and gathered regularly to pay honors to those gods, holding such all-Greek festivals as the Olympic games. Moreover, most of them shared a common language. Some progress had even been made toward establishing political unions, such as the already-noted Peloponnesian League. The first important practical demonstration of the need for unity, however, came in the fifth century,

when the rising Persian Empire threatened to engulf the Greek city-states.

The Persian Empire began to emerge in 550 B.C. Very quickly great conquerors like Cyrus and Cambyses destroyed the chief political powers in the Near East. Their expansion westward carried Persian rule to the shores of the Aegean Sea in Asia Minor. Several Greek city-states in this area were forced to accept Persian overlordship. Persian rule, especially as established by Darius (521–486 B.C.), was not unduly harsh. However, it seemed burdensome to the Greek city-states, so long accustomed to independence or to the easy overlordship of Lydia. They especially resented the heavy tribute demanded by Darius and the Persian intervention in city-state politics. The city-states in European Greece sympathized with their captured fellow Greeks, viewing the Persians as a threat to the independence of all Greek cities. They became especially alarmed when Darius invaded Europe in 512 B.C. and established his rule in the area called Thrace, lying north of the Aegean. This expansion convinced many Greeks that Persia was intent upon conquering the whole civilized world.

Hostility between Greeks and Persians grew rapidly after 499 B.C., when the Greek cities in Asia Minor revolted against the Persians. The rebels called on the European Greeks for aid and received it from Athens and Eretria. Darius crushed the rebellion, however, and determined to punish those who came from Greece to make trouble in his empire.

Developments in certain Greek city-states in the ten years following 500 B.C. helped to increase ill feeling between Greeks and Persians. One of the Spartan kings of the period, Cleomenes, was seeking to foster greater Greek unity under Spartan leadership. He was strongly anti-Persian and felt that the Persian threat, properly exploited, could help unite the Greeks. Meanwhile in Athens a political struggle was in progress. Some factions, especially the democratic party, led by Themistocles, and the commercial interests, led by Miltiades, were openly anti-Persian. Probably they were willing to risk a war, the democrats hoping to prove that Athens under their system of government was capable of winning a war and the commercial interests hoping to drive the Persians out of the rich trading areas of the Aegean and Black seas. Other parties, especially the supporters of the family of Pisistratus, hoped for a successful Persian attack, which would restore Pisistratus's son, Hippias, as tyrant. Hippias had fled to Asia when he was ousted in 510 B.C. and was still present at Darius's court. The open neutrality of many Greek city-states encouraged the Persians to believe that an attack on Greece might be successful.

Amid these worsening relationships Darius finally decided to attack. In 490 B.C. he sent a fleet across the Aegean to punish Athens and Eretria for intervention in the revolt of the Greek city-states under Persian control. After Eretria was captured, Persian troops landed in eastern Attica near Marathon. The Persian fleet sailed around the southern tip of Attica and approached the city of Athens, hoping to seize it— with the help of traitors inside the city— while the Persian army at Marathon was crushing the Athenian army. Athens seemed doomed. She appealed to other Greeks for aid, but almost none was forthcoming. Especially serious was the Spartan refusal to aid, on the plea that the moon was not right for sending troops abroad. The Athenian army saved the day by defeating the Persians at Marathon; under the leadership of Miltiades the Athenians outfought a larger Persian army. Once the army was beaten, the Persian fleet withdrew to Asia. The battle of Marathon raised the confidence of the whole Greek world and exalted Athens as the savior of Greece.

The Persians were unable to resume the war for ten years, detained by revolts within the empire and by the accession of a new king, Xerxes I. The Greeks meanwhile felt that the attack would be renewed and made better preparations. In Athens Themistocles, who had emerged as the chief leader, convinced the Athenians that they must build a strong fleet if they wished to stop the oncoming Persian attack. When Xerxes finally began organizing his resources for an even greater attack than the one in 490, other Greek city-states showed a willingness to co-operate. At a meeting of the Greeks in 481 B.C., Athens and Sparta, joined by many other cities, formed a league and agreed to wage a common war.

Early in 480 B.C. Xerxes began to move his huge army overland from Asia Minor across the straits and down through Greece. Once again the army was supported by a large fleet. The Greek league decided to make a stand at Thermopylae, where a narrow pass supplied a promising place to check the Persian army and where the sea lanes could be advantageously blocked by the Greek fleet. This plan failed when Greek traitors revealed to the Persians a passage that allowed the defenders of Thermopylae to be outflanked. A small band of Spartans sacrificed themselves trying to stop the Persians. Once past Thermopylae the Persians flooded into central Greece. Although Athens was captured and destroyed, most of her citizens fled to safety. Moreover, the Greek fleet was still intact and the bulk of the Greek armies had not yet been committed to battle. Nonetheless the future looked dim.

At this point Themistocles took charge of the war. Without the approval of his allies he enticed the Persian fleet into a decisive battle at Salamis, an island off the coast of Attica. The Greek fleet caught the Persians off balance and delivered a crippling defeat. Xerxes himself, who witnessed this battle from a promontory on the Attican coast, saw his chances of victory fade as the Persian fleet retreated to Asia, for without control of the seas he could not supply his forces.

His armies spent the winter of 480–479 B.C. in northern Greece and undertook a new campaign in the spring of 479 B.C. This time a sizable Greek army moved out to meet the Persians and defeated them at Plataea. In the meantime the Greeks sailed boldly across the Aegean and destroyed what was left of the Persian fleet at Mycale. This was a signal for the Greek cities in Asia Minor to revolt once again. Xerxes could do nothing but recall his armies from Europe, realizing that the Greek fleet might now cut the path of escape in the straits. The jubilant Greeks had demonstrated their vitality against even so great a foe as Persia. By acting together they had saved themselves.

2. Confederacy of Delos

The spirit of unity survived the withdrawal of the Persians in 479 B.C. Athens was the leading power in maintaining it, especially after Sparta showed an unwillingness to commit her strength to projects far removed from Peloponnesus. Under the leadership of two Athenian statesmen, Cimon and Aristides, steps were taken to establish a voluntary league to continue the war against Persia. Numerous cities joined this league, pledging themselves to contribute ships or money, according to their ability. The treasury of the league was to be kept at a shrine on the island of Delos, and annual meetings were provided to decide policy. Aristides was entrusted with the task of assessing the dues of each city and did so with such fairness that he was called "Aristides the Just." Cimon was to act as commander of the combined forces. No city-state was required to surrender its own sovereignty, thus protecting the sacred independence of each city.

The combined forces of the league enjoyed immediate success under the brilliant leadership of Cimon. Within about ten years all the Greek city-states in Asia Minor had been freed from Persian rule, while the Aegean and the straits area were cleared of Persian naval power. Athens was clearly the most powerful city in the league. She conducted herself with marked restraint in her relationships with her fellow city-states. Cimon's policy was conciliatory even toward non-members such as Sparta, although some elements within Athens resented his compromising attitude. Seldom before or after did the Greek world present a more united front than during the first years after the victory over the Persians.

3. The Athenian Empire

This happy condition did not last long. Athens was responsible for altering the situation. As the danger from Persia receded, some members of the Confederacy of Delos desired to withdraw. Athens was unwilling to allow this to happen. Her leaders and many of her citizens saw that Athenian sea power, developed to check the Persians, could be turned to commercial advantage. Instead of conducting herself as one among equals Athens slowly began to convert the league into an empire under her own control and to use its resources for her own ends. She refused to allow members to withdraw, used territories won by league forces to establish her own colonies, and forced cities not yet in the league to join. Member nations that insisted upon withdrawing were subdued by force. The populace in democratic Athens demanded that Athenian interests be put first, and the people had their way.

Athenian imperialism reached its full tide with the emergence of Pericles as the leader of the city in 461 B.C. Pericles came to power in the wake of the downfall of Cimon, who had tried to restrain Athenian imperialism. In 462 B.C. Cimon sent Athenian aid to Sparta, which had suffered a serious earthquake and a helot uprising.

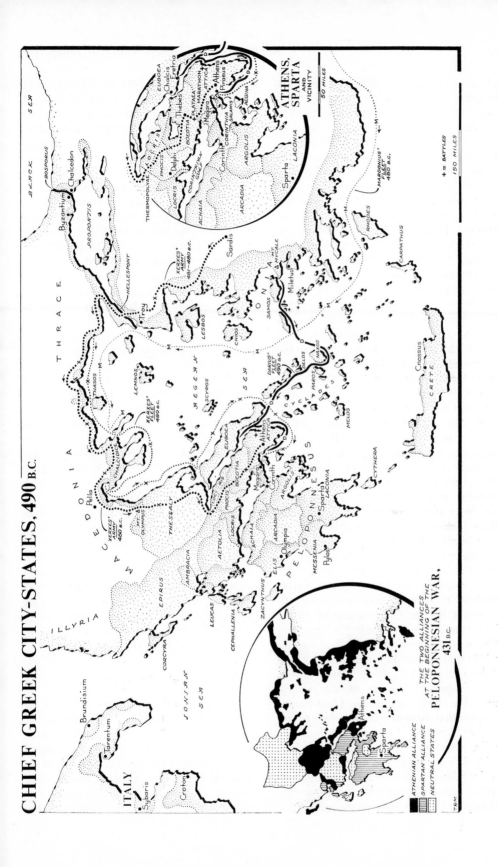

CHIEF GREEK CITY-STATES, 490 B.C.

ATHENS, SPARTA AND VICINITY

50 MILES

EUBOEA
Chalcis
Eretria
Thebes
BOEOTIA
PLATAEA
MARATHON
Athens
Megara
Piraeus
CORINTHIA
Corinth
Salamis
AEGINA
ARGOLIS
LACONIA
Sparta
ARCADIA
ACHAIA
LOCRIS
PHOCIS
Delphi
THERMOPYLAE
MARDONIUS' FLEET 490 B.C.

+ = BATTLES
150 MILES

BLACK SEA
BOSPORUS
Chalcedon
Byzantium
PROPONTIS
HELLESPONT
Troy
THRACE
MACEDONIA
Pella
MT. OLYMPUS
THESSALY
EPIRUS
ILLYRIA
CORCYRA
LEUCAS
CEPHALLENIA
ZACYNTHUS
AMBRACIA
AETOLIA
LOCRIS
PHOCIS
BOEOTIA
Megara
Athens
ATTICA
Corinth
ARGOLIS
ARCADIA
ELIS
Olympia
ACHAIA
MESSENIA
Pylos
Sparta
LACONIA
PELOPONNESUS
CYTHERA

XERXES' ARMY 481-480 B.C.
Sardis
IONIA
Miletus
SAMOS
MYCALE
CHIOS
LESBOS
LEMNOS
THASOS
CHALCIDICE
SCYROS
EUBOEA
DELOS
NAXOS
PAROS
CYCLADES
MELOS
RHODES
CARPATHUS
Cnossus
CRETE
AEGEAN SEA
XERXES' FLEET 480 B.C.
DARIUS' FLEET 490 B.C.

IONIAN SEA
ITALY
Brundisium
Tarentum
Croton
Sybaris

THE TWO ALLIANCES AT THE BEGINNING OF THE PELOPONNESIAN WAR, 431 B.C.

Athens
Sparta

ATHENIAN ALLIANCE
SPARTAN ALLIANCE
NEUTRAL STATES

When the Spartans rebuffed Athenian aid, the angry populace exiled Cimon in favor of the anti-Spartan, democratic party led by Pericles.

Since Pericles was a convinced democrat, he pursued a policy that he knew was popular; he was also an Athenian patriot who thought that Athenian prosperity and power were all-important. Once in power he launched a two-pronged drive to spread Athenian influence. In Greece he used every method available to force more cities into the Confederacy of Delos under Athenian control. He supported revolts against non-democratic governments, tried to entice the members of the Peloponnesian League to abandon Sparta, and used Athenian sea power to bottle up such trading powers as Corinth. Meanwhile Pericles renewed the assault on Persia, carrying the struggle into the Eastern Mediterranean. In both his offensives Pericles enjoyed some success. But about 450 B.C. it became obvious that Athens was overextending her power, and in spite of popular opposition Pericles arranged peace treaties with both Persia and Sparta. In a treaty of 448 B.C. Persia and Athens agreed to respect each other's spheres of influence. Persia promised to refrain from attacks on the Greeks in Asia Minor, leaving them open to Athenian control, while Athens promised to stop attacking Persian territory. In a treaty of 445 B.C., called the Thirty Years' Truce, Sparta and Athens reached a similar agreement. Sparta promised to refrain from interfering in the affairs of the Confederacy of Delos, while Athens agreed to halt her aggressive policy among Greek cities still free and especially those in the Peloponnesian League.

These treaties left Athens with a considerable empire, consisting of the several hundred communities in the Confederacy of Delos that Athens was now free to exploit. She continued to collect tribute annually, although the Persian danger had vanished. The money was now used in Athens for whatever the Athenians chose, including such things as beautifying the city and paying the common people salaries for serving in the government. Athens forced many of the league members to institute democratic governments, hoping that such governments would be more manageable. She forced subject cities to use her money and her weights and measures. By any standard of judgment she treated these formerly independent cities as her subjects. And she did this for her own profits.

Although most of the cities in the league actually benefited economically, their hatred for Athens increased steadily, for Athens had deprived them of their greatest privilege—independence. Not many years before, Athens had led the Greek world in a struggle to save the independence of Greek city-states from the Persians. Now she was acting like the Persians. Athens made no attempt to compensate her subjects for limitations on their freedom. They were not permitted to become citizens of Athens and they were allowed no representation in the Athenian government. Since the Athenian constitution was based on the principle of direct participation by the citizens, the principle of representation was foreign to any Athenian and to most Greeks. Gradually a tide of revulsion against Athens, springing mainly from free city-states that feared falling into her clutches, arose throughout the Greek world, which now began to look toward Sparta as a champion of freedom. This was a rather strange development, considering Sparta's own record of domination over the cities of Peloponnesus. The anti-Athenian sentiment heralded a serious war in which Greek assaulted Greek, unmindful of the many things the city-states had in common.

4. Peloponnesian War, 431–404 B.C.

The uneasy peace in the Greek world was finally shattered in 431 B.C. by the outbreak of the Peloponnesian War, which was born out of the increasing hostility against Athens. The immediate cause of the war was the success of a few cities, and especially Corinth, in convincing Sparta that Athens was violating the Thirty Years'

Truce of 445 B.C., thereby threatening the independence of all Greek cities. Athens, still led by Pericles, was not unwilling to join the issue, probably feeling that a showdown was inevitable. She had a large fleet and huge financial resources to pit against the superior land forces of Sparta and her allies. Pericles was confident that the Spartans were incapable of mounting a campaign that would strike at the real sources of Athenian power—her maritime empire.

The first ten years of the war were indecisive. Athens began by pursuing a strategy of refusing to fight on land. She withdrew her troops and her population within the city walls, against which the Spartan armies were powerless. In the meantime the Athenian fleet harassed the shores of Peloponnesus, seeking to cause enough damage to make Sparta and her allies war-weary. This strategy worked for a time, but a few years after the war opened, conditions began to change. The Athenian population, cooped up in the city, suffered terribly from a serious plague. Pericles was himself a victim in 429 B.C., his death being a costly loss. The populace began to demand a bolder military policy, insisting that the Athenians attack the Spartan armies. A new leader, Cleon, emerged to answer this demand by leading the Athenian armies abroad. Sparta produced a general named Brasidas, who convinced the conservative Spartans that they must strike at the Athenian Empire if they expected to defeat the city. Brasidas was allowed to take an army into the territory around the northern Aegean to help those cities willing to revolt against Athens. Cleon's aggressiveness was not especially successful. Athens did not possess the strength to defeat Spartan armies, and suffered severe and costly defeats, while the expenses entailed by the war placed a heavy burden on the Athenians. Brasidas, on the other hand, enjoyed considerable success, although many Spartans disliked sending their troops so far from home. In 422 B.C., however, both Brasidas and Cleon were killed in battle. This gave the Athenian peace party and the Spartan conservatives a chance to put an end to the war. In 421 B.C. a Fifty Year Truce was agreed upon between Athens and Sparta. Both contestants agreed to return to the situation that existed before the war. Great joy greeted the peace, although it was obvious to some that nothing had really been settled. Athens still had her empire and would obviously resume her former aggressiveness.

The truce lasted only until 415 B.C. Again Athens was responsible for ending the truce. The populace, led by the brilliant but overly ambitious Alcibiades, resumed an aggressive attitude toward other cities, arousing the old fears among the Greeks. Athenian ambitions culminated in an ill-conceived expedition against the great Greek city of Syracuse in Sicily, where the Athenians suffered a disastrous defeat after a two-year campaign (415–413 B.C.). Even worse, her attack on Syracuse provoked Sparta and her allies to renew the war against an Athens seriously weakened by the Sicilian venture.

After 413 B.C. the fortunes of Athens declined steadily. The main scene of the war shifted to the Aegean Sea, where the Spartans proceeded to destroy Athenian sea power while encouraging the cities of the Confederacy of Delos to revolt. At the same time, Sparta allied herself with the Persian king, who supplied money and ships in return for Spartan permission to re-establish Persian control over the Greek cities in Asia Minor. Athens occasionally won an isolated victory, but slowly the net of Spartan-Persian power closed around her. Finally in 404 B.C. she surrendered. The victors forced her to tear down her walls, to destroy all but twelve of her ships, and to submit to a government of oligarchs who were guarded by a Spartan army stationed in the city. Although these Thirty Tyrants, as the Athenians called them, were ousted in 403 B.C. and democratic government restored, Athens never recovered her former power. The mighty city-state that had united and led the Greeks against the Persians was humbled, the victim of her own attempt to reduce the other city-states to a subordinate position.

5. The Decline of the City-States, 404–336 B.C.

The defeat of Athens in no way solved the problem of intercity rivalry. The Peloponnesian War, which left a legacy of deep hatred, had caused other problems as well. Trade, the source of much wealth, had been badly disturbed, and numerous areas of Greece had been laid waste. Moreover, in many cities the declining economic situation bred serious class struggles. Often the lower classes were prevented from stating their case because democracy had suffered a heavy blow with the defeat of its champion, Athens. Many Greeks, especially the intellectual leaders, were beset by pessimism and sought escape from their civic responsibilities in individual pursuits, thereby depriving the Greek city-states of the leadership they had enjoyed in earlier centuries.

The majority of the Greeks failed to realize what was happening. They persisted in engaging one another in fruitless struggles that merely compounded the problems caused by the Peloponnesian War. At the end of the Peloponnesian War, Sparta was the greatest power in Greece. Her conduct was even more dishonorable than had been that of Athens. She pursued a reactionary policy of imposing oligarchical government on any Greek city-state she could bully into submission. When the Greek world protested her narrow and often brutal policy, she turned to Persia for help. The Persians were only too glad to assist her, thereby gaining the mastery over Greece that Persian armies had not been able to win a century earlier. Sparta's collaboration with Persia only increased the hatred of the other Greeks for the Spartans.

The resentment against Sparta led to a new series of wars. Thebes became the champion of city-state independence. Under her only great statesman, Epaminondas, Thebes smashed the declining power

of Sparta in a single battle in 371 B.C. Sparta rapidly sank to a second-rate power, her proud citizen-soldiers now having been reduced to a handful and her prestige gone. Thebes, however, was ill-suited to assume leadership in the Greek world. She established a new league under her control but was never able to extend it to all Greece. She too succumbed to the lure of Persian money in the attempt to ensure her own supremacy, but even Persian assistance was insufficient. A new coalition of cities, led once again by Athens, inflicted a fatal defeat on Thebes in 362 B.C., ending her dominance.

After 362 B.C. the numerous Greek city-states indulged in incessant wars out of which no decisive results emerged. It would be useless to follow these struggles in detail. In general they sapped the remaining strength of the Greeks at a time when weakness was especially dangerous. For on the northern fringe of the Greek world a powerful giant, the semi-barbaric kingdom of Macedon, was casting ambitious eyes southward.

Before dealing with the advance of Macedon into Greece and its tragic consequences, it must be noted that some Greeks became aware of the dangers involved in the intercity warfare and intrigue. They raised eloquent appeals for some kind of Greek union that would stop warfare and protect Greece from foreigners. Some of them, like the Athenian orator and statesman Demosthenes, argued that Athens should take the lead in forming a confederation, but his appeal was not effective in view of Athens's past role as a head of a confederacy. Others turned northward and began to urge the Macedonian king to serve as the head of a Greek confederation. But this idea was also coldly received, since to invite a foreigner into Greece was looked upon as treasonable. In general the movement for Panhellenism was a lost cause. The Greek city-states were too accustomed to total independence to surrender their sovereignty to a super-organization dedicated to peace and common action. Such great philosophers as Plato and Aristotle, who lived during the fourth century, vigorously maintained that only the traditional small city-state was fit for the Greeks. With this mood prevalent, nothing was done by the Greeks to put a stop to their own quarrels.

6. Macedonian Conquest of Greece

The Greek city-states, incapable of checking their own struggles, grew increasingly ripe for conquest by some outside power. That conqueror rather unexpectedly turned out to be Macedon. Macedon had not had a particularly brilliant history before the fourth century. The land was poor and inhabited by unruly peoples who resisted organization. Moreover the Macedonians were far inferior to the Greeks culturally. What little cultural advance there was came as a result of borrowing from the Greeks. Certainly such a backward state was not viewed with any great alarm by most of the Greeks.

The situation in Macedon changed rapidly as a result of the leadership of Philip II, king from 359–336 B.C. Philip was a masterful political leader, skilled both as a diplomat and as a general, with a clear understanding of the problems besetting the Greek world and a grasp of the potential strength of his own restless subjects. Equally significant was the fact that he genuinely admired Greek culture and wished to preserve it. Once he became king, he turned his energies toward organizing his own kingdom, his first concern being the Macedonian army. Within a short time he welded his wild subjects into a disciplined, loyal, and well-trained army, and he spared no efforts to secure an income sufficient to maintain it. The victories won by this force strengthened the loyalty of the whole Macedonian population toward the king.

Philip's own love of all things Greek, along with his personal ambition, soon drew him into Greek affairs. Finding the Greeks engaged in almost constant warfare,

Philip used this situation as a means of thrusting himself into Greek political life. His money and his army made him a valuable ally for any Greek city engaged in a war with its neighbors. He was not above intriguing to incite wars in Greece so that his services would be called upon. Wherever he became involved, Philip ended with the upper hand, having isolated individual cities and then forced them into dependence on him. Gradually the confusion in the Greek world began to clear as the Greeks realized the strength of Macedon and as Philip's growing mastery made itself felt. Athens emerged as the champion of the Greeks against Macedon and tried desperately to rally the rest of the Greeks to that cause.

The struggle was one-sided from the beginning. Athens was actually ill-fitted for the heavy burden of leadership of the Greeks. Internal politics crippled her diplomatic efforts, and the Athenian population, constantly encouraged by demagogues, was usually more intent on immediate economic and social gains than on a struggle against a distant foreign power. The chief leader of the party that realized the danger of Macedon was Demosthenes, whose eloquent pleas to the Athenian population to wake up to the threat from the north can still be read in his *Philippics*. On occasion Demosthenes did succeed in persuading the Athenians to send aid to Greek cities besieged by Philip, but usually this aid was too late, and always it was too little. Demosthenes's efforts to form a Greek union fared little better. Slowly Philip advanced, finally forcing the Athenian alliance to commit itself to battle at Chaeronea in 338 B.C. In a single engagement the last strength of the Greeks was destroyed by Philip's well-trained army. Greece lay at his feet to be dealt with as he chose.

Philip II, probably inspired by his deep respect for Greek civilization, treated his victims with extreme mildness. He did, however, end the old order in Greece. One of his first moves was to call a meeting of all Greek city-states in 338 B.C. and form a Hellenic league. Members of this league were theoretically entitled to complete independence, but in fact crucial restrictions were placed upon that freedom. No city was allowed to change its existing form of government, and without freedom to change its government a city-state certainly was no longer the city-state of old. The league held regular meetings at which each city had representatives to debate and decide league policy. Finally, a common army and navy were created, with each state contributing according to its ability. Although Macedon was not a member of the league, Philip required that the league sign a treaty of alliance with Macedon, thereby giving the Macedonian king an important voice in its decisions.

Philip dictated the first undertaking of the Hellenic league, which had actually been formed with the purpose of waging war on Persia. But he did not live to lead the union of Greeks and Macedonians in an Asian campaign. One of his own soldiers assassinated him in 336 B.C., perhaps at the behest of his wife, who did not fully approve of Philip's lack of respect for the institution of marriage.

Philip II was certainly one of the most far-seeing statesmen of the fourth century. He was aware of the folly of the rivalry that had kept the Greek cities in a state of warfare for nearly a century. To end this, he used the superior strength of Macedon to force the Greeks into a union sufficiently strong to check the strife among the cities. By penalizing revolutionists he tried to discourage the endless struggles that plagued each city internally. Finally, he sought to divert the martial characteristics of the Greeks into a war against Persia. These pol-

icies mark a turning point in Greek history. Philip II has seldom been given full credit, because he had the good fortune to produce a son, Alexander, who put into practice the policies Philip conceived.

7. Significance of the City-State

The fateful course toward self-destruction followed by the Greek city-states during the fifth and fourth centuries B.C. does not make for happy reading. The Greeks never found the political talent that would solve the problem of regulating relationships among independent, proud, self-contained political units. Their failure meant constant warfare, which only weakened the city-states and prepared them for conquest by foreigners. That conquest ended for all time the Greek city-state polity, since the conqueror demanded that each city-state surrender part of its independence.

But during its day of glory the city-state had produced results that offset its failure. For the first time in human history large numbers of men were encouraged to show their abilities and to develop their talents. The age-old political systems where the masses of men obeyed a few masters and fitted themselves into society as they were ordered had been challenged. The Greeks demonstrated in their city-states that men did not need to be slaves to a few. Mankind never forgot the ideals pursued in the Greek city-states, where a conscious effort was made to develop the excellence that was presumed to be in every man simply because he was a man. This demonstration of the qualities possessed by even the common man certainly overshadowed the failure of the Greek city-states to find a means of getting along with one another.

SUGGESTED READING

M. L. W. Laistner, A History of the Greek World from 479 to 323 B.C. 2nd ed. (1947). A thorough survey of the political history of the period covered in this chapter. It will be useful to any reader desiring to follow develop-

ments in greater detail than has been possible in the text chapter.

* Herodotus, The Persian Wars (many editions; a convenient and especially good one is the translation by Aubrey de Selincourt in the

Penguin Classics). This classic treatment by a fifth-century-B.C. Greek historian offers the best approach to the era of the Persian Wars. Herodotus provides not only a dramatic account of the wars but also an insight into the Greek point of view at that time.

* Thucydides, *The Peloponnesian War* (many editions; an excellent one has been published in the Penguin Classics, translated by Rex Warner). This is one of the world's great pieces of historical literature. Its objective description of the Peloponnesian Wars tells a gripping story. The philosophical turn of Thucydides's treatment makes this book an excellent reflection of the Greek outlook on life. It ought to be one of the first Greek works that a student reads; there is no better time to read it than while dealing with the historical period covered in the work.

Demosthenes, *Public Orations*, tr. by A. W. Packard-Cambridge, 2 vols. (1912). A sampling of the speeches of this fourth-century Athenian statesman will supply the best reflection of the problems of the difficult era just before the Macedonian conquest of Greece.

CHAPTER 7

Greek Culture

THE GREEK city-states, whose strength and weakness we have traced in the preceding chapters, must now be approached from a different viewpoint. They provided the setting and the stimulus for one of the greatest cultural upsurges in the history of the world. Our treatment of the cultural life of the Greeks can be only suggestive, since the Greeks spawned new ideas and art forms in such great numbers that a lifetime of study would not comprehend the full meaning of the Greek contribution to later civilizations.

Although the roots of Greek cultural life go far back into Greek history, it was not until about 800 B.C. that distinctively Greek literary and artistic works began to appear. After 800 B.C., however, cultural progress was rapid; overseas colonization, rapid expansion of trade, and political innovation stimulated and encouraged bold experimentation in literature, art, science, and philosophy, full of youthful exuberance and a searching quest for new ideas. By the fifth century Greek cultural life was in its golden age. Within the brief span of a century the Greeks, especially the Athenians, produced masterpieces still included among the greatest monuments of human creativity. Toward the end of the fifth century notes of discord and confusion entered Greek cultural life, and, although important works were still being produced in the fourth century, particularly in philosophy, Greek culture had passed its peak.

1. Greek Religion

Greek culture was never dominated by religion to the extent that Near Eastern civilizations were; in fact one of the unique features of the Greek way of life was the freedom that many Greeks felt to think and express themselves on matters other than religion. However, religion played a significant role in the development of their culture by providing a common starting point for artists and thinkers and by posing problems that led them on in their pursuit of new ideas.

Long before Greek art, literature, or philosophy took shape, the Greek people had arrived at a well-developed body of religious beliefs. They believed in a family of gods (often called the pantheon) who shared in guiding the destiny of the world. An elaborate mythology developed about these gods. They were conceived of as magnified human beings, leading a joyful existence atop Mount Olympus under the supervision of a kind of divine father called Zeus. The Olympian gods mingled freely with man and took part in shaping daily affairs. Although the Greeks believed that these gods had great power, they were not greatly to be feared. Men felt at home with gods so nearly like themselves.

The worship of the Olympian gods grew steadily more elaborate. To keep their gods happy, the Greeks made sacrifices, built temples, wrote hymns, and organized splendid ceremonies. Much of Greek art and literature originated as a form of religious worship. Since each Greek city-state accepted one of the Olympian deities as its patron, worship was usually a public affair and an important source of civic pride. Even Panhellenic ceremonies, like the Olympian games first held in 776 B.C. in honor of Zeus, were organized to praise the gods. Many spots in Greece were believed to be especially sacred to certain gods and therefore became public shrines accessible to all Greeks. Typical of such shrines was that of Apollo at Delphi, where Greeks came to consult the oracle through which Apollo gave advice on everything from personal problems to great political issues.

Alongside the stimulating public religion centering around the Olympian pantheon, there developed more intimate, personal mystery religions. The mystery religions centered around the worship of gods who had died and risen from the dead. Dionysus was by far the most popular such god, his cult becoming one of the major religious movements in the Greek world. Individuals won the favor of such deities by an elaborate, highly emotional purification ritual, and they retained that favor by leading a pure moral life. The chief attraction of the mystery religions seemed to lie in the close personal relationship felt by the worshipper to the god and in the ethical teachings associated with adherence to the god. Although the early mystery religions were often so unrestrained that respectable people shied away from them, they were gradually disciplined until they became a regular part of Greek life. Their importance lay in their awakening the emotional side of Greek life and in their focusing attention on the individual and his problems.

These religious systems always remained a part of Greek life, keeping men conscious of some higher force guiding their destiny. However, the Greeks never allowed their thought to be completely occupied with religion. Their humane, kindly gods, never far removed from life on earth, provided the Greeks with a cheerful, hopeful outlook and a confident trust that man could achieve qualities nearly equal to the gods dwelling close by, gods who were much like men in their basic nature.

2. Literature

Greek literature illustrates how religion served as a base upon which Greek culture was built. Although it is nearly incomprehensible without a familiarity with Greek mythology, it represents a probing into human problems that far transcends conventional Greek religious viewpoints.

The earliest and most famous Greek literary masterpieces were the two epic poems of Homer, the *Iliad* and the *Odyssey*, telling of the deeds of the Greek heroes who in the twelfth century B.C. fought the Trojans to avenge the theft of Helen, a Greek queen, by a Trojan prince, Paris. The *Iliad* describes the events of a few weeks out of the ten-year siege of Troy. Its plot centers around a quarrel between two Greek heroes, Achilles and Agamemnon, arising from their inflated pride. After numerous dramatic incidents and the intervention of the gods, the heroes overcome their pride and return to their duty, which lies in fighting the Trojans. Much of the appeal of the *Iliad* derives from Homer's vivid descriptive powers. However, behind the action lies a deep philosophical note. Homer's mind is constantly at work trying to convince his readers that men, no matter how mighty, must abide by the rules of the gods. They can disregard those rules if they choose, but they must pay a price for their freedom.

The *Odyssey* is an account of the long journey home of one of the heroes of the Trojan war, Ulysses, who takes ten years to complete his travels. His journey leads him to strange, exotic places and involves him in wonderful adventures. Only his cleverness and intelligence permit him to escape the clutches of his foes and to return finally to the arms of his faithful wife, Penelope, who had had her wits tested to the extreme in trying to escape her greedy wooers.

For a long time after Homer's death

(about 800 B.C.) his art cast a spell over Greek literature. Numerous epics were produced in imitation of the master's works, but not until about 600 B.C. did Greek writers begin to explore new literary themes and styles. The result was a large amount of lyric poetry in which writers gave vent to their personal feelings about man, nature, social problems, and almost any other conceivable subject. The individual and his inner self, not the adventures of warriors and gods, supplied the inspiration for this poetry. The passionate love songs of the poetess Sappho (about 600 B.C.) illustrate the new poetry. Probably the greatest lyricist was Pindar (about 518–438 B.C.), who managed to write moving inspirational poetry about a subject that seemed to offer little promise—the victorious athletes at the great religious festivals. The majesty of his language made sweaty runners and boxers symbols of ideal manhood.

The grand, dramatic style of Homer and the personal touch of the lyricists merged in the fifth century to produce the tragic dramas that represent Greek literature at its best. The drama originated as a religious ceremony at which attempts were made to represent the actions of the gods by having actors go through certain motions. Shortly before 500 B.C. writers began to take an interest in elaborating these religious ceremonies; they wrote speeches for the actors and composed choral pieces that reflected their own attitudes and feelings toward the action. Cities began offering prizes for such dramas and producing the plays for the public. The dramas retained religious stories as the basis of the plot, but the plots became a vehicle used by dramatists to expound their views about man and his fate.

Three tragic dramatists dominated the fifth century, and their works still rank among the world's dramatic masterpieces. They were Aeschylus (525–456 B.C.), Sophocles (496–406 B.C.), and Euripides (480–406 B.C.). All three built their plots around stories from mythology with which their audiences were familiar, but each dramatist achieved a different effect with this material. Aeschylus dramatized the tragic consequences that result when men transgress the dictates of the divine. For instance, his cycle of three plays called the *Oresteia* centers on the violent deaths of Agamemnon and his family resulting from the fact that Agamemnon and his ancestors were guilty of slaying their blood kin. Out of the action of these plays one has impressed upon him a powerful moral lesson —that fate will inevitably overtake men who defy the gods. Sophocles focuses his attention on the effects of fate on human beings. Each of his plays is an exploration into human suffering and its uplifting effect on man. In his *Antigone*, for instance, the heroine is ennobled by her tragic experience of being torn between duty to the gods and to the state. Euripides employs tragedy primarily to ask questions; his attitude is skeptical. He presents the gods in a way that makes one wonder whether they are man's benefactors or tyrants. His treatment of men caught in tragic situations arouses pity for human weaknesses. His plays present a fuller picture of man's whole nature than do those of Aeschylus or Sophocles, but they never attribute so much nobility to man. From the works of these three writers a discerning reader can catch a glimpse of almost every facet of human nature, from the most sublime contemplation of the divine to the basest human passion.

The Greeks produced comic drama as effective in its own way as the great tragedies. Comedy, like tragedy, began as a part of religious ceremonies, but by the fifth century comedy became independent of religious ceremony and was performed as a distinctive art for the purpose of educating audiences on current affairs by making them laugh. Aristophanes (about 445–385 B.C.), a conservative Athenian, was the leading writer of comedy. His many works heaped fun on the politicians, artists, democratic institutions, and customs of the Athens of his day.

THE ACROPOLIS. This view of the Acropolis, from the west, shows clearly why the Acropolis formed the hub around which the city of Athens developed. The Parthenon, a building of beautiful proportions and marvelous simplicity, dominates the hill, as was the case in ancient Athens. To its left is the Erectheum, a temple to Athena built at the end of the fifth century, which consists of several sacred chambers, each with its own entrance. On the left is the Propylaea, the entrance to the Acropolis. This massive structure was approached by a great stairway which highlighted the transition from the outer world of the city to the sacred precincts of the Acropolis. (*Philip Gendreau, New York*)

Prose literature, long overshadowed by poetry, finally emerged in the fifth century. The best prose was devoted to history. Two outstanding historians, Herodotus and Thucydides, graced the literary scene in fifth-century Greece, not only producing great pieces of literature but also introducing scientific history to the world. Herodotus (about 484–425 B.C.) wrote a history of the war between the Greeks and Persia. He tried hard to make his account accurate, traveling extensively and searching through written records for evidence concerning the causes and the events of the Persian wars. His researches produced an immense collection of fact and fiction pertaining to both Persians and Greeks. Herodotus usually tried to sift his material to arrive at the truth; however, he was too good a storyteller to leave out colorful material whether true or not. His finished work was therefore spiced with hundreds of anecdotes and stories, many quite fantastic, intended to illustrate the qualities of the two peoples involved in the war. His significance lies in the fact that he tried to discover the truth about the past, insisting that this is the historian's job.

The masterpiece of Thucydides (about 470–400 B.C.) was a *History of the Peloponnesian War*. He was an Athenian who served as a naval commander in this war but suffered exile as a result of losing a battle. While in exile he wrote his history, managing to avoid any personal rancor stemming from his harsh treatment by his fellow citizens. With great industry and complete objectivity he searched out and reported the details of the military campaigns and the political maneuvers associated with the war. Thucydides was convinced that this was the greatest war in

Greek history, and his work is marked by deep seriousness. He tries to let the events of the war illustrate the folly, the nobility, the chicanery, and the bravery of which men under stress are capable. By successfully illustrating what war in any age can do to men and to political institutions, Thucydides did what every modern historian yearns to do: to make the truth about the past enrich our understanding of human beings.

3. Art

Greek art, reaching its peak in the fifth and fourth centuries, reflected a spirit akin

to create works distinctively Greek. Within two centuries architects had established a basic style centering around simple rectangular buildings surrounded by columns. Sculptors had focused their attentions on portrayal of the human form, seeking to endow the natural forms of the human body with a quality of idealism. Architects and sculptors received encouragement because of the growing desire to beautify cities and of elaboration of religious worship. As a consequence Greek art became predominately public art, dedicated to the life of the city and to the gods who protected the city.

THE THESEUM. This is one of the best-preserved temples of the Greek world. It exemplifies the Doric style, the chief features of which are simple columns topped by undecorated capitals and simplicity in the structural design above the columns. It can be seen clearly in this picture that the columns surround an inner wall. Within are the sacred chambers of the temple. This basic ground plan for temples changed very little throughout Greek history. The Parthenon, essentially the same as the Theseum in its basic design, can be seen in the distance at the left in this photograph. (*Philip Gendreau, New York*)

to that of the contemporary literary works. Behind the art of the golden age lay a long period of experimentation. Art historians trace Greek art far back into Greek history, noting that at an early date foreign models, especially Cretan, Asian, and Egyptian, exercised a strong influence. By the beginning of the seventh century Greek artists began

Athens was the mecca of great artists during the fifth and fourth centuries; her monuments offer the best examples of Greek art. Unquestionably the crowning glory of Athens was the Acropolis, a hill within the city upon which were built three major temples, the Parthenon, the Erechtheum, and the temple to Victorious

THE TEMPLE OF ATHENA NIKE. This temple was constructed on the Acropolis when Athens was at the peak of her power in the Greek world. It was dedicated to Athena in her role as goddess of victory and thus was a monument to Athenian might. Built in the Ionic style, it is one of the most charming monuments of Greek culture. Its well-proportioned columns, topped by capitals with their typical Ionic scroll decorations, give to the structure a graceful quality, and the small chamber behind the pillars provided a delightful setting for a statue of Athena. The reliefs on the front frieze show a grouping of the gods around Athena, in the center; reliefs on the sides of the temple deal with the Athenian victories over the Persians. (*Philip Gendreau, New York*)

THE THREE FATES. These figures, now somewhat damaged, were possibly designed by Phidias and formed part of a frieze on the east pediment of the Parthenon. The entire composition dealt with the birth of Athena, whose figure occupied the center of the pediment. Within a triangular space the sculptor achieved remarkable balance and symmetry without distorting the bodies, and his skillful use of drapery gives a sense of relaxation and contentment. (*Courtesy, The British Museum*)

Athena. A splendid gate and stairway, called the Propylaea, gave access to the Acropolis.

The Parthenon, still standing in a ruined state, was the noblest of the temples. Built in honor of Athena, this structure embodies all the Greek architectural ideas. It is of moderate size, measuring 228 by 101 feet. Its rectangular shape and accentuated horizontal lines give it the appearance of dignity and simplicity. The inner chamber is surrounded by simple, unadorned columns (called Doric columns), seventeen on each side and eight on each end, which support the roof. The number and size of the columns leave the impression of perfect unity. To the building was added a series of dignified statues and relief works that gave a harmonious decorative touch. Many devices were employed by the architects to achieve harmony, balance, and unity. The columns all lean inward slightly and are thickened in the middle to offset the optical illusion that makes a straight column seem to tip outward when viewed from below. The middle of every long horizontal line in or around the temple is slightly higher than the ends to avoid the impression of sagging.

The other Acropolis temples and the Propylaea, all built after the Parthenon, incorporate the same features—horizontal lines, carefully calculated proportions, and technical perfection. The only basic departure was the tendency to make the columns slightly more slender and ornate (in the Ionic style), adding an element of grace lacking in the rather severe Parthenon.

Other cities built similar temples, although none quite equals the Acropolis group for total effect. The many public buildings constructed in Athens and other cities incorporated the principles employed in temple construction, adding to the simple beauty of the city. Most such buildings have disappeared, making it difficult to do more than guess at their appearances.

Greek sculpture was primarily dedicated to the adornment of temples. The most representative sculptors are Phidias (about 500–432 B.C.), Polyclitus (about 452–412 B.C.), and Praxiteles (about 400–320 B.C.), although there were numerous other important sculptors. Phidias designed the

sculpture adorning the Parthenon and executed some of the individual pieces. Of
the surviving sculpture of the Parthenon,
all of it relief work, it is difficult to tell
whether any particular piece is the work
of Phidias or of someone working under his
direction. Phidias's monumental statues in
the round have all been lost. Polyclitus devoted his talents chiefly to shaping bronze
statues of young men, seeking to create the
perfect human form. Praxiteles created
splendid versions of the gods in human
form. The work of all these sculptors concentrated on the human body and was remarkably lifelike. However, of the three
sculptors none was content to copy nature.

All idealized humanity, creating the perfect human body without flaw. Their figures are dignified, quiet, and perfectly pro-
portioned. However, other Greek artists
could portray violent action; for instance,
Myron (fifth century), in his statue of the
discus thrower, manages to catch the body
at a moment of tension just before the cast
and seems to show the energy stored up in
the body. When looking at any of the statues of the Greek sculptors the viewer feels
that he finally sees man as he should be,
although he is aware that he has never seen
such perfect men. Greek sculpture catches
a glimpse of the ideal human being while
managing to keep close to the earth.

HORSEMEN FROM THE FRIEZE OF THE PARTHENON. This scene was designed by Phidias and executed by skilled artisans under his direction. It is only a small section of the frieze that runs completely around the inside of the Parthenon depicting vast numbers of figures in a gigantic procession in honor of Athena. The artist endeavored to make the figures represent the various types of
citizens found in Athens, and thus each figure is idealized. However, the sculptor has succeeded
in creating a sense of movement and life that makes the entire frieze seem to be a portrayal
of the humanity of Athens at its best. (*Alinari Photo*)

HERMES AND THE INFANT DIONYSUS, BY PRAX-
ITELES. This statue illustrates some of the basic
features of Greek sculpture. The gods are used
as subject matter and portrayed in idealized human form, creating the impression of physical
perfection and mental stability. (*Alinari Photo*)

4. Philosophy

The Greek genius burned brightest in
the realm of philosophical and scientific
speculation, leaving a heritage that has
shaped thinking in the West up to the present. Until the sixth century B.C. most
Greeks were content to accept the explanations offered by their mythology concerning
the nature of the universe and man's place
in it. Then there occurred a revulsion
against the naïve and contradictory concepts of mythology. With breath-taking

boldness Greek thinkers plunged into some
of the most fundamental questions facing
mankind and emerged with bold answers.

Throughout the sixth and the fifth centuries a series of philosophers grappled
with one basic question—what was the fundamental force lying behind and giving
unity to the universe? Rejecting religious
explanations, these philosophers sought to
give rational answers. One school of thinkers based its answer on a materialistic
concept, concluding that such obvious elements as fire, water, and air served as the
basic substance out of which all other
things originated. This materialistic tradition continued to be refined until in the
early fourth century the philosopher De-
mocritus expounded an atomic theory ac-

SOPHOCLES. This bust of the Athenian playwright reveals the same calm, philosophical outlook that emerges in his great tragedies. (*Alinari
Photo*)

cording to which the universe is composed of tiny atoms floating at random in space. By mere chance these atoms compose themselves into beings and objects and by the same chance decompose into floating particles again. Another school of philosophers rejected materialism. Following the lead of Heraclitus (sixth–fifth centuries), who insisted that change occurred constantly in the material world, these philosophers argued that a non-material, changeless being, endowed with perfect intelligence, supplied the creative force of order in the universe.

Only toward the end of the fifth century did the search for a rational explanation of the basic nature of the universe lose its attraction among Greek thinkers. Those who had engaged in that search had made a notable contribution to intellectual history. They had boldly assumed that the human mind has the power to understand the world's mysteries; they were no longer content to await revelation from the gods or to live in ignorance. Their efforts freed human reason and gave birth to philosophy.

About the middle of the fifth century philosophical inquiry shifted from speculation about the fundamental nature of the universe to an examination of man's place in it. The Sophists, although they were primarily teachers whose interest in philosophy was a by-product of their ideas on education, led the way. Protagoras (485–410 B.C.), a famous teacher in Periclean Athens, was chiefly responsible for the basic orientation of the Sophists. He rejected speculative philosophy on the grounds that it could not discover objective truth. He even denied that such truth existed, arguing that man is the measure of all things. Human reason, he said, should be dedicated to a search for the kind of knowledge that would be useful to man. He therefore spent his time instructing Athenians in those things that would fit them for citizenship in a democratic society—public speaking, politics, grammar, and the art of being respectable. Greece soon swarmed with disciples of this philosophy, who delivered a withering attack on all things that were accepted as the truth, preached that truth was a relative matter, and encouraged their audiences to live by any rules of conduct that proved beneficial and workable. The Sophists as a group were condemned, with partial justice, as skeptics, troublemakers, and destroyers of morality. However, they made the Greeks more aware of human problems than had those earlier thinkers who were constantly preoccupied with a search for the deepest secrets of the universe. They also prepared the way for Socrates, Plato, and Aristotle, whose philosophical work reflected the new humanism without abandoning the search for ultimate truth.

Probably no one was better known in Athens just before 400 B.C. than a homely, dumpy little stonecutter named Socrates (about 469–399 B.C.). Socrates left no writings, but from his pupils (especially Plato) we can grasp his basic ideas. He believed that objective truth did exist. Man was prevented from discovering it by his own ignorance. Socrates made it his business to purge man's mind of prejudice. His method consisted of asking questions until he had exposed the error of those who claimed to know something. Once having cleared the mind of its errors, Socrates believed that further questioning would reveal the truth. He insisted that precise definition and exact logic were necessary if the truth were to be discovered. Behind all Socrates's questions lay a firm conviction: knowledge alone will serve as a guide to a good life. Socrates's annoying questions finally got him into trouble with the state. In 399 B.C. he was accused of corrupting the youth of Athens and was sentenced to death. Although given a chance to escape, he chose to abide by the state's decision and drank poison, still convinced that the highest virtue consisted of pursuing knowledge, no matter what the consequences.

Plato (427–346 B.C.) carried on the work of Socrates, his master. He was an Athenian whose career spanned a tragic era filled with defeats for Athens and with constant civil strife, all of which discouraged him. Most of his life was spent as a teacher in a school called the Academy, which he founded. His voluminous works, written as dialogues, offer a wide, sometimes confusing record of his thought. All his philosophy is concerned with a single goal—finding the final truth. Plato concludes that ideas are the only real things and that the world of truth is a spiritual world. Material objects are imperfect reflections of the ideal world. By using his mental faculties man can with great difficulty grasp some knowledge of the perfect world of ideas.

Although usually preoccupied with his theory of ideas, Plato was too much a Greek to neglect human affairs. He sought constantly to apply his basic concept to problems of conduct. His best-known dialogue, *The Republic*, illustrates his attack on human problems. This work is devoted to the problem of the state and government. Plato assumes that the purpose of the state is to achieve justice, the ideal state being an earthly embodiment of the perfect idea of justice. He then seeks to define justice, concluding that justice consists in each man's doing that for which he is best fitted. The ideal state is the one in which every man holds that station and does that job for which he is qualified. Such a state, Plato argues, must be ruled by a philosopher-king who will be wise enough to know and recognize the talents of his subjects and put these talents to work. The philosopher-king must train the lower classes to do their jobs and must keep them from learning those things that will distract them from their jobs. A completely socialistic economy controlled by the wise king must be instituted so that each will be rewarded according to his merits and so that competition and greed can be eliminated from society. In short, the perfect society is a dictatorial state run by wise men who know each citizen's talents and have the power to put those talents to work. Only in this way will justice be attained.

Aristotle (384–322 B.C.), a product of Plato's Academy, was not willing always to

remain under the sway of his master. Born in Macedon and educated in Athens, he spent several years as tutor for the young Alexander of Macedon. Later he returned to Athens and founded his own school, the Lyceum. During his career as a teacher Aristotle composed numerous philosophical tracts, ranging over almost the whole field of human knowledge. His works usually attempted to systematize and organize knowledge in whatever field he was treating. Aristotle's philosophical concepts rested on a basis different from that of Plato's. In one of his chief works, *Metaphysics*, he maintained that reality consisted of a combination of both ideas and matter. Each object we see consists of matter plus idea or form, the latter making the matter whatever thing it is. Since each object contains some of the ideal world, Aristotle saw no reason for spurning the natural world. He believed that every object has been created to serve some purpose. The philosopher can learn the truth only by studying individual objects of the natural world to see how each fits into an ideal scheme of things.

In most of his works, many of which deal with scientific subjects, Aristotle pursued the course laid down in the *Metaphysics*. He tried to accumulate all the detailed knowledge he could about the natural world and to classify it into a system that would explain how the total natural world operates. In his chief work on political theory, *Politics*, he supplies an illustration of his method. On the basis of a study of the history and organization of over 150 Greek city-states, he generalized about the nature and function of the state, concluding that the state is a natural grouping of men for the purpose of promoting virtue. Man is a political animal and cannot fulfill his true nature unless he is a member of a state. In his *Ethics*, Aristotle asked how man should conduct his individual life and concluded that happiness is the proper goal of every human action. He argued that man is happy and therefore good if he controls his passions by use of his reason and if he seeks a mean between extremes. Although Aristotle's principal method is inductive, proceeding from detailed observations of particulars to general conclusions and although he was the most influential exponent of that method among the Greeks, he is also the founder of formal logic. As the last great thinker of Greece, Aristotle was perhaps the most mature and comprehensive.

5. Science

Aristotle's scientific works were the culmination of a sustained and highly significant interest in science on the part of the Greeks, reaching back at least two centuries before Aristotle. Greek thinkers made no clear-cut distinction between science and philosophy; it is therefore difficult to treat science as a thing apart from philosophy. Nearly all thinkers derived their conclusions from observations of nature. From the sixth century on, the Greeks steadily accumulated new knowledge about the natural world. Much of this knowledge derived from observations that they themselves made; other knowledge came from ancient Babylonia and Egypt, from whom the Greeks borrowed extensively.

Typical of the Greek interest in observation was Hippocrates (460–377 B.C.), a leading physician whose famous oath defining the responsibilities of a physician can be seen in nearly every American doctor's office. He insisted that nothing could be known about sickness except through observation of sick people and through a search for the natural causes of their sickness. He repudiated the traditional belief that sickness was due to evil spirits, and taught that it was a result of natural causes. Hippocrates had numerous followers who took the same approach and accumulated an extensive body of knowledge about the human body and its working.

Other Greeks devoted their energies to compiling information relating to astronomy, physics, geography, botany, and zoology. Their collective efforts allow us to credit the Greeks with the discovery of the scientific method, which relies on observation as the source of knowledge about nature.

Because they lacked instruments for precise observation and measurement there were limits beyond which Greek scientists were unable to go. And they often made glaring errors in interpreting their observations. Moreover, few Greek scientists were interested in using their knowledge for practical purposes. Scientific knowledge was used chiefly by philosophers who sought to illustrate the operation of the universe by observing how it worked. Aristotle represents the typical point of view of a Greek scientist; his wide knowledge of nature was useful to him only as it illuminated philosophical speculation, never as it applied to improving the physical and material lot of human society.

6. The Greek Mind

Any review of the brilliant work of the Greeks in activities ranging through literature, art, philosophy, and science raises one final question: Did all the leaders of Greek cultural life, whatever their specific interests, share any common ideas and viewpoints that, taken together, might characterize the Greek approach to life? The following basic concepts are offered in answer to that question, although generalization is always dangerous when so many men of such varied talents are in question.

Greek thought was intensely *humanistic*, placing man on a pedestal for admiration and idealization. Most Greeks believed that the world had been created for man's happiness. They therefore were certain that man was in *harmony with nature* and had no need to struggle against nature, try to escape it, or shrink from it in fear. The Greeks were *rationalistic*, placing a powerful trust in man's ability to understand nature's mysteries through his own intelligence and to act on the basis of his sound judgment to solve any problems that might beset him. Greek thought insisted upon *restraint* and *balance*, feeling that nothing was worse than excess in any shape or form.

The keenest Greek intellects were inquisitive and searching, never content to accept the obvious or the traditional at full face value. This *spirit of inquiry* constantly pushed them into new fields in every aspect of life, adding an element of *boldness* as a characteristic feature of the Greek way of life. Most Greek intellectual leaders were intensely interested in *society as a whole*, especially in the society of a city-state community, and were ready to offer their talents to the community instead of pursuing individual and introspective ends. Finally, the Greek mind sought *order and symmetry* in all things, being unwilling to tolerate disorder in thought or art.

No one would insist that the ideals expressed by a few intellectual giants and artistic geniuses were attained by all Greeks.

Greek history is full of cases in which the ideals set down above were violated or denied. Probably most Greeks, engaged in the routine of daily life, seldom paused to think what their civilization really meant to them, just as most modern men seldom dwell on this question. Even if the Greeks as a whole did not attain or even understand fully what their intellectual leaders set up as ideals for the good life, at least those ideals were clearly expressed and presented to them in poetry, drama, history, sculpture, architecture, and philosophy. The values ingrained in the great artistic and philosophical works of the Greeks became a model of civilized life for numerous peoples who rose to prominence in the Mediterranean area after the Greeks had lost their leadership.

SUGGESTED READING

Herbert Newell Couch, *Classical Civilization: Greece*, 2nd ed. (1951). An excellent introduction to Greek cultural life in its proper historical and chronological setting. The descriptions of Greek art, literature, philosophy, and religion are concise, readable, and judicious. The book also contains excellent illustrations.

* Edith Hamilton, *The Greek Way to Western Civilization* (Mentor). Published earlier in a hardback edition under the title *The Greek Way* (1930). A provocative discussion of some of the unique features of Greek civilization. Miss Hamilton tends to idealize the Greeks but stimulates a deeper appreciation of Greek culture.

* Gilbert Murray, *Five Stages of Greek Religion* (Anchor). Also available in a hardback edition, 2nd ed. (1925). A well-known description of the evolution of Greek religious thought down to the time of the victory of Christianity. The book gives an especially good description of the nature of the Greek mystery religions.

H. J. Rose, *Ancient Greek Religion* (n.d.). A brief study concentrating on a description of the major aspects of Greek religion, including the nature of the Greek gods, the relationship between religion and city-state life, and Greek criticism of their own religion.

* Robert Graves, *The Greek Myths*, 2 vols. (Penguin). An excellent summary of the stories told by the Greeks about their gods,

compiled by a highly skilled writer of history and fiction. Not only will a student find these stories fascinating but also he will gain an acquaintance with the mythical figures that have been used by artists and writers ever since Greek times. Graves's rendering of the Greek myths supplants the older Bulfinch's *Mythology*, which was a source of information concerning Greek myths for several generations of students of the classics.

* Eduard Zeller, *Outlines of the History of Greek Philosophy* (Meridian). Also available in a hardback edition, tr. by L. R. Palmer, 13th ed. (1931). A standard introduction to the history of Greek philosophy. This book will acquaint the student with the chief philosophers in Greece.

M. Hadas, *A History of Greek Literature* (1950). A thorough survey of the history of Greek literature highlighted by sound characterization of the accomplishments of all of the chief Greek authors. This book is especially useful for any student who wishes to read about a particular author.

A convenient way to sample Greek literature is to turn to some anthologies. Among those that are well done and easily accessible are: * W. H. Auden, ed., *The Portable Greek Reader* (Viking paperback); George Howe and Gustave Adolphus Harrer, eds., *Greek Literature in Translation* (1924); and Charles Theophilus Murphy, Kevin Guinagh, and

Whitney Jennings Oates, eds., *Greek and Roman Classics in Translation* (1947). A sampling from these anthologies might persuade a reader to undertake reading some Greek authors in their entirety. The works listed below are recommended as a starting point in the vast field of classical Greek literature.

* Homer, *Iliad* and *Odyssey*, tr. by E. V. Rieu (Penguin). These excellent renderings in modern English of Homer's epic poems will serve as an excellent starting point for any reader's study of Greek literature.

* L. R. Lind, ed., *Ten Greek Plays in Contemporary Translations* (Riverside Editions). An inexpensive collection of representative works by Aeschylus, Sophocles, Euripides, and Aristophanes. The plays included in this collection will perhaps encourage the reader to turn to other plays by these same authors. Most of their other works are available in inexpensive paperback editions.

* Scott Buchanan, ed., *The Portable Plato* (Viking). Contains a representative selection of Plato's writings, including *Protagoras*, *Phaedo*, *Symposium*, and *The Republic*. Certainly the most important of these is Plato's masterful tract on political theory, *The Republic*.

Richard McKeon, ed., *The Basic Works of Aristotle* (1941). This is but one of many compilations made from Aristotle's huge body of writings. Professor McKeon has supplied an excellent selection from Aristotle's works. Especially recommended are *Politics*, *Nicomachean Ethics*, and *Poetics*.

CHAPTER 8

---◆---

Greek Imperialism: The Hellenistic World,
336–31 B.C.

THE MARCH of Philip's Macedonian soldiers into Greece in 338 B.C. by no means spelled the doom of Greek civilization. Rather the Greeks were launched on a new venture that increased their significance in world history. Under Macedonian leadership they swept eastward and southward into Asia and Africa, transporting their institutions and ideas into the Near East. As a result the Greek and the Near Eastern civilizations mixed, producing a culture that we call Hellenistic to distinguish it from Greek culture of the classical age.

1. Alexander the Great

The military and political genius of Alexander the Great was chiefly responsible for launching the Greeks on this new phase of their history. Endowed with numerous qualities of greatness—intelligence, ambition, industry, imagination, physical attractiveness, boldness, an iron will—Alexander has never ceased to fascinate students of history. Although a Macedonian by birth, he was a Greek in spirit. His education under Aristotle had instilled in him a thorough knowledge and a fanatical admiration of Greek civilization. His conviction that the Greek way represented the ultimate in human excellence, abetted by

strong ambition, served as the driving force of his fabulous career.

Alexander was twenty when his father was murdered in 336 B.C. Philip had charted the immediate future for his son. Besides being king of Macedon, Alexander was master of the Greek city-states in his role as head of the Hellenic League. Philip had made preparations for a war against Greece's ancient foe, Persia, perhaps hoping to win the approval of all Greeks by rallying them in a crusade. It was this war that absorbed Alexander's interests. He delayed launching it only long enough to strengthen his authority in the Greek Peninsula by smashing an anti-Macedonian rebellion led by Thebes and Athens.

In 334 B.C. he led his Macedonian-Greek army into Asia Minor in order to attack Persia. Although Persia possessed a huge empire, a rich treasury, and a large military force, Alexander was victorious from the beginning. In the battles of Granicus (334 B.C.), Issus (333 B.C.), and Gaugamela (Arbela, 331 B.C.) he virtually annihilated the Persian army. In the intervals between these battles he occupied Asia Minor, the Tigris-Euphrates Valley, Syria-Palestine, and Egypt. Included in his prizes were the chief strongholds of Persian power at Babylon, Susa, and Persepolis. By 330 B.C. Alexander had achieved what he had

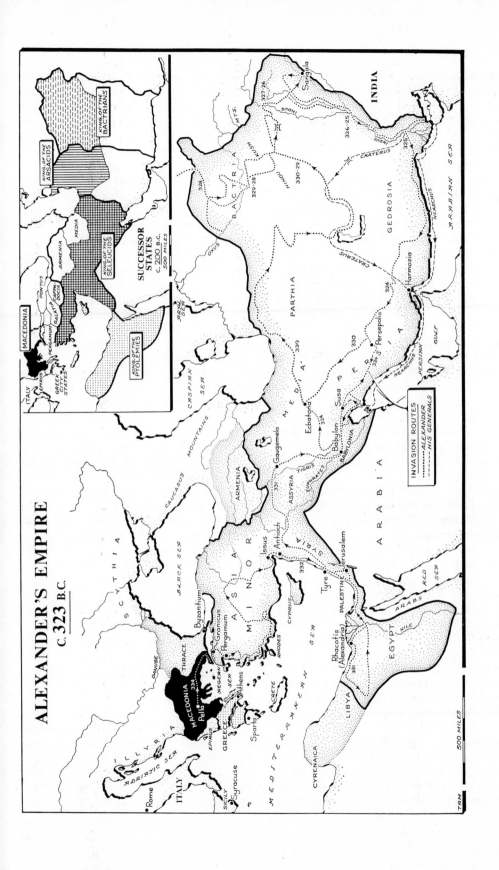

ALEXANDER'S EMPIRE

C. 323 B.C.

INVASION ROUTES
ALEXANDER
HIS GENERALS

500 MILES

Inset map:

MACEDONIA

KING OF THE ARSACIDS

KING OF THE SELEUCIDS

KING OF THE PTOLEMIES

KING OF THE BACTRIANS

SUCCESSOR STATES
C. 200 B.C.

500 MILES

Labels on main map:

ITALY · Rome · Syracuse · SICILY

ILLYRIA · ADRIATIC SEA · EPIRUS · GREECE · Sparta · CRETE

MACEDONIA · Pella · THRACE · 334 · Byzantium · AEGEAN SEA · Athens

SCYTHIA · BLACK SEA · Granicus · Pergamum · CAUCASUS MOUNTAINS

ARMENIA · ASIA MINOR · RHODES · CYPRUS · SYRIA · Antioch · Issus · Tyre · PALESTINE · Jerusalem

MEDITERRANEAN SEA · CYRENAICA · LIBYA · Phacolis (Alexandria) · EGYPT · NILE · 331

ARABS · RED SEA · ARABIA

CASPIAN SEA · MEDIA · Ecbatana · 330 · Gaugamela · 331 · ASSYRIA · TIGRIS · EUPHRATES · Babylon · BABYLONIA · Susa · 324

PERSIA · Persepolis · 330 · PERSIAN GULF · NEARCHUS · Harmozia · 324

PARTHIA · OXUS · BACTRIA · HINDU KUSH MTS. · 328 · 329–28 · 330–29

INDIA · Sangala · 327–26 · INDUS · 326–25 · 325 · CRATERUS · GEDROSIA · ARABIAN SEA

TRM

set out to do; he had crushed the ancient enemy of Greek civilization. This spectacular success was due to several factors—Alexander's well-disciplined foot soldiers, his strong cavalry, his own brilliant and bold generalship, and the poor quality of Persian leadership.

His restless genius would permit no pause. Ostensibly in pursuit of King Darius III, Alexander drove eastward from the chief Persian cities he had just conquered. The assassination of Darius by the Persians did not satisfy Alexander. Battling vast distances, native resistance, and defection in his own ranks, he pushed across Iran and the Hindu Kush Mountains into Bactria and eventually India, claiming all this territory as his and leaving behind newly founded cities as centers of Greek power. Beyond the Indus Valley his troops refused to go. Alexander, therefore, turned back westward through southern Persia and into Babylon, where he fell ill and died in June 323 B.C. at the age of thirty-three. Tradition has it that he was planning new conquests, including Arabia, Carthage, and Central Asia beyond the Caspian.

A career so short and so completely occupied with military campaigns left Alexander little time to face the problems of ruling his vast conquests. Probably he had no definite plans when he launched his campaign, forming his policies as circumstances arose. But before he died he had established certain broad principles of policy that guided his successors. As his career progressed, Alexander had conducted himself more and more like a divine autocrat, departing radically from the Greek ideal of a citizen-ruled state. Seeing that Greeks alone could not rule his vast empire, Alexander began to employ the talents of the conquered peoples. Persians were employed in some army and administrative posts. Alexander himself and many of his soldiers had married native women, suggesting that Alexander hoped for a merger of the many national groups under his rule. However, this point must not be pushed too far. From the beginning of his

career Alexander had insisted that the Greeks would remain politically, economically, and culturally supreme within his empire. High positions in the army and the civil administration were reserved for Greeks; non-Greeks would remain useful subordinates. In Alexander's eyes Greek dominance of the Near East was a goal much more worth attaining than that of amalgamating the East and West racially, culturally, or politically.

Alexander's death left most of his policies far from fulfilled, and it has often been said that his death was timely for the benefit of his fame, since his reputation might have suffered had he lived to face the task of holding his empire together. The Greek masters sat uneasily atop their vast domain. Greek culture was not firmly planted in the conquered territory, although many Greeks had migrated to the new cities built by Alexander and had become missionaries of the Greek way of life. Furthermore, Alexander left no heir capable of capitalizing on the magic of his name. Aside from his conquests his positive achievements were few. Yet no historian would deny his great importance. His influence lay chiefly in what later generations thought he was trying to do. He established for Greek society the ideal that a statesman of ability could create a government capable of bringing peace, harmony, and prosperity to all men living within a vast empire. He also convinced his successors that a great ruler could uplift his subjects by Hellenizing them. The struggle to attain these goals motivated much of the history of the Mediterranean world for centuries after Alexander's death.

2. Political Fate of Alexander's Empire, 323–31 B.C.

Politically Alexander's empire fared badly during the three centuries after his death. It split into numerous small states that engaged one another in constant warfare, a situation that hardly promoted Alexander's ideal of peace and harmony. Piece by piece Alexander's conquests were snatched away from his successors. Eventually the prize portions—those territories bordering on the Eastern Mediterranean from Macedon to Egypt—fell to Rome.

Immediately after Alexander's death a few of his generals tried to keep his empire united under a single king. Other generals fought this policy and eventually won the day. By 275 B.C. three major kingdoms, each ruled by its own king, had been established. In Egypt, Ptolemy set himself up as successor of the ancient pharaohs. In Macedon, Antigonus established his power as king, claiming both Macedon and the Greek Peninsula as his. Seleucus founded the third kingdom, claiming Asia Minor and all the territory from there to India. Numerous smaller kingdoms had also begun to emerge, often at the expense of the larger ones.

Only the briefest summary of the history of these kingdoms can be undertaken here. Macedonian political history was largely occupied with the problem of the relationship between the Macedonian kings and the Greek city-states. Antigonus and his successors insisted upon making the old city-states subordinate to Macedonian interests. The Greeks fought back with great persistence but not too much success. Many of the cities joined leagues in an attempt to hold off Macedonian power, the chief being the Aetolian League in northern Greece and the Achaean League in Peloponnesus. Even these leagues did not overcome the spirit of independence among the locally patriotic members, and resistance to the Macedonians was always weakened by quarrels among the Greeks themselves. Although the Macedonians were usually able to exert considerable influence over Greek affairs, this task absorbed all their energy, and eventually it brought on the downfall of Macedon. Shortly before 200 B.C. the Greeks appealed for Roman help against Macedon. In the ensuing wars Roman armies overran both Macedon and Greece, incorporating both areas into the Roman Empire.

The Ptolemaic kingdom of Egypt was the most stable and the longest-lasting of the successor states of Alexander, finally being conquered by Rome in 31 B.C. The Ptolemies ruled over a homogeneous population, a fact that reduced internal dissension. The chief goals of Egypt were to absorb Syria and Palestine and to be the strongest sea power in the Eastern Mediterranean. These goals involved her in constant war with the Seleucid kingdom. After Rome became prominent in the Near East, about 200 B.C., Egypt declined rapidly. The Egyptian people grew restive under the Greek Ptolemies, who made themselves Roman puppets in order to retain their power, and eventually Rome simply annexed Egypt.

The Seleucid kingdom had the stormiest history of all the successor states. Its gravest problem lay in trying to hold together different peoples scattered over a vast territory. Within a few years after Alexander's death all the territory east of the Tigris-Euphrates Valley shook off Seleucid control and split into independent kingdoms, the chief ones being Bactria and Parthia. From then onward the Seleucid kings strained every resource to hold Mesopotamia, Syria, Palestine, and Asia Minor. The most vulnerable of these proved to be Asia Minor, where Greek city-states, led by Pergamum, sought to carve out kingdoms free from the Seleucids, eventually calling Rome into Asia Minor to aid their cause. Rome did not stop until she overthrew the last Seleucid ruler in 63 B.C.

If Alexander's dream of a single empire came to nothing, so also did any hope of a single system of government for all people. The Hellenistic period saw almost as many systems of governments as there were states.

In spite of the variety, certain significant developments in the art of government occurred. The acceptance by the Greeks of monarchical government was undoubtedly the chief one. Even before Alexander's time many elements of Greek society began to abandon the idea that all men were capable of ruling, in favor of the idea that a hero, a philosopher-king, a superman alone could provide good government. The success of men like Philip and Alexander served as a practical demonstration of the validity of that idea. During the Hellenistic period the idea was put into action, monarchy becoming the typical form of government among the Greek rulers of the Near East. In most Hellenistic kingdoms the king's power was personal. He was a man who had won his position by strength of arms, virtue, and the blessings of the gods. Through his abilities he could bestow blessings upon his people. No constitution limited his power; only his personality and ability determined his conduct. In practical terms the typical Hellenistic king was absolute, and his chief task was to convince his subjects of his greatness by deeds and by a constant display of splendor.

To assist in exercising his vast powers, each Hellenistic king developed a highly centralized bureaucracy and maintained an elaborate court that swarmed with friends, wives, mistresses, favor seekers, and officials of all ranks. Well-defined departments of administration, concerned with finances, justice, record-keeping, and war, functioned under the eye of the king or his chief ministers. High offices in Hellenistic bureaucracies were reserved for Greeks, although natives filled lower positions. In establishing centralized, bureaucratic states the Greek masters of the Near East borrowed from the political practices of their predecessors, especially the Persians and the Egyptians.

While absolutist, bureaucratic monarchy gained the upper hand among the Hellenistic Greeks, the older city-state polity persisted with considerable vitality, especially in Greece and Asia Minor. Tyrannies, autocracies, and democracies operated everywhere. Assemblies, elected officials, councils of elders, popular courts, and citizen armies continued as of old. Some cities even showed an ability to innovate. For instance, the Aetolian and Achaean leagues marked the creation of confederations on a voluntary basis, something the earlier Greeks had never been able to accomplish. But if the city-states lived on, they were overshadowed by monarchy in the Hellenistic age. In war, in city beautification, in art patronage, and in economic activity the Athenians or Spar-

tans could not match the Seleucids or the Ptolemies.

For all its confusion, the Hellenistic period was important politically. The Greeks learned to conduct monarchical government as a substitute for their city-state polity. They put together larger states. They experimented with techniques aimed at allowing local autonomy within a larger political framework. And eventually they handed on to Rome a precious political tradition, enriched by their own experience as rulers of the Near East.

3. Hellenistic Prosperity

Greek rule in the Hellenistic world resulted in vigorous economic growth, so that one of the highlights of the period was an amazing prosperity. Alexander's conquests might well be compared to Columbus's discovery in that it opened up for Greek exploitation a vast territory endowed with great riches, just as Columbus's discovery supplied Europeans with new wealth and new lands to exploit. The Greeks migrated from their native cities in large numbers and applied themselves with vigor to the exploitation of these new lands. All over the Near East they found a native population accustomed to economic domination by a narrow ruling group and, therefore, were able to seize economic control without too much resistance. In many areas of the Hellenistic world well-organized agriculture, skilled industry, and well-developed trading systems already existed, again supplying openings for Greek enterprise. The energetic Greeks missed few of these opportunities. Agriculture, industry, and commerce all expanded under their management.

Agriculture continued to be the basic source of wealth in the Near East, but Greek control resulted in more efficient exploitation of the land. Irrigation systems, fertilizers, crop rotation, and new kinds of crops all combined to step up production. Nonetheless Greek rule did not fundamentally change ancient farming life in the Near East.

The chief advance lay in trade and industry. The Greeks displayed tremendous energy in exploiting the markets and the products put at their disposal when they conquered the Near East. Extensive capital came into their hands as a result of their seizure of the vast wealth stored in the treasury of the Persian king and of that controlled by the rich all over the Near East. The Greeks put this capital to work in large-scale trading and industrial ventures, their activities centering chiefly in the great seaboard cities of the Eastern Mediterranean. The Hellenistic kings led in this activity, creating state monopolies for the exchange and production of many products. They also helped trade by clearing the seas of pirates, keeping roads safe, building canals and harbors, improving marketing facilities in their cities, and establishing sound money systems. But private entrepeneurs were by no means absent in trade and industry; every important city was full of enterprising manufacturers, active traders, and skilled artisans.

Hellenistic prosperity was certainly one of the chief consequences of Alexander's conquests. However, that prosperity benefited only a few in Hellenistic society—princes, civil servants, landowners, great merchants, and priests. The mass of the population on the farms and in the cities still labored for small gain. The Greeks who spread over the Near East were usually predominant in the favored upper classes, the natives generally falling into the camp of the economically oppressed. As the Hellenistic era progressed, this gap between rich and poor caused increasing social conflict. Moreover, Hellenistic prosperity was not evenly distributed geographically. The great centers of wealth existed in a belt stretching from Asia Minor to Egypt. Here were the great cities, like Alexandria and Antioch, the best farms, the chief trade routes, the most skilled workers, and the most capital. Greece itself suffered a constant impoverishment during the Hellenistic age as economic leadership moved eastward and southward. This situation bred deep hostility and boded ill

for the long-run stability of Hellenistic society.

4. Literature and Art

The three centuries following Alexander's conquests mark an important era in cultural history. The Greeks were convinced that they had conquered "barbarians." No matter how deeply they became involved with Asians, they retained their feeling of superiority and sought to impress their ideas on their subjects. Nevertheless expansion brought the Greeks face to face with new ideas and made them aware of their own limitations. The result was a new outburst of activity in art, literature, and philosophy, which broadened older Greek culture without destroying its basic features.

In literature the Hellenistic age was not especially creative, although the quantity of output was tremendous. Epic poems, tragedies, comedies, lyrics, histories, and philosophical tracts were produced in great numbers, but very few of these works except the philosophical writings equaled in quality and originality those of the masters of the classical age of Greek civilization. Most writers, especially in poetic composition, concerned themselves chiefly with style, working over old subject matter in an attempt to achieve stylistic perfection. This preoccupation with style had an important bearing on later history, since it was the Hellenistic Greeks whom the Romans imitated in developing their literary styles.

The Hellenistic age produced a multitude of scholars who spent their lives reconstructing earlier literary masterpieces and writing extensive commentaries on them. These scholars congregated at a few great cities like Alexandria and Pergamum. With the help of their kings they collected huge libraries containing books from all over Greece and the Near East. Later ages owed an important debt to these scholars for preserving the bulk of classical literature. In an age before the use of printing, when only a few copies of any work were produced, it was easy to lose literary pieces or to have them

APHRODITE OF MELOS (VENUS DE MILO). This
statue dates from the Hellenistic era, probably
the third century B.C. The artistic ideals set by
Phidias and Praxiteles during the golden age of
Greek sculpture were still influential at this period. However, Hellenistic art was characterized
by a greater degree of realism than classical
Greek art. The feeling conveyed here is that the
figure portrayed is that of some actual woman,
rather than an idealization of the female form.
(*Archives Photographiques, Paris*)

corrupted by careless copying. The patient
yet unspectacular work of Hellenistic scholars prevented the loss of many classical
Greek authors and of important parts of the
literary tradition of the non-Greek Near
Eastern peoples.

The artists of the Hellenistic period were
no less active than the literary men. Again
classical Greek models exerted a powerful
influence, completely overshadowing the artistic traditions of the Near East. Architecture enjoyed a great boom because of the
numerous new cities built by the Greeks
and because of the desire of Greek kings
and rich merchants to display their power
and wealth. The new cities were filled with
the traditional buildings—temples, gymna-
siums, theaters, and buildings for conducting public business. There was a tendency
to stress size and ornateness in these buildings, although their basic architectural style
followed the pattern of the classical age.
Most Hellenistic cities were much better
planned than were older Greek cities, with
emphasis on wide streets, adequate water
supplies, commercial conveniences, and
parks. As a result, cities like Alexandria were
more impressive than older cities like Athens.

Much Hellenistic sculpture was mere
copying of the masters of fifth-century
Greece. However, some of this work took on
important new features. In place of the
classic quest to create idealized perfection
in portraying a subject, Hellenistic sculptors
tended toward realism. They came down
into the streets for their subjects instead of
ascending to the abode of the gods. Children, old people, common laborers, and barbarians occupied their attention. In place of
the restraint and reasonableness of classic
sculpture Hellenistic artists gave vent to
emotions, seeking to portray action and violence, passion, sorrow, and suffering. Often
they overdid themselves, leading to showi-
ness. Occasionally, however, a Hellenistic
artist caught the full spirit of the classical
style, as the famous *Winged Victory of
Samothrace* or the *Aphrodite of Melos*
(more commonly known as the *Venus de
Milo*) illustrate so well.

5. Philosophy and Science

The major contributions of the Hellenistic age were in the fields of science and
philosophy, which had been opened by the

pioneering Greeks in the sixth, fifth, and fourth centuries. Often the Hellenistic thinkers moved beyond their predecessors, a development that seldom occurred in the fields of literature and art.

Pre-Alexandrian Greeks, like Hippocrates and Aristotle, had introduced the concept that nature can best be understood by observing it, and they had begun to classify knowledge. Alexander's conquest put the Greeks in touch with a huge body of new data, which was carefully catalogued and from which scientists attempted to derive new laws about the world. The general use of Greek as the language of learning permitted scientific advances to spread widely. Royal patronage, especially by the Ptolemies, who built a great library and museum at Alexandria, helped to create an interest in science and to provide the necessary facilities. In this favorable climate the quest for knowledge about the natural world was actively pursued.

It will serve our purposes to mention a few of the great scientific names of the age, letting their work illustrate the efforts of the many who worked in science. For instance, geography was of great interest in the Hellenistic period. The new geography was summed up by Eratosthenes (about 275–200 B.C.), who worked at Alexandria. Using observations from a variety of sources, he reached many important conclusions. He calculated the circumference of the earth as 24,662 miles, 195 miles less than the actual figure. On the basis of his study of tides he insisted that the Atlantic and Indian oceans were joined and that India could be reached by sailing around Africa. He made maps using lines of longitude and latitude and divided the earth into zones still used by geographers. Seleucus (second century B.C.), along with others, studied the tides and came close to relating them to the gravitational force of the moon.

Astronomy likewise attracted attention. The two greatest names were Aristarchus (about 310–230 B.C.) and Hipparchus (about 185–120 B.C.). Both men worked from observations, many of which had

AN OLD MARKET WOMAN. This statue of the second century B.C. reflects the realism and emotionalism expressed in Hellenistic art. The lined face, the stooped posture, the halting step mark a radical departure from the idealization of humanity characteristic of classical Greece. (*Courtesy of The Metropolitan Museum of Art*)

been made by Babylonians of an earlier period. Aristarchus insisted that the earth revolved around the sun. Hipparchus denied this, and his opinion carried the day. Hipparchus also did work in calculating the length of the year. Both of these great astronomers tried to calculate the size of the sun and its distance from the earth, but with little success.

In mathematics the Hellenistic age was especially fertile. Euclid (323–285 B.C.) compiled a standard textbook of geometry that is still used as a basic text. Archimedes (287–212 B.C.) calculated the value of π (the ratio between the circumference and the diameter of a circle). He also devised a system for expressing large numbers, solved the problem of the relative volumes of a cylinder and a sphere, and laid the foundations for calculus. Trigonometry was perfected by Hipparchus, already mentioned above, and a fundamental work on conic sections was done by Apollonius of Perga (third century).

Scientific medicine was of great interest to the scholars of this period. Following the lead of Hippocrates, Hellenistic physicians made important progress in anatomy and physiology. Among the chief accomplishments of these men were the discovery of the nerves and the exploration of the function of arteries and the brain. Surgery advanced considerably; so did the use of medicines as a healing art.

Physics, chemistry, zoology, and botany were not of such great interest to the Hellenistic age. Archimedes, however, discovered the laws governing floating bodies and developed the theory of the lever; and Theophrastus (about 372–287 B.C.) wrote an important work on botany.

Most of the important work of Hellenistic scientists had been completed by the end of the second century B.C. Thereafter interest shifted to magic, astrology, and empty repetition of past accomplishments. The Hellenistic Greeks, like their predecessors in classical Greece, were limited in their scientific progress by lack of proper instruments. And there was still no widespread interest in the practical application of scientific ideas during the Hellenistic period, although a few scientists did distinguish themselves as inventors. Archimedes, for instance, invented the windlass, the double pulley, the endless screw, and several devices for defending his native city, Syracuse, against Roman attack.

The last significant development in ancient science came when certain scholars of the first and second centuries A.D. compiled great encyclopedias summarizing earlier scientific work. Among these works were those of Ptolemy (about A.D. 85–160) in astronomy and geography, Strabo (about 63 B.C.–A.D. 21) in geography, and Galen (A.D. 131–210) in medicine. The works of these men served as scientific guides until early modern times. As a result of their compilations Hellenistic science exerted enormous influence over later thinking.

For vigor and creativity Hellenistic science was rivaled by Hellenistic philosophy. In Athens the Academy of Plato continued to operate, serving in theory at least the ideals of the great master. Aristotle's work was carried on by the Peripatetics, who likewise maintained a school in Athens. However, the search for truth was not the chief interest of the Hellenistic age. The disciples of Plato and Aristotle found their work challenged by new schools of philosophy, interested chiefly in the problem of human conduct and seeking to derive ethical principles from the speculations of earlier philosophers.

Epicurus (about 341–270 B.C.), one of the chief representatives of this new point of view, built his ethical concepts on a strictly materialistic basis. He taught that the universe consisted of atoms, which by chance formed themselves into beings and things. The gods, if they existed, had nothing to do with this process and therefore need be of no concern to men. Given such a world, men should concern themselves only with happiness and pleasure. Epicurus argued that mere physical pleasure is not the path to happiness. Those things that will bring a peaceful, undisturbed mind alone can make a man truly happy. Epicurus pleaded with his disciples to withdraw into themselves, avoiding excessive wealth, involvement in politics, superstition, and too great contact with the world. Each individual ought to create a world of his own in which there is a minimum of strife, worry, or concern over the future. This philosophy was welcome to many educated men of the

Hellenistic period who saw little use in struggling in a world where great kings and great wealth determined most things. It offered a logical reason for escaping to a refined, enlightened, unburdened privacy. Although some disciples of Epicurus turned his teachings into an excuse for seeking purely physical pleasure, most Epicureans were admirable men, learned and refined, obedient to public authority, calm, and long-suffering.

Even more influential in shaping the moral atmosphere of the Hellenistic age were the Stoics, whose founder, Zeno (336–264 B.C.), taught in Athens while Epicurus was there. Stoicism was based on Zeno's conviction that the universe is ruled by a Divine Reason, which determines the fashion in which nature operates. For many Stoics this Divine Reason is a great god, overshadowing all other gods and providing a unity within the universe. This Stoic deity had ordained a perfect world; harmony and order would result if the laws of nature were adhered to by all creatures in the universe. Man's moral duty is thus clear. He must use his reason to attune himself and his actions to the unchanging laws of nature arising from Divine Reason. He must bear all misfortune with patience, since everything that happens has been ordained by an all-knowing Providence. And he must bear his good fortune without pride, since he is not responsible for it. The Stoic was schooled to adjust his life to fit circumstances; his life was a pilgrimage in which he disciplined himself to accept whatever came.

6. Hellenistic Religion

There was one notable exception to the general advancement and enrichment of Greek culture during the Hellenistic period. Older Greek religious ideas came into competition with Asian religions and suffered

an eclipse. This process had begun before Alexander's time when the mystery religions invaded Greece. During the Hellenistic period these religions steadily gained ground. Even the Greeks in the Near East were attracted to them, sometimes surrendering completely but more often trying to blend Asian religious ideas with their own philosophical concepts. All of the many mystery religions in the Hellenistic era had a few basic concepts in common. They provided a savior whose chief gift to man was eternal salvation. They tended toward monotheism. The mystery gods were universal gods, caring not where a man lived or who he was. Any individual who submitted to the purification rites could win favor with the mystery gods solely on the basis of his good conduct.

The mystery religions exercised a powerful influence on the Greeks as the Hellenistic age wore on. More and more, science and philosophy were put to the service of these religions. Scientific astronomy was transformed into astrology, the "scientist" studying the stars in order to know the future rather than to find new information, while the philosophers' quest for an understanding of the universe became an attempt to achieve contact with the powerful deities of the mystery cults. In this sense the peoples of the Near East conquered the Greeks during the Hellenistic period. A real possibility existed that some of the finest achievements of the Greeks would be swallowed up and twisted out of shape as a result of their losing encounter with Near Eastern religious ideas. This trend was checked at least temporarily by the emergence of Rome as a new champion of Greek civilization. Under Roman auspices Greek culture in a Latinized form enjoyed a renaissance and increased its geographical sway considerably by spreading to the Western Mediterranean world.

SUGGESTED READING

Arrian, *The Anabasis of Alexander* (many editions; a good one by F. R. B. Godolphin, ed., *The Greek Historians*, 2 vols. [1942]). A colorful account by a historian of the second century A.D. that serves as the chief ancient source for the career of Alexander the Great.

* W. W. Tarn, *Alexander the Great* (Beacon). Published in 1948 in a two-volume hardback edition. This is a beautifully written description of Alexander's career. Tarn especially stresses Alexander's importance as the creator of the ideas of brotherhood and unity.

A. R. Burn, *Alexander the Great and the Hellenistic Empire* (1948). A short, popularly written biography, so well constructed that it reads like a novel. The book ends with a stimulating discussion of Alexander's effect on world history.

Charles Alexander Robinson, *Alexander the Great: The Meeting of East and West in World Government and Brotherhood* (1947). A clear, well-constructed story of Alexander's career, marred slightly by the author's repeated complaint that Alexander was so busy conquering the world that he never did anything about his ideal of world brotherhood.

M. Cary, *A History of the Greek World from 323 to 146 B.C.*, 2nd ed., rev. (1951). A detailed political history of the complicated period in the Near East from Alexander's death down to Rome's emergence as the dominant power in the Near East. The author does an excellent job of presenting a clear picture of the political affairs in the various independent states that developed after Alexander's death.

W. W. Tarn and G. T. Griffith, *Hellenistic Civilization*, 3rd ed. (1952). A good description of all phases of Hellenistic civilization from 323 to 31 B.C. Political, economic, religious, and cultural matters are treated topically.

George Sarton, *A History of Science*, Vols. I and II (1952, 1959). The appropriate sections of these carefully prepared volumes on ancient science will supply a thorough introduction to the important subject of Greek and Hellenistic science.

Whitney J. Oates, ed., *The Stoic and Epicurean Philosophers* (1940). A collection of nearly all the writings of the early Stoic and Epicurean philosophers of the Hellenistic period. These writings furnish the best introduction to the ideas of these two schools of thought, so important in Hellenistic and Roman times.

* Frederick C. Grant, ed., *Hellenistic Religions: The Age of Syncreticism* (Liberal Arts Press paperback). The author presents a clear picture of the nature of the religious development of the Greek and Near Eastern world after the death of Alexander.

CHAPTER 9

The Rise of Rome to Domination of the Mediterranean World

THE GREEK failure to establish order permanently in the Eastern Mediterranean opened the way for the emergence of a new power there. By the end of the third century B.C., when Rome began to replace the Hellenistic states as the dominant power in the Mediterranean world, she already had a long history behind her.

1. The Early Italians

At a very ancient date Italy was inhabited by a primitive hunting people whose way of life was similar to that of hunting peoples all over the Mediterranean basin. Sometime before 3000 B.C. Italy was overrun by a short, dark people who had migrated from North Africa, probably to escape the rigors of the desert. These invaders introduced primitive agriculture into Italy.

About 2000 B.C. still more invaders began to enter Italy, this time from the north. These new invaders were Indo-Europeans. During the next thousand years several waves of these invaders pushed deep into Italy and fused with the older population to create the basic Italic racial stock. The Indo-Europeans arrived as conquerors, establishing themselves as political masters over much of Italy and imposing their language on the ancient inhabitants. The invaders also brought more advanced agricultural techniques and a knowledge of the use of copper, bronze, and iron. As a consequence Italy advanced toward a higher stage of civilization, although she still lagged far behind other peoples in the Mediterranean.

The backward Italic population was powerfully stimulated by the appearance on Italian shores of two highly civilized peoples—the Etruscans and the Greeks. The Etruscans came to Italy about 900 B.C., probably from Asia Minor, and eventually established political supremacy over western Italy from the Po Valley to Naples. Between about 750 and 500 B.C. the Greeks planted numerous colonies in southern Italy and Sicily. Both Etruscans and Greeks introduced the Italic peoples to new political institutions and economic techniques, fresh religious ideas, and advanced artistic and intellectual concepts.

2. The Foundation and Early History of Rome to 509 B.C.

Rome, originally one insignificant city among many in Italy, emerged out of this background. The founding of the city was quite different from that related in the familiar legend of Romulus and Remus. Rome was founded about 1000 B.C. by people speaking an Indo-European language. They were attracted to the location because it was easily defensible, the low-lying hills along the Tiber River and a convenient ford in the river making the spot ideal. In the beginning several villages existed independently on these hills, and for several centuries after their establishment little progress was made.

The first turning point in Rome's history came about 650 B.C., when the Etruscans, advancing southward from Tuscany, conquered the villages lying along the Tiber. Although we know very little about the details of Roman history under Etruscan rule, it is clear that the new masters of Rome exercised a lasting influence over the old population. The Etruscans united the several villages that occupied the site of Rome into a single city-state under a strong monarch. Two well-defined classes, the patricians and the plebeians, emerged. The patricians were distinguished by high birth and wealth, and were organized into clans, the heads of which exercised nearly complete control over the members and played an important role in political affairs as advisers of the kings. The patricians protected their position by refusing to allow intermarriage with plebeians. The plebeians—the rest of the population—were destined to a low place in society by their poverty and their exclusion from the great clans, although many of them managed to offset their lowly position by becoming clients of powerful patricians, performing some service for their patrons in return for protection and the means of livelihood. The Etruscans also taught the Romans new technical skills that increased the wealth of the native population. For the first time improved farming techniques, trading practices, and manufacturing skills were brought into the previously backward city.

In spite of the Etruscan contributions the Romans were not content to remain under Etruscan domination. Shortly before 500 B.C. Etruscan power was challenged by her conquered subjects throughout western Italy. Rome joined this rebellion, and in 509 B.C. her aristocrats led a successful revolution. The place of the Etruscan king was taken by two consuls elected annually from the patrician ranks. This revolt marked the beginning of the Roman Republic, an event long celebrated by the Romans as the greatest event in their history.

3. The Early Republic, 509–265 B.C.

In the two and a half centuries following the founding of the republic Rome was put to a severe test, for she was almost constantly at war during these years. So successful was she in these defensive wars that she ended by conquering most of Italy. While defending herself successfully she also perfected her republican government in a way that satisfied her citizens and made them dedicated patriots.

From 509 to about 350 B.C. Rome's position was most desperate. The fall of the Etruscans caused chaos in central Italy. The former subjects of the Etruscans battled one another, each trying to seize a lion's share of the spoils. Added to these wars were the repeated assaults on the lowland areas of west central Italy by tough mountain tribes from eastern Italy, previously held in check by the Etruscan might. A new foreign invader, the Gauls, who poured into Italy about 400 B.C., added to the confusion. Rome was usually at the center of these wars, fighting valiantly for survival, which often was in doubt. Only the gallantry of her citizens prevented the permanent ruin of the city.

Not until nearly 350 B.C. did some order begin to emerge again in a wide area around Rome. To a large extent Rome was responsible for this new order. Several neighboring communities began to look to her as a champion against the dreaded mountaineers. Rome met this challenge by assuming the responsibility for defending some of them. However, her rising prestige frightened other neighbors, some of whom had long been Rome's allies. Their attempts to check Rome resulted in a series of wars between 343 and 336 B.C., which ended with most of Latium and parts of Campania under Roman domination.

Spurning the usual methods of brutal subjugation and exploitation of conquered peoples, the Romans treated their new subjects in a fashion unique in antiquity. Some groups were immediately pacified by being given Roman citizenship. Other communities were allowed to keep control over local affairs but had to permit Rome to manage their foreign relationships. They also had to send troops to Rome's aid in time of war. These peoples were allowed to trade in Rome and to intermarry with Romans. It was clearly implied that these allies could have citizenship as soon as they demonstrated their loyalty and their fitness to participate in Roman political and social life. This intelligent treatment of conquered subjects soon paid off richly, and Rome gained the devoted support of most of these allies.

Her conquest of Latium and Campania imposed new and larger responsibilities on Rome. Upon her now rested the whole burden of holding off the hill peoples. Beginning as early as 326 B.C., the struggle between Rome and these invaders got under way in earnest, lasting almost continuously until 265 B.C. The superior armies of the Romans relentlessly pursued these foes until they were subdued. Luckily Rome seldom had to fight all her foes in Italy at once. Her skillful diplomacy succeeded in dividing them, a job not too difficult since peoples as diverse as Etruscan princes, Samnite barbarians, and Greek city-states had little in common. By 265 B.C. Rome had established her supremacy over all of Italy south of the Apennine Mountains. Fighting constantly to defend herself, she had conquered Italy and was mistress over a huge number of allies.

Many things account for this victory, including Rome's central position in Italy, her ability to make loyal allies out of conquered people, and her military genius. But perhaps the real key to her victory was the stable and just system of government that developed during this period of conquest. When Rome threw off Etruscan rule, political power fell into the hands of the narrow patrician aristocracy, which seemed determined to exploit its power for selfish purposes. During succeeding years, however, these patricians slowly surrendered their monopoly on power and wealth and agreed to share it with the citizen body at large, mainly because the sturdy plebeian farmers were needed as warriors to defend the city.

The long course of events leading to the modification of the early republic is referred to as the "Struggle of the Orders." Step by step the plebeians were given greater rights and powers in ruling the city. They were taken into the army. The law was codified for their protection. New assemblies were created to permit the voice of the whole citizen body to override or at least to guide the patrician minority. Special officials, called *tribunes*, possessing powers to veto the acts of the regular government, were created to protect the interests of the plebeians. One by one the elective offices of state were opened to plebeian and patrician alike. Laws were passed protecting debtors from unjust interest rates and preventing the patricians from monopolizing land. Intermarriage between plebeians and patricians was legalized. The final result of this political and social ferment can best be seen by examining Roman government and society in 265 B.C.

Theoretically the Roman Republic was ruled by the citizen body in 265 B.C. The citizens exercised their control through their right to participate in the deliberations of the popular assemblies, of which two were especially important. One was the Assembly of Centuries. Since it was based on a classification of the citizens on the basis of their financial ability to arm themselves for service in the army, the extremely rich were able to dominate it. However, all citizens were permitted to participate in the deliberations of this body, which had the power to pass laws and to elect most officials. The other important assembly was the Assembly of Tribes, which had been created early in the history of the republic exclusively for the purpose of giving plebeians a chance to express their complaints, although patricians were eventually admitted. The assembly was constructed by dividing the territory of the Roman city-state in thirty-five districts, or tribes. All citizens in each district were eligible to participate in assembly meetings and vote with their fellow tribe members. This body eventually gained the power to pass laws binding on the whole state. It was presided over by the tribunes who were elected from the plebeian class and who had the power to veto any act of the government at any time.

Although in theory the people were supreme, in practice the republic of 265 B.C. was ruled by a rather small group of wealthy aristocrats. These aristocrats controlled two parts of the governmental system absolutely, namely, the magistrates and the Senate. The magistracy consisted of all the elected officials charged with conducting the affairs of state. The chief officials were the two consuls, theoretically charged with the management of all civil and military affairs. The consuls were assisted by lesser officials performing specific functions. The *praetors* were elected to oversee the administration of justice. The *quaestors* were charged with handling financial matters. The *aediles* managed the policing of the city, the repairing of roads and buildings, and the providing of food for the city. All these officials were elected for one-year terms. Censors were elected every five years to classify the citizens for military service and to judge the moral fitness of citizens for public functions. In times of grave crisis a dictator was selected to rule the state; his term was limited to six months. According to law any citizen was eligible for these offices, but since there was no pay for officeholding and electioneering was expensive, few men of humble means aspired to high office and even fewer gained it.

Still more powerful than the magistrates was the Senate, a body of about three hundred men, already ancient by 265 B.C. Members of the Senate served for life. New members were recruited almost exclusively from the ranks of ex-magistrates. Election to the consulship or praetorship automatically

qualified a man for the Senate. Since the magistrates came almost exclusively from the wealthy class, the Senate was dominated by this group. The composition of the Senate is easier to describe than its powers, which though vague were very extensive. The Senate was in theory an advisory body, dedicated to making use of the political wisdom in the city-state to aid the magistrates and the people to decide wisely on public matters. However, in their capacity as advisers the senators virtually ran the state. Decisions relating to finances, war, peace, and internal affairs were never made without consultation with the Senate, whose decisions virtually had the effect of law and were usually accepted by the magistrates and the assemblies without question.

With the magistrates and the Senate controlled by wealthy men, usually of prominent families, it is clear that the republic was an aristocracy. The citizenry as a whole had considerable powers yet seldom exercised them. Most Romans were content to entrust the fate of the city to this aristocracy, satisfied that the aristocrats could be curbed if they abused their power. Certainly the history of Rome from 509 to 265 B.C. indicates that the trust was not misplaced: the aristocrats led Rome competently during her rise to mastery of Italy. Not guilty of any prolonged periods of abuse of power, they usually were sensitive to popular resistance and willing to make changes to satisfy popular demands for better treatment. Convinced that the aristocratic leaders were competent, extremely civic-minded, and not excessively greedy, the citizen body was content to approve and obey their orders. Not only did Rome's aristocratic republic satisfy her citizens, but it also proved to be a government capable of following a consistent policy to a successful conclusion. While satisfying the demands of most citizens well enough to encourage a deep respect for the city-state, the government of the republic also managed to avoid much of the wavering, fickle policy decisions that harmed so many of the more democratic Greek city-states. The Romans

had reason to speak with reverence throughout the remainder of their history about
the excellence of their early republic.

4. Overseas Expansion: The Punic Wars, 264–201 B.C.

Rome's increasing mastery over Italy in
the period preceding 265 B.C. brought about
an important change in her position in the
Mediterranean world. Although her people
did not fully realize it, she was becoming
a major power. For many years after 265
B.C. most of Rome's attention and energy
were directed toward establishing her place
among the other Mediterranean powers;
she ended by conquering them and welding
them into a vast empire.

The first important Roman encounter
with a major overseas power was perhaps
the most decisive. This clash came with the
African city of Carthage, a worthy com-
petitor. Carthage was an ancient Phoenician
colony that had gone its own way after
Phoenicia was conquered by the Assyrians
in the eighth century B.C. In the succeeding
centuries Carthage had created a thriving
commercial empire in the Western Mediterranean and had become the greatest power
in that area. Rome up to 265 B.C. had shown
little concern over Carthage's power and on
several occasions had signed peaceful alliances with Carthage, usually admitting in
these treaties that Carthage was entitled to
control the Western Mediterranean.

By 265 B.C. Carthage was making an effort to absorb all of Sicily in her empire
at the expense of the Greek city-states located there. One of these cities appealed
to Rome. This posed a serious problem for
the Roman authorities. One Roman account
of this event said that the Senate at first refused to allow Rome to become involved,
but the people, enticed by the promise of
rich spoils, overrode the Senate. This is
probably an oversimplification of the events.
A Carthaginian stronghold so close to Roman territory would constitute a grave danger, and, since the aggressive Carthaginians
were certain to cause trouble among Rome's

recently conquered allies in southern Italy,
Roman self-interest dictated that she check
Carthaginian expansion. Therefore, in 264
B.C. Rome decided to help the Greek city-
states in Sicily. This decision meant war
with Carthage.

The first Punic War (264–241 B.C.) centered around a struggle for Sicily. In the
early stages of the war Rome sent several
armies to Sicily but always found victory
eluding her because Carthage controlled the
sea routes and the key seaports in Sicily.
Rome was finally driven to build a navy to
offset Carthage's advantage. Almost miraculously the Romans learned to be fairly competent sailors, capable of challenging the
Carthaginian fleet. So bold did the Roman
sailors become that they undertook an invasion of Africa in 255 B.C. This move
ended in disaster when the Roman fleet was
caught in a storm and suffered staggering
losses. Without an adequate fleet Rome
found all efforts to drive the Carthaginians
out of their Sicilian holdings futile. Not until 241 B.C., and then only after a supreme
effort to raise money, was Rome able again
to put an adequate fleet to sea. When the
Carthaginians began to feel the revived Roman sea power, they sued for peace. Rome
annexed Sicily and received a sizable money
payment from her recent foe.

The first Punic War by no means settled
things between Rome and Carthage. In the
years that followed the peace of 241 B.C.
Carthage turned her energies to rebuilding
her strength for another showdown. Under
the leadership of Hamilcar Barca, Spain was
made the base for the next war. Hamilcar
successfully subdued the native Spanish
population, collected a huge war chest from
tribute, and recruited and trained an excellent army of the Spanish natives. After his
death in 229 B.C. his policy was carried on
first by his son-in-law and later by his brilliant son, Hannibal. Rome was able to do
little to counteract this threat, being fully
occupied in beating back several peoples
who had tried to invade Italy while she was
engaged in the first Punic War. And so a
determined Carthage and a busy Rome

headed for a new war, which finally began in 218 B.C. when Hannibal attacked a Roman ally in Spain.

The second Punic War (218–201 B.C.) was certainly the sternest military test Rome ever met. The genius of Hannibal was in large part responsible for Carthage's valiant struggle. Before the war began Hannibal had settled upon his strategy. He decided to invade Italy, hoping to encourage Rome's allies to desert her. Isolated, Rome would be an easy target. Rome, on the other hand, hoped to end the war quickly by invading Africa and Spain, but her plans were wrecked by Hannibal's remarkable feat of leading his army from Spain over the Alps into Italy, eluding the forces sent by Rome to stop him. Once in Italy, Hannibal proved unbeatable on the field of battle, for on three different occasions in 218 and 216 B.C. the Romans challenged him with large armies, only to be defeated disastrously each time. The last of these battles, Cannae, convinced the Romans that Hannibal was superior in open battle. They therefore adopted a policy of harassing his army, otherwise leaving him free to do as he pleased in Italy. For fifteen years Hannibal maintained an army on Italian soil, spreading destruction up and down the peninsula. This indeed was a remarkable feat, especially in view of the fact that he received almost no replacements or supplies from Carthage. It is no wonder that the Romans held this genius in awe. But Hannibal did not succeed. No matter how hard he tried he could not compel or persuade more than a few of Rome's Italian allies to desert her. As a consequence he did not succeed in isolating Rome and never found an opportunity to attack the city.

While holding Hannibal at bay after the disasters of 218 and 216 B.C., Rome undertook the long struggle to crush Carthage. She fought on many fronts, actually winning the war outside Italy. Large armies were sent to Spain, where Carthaginian power was slowly crushed, cutting Hannibal off from hope of reinforcements. Another Roman force was dispatched to Sicily to choke off a rebellion in support of Carthage. Meanwhile Roman naval units patrolled the Western Mediterranean and the Adriatic, keeping Carthage from sending aid to Hannibal from Africa and preventing Hannibal from getting help from his ally, the king of Macedon. At the same time Roman diplomacy encouraged African peoples to attack Carthaginian territory. The culmination of Rome's counteroffensive came in 205 B.C., when she landed a large army in Africa under Scipio Africanus, a young general who had demonstrated great ability in the war in Spain. Scipio's successes soon brought Carthage itself under attack. To save the city, Hannibal was recalled from Italy in 203 B.C., thus ending his hopes of bringing Rome to ruin on Italian soil. Even the great Hannibal could no longer stem the tide. He met Scipio in a battle in 202 B.C. at Zama, where he suffered a complete defeat, having finally encountered a Roman general who was his equal.

After Zama, Carthage sued for peace. She was forced to surrender Spain to Rome, her navy was destroyed, a heavy fine to be paid over the next fifty years was imposed upon her, and Carthage agreed never again to wage war outside Africa and in Africa only with Rome's permission. Part of her territory in Africa was turned over to Numidia, a state that Rome hoped would balance Carthage in Africa. Thus was Carthage reduced to a minor power. Victorious Rome was mistress of the Western Mediterranean!

5. Overseas Expansion: Domination of the East, 200–133 B.C.

Rome had seldom been concerned with the Eastern Mediterranean world prior to the second Punic War, but her rising power made it impossible to avoid that turbulent area forever. This was especially true because a crisis was developing in that area by 200 B.C. All during the third century B.C. an uneasy balance of power existed among the several states of the East. The three major powers were Macedon, the Seleucid Empire, and Egypt. Scattered among these three were many small powers, including Athens, the Aetolian League, the Achaean League, Rhodes, and Pergamum. As the third century drew to a close the balance among these states was upset by two factors. First, Egypt grew woefully weak under the poor rule of the Ptolemaic dynasty. Second, a pair of ambitious kings ruled in the other two kingdoms: Philip V in Macedon and Antiochus III in the Seleucid Empire. Each hoped to capitalize on Egypt's decline by conquering her and most of the other independent states in the Near East. Their aggressive policy frightened all the other states of the whole area. In frantic search for assistance everyone turned to the new star rising in the West: Rome.

Rome hesitated for a moment as the appeals from the East descended on her in 201–200 B.C. She was tired of war, nearly bankrupt, suffering from extensive devastation in Italy, and ignorant of affairs in the East. However, powerful forces drove her toward intervention. Philip V of Macedon had allied himself with Hannibal during the second Punic War. He was clearly a danger to Rome. Even more important, many Romans had become ardent admirers of the Greeks during the third century. This was especially true of the Roman aristocracy; no less a figure than Scipio Africanus was prominent in this Hellenizing movement. For such men it was urgent that something be done to save the Greek city-states from Macedonian aggression. Fear of Philip and the desire to help his victims outweighed the arguments against war. Therefore, in 200 B.C. Rome declared war on Philip V.

The campaign lasted only four years. Macedon was no match for Rome. In the Roman-dictated peace settlement Philip V was required to evacuate all Greece and confine himself to his old kingdom. Rome then preceded to restore the independence of the Greek city-states Philip V had conquered. In a few cases she intervened in city-state governments to create order, but in general she tried to give each Greek city-state its way. Having "freed" the Greeks, Rome withdrew, asking nothing. She had

fought an expensive war only to champion the much-admired Greeks.

If, however, Rome thought that her trouble in the East was over, she was sadly mistaken. Antiochus III had sat by innocently as his fellow culprit, Philip V, was beaten. Once the Romans left, he returned to his aggressive ways, convinced that his hour had struck. Included among his possible victims were many Greek communities, who again clamored for Rome's help. In 192 B.C. Antiochus sent his armies into Greece, urged on by a few Greek cities who disliked the Roman settlement of 196 B.C. Rome could only answer this challenge with force. Antiochus fared no better than had Philip V. Roman legions drove him out of Greece and pursued him into Asia Minor, where they inflicted a crushing defeat. By 189 B.C. Antiochus gave up. Once again Rome tried to set the Near East to order. Antiochus was required to keep out of Asia Minor in the future. His navy was destroyed, and a staggering fine was imposed on him. In Asia Minor, Rome turned over large territories to Pergamum and Rhodes, intending to support them as the dominant powers of Asia Minor. Most of the Greek cities were again given independence, although those who had aided Antiochus were fined and deprived of some territory, and again Rome took nothing except the fines she had imposed.

Both Macedon and the Seleucid state had now been reduced to secondary importance, and the threat in the East seemed to have vanished. However, the trouble had only started. The old balance of power had been destroyed, and with it went all semblance of order. Warfare between petty states became chronic. Each squabble was eventually called to Rome's attention. The years after 189 B.C. revealed that a new order was urgently needed in the East. With great reluctance Rome accepted the only possible solution— she must conquer and rule the East. Even the Greeks whom she admired so greatly proved treacherous, quarrelsome, and unreliable.

The first evidence of her more severe

policy came in 171–167 B.C., when Macedon began another war, joined by many
Greek cities. Their combined efforts were
easily defeated by the Roman army. Rome
virtually took over Macedon at the end of
this war, leaving her only nominal independence. Roman armies marched through
Greece, executing pro-Macedonians, deport-
ing hostages to Italy, and enslaving suspected troublemakers. A few years later a
minor disturbance in Macedon resulted in
the annexation of the whole territory as a
Roman province to be ruled by a Roman
governor. Trouble in Greece resulted in
stern reprisals, culminating in 146 B.C. with
the complete destruction of Corinth as an
example to the Greeks. By that date Rome
had managed to force pro-Roman governments on most Greek cities and to cow the
anti-Romans into submission. Although
technically free, most Greek cities were Roman dependents.

Rome's allies in Asia Minor had proved
equally unreliable and harsh measures had
to be taken against them. Finally in 133
B.C. Rome took over the key kingdom of
Pergamum in Asia Minor as a province. The
king of Pergamum had willed his kingdom
to Rome prior to that, probably in the hope
of getting Rome to protect his state from
his many foes. Once established in Asia
Minor, Rome would obviously have to extend her sway to protect herself. No one
was in any position to stay her advance,
since between 200 B.C. and 133 B.C. she
eliminated the chief Near Eastern powers.

While concentrating her attention chiefly
on the East between 200 and 133 B.C. Rome
continued to solidify her power in the West.
The occupation of Spain was begun and an
attempt was made to organize that land under a provincial organization. The territory
lying between the Alps and the Apennines,
called Cisalpine Gaul, which had revolted
in the course of the second Punic War,
was recovered and reorganized. Carthage was
not a serious threat to Rome after the second Punic War, but the old hatred and fear
of this ancient enemy continued to haunt
Rome long after 201 B.C., leading the Romans to magnify every act of Carthage far
beyond its importance. With politicians
shouting "Carthage must be destroyed" as a
solution to nearly all of Rome's problems,
it was only a matter of time until mighty
Rome took full vengeance on her old foe.
For no good reason Rome declared war on
Carthage in 149 B.C. In 146 B.C. the city
was captured, destroyed completely, the site
sown with salt, and Carthage's territory annexed as a Roman province.

The passing of her most formidable foe
was a fitting symbol of Rome's position in
the Mediterranean world as the second century B.C neared its close. She had grown
from a tiny village to the leading power in
the Mediterranean world. But her conquests immediately posed a new problem:
Now that her authority was predominant,
how would she use it?

SUGGESTED READING

M. Rostovtzeff, *A History of the Ancient World*,
Vol. II: *Rome* (1927). A stimulating survey
of the whole span of Roman history, useful
for this and the following chapters on Rome.
The volume is made even more valuable by
excellent illustrations.

Howard Hayes Scullard, *History of the Roman
World from 753 B.C. to 146 B.C.*, 2nd ed.,
rev. (1951). A detailed, thoroughly scholarly
survey of Roman history down to 146 B.C.
The volume concentrates chiefly on political
history and is especially useful for the clear
picture it supplies of the development of the
Roman republican system of government.

Tenney Frank, *Roman Imperialism* (1914). A
brilliant discussion of Rome's rise to power in
the Mediterranean world, especially useful for
the light it throws on Rome's motives and
methods in matters concerned with expansion.

Leon Homo, *Roman Political Institutions from
City to State*, tr. by M. R. Dobie (1929).
A thorough although sometimes difficult discussion of the development of the Roman system of government. The book contains mate-

rial for the whole of Roman history and is
therefore useful for Chapters 10 and 11 as
as well as for this chapter.

Frank Frost Abbott, *A History and Description
of Roman Political Institutions*, 3rd ed.
(1911). A concise yet complete discussion of
the Roman constitution. The book is divided
into two sections. The first treats the development of the Roman system of government
chronologically; the second describes the nature of the chief political institutions once
each had reached its full development.

H. M. D. Parker, *The Roman Legions* (1928).
A full discussion of the nature of the Roman
army and of its development.

G. P. Baker, *Hannibal* (1929). A well-written
evaluation of the great Carthaginian general
and his place in history.

B. H. Liddell-Hart, *A Greater than Napoleon:
Scipio Africanus* (1927). A readable biography
emphasizing, as the title suggests, Scipio's military greatness.

Polybius, *The Histories* (several editions; an excellent one in the Loeb Classical Library, tr.
by W. R. Paton, 6 vols. [1922–27]). Polybius,
a Greek who lived in Rome for part of his life
as an intimate friend of Scipio Aemilianus,
grandson of Scipio Africanus, supplies the best
information about the Punic Wars. His account will serve as an excellent introduction
to those wars and their effect on Rome.

Livy, *History of Rome* (many editions; the most
available good one is in the Loeb Classical
Library, tr. by B. O. Foster, 13 vols.
[1919 ff.]). Livy wrote his great history between 27 B.C. and A.D. 17. Its early books set
down in a dramatic fashion the stories that
the Romans themselves believed about their
own origins. Only by reading these accounts
can one grasp the meaning of certain attitudes
the Romans held toward political life and civil
responsibility.

* Plutarch, *Lives* (many editions; there is a good
one in the Modern Library series). The biographies of Romulus, Camillus, Fabius, Aemil-
ius Paulus, and Coriolanus are useful in supplying information concerning the legends of
early Roman history.

CHAPTER 10

The Failure of the Roman Republic, 133–31 B.C.

Rome's triumphant march to supremacy in the Mediterranean area by 133 B.C. seemed to indicate that all was well with the Roman Republic. Her constitution seemed sound, her institutions adequate, and her citizens satisfied. This outward appearance of the republic was misleading. The Romans had been neglecting serious problems that began to appear much earlier, and eventually they had to be faced. The history of Rome for a century after 133 B.C. was dominated by the upheavals caused by these problems, and as the century passed it became obvious that Rome's old form of government was obsolete and that fundamental changes had to be made.

1. Problems of a World Power

Rome's wars and conquests created problems of major proportions. The defense of vast frontiers required large armies and heavy expenses on a permanent basis. Administrative direction was needed to maintain law and order in areas where Rome had destroyed old governments. Rome's allies in Italy who had fought loyally to help her expand and who had not received adequate reward were becoming increasingly restless and hostile. Thousands of Roman citizens were uprooted, a factor especially true of the small farmer-citizens of Italy, long the back-bone of the Republic. Some left their farms to fight, never to return to the old way of life. Others were ruined economically when Rome began to collect large amounts of grain as tribute from her conquered subjects outside of Italy, and the small farmers who could not compete with this cheap grain were forced off their land and into the city, where they had to depend upon the state or some rich man for support. A new class of wealthy capitalists emerged from Rome's wars of conquest, their wealth coming chiefly from supplying the armies and from collecting tribute from Rome's new subjects. This new class sought political power to go with their wealth. They also sought more wealth, chiefly by investing their capital in land in Italy and turning it to the production of profitable crops, such as olives and grapes. They imported slaves from abroad as labor, depriving many citizens of a livelihood and placing a stigma on manual labor. Many citizens who had become acquainted with new ideas as a result of their experience abroad as warriors, governors, and tax collectors were less willing to live under old moral and social restraints. In short, from every side, political and economic problems, social stresses, and intellectual ferment were loosed on Rome as her armies conquered the Mediterranean world.

Most Romans paid little attention to

those problems prior to 133 B.C. Their system of government remained essentially what it had been before her armies began their successful march to world domination. Power was still concentrated in the hands of a narrow aristocracy entrenched in the Senate. In fact, during the terrible crises of the wars against Carthage and the Eastern kingdoms, this narrow minority actually increased its hold on Roman society. Most citizens, who did not understand complicated foreign affairs and did not have time to follow the intricate negotiations that accompanied Rome's expansion, gladly let the senators take over the state. By 133 B.C. this group claimed its monopoly on power as its right. The senators concerned themselves with little else except protecting their power and using it to increase their wealth. The needs and problems of other classes, constantly growing more serious, were of little concern to them. Moreover, they made no attempt to develop instruments of government to guard the frontiers and to rule the provinces justly and peaceably. At the very moment when major problems were emerging in Roman society, Roman political institutions were thus becoming more inflexible, more involved with class privileges than ever before, more incapable of facing the major issues of the day. In the face of this situation Rome was due for internal trouble. In 133 B.C. that trouble began, and it did not cease until Rome's republican form of government lay in ruins.

2. The Parties at War, 133–79 B.C.

The first phase in the decline of the republic was a violent party struggle for control of Roman government. On one side was the old ruling clique, calling themselves the *optimates* and standing for the supremacy of a few. Opposed was the party made up of the poor and the middle class, the *populares*. The populares were usually led by strong leaders (often of aristocratic origin) who realized that reforms were necessary but who were spurned by the Senate. These reformers turned to the people, where final authority theoretically lay, in search of support to carry out their programs.

The first sharp struggle between these parties arose between 133 and 121 B.C. The populares were led by the brothers Tiberius and Gaius Gracchus, known as the Gracchi. Although from the aristocratic class, these men were deeply troubled by the decline of Rome's small farmers. Tiberius, elected tribune in 133 B.C., proposed that land belonging to the state be granted to the landless residents of Rome. Since most of the public land was already in the hands of rich senators who had leased it on highly favorable terms, Tiberius's proposal was turned down by the Senate. Tiberius then went to the people in the Assembly of Tribes, where his proposal was enthusiastically approved. Rather than accept the will of the people the Senate resorted to violence, murdering Tiberius on the pretext that he was trying to be a dictator. Ten years later Gaius Gracchus took up the same cause, adding new ideas to attract a larger following. As tribune he persuaded the Assembly of Tribes to pass new land laws, to provide cheap grain for the city masses, and to establish colonies to care for impoverished Romans. His legislation also granted extensive privileges in tax collection to the non-noble capitalists (called *equites*), whom Gaius wanted to rally to the populares cause. The senators fought Gaius bitterly, but he prevailed through the popular assembly. His success sealed his doom, however, for the Senate again resorted to violence and Gaius was killed in 121 B.C. Although the careers of the Gracchi had ended tragically, their leadership had once again reminded the populace of Rome of its powers and had seriously challenged the senatorial monopoly. The Senate had not heeded the demands or respected the rights of the people. Concerned only with saving its power, it resorted to violence as a means of removing those who threatened it. Such methods certainly made it doubtful that the Senate was capable of dealing with Rome's complex problems in an intelligent way.

The death of Gaius Gracchus left the

populares leaderless for a decade. The Senate held power but unfortunately showed no deeper insight into Rome's problems. Inevitably a new crisis arose. It began in 118 B.C., when Rome became involved in a struggle for power within the kingdom of Numidia in Africa. This complicated affair led to charges that certain senators had been bribed to favor a Numidian prince named Jugurtha. The Roman public became so enraged that war was declared in 111 B.C. Senatorial bungling and corruption, resulting in the disgraceful surrender of several Roman armies, aroused Roman feelings to an even greater extent. Something had to be done to save Rome's honor.

A new popular hero arose to turn popular fury against the Senate. The man of the hour was a peasant's son, Marius, (about 155–86 B.C.), who had served in the army against Jugurtha. In 108 B.C. Marius ran for consul, building his campaign around violent charges against the Senate. Although the Senate fought him bitterly, he was easily elected to serve for the year 107 B.C. with a mandate to end the African mess. Once in office Marius took a bold and fateful step. He privately recruited an army of volunteers to fight in Africa, promising to reward them once the war was over. His control of a private army virtually put him beyond the reach of the Senate, which could no longer safely rely on assassination as a convenient way of disposing of a leader threatening its power.

Marius quickly justified the trust placed in him by crushing Jugurtha in 105 B.C. So great was his reputation that he was re-elected consul during the years 104–101 B.C. to fight Germanic tribes threatening to invade Italy from the north. Again he was successful, "saving" Rome in a time of great danger. The military danger over, Marius had one more task: to reward his veterans at the expense of the state. Thus he stood for election as consul once again in 100 B.C., coupling broad promises to the populace with coercion by his veterans to persuade people to vote for him. This combination assured his election and allowed

him to inaugurate a broad program favoring all elements of his party. However, Marius proved inept as a political leader. Before his term of office was finished, his party fell apart and he lost his great prestige. The optimates came back to power, having seen what even an unskilled politician could do to control Rome when backed by an army.

The next decade passed quietly, albeit the populace seethed with discontent and the senatorial rulers suppressed every effort to remedy the causes of trouble. In 90 B.C. another storm broke over Rome, opening a new era of strife. The occasion was a great rebellion of Italian allies who demanded Roman citizenship. The Senate met this crisis by entrusting an obscure nobleman named Sulla (138–78 B.C.) with an army and by eventually conceding citizenship to the allies. By 87 B.C. the allies were crushed. However, the revolt had caused still another threat to appear in the Eastern provinces, where the king of Pontus, Mithradates, undertook a war to liberate the East from Roman rule. He was widely accepted by the native population as a savior, and an army had to be sent against him. Rome was plunged into a civil struggle to decide who would command that army. The Senate wanted Sulla to go, feeling that he was "safe." The populares clamored for Marius. The question was settled only when Sulla marched the army that he had been using to defeat the rebellious Italian allies into Rome and secured the Asiatic command by force, a procedure that was hardly constitutional or customary.

Sulla was in the East until 83 B.C. He forced Mithradates to return to his kingdom and thus retrieved the Eastern provinces, but he made no final settlement. His eye was on Rome, where the Marians had forced their way back to power, the Senate being powerless to stop them once Sulla's army had left Italy. Sulla spent considerable time pillaging the East as a preparation for the eventual struggle for power. Finally in 83 B.C. he landed in Italy and marched on Rome, where the Marians, lacking in strong leadership since Marius's death in 86 B.C., were routed.

To re-establish order in Rome, Sulla assumed the office of dictator and undertook a program aimed at restoring the authority of the Senate. He brutally executed scores of populares leaders and virtually eliminated the powers of the tribunes and the Assembly of Tribes, although he did make some concessions to the equites by creating new seats in the Senate and filling them from this class. Having restored the Senate, Sulla retired from public life in 79 B.C. to enjoy the wealth he had accumulated. He obviously hoped that the Senate could find means of solving other problems now that it was free of rabble-rousers and the demanding voice of the Roman people.

Although it might seem that Sulla's restoration of the Senate left the situation just where it was in 133 B.C., his retirement actually ended an era. The Senate was in power in 79 B.C., not because of its own virtues or prestige, but because a successful military leader decreed so. The senators had earned the hatred and mistrust of many citizens by their bungling, violently reactionary actions of the past half century and they thus sat uneasily at the summit of power. It was clear that bold individuals, properly armed, might topple the Senate as easily as Sulla had restored it. The long, bitter, indecisive clash between the optimates and the populares favored the rise of such individuals who did not need to respect the law if they did not wish. The republican form of government had suffered a mortal wound.

3. The Era of the Strong Men, 79–44 B.C.

The Senate quickly proved itself unworthy of Sulla's confidence. Between 79 and 70 B.C. a series of civil wars, slave revolts, scandals, and foreign attacks disturbed the political scene. Each of these crises provided a chance for ambitious individuals to make a reputation for themselves and to lay the groundwork for great careers. Among the most prominent figures of this period were Pompey, Marcus Licinius Crassus, Julius Caesar, and Cicero. None of them had much hope of becoming important if the senatorial aristocrats continued to rule. However, by skillful maneuvering in times of crisis they managed to become indispensable to the state and thus the real rulers of Rome.

Pompey (106–48 B.C.) was the first of the new leaders to gain the upper hand. Acting behind the scenes, he got the Senate and the people to vote him two important military commands. In 67 B.C. he was granted vast powers to clear the Mediterranean of pirates, and in 66 B.C. he was given even greater power to deal with Mithradates, who was again on the rampage in the East. Pompey hunted down the pirates in a matter of months. In 66 B.C. he turned to a pursuit of Mithradates and very shortly eliminated him. While in the East, Pompey undertook important steps for which he had no authority: conquering new territories around the eastern end of the Mediterranean, organizing new provinces, cleaning up the administration of the old provinces, and putting his trusted followers in key spots. By 63 B.C. he was virtually the ruler of the East, having paid almost no attention to the regular government in Rome.

Pompey's rise to power did not go unchallenged. Back in Rome other aspiring politicians tried everything in their power to offset Pompey. The chief figure was Crassus (about 115–53 B.C.), a rich capitalist who had recently acquired a valuable ally in the person of Julius Caesar (100–44 B.C.), still a young man. Crassus and Caesar spent huge sums of money in an attempt to get the people of Rome to vote them armies and authority like those Pompey possessed. They engineered a series of conspiracies in the hope of creating the need for someone to protect Rome. The senators usually tried to block them, although Crassus's money won him friends even in the Senate. One of the biggest obstacles was Cicero (106–43 B.C.), who used his considerable political skill in an effort to work out an alliance between Pompey and the

THREE ROMAN STATESMEN. Julius Caesar, Cicero, and Pompey, the three statesmen so skillfully depicted here, dominated the political scene in Rome between 70 and 42 B.C., and their faces were as well known as are those of today's world leaders. Each played a crucial role in the decline of the Roman Republic and the institution of one-man rule for the vast empire that the Romans controlled by that time. The busts serve as good examples of the skill of Roman sculptors in portraying individuals realistically. (*Alinari Photo*)

Senate for the purpose of safeguarding the old order. Especially during his term as consul in 63 B.C. Cicero blocked the ambitions of Crassus and his companions, and for the rest of his life he talked about how he had saved the republic in 63 B.C.

Pompey brought matters to a climax by returning to Italy in 62 B.C. Everyone expected that he would do as Sulla had done, using his armies to seize Rome. But Pompey surprised everyone by disbanding his army, asking only that the Senate reward his veterans and legalize his settlement in the East. Why he acted in this fashion is a mystery. Probably he hoped that the Senate would recognize him as a great man and come to him requesting his advice about running the state.

Pompey's plans, whatever they were, were frustrated by the stubborn refusal of the Senate to grant his wishes. Julius Caesar did have a solution. At his suggestion Pompey and Crassus joined him in forming the First Triumvirate. The three agreed to take control of the government. Caesar was to be elected consul. Once in office he would force through legislation giving Pompey what he had already asked and granting Crassus permission to exploit the provinces more easily. Crassus's money, Pompey's veterans, and Caesar's abilities as a vote getter were an unbeatable combination. Caesar was elected consul for the year 59 B.C. and pushed through legislation favorable to all the triumvirs. Hardly a whisper of protest was raised.

Having finished his term as consul, Caesar went to Gaul as proconsul. There he remained from 58 to 49 B.C., during which years he conquered Gaul and added it to the empire. He also gained experience as a general and strengthened his personal power by creating an army fanatically dedicated to him personally. Moreover his Gallic experience was his making as a statesman. Away from Rome's petty politics, he began to see Rome as an imperial power faced with the problem of ruling millions of subjects.

The Triumvirate held together uneasily for part of these years. Caesar did his best to keep Pompey and Crassus on friendly terms, which was not an easy task, since these ambitious men were anxious to get on with their personal dreams of glory. But when Crassus was killed in 53 B.C. while leading a war against the Parthians in the East, a showdown between Pompey and Caesar was inevitable. Pompey, posing as champion of the Senate, gradually increased his personal powers after 53 B.C., and vast powers were voted to him, giving him almost dictatorial powers over most of the empire. Finally he made his move, trying to remove Caesar from his Gallic command. Caesar, knowing that he was doomed if Pompey succeeded, struck for a decision. In 49 B.C. he led his legions into Italy, plunging Rome into a full-scale war between two masters who between them controlled most of the Roman Empire.

Caesar's seasoned veterans, skillfully led by their popular general, made short work of Pompey's forces. First in Italy, then in Spain, and finally in the Greek Peninsula, Pompey's armies were smashed. Pompey tried to escape by fleeing to Egypt, but he was murdered there in 48 B.C. by Egyptians who hoped to win Caesar's favor. Caesar used this crime against a Roman citizen as an excuse to intervene in Egyptian politics, where a struggle for control of the crown was going on within the ruling family of the Ptolemies. Caesar decided to support the claims of Cleopatra against her brother. Perhaps his decision was hastened by the fact that he had become Cleopatra's lover, but Caesar may well have had another motive. Egypt, fabulously rich, was the last important Eastern kingdom still not under Roman control. By putting a young princess, attached to him sentimentally, on the throne, he might be able to control the destiny of Egypt and tap its resources. Thus he dallied in Egypt nearly a year, leaving only when Cleopatra was in control of Egypt as queen. During 47 and 46 B.C. Caesar continued his march through the empire, hunting down the last of Pompey's allies. In 46 B.C. he returned to Rome, undisputed military master of the Roman world.

Caesar was now faced with the problem of ruling what he had won with the sword. It is not clear whether Caesar formulated a full program of reform; perhaps he did not have time to do so before his untimely death less than two years after his victory. Some things, however, are fairly clear. Caesar intended to concentrate in his own hands powers and honors that would raise him above all other citizens. He "persuaded" the Senate and people to make him consul, tribune, high priest, and censor all at once, not to mention still other honors. From time to time he was granted special powers to deal with special problems. He even went so far as to allow his most enthusiastic supporters to hint that he was divine.

Caesar hoped to use these powers to solve the major problems causing trouble. He undertook to reduce the number of people in Rome dependent on the dole by providing extensive public works projects and by sending Romans to the provinces as colonists. He provided a police force for the city of Rome, thereby ending the mob violence and gangsterism that had had such a dire effect on political life during the preceding years. Steps were taken to aid the Italian farmers. More orderly institutions of local government were established in many towns throughout Italy. Regulations were put into effect to curb provincial tax collectors and governors, ending many of the abuses that provincials had been forced to suffer under the old republican system. Caesar in the meantime tried to conduct himself personally so as to appear to be the benefactor of all classes and therefore responsible for the welfare of all. Certainly he was anxious to achieve as wide a popularity as possible. But personal power was not all he desired; he hoped to use that power to build a new Rome.

Many Romans, however, were not won over by Caesar's program. Especially among the aristocrats there was an awareness that he was intent on destroying the old republican order, and these conservatives became obsessed with the idea of stopping him. Completely helpless to achieve that goal in a legal way, these would-be saviors of the republic resorted to assassination, cutting Caesar down in 44 B.C. as he entered the Senate chamber. But murdering Caesar proved not to be an effective way of ending his influence.

4. The Struggle for Succession, 44–31 B.C.

The conspirators who killed Caesar had no plan of action once they had eliminated the real ruler of the state; they mistakenly supposed that his passing would result in the restoration of the old republic. This was a bad miscalculation, since Caesar's death led only to a struggle to find a successor. Fourteen years of civil war were necessary to produce another individual whose power was equal to Caesar's.

There were numerous candidates for Caesar's mantle, two of whom became the chief protagonists between 44 and 31 B.C. One was Mark Antony (about 83–30 B.C.), who had served Caesar as a military commander for some time and was thus a man of considerable experience. He rose to a powerful position immediately after Caesar's death by a skillful use of propaganda and of Caesar's troops and wealth. The other important figure was an eighteen-year-old lad named Octavian, whom Caesar had adopted as his son and legal heir. Octavian entered Rome soon after Caesar's death and immediately began to attract a following. The Senate, guided chiefly by Cicero, could do little to control this pair, especially after they joined hands in 43 B.C. with a third general, Lepidus, to form the Second Triumvirate for the purpose of restoring order and punishing Caesar's murderers. Within a year most of the senatorial party, including Cicero, had been eliminated by a brutal proscription and by a successful military campaign against the armies raised by Caesar's assassins.

After 42 B.C. Antony and Octavian continued the pose of ruling Rome jointly. Actually each was preparing to eliminate the other, although the final struggle was delayed for ten years. Antony spent these years in the East under the guise of restoring order. His prestige among Romans declined rapidly during these years, especially after he fell into the clutches of Cleopatra and allowed himself to be used to promote her grandiose schemes for expanding Egyptian influence in the East. By 33 B.C. Antony went so far as to marry Cleopatra and give his approval to a scheme whereby Roman territory was granted to the children of Cleopatra sired by Caesar and Antony. It was bad enough that Antony already had a Roman wife—no less a person than Octavian's sister. But to surrender Roman lands to an Eastern queen made him seem a traitor. In 36 B.C. he made a vain attempt to restore his waning prestige by leading a war against the Parthians, only to suffer a humiliating defeat.

Octavian made better use of his time. He skillfully disposed of numerous Italian problems that might have defeated a weaker man. While establishing a solid hold on the Western provinces he conducted a powerful propaganda program picturing Antony as a madman, a traitor, and a stupid victim of a crafty Eastern harlot. Gradually he created the impression that he was the upholder of Rome's honor against the wicked schemes of Antony and Cleopatra. Finally, in 32 B.C., he refused to continue his joint rule with Antony and declared war on Cleopatra. The decisive engagement was fought at Actium, in Greece, in 31 B.C., where Octavian's fleet won an easy victory over the demoralized forces of Antony and Cleopatra. Octavian pursued his enemies back to Egypt, where Cleopatra made one final attempt to capture Rome by entrancing Rome's leaders. When Octavian would have none of her favors, Cleopatra committed suicide, as Antony had already done. This left Octavian undisputed ruler of Rome, his sword having raised him to the position held by Caesar in 46 B.C.

5. Consequences of the Civil Wars

Octavian's victory in 31 B.C. ended the civil wars and began an era of peace and order, as we shall see in the following chapter. Before looking to the new age a word is necessary about the impact of the century of civil war on Roman society. Unless we realize its revolutionary effects, we cannot appreciate the importance of the era extending from 133 to 31 B.C.

The era of the civil wars resulted in a social upheaval that especially affected the staunchest supporters of the old order. The incessant warfare, accompanied by proscriptions and confiscation of property, virtually destroyed the old aristocracy. The bids of ambitious politicians for popular support undermined the morale of the city masses, who turned from respect for the old institutions to hopes for material rewards. The turmoil of the century presented a golden opportunity for ambitious, ruthless, yet able men, even of low birth, to gain wealth and political power. These men, who were willing to accept new ideas and institutions as long as their new wealth and prestige were recognized, were the greatest beneficiaries of the civil wars.

The civil wars also drastically altered the thinking of most Romans, causing them to lose interest in the old political and social order. Many grew weary of war and murder and political intrigue. They became increasingly interested in anything that would give them peace and security. A wave of pessimism and hopelessness spread through Roman society during the civil wars, indicating that Romans had lost faith in what had once been things of value. People turned to pleasure-seeking, to new religions, and to foreign philosophies in search of something to live by in the midst of daily violence. Under such circumstances fewer men were willing to fight for the old order, which meant nothing but suffering and insecurity. Those who had new ideas found an increasing audience. The civil wars, involving the whole Roman Empire and its millions of residents, broadened the vision of many Romans beyond the confines of the city walls. The old, narrow Roman patriotism seemed senseless in view of the extensive world within which Romans now operated and of the millions of provincials upon whom Roman politicians often depended to get into power. These more broad-minded Romans could hardly be expected to fight to preserve a way of life confined to Rome itself.

The period from 133 to 31 B.C. proved still another thing: The traditional system of government simply could not cope with existing problems. Annually elected officials, a Senate of aristocrats, and a popular assembly attended by small numbers of people living in and around Rome failed on numerous occasions to deal adequately with such problems as defending Rome's extensive frontiers, maintaining peace among millions of subjects, supplying grain to the residents of Rome, and keeping order in the city. In a practical way the civil wars proved to even the most conservative that the old government was outmoded and must be replaced if Rome were to survive as mistress of the Mediterranean. The civil wars showed just as clearly that only capable individuals possessing extensive powers could cope effectively with Rome's chief political problems. In spite of their disrespect for the law and their heavy-handed methods, a Marius, a Sulla, a Pompey, and a Caesar achieved something positive in this wild century, whereas all others failed.

In view of these fundamental changes in the midst of the frenzied, brutal struggles for power from 133 to 31 B.C., we are certainly justified in saying that a revolution had occurred by 31 B.C. The republican form of government, under which a group of aristocratic senators (with the approval of the citizens of Rome) had decided political issues, was replaced by a system of government whereby one man guided political life in the vast empire stretching around the Mediterranean.

SUGGESTED READING

Frank Burr Marsh, *A History of the Roman World from 146 to 30 B.C.*, rev. ed. (1953). A good, readable account stressing political history. Useful for any student who would appreciate a detailed discussion of political affairs in this crucial period that marked the collapse of the Roman republican system of government.

R. E. Smith, *The Failure of the Roman Republic* (1955). A short but penetrating discussion of the major factors bringing about the downfall of the republic. The book is especially good in isolating the destructive political forces at work in Roman society in the last two centuries before Christ.

* F. R. Cowell, *Cicero and the Roman Republic* (Penguin). Originally published in a hardback edition in 1948. An attempt to survey the complex factors that brought about the fall of the republic, with Cicero's career serving as the central point around which the discussion develops. Excellent for anyone interested in an interpretation of the political affairs of the first century B.C.

Charles Oman, *Seven Roman Statesmen of the Later Republic* (1902). Short biographical sketches of the Gracchi, Marius, Sulla, Pompey, Crassus, and Cato the Younger. In reviewing the lives of these men the author succeeds in covering most of the important political events of the era from 133–44 B.C.

G. P. Baker, *Sulla the Fortunate: The Great Dictator* (1927). A well-done portrait of a brilliant Roman personality who is considered by the author to be one of Rome's most important statesmen.

John Buchan, *Julius Caesar* (1936). A short biography emphasizing Caesar's contributions in administration and lawgiving as well as in military affairs. The book draws a clear picture of Caesar's character.

Tenney Frank, *An Economic History of Rome*, 2nd ed., rev. (1927). The early chapters of this excellent book will acquaint the reader with the major economic problems affecting the Roman Republic and contributing to its downfall.

W. Warde Fowler, *Social Life at Rome in the Age of Cicero* (1909). A well-written social history that presents a clear picture of Roman society at the end of the republican period. The work relies heavily on Cicero's letters to reconstruct the social history of the period.

* Plutarch, *Lives* (many editions; a good one is in the Modern Library series). The short biographies of the leading figures of the second and first century B.C. by a Greek writer who lived in the second century A.D. make lively and instructive reading. See especially the biographies of Marius, Sulla, Lucullus, Crassus, Pompey, Caesar, Cato the Younger, Tiberius and Gaius Gracchus, Cicero, and Antony.

Cicero, *Orations* and *Letters* (many editions; a good one is in the Loeb Classical Library). One of the best sources for the history of the first century B.C. is the voluminous body of writing produced by Cicero. His orations, which touch on many of the great political events of Cicero's day, make especially fascinating reading. Cicero rewrote most of them after he delivered them but before he published them. It is a real test of intelligence to discover what he really said before the Senate and people. His *Letters*, of which there are several hundred, present much more candid views of the era.

CHAPTER II

The Roman Empire, 31 B.C.—A.D. 180

THE EIGHTEENTH-CENTURY English historian Edward Gibbon wrote that, if he had to choose a period when the condition of the human race was happiest, he would without hesitation name the period between A.D 96 and 180. Perhaps Gibbon's statement is exaggerated, but it does supply the theme to be dealt with in this chapter. During the first and second centuries A.D. the Romans made their most notable contribution to civilization by creating a system of government that brought peace and prosperity to a huge territory around the Mediterranean.

1. The Foundations of the Imperial Order: The Work of Augustus, 31 B.C.–A.D. 14

The victor at Actium, soon to be known by his title, Augustus, laid the basis for the new order. Augustus was not a flashy, brilliant, Caesar-like figure. His strength lay in patience, tact, realism, industry, and political intelligence. Working methodically and carefully throughout his forty-five-year reign, Augustus put together bit by bit the main components of the Roman imperial system.

When he defeated Antony and Cleopatra, Augustus was supreme by virtue of conquest. Realizing that mere military might would not endure, he sought to establish his own position on a sounder basis. He began this process in 27 B.C. by dramatically surrendering all his power to the Senate and people, insisting that he was restoring the republic. Impressed by this noble gesture and fearful lest the dreaded civil wars would break out again, the Senate hastened to bestow on Augustus vast powers. These powers gave Augustus control of the popular assemblies, the full authority of the consuls, command over all Roman armies, control over the state religion, and complete authority to govern most of the provinces. Within a short time Augustus was voted several honors that exalted him above all citizens. He was made chief senator, *augustus* (most revered one), *imperator* (victorious general), and "father of his country." With the passing of the years the idea was gradually spread about that Augustus was in some vague way divine or at least especially blessed by the gods. By virtue of all these grants of offices, titles, and honors Augustus became the *princeps*, or the *first* Roman, the possessor of more power and prestige than any individual or group. This exaltation occurred, however, in a very special way. Augustus had been given his powers legally by the Senate and the people. He was not king or dictator or tyrant; he was *princeps*, the first and best Roman, guilty of no illegal seizure of power. All his powers could be removed. Augustus had become head of the state without creating the impression of having seized powers or destroyed the ancient institutions and customs of the republic.

Armed with these great powers, Augustus turned his efforts toward reconstructing the ravaged social order of Rome. His chief concern was with the condition of the Roman citizen body, that relatively small group in Italy that must rule the vast territory of the empire. Augustus tried to redefine the ancient class structure and to assign to each class a specific task. Rigid requirements were set up for senatorial standing, and the senators were assigned a large share in governmental affairs. They were to hold the chief elective offices in the state, to advise the princeps, to serve as governors of specified provinces, and to fill high military and civil posts in the provinces where Augustus was in charge. Augustus hoped to make the Senate what it had traditionally been—a loyal, patriotic élite supplying leadership to Rome and sharing decisions with the princeps. The equestrian order (equites), made up chiefly of rich traders and industrialists, was also clearly defined and given honorable status. New positions in the army, the taxation system, and the judicial system were entrusted to this class; thus this class served to supply bureaucrats to assist the princeps. For the plebeians Augustus hoped to provide order and security. He concentrated on supplying cheap grain, police supervision, and entertainment for Rome's huge population, and economic security for the farmers of Italy. However, he left little political power in plebeian hands. The chief civic duty of the plebeians was to serve in the army as professional soldiers.

To improve the morale and the patriotism of the citizen body, Augustus encouraged a revival of the ancient Roman religion, patronized writers who turned out masses of propaganda exalting Rome's past, and arranged for the passage of numerous laws aimed at checking what Augustus thought of as softening vices—luxury, sexual irregularities, divorce, childless marriages, gambling, and drinking. He also spent immense sums beautifying Rome and providing public services in the hope that the citizens would feel a resurgence of pride in the capital of the civilized world.

AUGUSTUS AS EMPEROR. This majestic statue of Augustus, created during his reign, was intended to idealize and exalt Rome's first citizen. The facial expression, the posture, the hand outstretched in a gesture of command, and the symbolic decorations on the armor all express power, vigor, and confidence. Like many artists of the Augustan age in Roman history, the sculptor of this statue was intent on popularizing and exalting the man who had restored peace to the Roman world after the troubled times of the late republic. (*Alinari Photo*)

The provinces occupied much of Augustus's attention; perhaps his provisions for handling the provinces were his most enduring work. To ensure peace in and defense for the provinces, Augustus overhauled the military machine completely. He began the creation of a professional army made up of men recruited for long terms of service. The heart of the army consisted of Roman citizens, although auxiliary units were recruited among non-citizens in the provinces. Careful discipline, regular pay, and adequate pensions were provided. The army was commanded by of-

ROMAN RELIEF DEPICTING THE FAMILY OF AUGUSTUS. This relief from the frieze of an altar of peace (Ara Pacis) built by Augustus to commemorate the restoration of peace within the empire illustrates the skill of Roman artists in serving political purposes. The sobriety and dignity of the various members of the family of Augustus pictured here was intended to depict the excellence of the family. This relief might be compared with those of the Assyrians (see p. 45) and of the Greeks (see p. 85). (*Alinari Photo*)

ficers responsible to the princeps. The chief job of the army was to defend the frontiers and most units were stationed there, far from the political center of the empire. Only the Praetorian Guard, consisting of about nine thousand picked troops, was garrisoned in Italy. Except for one or two cases Augustus gave up the idea of offensive war and expansion and began the process of fixing a clear boundary between the Roman and non-Roman world. The army's job was to hold that frontier and to strike down any elements within the empire who tried to escape Roman domination.

Having provided for peace and defense in the provinces, Augustus attempted to improve Roman administration in them. By virtue of his proconsular powers he was governor of all but a few provinces that had been entrusted to the Senate, and he began to develop a regular provincial administration that he himself supervised. He selected legates to represent him in each province, and he watched carefully over their conduct. The legates were paid adequate salaries and thus had no need illegally to oppress their subjects. No legate was given a chance to gain military fame, all military glory being credited to the princeps, who was commander of all forces. The task of collecting taxes was completely removed from the legates' hands. Augustus sent into each province a procurator, usually of equestrian rank, to collect taxes and render account to the princeps. Under the careful eye of Augustus this set of administrative and financial officials almost immediately brought order to the provinces. The notorious corruption, oppression, and violence from which the provincials had suffered during the late republican period disappeared, to be replaced by the Roman peace. However, Augustus had no intention of exerting Roman control over every aspect of provincial life. Wherever possible he encouraged local communities, and especially city-states, to handle as many local affairs as possible.

As Augustus progressed step by step with his work, one final question faced him. What would happen when he died? His whole program centered around the concentration of vast powers in the hands of one man. Yet Augustus had no legal right to transmit his powers. Only the Senate and people could do so. Augustus began early to

try to assure his succession without seeming to be dictatorial. He attempted to combine two distinct ideas. He wanted his successor to be a member of his own family so that the second princeps would enjoy prestige as a descendant of Caesar and Augustus. He also sought before he died to establish his successor in important posts, thus permitting him to acquire the experience needed to administer the vast empire. Augustus had no sons. His only daughter, Julia, was three times married to potential heirs. Augustus outlived two of her three husbands and her two elder sons. Finally he chose as his heir his adopted son, Tiberius, whose mother was Augustus's second wife. Tiberius became Julia's third husband and after A.D. 4 was granted ever greater powers by Augustus. When the princeps died in A.D. 14, Tiberius was ready to assume full authority.

This quick summary will suggest the sig-

ROMAN RELIEF DEPICTING THE BOUNTY OF NATURE. Another section from Augustus's altar of peace demonstrates an attempt to propagandize the joys of the first emperor's regime. In this scene a goddess is flanked by figures representing the fields and the waters and surrounded by symbols of the bounty of nature waiting for these who seek her wealth. The treatment of the subject clearly reflects Greek artistic influences at work in Rome. The same effort to underscore the fecundity of nature can be seen in the literature of the Augustan age. (*Alinari Photo*)

nificance of Augustus's career. It would be foolish to say that he was inspired by any philosopher's concept of the best kind of government. He was a patient, realistic statesman. He came to power at the end of a century of bloody civil war that had nearly ruined Rome and that had shown that one-man rule was necessary to restore order. Knowing that many Romans would fight out-and-out dictatorship, he tried to find means of establishing one-man rule within the framework of the old system of government. Out of this emerged the office of princeps, whose holder shared power with the Senate and people. Armed with adequate powers, Augustus tried to do whatever possible to restore order among the citizen body, to control the army, to pacify the provincials, to defend the frontier, and to restore prosperity. In most cases his decisions guided Roman policy for the next two centuries and formed the basis of Rome's excellent imperial government.

2. Solidifying the Augustan Principate, A.D. 14–96

Admiration for Augustus should not lead us to think that he had solved all of Rome's problems. Between his death and the end of the first century the principate underwent a period of tremendous stress and strong opposition. Outwardly the history of this period was marked chiefly by the very thing Augustus wished to avoid: a clash between the princeps and the Senate, one that threatened to reopen the civil wars. Although this did not happen, Rome was in almost incessant turmoil.

One of the factors contributing to the tension was the difficulty of finding rulers fitted to the task of exerting tremendous power while appearing to respect the powers Augustus had left to the Senate and the people. Nearly all of Augustus's successors down to A.D. 96 were men of limited abilities who acted in a way that brought accusations of tyranny and violent opposition from the Senate. The first four successors were all related to Augustus, but this did not save them from trouble. Tiberius (A.D. 14–37) was a cold, suspicious, disillusioned man who repeatedly made brutal assaults on those he suspected of trying to undermine his position. Caligula (A.D. 37–41) was a man lacking completely in political sense; perhaps he was even mad. Claudius (A.D. 41–54) was a scholarly man whose chief interests lay outside Roman aristocratic society; to many he seemed something less than a real Roman and thus enjoyed little respect. Worst of all was Nero (A.D. 54–68). Cruel, vain, wasteful, he kept Rome in a turmoil in his attempts to satisfy his own desires. He was eventually ousted from office, avoiding assassination by killing himself, but only after he had killed his mother and two wives, disposed of numerous senators, persecuted Christians, made a fool of himself posing as an artist, and emptied the treasury in order to indulge his personal whims. With Nero's passing the family of Augustus was discredited, and the office of princeps forcefully seized by Vespasian (A.D. 69–79), an Italian who had spent most of his life in the army. He and his sons, Titus (A.D. 79–81) and Domitian (A.D. 81–96), were men of considerable ability, but they had little respect for the Senate. The members of this dynasty appeared to many aristocrats as worse tyrants than Augustus's relatives had been.

The unhealthy turmoil of the first century after Augustus was also due in part to the confused succession problem. Augustus had established conflicting principles. Theoretically the Senate and people chose the princeps, but Augustus had tried to make his position hereditary. Constant plotting resulted from this confusion. Between A.D. 14 and 68 some of Augustus's numerous relatives were always plotting against the princeps in office. These plots usually involved senators, who theoretically had the power to choose the princeps. They invariably ended in the elimination of either the princeps or the plotters, causing no end of suspicion and hatred. With Nero's death the Roman army stepped into the picture. During the years A.D. 68–69 actual war was waged by various legions seeking to establish a favorite general. Vespasian was the eventual victor, making it obvious that the Senate had little to say about the succession. He sought to establish a hereditary succession, but this solution was not satisfactory in terms of the Augustan ideal.

The plots, murders, and quarrels that loom so large in this period were, in reality, only an interesting if somewhat gory side show. Between A.D. 14 and 96 the system that Augustus established took permanent root. Some of the emperors—Tiberius, Claudius, and Vespasian—were able statesmen whose chief accomplishments were to increase the power of the princeps and to perfect the means of exercising that power. The powers Augustus had left to the Senate were slowly taken over by the princeps, usually because the Senate failed to exercise its power effectively. As the Senate was removed from active participation in political life, an organized bureaucracy was developed to replace it, thus supplying the princeps with a corps of loyal, disciplined servants devoted to the state. The frontiers were ably defended and on occasion extended, as when Claudius conquered Britain. The provinces, far removed from the storms raging in Rome, were well administered. Several rulers extended citizenship to many provincials, thereby adding to the manpower available to Rome. Vast public works were undertaken in Rome, Italy, and the provinces, earning for their sponsors the good will of the citizens. Trade, industry, and agriculture were given every possible encouragement by the rulers, causing a new level of prosperity. To the bulk of the Roman world—and even to the senators by the end of the period—an inevitable conclusion had to be accepted: Rule by a powerful princeps meant order and justice, prosperity and security. Only a fool would oppose the princeps. The events of the first century after Christ proved beyond a doubt that everyone's welfare depended on the orderly exercise of extensive power by an able princeps.

3. The Empire at its Peak: The "Good Emperors," A.D. 96–180

With the passing of Domitian opposition to the principate virtually disappeared, most people having accepted the necessity for one-man rule and having grown to appreciate its advantages. From the Atlantic to the Euphrates, from Central Europe to deep into Africa, the Roman peace became a reality. In brief, the history of the period A.D. 96–180 consists of a few ingredients— excellent rulers, just administration, benevolent concern with the general welfare, internal peace, growing material prosperity, and stout defense of the frontiers.

Seldom has any era produced rulers more highly praised than the five men who ruled from A.D. 96–180. Nerva (A.D. 96–98) was an elderly man when chosen to succeed the tyrannical Domitian. His short reign convinced everyone that a new day was at hand. Before he died he selected as his heir a native of Spain, Trajan (A.D. 98–117). This forceful, energetic ruler won the admiration of the whole Roman world by his respect for the Roman aristocracy, his brilliant military exploits, and his sound, honest administration. Hadrian (A.D. 117–138) was a cultured humanitarian who spent most of his reign in incessant travel throughout the empire, promoting the cause of peace and material well-being. Antoninus (A.D. 138–161), by the excellence of his character and intellect, earned the title of "Pius" from the Senate. The crowning glory of the era was Marcus Aurelius (A.D. 161–180), a noted Stoic philosopher who brought a deep sense of duty, willingness to work, and nobility of purpose to the Roman political scene. So outstanding were these five rulers that later generations referred to them as the "good emperors."

The program followed by these emperors was generally consistent. Rather early in his reign each took special care to select a successor, seeking out a man of ability, adopting him as a son, and then slowly increasing the power entrusted to the successor until at the death of the old emperor, the heir

PICTS

(IRELAND)

NORTH SEA

BRITAIN

0°

BALTIC SEA

ATLANTIC

OCEAN

12 B.C. TO 9 A.D.

ELBE

Cologne

G E R M A N I A

BELGICA

GERMANS

LUGUDUNENSIS

SEINE

RHINE

G A U L

LOIRE

AQUITANIA

Lyons

RHONE

NARBONENSIS

ALPS

RAETIA

DANUBE

Vienna

NORICUM

PANNONIA

TARRACONENSIS

PYRENEES MTS

CISALPINE
GAUL

APENNINE MTS

PO

ILLYRICUM

SPAIN

EBRO

Marseilles

ADRIATIC SEA

LUSITANIA

CORSICA

ETRUSCANS

TYRRHENIAN SEA

Rome

LATINS

SAMNITES

BAETICA

BALEARIC IS.

SARDINIA

ITALY

Naples

Cannae

Tarentum

M

(EPIRUS)

Actium

MAURETANIA

Carthage

Zama

M E D

SICILY

Syracuse

NUMIDIA

MOORS

G R E E C E

AFRICA

CYR

TRM

SARMATIANS

DACIA (107–275 A.D.)

MOESIA

THRACE

BLACK SEA

BITHYNIA

Byzantium

PONTUS

CAUCASUS MTS.

COLCHIS

CASPIAN SEA

ARMENIA (115–117 A.D.)

PARTHIAN EMPIRE

ON

(GREECE)

AEGEAN SEA

Athens

inth

ACHAIA

Sparta

ASIA

Pergamum

Smyrna

Ephesus

RHODES

CRETE

GALATIA

CAPPADOCIA

Tarsus

CILICIA

LYCIA AND PAMPHYLIA

CYPRUS

Antioch

ASSYRIA

MESOPOTAMIA (115–117 A.D.)

TIGRIS

EUPHRATES

PERSIAN GULF

SYRIA

Damascus

Tyre

A N S E A

Jerusalem

JUDEA

ARABIA

Alexandria

EGYPT

NILE

RED SEA

40°E

40°N

40°E

THE
**ROMAN
EMPIRE**
AT ITS HEIGHT
117 A.D.

500 MILES

was powerfully placed and widely experienced. Thus the succession question was solved. All these emperors were tactful and respectful toward the senatorial class, avoiding any charge of tyranny. The senators, who were given most of the high offices and were continually consulted, became staunch supporters of the principate, even though their independent power was extremely limited. The "good emperors" steadily developed the imperial bureaucracy, creating a disciplined body of administrators who gained by serving the state well. The emperors secured the enactment of legislation affecting all parts of the empire and slowly created a unified body of law for the whole empire. The interests of the provinces were guarded and promoted. Citizenship was granted to an ever-larger number of provincials, and humanitarian projects for the aid of the downtrodden members of the empire were repeatedly inaugurated. Public works—roads, aqueducts, harbor facilities, temples—were built at imperial expense. The army was kept in readiness. The economic welfare of the whole empire was the constant concern of the rulers. All the rulers showed a broad tolerance for different segments of the population, allowing local groups extensive freedom as long as that freedom did not threaten the peace. Since the services of the imperial government were costly, the "good emperors" worked tirelessly to establish a sound financial system that would provide adequate income and sound, worth-while expenditures. All these efforts on the part of the emperors slowly bound the fifty million or so residents [1] of the empire into a commonwealth guided from Rome by a benevolent ruler and his disciplined civil servants, enjoying a rule of law, partaking at least to some degree in the general economic prosperity, and safe from war and injustice.

[1] Population figures for ancient Rome are at best guesses and none too reliable. Some authorities would put the population of the empire as high as 70,000,000 for the second century of the Christian era.

Only one ominous cloud cast a shadow over this otherwise-peaceful scene—the frontier question. Rome's army of about 350,000 men was spread too thinly along her long frontier for safety. The "good emperors" wrestled constantly with the problem. Trajan tried to safeguard the frontier from the Germans and the Parthians by conquering Dacia and the Tigris-Euphrates Valley. Hadrian reversed this aggressive policy, trusting to strong defense and diplomacy. But the time of Marcus Aurelius, however, the problem had still not been solved, and this peace-loving philosopher was forced to spend much of his reign fighting Germans, who broke across the Danube frontier and penetrated deeply into Roman territory. When he died in A.D. 180, only an uneasy peace prevailed along the extensive frontier.

4. The Imperial Government of the Second Century

A brief review of the structure of the imperial government will help to explain why it pacified the Roman Empire.

Throughout the second century, theory still insisted that the Senate and the Roman people had final authority in the state, and that the ancient republican machinery of government continued to operate: the Senate met regularly; elections were held for the ancient offices; on occasion the assemblies met. However, all this was but a façade. In fact these organizations had but one function, to approve and legalize the authority of the princeps. The princeps, or emperor (derived from the title "imperator," the honor voted by soldiers to their victorious general), had a virtual monopoly on executive, legislative, and judicial powers. These powers were legally voted each emperor at the beginning of his reign. The key powers held by the emperor were his command over all military forces, his control of all revenues, and his power to control legislation. Most emperors enjoyed even greater authority than that voted by the Senate and the people. Each had huge personal fortunes. Each held titles that exalted him above all others, and most of them were believed to be especially blessed by the gods, if not actually divine.

The emperors exercised their vast powers through the army and a well-developed bureaucracy centralized in Rome. The bureaucracy was divided into great departments, each headed by experienced, able officials. Under each head stood numerous grades of officials with carefully defined functions, ranks, and rewards. The top levels of the bureaucracy were manned by senators and equestrians, while the lower ranks were filled chiefly with educated plebeians. Romans, Italians, and provincials alike were accepted in the civil service, making it an extremely cosmopolitan body. The "good emperors" maintained close guard over the bureaucrats, ensuring honest, efficient conduct of public business.

The army had changed little since Augustus's time, although by the second century more provincials were recruited, thus lessening the role of Roman citizens. The emperors of the second century bent every effort to get good commanders and to provide adequate training, pay, and pensions, thereby gaining the loyalty of the troops. The legions defended the frontier adequately, attacked Rome's enemies when necessary, and crushed rebels within the empire.

The bureaucracy and the army were expensive, necessitating careful attention on the part of the emperors to public finances. These efforts were generally successful; the imperial government was usually solvent.

The provinces were carefully ruled by governors assigned by the princeps. Imperial troops watched over the people living in each province, while imperial tax collectors gathered what was due the Roman government. The second-century emperors followed Augustus's principle of allowing as much local freedom as possible, and throughout the empire city-states were encouraged to regulate their own affairs. The emperors tried to create hundreds of small Romes for the purpose of supplying local

government. Each city-state and its surrounding territory was ruled by a body of local aristocrats (called *curiales*) who made up a local senate. These senates elected local magistrates, collected local taxes, assumed responsibility for policing and beautifying the city, held courts, and did the many other things necessary to sound government. As a matter of fact, these city-state governments bore the brunt of day-by-day political life, the Roman governors and armies merely standing by to keep order and protect them. There can be little doubt that the Romans were inspired to this policy by the model of the Greeks. They believed that the city-state was the ideal political institution and encouraged the residents of each city to be patriots concerned with the well-being of their city. Where city-states did not already exist— especially in the Western provinces—the Romans founded as many as possible. The second century was truly the culminating age of city-state polity; the whole vast Roman Empire was becoming a federation of nearly autonomous city-states kept at peace by the mighty princeps who ruled in Rome.

It must not be thought, however, that the imperial government was always aloof from local affairs. Numerous cases could be cited where emperors intervened in local affairs and regulated matters contrary to local wishes. Once Rome did intervene, the small cities had little hope of defending themselves. They had no power to match that of the princeps.

It is beyond question that by the second century A.D. Rome possessed the essentials of autocratic government. A Trajan or a Hadrian could do about anything he desired. However, Roman government of the second century was not despotic; seldom have men with such great power ruled so benevolently or humanely. This calls for a word of explanation. The emperors of the second century were strongly motivated by rather well-defined ideas of what constituted good government and the duty of a ruler. They believed that power entailed duty, that power existed so that humanity could be served. The excellence of government could be judged only by the good it caused. A strong sense of service to humanity thus kept the emperors from abusing their nearly unlimited power. This political philosophy was based to a large degree on the Stoic ideas to which most second-century emperors were devoted, but no less on the theories of men like Plato and to the political practices of men like Alexander the Great. The emperors were also bound by the deep Roman respect for law. The task of an emperor was to operate within the framework of the law, limiting and shaping his powers to fit it. This deep sense of duty and respect for the law gave Roman government an aspect that ought not to be forgotten in evaluating second-century Roman society. A strong idealism literally drove emperors and their thousands of servants to bring the highest degree of peace to as many people as possible. Good government to these men was the first need for civilized life.

5. Life in the Empire in the Second Century

What were the effects of the Roman imperial government on the population of the empire?

From the viewpoint of material well-being the internal peace was a blessing. For most people farming was the chief means of livelihood, and the demands of the great cities and of the Roman armies assured a fair degree of agricultural prosperity. Especially flourishing were the large estates, whose owners had sufficient capital to engage in the large-scale production of grapes, olives, livestock, and grain. The real key to prosperity, however, was the expansion of trade and industry. The reduction of artificial trade barriers, the sound money system, the good roads, and the well-policed seaways encouraged the movement of goods to every corner of the empire. In fact Roman traders did not even confine their efforts to the vast areas within imperial boundaries; they also developed important connections with India and China. Although most commercial activity was in grain, wine, oil, and other agricultural products, some of it was in a variety of manufactured goods, turned out by thousands of artisans throughout the empire. The Eastern cities led in quality and quantity of industrial production, but a notable increase in production occurred in the previously barbarous areas of the West. This combination of a sound agricultural system, extensive trade, and active industry assured a considerable portion of the population a decent livelihood; a small segment of the population even gained vast wealth.

Under the empire the Roman social system regained its stability, the chief social groups settling down to a secure and orderly existence. The cities were the centers of social life and Rome, of course, the hub of the whole empire. But many other cities, such as Alexandria, Antioch, Corinth, and Ephesus, were worthy rivals. An aristocracy, made up of wealthy landowners, successful traders, and high state officials, dominated life in the cities. These groups used their wealth to ensure themselves all imaginable comforts—fine houses, expensive food and clothing, abundant servants, good education, costly entertainment. Although they sometimes indulged in excesses and were always keenly conscious of their social superiority, the aristocracy of the Roman world took an active interest in aiding the poor and in improving the city in which they lived. Furthermore, the aristocracy was never a closed caste; members of the lower classes could move up to the highest social positions.

Below the aristocrats was ranked a bewildering array of city dwellers: shopkeepers, peddlers, hired laborers, minor officials, slaves, and throngs of idle men. Among the lower classes life was probably poverty-ridden, although there were many groups, especially among the shop owners and officials, that managed well enough. The very poor lived in miserably crowded quarters and possessed a minimum of worldly comforts. Often they depended upon the largesse of the state or a rich aristocrat for a livelihood. Nonetheless, city life with its pageants, its public shows, its splendid buildings, and its religious ceremonies was probably exciting. Slaves were always numerous in imperial cities. Needless to say the condition of a slave was not especially happy, although there is considerable evidence to suggest that many slaveowners were decent toward their slaves. Slavery had the usual bad effect of making labor disgraceful, so that every city was always plagued by idle freemen.

Probably the group that received the least benefit in Roman imperial society was the agricultural laborers. Isolated from the cities, they were cut off from the vital centers of Roman life. Their social lot tended to worsen during the first two centuries A.D. More and more farmers were reduced to the rank of tenant farmers (called *coloni*), meaning that they were forced to farm someone else's land, turning over to the owner a large share of the produce while keeping only a bare minimum for themselves. These people, many of whom had once been small landowners, were steadily becoming dependent upon landlords, losing almost all their freedom in the process. In effect, they were carrying the burden of high Roman society on their backs with very little recompense in the form of a better life.

Even the briefest examination of imperial society in the first and second centuries A.D. forces us to make certain reservations in praising the excellence of the Roman imperial regime. Obviously the Roman government did not create a material paradise for all its subjects. Poverty flourished alongside riches; economic oppression and exploitation were always present in Roman society. The existence of inequality and poverty among a large element of the population considerably dims the glory of the empire. Probably it is only safe to say that during the first and second centuries more people around the whole Mediterranean basin enjoyed economic security, justice, and the protection of a benevolent state than ever had been the case before. Roman society was always fundamentally aristocratic in its organization and orientation, which implies that the fate of the lower classes was not the major concern of those who dominated society.

One of the chief social results of the Roman imperial order was the speed with which all kinds of barriers tumbled within the empire. The distinction between Roman and non-Roman slowly faded as provincials gained citizenship, wealth, and the privilege of becoming government servants. The gulf between national groups faded away because of the free movement of peoples. The distinction between civilized and barbarian vanished because of Rome's attempts to civilize all her subjects. Religions, philosophies, art forms, and ideas fused in an empire where toleration was a byword of rulers. Many people, especially those previously suffering from a low level of civilization, benefited from this mixing process. Under Roman imperial rule the Mediterranean tended to become one world racially, religiously, culturally, and economically. The Romans provided the chief bond of unity by creating a centralized, humane system of government. This system of government was their major contribution to the history of civilization.

SUGGESTED READING

Martin P. Charlesworth, *The Roman Empire* (1951). A brief survey of the history of the Roman Empire from the time of Augustus until the fall of the empire. The author has succeeded in featuring the essential points about imperial history in spite of the brevity of his treatment.

Edward T. Salmon, *History of the Roman World from 30 B.C. to A.D. 138*, 2nd ed. (1950); and H. M. D. Parker, *A History of* the Roman World from A.D. 138 to 337 (1939). These two volumes, successive parts of a series, will furnish a detailed account of the political history of the three centuries from Augustus's reign to the end of that of Constantine. They are especially useful for the clear picture they supply of the evolution of political institutions.

John Buchan, *Augustus* (1937). A sound, well-written summary of the career of Augustus and an evaluation of his contribution to Roman history.

Bernard W. Henderson, *Five Roman Emperors* (1927). Brief studies of the emperors Vespasian, Titus, Domitian, Nerva, and Trajan. These studies supply a good picture of Roman life at the beginning of the second century A.D., when Rome was near the peak of its power.

Theodor Mommsen, *The Provinces of the Roman Empire from Caesar to Diocletian*, 2 vols., 2nd ed. (1909). Any reader who wishes to understand the way the Romans ruled their subjects in the provinces must sample this classic work on the subject.

Victor Chapot, *The Roman World*, tr. by E. A. Parker (1928). A study written for non-specialized readers surveying the Roman provincial organization and life in the Roman provinces. The book provides an excellent over-all picture of life around the whole Mediterranean in the first centuries of the Christian era, when Rome was at the peak of her power.

Jérôme Carcopino, *Daily Life in Ancient Rome*, tr. by E. O. Lorimer (1941). A lively, easy-to-read description of social conditions in imperial times which brings out the brilliance of Roman society as well as its sordid aspects.

* Samuel Dill, *Roman Society from Nero to Marcus Aurelius* (Meridian). Also available in a hardback edition, 2nd ed. (1925). A scholarly work treating social conditions in the first and second centuries after Christ. This book requires careful reading, but it contains a vast amount of material clarifying the nature of Roman society at the height of the empire.

* Tacitus, *Histories* and *Annals* (many editions; a good one is the Modern Library edition, which contains both works in a single volume). Although Tacitus was a disgruntled conservative writer of the second century A.D., his histories contain the clearest picture of developments in Rome during the first century A.D. Generally he is not favorable to the emperors and their slow suppression of the Senate; thus his work is colored and prejudiced. However, it is always lively and filled with intimate details about life at the imperial court.

* Suetonius, *The Twelve Caesars* (many editions; an excellent translation has been made by Robert Graves for Penguin Books). Suetonius (about A.D. 75–160) wrote a series of sketches of the lives of all the emperors from Julius Caesar to Domitian. Although the biographies are not always first-rate, each contains large amounts of interesting material illustrating the habits and actions of the emperors.

Henryk Sienkiewicz, *Quo Vadis*, tr. by S. A. Binion and S. Malevsky (1924). This classic novel unfolds an accurate picture of life in Rome in the times of Nero.

* Marcus Aurelius, *Meditations* (many editions; there is a good one in Meridian paperbacks). The reflections on his own life by one of the greatest of the Roman emperors. Marcus Aurelius was a Stoic, making his *Meditations* an important illustration of Stoic philosophy. The edition cited also contains Epictetus's *Enchiridion*, which is another classic exposition on Stoicism, written by a Greek slave.

* Marguerite Yourcenar, *Hadrian's Memoirs* (Anchor). This work of fiction represents a brilliant attempt to reconstruct what the Emperor Hadrian (A.D. 117–138) might have written in his memoirs. The author has succeeded in creating a stimulating picture of a highly sensitive and intelligent man placed in a position of tremendous responsibility, just as was probably the case with Hadrian when he ruled the Roman world.

CHAPTER 12

———◄◆►———

Roman Culture

DURING the same era that the Romans were perfecting the imperial government that served the Mediterranean world, they also produced their greatest cultural achievement. Rome played a dual role in cultural history. In certain fields, especially in art, philosophy, and abstract scientific thought, the Romans were not creators capable of striking out in new directions. Their role in these fields was primarily one of borrowing from the Greek tradition, adapting that tradition, and disseminating the product among others, especially in Western Europe. In this role the Romans helped to keep alive the Greek tradition. However, the Romans were not entirely imitators, not completely captivated by Greek models. They were capable of making major contributions in literature, architecture, engineering, and law. Their contributions in these phases of cultural history were sufficient to assure them an important place in cultural history.

1. The Preparation for the Golden Age

Until about 250 B.C. the Romans achieved little culturally; during these centuries they seemed destined to be ranked among the culturally backward, even in Italy. However, these centuries cannot be simply dismissed. They were vital because they resulted in the formation of a certain outlook on life—including cultural matters —that was to determine Roman thought

for centuries after. The early experiences of the Romans created a practical, down-to-earth, conservative people who had little interest in or time for intellectual and aesthetic matters. Virtues that the Romans came to admire were sobriety, industry, integrity, piety, and a strong sense of responsibility toward family, state, and the gods. Original, creative poets, artists, and philosophers did not flourish in this atmosphere.

This early Roman outlook on life was shaped by four major forces—family life, agriculture, warfare, and religion. The powerfully entrenched family structure was dominantly patriarchal. Fathers, who themselves possessed a strong sense of responsibility toward their kinsmen, impressed on other members of the family the need for discipline, obedience, and respect for authority and tradition. Farm life made the early Romans a practical, realistic people, willing to work, and content to live simply and frugally. Constant warfare in defense of Rome deepened the sense of duty and strengthened discipline. But religion had the most profound effect on the thought and actions of the early Romans. Their belief that every aspect of life was controlled by numerous gods and spirits instilled in them a deep piety and a sense of dependence on outside forces. The chief Roman gods at this early date were household and agricultural deities: Janus, the god of the doorway; Vesta, the goddess of the hearth;

and the *lares* and *penates,* which were spirits guarding the productive powers of the family and its lands. Almost as significant were the deities who protected civic life, headed by Jupiter and his wife Juno. Conciliating these spirits was life's chief burden, to which the Romans took a business-like attitude, approaching the gods with dignity and reserve. Religious worship consisted chiefly of making sacrificial offerings to the various gods and of repeating long-established prayers in their honor. The head of each family led in the worship of the family and household gods. The ceremonies in honor of civic gods were conducted by priests who placed great emphasis on the correct performance of traditional ceremonies and the proper utterance of ancient prayers. Even the least deviation from the proper pattern might anger the gods and bring great misfortune on their worshippers. This devotion to formalism discouraged religious speculation and emotionalism among the Romans. Instead, their kind of religious practice instilled a strong sense of propriety and dignity.

Family, farm, battlefield, and altar thus worked together to establish the early Roman outlook and character. The best Roman was a sensible, unemotional, hard-working, disciplined man, willing to accept the world as it was, not especially eager to seek out new things and usually indifferent to speculation. Such men were not apt to be creators. However, they could learn from others, and they could teach others.

2. The Hellenistic Tidal Wave

Beginning with the conquest of the Greek cities of southern Italy in the first half of the third century and continuing until the end of the second century B.C., these simple Romans experienced a cultural revolution. As a result of their relationships with the Italian Greeks, of their wars in the East, and of the importation of many Greek slaves into Italy, the Romans slowly became aware of the cultural heritage of the Greek world. They were so impressed that during the

third and second centuries B.C. they were literally conquered by the culture of the peoples they were themselves conquering politically.

One of the consequences of this experience was the adoption of a new educational system. Previously the young Roman had been educated at home by his father. He was taught family customs, the principles of Roman law, farming, civic duties, and religion. That system was now replaced. In every respectable Roman household educated Greek slaves were employed to teach young men to read Greek and to introduce them to Greek literature and philosophy. Rather quickly a considerable number of Romans absorbed Greek thought in all its form.

Their fascination with Greek culture soon spurred Romans to try their hand at imitating the Greeks. Greek influence was clearly evident in literature. Epic poems, comedies, tragedies, histories, and even philosophical tracts were produced in the Latin tongue. Most early Roman authors usually copied Greek literary styles slavishly and filled their works with Greek subject matter. Nevertheless, in their attempts to imitate the Greeks, the Romans progressed rapidly toward the perfection of the Latin language for literary expression and laid the groundwork for an independent Latin literature.

In art the Romans were even more deeply impressed by Greek models. During the wars in the East huge numbers of art pieces were pilfered to decorate Roman villas. Those who could not steal what they wanted hired Eastern artists to turn out copies of Greek art objects. Greek styles of architecture were applied to civic buildings in Rome. Private dwellings were built and decorated in styles used in the East. Rome was transformed physically into a Hellenistic city. Her populace became accustomed to seeing beauty in only those things modeled on the Greek style.

Even the masses in Rome felt the impact of Greek influences, being touched chiefly through religion. The terrible strain of the

wars of conquest left many people intellectually and emotionally lost. The formal unemotional religion of Rome offered little
satisfaction. The Eastern religions did.
Throughout this whole period new gods
and new rituals were taken from the Greek
civic religions and added to public religious
life in Rome, but even these additions did
not satisfy many Romans. From Eastern
slaves they learned about even more exciting religions like the worship of Dionysus
or Cybele or Isis. These religions were all
essentially alike, promising life after death
to all, emphasizing personal morality, and
involving a highly emotional ritual that furnished an outlet for personal feelings. All
over Italy people joined the Greek and
Asian cults in large numbers.

By 100 B.C. the Romans had become
ardent disciples of Hellenism. The old,
simple outlook had been replaced by new
ideals and attitudes derived from Greek
art, literature, and philosophy. Some Romans, however, fought against this intellectual revolution. Typical of these conservatives was Cato the Elder, a second-
century statesman, who spent his life
preaching against the Greek way. He argued
that Rome was being ruined by the loss of
her ancient virtues—sobriety, industry, respect for the old gods, patriotism. However, Cato was fighting for a losing cause.
Rome had chosen to be cultural heir to
Greece.

During the first century B.C. the Romans
began to put their own stamp on what
they had borrowed. Always using Greek art
forms and ideas as their starting points,
Roman writers, artists, and thinkers began
to add a distinctive Roman touch to their
work. The greatest cultural achievements of
the Romans were produced in the years
between 100 B.C. and A.D. 180, especially
after the accession of Augustus in 31 B.C.
Peaceful conditions, imperial patronage,
and Augustus's attempt to regenerate Roman society inspired poets, artists, and
philosophers to supreme efforts. After Augustus's death there was a brief slackening.
The "golden age" had passed. But a second

period of considerable activity, often called
the "silver age," took place under the "good
emperors" (A.D. 96–180). During these
three centuries the Romans added enough
to what they had borrowed from Greece to
permit us to call the product "Graeco-Roman culture."

3. Literature

Roman intellectual and artistic talents
emerge clearly in literature, the chief examples of which were produced between
the first century B.C. and the middle of the
second century A.D. Roman writers were
deeply in debt to the Greeks for both style
and content, and Roman literature lacks the
freshness of Greek literature. However, the
Romans possessed virtues of their own. The
greatest writers were men of strong convictions, seriousness, a sense of realism, and an
urge to instruct and uplift their readers.

Nearly everyone would agree that Rome's
greatest literary light was Vergil (70–19
B.C.). Born in rural Italy, Vergil grew to
manhood during the last years of the civil
wars. Eventually he attracted the attention
of Augustus, who, by becoming Vergil's
patron, permitted him to devote the last
years of his life to writing. Vergil turned
his talent to the service of Augustus, seeking
to glorify the new order, but doing so with
majesty and dignity. His masterpiece was
an epic poem, the *Aeneid*, which was an attempt to glorify Rome and to show that her
rise to mastery was divinely ordered. The
plot centers on the adventures of a Trojan
hero, Aeneas, who after the fall of Troy
was ordered by the gods to establish in Italy
a new city destined to rule the world. The
noble Aeneas—an ideal Roman—under-
goes a series of supreme tests but obeys his
orders. Vergil glorifies the virtues he believed to be responsible for Roman greatness—piety, bravery, self-control, diligence,
sobriety. Here is the old Roman character
enshrined as the foundation of the new
Augustan order. Never was the Roman ideal
of the virtuous patriot set forth with more
force.

Two other poets, Catullus and Horace, illustrate another side of Roman poetry. Catullus (about 85–54 B.C.) was a product of high society in the late republican period. His life was lived amid a dissolute, pleasure-seeking crowd of young nobles. Among his many adventures was a love affair with a noble lady who was already married and who eventually jilted him. His love and eventual disappointment inspired Catullus to pour forth powerful lyric poetry, full of all the emotions one might expect from a jilted lover. Horace (65–8 B.C.) was likewise a lyric poet. He enjoyed the patronage of Augustus and was second only to Vergil in influence. His best work, the *Odes*, represent his personal reactions to hundreds of situations he met in his lifetime. He expresses every shade of feeling from deep seriousness to light frivolity. Although he lacked the fire and passion of Catullus, Horace spoke to a wider circle, his poems reflecting the reactions of an educated, humane Roman to life as a whole—a great spirit looking at the world about him with sanity, intelligence, and wit. In his own day he was, and still remains, the ideal of a civilized man. Catullus and Horace together represent the Roman individual's ability to see, feel, and appreciate life in all its aspects.

Lucretius (about 95–55 B.C.) demonstrated still another aspect of Roman poetic genius. A contemporary of Catullus, he lived through and suffered spiritually the civil-war era. He found his personal salvation in Epicurean philosophy, which he undertook to explain in a long poem called *On the Nature of Things*. With almost missionary zeal Lucretius put poetry to the service of instruction. He made a noble plea to educated Romans to seek in philosophy the bases of moral regeneration. He urged his readers to dedicate their lives to the pleasure of seeking truth about nature and man's place in it. Seldom has a poet shown greater moral earnestness, idealism, and dignity than did Lucretius. His poem was a monument to the moral seriousness that characterized the enlightened Roman.

Among the lesser poets of Rome were Ovid (43 B.C.–A.D. 17), who entertained Augustan high society with his *Art of Love*, a frivolous but amusing poem on the art of seduction, and his *Metamorphoses*, an entertaining, lively rendering of Greek mythological stories into Latin; and Martial (about A.D. 38–102) and Juvenal (about A.D. 55–140), both of whom revealed the shortcomings of Roman society in their brilliant satires. These and others illustrate that the poetic genius was not a monopoly of a few extraordinary Romans like Vergil, Horace, Catullus, and Lucretius. Having found their inspiration in Greek models, the Romans produced poetry filled with idealism, touched with deep insight into human strength and weakness, and dedicated to enlightening humanity. Enshrined in that poetry were the noblest thoughts of the Greeks expressed with the dignity and good sense of educated Romans.

The Romans were equally adept at prose writing. Cicero (106–43 B.C.) was the most famous prose writer in Roman history. Although an active statesman, this genius found time to produce a wide variety of writing, of which his speeches form a large part. As a lawyer and a magistrate Cicero was constantly engaged in argumentation. Indeed, he made it an art; his polished speeches are masterpieces in the use of words to persuade. In addition Cicero wrote two important essays on political theory, *Republic* and *Laws*, defending the Roman republican institutions but pleading for the establishment of a first citizen to guide the state. He also wrote several philosophical tracts that popularized and made abstract Greek thought understandable to Roman readers. His numerous *Letters* supply a brilliant picture of Roman politics and society in the first century B.C. This eloquent, learned Roman made Latin prose a language capable of expressing any idea. He demonstrated an intellect alive to real problems and confident that the human mind could cope with all situations.

Few prose writers represented such a universal genius as did Cicero. Others were more specialized. History was of especial interest to the Romans. Perhaps Rome's greatest historian was Livy (59 B.C.–A.D. 17), another man inspired to write by the Augustan regime, who wrote the immense *History of the Roman Republic*, covering the period from 753 B.C. to A.D. 9. Although a large part of the work has been lost, it is quite clear from what is left that Livy believed that Rome had a great historical mission and that he wished to instruct his readers on that subject. Livy was not a scientific historian, interested only in the truth; his work was a conglomeration of truth and fiction put together to teach a lesson. None-

theless it presented with great dramatic impact the men and events that made Rome great over seven centuries. Patriotism, a sense of duty, sobriety, and moral excellence were put forward as the marks of Roman greatness.

Less monumental but equally artistic was Tacitus (about A.D. 55–117), who wrote about Roman history after Augustus. His *Histories* and *Annals* covered large portions of the period A.D. 14–96. Although Tacitus was a man of senatorial and republican sentiments, prejudiced against the successors of Augustus, he wrote with brilliance and deep moral sense. Another of his

MAISON CARÉE. This splendid temple built in the provincial city of Nîmes in Gaul during the first century A.D. is typical of the style of architecture most often employed by the Romans in their temples. The ornate Corinthian columns (contrast with the Doric and Ionian orders illustrated on pp. 82 and 83), the pediment, the friezes, and the cornices all show strong Greek influences. It was due chiefly to the Roman willingness to spread Greek civilization that such a structure could be built in Gaul, which had been a land of barbarians until shortly before this temple was built. (*Archives Photographiques, Paris*)

works, *Germania*, presented important information about the German barbarians who were soon to play a larger part in Roman life. Suetonius (about A.D. 75–150) vividly presented a wealth of interesting material about the Roman emperors from Julius Caesar to Domitian in his *Lives of the Twelve Caesars*. Greek writers swelled the body of excellent histories written in the period under consideration. Plutarch (about A.D. 46–120), using biography as a means of moral instruction, provided a brilliant series of biographies of Greek and Roman men in his *Parallel Lives*. Several Romans produced personal memoirs that were of the nature of histories. Probably the best examples were Julius Caesar's *Commentaries on the Gallic Wars* and Marcus Aurelius's *Meditations*.

Doubtless the reader has noted that no mention has been made of certain kinds of literature. Drama never took deep roots in Rome, although many attempts were made to imitate the magnificent Greek drama. Only occasionally did a fiction writer grace the Roman literary scene. Perhaps these gaps in the literary picture tell a great deal. They suggest that the creation of highly imaginative literature was foreign to the Romans, who had to be tied to reality—to history, to current moral problems, to personal experiences.

This review of Roman literature, touching on only a handful of the best writers, should leave no doubt that Rome could stand independently in the history of literature, for her writers handled great subjects in a powerful style, and countless generations in Western Europe in the centuries following Rome's fall were to be introduced to a civilized view of life by reading the men we have cited.

THE PANTHEON. This remarkable structure, built in Rome in the second century A.D., is the largest round temple ever built, and still stands today. Its massive concrete walls support a dome that is 142 feet in diameter. The construction of a dome of such proportions is indeed a tribute to the superior Roman engineering skill. Greek influence is clearly obvious in the columned porch in front, which was built earlier than the rotunda behind it. The structure as a whole marks a union of the Greek and the Roman contributions to architectural design. (*The Bettmann Archive*)

PONT DU GARD. This impressive monument of Roman engineering skill was built across the River Gard near Nîmes in Gaul. Rising 160 feet above the river bed, it served as both an aqueduct and a bridge. The bridge is about 900 feet long, and the span of each of the large arches is approximately 80 feet. Roman architects and engineers have seldom been excelled in the use of the arch. (*Archives Photographiques, Paris*)

4. Art

Rome's most splendid artistic work was in the field of architecture. The style was eclectic, although Greek models were most important. However, the Romans added important elements to what they borrowed. They developed concrete as a building material, using it to form the basic structure of most of the large buildings. They also perfected and put to new uses the arch and the dome, which had been developed earlier in the ancient Near East. These technical advances permitted the Romans to construct larger buildings and to depart from the horizontal lines that characterized Greek architecture.

As builders the Romans achieved their most impressive and creative results in buildings intended to serve worldly, public ends. They were not, like the Greeks, great

temple builders. Most Roman temples closely imitated Greeks models, differing only by being more ornate. However, the Romans did create their own temple styles. The Pantheon, built in Rome in the second century A.D., is the greatest round temple ever built. Its domed roof, made of stone, is 142 feet in diameter, and is supported by massive concrete walls built around a rotunda under the dome. A rectangular porch, the roof of which is supported by Greek columns, leads into the rotunda, supplying a pleasing mixture of Greek and Roman architectural ideas.

Much more distinctly Roman were the public baths, amphitheaters, aqueducts, bridges, meeting halls (basilicas), and palaces that appeared in Rome and in many provincial cities during the two centuries following Augustus. The famous Colosseum at Rome, about half of which still stands,

THE COLOSSEUM. The outer walls of this huge structure surround an amphitheater where the famous gladiatorial combats and other games were held during much of the Roman period. Built in Rome near the end of the first century A.D., the Colosseum measures 617 by 512 feet on the outside. The wall shown here is 160 feet high. Note especially the skillful use of the arch and of the blank wall to top the structure. The columns on the outside of the structure are for decorative purposes only; they bear none of the weight of the structure. From the arena floor, seats rise row upon row to approximately the level of the third tier of arches. (*Italian State Tourist Office*)

illustrates the Roman architectural genius. Built to serve the large audiences who loved the games, this concrete structure measures approximately 617 by 512 feet on the outside. The outer wall rises about 160 feet and consists of three tiers of arcades topped by a blank wall. The arcades of each tier are decorated with columns executed in the Greek style; however, these columns are purely decorative, having nothing to do with the structure of the building. Inside the Colosseum is an arena from which rises tier after tier of seats, each giving a good view of the scene of the action. Underneath the structure is an intricate network of arched passageways and rooms, all accessible to the arena.

The Roman basilica, built in great numbers in cities all over the empire, is especially significant in architectural history be-

cause it served as a model for early Christian churches and for most Christian architecture for many centuries after the fall of Rome. The basilica was essentially a long hall flanked by side aisles. The walls of the main hall were built higher than the side aisles, allowing windows to be cut high in the walls. The Romans made skillful use of the arch in covering these halls; for instance, in the Basilica of Maxentius (early fourth century A.D.) a concrete roof was put over a main aisle eighty feet wide. Roman baths, which consisted of a great central court surrounded by numerous smaller rooms, made skillful use of arched vaults and passageways to achieve great size. All of these buildings are especially impressive because of their size, reflecting the power and the wealth of the people who built them.

Roman sculpture showed less independ-

THE ROMAN FORUM. One of the great achievements of Roman architecture was the building of a harmonious group of public buildings called a forum. Here is a view of the ruins of the forum of Republican Rome, where most of the political struggles of the period centered. The columns at the right and left are the remains of temples, and in the background are ruins of other public buildings. In the center is the triumphal arch of the Emperor Septimus Severus (reigned A.D. 193–211), built later than most of the other structures shown. The building in the left background is modern. (*Italian State Tourist Office*)

THE ARCH OF TITUS. This triumphal arch commemorating the victory of the Emperor Titus over the Jews in A.D. 70 is typical of the means chosen by Roman rulers to commemorate their deeds. Built over one of the most important streets in the heart of Rome, the arch was decorated with scenes reminding all who passed of the feats of its builder, with suitable inscriptions telling of his works. (*United Press International Photo*)

ent genius than did architecture. Greek models exerted an especially powerful influence over Roman sculptors. Although almost every form of sculpture was produced in great quantity everywhere in the empire, the best work done by the Romans was in portraiture and relief work treating historical incidents. In both of these forms the Roman artists worked stone into realistic portrayals of a personality or an event. Even statues of emperors were extremely lifelike, accentuating the dignity and manliness of their subjects, but avoiding excessive idealization. The historical scenes carved on triumphal arches or the walls of public buildings are almost photographic. The Romans showed little interest in the idealization of reality, the trademark of Greek

sculpture. What little we know of Roman painting, used chiefly to decorate buildings, reflects this same sense of realism. This trait of Roman art was in keeping with the practical earthiness of Romans.

5. Philosophy, Science, and Religion

Roman philosophy was chiefly engaged in digesting and explaining those portions of the Greek philosophical tradition that seemed applicable to Roman problems, especially political and ethical problems. Roman philosophers carried on the trend already established in the Hellenistic period, concentrating on the application of philosophical principles rather than on further speculations. Rome's greatest accomplishment was, therefore, the transmission of at least a part of the Greek philosophical tradition to areas where it was unknown, especially Western Europe.

Four figures represent the main currents in Roman philosophy. Cicero was an eclectic philosopher, borrowing from many Greek schools of thought and working out a set of ideas that he felt were fitted to Roman society in the first century B.C. Lucretius was a disciple of Epicurus, making a powerful plea for intelligent Romans to adopt an outlook based on a materialistic concept of the universe. From Epicureanism he sought to justify a life of learning and withdrawal from the world, arguing that this alone was the true source of pleasure. Not all Epicureans, however, followed Lucretius's path; many Romans used Epicurean materialism as an excuse for a life of sensuous pleasure. Seneca (about 4 B.C.– A.D. 65) and Marcus Aurelius (A.D. 121– 180) were advocates of Stoicism, seeking to apply Zeno's concepts to Roman life in the great days of the empire. On the basis of Zeno's teaching that the universe was governed by a super intelligence, they advocated reasonableness as the aim of life. From reasonableness would spring all the Stoic virtues—humanitarianism, tolerance, devotion to duty, humility, and resignation to hardship. By arguing for the need of one

RELIEF FROM THE ARCH OF TITUS. Well-executed reliefs decorate the inside of the Arch of Titus. This scene shows the Romans bearing the spoils away from Jerusalem after its capture by Titus. The main object here is a candelabra used by the Jews in their religious ceremonies. Note the amount of detail included by the sculptor. (*Alinari Photo*)

state and one law the Stoics also helped to justify the Roman imperial government. Stoicism was especially popular in the first and second centuries A.D., when most educated men subscribed to it seriously as a guide in their daily lives.

Pure science made little progress during the Roman era. A few people, including Pliny the Elder, Galen, and Ptolemy, compiled great collections of scientific knowledge, chiefly from Greek sources, much of which was made available in Latin and thus transmitted to Western Europe in later ages. Although little interested in pure science, the Romans were highly skilled in putting existing scientific knowledge to practical use. Rome's engineers were unequaled in antiquity; her roads, aqueducts, and bridges have withstood the ages. The technical skills developed by engineers and artisans formed a precious heritage handed on to later generations; perhaps this heritage was as important to Western Europe as was the literary, artistic, and philosophical tradition transmitted by Rome.

While the educated upper class of imperial society absorbed and assimilated Greek philosophical and scientific knowledge, the bulk of society continued to find their chief source of satisfaction in religion. The most important development of the era from 100 B.C. to A.D. 180 in the field of religion was the growing popularity of Eastern mystery religions. The ancient Italian religion continued to decline, in spite of Augustus's efforts to revive it and of the poets' praises for it. Many intellectuals were atheists and openly scoffed at the old religion.

Some of the emperors tried to institute a new religion centering around worship of the emperor, but this movement did not appeal to most Romans, who preferred the emotional, personal Asian religions, which gave them a savior and promised them a happy life after death. These cults, already established in the East, gained an ever-increasing following in the western part of the empire. The tolerance of the imperial government aided their spread immeasurably. As we shall see, Christianity began its conquest of the Roman world during this period. Despite the enthusiasm of the converts some drastic results accompanied the spread of the Eastern religions. All of them tended to lessen the interest of their adherents in Roman public life and to concentrate attention on personal problems and life after death, thus making it more difficult for Rome to control her citizens. The spread of Eastern religions marked the beginning of Rome's decline.

6. Law

Perhaps Rome's most enduring cultural monument was her law. Although the evolution of Roman law was not confined to the period between 100 B.C. and A.D. 180, certain developments occurred in this era that decided its final character.

The Romans, unable to conceive of a state without a legal basis, had been concerned with law from the beginning of their history. In this respect they were not unique; other ancient political communities, such as the Hebrews, the Babylonians, and the Greeks, had a similar idea. Roman law was unique, however, in that it continued to grow century after century. Unwritten custom was constantly modified by the legislation of the assemblies during the republican period. Even more important was the custom of allowing the chief judicial official of the republic, the praetor, to pronounce his interpretation of the law at the beginning of his term. There thus developed by the end of the republic a vast body of judge-made law. Moreover, in the republi-

can period the Romans began to develop a body of law for their non-citizen subject peoples. This body of law became a kind of international law (*lex gentium*). Proclaimed by provincial governors and praetors elected to judge cases involving foreigners, it was built on legal ideas derived from the laws of subject people, on Roman legal principles, and on the common sense of the judges. By the end of the republic a huge although somewhat confused body of law had thus been accumulated.

In the period from 100 B.C. to A.D. 180 an effort was made to codify this law into a single, systematic body. This move was prompted by many forces. The new imperial government, itself moving toward a unified administration, saw in a unified law a means of exercising authority. The general trend toward removing the distinctions between Romans and non-Romans suggested a single law to fit a unified people. The extensive legislation by the emperors tended to create uniformity. Stoic philosophy, with its emphasis on a universal law of nature, prompted men to think in terms of a consistent body of law for all society. These forces produced during the first and second centuries a series of notable legal authorities who devoted their lives to the study and unification of the law, usually with the wholehearted support of the rulers. Their writings became the basis of legal education, so that most lawyers and public administrators adopted a similar view. Giving Roman law its fundamental features, the great jurists sought to relate human laws to deeper principles of natural law, thus giving the legal system a theoretical basis outside human whim and fancy. They sought to make the law consistent but flexible, recognizing the need for rational application of general principles to current problems. In effect, the jurists argued that the law was not yet perfect and that a continued effort must be made to bring it nearer perfection. By the end of the second century A.D. the Roman jurists had by no means completed the unification and standardization of Roman law; that would be done only in the sixth century by the Emperor Justinian. But they had established its basic principles. Although law could be derived from many sources, it must be related to the universal order of things, i.e., to the natural law. It must be supple enough to bend to changing conditions, yet firmly enough based on principle to avoid manipulation by unscrupulous men. It must serve the needs of all men and not a narrow segment of the population. These principles have survived until the present as the highest ideals of all legal systems.

7. The Romans as Spreaders of Culture

One final achievement that must be credited to the Romans is perhaps more important than anything else in their cultural history. The Romans developed a special talent for spreading their culture to culturally backward peoples. From the first century B.C. onward large areas in the western part of the empire were transformed rapidly into images of Rome. This transformation was of inestimable importance for the future of Western Europe. It represented the first step in the elevation of Western European peoples from barbarism and made it possible for them to play a more important role in history.

Rome's way of impressing her civilization on backward peoples was a complicated one. The uplifting of her subjects was the work of many agents working in many ways. Roman soldiers, officials, and merchants, moving freely about the whole empire, were agents of civilization. The Roman government founded towns in far-flung areas of the empire and encouraged Romans to live there. The Roman imperial government encouraged provincials to familiarize themselves with Roman ways in order to facilitate administrative relations. Latin and Greek, the administrative languages of the empire, soon became known to the barbarians, who thus gained direct knowledge of the Graeco-Roman literary tradition. Roman emperors built roads, aqueducts, temples, and public buildings throughout the provinces, impressing upon even the least advanced the majesty of Rome and prompting them to imitate. The freedom given to scholars, religious missionaries, philosophers, and artists encouraged them to seek out the barbarians. Rome opened her doors to men with artistic and intellectual talents from all corners of the empire, thus turning all eyes toward a common cultural center and providing a channel for the spread of Roman culture.

To trace the spreading circle of Roman culture into the heart of ancient centers of barbarism would require a detailed history of a dozen provinces and a hundred cities. Suffice it here to say that the marks of Roman culture remain. The French and Spanish tongues, for instance, are direct descendants of the Latin learned in these areas in the first and second centuries. When one comes across an elaborate bath in the city of Bath in Western England or a great amphitheater in Gaul or a Roman bridge at one of a dozen places, he realizes the extent of the Romanization of the Western provinces. Luckily for the inhabitants of Spain, France, Britain, or North Africa the Romans did not adopt the Greek attitude of looking down on foreigners. Instead the Romans gave their best to all comers, spreading civilization over a large area of the world previously caught in the clutches of barbarism.

SUGGESTED READING

Russel M. Geer, *Classical Civilization; Rome*, 2nd ed. (1950). A concise, well-organized survey of Roman cultural life, especially good on Roman art. This is a companion volume to the Couch book cited in the bibliography for Chapter 7. The two volumes make an excellent introduction to classical culture.

* Edith Hamilton, *The Roman Way to Western Civilization* (Mentor). Originally published under the title *The Roman Way* (1932). A

lively discussion of the nature of the Roman outlook on life, illustrated by generous quotations from Roman literature. A good introduction to the problem of evaluating Rome's role in the development of Western European society.

Albert Grenier, *The Roman Spirit in Religion, Thought, and Art*, tr. by M. R. Dobie (1926). A more profound attempt to paint a general picture of Roman character and thought than the Edith Hamilton book cited above.

Michael Grant, *Roman Literature* (1954). A relatively brief yet thorough discussion of the development of Roman literature. The author succeeds in highlighting the chief authors and the chief literary forms that characterize Roman literature.

J. Declareuil, *Rome the Law-Giver*, tr. by E. A. Parker (1927). An excellent discussion of Roman law, stressing especially its uniqueness. The book is not easy to read, but it will be rewarding for any reader interested in a full understanding of what was probably Rome's greatest contribution to later history.

H. F. Jolowicz, *Historical Introduction to the Study of Roman Law*, 2nd ed. (1952). A detailed, often extremely technical discussion of Roman law, especially recommended for anyone interested in law as a profession and willing to dig into a difficult book in search of a complete picture of the development of Roman law.

Herbert Jennings Rose, *Ancient Roman Religion* (1948). A short introduction to Roman religion, stressing especially the basic Roman concepts of deity, the religious duties of man, and the relation of religion to Roman public life.

Franz Altheim, *A History of Roman Religion*, tr. by Harold Mattingly (1938). A more thorough and detailed discussion of Roman religion than the Rose book. This book is recommended to all readers interested in the religious scene out of which Christianity emerged. A mastery of Altheim's book will help to clarify many complicated questions connected with the rise of Christianity.

Kevin Guinagh and Alfred P. Darjahn, *Latin Literature in Translation* (1942). A convenient anthology that will serve to introduce the reader to a representative selection of Roman literature. It may suggest to the reader some author or work to be read in entirety. The four authors listed below are recommended; to them should be added the writings of Livy, Polybius, Cicero, Tacitus, and Suetonius cited in previous chapters.

* Vergil, *Aeneid* (numerous editions; a good one is the translation by C. Day Lewis, Anchor). An epic poem dealing with the founding of Rome and her subsequent rise to greatness by the greatest of all the Latin poets.

* Caesar, *Conquest of Gaul*, tr. by S. A. Handford (Penguin). Julius Caesar's own account of his adventures in Gaul is a skillful mixture of history and propaganda, reflecting the powerful mind of an important Roman.

* Lucretius, *On the Nature of Things* (many editions; a suitable one is the edition in Everyman Library or that in Penguin). A long poetic discussion of Epicurean philosophy.

* Ovid, *The Metamorphoses*, tr. by Rolfe Humphries (Indiana University Press paperback). A poetic rendering of the chief religious myths that circulated in the Roman world.

SECTION 3

The Fall of

Graeco-Roman Civilization,

A.D. *180–500*

During the second century A.D. Graeco-Roman civilization had held unchallenged sway over the Mediterranean basin, extending its influence inland from the sea into three continents—Europe, Asia, and Africa. The political genius of the Romans, expressing itself through the imperial system of government, had furnished the key to the wide dispersion of the Graeco-Roman way of life. Greek literature, art, philosophy, and science, adapted by the Romans, had served as another vital force unifying and enlivening that world. Under these two influences one of the most magnificent eras in human history had unfolded itself.

As the second century drew to a close, however, Graeco-Roman civilization began to decline. Although this civilization was endowed with sufficient reserve strength to withstand great shock, the decline ran its relentless course. Within three centuries Graeco-Roman civilization was virtually dead, eaten away by sicknesses from within and torn apart by the assaults of barbarian outsiders. The final disintegration of this civilization forced large numbers of people in the Mediterranean world to construct new ways of life.

CHAPTER 13

The Decline of the Roman Empire
and the Rise of Christianity

THE CENTURY following the death of Marcus Aurelius in A.D. 180 was highlighted by a serious crisis manifesting itself in a rash of civil wars that sapped the strength of the imperial government. At the same time economic and social maladjustments, together with intellectual and spiritual confusion, slowly ate away at the foundations of Graeco-Roman society. These tragic developments must now be analyzed with some care.

1. The Political Crisis, A.D. 180–285

The most pressing political problem of the third century was that of the imperial succession. During the period of the "good emperors" (A.D. 96–180) each ruler had chosen an able, experienced man to succeed him. Marcus Aurelius repudiated that principle by selecting his son, Commodus (A.D. 180–192), who was completely incompetent. He devoted most of his energies to training gladiators, neglecting defense, finances, justice, and sound administration. When voices were raised in protest, Commodus brutally silenced them. His tyranny finally resulted in his murder by the Praetorian Guard. From that moment on the army and its ambitious generals dominated Roman politics. A military despotism had replaced the enlightened rule of the great emperors.

There would be little point in tracing in detail the terrible struggles caused by the competition of generals for the imperial crown. The general pattern was always the same. At the death of an emperor various units of the army proclaimed their own successors. These candidates then went to war with one another, until one of them eventually emerged victorious. No sooner had the successful candidate established himself than plots began to form in the army to unseat him. These plots brought on new civil wars and usually ended in assassination; it was a rare emperor who died of natural causes in the third century. Civil war had replaced the Pax Romana of the second century.

While the civil wars raged, the political structure of the empire underwent a fundamental change. The emperors of the third century were entirely different from those of the second. Almost all of them were professional soldiers with little knowledge of the intricate problems of civil administration and not much concern for the civilian population. Many were natives of the frontier provinces of the empire with little respect for Rome's political and cultural heritage. Their sole interest was in the exploitation of the empire for the benefit of the army. Favors of all kinds were showered on the insatiable soldiers. Discipline was relaxed and the task of defending the frontiers forgotten. The military became a pampered caste preying on the population. Even more significant, the third-century emperors more and more relied upon their army colleagues to fill the chief governmental posts, the old senatorial aristocracy and the middle-class equestrians being pushed out of high office, often in none too gentle a fashion. The Augustan political system, involving co-operation between princeps and aristocracy, was replaced by naked despotism based on armed force.

The militaristic regime led to other evil consequences. When state expenses grew much more rapidly than income, chiefly because of constant warfare and liberal grants to the army, the emperors of the third century debased the coinage, thus causing inflation. They also imposed a crushing tax burden on the whole population, and when money income was still not equal to their needs, they requisitioned goods and services from their subjects, paying little attention to the justice of their demands. These requisitions on the citizen body led to the regimentation of society, the freezing of peasants and artisans in their jobs. More and more the imperial government intruded into the political life of the city-states, forcing local aristocracies (curiales) to raise the heavy taxes or pay out of their own pockets. To be associated with city government became the worst job in the empire. Gradually the curiales were ruined, eliminating one of the strongest political elements in the Roman world. The need for money also brought about a drastic increase in the bureaucracy, hordes of tax collectors and imperial agents intruding into every corner of the empire. Since emperors came and went rapidly, the bureaucracy lacked real direction and became a rapacious, corrupt body.

Added to the internal crisis in the empire was heavier pressure on its frontiers. Hardly a year passed without an assault from some enemy, usually the Germans and the Persians. In part these attacks were fostered by the internal troubles, but they were rendered more serious by factors beyond Roman control. A new dynasty in Persia strengthened that kingdom to the point where she was able to threaten all of Rome's holdings in Asia. Hordes of Germans, moving southward in Central Europe, tended to coalesce into larger groups, ever more difficult to restrain from crossing the thinly defended frontier. To maintain the frontier under these increasing pressures, the Romans were forced to enlarge their armies and to make heavier demands on the civilian population. Even so large areas of the frontier were devastated and depopulated by the constant warfare. By A.D. 285 the Roman Empire stood like a beleaguered fortress.

2. Economic, Social, and Cultural Decline

In this difficult era Rome's problems were not only political and military. Her people suffered serious economic and social dislocations. Although some of these problems predated the era from A.D. 180 to 285, they were all made worse by the chaos of these years.

The period was one of declining economic prosperity. The causes are too complex and the information too scanty to allow any easy explanation. Agricultural production, if not actually decreasing, was barely holding its own. The continued spread of the large-estate system, with its increases in tenant farming, may have been partially responsible. But the devastating civil and foreign wars also hurt farming, especially along the frontier, where large areas were actually turned over to barbarians, who were far from being efficient farmers. Moreover, the best evidence suggests a shortage of farm labor, perhaps due to a declining population.

Trade and industry suffered even greater depression. Trade declined in part because of the growing self-sufficiency of those backward parts of the empire that had once depended on traders to supply their needs from distant points. For instance, the development of industry in places like Gaul and Spain during the peaceful second century made it less necessary for these peoples to import products from the East. Trade suffered worse, however, from political anarchy. The collapse of the imperial money system through debasement of the currency took away a basic requirement for active trade—a sound system of exchange. Heavy taxation bore especially hard on the trading classes, whose wealth could be most easily seized. The lawlessness, banditry, and piracy that accompanied the civil wars interfered with the movement of goods. State regimentation of trade and industry to serve military needs often acted to restrict and limit economic growth. The end of the Roman geographical expansion offered no new territories to exploit, again checking the growth of trade and industry.

Social transformations of no less significance took place in the third century. The urban aristocracies who had upheld Graeco-Roman civilization were on the decline. While the military despots ousted most of the great nobles of Rome and Italy from key places in government, the aristocrats of cities in all corners of the empire were crushed beneath the burden of taxation and gradually deprived of their control over local affairs by bureaucrats very often coming up from the lower classes through the army. Roman society could ill afford the crushing of a class that had always carried the chief burden of government and whose members were the main pillars of Graeco-Roman civilization. Had the lower classes benefited from the decline of the old aristocracy, the loss would not have been so serious. Such was not the case. Both agricultural and urban lower-class elements were increasingly regimented and socially debased. The peasants were forced to become hereditary servants of great landowners and surrendered a large part of their income and their labor to their masters. The craftsmen and laborers in the cities were compelled by the state to remain in one trade and to bring their sons up in that trade.

Only one element of the Roman population saw its position bettered socially—the army. A soldier of ability could work himself up to a high position in the state, becoming eventually an aristocrat in power and wealth. Even a member of the lower ranks of the army had all kinds of benefits bestowed on him by generals anxious to win or keep his favor. This development had an evil effect in society, since on an ever-increasing scale troops were recruited from the most primitive areas of the empire. Often even barbarians were taken into the army to fill the constantly depleted ranks. These people, little acquainted with Roman ideals and institutions, took over the leadership of society. They could hardly help barbarizing Roman life. And they could hardly be expected to uphold the ancient order as well as those better acquainted with it.

The political, social, and economic turmoil of the third century created an atmosphere that obviously was not suited for cultural and intellectual activity of a high order, and the record in these fields was not especially impressive. Writers, artists, and thinkers merely imitated the past, and their works, although plentiful, show definite signs of stagnation and sterility. There seemed nothing new to say.

These troubled times drove dispirited men to the gods, new and old, for hope. Even the philosophers turned more and more to philosophical systems like Neo-Platonism, which denied the importance of this world and asked its adherents to seek to join themselves spiritually with an eternal, non-material force. The Eastern mystery religions were the chief refuge of the masses. Superstition, magic, astrology, and prophecy all flourished among a people thirsting for relief from the sad scene unfolding about them. So important was this whole matter of the loss of faith in Graeco-Roman ideals that we need to pause here to analyze the emergence of one new set of ideals that not only made great progress in the empire in the third century but that also was destined to reshape the history of a large part of the world.

3. The Rise of Christianity: Beginnings

Few subjects have been more thoroughly discussed than the story of the first three centuries of Christianity. It will suffice for our purpose here if we can understand how Christianity offered the citizens of the great Roman Empire something to satisfy them and turn their minds and hearts to the service of ideals other than those offered by Graeco-Roman civilization.

Christianity certainly did not start its career as if it would sweep across the Graeco-Roman world and beyond. It began as a splinter movement among the Jews, who had long been looked upon with suspicion by a large part of the Graeco-Roman populace. Since the destruction of the Hebrew state in the sixth century B.C. the Jews had dreamed of the day when they would regain their political freedom. Their ancient religion held them together despite their failure to re-establish an independent nation and their dispersion throughout the Mediterranean world. With the passing of the centuries the Jews more and more placed their hope in a God-sent Messiah who would deliver them from their oppressors, a hope that had reached a fever pitch by the time the Romans conquered Palestine in the first century B.C. Although the Romans were extremely tolerant toward the religion of the Jews, their suspicion was aroused by talk of the Messiah, which led them to believe that the Jews were bent on revolution. Chafing under Roman rule, the Jews quarreled among themselves about what to do. Some felt that they must compromise with Rome, accepting Roman rule in exchange for religious freedom. Others refused to compromise, insisting on a rigid observance of ancient Jewish law as a mark of uniqueness. Still others agitated for immediate and bloody war on Rome, believing that God would once again deliver His chosen people.

Into this complex scene came Christ. His career is too well known to require summarization here, but it must be realized that his preaching exerted a tremendous influence on the Jews. Christ pronounced the coming of a new kingdom for which his audience must prepare itself by repentance and spiritual regeneration. He did not ask that his followers break with their Jewish tradition. Instead he preached that they should go beyond it by substituting love of God and of man for conformance with the ritualistic laws of Judaism. To those sinful men who accepted his call for regeneration Christ promised eternal happiness, asking that his followers have faith that God was filled with love for them. He soon won an enthusiastic following, but he also aroused enmity among the Jews. His scathing attack on the formalism and the materialism of Jewish religious leaders turned them against him and brought forth the charge that he was trying to destroy Judaism. Furthermore, many of his most enthusiastic followers deserted him when he made it clear that his mission was not to create or rule an earthly kingdom and that he would not take up the sword to liberate the Jews. This hostility ended in his crucifixion.

His death was followed by a development of the utmost importance. A very few of his stoutest followers were convinced that Christ arose from the dead, returned among them, and commanded them to carry on what he had begun. The Resurrection was to these disciples proof that Christ was the Son of God and that he had brought to mankind a new revelation. This belief led his disciples to proclaim a new religion.

The first Christian community in Jerusalem had little success. However, the Christians soon widened their views. The idea of converting all men to Christianity became a compelling passion. St. Paul was the leading force in this crucial development. A Jew born in Tarsus, Paul was familiar with Graeco-Roman thought and was convinced that Christ's message was for the Gentiles as well as for the Jews. This inspiration launched him on a long career of preaching in Asia Minor, Greece, and Rome. He emphasized those ideas of Christ which had universal application—love of God and man, moral rebirth through faith, and eternal salvation as a reward for belief in Christ and for high moral life. He insisted that Christians need not follow in detail the requirements of Jewish law, which to him were merely outward signs of piety. By the time of his martyrdom (perhaps A.D. 67) many others were seeking converts among Jews and Gentiles alike. Christianity and Judaism had begun to part company.

4. The Rise of Christianity: Spread to the End of the Third Century

Once launched, Christianity grew steadily. The manner in which it spread is largely veiled from our view. Many dedicated missionaries preached the word under all kinds of conditions. Converts convinced others to join the fold. The great cities of the empire, especially in the East, were the chief centers of Christianity. The lower classes were more often attracted, although from an early date members of the upper classes also became converts. By the end of the third century the number of Christians was already extensive, although not a majority in the empire.

The progress of Christianity was not automatic and painless. The Roman government from time to time persecuted Christians. Usually these persecutions were not prompted by religious motives. The Christians were accused of political crimes. Their refusal to worship state gods and their development of a church organization without approval of the Roman government made it appear that they were not loyal to the empire. Usually the persecutions were local and temporary, although in the third century attempts were made to exterminate Christians everywhere. Roman intellectuals poured scorn on Christianity, accusing it of being simple, superstitious, and illogical. Among the masses there spread the vilest sort of rumors about the immoral, brutal practices of Christianity.

Christianity had strong competitors from other oriental mystery religions, which likewise provided saviors, loving gods, immortality, and satisfying ritual. At the same time Christianity suffered from internal disputes over such questions as the relationship between Christianity and Judaism, the exact nature of Christ, his relationship to

God, the details of Christian morality, and the manner in which Christians should worship. Solutions to these disputes were never easy and inevitably set Christians against one another.

5. The Rise of Christianity: Reasons for Its Success

Yet Christianity grew. Its success was due to many factors, stemming from conditions in the empire and from the nature of Christianity itself. Christianity showed a remarkable flexibility during its early years, adapting itself to the religious needs of the age while retaining its individual characteristics. Perhaps the following developments were chiefly responsible for the advance of Christianity, although one must always admit that there is a danger of oversimplification in so complex a matter.

Conditions in the Roman Empire were favorable to the growth of a new religion. The empire was knit together so that movement of ideas was easy. In spite of isolated cases of persecution an atmosphere of tolerance generally prevailed. The ever-growing power of centralized Roman government and the decline of city-states inclined individuals to abandon social goals and to seek personal, spiritual, and emotional satisfactions, while the chaos of the third century made the need for personal relief even more urgent. The emergence of a single state uniting many peoples into one society suggested the need for a religion that would apply to all men regardless of origin or class. Admittedly, the other great religions enjoyed these same advantages. Nonetheless, Christianity came into existence at a moment that was ripe.

Another source of Christian strength lay in its appeal as a religion. No matter how far one may push the search for an explanation of Christian expansion, one must always remember that Christianity won converts primarily because its teachings answered their deepest religious yearning. Such ideas as the existence of one almighty, loving, merciful God, His sacrifice of His son to redeem men, eternal salvation based on individual worth, damnation for sinners, and universal brotherhood fitted together to supply a powerful answer to those seeking to know about God's ways toward men. The humanity of Christ, living here on earth not so long ago, gave an intimacy to Christianity that other religions lacked. Moreover, Christian teachings were dramatically and simply presented in the New Testament, which began to take form immediately after Christ's death; no other religion in the Roman world possessed so effective a sacred literature.

Another basic source of strength was the church organization that took shape during the first three centuries after Christ. The earliest church organization was simple. Christians in a community met for worship, partook of a common meal, and joined together in prayer and song. Certain individuals, especially those who had been close to Christ, were recognized as natural leaders and served as instructors to others. Some of these leaders, like Paul and Peter, were accepted by many different communities. Later in the first century a few communities began to look to local figures for guidance and leadership, and titles like bishop, presbyter, and elder appeared. With the passage of time disputes within the Christian body, persecutions, and increasing wealth led to new problems demanding stronger authority. In answer to these problems authority began to settle in the hands of bishops, who undertook to settle matters of discipline, doctrine, property, and worship. The bishop's authority almost always coincided with the boundaries of a city-state, indicating that the Christians were imitating the political organization of the Roman Empire. In some of the larger cities of the empire, where the burden was too great for one man, subordinates were appointed to assist the bishop. For instance, in a city that had several churches, presbyters, or priests, were put in charge of each church, but all the priests remained under the authority of the bishop. In effect, the Christian world was evolving rapidly toward

a division into self-contained, self-governing units, each of which had a machinery for discipline, uniform instruction, and adequate resources to carry on its activities in an organized fashion.

Christians never lost sight of their bonds of unity, however. While many churches existed, there was an awareness of oneness. Church organization reflected this idea. At first the great prestige of Christ's disciples and the early missionary leaders served to tie the scattered communities together. Later, bishops from rather extensive areas met to decide common problems and to apply these decisions in each locality, thus establishing church councils with legislative and judicial powers. Before the end of the third century A.D. there was already an urge to establish a final authority who could lay down doctrine and enforce obedience. Already some of the chief bishops, such as those of Jerusalem, Antioch, Alexandria, and Rome, were exerting considerable influence. The bishop of Rome was especially influential. He naturally gained prestige because of Rome's position as capital of the empire. Furthermore, an important doctrine, called the Petrine theory, had begun to take shape to buttress the power of the bishop of Rome. According to this doctrine Christ had granted to Peter a special place as his vicar on earth. Peter had chosen Rome as the seat of that power, and his successors as bishops of Rome exercised the same authority. By A.D. 285 the Christian world had by no means accepted a single head, but a strong current was running that way. A kind of second Roman Empire was being born, subdivided into well-governed local units. No other religion could boast such an organization.

Early Christianity increased its appeal, especially to the educated classes, by developing a systematic, reasoned statement of fundamental beliefs. Two forces drove Christian thinkers on in this task: the need to answer accusations by their non-Christian critics and the need to iron out differences on basic teachings within the ranks of the Christian camp. The early theologians tended to discuss and define Christian teachings in terms that educated Romans could understand, borrowing heavily from Graeco-Roman philosophical teachings to express their ideas. Although this early theology retained the essential features of Christianity, it came more and more to incorporate Graeco-Roman ideas. As this process continued, Christianity became more attractive to the educated and escaped the charge of being illogical and simple.

For those who were not capable of absorbing the lofty ideas of the theologians Christianity had something else to offer. Growing in a society accustomed to splendid religious pageants, to highly emotional practices of worship, and to a constant round of non-religious spectacles provided in the circuses, the Christians developed a ritual that could compete on equal terms. To a large extent this involved adapting existing usages to Christian ceremonies. Christian worship, which originally consisted of meetings in private dwellings for a common meal imitating the last supper of Christ and for prayers, gradually became more elaborate. Churches were built and decorated with art inspired by Christian doctrine. Services were conducted by a clergy in elaborate attire. The common meal became the center of a ritual that emphasized Christ's sacrifice, thus instituting the Mass. Prayer and music became more elaborate, and ceremonies were instituted for such events as baptism, marriage, and burial. Holidays commemorating the highlights of Christ's career and the death of early martyrs were celebrated. The Christians had their own heroes in the saints and martyrs. In short, the development of an elaborate ritual made Christian worship as spectacular and as impressive as that of any other religion or that of the secular pageants. Although modern men sometimes scoff at this aspect of religious life, there can be little doubt that the ability of Christians to develop an elaborate ritual increased its appeal, especially to the vast majority of men for whom religion is more a matter of feeling than of thought.

The Christian movement also developed a strong social consciousness. Christ's career repeatedly exemplified the need for charity and kindness in dealing with others. This idea received expression in Christian practice almost from the beginning. Christians poured out their resources to help the sick, the poor, the criminals, the slaves, children, widows, and hundreds of others who suffered misfortune in Roman society. In spite of their belief that happiness came in the hereafter, the early Christians did not close their eyes to earthly affairs. Anyone could find help within the Christian body—a matter of no small importance to those who suffered ruin in the declining days of Rome.

The steady progress of Christianity against major opposition may now be a little more understandable. Impelled by the powerful message transmitted by Christ, the early Christians fitted themselves to their work with amazing skill. In the name of God they turned all things to religious ends. No other agency, religious or nonreligious, demonstrated such vitality during the three centuries from Christ's birth.

Now we can ask the questions that prompted us to study the growth of Christianity. Did its growth mark the decline of Graeco-Roman civilization? Was the Christian of the third century a good Roman? Answers to these questions are difficult. In many ways the Christian was a good Roman. He performed his duties as long as he was not required to deny his God. He paid his taxes and obeyed the emperor, usually conducting himself in a way that was above criticism. He tried his best to help the unfortunate members of his community. He read books on Christian theology that contained huge portions of Graeco-Roman philosophy. He worshipped in a fashion that was not too much different from non-Christian worship. At least the Christian was not an open rebel, bent on pulling down the established order.

Yet in more important ways the Christian was not a good Roman. He might be in the Roman Empire, but his allegiance lay elsewhere. He served a God who would tolerate no rivals, including Roman emperors who claimed divinity. Believing that his God disapproved of the ways of non-Christian men, he tended to shy away from involvement in worldly affairs. His strong sense of sin led him to regard the world, including the Roman Empire, as hardly worth saving. Awe before his God made him put small trust in human reason or in man's ability to create a paradise on earth. Graeco-Roman civilization was built entirely on the concept that earthly life, if reasonably conducted, could be nearly perfect. The Christian, a man of faith, could hardly be expected to serve such an ideal. The Christian was a devoted, disciplined member of an organization existing independently of the Roman state. His "citizenship" was in the Church, and the Church served his needs better than did the Roman state. Through art, literature, and religious services the Church kept constantly before his eyes and his mind a series of symbols and arguments that made him feel his separateness and his uniqueness. Every Christian convert

meant one less Roman citizen in the fullest sense of the word.

What has just been said about the Christians applies to a lesser degree to the adherents of the other Eastern religions of the third century. The followers of Mithra, Isis, the Unconquerable Sun, and Dionysus all found new ends to serve and gave all their energies in service. These new religions ate away the heart of the worldly, politically oriented thinking of Graeco-Roman civilization. When men began serving these deities to gain an eternal reward, they lost interest in serving the emperor for worldly prizes.

As the third century drew to a close, Rome and all it stood for seemed destined for quick destruction. Political chaos, external assaults, economic decline, social turmoil, and desertion to foreign religions, all coincided to strain the imperial structure to the utmost. The history of the third century gave little sign of eventual recovery. Seldom had Roman leadership seemed less inspired and more selfish and brutal. Men might well ask, as some did, if the end was not near for Rome.

SUGGESTED READING

* Solomon Katz, *The Decline of Rome and the Rise of Medieval Europe* (Cornell). A brief examination of the problems connected with the decline of Rome.
* F. W. Wallbank, *The Decline of the Roman Empire in the West* (Schuman's college paperbacks). Another brief study of the cause of the decline of the Roman Empire, successfully summarizing the best scholarship on the subject.
Arnold Toynbee, *A Study of History*, 10 vols. (1934–54), Vol. I, pp. 22–84. This brief passage in a monumental ten-volume survey of history presents several provocative ideas on the problem of the fall of Rome.
* Erwin R. Goodenough, *The Church in the Roman Empire* (Berkshire Series). A very brief but accurate account of the rise and spread of Christianity under the Roman Empire.
Kenneth Scott Latourette, *A History of Christianity* (1953), pp. 3–235. A well-organized, brief, and fair description of the spread of

Christianity in the Roman world down to about A.D. 500 by a Protestant author. This work is further recommended for its up-to-date bibliographies on the many subjects connected with early Christian history.
Philip Hughes, *A History of the Church*, 3 vols. (1935–47; 2nd ed. of Vols. I and II, 1949). A Roman Catholic interpretation of early Christian history. Volume I of this work traces the spread of Christianity down to about A.D. 300. The author writes well and does not allow his work to be marred by sectarian viewpoints.
H. Lietzmann, *A History of the Early Church*, 4 vols. (1949–52; 2nd ed. of Vol. II, 1950). A detailed account of the history of the early Christian period by one of Germany's greatest scholars. The author brings into the picture in a well-organized fashion problems of organization, doctrine, morality, and social conditions in so far as these matters relate to early Christian history.
Louis Duchesne, *Early History of the Christian*

Church, 3 vols. (1909–24). A detailed history of the early church by a Roman Catholic author. Any student seriously interested in church history ought to read either the Lietzmann or the Duchesne volumes or both.

Arthur Cushman McGiffert, *A History of Christian Thought*, 2 vols. (1932–33), Vol. I. A thorough, readable survey of the complicated problem of Christian dogma as it developed in the early centuries of church history.

* Charles Norris Cochrane, *Christianity and Classical Culture* (Galaxy). Published originally in a hardback edition in 1944. A challenging book for any serious reader who wishes to get to the heart of the differences between classical and Christian ideas and who wishes to observe the conflict between the two systems of thought, especially in the third and fourth centuries. Valuable for its discussion of the Christian attitude toward the state.

CHAPTER 14

---❖---

The Destruction of the Roman Empire,

A.D. *285–500*

In A.D. 285 a general named Diocletian seized the imperial throne by force. In itself this was not a startling event; the rise and fall of generals had been a regular occurrence during the preceding century. However, Diocletian was different. He and his most important successor, Constantine, undertook a thorough reform of the empire in an attempt to check the decline into which it had fallen. Their work gave the empire a reprieve during the fourth century. But their efforts were ultimately in vain. By the opening of the fifth century the empire had lost all its vitality. During that century the barbarian Germans smashed it to pieces.

1. Reforms of Diocletian and Constantine

Once he had seized the imperial throne, Diocletian (A.D. 285–305) vigorously undertook a thorough reform of the government. Sensing that the many problems besetting the empire were too difficult for a single man to handle, he decided to share the office of emperor with three others. To himself and another Diocletian assigned the title of "Augustus"; and to each Augustus a subordinate called a "Caesar." The imperial territory was also divided into four parts, each ruler being entrusted with the power to defend and govern a territory of his own. Diocletian had no intention of per-

manently dividing the empire, however; the Augusti and the Caesars ruled jointly. He hoped that this reorganization would do more than make available additional leaders to face the grave problems of the period. The system was also intended to settle the succession question. When an Augustus died, his Caesar would succeed and would appoint another Caesar.

Diocletian tried to supply the emperors with the resources to cope with the problems in their territories. The army was increased in size and reorganized to provide mobile field armies that could be shifted from place to place as needed to supplement the frontier garrisons. The bureaucracy was reorganized and increased in size to supply more complete control over the population. The provincial administration was more tightly organized in order to centralize authority and ensure uniformity of administration. Finally, new sources of income were provided to meet the costs of larger armies and of a growing bureaucracy.

To meet the rising costs of government necessitated by supporting four courts, by the enlargement of the army, and by the increased bureaucracy, Diocletian created a regimented economy. In 301 he decreed a system of fixed prices and wages, hoping to check the inflationary pressure of the preceding century. Although money taxes continued to be levied, Diocletion placed his greatest trust in a system by which citizens of the empire supplied goods and services directly to the government. All the land of the empire was divided into taxable units, and each unit was required to turn over a fixed amount of produce to the state. Industrial producers were likewise required to supply the state from their shops. Shipowners, caravan operators, and anyone else who could provide services had to work for the state.

To keep producers on their jobs, Diocletian froze the population in various occupations. Peasants, artisans, traders, shippers, bureaucrats, and many others were not permitted to change their occupations. Sons had to step into their fathers' shoes. Even the upper classes were subject to this regimentation. Landowners and members of the urban aristocracy were assigned the burden of collecting taxes and required personally to make up any shortages. Citizens of the Roman Empire now had one end for which to live—all had to serve the state.

Diocletian's intentions were clear: to create a militarized state, the rulers of which would be generals commanding armies large enough to defend the frontiers, and administrators commanding a bureaucratic structure capable of compelling the civilian population to labor for the state. To strengthen this system, Diocletian sought to create a new image of the emperor. Following oriental precedents, he tried to make the imperial office sacred and mysterious. He seldom appeared in public. An elaborate ritual was established in his court, designed to remove the ruler from easy access and to exalt him above all other men. Gone were the days of a benevolent, humane princeps like Hadrian or Marcus Aurelius; the new emperor was lord over all he surveyed. The Roman Empire was ruled by despots with absolute power, each the complete master of millions of subjects.

When Diocletian abdicated in 305, events proved that his scheme for regulating the succession was a failure. A whole new series of civil wars spread over the empire and ended only when Constantine finally fought his way to complete control of the empire, a goal he did not accomplish finally until 324. Constantine was a worthy successor to Diocletian and carried on most of the latter's policies. He strengthened the armies, tightened bureaucratic control, further regimented the Roman economy and populace, and took even more power into his own hands. Through his efforts the absolutist, bureaucratic, militaristic state was given permanent form.

Constantine added his own particular touches to the new order. In 313 he issued the Edict of Milan, a decree that gave the Christians a legal right to practice their religion in the western part of the empire, over which Constantine was then supreme. His action may have been preceded by his own conversion. While fighting for power in 311, Constantine claimed to have seen a cross in the sky and to have been promised in a dream that victory would be his if he took the cross as an insignia for his army. Some of his contemporaries interpreted this event as marking the conversion of Constantine to Christianity. Perhaps his conversion was not so simple as that. Even before his reign there were many signs that the Eastern religions, including Christianity, were so powerful that they had to be taken into consideration by rulers. A violent but unsuccessful persecution of the Christians under Diocletian demonstrated the great strength of this religion, and Constantine must have realized that the Christians, if won over his cause, could offer him valuable support. Since his mother was a Christian, he may have been strongly inclined toward this religion before his sudden "conversion." Perhaps he even hoped that the new religion would serve as a source of inspiration to revive the nearly dead Roman spirit of patriotism. A Rome dedicated to the service of the Christian God and ruled by a Christian emperor might be more attractive to its citizens than the old Rome. Whatever his motives, Constantine's conversion and his legalization of Christianity in at least part of the empire were events of great significance.

While he ruled, Constantine never went so far as to outlaw the other religions flourishing in the empire, although he did make it more difficult for them to exist legally. He showered numerous favors on Christians, making of them a favored group in the empire. Clergymen entered the councils of state as imperial advisers, and extensive legislation reflected Christian teachings in matters such as slavery and marriage. Under these circumstances Christianity grew rapidly toward becoming the chief religion of the empire. Constantine certainly hoped that this closer identification of Christianity and the Roman state would strengthen the latter and help it to recover its old vigor.

Another important act of Constantine's was to move his capital from Rome to the new city of Constantinople (330). This action, dictated by the strong defensibility of the new city and by Constantine's desire to be closer to the rich East from whence the chief resources of the state were gleaned, signified to many the end of Roman rule and the beginning of Eastern domination of the Mediterranean world. The city on the Tiber that had created the vast empire was now little more than an outlying province. All that Rome had stood for was spurned by a despot who preferred to live in the East, to worship an Eastern God, and to be fawned over by Eastern slaves. For many it had become difficult to speak of a Roman Empire. Diocletian and Constantine had literally turned the world around, allowing the East to conquer the West.

2. The Fourth-Century Lull Before The Storm

The reforms of Diocletian and Constantine worked well enough to keep the empire intact and prosperous until the end of the fourth century. Certainly things were better than in the third century. There was a fairly regular succession of emperors based on a hereditary principle with little civil strife. Agriculture, trade, and industry held their own, albeit under rigid state control. The armies were supplied and the bureaucrats paid.

Yet the calm was misleading. Imperial strength was being sapped. The absolutist state, which Diocletian and Constantine had hoped would be able to meet all problems, became a monster consuming the wealth of the empire and killing the spirit of its subjects. The bureaucracy grew costly, corrupt, and inefficient. Rigid control of the economy killed off economic expansion and deepened the depression. The army fell increasingly into the hands of barbarian troops whose generals moved into key places in government.

Christianity continued its conquest of the empire until finally Emperor Theodosius (379–395) made it the state religion and outlawed all others. However, this new religion did not become a bond of unity or a source of patriotism, and divisions within the Christian ranks were responsible for all kinds of disorders. For instance, during the reign of Constantine the Christians divided into two factions, Arian and Orthodox, over the question of the Trinity. The Arians, troubled by the danger of worshipping more than one God and puzzled by the intricate problem of the relation of the Father and the Son, sought to exalt the power of the Father by making the Son subordinate to Him and denying the absolute divinity of Christ. The Orthodox spokesmen insisted that the Son was coequal with the Father and that the two plus the Holy Spirit formed a unity. An attempt to settle this quarrel was made at the Council of Nicaea in 325. Churchmen from all over the empire gathered under the auspices of Constantine and agreed upon the Nicene Creed as a basic definition of the Christian position on the nature of Christ. This creed marked a victory for the Orthodox position over that of the Arians. However, in spite of the agreement reached in 325, the quarrel continued to rage for a century, involving the imperial government, setting Christian against Christian, and causing persecutions of one side by the other.

By the end of the fourth century signs of

an impending crisis appeared. They came from Central Europe, the homeland of the Germanic barbarians who had for so long plagued the empire. German pressure on the frontier continued throughout the fourth century. Many small groups actually penetrated the empire, usually as recruits in the army or as settlers on vacant land along the frontier. About 370 a wild horde of Asiatics, the Huns, swept across southern Russia toward Central Europe. When they reached the Black Sea area, they encountered two Germanic nations, the Ostrogoths and the Visigoths. The former group was conquered, while the terror-stricken Visigoths begged permission to migrate across the Danube into Roman territory. Their request was granted. The Visigoths were allowed to keep their own king and were promised lands by the imperial government. When the imperial government failed to provide for their needs, the Visigoths rose in revolt. The Emperor Valens marched against them but suffered a smashing defeat at Adrianople in 378. Rome now had a barbarian nation within her boundaries which she could neither control nor destroy. The day of reckoning was at hand.

3. The Barbarian Germans

Our limited information about the Germans prior to the fourth century A.D. reveals that they were barbarians. Their basic political institution was the tribe, composed of a number of clans and headed by a tribal chief. The heads of the clans exerted a tremendous influence over their relatives and played a major role in advising the tribal chief. The tribe concerned itself chiefly with war and with religious worship, most other matters falling under the control of the clans, and every tribe had an extensive body of customary law, which was vigorously observed. The Germans were previously hunters and herders, although by the third century agriculture was spreading among them. Trade and industry played a minor role in tribal life. Religiously, the Germans worshipped many gods, including especially the forces of nature. They believed that these gods controlled the material welfare of men, and their chief religious concern was to make the gods happy by sacrifices and prayers. The Germans possessed no written language; what "literature" they had, mostly stories about the deeds of the gods and heroes, was orally transmitted.

By the fourth century the simple life of the Germanic barbarians was changing. Small tribal groups were being unified into "nations" ruled over by elected kings, a development making it easier for a single Germanic ruler to mount heavy attacks on the frontier and making it more difficult for Rome to play tribe against tribe. Within Germanic society there was also developing a unique institution—the war band (*comitatus*)—consisting of voluntary unions of warriors who pledged themselves on oath to follow the lead of their chief, who in turn pledged to lead them in profitable ventures and share the booty. These warriors became a kind of aristocracy, practicing war as a way of life and gaining tremendous proficiency in fighting. Furthermore, the Germans, who were becoming more and more interested in agriculture, felt a great hunger for farm land. Since land was short in the heavy forests of central Europe, many nations and tribes moved southward toward Roman territory.

Between Germans and Romans there was no deep-seated hatred. The Germans were ardent admirers of Graeco-Roman civilization, desiring nothing more than to settle in the empire and to become "civilized." The Romans on their side respected the Germans for their splendid physical features, their fighting prowess, and their moral excellence. For many centuries before the fourth century the two peoples had been in close contact, fighting, trading, and living side by side. The Romans had from at least the time of Augustus established a set frontier, permitting Germans to cross that frontier as long as Rome could control the movement, and, as has been noted previously, large numbers of Germans entered the Roman armies and settled on Roman

GERMANIC BARBARIANS ATTACKING A ROMAN FORT. This relief from the Column of Trajan, a monument erected in Rome to commemorate the conquest of Dacia by the Emperor Trajan (reigned A.D. 98–117), shows Germanic warriors assaulting a Roman fortification. Attacks such as these eventually broke through Rome's frontiers, but for nearly four centuries after the time of Augustus the Roman population lived with the assurance that the frontier garrisons, such as the one shown here, would hold back the barbarians. (*Alinari Photo*)

soil as farmers. These migrants quickly became Romanized and often rose to high places in Roman society. Influences from the Roman world also sifted across the frontier into Germany. For instance, during the fourth century many Goths were converted to Christianity by Ulfilas, himself a Goth but educated in Constantinople. Ulfilas provided a Gothic version of the Bible for his converts and actually created a written language for that purpose.

This relationship depended on Roman strength. Was the Visigothic victory at Adrianople in 378 a sign that Rome could no longer control the Germans? Events were soon to decide the issue and with it the fate of the empire.

4. The Fall of the Empire

The crisis caused by the Visigothic problem was faced with vigor by the last great emperor, Theodosius (reigned 379–395). He kept the Visigoths in check by granting them the status of *foederati*, or allies, meaning that they were assigned lands in the empire in return for supplying troops for the Roman army. He struggled valiantly with rival contenders for his throne and eventually eliminated most of them. The elaborate machinery of state was kept running, permitting a continued defense of the frontiers.

His passing, however, spelled the beginning of the end of the uneasy calm lying over the empire since the time of Diocletian and Constantine. Theodosius was succeeded by two sons, one assigned the western section of the empire and the other the eastern. Neither had any ability or much interest in the problems of state and allowed the direction of affairs to fall into the hands of powerful generals, most of whom were Germanic in origin. This situation set off a series of power struggles in which the generals sought to manipulate affairs for their own advantage.

The stricken empire, caught up in endless intrigue, proved an easy prey for the barbarians. As the fifth century opened, the Visigoths, firmly entrenched in the Balkans, were playing a dangerous game of selling their services to either the emperor in the West or the one in the East. Eventually they turned against Italy, having been promised by the emperor in the East whatever new lands they might conquer. In 410, Rome was captured and sacked by the first foreign army to take the city in nearly eight hundred years. To defend Italy against Visigoth attacks, the emperor in the West withdrew troops from the British, Rhine, and Danube frontiers. Thereupon other Germans poured across the frontier and plunged into the heart of the empire at will.

In pursuit of land for permanent settlement the Germanic nations proceeded to dismember the western part of the empire, taking over large areas and imposing their own rule. Whenever they occupied lands of their choice, their kings and warrior nobles became the the real rulers over Germans and Romans alike. A series of new kingdoms, independent in fact, replaced the previously unified empire. During the fifth century Anglian, Saxon, and Jutish invaders from the continent established several petty kingdoms in Britain and destroyed all signs of Roman control there. The Vandals crossed Gaul and Spain to establish themselves in the rich Roman provinces in Africa. The Visigoths, after sacking Rome, eventually left Italy to occupy Spain and southern Gaul, while Franks, Burgundians, and Alemanni partitioned the rest of Gaul. Other Germanic groups ravaged the territory south of the Danube, turning it into a no-man's land politically. Even Italy finally fell victim when the Ostrogoths seized it in 493 and established their king, Theodoric, as the ruler of the whole peninsula. The Germans also hurled themselves at the eastern part of the empire, but Constantinople proved too formidable a fortress to by-pass or to conquer, thus saving the Asian and Egyptian provinces from falling to the barbarians.

Under the successful blows of the invaders the old government in the West slowly dissolved. Some of the generals serving the Western rulers fought valiantly to check the invasions and negotiated desperately to turn German against German. Each Germanic nation was usually persuaded to sign a treaty with the Roman government, accepting the status of foederatus and recognizing Roman overlordship in a legal sense. In practice, however, Rome's allies became independent in the areas assigned to them. Their kings became the real rulers, taking over the responsibility for maintaining order, collecting taxes for their own use, conducting independent foreign policies, and grasping for more land. Roman bureaucracy broke down, imperial income dwindled to nothing, and the authority of the successors of Augustus disappeared. By 476 the political reality in the West was recognized. A German general, Odoacer, deposed the last Western emperor, turning the insignia of imperial office over to the emperor in Constantinople with the advice that there was no longer need for an emperor in the West. In theory the empire was united under the ruler in Constantinople. In practice the Eastern emperor had no control over the West. Many Germanic kings ruled there, each in his own territory and each independently.

5. The Aftermath

The Germanic invasions of the fifth century had consequences much more far-reaching than the political changes traced in the preceding section. Every aspect of life in the empire, and especially in the western part of

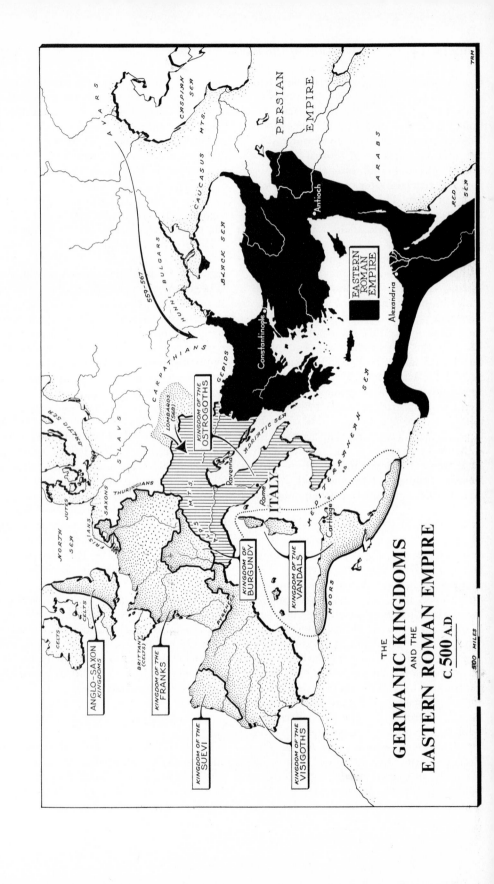

THE
GERMANIC KINGDOMS
AND THE
EASTERN ROMAN EMPIRE
C. 500 A.D.

500 MILES

EASTERN
ROMAN
EMPIRE

ANGLO-SAXON
KINGDOMS

BRITTANY
(CELTS)

KINGDOM OF THE
FRANKS

KINGDOM OF THE
SUÈVI

KINGDOM OF THE
VISIGOTHS

KINGDOM OF
BURGUNDY

KINGDOM OF THE
VANDALS

KINGDOM OF THE
OSTROGOTHS

LOMBARDS
(568)

ITALY

Ravenna

Rome

Carthage

MOORS

PYRENEES

ALPS MTS.

THURINGIANS

SAXONS

FRISIANS

JUTES

NORTH
SEA

CELTS

CELTS

BALTIC SEA

SLAVS

CARPATHIANS

GEPIDS

ADRIATIC SEA

MEDITERRANEAN SEA

HUN-BULGARS

559-567

AVARS

CASPIAN SEA

CAUCASUS MTS.

BLACK SEA

Constantinople

PERSIAN
EMPIRE

ARABS

Antioch

RED SEA

Alexandria

TRM

the empire, was affected in a way that signified the end of Graeco-Roman civilization. Although the Germans would have preferred to participate in rather than to destroy that civilization, their presence in the empire hastened its fall.

The most obvious by-product of the invasions was the dissolution of the imperial administration in the West. Gone were the mighty emperors, their armies, their bureaucrats, their courts, their public projects, and everything else associated with imperial government. Although that government had become oppressive and inefficient in the century before the invasions, its destruction could not help but change conditions for the Roman population. The new masters of the West, the Germanic kings and their warriors, were not fitted to conduct government after the fashion of the Roman emperors. Some of them tried to do so but seldom succeeded. A tragic political chaos unsettled the West.

Economically the invasion was followed by increasing impoverishment. The invaders were not wholly responsible for this depression, since it had begun long before their arrival. Nonetheless, the wars they caused and the destruction of the Roman government speeded up economic decline. The new Germanic overlords were primarily interested in land, and reversion to an agricultural economy was rapid. Cities especially suffered a disastrous decline, some of them shrinking to a fraction of their old population. Roman landholders, although sometimes ousted from their property by German warriors, bent their efforts to enlarge their holdings amid the confusion. Peasants were glad to serve great landowners in return for whatever protection the landowners, German or Roman, could offer. Most of the owners of large estates tried to become self-sufficient during these troubled times with the result that the western part of the empire broke up into thousands of tiny self-contained units that had less and less economic interchange with each other. This system drove standards of living down almost to subsistence levels.

Culturally also the invasion era was marked by decline. The new rulers tried to absorb Roman civilization by learning Latin, by patronizing artists, and by adopting Roman dress and manners. Educated Romans in Italy, Gaul, Spain, and Africa continued to read their classics, to study philosophy, and even to write. However, the Graeco-Roman spirit was crushed. The cities, long the true centers of civilized life, were dying, and the impact of the invasions disheartened the creative elements in society. The agricultural population was too provincial to shoulder the burden of upholding the literary, artistic, scientific, and philosophical traditions of the old order. Try as they might, the Germans could do no better than imitate. The old barbarism showed through their thin veneer of civilized life.

One must, however, be cautious in assigning to the Germanic invasions too great a significance. Destruction of life and property was not excessive, and in most cases the Germans and Romans settled down peacefully side by side. Moreover, the Germans were not numerous enough to be responsible for everything that happened. The chief features of fifth-century history—the disintegration of the imperial government, economic decline, and cultural stagnation—had all begun before the Germans invaded the empire in mass. The invasions were simply the final chapter in a long process of decline.

6. Christianity in the Late Empire

The final destruction of the Roman Empire had one consequence that needs special attention, namely, the strengthening of Christianity. From Constantine's time onward Christianity enjoyed a rapid growth. With the state supporting Christianity the bulk of the population of the empire was converted. Church wealth increased rapidly, and churchmen were raised to high offices of state. It is not stretching the point to say that by A.D. 400 the Roman Empire had become a Christian Roman Empire. These successes posed new problems for the Christians. Discipline declined badly because of the avalanche of conversions, and several

INTERIOR OF AN EARLY CHRISTIAN CHURCH. The church of S. Apollinare Nuovo in Ravenna, Italy, is a basilica, a Roman architectural style put to Christian use. The structure is almost a replica of the public meeting halls built by the Romans. The central hall (nave) has high walls supported by columns; lower ceilings on the side aisles allow windows to be cut in the upper walls of the nave. Both the center and side aisles have vaulted roofs of concrete, which the Romans were especially adept at building. Paintings and mosaics (see facing page) decorate the interior of the church. (*Alinari Photo*)

heretical movements tended to split the Christian world apart. Now that the unifying force of fighting pagan religions and a hostile state had ceased to exist, the Christians took to fighting one another. Perhaps the gravest danger of the new era was that of state control over the church. The emperors tended to treat the church as a branch of government to be used for political purposes. This involvement of the church in political affairs and the tendency to subordinate religious considerations to political ends were serious threats to the power of Christians to control themselves. And, by allying itself so closely with the Roman Empire, Christianity seemed to be running the risk

of falling with that empire, of becoming so "Roman" that it could live nowhere else except in the empire.

The fifth century, with all its tragic events, demonstrated nonetheless that Christianity had enough vitality and independence to survive the collapse of the Roman world. Church organization survived the ordeal of the invasions almost intact; as a matter of fact, its power was probably greater than ever before. In many parts of the Western empire bishops and their subordinates strengthened their authority by replacing the imperial governors in such fundamental tasks as keeping order, administering justice, and caring for the unfortunate. The church's

EARLY CHRISTIAN MOSAICS. This magnificent mosaic, made by fixing thousands of different colored pieces of stone into wet plaster, is in the church of S. Apollinare Nuovo in Ravenna, Italy. It illustrates themes that dominate early Christian art: in the center are figures representing the prophets, below are the saints, and at the top of the photograph is a scene showing Peter denying Christ. Note also the geometric designs used as a decorative element. (*Alinari Photo*)

wealth also increased, chiefly in the form of landed estates. Before the end of the fifth century most of the Germanic invaders had accepted Christianity to replace their ancient religions, thus becoming members of at least one organization to which most of the old Roman population belonged. The Germanic rulers continued to give Christianity the same state support that the late Roman emperors had.

Probably the most important role played by the Christians during this era was that of cultural leadership. Church building provided most of the outlet for architects. Churches were decorated with paintings, murals, and statues dedicated to the portrayal of the Christian message, leaving behind most of the themes of classical artists. Some of the most inspired poetry of the fourth and fifth centuries was written by Christians. St. Jerome's translation of the Bible into Latin, called the Vulgate, ensured that Latin would survive as the language of the Church and that the Christians would retain ties with Graeco-Roman civilization.

The greatest intellectual figure of the period was St. Augustine (A.D. 354–430), an African bishop who wrote two books destined to have a great influence on the future. In one, entitled the *Confessions*, Augustine related how, after trying nearly every system of philosophy and religion of the ancient world, he eventually found that Christianity alone offered a satisfactory answer to his problems, and by arguing for the necessity of faith he set up a new ideal of what constituted a truly enlightened man. Another book, *City of God*, contained an even more powerful and unique message. Augustine wrote the book to answer certain pagans who charged that the Visigoths had been able to sack Rome in 410 because the old gods were angry at the Romans for becoming Christians. Augustine insisted that such was not the case, that the fall of Rome was only a step in the unfolding of God's plan for the universe. God, he said, had ordained two cities, that of God and that of men. The perfect City of God can exist only in the other world, a goal for

which believing men must work. On earth exists the sinful city of men, of which Rome was a part. The coming of Christ meant that Rome must pass away so that men could serve in an earthly embodiment of the City of God. This earthly institution, more godly and consequently more worthy than Rome, is the Christian Church. Thus Augustine did not despair over the fall of Rome; to him it was a step toward a better world, a Christian world more noble than anything from the Graeco-Roman past.

Augustine's ideas became the most powerful in the West from the fifth century onward. He had produced a Christian interpretation of the universe that could compete with the philosophies that had long dominated Graeco-Roman thought, and despite extensive borrowings from his pagan predecessors he had created a new viewpoint toward human existence and its purpose.

While Augustine was arguing his case philosophically, other Christian spokesmen were bringing Christian teaching into practical affairs. For instance, St. Ambrose (about A.D. 340–397), bishop of Milan, preached constantly on the subject of sound moral principles to guide Christian life, praising a standard of behavior different from that taught by adherents of Graeco-Roman civilization. These great church fathers of the fourth and fifth centuries had become the intellectual and moral spokesmen of a large part of the civilized world. No representative of Graeco-Roman civilization could match their vigor, their grasp of reality, their zeal, or their persuasiveness.

Perhaps it is to the years between the dismissal of the last Roman emperor in the West (A.D. 476) and the capture of Italy by the Ostrogoths (A.D. 493) that we can best assign the death of Graeco-Roman civilization. The Romans had created a magnificent political order dedicated to the peace, well-being, and enlightenment of about fifty million people, but they had failed to maintain it. Barbarian Germans from beyond the borders of the empire struck the final blow against the paralyzed empire, wresting away huge territories for their own. From within, the Christians emerged victorious to impose their ideas on the populace. The barbarians and the Christians now held the key to the future. However, the Graeco-Roman tradition was to remain a force affecting the future. When the Roman Empire collapsed, it left behind monuments that would serve as guides to its heirs—a magnificent literature, a great art, model forms of govern-

ment, a legal system, economic institutions and techniques, moral precepts, philosophical ideals, scientific knowledge, and countless other achievements. In a sense Greece and Rome did not really die. Little that has happened in the Western world since 476 or 493 makes much sense unless one remembers Graeco-Roman civilization as its background.

SUGGESTED READING

Edward Gibbon, *The History of the Decline and Fall of the Roman Empire*, ed. J. B. Bury, 7 vols. (1897–1900); there is also a convenient edition in the Modern Library. This famous study of the passing of Rome and the emergence of the Middle Ages, first published in the last quarter of the eighteenth century, will capture the fancy of any student of history. Written in a grand style, it is full of the intricate details that make up the history of the late imperial period. Gibbon was an ardent admirer of the Graeco-Roman civilization, whose fall he was describing; therefore, he writes of the fall of Rome with a feeling that a great age was passing away forever in favor of a period characterized by ignorance, barbarism, and superstition. He is especially critical of Christianity; perhaps the reader with limited time would find Gibbon's famous Chapters 15 and 16, dealing with early Christianity, a good introduction to this famous work. However, every educated man ought sometime in his lifetime to read all of Gibbon.

A. H. M. Jones, *Constantine and the Conversion of Europe* (1949). A brief treatment of the complicated problem of the transition of Roman society from paganism to Christianity, the discussion being centered around the career of Constantine. The book manages to clarify the great issues of the critical years around A.D. 300.

* Jacob Burckhardt, *The Age of Constantine the Great*, tr. by M. Hadas (Anchor). A study, first published in 1867, of Constantine's conversion by one of the great European historians of the nineteenth century.

Hugh Pope, *Saint Augustine of Hippo* (1949). A readable biography of one of the chief figures in all Christian history. This book sup-

plies a clear statement of most of Augustine's major philosophical concepts.

F. Homes Dudden, *The Life and Times of St. Ambrose*, 2 vols. (1935). An excellent biography of one of the major religious figures of the fourth century. The study makes especially clear the contributions of Ambrose to the development of the Western European Church while also succeeding in portraying the individual personality of this great Church father.

Samuel Dill, *Roman Society in the Last Century of the Western Empire*, 2nd ed., rev. (1921). A scholarly picture of social and intellectual aspects of Roman society in the fifth century.

J. B. Bury, *The Invasion of Europe by the Barbarians* (1928). A standard work on the Germanic invasions, presenting a complete account of the invasions and their impact on the Roman Empire.

* Tacitus, *Germania* (many editions; a satisfactory one is the translation by H. Mattingly in the Penguin series). This brief essay by a second-century Roman historian supplies the best picture we possess of the condition of early Germanic society prior to the invasions of the Roman Empire. Tacitus's work is marred by his tendency to idealize the Germans and must be used with care.

* Augustine, *Confessions* (many editions; a good translation is by Edward B. Pusey in the Modern Library series), and *City of God*, tr. by Marcus Dods, 2 vols. (Hafner Library of Classics, 1948). These two works by the greatest of the early Church fathers will provide an introduction to early Christian thought. The *Confessions* is a moving account of Augustine's conversion to Christianity. The *City of God* presents an early Christian version of the ultimate destiny of the world and man.

SECTION 4

The Early Middle Ages, 500–1000:

Struggle Toward a New Order

T he fall of the Roman Empire marks the end of the political, economic, and cultural unity of the Mediterranean world. During the centuries that followed Rome's fall three new civilizations emerged, each absorbing a part of the Roman world and each extending beyond its boundaries into "new" territory. One of these civilizations had its center at Constantinople, where Graeco-Roman civilization suffered the least change. This civilization, called Byzantine, exerted its chief influence in Asia Minor, the Balkans, and European Russia. The second new civilization, called Moslem or Islamic, arose in the Arabian Desert, spreading eastward to India and westward across North Africa into Spain. Its chief driving force was a new religion, Mohammedanism. The third new civilization was created by the Germanic invaders of the Roman Empire. Gaul and Italy formed its center, but its influence eventually reached into Germany, England, Scandinavia, Spain, and the western portions of the Slavic world.

Each of these three civilizations took shape during the five hundred years from about A.D. 500 to 1000. The history of their foundations will be the chief concern of this section. Although our attention will focus on the development of the new Western European civilization, the basic history of the other two must be recounted briefly in order that we may understand their effect on Western Europe. The interaction among these three civilizations is still today a prime factor in world affairs.

CHAPTER 15

Western Europe's Neighbors: The Byzantine and Moslem Empires

WESTERN European civilization grew slowly in the early Middle Ages in the shadow of the more powerful and more advanced Byzantine and Moslem cultures. These two cultures are worthy of considerable discussion, since each had its own complicated political history, its own institutional development, and its own cultural and religious life. Here, however, we can only present a brief characterization of these civilizations with special emphasis on those elements that had bearing on Western Europe.

1. Byzantine Civilization: Its Origins and Political History Until About 1100

Byzantine civilization was born in the era of turmoil that marked the breakup of the old Roman Empire. Perhaps it can best be considered as the direct survival of the old imperial order in the Eastern provinces.

Even though Constantine had moved the imperial capital to Constantinople in 330 and in spite of the fact that Germanic invaders had seized most of the Western provinces of the empire during the fifth century, not until the sixth century did it become clear that the ancient Roman Empire was split beyond repair. The reign of Justinian (527-565), who might be called the last Roman emperor and the first Byzantine em-

peror, revealed that the East and the West were parting ways. His reign was devoted chiefly to the vast project of restoring his authority over the Western provinces, which were held by the Germans. This project demanded a major war. However, the best that Justinian's armies could do was to recapture North Africa from the Vandals and Italy from the Ostrogoths. Gaul, Spain, England, and the Danube provinces remained in Germanic hands. Even the victories in Africa and Italy proved too costly. While Justinian was trying to reconquer the West, the Persians attacked the imperial territories in Syria and Palestine and threatened to cause a disaster there. A concentration of imperial forces on that frontier was absolutely necessary; the West would have to be abandoned to the Germans while the emperors at Constantinople contented themselves with a smaller state made up of Greeks and Near Eastern peoples.

Events in Justinian's reign suggested in other ways that a distinctive way of life was emerging in the territory ruled from Constantinople. Justinian took important steps to perfect a system of absolutist monarchy, which contrasted vividly with the almost primitive governments established by the Germans in the West. His chief effort in this direction was a codification of Roman law. This important legal work consisted of

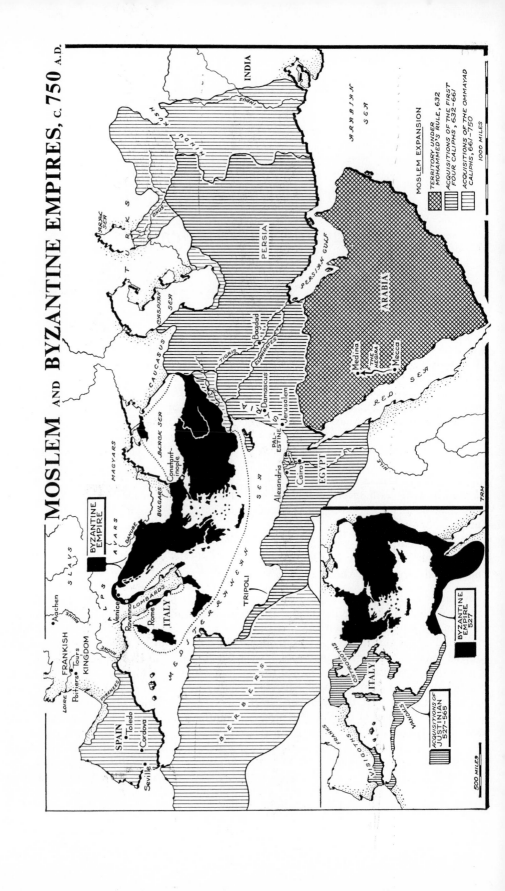

MOSLEM AND BYZANTINE EMPIRES, C. 750 A.D.

MOSLEM EXPANSION

TERRITORY UNDER THE FIRST FOUR CALIPHS, 632-661

ACQUISITIONS OF THE OMMAYAD CALIPHS, 661-750

1000 MILES

BYZANTINE EMPIRE

INDIA

ARABIAN SEA

PERSIA

ARABIA

Bagdad

PERSIAN GULF

Medina
THE HEGIRA
Mecca

RED SEA

TIGRIS

EUPHRATES

HINDU KUSH

INDUS

OXUS

ARANG SEA

T U R K S

CAUCASUS

Damascus

Jerusalem
PAL-
ESTINE

Cairo

EGYPT

Alexandria

NILE

BLACK SEA

Constant-
inople

MAGYARS

BULGARS

AVARS

DANUBE

SLAVS

ALPS

Aachen

FRANKISH
KINGDOM

Poitiers Tours

RHONE

LOIRE

Venice
Ravenna

LOMBARDS

Rome

ITALY

TRIPOLI

B E R B E R S

M E D I T E R R A N E A N   S E A

PYRENEES

SPAIN

Toledo

Cordova

Seville

500 MILES

ACQUISITIONS OF JUSTINIAN 527-565

BYZANTINE EMPIRE 527

OSTROGOTHS

ITALY

VANDALS

FRANKS

VISIGOTHS

TRM

shaping the long legal tradition of Rome to fit the needs of an all-powerful ruler. In the process Justinian's lawyers incorporated into the code legal principles and precedents that became important guides for later ages.

Violent religious quarrels forced the emperor to issue edicts defining dogma and to appoint clergymen who would accept his decisions. The result was a church whose organization and authority extended only so far as the boundaries of Justinian's empire. A Greek church, closely identified with the Byzantine state, was being born.

Justinian's reign also saw the birth of a distinctive Byzantine culture, strongly colored by Greek influences and little affected by Latin traditions. For instance, Santa Sophia in Constantinople, a magnificent church built by Justinian, represented a clear break with the Graeco-Roman styles of architecture and heralded the arrival of a distinctive Byzantine culture.

Byzantine political history from Justinian's reign until the beginning of the Crusades (1095) would fill a thick volume with a rich panorama of wars, intrigues, intricate diplomacy, and great leaders. Unquestionably the chief theme of that history was the desperate military and diplomatic struggle of the Byzantine state to survive in the face of constant attack from beyond her frontiers. Persians, Arabs, and Seljuk Turks slashed at the empire from the east. Avars, Bulgars, and Slavs pushed into the Balkans and threatened Constantinople from the northwest. Western Europeans nibbled away at the western extremities of the empire. These assaults, stretching over nearly five centuries, constantly reduced the size of the empire. The Moslem Arabs seized Syria, Palestine, and North Africa during the seventh century and on more than one occasion held parts of Asia Minor. During the seventh, eighth, and ninth centuries the Avars, Bulgars, and Slavs penetrated deep into the Balkans and nearly exterminated the Greek elements in that area. Piece by piece Byzantine possessions in Italy were absorbed by various Western European groups, including the Lombards, the Vene-

tians, and the Normans. By the end of the eleventh century the Byzantine Empire consisted only of Asia Minor, a part of the Balkan Peninsula, and the Aegean Islands.

2. Byzantine Civilization: Political, Economic, Religious, and Cultural Life

The ability of the Byzantine Empire to resist these repeated blows stemmed chiefly from the strength of her government and from her vast economic resources. The Byzantine government was an absolute monarchy. The emperor in theory possessed complete power to do what he wished with his subjects. At his court in Constantinople the emperor lived in splendor befitting his claims to power, the ritual of his court rivaling anything we have previously seen in the ancient Near East. He commanded a horde of civil servants at his court, to each of whom was assigned a specialized function, a rank, and a salary. The empire was divided into a number of districts, called *themes*, where officials representing the emperor recruited troops, collected taxes, maintained order, judged cases, and enforced imperial edicts. The emperor's power was buttressed by a well-organized army and navy, an efficient system of taxation, and the services of the Eastern church.

In a real sense this system of government was a continuation of that of the late Roman Empire. Probably the Byzantine emperor was even stronger than Diocletian, since the Byzantine imperial office had stronger religious sanction. The emperor was looked upon as an agent of God, given his office so that he might maintain peace and order among the Christian population of his state. On many occasions the efficient operation of this government was impeded by ambitious generals, greedy bureaucrats, dissatisfied churchmen, scheming empresses and courtiers, self-centered landowners, and even the mobs of Constantinople. However, none of them ever completely paralyzed the imperial government; it always had the ability to restore order and man the imperial defenses.

Byzantine economic strength played an equally vital role in the long struggle for survival. The agricultural system formed the backbone of the Byzantine economy. Large estates, farmed by tenants, were predominant, although many small landowners existed in various parts of the empire and were usually protected by the imperial government. The state took a vital interest in keeping agricultural production at a high level so that taxes could be collected from the farmers, whether large or small, landowner or tenant. Aside from agriculture the empire enjoyed a tremendous commercial and industrial activity, and for many centuries Constantinople was the world's chief trading and industrial center. Goods entered her markets from all directions, while her shops produced a variety of high-quality products in demand throughout the Mediterranean world. All commerce and industry were rigidly controlled by the state. Wages, prices, and profits were carefully fixed. Artisans and traders were compelled to remain in their trades and hand them on to their sons. Everyone paid heavy taxes to the state. The imperial government itself monopolized many lucrative businesses.

A strong government and a prosperous economy do not, however, fully explain the vitality of the Byzantine Empire. Byzantine life was strongly affected by Christianity, which helped to shape nearly every institution and every activity in this society. In many important ways a Christian of the Byzantine Empire was like a Christian anywhere, holding to the same basic beliefs and conducting himself by the same standards of conduct. However, with the passage of time, Christianity underwent unique developments within the Byzantine Empire, giving rise to what is now called the Greek Orthodox Church.

The Greek Orthodox Church was always more completely controlled by and subjected to the state than the church in Western Europe. Since the emperor was both caesar and pope, scholars have coined the term *caesaropapism* to describe this distinctive feature of Byzantine religious life. The emperor appointed clergymen, defined dogma, settled theological disputes, imposed discipline on clergymen and laymen, and used the wealth of the church to serve the purposes of the state. Byzantine religious life was also distinguished by its intense interest in questions of dogma. Quarrels over such problems as the nature of Christ and his relationship to God aroused strong feelings in everyone from the most learned monk to the lowliest artisan and peasant and led to serious political crises on more than one occasion in Byzantine history. Greek Orthodox religion placed a tremendous emphasis on rituals and a deep trust in the power of these rites to effect the salvation of the souls of those who practiced them. Attempts were made to check this tendency, and it was the chief issue of the religious struggle that raged during the seventh and eighth centuries. Several emperors and a part of the clergy attempted to remove all statues (called icons) from the churches, insisting that Christians were worshipping these instead of God. These "puritans" made little progress, however, so that after the ninth century ritualism became a characteristic feature of religious life in the empire. Byzantine religious life also gave a prominent place to mysticism and emotionalism, that is, to those kinds of religious experiences in which believers were convinced that they could reach and commune directly with God. Byzantine monasteries were the chief centers of this type of religious life, and numerous monks exercised a powerful influence on the population.

As early as the seventh century bitter quarrels between Christians in the East and in the West over dogma, ritual, and church government created a growing gap between the Byzantine and Western worlds, which no amount of compromise ever closed. By 1054, when the pope at Rome pronounced that the adherents of the Byzantine Church were schismatics, the breech became irreparable.

This religious split took on greater significance in view of the success enjoyed by the Byzantine Church in missionary affairs.

From almost the beginning of Byzantine history Greek missionaries, strongly backed by the imperial government, began to penetrate the vast world of the Slavs in Central and Eastern Europe. Eventually most of the Slavs in the Balkan Peninsula and in Russia were converted to Christianity. Although these converts were permitted to organize their own churches and to utilize their native languages in their services, Byzantine religious practices, political ideas, and social concepts spread among them. This process helped to divide part of the Slavs from Western Europe and to create barriers that have not yet disappeared.

The Byzantine Empire gradually developed its own cultural life. Often the Byzantine accomplishments in this field have been overlooked. Perhaps the explanation

for this neglect lies in the fact that Byzantine cultural activity was devoted chiefly to the preservation of the classical tradition of Greece and Rome and the adaptation of that tradition to Christian teachings. Byzantine society always contained a large group of educated men conversant with the great literary, scientific, and philosophical masterpieces of classical Greece, which continued to serve as the bases of the educational system. The influence of classical Greek literature tended to make Byzantine writing imitative and not especially creative. Theological writers were probably the most creative figures in Byzantine society, although Byzantine historians also produced excellent works, marred only by a tendency to partisanship.

Byzantine art was much more creative

ISTANBUL (CONSTANTINOPLE). This is a modern view of the city that was the center of the Byzantine Empire and one of the chief cities of the medieval world. The streets were filled with the shops of artisans and the bazaars of merchants whose efforts brought wealth to the empire. At the left is the great church of Santa Sophia, which was made a Moslem mosque after the fall of the city to the Ottoman Turks in 1453. Clearly visible is the huge dome, its chief architectural feature. The tremendous size of this chief example of Byzantine architecture is suggested by comparison with the surrounding buildings. The mosques of the Sultan Mahmoud (center) and the Sultan Ahmed (right), built by the Turks after the fall of the Byzantine Empire, illustrate that the Byzantine style lived on. In the background is the Sea of Marmora and the shores of Asia. (*Philip Gendreau, New York*)

and more distinctive than Byzantine literature and learning. Byzantine architecture,
distinguished by the fusion of Graeco-
Roman and Persian styles, was pre-eminent
among the arts. The chief monuments of
Byzantine architecture were the churches,
of which Santa Sophia in Constantinople
was by far the most impressive example.
Built by Justinian in the sixth century, this
church combined the rectangular style of
Graeco-Roman buildings with the Persian
dome. The great dome of Santa Sophia, rising about 180 feet above the floor of the
church, rests in imposing grandeur on the
tops of four arches springing from four great
pillars that form a central square in the
building. This type of structure became a
model for most Byzantine churches. Santa
Sophia represented another characteristic of
Byzantine art—a love of decoration. The
inside of the church was adorned with a
brilliant array of precious metals, mosaics,
paintings, and jewels. Especially unique were
Byzantine mosaics, made by setting multi-
colored stones in plaster to form designs.
The decorators were never especially concerned with creating realistic, natural effects; their mosaics, painting, and sculpture were symbolical, seeking to convey some
spiritual message rather than to portray natural scenes. Byzantine artists, however, did
not concentrate all their talents on religious
themes; Byzantium was noted for its skillful jewel makers, goldsmiths, silversmiths,
manuscript illuminators, and workers in almost all the other minor arts. In every kind
of art the same features predominated—fusion of Graeco-Roman and oriental motifs
and styles, love of decoration and color, and
preoccupation with symbolism.

3. Moslem Civilization: Origin and Expansion

Western Europe's second important
neighbor was the Moslem Empire, born in
the Arabian Desert and eventually expanding to embrace a huge area in Africa, Asia,
and Europe. Certainly no one living in the
Near East about 600 would have guessed

that the Arabs were destined to play an important role in history. Badly divided into
hundreds of warring tribes and still wresting a meager living from the desert wastes,
they seemed little more than barbarians by
comparison with the residents of the Byzantine or the Persian empires which bordered
on the Arabian Desert. Only a few Arabs
in trading centers like Mecca were aware of
these great civilizations, and these few city
dwellers, busy with trading ventures, hardly
seemed capable of transforming the desert
dwellers into a major force in the Near East.

A single figure, Mohammed, changed all
this; his religious leadership jolted the Arab
world out of its backwardness and isolation.
He was born in Mecca about 570. As a
young man he became a trader, serving as an
agent for a rich widow whom he later married. As a part of his job Mohammed traveled abroad and was in constant contact
with foreign merchants who came along the
caravan routes to Mecca. These associations
probably acquainted him with men of different religions and aroused his interest in
religious movements such as Christianity,
Judaism, and Zoroastrianism.

When Mohammed was about forty, he
suddenly made an amazing claim. He insisted that the Arab god, Allah, had spoken
directly to him and had told him that he
was Allah's prophet. From then on he dedicated himself to convincing others that
Allah had shown him the way to righteousness and truth, and by the time of his death
he had made many converts.

What did Allah reveal to his prophet?
After Mohammed's death some of his associates compiled a book containing what was
recorded or could be recalled of the prophet's revelations from Allah. This book, called
the Koran, became the source of truth for
Mohammed's followers and serves as the best
source of his teachings. His message was
simple and in many ways not especially
new to anyone except the Arabs. Many of
his teachings were so closely related to Christian and Jewish teachings that it is virtually
certain that Mohammed merely borrowed
ideas from these well-established religions.

Mohammed insisted that there was but one god, Allah; he demanded that his followers reject their worship of many gods for monotheism. He taught that Allah had revealed himself bit by bit down through the ages, the Jewish prophets and Christ all being accepted as agents of Allah. However, Mohammed was the last and greatest prophet, superseding all others. Older religions were therefore inferior, and Mohammedanism was destined to conquer the world. Allah was pictured in the Koran as an almighty deity who required complete submission to his will. Therefore every true follower of Allah must regulate his life accordingly. Those who believed in Allah and who obeyed his orders would gain a happy life after death while the disobedient and wicked would be damned forever.

To these simple articles of faith Mohammed added a list of duties required of all the faithful. All must pray five times daily while facing Mecca. All must give of their wealth to support the poor. Each Moslem must fast during one month of each year. And everyone must, if possible, make a pilgrimage to Mecca once in a lifetime. Mohammed also laid down strict rules regulating diet and marriage, prohibiting drinking and gambling, and demanding of each Moslem honesty, fair play, and respect for others. This code of conduct injected a strong ethical vein into the new religion. Each man was personally responsible to Allah for his conduct; Mohammed created no church, no clergymen, no sacraments to assist in gaining Allah's favor.

At first the teachings of the new prophet fell on deaf ears in Mecca; several years of preaching netted only a few converts. In fact Mohammed won many more enemies than followers. By 622 these foes forced him to flee to Yathrib (later renamed Medina, which means "City of the Prophet"), a city north of Mecca. This flight, called the Hegira, marked a turning point in the history of the new religion. Feeling himself spurned and convinced that the will of Allah had been defied by the Meccans, Mohammed began to shape a following dedicated

to the punishment of sinners and to the spread of the true religion by force of arms. He molded his converts, mostly Arab nomads from in and around Medina, into an armed political following, held together and inspired to obedience by the commands of the prophet. More and more Mohammed's revelations took the form of political and social legislation destined to create a warrior nation. By 630 his following was great enough to recapture Mecca, a feat that impressed many Arab tribes and caused them to join the prophet. When he died in 632, Mohammed was the leader of a large following of Arabs whose primitive tribalism had been overcome by their willingness to obey Allah and his spokesman.

Almost immediately this new Arab "nation" burst out of Arabia and began a series of spectacular military conquests. In 732, exactly a century after Mohammed's death, an Arab army fought a battle at Tours in central France, having advanced through Egypt, North Africa, and Spain to reach Gaul. Although they were defeated in this battle by the Frankish leader, Charles Martel, the Moslem Arabs had already established their control over all the territory from Egypt to the Pyrenees in Spain. Other armies engulfed Palestine, Syria, and Persia, and advanced to the Indus Valley in India. Some ancient states, like Persia, were wiped off the map. Others, like the Byzantine Empire, were nearly done to death by the ferocious assault of the Arabs and lost valuable territories in the course of these attacks. By the end of the eighth century Moslem expansion came to a temporary halt, primarily because of the determined resistance of the Byzantine Empire. However, the Moslems long remained an aggressive force, constantly threatening their neighbors.

4. Moslem Civilization: Political, Economic, and Cultural Features

The rapid expansion of the Arabs had a profound effect on the Near East. First of all, a new political order was established to rule over the huge territories won by arms.

When Mohammed died his associates established a single ruler for this empire. The new leader was called the "caliph," a title that signified that its holder was a representative of Mohammed and thus a religious as well as a political leader; and Moslem rulers always retained their religious authority. The first caliphs were drawn from Mohammed's close associates or relatives, bitter quarrels arising each time a new ruler was selected. In 661 power was seized by an important military leader whose descendants ruled until 750. This dynasty, called the Omayyads, or Ommiads, established its capital at Damascus in Syria. The Omayyad rulers were able administrators. Imitating Byzantine ideas, they created a system of government based on a centralized court, a bureaucracy, an efficient tax system, and a strong army and navy. Thus the caliph's power no longer derived completely from his religious authority.

In 750 the Omayyads were overthrown and the caliphate fell into the hands of the Abbasids, who ruled until 1258. These new rulers insisted that all Moslems, Arabs and non-Arabs, were equal, and recruited civil servants from all over the vast empire. The capital was shifted from Damascus. The new center, Bagdad, located on the Tigris River, became one of the world's greatest cities. The Abbasid dynasty reached its peak in the late eighth and early ninth centuries, the most famous caliph being Harun al-Rashid (reigned 786–809), immortalized in the *Arabian Nights*. The caliphs of this era ruled in the best style of oriental despotism, using their governmental machinery and their religious authority to command the obedience of millions of subjects. By the end of the ninth century the Abbasids began to decline. This weakening of the central government caused a rapid split of the empire. Independent caliphs established themselves in Spain, North Africa, Syria, and India, ending the political unity in the Moslem Empire. The various caliphates soon fell to fighting each other. Seeking to protect itself against these rivals, the Abbasid family increasingly placed its trust in Seljuk

Turkish soldiers, who by 1055 had become the real masters of Bagdad. These barbarians from Central Asia became another disruptive element in the Moslem political world. Everything considered, one must conclude that the Moslem world was never so well-organized politically as the Roman Empire and its successor, the Byzantine Empire. Neither the Arabs nor the non-Arabs within the empire were capable of fashioning a stable, lasting political order.

The expansion of the Arabs promoted a significant economic revival. The key to this new prosperity was a network of trade routes, stretching from Spain to India and China, over which materials and manufactured goods moved freely. Great cities like Cordova in Spain, Damascus, Bagdad, and Alexandria, whose merchants and artisans were seldom restricted by Moslem governments, became teeming centers of production. The wealth of the Moslem world at this time exceeded even that of the Byzantine world, and far outstripped that of Western Europe, which still depended upon a backward, agricultural economy.

However, neither the political nor the economic changes that accompanied the rise of the Moslem Empire were as significant in establishing the main features of Moslem civilization as were religious and cultural developments. The religion of Mohammed demonstrated an amazing power to win converts. Its success did not usually depend on forceful conversion, since Arab conquerors seldom insisted that their subjects accept the new religion. At first most Christians, Jews, Zoroastrians, and Hindus continued to worship as they had in the past. The Moslem conquerors demanded only that their non-Moslem subjects pay a special tax for the privilege of retaining their old religion and accept exclusion from Moslem governmental positions. As the years passed, however, most devotees of non-Moslem religions were converted to the Moslem faith. Perhaps the tax penalty was too great a burden. Perhaps the exclusion from high positions was unbearable. Unquestionably the Moslem religion had an appeal to everyone.

Jews, Christians, and other groups slowly vanished; the overwhelming majority of men in the vast area stretching from Spain to India became Moslems without struggle or protest. An extensive community believing in the same God, worshipping in the same simple fashion, and observing a single moral code came into existence. Political divisions might fragment that community, but nothing ever succeeded in destroying the religious ties that held the followers of Mohammed together. Even to this day Moslem religious unity is a prime factor in world affairs.

Moslem expansion also brought about a tremendous cultural revival and resulted in a cultural unification of the empire. The conquests of the semi-civilized Arabs who moved out of their desert homeland in the seventh and eighth century brought together into a single society nearly all of the world's chief cultural traditions: Graeco-Roman, Persian, Babylonian, Egyptian, Germanic, Jewish, Indian, and Arabic. Out of these many cultures a new culture arose, retaining aspects of each of the older traditions. The religious convictions of the Moslems supplied the unifying force in the new society. Since Mohammed had forbidden the translation of the Koran into any other language, all Moslems had to learn Arabic; and, since the Koran contained the final truth, it was necessary to reconcile the knowledge of older cultures with Moslem religious teachings. Finally, the bringing together of the older traditions revealed contradictions and differences, requiring that these diverse traditions be found mutually compatible. The labors devoted to these tasks resulted in a brilliant outburst of writing and scholarship, practically all the literature of the empire's many peoples being translated into Arabic. The Moslems could rightly claim to be the cultural heirs of all the ages.

Many authorities would agree that the greatest Moslem achievements were in philosophy and science. Moslem philosophers devoted their efforts chiefly to the task of reconciling Greek philosophy with the teachings of the Koran. When the philosophical writings of the Greeks were translated into Arabic, huge commentaries were composed showing how the principles of Greek philosophy explained and enlarged upon the teachings of the Koran.

In science the Moslems' efforts were even more spectacular. Huge collections of scientific information deriving from Greek, Indian, Persian, Babylonian, and Egyptian sources were compiled. As a result Moslem scientists possessed a larger body of reliable scientific knowledge than did scientists anywhere in the world until modern times. And they made this knowledge available to a large circle of educated men by putting it into Arabic, the language of the whole Moslem world. Moreover, Moslem scientists made many original contributions and were amazingly successful in finding practical applications for their new knowledge.

In mathematics the Indian numerical system was adopted and the use of the zero was added, creating the Arabic system of numbers which is used almost universally today. A Moslem, al Khwarizmi (about 780–850), combined Greek and Indian mathematical ideas to create algebra. Astronomy advanced tremendously as a result of joining the knowledge of Greeks such as Ptolemy with that of Persian and Babylonian astronomers. The works of great medical writers like al Razi (865–925) and Avicenna (980–1037) represent compilations from numerous sources. Moslem doctors studied diseases in hospitals, dissected bodies, and experimented with drugs, thereby adding tremendously to the existing body of medical knowledge. Astronomers, geographers, and physicists followed the same course. Moslem science thus represents a considerable advance in human knowledge.

Moslem literature also demonstrated great vigor and variety. The colorful, imaginative, emotional literature is best exemplified by the poetry of Omar Khayyám and the fascinating stories of the famous *Arabian Nights*. The latter work is especially typical of Moslem literature in that it consisted of stories collected from nearly all the peoples over whom the Arabs ruled.

THE SULEIMAN MOSQUE, DAMASCUS. The mosque is primarily a place of prayer for faithful Moslems, who are summoned to prayer by a call issued from the minarets rising above the main structure. Sermons are also delivered in them, especially on Fridays. These slender, graceful minarets, the rounded dome, the slightly pointed arches, the simple columns, the geometric decorative patterns are typical features of Moslem architecture and represent a synthesis of many artistic traditions—classical Greek, Persian, Byzantine, and Arabic. (*Philip Gendreau, New York*)

The distinctive Moslem architectural style, illustrated by great mosques and palaces, especially the mosques, combines aspects of several earlier architectural traditions. Before each mosque was an open court containing a purification fountain for the use of the faithful and surrounded by a covered passageway. The mosque itself was simply a large prayer room, usually containing little more than a pulpit from which the Koran could be read. As a rule the mosque was covered by a dome very similar to those in Byzantine churches, above which on several sides rose graceful minarets (towers) from which the call to prayer was issued. Many mosques made effective use of the horseshoe arch to create doorways and windows. The mosques were usually stark and severe on the outside, but brilliant decorations were employed to brighten the inside. Since Moslem religious teaching prohibited the use of human and animal forms in art, Moslem artists relied chiefly on floral designs, geometric patterns, and brilliant colors to relieve the bare stonework.

5. Western Europe and Her Eastern Neighbors

The brilliance and vitality of the Byzantine and the Moslem civilizations found little competition from the Germanic-Roman portion of the old Roman Empire. Western Europe lagged far behind them until at least the twelfth century. This situation had a profound effect on Western Europe, and, before moving ahead to the history of the West, a few words must be said about the nature of the relationship between the West and her more mature neighbors.

Outwardly considerable hostility marked this relationship. During most of the early Middle Ages both the Byzantine Empire and the Moslem world posed threats to the West, although the Moslem danger was much the greater. Religious differences promoted discord. Christians in the West, who looked upon the Moslems as infidels, believed any atrocity story told about them. The Christians in the Byzantine Empire were distrusted almost as much. Language differences also created a difficult barrier.

At first glance one might suspect that the West was cut off from the Byzantines and Moslems and was little influenced by them. However, over this gulf passed strong influences that played a crucial role in shaping the infant culture emerging in Western Europe during the dark centuries that followed the fall of Rome. From both Byzantines and Moslems the Western Europeans derived an extensive body of technical knowledge, especially with respect to manufacturing and commercial practices. Almost all the luxury items that added to the refinement of life in Western Europe during the Middle Ages were introduced to the West from one or the other of the civilizations of the Near East. Western Europe inherited the Roman law from the Byzantine Empire. The first distinctive architectural style to develop in the West in the Middle Ages (the Romanesque) developed from Byzantine models, as did the sculptural and painting styles used to decorate the churches built in the Romanesque style. Throughout the Middle Ages and into the Renaissance, Western European scholars learned about the splendid culture of ancient Greece from those who played a vital role in preserving it in Constantinople. Moslem cultural influences were nearly as strong in medieval Europe. A large body of philosophical and scientific knowledge passed into Western European hands as a result of the meeting of Christians and Moslems in Spain. This knowledge provided the chief leaven in the resurgence of Western European culture in the twelfth and thirteenth centuries. Finally, European literature received a priceless heritage from the love poetry of the Moslems.

In short, during its youthful centuries no aspect of Western European civilization escaped the subtle influence of the East. In recent centuries, when the West has materially outstripped the peoples of the Near East, this debt has often been forgotten by Westerners, although not by the heirs of the Byzantine and Moslem civilizations.

SUGGESTED READING

Alexander A. Vasiliev, *History of the Byzantine Empire 324–1453*, 2nd ed., rev. (1952). A complete survey of Byzantine history, difficult but rewarding.

Norman H. Baynes, *The Byzantine Empire* (1925). A brief introduction to Byzantine civilization from a topical point of view.

* P. N. Ure, *Justinian and His Age* (Penguin). An excellent description of Byzantine society during its early stages. The great Justinian provides an attractive center around which the discussion is built.

* Steven Runciman, *Byzantine Civilization* (Meridian). A broad treatment of Byzantine civilization from 330 to 1453, concentrating primarily on institutions, cultural affairs, religion, and social conditions. Although such a vast subject leads to inadequate treatment of some topics, this volume probably provides the best introduction available to Byzantine civilization.

Charles Diehl, *Byzantine Portraits* (1927). This book, written by one of the greatest scholars of Byzantine history, attempts to present a picture of Byzantine society by selecting representative figures from that society and then drawing character sketches of those selected. The result provides a fascinating glimpse of the Byzantine world.

* H. A. R. Gibb, *Mohammedanism: An Historical Survey* (Mentor). A short survey of the career and teachings of Mohammed and of the evolution of those ideas in later ages.

* A. Guillaume, *Islam* (Penguin). A short, stimulating discussion of the Moslem religion, concentrating on the teachings of Mohammed and the evolution of his ideas through the centuries.

Philip K. Hitti, *History of the Arabs from the Earliest Times to the Present*, 6th ed. (1956). A full-scale history of the Moslems, useful for anyone interested in tracing the rise of the Arab Empire and the history of that empire down to the present. The volume also contains a discussion of Moslem cultural life.

Carl Brockelmann, *History of the Islamic Peoples*, tr. by Joel Carmichael and Moshe Perlman (1947). This excellent study extends from the time of Mohammed to the beginning of World War II, presenting a clear picture of political and cultural developments in the Moslem world. It requires careful and patient reading but will provide an intelligent, balanced picture of Moslem history.

* *The Koran* (many editions; a good one is the translation by N. J. Dawood in the Penguin series). Every reader should become acquainted with the sacred book of the Moslem religion in order to appreciate the spirit of the religion founded by Mohammed.

CHAPTER 16

The Barbarian West, 500–750

AGAINST the background of the brilliant Byzantine and Moslem civilizations Western Europe presented a sorry picture in the early Middle Ages. After 500 the West was plunged into a dark age. Strife, confusion, and decline dominated in all phases of life. However, in the midst of the barbarism creative forces were at work. By 750 new ideas and institutions, destined to play a chief role in Europe's history for many centuries as the bases of a more stable and creative society, had begun to develop.

1. Political Developments

Much of the confusion of the period from 500 to 750 resulted from the absence of sound political institutions. In 500 the Germans, making up only a small minority of the total population, were the masters of Western and Central Europe by right of conquest. They had divided the imperial territory in the West into several independent states, thereby ending the political unity that had characterized Roman rule. Upon the rulers of each of these states fell the responsibility of building a political system to replace that of Rome. That responsibility was a heavy one for the new lords of Western Europe, who had never ruled states as large as those they now possessed. Moreover, the boundaries between states were indistinct, and each state contained diverse population elements that had previously enjoyed political independence and had lived under different systems of law. Political chaos was inevitable under these conditions.

The Germanic rulers added to the chaos by persisting in their ancient custom of fighting for new lands, thus writing a bloody record of warfare across the period from 500 to 750. This warfare caused untold suffering and resulted in constant changes in the political map of Europe. Some of the Germanic kingdoms, too weak to stand up under unrelenting pressure, vanished completely. While the Germanic states clawed at one another, the rampaging Moslems took North Africa and Spain from German rulers, and Slavic hordes inched westward in Central Europe. By 750 only three major Germanic groups still survived. On the continent the Franks had swallowed up several other Germanic kingdoms to create a large state centered in Gaul. The Lombards, who had invaded Italy in 568, were in control of most of that peninsula. In what is today England the Angles, Saxons, and Jutes had formed seven small kingdoms.[1]

The rise of the Franks was the most significant result of the struggles among the Germans. At the end of the fifth century the Franks were transformed into a crushing military force by the leadership of their first great king, Clovis (reigned 486–511). When Clovis became king, his people occupied only a small territory astride the Rhine River in northern Gaul, but this

---

[1] Scotland, Wales, and Ireland were held by non-Germanic peoples, chiefly Celts.

cruel, ruthless barbarian launched a series of wars that soon made the Franks the mightiest power in the West. His successors carried on his militaristic policy, so that in about a half century the Franks had destroyed and absorbed the other kingdoms in Gaul. They then turned their armies eastward, extending their boundaries across the Rhine to include territories that had not been part of the Roman Empire. These conquests shaped a kingdom that embraced peoples with both Roman and German cultural backgrounds, and here more than anywhere else Roman and German ideas and practices were forced to mix, a process out of which emerged Europe's most fundamental institutions. Frankish expansion also created a state strong enough to block further barbarian invasions for several centuries. The end of invasions was a blessing for Europe, bringing to a close one of the major causes of political instability.

As the political map of Europe slowly took shape, the rulers of each Germanic kingdom tried to build workable institutions of government within their states. This process created even more disorder than did the competition among the states. Every state suffered from violence, civil war, injustice, and murder—sure signs that the German rulers did not provide good government. However, in the kingdoms that survived until 750 the bases for workable government were slowly established.

The pattern of government painfully evolving in Western Europe can be seen best in Frankish history. The Franks sought to restore order in their state by instituting an absolute monarchy. Beginning with the reign of Clovis, the Frankish king assumed the role of supreme lawgiver, final judge, sole commander of the armies, and religious director over all his subjects, Roman and German alike. To execute these vast powers, the monarch created a court of officials, many of whom bore old Roman titles and were assigned duties comparable to Roman bureaucrats. To exercise his will over his subjects on a local level, the king retained the old Roman territorial divisions of Gaul

as the units of local administration. Each district, now called a county, was governed by a count who was appointed by and responsible to the king. The count was charged with holding regular courts, keeping order, improving public facilities, collecting taxes, and raising army contingents. Outwardly Roman political institutions were being carried on by the Germans.

This grandiose attempt to perpetuate the Roman tradition had one positive effect on the political life of the West. It established monarchy as an important and necessary political institution. The more capable members of the Merovingian dynasty,[2] like Clovis, were able to exercise some of the powers they claimed and thus provided their subjects with peace, order, and justice. By doing this they began the slow process of defining the functions of kingship in the new order. Furthermore, the royal family served as a symbol of unity for all the peoples in the kingdom. To see the king traveling through the land, to hear of his exploits as head of the army, and to witness the pompous ceremonies of court life offered the Franks virtually the only evidence that they belonged to a state. Their king served as the visible sign of public life and group solidarity at a moment when poor communications and cultural differences created tremendous obstacles to political unity.

However, the Merovingians never enjoyed the real power of Roman emperors. Many factors explain their failure. Most of them relied heavily on force to gain their ends and appeared to many as bloodthirsty tyrants. They seldom tried to perform positive services for their subjects, since most of them had only a vague concept of public welfare. They persisted in following the ancient Germanic custom of treating their state as private property to be divided among all male heirs of each king at his death. This practice led to family quarrels that constantly disturbed the peace of the kingdom and dis-

[2] The family of Clovis and his successors was called the Merovingian dynasty. It ruled the Franks until 751.

tracted the kings from constructive activity. Finally, the Merovingian kings lacked the financial resources necessary to conduct good government, and the differences in laws, customs, religious practices, languages, and cultural levels among their subjects made it impossible for even the most able Merovingian to find a single policy suitable to all.

Having failed to establish a system of absolute monarchy in which the king exercised complete power, the Merovingian rulers were eventually forced to share their political power with the great landowners. The emergence of the landed nobility as the possessors of political power was the chief development of the era, laying the groundwork for the feudal system. The increasing political power of this class resulted chiefly from the failure of the Merovingian kings to create a workable taxation system. Always lacking money income to run their government, the kings were forced to call upon their subjects for personal service to the state. For instance, the Merovingians could not afford to outfit and support armies from their income. When, therefore, an army was needed, they asked their subjects to supply their own horses, armor, and food. Similarly, the kings could not pay salaries to public officials and had to ask officers to serve at their own expense. Under these circumstances only the great landowners could afford to serve the crown, and in return for their services they received grants of land from the royal estates and sometimes the right to govern their private estates as they saw fit. This process resulted in the gradual separation of the bulk of the Frankish population from the authority of the central government, and the creation of many private governments. The kings usually tried to ensure the loyalty of the landowners by requiring each to swear a special oath of allegiance to the crown. This procedure placed the nobles in a special category above the bulk of the population and forced the king to devote most of his attention to maintaining his position against the powerful nobles.

The growing power of the nobles was the source of tremendous strife in the Merovingian kingdom. The system was so new that the line between the king's authority and the landowner's authority was indefinite. The kings struggled to keep their land and political authority, while the nobles practiced every guile to gain stronger positions. Civil war resulted, usually ending with the landowners gaining more power, since the kings were forced to give away their own lands to try to buy the support of some nobles against others who were attacking royal power. However, the victorious landowners did not think of abolishing kingship, since much of their wealth and power was derived from royal authority.

In 750 the political picture in the rest of Western Europe was equally somber. Good government had been replaced by civil war, by the irresponsible rule of great landowners, and by nearly powerless kings. But in the midst of this chaos the basic political institutions that would dominate Europe for several centuries were being shaped. Monarchy, however shadowy, was established as a symbol of public authority and as a unifying force for a large group of people. The landowners monopolized political rights and offices and controlled large elements of the population through the private governments they had constructed on their own estates. This was a poor substitute for Rome's mighty government, but its full possibilities had not yet been exploited.

2. Economic Life

Between 500 and 750 Western Europe was plunged even more deeply in the depression that had begun in late Roman times.

The major economic catastrophe of the early Middle Ages was the progressive strangulation of commerce. The Germanic invasions had hastened this decline by increasing the political turmoil in the West, and, moreover, the barbarian rulers were little interested in trading ventures. The final blow came in the seventh century when the Moslems seized control of the Mediterranean and virtually ended sea communications between East and West. City life, the trading and artisan class, money economy, and a large array of technical skills virtually disappeared in the West, and such losses were reflected in a constantly declining standard of living.

To meet its needs, Europe's population turned almost exclusively to an agricultural economy. Land became the measure of a man's position and power, and those who controlled land dominated society. For those who were unable to own land there was nothing left except to become toilers on the soil, dependent upon landowners; no longer was the life of the trader or the artisan open to them.

Agricultural life assumed a definite organization by 750. The tendency toward the formation of large estates, which was begun in Roman times, continued and spread. The small, independent farmer virtually disappeared, a large landholder absorbing his holding into a great estate. The nobles usually lived on their land and made it produce everything they needed. Labor was supplied for the most part by tenants whom the landowner bound permanently to the soil. There were slaves on many estates, although the institution of slavery tended to disappear as a result of Church opposition. Tenants were usually given a piece of land for themselves, but they also farmed part of the owner's land and paid rents in produce. Each estate, tending to become self-sufficient, had little need for outside contacts.

Gone were the bustling cities, the skilled artisans, the fine products, and the extensive public and private displays of wealth that had characterized Roman society, and the European economy permitted almost no accumulation of wealth to be invested in growth and expansion. In spite of the dreariness of this picture, however, the Europeans had discovered a means of feeding and clothing themselves. For many centuries the large estate with its landowner and its peasant residents would supply the material needs of the West.

3. The Church

Western society needed more than the rebuilding of its political and economic structure. The passing of Rome witnessed the virtual destruction of moral, spiritual, and cultural values, necessitating reconstruction on this level of life. To the Church fell the lot of struggling against moral, spiritual, and cultural barbarism, which threatened to engulf Western Europe in the wake of the fall of Rome. It was especially fitted for this task because it had survived the fall of Rome better than had any other institution, carrying over into the new age an appealing, satisfying religious message plus large elements of Graeco-Roman culture that found their way into its organization, theology, liturgy, and moral code.

The Church itself was faced with great adversity between 500 and 750. In the West it lost the beneficial support of the Roman government. Most German rulers, having been Christianized before or very early in this period, sought to aid the Church but often harmed it by their brutal methods and their political ineptness. Under their influence the Church broke into units that coincided with the boundaries of the Germanic states, and that usually disregarded one another, thereby threatening the unity of Western Christendom. Moreover, by 750 differences in theology, ritual, and organization had already separated the Greek and Latin churches, and as the Christian world split and divided its energies, the assaults of Moslems and Slavs rolled back its frontiers.

Even more dangerous was the decay of religious life within the Western Church. Christian leadership deteriorated badly. The bishops, who were the most important Church officials, were especially lax in serving religious ends. Most of their energy was devoted to increasing Church lands. As the possessors of large land holdings, the bishops had political duties thrust upon them, just as did other landlords. And in the unholy competition for the office of bishop, with its land and political power, the strong usually won over the pious. The typical bishop of the age was a warlike, quarrelsome, greedy, worldly figure, forever fighting and seeking power. Seldom did he concern himself with spiritual affairs. As a consequence discipline in the lower ranks of the clergy also suffered. The typical priest who dealt directly with the people was unlettered, ignorant of the rudiments of doctrine, unfamiliar with liturgy, and lax in moral life.

Religious life in general reflected the inferior leadership. Recently converted pagans mixed their old religious ideas with Christianity to create beliefs and practices of the most amazing kinds. Crude superstitions gripped the minds of many Christians. Most of them still understood vaguely such ideas as original sin, the Incarnation, the Redemption, free will, and the rewards of the good life. However, their daily religious life was dominated by efforts to avoid Satan's hordes, who plagued mankind at every turn and had to be defeated by miracles, magic, and the intervention of the saints. Moral conditions degenerated badly. The Church writers of the period complained bitterly about sexual promiscuity, crimes of violence, thieving, and general unruliness among Christians. The whole population was badly in need of instruction and discipline, neither of which was forthcoming from the degraded clergy.

Few of these difficulties had been corrected by 750. Nonetheless revitalization had begun and the Church was well on the way to becoming the dominant institution in Western society.

One of the most significant features of the period was the Church's continued ability to win new converts. We have already noted that some of the Germans accepted Christianity as soon as they came into contact with Roman civilization. After the fall of Rome, Christianity continued to spread among them. Just as this period opened, Clovis and his Franks were converted (496), thus bringing into the Christian camp the Germanic nation destined to

dominate the West. Backed by the Franks, missionaries in the sixth and seventh centuries pushed the Christian frontier slowly eastward from the Rhine. About the same time the Anglo-Saxons in Britain were converted by Roman and Irish missionaries. The Irish had been converted in the fourth century and had remained a Christian stronghold during the troubled period of the Germanic invasions. In the first half of the eighth century English missionaries crossed to the continent to win new converts on the northern and eastern frontiers of the Frankish kingdom. The conversion of almost all of the Germans meant that the population of the West lived under the influence of at least one unifying force. In fact religious unity had by 750 become a powerful substitute for the political and cultural unity of the Roman Empire.

A second positive achievement of the Church was its growing participation in activities that were not strictly religious. The Church, living in a world of weak governments, often shouldered the burden of caring for the weak in society—widows, orphans, cripples, slaves, and prisoners. It maintained the only hospitals and schools available. It injected some of its ideas of justice and mercy into the harsh law codes of the era, thus powerfully influencing the administration of justice. Each time the Church intervened in these matters, its prestige as a social agency and its influence over society increased. These activities set new standards of social welfare that were to serve as models in reawakening the social consciousness of society in general.

However, the Church's greatest accomplishment in this period was its ability to perfect institutions capable of attacking the weaknesses within its own body—corruptness and worldliness among the clergy, moral laxness, ignorance, and lack of discipline. Especially important were two institutions that evolved rapidly between 500 and 750: the Roman papacy and the Benedictine monastic order.

The bishop of Rome, more commonly designated as the pope (which is a word derived from the Italian word for father), had begun to emerge as a powerful figure in Christendom long before 500. From an early date many Christians accepted the bishops of Rome as the chief representatives of Christ on earth, a belief based on what is called the Petrine theory, which says that Christ had designated Peter as his representative on earth and that that commission applied to Peter's successors as bishop of Rome. Because the bishops of Rome had also gained wealth and prestige after the fall of the Roman imperial government in the West, their decisions were often accepted in settling disputes within the Church over discipline and dogma. However, conditions in the early sixth century seriously affected the position of the pope. Political chaos in Italy offered the gravest danger. The Ostrogoths, who ruled Italy in 500, were Arians (did not accept the doctrine of the trinity) and thus averse to obeying the pope. When, later, Justinian destroyed the power of the Ostrogoths, the pope fell under the authority of the Eastern emperor, whose Greek orientation tended to reduce the importance of Rome in favor of Constantinople. Still later, in 568, the Lombards seized most of Italy from the Byzantines, thus opening up an era of bloody struggle between Lombards and Byzantines that made it nearly impossible for the pope to act positively. Finally, the influence of the pope was diminished in other Germanic kingdoms in the West as kings and bishops seized control of religious life and made it serve their own ends.

The recovery of the papacy was sparked by the genius of the first great churchman of the Middle Ages, Pope Gregory I, the Great (590–604). Descended from a noble Roman family and educated for a political career, Gregory rejected worldly affairs to become a monk. Eventually he left his monastic life to serve as a papal diplomat in Constantinople and then to become pope. Coupling a deep religious fervor with a hardheaded business sense, Gregory quickly established himself as one of the truly constructive figures of the age. Essen-

tially his policy consisted of making the pope politically and economically independent while at the same time asserting the authority of the papal office as the fountainhead of spiritual life in the Christian world.

Gregory was convinced that political and economic independence could come only if the pope possessed wealth. He therefore devoted himself to the sound administration of papal property in Italy, taking an active part in the management of his estates, collecting everything due him, goading his agents into farming better, and acquiring new lands whenever possible. Gregory used his income to establish full control over the city of Rome, turning it into a little state ruled by the pope. On the basis of his political power Gregory began to act as an independent agent in the incessant struggles between the Lombards and Byzantines. By playing one side against the other he managed to enhance his position in Italy. He had begun the process of creating an independent papal state with resources sufficient to make its power felt in ever-wider circles.

Gregory was not, however, simply a wily politician and administrator. His greatest fame came as a spiritual leader with a simple and clear message especially suited for the culturally backward Christians of Western Europe. During his busy pontificate he found time to write important books on theology and church administration. His powerful sermons, circulated in manuscript form, served as examples to revive the art of preaching in the West. He took important steps to improve the church liturgy. He sought to bestir princes and clergymen to reform their lives. Perhaps his most spectacular achievement as a spiritual leader was his sponsorship of the conversion of England, a program that allowed him to organize the new church of England under papal guidance. Rome took on new glory as the center of Christianity, and the pope's word began to serve in Western Europe as a final guide in spiritual matters.

Gregory's successors continued his policy,

although not so brilliantly. As a consequence, papal political independence and economic strength increased. Popes continued to speak out on theological and disciplinary matters, and the papacy became the authority for Western Christendom. Obviously a new force of unity and discipline was emerging, although by 750 it had not yet achieved complete domination of the Christian world in the West.

Monasticism had also appeared in Western Europe before 500, but was by that date badly in need of revitalization. The West produced another churchman able to handle this new problem. Benedict of Nursia (480–543) stands alongside Gregory the Great as a builder. He too was an aristocratic Italian who abandoned his worldly career to become a hermit, but his rigid practices and holiness as a hermit attracted so much attention that he was forced to create a monastery for the monks who gathered around him. At Monte Cassino, a village between Rome and Naples, he built his monastic house. There he put into practice the Benedictine rule as the governing regulation for his monastery. The rule was so practical, so sensible, and so well fitted to the needs of the period that by 750 it had spread all over the West and had begun to play an important role in revitalizing the whole Christian world.

The Benedictine rule contained several basic principles that explain its success. It established the idea that a community of men could serve God better than a single individual. Such a community must, however, be made up of selected members. The rule laid down rigorous tests for the sincerity of prospective members. After a long testing period each new member was required to take vows, promising to renounce all personal wealth, to remain chaste, and to obey his superiors. These vows created a complete loyalty to the monastery and obligated the monk to avoid the chief sins of clergymen of the era—greed for wealth, luxury, sexual laxity, and disregard for authority. Since the monks were to live as a community, a government was necessary,

and the rule entrusted absolute authority to an abbot, a sensible move in view of the desperate need for discipline in the church. Probably the most important part of the rule was its provision for an orderly daily routine. Benedict assigned to his monks three kinds of activity. The most important was the worship of God, eight religious services being established for each day. This seems an outrageous burden to the modern worshipper; however, it was a sensible requirement when measured alongside some monastic practices of the day, such as spending one's life atop a pole as an act of worship. The second kind of activity required of Benedictine monks was four to eight hours of manual labor a day, depending on the season. That labor included cooking, field work, clerical work, the crafts, and teaching, depending on the talents of each monk. Finally, each monk was required to devote a part of each day to study.

Having provided for the selection, discipline, and occupation of his monks, Benedict wrote one final principle into his rule —moderation. Repeatedly he cautioned against too strict discipline, advising the abbot to temper his rule with mercy. Benedict made allowances for human nature, realizing that man might achieve some degree of godliness but that he could never be perfect. This spirit of moderation permitted a flexibility in the typical Benedictine monastery that allowed it to fit nearly every circumstance.

Benedict's rule was adopted over most of Western Europe,[3] "schools for the service of God," as Benedict called his establishments, appearing everywhere. These monasteries not only served as places of withdrawal from barbarized society for those Christians who desired to perfect their lives, but also produced large numbers of men and women who stood out as ideal Christians. Their services to society were immense. Monks carved new estates out of Europe's wilderness and made them into the best-managed economic institutions in

[3] Eventually the rule was adapted to serve for nunneries.

the West. They taught backward peoples all kinds of technical skills. They showed bewildered Christians the proper performance of Church rituals. They instructed the ignorant in the basic tenets of the faith. Their devotion, charity, and purity of life served to inspire others to reform. They bore the brunt of missionary work, their bravery and sacrifices in the face of paganism serving as the most inspiring Christian acts of the period. Again, in the midst of Europe's darkness, a new institution had been created, capable of making inroads into the most serious evils of the sixth, seventh, and eighth centuries.

4. Cultural and Intellectual Activity

The most significant achievement of the Benedictine monks, however, was their contribution in the struggle to keep alive a cultural life in Western Europe. The barbarian invasions had hastened the death of Graeco-Roman cultural life and introduced a cultural dark age that threatened to extinguish all signs of learning and art.

The Church almost singlehandedly kept the Graeco-Roman artistic and intellectual heritage from completely disappearing. Most of its efforts were unspectacular and sometimes uninteresting, but they were of tremendous importance to Europe's later cultural development. The monasteries of the West performed the most valuable service by saving a few scraps of Rome's culture. Benedictine monks, taking seriously their master's injunction to serve God by study, tediously copied the works of classical authors and of the Church fathers in order to build up little libraries for the use of fellow monks. These efforts permitted later generations to read most of the Roman classical authors whose works might otherwise have disappeared. Monks compiled Latin grammars and painfully taught the language to their disciples, thus keeping Latin alive as the language of learning and public affairs and retaining a link with the classical past. They put together simple textbooks in rhetoric, mathematics, and logic. Occasionally

a monk wrote down his interpretations of the document he was copying, trying by his scholarly efforts to make its contents understandable to his contemporaries. Some bolder spirits of the age attempted to imitate classical models and produced an occasional original poem or hymn. Outside the monasteries, bishops, inspired by a desire to honor God in any and all ways, kept alive traditions of architecture and decorative arts by providing for church building. This intellectual and artistic activity seldom had much effect on lay society, which sank into almost complete ignorance. However, it did succeed in preserving a tradition of writing, scholarship, and artistic effort. Equally important was the fact that cultural activity became the monopoly of the Church and took on a definite ecclesiastical coloration.

The preservation of the Latin tradition did not completely dominate the intellectual and artistic life of the age. A few creative figures managed to rise above the almost universal stagnation and produce works of art and intellect worthy of note. Gregory the Great, for instance, wrote theological works that served for a long time as models in this field. A Frankish bishop, Gregory of Tours (about 538–593), in his *History of the Franks* demonstrated a real ability to compile and organize historical material. The most outstanding intellectual figure of the age was an English monk, Bede (673–735), whose theological, historical, and biographical writings greatly impressed his generation and set high standards of style. Especially in the Irish monasteries, which had escaped the rigors of the Germanic invasions, was the tradition of creative writing and original scholarship sustained. The Irish monks, coming to England and the continent as missionaries, spread their works there. Perhaps most amazing of all is the fact that even the Germanic element in Western society, usually completely dominated by Latin culture, could create original works. The magnificent Anglo-Saxon epic, *Beowulf*, was written in this age.

As the Western world passed the middle of the eighth century, it had by no means emerged from its dark age. Two and a half centuries of barbarism had left their marks on the European population. Habits of violence, dismal ignorance, widespread poverty, and moral decadence hung over the West for many centuries. Nonetheless, compact political units, monarchy, a politically conscious nobility, large estates, a stabilized peasantry, an active Church, the papacy, Benedictine monasticism, and a small but priceless treasury of Graeco-Roman culture promised to counteract barbarism. The future of Western European civilization depended to a great extent on these forces.

SUGGESTED READING

* R. F. Arragon, *The Transition from the Ancient to the Medieval World* (Berkshire Series, 1936). A short book that successfully summarizes the most recent scholarship pertaining to the problem of the passing of Graeco-Roman civilization and the beginning of a new order in Western Europe.

H. St. L. B. Moss, *The Birth of the Middle Ages, 395–814* (1935). A clearly presented account of the major events connected with the fall of Rome, the Germanic invasions, and the post-invasion period in Western Europe.

* Christopher Dawson, *The Making of Europe* (Meridian). Originally published in a hardback edition in 1932. A stimulating discussion of the importance of the early Middle Ages in the formation of Western European civilization. Dawson especially highlights the role of the Church in shaping the new civilization.

* Edward Kennard Rand, *Founders of the Middle Ages* (Dover). Originally published in a hardback edition in 1928. A thorough discussion of the Church fathers and their importance in laying the intellectual basis for Western European civilization during the early Middle Ages. The emphasis is placed especially on the role of the Church fathers as transmitters of classical ideas to the barbarian world.

Samuel Dill, *Roman Society in Gaul in the Merovingian Age* (1926). A detailed study of social and intellectual conditions in Gaul in the troubled Merovingian era, when nearly the last vestiges of Roman civilization were being crushed amid the violence and poverty of barbarian society.

F. Homes Dudden, *Gregory the Great, His place in History and Thought*, 2 vols. (1905). A thorough study of the life of one of the chief men of the sixth century, making it clear through numerous extracts from Gregory's own writings how great was his contribution to Western European life.

* Justin McCann, *St. Benedict* (Image). Published in a hardback edition in 1937. An excellent study of Benedict's life; the book is brief, yet it covers adequately all phases of Benedict's career.

James T. Shotwell and Louise Ropes Loomis, eds., *The See of Peter* (1927). A collection of all the historical sources relevant to the early papacy. This book will provide its readers an excellent opportunity to experience at first hand the problems a medieval historian must face in ascertaining the meaning and reliability of source materials.

Benedict of Nursia, *Rule*, tr. in E. F. Henderson, ed., *Select Historical Documents of the Middle Ages* (1896). This document became the guide for the establishment of monasteries all over Western Europe after the middle of the sixth century.

Gregory of Tours, *History of the Franks*, tr. by O. M. Dalton, 2 vols. (1927). The chief source of information about the Merovingian rulers of Gaul by a bishop who lived in the difficult years of the sixth century. The book will supply a first-hand account of the disorders occurring in Western Europe after the fall of Rome.

* *Beowulf* (many editions; a satisfactory one is the translation by David Wright in the Penguin series). An epic poem stemming from the early history of the Anglo-Saxons before this group conquered England. The poem will illustrate the Germanic mentality in the early stages of the formation of Western European society.

CHAPTER 17

The First Revival of Western Europe,
750–1000

IN 750 the situation in Western Europe was anything but promising. Despite the constructive steps noted in the previous chapter, civil wars, foreign invaders, ignorance, and poverty threatened to prolong the chaos indefinitely. At this grim hour, however, Western Europe enjoyed a brief upsurge. On the continent a few rulers of the Carolingian family in the Frankish kingdom, supported by a handful of inspired clergymen, sought to give society new goals and to provide leadership to carry men toward these goals. In England at a somewhat later date the kings of Wessex played a comparable role. The efforts of the Carolingians were abortive; those of the English kings were only partly successful. However, in both cases, an important heritage was left for later generations.

1. The Rise of the Carolingians

The Carolingian family rose to prominence during the seventh century. Originally this family had joined other ambitious families in undermining the authority of the Merovingian kings of the Franks, gaining huge estates in the process. Toward the end of the seventh century, however, the Carolingians gained hereditary control of the office of mayor of the palace, one of the chief offices in the Merovingian kingdom,

and as mayors of the palace they became champions of strong central government, using their wealth and ability to strengthen the weak Merovingian kings they served.

Charles Martel, who was mayor of the palace 714–741, and Pepin the Short, who held the office from 741 to 751, were so successful that they became the strongest men in Western Europe, far overshadowing the kings they served. The program of Charles and Pepin was essentially simple, yet it struck directly at the chief evils of the period. Both men waged incessant and successful war against the turbulent, greedy nobles who caused so much trouble for the Merovingian rulers of the Frankish kingdom. Both defended the frontiers against hostile invaders, and Charles Martel gained undying fame by defeating at Tours in 732 a Moslem army that had invaded the Frankish kingdom from Spain. Both tried to improve the royal administration so that justice might be rendered, taxes collected, and the weak protected. Both showed every inclination to win the support of the Church by helping missionaries, by trying to reform the clergy, and by seeking to improve the quality of religious life throughout the Frankish kingdom.

While doing all these things Charles and Pepin were still only servants of the "do nothing" kings of the Merovingian dynasty.

As the years passed, it became clear to everyone that the legal kings were less than useful and that the real power lay in the hands of the mayors of the palace. It was they who raised armies, administered justice, defended the frontiers, appointed officials, and made laws. Finally Pepin undertook to do something about this illogical situation. He took steps to transfer the Frankish crown from the Merovingian family to his own.

Feeling that it might be dangerous to unseat forceably the ancient Merovingian dynasty, Pepin sought a higher authority to sanction his bold act. His choice was a momentous one: he turned to the pope. In 749 he sent an envoy to Rome to ask Pope Zacharias if it were not right that one who really exercised power should wear the crown. When Zacharias approved, Pepin deposed the Merovingian king and had himself elected. When he was crowned in 751, a papal legate was present to anoint him, indicating that, in the eyes of the Church, Pepin was king by the grace of God.

These dramatic events led to others equally significant. Zacharias had been favorable to Pepin's request largely because the papacy desperately needed assistance. Since the days of Gregory the Great (590–604) the papacy had been struggling to retain its possessions in central Italy as a guarantee of independence. By 750 these possessions were threatened by the Lombard kings of Italy. Even before 750 the popes had begun to plead for help from the Frankish mayors of the palace. In 753 Pope Stephen II, strengthened by the fact that his predecessor had helped Pepin acquire his crown, made a journey to the Frankish court to secure a protector. After long negotiations an agreement, called the Donation of Pepin, was reached. Pepin promised to ensure papal control over specified territories in Italy, some of which the Lombards already held. To establish a legal claim to these territories, Stephen apparently confronted Pepin with a document known as the Donation of Constantine.

This document, probably compiled at the papal court just before Stephen's departure for the Frankish kingdom, claimed to be a deed in which the Emperor Constantine, who died in A.D. 337, granted to Pope Sylvester complete control over the western part of the Roman Empire, especially Rome and Italy. Constantine was allegedly prompted to this action by virtue of the fact that the pope had cured him of leprosy. In return for the aid of the Frankish king Stephen bestowed on Pepin the somewhat vague title of "patrician of Rome," signifying Pepin's role as protector of the papacy and of the papal state. Pepin then made two campaigns into Italy and forced the Lombards to surrender some of the territories claimed by the papacy.

The alliance of the Franks and the papacy was truly a landmark. Germanic monarchy and the head of the Christian Church had now cast their lots together. The Frankish kings now ruled by the grace of God bestowed through the papacy. They had assumed the responsibility of safeguarding their realm against all enemies of Christianity and of encouraging their subjects to become more perfect Christians. They had placed themselves under the guidance of the papacy, which claimed the power to lead the Christian world toward perfection. At the same time the papacy, now backed by strong protectors, had lifted itself to a new position of authority.

2. The Reign of Charlemagne (768–814)

The work of Charles Martel and Pepin the Short was carried on by Charlemagne (reigned 768–814). This energetic, talented ruler was first of all a successful war lord. His long reign was highlighted by a series of campaigns that added important territories to the Frankish realm and threw back its attackers. Charlemagne's first notable success came in 774, when he defeated the Lombard king of Italy and annexed all the peninsula except the Byzantine territories in the south and the papal states over which he was already protector. Even before dis-

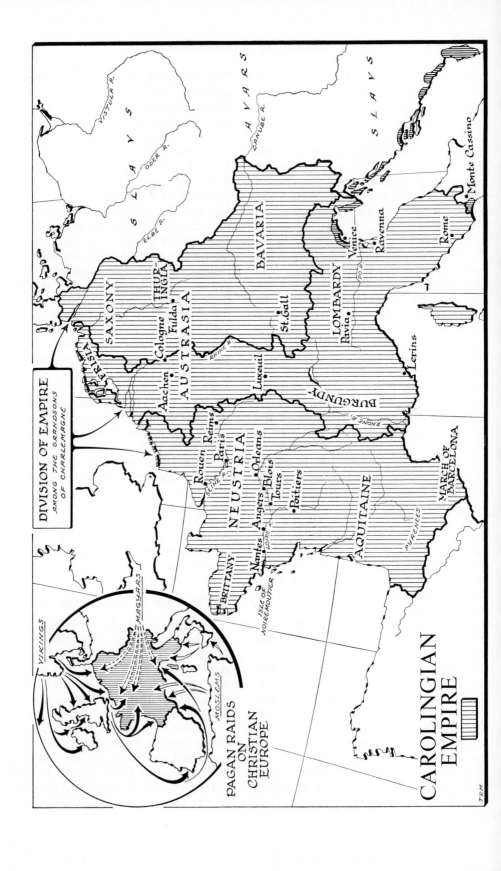

DIVISION OF EMPIRE
AMONG THE GRANDSONS
OF CHARLEMAGNE

PAGAN RAIDS
ON
CHRISTIAN
EUROPE

VIKINGS

MAGYARS

MOSLEMS

CAROLINGIAN
EMPIRE

SLAVS

AVARS

SLAVS

VISTULA R.

ODER R.

ELBE R.

DANUBE R.

SAXONY

THUR-
INGIA

FRISIA

Cologne

Fulda

Aachen

AUSTRASIA

RHINE R.

St. Gall

BAVARIA

Luxeuil

BURGUNDY

LOMBARDY

Pavia

PO R.

Venice

Ravenna

Rome

Monte Cassino

Lérins

Rouen

Reims

Paris

SEINE R.

NEUSTRIA

Orleans

Blois

Angers

Tours

Poitiers

LOIRE R.

Nantes

BRITTANY

ISLE OF
NOIRMOUTIER

AQUITAINE

PYRENEES

RHONE R.

MARCH OF
BARCELONA

T.R.M.

posing of the Lombards, Charlemagne launched an attack on the Saxons who lived on the northeastern frontier of the Frankish kingdom, finally subduing them after twenty years of struggle and forcing them to accept Christianity. His armies also drove down the Danube into the land of the Avars and the Slavs, where another large territory was annexed. He even tried his military strength against the Moslems in Spain, eventually managing to win a narrow strip of land south of the Pyrenees. These successful aggressive wars, coupled with a stout defense at home, permitted Charlemagne to rule over the largest state in the West since the fall of Rome. In all his wars Charlemagne managed to create the impression that he was not merely serving his own greed, but rather overpowering barbarians, pagans, and infidels, thereby saving his Christian subjects from grave danger. Popes, poets, and nobles addressed him as "the strong right arm of God."

Charlemagne tried to be a good and just ruler as well as a conqueror. He made few innovations in the system of government that his family had taken over from the Merovingians, assuming their powers and utilizing a court of officials similar to theirs. Charlemagne supported himself and his court chiefly by the careful use of royal lands, anything like a system of taxation having virtually disappeared. The king's commands were executed locally by counts and dukes appointed by the king. Charlemagne tried to keep track of his government by the use of special officials, called *missi*, sent out from his court periodically to see how royal officials were conducting themselves.

Charlemagne's great distinction as a ruler lay in what he tried to achieve within this old system of government. More than anything else he sought to institute a regime of order and justice. The counts and dukes were instructed to quiet the turbulent nobles and to render protection to the weak and helpless. Tremendous emphasis was placed on safeguarding each man's rights under the law to which he was born. Char-

lemagne sought to supplement the existing legal systems by issuing edicts (capitularies) affecting nearly every phase of life. For at least the length of his reign Charlemagne once again made monarchy stand for justice, protection, and order.

Realizing that the only thing all his subjects had in common was religion, Charlemagne was especially concerned with the condition of the Church. He took the position that he had a duty to strengthen it in its important task of saving souls. He was an ardent champion of the expansion of Christianity, encouraging missionaries and even using force to compel pagans to accept baptism. He also continued the vigorous reform movement begun by Pepin. With the advice of the higher clergy he enacted a large body of law aimed at strengthening Church organization, protecting Church property, imposing higher moral and educational standards on the clergy, establishing uniform doctrines and rituals, and destroying pagan superstitions. At least on the surface the Church took on new vigor under the guiding hand of Charlemagne. The king was hailed as the best servant of the Lord and credited with leading his people toward true citizenship in the City of God.

The high point of Charlemagne's career and, to many of his contemporaries, the culmination of his efforts as a warrior, lawgiver, and champion of the true faith came on Christmas Day, 800. While Charlemagne was attending a mass in St. Peter's church in Rome, Pope Leo III placed a golden crown on his head and the crowd hailed him as "Augustus, crowned by God, the great and peace-bringing Emperor of the Romans." Einhard, Charlemagne's biographer, claimed that the king was surprised by Leo's action and did not want the new title. Perhaps this was only polite modesty. Certainly the coronation of 800 was in keeping with Carolingian policy and with Charlemagne's position. He needed a more dignified title to designate his role as conqueror, ruler of many different people, lawgiver, protector of the weak, and champion of the Church and the papacy. In the

CHARLEMAGNE. This bronze statue, dating from the Carolingian period, is usually considered to be a representation of Charlemagne. If this is true, it represents the oldest existing portrayal of that great conqueror and emperor. (*Archives Photographiques, Paris*)

opinion of his advisers—and probably in his own—Charlemagne had done greater things than any previous ruler since the fall of Rome. His title ought to reflect his greatness. The answer was to create a Christian empire with the ideal Christian prince, Charlemagne, at its head.

In a sense the coronation of 800 was an attempt to revive the dead Roman Empire in Western Europe; Charlemagne was often hailed as a new Constantine. However, the Carolingian Empire was clearly distinct from the Roman Empire. Territorially it came nowhere near embracing the old Roman imperial territory even in the West. Also, the Carolingian Empire was based on ideas distinct from those lying behind the Roman imperial system. Those who insti-

tuted the new empire, especially the churchmen who played a key role in advising Charlemagne, were prompted by Christian idealism. They were convinced that it was God's will that all Christians should be joined in a single earthly commonwealth under a Christian prince. They argued that Charlemagne, a tested champion of the faith, was the only prince capable of ruling such a state. The emperor in Constantinople still maintained the fiction of ruling the West and of protecting the Church but had proved incapable of defending anyone in the West. By reviving the imperial office and by crowning a Germanic ruler the West could pursue its own vision of the City of God on earth, shaped in the image of the Roman Empire but sanctified by the blessing of the Church.

Charlemagne ruled fourteen years as emperor. His actions indicate that he took his new title seriously. He conducted a skillful diplomatic drive that compelled the Eastern emperor to recognize his new title. This was a touchy problem in view of the vaunted claims of the ruler at Constantinople with respect to the West. Charlemagne also legislated more extensively than before, especially in religious matters, and assumed many of the trappings of the imperial office. When he died in 814 he left behind a large, well-ruled state that had moved far in the direction of unity based on acceptance of one emperor and one religion.

3. The Disintegration of the Carolingian Empire

For a variety of reasons Charlemagne's empire broke up almost immediately after his death. Charlemagne had not succeeded in developing permanent governmental institutions capable of surviving after his powerful personality had been removed. To secure assistance in carrying out the functions of government within his empire, Charlemagne had been forced to grant large blocks of lands to the nobles in return for military service, often conceding authority to exercise governmental powers over the lands he had granted. Such grants of governmental authority, called immunities, were made on the assumption that the nobles would be guided in their actions by the example of the great emperor, and Charlemagne tried to keep these men faithful to him by making them swear that they were his vassals. But this arrangement could work for the benefit of the emperor only if he were forceful enough to keep his widely scattered, wealthy vassals under close watch. This was a tremendous burden, one that most of Charlemagne's successors could not successfully assume.

Moreover, Charlemagne's empire was never unified in a real sense. Germans, Romans, and Slavs were still divided by language differences, and in spite of all Charlemagne's legislation numerous different law codes still existed within the empire. The different cultural backgrounds to which his subjects were heirs could not be wished out of existence. Neither the Christian religion nor the commands of an emperor were powerful enough to bridge the gap between groups as diverse as the newly conquered and converted Saxons and the residents of proud old Rome.

The Church, upon which Charlemagne relied so heavily to inspire and guide his subjects to obey and to serve, was actually a doubtful ally. Its leaders in Rome and in the great bishoprics and monasteries scattered over the empire were uneasy about Charlemagne's interference in church affairs. While aspiring to the same end that he did, namely, an earthly society dedicated to the service of God, many churchmen preferred to lead society themselves rather than to bend before a layman.

Charlemagne's empire was threatened by powerful external foes. On the south were the aggressive Moslems, especially strong in sea power, against which the Franks had little defense. On the east the Slavs, under the pressure of the Magyars, new invaders from Asia, pushed relentlessly westward. Finally, the Vikings or Norsemen (comprising Danes, Swedes, and Norwegians) threatened on the north. The Vikings, virtually strangers to Western Europe in the early ninth century, quickly became the greatest danger.

The Vikings were still barbarians and heathens. They had long dwelt along the wild coasts of Scandinavia, surviving chiefly by fishing and piracy. These occupations made them skilled seamen. Politically, strong clans played a dominant role, although by 800 loose kingdoms were in the process of formation. In the ninth century, for reasons hard to discern, the Vikings began to expand. Traveling by sea in small groups, they spread over an immense area, touching Ireland, England, the whole Atlantic coast of Europe, the southern shores of the North and Baltic seas, Russia, Iceland, Greenland, and probably North America. Following the rivers, they penetrated far inland in Western Europe, England, and Russia. Wherever they went, they pillaged the land and hauled off vast quantities of loot. Eventually in the late ninth and tenth centuries some of them began to settle permanently in the lands they had been raiding, especially in England, Ireland, France, and Russia, and piracy gave way to trade. The Vikings slowly accepted the religion and culture of Western Europeans. As we shall see later, they became one of the most creative groups in Western Europe, especially in the eleventh and twelfth centuries. However, all this was too late to spare the Carolingian Empire. Charlemagne's successors had to face the full fury of the destructive raids and found no effective defense against the dreaded raiding parties.

Perhaps these difficulties could have been offset had there been more Charlemagnes, but this was too much to expect. Charlemagne's successor, Louis (814–840), demonstrated the lack of leadership that would plague the empire throughout the ninth century. Louis's chief interest lay in religious matters, and he permitted powerful churchmen to assume authority at the expense of the emperor. His policy earned him the title "Pious" but gave him no help in dealing with the chief problem of his reign—providing for his four sons (one of whom died before him). As early as 817 Louis began making divisions of the empire for their benefit, but this did not prevent them from revolting against him. All the enemies of unity and strong government joined Louis's rebellious sons.

Before his death Louis did provide a "kingdom" for each of his three surviving sons and granted to his eldest, Lothair, the title of emperor with a vague authority over the others. Almost immediately the younger sons declared war on Lothair and in 843 forced him to sign the Treaty of Verdun. This document legalized the division of the empire into three parts: a kingdom embracing most of modern France, a kingdom of Germany, and a kingdom of Lotharingia (Lorraine) consisting of a narrow band stretching between the west and east kingdoms from the North Sea to Italy. Almost immediately the eastern and western Frankish kingdoms began to turn the middle kingdom into a battleground, each seeking to annex it. Eventually further divisions occurred, creating the kingdoms of Italy and Burgundy.

After 843 each kingdom had its own history. Carolingian unity was gone forever. Most of the energies of the Carolingians who ruled these several kingdoms were absorbed in snatching bits of territory from their relatives. The resulting petty wars left little time for problems of religion, justice, internal order, and defense against the mounting attacks of outsiders. The later Carolingians continued the practice of buying support by granting new lands to nobles. This constant diminution of royal estates eventually left the Carolingian rulers powerless to curb the nobility.

High churchmen usually supported the later Carolingian kings and tried to keep alive the old imperial ideal as it had existed under Charlemagne, and the kings showed their gratitude by heaping rich endowments on the Church. But in the long run ecclesiastical support of the Carolingian family worked against the interests of the rulers.

The Church became bolder and bolder in its claims to supremacy over the state. By the middle of the ninth century the pope was openly claiming a superior authority over all Christians—including kings. Pope Nicholas I (858–867) actually tried to exercise these claims by interfering in the private lives of the kings, while at the same time carrying on extensive diplomatic negotiations in an attempt to halt the civil wars raging everywhere, legislating for the whole church, and taking the lead in spreading Christianity. The spirit of independence on the part of the Church took much of the glory away from the last Carolingian rulers.

By 900 the Carolingian dynasty was thoroughly discredited and the empire divided beyond repair. Invaders pillaged Western Europe almost at will. Landed nobles tightened their holds on their small principalities and compelled the lower classes to submit to their petty domination. Even the Church, the last bastion of unity, suffered fragmentation. The feudal age had arrived. The dream of Charlemagne and his advisers to make Western Europe a single political unit had not been fulfilled.

These obvious failures must not hide the deeper significance of the Carolingian era. The overambitious Carolingian Empire represented a youthful attempt by some Western Europeans to give expression to the uniqueness of the West. Germanic rulers—represented by Charlemagne—demonstrated a deepened awareness of a responsibility other than conquering lands for their own private profit. It is not without significance that Charlemagne became the hero of numerous legends eagerly read during the centuries following his death. He became the ideal prince for medieval Western Europe. His attempt to unify Europe politically was destined to inspire the actions of numerous later medieval kings. Several of the chief kingdoms of Europe, especially France, Germany, and Italy, traced their origin to the Carolingian period and considered themselves successors of the Carolingian kingdom. Certain Carolingian techniques of government, especially the practice of creating lord-vassal ties to define the relationship between ruler and ruled, long served as the basis for political life in these successor states. Carolingian law codes persisted for many centuries as the basis of justice in some areas of Western Europe. Under its Carolingian champions the Western Church moved further from dependence on and co-operation with the Greek Orthodox Church, succeeded in imposing a considerable degree of doctrinal and liturgical uniformity throughout the West, and gained important ground in creating an independent state in Italy. The papal role in sanctifying the Carolingians first as kings of the Franks and then as emperors established a significant precedent for the fundamental medieval idea that the state must have the blessing of the Church. The revival of the idea of empire dramatically reaffirmed the tie between Western Europe and classical Rome. As we shall see in the next section, the renewed interest in Roman civilization brought about an upsurge of intellectual activity during the Carolingian period. This Carolingian renaissance was the first of several that brought Western Europeans into more intimate contact with the classical civilizations of Greece and Rome. The true significance of the Carolingian era must thus be sought in the world of ideas. It was a period when some Western Europeans tried to define what they wanted politically, socially, religiously, and culturally. Although few of the ends pursued were attained at the time, much of later medieval history consists of working out the details of ideas brought forth in the Carolingian period.

4. The Carolingian Renaissance

The sad fate of the Carolingian Empire was slightly offset by a highly significant cultural revival. We have already indicated that the era from the fall of Rome until the eighth century was one of cultural stagnation. During the last half of the eighth and the first half of the ninth centuries a serious attempt was made to revive literature, learning, and the arts. Charlemagne was more responsible than anyone else for this revival. He felt strongly the need for more educated men to assist in running his state and his Church. Many churchmen shared his view and eagerly followed his leadership.

Charlemagne's contribution to this renaissance lay primarily in his encouragement of education. He created a palace school where were congregated some of the best minds of the period, recruited from England, Ireland, Spain, and Italy, as well as from the land of the Franks. By far the most notable luminary of the palace school was the Englishman Alcuin, who set a high standard for the study of theology and classical Roman literature. Charlemagne and his learned courtiers encouraged the establishment of schools at monasteries and bishop's churches all over the empire, endowing such institutions liberally and lending aid in the recruitment of teachers.

Educated men of the Carolingian period devoted their chief efforts to a study of the past. The Bible was studied carefully and commented upon copiously. So were the writings of the church fathers. Every important school acquired copies of the writings of the great Latin writers, thus establishing small libraries. They carefully studied the style and content of these masterpieces. They wrote long commentaries trying to explain the works to their contemporaries. Latin grammar was also studied carefully.

Inspired by the example of classical Roman and early Christian writers, many Carolingian scholars tried their own hands at writing. As a result a considerable body of poetry, history, biography, letters, and theological tracts was produced. None of these works would be ranked among the world's literary masterpieces. Some, however, have real merit. As previously noted, one of Charlemagne's courtiers, Einhard, wrote an excellent biography of the emperor. Alcuin compiled several useful textbooks in grammar and logic. An Italian, Paul the Lombard, wrote the well-organized *History of*

THE VIRGIN ENTHRONED. Produced in the tenth century, this ivory carving is typical of a style of art that flourished during the Carolingian period. This portrayal of the Virgin possesses a quality of vigor and vitality which suggests that the barbarian invasions of Western Europe had a strong effect on the plastic arts. It will be interesting to observe the development in the portrayal of the Virgin by Christian artists in later periods. (*Courtesy of The Metropolitan Museum of Art*)

the Lombards. The most competent theologian in the West since Gregory the Great was an Irishman, John Scotus Erigena, who lived in the kingdom of the West Franks from about 850 to 875. Taken together, the Carolingian scholarly and literary output, most of it produced between 775 and 875, represented a notable burst of cultural activity in an age whose general feature was cultural stagnation.

5. England in the Early Middle Ages

While the Carolingians were shaping much of Western Europe, the small Anglo-

Saxon kingdoms of England were likewise undergoing an important transformation. After a long period of fruitless warfare these kingdoms began to coalesce, chiefly as a result of two outside forces—Christianity and the Viking menace.

England had been Christianized in Roman times, but the Anglo-Saxon invaders wiped out Christianity in the territories they occupied. Late in the sixth century missionaries began to penetrate England both from Rome and from Ireland. Within a century the Anglo-Saxons were converted, and a common religion prevailed throughout the different kingdoms. For a brief period in the seventh century Roman and Irish missionaries clashed bitterly for the right to dominate England. Rome won, assuring uniformity of organization, ritual, and doctrine and putting the English in touch with the mainstream of continental religious life.

However, the second force bringing about unity in England, the terrible threat of the Vikings, was the more important. No area suffered more from their pillaging, especially during the first half of the ninth century. Some Vikings even settled permanently in England, occupying a large territory in the northeast known as the Danelaw (i.e., the land where Danish law was supreme). Several of the old Anglo-Saxon kingdoms were swallowed up by the invaders.

The kingdom of Wessex became the center of resistance and eventually of counterattack against the Vikings. The reign of Alfred the Great (871–899) was the decisive period. Alfred was a crafty, determined war leader. He not only stopped Viking expansion but also laid the groundwork for the reconquest of the Danelaw. His leadership also served to revitalize the church and dormant English intellectual life, and both of these accomplishments helped to stir up the English against foreigners. During the tenth century Alfred's heirs rewon the Danelaw, pushing the English frontier to about the present boundary between England and Scotland. All the conquered territory and its peoples, including the Danes, were made subjects of a single king, who was no longer king of Wessex but king of England.

The unification of England necessitated a single governmental system for all England. This system of government, based on institutions that had existed in England since the arrival of the Anglo-Saxons in the early fifth century, assumed its final shape by 1000. A single king, claiming to be supreme judge, leader of the army, head of the church, and lawgiver, ruled over the land. Actually, royal power was limited, since the kings lacked effective means of exercising the authority they claimed. The central government consisted chiefly of household officials who cared for the kings' personal needs. Each king supported himself and his court chiefly from the income derived from royal estates. On rare occasions the king could levy a direct tax on his subjects; for instance, several kings collected the Danegeld, levied first in 991 to buy off Viking raiders. But ordinarily this was not possible. For military support the kings depended heavily on knights to whom land had been granted, although the king could summon all freemen to serve in the army (called the *fyrd*). The king was advised on matters of great importance by the *witan*, an assembly of great nobles and churchmen that in a general way was held to represent all freemen. Usually the witan was taken into the king's counsel on matters such as waging war or enacting new laws. However, a strong king could do any of these things without the help of the witan. The whole complex of institutions sur-rounding the king—household officials, fyrd, royal knights, and witan—made the central government an institution of considerable importance, but certainly not strong enough to control political life in all England.

Much more significant in tenth-century England was the system of local government that had long been evolving. England was divided into shires, of which there were about forty in the tenth century. The king was represented in each shire by three officials—the earl, the sheriff, and the bishop. The earl was most important in rank and prestige, but the sheriff usually conducted most of the royal business. In each shire a court was held twice a year, and all freemen were expected to attend. At this court the king's orders were proclaimed and all civil and criminal cases were handled. Any freeman could bring his complaints to the court. The law administered in these courts was customary law, dating from far back in Anglo-Saxon history and known by the local landlords who sat in the court. Each shire was subdivided into smaller units called *hundreds,* where courts met monthly to deal with minor cases. A royal official presided over these courts. The agricultural villages also had their own courts and customs; great landowners usually conducted these courts. As a rule the business of the Church was conducted in the shire and hundred courts. This network of local institutions, tied to the central government through royal officials but also self-sufficient to a large extent, provided an element of orderly political life in England that was sometimes lacking on the continent.

SUGGESTED READING

Richard Winston, *Charlemagne: From the Hammer to the Cross* (1954). The latest biography in English of the central figure in Carolingian history. This book supplies a good summary of Charlemagne's career and some balanced judgments with respect to his role in Western European history.

* Henri Pirenne, *Mohammed and Charlemagne* (Meridian). First published in English in 1939. An important although much-debated study seeking to show how the Moslem seizure of the Mediterranean powerfully affected Western Europe.

M. L. W. Laistner, *Thought and Letters in Western Europe,* A.D. 500 *to* 900, new ed., rev. (1957). A brilliant book that provides an excellent discussion and evaluation of the Carolingian renaissance and of the cultural developments that lay behind it.

Einhard, *Life of Charlemagne*, included in A. J. Grant, ed., *Early Lives of Charlemagne* (1907). A short biography by a contemporary of Charlemagne, especially good for the insights it provides into the habits and character of the great warrior-statesman who dominated Europe in the era around 800.

Eleanor Shipley Duckett, *Alcuin, Friend of Charlemagne: His World and His Work* (1951). A valuable guide for a reader seeking to understand the intellectual activity that centered around Charlemagne's court.

Axel Olrik, *Viking Civilization* (1930). This volume presents a brief history of the Vikings and a clear description of the chief features of Viking culture, especially as that culture is reflected in the Sagas.

Charles Homer Haskins, *The Normans in European History* (1915). A reader who has become interested in the Norsemen as a result of encountering them as raiders of Europe in the ninth century may enjoy following up on some of these raiders in later history. This book provides an excellent account of the ef-reflected in the sagas.

Eleanor Shipley Duckett, *Alfred the Great* (1956). A brief, dramatic presentation of the career of England's greatest king during the early Middle Ages.

CHAPTER 18

The Emergence of the Feudal and Manorial Systems

THE COLLAPSE of the Carolingian Empire forced Western Europeans to fall back on more workable political, social, and economic foundations. Two basic institutions characterized the new order: feudalism and manorialism. Both institutions represent the final product of the long search for order that had been going on since the fall of Rome, and they became the basis upon which Western European society was built during later centuries.

1. The Origins and Nature of Feudalism

Seeking a workable substitute to replace the Carolingian governmental system, Europeans turned in desperation toward the establishment of personal agreements between individuals. In essence that was what the feudal system was. It consisted of private contracts whereby one man willingly accepted the status of being an honorable dependent of another. By the terms of such agreements each party pledged himself to do certain things of a political nature for the other. These private contracts were sealed and guaranteed by grants of land that provided the parties involved with the means to fulfill their obligations.

The origins of this system of private contract were very ancient. Both the Germans and the Romans had long ago developed systems of personal dependence in which individuals pledged themselves to perform services for others in return for some favor. The Romans had also developed a system of landholding based on use of land instead of outright ownership. These early institutions of personal dependence and land tenure became more widespread in Western Europe after the Germanic invasions. To escape the turmoil of the Merovingian era, many men were glad to find a protector to whom they could swear allegiance and render personal services. Others were willing to turn the title to their land over to someone capable of protecting it as long as they were allowed the use of the land.

During the Carolingian period even kings began using these practices, thus giving them clear legal status. The great men in the kingdom swore oaths of allegiance to the Carolingian rulers, and lesser men likewise bound themselves to more powerful landholders, thus creating, in the terminology of the period, a system of lords and their dependent vassals. Grants of land, called benefices or fiefs, were made in return for military aid and political services. The kings even went so far as to grant immunities to those who received land from them, meaning that the king gave landholders permission to exercise the power of government on their lands, which henceforth would be immune from royal control.

The Church also used the practice of granting benefices as a means of exploiting its ever-increasing amount of land and of securing the forces necessary to protect its holdings.

The eclipse of workable government in the ninth century forced society to depend almost entirely on these ancient usages. Amid the civil wars and the invasions that accompanied the breakup of the Carolingian state all men who had any freedom of choice hastened to become vassals of anyone who could protect them. Strong individuals, anxious to acquire vassals who would serve as soldiers, were eager to grant their lands in return for military service. With no other effective form of government in operation, the holders of land simply assumed the right to provide government for it. Europe was thus divided into hundreds of tiny private states ruled by the persons who held the land at the moment. The relationships between the people involved were governed wholly by the terms of their private agreement; there was no such thing as public law.

One important point must be added. Long before the ninth century the bulk of the peasant population had already become associated with the manors (self-sufficient agricultural estates) dotting the map of Europe, being attached to the land in such a way that they had no freedom to choose another lot. As a consequence they were not, properly speaking, participants in the feudal system. The status of lords and vassals was reserved to an aristocratic class, the members of which were capable of performing honorable services like fighting and governing. Fiefs were granted only to members of this noble class. The feudal system was therefore a political system affecting the relationship of a small class of nobles. These same nobles ruled over the peasant population on a basis that will be described in the discussion of the manorial system.

2. The Feudal Contract

A definite ritual developed to signify the creation of a feudal contract. Kneeling before a lord, the lesser noble placed his hands between those of the lord and declared himself the lord's "man" or vassal. The lord then lifted the new vassal to his feet and kissed him as a sign of acceptance. This process was called *homage*. The vassal then swore an *oath of fealty*, thereby binding himself religiously to live up to his obligations. The lord thereupon gave to the vassal some object like a banner, a clod of dirt, or a ring. This was called *investiture*. It symbolized the granting of a fief, usually a piece of land, by the lord to the vassal. By the three acts of homage, fealty, and investiture two individuals bound themselves together in a way that gave to each important rights and imposed on each duties that controlled his political and social activities to a large degree.

The relationship between lord and vassal was intended to last until one party died, unless either broke the contract by some illegal act. By the time the feudal system had reached its full development in the tenth century, the whole arrangement had become hereditary. When a lord died, his eldest son took his place, receiving homage and fealty from his father's vassals and investing them with their fiefs. When a vassal died, his lord accepted his son as a vassal and permitted him to retain the fief of his father. Under these arrangements lord-vassal relationships continued for generations in the same families.

The exact obligations of each party differed to such an extent that it is difficult to describe them accurately. Generally, however, there were certain basic duties for each party. The lord obligated himself to protect his vassal and give him justice. In an age when there was no effective central government this meant that a lord was obligated to use his army to protect a vassal against attack. It also meant that the lord had to maintain a court where the vassal could appear and receive a hearing for any grievances he might have. Put briefly, it imposed on the lord the grave responsibility of running a small-scale government for his vassals.

The vassal's duties were usually more specific. His first obligation was *military service* as an armed knight for forty days a year at his own expense. The vassal also owed *counsel and advice* to his lord, meaning that he had to appear at the lord's court when summoned and to perform any political duties the lord might require. The third obligation of a vassal was to give *aids*. This meant that under certain conditions a vassal had to make a specified money payment to his lord. Usually there were three cases when an aid was required: the ransom of a lord who had become a prisoner of war, the knighting of a lord's eldest son, and the marriage of his eldest daughter. A lord might require other aids from his vassals, but usually only with their consent. A fourth duty that befell a vassal was that of *hospitality*, that is, to entertain his lord and the lord's party when the lord happened to travel through the fief; this could be a great burden when the lord came often with a big following and stayed long. Finally, a vassal's heir usually had to pay an inheritance tax, called a *relief*, when he succeeded his father as vassal and fief holder. In addition, the vassal had to maintain the fief in good condition, since it did not really belong to him. He had to recognize the lord's right of guardianship of the vassal's eventual heir and approval of the marriage of his daughter since her husband might someday become heir to the fief and to the status of vassal. He was obliged to recognize that if he died without heirs the fief was to revert to the lord. And the vassal was expected to conduct himself honorably and loyally so as not to disgrace his lord.

How were these mutual obligations enforced? When a contract is made in present-day society, the state stands above the parties as the enforcing agency. In the tenth century there was no state capable of enforcing feudal contracts. Enforcement was a matter to be settled by lords and vassals. The lord maintained a court before which unworthy vassals could be summoned and judged. Every vassal had the right to bring complaints against his lord and gain redress or be freed from his duties as a vassal. In numerous cases these courts did act as enforcing agencies upholding feudal contracts, but force was always a last recourse. A lord could march against a rebellious vassal, and a vassal could raise the standard of revolt against an unjust or unfaithful lord. Such wars were numerous in the feudal age and often caused considerable suffering among all elements of society. It would be wrong, however, to picture feudal lords and vassals as seeking any opportunity to start a brawl. In a society that knew no other workable political system lords were anxious to keep their vassals and gain their services. And vassals were equally anxious to enjoy the protection of a lord, even though he might not be a paragon of virtue, for it was from him alone that they received protection and justice. Thus it was to the mutual advantage of each party to live up to the terms of the contract. And then it must be remembered that the contract was sealed by an oath of fealty. In an age when men took religion seriously there was a good deal of reluctance to break a promise sealed in the presence of God.

3. Feudalism and the State

In theory the feudal system was an ideal way of governing a state of any size. The king was the supreme lord and theoretical owner of all the land in the kingdom. At his own pleasure he had granted out his land as fiefs to men who became his vassals. Each owed him the services previously described. Perhaps the king had also granted his greater vassals rights of immunity, which permitted them to exercise the powers of government over their fiefs. The great vassals of a king could then subdivide their holdings into smaller fiefs and grant them to other men willing to become vassals. This process of division could be continued until land had been subdivided into fiefs so small that they would support a single vassal and allow him to provide arms to maintain himself as a knight. In theory a vast hierarchy was constructed, with a king at the top and with each rank downward owing allegiance and services to an authority above. That theoretical hierarchy might be illustrated by the following diagram.

ments had been established, several interesting situations could arise. Suppose A and D went to war. Whom would F serve, since he owed military service to each? We can see clearly that the orderly hierarchy would be broken down. Suppose that by all his deals F acquired control over more land than any of his lords—A, B, C, D, or E. Who would be master of the situation then? Obviously the vassal would be in a position

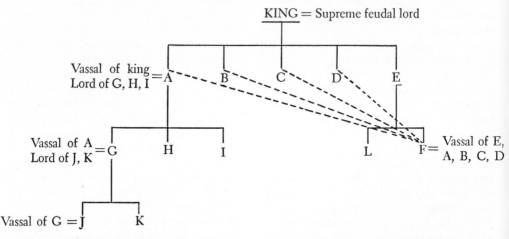

In practice the feudal system did not work so smoothly. First, the king's authority was only theoretical. If he should grant too much of his land, he had no means at his disposal to enforce his authority over his vassals. Although they owed him services, there was little he could do to force them to render those services if he had no means of backing up his orders. The same fate might befall any lord in the feudal hierarchy if he granted away too much of his land to vassals.

Another situation that upset the feudal hierarchy was the process of subinfeudation. There was nothing to keep a vassal of one lord from becoming the vassal of and accepting a fief from another lord. To illustrate the confusion that resulted from this practice, let us return to the diagram above. Vassal F, an ambitious, capable man, dissatisfied with his status as a simple vassal of E, also does homage to A, B, C, and D in return for fiefs from each one, owing services for each of these fiefs. Once these agree-

to defy his lords and turn the feudal hierarchy upside down. The reader can work out other possible arrangements of the parties in our diagram. He can see clearly that subinfeudation created conflicting allegiances and confusing alignments that destroyed the theoretical hierarchy, thus making it impossible for feudalism to operate effectively for the control of a large state.

In view of these considerations it can be seen that the feudal system seriously impeded the growth of extensive kingdoms. By about 900 the feudal system had worked its most serious effects on those kingdoms that had emerged out of the division of the Carolingian Empire—the kingdom of the West Franks (France), the kingdom of the East Franks (Germany), the kingdom of Italy, and the kingdom of Burgundy (or Arles). Theoretically the king of each of these states possessed extensive powers to legislate, dispense justice, collect taxes, maintain armies, and command the services of his subjects. Actually, each had divided his kingdom into numerous fiefs, which he had granted to vassals in return for services. Often the royal vassals were granted or had usurped extensive immunities from royal authority, thereby acquiring the right to exercise political power on their own within their fiefs. This granting of fiefs divided each kingdom into a confusing array of counties, duchies, viscounties, marches, and comparable principalities. Most of the larger fiefs granted by the kings were further subdivided, the direct vassals of the kings acquiring vassals of their own. Among the vassals and subvassals in each of the kingdoms there existed a bewildering array of cross relationships that blurred clear lines of authority or allegiance. Some of the great vassals of the kings managed to maintain authority over their subvassals, thereby creating well-governed feudal principalities functioning on the basis of the rights and obligations contained in feudal contracts. However, other great fief holders were just as ineffective as the kings in controlling their vassals. In a practical sense, then, the feudal system led over much of Europe to a regime of small principalities, each having its own law, its own feudal hierarchy, and its own manner of handling political problems. The great kingdoms were not functioning, organic states, headed by monarchs exercising effective political power. Instead they were communities of individuals tied together by interdependency as lords and vassals. Within these communities individuals acquired the right to exercise political powers over the land they controlled. Each kingdom was thus a collection of private governments, each of which might, but often did not, respect the authority of the king who was theoretically lord of all.

4. Feudalism and the Church

Feudalism had a drastic effect on another vital institution in Western society: the Church. Under the guidance of the great Carolingian rulers of the eighth and early ninth century the Church had enjoyed a tremendous upsurge in power and influence, owing to better organization, a reform of the clergy, and a standardization of ritual and doctrine. The coming of feudalism undid most of this work and pushed the Church into one of its worst periods of decay and inefficiency.

The difficulties of the Church in feudal society stemmed from its position as a great landholder. Much of the Church's land had been acquired in the form of grants from kings. The Carolingian rulers had been especially generous. However, they expected the officials of the Church who received land to render services as did any other recipient of royal lands. Bishops and abbots had to become vassals of the kings and fulfill their obligations as vassals. The great Church officials were not even averse to receiving fiefs from powerful laymen other than the king and accepting positions as vassals of these lords. Once having acquired large fiefs, Church officials acted as did other landholders of the feudal age. They granted their lands out as fiefs, thus becoming lords in their own turn. As lords they had to concern themselves with protecting their vassals, holding courts, and protecting their interests in general.

There is little use in condemning Church officials for this conduct. In the feudal age those who had no land had no power. And those who had no lords to protect them or vassals to serve them did not long survive. Churchmen were only adapting themselves to the times. However, the results were tragic. The ruling officials of the Church became completely preoccupied with secular matters at the expense of their religious duties. Laymen who granted fiefs to Church officials wanted to be sure that the fief fell into capable hands. They refused to invest any bishop or abbot with a fief unless he had the qualities befitting a good vassal. In effect this meant that laymen controlled elections to high offices. These offices came to be filled with good fighters and good administrators who had little interest in religious problems. Once in office, such officials devoted most of their time to ruling their own vassals and engaging in war and politics. The whole top level of the church organization was dominated by men who were laymen and feudal nobles at heart. They neglected discipline, education, charity, moral conduct, and all the other matters properly associated with running a religious establishment. The lower clergy sank into ignorance. Religious life in lay society suffered an assortment of evils worse than in any other age in Christian history. Even the pope, who was the head of the Church, did not escape. During the tenth century the papal office was filled with men chosen by powerful feudal lords in central Italy. Most of these popes were only tools of these nobles and were looked upon with contempt by Christians in the rest of Western Europe.

5. The Feudal Nobility

The emergence of the feudal system created a clearly defined noble class into which the lower classes seldom entered. This class was governed by its own laws. Its members concerned themselves with government and warfare but did not perform manual labor. However, the chief distinction of this class lay in its unique way of life, so fascinating that it still catches the imagination.

Perhaps the best way to picture the feudal way of life is to follow the career of a typical noble from his youth onward. If his father were important enough, our noble would probably be born in a castle designed primarily to serve as a defensive stronghold in an age of almost constant warfare. Feudal nobles of lesser means usually lived in manor houses built on the land from which the noble gained his living. By the time he was seven, the noble youth began his education as a member of the feudal class. He was usually sent to serve some other noble; often the father placed his son in the court of his lord. First as a page and then as a squire, the youth learned the ways of the feudal class. He was taught the difficult art of fighting on horseback in full armor, the rudiments of the Christian religion, and the proper etiquette. He observed at first

hand the operation of feudal justice and the management of feudal estates. Most important, he had impressed on him the moral code of his class, called chivalry. He was taught to be loyal to his companions, to be honorable in fulfilling any obligations he assumed, to be brave, to be truthful, to respect the Church, and to protect the weak. As feudal morality developed, chivalry eventually included a code of behavior with respect to women. A chivalrous gentleman was taught to protect and honor all women, but especially some particular lady with whom he had formed a romantic attachment. This lady need not be his future wife; she became to the chivalrous gentleman a kind of ideal in whose service and for whose honor he could perform great deeds.

By the time he was twenty-one, the young noble would have completed his education. He then experienced the greatest event of his life—his knighting. In an elaborate ceremony in which the Church participated, he was invested with arms and other insignia of his class. He was now ready for a career as a noble. Sometime during these years our noble would have taken a wife, also of noble birth. He probably had little to say about this matter, marriages being arranged by fathers with an eye for gaining new lands, new vassals, or some other political and economic advantage. The newly dubbed knight often served his father's lord in the years immediately following his knighting. He spent his days hunting, feasting, and engaging in the exciting mock warfare of the tournaments. Occasionally a real war required his services. Eventually the gentleman's father would die, whereupon the son inherited his father's position, becoming a vassal to the lord or lords whom his father had served and accepting as vassals all those who had been his father's vassals. He would move into his father's castle or manor house and take over his father's land. By this time he hoped to have a son of his own who could be started through the process we have just described.

Most of the information we have about the daily life of the feudal nobility suggests that they lived a crude, rough, violent life.

A Medieval Fortress. This fortress at Carcassone in southern France, built chiefly during the twelfth and thirteenth centuries, was one of the most powerful strongholds in all medieval Europe. Its heavy gates, deep moat, double walls, and fortified towers exemplify military defenses during the feudal age. (*Courtesy, French Government Tourist Office*)

The nobles ate and drank heavily. Their living quarters were cold, dark, and poorly furnished. They were quick to anger and to resort to violence. They enjoyed hunting and gambling more than was good for them. Their appreciation of the arts was confined to dancing, epic poems about great warriors, and songs with an earthy flavor. They were religious only in the sense that they believed in God and attended religious ceremonies. Only slowly were the manners of the nobles refined and their mode of living made more luxurious.

6. The Manorial System

Below the feudal nobility, and supporting them, labored the great mass of the medieval population. Their lives were bound up completely in the manorial system. In trying to understand this institution two things must always be kept in mind. First, the manor was a unit of land organized so that it would produce nearly everything required to support its lord and the laborers who worked on it. Second, it was a system of government through which order and justice were supplied to all those who lived on it.

The typical manor consisted of several hundred acres, its size being determined by the need for self-sufficiency. A workable manor had to have arable land for raising crops, meadowland for hay and pasture, woodland for fuel and building material, and a natural water supply. A feudal noble might be able to carve several such self-sufficient units out of his fief, the size of the fief having little to do with the size of the manor.

Of the tillable land on each manor from one third to one half was set aside for the lord's support. The rest was divided into small tenancies and allotted to the peasants for their own support. The non-tillable land, like meadows, pastures, and woods, was exploited in common, the individual's share being determined by custom. In the actual farming of the land the open field system was used. The land was divided into open fields of considerable size. Each large field was subdivided into strips of about an acre. The lord reserved some of these strips in each large field to himself and assigned others in each field to each tenant. In this way everyone got a share of good and bad land.

Farming techniques were crude. Most labor was done by hand, since few peasants could support heavy-eating oxen. Teams of oxen for heavy jobs like plowing and hauling farm equipment were communally owned. Most labor was performed as a common effort. To protect the fertility of the soil, the three-field system was employed over much of Europe. The arable land of each manor was divided into three open fields, lord and tenants having strips in each. Every year one field lay fallow, a second was planted to wheat in the fall, and a third to barley or rye in the spring. A regular rotation followed in succeeding years. In spite of this system of rotation yields were small. Aside from the crop-growing land each manor produced hay from its meadows and had facilities for pasturing a limited number of animals. Pigs and goats were especially popular because they could live off the woods and wasteland. Some peasants raised a few vegetables in the meager plots surrounding their huts.

Food and animals were not the only things produced on a manor; most manufactured goods had to be made there, since there was little trade. Although specialized artisans such as blacksmiths, carpenters, and masons sometimes plied their trades on the manors, the peasants were generally required to make and to repair the equip-

ment, buildings, and furnishings needed to sustain life. Women, including noble ladies, were skilled at making clothing, preserving food, concocting medicine, and a dozen other things. As a result the manor had little need for the outside world; it was self-sufficient.

The center of a manor was a village containing a manor house, peasant huts, a church, granaries, a mill, a bakery, and the like. This village was more than a collection of buildings. It was a community containing a government and a social system. Its governor was the manorial lord, whose position was defined by the feudal society. He had his obligations as a vassal and possibly as a lord. On his manor he was master. Perhaps only the Church could control his activity, although the Church's influence consisted chiefly in persuasion. If the lord lived on the manor, he usually exercised his power in person. If he lived elsewhere, he entrusted the management of his manor to a steward. Each manor had its own governmental institutions—a court, a law based on ancient customs, and a police force. Manorial law or custom usually consisted of a vast body of tradition defining every aspect of the relationship between a manorial lord and his subjects.

The peasant inhabitants of a manor were divided into numerous classes depending upon their obligations to the lord. Perhaps it is not too important to inquire into the fine legal distinctions within the ranks of the peasantry, since all peasants lived much alike. Most of them in the tenth and eleventh century were serfs, bound to the soil and at the mercy of their lord. The only thing that distinguished a serf from a slave was the fact that the serf could not be parted from the soil of which he was a part. Some peasants were not actually serfs but freemen (villeins) who had rented land from a lord in return for specified services and payments. However, their general economic and social condition differed very little from that of the serfs.

The main job of all peasants was to work the land of their lord. Custom usually dic-

MEDIEVAL PEASANTS AT WORK. These manuscript illustrations made during the later Middle Ages show the activities of typical peasants, and give some idea of the agricultural techniques employed. Since so little was written about the medieval peasant, a careful study of a large number of such manuscript illustrations provides one of the best ways of grasping the essence of manorial life in the Middle Ages. (*Above, The Bettmann Archive; below, Walters Art Gallery, Baltimore*)

tated that a serf had to devote three days a week to working for the lord; many free tenants also were required to labor for the lord as partial payment of their rent. From time to time extra work, called boon work, could be required in order to accomplish such things as repair of buildings and building of roads. What time the peasant had left was devoted to the cultivation of his own land, from which he derived his living. Usually the lord collected a share of all the produce raised; this is but another way of saying that every peasant was taxed heavily. The peasants were also required to pay for the use of bakeries and mills provided by the lord, and for hunting in his forest. Almost everywhere lords collected a death tax (*heriot*), usually the best animal the peasant possessed. The function of a medieval serf was thus clear; his job was to labor on the land for the profit of the lord who controlled it. In return he got permanent use of a few acres of land from which he had to derive his own livelihood. Anything he gained beyond a bare livelihood could be taken from him by his lord.

There were, however, limits on the extent to which peasants could be exploited. The lord of the manor was dependent upon their co-operation. Extreme cruelty might well upset the functioning of the manorial economy, causing the lord to lose his income and thus ruining him in the feudal society in which he was a member. He had to act with some justice and benevolence toward those who were actually little more than slaves. He had to keep them alive, healthy, and reasonably contented. This is not to deny that the medieval peasant lived a hard life. But it was softened somewhat by the benevolence of a paternalistic lord who needed the help of the serfs under his jurisdiction. The manorial system was capable of supplying security to the serf in a society that tended to be insecure, and the assurance that there was a permanent place for him on the manor must have been a source of contentment for most serfs. Within his family and among his friends in the manorial village the medieval serf probably found some pleasures to compensate for his long hours of labor and his low standard of living.

SUGGESTED READING

* Carl Stephenson, *Mediaeval Feudalism* (Cornell). The best brief discussion of the nature of the feudal order. The author not only deals with fundamental feudal practices but also presents a clear picture of chivalry, the noble class, and the effects of feudalism on political life in Europe.

F. L. Ganshof, *Feudalism*, tr. by Philip Grierson (1952). A short discussion of the development of feudalism from the Merovingian period to the thirteenth century. The book is especially good for its clear definitions of basic feudal terminology. The author employs ample illustrative material to give concreteness to his definitions.

P. Boissonnade, *Life and Work in Medieval Europe*, tr. by Eileen Power (1927). An excellent and full discussion touching many phases of medieval social history.

* N. Neilson, *Medieval Agrarian Economy* (Berkshire Series, 1936). A brief but excellent discussion of the main features of medieval manorialism.

H. S. Bennett, *Life on an English Manor* (1937). A detailed description of an English manor in the Middle Ages, especially good for its portrayal of the peasant's condition.

William Stearns Davis, *Life on a Mediaeval Barony* (1923). An interesting although somewhat oversimplified study of a sample French fief, giving a picture of feudal manorial society in the Middle Ages.

* Sidney Painter, *Mediaeval Society* (Cornell). A brief but sharply drawn picture of the chief medieval classes and their manner of life.

* Eileen Power, *Medieval People* (Anchor). Published originally as a hardback edition in 1924. A delightful description of medieval society in which the author has selected typical representatives of the major social groups in medieval society and has then drawn imaginative sketches of their manner of life.

* *The Song of Roland*, tr. by Charles Scott Moncrieff (1931). Also many other editions. This epic poem, written about 1100 to recount the exploits of Charlemagne and his followers in their attack on the Moslems in Spain, provides the best insight into the ideals of the feudal nobility. Moreover, this book tells a good story well.

SECTION 5

---◆---

The High Middle Ages, 1000–1300:

The Revival of Europe

T he belief circulated widely in Europe after the breakup of the Carolingian Empire that the world would come to an end in the year 1000. According to one medieval writer, when that fateful year passed uneventfully, Europeans suddenly threw themselves with great energy into rebuilding. This bit of medieval legend actually reflects an important fact about Western European history. Somewhere around 1000 Western Europe did begin to revive. Building upon the feudal order, the manorial system, and a common religion, the Europeans shaped new political institutions, expanded their economy, revitalized the church, and produced a vigorous distinctive culture. Their new wealth and organization permitted them to turn back the tide of invasion that had so long threatened Europe; the contraction that had been so long a feature of Western European history gave way to expansion. This period of creative activity embraced about three centuries—from 1000 to 1300; it is often referred to as the High Middle Ages.

CHAPTER 19

Germany and Italy:

The Holy Roman Empire to 1273

THE POLITICAL history of Europe from 1000 to 1300 is chiefly a story of the building from a feudal base of new states and new institutions of government. The most spectacular attempt to reconstruct political life occurred in Germany, but the attempt ended in a tragic failure that doomed the Germans to play a secondary role in European political history until the modern period.

1. The Last Carolingians

The kingdom of the East Franks, or Germany, was created as an independent political unit by the Treaty of Verdun in 843, when the sons of Louis the Pious carved the Carolingian Empire into three parts. For almost a century after that division the new kingdoms suffered from the growing political disorder that was spreading over all Europe. In Germany that disorder took the form of the division of the kingdom into small principalities whose boundaries corresponded roughly with those of the ancient Germanic nations that had existed before the Frankish rulers of the Merovingian and Carolingian houses conquered the land east of the Rhine. The later Carolingians failed to maintain control over the counts and dukes who ruled these principalities, the chief of which were Saxony, Bavaria, Franconia, Swabia, and Lorraine. The princes steadily took over royal governmental functions, revolted against any attempt by the king to interfere, and fought with one another for more land. Under these circumstances the Carolingian kings were gradually reduced to figureheads. By 911 the great dukes had repudiated the Carolingian idea of strong government by electing as king one of their own breed, Conrad, the duke of Franconia. The title of king had been reduced to an honor to be passed among the great families of Germany.

The weakness of the last Carolingians and the subdivision of Germany brought on another grave crisis—foreign invasion. In the last years of the ninth and the early years of the tenth centuries Germany was devastated by raiding Norsemen and Magyars. The latter, representing another assault on Europe by Asiatic nomads, were especially destructive. The frontier defenses that Charlemagne had constructed and maintained were now but a memory; only those who could organize a local defense under a local landowner were safe.

2. The Saxon Dynasty and the Renewal of the Holy Roman Empire

The disintegration of Germany was suddenly checked during the course of the tenth century. The credit for this accomplishment rests with a family of rulers springing from Saxony. When Conrad died in 919 his greatest foe, Henry, duke of Saxony, was elected king. As Henry I (919–936) he created a solid basis from which his son, Otto I (936–973), could make Germany the greatest kingdom in Europe. Otto was a man of great vigor and vision, and upon becoming king he set himself to the task of becoming the effective ruler of Germany. The most pressing problem was to curb the independence of the great dukes. After years of struggle Otto succeeded, but only after uprooting some of the old ducal families and replacing them with more obedient vassals, often his own relatives.

In the meantime Otto continued his father's policy of checking the Magyar invasions. His efforts were rewarded in 955 at the great battle of Lechfeld; the royal armies smashed the Magyar horde so completely that it never again seriously threatened Germany. Otto was hailed as the savior of Germany and Christendom. Not content to trust the future to one military victory, Otto began a policy of eastward expansion that continued for centuries, generating no end of trouble between Germans and Slavs.

While curbing the nobles and beating back invaders Otto made another decision of momentous importance. Searching for someone to help him with the pressing problems of administering his kingdom, he chose to form an intimate political alliance with the clergy. Convinced that clergymen were more loyal to the idea of monarchy than lay nobles, he decided to rely largely upon church officials for the performance of the services he needed to rule Germany. To secure their services, Otto made large grants of land on what amounted to a feudal basis. Ecclesiastical principalities were created in every corner of Germany. In return for his generosity Otto secured the military and political services he needed, leaving him to a degree independent of lay nobles and in a better position to curb their ambitions. To make this policy work, Otto had to be sure that the right kind of men filled ecclesiasti-

cal offices. This consideration forced him to assume the power to elect the clergymen (this was called lay investiture) who were to receive his lands and to serve him. The German church was thus converted into an institution serving the monarchy.

Dedicated to uniting and defending his kingdom and served well by his ecclesiastical servants, Otto made German monarchy the strongest in tenth-century Europe—so strong that he could entertain new dreams of power and greatness. These dreams led him to Italy and to a revival of the Carolingian idea of a European empire. Italy by the middle of the tenth century was in complete chaos. Dozens of ambitious princes were struggling to create independent principalities as a substitute for the united kingdom that had been established during the breakup of the Carolingian Empire. When this internal competition led the Magyars and the Moslems to attack, many Italian powers pleaded for Otto's intervention. Not the least important of these were the popes, who suffered badly as captives of local Roman aristocrats and sought a liberator who would restore papal independence. Otto did not remain unconcerned about the situation in Italy. During an initial venture in 951 he assumed the vague title of "King of Italy," but he did not clarify his position until 961-962, when he again marched into Italy, captured Rome, and got Pope John XII to crown him Holy Roman Emperor, thus assuming the title that the Carolingians had once held.

Having secured control over all but the southern portion of Italy, Otto now had to make his power permanent. He proceeded as he had in Germany. Quarrelsome aristocrats were forced to admit his authority and obey his commands a vassals. Great church-men in Italy served as his chief allies. Especially important was Otto's treatment of the papacy. John XII had hoped to find an ally so occupied in distant places that he would allow the pope to rule central Italy independently. Otto had no such idea; he expected the bishop of Rome to serve him as other churchmen did. When John refused to accept a subservient position, Otto deposed him and arranged the election of a more pliant successor. The emperor further imposed the rule that no pope would be elected without the consent of the emperor. Although Otto had to spend most of the remaining years of his reign intervening in Roman affairs to make this rule stick, he succeeded. The emperor was supreme, even over the pope.

Thus was reestablished the Holy Roman Empire, embracing Germany and Italy and claiming a vague authority over all Christian princes in the West. Otto's intention was certainly good—to restore order in Germany and Italy, to check the usurpation of power by selfish landowners, and to stop the attacks by outsiders. He left his heirs a heavy burden to bear, but he had made the German ruler the greatest figure in Europe—the Holy Roman Emperor, master of Germany and Italy, heir of Charlemagne.

3. Otto's Successors and the Gathering Opposition

From Otto's death in 973 until 1056 a succession of five emperors continued the main lines of Otto's policies with considerable success. They kept up the struggle with the great nobles scattered over Germany and Italy, retained a tight control over the great Church officials, including the pope, and exerted strong pressure to the east with such success that by 1056 Poland, Bohemia, and Hungary all recognized German overlordship. German influence was strong even in Western Europe. And although the old dream of a Europe united under one emperor was not fulfilled, the Holy Roman Empire under German rule was by 1056 an extensive and influential state, far excelling contemporary kingdoms in France, England, or Spain.

The power of the German emperors was, however, opposed by many foes. These enemies slowly gathered strength in the latter part of the tenth and early eleventh centuries. As might be suspected, feudal nobles in Germany and Italy never accepted Otto

the Great and his successors happily. They resented royal authority and royal taxation, desiring a king who would allow them greater independence.

In northern Italy another enemy of German overlordship rapidly gained strength during the eleventh century. The Italian towns, waxing rich as the leaders in the revival of commerce that was beginning in Europe, hated to be dominated by the Italian bishops who were the chief agents of the German kings in Italy and who had no sympathy for trade and no appreciation of commercial problems. The towns wanted to control their own political destinies so that they could pursue their commercial interests without restraint.

Another situation in Italy seriously threatened German power. A group of Norman warriors, descendants of the Viking invaders who seized the territory of Normandy in France early in the tenth century, had migrated to southern Italy and Sicily. By early in the eleventh century, having created well-organized states for themselves there, they turned northward with the idea of seizing all of Italy and thus came into conflict with the Holy Roman Emperors. Their enmity, coupled with that of the Slavs to the east and the French to the west, confronted the Holy Roman Emperors with the grave danger of foreign attacks on their sprawling empire and challenged their claims to universal authority.

These foes, threatening as they were, were slight compared with the resurgent Church. Repeatedly it has been stressed that the Holy Roman Empire was based on the ability of the emperor to exploit the services of loyal churchmen. This grew steadily more difficult in the eleventh century as the Church strove to gain its independence from the lay control under which it had suffered since the emergence of the feudal system.

A fundamental reform movement pointing to this end had started in a monastery founded at Cluny in France in 910. In this new monastery great stress was placed on the strict observance of the old Benedictine rule. Even more important, the new monastery was completely free from lay control. Its fame spread far and wide, until eventually over three hundred monasteries in Europe belonged to the Cluniac Order. The Cluniac Order vigorously promoted two basic ideas—moral purity of the clergy and independence of the Church from lay control. Put another way, the Cluniac monks became the chief preachers against the feudalization of the Church.

From the monasteries the reforming spirit of Cluny spread abroad. Many bishops accepted its ideals, especially in connection with corruption among the clergymen under their authority. Important laymen also became enthusiastic supporters of the idea of Church reform. Among those none was more ardent than the Emperor Henry III (1039–56). Henry's enthusiasm went so far that he installed a dedicated reformer, Leo IX (1049–54), as pope. This was a fateful event in German history. Once the reformers were established in Rome they began to have exalted ideas about purifying and strengthening the papacy and the Church all over Europe.

The principal figure driving the papacy toward the leadership of the reform movement and toward re-establishing the independence of the Church was Hildebrand, who served as a power behind the papal throne for many years before becoming Pope Gregory VII in 1073. He was strongly convinced that God had created man to seek salvation and had instituted the Church as the sole means whereby salvation could be gained. The Church had at its head the successor of St. Peter, the pope at Rome, whose responsibility was to make the Church a perfect instrument for saving souls. Since salvation was the chief business of man, the Church must be superior to all other kinds of authority and the pope must be the head of all society.

During many years Hildebrand and the popes he served shaped their attack on the evils in the Church that seemed to hinder the attainment of this ideal and on the laymen who controlled the Church everywhere in Europe. Legislation began to issue from

Rome against the immorality and corruption afflicting the clergy, especially against simony (buying church offices) and violation of the law of celibacy. Slowly the popes began to shape a machinery to enforce this legislation all over Europe. In 1059 a papal decree provided that henceforth new popes would be chosen by the college of cardinals, made up of clergymen holding certain churches in the city of Rome. The emperor, long accustomed to selecting popes, was no longer to have a voice except to approve what the cardinals did. The revitalized papacy did not neglect more mundane matters, either. Also in 1059 a formal alliance was established between the papacy and the Normans in southern Italy. The pope gave the Normans the right to possess certain lands in return for their promise to protect the papacy.

Naturally, opposition began to grow throughout Europe against these papal actions. Immoral clergymen, especially those guilty of simony, began to squirm at the talk of moral reform. Many sincere bishops and abbots, long accustomed to local independence, resented Rome's interference in their local affairs. Laymen were uneasy at the prospect of losing the right to appoint Church officials and with it control over the Church's extensive lands. If the popes were successful, the whole feudal order was endangered. No one was more alarmed, however, than the Holy Roman emperors, who relied on a subservient Church as a chief source of power.

This opposition did not daunt Hildebrand, who upon his election to the papacy as Gregory VII struck hard to carry on the reform. The legislation against corrupt clergymen became stronger; Gregory went so far as to begin deposing bishops whom he judged guilty. In 1075 he decreed that henceforth lay investiture, that is, the filling of a Church office by a layman, was prohibited. As was to be expected, one of the first violators of this decree was the Holy Roman Emperor, Henry IV (1056–1106). Gregory VII took an unprecedented step: he excommunicated Henry IV. With this act the struggle for supremacy of the Church against the empire was clearly set forth. And the Church soon found it could count on other foes of the empire.

4. The Investiture Struggle and Its Consequences, 1076–1152

At the time the papacy was declaring its headship over the Church and beginning to free itself from lay control, the German emperor was temporarily incapable of decisive action. Henry III had died in 1056, leaving a young son, Henry IV, who did not come of age until 1065. While he was a minor, numerous German and Italian nobles revolted in hopes of weakening the royal power, and once he began to rule Henry IV had to spend several years restoring order. In doing this he demonstrated that he was a man of great ability, hardly to be frightened by the proclamations of the popes at Rome. Thus he paid no attention to Gregory's prohibition of lay investiture and proceeded to elect men of his own choice to Church offices. When Gregory warned him in 1076, Henry IV wrote the pope, accusing him of having gained office illegally and of being unfit to be a pope. Gregory's answer was to excommunicate Henry, deprive him of his royal power, and free all his subjects of their feudal vows. He also invited the Germans to elect a new king. They were happy to comply, giving Henry a year to remove the excommunication or be replaced by a new king chosen by the nobles.

Henry IV was not one to be put to flight easily. His next step was as surprising as Gregory's. With his kingdom slipping away from him, he left Germany for Italy. In January 1077 he appeared at Canossa, where Gregory was staying. Barefoot and dressed in coarse clothes, he approached the pope for forgiveness. Gregory was in a difficult spot. If he forgave Henry, the king could return to Germany and suppress his rebellious subjects, having been purified by none less than the pope himself. If he refused to forgive a repentant sinner, he was obviously an unworthy clergyman. Gregory soon reached

a decision; he absolved Henry. In doing so he risked alienating papal supporters in Germany. But at least the papacy had won a great moral victory: the greatest ruler of Europe had come crawling for forgiveness.

Henry IV made good use of his return to grace. Having restored his position in Germany by force of arms, he turned on Italy, captured Rome, drove Gregory into exile (where he died in 1085), elected another pope, and had himself crowned emperor in 1084. These bold actions were carried out in spite of another excommunication by Gregory. But Henry's victory was a hollow one. The papacy had challenged his authority, and for their own reasons others took up the challenge. In time all Germany and Italy became a seething chaos of political struggle. Although Henry IV defended his power valiantly, he ended his reign virtually a fugitive from rebellious nobles, including his own sons, in his own kingdom.

His next three successors, ruling until 1152, fared little better. Effective control over Italy virtually disappeared, the independent towns, nobles, and the papacy doing about as they pleased. The imperial crown tended to become a pawn of warring noble factions, election going to a prince who seemed least likely to exert much power. In 1122 the emperors made their peace with the Church by signing the Concordat of Worms, which provided that election to ecclesiastical offices be made by the Church while the lands and secular powers going with the office be invested by the crown. This settlement actually gave the kings a chance to veto officials chosen by the Church, since bishops and abbots could not get along without lands. Gregory VII would probably not have been satisfied with this compromise, but it did signify that the emperor's control over the Church was not so complete as it once had been.

The investiture struggle resulted in another and more serious setback to imperial power in the first half of the twelfth century—the rapid progress of feudalism in Germany. Seeking desperately for allies during this period of struggle, the kings often gave in to the demands of aristocrats for lands and privileges. The disorders also drove many lesser men to seek the protection of greater ones. A kingdom that had avoided the worst evils of feudalism in the tenth century by constructing a strong monarchy was now rapidly acquiring a feudal structure.

5. The Hohenstaufens, 1152–1250

In spite of its feeble appearance in the middle of the twelfth century the Holy Roman Empire was not yet finished. A new dynasty, the Hohenstaufens, produced three men of vision and ability who again took up the struggle to build the empire on a sound basis.

The first of these was Frederick I, also known as Frederick Barbarossa (1152–90). He was elected German king in 1152 because some of the warring factions of nobles in Germany were tired of disorder. Since Frederick was closely connected by family ties with the two most powerful factions, the Welfs and the Hohenstaufens, many hoped that he could pacify their clashes and end the warfare that had torn Germany apart since the beginning of the investiture struggle.

Frederick I attacked the German problem vigorously. To put an end to petty warfare, he increased the power of the greatest nobles and let them curb the troublesome lesser nobles. For instance, Frederick allowed his greatest rival, Henry of Saxony, leader of the Welfs, to control both Saxony and Bavaria and gave him a free hand to extend his power eastward into the Slavic world. Frederick sought to remain superior to these great princes by increasing his own private lands and by administering them effectively for his own benefit. He began developing a body of non-feudal civil servants to assist him in administering his own lands and in guarding his royal rights throughout Germany. He also returned to the old Ottonian policy of making the German church serve him, a policy that demanded that he control elections to Church offices.

Not content to rule Germany, Frederick soon plunged into Italian politics in the hope of restoring control there. In 1155 he was crowned emperor by the pope, who needed protection at the moment. Frederick made it clear to everyone that he had no intention of allowing the papacy to dominate him or to limit his powers to control the Church in his empire. He also demonstrated his determination to rule Italy. In 1158 he summoned representatives of the Italian towns to a meeting at Roncaglia and laid down a new set of rules to govern relationships between emperor and towns. The towns were to pay regular taxes, accept imperial officials as their rulers, and permit the emperor to coin money and regulate commerce. For at least a century before 1158 the Italian towns had been proceeding toward independence; now at one stroke their independence was to be wiped out.

Once Frederick had made his policy clear, the storm broke, and for more than twenty years Frederick was forced to fight an imposing array of enemies. The papacy stood at the head of these foes. Pope Alexander III (1159–81), a true heir of Gregory VII, was the main protagonist, battling with great skill to uphold the independence and superiority of the Church. Frederick sought to offset Alexander's opposition by electing another pope. But most of Europe supported Alexander, and eventually he gained recognition, even in Germany, as the rightful pope. With papal encouragement the Italian towns formed the Lombard League to resist Frederick, and once again the Norman kingdom in Italy was rallied to oppose the emperor. And, of course, the German nobles, still refusing to accept a strong king, used every chance available to limit and defy Frederick's authority.

Frederick battled this alliance with great skill, yet he failed to emerge victorious, being forced to settle for a compromise. In 1176 he suffered a crushing military defeat at the hands of the Lombard League, a catastrophe brought on in part by the refusal of his great vassals in Germany to supply troops. By 1177 he gave up his at-

THE
HOLY ROMAN EMPIRE
UNDER THE HOHENSTAUFEN
1138-1254

tempt to establish a German pope and recognized Alexander III. In 1183, at the Peace
of Constance, the Italian towns came to
terms, recognizing Frederick's overlordship
in return for certain specific rights, such as
those of choosing their own officials and
levying their own taxes. In 1186 Frederick
arranged for the marriage of his son, Henry,
to the heiress of the Norman kingdom of
Sicily, a diplomatic triumph that removed
one of the most persistent foes of the emperor's power in Italy. Frederick had not
gained full control of Italy, nor had he subdued the papacy. However, his power was
still extensive in Italy and his position as
emperor was still intact.

Frederick's long-standing policy of trying
to live with a few great princes in Germany
did not prove completely successful. Eventually he had to smash the chief of these
nobles, Henry of Saxony. Thereafter Frederick decided to break up the large principalities that had long been a feature of
Germany, granting the territory to many lesser nobles instead of a few great ones. This
step relieved him of immediate danger, but
in the long run, by further promoting the
feudalization of Germany, proved fatal.

Frederick decided to crown his illustrious
reign by leading the Third Crusade, such
an act being expected of every great prince
of the twelfth century. In 1190, before he
had reached the Holy Land, he was drowned.
Thus ended the career of a man whose personal energy and political ability had revived
imperial prestige. He had bent all his efforts
toward the aim of defining clearly his imperial rights and creating means of exercising
them. Realizing that he must live with the
feudal system, he had attempted to compel
his vassals in Germany to respect their obligations while he respected their privileges. To achieve this end, he had tried to
gain sufficient lands for himself to maintain
his power over his vassals. In Italy he had
sought to check the continued usurpation of
imperial power by the towns and to gain
strength by capitalizing on their wealth.
With respect to the Church he insisted upon
his supremacy over the pope and his rights

to exercise control over ecclesiastical offices
to which royal lands were attached. Upon
these bases he had hoped to rebuild the
fortunes of the Holy Roman Empire, which
had been so badly shattered by the investiture struggle.

Frederick's son, Henry VI (1190–97),
took up his father's work and seemed for a
time destined to be the greatest of all emperors. Germany was far from peaceful under
her new king; his presence was actually required every minute in Germany to curb the
feudal nobles. However, Henry VI was attracted to Italy. His chief problem lay in
securing Sicily, which his wife was entitled to
inherit. In this he succeeded, but only after a
long war. But then, instead of confining himself to the hard business of ruling his possessions in Germany and Italy, Henry VI became enmeshed in a series of schemes to
extend his power: German control over the
Mediterranean, a German crusade to seize
the Holy Land, an attempt to make the kings
of France and Spain his vassals. As his vast
schemes unfolded, Henry's foes once again
began to join hands. Only a premature death
in 1197 relieved him of paying the price for
his ambition.

For the next several years the fate of the
Holy Roman Empire was decided by Pope
Innocent III (1198–1216), the most powerful of all medieval popes. When Henry VI
died, he left an infant son, Frederick, who
was placed under the guardianship of Innocent III by his mother before her death
in 1198. Innocent was determined that this
prince would not rule Germany and Sicily
except on papal terms. In Germany he encouraged a civil war that pitted rival candidates for the crown one against another.
This war was kept going almost incessantly
until 1212. During this interval Innocent
had little to fear from the aspirants to the
imperial crown; they were too busy in Germany. Papal diplomacy encouraged the
northern Italian towns and the princes of
central Italy to throw off German control.
Meanwhile Innocent controlled the Norman
state himself as guardian of Frederick. It
seemed that the pope had finally acquired

the overlordship of which Gregory VII had dreamed.

In 1212 Innocent decided to use his ward to impose papal control on Germany. Securing the aid of the king of France, he made Frederick II king of Germany and, eventually, Holy Roman Emperor. Frederick paid for papal help by making important concessions that returned control of the German church to the papacy, thus reversing a condition that had existed since Otto the Great's time.

Frederick II was not destined to remain a docile servant of the papacy. Until his death in 1250 he took up the battle once more for a strong Holy Roman Empire. Beyond a doubt he was one of the most capable men of the Middle Ages—well educated, ruthless, a patron of the arts and sciences, uninhibited by religious scruples, and above all ambitious.

Frederick II was not really interested in Germany; Sicily was his true homeland. After becoming ruler of Germany he remained there until 1220. He spent these years surrendering the royal power that his predecessors had carefully nourished. We have already noted how he gave up control of the Church to the papacy. To the great feudal princes he was equally generous. Their fiefs were made hereditary, and they were given full rights of government over the fiefs. Even the German towns were put under feudal control. In effect, Frederick abdicated his power in Germany.

His surrender in Germany was prompted by a desire to make Sicily his base of operations. Frederick devoted his career to building in Sicily a Byzantine-like, centralized, bureaucratic state where his power was absolute. From this base he hoped to extend his power over all Italy, replacing feudal chaos with orderly centralized government. This program reopened the ancient hostilities. For thirty years popes, townsmen, and nobles in Italy pitted themselves against Frederick in a ruinous struggle. Frederick held his own, but he did not win. He lacked the resources to overpower his Italian foes. The papal prestige was too extensive over all Europe to permit Frederick to form an anti-papal alliance. Moreover Germany was beyond recall and offered no help to its absent king. Frederick II died in 1250 even further from effective control of his empire than his predecessors had been.

In the period from Frederick's death in 1250 until 1273, known as the Interregnum, the power of the emperor was virtually destroyed. The German nobles refused to consider electing a strong king. Their final choice in 1273—a certain Rudolph, count of Hapsburg—was qualified chiefly by his lack of strength. The feudal lords were masters of Germany. Meanwhile, in Italy a French prince, Charles of Anjou, accepted a papal invitation to take over Sicily and accomplished the mission in 1266. In the rest of Italy each town, each churchman, each feudal lord went his own way. There was no central authority guiding Italian politics any longer. The Slavic kingdoms that had long been under strong German influence were also free to go their own way. In fact all of Europe was free from the prospect of being put under the control of a single ruler calling himself Holy Roman Emperor.

After a notable start in the tenth century the German rulers had had little success in creating a strong state. Perhaps their trouble lay in trying to be emperors. When they took that title they proclaimed to the world that their power was superior to that of all other rulers. Many elements of European society were unwilling to admit this and resisted the Holy Roman Emperors. The papacy, the most persistent and determined foe of the empire, was to a large degree responsible for the failure of the Germans to weld together a strong state. The resistance kept the emperors so fully occupied that they were never able to create instruments of government that would allow them to exercise the power they claimed. The Holy Roman Empire was a structure built on quicksand, doomed from its inception because it assumed that emperors could rule men who had very few things in common. Probably the German rulers would have built a sounder political structure had they stuck to Germany, building political institutions to fit the situation there. In any case their failure doomed Germany and Italy to disunity and caused these areas to lag politically behind the other Western European states, which succeeded better in creating workable political systems during the Middle Ages.

————•◦•————

SUGGESTED READING

Z. N. Brooke, A *History of Europe from 911 to 1198*, 3rd ed. (1951); and C. W. Previté-Orton, A *History of Europe from 1198 to 1378*, 3rd ed., rev. (1951). These two volumes, part of a four-volume series, will supply the serious reader with additional details on the political history of continental Europe during the period of the high Middle Ages (i.e., about 900–1300).

* Sidney Painter, *The Rise of the Feudal Monarchies* (Cornell). Part of this brief volume (Chapter III) gives a good summary of the history of the Holy Roman Empire during the Middle Ages.

James Bryce, *The Holy Roman Empire*, rev. ed. (1904). This classic discussion of the Holy Roman Empire extends far beyond the period covered in this chapter. However, the early chapters of the book provide a stimulating discussion of the basic ideas inspiring the revival of the Roman Empire in medieval Western Europe.

Geoffrey Barraclough, *The Origins of Modern Germany*, 2nd ed. (1947). The best study in English of the evolution of the Holy Roman Empire from the end of the Carolingian period to the end of the thirteenth century.

The book, however, presupposes some knowledge of German history.

A. J. Macdonald, *Hildebrand: A Life of Gregory VII* (1932). A well-written biography into which the author has incorporated a large number of extracts from Gregory's writings to illustrate the papal position in the struggle over lay investiture.

Gertrude Elizabeth Slaughter, *The Amazing Frederic* (1937). A lively biography of Frederick II somewhat distorted by the author's attempt to "modernize" Frederick II and to make him the originator of new things. The book is relatively short, necessitating an oversimplification of some issues.

Ernst Kantorowicz, *Frederick the Second, 1194–1250* (1931). A brilliant biography that not only recounts the career of an important emperor but also throws light on conditions throughout the medieval world in the thirteenth century.

The Correspondence of Gregory VII, tr. by Ephraim Emerton (1932). An excellent selection from the letters of Gregory VII illustrating the papal position in the struggle against emperors that raged in the eleventh, twelfth, and thirteenth centuries.

CHAPTER 20

The Emergence of Feudal Monarchy
in France and Spain

THE POLITICAL history of France and Spain during the high Middle Ages offers nothing so spectacular as the Holy Roman Empire. Yet each of these countries created a more permanent political structure. Kings, exploiting their feudal rights, slowly built up the royal power, which they used to exercise unified control over states of limited but manageable size. By 1300 their actual powers far exceeded the vaunted claims of the Holy Roman Emperors, who had failed to construct effective governmental institutions to back up their claims to power.

1. The Last Carolingians in France to 987

Like Germany, France was created as a separate kingdom by the Treaty of Verdun in 843, when the sons of Louis the Pious divided the Carolingian Empire. And, as in Germany, subsequent Carolingian rule was ineffective. The Carolingian rulers failed most dismally in defending their kingdom. During the late ninth and early tenth centuries the Norsemen raided the kingdom at will. In southern France, Moslems joined the attack. The burden of defense fell on local leaders. The Carolingian rulers also gave away extensive royal lands to vassals or stood by idly while those vassals took over royal lands. Thus the ruling family became steadily poorer, eventually having only a single city, Laon, left in all France as their own. The functions of government that the Carolingians had once provided were no longer performed by the kings but were usurped by royal vassals.

During the years down to the end of the Carolingian dynasty in 987 feudalism took deeper roots in France than anywhere else in Europe. A king was elected for the whole of France and he was recognized in a vague sort of way as the highest lord of the kingdom. Real power, however, had settled into the hands of great vassals who held extensive fiefs from the crown and enjoyed the right to rule them. Although the holders of these fiefs admitted that they were vassals of the king, they seldom rendered their obligations to him as vassals should. The king, lacking in land, was in no position to collect what was due him. Perhaps we should recall that in Germany long before 987 Otto the Great had stopped the breakup of his kingdom, crushed its invaders, and seized Italy. What a contrast with the kings of France, literally hiding out in their one city while the feudal lords and vassals did as they pleased throughout the realm!

2. The First Capetians, 987–1108

In 987 the French nobles and churchmen ousted the dying Carolingian house, electing as their king one of the chief feudal lords of

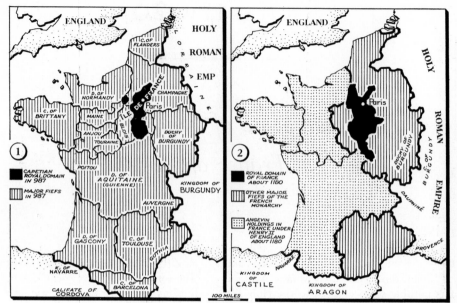

CONSOLIDATION OF FRANCE,

the day, Hugh Capet, count of Paris, whose feudal holdings were extensive in central France. This was really a final victory for feudalism, since Hugh Capet and his immediate successors showed little interest in ruling France.

The first four Capetians were distinguished chiefly for their long lives, the four of them ruling until 1108. During these years the feudalization of France progressed unchecked. The great Carolingian principalities continued while new fiefs were created at the expense of the Capetians. Their extensive lands were diminished until by 1106 the royal domain consisted only of a tiny island of territory, called the Île de France, surrounded by more powerful feudal principalities. Even within that territory, extending from Paris to Orléans, the Capetians were challenged by numerous petty vassals who had established hereditary fiefs and defied the authority of their lord, the king of France.

If the Capetians could not control their petty vassals in their own domain, one could hardly expect them to control the hundreds of other principalities comprising the rest of France, some of them far larger and richer than the royal domain. Among the major fiefs were the county of Flanders, the duchy of Normandy, the duchy of Brittany, the duchy of Aquitaine, the county of Toulouse, the duchy of Gascony, the county of Barcelona, the duchy of Burgundy, the county of Anjou, the county of Blois, and the county of Champagne. There were also hundreds of smaller fiefs and ecclesiastical estates scattered over France to complicate the scene further.

It is difficult to generalize about the situation within each of these feudal principalities. In general, all were feudalized, the great dukes and counts having granted their lands to lesser vassals in return for feudal services. In some principalities, especially Flanders and Normandy, the counts and dukes kept strict control over their vassals, thereby creating well-governed principalities. The duke of Normandy, for instance, had perfected the means of making all his vassals render their dues promptly and fully. As a result he commanded a strong army, maintained an efficient system of courts, kept the peace, and controlled the Church in his duchy.

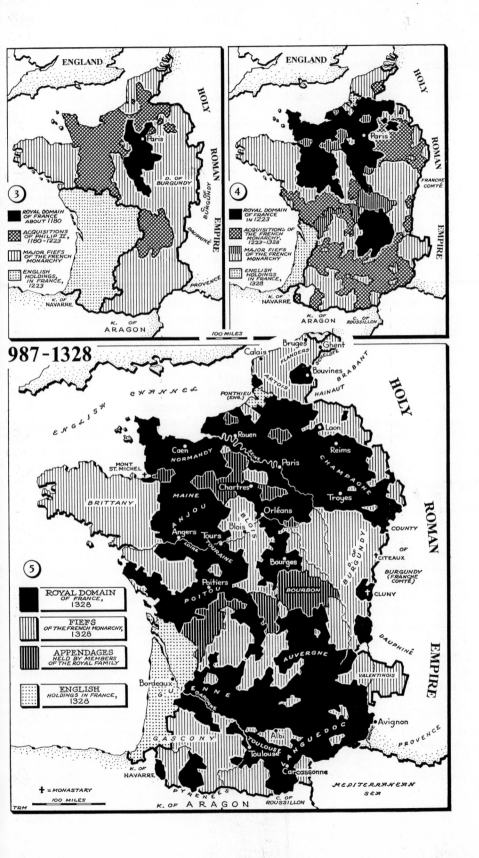

3

ENGLAND

HOLY

ROMAN

EMPIRE

Paris

D. OF
BURGUNDY

PROVENCE

K. OF
NAVARRE

K. OF
ARAGON

- ROYAL DOMAIN
  OF FRANCE
  ABOUT 1180
- ACQUISITIONS
  OF PHILIP II,
  1180-1223
- MAJOR FIEFS
  OF THE FRENCH
  MONARCHY
- ENGLISH
  HOLDINGS
  IN FRANCE,
  1223

4

ENGLAND

HOLY

ROMAN

EMPIRE

Paris

FRANCHE
COMTÉ

K. OF
NAVARRE

K. OF
ARAGON

C. OF
ROUSSILLON

- ROYAL DOMAIN
  OF FRANCE
  IN 1223
- ACQUISITIONS OF
  THE FRENCH
  MONARCHY,
  1223-1328
- MAJOR FIEFS
  OF THE FRENCH
  MONARCHY
- ENGLISH
  HOLDINGS
  IN FRANCE,
  1328

100 MILES

987-1328

ENGLISH CHANNEL

Calais

Bruges

Ghent

FLANDERS

SCHELDT

BRABANT

Artois

Bouvines

PONTHIEU
(ENG.)

HAINAUT

HOLY

Rouen

Laon

ROMAN

Caen

NORMANDY

SEINE

Reims

MONT
ST. MICHEL

Paris

CHAMPAGNE

Chartres

Troyes

BRITTANY

MAINE

Orléans

BURGUNDY

COUNTY

ANJOU

BLOIS

OF

CITEAUX

Angers

Tours

Bourges

BURGUNDY
(FRANCHE
COMTÉ)

LOIRE

TOURAINE

CLUNY

Poitiers

BOURBON

POITOU

EMPIRE

5

- ROYAL DOMAIN
  OF FRANCE,
  1328
- FIEFS
  OF THE FRENCH MONARCHY,
  1328
- APPENDAGES
  HELD BY MEMBERS
  OF THE ROYAL FAMILY
- ENGLISH
  HOLDINGS IN FRANCE,
  1328

Bordeaux
G.

AUVERGNE

DAUPHINÉ

VALENTINOIS

Avignon

GASCONY

GARONNE

LANGUEDOC

PROVENCE

TOULOUSE

Albi

Toulouse

Carcassonne

MEDITERRANEAN
SEA

+ = MONASTARY

100 MILES

K. OF
NAVARRE

PYRENEES

C. OF
ROUSSILLON

K. OF ARAGON

TRM

In some other principalities, like Aquitaine and Burgundy, the duke or count was a figurehead, real power being held by numerous and unruly vassals to whom fiefs had been granted.

Theoretically the Capetian king of France was feudal lord of all the great fiefs. The counts and dukes were his vassals and owed him military service, court service, aids, hospitality, and relief. In spite of their theoretical rights over their vassals the early Capetians were powerless to control them. Since the tiny territory controlled by the king was surrounded by virtually independent principalities much greater in size and richer in resources, it was almost a miracle that the early Capetians managed to keep the monarchy alive and to retain the royal title as a hereditary privilege. Tradition, however, worked for the Capetians; France had had a king since the days of the Germanic invasions, and it seemed natural to even the most ambitious feudal lord that she continue to have one. Moreover, the Church stoutly supported the early Capetians, lending its great moral force to the idea that the Capetians were greater than all their vassals.

3. The Consolidation of France

Between 1108 and 1223 the position of the Capetians improved rapidly. By the end of this era the king of France was the most powerful figure in France instead of the insignificant force he had been in the eleventh century. The story of the revival of French monarchy centers primarily around the successful efforts of a group of intelligent, industrious, and persistent kings to exploit their rights as feudal lords over the great fiefs of France.

Louis VI (1108-37) took the first steps toward increasing royal power. His most enduring achievement was not especially spectacular. He devoted the greater part of his reign to a struggle to subdue the petty feudal lords in the Île de France, that is, in the king's own domain. Louis forced them to end their lawlessness and render their dues

to the king. When necessary he ruthlessly crushed his vassals and confiscated their fiefs. To administer the Île de France, he gathered around him loyal servants, some of them drawn from the non-noble classes, and assigned them governmental duties.

Although Louis VI was chiefly involved in a struggle to become master of his own small domain, he seldom missed an opportunity to claim his rights with respect to his great vassals scattered over France. He tried to exercise his right as judge in their disputes, and he claimed the privilege of having a voice in the selection of men who would inherit the great fiefs. Occasionally he used arms to defend his vassals when attacked by others, gaining thereby a reputation as a protector of the weak. He engaged in a constant diplomatic game to play one combination of great vassals off against another so as to safeguard the royal position. The king of France was making his presence known in all France. Nowhere was this better illustrated than by the decision of the duke of Aquitaine as death approached to entrust his daughter and heiress, Eleanor, to the protection of King Louis. Louis promptly married the princess to his son, thereby setting the stage for the annexation of the great duchy of Aquitaine to the royal domain.

Louis VI's son, Louis VII (1137-80), was not so able or clearheaded as his father. Although, with the help of his father's advisers, he continued to maintain a firm grip on the Île de France, the resources of which were the basis of the power of the king, he tried to move too fast in other directions. He challenged some of his vassals when he really had no hope of subduing them. He failed to exploit the advantages that resulted when he gained possession of the duchy of Aquitaine through his marriage with Eleanor. The unruly vassals in this huge territory defied the king at every turn. Louis lacked the energy and the resources to beat them into submission, as his father had done in the Île de France. Even his participation in the Second Crusade was disastrous. He not only won no glory but also lost his valuable wife. The gay, romantic Eleanor, bored with her dull and pious husband, was rumored to have engaged in amorous adventures with some of the more glamorous knights who accompanied her and her husband to the Holy Land. Such unholy conduct on so holy a mission was too much for the pious Louis. Moreover, the marriage had produced no sons, a situation that a good Capetian could not tolerate. Louis therefore arranged for dissolving the marriage on his return. The dissolution of the marriage threatened the future of France. Eleanor, who married Henry of Anjou immediately after the dissolution, handed Aquitaine over to her new husband. This dashing, able prince was rapidly becoming one of the most powerful figures in Europe and a direct threat to the Capetian kings.

The attempts of the Capetians to parry Angevin power became the central theme of French history in Louis VII's time. Eventual success for the Capetians in this struggle was the making of a strong France. Anjou was an ancient fief lying southwest of the Île de France. Its counts during the eleventh century were aggressive men, warring constantly to enlarge their holdings; by the twelfth century they had succeeded in establishing one of the most powerful principalities in France. Count Geoffrey was especially successful in adding new territory, his chief acquisitions being Normandy and Brittany, which he gained by marrying the daughter of the king of England, Henry I, who was also duke of Normandy. When Geoffrey died in 1151 he left to his son Henry a huge territory consisting of Anjou, Normandy, and Brittany. This was the same Henry who married Eleanor in 1152, thereby adding Aquitaine to his already extensive holdings. For all these territories Henry was theoretically the vassal of Louis VII of France. In 1154 Henry became King Henry II of England by inheritance, making him an even greater power. The Angevin "empire" embraced all western France as well as England. Its new ruler was an ambitious figure, intent upon expanding his holdings and unwilling to bow before any-

one, not even his feudal lord, the king of France. The French crown was obviously in grave danger.

Louis VII did his best to restrain the Angevins, but he was no match for Henry II in open warfare or diplomacy. Philip II, or Philip Augustus, the next French king (1180–1223), met the Angevin problem more successfully. Before his long reign ended, Philip had seized the most valuable parts of the Angevin holdings and had made them a part of the lands of the king of France. His success marked the turning point in the history of medieval French monarchy. The kings became the strongest force in France, finally capable of curbing feudal disorder. For his work Philip II must be counted one of the great figures in France's history.

Philip II achieved his goal chiefly by warfare. As long as Henry II lived, Philip bided his time, realizing the great ability of this man. But after Henry II's death in 1189 war between Philip II and his vassals, Richard I and John of England, the sons and successors of Henry, was incessant. Militarily Richard was a match for Philip, but John was not. John's French vassals, disaffected by his tyranny, were glad to support Philip, who posed as a righteous feudal lord protecting the sanctity of the feudal contract. In England, John outraged his subjects and the Church, as we shall see in a later connection. Exploiting John's troubles and handling his military resources with great skill, Philip waged a successful struggle that culminated in 1214 at the Battle of Bouvines, where Philip crushed the armies of John and his ally, Otto of Germany. (Philip was aided by Pope Innocent III and his young protégé, Frederick of Hohenstaufen, who won control of Germany by this same battle. See p. 233.) After the Battle of Bouvines, Philip was able to annex key territories held by the English king north of the Loire, including the duchy of Normandy and the county of Anjou. These territories became a part of the royal domain and were no longer ruled by vassals of the king of France. Philip was now master of a solid block of territory in northern France consisting of his new conquests, the Île de France, and other smaller territories that the kings of France had been picking up. The duchy of Brittany, previously controlled by the English king, became a fief held directly from the French king and therefore no longer under English domination. Philip's vassals would think twice before attacking a lord armed with the resources of so large a territory.

Philip's military victories over his Angevin vassals would have been sufficient to ensure his importance in French history. However, he added still more glory to his name by laying the foundations for a system of government suited to ruling his new conquests. We shall return to this subject below, since his contributions are part of a longer story involving other French kings. Suffice it to say here that Philip worked chiefly within a feudal framework, just as he had used feudal rights to curb the Angevin ambitions. He began building a judicial system, a trained civil service, and a financial system—all of which were as vital to France as the armies Philip had mustered to curb his unruly vassals. The king's judges and the king's civil servants, fortified by the king's treasury, soon proved capable of ending the misgovernment and disorder that had beset France since the feudal system had taken over.

4. The Last Capetians, 1223–1328

The Capetian dynasty ruled France for a century after the decisive reign of Philip Augustus. During that century French history was dominated by the two themes we have already emphasized: addition of new territories to the royal domain and perfection of the monarchical government.

The territories added to the royal domain after Philip II's death were won with comparative ease. The county of Toulouse was annexed by Louis IX (1226–70) through a marriage arrangement. Even before it was annexed, the king had become all-powerful in this rich county when, at the insistence of the Church, he had furnished the bulk of the armed force used to root out the hereti-

cal Cathari, or Albigensians (see p. 262). Another marriage arranged by Philip III (1270–85) brought the county of Champagne to the Capetians. Important territories in the old duchy of Aquitaine were forceably seized at the expense of the king of England. Numerous smaller territories were conquered, purchased, or confiscated to extend further the royal domain. When the Capetian dynasty ended in 1328 only Flanders, Brittany, parts of Aquitaine, and Burgundy remained as independent fiefs; the rest of France belonged to the Capetian kings.

While the kings of the thirteenth and early fourteenth centuries were rounding out their territorial control over France, they were also proceeding rapidly with the organization of a stronger and more centralized government. The three kings chiefly responsible for this progress were Philip II, Louis IX (1226–70), and Philip IV, also known as Philip the Fair (1285–1314).

These great constitution builders worked from a primarily feudal foundation. According to feudal theory, the king, as supreme feudal lord, had an obligation to protect his vassals, to judge them, and to demand their services for governmental activities. The early Capetians sought to fulfill their obligations through a royal court, called the *curia regis*, made up of the king's vassals. This body served primarily as a court of justice where vassals were heard and their cases decided. It also served as an advisory body to the king. For a long time it was poorly attended and its decisions little respected because the king lacked the power to enforce them. The early Capetians were also served by a seneschal, a constable, a chaplain, and a chancellor, who cared for the personal needs of the kings. This group was called the royal household. A small group of provosts managed the royal estates, from which the king derived his living.

One of the chief accomplishments of Philip II, Louis IX, and Philip IV was the building of an effective central government out of these primitive institutions. Philip II began this process by steadily increasing the amount of business put before the curia regis. Although the body still consisted chiefly of feudal vassals, he began adding non-feudal administrators (especially trained lawyers) of his own choice. In time the royal household, which was now staffed by men of the king's choice rather than by hereditary officeholders, was merged with the curia regis to form a single judicial and administrative body serving the king. Paris became the fixed seat of royal government, permitting records to be kept as the basis for conducting the king's business.

Louis IX and Philip IV pushed this development along rapidly. They constantly increased the business of the curia and added trained personnel to its composition. The chief development of their reigns was the division of the curia regis into specialized departments. The administration of justice was handled by a section called the *Parlement de Paris*, made up chiefly of lawyers who spent their lives administering the law. The Parlement de Paris was further divided into specialized courts, each handling a different kind of case. A second division was the *chambre des comptes*, which dealt exclusively with financial matters, especially the collection of taxes. A small circle of members of the curia regis also acted as the *Conseil* to meet with the king to advise him on administration. Specialization within the central government allowed for more skilled administration, better use of administrative talent, and the handling of a greater volume of business. By the reign of Philip IV this central government, headed by the king and those in charge of the specialized departments and backed by an army of lesser civil servants, was fully informed of what was going on in France and capable of making its power felt over most of the country.

The problem of making royal authority effective throughout France, always serious, became monumental when the king added huge pieces of territory to his domain. Philip II attacked this problem by the extensive use of officials known as *baillis* (bailiffs). Usually selected from the non-noble personnel of his court, these officials were assigned to specific areas in the royal domain. They held courts in cases where the king was a party, maintained police regulations, collected taxes, and punished lawbreakers. Their pay consisted either of a part of the fees and taxes they collected or of the income from a Church office that the king controlled. Since they were not given land, they did not become feudalized. Succeeding kings increased the number of bailiffs, broadened their powers, and laid down more careful regulations to guide them. Louis IX established special officers, called *enquêteurs*, whose job it was to check on the conduct of the bailiffs and report any misconduct to the king. This corps of officials, installed all over France and backed by royal authority, constantly assumed political functions once exercised by feudal lords and churchmen. However, the thirteenth-century monarchs always paid due respect to the rights of their vassals; thus the French monarchy continued to retain its feudal characteristics. Repeatedly during the thirteenth century the kings gave assurances to the nobles that their privileges would be respected by the crown and its officials.

The increasing size of the court and its broadening functions placed a heavy financial burden on the king. Philip II gave serious attention to this problem. His chief source of income still came from his own properties, and he collected all feudal dues coming to him with increasing care. Often he was willing to permit his vassals to make a money payment in place of rendering personal services. In emergencies direct taxes, such as the Saladin's tithe (a tax levied on property to finance the Third Crusade), were levied. Louis IX and Philip IV levied taxes on the towns and the Church regularly. Forced loans were exacted from foreigners (especially Jews). Philip IV even resorted to methods such as confiscating the wealth of the Knights Templars, a rich monastic order that had originated during the early period of the Crusades, and debasing the currency regularly to gain income. These methods, exploited by the financial experts of the chambre des comptes, permitted the kings to get by financially, but as the Capetian dynasty approached its end, this major problem of finances had still not been solved.

While extending their tentacles over all France and perfecting the central government, the Capetians early in the fourteenth century instituted another practice that strengthened their position. They began to summon representatives of various classes (estates) from all over their realm to advise them and approve their decisions. On three different occasions during the reign of Philip IV (in 1302, 1308, and 1314), townsmen were summoned, along with nobles and clergymen, to meet the king and discuss serious issues facing the nation. These meetings came to be known as Estates General. Such meetings of nobles, clergy, and townsmen, which always ended in approval of what the king proposed, added tremendous weight to royal power. The whole nation seemed to approve of what the king was doing. Philip IV was careful to keep the Estates General under control so that it did not develop independent powers, a custom that well served many later French kings with absolutist ideas. Nonetheless, the institution was important in uniting Frenchmen of all classes under a single government.

By the beginning of the fourteenth century the French monarchy was an imposing structure, built on solid moorings—a centralized administration, a functioning judicial system, efficient local government, fairly adequate finances, and a means of influencing and controlling through the Estates General the opinions of the classes that mattered. An efficient king like Philip IV could exercise nearly absolute power by the skillful operation of this system. However, the French monarchy was more than an efficient administrative machine. It was an institution with immense prestige inside and outside France. The greatest French kings had a quality that made them stand out in thirteenth-century Europe. Louis IX, eventually sainted by the Church, illustrates this feature of French monarchy. He was beloved by all his subjects, chiefly because of his interest in justice for all men. He was a friend of

the Church. He was a gallant, if not very successful, crusader, ending his life in the perfect Christian fashion—fighting infidels. He was famed as Europe's peacemaker. He tried valiantly to improve the moral life of his subjects, going so far as to make laws prohibiting swearing and private warfare. He was an ideal son, husband, and father by the standards of his day. All these factors combined to earn Louis the respect and trust of his people, thereby increasing his authority tremendously. Monarchy had become an effective symbol binding France together.

Our mention of Louis's sainthood raises the question of the relationship of the French monarchy with the Church. Until the French king was strong enough to defy the Church, the relationship was peaceful, and no deep-seated quarrel with the Church distracted the French kings from their affairs, as was the case in Germany. The Church was one of the chief supporters of the early Capetians and had encouraged them to curb the feudal disorders, which affected the Church adversely. When the problem of lay investiture arose, the Capetians solved the question by permitting the Church to choose its own officials while the king invested the official with the fiefs that went along with the office. The French kings performed numerous acts that pleased the Church and especially the papacy. They sided with Rome against the Holy Roman emperors and sometimes gave the pope vital aid in his struggles with the emperors. They helped reform the clergy. From France came most of the crusaders. Rich gifts were bestowed on the Church by the French monarchy. All these factors made for good feelings up until nearly the end of the high Middle Ages, although as the Capetians began to grow stronger in the twelfth century, they exploited the Church for their own purposes by filling its offices with their friends and by tapping its wealth.

This generally happy relationship was shattered by Philip IV. He became involved in a quarrel with Pope Boniface VIII (1294–1303) over the extent of the king's power to tax Church property and to judge clergy-men. When Philip defied the papal commands on these matters, Boniface VIII unloosed all his weapons against the French king. Philip routed his foe by using his extensive royal powers to turn public opinion against Rome, to force the French clergy to follow his orders, and to send into Italy an expedition to capture the pope. The mighty head of the Church, who had more than held his own against Holy Roman emperors, had met his match. The explanation is simple. By the early fourteenth century the French king possessed the kind of power that the papacy could not dissolve. The popes could find no great crowds of dissatisfied subjects in France to turn against the king, as they had in the Holy Roman Empire.

5. The Growth of Feudal Monarchy in Spain

While the French kings were shaping a workable monarchy out of feudal chaos, Spain was undergoing a comparable process. The development of monarchy in Spain took its own peculiar course owing chiefly to the task of reconquering the land from the Moslems (or Moors, as they are called in Spanish history).

When the Moors conquered Spain in the eighth century, they failed to subdue the Christians in the mountainous areas of northern Spain, who soon undertook a war against the Moslems which stretched out into a perpetual crusade. The Reconquista, as this crusade was called, started slowly but gathered speed in the eleventh and twelfth centuries as strong reinforcements from France flooded into Spain. It reached its culmination in the thirteenth century when the Moors were confined to a narrow area in southern Spain called Granada. Out of this religious warfare were shaped four kingdoms—Castile, Aragon, Portugal, and Navarre, each with its own king and its own system of institutions. Warfare against the Moors engrained combativeness in the souls of the inhabitants of these kingdoms. Often

they warred with each other to complicate further the torturous process of bringing these four kingdoms into existence. However, the Reconquista gave to each of these kingdoms a certain solidarity born of war against a common foe.

Each kingdom developed its own system of government, although all had certain basic similarities. Monarchy was, of course, the basic institution, the various kings claiming extensive powers over society. The Spanish kings steadily gained prestige as a result of their leadership of the Reconquista. The Church championed their cause. The profits they gained at the expense of the Moors constantly supplied them with resources to bolster their power. Newly conquered lands gave them a chance to settle people as farmers or townsmen under conditions that allowed the king to retain his authority. These factors retarded the coming of the feudal system, and Spain was never as thoroughly feudalized as France. Eventually, however, feudal practices not unlike those of France did develop. Hereditary fiefs were granted to nobles in return for services, and some of the vassals gained a large degree of immunity from royal control.

The Spanish monarchs worked incessantly to make their power more effective. Particularly during the thirteenth century they sought to develop centralized administrations, specialized civil servants, well-organized financial systems, and effective courts. Several thirteenth-century kings of Aragon and Castile legislated extensively in an attempt to define royal powers and rights. Such legislation usually assigned to the kings extensive authority. Local officials of the king, comparable to the French bailiffs, were appointed and put under rigid royal supervision.

Nobles and townsmen resisted royal attempts to monopolize power. By every means at their disposal the landed nobles sought to protect their privileges and independence against royal officials. The chartered towns, many of which were founded by the kings, were equally jealous in protecting their liberties. In the long run the

Spanish monarchy was checked, being compelled to admit limitations on its powers and to allow considerable independence to nobles and towns. Still, one must concede that Spanish monarchs retained much authority to check internal disorder, to provide justice, and to protect the whole population. This balance between monarchy and specially privileged groups was symbolized by an institution that became a regular part of government in the twelfth and thirteenth centuries. This was the Cortes, a representative body composed of nobles, clergymen, and representatives of the towns. Before the end of the thirteenth century these bodies were being summoned in all the kingdoms to consult with the king. Custom had already sanctioned the right of the Cortes to approve new taxes, to address petitions to the king for redressing wrongs, and to be consulted in matters of war and peace. Nowhere else in Europe, with the possible exception of England, was there such a well-defined institution for curbing the authority of kings and confronting them with the desires of the vested interests in their realms.

The long struggles to enlarge the royal domain in France and to drive back the Moslems in Spain, coupled with the patient work of many kings to build workable institutions of government, paid off handsomely by 1300. In both France and Spain a solution had finally been reached for a problem that had persisted since the fall of Rome, namely, how to create stable, orderly, just government. In both areas the major evils of the feudal system had been corrected or curbed. Royal government had provided effective means for large groups of people to live together peacefully and on the basis of law.

The answer had been found in establishing feudal monarchies. The king as supreme feudal lord exercised those powers and rights that were his under the feudal system. He respected the rights and privileges of such privileged groups as nobles, the Church, and the towns. A common authority—the king—had bound diverse feudal groups together into compact states.

SUGGESTED READING

* Sidney Painter, *The Rise of the Feudal Monarchies* (Cornell). Chapter I of this brief volume supplies an introduction to the emergence of a unified France in the Middle Ages.

Ch. Petit-Dutaillis, *The Feudal Monarchy in France and England from the Tenth to the Thirteenth Century* (1936). A comprehensive treatment of the growth of French monarchy, especially good for its descriptions of the chief institutions of the central government.

Achille Luchaire, *Social France at the Time of Philip Augustus* (1912). A scholarly treatment of all aspects of life in twelfth-century France by one of France's greatest medievalists.

* Amy R. Kelly, *Eleanor of Aquitaine and the Four Kings* (Vintage). Published in a hardback edition in 1950. A lively treatment of an especially lively subject. Perhaps no clearer picture of the turbulence of feudal France can be found than that which emerges from a full study of Eleanor and her associations with the great men of the twelfth century.

Urban T. Holmes, *Daily Living in the Twelfth Century* (1952). An excellent portrayal of life in Paris in the twelfth century, centering around the activities of a student who came from England to France.

Rafael Altamira y Crevea, *A History of Spain from the Beginnings to the Present Day*, tr. by Muna Lee (1949). The early sections of this book supply a brief but accurate account of Spanish history in the period of the *Reconquista* and of the formation of the first Spanish kingdoms.

The History of St. Louis by Jean, Sire de Joinville, tr. by Joan Evans (1938). A splendid picture of the times of St. Louis IX by a contemporary admirer. Jean de Joinville was a French nobleman who accompanied Louis on his Egyptian crusade.

* *The Poem of the Cid: A Prose Translation*, tr. by Lesley Byrd Simpson (University of California Press paperback). Spain's great medieval epic poem, centering around the career of a knightly crusader engaged in the wars against the Moslems. From this poem we learn of the birth of Spanish patriotism as well as the nature of Spanish feudal society.

CHAPTER 21

The Rise of Feudal Monarchy in England

L IKE France, Germany, Italy, and Spain, England underwent an important political transformation during the eleventh, twelfth, and thirteenth centuries. Although her political history paralleled that of France, significant differences emerged, with important consequences for the future.

1. The Norman Conquest

The medieval histories of France, Germany, and Italy had a common starting point in the division of Charlemagne's empire. England did not share that experience. We have already discussed (see pp. 208–9) the unification of England by King Alfred of Wessex and his successors and the establishment during the tenth century of a system of royal government based on ancient Germanic institutions. Nonetheless, by 1000 England was suffering from many of the same political difficulties as the rest of Europe. Her Anglo-Saxon kings were incapable of maintaining effective control over all their kingdom. Feudal practices were emerging as a substitute for effective royal control. Earls and sheriffs, supposedly servants of the kings, steadily secured rights of private government. Kings granted royal lands to *thegns* who pledged to give military service but often defied the kings. Many freemen were compelled to become vassals of rich and powerful nobles. Although the trend toward decentralization had by no means gone so far as in France, Anglo-Saxon monarchy was far from healthy.

The decline of Anglo-Saxon monarchy opened the way for new assaults by the Vikings, spearheaded by the Danes. The invaders were so successful that from 1017–35, a Dane, Cnut (or Canute), ruled as king of England. After his death an Anglo-Saxon, Edward the Confessor, regained the throne. Edward's reign was troubled, not only by the threat of new Danish attacks, but also by the ambitions of powerful nobles, the chief of whom was Earl Godwin, who schemed to make his son, Harold, king. Edward, who was related to the Norman dukes by marriage and who had spent much of his early life in Normandy as an exile, came more and more to rely on William, Duke of Normandy, for support. This ambitious and powerful duke, a descendant of Viking warriors who had settled in France in the early tenth century, was only too happy to fish in England's troubled waters and laid plans to seize England's throne himself. When Edward died in 1066, Harold was elected king, but William moved to dispute by force Harold's accession, claiming that Edward had designated him as heir. His Norman knights met the Anglo-Saxon army near Hastings in 1066. When the battle was ended Harold was dead and William was master.

2. Reign of William I (1066–87)

William's position was far from secure immediately after the Battle of Hastings in 1066. He and his few knights were foreigners surrounded by hostile Anglo-Saxons.

Danish invasions were still a threat. To survive, William had to fashion tools of power capable of subduing those who resisted him and of perpetuating his authority for his heirs. This he did in a way that shaped England's future for a long time.

From the moment of his coronation William made it clear that he did not intend to revolutionize England. In his coronation oath he promised to observe all ancient Anglo-Saxon customs. This act not only pacified some of the opposition to his rule but also put William in a position to claim the powers of his Anglo-Saxon predecessors. In this sense the Norman Conquest signified a continuation of what had always existed under Anglo-Saxon kings.

William was not content to remain as weak as his Anglo-Saxon predecessors. To bolster his position, he introduced a full-fledged feudal system into England. As the conquest progressed (not until 1071 was the last resistance crushed), William claimed possession of all English soil. First, he set aside extensive lands for his own domain. He then made liberal grants to the Church, a gesture that won him the loyalty of that powerful institution. Finally, he granted fiefs to his Norman followers and to loyal Anglo-Saxons. Those who received grants became his vassals and were required to render the customary services in return for for their land. Most of the direct vassals of William (usually called tenants in chief or barons) received fiefs large enough so that the services of many knights were due from each. This required a further division, the direct vassals of the king becoming lords over their own vassals. William encouraged this. He insisted, however, that lesser vassals owed their first allegiance to the king and not to their immediate overlord. The evils of subinfeudation were thus avoided to the advantage of the king. As a result of the introduction of feudalism William acquired the services of about five thousand knights, more than enough to make him master of England, to check potential Anglo-Saxon uprisings, and to defend England from invaders.

William revitalized the central government in order to control his new kingdom more effectively. The old *witan* was replaced by a feudal body called the *curia regis*, at whose meetings the barons and high churchmen were expected to render court service, judge cases, and advise the king. William wisely retained the Anglo-Saxon system of local government; both shire and hundred courts continued administering law in the ancient way. But William exercised closer control over the shire courts than had his predecessors, usually entrusting the office of sheriff to loyal vassals. Naturally the great barons demanded the right to hold feudal courts for their vassals, resulting in the growth of feudal law and feudal courts. However, feudal law affected only the nobility involved in feudal contracts.

To support his government financially, William relied chiefly on the income from his own domain, but no other source of income was overlooked. William, for instance, continued to collect the Danegeld, probably being the only king in all Europe powerful enough to collect a direct tax on other than an emergency basis. In 1086 he caused a great survey to be made of the property of Englishmen, seeking to discover whether any income was escaping the king. This survey, the results of which were incorporated in what was called the Domesday Book, was made by royal officials who systematically held inquests from county to county and manor to manor up and down the whole land. According to a chronicle, "there was no cow, ox, or swine not set down."

Not overlooking any possible source of power and prestige, William gave considerable attention to religious affairs. The Anglo-Saxon Church just prior to the conquest was badly in need of reform, and, to get papal blessing for his attack on England, William had promised to undertake this reform. He fulfilled his promise, entrusting the task to a Norman, Lanfranc. Lanfranc was made archbishop of Canterbury and soon set about improving the moral life of the English clergy, building new churches, and finding better-educated men to fill Church offices. William permitted the Church to have its own courts instead of following the old custom of settling Church affairs in the shire court, but he continued to play a major role in Church affairs himself, chiefly by controlling the elections of high officials and by restraining papal intervention. Indeed, he ran the risk of a quarrel with the papacy, but he gained a powerful political weapon by controlling the religious organization in his kingdom.

For a considerable portion of the old Anglo-Saxon population the Norman Conquest meant important changes. Many Anglo-Saxon nobles were destroyed; those who survived adopted the ways of the newcomers rather quickly. French became the language of the nobility. New ideas in art, literature, and philosophy, the Romanesque style of architecture, epic poetry so popular among the French nobles, and the new theological discussions arising in Europe flooded into England from the continent, tending to submerge the older cultural life of the Anglo-Saxons. The new Norman nobility, enriched by large grants of land, quickly introduced the manorial system into England, reducing many Anglo-Saxon *ceorls* (freemen having small landholdings) to the rank of serf and making them dependents of manorial lords. Although this process had begun before the Normans came, its rapid spread made the Normans seem oppressive to many Anglo-Saxons. In the broadest sense the conquest made England more nearly like the rest of Europe than she had been. In this process some desirable features of Anglo-Saxon society were destroyed, but England probably gained more than she lost in terms of efficient government, new ideas, and new contacts with Europe.

3. The Building of the Medieval English Constitution

William the Conqueror's political genius might have been wasted had capable successors not continued his work. In the century following his death, however, four capable kings, each with unique talents, guided England's destiny, making the century one of the most significant in English history. William II (1087–1100) was a rough, brutal, immoral tyrant, whose chief contribution lay in his ruthless curbing of the ambitious feudal lords whom the Conqueror established in England. Henry I (1100–35) was the opposite, a quiet, prudent, tight-fisted administrator, willing to labor patiently at the task of running the government he headed. Henry II (1154–89), the greatest of all these kings, was a restless, energetic genius, bent on ruling instead of merely reigning. Richard I, the Lion-Hearted (1189–99), was one of the flashiest men of his age, the ideal knight whose exploits as a crusader stirred the imagination of England and of all Europe. These men together achieved many things we can only mention. They expanded English influence in Wales and Scotland. Henry II ruled over half of France as well as England, completely overshadowing his rivals, the kings of France, and threatening their very existence. Richard played a leading role in the Third Crusade and at least tried to extend England's influence into Mediterranean affairs. None of these achievements can compare, however, to the steady perfection of the English system of government.

One of the chief constitutional developments during the twelfth century was the formation of an effective central administration manned by officials who made a career of serving the king. The old curia regis, which was merely a feudal court made up of royal vassals, was modified to achieve this end. Beginning with Henry I and continuing with Henry II, the king began to call upon certain members of the curia regis to remain constantly in his service instead of returning to their private affairs after the brief meetings of the entire body. This small council soon became a body of specialists in administration. One group of these specialists, known as the Exchequer, devoted full time to administering finances, keeping permanent records, trying judicial cases involving taxation, and overseeing the delivery of money collected by the king's local officials. A separate officer, the treasurer, was created to guard the actual money collected by the Exchequer officials and to make payments from that money on the king's orders. Another group, known as the Chancery, concentrated on composing and registering royal orders and correspondence to which they affixed the royal seal; this branch of the royal government was headed by an official called the chancellor. Other men, specially trained in law, began to devote full time to handling all legal matters needing the king's attention. Each of these great branches of government quickly added large numbers of lesser officials, usually drawn from the non-noble classes of society. By the end of the twelfth century the English king was served by a more fully developed bureaucracy than any other king in Western Europe. So efficient were these officials that Richard the Lion-Hearted was able to spend several years abroad during the Third Crusade without suffering any loss of power.

Finances were always foremost in the minds of England's kings in the late eleventh and twelfth centuries. Again the kings built on the rights they derived from Anglo-Saxon times and from their position as feudal lords of all England. Royal property still provided most of the income. All feudal dues coming to the kings were collected promptly and efficiently; the financial specialists associated with the royal court permitted little that was due to escape. As we shall see, the king took over an ever-increasing amount of judicial business, which returned lucrative fines and fees. By 1200 English kings were even able to levy direct taxes on land and personal property with increasing regularity. William I made regular use of the Danegeld, which was a tax on land first imposed in 991 to raise money to buy off Viking invaders. The Danegeld was abandoned before 1200, but all William's successors collected some kind of direct tax on land. Henry II introduced a new concept of taxation when he began taxing incomes and personal property. The first such tax was levied in 1166 to assist crusaders. In 1188 the famous Saladin tithe was imposed to support Henry II's proposed participation in the Third Crusade. This levy, consisting of a tenth of the value of incomes and personal property, served as a precedent for the king's right to ask for special income in times of crisis. The increasing income from all these sources was an invaluable asset to the kings in expanding their activities and freeing them from dependence on their vassals for services.

Beyond all doubt the most important development of the twelfth century was the formation of a royal judicial system. Henry I and Henry II were the leading figures in the legal innovations of the period. The existing legal system in England was a bewildering maze. Courts were conducted by the king, by his local representatives, by feudal lords, by manorial lords, by the Church, and by the independent towns. In each set of courts different systems of laws, different procedures of determining guilt, and different systems of punishment were followed, creating a chaos almost beyond description. During the twelfth century the kings and their legal advisers took the initiative in ending some of this confusion and in establishing a law common to all citizens.

One of the chief concerns of Henry I and Henry II was to increase the number of royal courts, to man them with expert judges, and to encourage these judges to apply a unified legal code. Henry I began the practice of sending itinerant judges to various parts of England to try cases involving the king's interests, and by Henry II's reign this practice had become regular. At set intervals, announced in advance, royal judges appeared in the shire courts to try cases. After making their circuits, these judges returned to the king's court, where they could compare notes. As a result they were soon deciding cases on the basis of a common set of principles. Henry II established the first of England's great central courts, setting up at Westminster a group of men who sat permanently to handle many cases previously heard by the curia regis. Soon this body began to divide into specialized courts like the court of common pleas and the court of the king's bench. The decisions of these central courts became a guide for the activities of itinerant judges and contributed greatly to uniformity in the royal legal system. The need for judges caused a tremendous interest in legal education, which had the effect of further standardizing legal concepts and produced an extensive literature reflecting a search for new ideas, especially in the Roman law.

Both Henry I and Henry II worked feverishly to expand the jurisdiction of the king's courts. This required depriving feudal lords, the Church, manorial courts, and town courts of some of their ancient rights of justice. In this stirring battle the kings and their lawyer-servants of twelfth-century England showed the greatest ingenuity. In criminal cases the kings usually increased their jurisdiction by legislation that defined new crimes against the king's peace and ordered royal judges to punish violators. No one complained too loudly, since all society was happy to see violence curbed. In civil cases, chiefly involving disputes over property, the problem of increasing royal jurisdiction was more complicated and met with greater opposition, especially from feudal lords, long accustomed to dealing with property disputes in their own courts. Insisting that it was wrong for a man to lose his property unjustly (who would disagree?), the king made it known that anyone who felt that he had been unfairly treated could appeal to the king. All he had to do was to purchase a writ ordering a royal inquiry into his case. The fertile minds of the royal lawyers soon devised writs that applied to almost every conceivable kind of property dispute. By purchasing a writ the man with a complaint brought a royal judge to inquire into his case. On the basis of that inquiry the judge ordered justice to be done. In effect, purchasing a writ amounted to transferring a civil dispute to royal courts and taking it away from feudal or manorial courts.

To encourage the use of royal courts, Henry II and his lawyers made important innovations that assured speedier and more

efficient judgments. Well-trained experts who excelled feudal barons in their knowledge of the law served as royal judges and lawyers. Court sessions were held regularly when scheduled. Fees were clearly fixed. Corruption and bribery among royal judges were severely punished.

Even more significant, however, was the introduction of the jury system in criminal cases. Long before Henry II's reign groups of men had been called together by the king or his officials and required under oath to tell what they knew about some public question. After 1164 Henry applied this idea to criminal cases by ordering his sheriffs to call together a group of men from an area where a crime had been committed and to question them under oath concerning what they knew about the crime. On the basis of this testimony sheriffs could then proceed to apprehend the suspected criminals and put them to trial. Such a jury, called a presentment or grand jury, proved efficient in the speedy apprehension of criminals. By the thirteenth century such groups of men, known as petit juries, were used to decide guilt or innocence.

To most Englishmen the jury system was far fairer and more efficient than the old trials by ordeal or battle. And this innovation, together with the other steps taken to improve judicial efficiency, made royal courts popular. Indeed, nothing increased the prestige of the English monarchy more than did the expansion of royal justice. A single, common law for all the land was virtually a fact by the thirteenth century.

Naturally the feudal barons and the Church resented the increasing authority of the kings. Feudal resistance prior to 1200 usually took the form of an occasional revolt that the kings handled easily. The Church was a stouter foe. From William I's reign to that of Richard I the English crown and the Church wrestled with one another for power, although the struggle reached nowhere near the proportions it did in Germany, probably because the English king's power was more solidly established than was the emperor's. As previously noted, William I made himself popular with the Church by helping to reform it and by granting it extensive lands. However, he clearly established the idea that he expected to exercise control over the filling of high Church offices and over a portion of the Church's wealth. The English clergy, backed by the papacy, first challenged the king's claim to appoint Church officials. The main phase of this quarrel pitted William II against Anselm, archbishop of Canterbury. This quarrel was resolved by the Compromise of Bec in 1106, which allowed the Church to elect its own officials while reserving to the king the privilege of investing the newly elected officials with their lands. This satisfied both king and Church for a time.

However, in the reign of Henry II a new quarrel arose. Henry's choice for the archbishopric of Canterbury fell on one of his most trusted royal servants, Thomas à Becket. Once in possession of his office Becket became an ardent champion of the rights of the Church. When Henry tried to compel clergymen accused of a crime to face trial in royal courts, Becket defied him, claiming that clergymen could be tried only in Church courts. After the quarrel dragged on for several years, the hot-tempered Henry declared that he would like to see Becket dead. A group of Henry's youthful men took the king at his word and murdered Becket at the altar of Canterbury Cathedral. Confronted by a martyr, Henry was forced to concede considerable independence to the Church in judicial affairs and to do public penance for his share in the murder of Becket. In spite of these cases in which the Church held its own against the power of the king, royal influence over the English church was extensive, and usually the Church supported strong monarchy. Just as in France—and in strong contrast with Germany—English monarchy and the Church benefited from mutual support.

As the twelfth century closed, English kings enjoyed an enviable position. They had built a strong government chiefly by exploiting their feudal rights and curbing those elements of English society that favored local exercise of power. Like their counterparts in France and Spain—and at an earlier date—they had removed many of the political evils of the feudal order.

4. Limitations on the Growth of Royal Power, 1199–1272

In spite of the great advance of royal power in the twelfth century, English monarchy was not yet able to exercise absolute authority. During the thirteenth century the barons, supported by the clergy and the rising middle class, reasserted themselves and established a principle inherent in feudal monarchy: The crown was forced to concede that its power was limited by the law and that it could not do certain things without the approval of the privileged interests.

The reign of John (1199–1216) marked a definite turning point in the progress of royal power. This obstinate, short-tempered tyrant, lacking completely in good sense, brought much of his trouble on himself, although it was his misfortune to have as foes two of the most powerful figures in the Middle Ages, Philip II of France and Pope Innocent III. Faced by these giants, John was driven into a series of crises that turned his subjects against him and led to certain highly significant constitutional developments.

The first great blow was dealt by Philip II. We have already observed how Philip enmeshed John in a war in which the prize was the chief English holdings in France. And we also noted how Philip wrested away the English possessions north of the Loire, leaving only remote Aquitaine in English hands (see pp. 239–40). Failure in war was a tragedy for a medieval king; John's subjects were convinced that they were ruled by a man hardly worthy of the crown.

Hard on the heels of the loss of his chief French possessions came a second humiliation. In 1205 John became involved in a quarrel with Innocent III over the appointment of an archbishop of Canterbury. This quarrel dragged on until 1213, when Innocent excommunicated John, put England under interdict, thereby suspending all regular church services, and encouraged Philip II to seize the English throne. To avoid the loss of his throne, John surrendered to Innocent's demands. He even went so far as to turn England over to the pope and then receive it back as a fief, becoming a papal vassal in the process. In reality this was not an especially important transaction, since John was still king. Nevertheless, it did nothing to increase John's prestige in England.

While suffering these rebuffs from France and the papacy John committed a series of unjust and oppressive acts that enraged his own subjects. Most of the powerful barons and churchmen of England rebelled in 1214 and refused to lay down their arms until a year later, when John put his name to the Magna Carta.

The Magna Carta consisted primarily of a long list of specific feudal customs and Church privileges that John promised to observe. A few provisions, however, guaranteed the towns their ancient rights, thus bringing a small portion of the non-noble population into the scene. In general, what the feudal lords, churchmen, and townsmen sought was protection against excessive taxation and guarantees that royal justice would not be expanded excessively. The charter was thus conservative, seeking to check the growth of royal power, which had been so beneficial to England since the conquest. However, the framers of the charter indicated their willingness to accept a strong central government as a necessary element in English life. They were hardly proponents of a return to feudal chaos. They simply insisted that there was a point, defined by law and custom, beyond which royal power must not go. In the clear statement of this principle, not in its specific provisions, lay the importance of the Magna Carta, which has repeatedly served as a precedent for limiting royal power in England until the present.

The clash begun under John continued during the long reign of his son Henry III (1216–72). Henry III was a weak king, extravagant and prone to choose bad advisers,

most of whom were destitute Frenchmen brought to England by his French wife and by his mother, who married a Frenchman after King John's death. Under the strong influence of the papacy Henry allowed the Church to exact heavy dues from England and to fill English church offices with foreign clergymen. And in the hope of regaining England's possessions in France he also allowed himself to become involved in costly wars against a stronger foe.

A considerable number of nobles and churchmen opposed Henry on these matters and found ways of deterring him. Early in his reign he reissued the Magna Carta at the insistence of the nobles, and from time to time some of his foreign advisers were ousted because of baronial pressure. Toward the end of the reign the opposition took more significant steps. In 1258 the barons attempted to create a council of nobles to reform royal government. When this move failed, chiefly because the nobles could not agree on what to do after a council had been set up, they resorted to arms. Under the leadership of Simon de Montfort the nobles, backed by the clergy and towns, waged war against Henry III in 1264 and 1265 and gained the upper hand. Once in control of the government, in 1265 Simon de Montfort and his colleagues tried to secure the backing of all England by summoning the nobles, the clergy, and two representatives from each town and shire to meet as a Parliament. This step, although of great importance for later history, did not save the ruling nobles. In the same year Henry III's son, Edward, mustered the royal forces and crushed the rebel nobles, again making the king master.

5. The Reign of Edward I (1272–1307)

After 1265 a new spirit pervaded England. The highly competent Edward I (1272–1307) apparently realized the issues at stake in the struggle. None of the nobles who opposed John and Henry III ever denied the need for strong monarchy or for the basic institutions through which the king exercised his power. Their protest was against the misuse of royal government and the abuse of ancient rights by kings and their officials. They insisted that royal government had to be conducted to serve the interests of at least a portion of England's people and not merely for the pleasure and profit of the king and his cronies.

Edward I's reign represented an attempt to strengthen the central government by taking these views into account. Edward first of all maintained a watchful eye over the administrative and judicial system he had inherited from his predecessors. Local officials were rigorously supervised, and expert civil servants were chosen to man the chief governmental posts. Effective administration removed many of the complaints that the nobles, clergy, and townsmen had previously raised. Secondly, a series of fundamental laws was enacted, defining more clearly the rights of the crown and the manner in which it would exercise its powers. In general, this legislation, which earned Edward the honor of being called England's Justinian, further limited the power of feudal lords and the Church, while expanding that of the king and his courts. Edward's aggressive legislation raised protests, but his political skill usually disarmed the criticism before it became dangerous.

Edward's chief means of avoiding opposition and one of the chief developments in English history was the regular use of Parliament as a means of taking the important elements of the population into consideration in ruling England. Advisory bodies, like the Anglo-Saxon witan and the Norman curia regis, had long played a part in English life. These groups, however, represented only those individuals having a feudal obligation to serve the king by advising him. During the reign of Henry III a new prac-

tice was instituted. As noted above, Simon de Montfort, seeking the widest possible support for the reforms he was trying to force on the king, summoned in 1265 representatives of the shires and the towns to join with the feudal barons and churchmen in a meeting. And later Edward I clearly sanctioned this precedent in his Model Parliament of 1295. He commanded that each county and each town select two representatives to Parliament to take counsel with the barons and ecclesiastical lords. Such a body was soon accepted as having the power to speak for all Englishmen. Edward called Parliament to serve his own purposes, and especially to get extra money or to have approved some piece of legislation that promised to irk part of the population. At first the organization and the powers of Parliament were vague; not for at least another century did it divide into the Houses of Lords and Commons and establish its rights to approve taxes, to initiate legislation, and to censure or even depose the king. The importance of Edward's innovation in establishing Parliament lay in his recognition of the fact that he had to listen to the demands of his subjects and in his willingness to create an institution that gave his subjects a voice in government.

Edward's death in 1307 heralded the end of one age and the beginning of another. His career, built upon the work of his predecessors, left England with a sound set of political institutions that permitted the king to supply justice and order to all his subjects while still allowing them to retain part of the rights and privileges they claimed. The chaos that threatened to engulf England before 1066 had been replaced by a solidly established monarchy whose authority was widely accepted yet limited by law and ancient custom.

SUGGESTED READING

* George Macaulay Trevelyan, *History of England*, 3 vols. (Anchor). Originally published as a single volume in 1926; 3rd ed., 1952. A brilliantly written survey of all English history. Books I and II of the first volume of the paperback edition cover English history from Anglo-Saxon times down to the middle of the thirteenth century.

H. W. C. Davis, *England under the Normans and Angevins, 1066–1272*, 13th ed. (1949). A thorough treatment of the political history of England from the Conquest to the end of the thirteenth century.

* Sidney Painter, *The Rise of the Feudal Monarchies* (Cornell). Chapter II of this short volume gives a concise survey of medieval English history, stressing the key constitutional developments accompanying the establishment of strong monarchy.

Ch. Petit-Dutaillis, *The Feudal Monarchy in France and England from the Tenth to the Thirteenth Century* (1936). An excellent treatment of the development of the central government of England, much more detailed than Painter's treatment, cited above.

Frederick Pollock and Frederick William Maitland, *The History of the English Law before the Time of Edward I*, 2nd ed., 2 vols. (1923). A classic treatment of the early development of English law. This is not an easy book to master, but it is of immense value in understanding the background of the modern legal systems of England and the United States. It is especially recommended for those who intend to study law.

* D. M. Stenton, *English Society in the Early Middle Ages*, 2nd ed. (Penguin). An excellent survey of social conditions in England during the eleventh, twelfth, and thirteenth centuries.

Sidney Dark, *St. Thomas of Canterbury* (1927). A clear picture of English life in the twelfth century can be gained from this well-written biography of one of the chief religious leaders of this period.

Carl Stephenson and Frederick George Marcham, eds., *Sources of English Constitutional History* (1937). An excellent collection of original documents illustrating the development of the English government. Included in the collection is a translation of the Magna Carta.

CHAPTER 22

The Revival and Triumph of the Church

WHILE emperors and kings were consolidating their authority, a comparable consolidation was occurring in the religious structure of Western Europe. Impelled by a variety of motives, not the least of which was an urge to create the City of God on earth, able churchmen during the eleventh and twelfth centuries launched a vast program to improve the Church's organization, to define its teachings, to discipline its members, and to probe more deeply into the meaning of the Christian message. Their efforts were so successful that by the thirteenth century the Church controlled much of Western European life.

1. The Church in the Tenth Century

The magnitude of the effort to revive the Church can only be appreciated by understanding the dismal religious situation in the tenth century. The papacy had fallen into a helpless dependence on the feudal nobles of Italy, losing most of its moral and spiritual authority in the process. Most of the higher clergy in Europe were so thoroughly enmeshed in the feudal system as vassals, lords, landowners, and warriors that they had little time for religious affairs. The lower clergy was sunk in ignorance and vice, seldom being subjected to any kind of discipline or education. The laity, although deeply religious, was poorly informed about Christian teachings and tended to fall into the worst kinds of superstitions.

There were, however, some bright spots, pointing toward a recovery and reform. As early as 910 the important new monastery founded at Cluny in France aimed straight at the heart of the church's trouble. Its founder, Duke William of Aquitaine, provided that the new monastery be free from lay control in any form, and strict adherence to the Benedictine rule resulted in an immediate improvement in the moral life of the monks. Cluny was quickly imitated all over Europe, serving as a model both for reforming existing monasteries and for establishing new houses. The abbot of Cluny, who was accepted as the head of numerous individual monasteries, created an order capable of imposing uniformity and discipline. The Cluniac spirit loosed a movement that soon caught up the whole Church and opened an assault on the many evils in tenth-century religious life.

2. Centralization of Church Organization

By the beginning of the eleventh century the reforming spirit had begun to stir the world outside monastic walls, and the Church grew steadily in power and prestige. In the thirteenth century the peak had been reached.

One of the major aspects of this growth was the perfection of a centralized organization that placed the whole ecclesiastical structure under the direct control of the Roman papacy. Gregory VII was a pioneer figure in this move. He dominated the papal office for nearly forty years, first as confidant and adviser of several popes and then as pope himself from 1073 to 1085. A man of strong principles, he proved a ferocious foe for those who resisted his plans. He believed that all human activity ought to be dedicated to the service of God and that the Church had been instituted to guide men in serving their Maker. The pope had the responsibility to lead the Church in this mission.

To restore papal leadership from the dismal depths to which it had sunk in the tenth century, Gregory believed that he had a twofold task. First, he must free the Church from lay control. This conviction led him to enter a long struggle with lay society over the investiture question, the most dramatic phase of which pitted Gregory against Henry IV, the Holy Roman Emperor. We need not review the details of that struggle, since we have discussed it in connection with the kingdoms involved. It went on long after Gregory's death. The Church never won a complete victory, being forced to agree to a compromise solution that allowed the Church to elect its own officials while reserving to laymen the right to invest the new official with the property connected with the office. However, this compromise elevated the Church to a position of equality with lay authorities and provided a freedom of action that allowed the Church to increase its role in society.

Gregory's second task was that of strengthening the Church's organization. Realizing that freedom from lay control imposed on the Church the burden of its own control, Gregory took steps to establish papal direction over the whole Church. The fundamental elements of a centralized ecclesiastical organization already existed; Gregory's task was to fashion a unified working system out of the pieces. Under his guidance a college of cardinals was instituted in 1059 to elect the pope and eliminate the Holy Roman emperors from this important function. Gregory also launched a legislative program aimed at eliminating marriage, simony (buying of Church offices), and other moral laxness among the clergy. Papal legates were sent everywhere to discover and correct such evils, although Rome reserved the right to handle difficult cases. Finally, Gregory paid special attention to papal finances, hoping to create a taxing system adequate to support the Church.

Gregory did not live to see his program succeed. However, his policy became that of his successors. Step by step through the twelfth and into the thirteenth centuries an ecclesiastical monarchy was built, making St. Peter's successors head of the Church in reality. This centralizing trend reached its culmination during the pontificate of Innocent III (1198–1216), probably the most powerful of all popes and certainly the most powerful figure of the thirteenth century. Innocent lacked none of Gregory's convictions with respect to the pope's God-given right to judge and direct the activities of all Christians, whatever their rank. Innocent was willing to concede that kings and lay governments were necessary in order to govern earthly society, but he insisted that princes must submit to the superior wisdom of the Church and its head, the pope.

Innocent was able to make papal influence felt widely in Western Europe because he stood as undisputed master of an organization that had been growing since Gregory VII's time. In Rome the pope commanded an extensive bureaucracy, called the curia, which was divided into specialized departments dealing with finances, correspondence and records, doctrinal affairs, and disciplinary matters. These departments were manned by well-educated experts. The curia maintained a network of communications reaching over all Europe. Papal legates traveled everywhere to direct church activities, to enforce papal orders, and to gather information. A huge body of judicial business flowed to Rome for final decision. In many areas the pope had acquired the right to fill local offices, allowing him to control the personnel who manned the key spots in the Church's organization. A huge income, derived from papal property, gifts, fees paid for use of papal courts, assessments on the faithful, levies on the income of lesser clergy, and numerous other sources, supported this vast organization.

Ranked under Innocent III was the age-old hierarchy of archbishops, bishops, and priests. By the thirteenth century the exact function of each branch of the clerical hierachy was carefully defined in canon law. Each archbishop and bishop headed a small-scale model of the papal curia, called a cathedral chapter, which directed the activities of parish priests who in turn supervised the religious life of laymen. Most of the great monastic orders had also been brought under papal control by the thirteenth century.

The chief occupation of this vast hierarchy was the saving of souls. During the thirteenth century the powerful church organization succeeded in imposing a high degree of uniformity in Europe's religious life. Christians participated in the same ceremonies, received the same sacraments, said the same prayers, and were taught the same doctrines. A single code of law, backed by an efficient court system, imposed a common discipline on all Christians. To ensure uniformity within the Church, the papacy had developed a special court called the Inquisition, first inaugurated by Innocent III. This court was armed with authority to discover heretics, secure from them an admission of guilt, and give them the choice of returning to orthodoxy or of death. Free to roam over all Europe, the Inquisition was a devastating weapon against anyone who balked at accepting the Church's authority.

The influence of Innocent III and his vast organization extended far beyond religious affairs. No pope ever played a more important role in political life than did Innocent, who was a masterful politician. To describe all his exploits would demand telling most of the political history of Western Europe in the early thirteenth century. We have already observed how Innocent manipulated affairs in Germany and Italy to weaken the Holy Roman Emperor and to make his own candidate, Frederick II, ruler of the empire. This was also the pope who humiliated John of England over the issue of filling the highest church office in England. After a long quarrel Innocent finally compelled Philip II of France to take back his second wife, whom he had repudiated the day after their marriage. Several lesser states were compelled or persuaded to accept the pope as their overlord, their kings becoming papal vassals. Innocent launched the Fourth Crusade and exercised considerable influence in Byzantine affairs when that crusade ended in the capture of Constantinople. The mighty pope was able to organize a crushing crusade against the heretical Albigensians in southern France by calling on the services of the French king and nobility to wield the sword. In exercising such wide political power Innocent made no distinction between religion and politics. He used religious weapons to gain political ends and political pressure to impose his spiritual leadership. When he spoke of his right to exercise "the fullness of power," Innocent meant complete mastery over all aspects of life.

3. Standardization of Canon Law and Doctrine

Organization alone did not solve all the Church's problems. Increasing centralization revealed that there was considerable confusion in the governing regulations and the teachings of the Church. In the eleventh and twelfth centuries there was a great surge of activity to remove the confusion.

One area of progress centered around the canon law. The Church possessed a large body of law, much of it dating from earlier periods. Many of its provisions were contradictory and some no longer applied to current situations. Moreover, new difficulties were constantly arising in this era of reform. Church lawyers tackled the problem with vigor. Guided by Scripture, papal decrees, the acts of councils, the writings of the early fathers, and the example of the Code of Justinian, they worked toward an extensive, consistent, and organized collection of canon law. The greatest canon lawyer of the era, Gratian, published his *Decretals* in 1140. This work immediately became the standard guide for church administration and discipline, and the basis upon which extensive legal comments were written. Among many other things Gratian's work defined the powers of each rank of the clergy, the jurisdiction of ecclesiastical courts, crimes against the Church and their punishment, the proper use of income and property, and the manner of conducting services. Throughout the work ran one predominant idea—the supremacy of the papacy in governing Church organization.

Church doctrines were even more confused than Church law. The teachings of the fathers were not adequately understood. And, as we shall see later, during the twelfth century Western Europeans began to gain a wider acquaintance with the philosophical and religious teachings of the classical Greeks, which often contradicted Christian teaching. This challenge was answered by the emergence of several vigorous theologians who worked successfully to define with precision the basic doctrines of the Church.

Probably the chief figure in the Church's struggle to standardize its doctrines was Abélard, a tempestuous twelfth-century scholar, constantly in trouble for his criticism of other scholars. Abélard's contribution to the development of systematic theology lay in establishing a method for eliminating confusion and contradiction. He dramatically called attention to the conflicting teachings of Scriptures, the fathers, and tradition on certain key theological questions. He insisted that only by the application of human reason could these differences be resolved. This method of clarifying revealed truth by the use of reason soon came to be known as scholasticism. Most theologians quickly adopted the method. During the thirteenth century a series of great scholastic philosophers, the chief of whom was Thomas Aquinas, worked toward a systematic description of the Church's teachings and eliminated most of the earlier confusion. Not only did Thomas Aquinas and his fellow theologians define doctrines more

clearly, but also they tried to weave all human knowledge into a single body related to the Church's teaching, giving the Church a single version of the truth that could be taught to all.

Leaving aside for a moment the larger implications and achievements of the scholastics, let us concentrate on the doctrines concerning salvation and the sacramental system that stood at the heart of the Church's teachings by the thirteenth century. None of these doctrines was new; most of them dated back to the early centuries of Church history. The theologians of the twelfth and thirteenth centuries merely supplied more precise definitions and, with the backing of the ecclesiastical hierarchy, imposed greater uniformity concerning these fundamental questions.

According to the thirteenth-century theologians, God had created man in order that he might eventually be saved, human life being but a testing period during which man proved his worthiness of salvation. A Christian could be saved only by virtue of the grace God bestowed on him. Grace was obtained by partaking of the sacraments, instituted by Christ as the essential part of His divine mission. According to Peter Lombard, a twelfth-century theologian, whose *Sentences* was the most widely read book on doctrine of the age, there were seven grace-giving sacraments. Prior to this there had been considerable disagreement on the exact number of sacraments. Baptism removed the stain of original sin, which all Christians inherited from Adam and Eve. Confirmation infused into a Christian the Holy Ghost, strengthening his faith and fortifying him against the devil. Extreme unction, administered to those in danger of death from sickness, supplied its recipients with grace to strengthen them spiritually at the time when they might face the Almighty and removed from their souls the stain of the minor (or venial) sins they had committed. Marriage sanctified the married state and family life. Holy orders or ordination, through which a layman was elevated to the rank of priest, supplied the clergyman with special powers required to perform his religious duties. This sacrament was administered by a bishop, whose authority, according to the Church's doctrine of apostolic succession, extended back in an uninterrupted line to the apostles. The Church taught that Christ had handed on to his apostles the powers to teach the faith, to forgive sin, and to consecrate the Eucharist. The apostles had in turn conferred these powers on certain bishops who by this act acquired the power to transmit them to their successors. Therefore, each ordained

THE CONSECRATION. This scene depicts a priest elevating the sacred host at the most solemn moment during the celebration of the Mass. According to the doctrine of transubstantiation the wafer, here being held aloft by the priest, is actually the body of Christ. In the belief of Christians, the real presence of Christ during the mass gave each individual a chance to approach the Lord, to ask his blessings, and to benefit from his grace. (*Walters Art Gallery, Baltimore*)

clergyman by receiving the sacrament of holy orders became a valid successor of Christ and the apostles in teaching the faith, forgiving sins, and consecrating the Eucharist at Mass. The Eucharist was the sacrament by which Christ himself was present to the faithful during the celebration of the Mass. The exact nature of this sacrament had long troubled theologians. It was not until 1215 at the Fourth Lateran Council, held under the direction of Innocent III, that the doctrine of transubstantiation was officially pronounced. According to this doctrine, Christ became truly present at the moment of the consecration under the appearance of bread and wine. His real presence was effected by a miraculous change in the substance of the bread and wine, although their external accidents (i.e., color, shape, taste, etc.) remained the same. Partaking of this sacrament by attending Mass and receiving Communion signified the receiving of Christ and the consequent infusion of grace into the soul. No punishment was greater than to be excommunicated, which meant being cut off from receiving the Eucharist. The last sacrament was penance, whereby a sinner who confessed his sins to a priest and felt sorrow for his sins would receive the forgiveness of God. Provided that he made some sacrifice or did some good work assigned by the priest, the penitent sinner who had confessed was relieved of all the punishments for his sins. The Fourth Lateran Council decreed that every Christian must confess at least once a year. These sacraments were administered by the clergy, meaning that the Church held the keys to the kingdom of heaven. No man could thus expect salvation without the services of the Church.

Since canon law and theology were formidable subjects, requiring extensive learning, the Church attempted to perfect its educational system. Episcopal and monastic schools flourished as never before, broadening their curricula and intensifying their studies. The chief educational innovation of the era was the founding of universities, which began to appear in the late twelfth century (which we shall see later). These Church-supported institutions provided scholars with an opportunity to devote all their time to study and teaching. Moreover, the universities and the episcopal and monastic schools gave the Church a powerful weapon in impressing its ideas on all of Europe: virtual monopoly of learning.

4. New Monastic and Popular Religious Movements

Not all the regenerative forces in the Church during the eleventh, twelfth, and thirteenth centuries were poured into perfecting organization, codifying law, and systematizing doctrine. Several vigorous movements sprang up seeking to find new meanings in Christianity and to put these ideas into practice. Most of this activity took the form of new monastic movements. However, there were important popular movements dedicated to the same end.

After the papacy and even laymen became the champions of independence for the Church and of higher moral standards for clergymen, the Cluniac movement lost its leadership, and emphasis in the monasteries shifted toward perfecting the inner life of individuals rather than correcting their external activities. This new spirit found its best expression in the Cistercian Order, founded in 1098 by a Benedictine monk who felt that the ancient rule was not being strictly observed. The new order was dedicated to extreme poverty, simplicity of worship, complete isolation from the world, hard labor, and rigid discipline. However, the Cistercian movement was more than a return to Benedictine purity. Owing largely to the influence of the greatest Cistercian, Bernard of Clairvaux, the order became a militant agency seeking to arouse all men to purity, piety, and devoted action for Christ. Bernard entered the order in 1113; until his death in 1153 he was the most influential figure in Western Europe. As a monastic leader he insisted that a monk could learn to know God directly only if he deprived himself of physical comforts and prayed

long and earnestly. A monk who had thus fortified himself would be a worthy opponent of the devil and could go into the world to fight sin and indifference without fear of corruption. This was exactly what Bernard did. During his long public career he was involved in nearly every important event in Europe. His preaching was instrumental in launching the Second Crusade. He became the papacy's chief support in hunting down corrupt clergymen; Bernard even turned his blasts against a pope or two. He was a ruthless and relentless foe of any unorthodox or heretical movement. He hounded Europe's kings constantly to improve their lives and their government. As a popular preacher he had no peer. He and other monks cast in his image—almost an army of puritanical, industrious, sober soldiers of Christ—penetrated into every corner of Europe urging men to be better Christians.

Although the Cistercians dominated monasticism during the twelfth century, other vigorous monastic movements contributed to the deepening current of religious life. Numerous hermits, living in isolated cells and making a virtue out of extreme poverty, fired the imagination of many with their sacrifices and their refusal to let the world distract them from God. A highly important order called the Augustinian canons was organized for the purpose of improving the moral quality of the clerks who assisted bishops in their administrative tasks. The new order put these clerks under a strict rule emphasizing poverty, prayer, and moral excellence, while allowing them to move about freely as preachers and administrators. The twelfth century saw the founding of the great crusading orders, the Templars, the Hospitalers, and the Teutonic Knights. These orders were made up of knights who took special vows fitting to their work as warriors against the infidel Moslems. Their rigid discipline, their zeal, and their extensive organization capable of supplying men and money from all over Europe made the crusading orders a powerful weapon during the early crusades. The military orders also organized numerous charitable works to help pious crusaders.

The thirteenth century produced two more new monastic orders, the Dominicans and the Franciscans, which represented the culmination of the trends apparent in the previous century and which marked the height of medieval spiritual striving. The Dominican order was the product of the fertile mind of a Spanish priest named Dominic (1170–1221). During a tour through southern France, where the Albigensian heresy was rampant, Dominic became convinced that orthodoxy would prevail only on condition that preachers learned in theology and free from all suspicion of excessive wealth mingled with the heretics. In 1215 he presented this idea to Innocent III, who authorized him to organize a new order dedicated to the destruction of heresy by preaching. Dominic immediately began to recruit members for his order. He required that all of them practice poverty, insisting that his monks live by begging. Even greater stress was placed on education. Each Dominican was put through a rigorous training program aimed at making him an expert theologian. Armed with their knowledge, the Black Friars of St. Dominic spread over Europe preaching to everyone. Typical of the new monasticism of the thirteenth century, the Dominicans did not live in isolated monasteries; instead they circulated freely among laymen. They very quickly established themselves as one of the strongest arms of papal power, especially useful in directing the Inquisition against heretics and controlling the teaching of theology in the great universities.

The inspiration for the Franciscan order was supplied by one of the most appealing figures in all history, Francis of Assisi (1182–1226). The son of a wealthy Italian merchant, Francis established in his youth a reputation as a playboy and jovial companion. But while still a young man he underwent a fundamental spiritual conversion that convinced him that he must imitate Christ. Because of his strange conduct his father disinherited him, whereupon Francis turned to a life of poverty, preaching, and the performance of charitable works. He stressed the need for love and repentance. Francis was especially effective as a preacher because of his personality, which exuded joy, lightheartedness, and a sympathy for all men. Almost immediately both men and women were converted by his simple message and his fascinating personality, surrendering their wealth, working or begging for a livelihood, and preaching a simple message of love for all.

Francis was always an obedient son of the Church. In 1210 he applied to Innocent III for permission to continue his work. Innocent hesitated, feeling that Francis's demands on his followers were too severe, and perhaps concerned lest the simple message of love and repentance would breed a crop of heretics with little regard for the elaborate machinery that the organized Church supplied for saving souls. Finally, however, he consented to Francis's request. Between 1210 and 1226, when Francis died, the order grew rapidly, spreading to nearly every part of Western Europe and even to areas outside Europe. Often the Franciscans met opposition from local clergymen because of their stirring sermons, their exaltation of poverty, and their ability to attract attention. The Franciscans flourished in spite of this opposition. Their fresh approach to religious life was welcome, especially among the masses.

The mendicant orders of begging friars were pillars of strength for the thirteenth-century Church. Each order was a controlling influence on the dynamic forces working in Europe and threatening the Church's power. The Dominican Order, emphasizing education and teaching, became the refuge of scholars and preachers, who studied, systematized, and propagated Christian doctrine with a vigor seldom seen in the earlier history of the Church. The simple disciples of Francis, preaching a message of repentance and love, provided an outlet for those dissatisfied with the rigorous, rather formal activities of the organized Church. The friars proved especially useful to the papacy, lending themselves to the containment and direction of theological speculation and popular religious life. Because of their flexible organization, which did not confine the friars to a fixed residence, the new orders were able to extend the Church's influence to those centers of thirteenth-century life where there was tremendous ferment—the cities, the universities, and the courts of the powerful kings. Their success demonstrated the Church's ability to make an appeal to almost any element of society.

The intensification of religious life was also felt outside the monastic orders, producing a variety of popular religious movements. Most of these began independently of the official Church, and many of them were eventually condemned as heretical. Some of the movements resulted from the activities of a single individual, hardly outlasting his career. The most significant manifestations of spontaneous religious sentiment, however, took the form of mass movements. The best examples were the Waldensians and the Cathari (or Albigensians).

The Waldensian movement grew out of the work of Peter Waldo, a rich French merchant who in 1173 gave away his wealth and took up a life of poverty in imitation of Christ. His dramatic decision attracted a large following. The Waldensians took as their only authority the New Testament, refusing to accept the dictates of popes and bishops, who were only men and who because of their wealth were not good Christians. Living in poverty, the Waldensians went among the people, preaching and praying in vernacular languages, condemning the ordinary clergy, and refusing to admit many of the current teachings of the Church. They developed their own clergy and their own religious services. Among their followers they insisted upon strict moral life, reflecting many of the ideas about sobriety, temperance, honesty, and simplicity of life that St. Bernard and his Cistercians were preaching. Although the Waldensians were per-

SAINT FRANCIS OF ASSISI, BY PISANO. This painting of the founder of the Franciscan Order catches the spirit of the simple, loving man of poverty who repudiated wealth and pleasure in favor of love for and service to his fellow men. Saint Francis was one of many medieval monks whose zeal to serve Christ brought about the constant regeneration of the Church. (*Alinari Photo*)

mitted to carry on their work for a while, eventually they were accused of heresy and attacked by the papacy and the Church hierarchy. Some Waldensian groups, especially in France, returned to orthodoxy. However, in northern Italy they survived persecution throughout the Middle Ages.

Far more radical were the Cathari, or Albigensians. This heresy originated in the Near East as early as the fourth century, probably as a result of the mixing of Christian and Zoroastrian ideas. It spread slowly westward across Asia Minor, through Bulgaria and Hungary, finally reaching northern Italy and southern France in the tenth century. The movement was most vigorous in southern France, although by 1200 it exerted influence throughout Europe. The Cathari believed that two powers, one good and the other evil, were constantly in combat for the world and for men. The power of good was a spiritual power, while the evil force was materialistic. Everything that had to do with the material world was to be avoided. Because the organized Church had wealth and dealt in worldly affairs, it was condemned; its clergy, its sacraments, its services were creations of the devil. The true Church was made up of those who completely denied the world and the flesh. True Cathari refused to marry, holding that even reproduction was evil. They ate no meat, milk, or eggs, which were the fruits of sexual union. They owned no property and refused to shed blood. The "perfect," as they called themselves, were certain that they were saved. Allowance was made, however, for weaker men. Second-grade Cathari, called "believers," were permitted to indulge more freely, although every "believer" hoped someday to become a "perfect." Since they repudiated the Church, the Cathari developed their own clergy, their own simple services, and their own rules of conduct. Needless to say, they were considered heretics from the beginning, and in the thirteenth century the papacy and the French monarchy delivered a ferocious assault that virtually eradicated the movement.

5. The Expansion of Christianity

Still another manifestation of religious vigor and of the Church's increasing power in the eleventh, twelfth, and thirteenth centuries was the expansion of the Christian world. Expansion took two forms: military crusading and missionary work. We shall return to military expansion later. While Christian armies were on the march, missionaries won notable successes on the northern and eastern fringes of Europe. Beginning in the late tenth century, Christianity advanced steadily among the Scandinavian countries, the home of the awesome Vikings. Missionaries from England carried the chief burden here. They received invaluable help from various Scandinavian kings, who were nearly always the first converts and who then worked hard to convert their subjects. From Scandinavia, Christianity was soon carried to Iceland by the Viking sailors. During the tenth and eleventh centuries Poland, Bohemia, and Hungary entered the Christian camp, converted chiefly through the efforts of German clergymen, actively backed by the strong arm of the Holy Roman Emperors. German missionaries also pushed slowly eastward along the Baltic Sea coast during the eleventh and twelfth centuries. The majority of the Russians were converted before 1100, although the Western Church could not take credit for this accomplishment, since Byzantine influence was all-powerful there. Wherever new converts were made by Western missionaries, Western religious institutions and practices were introduced. Through the Church the newly converted peoples were rapidly incorporated into the main stream of Western European civilization.

6. The Nature of the Church's Power in the Thirteenth Century: A Summary

The root of the Church's power in the thirteenth century lay in its successful effort to convince nearly all Western Europeans that it possessed the keys to heaven in its sacramental system. That fundamental teaching was presented to millions almost daily in the form of a standardized system of worship and ritual. Through a highly centralized organization the Church was able to enforce uniformity of belief, ritual,

THE LAST JUDGMENT. This scene of judgment day is carved above the central entrance of the cathedral of Bourges in France. The lower panel depicts the tombs of the dead being opened; above, the angel weighs the good in each man in his scales. Christ sits in his judgment seat at the top, surrounded by disciples. By attending Mass, partaking in the sacrament of the eucharist, and sharing in Divine Grace, men hoped to avoid joining the company on the right (center panel). (*Archives Photographiques, Paris*)

and conduct. Repeatedly the Church demonstrated its ability to expand its activities to embrace new problems. Through its hold on men's minds and hearts and because of its organization the Church played a major role in Europe's political and economic life. Perhaps it would be more accurate to say that the Church insisted with considerable success that political life and economic life were but different aspects of the service of God and must therefore be bent to serve religious ends as directed by the Church. Few things happened in which the Church did not have a voice; few problems arose for which it did not have an answer.

An over-all view of the Church's activity strongly suggests that the Church succeeded in bringing most of Western Europe's population very close to unity in thought and action. As members of the Roman Catholic Church all men were expected to adhere to one set of ideas, one code of conduct, one master. It would be impossible to judge to what extent the total population of Western Europe felt this unity, since we have no means of probing the innermost thoughts of people either in the past or the present. Outwardly the history of the thirteenth century suggests a general conformance to Church leadership. Some historians have concluded that this century marked a period in which Western European civilization came the closest to meaning one thing to all people and that never since have Europeans had so much in common. If this is true, then it was the Church that made it possible.

SUGGESTED READING

* Marshall W. Baldwin, *The Medieval Church* (Cornell). A brief review of medieval Church history that succeeds in highlighting the most important aspects of the Church's activity.

Kenneth Scott Latourette, *A History of Christianity* (1953), pp. 381–597. A more detailed discussion of Church history than the Baldwin book. Especially good for its up-to-date bibliographies on the many subjects connected with Church history.

Philip Hughes, *A History of the Church*, rev. ed. (1949), Vol. II. A longer history of the medieval Church; this volume covers the period from the fourth to the thirteenth century by a Roman Catholic author.

* Sidney R. Packard, *Europe and the Church under Innocent III* (Berkshire Series, 1927). An excellent short study of the Church during the brief period in the early thirteenth century when its power reached its peak. This book will serve especially well to show how the Church exercised its tremendous power.

* Summerfield Baldwin, *The Organization of Medieval Christianity* (Berkshire Series, 1929). A clear description of the major features of medieval Church organization, recommended to any reader who has difficulty in understanding the intricacies of Church organization.

William Barry, *The Papal Monarchy from St. Gregory the Great to Boniface VIII* (590–1303) (1902). A good treatment of the growth of the papacy and of the establishment of papal control over all aspects of Church life.

G. G. Coulton, *Five Centuries of Religion*, 4 vols. (1923–50). A vast collection of materials illustrating the nature of medieval religious life. Any reader will enjoy a random sampling of the material gathered in these volumes. Monasticism occupies most of the author's attention; generally he is not sympathetic toward the monks.

Herbert B. Workman, *Evolution of the Monastic Ideal from the Earliest Times to the Coming of the Friars* (1913). A sympathetic discussion of a subject of tremendous importance to medieval civilization but little appreciated today. The book is especially good in its discussion of the Benedictine movement.

Edward L. Cutts, *Parish Priests and Their People in the Middle Ages in England* (1914). A fairly adequate picture of parish life in the Middle Ages, a phase of religious life that is often neglected amid the activities of great popes, monks, and bishops.

Paul Sabatier, *The Life of St. Francis*, tr. by Louise Seymour Houghton (1930). A classic biography of this highly appealing figure; the book is extremely sympathetic toward St. Francis. Perhaps any reader will have difficulty avoiding the charm of Francis and therefore will overlook Sabatier's strong feeling for his subject.

L. Elliott Binns, *Innocent III* (1931). A brief, somewhat oversimplified summary of this great pope's career.

Watkin Williams, *Saint Bernard of Clairvaux*, 2nd ed. (1953). A well-done study of Bernard's career and a sound analysis of his influence on medieval history. The book is graced by numerous selections from Bernard's own writings.

Roger Lloyd, *Peter Abelard: The Orthodox Rebel*, 2nd ed., rev. (1947). A well-written biography not only covering the career of Abélard but also discussing adequately his role in medieval thought and in the history of the medieval Church.

Bede Jarrett, *Life of St. Dominic* (1170–1221) (1934). A sound biography of the founder of the Dominican order.

Arnold Toynbee, *A Study of History*, 10 vols. (1934–54), Vol. IV, 512–84. This passage, devoted to the nature of the power of the papacy in the thirteenth century and to the dangers inherent in that power, contains some especially brilliant suggestions on the position of the Church in medieval society.

———◆———

CHAPTER 23

The Expansion of Europe

THE RESTORATION of political order and the revitalization of the Church between 1000 and 1300 led Western Europeans to become increasingly aggressive toward the non-European world and to exploit the backward areas of Europe. Their expansive thrust operated in different ways. While merchants and artisans combined their skills to create new sources of wealth within Europe, European warriors and merchants moved beyond Europe's frontiers to capture new lands and to exploit new sources of wealth. At the same time landlords and peasants broke out of the old manorial boundaries to clear new lands. By 1300 the subtle working of these forces had wrought important changes within European society and had considerably altered the relationship between the European and non-European worlds.

1. Military Expansion: The Beginning of the Crusades

By the end of the tenth century many forces encouraged Western Europeans to attempt the conquest of foreign lands. The fury of the Viking, Magyar, and Moslem attacks had begun to lessen. The Vikings had settled in large numbers on European soil and were now lending their warlike talents for use against the non-European world. The Magyars had settled peacefully in Hungary. The great Moslem Empire of the Abassids was rapidly disintegrating, and struggles for

power were crippling its already weakened body. The Byzantine Empire, controlling Asia Minor, the Balkan Peninsula, and southern Italy, had passed its peak. The new states of Western Europe were beginning to take shape, putting an end to the worst of the feudal disorders and freeing a part of the warring nobility for activity other than fighting each other.

During the eleventh century Europeans began to capitalize on the changing situation. German princes, clergymen, and peasants moved eastward across the Elbe. Norman adventurers struck from France into southern Italy and Sicily, reducing the power there of the Byzantine Empire and the Moslems. Spanish warriors, backed by French knights, advanced southward in the Iberian Peninsula.

However, these unco-ordinated efforts did not tap Europe's full capacity for expansion. What was needed was a cause with which a larger segment of Europe's population could become identified. The Church supplied this cause by calling for a war on the Moslem infidels to win back the Holy Land and to crush these ancient foes of Christianity.

Pope Urban II launched the crusading movement with a speech at Clermont in France in 1095. He was prompted to act at this moment chiefly because of an appeal he had recently received from Alexius, the Byzantine emperor, pleading for European warriors to help the Byzantine Empire defend itself against the Seljuk Turks. These

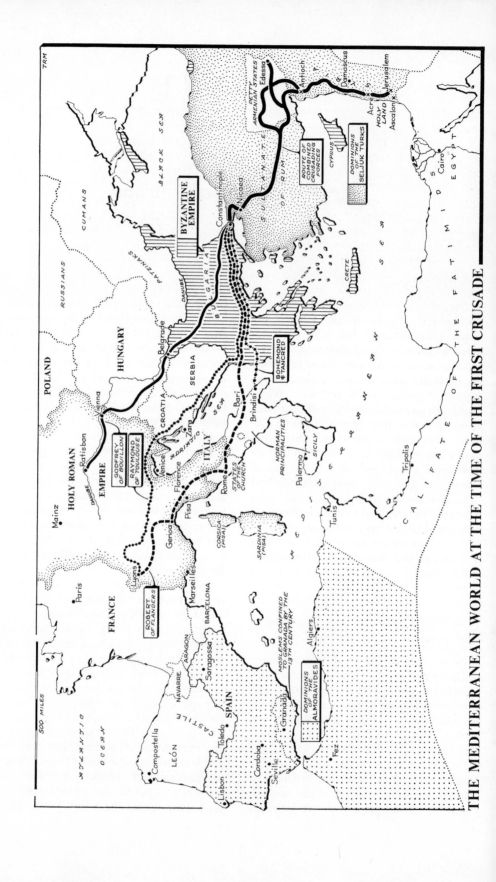

THE MEDITERRANEAN WORLD AT THE TIME OF THE FIRST CRUSADE

recent converts to Islam, advancing out of the East, had in 1071 defeated the Byzantines at the battle of Manzikert and had won virtual control of Asia Minor. Moreover, Urban II, still locked in a struggle with the Holy Roman Emperor, Henry IV, over the investiture question, needed some bold stroke to elevate papal prestige.

At Clermont, Urban called for an army of knights under papal leadership to be formed immediately. Although his appeal was greeted enthusiastically, especially in France, no single army was formed. Instead several important feudal nobles gathered separate armies. By the summer of 1096 these armies, totaling about fifteen thousand knights and foot soldiers, began to move toward Constantinople. They had been preceded by a poverty-stricken crowd of peasants and artisans stirred to crusading fervor by overenthusiastic preachers. These peasants succeeded only in arousing hostility among the peoples in the Balkan area and around Constantinople by their unruly conduct.

The crusading armies converged on Constantinople during the fall and winter of 1096. After protracted negotiations Alexius persuaded the crusading leaders to swear an oath of allegiance to him personally and to promise to return any conquered territories to his control. In the spring of 1097 the crusaders began their march across Asia Minor. One decisive battle at Dorylaeum brushed aside Turkish resistance and allowed the crusaders to pass on toward the Holy Land. Once in Syria the crusading army began to split up, chiefly because its leaders were anxious to assure their private fortunes. One group left the main body of the crusaders to establish control over Edessa and its surrounding territory. After the key city of Antioch had been captured in June, 1098, a Norman prince, Bohemond, refused to leave it, claiming it as his by right of conquest. It was not until July, 1099, that Jerusalem was captured by the remaining crusaders, who vented their fury on the Moslems by slaughtering hundreds of natives. This great victory made the First Crusade

a success. All Europe was exalted at the news that the valiant Christian warriors had planted the cross once again in the Holy City.

Once in possession of Jerusalem, Antioch, Edessa, and other key cities, the crusaders had to think of instituting a government. Disregarding their pledge to Alexius to serve as his vassals and the papal plan to create a state subordinate to Rome, the crusaders established a feudal monarchy similar to what they had left behind in Europe. In 1100 Baldwin of Edessa was elected king of the Latin Kingdom of Jerusalem. He created a series of fiefs that he granted to men willing to become his vassals. These great fief holders subdivided their holdings and acquired vassals of their own, creating a typical feudal hierarchy. The king ruled this kingdom with the advice of his vassals, who met regularly in a high court at Jerusalem. The native population was disturbed very little. Usually their previous local rulers continued to control them under the supervision of the Latin rulers.

The chief problem of the Latin Kingdom of Jerusalem was defense. The Latins tried hard to strengthen their position. They seized the chief seaports along the Mediterranean with aid from Italian navies. They built powerful castles at strategic locations in the Holy Land. Before 1130 they established the two great crusading orders, the Knights Templar and the Knights Hospitaler, made up of knights who had taken a vow to defend the Christians living in and coming to the Holy Land. Nevertheless, the Christian position was always weak. For nearly two centuries new crusades were launched in Europe to protect the Christian outpost in Jerusalem.

2. Later Crusades

The Second Crusade was inspired by the loss of Edessa in 1144. At the instigation of the pope and of St. Bernard of Clairvaux, Louis VII of France and Conrad of Germany led separate armies to the East. Both armies were virtually destroyed by Turkish armies in Asia Minor before reaching the Holy Land. When the two kings did arrive in the East with the remnants of their armies, their attempts to organize a successful attack on the Moslems were complete failures.

During the years following the Second Crusade a profound change occurred in the Moslem world. Under the skillful guidance of two Moslem leaders, Nureddin and Saladin, a unified Moslem state stretching from Syria into Egypt replaced the many small, quarreling principalities that had existed when the crusaders first attacked the Holy Land. In 1187 Saladin struck against the kingdom of Jerusalem and easily captured all the Christian holdings except Tyre, a few isolated castles, and the northern counties. Europe was deeply shocked. The pope called for a new crusade and received the promises of Henry II of England, Philip II of France, and Frederick Barbarossa of Germany to lead armies against Saladin. Frederick left first but was drowned en route; most of his army turned back after his death. Henry II also died, even before he could begin his march; however, his successor, Richard the Lion-Hearted, stepped into his place. He and Philip, almost always at odds, made their way to the East by 1191. Philip, anxious to snatch away Richard's French possessions, stayed on the scene only the minimum time. The colorful English king remained for over a year. After several inconclusive engagements with Saladin, he finally agreed to a truce by which the Christians were allowed to visit Jerusalem although the city remained in Moslem hands. The Third Crusade, which promised to be the greatest, did little to improve the Christian position in the East.

The Fourth Crusade was engineered by Innocent III, who wanted to add to his great stature by recovering the Holy Land. However, he soon lost control of this venture. Tempted by promises of trade concessions and of money made by Byzantine political leaders, the Venetians and some of the ambitious crusading knights diverted the crusading armies to an attack on Constantinople, which was captured and looted in 1204. The victorious crusaders immediately established a Latin Empire in Constantinople, electing a Flemish noble as emperor and a Venetian clergyman as patriarch of the Greek Orthodox Church, restored for the moment to union with the Roman Catholic Church. Innocent III forgot his anger at the crusaders and approved the whole procedure. The Latins ruled Constantinople until 1261. Although many nobles won rich fiefs in the Byzantine Empire, the chief beneficiaries were the Venetian merchants who gained valuable trading concessions that they continued to exploit until the seizure of Constantinople by the Turks in 1453.

After the Fourth Crusade the crusading movement deteriorated and lost most of its appeal. Innocent III organized the Fifth Crusade, although he died before it got under way in 1217. The armies of this crusade attacked Egypt, where, since Saladin's time, the chief center of Moslem power was located. The result of this attack was the capture of the key city of Damietta. The crusaders could have traded Damietta for Jerusalem, but ignorance and greed led them deeper into Egypt, where they permitted themselves to be trapped by a Nile flood and destroyed by the Moslems. Frederick II led the next crusade, chiefly because he wanted to secure possession of the Holy Land, to which he had a legal right by virtue of his marriage to the heiress of the kingdom of Jerusalem. Frederick's crusade was fraught with difficulties from its very beginning. Because of its leader's refusal to accept papal direction, he was in the bad graces of the papacy when he departed for the Holy Land. Once in the Holy Land he chose to gain his ends by diplomacy rather than by the sword. In 1229 he signed a treaty with the Moslems that restored Jerusalem to the Latins and provided for a cessation of war between Christians and Moslems. This indeed was a great victory, but the way it had been gained outraged many in the Christian West. When Frederick finally occupied Jerusalem, he himself was under a sentence of excommunication, and the city of Jerusalem was immediately placed under a papal interdict. This was hardly a fitting end for a successful crusade.

In 1244 the Moslems recaptured Jerusalem, indicating that the Latin defenders of the Holy Land were again weakening. Louis IX, the saintly king of France, made a feeble attempt in 1248–49 to relieve the pressure on the Latin holdings in Jerusalem by attacking Egypt, but his effort accomplished little. In the middle of the thirteenth century the Christians in the Holy Land received a brief reprieve by allying themselves with the Moslems to resist the threatened invasion of the Eastern Mediterranean area by the Mongol hordes, led by the successors of Genghis Khan. But when after 1260 the Mongol threat had passed, the Christians again fell to fighting with the Moslems. In 1291 the last Christian stronghold in the Holy Land was conquered. After nearly two hundred years the Latins had finally been ousted from Syria and Palestine.

Other movements akin to the Crusades were more successful. By the middle of the thirteenth century all of Spain except a strip in the extreme south (Granada) had been wrested from the Moslems. Germans had pushed deeper into the Slavic world, especially along the Baltic coast. One of the great crusading military orders, the Teutonic Knights, had shifted its activity to this area, and its conquests were quickly exploited by German priests, merchants, and peasants. At least some permanent gains for Western Europeans had resulted from the crusading movement.

3. Economic Expansion: The Revival of Trade and Industry

Europe's contacts with the East were not left entirely in the hands of the crusaders. Her merchants penetrated the East in increasing numbers, and their activities had even greater effects on European society than did the Crusades.

Although trade had never completely vanished from the European scene, it had sunk to a low level by the ninth and tenth centuries. In the tenth century commercial activity began to quicken, with the cities of northern Italy, especially Venice, leading the revival. The Venetians directed their activity toward Constantinople, exchanging raw materials for manufactured goods. Pisa and Genoa soon followed Venice's example. In the eleventh century their navies ended Moslem control over the Western Mediterranean. All these cities made considerable advances during the Crusades, winning valuable concessions in the great cities of the Byzantine and Moslem empires. By the thirteenth century the Italians were the dominant traders in the Mediterranean, acting as middlemen between Western Europe and the rich markets of the Near East.

Meanwhile, on the northern fringe of Europe another trading network was shaped. Viking pirates played the leading role here. Their raids carried them over a wide area of Europe. By way of the North Sea they reached France, England, and northern Germany. Through the Baltic they entered northern Germany and Russia, whose rivers carried them into the Black Sea and to Constantinople. Slowly these marauders learned that they could profit by hauling valuable products from Scandinavia to Western Europe, Russia, and Constantinople, by supplying Northern Europe with items from Constantinople, and by carrying Western European goods to the East. They thus opened a vast network of trade routes circling Western Europe on the north and east. By the eleventh century Flanders was rapidly becoming the center of northern trade.

At first these international trade routes, traveled by aggressive merchants from Italy, Flanders, and Scandinavia, affected Europe very little. However, before the tenth century ended merchants from Italy and Flanders began to penetrate inland. The Italians pushed across northern Italy, over the Alps into the Rhone and Rhine river valleys, and thus into the heart of France and Germany. Flemish traders penetrated England by the Thames; France and Germany by the Rhine, Scheldt, and Meuse valleys. In the twelfth century the great meeting place of the international traders was at the fairs in Champagne. Here, under the protection of the counts of Champagne, merchants came from everywhere to display their wares for sale to other merchants. An ever-growing crowd of local merchants was attracted to these fairs. By the end of the thirteenth century scarcely a corner of Europe had not felt the influence of traders and enjoyed the benefits of new products brought from afar by these enterprising souls.

At first European traders had been forced to exchange raw materials or precious metals for the highly desired manufactured goods and luxury items of the Eastern Mediterranean, but this condition did not last long. Increased trade stimulated the growth of industry in Western Europe and by the thirteenth century converted some sections into important manufacturing centers. It would be useless to try to catalogue all the products manufactured by European craftsmen in 1300, especially in Flanders and northern Italy, where industrial life was most highly developed. Certainly they had reached a point where Western European merchants could go abroad well provided with easily marketable articles. The expanding volume of industrial production hastened commercial expansion in another way. The artisans who concentrated on specialized production and the merchants who sold these goods depended for their food, clothing, and comforts on still other producers. Thus a heavy volume of local trade grew, simply supplying the needs of those engaged in trade and industry. Trading of this sort reached out to touch Europe's manors and ended their long isolation.

4. The Towns and the Middle Class

The revival of trade and industry gave great impetus to the growth of towns and helped to produce an urban middle class. City and town life had nearly disappeared in Western Europe during the centuries between the fall of Rome and about 1000. By 1300 this situation had changed entirely.

Numerous towns, populated chiefly by people who earned their livelihood from trade and industry, had appeared everywhere. Within each of these towns new institutions suited to the needs of merchants and artisans had emerged. This rapid development of town life added a completely new way of life to a society that had been predominantly agricultural, aristocratic, and clerical.

Medieval towns (that is, communities of merchants and artisans) usually grew up around older centers of population, such as episcopal centers or fortresses, especially those located on a river or an important road. Often merchants and artisans settled outside the walls of the older center, but as the commercial and industrial population increased the walls were often extended to include the new settlement. In many cases the market place in the new quarter of the town actually became the center of urban life. As a rule medieval towns were not large, and, although many new towns were created in Europe between the tenth and the thirteenth centuries, probably no more than 10 per cent of Europe's population lived in urban communities in 1300.

Wherever towns arose and whatever their size, their residents quickly discovered that the political and social rules that governed feudal and manorial society were ill suited to the needs of traders and artisans. Especially intolerable was the lack of personal freedom, which almost universally held for non-nobles. Almost from the beginning townsmen struggled for personal freedom, without which they could not move about and work as they pleased. Personal freedom could be gained in many ways: purchase, revolution, or free grant by king, feudal lord, or bishop. Whatever the means used, freedom was always a necessity for townsmen. By the end of the thirteenth century this struggle for personal freedom in the towns had resulted in the formation of a new class —the bourgeoisie—whose members were non-noble freemen, legally distinct from both aristocrats and serfs.

Townsmen could hardly flourish under the political and legal system that characterized feudal society. They could not, for instance, spend part of their time serving in a feudal army or tilling a lord's soil in payment for the bit of land they occupied in the town. Neither were they interested in holding any kind of feudal or manorial tenure. They needed to own property outright so that they could dispose of it for a profit when the opportunity arose. New laws and new forms of government were absolutely necessary in any town that hoped to flourish.

To meet these political and legal needs, most towns sought to obtain a charter from some authority, such as a feudal lord, a bishop, or a king. The charter granted the town and its residents a privileged status and permitted them to create their own political and legal institutions. It is difficult to generalize further about charters, since each was different, but usually a charter recognized the citizen body of the town as a corporation that would legally be treated as a person. The charters almost always granted personal freedom to the citizens of the town. Most charters carefully defined what the corporation owed to the granter of the charter. Almost always dues were to be paid in money instead of in personal services. Finally, most charters granted some degree of political freedom, thereby giving the townsmen permission to institute their own government. In a few cases, especially in Italy, towns gained complete political freedom and owed nothing to an outside authority. Such towns, called communes, were the exception. More commonly the townsmen had only the right to regulate local affairs while respecting some higher authority in matters not strictly local. This was especially true of towns chartered by a king. Few European kings were willing to let rich cities slip completely from their control; they thus granted charters rather freely.

In shaping political institutions the townsmen experimented considerably. In most towns there was some degree of popular participation in political life, authority being vested in an elected council that varied in size from town to town. In a commune the council usually possessed complete powers

to legislate, conduct courts, levy taxes, expend money for civic purposes, and negotiate with outside powers. Its only responsibility was to the citizens of the town. There was a tendency in many towns to establish officials, chosen either by the council or by the populace, to carry the chief burden of administration under the supervision of the council. These officials bore various titles—mayor, burgomaster, podesta. Judicial affairs were also entrusted to specially trained judges. In towns where the charter granted only limited freedom the townsmen often had to respect the authority of a royal official or a representative of a feudal lord who exercised many powers in judicial and financial matters. Whatever the form of government, the towns quickly created an elaborate new body of law regulating civic affairs. The bourgeoisie lived in an entirely different legal setting than did the feudal nobles, the clergy, and the serfs.

Not all the problems of the bourgeoisie were solved by the establishment of city governments and by the securing of personal freedom. Probably the gravest problem was the regulation of economic activity among merchants and artisans. The usual answer here was the establishment of guilds within each town. A guild was an association of men, engaged in a common commercial or manufacturing enterprise, who set up rules governing the conduct of that enterprise. The merchants in each town usually formed a merchant guild while the artisans formed several craft guilds, one for each trade. The merchant guilds existed primarily to protect the interests of merchants from outsiders and to restrain the merchants within a town from taking unfair advantage of one another. Each guild enacted specific rules governing prices to be charged, trading practices to be observed, and the conditions under which trade could be carried on. Most of these rules had one basic purpose—to give each merchant a share in the available trade without permitting anyone an unfair advantage. The craft guilds were not essentially different. They imposed regulations on their members concerning prices, quality of goods, conditions of labor, and quantity of production. Boys began their education in a craft by becoming apprentices to a master, working from two to seven years under his guidance and living in his household. The apprentice then became a journeyman who worked for hire until he had saved sufficient money and developed adequate skill to open his own shop and become a master. Before he acquired that rank he had to submit his workmanship to a rigid examination by the guild. This educational system permitted the guild to control the number of workers in each trade. Along with their regulative functions merchant and craft guilds had purely social functions. Each guild usually had its own guildhall, where banquets, pageants, and religious affairs were conducted for the entertainment and edification of the members. Each guild also aided its members when sickness or death struck a family.

Obviously the guilds placed considerable restriction upon the merchants and artisans. Usually they could count on the town governments to enforce their regulations and to oust any merchant or craftsman who refused to obey the rules. In spite of their restrictive, monopolistic activities the guilds played a vital role in the expansion of commerce and industry. Merchants and craftsmen of the Middle Ages lived in a society ruled by nobles and clergymen who had little sympathy with their activity. The guilds supplied protection and discipline for the merchants and artisans, restraining them from excessive profiteering and preventing them from destroying one another. Until central governments became strong enough to assume these burdens, the guilds were absolutely necessary for controlling and safeguarding the economic life of the artisans and merchants.

New business methods developed rapidly in the towns. The use of money as a measure of value and a means of exchange spread rapidly. Sound systems of coinage developed. This was especially true in Italy, and the use of Italian coins spread over all Europe. Eventually powerful kings took an interest in

sound money, and national money systems began to take shape. Along with money economy banks appeared. Banks lent money for interest, supplied bills of exchange to merchants who did not want to carry large amounts of coins with them, and provided places of deposit. Since the Church strenuously opposed the lending of money for interest (usury), the Jews usually handled such transactions. But in the twelfth century, with the growth of trade and industry, many Christians became involved. By the thirteenth century several rich Itailan merchant families and the great crusading orders, especially the Templars, conducted large-scale lending ventures. They were criticized by the Church but not with any great effect. Actually the Church began to modify its position on usury, conceding that anyone who lent at great risk ought to be compensated and that a borrower who did not pay his debt promptly ought to be penalized. Indeed, churchmen were among the best customers of Italian bankers, and paid high rates of interest for the convenience. Insurance was developed to protect merchants against almost any risk. Wholesaling became a regular practice in many cities. Bookkeeping systems were devised. In brief, a modern businessman would have been much at home among his medieval predecessors.

5. Effects of Expansion

Western European society was vitally affected by geographical, commercial, and industrial expansion. Western Europe's outward thrust certainly strengthened her position with respect to the non-European world. By 1300, important territories like the Iberian Peninsula, southern Italy and Sicily, and lands in Central Europe became permanent parts of Western Europe. Western Europeans had gained a large measure of control over the Mediterranean Sea. The Byzantine Empire had been dealt a serious blow by the crusaders. Europe's traders had established an important position in the great markets of the Near East and added immeasurably to the West's total wealth by their exploitation of these markets. In all these ways the Western Europeans weighed much more heavily in "world" affairs by 1300 than they had in 1000.

The tremendous expansion of trade and industry had wrought major changes in Europe's economy. The older system of self-sufficient manors began to dissolve under the impact of the money economy that had been introduced by the growth of commerce. Landholders who observed merchants and artisans growing wealthy sought to imitate them and began thinking of agricultural production for profit instead of self-sufficiency. To achieve this end, they tried to increase production so that they might have a surplus to sell in the cities. Whenever possible they collected rents from their lands in money rather than in produce. They spared nothing to clear forests and drain swamps in order to add new lands to their estates. With the traders and artisans busy creating new wealth and with the landlords joining hands, European economy enjoyed a considerable expansion. Signs of the new prosperity were everywhere by the thirteenth century. Bigger cities, bigger churches, richer houses and furnishings, more elaborate dress, better food—all testified to economic expansion and growth.

The most important change socially was the growing prominence of the bourgeoisie. Some of the most successful merchants and artisans had become wealthy enough to rival Europe's nobles for social leadership. The money of these newly rich could buy almost anything a noble possessed. The townsmen, often armed with better education and more experience in public affairs than the nobles, even entered political affairs, chiefly as servants of the kings. The monopoly that the nobles had long held on political life was threatened. The nobles of Europe answered this challenge by seeking to increase their wealth and by competing with the new middle class for political preference. The strictly feudal noble-warrior was passing away.

Even the peasants did not escape unaffected. The twelfth and thirteenth centuries witnessed a large-scale freeing of serfs, especially in France, England, Flanders, Italy, and Western Germany. This was partly caused by the new opportunities for serfs to accumulate a bit of wealth in money with which to purchase their freedom. A more important cause was the willingness of landlords to let their land out for money instead of collecting rents in produce and services. The peasant-renter whose dues were clearly established was no doubt better off economically than the serf. The lord was no longer in a position to commandeer all the peasant's wealth at will. On the other hand, the renter was much more on his own, for he could no longer rely on a paternalistic manorial lord to care for him in difficult times.

All of the changes noted above had the effect of breaking down the rigidity of the class structure of the early Middle Ages. Wealth became more important in determining one's status. Less depended upon birth.

The expansion of Europe resulted in broadened horizons for Western Europe's population. Crusaders brought back from the East new knowledge and new habits, and merchants acquainted the West with a whole new range of products. The increased travel that accompanied the expansion of trade brought the various parts of Europe more closely together. City life presented a cosmopolitan atmosphere for the meeting and exchange of knowledge and ideas, and the old localism was at least in part broken down by the movement and mingling that accompanied the expansion of Europe.

Finally, by the thirteenth century European society took on a new spirit of adventure, especially in the cities. The desire for the acquisition of wealth shook the staid agricultural society that so long had prevailed, and the affairs of this world attracted greater attention as it became a more exciting and somewhat more comfortable place in which to live.

SUGGESTED READING

* Richard A. Newhall, *The Crusades* (Berkshire Series, 1927). A good brief survey of the crusading movement, compressing a great deal of information into a short space.

Steven Runciman, *A History of the Crusades,* 3 vols. (1951–54). An excellent extensive history of the Crusades. The author enlivens his detailed study with interesting generalizations and suggestions about the impact of the Crusades on the medieval world.

Kenneth Setton, ed., *A History of the Crusades,* Vol. I (1955). This is the first volume of a proposed five-volume history of the Crusades being undertaken by a group of American scholars. Various authors have contributed to this volume.

Harold Lamb, *The Crusades: Iron Men and Saints* (1930) and *The Crusades: The Flame of Islam* (1931). These two popularly written accounts of the Crusades provide an excellent introduction to the subject. Some allowance must be made, however, for the fact the Mr. Lamb often colors the facts in the interest of readability.

August C. Krey, ed., *The First Crusade: The Accounts of Eye-Witnesses and Participants* (1921). A collection of judiciously selected source material relative to the First Crusade. Nothing will provide a better introduction to the spirit surrounding the crusading movement in its early stages than these firsthand accounts of its impact on Europe.

Fulcher of Chartres, *Chronicle of the First Crusade,* tr. by Martha Evelyn McGinty (1941). An eyewitness account of the First Crusade that supplies the color and excitement often missing in other descriptions written by authors not involved in the Crusade.

R. C. Smail, *Crusading Warfare, 1097–1193* (1956). A fascinating account of the art of warfare as practiced by Western European knights, Greek warriors, and Moslem soldiers during the era of the Crusades.

* Henri Pirenne, *Medieval Cities; Their Origins and the Revival of Trade,* tr. by Frank D. Halsey (Anchor). Published in a hardback edition in 1925. The best introduction to the problem of the revival of trade and the growth of the cities in the Middle Ages.

* Summerfield Baldwin, *Business in the Middle Ages* (Berkshire Series, 1937). A description of business methods during the Middle Ages.

CHAPTER 24

Intellectual, Literary, and Artistic Achievements

THE POLITICAL, economic, and religious developments between 1000 and 1300 that we have traced in the preceding chapters promoted and were accompanied by a vigorous burst of cultural activity. A new culture, bearing a unique medieval and a distinctive Western European stamp, was created. In literature, in philosophy, in art the leaders of the high Middle Ages gave demonstration of great creative powers.

1. The World of Learning: Theology, Philosophy, Science, and Social Thought

A major portion of the intellectual energies of medieval men was absorbed in a quest for a fuller understanding of the Christian faith. Out of this quest came one of the chief monuments of medieval culture: a body of theology and philosophy that attempted to clarify Christian doctrine and to relate all other branches of knowledge to Christian teaching.

Between the fifth and the eleventh centuries almost no significant theological works had been produced in Western Europe. However, in the eleventh century there was a revival of interest in theology. An ever-increasing amount of attention was devoted to the question of the extent to which human reason could be useful in grasping religious truth. Some conservative thinkers insisted that reason was dangerous and that everyone must rely on revelation as set forth in Scripture and in the writings of the early fathers for knowledge about God. Others, influenced chiefly by an increasing knowledge of classical Latin literature and troubled by the contradictions in Christian doctrine, argued that God had given man reason in order that he might seek the truth. These men began scrutinizing some of the doctrines of the Church in an attempt to find rational justification and proof of them.

The attempts of the eleventh-century scholars to clarify the use of reason in exploring religious authority reached a decisive point with the career of Peter Abelard (1079-1142). Even as a student this bold thinker disturbed the intellectual leaders of his generation; according to his own version of his life, he put his teachers at Paris to shame in philosophical dispute. His own career as a teacher was ruined by a love affair with one of his young pupils, Héloïse, and he was forced to spend the rest of his days wandering from monastery to monastery. However, through his writing and teaching he impressed certain fundamental ideas on his numerous students. Abelard argued that only through the use of reason could man come to a fuller understanding of God. He maintained that the truth consisted of concepts formed in the mind as a result of the study of the things God had created, such mental concepts being the nearest approximation to the perfect knowledge that is God. A philosopher's task is to organize in a logical fashion all that he knows so as to create in his mind an image of God's universe. A storm of protest was raised against Abélard's position on the validity of rationalism; however, his approach to theology quickly became the prevalent one.

Abelard's position seemed especially useful to thinkers during the twelfth and thirteenth centuries. They were challenged by a vast body of new knowledge coming from Latin and Greek sources. The study of Latin classics flourished in the cathedral and monastic schools of the twelfth century. Western Europeans also discovered the major scientific and philosophical works of ancient Greece. This knowledge came to the West through Moslem and Jewish scholars in Spain, who had translated many Greek philosophical works into Arabic. Large numbers of Greek works, along with Moslem and Jewish commentaries, were then translated into Latin. Aristotle especially captivated European scholars and became for many the final authority on logical methods and scientific knowledge. Only by careful, systematic study could this vast body of new, non-Christian knowledge, often contradictory to Christian teaching, be squared with Christian belief.

Many scholars, called collectively the scholastics, labored at the task of incorporating the new knowledge into the Christian frame of reference. By far the most influential was Thomas Aquinas (1225–74), an Italian Dominican who spent most of his life studying and teaching at the university in Paris. Thomas produced a huge body of theological writing during his life, running in one modern edition to thirty-four large volumes. His chief work was the *Summa Theologiae*, which is probably the best product of medieval thought. In this and all his works Thomas begins with the assumption that God created the universe in such a way that all its parts fit together and have a

single purpose. Every man has the duty to know God and His works. There are two paths to a knowledge of the truth: revelation and reason. The task of the human mind is to seek the truth by applying itself to those things that are the proper subjects for reason while accepting on faith those things that can be learned only by revelation. Thomas accepted on faith the creation, the Trinity, and the Incarnation. However, he applies his reason to many other problems such as the existence of God, immortality, the operation of the natural world, the nature of government, and ethics. He sees no possibility of conflict between revelation and reason, since there is but one truth. If there is a conflict, then it results from faulty reasoning.

Throughout his writings Aquinas relies heavily on Aristotle as his authority on subjects proper to human reason, although he always implies that the human mind can learn the truth by observation of the natural world. In his quest to square Aristotle's ideas and his own observations with revealed truth, Thomas's chief tool is logic. Following the rules of thinking formulated by Aristotle, he proceeds step by step through the whole realm of human knowledge and measures item after item against the revealed truth. Everything in Aquinas's system of thought is related to one single theme: what part each object of knowledge plays in God's universe. The final result of Aquinas's work is a synthesis of all knowledge into one vast structure glorifying God and demonstrating His power. For Aquinas and those who subscribed to his conclusions the human mind had found its fundamental task, namely, to glorify God by relating all knowledge from whatever source to His divine plan of things.

Obviously theology and philosophy, as conceived by Thomas Aquinas and the other scholastics, were all-embracing "sciences." Thus, to discover medieval political thought and scientific concepts, one must usually turn to the vast theological works turned out by the scholastics.

Medieval thinkers made little progress in

science. Their knowledge of the natural world consisted of a confused body of information derived from myths and legends and from the scientific works of the Greeks and the Arabs. All of this information was mixed together uncritically, giving rise to many errors about the natural world and its operation. Even in the thirteenth century, when European thinkers had at their disposal the excellent scientific works of the great Arab scholars, they made little effort to correct the current errors about nature or to advance toward new scientific knowledge. This lack of interest in discovering new scientific knowledge was largely due to the preoccupation of the scholastics with the task of relating all knowledge to the revealed truth. Those with any interest in science usually spent their time trying to work their knowledge into the vast summaries of thought that were the chief product of scholasticism. Occasionally, however, the Middle Ages did produce a figure with a true scientific spirit. Such was Roger Bacon (about 1214-94), an English Franciscan who wrote extensively on the necessity of conducting experiments to ascertain the truth about the natural world. He believed that most scholastics put too much trust in ancient authorities and thus perpetuated errors that a little observation and experimentation would correct. Although his work was not especially outstanding, Bacon himself engaged in experimentation, especially in optics. Actually, during the Middle Ages there was a steady increase in the practical knowledge relating to medicine, mechanics, and plant and animal life. But this information was accumulated without thought for scientific method as conceived of today. Typical of this kind of knowledge was that accumulated by medieval alchemists. While seeking to change base metals into gold, they managed to learn a great deal about the nature of metals and the way to handle them. However, they can hardly qualify as scientists.

The efforts of medieval political theorists were guided chiefly by religious concepts, their intention being to formulate political and social theories that corresponded to what they believed God's order for the universe to be. Thomas Aquinas provides a typical example of medieval political and social thought. He argued that the state is an institution willed by God as a necessary part of the universal scheme of things; it is therefore necessary and good. To function properly, the state must be made up of classes, each with a specific function. Peasants and artisans must work, nobles must rule, and priests must pray and administer the sacraments. Those who refuse to do their duty are guilty of defying God's will. Those who perform their duty are entitled to a fair share of the things of this world. The function of the state and the ruler is to see to it that each does his duty and that each gets his reward; this is justice. A tyrannical king, a merchant who charges unfair prices, a banker who charges interest, and a lazy or rebellious peasant are all guilty of injustice in that they are depriving someone in the community of his due. To the ruler falls the God-given responsibility of seeing that justice is done. Aquinas places upon the ruler the heavy responsibility of discovering the principles of natural law that God has ordained to regulate human society. No prince is free to do as he pleases; if he acts despotically, he is unfit to rule and may be deposed.

Our brief description of medieval thought demonstrates at least the over-all spirit of the Middle Ages. Moved by a strong belief that all knowledge is one because it stems from God, medieval scholars devoted their energies to an organization of knowledge into a single consistent structure. Not new knowledge, but the organization of existing knowledge was their constant objective. Out of this effort there emerged a strong interest in closely reasoned, highly organized thought. This rationalism was destined to play a major role in future thought in Western Europe. However, during the Middle Ages reason was always controlled, disciplined, and channeled by a conviction that there was a higher, more sacred truth—that which God had revealed to man. Therefore, human reason was not free to wander and seek where it would; it always had to test its findings against the teachings of Christianity.

2. The World of Learning: Education

Much of the learning we have discussed would have been impossible without a sound educational system. One of the chief accomplishments of the high Middle Ages was the development of such a system.

During the eleventh and twelfth centuries the monastic and episcopal schools, many of them dating from the Carolingian period, experienced a brilliant revival. The reformed Church wanted better-educated clergymen; the kings, more capable administrators. The revival took the form of a more thorough training in the seven liberal arts, which had long been the basis of education. Three of the arts (called the *trivium*) —grammar, rhetoric, and dialectic—especially caught the interest of the age, the classical Latin authors and Aristotle supplying the bulk of the material studied. The other four arts (the *quadrivium*)—arithmetic, geometry, astronomy, and music—were broadened as a result of Greek and Moslem knowledge but were never so eagerly pursued as literary studies and logic.

By the end of the twelfth century the cathedral and monastic schools were no longer large or advanced enough to satisfy the learned world. The demand for more advanced education was met by establishing universities.[1] The first were specialized institutions. At Salerno in Sicily and Montpellier in France medicine was emphasized. Bologna was famous as a law school, while theology was the chief interest at Paris.

[1] The exact date of the foundation of the earliest universities is difficult to ascertain. Most of them grew gradually to the status of a university. The University of Paris was granted legal status by the king of France in 1200, although an important institution of learning had existed there at least a century earlier. Bologna became a university in the period from 1150–1200. A school of medicine existed in Salerno in the tenth century. Oxford and Cambridge were established early in the thirteenth century.

Universities were founded by the action of either students or faculty, who organized themselves into corporations or guilds and assumed powers of self-government. At Bologna the students took the initiative in forming a corporation because they felt the need for protection against the townsmen. At Paris, on the other hand, the teachers of the arts in the Paris episcopal school broke away from the control of the bishop and founded a self-governing body, and later faculties of law, theology, and medicine were added. A rector was elected as head of each faculty, the rector of the arts faculty being the head of the university.

Each university had as the basis for its curriculum the study of the seven liberal arts, and maintained a faculty for the teaching of the arts. The arts program, often lasting six or eight years, usually culminated in the grant of a master of arts degree, which entitled its holder to teach. Eventually a bachelor of arts degree was instituted, requiring four or five years of study but not entitling its holder to teach. The doctor's degree was taken in theology, law, or medicine. Advanced study in these specialized fields was usually begun after the master's degree had been earned. At Paris the doctor's degree in theology required at least thirteen years of study.

Teaching in medieval universities consisted chiefly of commenting on texts. Students who could afford to buy a manuscript copy of the authority under discussion made notes of the teacher's comments in the margins of his text. Those without a text tried to copy the text as the master read it. Examinations, coming at the end of his four or six or thirteen years, depending on the student's curriculum, were designed to test the student's ability to take a text or thesis and expound on it. Success depended upon a good memory and the ability to reason closely. Often the masters prodded the student to test his ability to think with facility by subjecting him to rigorous questioning.

At first most universities had no buildings. Classes were held in rented halls, while students took lodgings in private homes. During the thirteenth century men of means, perhaps moved by the miserable conditions under which some students lived, began to endow establishments for housing and feeding students. Such establishments, called colleges, became the centers of most educational activities. The first such institution was the Sorbonne at Paris, endowed in 1258 by Robert de Sorbon, a rich merchant. University authorities assumed responsibility for disciplining students. Usually students and faculty were considered members of the clergy and were thus under the jurisdiction of church courts. This led to endless conflicts between townsmen (who had to tolerate students without being able to control them) and the university community.

3. Literature

The theologians, philosophers, and teachers who haunted the universities set the over-all tone of medieval culture. However, they did not monopolize the scene. A varied and brilliant literature flourished alongside the learned works in theology and philosophy. This literature was impregnated with the values defined by the theologians, but it was intended to entertain and instruct a far larger audience. Although Latin remained a living language throughout the Middle Ages, much of the literary production was in the languages spoken by the common people of the various countries of Europe. These vernacular languages are the forerunners of the languages spoken in European countries today.

During the high Middle Ages there was a large body of literature produced in Latin, most of it religious. Especially excellent was the Latin poetry written to express personal feelings about a wide range of religious themes. Some of this poetry supplies the best information we have for measuring the intensity of medieval religious emotions. Non-religious themes were also treated in Latin. For example, the Goliardic verse, produced by wandering students, dealt with taverns, love affairs, gambling debts, and numerous other worldly subjects. There was

also a vast body of historical and biographical literature written in Latin. On the whole, however, Latin literature was not the best product of medieval writers. Latin was the language of learning and unknown to most men. Folk stories and tales of love and battle were in the native tongues, which proved especially effective for expressing ideas and feelings on nonreligious themes.

Most vernacular literature was produced to suit the tastes of Europe's feudal nobility. One of the earliest forms of such literature was the epic, or, as it is sometimes called, the *chanson de geste*. An epic is a poetic account of the deeds of great warriors. The plot of the medieval epic was usually based on an oral tradition deriving from primitive Germanic society, but many feudal and Christian ideas were incorporated, making of each epic a mirror of the ideals and the customs of feudal society in the eleventh and twelfth centuries. The best known and one of the earliest epics was the *Song of Roland*, written about 1100 in France. The subject of the poem is Charlemagne's expedition to Spain in 778 to attack the Moslems. However, the hero, Roland, becomes in the poem a model knight of the late eleventh century. The poem glorifies war, loyalty of vassals, hatred of the Moslems, and physical prowess. Roland, a rash, violent man, guided by courage, simple faith in God, and deep loyalty, is what every knight ought to be. As counterparts of the *Song of Roland*, Germany had the *Nibelungenlied*, Scandinavia the *Sagas*, and Spain *The Song of the Cid*, to mention but a few of the best epics. Nowhere can one find a better reflection of the ideals of feudal society than in these poems recited by minstrels for the entertainment of rough, unlettered warriors.

Late in the eleventh century another kind of poetry emerged, developing first in Provence in southern France and then spreading over most of Europe. This was lyric poetry centering chiefly around the theme of love. Its creators, the troubadors, became the most popular poets of the twelfth century. Although troubador poetry appealed chiefly to the feudal nobility, it contrasted sharply with the action-filled, bloody epics. Its basic theme was the effect on a knight of love for a lady. In the troubador verse the knight pours forth his innermost feelings as he seeks and wins the affection of his lady. Obviously the knightly ideal had changed. The knight is no longer the doughty warrior of the epics, but rather a creature of dreams and emotions. His loyalty to his feudal lord has been replaced by romantic loyalty to a lady. In order to succeed in love the knight has to acquire a whole new set of virtues and skills that, taken together, make up the code of chivalry. The knight of the troubadour poetry inclines toward refinement, formal manners, and gentility.

Before the end of the twelfth century the epic and lyric traditions had merged to produce a third type of vernacular literature, the romance. Romances were stories combining love with high adventure, written to entertain nobles. The love theme was treated with exaggerated passion and yearning. The adventure element centered around three broad themes: the deeds of Charlemagne, the adventures of King Arthur and his knights, and the actions of Greek and Roman heroes. These basic plots were treated with complete disregard for historical accuracy. A reader might find Alexander the Great fighting the Seljuk Turks, attending Mass, and engaging in a tournament. Such flights of imagination did not trouble the romance writers, since their aim was to create an idealized and entertaining picture of refined feudal society. Many of the romances were run-of-the-mill productions, comparable to the bulk of modern novels and movies. A few writers, however, especially the Frenchman Chrétien de Troyes, and the Germans Gottfried von Strassburg and Wolfram von Eschenbach, managed to endow such heroes and heroines as Lancelot, Tristram, Parsifal, Isolde, and Guinevere with real personalities and to make of their loves and adventures stories of enduring qualities.

While the epics, lyrics, and romances were being written, sung, and read by no-

bles, the middle class produced a literature suited to its tastes and situation. Especially popular in the towns were dramas and *fabliaux*. Medieval drama had its origin as a part of church liturgy, attempts being made to dramatize certain parts of the services. Eventually the presentation of these plays moved outside the church into the market place. By the thirteenth century the guilds had taken over the responsibility for producing and acting these dramas on the occasion of religious festivals. Several types of plays were popular: mystery plays, enacting scenes from the Bible; miracle plays, treating the highlights of saints' lives; morality plays, seeking to teach a lesson by personifying human virtues and vices. Often the stories dramatized in medieval plays were already familiar to the audience, whose chief interest was in seeing how well the actors could portray their parts as God or Noah or the devil.

The *fabliaux* were short tales recited in public squares for the entertainment of the crowds. The subject matter could be almost anything. Whatever the subject, the *fabliaux* were always close to city life, faithfully representing everyday events in the lives of ordinary people. They were often filled with vulgar humor and satire directed especially at priests and women. The most famous collection of such literature was the *Romance of Reynard the Fox*, made up of many stories in which animals symbolize people and human characteristics.

Of the many writers during the high Middle Ages one genius, Dante Alighieri (1265–1321), towers above all others. He was to the literary world what Thomas Aquinas was to theology. Dante was a product of Florence, actively engaging in political life in that city and eventually suffering exile. Although he resented his fate bitterly, his exile was fortunate in that it allowed him to produce the *Divine Comedy*, one of the great masterpieces of world literature.

Outwardly the *Divine Comedy* is Dante's account of his journey through hell, purgatory, and heaven. Guided through the first two by Vergil, and through heaven by Beatrice, Dante is permitted to see all things from the depths of hell to God Himself. The poem, however, is much more than a well-written adventure story. Dante is a philosopher, presenting with consummate skill the medieval idea that all things in the universe are ordered under God and according to His will. He is a mystic, yearning to the depths of his soul to catch a glimpse of God. He is a love poet, expressing his sentiments as skillfully as any troubador. (Beatrice, his guide in heaven, is a symbol of human love, which purifies and uplifts man.) Dante is a scientist, weaving into his poem many medieval ideas about the structure of the physical universe. He is a lover of Greek and Roman classics, praising the men of the ancient world who produced them, although he has to condemn them to hell as non-Christians. He is a keen political observer, full of fierce partisanship. His hell is crowded with men guilty of what Dante believes to have been political crimes. During the course of his long journey from the gates of hell to its very pit, where Lucifer chews three great traitors, Brutus, Cassius, and Judas, Dante discusses with Vergil nearly every kind of sin, showing a deep understanding of human nature and its weaknesses. Few artists have grasped human life and human aspirations more fully or written of them with greater artistry. This greatest medieval writer wraps up in one masterful poem all the many threads that run through medieval literature as a whole.

4. Medieval Art

Medieval artists created monuments no less impressive and no less illustrative of the medieval spirit than did scholars like Thomas Aquinas or writers like Dante. Church building absorbed the best artistic talent of the Middle Ages. However, the construction of churches was more than an architectural undertaking. Every church was a complete museum, filled with sculpture, painting, wood carving, glasswork, metalwork, and decorative handwriting. No amount of description can ever convey a true

impression of the total artistic effect created by a medieval church in its entirety. Only by seeing monuments such as Notre Dame in Paris and the cathedrals at Chartres, Amiens, and Rheims can one appreciate the quality and spirit of medieval art.

Since medieval architectural style evolved over a long period of time, it is difficult to treat the subject simply. The basic form of church architecture developed from the Roman basilica, which was simply a long meeting hall with a semicircular *apse* at the rear to provide a place for conducting meetings. The early Christians placed their altars in the apse and used the rest of the hall, called the *nave*, for seating the faithful. Side aisles were built along the nave and around the apse. A lateral aisle, called the *transept*, was often built across the nave just in front of the apse, so that the early church took the form of a cross. The walls of the nave were built higher than those of the side aisles, permitting windows to be cut high in the nave walls to admit light.

The basic structure was slowly and painfully evolved until finally large structures of stone could be built. The first such large churches appeared in Western Europe in the tenth and eleventh centuries, being built in a style called Romanesque. The distinctive feature of Romanesque architecture was the use of round arches as a means of putting a stone roof over the church. Barrel vaults were used the full length of the nave, while cross vaults were evolved to cover the area where the nave and transept crossed. Since the stone roof exerted a tremendous downward and outward thrust, Romanesque churches had heavy walls and a minimum of windows. Wherever the walls were pierced, massive piers had to be constructed; and these piers had to be supported with equally strong arches to bear the weight from above. Thus, the typical Romanesque church tended to resemble a dark, gloomy tunnel, as can be seen in the churches at Poitiers and Mainz. Even the employment of bright paints for decoration could not dispel the atmosphere of gloom and mystery.

EXTERIOR OF A ROMANESQUE CHURCH. The church of Notre Dame la Grande in Poitiers, France, was built during the eleventh and twelfth centuries and illustrates the main features of the Romanesque style of architecture. Note the rounded arches, massive columns, heavy walls, and the elaborate decorations of carved stonework in nearly every available space on the façade of the church. As can be expected, the interior of this structure is dark and confining. One senses a certain resemblance to a military fortification, perhaps because the Romanesque style flourished during the era when feudalism was at its peak. (*Courtesy, French Government Tourist Office*)

Driven by a desire for height and light, architects continually experimented with the Romanesque style. By the late twelfth century they began to find the answer in the pointed arch and the ribbed vault. Thus was born the Gothic style, appearing first in northern France and then spreading over most of Europe. The pointed arch had the effect of carrying the thrust downward, while the ribbed vault allowed the architect to concentrate the thrust at a few spots. By combining pointed arches, ribbed vaults,

INTERIOR OF A ROMANESQUE CHURCH. The Benedictine abbey church of Saint-Sernin at Toulouse, France, begun late in the eleventh century and completed during the twelfth, is one of the best preserved and largest Romanesque structures in Europe. This view along the nave toward the altar highlights the characteristic features of the Romanesque style: rounded arches, heavy columns, and relatively small window space above the chief arches. Side aisles run along each side of the nave. This church has great height for a Romanesque structure. (*Archives Photographiques, Paris*)

EXTERIOR OF A GOTHIC CHURCH. This thirteenth-century French cathedral at Reims is characteristic of a Gothic church. Although in this photograph repair scaffolding is shown on the left, the symmetry of the façade is evident. The high pointed arches carry the eye upward and give the impression that the building is a vast skeleton of stone arches and their supporting columns. The sides of the structure are supported by great buttresses, with large windows between. The large round stained glass window in the façade creates a brilliant effect inside the church. Note also the numerous statues decorating the front of the building. These statues served as a source of education in the Christian faith for all who approached the church. (*Courtesy, French Government Tourist Office*)

and columns, tremendously tall skeletons of stone could be built, their enormous weight flowing to the earth through a series of slender pillars. The outward thrust, likewise concentrated at a few spots, was offset by thickening the columns on the outside of the building or by building flying buttresses, pillars set away from the main building and joined to it by bracing arches high above the ground. Once the skeleton was constructed, thin walls, supporting nothing but their own weight, could be filled in between the pillars. These walls could be pierced by as many windows as the architect wanted.

Nothing is more characteristic of Gothic architecture than the numerous high, pointed windows, often interlaced with delicate stonework for decorative purposes. In contrast with Romanesque churches, Gothic churches were full of light. The windows were usually made of colored stained glass that caught the outside light and poured it into the church with a brilliance that defies description. It has often been said that Gothic architecture symbolized medieval man's striving to reach God. Certainly everything in these churches carries the eye upward toward the light.

Nearly every other art was put to work to decorate medieval churches. Sculpture predominated in the decoration of most cathedrals, especially in the great doorways at the fronts and sides of the churches. Most church sculpture represented in stone the basic teachings of the Church—the stories from the Bible, incidents in Christ's life, or deeds of the saints. During the Romanesque period sculpture tended to be stiff, distorted, and highly symbolical; the artist was chiefly concerned with transmitting a religious idea. Gothic sculptors achieved a greater degree of realism, espe-

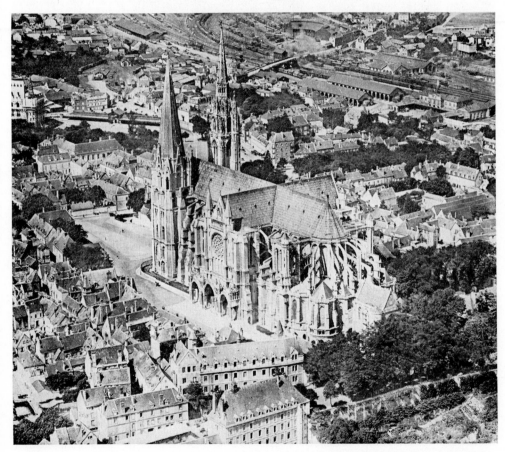

A Gothic Church and the Surrounding City. This view of the south side of the cathedral of Chartres in France, sometimes called the finest of all the Gothic churches, illustrates dramatically how a great church towered above and dominated a medieval city. Flying buttresses at the sides support the outward thrust of the structure. The twin steeples, typical of Gothic churches, are of different styles, the near one being built earlier than that on the right, which is more ornate. (*Photo from European*)

INTERIOR OF A GOTHIC CHURCH. The cathedral of Amiens, in France, seen looking from the altar at the east end toward the great center entrance, above which there is a beautiful stained glass window. Such great height was achieved by using the pointed arch and the ribbed vault to carry the weight downward on relatively small columns. Large windows in the upper wall afford abundant light. Note the intricate carving at the tops of even the highest columns. The nave is flanked by aisles that rise to the top of the lower tier of arches. (*Archives Photographiques, Paris*)

cially in treating the human figure. Painting (usually in the form of frescoes), stained glass, and wood carving, like the sculpture of the period, were devoted primarily to religious themes. Herein lay the essential element of medieval art. Its intention was to illustrate moral lessons for the unlettered masses who passed in and out of the churches. Artists did not strive for an exact duplication of the natural world, but sought to get across their religious message. The devil and his legions bear a resemblance to earthly men, but they are always more horrible and grotesque. Christ, the Virgin, the angels, and the saints are also human, but they are idealized. The art of the churches therefore presented a reflection of another world—the world of the spirit—toward which man must aspire.

The great cathedrals commanded the best artistic talent and the bulk of the wealth that medieval society had to devote to art. However, there were other lines of artistic pursuit, most of which imitated styles and techniques borrowed from church building. Feudal castles were built in many places. Their characteristic feature was massiveness, little attention being paid to elegance. The Romanesque style was especially suited for such buildings. In the towns, especially from the thirteenth century onward, beautiful town halls and guildhalls were con-

MEDIEVAL SCULPTURE. This scene, picturing the descent of the Holy Ghost on Pentecost, is carved above the main portal of the Romanesque church at Vézelay, in France. Compositions of this type adorned the entrance of nearly every church built in the Middle Ages. The lines extending from Christ's hands to the heads of the apostles symbolize the imparting of the divine spirit. The other figures of the composition have baffled authorities; a careful study will show that there are many fantastic creatures pictured. Perhaps the artist intended to indicate that the gospel was preached everywhere and therefore brought into his work all manner of creatures. Medieval men accepted without question the existence of fantastic creatures which dwelled in strange lands. (*Archives Photographiques, Paris*)

STATUE OF CHRIST TEACHING. This appealing figure of Christ teaching greets all who enter the south portal of the cathedral of Chartres in France. It represents the ability of medieval artists to treat the human figure with some degree of realism while retaining a strong religious feeling. The figure has dignity and solemnity without being cold or remote. One senses that this representation of Christ could become a beloved sight to those entering the church and could arouse in them a strong Christian feeling. (*Archives Photographiques, Paris*)

STATUE REPRESENTING THE VICE OF INCON-
STANCY. Medieval artists and writers were fond
of personifying virtues and vices in order to render their lessons more concrete. This artist's conception of the vice of inconstancy appears on the
cathedral of Chartres. Directly above is another
figure, much more pleasing, representing the virtue of constancy. Such figures appear in numerous
places in every medieval church. (*Archives Photographiques, Paris*)

STATUE OF THE VIRGIN. This beautiful work in
the Gothic style, often called the "Golden Virgin," stands at the portal to the south transept
of the cathedral of Amiens. The youthful face,
the loving smile, the tender grasp of the child,
and the relaxed posture of the body suggest the
artist's awareness of a mother's love for her child.
(*Archives Photographiques, Paris*)

structed, putting Gothic principles to new
uses. None ever rivaled churches in size and
beauty, but some of them were impressive
signs that the Church never completely absorbed artistic energies.

5. The Underlying Spirit of Medieval Culture—A Summary

Our attention has ranged far and wide in
the preceding pages. Perhaps we ought to
conclude by searching for something to tie
together the many cultural trends that
reached their culmination in the thirteenth
century. Certainly it is not easy to find a
common denominator for Thomas Aquinas,
Dante, the architects and sculptors who
built the churches at Poitiers, Amiens, and
Chartres, the troubadors, the romance writers, and the authors of *fabliaux*. The cul-

tural life of the high Middle Ages was marked by diversity and variety. One need not search far in medieval cultural life to find signs of nearly every attitude or idea present even in modern society, a fact that has led some scholars to insist that modern Western European culture was born in the eleventh, twelfth, and thirteenth centuries.

However, medieval culture has its own distinctive flavor. Most medieval art and thought are permeated by a quest for truth and light outside and beyond the world in which men live. This ever-present reaching out of the mind and the imagination sprang from the almost universally accepted belief that God controlled the universe and that it was man's duty to know and worship Him. The artist and the writer stood in awe of God and used their talents humbly to see, know, and serve Him. Medieval culture, viewed as a whole, therefore, has an atmosphere of otherworldliness and of surrender to a power beyond human understanding.

Yet, intertwined with this aspiration toward the infinite and with the humble sub-mission to the divine, there is a warm, sympathetic feeling for humankind. Medieval men believed that man was God's finest creation. Artists and writers were never disdainful of human powers and potentialities. They took joy in presenting man as he was and wrestled constantly with the problem of understanding human nature more fully.

Medieval genius shines most brilliantly when it attempts to synthesize these two outlooks. Medieval men never felt that otherworldliness and secularism, spirituality and humanism were exclusive terms. Medieval culture was most clearly distinguished by its attempts to make human knowledge and emotion at one with God. Thinkers and artists respected their own powers enough to believe that they could reach out toward God—by building cathedrals higher or by putting together greater *summae* of knowledge or by traveling in poetic fancy to meet God face to face. Yet they were men of great enough faith to believe that their quest would lead them to a power infinitely greater than themselves—to God.

SUGGESTED READING

F. B. Artz, *The Mind of the Middle Ages*, A.D. 200–1500: *An Historical Survey*, 2nd ed. (1954). This volume will serve as an introduction to the complex problem of medieval cultural life. Its excellent bibliographies will help the reader to find books on specialized subjects related to medieval cultural life.

H. O. Taylor, *The Medieval Mind*, 4th ed., 2 vols. (1949). This monumental study is still the best treatment of the whole subject of medieval thought. It is well written, imaginative, and thought-provoking. The author illustrates his points with numerous selections from medieval literature.

* Charles Homer Haskins, *The Rise of the Universities* (Cornell). Published in a hardback edition in 1923. A brief introduction to the history of the early medieval universities, presenting a clear picture of their organization, their program, and their relationship with the rest of society.

University Records and Life in the Middle Ages, tr. by Lynn Thorndike (1944). A delightful collection of materials dealing with nearly every aspect of medieval university life, most of it written by men connected with these universities. From this collection one can get a full picture of the curriculum, government, discipline, teaching methods, and student life in medieval universities.

Étienne Gilson, *History of Christian Philosophy in the Middle Ages* (1955). A detailed survey of medieval philosophy by one of the most distinguished of modern students of medieval philosophy. Gilson maintains that medieval thinkers made a major contribution to the development of Western European philosophy.

* G. K. Chesterton, *St. Thomas Aquinas* (Image). Written for popular reading, this sympathetic discussion of Aquinas's life and philosophy serves as a good introduction to one of the chief figures of the Middle Ages and one of the major philosophers in the whole Western European tradition. Chesterton's literary skill adds to the charm of the book. No biography, however, will supply as good an introduction to Thomas Aquinas as will his own writings, selections from which are available in many editions.

* Anne Freemantle, ed., *The Age of Belief; the*

Medieval Philosophers (Mentor). An excellent selection of representative writings by the major medieval philosophers.

Ewart Lewis, *Medieval Political Ideas*, 2 vols. (1954). A thorough study of the development of political theory in the Middle Ages. The book is organized topically, permitting a reader to find rather easily a discussion of specific aspects of political theory. The author quotes copiously from medieval writers.

Charles Rufus Morey, *Mediaeval Art* (1942). A thorough yet not too technical discussion of medieval sculpture and painting. The value of the book is increased by its excellent illustrations.

* Henry Adams, *Mont Saint Michel and Chartres* (Anchor). Published in a hardback edition in 1904. One of the most moving interpretations of the Middle Ages ever written. Mr. Adams, one of America's chief literary lights, uses his writing skill to weave a magic spell about two medieval architectural monuments, making them serve as symbols of the medieval outlook on life.

Charles Williams Jones, *Medieval Literature in Translation* (1950). This volume offers a representative selection of medieval literature. It should certainly be supplemented by reading in their entirety a few medieval "classics." Besides those mentioned in previous chapters the five titles below are especially recommended as good examples of medieval literature.

* Dante, *The Divine Comedy*. Many editions; a good translation is by Paoli Milani in *The Portable Dante* (Viking). This poetic rendering of the story of Dante's journey through hell, purgatory, and heaven presents an excellent summary of medieval ideas and values.

The Letters of Abélard and Héloïse, tr. by C. K. Scott-Moncrieff (1926). A touching picture of two medieval lovers forced to separate, as presented in their letters to one another.

* *The Romance of Tristan and Iseult*, tr. by Joseph Bedier (Anchor). Probably the best of the medieval romances, illustrating the blending of love themes and adventure so characteristic of a vast body of literature produced for feudal society.

John Addington Symonds, *Wine, Women, and Song* (1925). A delightful collection of medieval lyric poetry dedicated to the themes suggested by the title. This work will demonstrate that medieval men did not devote all their thoughts to prayer.

The Romance of the Rose by W. Lorris and J. Clopinel, tr. and ed. by F. S. Ellis, 3 vols. (1926–28). A long poem cast in allegorical form, illustrative of the moral ideas of thirteenth-century medieval society.

SECTION 6

The Late Middle Ages,

1300–1500

I n the preceding section we examined those developments which carried medieval civilization to its high point in the thirteenth century. Even by 1300 there were signs that Western Europe would not long remain on the plateau reached in the thirteenth century. Dynamic new forces ate away at the foundations of the medieval order and pointed toward a new age. The fourteenth and fifteenth centuries were marked by the disintegration of all that characterized the medieval world and by the simultaneous emergence of ideas and institutions that would eventually shape a new order. These two centuries were thus partly medieval and partly modern. On the one hand, they were dreary centuries, filled with decadence and decline; on the other, they teemed with exhilarating forces of rebirth and revolution.

In a later discussion we will return to the new forces that arose during the fourteenth and fifteenth centuries. The following two chapters will deal chiefly with the decline of medieval institutions and ideas. Our task will be to observe the failure of such typical medieval institutions as the great empires, feudal monarchies, the universal church, the monopolistic guilds, the manorial system, and scholasticism. In almost every case these medieval institutions, stricken by their inability to contain and channel dynamic new forces, rotted from within.

CHAPTER 25

Political, Economic, and Social Tensions

POLITICALLY the fourteenth and fifteenth centuries were filled with disorder. Such typically medieval institutions as the Holy Roman Empire, the Byzantine Empire, the feudal monarchies of England, France, and Spain failed to cope with new political problems. Their inadequacies bred civil strife, class struggles, international wars, and internal injustices everywhere in Western Europe. Behind much of this political trouble lay economic and social problems arising from the growing failure of medieval agricultural and commercial institutions.

1. The Decline of the Holy Roman Empire

The most obvious case of the failure of a medieval political institution was the Holy Roman Empire. From about 950 to 1250 a series of German rulers joined Germany, Italy, and the western fringes of the Slavic world to form the largest and most powerful state in Europe. A host of foes, led by the papacy, resisted the attempts to join Germany and Italy and finally defeated the German rulers after 1250. The death of the last great emperor, Frederick II, in that year marked the beginning of the end.

In Germany a bitter civil war, centering around the succession question, followed Frederick's death. During this war nobles, clergy, and townsmen successfully established their independence from central authority. In 1273 the long struggle for the crown ended with the election of Rudolph of Hapsburg (1273–91), whose chief recommendation was his lack of strength. Rudolph confined his efforts to increasing his family holdings in the area of modern Austria. His success in this venture caused the princes of Germany to repudiate the Hapsburgs in 1308 in favor of a prince from Luxemburg. In 1313 a ruler from the house of Wittelsbach of Bavaria was elected out of fear that the house of Luxemburg was getting too strong. The German nobles demonstrated that they would not tolerate a strong ruler. Those who desired to be emperor of Germany quickly caught on; although they used the imperial office to improve the standing of their family and to acquire title to rich provinces, they did little to disturb the independence of other princes.

This trend was finally given legal definition. In 1347 Charles IV of Luxemburg was elected ruler. His most important act was to promulgate in 1356 the famous Golden Bull, designed to establish a constitution for Germany that would recognize the existing situation. This document provided that in future the Holy Roman Emperor would be elected by seven German princes designated as the electors. These electors were the archbishops of Cologne, Trier, and Mainz, and the princes of Saxony, Brandenburg, the Palatinate, and Bohemia. The papacy was excluded from the election process, which was now a strictly German affair. Each of the electors was granted almost complete independence within his own territory. In evaluating Charles IV's action perhaps the words of Lord Bryce are most fitting: "He legalized anarchy and called it a constitution." The Golden Bull made the German crown a pawn in the hands of a select group of independent princes, who had the power to demand all kinds of concessions from any individual who hoped to be emperor.

After 1356 Germany progressed rapidly toward decentralization. Other princes demanded and gained the same kind of independence enjoyed by the electors. Germany was not a real kingdom; it was a confederation of independent states. The emperor had no real power. He could call together the princes, churchmen, and representatives of the towns in meetings called diets. Usually such meetings achieved little, since the emperor lacked any means of enforcing decisions. He had no national army, no tax system, and no court system with which to make his influence felt. As previously noted, most of the emperors devoted their attentions to increasing their holdings. For instance, the Hapsburgs, who ascended the imperial throne again in 1438, acquired tremendous possessions and became one of the great families of Europe. As emperors of Germany, however, they enjoyed little power. Within their small principalities many princes created stable, well-organized political systems. Germany was not a lawless, ungoverned land by any means. But she did lack unity, and for this she was to pay a heavy price in early modern times, when she had to meet the competition of the large national states that emerged elsewhere in Europe.

In Italy the trend toward decentralization after 1250 was even more pronounced than in Germany. Italy lacked even a weak king as a symbol of unity. There emerged a welter of independent states of every conceivable kind to confuse the picture. In the north the self-governing towns, exemplified by Venice, Milan, Genoa, Pisa, and Florence, dominated the scene. These cities tended to develop systems of government

in which one strong man or a small clique of rich men monopolized political power. Often such autocratic governments bred social strife within the cities, leading to innumerable cases of civil war and mob violence. Moreover, the bitter competition among the cities of northern Italy for economic gain and additional territory resulted in almost incessant intercity warfare after 1300. Central Italy was dominated by the papacy, although papal overlordship was bitterly resented, leading again to perpetual warfare. As the Middle Ages drew to a close, the papacy succeeded in creating a dictatorial governmental system within the Papal States that curbed disorder. In so doing, however, the papacy neglected its spiritual leadership and lost much of its influence in the rest of Europe. Southern Italy became a pawn of several European powers, especially France and the Spanish kingdom of Aragon. Since nothing whatsoever existed to unite, direct, and curb these hundreds of small principalities, the breakup of the Holy Roman Empire doomed Italy to extreme division and endless strife.

2. The Failure of Feudal Monarchy in France, England, and Spain

After 1300 England, France, and the kingdoms of the Spanish Peninsula encountered troubles nearly as serious as those of the Holy Roman Empire. It will be recalled that up to 1300 these states had developed well-organized feudal monarchies, in which kings shared political power with such vested interests as the nobles, the Church, and the towns. As the fourteenth century progressed, these feudal monarchies began to show signs of weakness. Kings were not content to share power. Nobles, clergy, and townsmen were unwilling to surrender more of their privileges. Problems arose that transcended class interest, especially wars and economic crises. Kings lacked the power and the resources to solve these problems. Vested interests were not blessed with vision great enough to face them. The result was a lack of harmony in each kingdom, sometimes bursting forth in civil war. This strife slowly broke down the essential features of feudal monarchy and left kings free to increase their powers. As 1500 approached, new national states were born to replace feudal states, and when these national states came into existence, the medieval period was ended.

The evolution of France and England from 1300 to 1500 must be dealt with as a unit because the histories of these nations center around a single event, the Hundred Years' War (1337–1453). This struggle began as a result of the actions of Edward III (1327–77) of England. He was fearful of losing the French province of Guienne, which he held as a vassal from the king of France. For a long time the French kings had followed a policy of absorbing the lands of their vassals and thus enlarging the holdings of the French crown. Edward was also worried lest the French king take over the province of Flanders. French control over this center of the woolen industry would have been an economic blow to England, which furnished most of the raw wool for the Flemish shops. Such a loss would have been disastrous to the English treasury, since a good deal of the royal income was derived from export duties on wool. The French kings had also been encouraging the Scots to resist English rule.

The moment was ripe for a blow against France. In 1328 the last member of the Capetian house had died. Philip of Valois succeeded to the throne as Philip VI. He and his successors were men of small ability who equated kingship with romantic notions about chivalry and showed little interest in performing the numerous administrative tasks associated with ruling their state. So Edward struck boldly. After careful steps to create a good army and to build up a system of alliances against the king of France, he announced in 1337 that he was claiming the French throne on the grounds that he had a superior hereditary claim to the throne, since he was the grandson of Philip IV while Philip VI was only a nephew. Philip VI answered this claim by pronouncing Edward a rebellious vassal and by confiscating the fief of Guienne.

The first phase of the Hundred Years' War lasted until 1360, and was nearly fatal to France. English ships won control of the English Channel. English armies, made up largely of non-noble bowmen and pikemen, cut to pieces the flower of French feudal nobility in two great battles at Crécy (1346) and Poitiers (1356). Between times English armies ravaged French soil and spread chaos through the land. The French monarchy was powerless to check this disaster. The crowning blow came at the battle of Poitiers when King John of France (1350–64) was captured and carried off to England.

Without a king France was plunged into a desperate crisis. John's son, Charles, tried to carry on as regent, but his authority was challenged on every side. The Estates-General, led by a Parisian merchant, Étienne Marcel, undertook extensive reforms aimed at curbing royal taxation, correcting abuses in the royal government, and putting controls on royal civil servants. A peasant revolt broke out in protest against taxes and war losses. Bands of soldiers ran wild over France. The nobles sought greedily to extend their privileges. Charles finally crushed the rebellious Estates-General by force, while the terrified nobles smashed the peasants. John bought his release by signing a humiliating peace with the English in 1360, in which Edward III was given full title to Guienne. France had been reduced greatly in power, chiefly because her kings could not ward off a foreign foe and control dissatisfied elements within the kingdom.

The next phase of the war, extending from 1364 to 1415, was marked by little decisive fighting but by tremendous internal dissension in each kingdom. France enjoyed a brief recovery under the rule of Charles V (1364–80), who succeeded in rebuilding France's military strength and increasing royal income. Using these resources skillfully, he slowly weakened England's hold on Guienne and threatened to drive her out of France. However, his work was not continued by his successor, Charles VI (1380–

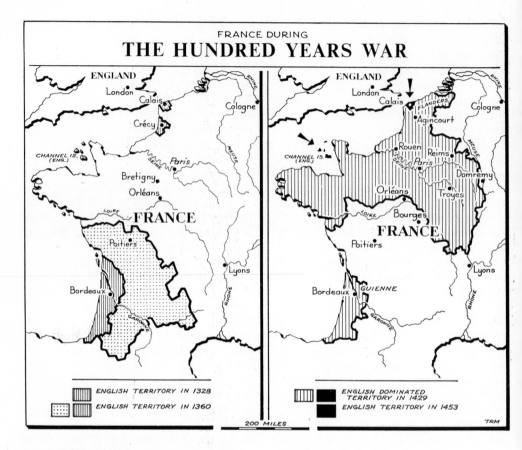

FRANCE DURING
THE HUNDRED YEARS WAR

ENGLAND
London
Calais
Crécy
CHANNEL IS. (ENG.)
Bretigny
Paris
Orléans
FRANCE
Poitiers
Bordeaux
Cologne
Lyons

| | ENGLISH TERRITORY IN 1328 |
| | ENGLISH TERRITORY IN 1360 |

ENGLAND
London
Calais
FLANDERS
Agincourt
Rouen
Reims
CHANNEL IS. (ENG.)
Paris
Domremy
Orléans
Troyes
Bourges
FRANCE
Poitiers
Bordeaux
GUIENNE
Cologne
Lyons

| | ENGLISH DOMINATED TERRITORY IN 1429 |
| | ENGLISH TERRITORY IN 1453 |

200 MILES   TRM

1422). This pitiful figure became a helpless victim of the French nobility. When Charles VI became king, he was still a minor. A regency, dominated by the young king's greedy uncles, of whom Philip, duke of Burgundy, was the most powerful, was placed in control of the kingdom. Charles succeeded in ridding himself of the influence of his uncles for a brief period after he reached his majority, only to fall under the spell of his brother Louis, duke of Orléans. While still a young man, Charles began to suffer from spells of insanity. Each attack required the reinstitution of a regency. The Burgundians and the Armagnacs (partisans of the duke of Orléans) competed bitterly for control of the regency and control of the kingdom. By the early fifteenth century their rivalry divided the nobility of France into two great camps engaged in a ruinous civil war. Efficient administration broke down

completely during this hate-filled struggle. Peasant revolts, civil strife in the towns, and private warfare added to the confusion. France got a chance to see the complete inefficiency of the feudal nobles as rulers. Without a strong king to curb them they plunged France into a disgusting display of violence, greed, and selfishness. The final proof of the political bankruptcy of the nobility came when the Burgundians and the Armagnacs each began to dicker with the English to help destroy the other.

England was hardly less troubled during these years from 1360 to 1415. The old hero of the first years of the struggle against France, Edward III, ruled until 1377 amid increasing trouble. His reign was highly significant because of the rapid growth of Parliament. Edward's chief interest was always in waging war against France, but for this he needed money, and the easiest way to get it was to call Parliament. Frequent meetings of Parliament resulted in the rapid development of parliamentary organization. The House of Lords, comprising the great feudal barons and high churchmen, separated from the House of Commons, made up of townsmen and of the lesser gentry representing the counties. Each house perfected rules regulating conduct of business and steadily increased its powers. Edward usually agreed to parliamentary demands because he wanted money. Aside from extensive control over taxation Parliament began to gain a voice in spending money, in controlling royal officials, and in initiating legislation. By the time of Edward's death Parliament had become a vital factor in English political life. However, its future was not yet charted. Obviously it could curb royal power, but no one knew whether Parliament would use its power to weaken monarchy beyond a safe point, and it was not yet possible to tell whether the interests represented in Parliament would co-operate for the common good or would use their power to further private instead of national interests.

Edward's successor, Richard II (1377-99), certainly felt the new power of Parliament. His stormy reign was filled with civil strife arising from dissatisfaction with royal government. A great peasant revolt broke out in 1381 and had to be crushed by force. The nobles, acting in Parliament, tried hard to limit royal power, and when Richard resisted their efforts he was charged with tyranny and in 1399 was deposed by Parliament. Henry IV (1399–1413) was elected in his place. This was an event of tremendous importance, since it made the monarch more than ever responsible to Parliament. However, Parliament was neither capable of directing royal government adequately itself nor willing to trust the king to do so. The reign of Henry IV saw a tragic current begin to run in England. Almost constant civil war raged, led by great nobles who refused to recognize Henry IV as king. What these nobles wanted was someone sitting on England's throne who would favor their selfish interests. Parliament became a convenient place to agitate for a change of kings or for control over the present king, although the battlefield might be the final scene of decision. Just as in France, the nobles were making a bid to retain their power, their aim being to achieve this end by controlling the king.

Henry V (1413–22) hastened both England and France along their troubled path by reopening the Hundred Years' War. Desirous of giving his nobles something to think about other than curbing his authority and assured that he would find support among France's warring factions, he invaded France in 1415. His avowed aim was to seize the French throne. His campaign opened brilliantly when he crushed a French army of knights at Agincourt in 1415 and then captured a series of key cities in west-central France. Instead of rallying to defend France the Burgundians and Armagnacs tried to use the English to destroy one another. Eventually the Burgundians allied openly with the English, permitting Henry V to force the humiliating Treaty of Troyes on Charles VI in 1420. By its terms Henry married Catherine, the daughter of Charles. He or his successor was to become king of France when Charles died; until that time he would act as regent for the mad Charles. Most of France north of the Loire River was in English hands. A great nation seemed about to be exterminated.

Both Henry V and Charles VI died in 1422, leaving Henry's nine-month-old son, Henry VI, to inherit both thrones. The English were not destined to enjoy dominance over France for long. France made a spectacular recovery from the disasters of the early fifteenth century. A new, hard-to-define feeling provided the inspiration for her recovery—the feeling of patriotism, of love for France and hatred for foreigners. The chief beneficiary was the son of Charles VI, soon to be known as King Charles VII. After 1420 he had fled to southern France as a virtual prisoner of the Armagnac faction. For some years he lived at Bourges, despairing of ever becoming king of France, as was his right. Then there appeared before him a simple peasant girl, Joan of Arc, claiming that God had revealed to her that Charles must free France from the English and assume his rightful place as head of the French kingdom. Her pleas bestirred the dispirited Charles and pumped new confidence into the French soldiers loyal to Charles. Joan herself led an army that captured Orléans in 1429, the first French victory for many years. From 1429 to 1453 the French won victory after victory until the English held only the city of Calais in France. Joan did not live to see these victories. In 1430 she was captured by Burgundian troops, turned over to the English, tried by the Church for heresy, and burned at the stake in Rouen in 1431. Yet, as a symbol of France, the maid of Lorraine lived on to rally the French population to a common purpose.

However, the French victory was based on more than patriotism. During the reign of Charles VII there was a great revival of royal power. A strong, well-trained army, equipped with new weapons, was created and paid for by the king, who thus ended his dependence on useless feudal armies such as had been slaughtered at Crécy, Poitiers, and Agincourt. In 1439 the Estates-General voted Charles VII the power to impose a direct tax on persons, called the *taille*, without any consultation or further authorization. And since the king was winning victory after victory, no one was in a position to protest the growth of royal authority. Even the great nobles bowed before royal will. Charles VII became the focal point of political life. The bitter taste of defeat, of disorder, of irresponsibility on the part of great nobles compelled everyone in turn to the king for leadership. Charles VII was not a strong ruler; he did not make full use of his opportunity. However, when he died in 1461, his son, Louis XI, inherited elements of strength that were of vast significance—a strong army, the power to tax at will, a patriotic people, and the bitter memory of what royal weakness and feudal selfishness could mean to France. His ac-

cession marked the beginning of a new era.

England was in a less happy state. Strife among rival factions of nobles struggling to dominate weak kings finally led to a destructive civil war called the War of the Roses. This struggle had its origins during the tragic reign of Henry VI (1422–61). When he became king he was only an infant, a situation demanding a long regency. When he did reach his majority, he continued to be dominated by noble factions motivated chiefly by personal ambitions. The final blow was an attack of insanity. Two major factions of nobles, the Lancastrians and the Yorkists, locked in a deadly struggle for control of the government. While this civil war raged, the regular processes of orderly government were forgotten. Tyranny, intrigue, murder, confiscation of property, and pursuit of private ends were the order of the day. The Yorkists held the throne from 1461 to 1485. Finally in 1485, Henry Tudor, a Lancastrian, defeated Richard III in a pitched battle at Bosworth Field and assumed the crown as Henry VII. The nation was sick of civil war and disorder and was willing to follow anyone who promised to restore peace and security. The old noble factions had been decimated. Henry was, therefore, free to do with England almost anything he pleased. He used the opportunity to end the feudal state and to create a strong central government that united the English people into a nation.

In the Spanish Peninsula several well-defined monarchies—Aragon, Castile, and Portugal being the chief ones—had been shaped out of territories won by Christian warriors fighting the Moslems between the tenth and the thirteenth centuries. By 1300 the holy war against the Moslems ceased to be the significant factor in Spanish affairs, the Moslems having been confined to the narrow territory of Granada. The Christian kingdoms then turned on one another, competing bitterly for territory. Added to these wars was the almost constant civil strife within each kingdom. The struggles in Spain were but replicas of the Anglo-French struggle and of the civil wars in these kingdoms.

Spanish nobles, churchmen, and townsmen were as anxious as their counterparts in England and France to curb royal power, and the kings tried to expand their authority. All these senseless quarrels finally ended when in 1469 the heiress of Castile, Isabella, married Ferdinand, the heir of Aragon. By 1479, when this couple had succeeded to both thrones, they quickly took steps to end the strife and unify their lands into a single national state. In Portugal a steady consolidation of power in royal hands occurred in the fifteenth century. Portuguese kings did not meet such violent resistance as did the kings of the other Spanish kingdoms. They gained considerable support within Portugal because of their heroic struggle to prevent Castile from absorbing Portugal. The Portuguese kings also promoted the commercial interests in their kingdom. Throughout the fifteenth century Portuguese merchants with royal backing expanded southward along the African coast and found lucrative markets.

3. Eastern Europe and the Mediterranean World

In Eastern and Southeastern Europe the decline of the Holy Roman Empire and the collapse of the Byzantine Empire heralded a new political order. The Byzantine Empire never fully recovered from the attacks of the Seljuk Turks in the late eleventh century and the capture of Constantinople by Western Europeans in 1204 during the Fourth Crusade. After the Europeans were finally ousted in 1261 and Greek emperors assumed power, a fatal illness seemed to settle over the empire. Civil strife slowly sapped the strong imperial government. The Italian city-states, led by Venice, deprived the empire of much of its trade, and bit by bit the territory of the Byzantine Empire was pared away, especially by the Ottoman Turks. The emperors of the fourteenth and fifteenth centuries appealed desperately to the West for help but received little, since Western Europeans were too enmeshed in their own rivalries. Finally

in 1453 Constantinople was captured by the Ottoman Turks, ending forever the power that had so long shielded Western Europe and supplied Europeans with inspiration and models in scholarship, the arts, industry, and trade.

The victory of the Ottoman Turks at Constantinople in 1453 signified more than the fall of the Byzantine Empire. It marked the reappearance of an aggressive Moslem force threatening Western Christendom, a danger that had not existed for a long time. We previously noted that the Abbasid dynasty (750–1258) had been incapable of maintaining political control over the vast Moslem Empire. The disintegration of the Moslem Empire and the resulting internal rivalries removed most of the pressure of Moslem expansion and prepared the way for the European counterattack during the Crusades. Vast upheavals continued to shake the Moslem world after the crusading movement had subsided, and the chief cause of these upheavals was the intrusion of non-Moslem Asiatics into the Moslem world. In the thirteenth century a Mongol horde led by Genghis Khan and his successors raced westward to build an empire that reached into western Russia, Asia Minor, and Syria. The already-weak Abbasid dynasty disappeared before this avalanche. When, however, by the end of the thirteenth century the Mongol Empire began to recede, its Moslem portions broke into rival principalities, and one of the most powerful was that of the Ottoman Turks in Asia Minor. The Ottoman Turks were Asiatic nomads, distantly related to the Seljuk Turks, whose earlier attacks on the Byzantine Empire in Asia Minor played a part in the crusading movement in Western Europe. The Ottomans were permitted to settle in Asia Minor in the thirteenth century by the Seljuk Turks, who still maintained an important state there. Within a short time the Ottomans had established their independence, their first great ruler being Osmanli, or Othman (1290–1326), from whence the term "Ottoman." The new state began to expand almost immediately, chiefly at the expense of Byzantine possessions in western Asia Minor. By the end of the fourteenth century the Ottomans had taken over Asia Minor and had begun to attack Byzantine territory in the Balkans. The Ottomans had become Moslems even before they first settled in Asia Minor.

Early in the fifteenth century Ottoman power was nearly destroyed by a new threat from the east in the person of Tamerlane, a Mongol warrior who sought to reconstruct the empire of Genghis Khan. However, Tamerlane's death in 1405 was followed by a sudden collapse of his empire. The Ottomans soon recovered from the defeats inflicted on them by Tamerlane and returned to their attack on the Byzantine Empire, seizing Constantinople in 1453. Early in the next century they conquered Syria, Palestine, and Egypt, creating a huge state that stretched from the Danube to the Nile. Flying the flag of Mohammedanism, rich in material resources, and possessing an excellent army and navy, the Ottomans loomed as a major threat to Western Europe as the Middle Ages ended. No great power like the Byzantine Empire existed to resist this menace; Western Europeans had to face it on their own.

The Eastern and Central European area began to assume its modern shape in the wake of the decline of the Holy Roman and Byzantine empires during the late Middle Ages. Lithuanians, Poles, Bohemians, and Hungarians gained a greater degree of freedom from German domination and Byzantine influence than they had ever before enjoyed, heralding the appearance of new national states. Kings became the rallying points for the patriotic sentiments of these peoples. However, none of these states possessed highly developed political institutions as the Middle Ages closed.

Farther east the Russians slowly freed themselves from the Mongol invaders who had seized much of Russia during the thirteenth century. The Mongol khans (emperors) had made no attempt to establish their own system of government in Russia. Instead they forced the numerous conquered Russian princes to become tribute-paying subordinates of the khans, responsible for collecting tribute from the Russian populace. In the fourteenth century the princes of Moscow gained the privilege of collecting tribute in the name of the khans from all the other Russian princes. Using this right skillfully, the Muscovites began to establish a strong state at the expense of the other Russian principalities. Early in the fifteenth century they rejected the overlordship of the khans, whose power was rapidly deteriorating, and started a series of wars for the purpose of Muscovite expansion and liberation from the Mongols. Under Ivan III (reigned 1462–1505) the Mongol hold on Russia was finally broken, and Ivan was powerful enough to compel most Russian princes to accept his authority. After the fall of Constantinople in 1453 the Muscovites claimed that they were the heirs of the Byzantine tradition and the protectors of the Greek Orthodox religion. Ivan III began calling himself "tsar," which implied that he was the successor of the Roman caesars. This sense of protecting an ancient heritage gave Russia a new mission and a feeling of uniqueness that would help to solidify her people into a powerful nation in the future.

4. Economic and Social Tensions

Responsible for a part of the political difficulties we have just traced were basic economic and social problems besetting most areas of Europe. The economic system that had flourished in the twelfth and thirteenth centuries ceased to be entirely adequate and was slowly being superseded by new institutions. Social disequilibrium accompanied economic difficulties.

The most vital factor in the prosperity of the twelfth and thirteenth centuries had been *expanding* trade. In the fourteenth and fifteenth centuries many factors combined to cause a leveling off of commercial expansion. The incessant warfare of these centuries upset established trade processes. Europe's population ceased growing because of recurrent famines and the horrible Black Death, which between 1347 and 1350 wiped out nearly one third of the population. The rise of the Ottoman power made it more difficult for Western Europeans to penetrate new geographical areas. There was a shortage of capital. The independent cities that had been the sources of medieval commercial growth lacked the manpower, the wealth, and the political power to offset these numerous difficulties. Co-operation was nearly impossible for them. This is not to imply that the fourteenth and fifteenth centuries enjoyed none of the benefits of trade, for trade did flourish and many grew rich from it. However, trade did not grow so fast as it previously had.

Industry experienced a comparable constriction. The existing productive system was the biggest barrier to industrial growth. The guild system, which had once promoted the growth of industry, grew increasingly restrictive. Seeking to protect their monopoly on production in each city, the guilds passed rules excluding the products of outsiders. They barred technical changes that seemed to threaten their members, and they excluded new members or reduced them to inferior rank in the guilds. Often their pricing arrangements were unrealistic. Such practices curtailed production and discouraged expansion into new areas of production.

Agricultural production, the basis of Europe's economy, also underwent changes. The manorial system continued to break up, the serfs becoming tenants rendering payments in money instead of in services and produce for the plots of land they rented. This transition caused considerable disturbance, chiefly in the form of peasant revolts. In general, agricultural production probably did not increase greatly, owing chiefly to political disorder, the Black Death, and the decline of the population. The opening of new lands that had highlighted the twelfth and thirteenth centuries nearly ceased in the late Middle Ages.

Significant social disturbances followed in the wake of economic tension and political disturbances. Every class experienced some fundamental change. The landowning feudal nobility discredited themselves politically as a result of their selfish, obstructive attempts to seize power and to impede the development of strong monarchy. Their position as the wealthiest element in society was challenged by the rising capitalists in commerce and industry, and in warfare they were being replaced by non-noble professional soldiers. Seeking to retain their social pre-eminence, the nobility turned to political intrigue, ruthless exploitation of their lands, and the costly indulgence in a pompous mode of life—none of which won them many friends.

Although most peasants in the western areas of Europe continued to escape from serfdom, they were thrown more and more on their own economically. As renters they could no longer appeal to a kindly manorial lord in times of war and famine. Many landlords, seeking to squeeze every penny out of their tenants, continued to collect most of the old dues that peasants had once owed as serfs. Taxes levied by kings to fight expensive wars fell heavily on the peasants, and the wars that the peasants thus paid for often ravaged their farms, especially in France, Italy, and Germany. Peasants expressed their discontent by rebelling frequently, only to be crushed by brute force exerted by kings, nobles, and clergymen.

Equally unhappy were certain elements of the middle class, especially in Flanders and Italy, where capitalistically organized industry increasingly dominated the scene. Many artisans were reduced to the ranks of laborers for hire, working for the entrepreneurs who bought raw materials in bulk and produced finished products in great quantities. These artisans often lost the political power they had enjoyed in the twelfth and thirteenth centuries when the towns were struggling for independence. The rich entrepreneurs more and more dominated political life in the cities. The monopolistic guilds tended to exclude artisans from the trades, leaving many people with little means of earning a livelihood. The laborers and the unemployed frequently resorted to mob violence, but with no more success than the peasants. The towns, which once had made men free, were no longer havens for the oppressed.

The class making the greatest advance in the fourteenth and fifteenth centuries comprised the capitalistic leaders of trade and industry. This was particularly the case in northern Italy and Flanders, although the generalization also holds for France, England, and parts of Germany and Spain. Often the members of this new class refused to carry on business within the framework of the old guild structure and felt no need to confine their activities to a single city. Their boldness in such fields as banking, moneylending, and the woolen industry netted them huge fortunes. Politically they seized control of most city governments and found increasing favor with kings. Culturally they were able to patronize the advancing

cause of the humanists and to set standards in fashion. The complete victory of the new middle class lay in the future, but its presence was already felt in the society of the late Middle Ages.

More and more it became obvious that the solution to the economic and social problems of the fourteenth and fifteenth centuries lay with a stronger central government. Peasants, capitalists, industrial workers—all regarded kings as champions of their cause and pressed the central government to assume great control over trade, industry, agriculture, and the class structure. In countries such as England and France kings responded to this pressure and began regulating economic and social conditions on a national scale. This trend was proof of the passing of medieval society, which had been built on social stratification, economic localism, and group protection of vested interests.

SUGGESTED READING

C. Previté-Orton, A History of Europe from 1198 to 1378, 3rd ed., rev. (1951); and W. T. Waugh, A History of Europe from 1378 to 1494, 3rd ed. (1949). These two volumes, consecutive parts of a series, provide full details on the political history of Western Europe in the late Middle Ages.

E. P. Cheyney, The Dawn of a New Era, 1250–1453 (1936). The author of this volume has tried the difficult task of viewing the political, social, economic, religious, and cultural developments of Europe as a whole in the late Middle Ages.

É. Perroy, The Hundred Years War (1951). This book not only supplies a detailed account of the military aspects of the Hundred Years' War, but also provides a good history of France in the late Middle Ages.

* A. R. Myers, England in the Later Middle Ages (Penguin). An excellent description of social conditions in fourteenth- and fifteenth-century England, showing clearly some of the forces that hastened the downfall of medieval society.

George Lee Haskins, The Growth of English Representative Government (1948). This volume traces the history of Parliament down to the early seventeenth century. The author does a remarkable job of summarizing the ideas of

numerous specialists, making his work a clear, concise survey of a complicated subject.

James Bryce, The Holy Roman Empire, rev. ed. (1904). This previously cited classic presents a clear picture of the decline of the Holy Roman Empire after 1250.

Geoffrey Barraclough, The Origins of Modern Germany, 2nd ed. (1947). The most up-to-date discussion in English of German political evolution, especially good in summarizing the latest scholarship pertaining to the decline of the Holy Roman Empire.

Herbert Heaton, Economic History of Europe, rev. ed. (1948). The early chapters of this general survey of European economic history will supply important information on the economic problems and changes affecting Europe in the late Middle Ages.

Harold Lamb, Genghis Khan and the Mongol Horde (1954). A brilliantly presented account of the impact of the Mongols on the European world. The author is especially skillful at bringing to life the main characters involved in the story of Mongol expansion.

Helen Zimmern, The Hansa Towns (1889). An old but still interesting treatment of the Hanseatic League and its role in late medieval history.

Jean Froissart, The Chronicles, adapted by H. P. Dunster (1906). This chronicle of the Hundred Years' War provides a fascinating insight into the lack of political intelligence of the French nobility of the early fifteenth century. Froissart portrays the Hundred Years' War as a series of romantic episodes by chivalrous knights without any realization of the political, social, and economic issues involved.

William Langland, *The Vision of Piers Plowman*, ed. by Henry W. Wells (1945). This fourteenth-century English poem reflects the deep religious sentiments and the growing sense of social criticism prevalent in the lower classes, especially the peasantry, in late medieval society.

———— ◆ ————

CHAPTER 26

The Decline of the Church

THE TENSIONS that beset Western European political, social, and economic institutions in the fourteenth and fifteenth centuries afflicted the Church even more severely. After 1300 this powerful institution, which had earlier influenced all aspects of human activity and supplied the common denominator for every element of European society, found itself increasingly incapable of guiding men. Its teachings, its system of government, and its leaders were subjected to merciless criticism and to open defiance. The previously potent Church failed to discover new resources with which to meet these criticisms, thereby dooming itself to a reactionary role in society.

1. The Decline of the Papacy

The decline of the Church in the fourteenth and fifteenth centuries was most obvious in the case of the papacy. We have noted that during the thirteenth century the papacy was amazingly successful in taking control of the Church, creating a religious monarchy in which a single man guided the beliefs, the morals, and the worship of most Europeans. The centralization of religious life under a single ruler meant that the vigor of the Church depended to a large extent upon the forcefulness of that leadership. After 1300 the papacy suffered repeated setbacks, until by 1500 papal prestige was little respected anywhere in Western Europe.

The first serious setback for the papacy came at the hands of the kings of England and France, Edward I and Philip IV. These rulers both sought to impose taxation on the Church in their kingdoms in order to fight a war against each other. Pope Boniface VIII (1294–1303) insisted that the Church's property was exempt from lay control and issued a papal bull, called *Clericis Laicos*, in which he maintained that only with papal consent could any taxes be laid upon the Church. Edward and Philip defied Boniface and took steps to cut off all revenues from their kingdoms to Rome. Boniface had to retreat from his position, something the bishops of Rome were not accustomed to do. Before long he was involved in a new quarrel with Philip IV, this time over the question of the proper courts for trying clergymen. Again the strong-minded pope stated his case in a way that outraged Philip. In the bull *Unam Sanctam*, Boniface insisted that the French king and all men must subject themselves to the pope if they were to be saved. Philip counterattacked violently. He turned public opinion in France against the pope, called a meeting of the Estates-General, and finally sent some of his henchmen to Italy to capture Boniface. Philip's agents were successful, and the pope escaped what might have been an even more painful defeat by dying, perhaps as a result of the strain resulting from his capture by Philip's agents. No one could mistake the importance of these events: the pope had suffered a humiliating defeat at the hands of a strong political leader unwilling to accept papal guidance in the running of his kingdom.

Philip IV capitalized on his victory by arranging for the election of a Frenchman as pope. The new pope took up residence at Avignon, a city on the Rhone River lying just outside the boundaries of the French kingdom. From 1305 to 1377 this city remained the residence of the papacy. During these years of what the Italian writer and humanist Petrarch called the "Babylonian Captivity" the popes were virtually captives of the French king, and many Europeans regarded them as unworthy of the title of head of the universal Church. The English, for instance, who were engaged in the Hundred Years' War with the French, took steps to abolish papal control over ecclesiastical affairs. Few would criticize the English for removing from their midst the agents and the influence of one who was a pawn of England's enemy. The German emperors and many German princes were equally defiant. Many Christians were troubled by the fact that the pope's claim to power was based on succession to St. Peter as bishop of Rome, not Avignon. The Babylonian Captivity caused scholars and writers to raise the whole question of Church government and to arrive at answers that challenged papal supremacy.

The Avignon popes were not idle during these years, however. Realizing that papal prestige was being challenged, they worked to increase their command over the organization and the resources of the Church. Several of them were skilled administrators who succeeded in pushing papal control over the Church organization to its greatest height. They increased the number of Church offices which they could fill with their own appointees. They collected old Church taxes with great vigor and even discovered new sources of income. They steadily increased the number of judicial cases that had to be appealed to Rome and derived a huge income from this activity. They enlarged the papal bureaucracy beyond anything previously known. In terms of income, number of subordinates controlled, and amount of business handled, the popes at Avignon were actually the most powerful men in Europe.

However, this emphasis on administrative, financial, and judicial affairs did the papacy more harm than good in terms of prestige. Abuses of the worst kind began to plague the papal government. The increasing horde of papal bureaucrats engaged in every type of corruption, such as selling offices and accepting bribes. Knowing that favors were for sale, crowds of opportunists descended on Avignon. Many buyers of Church offices were interested only in income, never going near the office they had purchased. Absenteeism thus became a plague on the Church. Bishops and abbots in all parts of Europe resented papal interference in local church affairs and tried to escape papal control, often by turning to their kings, who gladly protected them—for a price. Papal taxation aroused bitterness everywhere. Edward III of England reflected the dislike for the money-grabbing popes when he said: "The successor of the Apostles was ordered to lead the Lord's sheep to the pasture, not to fleece them." Much of this wealth was spent for luxurious living by the clergymen who managed to get their hands on it, arousing the bitter anger of the many in Europe whose lot was poverty. The popes at Avignon were not entirely responsible for this corruption and moral laxness; any huge organization has to face such a problem. But the popes did nothing to correct it. As a consequence many placed the blame on the popes. Religion had become a profitable financial venture; religious leaders appeared to be greedy profiteers, little interested in saving souls. A thorough house cleaning was in order. However, the Avignon popes never found the energy to begin such a reform.

The Babylonian Captivity finally ended in 1377 with the return of the pope to Rome. This move only heralded a greater tragedy for the papacy. The return of the pope to Rome led to the election by a part of the college of cardinals of a second pope, who continued to live at Avignon. Thus began the Great Schism, which lasted until 1417. For forty years the Church was headed by at least two and sometimes three popes. This intolerable situation upset religious life all over Europe. Two administrative systems, two systems of taxation, two systems of Church courts were created, leaving everyone at a loss to know which was the right one. Corruption became twice as bad. Rival popes played politics more furiously than ever before, each seeking to gain enough allies to oust the other. Many Europeans— and especially princes—thought in terms of obeying the pope who offered the best political "deal." Few took seriously the papal claim to be spiritual leader of Europe; popes who competed with one another and encouraged the division of Christendom seemed little better than greedy politicians. The Schism was a costly chapter in the history of the Church.

Before the Schism was many years old, serious men began to search for a way of ending the division. Eventually it was generally agreed that a council should be called in which churchmen from all of Europe would meet to end the Schism and reform the clergy. This revolutionary idea, threatening the whole concept of papal supremacy and the traditional idea of a Church ruled from the top down, increased the confusion in church affairs during the first part of the fifteenth century. Four councils were held between 1409 and 1449. Each was a stormy affair, marked by interminable negotiations. In general, the conciliar movement was a failure in terms of finding a new way of governing the Church, although the second council, held at Constance (1414–18) did end the Schism and re-establish a single pope. Thereafter the popes generally devoted their energies to controlling the councils and ending this dangerous threat to papal authority. Since the councils were often split by quarrels among clergymen representing different nations, papal control was not too difficult to maintain.

Probably the greatest failure of the councils of the fifteenth century was their inability to reform the whole Church. Although many clergymen desired reform and tried to enact reforming legislation at the church councils, they never succeeded in making church councils an effective means of putting their wishes into a practical program of action. When the last council disbanded in 1449, most people had lost confidence in such a device as a means of revitalizing the Church. The greatest influence of the conciliar movement was indirect. It raised the whole question of Church organization and caused many to conclude that the papacy was not necessarily sacred.

The popes of the last half of the fifteenth century sacrificed the final bit of papal influence by pursuing policies that were far removed from religious leadership. They concentrated on strengthening their control over the Papal States in Italy and competing in the many power struggles raging in Italy in this period. To all outward appearances each was a secular prince, scheming, bribing, and brawling to get what he desired for himself, his family, and his friends. Each of them enjoyed a life of luxury rivaling that of any prince in Europe. A few of them lived in a way that was absolutely scandalous, and several became patrons to Renaissance artists and writers who were openly repudiating Christianity in favor of paganism. Since the political activities and the luxury of the papal court were expensive, causing increased financial exactions and increasingly flagrant abuses to gain wealth, corruption became more rampant than ever before. Any thought of reforming the Church slipped farther into the background.

Every activity of the popes of this period pointed to a single conclusion: the papacy no longer enjoyed respect among most Christians. No one would deny that the popes were powerful in terms of wealth and political resources. What the popes had lost was the moral authority that had been their chief source of influence in the thirteenth century, and without that moral authority the papacy became a liability to the Church.

2. Decline of the Clergy

Although the prolonged decay of the papacy was a shattering blow to the strength of the Church, it was not the only source of decline. Hardly less significant was the steady decay of the whole body of the clergy. A large part of the vitality of the earlier Church had depended upon the work of disciplined, serious, and well-trained monks, priests, abbots, and bishops. After 1300 clergymen in general conducted themselves in ways that brought criticism on the Church and reduced their ability to control their flocks.

Especially pronounced was the decline of monasticism. Before 1300 reform movements had repeatedly begun in the monasteries; very often new monastic orders had been founded primarily for the purpose of purifying the Church. Between 1300 and 1500 not a single new monastic order of any importance was established in Western Europe, and the older monastic institutions became increasingly corrupt. Monasteries were no longer a refuge for the dedicated or a stage from which the zealous could launch their efforts to cleanse and purify religious life. The Franciscans and the Dominicans forgot their ideals about poverty and service and turned instead to the pursuit of wealth and power. Lesser orders followed suit. Strict rules about moral purity and piety were relaxed to the point where monks and nuns openly broke their vows. Little attention was paid to the kind of recruits entering monasteries; many were populated by aristocratic ladies who could not find husbands, younger sons without land, and commoners who wanted to escape work. Monastic government fell into the hands of absentee abbots who thought only of capturing the monastic incomes. Of course not all monks were guilty of this laxness and this lack of fervor for religious affairs. However, the culprits, as usual, got most of the publicity. One needs to read only a little of the literature of the fourteenth and fifteenth centuries to realize that monasticism was held in low repute. No longer did monastic life signify holiness, zeal, and moral excellence. It epitomized rather laziness, greed, immorality, and hypocrisy.

The secular clergy, charged with the Church's business in the everyday world, was equally plagued by corruption and moral laxness. Bishops were better known for their political activities and their wealth than for their interest in administering to their flocks. Many of them purchased their offices, paying prices that left them little choice but to spend their time wringing money out of their subjects. Some held several offices at once, making it impossible for them to perform the duties of any. Absenteeism was a common thing, many bishops and priests preferring life at Avignon or at a royal court to life in their episcopal sees or parishes. Absentee clergymen often turned their religious duties over to ignorant clerks who served for a small price but who were incapable of guiding religious activities. Heavy papal taxes tempted bishops and lesser clergymen to devote their energies to shady financial practices. Church services, instruction, confessions, preaching, and counseling were slighted, leaving people with religious problems lost and unhappy.

Although the decay of the clergy called for reform and although many Christians were aware of this need, little was done prior to 1500. The Church was organized in such a way that effective reform had to come from above, but we have already seen the conditions that made it impossible for the papacy to purge the ranks of the clergymen.

3. Old Religious Practices and New Religious Ideas

The Church of the later Middle Ages suffered another setback stemming from its inability to put to its service certain new religious ideas that welled up in Western European society. Prior to 1300 most Europeans had accepted and found satisfaction in a basic set of religious ideas discussed in a previous chapter. Fundamentally, this belief centered around the idea that Christ had instituted a Church that held the keys to heaven in the sacraments it administered. Man's duty was to accept the gift from the Church. By 1300 the theologians and canon lawyers insisted that this was *the* way to salvation. After 1300 few church leaders gave much thought to the meaning of the Christian message. Roman Catholic belief and the religious practices based on it fell into a rather unbending, formal pattern that became increasingly mechanical. Most churchmen were content to equate piety with going through the motions of attending services, receiving the sacraments, and obeying the clergy.

During the last two centuries of the Middle Ages dissatisfaction with this situation was demonstrated in many ways, one of the most important of which was an increase in the number of mystics, i.e., persons who believe that they can experience and know God directly through intuitive powers. Mysticism was present throughout the whole Middle Ages; for instance, St. Bernard and St. Francis of Assisi were mystics. But the fourteenth and fifteenth centuries produced an especially large number. Many were simple men and women who never wore clerical garb. Several of them attracted great attention by recounting their visions of God and by teaching fresh ideas about His will toward men. We have already noted how a French peasant girl, Joan of Arc, impressed those she met. Dozens of comparable figures might also be listed. None was more prominent than Catherine of Siena (1347–80). At an early age she spoke of visions of Christ and vowed to remain unmarried in order to serve Him. For many years during her youth she devoted herself to prayer and physical deprivation, believing that this would bring her closer to Christ. Eventually she turned her energies to helping the poor, the sick, the criminals, and the downhearted. She also found time to agitate for Church reform and to try to conciliate political quarrels in Italy. When death ended her career at the age of thirty-three, many believed her to be a saint possessed with powers to heal and to com-

mune personally with Christ. Although she was never seriously at odds with the Church, Catherine certainly added elements to Christianity with which contemporary bishops, priests, monks, and popes were not acquainted. Nearly every country in Europe produced mystics like Catherine. These figures and their followers, although still Roman Catholics, were going beyond the Church's official cult.

The activities of the mystics led to the development of group movements that operated almost independently of the official Church. These movements were especially strong in Germany and the Low Countries. Perhaps the best example was the Brethren of the Common Life (and its female counterpart, the Sisters of the Common Life). This organization was the outgrowth of the teachings of a long series of mystics whose message centered around a new kind of piety that came from prayer, love, and direct communion with God. Devotees of this idea founded communities where all members pooled their earnings, engaged in common prayer, confessed their sins to one another, cared for the unfortunates about them, educated their children, and even produced their own devotional literature. One of the best examples of their literature, still read today as a spiritual guide, was Thomas à Kempis's *The Imitation of Christ*. The many communities of Brethren seldom strayed into heresy, but their piety, their puritanical life, their communal spirit, and their mysticism set them apart from traditional and conventional religious life within the main body of the Church. It is not therefore surprising that some of the most important later reformers of the Church were educated in their schools or that the Brethren were often attacked for spreading dangerous ideas.

More radical than the mystics and the new communal movements were the reformers—usually called heretics by the Church—who spoke forth openly and whose words provoked many to violent action against the Church. Some of these reformers were intellectual figures who devoted their time to writing criticisms of the Church. Typical was Marsiglio of Padua, whose devastating book, *The Defender of the Peace*, appeared in 1324. Its thesis was that the secular state ought to be independent of the Church. The Church was obligated to fulfill certain spiritual duties, but was not entitled to exercise any secular powers. Marsiglio advocated that it be deprived of its wealth and relegated to the role of a branch of government, subservient to the ruler of the state. Perhaps even more revolutionary was his view that the pope's claim to rule the Church was a fiction, not in accord with Christ's instructions. Marsiglio argued that the "Church" as a community of all Christians should be ruled by a council representing all elements in Christian society, not by a hierarchy of officials headed by the pope. This idea was soon to be put into effect in the conciliar movement. Marsiglio's ideas influenced many others. Such thinkers were clearly undermining the older opinion with respect to the place of religious affairs and of the Church in society.

Somewhat later an Englishman, John Wycliffe (1320–84), delivered an even heavier attack on the Church. This Oxford scholar and teacher entered the ranks of rebellion only during the last part of his life after having spent years studying most phases of Roman Catholic teaching. In his first attacks on the Church he argued that the Church had abused its right to hold property and that all Church property should be confiscated by the state. This suggestion was eagerly welcomed by many Englishmen who wanted such property for themselves or who were tired of seeing the papacy milk the English to support the corrupt papal court at Avignon. Later Wycliffe advocated the destruction of the whole clerical hierarchy on the grounds that it was not necessary. He insisted that salvation depended, not on clergymen, but upon the power of God. Here, of course, he was striking at the fundamental belief upon which the medieval Church was built.

Holding that every man was his own priest, Wycliffe also attacked many of the religious practices of the Church, including elaborate ritual, prayers to saints, veneration of relics, pilgrimages, and the like. Wycliffe even questioned the validity of the sacraments. He argued that Scripture alone must be the authority for Christian doctrine and practice. In line with this idea he translated the Scriptures into English and encouraged all men to read it. Running throughout his writings was the argument that the ruler should take religious affairs in hand to bring about necessary reforms.

Although Wycliffe was soon condemned as a heretic and forced to leave Oxford, his teachings attracted many followers, known as the Lollards, and for many years Lollard preachers agitated for their master's ideas in England. In time, however, they came to challenge all authority, and the English kings of the fifteenth century joined the Roman Catholic clergy in hunting them down and destroying their movement.

Wycliffe's ideas had their most powerful effect, not in England, but in Bohemia. The leading disciple there was John Huss (about 1373–1415), a priest who taught at the University of Prague. His preaching of Wycliffe's radical ideas raised a protest from the Bohemian clergy and ruling faction. Since most of this element was German and was passionately hated by the native population, Huss became a national hero of the Bohemians. Religious revolt mixed with patriotism proved to be explosive. The teachings of Huss were brought to the attention of the papacy, and the agitator was excommunicated as a heretic. He finally consented to journey to the Council of Constance under a promise of safe-conduct from the German emperor. Once at Constance, Huss was imprisoned, tried, and executed as a heretic in 1415. A tremendous rebellion broke out immediately in Bohemia and raged until 1436. Crusade after crusade was preached by the papacy against the Hussites; several German armies, led by an emperor who was anxious to reclaim Bohemia, were soundly thrashed by the fanatical Bohemians. Eventually peace was restored by granting certain concessions of a religious nature to the Hussites. However, a faction of the followers of Huss and Wycliffe, called the Taborites, was not satisfied by these concessions and became practically a church apart during the last years of the Middle Ages.

Clearly Europe was in a state of religious ferment. Neither the gentle mystics nor the fiery-tongued rebels were at home in the Roman Catholic Church. They had begun to strike out in all directions, questioning ritual, devotional practices, organization, and dogma. But the institution that claimed to care for men's souls either ignored or ruthlessly crushed them. This failure to meet religious problems was but another sign of the decay of the Church.

4. Failure of the Intellectual Leadership of the Church

In a previous chapter we noted that one of the main sources of strength of the medieval Church was its ability to command the best intellects, thus creating a world of learning that supported and justified the teachings of the Church. The great scholastic philosophers of the thirteenth century, especially Thomas Aquinas, represented this leadership. In essence their work consisted of demonstrating to their age that the truth revealed by God squared with the truth discovered by man's reason. During the fourteenth and fifteenth centuries the scholastics lost their dominance over the intellectual world. Their efforts became increasingly sterile. Other thinkers with different ideas, not so favorable to the Church, moved slowly to the forefront.

The history of philosophy and theology of the later Middle Ages is an arid desert into which we need not venture, but one philosopher must be mentioned because of his destructive assault on thirteenth-century scholasticism. He was William of Ockham (about 1300–49), an English Franciscan. The central idea in his extensive theological writings was that matters of faith could not be demonstrated by human reason. Such things as the existence of God and the immortality of the soul came to a man only by

intuition, by a mystical process. William's position was soon accepted at the great universities like Paris and Oxford. Faith and reason now became two distinct and unrelated spheres of intellectual activity, instead of complementary routes to a single truth, as Aquinas had taught. Since few believed that reason could discover knowledge about God, about all there was left for the "philosophers" was to split hairs in logical arguments pertaining to nothing; one favorite project was arguing about how many angels could stand on the head of a pin. No wonder that increasingly in the fourteenth and fifteenth centuries the scholastics became the butt of nearly everyone's jokes and the targets of bitter criticism.

Serious thinkers could not, of course, be expected to be satisfied with the silly projects left to human reasoning by the later scholastics. Since reason no longer had any relevance to religious questions, thinking men focused their minds on other activities. Political theorists, like Marsiglio of Padua, turned their thoughts to new ideas about the government of Church and state and came up with ideas damaging to the cause of the Church. Recall what Wycliffe and Huss concluded in their thoughts about the Church. The later Middle Ages also witnessed a growing interest in science. Since reason was not fit to consider religious truths, it was applied to earthly objects. Scholars at the universities of Paris and Oxford produced a considerable body of scientific observation and scrutinized Greek scientific writing rather carefully, laying the groundwork for the revolutionary scientific discoveries of Copernicus, Galileo, and others in the sixteenth and seventeenth centuries.

5. The Pressure of New Forces on the Church

So far we have noted the sure signs of decay *within* the Church—decline of leadership, corruption, inflexibility in dogma and ritual, lack of strength to reform, and loss of intellectual vigor. This does not tell the whole story. While the Church was faltering internally, new, non-religious forces were crowding into the scene to challenge its leadership. This is not the place to analyze these new forces in detail; they will be discussed later. They must be mentioned here, however, merely to round out the picture of the decline of the Church.

The new, aggressive national states certainly harassed the Church in the later Middle Ages. The rulers of these states were determined to control any institution that challenged their dominance or that might be useful to them. Everywhere the princes, although still Catholic, sought to limit and dominate the Church. In England a series of laws was enacted to exclude the papacy from taxing the Church's property and from controlling Church offices. The king and Parliament alike joined in this activity. In France the royal government worked steadily, often with the help of the French clergy, to establish a "French" church, independent of the papacy and subservient to the crown. In Spain late in the fifteenth century the monarchs even undertook to reform the Church independently of the papacy. As 1500 approached, "national" churches, dominated by kings, were becoming a reality at the expense of the previously self-sufficient universal Church.

The middle class, accepting a capitalistic philosophy, was likewise challenging the Church's social and economic teachings. Many capitalists would have liked to see the Church's wealth put to a different use. Most of them paid no attention to religious arguments against charging interest or on behalf of fair prices. To these men the Church was reactionary and deserved to be deprived of its position of power and its wealth.

Finally, a new breed of thinkers and artists, called the humanists, was emerging to criticize and repudiate most of the teachings of the Church. The humanists, flourishing especially in Italy, were interested in the joys and wonders of the physical world and often rejected the spiritually oriented views characteristic of the Church-dominated culture of the high Middle Ages.

Realizing that a combination of internal difficulties and the challenge of new forces undermined the power and influence of the Church in the late Middle Ages, one can no longer doubt that an epoch was ending. Admittedly the breakup of the medieval empires, the decline of feudal institutions, the dislocation of the medieval class structure, the failure of manorialism and the guild system—all point toward the passing of medieval civilization. However, the Church stood above all these as the essential factor in medieval civilization. For centuries it had played the leading role in determining what men thought and how they acted. Without its presence atop Western European society medieval civilization is inconceivable. The decline of the church marked the passing of the medieval epoch in Western European history.

SUGGESTED READING

Kenneth Scott Latourette, A *History of Christianity* (1953), pp. 601–89. These few pages provide a well-rounded, balanced, and judicious summary of the difficulties and failures of the Church between 1300 and 1500. Complete and up-to-date bibliographies are included.

Philip Hughes, A *History of the Church*, Vol. III (1947). An excellent longer treatment of the era from Thomas Aquinas to Martin Luther by a Roman Catholic historian.

Alexander Clarence Flick, *The Decline of the Medieval Church*, 2 vols. (1930). Another longer treatment of the Church in the late Middle Ages with heavy emphasis on the Avignon papacy, the Schism, and the conciliar movement.

* J. Huizinga, *The Waning of the Middle Ages* (Anchor). Available in a hardback edition, 1924. A brilliant study that attempts to show how the chief values of medieval society decayed and became distorted in the late Middle Ages.

Herbert B. Workman, *John Wyclif; a Study of the English Medieval Church*, 2 vols. (1926). A detailed study of the career of one of the bitterest critics of the late medieval Church.

T. S. R. Boase, *Boniface VIII* (1933). An adequate biography of the career of the pope whose actions precipitated a series of crises that nearly wrecked the papacy in the late Middle Ages. The book presents a dramatic description of Boniface's struggle with Philip IV of France.

J. M. Clark, *The Great German Mystics: Eckhart, Tauler, and Suso* (1949). A thorough treatment of mysticism and its implications in the religious history of the late Middle Ages.

* Thomas à Kempis, *The Imitation of Christ* (numerous editions; a suitable one is the translation by Harold C. Gardiner in Image paperbacks). This work by a fifteenth-century author serves as the best introduction to the religious ideas of the late medieval mystics, who played such an important role in the religious evolution of the fourteenth and fifteenth centuries.

* Chaucer, *Canterbury Tales* (numerous editions; an excellent one from the point of view of readability is edited by Nevill Coghill in Penguin paperbacks). This classic provides not only interesting reading but also a good picture of the state of mind of several different classes in about 1400.

SECTION 7

The Beginning of Modern Times—

Fifteenth and Sixteenth Centuries

Four major developments (sometimes called revolutions) ushered in the modern era. In the political realm, feudalism gave way to the national state as the dominant unit of organization. A great expansion of commerce gave rise to our modern capitalistic economy and to the Europeanization of much of the rest of the globe. A renaissance or rebirth of secularism occurred in the fields of intellect and art. The Protestant and Roman Catholic reformations brought to an end the religious unity of Western Christendom. These four developments were especially pronounced in the fifteenth and sixteenth centuries. Therefore, it may be useful, if somewhat oversimplifying, to conceive of the fifteenth as a century of transition, and the sixteenth as the first century of modern times.

CHAPTER 27

————— ◆◆ —————

The Rise of National States

I N FIFTEENTH-CENTURY Europe at least four royal monarchs succeeded in creating powerful national states. They did so at the expense of rival feudal barons who had fallen upon hard times. The longbow and gunpowder had begun to destroy the fighting effectiveness of these mounted armored knights as early as the fourteenth century. At the same time reviving commerce, bringing with it a money economy and a prosperous middle class, undermined the economic monopoly of the landowning aristocracy. The kings made use of the new, moneyed class and with its support hired standing armies armed with the new weapons. Against such royal armies the feudal barons were unable to stand.

Another factor that aided the royal monarchs in the building of their nation-states was the rise of a national consciousness based primarily upon language. In each of the lands that are now Spain, Portugal, France, England, Germany, and Italy one dialect in the hands of able writers like Chaucer and Dante came to dominate over all others. Once established, these national vernaculars became the instruments for propagating common traditions, customs, and achievements on which national pride and loyalty were built.

Although other factors retarded unification in Italy and Germany until the nineteenth century, Spain, Portugal, France, and England were already well on their way to becoming powerful national states in the late fifteenth century.

1. Spain

The most powerful and influential of the new national states at the opening of the modern era was Spain. The energy and enthusiasm that Spain displayed at this time may be attributed in part, at least, to her long and finally successful struggle against the Moors. By the middle of the thirteenth century the Moors had been driven out of the entire Iberian Peninsula except for the southernmost province of Granada. Furthermore, the numerous medieval feudal holdings in what is now Spain had been consolidated into four large kingdoms—Castile, Aragon, Granada, and Navarre (south of the Pyrenees). The marriage of Ferdinand of Aragon and Isabella of Castile in 1469 united for all practical purposes the two largest kingdoms. During their reign (1474–1516) [1] Granada and Navarre were conquered. Thus, within the forty-seven-year span from 1469 to 1516 the Spanish national state was created.

Ferdinand and Isabella strove incessantly for political and religious unity. In order to suppress further the jealous nobility, they allied themselves with the middle class, leaning heavily upon it for financial and ad-

[1] Isabella ruled Castile from 1474 to 1504, and Ferdinand ruled Aragon from 1479 to 1516.

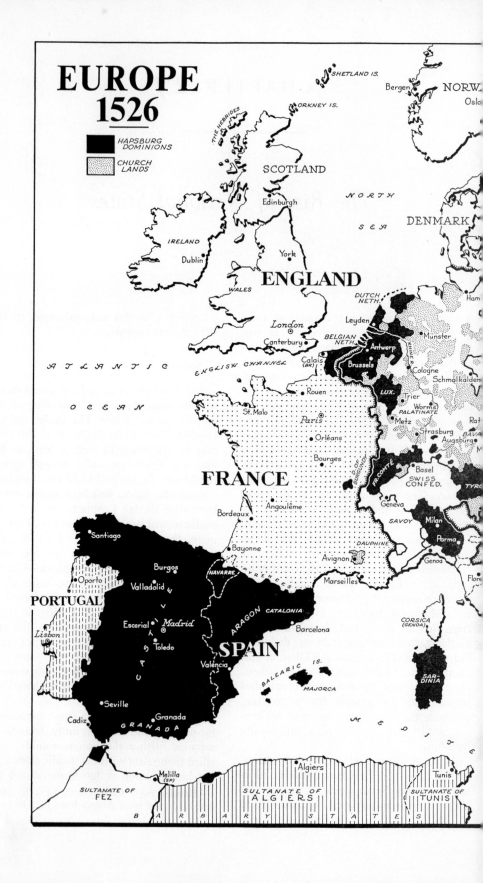

EUROPE
1526

■ HAPSBURG
DOMINIONS
▨ CHURCH
LANDS

SHETLAND IS.

Bergen
Oslo
NORW
THE HEBRIDES
ORKNEY IS.
SCOTLAND
NORTH
SEA
DENMARK
Edinburgh
IRELAND
Dublin
York
ENGLAND
Ham
WALES
DUTCH
NETH.
Leyden
Münster
London
BELGIAN
NETH.
Antwerp
Canterbury
Calais
(BR)
Brussels
Cologne
Schmolkalden
ATLANTIC
ENGLISH CHANNEL
LUX.
Rouen
Trier
Worms
PALATINATE
St. Malo
Metz
Rat
OCEAN
Paris
Strasburg
BAVA
Orléans
Augsburg
M
Bourges
Bordeaux
Angoulème
FRANCE
D. OF BURGUNDY
Basel
SWISS
CONFED.
TYR
Geneva
FR. COMTÉ
SAVOY
Milan
Bayonne
DAUPHINE
Parma
NAVARRE
Avignon
Genoa
Santiago
Burgos
PYRENEES
Marseilles
Flor
Oporto
Valladolid
ARAGON
CATALONIA
CORSICA
(GENOA)
PORTUGAL
Escorial
Madrid
Barcelona
Lisbon
Toledo
SPAIN
Valencia
BALEARIC IS.
SARDINIA
Seville
Granada
MAJORCA
Cadiz
GRANADA
M
E
D
I
Algiers
Tunis
Melilla
(SP)
SULTANATE OF
FEZ
SULTANATE OF
ALGIERS
SULTANATE OF
TUNIS
BARBARY STATES

FINLAND

SWEDEN

Helsingfors

500 MILES

Stockholm

Novgorod

ESTONIA

Moscow
⊙

LIVONIA

RUSSIA
(MUSCOVY)

Riga

COURLAND

BOUNDARY OF
HOLY ROMAN
EMPIRE

•Vilna

PRUSSIA

Danzig

LITHUANIA

VISTULA R.

Warsaw

POLAND

POLAND

•Kiev

Breslau

SILESIA

Cracow

Lemberg

GALICIA

PODOLIA

DNIESTER R.

YEDISAN

KHANATE
OF THE CRIMEA

BOHEMIA

MORAVIA

CARPATHIAN

AUSTRIA

Vienna

Budapest

MOLDAVIA

CRIMEA

H U N G A R Y

TRANSYLVANIA

TISZA R.

Mohacs

DANUBE R.

WALLACHIA

BLACK SEA

Belgrade

Bucharest

DANUBE R.

CROATIAN
MIL. FRP.

BOSNIA

OTTOMAN

EMPIRE

DALMATIA

MONTE-
NEGRO

Sofia

Adrianople

STATES

ADRIATIC SEA

ALBANIA

Salonica

Constantinople

Naples

NAPLES

IONIAN
IS.
(VENICE)

Lepanto

AEGEAN SEA

GREECE

Smyrna

CHIOS
(GENOA)

TO
ARAGON

Palermo

MOREA

(VENICE)

RHODES
(TURKISH)

CYPRUS
(VENICE)

SICILY

TYRRHENIAN SEA

MALTA
(KNIGHTS
OF ST. JOHN)

CRETE
(VENICE)

TRM

ministrative assistance. In return the joint sovereigns did everything in their power to advance the fortunes of the merchants. Vigorous enforcement of law and order, stabilization of the currency, building of roads and bridges, tariff protection of home industries —all served to advance the economic prosperity of Spain in general and the middle class in particular. The climax of this commercial expansion came in 1492 with the discovery of the New World in the name of Spain. The ensuing profits and loot further strengthened the hands of the Spanish sovereigns by freeing them from dependence upon the Cortes (representative bodies that had grown up in both Castile and Aragon during the Middle Ages) for funds.

In religious as well as political affairs Ferdinand and Isabella sought and attained virtually complete unity for their country. Against the two non-Christian groups in their realm, the Jews and the Moslems, the "Catholic Sovereigns" waged a campaign of conversion or extermination. The Jews had long been the object of hatred and persecution in Christian Europe. In part this hatred derived from religious differences, but there was also an economic factor. Church laws against usury had given to the Jews a monopoly on moneylending, which high rates of interest rendered very profitable. The envy and hatred of the Christians led to periodic outbreaks of violence. In the late fourteenth century an outbreak of unusual severity forced many Spanish Jews to seek safety in outward conversion. But these Marranos, as the pseudo-converts were called, were the objects of increasing suspicion. Finally Ferdinand and Isabella, yielding to the persuasion of Dominican fanatics, permitted the Inquisition to be introduced into Spain. At the mercy of this dread church court, the Marranos were terrorized by imprisonment, torture, and loss of life and property. In 1492 the remaining Jews were ordered to leave the country. The exiles thus banished (estimated to be in the neighborhood of one hundred and fifty thousand) took much of their wealth and all of their economic energy and skills with them.

Shortly afterward the Moslems suffered a similar fate. Upon surrendering their last stronghold in Granada, in 1492, they had been promised religious freedom in return for submission to the political authority of the Spanish crown. However, again the "Catholic Sovereigns" yielded to the increasing pressure of religious intolerance, and in 1502 the Moslems were ordered to accept Christianity or leave Spain. Although thousands did leave, even more thousands remained and went through the farce of outward conversion. But these "converts," called Moriscos, only delayed their fate. In the two succeeding reigns they too were persecuted and expelled. A little later the Inquisition was also used to rid Spain of Protestantism. Spain, then, was unified religiously, but at an economic and intellectual cost that was to blight her future. Nevertheless, territorially consolidated and politically unified by Ferdinand and Isabella, enriched by the wealth of the New World, and inspired by the crusading zeal of a purified and triumphant religion, Spain was to be the most powerful and influential of the new national states during the first century of the modern era.

2. Portugal

Next to Spain the most prosperous and energetic state in the sixteenth century was Portugal. That little state appears to be almost an accident of history. Its origin can be traced back to the eleventh century, when, in return for his services in the struggle against the Moors, Count Henry of Burgundy was granted a fief in the vicinity of Oporto by the king of León. Count Henry and his doughty successors not only asserted and achieved their independence from Spanish overlords, but by driving the Moors steadily southward carved out for themselves the sizable state of Portugal. Meanwhile the Portuguese dialect was developing into a national language somewhat different from the Spanish.

Hemmed in by their larger Spanish neighbors by land, the Portuguese turned to the sea. In the fifteenth century such navigators as Prince Henry, Diaz, and Vasco da Gama carried the Portuguese flag around the Cape of Good Hope to India and laid the foundation for a vast empire. As a result of the papal Line of Demarcation (1493) and the Treaty of Tordesillas with Spain, Portugal obtained a monopoly on trade with the East around the Cape. From this trade she amassed more wealth than Spain extracted from the New World. However, so many of Portugal's able merchants and administrators went out to the Eastern empire to make their names and fortunes that her sparse reserves of talent were depleted at home.

Like Spain, Portugal persecuted and expelled her Jews, Moslems, and Protestants. And like Spain her brilliance rapidly waned after the sixteenth century.

3. France

The reign of Louis XI (1461–83) may be said to mark the beginning of France as a modern national state. This crafty "spider king" came to the throne of France eight years after the end of the Hundred Years' War with England. His predecessor had used the war emergency to obtain a land tax (taille) and a standing army for the crown. During the last phase of the war a great upsurge of French national spirit under the leadership of Joan of Arc made possible, at long last, the expulsion of the English invaders. These things Louis XI inherited and put to clever use. First of all he set out to crush the power of the feudal nobility who had taken advantage of the royal distress during the Hundred Years' War to assert their virtual independence of the crown. By craft and by direct military force he broke up the league that the insubordinate nobility formed against him and reduced the individual nobles to submission. In order to achieve this difficult task, Louis utilized the rising middle class. In return for its support he placed many members of this class in his councils and key administrative posts and did what he could to foster commerce and industry. Roads, harbors, and waterways

were improved. Shipbuilding, commerce, and industry were encouraged by royal subsidies and protective regulations.

Louis XI virtually completed the territorial consolidation of the French national state. He brought province after province under direct royal control until by the end of his reign France had acquired all of its modern territory except the northwesternmost peninsula of Brittany (which was acquired by Louis's son) and a few territories along her fluid northeastern frontier. This expansive movement brought Louis XI into conflict with Charles the Bold of Burgundy. Charles the Bold (perhaps "the Rash" would have been a more accurate title) had inherited many rich and strategically located territories that included the Netherlands, the duchy of Burgundy, and the free county of Burgundy. These he hoped to consolidate into a great national state—the old Middle Kingdom of Charlemagne's grandson Lothair—between France and Germany. Had he succeeded in doing so, the course of history might have been changed significantly. However, Charles the Bold and his successor, Mary of Burgundy, were no match for the "spider king." Charles was killed battling the Swiss, and Mary was unable to prevent Louis XI from seizing the duchy of Burgundy, Picardy, and part of Flanders. (The abortive Burgundian "Middle Kingdom" has been a battleground between France and Germany throughout much of the modern period.) Thus consolidated and enlarged, France was to play a dominant role in European affairs in the centuries which followed.

Louis XI's schemes did not include betterment of the condition of the lower classes. Having paid for his ambitious program with heavy taxes with little tangible benefit in return, the lower classes rejoiced at his death.

4. England

Modern times, so far as English history is concerned, may be said to have begun with the reign of Henry VII (1485–1509), the first of the Tudor dynasty. The political unity of the English national state had been brought about as early as 1066 by William the Conqueror (aided to a considerable degree by geography). However, the feudal system, with its decentralization of administration and society, the Hundred Years' War with France (1337–1453), and the Wars of the Roses (1453–85) between the rival houses of Lancaster and York, had by the last quarter of the fifteenth century brought England to a state of political turmoil bordering on anarchy. Henry Tudor acquired the English throne by victory on the battlefield over the Yorkish king, Richard III, who was slain. Himself a member of the Lancastrian family, Henry ended the bloody dynastic feud by marrying Elizabeth of York.

The most pressing task confronting the strong-willed new monarch was the suppression of the turbulent nobility. The great feudal barons had taken advantage of the three decades of civil war and of the long rule of a weak king prior to the war to defy royal authority. They retained their own private armies and overawed the local courts. At once and with great vigor Henry VII proceeded to enforce the laws against livery and maintenance,[2] thereby destroying the illegal feudal armies. Since the regular local courts were too weak to proceed against the insubordinate nobility, Henry set up his own Court of Star Chamber, which, backed by the royal army, was able to overawe the most powerful barons and bring them to justice and to submission to the crown.

In these undertakings Henry VII had the wholehearted support of the lesser gentry and the middle and lower classes, all of whom yearned for peace and order. The middle class, particularly, desired stability for the sake of its growing business activities, and it was with this class that the Tudors allied themselves. Henry selected many of

[2] So called from the practice of the peasantry wearing the lord's badge or livery, signifying membership in his private army, in return for the lord's promise to maintain (support) them in courts of justice.

his counselors and administrators from the ranks of the bourgeoisie. He made favorable commercial treaties with the Netherlands, Denmark, and even with Venice, the jealous queen of the rich Eastern Mediterranean trade. Navigation acts were passed to protect English shippers. Henry's frugality and careful collection and handling of revenues not only were good business but freed the king of dependence upon Parliament for funds.

Henry VII, unlike Louis XI of France, attempted to protect the interests of the English peasants, who were being forced off the land by the enclosure movements. The landed nobility, taking advantage of the brisk demand for wool, were turning their farming lands into sheep runs. Thousands of dispossessed peasants roamed the countryside as beggars or drifted to the cities looking for work at any price. Laws passed to protect the peasants from dispossession proved to be largely ineffective, however, as anyone traveling through the lush green and largely untilled English countryside can observe today.

Henry VII died in 1509, prematurely worn out by his arduous labors. But he passed along to his glamorous son, Henry VIII, a united and orderly national state and a well-filled treasury. And under his granddaughter, Elizabeth, England rose to a position of first-rate importance in European and world affairs.

5. Failure of the Germanies and Italy to Attain National Statehood

Although Germany and Italy have played a vital role in modern European history, they did not achieve political unity at the opening of the modern period. Their failure to do so did not prevent them from contributing their share to the world's culture. It did, however, create political maladjustments that account for much of Europe's modern turmoil, particularly in the twentieth century.

During the fifteenth century, when the Spanish, Portuguese, French, and English peoples were becoming united under powerful national monarchs, the German-speaking people were split up into more than three hundred virtually independent units. The only political bond between them was the impotent government of the Holy Roman Empire. This ramshackle institution— a survival of the state set up by Charlemagne in 800 and revived by Otto the Great in 962—purported to be a restoration of the old Roman Empire, but it never was. In the Middle Ages, when the Spanish, Portuguese, French, and English sovereigns were consolidating their territories and their authority, the German emperors were frittering away their time and energy trying hopelessly to bring Italy under their control. While they were away from Germany on these quixotic ventures, the local feudal barons conspired against them, consolidated their own power, and built up hereditary states of their own within the empire. Meanwhile, territory after territory slipped from under the emperor's control until by the opening of the modern period the Holy Roman Empire included for all practical purposes only the German-speaking states.

Eventually seven of the emperors' most prominent subjects gained the right to elect him. This elective feature not only diminished the prestige of the emperor but forced candidates to bribe the electors and bargain and promise away any chance of strengthening the office. Since the emperor had no sure income, he had no military force with which to enforce his will. Even to defend the empire, he was forced to call upon his subject princes to furnish troops. The law-making and taxing power lay in the hands of the Diet, which was composed of three houses: the house of electors, the house of lesser princes, and the house of representatives of the free imperial cities. The Diet had no regular time or place of meeting, and was seldom able to reach agreement on any important question. In the late fifteenth century an imperial court was set up to settle disputes between member states. However, lacking any means of enforcing its decisions, this instrument too proved ineffective.

The one factor that gave any semblance of vitality to the Holy Roman Empire was the Hapsburg family. A Hapsburg was first elected emperor in 1273. After 1438, with only one brief exception, no one but a Hapsburg was elected until the empire finally died at the hand of Napoleon in 1806. By marriage and diplomacy the Hapsburgs expanded their original Austrian lands until they possessed at the opening of the modern period one of the largest and richest dynastic estates in Europe. Although, therefore, the Holy Roman Emperor as emperor was virtually powerless, as head of the house of Hapsburg he was one of the most influential of monarchs. Nevertheless, all efforts of the Hapsburgs to strengthen the central government of the empire foundered on the rocks of German particularism—the selfish local interests of the jealous princes. In and around this political vacuum much modern European and world history has centered.

Italy's modern history has paralleled to a considerable degree that of Germany. At the opening of the modern period the Italian Peninsula was divided into six major independent states without even the pretense of a Holy Roman Empire to unite them. The six were The Kingdom of the Two Sicilies (sometimes called Naples), the Papal States, Florence (Tuscany), Venice, Milan, and Piedmont. The Kingdom of the Two Sicilies, the poorest and most backward of the Italian states, occupied the southern third of the peninsula and the large island of Sicily. During the fifteenth and sixteenth centuries it was a bone of contention over which France and Spain repeatedly fought. The Papal States occupied the central portion of the peninsula. These states were ruled by the pope, not only as supreme pontiff, but also as political head. The popes based their claims to political rule over these states upon the Donation of Pepin, the father of Charlemagne, who drove out the Lombards and gave the territory to the pope in 756. Florence and Venice, republics in name, were dominated by rich commercial and banking families. Milan, an-

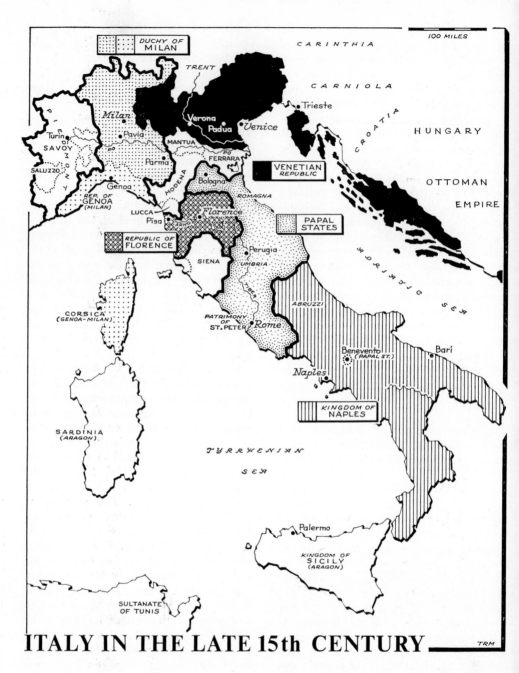

ITALY IN THE LATE 15th CENTURY

other thriving center of commerce, was ruled by an autocratic duke. Piedmont, occupying the northwesternmost portion of the peninsula, was the property of the house of Savoy. This mountainous state, which eventually assumed leadership in the unification of Italy, played a relatively minor role in Italian affairs before the nineteenth century.

An important factor accounting for Italian disunity in the first centuries of the modern era was the presence of the Papal States in the strategic center of the peninsula. Fearing the loss of their territories to a national monarch, the popes successfully blocked all efforts to set up an Italian national state until the middle of the nineteenth century. A second factor was the long tradition of independence and the great commercial prosperity in the thirteenth, fourteenth, and fifteenth centuries of Florence, Venice, and Milan, where a spirit of local rather than national pride and loyalty was encouraged.

Like the Germans, the Italian people in their condition of political disunity were to produce their share or more of the world's top literature, philosophy, and art. But also like their northern neighbors, their political division and weakness in an age of powerful national states was to be a standing invitation to aggression against them.

6. International Rivalries in the Age of Charles V, 1516–56

The rise of national states failed to bring peace to Europe. The national monarchs, supported by the bourgeoisie, had justified their own aggrandizement on the grounds that it was necessary to end the interminable feudal wars, and they had in fact established a large measure of internal law and order. However, the little feudal wars were followed by big national and dynastic wars. Throughout the first modern century—the sixteenth—international strife centered around the house of Hapsburg.

During most of the first half of the century the house of Hapsburg was headed by Emperor Charles V. Charles V inherited from his parents and four grandparents an array of territories and claims that have been exceeded in history only by those of his son, Philip II. This is the family tree of Charles:

From his grandfather Maximilian he inherited the Hapsburg provinces of Austria, Tyrol, Styria, Carinthia, and Carniola, to which were added in Charles's lifetime Hungary, Bohemia, Moravia, and Silesia. As a Hapsburg, he also inherited an inside track on the imperial crown of the Holy Roman Empire. From his grandmother Mary he inherited the Burgundian lands: the free county of Burgundy (Franche Comté), the Netherlands, Luxemburg, Flanders, Artois, and claims to the duchy of Burgundy and Picardy, which had been seized by Louis XI. From his grandfather Ferdinand he received Aragon, Minorca, Majorca, Sardinia, and The Kingdom of the Two Sicilies. From his grandmother Isabella he received Castile and a claim to the entire Western Hemisphere based upon the papal Line of Demarcation (1493). And from Ferdinand and Isabella jointly, he inherited Granada and Spanish Navarre. The student of world history will find it profitable at this point to locate all of these territories (see map pp. 322–3).

The very size of Charles V's far-flung holdings spelled perpetual trouble. The language problem alone was appalling. To this were added differences in local customs, tastes, and eventually religion. Moreover, Charles V was sure to become involved in all the major international conflicts of Europe. Born and reared in the Netherlands, Charles got himself accepted in Spain only after serious opposition and open revolt. His efforts to strengthen the government of the Holy Roman Empire and to raise money and troops there were stymied by the local German princes. Finally, the Lutheran revolt further split the empire and shattered completely the personal power of Charles in the Germanies.

Charles V found himself perpetually at

Maximilian of Hapsburg ⎫
Mary of Burgundy   ⎬ Philip the Handsome ⎫
                                                ⎬ Charles V
Ferdinand of Aragon ⎫   ⎪
Isabella of Castile ⎬ Joanna the Mad ⎭

war with Francis I of France. Each feared the other's power. Francis vigorously contested Charles's election to the Holy Roman emperorship. They fought over conflicting territorial claims in Italy, the Burgundian lands, and along the French-Spanish border. Charles won nearly all of the battles, but was never able to make his victories stick. The result was a stalemate.

The relations between Charles of Hapsburg and England were limited to a personal family quarrel. When Henry VIII sought an annulment of his marriage to Catherine of Aragon, the aunt of Charles V, Charles used his influence with the pope to block the proceedings, thus touching off a chain of events that ended with the separation of England from the Roman Catholic Church. It was under Charles's son, Philip II, that affairs between Spain and England were brought to a showdown.

Among Charles V's more constructive achievements were his marriage to Isabella of Portugal, which brought about a brief union of Spain and Portugal under Philip II, and his repulse of the Ottoman Turks. Early in the sixteenth century, the Turks under Suleiman the Magnificent swept across Hungary and laid seige to Vienna in the heart of Christendom. It was feared that all Western Christendom might fall to the invincible Moslem Turks. At this point Charles V rallied the forces of the empire and the Hapsburg provinces, raised the siege of Vienna, and drove the Turks back into Hungary. He also defeated and humbled the Moslem Barbary pirates in the Western Mediterranean.

In 1555 Charles V began to divide his holdings between his son, Philip II, and his brother, Ferdinand. To Philip he gave the Burgundian provinces and Spain, with her appanages in Italy, the Mediterranean, and the New World. To Ferdinand he handed the Austrian provinces and successfully promoted his candidacy to the crown of the Holy Roman Empire. Henceforth there were two branches of the Hapsburg dynasty —Austrian and Spanish—both of which would long continue to play important roles in European and world history.

7. Summary—The Political Map of Europe in 1500

At the beginning of the modern period, then, four powerful national monarchies, Spain, Portugal, France, and England, had emerged to dominate the European political scene. Germany and Italy were divided into many small states. The German states and Slavic Czech-speaking Bohemia were in the Holy Roman Empire. The Netherlands, owned by the Hapsburgs, were a part of the empire. Switzerland, nominally in the empire, was in reality an independent confederation of semi-autonomous cantons. Elsewhere in Europe clannish Scotland was still independent, and England's control over Ireland was only tenuous. Denmark owned Norway and was in temporary union with Sweden, but Scandinavia had too few people and resources to count for much in international politics. Poland, including Lithuania, occupied a large stretch of territory east of the Germanies, but her anemic government made her impotent at home and abroad. Russia, under Ivan III, had just thrown off the Tartar yoke and as yet counted for little in European or world affairs. The Balkan Peninsula was a part of the Ottoman Empire. Hungary was a battlefield fought over by the Hapsburg dynasty and the Ottoman Turks. It was the four new national states that represented the political wave that the rest of Europe and most of the world would eventually follow. The new national states, though quelling much lawlessness and feudal turbulence, did not bring peace, but rather wars on a larger scale. The reign of Charles V illustrates the working of the new political system.

SUGGESTED READING

R. B. Merriman, *The Rise of the Spanish Empire in the Old World and the New*, 4 vols. (1918), Vol. II. Volume II of this scholarly and readable work deals with the reigns of Ferdinand and Isabella, when the Spanish national state was created.

Comines, *The History of Comines*, tr. by Thomas Danett (1897). Comines was in the service of both Louis XI of France and Charles the Bold of Burgundy. His vivid eye-witness account is the chief historical source for their momentous struggle, which decided the question of the emergence of either a powerful French nation or a dominant "middle kingdom" of Burgundy.

Conyers Read, *The Tudors: Personalities and Practical Politics in the 16th century* (1936). The story of England's emergence as a powerful national monarchy by a leading American authority on the subject.

James Bryce, *The Holy Roman Empire* (1904). Still an excellent work on the Germanies in the late medieval and early modern period, when they failed to achieve national statehood.

Geoffrey Barraclough, *The Origins of Modern Germany* (1949). Has good chapters on the early modern period, showing its significance for later German history.

Ferdinand Schevill, *History of Florence from the Founding of the City through the Renaissance* (1936). The history of one of the richest and most colorful of the Italian city-states through the time of its greatest glory. Loyalty to the brilliant city-states helps to explain the failure of Italy to attain national unity before the late nineteenth century.

Edward Armstrong, *Emperor Charles V*, 2 vols. (1902). The standard biography of the leading European political figure at the opening of the modern period. Much of Western history during the first half of the sixteenth century centered around Charles V.

Charles Reade, *The Cloister and the Hearth* (1949); originally published in 1861. The hero of this melodramatic novel is the natural father of Erasmus. The novel presents a fascinating picture of life in Europe at the dawn of the modern era, based on excellent historical research.

Paul Murray Kendall, *Warwick the Kingmaker* (1957). A vivid biography of one of the last great feudal barons. The Earl of Warwick was a dominant figure during the Wars of the Roses, when medieval feudalism was crumbling and modern national monarchies were emerging.

CHAPTER 28

The Rise of Modern Capitalism

THE RISE of the modern national state was closely associated with the rise of modern capitalistic economy. The royal monarchs who created the national states made great use of the rising middle class in overcoming the feudal aristocracy. The strength of this middle class lay in its capitalistic wealth. The term *capitalism*, stripped to its barest essentials, may be defined as a system of putting money to work to make more money. It involves, among other things, private property, the profit motive, a substantial amount of free enterprise and individual initiative, the hiring of labor, and the lending of money for interest.

1. Roots and Beginnings of Modern Capitalism

Although we are likely to think of capitalism as a typically modern system of economy, it reached a fairly high development in ancient Greece and Rome. The reader will recall from earlier chapters that trading, banking, and production of certain wares on a capitalistic basis thrived in and among the Greek city-states, particularly in the Hellenistic age. Capitalism developed to a higher degree in the Roman world. For many centuries all roads and all ship lanes in the Western world led to Rome and were protected by Rome. Interest rates came down, and the standard of living went up.

However, the reader will also recall that, with the breakdown of the Roman Empire, capitalistic practices virtually disappeared. Early medieval economy, like early medieval government, was decentralized. Each manorial estate produced almost all of its own needs. Agriculture was collectivist or cooperative. Commerce was a mere trickle of luxuries for the rich and necessities such as iron, implements, and salt. The Church insisted upon the "fair price" rather than competitive pricing, and since it also forbade the lending of money for interest (usury), the Jews monopolized what small-scale lending of money there was.

During the course of the Middle Ages commercial activities and capitalistic practices began to revive. A slight increase may be observed as early as the eleventh century. By the thirteenth century a pronounced recovery was under way. The Crusades contributed significantly to this revival. The huge movement of men and supplies from Western Europe to the Holy Land enriched the merchants and shippers of Venice and other Italian cities. Many of these set up permanent trading posts in the Near East and introduced the luxuries of the materially more advanced Moslem and Byzantine world to Western Europe. The Fourth Crusade, which the Venetians diverted to the looting of Constantinople, was particularly fruitful for the rising Western capitalism. The Venetians seized, not only a great hoard of gold and silver in the stricken Eastern imperial capital, but also three eighths of the territory of the Byzantine Empire itself. This wealth flowed into the stream of Western European commerce.

Foremost among the centers of this newly revived commerce and capitalism were the city-states of northern Italy, such as Venice, Genoa, Florence, and Milan. Venice was the queen of the Mediterranean in the thirteenth, fourteenth, and fifteenth centuries. After her chief rival, Genoa, was eliminated in the fourteenth century, she enjoyed a virtual monopoly over the lucrative trade with the East. At the peak of her prosperity her merchant marine numbered some thirty thousand sailors. Milan was the starting point of the overland traffic across the Alps to Northern Europe. In the late fourteenth century she gained control of the port city of Genoa. Florence manufactured large quantities of fine woolen textiles on a capitalistic basis, and in the fourteenth and fifteenth centuries was the banking capital of the Western world. The Medici family alone possessed at one time some two hundred branch banks scattered throughout Western and Central Europe.

In Northern Europe the Hanseatic League, composed of some eighty German Baltic and North Sea cities, enjoyed a brisk trade in such commodities as fish, furs, grain, and timber. In South Germany and the Rhine Valley numerous trading centers such as Augsburg, Nuremberg, and Cologne sprang up along the overland route between Italy and Northern Europe. Finally, the Netherlands, Paris, and London shared in this early period of revived commercialism.

By the end of the fifteenth century, however, the further growth of European commerce was threatened by a number of obstacles that little feudal fiefs and independent cities were not able to overcome. One was the expense of overland trade routes between Europe and the East, especially after Moslem middlemen had taken their share of the profits. Another was the inadequacy of the gold and silver supply to serve as a satis-

factory medium of exchange. A third was the restrictive practices of the guilds. All of these obstacles were soon to be brushed aside.

2. The Age of Discovery

In the late fifteenth and early sixteenth centuries European mariners made a series of daring voyages, discovering not only the New World, but also new and much better routes to the East. These voyages were promoted by the governments and subjects of the four national monarchies along the Atlantic coast. The principal motive was a desire to by-pass the Venetians, the Moslems, and the land barriers that separated them from the riches of the East. Other motives were Christian missionary zeal and a spirit of adventure kindled by the renaissance of interest in the secular world. The results were momentous. The age of discovery opened up an era of capitalistic economy vaster in scale than anything yet dreamed of and brought most of the rest of the world under the domination of Europe.

The first to begin the fifteenth-century explorations were the Portuguese. Prince Henry the Navigator, who as the younger son of the king was not immediately in line for the crown, devoted his talents and influence to navigation. He set up a school for mariners, which numbered Christopher Columbus among its students. Prince Henry's sailors pushed farther and farther down the west coast of Africa until, by the time of their master's death in 1460, they had reached the westernmost bulge at Cape Verde. In 1488 Diaz rounded the cape, soon to be named Good Hope; and in 1498 Vasco da Gama, in what was probably the greatest voyage in the history of navigation, reached India, the object of all the mariners' quests. Vasco da Gama was out of sight of land ninety days—three times as long as Columbus on his voyage to the New World. That the Portuguese knew what they were up to is proved by the fact that Vasco da Gama's return cargo sold for sixty times the cost of

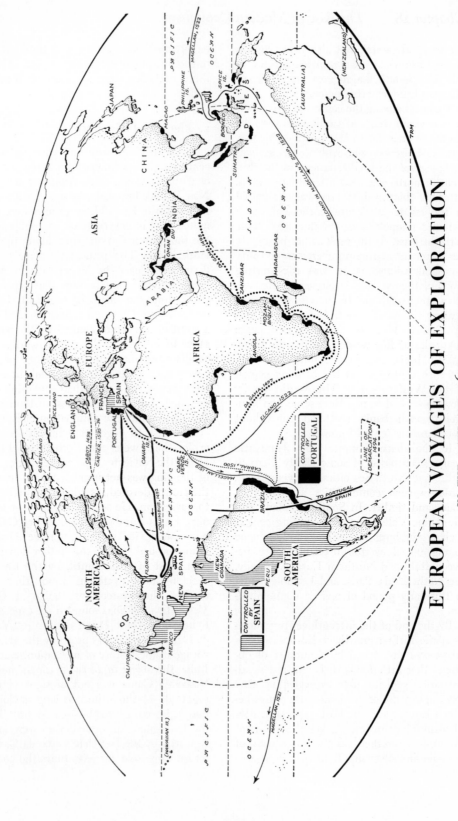

EUROPEAN VOYAGES OF EXPLORATION

IN THE 15TH AND 16TH CENTURIES

the expedition. These glad tidings sent a host of Portuguese adventurers hurrying to the East Indies, where they carved out a huge commercial and political empire.[1] One of these adventurers, Cabral, swinging too far westward, touched the eastern bulge of South America, thus laying the basis for Portugal's claim to Brazil. With the discovery of an all-water route to the East the commerce of the Italian city-states soon withered. So did that along the overland route from Italy across Germany.

Meanwhile, Spain was sending her mariners westward, for by the late fifteenth century most educated people in Western Europe assumed that the earth was round, al-

[1] For conditions in Southern Asia at the time of the European intrusion see pp. 424–8.

though they greatly underestimated its size. It was, therefore, believed by many navigators that the East Indies could be reached by sailing west. Columbus was the first European to attempt it. (Nothing had come of the tenth-century voyages to Greenland and northern America of the roving Norsemen, Eric the Red and Leif Ericson.) Almost every American schoolboy and schoolgirl knows the story of Columbus. Many even assume that American history begins with Columbus rather than with the civilizations of ancient Egypt and Mesopotamia. Columbus was born in Genoa but moved to Portugal, where he studied in the school of Prince Henry the Navigator. When, however, Portugal failed to support his westward voyage, he turned to Queen Isabella of

THE RETURN OF CHRISTOPHER COLUMBUS FROM THE NEW WORLD, BY DELACROIX. This painting depicts Columbus reporting to the Spanish sovereigns, Ferdinand and Isabella. The voyages of Columbus and his contemporaries led to the Europeanization of much of the world and facilitated the rise of capitalism in Europe. (*Toledo Museum of Art, Thomas A. De Vilbliss Bequest*)

Castile, who gave him the necessary backing. His three ships touched a West Indian island on October 12, 1492. Thinking that the West Indies were islands off the east coast of Asia, Columbus made three further voyages in the hope of by-passing these barriers and sailing on to his real goal, the East Indies. Instead he was turned back by the South and Central American mainlands. He died disappointed, not realizing the greatness of his achievement.

But others soon realized it, and in the first half of the sixteenth century Spanish expeditions to the New World were the order of the day. As previously noted the pope in 1493 had drawn a line of demarcation dividing the non-Christian world between Spain and Portugal. Since all of the Western Hemisphere except the eastern part of Brazil and Greenland fell to Spain, the Spanish sailors continued to bend their sails westward. Ponce de León, De Soto, and Coronado explored the southern part of what is now the United States. Balboa crossed the Isthmus of Panama and looked out upon the Pacific Ocean. In 1519 Magellan set out around the world by way of the Strait of Magellan. Although he himself was killed in the Philippines, one of his ships completed the circuit. In the same year Cortez began the conquest of the Aztec Empire in Mexico. In 1531–32 Pizarro conquered the Inca Indians in Peru.

The other two new national states, England and France, were relatively inactive in discovery and exploration during the fifteenth and early sixteenth centuries. Their turn was to come later. The English crown did, however, sponsor voyages to northern North America by the Italian mariner, John Cabot, in 1497–98. These voyages became the basis for England's claims to North America, where she later built a great empire. The French government sponsored Jacques Cartier, who in 1535 sailed up the St. Lawrence to Montreal and claimed Canada for France. Nonetheless, it was not until the seventeenth century that Spain and Portugal were replaced as the world's leading imperial and commercial powers.

3. The Founding of the Spanish New World Empire

Although most of the Western Hemisphere at the beginning of the sixteenth century was sparsely inhabited by primitive and often savage Indian tribes, the Spaniards did find two rich and colorful civilizations: those of the Aztecs in Mexico and the Incas in Peru.

The American aborigines are clearly members of the Mongoloid branch of the human family. They are generally believed to have come from Asia across the Bering Strait, perhaps as long as forty thousand years ago. It must have taken them quite a time to push down to the southern tip of South America.

The first of these primitive tribes to build a highly civilized society were the Mayas. They are believed to have come into what is now Guatemala and the Yucatán Peninsula of southeast Mexico from the northwest about 1000 B.C. Their civilization reached its height between A.D. 400 and 600. It was a city-state civilization resembling in many respects that of ancient Greece approximately a thousand years earlier. Their writing, most of which has been lost, was a combination of pictures and ideographs. Their best art was brightly colored pottery, gems, gold and silver ware, and sculpture. Probably their most remarkable creations were a system of mathematics based on the decimal (actually vigesimal) system and a calendar based upon astronomy, both of which were in advance of those used in contemporary Europe. Their massively walled stone cities were connected by elaborately paved roads. These cities, however, were continually warring with each other like those of Greece, and in the twelfth century the less-civilized but better-organized Toltecs from the north conquered the Maya city-states much as Philip of Macedon conquered the Greeks.

In the fourteenth century the warlike Aztecs came down from the north and founded a city on an island in Lake Tezcoco —the present Mexico City. From this base

Pizarro's First Sight of the Inca Empire, by C. W. Jefferys. With a small band of well-armed Spanish soldiers, Pizarro in 1532 conquered the fabulously rich and colorful Inca Empire in South America. (*Reproduced from Volume I, The Pageant of America. Copyright Yale University Press.*)

they conquered and organized a military empire or confederacy comprising most of what is now southern Mexico. The Aztecs were the Romans of the New World, and like the Romans they acquired most of their culture from the earlier civilization (Mayas). Theirs was the gift of military and political organization. They developed an elaborate, though stern, system of justice. Their religion was important and highly organized. Several thousand priests, both regular and secular, tended the impressive temple and supervised education and morals. The numerous gods, taken mostly from the Mayas, were headed by the terrible war god, whose unquenchable thirst for blood demanded human sacrifice, usually prisoners of war. And yet the rank and file Aztecs were gentle lovers of poetry and art. A flourishing commerce, agriculture, and mining added to the wealth obtained by their conquests.

An even more colorful civilization was that of the Incas in the Andean Plateau of South America. In the eleventh century the

Inca Indians began to extend their sway over their neighbors until their empire covered an area fifteen hundred miles long and three hundred miles wide—including present-day Ecuador, Peru, and parts of Bolivia and Chile. An elaborate system of roads and communications tied this vast and lofty empire together. Incan society was a combination of benevolent despotism and socialism. The all-powerful Inca was treated as a god. However, he had a body of advisers and administrators chosen from the upper classes. All land and all production were owned and directed by the state. The regimented lower classes did all the work under close supervision and shared from the common stores. A high degree of specialization was practiced. Agriculture was well advanced, huge terracing and irrigation projects having been developed to overcome the difficulties of the Andean terrain. Religious worship, particularly of the sun god, was a beautiful and important feature of national life. Although Incan writing was backward, its art was well advanced.

Outstanding were pottery, architecture, textiles, and gold and silver objects of ornamentation.

Cortez with a band of some six hundred soldiers and eighteen horses overcame the Aztecs by a combination of treachery and superior weapons. He took advantage of the Aztec belief that the Spaniards were ancient gods whose return had long been expected. Once inside the capital city the Spaniards were too strong to be expelled. They slaughtered and looted the poorly armed Aztecs without mercy. Even more spectacular was the conquest of the Incas. Pizarro enticed the Incan emperor into a conference. At a given signal Pizarro's small but well-armed band of Spanish soldiers fell upon the splendidly dressed but primitively armed Incan troops and slew them by the thousands. Not a Spaniard lost his life. Pizarro promised to free the Incan chieftain in return for a ransom of gold objects sufficient to fill a room seventeen by twenty-two feet to a height of nine feet, plus a larger amount of silver. This ransom was collected and paid, but Pizarro, who never really intended to free the emperor, had him put to death anyway. When this gold and silver, an estimated ten million dollars' worth, reached Spain, the money shortage in Europe was over.

Throughout the sixteenth century Spaniards flocked to the New World. By 1607, when the first permanent English colony was founded in the New World, a quarter of a million Spaniards had settled in the vast Spanish Empire stretching from San Francisco Bay to Cape Horn. A number of distinguished churches and cathedrals had been erected, and two thriving universities had been founded, one at Mexico City, the other at Lima in Peru. The native civilizations had been almost wholly destroyed and replaced by the Christian civilization of Spain. Meanwhile, the Portuguese, in addition to reaping a golden harvest from their commerce with the East, were duplicating on a smaller scale in Brazil the feats of Spain.

4. The Commercial Revolution

The discovery of the New World and of all-water routes to the Far East resulted in an expansion of European commerce and commercial capitalism on such a scale that the term *Commercial Revolution* may accurately be used to describe it. As the main routes shifted from the Mediterranean to the Atlantic, the stranded Italian and German cities decayed, and new commercial centers to the west began to flourish. Strangely enough, Spain, surfeited with gold and silver from Mexico and Peru, never developed a thriving commercial capitalism. And although Lisbon became the first great terminus of goods pouring in from the East, the Portuguese, like the Spanish, were so preoccupied with their vast overseas empire that they neglected the marketing opportunities in Europe itself.

These lucrative opportunities were first seized by the Dutch. Enterprising Dutch merchants purchased the goods in Lisbon, shipped them to the Netherlands, and sold them at a nice profit throughout Northern and Western Europe. In the sixteenth century Antwerp, with its excellent harbor and location, was the most thriving commercial center in Europe. In the seventeenth century, following the sack of Antwerp in 1585 by Spanish troops, Amsterdam and London rose to the top of the commercial world. The little Dutch Netherlands even took advantage of their newly won independence from Spain and of Portugal's temporary conquest by Spain in 1580 to seize the best part of Portugal's Eastern Empire.

Another phase of the commercial revolution was the advent into the channels of commerce of more bounteous supplies of commodities. Spices, coffee, tea, sugar, dyes, tropical fruits, fine textiles, tapestries, and precious stones, long known but in scarce supply and too expensive for all but the very rich, now came into Europe in ever increasing volume. From the New World came potatoes, corn, tobacco, and chocolate (all of which were previously unknown in Europe), new dyes and medicines, gold and silver.

A different kind of new product—Negro slaves—also helped to swell the rising stream of commerce. This most nefarious traffic of modern times was first begun by the ship captains of Prince Henry the Navigator. It was later taken over by the Spaniards to supply labor for their empire in the New World. When the Spanish discovered that the native Indians were poor slave laborers, they turned to tropical Africa. Thousands of Negroes were captured or bought from local chieftains and crowded into the holds of ships. Many of them died during the crossings, but the survivors sold like cattle for a high price in the New World markets. So heavy was this immensely profitable traffic that the racial and social complex of the New World society was quickly and drastically altered.

New types of business organization were developed to accommodate the expanding volume of commerce. Chartered companies were organized to by-pass the medieval guilds, which were unable or unwilling to meet the new demands. The first chartered companies were called regulated companies. A group of merchants would voluntarily band together under a government license or charter for the purpose of exploiting a certain market. While co-operating to the extent of limiting competition and providing mutual protection, the individual members of the company carried on their own private operations. Since some members tended to chisel on the others and since reorganization was required upon the death or defection of a member, a more efficient type of organization was sought.

In the early seventeenth century the joint-stock company began to replace the regulated companies. The members of a joint-stock company pooled their resources, hired or elected their management, and shared in the profits in proportion to the amount of stock owned. In this way competition within the company was eliminated and permanence was achieved by selling or buying the stock of changing personnel. Moreover, unlimited amounts of capital could be raised by selling stock. This type of business organization has never been improved upon for large-scale efficiency, as present-day joint-stock companies such as General Motors, Standard Oil, and United States Steel demonstrate.

Two of the earliest joint-stock companies were the British East India Company, founded in 1600, and the Dutch East India Company, founded two years later. The British company was given, not only a trading monopoly over British India, but political control as well. The Dutch company was given a monopoly over all Dutch trade east of the Cape of Good Hope. Profits of 300 per cent were not uncommon for these giant companies. The annual profits of the Dutch East India Company never fell below 12 per cent over a period of two hundred years.

Although there was some expansion of industrial capitalism in the age of the Commercial Revolution, it was relatively slight until means had been found to overcome or evade the obstruction of the monopolistic craft guilds. Wherever the production of goods was done on a capitalistic basis, the domestic or "putting out" system was generally used. Capitalistic entrepreneurs would purchase the raw materials and distribute them to craftsmen, who would do the piecework in their cottages. Then the entrepreneur would collect the finished products, pay the cottagers for their work, and market the goods at a profit. While this system had certain advantages, it limited the volume of production. Until the coming of the machine and the factory system in the late eighteenth and early nineteenth centuries, therefore, large-scale capitalism was to remain commercial rather than industrial.

Banking expanded in proportion to commerce. The Fugger family of Augsburg occupied in the sixteenth century the place in the financial world that the Medicis of Florence had held in the fifteenth. Jacob (the

Rich) Fugger loaned Charles V the money with which he bribed his way to the emperorship of the Holy Roman Empire. He also loaned the Archbishop of Mainz the money with which he purchased his archbishopric; and it was the selling of indulgences by this archbishop in order to repay the loan that touched off the Protestant Reformation. In the seventeenth century the Bank of Amsterdam and the Bank of England were founded on a semi-national basis. Both of these banks were really private joint-stock companies, but in return for certain monopolies, such as the handling of government funds and the issuance of currency, they were obliged to accept a degree of government regulation. Banks of this size were able to mobilize sums of money and credit sufficient, not only to launch and control large-scale commercial ventures, but also to influence government and religion as well.

5. New Commercial Policy— Mercantilism

Governments attempted to exercise some control over economic developments. From the beginning of the Age of Discovery in the late fifteenth century until the end of the eighteenth century all of the governments of Western Europe except the Dutch Netherlands pursued a policy that has come to be called *mercantilism*. Mercantilism was, in essence, economic nationalism. While the monarchs of the new national states were consolidating their political power, they were also attempting to unify and centralize their national economies. Efforts were made to standardize national currencies and weights and measurements. Internal commerce was encouraged by improving communications and reducing or removing internal tariff barriers. These efforts were only partially successful. More attention was paid to the aggrandizement of each nation's economy at the expense of its neighbors. The basic assumption of mercantilist theory was that gold and silver are the true measure of national prosperity and power. Gold and silver, the mercantilists

believed, in addition to being convenient mediums of exchange could purchase anything—consumer goods, armies, navies, and administrative personnel. Spain's good luck in Mexico and Peru and her sixteenth-century brilliance and influence undoubtedly strengthened this view.

Spain alone was fortunate enough to come upon the gold and silver directly. All the other states had to devise more roundabout means of acquiring the precious metals. The favorite device was to seek a favorable balance of trade. The importation of expensive manufactured goods was discouraged by high tariffs, whereas the exportation of manufactures was encouraged, if need be, by subsidies. The reverse was true of inexpensive raw materials. The national aim was to buy low and sell high. Colonies were sought as sources of raw materials and markets for manufactured goods. But the colonies were not to be permitted to compete with the manufacturers and shippers of the mother country. Navies were advocated for the protection of the colonies. Sometimes the mercantilists closely regulated a nation's manufactures with a view to maintaining a reputation abroad for high quality. This phase of mercantilism reached its highest development in France in the seventeenth century under Louis XIV's economic minister, Colbert. It was not until the latter part of the eighteenth century that the British economist, Adam Smith, and the French physiocrats began to undermine public faith in the validity of mercantilist principles and to prepare the way for an era of *laissez faire*, or free trade.

6. Political and Social Consequences

The immediate political consequence of the rise of modern capitalistic economy in Western Europe was the strengthening of royal absolutism. The monarchs made use of the merchants and bankers in order to increase their own power at the expense of the rival nobility. More money was now available for the royal treasury and the royal army. The middle classes, of course, shared the benefits of their alliance with the royal monarchs. Many members of the bourgeoisie were appointed to key positions in the royal administrations. With their increased wealth came increased social and political influence.

As the power of the national monarchs and the middle classes grew, the position of the nobility declined. Their wealth and power were based upon land, and now money talked louder than land. Their castles and their armor also had become obsolete. A severe inflation brought on by the great influx of gold and silver into Europe further hurt the nobility in relation to the moneyed bourgeoisie. Not overnight, but slowly, and with occasional setbacks, over the decades and centuries, the nobility of Western Europe was displaced by the middle classes in political and social influence. Only in England and the Netherlands did the nobility save itself by going into business.

The triumph of the capitalistic middle class did not bring an immediate improvement in the condition of the lower classes. Indeed, the *nouveaux riches* often proved to be harsher taskmasters than the older aristocracy, who had had time to learn that power brings responsibility. The urban wage earners, no longer protected by the guilds, were especially hard hit by the inflation. In France and England some peasants who had converted their feudal dues to money payments profited, but most of the peasants in Western Europe and all of those in Central and Eastern Europe suffered from the inflation and the general loss of feudal security. The distressed landlords were likely to pass their hardships along to the peasantry. Peasant revolts were common throughout Europe in the sixteenth century. However, the rise of the middle class and the disappearance of feudal class lines produced a more fluid social structure and made possible the future growth of democracy. Money is more easily acquired by the commoner than is blue blood or title.

7. The Europeanization of the Globe

Europe's Age of Discovery and the rise of modern capitalistic economy were as momentous for the rest of the world as they were for Europe itself. Much of the Western Hemisphere, Southern Asia, and the coastal areas of Africa were quickly brought under European domination. This amazing expansion continued until by the end of the nineteenth century practically the entire world was dominated by Europe and European civilization. Spanish, Portuguese, English, French, and Dutch colonists, followed later by the nationals of all the other European countries, flocked to the New World, taking their Western Christian culture with them. The brilliant Aztec and Incan civilizations of Mexico and Peru were destroyed. The more primitive tribes of American Indians were exterminated, absorbed, or confined to reservations. The Moslem, Hindu, Buddhist, and Confucian civilizations of Asia and Africa were virtually enslaved by the aggressive European imperialists. Modern European history is therefore world history, and the details of European expansion (and eventual contraction) constitute a considerable portion of the history of Western civilization in the modern era.

Thus we see Europe's static, agricultural, collectivist, "fair price" economy transferred into a dynamic, urban, competitive, profit-motivated economy. The rise of capitalism not only changed the nature of European society; it also provided much of the explosive force that enabled tiny Europe to dominate most of the rest of the world.

SUGGESTED READING

Herbert Heaton, *Economic History of Europe* (1948). One of the best general economic histories of Europe.

J. Streider, *Jacob Fugger the Rich* (1931). The story of one of the leading financial tycoons of the early period of modern capitalism. The Augsburg banker was so rich that he was able to sway international politics and religion in the early sixteenth century.

* Richard Hakluyt, *Principal Navigations, Voyages, Traffiques and Discoveries of the English Nation* (Everyman's Library). Original 2nd edition: 1598–1600. A major contemporary account of the age of discovery. Interestingly written.

S. E. Morison, *Admiral of the Ocean Sea*, 2 vols. (1942). The best biography of Christopher Columbus. Combines great scholarship and fine writing. Before writing the book Professor Morison sailed the route followed by Columbus on his first voyage to America.

* W. H. Prescott, *The Conquest of Mexico* (Modern Library). This is history at its best, combining excellent scholarship, literary skill, and romance.

W. H. Prescott, *The Conquest of Peru*, 2 vols. (1880). Originally published in 1847. Possibly even more fascinating than *The Conquest of Mexico*.

* Charles Kingsley, *Westward Ho!* (Everyman's Library). A classic novel depicting the spirit of the times of Queen Elizabeth and Philip II, when England and Spain were struggling for the mastery of the seas and the New World. Much historical research went into the writing of this melodrama.

* L. B. Packard, *The Commercial Revolution, 1400–1776* (Berkshire). This is a little gem. Brief and lucid.

CHAPTER 29

The Italian Renaissance

THE TERM *renaissance* means rebirth, and in the development of Western civilization it designates particularly the rebirth of a secular civilization, inspired in large measure by that which had flourished in pagan Greece and Rome and declined with the rise of Christianity. However, *rebirth* is too sharp a word. Secular interests had never completely died out, even at the peak of the prestige of the Christian Church in the Middle Ages; and the revival of secular interests was a gradual process that took place over a long span of time. Furthermore, the Renaissance was not merely a return to pre-Christian culture. New elements that had not existed previously were added. It would be better to regard the Renaissance as an intensification of the secular spirit in Western European thought, literature, and art during the fourteenth, fifteenth, and sixteenth centuries. The key word here is *secular*, meaning that which pertains to this physical world as contrasted with the sacred things of the spirit. The Renaissance began in Italy, where many monumental reminders of the glory that was Greece and the grandeur that was Rome remained through the Middle Ages.

1. General Nature

Probably the most basic of the secular attitudes that characterized the Renaissance was humanistic. Humanism, as the name suggests, makes man and not God the chief center of interest. In a period dominated by humanistic concepts the arts, the sciences, and all forms of intellectual and practical activity tend to be directed toward the scrutiny of man. Theology, concerned with the nature of God, tends to give way to a philosophy that is interested in questions pertaining to the nature and condition of man. During the Italian Renaissance man, not God, was enthroned as lord of the universe. In this respect Renaissance thought was like that of pagan Greece and Rome and unlike that of the Christian-dominated Middle Ages. The medieval Christian theologians distrusted the flesh as an enemy of the spirit, and human wisdom as a frail thing unable to perceive divine truth by rational processes unless it is guided by Christian inspiration. But men of the Renaissance, like their Greek and Roman kinsmen, glorified the human form as a thing of beauty and the human intellect as capable of discovering all truth worth knowing.

Humanism extols not only mankind in general but also individual man. Individualism, therefore, was another important facet of the secular spirit of the Renaissance. In this respect the difference between the medieval and the Renaissance spirit was primarily one of degree. Probably no influence in history has done more than Christianity to elevate the dignity of the individual soul and the individual personality. Christianity taught that even when a sparrow falls God sees and is concerned. How much more then is He concerned for every man, made by Him in His own image and for His own glory. But the medieval churchmen were fearful of the deadliest of all the sins—pride. Therefore, they taught that the individual ego must be carefully held in check. Medieval monasticism went so far as to attempt to suppress the individual ego altogether and submerge it in the group. In practice, then, medieval Christianity, like medieval economy, tended to be collectivist. Accordingly, church artists and writers usually did not sign their names to their work, which was supposed to contribute to the greater glory of God, not of the individual artist or writer. Renaissance individualism, like that of Rome, was of the lusty variety. One could hardly imagine a Michelangelo or a Boccaccio not signing his name. This kind of individualism also gave rise, as in ancient Rome, to excessive men. No more boastfully egotistical individual can be found in history than Benvenuto Cellini, liar, thief, murderer, rapist, and one of the most gifted artists of the Renaissance era.

That a Cellini should be not only tolerated but also honored by his contemporaries may be further explained by the fact that he represented another cardinal principle of the Renaissance ideal—versatility. We are reminded of Pericles's all-round man of Athens of the fifth century B.C. and of the broadly educated Roman patrician. The educated man of the Middle Ages was usually a specialist—a theologian or a church artist or administrator. Some of the Renaissance schoolmasters taught many subjects in addition to the traditional formal ones—dancing, fencing, poetry, and vernacular languages, to mention a few. Many of the Renaissance universities secularized and broadened the old theology-oriented seven liberal arts and made much greater use of pagan classical literature and philosophy in the curriculum. One of the most popular books in Europe in the sixteenth century was Castiglione's *Book of the Courtier*. The ideal courtier, said Castiglione, is not only a gentleman and a scholar, but also a man of action—a soldier and an athlete. Prob-

ably the best illustration of versatility that could be found in any age is Leonardo da Vinci. This renowned Renaissance figure, one of the most celebrated painters of all time, was also an able sculptor, architect, mathematician, philosopher, inventor, botanist, anatomist, geologist, and engineer.

Finally, the secular Renaissance civilization was urban—again like that of ancient Greece and Rome, but unlike that of the Middle Ages, which was rural. Renaissance writers and artists were more often than not sustained by rich merchants and bankers, first in the revived commercial cities of Italy and later in those of Northern Europe.

2. Literature

These secular characteristics of the Renaissance spirit are richly illustrated by the Italian literature of the fourteenth century. The best of the literature was produced by the Tuscan Triumvirate—so called because it consisted of three men who were natives of Florence in the old Etruscan province of Tuscany. The first voice of the Italian Renaissance was Dante Alighieri (1265–1321). In an earlier chapter (see pp. 280–1) we have already studied Dante as the greatest of the late medieval writers. His masterpiece, the *Divine Comedy*, takes us through purgatory, hell, and heaven, and is so full of medieval Christian lore and theology that it has been called St. Thomas Aquinas's *Summa Theologiae* in poetic garb. Nevertheless, there is so much of the secular spirit in the *Divine Comedy* and in Dante's other writings that he belongs also to the Renaissance. In the "Inferno" portion of the *Divine Comedy*, Dante paints for us vivid, sensuous pen pictures that smack of this world rather than the next. The blazing fires and sulphurous fumes of hell, the cries of lament and curses of the damned come alive in our imagination. Furthermore, the author venerates such pagan classical writers as Vergil and Cicero to a much greater degree than had the medievalists (although a number of medieval writers had tried to make Vergil a Christian).

Dante's other major writings are entirely secular. His love lyrics, written in his native Tuscan vernacular and addressed to Beatrice, are among the most beautiful in any language. In fact Dante's writings greatly enriched the Florentine dialect and raised it eventually to the status of the national language of Italy.

Dante was a Renaissance man also in that he was versatile; he was a man of public affairs as well as of letters. An active participant in the turbulent politics of Renaissance Italy, he was exiled from his native Florence when his faction lost out. Dante even went so far as to fill hell in the *Divine Comedy* with his political enemies. His political treatise, *De Monarchia*, argues for a united Italy under the leadership of the Holy Roman Emperor.

Petrarch (1304–74), the second of the Tuscan Triumvirate, like Dante wrote beautiful love lyrics in the Tuscan vernacular. His exquisite odes and sonnets were poured out to Laura, a noble lady whom he saw at Mass but never met. He goes on rapturously about Laura's bosom, arms, face, and feet with most unmedieval abandon. The sonnet is Petrarch's own invention.

Boccaccio (1313–75) did for Italian prose what Dante and Petrarch did for Italian poetry. In his *Decameron*, a collection of one hundred tales or novelettes, Boccaccio makes no pretense of using Christian restraint. He relates bawdy romances with skill and grace, condoning and even glorifying the seamy side of human nature. Here we have open revolt against the medieval ideal.

3. Humanism

Toward the end of the fourteenth century, original Italian Renaissance literature was stifled by the rise of humanism. Italian humanism was a movement consisting of two rather distinct phases. One phase was the passionate quest for Greek and Latin literary manuscripts. The other was the development of a many-sided secular philosophy of life.

The search for classical literary manuscripts conflicted with the creation of original Italian literature by siphoning off the interest and energy of the writers. This conflict is illustrated by Petrarch, who rather early in life ceased writing what he called his "worthless" lyrics in order to discover lost classical manuscripts and to copy their style. He did succeed in bringing to light many priceless classical literary gems, but his epic *Africa* (relating the exploits of Scipio Africanus), written in Latin after the style of Vergil's *Aeneid*, is all but forgotten.

Petrarch interested Boccaccio in the recovery of Greek and Latin manuscripts, and the search soon became a fad. Popes, princes, rich merchants, and bankers subsidized the humanists, so-called because the pagan Greek and Latin literature dealt with human rather than divine affairs. (Likewise, studies concerned with classical literature and language, philosophy, and history came to be called the humanities.) In the fifteenth century Italy was busy with professional humanists hunting, copying, translating, and editing ancient manuscripts. Many of them were distinctly second-rate scholars. Spurning the use of the beautiful Italian vernacular in favor of Latin, and slavishly imitating the classical authors in both form and content, the humanists were a blight on original, spontaneous, creative writing. But in time the tendency of the Italian humanists to adopt the pagan vices without their accompanying virtues, and their snobbish scorn of the less learned, caused them to lose favor. The printing press, which became commonplace by the end of the fifteenth century, put most of the humanists out of a job.

Meanwhile, the content of the classical masterpieces was influencing the growth of a secular philosophy of life. This phase of humanism had many facets, such as the rise of the concept of the nonmoral state, the development of a critical or scientific attitude, and the revolt in private and social behavior against Christian moral restraints. Machiavelli, in his celebrated *The Prince*, suggested that Christian morals have no place in government. Since men are self-seeking animals and this is a dog-eat-dog world, the prince (or ruler or governing officials), to be effective, must be both unmoral and ruthless. The prince must assume that his own lieutenants, like all rival princes, are yearning and conspiring for his crown. Therefore, his own chief subjects must be set against each other and maneuvered into impotence. The foreign rivals must be deceived and treacherously attacked at the most favorable moment before they can do the same. While Machiavelli was trying to remedy the deplorable reality of a divided Italy overrun and pillaged by more powerful foreign enemies, he also reflected the thinking of a man-centered, secular age. Few books have had more influence on, or been more descriptive of, modern political thought and practice.

Another facet of the humanistic or secular view of life was the development of an analytical or scientific attitude. Lorenzo Valla did not hesitate to use his critical powers to prove by linguistics that the Donation of Constantine was a forgery. Nor did the scholarly and secular-minded pope raise any objections, although this was one of the documents upon which the papacy had based its claims to temporal power in the West. In fact Pope Nicholas V made Valla his secretary. By making this discovery Valla established himself as the father of modern critical historical scholarship. This spirit of critical inquiry was to bring about the first flowering of modern natural science in the seventeenth century.

A third product of the rise of a secular philosophy of life—the revolt against Christian restraints on private morals—is a facet of humanism illustrated by the fabulous career of Benvenuto Cellini. As mentioned earlier, this gifted Florentine—some say the greatest gold- and silversmith of all time —boasts loudly in his *Autobiography* of his lies, thefts, illicit loves, even of rape and murder. Here was humanism gone to seed. Admittedly Benvenuto Cellini is an extreme case, but the fact that such a character should have been honored in early sixteenth-century society indicates the degree to which Italian Renaissance society had departed from the medieval Christian ideal.

4. Art

The renaissance of secularism is vividly illustrated in the Italian visual arts of the fourteenth, fifteenth, and sixteenth centuries. Its impact is seen in painting, sculpture, and architecture alike. Medieval *painting* in Europe had been closely subservient to the Christian Church and its purposes. Human flesh was deliberately penalized in order that the spirit might shine forth unimpeded. The figures, nearly always saints, were stiff, haggard, flat, and elongated. The physical world too was blanked out with solid gold backgrounds. The styles were stereotyped.

In the early fourteenth century Giotto, a contemporary of Dante, began to break this medieval mold of artistic custom by humanizing his human figures and painting functional landscape backgrounds. Although his magnificent frescoes in the church of St. Francis at Assisi depicting the life of St. Francis were still rather flat, with diffused lighting, this did not make them less decorative—an artistic principle that the ancient Egyptian artists knew full well. True, Giotto's subject matter was almost entirely religious, but his treatment of it was such that the secular spirit made definite advances at the expense of the sacred. In the early fifteenth century Masaccio greatly developed the trends begun by Giotto a century earlier. He increased the illusion of depth by introducing atmospheric perspective and by further developing linear perspective. He also introduced the principle of the known light source, which thereafter replaced diffused light in painting. His nude human forms were further rounded and humanized. His landscape backgrounds were realistic and detailed. With Masaccio the transition from medieval to Renaissance painting was well-nigh completed and the stage set for such towering geniuses of the Italian high Renaissance as Leonardo da Vinci, Michelangelo, Raphael, and Titian.

THE FLIGHT INTO EGYPT, BY GIOTTO. In the early fourteenth century Giotto began to break with the medieval tradition in painting by humanizing his figures, depicting naturalistic backgrounds, and introducing perspective to suggest a third dimension. These features, though still but slightly developed, marked a transition from medieval to Renaissance painting. (*Alinari Photo*)

It would be difficult to find a more representative figure of the Italian Renaissance than Leonardo da Vinci (1452–1519). All the colorful facets of the secular spirit are richly illustrated by the career and work of this versatile genius. Attention has already been called to his many-sided interests and achievements. As a painter he is probably unsurpassed in any age. Leonardo was an illegitimate child, as were a remarkable number of the Renaissance greats. Vinci, his birthplace, is near Florence, where he grew up and launched his career. Some of his most productive years were spent in Milan in the employ of the duke. He finally followed King Francis I to France, where he died. Like most Renaissance artists, Leonardo dealt primarily with religious subject matter, but, like the others, his treatment of it was invariably secular and human. In his *Virgin of the Rocks*, for instance, Leonardo creates with exquisite grace and beauty the Virgin Mary and the Christ child. The Virgin, however, is the loveliest of women, and the Christ child is a plump and playful baby boy. The characters are human, not divine. The background is a strange rock formation, naturalistic enough to reveal a keen interest in this material earth, and yet arrestingly abnormal. The plant forms in the background are actually identifiable. Leonardo's *The Last Supper* depicts the reactions of the twelve disciples to Christ's words, "One of you shall betray Me." This celebrated fresco, exhibiting the artist's complete mastery of technique and draftsmanship, is essentially a study in human psychology—a subject in

THE VIRGIN OF THE ROCKS, BY LEONARDO DA VINCI. With Leonardo (1452–1519) Renaissance painting reached its peak. Although the subject matter is primarily religious, the treatment is secular. In this oil painting the Virgin is a beautiful woman, and the Christ child is a pudgy, playful boy. The arresting rock formation is authentic, and the plants are identifiable specimens. (*Archives Photographiques, Paris*)

which Leonardo always showed a special interest. The *Mona Lisa* is not even religious in subject matter; it is the portrait of a real woman. (Portrait painting, which was begun by Renaissance artists, reflects clearly the humanistic spirit of the time.) The mysterious *Mona Lisa* half smile—the mouth smiles but the eyes do not—so captivates the viewer that he is likely to overlook other features of the picture, including the hands, which are said to be the most sensitive ever painted. In the *Mona Lisa*, Leonardo, who appears to have been little interested in women in real life, is believed to be probing the universal human nature of womanhood.

Michelangelo (1475–1564) is second only to Leonardo da Vinci as a versatile Italian high Renaissance genius. Since sculpture was Michelangelo's first love, his painting is sometimes called "painted sculpture." His favorite subject was the virile, muscular male nude. Although a Florentine, much of his life was spent in Rome, where he labored in the service of the popes. His greatest painting—some say the greatest single painting of all time—was the ceiling fresco in the Vatican's Sistine Chapel. The hundreds of individual figures, representing nine scenes from the Book of Genesis, marvelously blend together into one harmonious whole. A subdued, blond cast adds to the religious atmosphere of the work. And yet the figures are all vibrant, muscular human beings, mostly male nudes. Later Michelangelo painted the *Last Judgment* as an altarpiece for the same chapel. The Christ in this picture is actually a terrifying, pagan giant, hardly the Jesus of Nazareth of the New Testament and the Christian Church.

Some critics believe Raphael (1483–1520) to be the greatest painter of all time; others say that he merely synthesized the original work of others. The output during his brief life was enormous. His favorite subjects were religious, but his Madonnas were very feminine, gracious women and his Christ childs pudgy and mischievous. His best-known paintings, the *Sistine Madonna* and the *Madonna of the Chair*, both of them in rich oils, well illustrate this secular treatment of a sacred theme. Many of Raphael's colorful portraits are of lay princes and tycoons. His monumental *School of Athens* reveals the veneration that Renaissance man felt for the pagan glory of Greece.

The fourth of the great painters of the Italian high Renaissance was Titian (1477–1576). A citizen of Venice, the most prosperous commercial city of the fifteenth century, Titian reflected the secular spirit of the Renaissance to an even greater degree than his three renowned contemporaries.[1] Although a considerable portion of his painting was of religious subjects, his concern was nearly always for the sheer pomp and pageantry of the Church rather than for matters of the spirit. But a large part of his subject matter was purely secular. The wealth and brilliance of Venice, overflowing with cargoes of luxurious fabrics, tapestries, and gems from the East, provided a challenging array of sensuous and colorful material for the artist to depict. And in the use of color, particularly the vivid yellows, reds, and blues, Titian had no peer. He always painted the hair of his women a reddish gold hue that has come to be called Titian. His portraits of some of the great lay personages of the sixteenth century, such as Francis I of France, and Charles V and Philip II of Spain, bring them alive for us today. With Titian the break with medieval painting, begun by Giotto and Masaccio, was completed.

In *sculpture* the name without a peer in any age is Michelangelo. It is true that in Michelangelo's favorite medium he had Roman copies of the sculpture of Hellenistic Greek masters such as Praxiteles and Scopas to guide and inspire him. But the gifted Florentine was no mere copier. The Greek masterpieces, for all their beauty and grace, were idealized types—half gods and half men. Michelangelo and his lesser-known immediate predecessors and contemporaries added a typically Renaissance characteristic to sculpture: individuality. The statues of

[1] There were many other brilliant names in Italian Renaissance painting such as Fra Filippo Lippi, Fra Angelico, Botticelli, and Tintoretto.

MOSES, BY MICHELANGELO. Man, not God, was glorified as lord and master of the universe by the sixteenth-century Renaissance artists. The treatment of Moses's beard illustrates Michelangelo's ability to distort for powerful effect. (*Alinari Photo*)

the Italian Renaissance are not only human beings but human individuals. Even Michelangelo's *Pietà*, which represents the mother of Jesus holding the dead body of her son in her lap and arms as she looks down piteously, is a study in human emotions. His *Moses* portrays the fierce and rugged strength of man, not God. Moses's beard, as crude as icicles beneath a water tank in January, displays the sculptor's ability deliberately to distort for effect. The three-dimensional medium of marble enabled Michelangelo to exploit to the full his favorite subject, the masculine nude. Numerous statues of David are used to convey, not only the virile muscular power, but also the agile grace of the male animal. His *Bound Slave* is a sublime portrayal of both the human form and the human spirit. Some critics think that the great sculptor's finest genius is displayed in the companion statues of two members of the Medici family—Lorenzo, the contemplative type, and Giuliano, the man of action. In these two pieces the master craftsman and artist exhibits every technique of sculpture. The work of Michelangelo is probably our best example of the Renaissance glorification of man as lord and master of the universe.

The subject of Renaissance sculpture cannot be dismissed without brief mention of the work of Benvenuto Cellini. His sculpturing in gold and silver was of an exquisite delicacy that has never been equaled. His most famous larger work is the bronze statue of Perseus holding up the Gorgon's head. In this amazing conglomeration of unrealities Cellini showed complete disregard of all accepted traditions and standards, and yet with most happy results. Such bold and original pioneering was typical of the self-confident, secular nature of the Renaissance mind.

Renaissance *architecture*, like Renaissance sculpture, drew heavily from Greek and Roman sources. From Greece by way of Rome came columns (now merely decorative) and horizontal lines; from Rome came the dome, the arches, and the massiveness that characterized Renaissance buildings. All of these features represented a revolt against the Gothic architecture of the later Middle Ages, although the Gothic had never gained much of a foothold in Italy anyway. The two greatest monuments of Italian Renaissance architecture are the Florence cathedral and St. Peter's church in Rome. St. Peter's cannot be called a cathedral,

SAINT PETER'S, ROME. This largest of all the Christian churches was built at a cost that helped to precipitate the Protestant revolt. The secular-minded Renaissance architects of St. Peter's were influenced by the styles of pagan Greece and Rome. (*The Bettmann Archive*)

since it has never been the seat of a bishop. The Florence cathedral, with its gigantic octagonal dome and ornate rectangular façade and bell tower, reflects the influence not only of ancient Rome but of Byzantine and Islamic art as well. The most grandiose achievement of Renaissance architecture is St. Peter's. This magnificent structure was to the Renaissance era what the Pyramids, the Parthenon, the Colosseum, and the Gothic cathedrals were to their respective epochs. It was built during the sixteenth and early seventeenth centuries at a cost that shook all Western Europe religiously and politically. Its numerous architects drew primarily upon pagan Greek and Roman sources for their inspiration. Even seventeenth-century baroque features eventually entered into its design. Raphael served for a time as chief architect. Michelangelo designed the distinctive dome. One has to step inside St. Peter's to appreciate the breath-taking grandeur of this awesome structure. Its lofty proportions and gigantic pillars, its brilliant paintings and sculptures, its gold, marble, and mosaic decorations all glorify the material things of this world rather than the spiritual aspects of this world and the next. Built by the popes of the Western Church, St. Peter's is really a temple dedicated to the sensuous beauty, earthly pride, and confidence of man that characterized the secular spirit of the Renaissance.

Music was another field of art in which the Italian Renaissance made many original contributions. The chief developments in Renaissance music occurred in the sixteenth century. Instrumental music became popular, and great improvements were made in the instruments. The harpsichord, forerunner of the piano, and the violin family of instruments came into existence. Musical techniques such as major and minor modes, counterpoint (the blending of two contrasting melodies), and polyphony (the interweaving of several melodic lines) rapidly developed. The most illustrious musician of the sixteenth century was Palestrina, chief musician to the pope, and probably the

greatest master of polyphonic music of all time. Although most of the music of the Renaissance still centered about the church, it was now more sensuous and versatile. Moreover, new and entirely secular forms appeared. The madrigal, popular throughout Europe in the late sixteenth century, was a musical rendition of stanzas of secular lyrical poetry. The Renaissance musicians laid the foundations for modern classical music in all its major forms—concerto, symphony, sonata, oratorio, opera. This development was to reach its climax in the eighteenth century with such masters as Bach, Handel, Mozart, and Beethoven.

5. Science

It was almost inevitable that a renewed interest in the material things of this earth, combined with optimism and confidence in the wisdom and self-sufficiency of man, should have resulted in scientific inquiry. Although the flowering of natural science did not occur until the seventeenth and eighteenth centuries, its seeding and sprouting took place in the soil of the Renaissance. Leonardo da Vinci had a scientific mind. His versatile interests and boundless energy caused him to make accurate observations and ponder deeply on such subjects as geology, anatomy, botany, and applied mechanics. His inventions, drawings, and scientific predictions impress us even today in this age of natural science.

The year 1543 saw the publication of two of history's most original and provocative scientific works—Copernicus's *Concerning the Revolutions of Heavenly Bodies* and Vesalius's *Concerning the Structure of the Human Body*—both in large measure products of the free atmosphere of the University of Padua. Copernicus was a Pole, and Vesalius was a Fleming. Both were attracted by the intellectual climate of Renaissance Italy, and both attacked long-accepted theories. Copernicus challenged the geocentric theory of Ptolemy (second century A.D.) that the earth is the center of the universe in favor of the heliocentric theory, according to which the sun is the center of the solar system, the earth being only one of many planets revolving around the sun. Vesalius assaulted the theories of Galen (also second century A.D.) concerning the structure of the human body, particularly the heart. Both books raised a storm of opposition, and both were popularly rejected. However, after a century of controversy, both books were to win the battle. Copernicus was to become the father of modern astronomy, Vesalius the father of modern anatomy and physiology. The rise of a spirit of scientific inquiry completed the downfall of medieval scholasticism. More important, the beginnings made by Leonardo, Copernicus, and Vesalius were to bring forth in the seventeenth century and after a veritable era of natural science.

6. Decline

The Italian Renaissance declined by degrees. By the end of the fourteenth century Italian Renaissance literature had given way to humanism, and by the end of the fifteenth century Italian humanism had outlived much of its usefulness. In the sixteenth century Italian Renaissance art was at its peak, but by the end of the century its vigor, too, had waned. Meanwhile, the center of the Renaissance spirit in thought and literature had shifted from Italy to Northern Europe. This shift closely paralleled that of commerce from the Mediterranean to the Atlantic. When Venice, Florence, and Milan were the most prosperous commercial and banking centers in Europe, they were at the same time the most vigorous seats of Renaissance culture.

As their economy stagnated with the shifting of the trade routes to the west, their cultural vigor likewise declined, although Italian art, heavily patronized by the Church, kept its momentum for several generations longer. Throughout history, scholarship, philosophy, and the arts have generally been charity cases, unable to support themselves by their own earning power.

Another factor that undoubtedly contributed to the decline of the Italian Renaissance was the revival of interest in religion, which resulted from the Protestant and the Roman Catholic reformations. This was a damper on the secular spirit. Italian humanism, which was more secular and pagan than Northern humanism, was particularly hard hit by the religious revival. It must be remembered also that the Renaissance was for the most part of, by, and for the elite only. The Italian humanists were particularly contemptuous of the masses. Other causes of the decline of the Italian Renaissance are obscure. One frequently reads that the invasion of Italy by the French, Spanish, and German armies and the general military and political instability of the period constituted important factors in the decline. This proposition, however, is difficult to prove. The ancient Greeks and modern Germans—to cite two parallel cases—produced their greatest culture before they became united—while they were split up into many little political units. Much of it was produced under conditions of foreign invasion or civil war. The causes of the decline of brilliant civilizations and epochs remain a challenge to the student of history.

SUGGESTED READING

* W. K. Ferguson, *The Renaissance* (Berkshire). An excellent brief survey.
* Jacob Burckhardt, *The Civilization of the Renaissance in Italy* (Harper Torchbook). A nineteenth-century classic, interpreting the Renaissance as the triumph of man the individual as lord and master of the universe. A very influential book.
* Dante Alighieri, *Divine Comedy* (Rinehart). Even a few stanzas of this masterpiece will reveal the universal genius of this early Renaissance poet. The subject matter is sacred, but

the sensuous treatment is largely in the secular vein characteristic of the Renaissance.

Giorgio Vasari, *Lives of the Most Eminent Painters, Sculptors, and Architects,* 10 vols. (1912–16). A major source for Renaissance art. Vasari was himself a sixteenth-century artist.

* D. Merejkowski, *The Romance of Leonardo* (Modern Library). Although this important work is highly entertaining fiction in form, it is based upon sound historical scholarship and is one of the best approaches to Leonardo and the spirit of the Renaissance.

Leonardo da Vinci, *The Notebooks of Leonardo da Vinci,* ed. by E. MacCurdy, 2 vols. (1938). The notebooks contain hundreds of drawings of the fabulous Leonardo—from art designs to steam engines and flying machines.

* Benvenuto Cellini, *Autobiography* (Bantam). This is a racy account of the illicit loves and adventures of one of the greatest artistic geniuses of the Renaissance period. Cellini represents the ultimate in the revolt against Christian ethics and standards by the secular man of the Italian Renaissance.

* Machiavelli, *The Prince and the Discourses* (Modern Library). These readable and highly influential tracts represent the Renaissance revolt against Christian ideals in the field of political theory. *The Prince* has been a bible for modern power politicians from sixteenth-century despots to twentieth-century dictators.

Lynn Thorndyke, *Science and Thought in the Fifteenth Century* (1929). A solid and standard work on a significant phase of the Renaissance.

CHAPTER 30

The Northern Renaissance

THE Northern Renaissance was in large measure an importation from Italy. Northern European scholars such as Chaucer had gone to Italy as early as the fourteenth century and imbibed the secular outlook of Petrarch and Boccaccio. By the late fifteenth century such inspirational journeys to Italy were commonplace. The rapid increase of commercial and capitalistic activity in Northern and Western Europe, following the shifting of trade routes from the Mediterranean to the Atlantic, facilitated the development of the Northern secular spirit.

1. General Nature

Not only was the Northern Renaissance later than the Italian Renaissance but it was also somewhat different in nature. Painting, sculpture, and architecture played a much less prominent role in the Northern Renaissance than in the Italian. Humanistic philosophy and literature, on the other hand, were relatively more important in Northern Europe than in Italy. Northern humanism itself, though an importation from Italy, was markedly different in nature. Whereas Italian humanism represented an open revolt of pagan secularism against Christian ideals, Northern humanism sought, for the most part, to humanize Christianity and thereby to reconcile the sacred and the secular.

2. Northern Humanism

The trend to secularism as a basic attitude toward life began in earnest in Northern Europe in the late fifteenth century. One of the first evangelists of the new man-centered faith was Johann Reuchlin, a professor at Heidelberg University. After a sojourn in Italy during which he became imbued with the ideas of the Italian humanists, Reuchlin undertook to introduce the new classical learning into Germany. Specifically he sought to broaden and enrich the university curriculum by establishing the study of the "un-Christian" Hebrew and Greek languages and literature. The Church and university interests vested in the medieval order of things attempted to thwart him, invoking the Inquisition to try him on grounds of heresy. Reuchlin fought back courageously and enlisted a large and enthusiastic following. Eventually the pope condemned Reuchlin to silence. However, the victory really lay with Reuchlin and his humanist supporters. The tactics and self-centered motives of the churchmen and scholastic pedagogues disgusted most of the genuine scholars and students of the day, and during the first few decades of the sixteenth century the new humanistic curriculum became established in all the major universities of Germany.

Meanwhile, in England a group of Ox-

ERASMUS OF ROTTERDAM, BY HOLBEIN. The scholarly and genial nature of Erasmus is skillfully portrayed by the northern Renaissance portrait painter, Hans Holbein. Known as "the prince of the humanists," Erasmus raised one of the most fundamental issues that have ever been debated concerning Western civilization when he attempted to humanize the Christian religion. (*Archives Photographiques, Paris*)

ford professors was accomplishing with less opposition much the same program that Reuchlin had fought for in Germany. John Colet was the most prominent member of this group. He, too, visited Renaissance Italy. In true Northern humanistic fashion he gave a rationalistic slant to his preaching and teaching of the Scriptures at Oxford. Probably the greatest of Colet's contributions to the new learning was the founding of St. Paul's grammar school in London, with a curriculum devoted largely to the pagan classics. To guarantee its secular orientation, he chose as trustees a guild of London merchants. St. Paul's soon became a model for many other such schools throughout England.

The most famous of all the early sixteenth-century English humanists was Sir Thomas More, Lord Chancellor of the Realm. More's *Utopia* (Nowhere), like Plato's *Republic*, blueprinted an earthly, not a heavenly, paradise. In picturing his ideal commonwealth More, by subtle implications, indicated the social, religious, and political evils of his own time. Utopia was a socialistic society where private property and profits were unknown. Much attention was given to public health and education. The economy was planned and co-operative. Iron was more valuable than gold because it was more useful. War was outlawed except in self-defense. Religious freedom was granted to all but atheists. Although More eventually was to accept death by beheading rather than to recognize Henry VIII as head of the English church in place of the pope, his ideal society was entirely secular. Man through his own wisdom would create his own perfect world here on earth.

Towering above all the other Northern humanists was Desiderius Erasmus (1466–1536), the intellectual dictator of the sixteenth century. In his efforts to humanize Christianity itself the "Prince of the Humanists" created the most fundamental issue that has ever been raised within Western Civilization: Are the basic faith, ideals, and standards of Western Civilization human or divine? Erasmus was born in Rotterdam in the Netherlands, the illegitimate son of a priest. Reared as an orphan, he was educated in a school run by the Brethren of the Common Life, a religious order that taught the Greek and Latin classics and emphasized simple inner piety rather than ritual and formal creed. (It is interesting and probably significant that Martin Luther, the great contemporary and adversary of Erasmus, also attended a school of the Brethren of the Common Life.) At the age of twenty-one Erasmus entered an Augustinian monastery (again like Luther) and was eventually ordained. Instead of serving as a priest, however, he spent every possible moment studying his beloved classics—a pursuit he was to continue at the Sorbonne and for the rest of his life. He came to be regarded as the most learned humanist of his generation.

Erasmus's vast erudition combined with his great personal charm made him a much-sought-after man. He was a popular figure around Paris. On a trip to England he added to his growing band of friends and followers many of the important personages of that land, including John Colet and Sir Thomas More. They persuaded him to begin writing. His first book was *Adages*, a collection of wise sayings of the Greeks and Romans together with his own comments. It was an immediate success, and other books soon followed. His greatest work was the *Praise of Folly*, in which he ridiculed with subtle humor and delightful satire the ignorance, superstition, credulity, and current practices of his day, particularly those connected with the Church. Wherever he went—France, England, Italy, Switzerland, Germany, the Netherlands—he was received with admiration and awe. No man so advanced the cause of Northern humanism by popularizing the study of the pagan Greek and Latin classics. He ended his glamorous career in Basel, Switzerland, as editor and adviser of the Froben press.

In addition to popularizing the new humanistic learning north of the Alps, Erasmus is significant in history for at least two other reasons—his influence on religious and social reform, and his efforts to humanize and intellectualize Christianity. He was at his best when laughing to scorn the abuses and superstitious practices of the Roman Catholic Church. The taking of money from the poor and ignorant masses by wealthy and corrupt churchmen, veneration of relics, and unquestioning belief in the miraculous were in the eyes of Erasmus beneath the contempt of enlightened men. But he was clever enough to sheathe his barbs with genial humor, thus making them more subtle and effective. Erasmus, however, was no Protestant. When Martin Luther first began his attacks on the Roman Catholic Church, Erasmus thought that he was merely seeking to correct glaring abuses and hailed him as a fellow spirit. But when Erasmus discovered that the German reformer was primarily interested in doctrinal reform and that

the Protestants were as dogmatic as the Roman Catholics (actually more so in the early sixteenth century), Erasmus would have nothing more to do with him. The great humanist, uninterested in religious dogma, found it more comfortable to remain in the Roman Catholic Church. The two men ended up hurling epithets at each other. Nevertheless, Erasmus's incessant attacks on the abuses in organized Christianity undoubtedly encouraged both the Protestant and the Roman Catholic reformations. His skillfully conducted lifelong crusade for tolerance, kindness, and reasonableness could not have failed to leave an imprint upon Western society and institutions in general.

Erasmus's efforts to humanize Christianity, however, are far more significant historically than his campaign to eradicate religious and social abuses. Since the fall of the Roman Empire the great common denominator of Western civilization has been the Christian religion. The vast majority of the members of Western society have subscribed even if they have not lived up to its creeds, ideals, and moral standards. Furthermore, the vitality of these creeds, ideals, and moral standards has derived, in large measure, from the belief that they are of divine origin and sanction. Indeed, it is difficult to conceive of Western civilization as it has developed thus far without this basic faith at its center. This is why Erasmus's questioning of the divine origin and nature of the Christian religion—his efforts to humanize it—is of such deep significance. Although the "Prince of the Humanists" never did specifically say so, the implication running through his writings is that Jesus was a human being—the greatest, best, and most charming man that ever lived, the man whom we should all try to emulate, but nevertheless man, not God. Erasmus would by-pass formal creed and dogma, ritual, organization, and priestcraft, and seek after the "historical" Christ. Now, all this is quite appealing to the rationalistic humanist, but it is not quite so simple as it first appears. The historical Christ is a most elusive figure. As a matter of fact, the only documentation we have for Christ is in the New Testament, and if we apply to it the same standards of critical analysis used for other historical documents, its evidence is by no means conclusive. And yet the secondary evidence—the word of mouth and written tradition—is overwhelming. Few historians today would deny the existence of Jesus of Nazareth. However, all we have to go on for the "historical Christ" is the New Testament and the early tradition, and the Christ of both these sources is not the Christ of Erasmus. He is a miracle-working Christ who claimed to be the son and image of God, to have the gift of eternal salvation, who "spake as no other man ever spake." Far simpler to reject Christ as did the Italian humanists than to humanize him. Erasmus's attempt to humanize Christianity not only was the ultimate in the renaissance of secularism, but it raised a question that is as much alive in the twentieth century as it was in the sixteenth.

3. The National Renaissance Literatures

The era of the Renaissance witnessed the flowering of national literatures. These literatures reflected the secular spirit in all its phases; they also reflected the rapidly growing national interests and traits. In both respects they constituted a sharp departure from the literature of the Middle Ages, which in the main (with noteworthy exceptions, of course) centered around religious subjects and was international in viewpoint. Although the national literatures of the Northern Renaissance owed a great deal to the Italian literature of the fourteenth century, they reached their prime much later—in the sixteenth and early seventeenth centuries. The most important literary development in this era was in England, France, and Spain.

English Renaissance literature began with Chaucer (1340–1400), who traveled to Italy, became acquainted with Boccaccio, and brought back to England the spirit and

much of the technique of the early Italian Renaissance writers. His *Canterbury Tales* are almost an Anglican *Decameron* in charming verse. Salty and very earthy characters from all walks of life parade past us on their way to Canterbury, their human frailties and sins of the flesh forgiven them by the author. Only hypocritical churchmen get the censure of the English Boccaccio, and even they with a light and subtle touch. Chaucer's artistic use of the Saxon dialect helped to establish it as the national language of all England. As in Italy, however, the century following Chaucer was rather barren in a literary sense; it was not until the mid-sixteenth century, the time of Queen Elizabeth I, that his plantings suddenly burst forth in full flower.

The reign of Queen Elizabeth I (1558–1603) was a period of great energy and optimism in England. To the rediscovery of the glamorous secular achievements of ancient Greece and Rome were added the discovery of the New World and of new routes to the riches of the Far East. Dauntless English seamen such as Drake, Gilbert, Hawkins, Grenville, and Howard first plundered the Spanish treasure ships, and then crushed the "Invincible Armada" of the world's chief military power, making England mistress of the seas for the next three centuries. English explorers boldly laid the foundations for a future empire in the East and in the West. England's commerce increased, and the standard of living for the middle and upper classes rose sharply. The Queen herself knew how to stimulate national pride centered around her own person. Because of these obvious factors and doubtless many more of a less tangible nature, England became "a nest of singing birds" such as the world has never seen or heard. Edmund Spenser's *Faerie Queen* glorified the versatile man of the Italian humanists, particularly the ideal set forth by Castiglione in his *Book of the Courtier*. Christopher Marlowe in his brief life wrote man-centered plays of such caliber that some critics think that he would have achieved the stature of Shakespeare had he lived. His *Tamburlaine the Great* and *Edward II* treat of the worldly drama of royal ambition. The central figure in *The Jew of Malta,* a forerunner of Shylock, is a product of the revived commercial capitalism. *Doctor Faustus* dramatizes the theme, later immortalized by Goethe, of the intellectual who in true Renaissance fashion sold his soul to the devil in return for earthly knowledge and pleasure.

Mightiest of all the artists of the English Renaissance was, of course, William Shakespeare (1564–1616). Shakespeare was born in the same year that Michelangelo died, a fact that ought to remind us that virtually the same set of circumstances that stimulated the Italian artists of the sixteenth century to design St. Peter's and paint the *Sistine Madonna* spurred the English artists to write the *Faerie Queen* and *Hamlet.* So little is known of Shakespeare's life that some have tried to attribute his matchless work to others. Shakespeare penned some of the world's most beautiful lyrical poetry. His most important work, however, was in the field of drama. Here he was heavily indebted to his contemporary, Christopher Marlowe, as well as to the ancient Greek and Roman dramatists. Marlowe developed the blank-verse form, which Shakespeare perfected. In his incomparable plays such as *Hamlet, Macbeth, Othello, King Lear, Merchant of Venice, As You Like It, Henry IV, Romeo and Juliet,* and *Julius Caesar* (to mention a few of the best known) Shakespeare displayed a mastery of every known technique of the dramatic art.

More importantly to the student of history, he exemplified and dramatized every facet of the secular spirit of the Renaissance. Secular man is Shakespeare's subject matter. Rugged, distinctive human personalities are the heroes and villains of his plays. No human emotion, aspiration, or psychological conflict escapes the eye of this analyst. On the whole, Shakespeare, unlike the Greek dramatists, makes man the master of his own fate. In addition to making man

the center of his universe Shakespeare illustrates the Renaissance spirit and times in other ways. Admiration for pagan Greece and Rome, a keen interest in new-found lands, the first stirrings of modern natural science, the commercial revolution and social problems arising from the emergence of the capitalistic middle class, the rise of national monarchy and a national patriotic spirit—all enter into the fabric of Shakespeare's plays. In spite of the fact that both the Protestant and the Roman Catholic reformations loomed large in the affairs of England and the rest of Western Europe just before and during Shakespeare's time, he showed little interest in matters of religion. In this respect, too, he was a true child of the Renaissance.

One of Shakespeare's most important contemporaries was Sir Francis Bacon. Though not in Shakespeare's class as an artist, Bacon was nontheless an intellectual giant. His father, Sir Nicholas Bacon, was one of the chief administrators and advisers of Queen Elizabeth, and Francis spent much of his life arduously seeking political fortune. Finally he succeeded, becoming Lord Chancellor of England, only to be convicted shortly of dishonesty, stripped of his powers, and for a time imprisoned. That his reputation and his own self-esteem could survive such fortune is indicative of the moral relativism of the Renaissance era. Bacon's intellectual interests were broad, and his knowledge encyclopedic. His *History of the Reign of Henry VII* is still an important source. His *Novum Organum* is one of the first important treatises on modern natural science. Bacon preached the absolute necessity of accurate and unbiased observation in the acquiring of scientific truth. His major contribution to Renaissance literature is his *Essays,* which he continued to polish and refine as long as he lived. The final result is fifty-eight gems of pithy, salty, practical, and very human wisdom.

The last of the giants of Elizabethan literature was Ben Jonson. This robust personality, a familiar figure in the bohemian taverns of London, could serve as a trooper in the English army and also write "Drink to me only with thine eyes." Jonson was first and foremost a connoisseur of classical literature. With exquisite plays reminiscent of the Greek dramatists he attempted unsuccessfully to reverse the trend toward cheap popularization and sensationalism that had characterized the English stage after the death of Shakespeare. Jonson's death in 1637 marked the end of the most glorious epoch in the history of the world's literature—England's greatest contribution to the Renaissance and the Renaissance spirit.

The two chief figures in *French* Renaissance literature were François Rabelais and Michel de Montaigne, both of whom lived in the sixteenth century. Rabelais was a renegade priest, a bored physician, and above all a loving student of the classics. Although he stumbled quite by accident and late in life upon his gift for writing, he turned out to be one of the greatest creative geniuses in the history of literature. His masterpieces are *Pantagruel* and *Gargantua*. They are fantasies about two completely unrestrained giants who wallow and revel unashamedly in all the sensuous and sensual pleasures known to man. These works are an open assault upon Christian moral standards and restraints. The wit is coarse, lewd, and sympathetic toward the frailties of human nature. Rabelais's rich imagery, his marvelous gift of expression, and his graceful artistry combine to make him one of the founding fathers of modern French prose. He has to share that honor, though, with his contemporary, John Calvin, whose lucid and incisive Protestant writings Rabelais hated no less than the works of the Roman Catholic theologians and the scholastic philosophers.

Montaigne was a prodigy born in the lap of luxury. By the age of thirty-seven he had received a university education, practiced law, served as a magistrate in his native Bordeaux, and retired to spend the rest of his life in study, contemplation, and writ-

ing. Like Rabelais he was an ardent lover of the classics. This, together with the fact that his mother was Jewish and his father Roman Catholic, probably accounts for his skepticism in matters of religion. The result of his life of study and reflection was his *Essays*. Montaigne was a skeptic and an Epicurean. To arrive at reliable truth, Montaigne believed, one must rid himself of all religious prejudice. He was a moral and spiritual relativist, rejecting all absolutes. Unlike his successors of the eighteenth-century Enlightenment, he distrusted the authority of human reason. Unable to replace the authority of Christian dogma with any other firm conviction, Montaigne was nearly always negative in his conclusions. But he immensely enjoyed this game of intellectual hide-and-seek. In fact Montaigne believed that the chief purpose of life is pleasure—not the "eat, drink, and be merry" pleasure of Rabelais, but urbane, sophisticated, restrained, intellectual pleasure. This marked him as a true Epicurean of the uncorrupted Greek school. The influence of Montaigne has been enormous—obviously upon essayists from Bacon to Emerson and later, but also upon the development of modern thought in general.

Standing out above all others in *Spanish* Renaissance literature are Miguel de Cervantes and Lope de Vega. Cervantes was a contemporary of Shakespeare, the two dying within a few days of each other in 1616. As with Shakespeare, Cervantes's early life was obscure. In time he became a soldier of fortune, fought heroically and was wounded in the great naval battle of Lepanto with the Turks, suffered a five-year imprisonment in Algeria, and finally served as a quartermaster for Spain's Invincible Armada. In poverty-stricken later life he settled down to write *Don Quixote*, called by some critics the greatest novel ever written. This top masterpiece of all Spanish literature relates with urbane grace and humor the adventures of a slightly addled knight who filled his noble head too full of the lore of chivalry, and of his groom, Sancho Panza. Sancho, a squat plebeian on a donkey, and Don Quixote, an emaciated knight on a tall, lean horse, go about Spain from one delightfully charming adventure to another. It is altogether necessary to read a few pages, almost any few pages, of this rollicking fantasy to appreciate the genius of Cervantes. Since all types and classes of people in all parts of Spain are lucidly portrayed, *Don Quixote* is the most valuable historical source in existence for life in sixteenth-century Spain. Cervantes's deeper purpose was to laugh out of existence what was left of medieval chivalry. He therefore did to feudal society what Erasmus and Rabelais were trying to do to medieval Christianity, and in much the same manner.

Lope de Vega was a contemporary of Ben Jonson. In sharp contrast with Cervantes, most of whose whole literary life and genius were centered on one masterpiece, Lope de Vega wrote a fabulous number of pieces of practically every known type of literature. His plays alone exceed in number those of any other writer, whether you accept the writer's own claim to twenty-two hundred or recognize only the seven hundred-odd plays that can be accounted for today. Secular man, pictured in every conceivable dramatic situation, is the hero of the great Spanish playwright. Lope de Vega was an ardent Spanish nationalist; he sailed with the Invincible Armada. Like the Elizabethans and other Northern Renaissance writers he thought that his country and the sixteenth and early seventeenth centuries were an exciting place and time to live.

Thus the writers of the Northern Renaissance had much in common. Their chief interests were contemporary man and the exciting, rapidly expanding material world around them. Their chief inspiration was the pagan classics of Greece and Rome. They were on the whole nationalistic and wrote in the new national vernaculars. Although the Protestant and Roman Catholic reformations were threatening to tear Western European society apart throughout the sixteenth century, the men of letters were in the main either apathetic or, as in the case of Rabelais and Montaigne, hostile to theology in general and to Christianity in particular.

4. Northern Renaissance Art

Northern Renaissance art did not equal either the Northern Renaissance literature or the Italian Renaissance art after which it was largely patterned. Nevertheless, it was by no means insignificant. The best Renaissance painters outside Italy were the Flemings (Belgians) and the Germans. The Van Eyck brothers, Hubert and Jan, lived in Ghent in the Flemish Netherlands in the early fifteenth century. Like Masaccio, their Italian contemporary, they brought to near completion the transition from medieval to Renaissance painting. Their greatest joint work is *Adoration of the Lamb*. Not the least of their contributions to painting was the development of oil as a medium. It was from them that Leonardo da Vinci got this priceless medium, which he perfected and without which he could not have painted the *Mona Lisa* or the *Virgin of the Rocks*.

In sixteenth-century Germany, Albert Dürer of Nuremberg and Hans Holbein the Younger of Augsburg were the leading painters. Dürer was primarily a master craftsman of delicate and graceful line. Probably for this reason, his woodcutting and engraving are better than his painting. In the former arts he is without a peer in any age. Holbein was a skillful sketcher and woodcutter, but he made his greatest contributions in the field of portrait painting. He painted several portraits of Erasmus and illustrated Erasmus's *Praise of Folly* with pen-and-ink drawings. Many of his most productive years were spent in England in the employ of Henry VIII. Among his greatest portraits are those of Henry VIII, Edward VI, Mary Tudor, and Sir Thomas More, all of whom live thereby in vivid likeness for us today. Both Dürer and Holbein were interested primarily in the contemporary things and people of the material world around them.

Renaissance artists did not produce many

architectural monuments outside Italy, probably because commercial capitalism had not yet sufficiently developed in Northern Europe to finance this more costly type of undertaking. The largest if not the most beautiful Renaissance structure outside Italy is the vast Escorial near Madrid, which Philip II of Spain built as a royal palace and mausoleum. Its rugged massiveness, rectangular shape, and horizontal lines typify the Renaissance style. Some of the best examples of Northern Renaissance architecture are the Renaissance wing of the Louvre in Paris, which is the world's largest and probably greatest art gallery, and some of the largest chateaux along France's Loire River. This architecture was essentially derivative; the French Renaissance chateaux were really fortresses being played with.

5. Printing With Movable Type

A major Renaissance contribution to the world of intellect and literature was the invention of printing with movable type. In ancient and medieval times manuscripts were written and copied in longhand on parchment or papyrus. Needless to say, this slow and costly process greatly retarded the dissemination of knowledge. In the fourteenth century printing from carved wooden blocks came into Western Europe from China by way of the Mohammedan world and Spain. This, too, however, was tedious, costly, and limited. From China likewise came paper, made of various fibers, silk, cotton, or flax. Paper was a great improvement over parchment or papyrus for purposes of mass production. (Even the art of printing by movable type itself was a Chinese invention, although this is not believed to have influenced its invention in the Western world.)

John Gutenberg set up the first practical printing press using movable type in the European world at Mainz in western Germany. The Gutenberg forty-two-line Bible printed in 1454 is the earliest known book to be printed by the new process. The invention was an immediate success and spread quickly to all the other countries of Western Europe. It is estimated that by the end of the fifteenth century more than twenty-five thousand separate editions and nearly ten million individual books had been printed. To appreciate the significance of the new invention in making knowledge available to the masses, the reader need only reflect for a few moments on the probable cost of this book if it were copied in longhand on parchment or printed from seven hundred handcarved wooden blocks at present-day wages. As a result of Gutenberg's invention and later improvements few people in the Western world today can excuse their ignorance of literature on the grounds that it is unavailable.

6. Significance of the Renaissance in History

In retrospect, then, it is apparent that the Renaissance was fundamentally a transition from the God-centered civilization of the Middle Ages to the man-centered, secular civilization of the modern period. In some measure it was a rebirth of the classical civilization of pagan Greece and Rome, but it was not merely that. There was much in the Renaissance that was fresh and original. The rediscovery of the brilliant culture of antiquity and the rising secular spirit with its confidence in man, versatility, egotism, materialism, and individuality combined to produce some of the most beautiful art and literature the world has ever known. In addition, the foundations were laid for the later rise of science. The Renaissance was also in large measure a revolt against Christianity, directly in Italy and somewhat indirectly in Northern Europe. That it did not destroy or palsy Christianity as a dynamic force in Western civilization is due to the Protestant and Roman Catholic reformations, which revitalized Christianity. To these great movements, which paralleled the Renaissance in its later stages and which were in part provoked by it, we must now turn.

SUGGESTED READING

J. H. Randall, *The Making of the Modern Mind* (1940). A highly readable intellectual history of modern Western civilization from its medieval roots to the twentieth century. Although Randall considers medieval Christianity to be the chief foundation for modern Western civilization, he equates Christian faith with alchemy; progress, with escape from Christian faith. Natural science is the hero of this book.

H. O. Taylor, *Thought and Expression in the Sixteenth Century*, 2 vols. (1930). A work of mature scholarship that the interested and ambitious student should find rewarding.

Preserved Smith, *Erasmus: A Study of His Life, Ideals, and Place in History* (1923). A sympathetic and scholarly biography of the "Prince of the Humanists."

Erasmus, *The Praise of Folly* (many editions). Originally published in 1509. This masterpiece of the chief of the Northern humanists had great influence on the intelligentsia of the sixteenth century. It is an excellent and enjoyable approach to the critical humanistic mind.

* Sir Thomas More, *Utopia* (Crofts). Another product of Northern humanistic thought of wide and continuing influence. It is fascinating reading.

* Rabelais, *Gargantua and Pantagruel* (Penguin). Rollicking fantasy by a first-rate literary genius who was in open revolt against Christian ideals and standards.

* Montaigne, *Autobiography* (Vintage). Montaigne was a cultivated sixteenth-century Epicurean. This book reflects his erudite, skeptical, and mildly tolerant humanistic mind. Many modern intellectuals have delighted in his life and thought.

* Cervantes, *Don Quixote* (Modern Library). This charming fantasy is sometimes called the world's greatest novel. Cervantes's discerning pen pictures of sixteenth-century Spaniards of all walks of life make *Don Quixote* an important source for social conditions at the time of the Renaissance. The student who begins to read this book will have difficulty putting it down.

CHAPTER 31

The Protestant Reformation

THE Protestant Reformation, or Protestant Revolt, as it is sometimes called, was primarily, though not entirely, a religious movement. Western Europeans of the sixteenth century were intensely interested in religion. The Church was still at the very center of their lives, and even the unlettered masses knew a good deal about matters of doctrine and ritual. The leaders of both the Protestant and the Roman Catholic reformations were certainly men whose lives were dedicated to religion.

1. Causes

In the late Middle Ages there developed within the ranks of the Roman Catholic Church a growing dissatisfaction with some fundamental doctrines (see pp. 311–14). The most dissatisfied elements had come to believe that the Roman Catholic Church had departed so far from the spirit and practices of the apostles and early fathers that it could no longer be considered God's appointed custodian of the Christian religion. They began to define *The Church* to mean the sum total of all those who put their faith in Christ, not any one specific institution.[1] The Scriptures alone, not the deci-

sions and traditions of the organized Church, became for these reformers the sole authoritative source for Christian dogma. Their growing conception of the Christian religion as a direct relationship between man and God tended to lessen the importance of the professional clergy and the sacraments of the Roman Catholic Church. They spoke of the priesthood of all believers. These ideas the reformers believed to be in harmony with those of St. Augustine and the early Church, as well as with those to be found in the Scriptures. They clashed sharply, however, with the beliefs and practices of the Roman Catholic hierarchy of the late Middle Ages. The two views could not be harmonized. This doctrinal split within the ranks of organized Western Christendom was the most fundamental of all the causes of the Reformation.

However, other factors contributed to the break within the Roman Catholic Church. Quite apart from matters of doctrine, many abuses had arisen in the Church during the fourteenth and fifteenth centuries when the

---

[1] The reformers disputed the Petrine doctrine upon which the popes based much of their claim to headship over the Christian Church. The popes claimed that, as bishops of Rome, they inherited the authority of St. Peter, the first bishop of Rome, whom Christ designated to head His Church. (". . . thou art Peter and upon this rock I will build my church . . . ," Matthew, 16:18.) The reformers maintained that in the original Greek the word for Peter is *petros*, meaning an individual stone, and that the word for rock is *petra*, meaning a large body of stone. Therefore, they assert, Christ did not mean to say that he would found his Church upon Peter, but upon the faith that Christ was the Son of the living God, which Peter had just affirmed.

Church was torn by the Babylonian Captivity, the Great Schism, and the struggles between the popes and the councils (see pp. 308–10). Ignorance and worldliness of the clergy, the sale of Church offices and services (simony), the favoring of relatives for lucrative Church offices (nepotism), the holding by one man of more offices than he could adequately serve (pluralism)—all were subjects of loud and growing complaint. Many of the higher clergy, even the popes, became infected with the secular spirit of the Renaissance. Often they displayed greater interest in humanistic pleasures and pursuits than in feeding their flocks. Eventually the Church hierarchy came to realize the seriousness of these abuses and took drastic steps to remedy them, but not until much of Western Christendom had left the Roman fold.

Politically the rise of national states and of local loyalty to them clashed with the international character of the Church. The national monarchs became increasingly jealous of the claims of the pope over their subjects. In many cases they supported native Protestant leaders and movements.

Economic motivation undoubtedly played a significant part. Church taxes drained away to Rome much wealth from the local economy. The rich tax-exempt lands of the Church all over Western Europe excited a great deal of envy. The Church's opposition to usury and its close alliance with the landed aristocracy antagonized the rising capitalistic classes.

Finally, the intellectual activities of the humanists weakened the hold of the Church on many minds. Erasmus and other humanists heaped mountains of ridicule upon what they considered to be superstitious beliefs of the Church. Their scholarly translations and critical textual studies exposed errors in the sacred documents upon which the Church based its claims. It must not be assumed, however, that the Protestants were more humanistic than the Roman Catholics. As a matter of fact, the sixteenth-century humanists found the Protestant leaders even more dogmatic and uncongenial than

the Roman Catholic hierarchy. However, the humanists unwittingly helped to bring about the Reformation by weakening the position of the Roman Catholic Church.

As early as the fourteenth century such reformers as John Wycliffe in England and John Huss in Bohemia had voiced their protests against the Roman Catholic Church. By the opening of the sixteenth century the religious, political, economic, and intellectual opposition to the Church as it then stood had reached explosive proportions. All that was needed for revolt was a dynamic personality to lead it and an incident to set it off.

2. Lutheranism

The Protestant Reformation was composed of three major distinct but related movements—Lutheranism, Calvinism, and Anglicanism. From these three main stems, and from several minor radical sects called Anabaptists, have sprung the hundreds of Protestant denominations that exist today. The Lutheran revolt was first in point of time.

Martin Luther (1483–1546) was a dynamic leader of men. Like so many great leaders he had a humble beginning. His father was a poor, though not poverty-stricken, miner of central Germany. Young Martin was chosen from among his numerous brothers and sisters to be educated. At a boarding school run by the mystic Brethren of the Common Life he, like his contemporary Erasmus, was introduced to a type of Christianity that emphasized simple piety rather than dogma and ritual. At Erfurt University he received a traditional liberal-arts education. He was an excellent student. However, upon the completion of his undergraduate course and just as he was ready to begin study of the law, he suddenly renounced the world and entered an Augustinian monastery. This decision was no passing whim. As a child Luther was much concerned over the fate of his soul, and throughout his university days religious yearning increased.

The young friar found no satisfaction for his hungry soul in the monastic life of the sixteenth-century Church. He scourged himself, donned the beggar's garb, and went out among his former fellow students with sunken cheeks and gleaming, feverish eyes. It was not until, on the advice of a perceptive supervisor of his monastic order, he began to read the writings of St. Augustine and St. Paul that Brother Martin found at last the answer to his lifelong quest. On reading in Paul's Letter to the Romans (1:17) "the just shall live by faith," it suddenly began to dawn upon Luther that here was the true means of salvation—not by good works, sacraments, and rituals, but by simple faith in Christ. Over a period of years he developed his theology based upon this fundamental concept. Gradually he regained his old radiance and energy.

In the meantime Luther became a charter member of the faculty of the newly founded University of Wittenberg in Saxony, where he was to remain for the rest of his life. For years he taught philosophy and theology, quite unaware that his belief in salvation by faith alone was in fundamental conflict with the dogma of his church. Students flocked from afar to listen to him.

One day a friar named John Tetzel came into the vicinity of Wittenberg selling indulgences. According to the doctrine of indulgences, which had grown up in the late Middle Ages, Christ and the saints, by their good works while on earth, had accumulated in heaven a treasury of excess merit, which the pope could apply to the credit of penitent sinners, thereby shortening for them or their loved ones their stay in purgatory. By the opening of the sixteenth century the dispensing of this extra sacramental means of grace had become a crying abuse, reflecting the growing worldliness of the Church. In the hands of unscrupulous commission merchants and pardon hawkers the dispensing of indulgences had become nothing less than a money-making venture. Huge sums, taken from the credulous all over Europe, were brought to Rome for the construction of St. Peter's Church or for other costly and ofttimes worldly papal projects. Here we have a good example of the religious, intellectual, political, and economic causes of the Reformation all rolled into one.

On October 31, 1517, Martin Luther posted on the church door in Wittenberg ninety-five theses or propositions concerning the doctrine of indulgences, which he proposed to be debated publicly. It did not once occur to him that this event would mark the beginning of an upheaval to subside only after almost half of Western Christendom had broken away from the Roman Catholic Church. He was astonished and at first dismayed to find himself suddenly the national hero of all the various disgruntled elements throughout Germany. When, however, two years later in a public debate at Leipzig Luther finally realized that his position was hopelessly at odds with that of the Church, he lost no time in making the break clean. He published a series of pamphlets in which he violently denounced the pope and his organization, and called upon the German princes to seize the property of the Church and make themselves the heads of the Christian Church in Germany.

A papal bull of excommunication (which Luther publicly burned) soon followed. A little later Emperor Charles V called the troublesome monk to appear before the Diet of the Holy Roman Empire at Worms. There Luther boldly refused to recant and was outlawed by the highest civil authority in Germany. Although Luther remained under this death sentence with a price on his head for the rest of his life, he was protected by his prince, the elector of Saxony, and by German public opinion.

By this time all Germany was in religious and social turmoil. Nearly everyone with a grievance of any kind was looking to Luther for leadership. Religious zealots, many of them calling themselves Anabaptists, began preaching individualistic and extremist doctrines in the name of Luther, and he found it necessary to repudiate them. Taking a somewhat more conservative stand, he decided that only those features of the Roman

Catholic Church that were repugnant to the Scriptures ought to be rejected. In the early stages of the conflict Erasmus and many other humanists thought that they saw in Luther a kindred spirit and agreed to join forces with him. However, this alliance was short-lived. Erasmus soon found Luther to be as dogmatic and uncompromising in matters of doctrine as the Roman Catholic theologians, if not more so. Erasmus was primarily interested in matters of the intellect, and Luther in those of religious faith. Erasmus found it more convenient and comfortable to remain in the Roman Church, which he had done so much to discredit. He and Luther ended their days hurling recriminations at each other.

Luther also found it necessary to break with a group of rebellious peasants in south Germany. The condition of the peasants was bad and growing worse. The landed aristocracy, themselves losing ground to the rising middle classes, were depriving their peasants of long-established manorial rights such as free use of meadow and woodlands. In 1524 widespread disturbances broke out in southwestern Germany. The next year the peasants published a list of moderate demands; when these demands were refused, the peasants revolted in the name of Luther, whom they believed to be in revolt against all oppressive authority. Luther, although very sympathetic with the peasants, pleaded with them to refrain from violence. This the peasants refused to do, and when they went on a bloody rampage, killing and burning in Luther's name, he repudiated them and called on the civil authorities to suppress the revolt by force. The alarmed authorities did so with a vengeance.

In the end both sides blamed Luther for the revolt and its painful results. South Germany has remained a Roman Catholic stronghold to this day. Luther was in favor of peaceful social reform, but he believed that successful reform depended upon a change of heart. In short, the first Protestant leader found it necessary quite early in the revolt to make it clear that Protestant Christianity was neither a humanistic philosophy

nor a materialistic social reform movement, nor yet a free-for-all for everyone to believe and preach anything he chose.

Luther's new religion, as he eventually formulated it, made the Scriptures the sole authoritative source of Christian dogma. That all might have access to the Bible, he translated it into German.[2] He conceived of the Church as that whole body of believers in Christ, not the Roman Catholic or any other specific organization. He abolished the hierarchy of pope, cardinals, and bishops, and reduced the importance of the clergy in general, proclaiming the priesthood of all believers. He made the various secular rulers the heads of the Christian Church in their territories. He abolished monasteries and the celibacy of the clergy. Luther himself married an ex-nun. The ritual of worship was made much simpler. Of the seven sacraments of the Roman Catholic Church, Luther kept only the two he found mentioned in the Bible: baptism and the Eucharist. He rejected the Roman Catholic doctrine of the Eucharist known as transubstantiation.[3] Luther interpreted the passages of the Scriptures that refer to the Holy Eucharist, or Lord's Supper, to mean that during the administration of the sacrament Christ's body somehow enters into the bread and the wine, but the bread and wine remain. He denied the Roman Catholic belief that a sacrifice is involved.

The Emperor Charles V was greatly distressed by this religious revolution, which further divided his scattered and chaotic empire. Although determined to suppress the Protestants, he was too busy with his wars against the French and the Turks to make much headway. Nine years of indecisive fighting between the Roman Catholics under

---

[2] Luther's translation was in such excellent German that it had great influence on the standardization of the modern literary German language.

[3] The New Catholic Dictionary defines transubstantiation as "the marvellous and singular changing of the entire substance of the bread into the entire substance of the Body of Christ and of the entire substance of the wine into His Blood."

Charles V and the Protestants ended in 1555 with the compromise Peace of Augsburg. Each of the more than three hundred German princes was left free to choose between Lutheranism and Roman Catholicism; his subjects were to abide by his choice. Luther himself died in 1546, just before the fighting began. Lutheranism triumphed in the northern half of Germany and soon spread to Denmark, Norway, Sweden, and the Baltic provinces (now Lithuania, Latvia, Estonia, and Finland), which were then under Swedish control. In addition, Lutheranism heavily influenced all later Protestant movements.

3. Calvinism

Calvin shares with Luther the position of first importance in the founding of Prot-

CALVIN AS A YOUNG MAN. This portrait of Calvin by an unknown painter reveals his intellectual keenness and his elegant bearing. Calvin was an uncompromising zealot for the Protestant faith. His enemies thought him a killjoy and a tyrant— a "Protestant Pope." His friends and followers considered him the most gentle and inspiring of men. (*Société du Musée Historique de la Réformation, Genève*)

estant Christianity. Born in France in 1509, the son of a lawyer and secretary to the bishop of Noyon, John Calvin was twenty-six years younger than Luther. Young Calvin had a radiant personality that made for warm friendships. Long association with aristocratic friends probably accounts for his elegant manners. His father sent him first to the University of Paris for a thorough grounding in the humanities and theology, and then to the best law schools in France, where Calvin ruined his health by overwork. Upon finishing his legal training, he entered upon a humanistic literary career and quickly showed signs of becoming a second Erasmus. Suddenly at the age of twenty-four he was converted to Protestant Christianity, probably as a result of reading Luther.

The zealous young reformer soon aroused the ire of the Roman Catholic authorities in France and of the French government and was forced to flee his native land on pain of death. Finding refuge in Basel, Switzerland, Calvin then spent the next two years writing the first edition of *The Institutes of the Christian Religion*. Published when Calvin was only twenty-six years of age, this theological treatise was to become the most influential writing in the history of Protestantism. Its precise and forceful logic reveals not only the fine legal training of the author but also one of the most powerful intellects in history. Its lucid and facile style had much the same influence on the formulation of the modern literary French language that Luther's translation of the Bible had on the German. It immediately made Calvin an important name in literary and theological circles.

Probably the most significant single contribution of Calvin to Christian theology is his sublime concept of the majesty of God. To the author of the *Institutes* the Divine Creator is so majestic and awe-inspiring and man so insignificant by comparison that salvation by election, or predestination, as it is more often called, seems to follow logically. According to Calvin, God in the beginning planned the whole universe to the end of time. For unfathomable reasons of His own God selected those human beings who would be saved and those who would be damned. He planted in the minds of the elect a saving faith in Christ and an insatiable desire to live the Christian life and to bring about the Kingdom of God on earth. In no other way could men acquire this faith and this desire. Calvin based this doctrine upon the Scriptures (particularly the writings of St. Paul), which he considered to be the sole authoritative source for Christian theology. St. Augustine, the most influential of the early Church fathers, and Luther also believed in salvation by election, but neither they nor anyone else had ever developed the doctrine so elaborately or given it such emphasis.

Shortly after the publication of the *Institutes*, Calvin went to Geneva. That city, like most of the rest of Switzerland, was in the throes of religious and political revolt brought on partly by the influence of Luther and the native Swiss reformer, Ulrich Zwingli (1484–1531). The Protestant leaders in Geneva immediately recognized in Calvin a natural leader and with difficulty persuaded the gifted but modest young man to remain there and make Geneva a model city of God on earth. Calvin, by sheer force of personality and intellect, soon rose to a position of virtual dictatorship over the city. He brought the town council, which was remarkably democratic and representative for the sixteenth century, under the dominance of a consistory composed of Protestant pastors and laymen. In other words, Geneva became a theocracy. Under Calvin's dynamic leadership the town council and the consistory set up a strict system of blue laws. Churchgoing was compulsory. Dancing, card-playing, theatergoing, drinking, gambling, and swearing—all were forbidden. Enforcement was vigorous, and penalties were severe, even for the sixteenth century. The most famous penalty imposed by Calvin's theocracy was the burning of Michael Servetus, an eccentric amateur scientist and theologian whom the Roman Catholic

Church had already condemned to death for heresy.[4] Servetus escaped his Catholic persecutors and came to Geneva for the purpose of destroying Calvin and his works. Calvin had warned him to stay away on pain of death, and when Servetus arrived he was seized, tried, convicted, and burned at the stake.

A strong minority in Geneva had no use for Calvin, for his theology, or for his blue laws. To them Calvin was a kill-joy, a bigot, and a tyrant. This verdict is the one that has found its way into most history textbooks. The majority of the Genevans, on the other hand, practically worshipped their leader; they considered him to be the most brilliant, inspiring, sympathetic, kindly, and gentle of men. Protestant Christians came from many countries to sit at the feet of Calvin and to study at the University of Geneva, which he founded. John Knox, who came all the way from Scotland to study under Calvin, called the Genevan theocracy "the most perfect school of life that was ever on earth since the days of the apostles."

Calvinist ritual was even simpler than that of the Lutherans. The worship service consisted of preaching, praying, and psalm-singing. Like Luther, Calvin retained only two of the seven sacraments—baptism and the Holy Eucharist, or Lord's Supper. But to Calvin, Christ was present only in spirit in the bread and wine, and only for the elect. Calvin patterned his system of church government after that of the very earliest church as described in the Bible (Acts of the Apostles). The local churches were governed by laymen called elders who were elected by the congregations. A measure of unity in faith and practices was maintained by means of a hierarchy of representative assemblies.

Calvinism gained control of most of Switzerland (Swiss Reformed), the Dutch Netherlands (Dutch Reformed), Scotland (Presbyterian), and the German Palatinate. It also had a strong minority following in

[4] The most serious of Servetus's heretical views was his denial of the Trinity, casting doubt upon the divinity of Christ.

England (the Puritans) and a smaller but vigorous following in France (the Huguenots). The Calvinists played a very important part in the founding of the United States, particularly the Puritans in New England, the Dutch Reformed in New York, and the Scotch-Irish Presbyterians along the frontiers of all the original states. Such well-known denominations in present-day America as the Congregationalists, the Presbyterians, and the Baptists are Calvinist in origin. The Calvinists were the most zealous and evangelical of all the major early Protestant groups. They made a strong appeal to the rising middle classes. Wherever they were found they were a powerful influence for the growth of democracy and for public education.

4. Anglicanism

The occasion, though not the cause, of the beginning of the Reformation in England was the desire of Henry VIII (1509–47) for a male heir. Catherine of Aragon, to whom he had been married for eighteen years, had provided him with only a daughter, Mary. When it became apparent that Catherine would have no more children, Henry decided to ask the pope to annul the marriage. The pope, however, was in no position to grant the annulment. The about-to-be-disgraced Catherine was the aunt of the Emperor Charles V, whose troops were at that very moment in control of the city of Rome. When the impetuous Henry realized that the pope was not going to accommodate him, he took matters into his own hands. At his bidding a subservient Parliament passed the Act of Supremacy, making the king of England, not the pope, head of the Church in England. Later the monasteries, strongholds of papal influence in England, were dissolved. Meanwhile, Thomas Cranmer, whom Henry made archbishop of Canterbury, had granted the annulment, and Henry had married Anne Boleyn. (He was to marry six times in all.) Henry was, of course, excommunicated by the pope.

But Henry VIII was no Protestant. In the

days before the annulment controversy the pope had given him the title "Defender of the Faith" for his anti-Lutheran writings. Now he had Parliament pass the Six Articles reaffirming the Catholic position on all the controversial doctrinal points except that of papal supremacy. Protestants, on the one hand, and on the other, Roman Catholics who refused to acknowledge the headship of Henry VIII in place of the pope were persecuted with equal severity. Death was the penalty for both.

It was during the reign of Henry VIII's young son, Edward VI (1547–53), that the Anglican Church first became Protestant. Archbishop Cranmer drew up a *Book of Common Prayer* and Forty-two Articles of faith that were definitely Calvinist in flavor. Edward VI was succeeded by his elder sister, Mary (1553–58), who was the daughter of Catherine of Aragon and a devout Roman Catholic. Mary's ambition was to restore her kingdom to the Roman Catholic fold. Her first step was to marry her cousin, Philip II of Spain, the most powerful champion of resurgent Roman Catholicism in all Europe. Next she asked and received papal forgiveness for her wayward people. Finally, Bloody Mary burned at the stake some three hundred Protestants, including Archbishop Cranmer. But Mary's marriage and her persecutions were extremely unpopular in England; in the long run her policies hurt rather than helped the Roman Catholic cause there.

Elizabeth I (1558–1603), the Protestant daughter of Anne Boleyn, followed Mary on the English throne. This high-spirited, cynical, and politically minded queen found theology tiresome. Her chief interest was to find a satisfactory compromise that would unify her people. During the course of her long reign the Anglican Church became definitely, but moderately and conservatively, Protestant. Cranmer's *Book of Common Prayer* was readopted with slight alterations. The Forty-two Articles of faith were changed to the Thirty-nine. Some of the more controversial doctrinal points such as the question of the real presence of Christ in the bread and wine were left purposely vague. Although celibacy of the clergy was abandoned, the episcopal system (government of the church by bishops and archbishops) was retained. A rather elaborate ritual was adopted. Two of the sacraments, baptism and the Eucharist, were retained.

Although the great majority of the English people appear to have accepted Elizabeth's compromise settlement, two groups remained dissatisfied. An extreme Calvinist element sought to "purify" the Anglican Church of all remaining traces of Roman Catholicism. These Puritans were to increase in strength until under Oliver Cromwell's leadership in the next century they gained temporary control of the country. The Roman Catholic minority, on the other hand, lost steadily in numbers. The support that some Roman Catholics gave to Philip II's attempt to conquer England and to the effort of Catholic Mary, Queen of Scots, to overthrow Elizabeth (see p. 376) tainted all of them with the suspicion of treason and played into Elizabeth's hands.

5. Summary

By the end of the third quarter of the sixteenth century, then, Protestantism had triumphed in the northern half of the Germanies, in Scandinavia, in the Baltic provinces, in most of Switzerland, in the Dutch Netherlands, Scotland, and England. In addition, it had gained a strong minority following in France, Poland, Bohemia, and Hungary. And, no matter how much the various Protestant denominations might disagree among themselves on minor details, they presented a solid front against the Roman Catholics. All Protestants rejected papal supremacy, the divine sanction of the Roman Church, the celibacy and indelible character of the priesthood, monasticism, and such other characteristic Roman Catholic doctrines as purgatory, transubstantiation, invocation of saints, and veneration of relics. These doctrinal differences between the Protestants and the Roman Catholics were fundamental, and no middle ground for a compromise was ever found. Nor was the Roman Church, notwithstanding its strong comeback, ever able to reconquer the territories in which the Protestants had gained a definite majority. The Reformation split Western Christendom into two sharply defined and hostile camps. In place of two major divisions into which Christianity had been separated since the early Middle Ages (Eastern Orthodox and Roman Catholic) there were now three.

SUGGESTED READING

Preserved Smith, *The Age of the Reformation* (1920). This is an erudite account not only of the Protestant and Roman Catholic reformations but also of the various facets of life and society in the Reformation era. Smith, an ardent admirer of Erasmus, is hostile to mystic Christianity in general and to Calvinism in particular.

Harold J. Grimm, *The Reformation Era, 1500–1650* (1954). An excellent survey incorporating up-to-date findings of scholars of the Reformation period. More objective than Preserved Smith.

T. M. Lindsay, *History of the Reformation*, 2 vols. (1906). A scholarly account sympathetic to Protestantism. Particularly good on theological issues.

* R. H. Bainton, *Here I Stand: A Life of Martin Luther* (Mentor). One of the best biographies of the great religious reformer, combining the latest scholarship with a journalistic style.

H. Grisar, *Luther, His Life and Work* (1950). A good Roman Catholic version by a German Jesuit.

Williston Walker, *John Calvin, the Organizer of Reformed Protestantism* (1906). Still the best single-volume biography of the often-misunderstood theologian and reformer.

H. M. Baird, *History of the Rise of the Huguenots of France*, 2 vols. (1907). A scholarly and colorful account of the struggles of the Calvinists to gain a foothold and survive in France.

T. M. Parker, *The English Reformation to 1558* (1950). An excellent short account.

A. F. Pollard, *Thomas Cranmer and the English Reformation* (1904). A scholarly treatment of the chief theologian of English Protestantism, written by a master of the history of Tudor England.

CHAPTER 32

The Roman Catholic Reformation

THE LOSS of half of Western Christendom by the Roman Catholic Church and the threatened loss of the rest touched off a reform movement within the Church. By the middle of the sixteenth century the Roman Catholic reform movement was well under way. The Church was revitalized, and a counteroffensive was launched against the Protestants, one that not only prevented their further encroachment on Roman Catholic domain but pushed them back a bit.

1. The Rise of a Reform Movement

Long before the revolt of Luther and Calvin there had been a demand for reform by many loyal Roman Catholics. In Spain, around the turn of the sixteenth century, Cardinal Ximenes had anticipated and forestalled a Protestant revolt by enforcing strict discipline upon the clergy and waging bitter warfare against heresy. However, in the rest of Western Christendom, the secular interests of the Renaissance popes and prelates and the popes' fears that a reform council might again challenge the absolute authority of the Holy See prevented effective action. Now, with state after state going over to the Protestants, countermeasures of a rather drastic nature became imperative. There arose two schools of thought concerning the proper course of action. One, led by the liberal Cardinal Contarini of Venice, advocated compromise and conciliation. Contarini eventually went so far as to meet

with Melanchthon, a close friend of Luther and an important figure in the Lutheran revolt, in earnest quest of an acceptable compromise. Nothing came of this meeting; in both camps powerful elements became convinced that the two religions were fundamentally incompatible. The other school of thought was led by the conservative Cardinal Caraffa of Naples. Caraffa believed that many corrupt practices in the Church needed to be reformed but that no compromise whatever should be made in the dogma. He believed that the Protestants were heretics and could reunite with the Roman Catholic Church only by recanting and submitting to the pope. This is the school of thought that triumphed, and Caraffa became Pope Paul IV. The upshot of this line of thinking was the calling of a Church council at Trent, an imperial city in northern Italy.

2. The Council of Trent

The Council of Trent, which was in session off and on for eighteen years from 1545 to 1563, was probably the most important council in the history of the Roman Catholic Church. The pope skillfully controlled its membership and voting procedure. The ultimate decisions of the council were in two categories: dogmatic and reformatory. In matters of faith or dogma all the traditional doctrines of the Church were reaffirmed and redefined, especially controversial ones such as the seven sacraments, transubstantiation, auricular confessions, celibacy of the clergy, monasticism, purgatory, invocation of the saints, veneration of relics, and indulgences. The dogmatic canons and decrees of the council concluded: "Anathema to [accursed be] all heretics! Anathema! Anathema! Anathema!" In the field of Church practices the council admitted the existence of much corruption and took stern measures to clean it up. Simony, nepotism, pluralism, and immorality and ignorance among the clergy were condemned. Schools for the education of the clergy were called for. The bishops were admonished to exercise closer supervision and discipline over the lower clergy. To implement its canons and decrees, the council endorsed the Inquisition, which had recently been set up in Rome to combat heresy, and inaugurated the Index of Forbidden Books to prevent the reading of heretical literature by unauthorized Roman Catholics. Both instruments were placed under papal control and supervision. The Index, periodically revised, has proved to be particularly effective. Thus the Roman Catholic Church at last spoke out with a voice clarion-clear, selected its weapons, and girded itself for more effective battle against the Protestants. At its service were the militant new Jesuit order and the world's greatest military power of the sixteenth century, Philip II's Spain.

3. The Society of Jesus

The founder of the Society of Jesus, Ignatius Loyola (1491–1556), was the equal of Luther and Calvin as a dynamic personality, organizer, and natural leader of men. He was a member of the Spanish lesser nobility. Until early middle life he was an obscure and ignorant soldier. In a battle with the French his leg was crushed by a cannon ball. Without benefit of anesthetic he had it set and, when it grew crooked, twice broken and twice reset. He remained a cripple for the rest of his life. During the months of agony and convalescence Loyola read lives of the Christian saints and underwent a deep spir-

LOYOLA, FROM A PAINTING BY RUBENS. Ignatius Loyola was the equal of Luther and Calvin as a dynamic personality and organizer. His militant Society of Jesus did much to revitalize the Roman Catholic Church. (*The Bettmann Archive*)

itual conversion. He determined to devote his tremendous energies and latent talents to the service of the Roman Catholic Church —to become a soldier of Christ, the Virgin Mary, and the pope. Since his first efforts only revealed his ignorance and got him into trouble with the clerical authorities, he set off for the University of Paris to begin his education. However, the dynamic Loyola was cut out, not as a scholar or theologian, but as a man of action. He soon began to attract a band of followers, with whom he organized the Society of Jesus.

The Jesuit Order, as the Society of Jesus is commonly known, was founded along military lines. A general, elected for life and residing in Rome, issues orders that are transmitted through a hierarchy of officials to the rank and file. Absolute and unquestioning obedience is the first requirement. Loyola admonished his followers, ". . . if she [the Church] shall have defined anything to be black which to our eyes appears to be white, we ought in like manner to pronounce it to be black." Members are urged to cut all earthly ties, even with family and friends, that might divide their loyalties or impede their wholehearted devotion to the work of the order. Applicants for membership are carefully screened. Only those of superior intelligence, sound health, and attractive appearance are chosen. Then follows a two-year testing time, a sort of officer-training school, during which the novices are severely tried and examined for signs of weakness of will or purpose. Those who survive are next given a long and rigorous education as scholastics in preparation for their specialized work. When found to be ready, they are admitted to full-fledged membership as coadjutors. They may now serve as priests, teachers, medics, diplomats, or in almost any other capacity suitable to their talents and training. Whatever their work, it is "all for the greater glory of God," which to the Jesuit means for all practical purposes the Roman Catholic Church. After years of service a few of the most outstanding are admitted to the highest circle. These select few take, in addition to the three Benedictine vows of poverty, chastity, and obedience, a fourth vow of special obedience to the pope. It is from this inner circle that all the high officers of the order are chosen.

For the spiritual guidance and inspiration of the members of the Society, Loyola wrote the *Spiritual Exercises*. In language rivaling Dante in vivid imagery, the *Exercises* guides the member through a solid month of concentrated meditation, a week each on the horrors of sin, the life of Christ to Palm Sunday, his suffering and crucifixion, and his resurrection and ascension. This remarkable work has proved to be a powerful stimulant in time of flagging zeal.

Loyola's high standards, far from deterring applicants, served as a challenge and an attraction. The Society of Jesus grew rapidly. As priests the Jesuits were nearly always the best trained, the most popular, and the most influential. As teachers they were usually more highly educated, devoted, and attrac-

tive than their competitors. They have always been keenly aware of the power of education, especially for the very young. "Give me the child, and I care not who has the man." The Jesuits soon got control of all education in most Roman Catholic countries.

These dedicated soldiers of Christ also made the best missionaries. In North and South America the dauntless Jesuits went among the Indians, risked and in many cases lost their lives, learned the languages of the natives, lived with them, and converted most of them to Roman Catholic Christianity. In the Far East, Francis Xavier, second only to Loyola himself in Jesuit history, converted tens of thousands.

Not the least important of Jesuit activities was that of gaining the confidence of kings, princes, and other high political personages, thereby influencing state policy. This militantly zealous order was a powerful stimulant to the wavering cause of Roman Catholicism. In Italy, Spain, Portugal, and Ireland, where Protestantism had only a weak foothold, the Jesuits stamped it out altogether. In France and Belgium they helped to turn the tide against the Protestants. In southern Germany, Poland, and the Austrian Hapsburg lands, all of which seemed to be on the point of going Protestant, the Jesuits reversed the trend and made those lands the strongholds of Roman Catholicism they are today.

4. The Crusade of Catholic Spain

Also at the service of the Roman Catholic Church in its counteroffensive against the Protestants was the world's greatest military power of the sixteenth century—the Spain of Philip II. Emperor Charles V had bequeathed the lion's share of his vast empire to his son Philip II (1556–98). In addition to Spain, Philip's inheritance included the Netherlands, Franche-Comté, The Kingdom of the Two Sicilies, Sardinia, the Balearic Islands, holdings along the west coast of Africa, and the Western Hemisphere. When in 1580 Philip conquered Portugal in the name of his Portuguese mother and became master (at least in name) of Portugal's huge Eastern empire, he exercised legal rule over more of the earth's surface than any other man in history.[1] Philip II, unlike his father, was a native and thoroughgoing Spaniard. The gold and silver now flowing in a steady stream from the New World and the lucrative commerce of the East Indies and of the busy Netherlands he utilized in the interests of Spain. The soldiers of the Spanish infantry were the best foot soldiers of the sixteenth century. Philip II was also a firm believer in the divine rights of monarchy. Ignoring the Cortes and the local rights of Aragon and tending personally to the myriads of details of government, the meticulous and stubborn Philip brought Spain under his sway to an extent that Ferdinand and Isabella and Charles V had never been able to do. Little wonder that the king of Spain was the most feared man in Western Christendom.

More important even than Spain in the mind of Philip II, however, was the Roman Catholic Church. He conceived it to be his chief mission in life to use the great wealth and power of Spain to restore the dominion of the Roman Church over all of Western Christendom. In the Netherlands, in England, and in France, Philip II threw the might of Spain on the side of the Roman Catholics in their counteroffensive against the Protestants.

Religion was only the chief among many causes of the revolt of the Netherlands against Spanish rule. Philip II, unlike his father, Charles V, was considered by the Netherlanders to be an unsympathetic foreigner who taxed their prosperous commerce and industry for the benefit of Spain. The absolutist monarch and his Spanish administrators also overrode the traditional political privileges of the nobles and the cities in the Netherlands. Nonetheless, religion was the first and foremost cause of dissension. Although the southern (Belgian) provinces of the Netherlands remained pre-

dominantly Roman Catholic, the northern (Dutch) provinces had by mid-sixteenth century become strongly Calvinist. Philip II, who would tolerate no heresy in his empire, took stern measures to stamp out Dutch Protestantism. The Inquisition was used to enforce the laws against heresy, and twelve new Roman Catholic bishoprics were added. In 1566 four hundred of the leading noblemen of the Netherlands presented a list of grievances to Philip's regent. When no relief was forthcoming, bands of Protestants began to deface Roman Catholic churches. Philip thereupon dispatched the Duke of Alva with 10,000 Spanish soldiers to reduce the Netherlands to submission. A six-year reign of terror followed. Thousands were put to death.

Far from being cowed, however, the Netherlands flew to arms. They found a brilliant leader in William of Orange, or William the Silent, as he came to be known. They took to the sea, playing havoc with Spanish commerce and communications. When, in 1580, Philip conquered and annexed Portugal, the hardy Dutch "Sea Beggars" seized the richest parts of the Portuguese Empire in the East Indies. In 1579 the ten Roman Catholic southern provinces, fearful of the growing power of the Protestant northern provinces, submitted to the Spanish yoke. The seven Calvinist northern (Dutch) provinces, however, banded together in the Union of Utrecht and continued the struggle for independence with renewed vigor. When in 1584 William the Silent was assassinated by a hireling of Philip II, other able leaders arose to take his place. Finally in 1609, eleven years after Philip's own death, Spain agreed to a twelve-year truce, and in 1648 Spain recognized the complete independence of the Dutch Netherlands, as the seven northern provinces are commonly called. The Dutch struggle for independence was heroic, bearing a strong resemblance to the revolution of the thirteen American colonies two centuries later. In the seventeenth century the little Dutch republic led the world in commerce and in painting and was second to none in science and philosophy.

[1] Sixty years later Portugal regained her independence.

Thus Philip II's crusade in the Netherlands was only partly successful. He saved the southern provinces for Spain for another century, and for the Roman Catholic Church, but the Dutch provinces were lost both to Spain and to the Church.

Most grandiose of all of Philip II's crusading efforts was his attempt to restore wayward England to the Roman Catholic fold. His first move was to marry England's Roman Catholic queen, Mary Tudor. This was done in 1554, two years before he began his own rule over the Spanish Empire. However, Mary's marriage to the king of a feared and hated rival power and her bloody persecutions of English Protestants only increased her own unpopularity and that of the Roman Catholic cause in England. Moreover, the marriage failed to produce a Roman Catholic heir. When unhappy Mary died in 1558, Philip sought to continue his influence in England by trying to marry her successor, Elizabeth. But Elizabeth was a Protestant and a high-spirited English patriot. She cleverly put off her dangerous Spanish suitor and eventually spurned him outright. Not to be deterred in his scheme to gain control of England, Philip, some years later, plotted the assassination of Elizabeth. Next in line for the English throne after Elizabeth was Roman Catholic Mary Stuart (Queen of Scots). Having been driven from Scotland by her Calvinist subjects, Mary threw herself on Elizabeth's mercy and was kept under detention. Only Elizabeth, then, stood between the English throne and another Roman Catholic queen. When Elizabeth discovered that Mary Stuart was a willing accomplice to Philip II's assassination plots, she at long last (1587) had her Scottish cousin beheaded. Meanwhile, Elizabeth was aiding the Dutch Protestant rebels and encouraging English sea dogs to plunder Spain's treasure ships sailing from her New World colonies—indeed, to plunder the colonies themselves.

When Philip II learned of the death of his candidate for the English throne, Mary Stuart, he undertook to conquer England with the Invincible Armada. In 1588 the Armada sailed forth—130 great galleons. It was to go first to the Netherlands, pick up an additional army of Spanish veterans, and transport them to England. The Spanish galleons were really ponderous armed transports. In the English Channel they met a somewhat larger number of smaller but swifter and more heavily armed English ships. The battle was really a massacre. The maneuvering English ships poured death and destruction into the almost helpless Spanish transports. Fire and storm added to the catastrophe. Less than a third of the ships ever reached Spain by way of northern Scotland, whither they had fled. In this battle England began to wrest the control of the seas from Spain. Philip II had not only failed to exterminate Protestantism in England, but the Roman Catholic cause there was now tainted with treason, and Protestantism was stronger than ever.

Philip II found it more profitable to crusade against the Moslem Turks than against the Protestants. In fact one of the few clear-cut successes of his career was the great naval victory over the Turks at Lepanto. Under the urging of the pope Venice, Genoa, and Spain amassed a fleet of more than two hundred vessels under the command of Philip's illegitimate half brother, Don Juan. In 1571 this fleet caught and annihilated the somewhat larger Turkish fleet off Lepanto on the coast of Greece. Never again were the Turks to menace Christendom by sea.

5. The Religious Wars in France

In France and Germany the Roman Catholic counteroffensive against Protestantism resulted in bitter religious wars in the late sixteenth and early seventeenth centuries. Crusading Spain participated in these wars, but here her role was relatively minor and indecisive. In France, Calvinism had made slow but steady progress during the reigns of Francis I (1515–47) and Henry II (1547–59) in spite of vigorous persecution by those Roman Catholic monarchs. By 1559 the Huguenots, as the French Calvinists were called, numbered possibly a tenth of the total population. However, since their ranks were made up largely of the prosperous bourgeoisie and the nobility, their influence was far greater than their numbers would indicate. Enmity between the Huguenots and the Roman Catholics, which had smoldered under the strong rule of Francis I and of Henry II, broke into open and consuming flame under Henry II's three weakling sons, who ruled in succession from 1559 to 1589. All three were dominated by their unscrupulous and ambitious mother, Catherine de Médicis. This situation invited political as well as religious faction and intrigue, and in the civil wars that followed politics and religion were intertwined.

The leadership of the Roman Catholic faction was assumed by the powerful Guise family; that of the Protestants by the influential Bourbon family, who were related to the royal line. The first eight years of fighting were ended in 1570 by an uneasy truce. However, Catherine de Médicis, fearful of the growing influence of the Huguenots, decided to exterminate them all. She was, of course, supported and urged on by the Guises. At a given signal at midnight, August 24, 1572 (St. Bartholomew's Day), the Roman Catholics in Paris fell to slaughtering the Protestants. The massacre soon spread to the provinces and went on for weeks. Thousands of Huguenots were slain. When news of the Massacre of St. Bartholomew reached Madrid, Philip II, who seldom smiled, smiled.

The ablest of the Huguenot leaders, young Henry (Bourbon) of Navarre, escaped and rallied the remaining Protestant forces for the war that was now renewed in earnest. The wealth and energy of the middle-class Huguenots, plus the brilliance of their dashing young leader, offset the superior numbers of the Roman Catholics. Eventually Henry III, the third son of Catherine de Médicis to rule France, organized a moderate Roman Catholic faction to stand between the uncompromising Guise faction and the Protestants. The struggle now became a three-cornered "War of the Three Henrys" (Henry, duke of Guise, Henry

of Navarre, and Henry III, king of France). Philip II of Spain threw his support to Henry, duke of Guise. Henry III, now regarding Henry, duke of Guise, as the greater menace to his own royal authority, had him assassinated in 1588. The next year an agent of the Guises assassinated Henry III. This left Protestant Henry of Navarre, by right of succession, King Henry IV of France. However, it was only when he abjured Protestantism four years later and went through the formality of becoming a Roman Catholic that the great majority of his subjects, who were Roman Catholics, allowed him to enter Paris and be legally crowned. "Paris is worth a Mass," he is alleged to have remarked. Five years later (1598) he issued his famous Edict of Nantes (see p. 388), which by granting toleration to the Protestant minority ended religious strife in France for nearly a century.

6. The Thirty Years' War in Germany

The Peace of Augsburg, 1555, which had brought to a close the first armed conflict in Germany between the Roman Catholics and the Lutherans, proved to be only an uneasy truce. Since the signing of the treaty, which recognized only Roman Catholics and Lutherans, the Calvinists had made strong headway in several states of the Holy Roman Empire and demanded equal recognition. Furthermore, lands of the Roman Catholic Church were constantly being secularized in Protestant areas in the Germanies in violation of the treaty. On the other hand, the Roman Catholics, becoming more aggressive as a result of the clarification of their position by the Council of Trent and the activities of the militant Jesuit Society, dreamed of exterminating Protestantism in the Holy Roman Empire and recovering all their lost lands and souls. The Protestants in alarm formed a defensive league. The Roman Catholics countered by forming a league of their own.

The increasing tension finally erupted into the Thirty Years' War (1618–48). In this war the religious issue was complicated

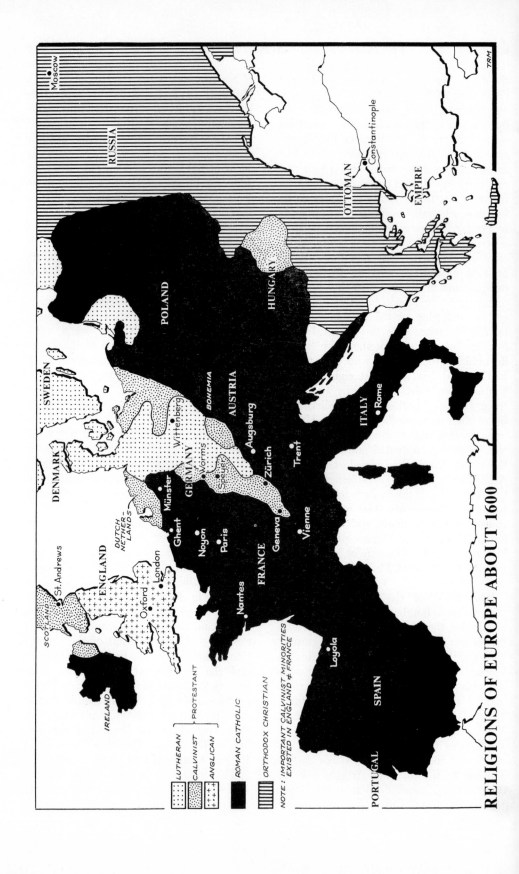

RELIGIONS OF EUROPE ABOUT 1600

LUTHERAN

CALVINIST   PROTESTANT

ANGLICAN

ROMAN CATHOLIC

ORTHODOX CHRISTIAN

NOTE: IMPORTANT CALVINIST MINORITIES
EXISTED IN ENGLAND ≠ FRANCE

Moscow

RUSSIA

Constantinople

OTTOMAN   EMPIRE

POLAND

HUNGARY

SWEDEN

BOHEMIA

AUSTRIA

DENMARK

Wittenberg

Augsburg

Worms

Speyer

Zürich

ITALY   •Rome

Trent

DUTCH-
NETHER-
LANDS

Münster

GERMANY

Ghent

Noyon

Paris

Geneva

Vienne

SCOTLAND

St. Andrews

ENGLAND

Oxford

London

FRANCE

Nantes

IRELAND

Loyola

SPAIN

PORTUGAL

TRM

and often confused by political and dynastic issues. The individual princes of the empire were struggling to maintain or even increase their independence of the emperor. The Hapsburg dynasty, both Austrian and Spanish, threatened to become so powerful that the apprehensive Bourbons of France entered the war against them. The upshot was that eventually the Roman Catholics, the Holy Roman Emperor, and the Hapsburg dynasty (the emperor was an Austrian Hapsburg) formed one faction against which were arrayed the Protestants, most of the individual princes of the Holy Roman Empire, and the Bourbons.

The long-brewing Thirty Years' War began in 1618 when a group of Bohemian noblemen, mostly Calvinists and fearful of losing both their religious and their political rights, declared their Hapsburg ruler deposed and chose the Calvinist elector of the Palatinate as their king. The Hapsburg Holy Roman Emperor, aided by the Roman Catholic League and by Hapsburg and Roman Catholic Spain, took the field and easily crushed both Bohemia and the Palatinate. Hundreds of Calvinist Bohemian noblemen were executed and their property confiscated. Protestantism was outlawed in Bohemia. The Calvinist Palatinate was annexed to Roman Catholic Bavaria. This quick and crushing victory by Roman Catholic and Imperial forces frightened not only the Protestant princes of northern Germany but also the Protestant neighboring states.

In 1625 Lutheran King Christian IV of Denmark, who held in Germany numerous bishoprics that had been illegally secularized, entered the war against the Roman Catholic and imperial forces. Christian IV was aided by English subsidies and numerous German Protestant princes. At this critical juncture a brilliant soldier of fortune, Albrecht von Wallenstein, offered his services to the emperor. This military genius raised a volunteer army of 50,000 adventurers of various nationalities whose only motivation was hope of plunder. Wallenstein's army, together with the regular imperial and Roman Catholic forces, de-

feated Christian IV and drove him out of Germany. The Danish king was deprived of all his German holdings except the duchy of Holstein. Upon the conclusion of this phase of the war in 1629 the victorious emperor issued the Edict of Restitution, restoring to the Roman Catholic Church all the lands illegally secularized since the Peace of Augsburg—more than a hundred tracts, large and small.

The whole Protestant world was now genuinely alarmed at the resurgent power of the Roman Catholics. The German princes were faced with the loss of their powers to the Holy Roman Emperor. The French Bourbons were concerned about the rapidly growing strength of the Hapsburgs. At this juncture another Protestant champion stepped forward—Gustavus Adolphus of Sweden. This Lutheran "Lion of the North" was a military leader of great ability. Furthermore, he was well backed by French gold; Cardinal Richelieu, who was then at the helm of the French government, placed the interests of his Bourbon masters above those of his church. Gustavus Adolphus marched and fought victoriously through the Germanies, gaining allies among the Protestant princes as he went. The Hapsburg emperor hastily recalled the ambitious Wallenstein, whom he had dismissed upon the conclusion of the Danish phase of the war. Two of the ablest military commanders of early modern times now faced each other. In the battle of Lützen (1632) Wallenstein was defeated, but Gustavus Adolphus had been killed and the victory was far from decisive. Fortunately for the Protestants, Wallenstein was dismissed and assassinated two years later. Since the Swedes had failed to turn the tide of the war, Richelieu in 1635 threw the full weight of France's military might directly into the fray. For thirteen more years the war dragged on until all participants were exhausted. The Treaty of Westphalia in 1648 finally brought the dismal struggle to a close.

In general, thanks largely to the intervention of France, the Roman Catholics, the

EUROPE
1648

AUSTRIAN HAPSBURGS

SPANISH MONARCHY

SWEDISH DOMINIONS

BRANDENBURG-PRUSSIA

CHURCH LANDS

SHETLAND IS.

Bergen

NORWAY

ORKNEY IS.

SCOTLAND

KINGDOM OF
DENMARK
AND
NORWAY

Edinburgh

NORTH SEA

DEN

SCHLESWIG

Belfast

IRELAND

ENGLAND

COMMONWEALTH,
1649-1660
UNITED KINGDOM,
1707

BOUNDARY OF
HOLY ROMAN
EMPIRE

HOLSTEIN
(SW.)

Dublin

Liverpool

UNITED
PROVINCES

Bremen

Ham

HANOVER

MINOR

GERMAN

STATES

Bristol

London

Amsterdam

Ryswick

Utrecht

Münster

Brussels
SPAN.

Cologne

ATLANTIC

ENGLISH CHANNEL

Rouen

NETH.

Trier

Metz PALAT.

Mainz

OCEAN

Rennes

Paris

LORRAINE

Strasburg

BA

Au

Nantes

Orleans

FRANCE

SWISS
CANTONS

Bordeaux

Lyons

SAVOY

PIEDMONT

Milan

REP.

Parma

Corunna

León

Montauban

Avignon

Genoa

Fl

TUSC

Oporto

NAVARRE

PYRENEES

Marseilles

CORSICA
(GENOA)

PORTUGAL
TO SPAIN, 1580-1640

Valladolid

Saragossa

ARAGON

CATALONIA

Lisbon

Escorial

Madrid

Barcelona

SAR-
DINIA

Mérida

Toledo

CASTILE

SPAIN

Valencia

BALEARIC IS.

MINORCA

MAJORCA

Seville

Murcia

MED

Malaga

Cadiz

Tangier
(PORT.)

GIBRALTAR

Ceuta
(SP.)

Algiers

Oran (SP.)

Tunis

FEZ
AND
MOROCCO

ALGERIA
(TURKISH)

TUNISIA
(TURKISH)

BARBARY STATES

TRM

SWEDEN

FINLAND

LAKE
LADOGA

R U S S I A

Helsingfors

INGRIA

Novgorod

Stockholm

ESTONIA

LIVONIA

VOLGA R.

Moscow

Riga

BALTIC SEA

COURLAND

Smolensk

BRANDENBURG-
PRUSSIA

EAST
PRUSSIA

LITHUANIA

tralsund

Danzig

Minsk

MERANIA

Stettin

POLAND

GREAT
POLAND

VISTULA R.

ODER R.

Warsaw

Kiev

Breslau

LITTLE
POLAND

DNIEPER R.

Prague

SILESIA

Cracow

Lemberg

GALICIA

PODOLIA

EMIA

CARPATHIA

DNIESTER R.

MORAVIA

YEDISAN

AUSTRIA

Vienna

ALPS

MOLDAVIA

BESSARABIA

CRIMEA

Budapest

H U N G A R Y

TRANSYLVANIA

K.H.K.

SLAVONIA

DANUBE R.

WALLACHIA

Bucharest

DOBRUJA

BLACK SEA

BOSNIA

Belgrade

DANUBE R.

SERBIA

Zara

OTTOMAN   EMPIRE

PAL
TES

MONTE-
NEGRO

BULGARIA

quila

ADRIATIC SEA

NAPLES

Naples

Bari

ALBANIA

RUMELIA

Constantinople

Salonica

DOM OF THE
SICILIES

IONIAN
IS.
(VENICE)

AEGEAN
SEA

GREECE

Smyrna

Athens

SICILY

I O N I A N   S E A

RHODES
(TURKISH)

CYPRUS
(TURKISH)

MALTA
(SP)

CRETE
(VENICE)

500 MILES

Holy Roman Emperor, and the Hapsburgs suffered a setback. Not only were the Roman Catholics thwarted in their efforts to exterminate Protestantism in the Germanies, but the Calvinists now gained equal status with the Lutherans and Roman Catholics in the Holy Roman Empire. The Edict of Restitution was nullified. The Holy Roman Empire practically fell apart. According to the terms of the Treaty of Westphalia, each of the more than three hundred individual princes could now make his own treaties. Three of the most important princes, the rulers of Brandenburg, Bavaria, and Saxony, made sizable additions to their territories. Sweden gained strategic territories along the German Baltic and North Sea coasts. France gained the important bishoprics and fortress cities of Metz, Toul, and Verdun, and the province of Alsace except for the free city of Strasbourg. These former imperial territories gave both Sweden and France a vote in the Diet of the Holy Roman Empire and a say in German affairs. The complete independence of Switzerland and the Dutch Netherlands was officially recognized. The Austrian Hapsburgs retained their hereditary possessions but lost prestige as emperors of the decrepit Holy Roman Empire. Also, their relative position declined as that of France rose. The Spanish Hapsburgs fared worse. After eleven more years of fighting with France they yielded a strip of the southern Netherlands and the Spanish border province of Roussillon to France. Spain's days of greatness were finished.

The immediate effect of the Thirty Years' War on the Germanies was disastrous. For three decades hostile German and foreign armies had tramped back and forth across Germany, killing, raping, and looting the defenseless inhabitants. In the wake of Wallenstein's army of 50,000, for instance, swarmed 150,000 camp followers bent on plunder. To the usual horrors of war was added religious fanaticism. Many years would be required for Germany to recover from these wounds.

The Thirty Years' War was the last and the bloodiest of the religious wars that accompanied the Roman Catholic Reformation. Although much religious strife and controversy still lay ahead, the religious map of Europe henceforth would change very little. In a real sense, then, 1648 marked the end of the era of the Protestant and Roman Catholic reformations. The Roman Catholic Church, by closing ranks, setting its house in order, and availing itself of the militant Jesuit Society, had checked the further spread of Protestantism in Europe but had been able to win back relatively little that had been lost. Western Christendom was now definitely split into two irreconcilable camps—Roman Catholic and Protestant. For many years after 1648 political rather than religious affairs would occupy the center of the stage in the Western world.

SUGGESTED READING

Pierre Janelle, *The Catholic Reformation* (1949). A sympathetic Roman Catholic account.

Paul Van Dyke, *Ignatius Loyola, the Founder of the Jesuits* (1926). A good biography of the most dynamic personality of the Roman Catholic Reformation.

H. C. Lea, *History of the Inquisition in Spain*, 4 vols. (1906–7). A classic on the subject. Scholarly and colorful.

* J. E. Neale, *Queen Elizabeth I* (Anchor). One of the best biographies of England's glamorous queen, who successfully resisted the advances of Catholic Spain.

Franklin Palm, *Calvinism and the Religious Wars* (1932). A good brief account of the religious wars in France.

J. L. Motley, *Rise of the Dutch Republic*, 3 vols. (1877). Brilliant account of the heroic struggle of the Dutch for independence.

Ruth Putnam, *William the Silent*, 2 vols. (1911). An excellent biography of the George Washington of the Dutch Netherlands.

C. V. Wedgwood, *The Thirty Years' War* (1938). Sound scholarship and good writing. Miss Wedgwood believes that the destructiveness of the Thirty Years' War in Germany has been greatly exaggerated by earlier historians.

SECTION 8

The Age of Royal Absolutism—

Seventeenth and Eighteenth Centuries

As we have seen, the kings of Spain, Portugal, France, and England gained the ascendancy over the feudal nobility in the late fifteenth century and welded the first four national states around their own persons. The trend toward absolute monarchy reached its peak in Spain and England in the sixteenth century; in most of the rest of Europe, particularly France, Prussia, and Russia, in the seventeenth and and eighteenth centuries. In general, the seventeenth was the century par excellence for royal absolutism, both in theory and practice. The reign of Louis XIV in France served as the perfect model. Among the major powers only England failed to follow the seventeenth-century pattern of royal absolutism. There Parliament, dominated by commercial interests, frustrated the absolutist ambitions of the Stuart kings and established its own supremacy.

France enjoyed hegemony in Europe throughout most of the seventeenth and eighteenth centuries. However, after a bitter struggle in the eighteenth century, she was forced to yield supremacy in India and North America to England, and her leadership in Europe was somewhat dimmed. The eighteenth century is also important as the period marking the rise in Central and Eastern Europe of two new military despotisms—Prussia and Russia.

The prestige enjoyed by the royalty and the aristocracy in this period was reflected in the classical literature and music, and the baroque painting, sculpture, and architecture.

CHAPTER 33

The Dominance of France: The Age of Louis XIV

FRANCE was the dominant nation in Europe throughout most of the seventeenth and eighteenth centuries, and the reign of Louis XIV represented the height of royal absolutism. All other monarchs strove to emulate the Sun King. The well-lighted stage across which he strode was set for him by three able predecessors—Henry IV, Richelieu, and Mazarin.

1. The Rise of France Under Henry IV, Richelieu, and Mazarin

When *Henry IV* became king of France in 1589, his country was torn and bleeding from a quarter century of bitter religious war. Respect for law and order had broken down. The feudal nobility had in many cases reasserted its own authority. The finances of the central government were in chaos. Roads and bridges were in disrepair. French prestige abroad was at a low ebb; even the city of Paris was garrisoned by the Spanish troops of Philip II.

Henry of Navarre, the first of the Bourbon dynasty to rule France, set out to change all this. The vigorous new king, now at his prime at the age of thirty-six, was debonair and witty, courageous, generous, and optimistic, and democratic in his social life. His slogan, "A chicken in the pot of every peasant for Sunday dinner," was more

than an idle phrase. Little wonder that *Henri Quatre* became the most popular monarch in French history. The romantic Henry had in the duke of Sully an able, methodical work horse to serve and to steady him. The most urgent task confronting Henry IV was to restore the authority of the central government. This he set out to do by vigorously suppressing brigandage and enforcing the law. The lesser nobility was brought to heel directly and quickly. The powerful nobility was dealt with more gingerly, but by the end of Henry's reign real headway had been made toward reducing the nobles to obedience to the central government.

Henry and Sully launched a comprehensive program of economic reconstruction. Agriculture and commerce benefited from the increased security of life and property, from the repair of roads, bridges, and harbors, and from the freeing of internal and external commerce of many obstructions and tariff barriers. Marshes were drained for farming. Better breeding methods were introduced. The peasants' livestock and implements were protected against seizure for debt or taxes. New industries producing glass, porcelain, lace, tapestries, and fine leather and textiles were subsidized and protected by the state. Silk culture, which has brought vast wealth to France, was introduced. In 1608 Champlain founded Quebec, the first French colony in the New World.

When Henry IV came to the throne, the government was in debt and the budget out of balance. Only about one fourth of the heavy taxes, from which the clergy and

CARDINAL RICHELIEU, BY CHAMPAIGNE. The imperious and ruthless Richelieu played a major role in making the royal power supreme in France, and France the supreme power in Europe. (*Archives Photographiques, Paris*)

the nobility were largely exempted, ever reached the national treasury. The rest fell into the pockets of the grafters and the tax farmers, i.e., the collectors who bid a fixed sum for the privilege of collecting the taxes and were permitted to keep all the money collected over and above the contracted amount. Sully was unable to change this vicious system, but he cleaned it up. By means of careful bookkeeping, efficient administration of expenditures, and elimination of corruption, he was able to show a surplus for the first time in many years.

Another major achievement of Henry's reign was the granting of religious toleration to the Huguenot minority. Although Henry abjured Protestantism in order to gain the acceptance of his nation, which was overwhelmingly Roman Catholic, the sympathy and probably the faith of this former leader of the Huguenots remained with the Calvinist minority. The Edict of Nantes, which Henry IV issued in 1598, granted not only complete freedom of conscience and limited public worship to the Huguenots but also civil and political equality. Moreover, they were given military control of some two hundred fortified cities and towns as a guarantee against future oppression. The Edict of Nantes stands as a handsome monument in the bloody and endless struggle for religious freedom—probably the most precious of civilization's possessions. It antedates the work of Roger Williams in Rhode Island by thirty-eight years.

Having laid the foundations for royal supremacy, economic health, and religious toleration, Henry IV devoted in the last years of his reign an increasing amount of attention to foreign affairs. He talked vaguely from time to time about a sort of league of nations for perpetual peace, but nothing came of it. His specific goal was to make France first secure and then supreme in Europe by weakening the power of the Spanish and Austrian Hapsburgs. He readied his armies for attack, but just as he was preparing to join them he was assassinated (1610) by a fanatical Roman Catholic who doubted his orthodoxy.

After fourteen years of retrogression under Henry IV's Italian wife, Marie de Médicis, and their young and inept son Louis XIII, *Cardinal Richelieu* gained active control over the government of France. Although technically a mere servant of the fickle Louis XIII, the masterful cardinal made himself so indispensable that for eighteen years (1624-42) he held firm control over French affairs. Handsome with his chiseled features, regal bearing, and red robes, Richelieu was a true Machiavellian —his heart as hard as flint. His twofold policy, from which he never veered, was to make the royal power supreme in France and France supreme in Europe.

Believing the high nobility and the Huguenots to be the chief threats to royal absolutism, Richelieu crushed them both. He boldly destroyed the castles of the nobles who remained defiant, disbanded their private armies, and hanged a number of the most recalcitrant. The special military and political privileges that the Huguenots enjoyed under the Edict of Nantes were considered by Richelieu to be intolerable, giving them the status of a state within a state. After a bloody two-year struggle he stripped the Huguenots of their military and political privileges, although he left their religious and civil liberties intact.

In order to by-pass all local political influence, which in some provinces was still strong, the dynamic minister divided all France into some thirty administrative districts called *généralités*, each of which was placed under the control of an *intendant*,[1] who was an agent of the crown. So absolute was the power of the intendants over local affairs, even of the most minute nature, that they soon came to be called the "thirty tyrants of France." They were chosen from the ranks of the bourgeoisie and were shifted around frequently lest they become too sympathetic with the people over whom they ruled. Thus was the absolute royal will extended to every nook and cranny of France.

Although Richelieu was a cardinal in the Roman Catholic Church, he did not hesitate to plunge France into the Thirty Years' War in Germany on the side of the Protestants. His purpose, of course, was to weaken the Hapsburgs, the chief rivals of the French Bourbons for European supremacy. As a result of Richelieu's intervention Protestantism in Germany was probably saved from extermination at the hands of the Roman Catholics, but the Hapsburgs were humiliated. When Richelieu died in 1642,

[1] The *intendants* existed before Richelieu's time, but he greatly increased their power and functions.

he had gone far toward bringing to fruition Henry IV's policies of royal supremacy in France and French supremacy in Europe. Richelieu, however, did not share Henry IV's concern for the common people. Their lot became harder under the imperious and ruthless cardinal. They rejoiced at the news of his death. And twentieth-century France is still saddled with an excessively centralized and bureaucratic administrative system whose agents are entrenched and ofttimes self-seeking—a system that owes much of its origin to Richelieu.

Richelieu was succeeded at the helm of the French ship of state by his protégé, *Cardinal Mazarin.* Louis XIII's death in 1643, one year after that of his great minister, Richelieu, left the throne to Louis XIV, a child of four. Mazarin played the same role in the early reign of Louis XIV that Richelieu had played during most of the reign of Louis XIII. From the death of Richelieu in 1642 until his own death in 1661 Mazarin vigorously pursued the policies of his predecessor. The Thirty Years' War was brought to a successful conclusion. All who opposed or challenged the absolute authority of the crown were summarily crushed.

Although the policies were the same, the methods of carrying them out were quite different. Whereas Richelieu was bold and forthright in dealing with even his most formidable enemies, the Italian-born Mazarin was treacherous, deceitful, and devious. He was hated even more intensely than Richelieu. The most noteworthy events during his administration were two uprisings, known as Frondes, against his tyranny. The Frondes were revolts of the disgruntled nobility, supported by various other rebellious elements, against the ever-increasing authority of the central government. At times it looked as if the rebels might succeed, but the crafty Mazarin was too much for them. The failure of the Frondes marked the last overt resistance to royal absolutism in France until the French Revolution in 1789. When Cardinal Mazarin died in 1661, he passed along to young Louis XIV a royal power that was at last absolute and a national state that was easily the first power of Europe.

2. Louis XIV and His Government

Louis XIV was twenty-three years of age when, in 1661, he stepped forth as the principal actor on the world's gaudiest stage— a stage set for him by Henry IV, Richelieu, and Mazarin. Young Louis was well fitted for the part. He had a sound body and a regal bearing. His lack of brilliance and of deep learning was more than offset by his large store of common sense, sharp memory, sense of responsibility, and capacity for hard, tedious work. From his Spanish mother, from Mazarin, and from his tutors he had gained the conviction that he was God's appointed vicegerent for France. In Bishop Bossuet he had at hand the most famous of all theorists and exponents of royal absolutism. Bossuet in numerous writings argued that absolute monarchy is the normal, the most efficient, the best, and the divinely ordained form of government for men. Furthermore, the royal monarch, the image of God and directly inspired by God, is above human reproach and accountable to God alone. These ideas were the culmination of the thinking of James I of England a half century earlier. As acted out by Louis le Grand they gained and held the ascendancy throughout the continent of Europe, and indeed far beyond the confines of Europe, during the late seventeenth and most of the eighteenth century.

Although Louis considered himself to be the state, he could not possibly perform all the functions of government personally, try as hard as he might. (The words *"L'état, c'est moi"* [I am the state] are often attributed to him.) Actually the great bulk of the decisions and details of government were handled by a series of councils and bureaus, and administered locally by the intendants. The functions of the chief councils, such as those of state, finances, dispatches, and the privy council, appear on paper to have been overlapping and ill-defined. As supervised by the industrious Louis XIV, however, the

system worked smoothly and efficiently. In fact it was the envy of his fellow monarchs and probably constituted his most constructive achievement. In the government of Louis XIV there was no semblance of popular participation. The role of the people was to serve and obey; in return they enjoyed reflected glory and received such benefits as the monarch might be willing and able to bestow upon them. The Estates-General was not called once during the seventy-two years of Louis XIV's reign or the fifty-nine-year rule of his successor.

3. Versailles

In line with Louis XIV's concept of divine-right absolutism he believed that he should have a palace worthy of God's chief vicegerent on earth. Hating tumultous Paris, congested and crowded with vulgar tradesmen, he selected Versailles, eleven miles southwest of the city, to be the new seat of government. There as many as thirty-five thousand workmen toiled for thirty years, turning the marshes and sandy wastes into the world's most splendid court. The cost was so staggering that Louis destroyed the records. The greatest artists in the land were employed in the creation of the palace and the grounds. The most costly marbles, glass, tapestries, paintings, and inlaid woods were used in profusion in the ornate baroque style of the period. Hundreds of acres of gardens, parks, walks, canals, and artificial lakes were laid out with mathematical precision. Playing fountains and myriads of marble statues formalized the landscape.

Around his court Louis XIV gathered the great nobles of France. Henry IV, Richelieu, and Mazarin had broken their power; Louis XIV turned them into court butterflies. The inevitable jostling for the king's attention, which was the one source of preferment, and the conflicting claims of so much titled rank necessitated the drawing up of an elaborate code of etiquette. The king was dressed and undressed, bathed, and fed by the highest noblemen in the land—all in strict ritual. The household

MOLIÈRE DINING WITH LOUIS XIV, BY GÉRÔME. Under Louis XIV royal absolutism and splendor reached a height never before or since achieved in Europe. The royal court at Versailles was not all glitter, however. Pictured here is a scene typical of France's "golden age" of classical literature and baroque art, when Louis XIV patronized many of the leading writers and artists. (*The Bettmann Archive*)

personnel consisted of ten thousand soldiers in brilliant uniforms and four thousand civilians. Little wonder that all the world's other monarchs were awed and that many attempted to imitate in miniature *Le Roi Soleil* (the Sun King). Nor was the pageant of Versailles mere glitter alone. Louis XIV subsidized or gathered around himself the leading French artists and literary figures. Mansard the architect and Lebrun the painter were the chief designer and decorator respectively of the palace. Corneille, Racine, Molière, La Fontaine, La Rochefoucauld, Saint-Simon, and Madame de Sévigné made Louis XIV's reign the golden age of French literature. (Their work will be discussed in Chapter 37.)

But there was a reverse side to the coin. The chateau was a show place, not a comfortable home for the king. It was cold, drafty, and inconvenient. The balls, parades, hunts, and social ritual were not sufficient to absorb the energy of the vivacious and ambitious nobility of France. The court seethed with gossip, scandal, and intrigue. Nor did the hard-toiling, heavily taxed French masses, who were supposed to enjoy the reflected glory of the monarch, always appreciate such extravagant glamour. Indeed, expressions of discontent were heard with increasing frequency.

4. Colbert and the French Economy

Louis XIV was fortunate to have at his command during the first half of his reign a prodigious manager of the nation's finances and economy. Jean Baptiste Colbert was an inordinately ambitious social climber who realized that, because of his bourgeois origin, his only means of advancement was through indispensable service to the king. An engine of efficiency, he toiled from dawn till dark, supervising the myriads of details of the French economy.

Colbert's first and probably his most difficult task was to balance the national budget, which had become badly unbalanced under Richelieu and Mazarin. The careful accounting of receipts and expenditures that Sully had inaugurated three quarters of a century earlier was resumed. Some of the debts that the government had contracted at extortionate rates of interest were canceled; on others the rates were reduced. Colbert, however, like Sully before him, was unable to change the pernicious system of tax farming. He had to be content with discharging and punishing the dishonest tax collectors. Neither was he able to abolish all internal customs duties, although he did free a large block of territory around Paris from these crippling barriers to commerce.

With Colbert mercantilism reached its peak. French industries were protected by prohibitive tariffs, while exports and new industries were subsidized. Raw materials, however, were strictly husbanded in France. Imperial and commercial activities in India and the vast interior of North America were vigorously promoted. It was at this time that Marquette, Joliet, and La Salle explored the Great Lakes and the Mississippi Valley for France. To protect this growing empire and the commerce with it, a large navy was built. But Colbert did not stop with these traditional mercantilist practices. In order to gain a world-wide reputation for the uniformly high quality of French products, all manufacturing was subjected to the most minute regulation and supervision. So many threads of such and such quality and color must go into every inch of this textile and that lace. A veritable army of inspectors enforced the regulations. This phase of mercantilism has come to be called Colbertism. It achieved its immediate end so far as quality and reputation were concerned, but it stifled initiative and retarded future industrial development. That Colbert was able to balance the budget and achieve general economic prosperity in the face of Louis XIV's lavish expenditures, including the building of Versailles, was a remarkable feat. It is well, however, that Colbert died in 1683, for the wars of aggression of Louis's later reign wrecked most of the great minister's work. With the exception of the Nether-

lands practically all of Europe copied Colbert's policies and techniques during the latter part of the seventeenth and most of the eighteenth centuries. This extreme mercantilism was the economic phase of royal absolutism.

5. Absolutism and Religion

It was virtually inevitable that Louis XIV's concepts of divine-right monarchy would have religious repercussions. First of all they ran counter to the claims of the pope. All his life Louis considered himself to be devoutly loyal to the Roman Catholic faith, as were the majority of his subjects. But when it came to matters of church administration—matters so important in French government and society—Louis was not willing to have his royal authority limited, even by Rome. Numerous conflicts between king and pope led to the calling of a great council of the French clergy in 1682. This council, under the domination of Bishop Bossuet, faithful servant of Louis XIV and famed exponent of the theory of royal absolutism, drew up a statement of *Gallican Liberties*, special privileges or freedoms of the French church from Roman domination. These were in essence: 1. A church council is superior to the pope. 2. The pope's jurisdiction is supreme only in matters of faith, and his rulings even here are applicable in France only after they have been accepted by the French clergy. 3. The traditional customs and practices of the French church shall be respected. The *Gallican Liberties* brought the French church to a position close to that of the English church under Henry VIII. They might even have led to eventual separation from Rome had not Louis XIV in later life fallen increasingly under the influence of the Jesuits and his pious mistress, Madame de Maintenon, who were able to rekindle his loyalty to the pope.

Louis's absolutism also ran afoul the Jansenists, so called because they were followers of a Belgian bishop, Cornelius Jansen. This group represented a puritan movement within the Roman Catholic Church. They had no intention of breaking away from the Church, to which they considered themselves entirely loyal. It was their wish to return to the teachings and practices of the Church in the days of St. Augustine. They emphasized predestination, inner piety, and the ascetic life. A number of intellectuals and people of means were attracted to their ranks, including the dramatist Racine and the eminent mathematician and philosopher Blaise Pascal. At Port Royal near Versailles a group of prominent Jansenists practiced a communal life and established an excellent school that attracted much favorable attention. It was probably fear for the reputation of their own schools that aroused the jealousy of the Jesuits, militant watchdogs over Roman Catholic orthodoxy and papal supremacy. After a long and bitter controversy the pope was persuaded to declare Jansenism heretical, though no bill of particulars was ever presented. Eventually the Jesuits also aroused against the Jansenists the animosity of Louis XIV, who could tolerate no deviation from his own views even in matters of religion. He outlawed the sect and destroyed its buildings. However, he was unable to destroy Jansenism itself, which has continued to exist to the present time.

The chief religious victims of Louis XIV's absolutism were the Huguenots. Ever since Richelieu had removed the military and political privileges that the French Calvinists had enjoyed under the Edict of Nantes, the Huguenots had lived quietly as good French citizens, clinging unobtrusively to their Protestant faith. Although the Huguenots numbered not more than one tenth of the total population of France, most of them were industrious, prosperous, and highly educated members of the middle class. The Jesuits had little difficulty kindling the ire of Louis XIV against these heretical subjects who had the audacity to consider the king's religion not good enough for themselves. The Huguenots were subjected to one of the cruelest persecutions in the bloody history of religious intolerance.

Barbarous regular army troops were quartered in Huguenot homes and instructed to live licentiously. Students familiar only with twentieth-century civilian armies will need to reflect a little to realize the significance of this move. Whole Huguenot communities would abjure their faith at the approach of the troops. Finally in 1685 the Edict of Nantes was totally revoked and the Protestant religion was outlawed. Although Huguenots were forbidden to emigrate, many—probably a quarter million—succeeded in doing so, taking much of their wealth and all of their economic knowledge and skills with them. Not only were these industrious citizens, the backbone of French commercial and industrial life, lost to France, but they greatly strengthened enemies of France such as England, the Dutch Netherlands, and Brandenburg, who welcomed them. Forbidden to enter the underpopulated French colonies, many Huguenots helped to people the English colonies in America.

6. Louis XIV's Wars of Aggression

The Sun King was not content to remain merely the most awesome single monarch in the world. France was not big enough to satisfy his vanity, ever inflated by the constant flattery of his courtiers. He began to covet a wider domain. Louis's immediate and expressed goal was to extend his rule to France's natural frontiers. Since the French boundaries were already delimited by mountains and sea on every side but the northeast, it was in that direction that Louis looked for expansion. He claimed that only the Rhine River would provide France with an adequate natural strategic boundary on that side. This was, of course, pure fiction; Louis was undoubtedly seeking an excuse for aggression. River valleys unite rather than separate people. Nor have rivers ever proved to be effective military barriers. A glance at the map (p. 394) will quickly reveal that an advance to the Rhine would involve France in war with most of Europe. Between the French frontier and the Rhine

GROWTH OF FRANCE UNDER LOUIS XIV

FRANCE
BEFORE LOUIS XIV

ACQUISITIONS OF
LOUIS XIV,
1643–1715

lay the Spanish Netherlands, much of the
Dutch Netherlands, Holy Roman Imperial
territory involving the Austrian Hapsburgs,
and many German states, including some
holdings of Brandenburg. England, too,
would be threatened, and the balance of
power upset. Nevertheless, Louis XIV felt
himself equal to the task of challenging and
defeating all those powers.

Louis's war minister, Louvois, is often
considered the father of modern militarism.
Louvois organized France's huge military
establishment on a scientific and business-
like basis, replete with supply depots and
hospitals. He introduced strict discipline,
uniforms, and marching drill. Louis's other
military aides were also distinguished. Vauban was one of the great designers of fortifi-

cations and of siege operations. It was a common saying that a city defended by Vauban was safe and that a city besieged by Vauban was doomed. Condé was an able and dashing leader of men, and Turenne a masterly planner of campaigns and battles. No combination of enemies could match this array of talent, and no single adversary could come close to France in wealth and resources.

Between 1667 and 1713, Louis XIV fought four wars of aggression. The first is known as the War of Devolution. Trumping up the ridiculous claim that in accordance with local inheritance laws the Spanish (Belgian) Netherlands devolved upon his Spanish wife, Louis unceremoniously sent French armies in to conquer those rich provinces. Since Spanish power had declined rapidly since the glorious days of Charles V and Philip II, Louis's armies captured one fortress city after another. The Dutch, however, took alarm and formed an alliance with England and Sweden to check the French menace. This array of power in addition to Spain caused Louis to accept a peace that granted him only a slice of the whole of the Spanish Netherlands.

The frustrated Grand Monarch determined to punish the upstart Dutch. In the seventeenth century the Dutch Netherlands possessed the largest and the most profitable commerce of any nation in the world. Having won their independence from Spain near the end of the sixteenth century and having taken advantage of Portugal's temporary conquest by Philip II to seize the best part of the Portuguese Empire in the East, the Dutch soon became the envy of all their neighbors. The seventeenth century was also the century of Rembrandt, Grotius, and Spinoza—the golden age of Dutch culture (see Chapter 37). It required an all-out effort of the English by sea and of the French by land to end this amazing Dutch supremacy. The interference of the Lowlanders in French affairs, the great wealth of the Dutch Netherlands, and their location straddling the Rhine were sufficient in Louis XIV's mind to justify attack. Having

detached Charles II of England and the king of Sweden from the Dutch alliance with lavish bribes, Louis sent the huge French armies under Condé and Turenne into the Netherlands. The cause of the Dutch seemed hopeless. In desperation they cut their dykes. Large portions of their land were flooded, but the French were held at bay. Meanwhile the threatening power of France frightened Spain, the Holy Roman Emperor, Brandenburg, and several small German states into joining the Dutch in alliance. Louis XIV won many victories over the allies, but when the English Parliament forced Charles II to break his agreement with the French king and join the alliance against him, Louis XIV decided that the time had come to make peace. Again hapless Spain was the loser, giving up to France the long-coveted Franche-Comté (free county of Burgundy) and another strip of the Spanish Netherlands.

At the end of the Dutch War (1678) Louis XIV stood at the peak of his power. He had defeated all the greatest military powers on the Western European continent and had gained valuable territories. But the tide was about to turn. Turenne was killed near the end of the Dutch War, and the aged Condé retired at the end of war. No comparable generals were found to replace them. Colbert's hard-won surplus and balanced budget were now things of the past, and French economy was suffering. All Europe had become alarmed by French aggression. However, Louis XIV was not statesman enough to perceive the realities of the present, not to speak of the immediate future. His ever-growing appetite for power and glory had hardly been whetted.

No sooner had the Dutch War ended than the insatiable Grand Monarch began trumping up false claims to various territories on France's eastern frontier and sending in his armed forces to occupy them. The result was another defensive alliance against Louis XIV composed of the Dutch Netherlands, Spain, Sweden, the Holy Roman Emperor, and a number of small German states. The heart and soul of the alliance was William of Orange, stadholder of Holland, and when the redoubtable Dutchman became King William III of England after the Glorious Revolution of 1688, England, too, was brought into alliance against Louis. The alliance was called the League of Augsburg, and the war that followed is known as the War of the League of Augsburg. After nine years of exhausting and fruitless struggle Louis XIV was forced to accept a peace that gave him only the city of Strasbourg.

But The Sun King, blinded by pride and greed, had still not learned his lesson. Before the last monarch of the Hapsburg line in Spain died in 1700, Louis XIV persuaded him to choose one of Louis's grandsons as king. The prospect of Spain and the Spanish Empire adjoined to the already inordinately powerful French monarchy frightened the other powers of Western Europe once more into forming an alliance against France. This alliance, known as the Grand Alliance, was also engineered by William III; it consisted of England, the Dutch Netherlands, Austria, Brandenburg, several small German states, Savoy, and Portugal. The ensuing War of Spanish Succession lasted twelve years (1701–13) and was the most destructive of all Louis XIV's wars. The allies, led by the brilliant duke of Marlborough (John Churchill, a direct forebear of Winston Churchill), administered to the French and Spanish armies a series of severe defeats. In 1713 Louis XIV, beaten and ex-

hausted, was forced to accept the Treaty of Utrecht. Although Louis's grandson was permitted to retain the Spanish throne, France yielded Newfoundland, Nova Scotia, and Hudson Bay to Great Britain.[2] Spain gave up Gibraltar and Minorca to Great Britain, and gave the Belgian Netherlands, Naples, Sardinia, and Milan to Austria. The duke of Savoy received the title of king and the Spanish island of Sicily (which he later exchanged with Austria for Sardinia). The Hohenzollern margrave of Brandenburg was granted the title "king in Prussia," and henceforth his state was called Prussia. Thus the houses of Savoy and Hohenzollern, which later were to create the Italian and the German nation, respectively, added greatly to their prestige. France was somewhat humbled. She was beginning to lose ground overseas to Great Britain, and in Europe had been halted short of the Rhine. But she was still the most powerful single nation in Europe.

Louis XIV lived only two years after the signing of the Treaty of Utrecht. He had long outlived his popularity. As the body of the grandest of all the absolute monarchs was drawn pompously through the streets of Paris, his abused people cursed and threw bottles at the coffin. A faint scent of revolution was already in the air.

[2] The term *Great Britain* replaced the term *England* in 1707 when England and Scotland were united.

SUGGESTED READING

A. J. Grant, *The French Monarchy*, 2 vols. (1914). A lucid brief history of France up to the time of the French Revolution.

P. F. Willert, *Henry of Navarre* (1902). Still the best biography of the gallant and debonair king who started France on the road to supremacy in Europe.

J. B. Perkins, *Richelieu and the Growth of the French Power* (1900). A scholarly study of the brilliant cardinal-statesman who stamped his imperious personality on the course of French history.

* Alexander Dumas, *The Three Musketeers*

(Penguin). This melodramatic novel, romanticizing French society of the mid-seventeenth century, when France was reaching the peak of her power and glory, has delighted generations of young and old alike. Cardinal Richelieu, vividly drawn, appears as a character in the novel.

* L. B. Packard, *The Age of Louis XIV* (Berkshire). An excellent, brief survey.

Albert Guérard, *The Life and Death of an Ideal: France in the Classical Age* (1928). An excellent synthesis of French civilization in the sixteenth, seventeenth, and eighteenth centuries with special emphasis on French classical literature.

* Voltaire, *The Age of Louis XIV* (Everyman's Library). Original English edition published in 1851. Voltaire was not only the intellectual dictator of the eighteenth century but also the first modern cultural historian. Voltaire shows how the brilliance of French culture in the latter half of the seventeenth century was reflected all over Europe.

Francis Steegmuller, *The Grand Mademoiselle* (1956). A novel, based on sound historical research, about the heiress to the vast Orléanist fortune (the richest woman in Europe) and a cousin of Louis XIV. This book captures the spirit of the royalty and top aristocracy when royal absolutism was at its peak.

A. J. Grant, *The Huguenots* (1934). A brief and highly readable account that carries the story through the dispersion of the Huguenots following the revocation of the Edict of Nantes.

CHAPTER 34

The Climax and Decline of Absolutism
in England

WHILE Henry IV, Richelieu, Mazarin, and the Sun King perfected royal absolutism in France and set an example for other continental powers, absolutism passed its peak and received a setback in England. Most of seventeenth-century English history centers around the struggle between absolutist monarchy and the partisans of limited monarchy, the latter eventually winning. This constitutional change played an important part in strengthening England's position as one of the great European powers toward the end of the seventeenth century. The English Revolution also exerted a significant influence on other parts of the world, long serving as a model in the struggle against absolutism.

1. Tudor Absolutism

Royal power reached its pinnacle in England during the Tudor period (1485–1603). The greatest Tudors, Henry VII, Henry VIII, and Elizabeth I, successfully concentrated the control of English society in their own hands. They brooked little criticism of their policies and summarily checked any efforts to weaken their domination over English political life.

In its essential features Tudor absolutism was not much different from that of Louis XIV. Although the great Tudor rulers seldom talked much about their power, they assumed that it was their prerogative to guide every phase of English society. As we have noted above (see pp. 325–6), Henry VII established the pattern of Tudor government, creating a centralized administration manned by advisers of his own choice, paying careful attention to financial matters so that his government had adequate resources, monopolizing the military resources of the state, perfecting local institutions of government, and establishing special courts to serve royal dictates. Henry VIII and Elizabeth continued to work within this framework. Their chief accomplishment was to expand the range of governmental activity and to enlarge the machinery of government. Religious life in England was placed under royal control. More thorough regulation of the nation's economic life was carried out. New financial resources were exploited to permit the government to expand its activities. A large part of the success of the Tudors was due to their ability to raise money without having to go to Parliament. The hard-working Tudor rulers, with the help of loyal and skilled advisers, had gained nearly complete control over England by 1603.

Tudor absolutism demanded a tremendous amount of skill on the part of the rulers. From the Middle Ages England had inherited a tradition of limitations on royal power. These limitations had taken shape in two highly significant institutions: Parliament and the common law. By never assaulting these institutions openly the Tudors managed to avoid the charge of tyranny. However, they worked with infinite patience and skill to get around the restrictions these institutions might have imposed. For instance, Parliament was consulted whenever any important and controversial legislation needed to be enacted. By personal persuasion, bribery, skillfully applied compulsion, and patronage the Tudors always managed to get Parliament to do exactly what they wanted. A good part of Tudor success sprang from the fact that their ideas for the good of England happily coincided with the interests of their subjects. Internal peace, religious reform, success in foreign wars were all popular; Englishmen did not think too seriously about how these goals were achieved. Few rulers have been more popular than Queen Elizabeth I, and it was easy for her to exercise tremendous power.

As the Tudor period neared its end, however, there were signs of discontent. Parliamentary leaders began to realize that they were being "managed." Dissenting religious groups, especially the growing numbers of Puritans, thought that the Church of England was in need of further reform. Independents wanted to abolish the state church and permit each congregation to govern itself. Commercial interests were anxious for England to take a more aggressive stand in exploiting overseas trade. Finally, since the danger of Spanish conquests of England lessened after 1588, there was less need to trust everything to the crown. All these factors heralded greater difficulties for future rulers of England.

2. The First Stuarts (1603–49)

"Good Queen Bess" finished her life still a beloved ruler. She left her throne to a distant cousin, James Stuart, king of Scotland. James I came to England with definite ideas about his rights as king but almost no knowledge of English political realities. He was a thorough absolutist, believing that

God had set him on the English throne with full authority to do as he pleased. Not only did he claim absolute power, but he was always ready to make an issue of the matter with anyone who even suggested that he modify his position.

James I immediately launched a program that bred bitter resistance. He absolutely refused to listen to the complaints of the Puritans and threatened to harry them out of the land if they did not abide by the regulations of the Church of England. He outraged public opinion by making peace with Spain, the Catholic power that within the memory of men had tried to invade England. By refusing to become involved in the Thirty Years' War, James seemed to many to signify the abandonment of the cause of Protestantism that Elizabeth had stoutly upheld. Early in his reign James began a running fight with Parliament over taxation. He demanded grants of money and then angrily dismissed Parliament when it balked. He turned to his own means of exacting money, some of which were illegal, to the minds of Englishmen. When the courts and the lawyers protested, James retaliated by dismissing several judges. At every turn the would-be absolutist encountered opposition. Yet he resolutely refused to make concessions.

Probably the chief development of James's reign was the growing tendency for discontent to focus in Parliament, especially in the House of Commons. The House of Commons, theoretically representing all England, was dominated by well-to-do country squires, commercial men, and lawyers. They were patriotic, religious, conservative men, but they were also men of political experience, intent on sharing in the governance of England. Already they had begun to realize that Parliament was an effective place to criticize the Crown. Nowhere else in Europe was there an institution so well fitted to stand against royal absolutism and publicize its shortcomings.

The struggle between the Crown and Parliament sharpened under Charles I (1625–49). During the first years of his reign

Charles called several parliaments, only to dismiss them for demanding that he alter his conduct, change his advisers, or get along on less money than he requested. The Parliament of 1628 was so bold as to greet the king's request for money with a document called the Petition of Right. It insisted that Charles had acted illegally by using martial law in peacetime, by arbitrary taxation, by imprisoning citizens without trial, and by housing soldiers with private citizens. These practices violated the law of the land, which even the king had no right to do. Parliamentary leaders now affirmed a principle upon which to base their opposition: the king must keep within the law. Charles accepted the document because he needed money. But he probably realized that he could not compromise his absolutism with parliamentary ideas. When his next Parliament (1629) started on the same tack, he sent his officers to disband it.

For eleven years Charles ruled without Parliament. Money was his gravest problem. Only by the strictest economies, by refraining from war, and by exploiting every source of revenue did he manage to survive. Without being able to meet in Parliament the opposition was largely paralyzed. However, the policies of Charles had earned him new enemies. His financial exactions, many of which were illegal or of questionable legality, outraged nearly everyone. The courts tried to check his attempts to gain money, but Charles used pressure to circumvent them and limit their independence. His gravest mistake was his religious policy. Under the guidance of William Laud, archbishop of Canterbury, a strong effort was made to compel adherence to Anglicanism and to weed out from the established church all signs of Puritanism. Independents and Puritans alike detested this policy, since it threatened the existence of their most cherished ideas. Even many Anglicans resented Laud's policy, which seemed to restore many features of Roman Catholicism to the Church of England.

Charles's attempt to rule without Parliament finally failed when Laud tried to force his religious ideas on Presbyterian Scotland, where Charles was also king. In 1639 the Scots leaped to arms to defend their religion. Charles had to have money to resist; the only place to get it was from Parliament. So in 1640 he called a new Parliament.

The first Parliament of 1640, called the Short Parliament, lasted only three weeks. Its leaders angered the king by their threats against his policy, and so the king dissolved it. However, as the Scots continued to press, Charles had to abandon the hope of ruling without Parliament. He summoned the so-called Long Parliament. Once seated, the Long Parliament proceeded to legislate an end to Stuart absolutism. It forced Charles to sacrifice his chief ministers, including Laud. It abolished all the extraordinary courts, including the Star Chamber and the Court of High Commission, which had long been tools with which absolutist kings had dodged the common law. An act was passed requiring the king to call Parliament every three years and curbing his power to dismiss Parliament. Severe limits were imposed on royal taxing power unless Parliament was consulted.

Up to this point Parliament had succeeded brilliantly in achieving what its leaders had long been preaching. However, it hit a snag on religion. A wide range of religious opinion, extending from radical ideas about ending Anglicanism "root and branch" to mild condemnations of Laud's policy, was represented in the Long Parliament. Charles sought to use this split as a way of restoring his control. While Parliament hesitated, he tried force to regain his mastery. In 1642 he sought to arrest the leaders of Parliament and thus render it powerless. His action was a call to arms. Charles had clearly demonstrated that he had no intention of honoring the work of the Long Parliament. That work would have to be defended by force.

3. The Civil War (1642–49)

When Charles took up arms in 1642, he represented himself as the champion of the old political and religious order against the

CHARLES I IN THE HOUSE OF COMMONS DEMANDING THE ARREST OF HAMPDEN, PYM, HOLLIS, HAZELRIG, AND STRODE, FROM A PAINTING BY COPLEY. Charles's rash attempt to arrest the opposition leaders precipitated the Puritan Revolution, which ended in the victory of Parliament over the king. (*Courtesy of the Trustees of the Boston Public Library*)

radical ideas of the Parliamentary madmen. For this reason he commanded a large following, known as the Cavaliers. Although all classes were represented, the Cavalier ranks were filled largely with great nobles and country squires from northern and western England. The Parliamentary faction, called the Roundheads, stood for a cause equally attractive—saving England from tyrannical, irresponsible government and from the destruction of the essentials of Protestantism. To this cause rallied many squires, most members of the middle class, and the Puritans. Neither side had an army in 1642. The navy joined the Parliamentary cause. So also did the populace of London, who gave the Roundheads a center for their activities. The Roundheads retained control of the regular organs of administration, which gave them one great advantage: they could vote and collect money.

The first phase of the war lasted through 1646. Charles won a few initial victories. Meanwhile, the Parliamentarians gathered the tools of final victory. Taxes were collected in an orderly fashion. In 1643 an arrangement was made with Scotland, bringing her forces into the war against the king in return for establishing Presbyterianism as the religious system for England. Probably most important of all was the ability of the Parliamentarians to create an effective army. For this Oliver Cromwell was responsible. This Puritan farmer first created a cavalry regiment of disciplined and deeply religious recruits, which proved its fighting quality by routing the Cavaliers. Cromwell's ideas were then applied to the whole army of the Parliamentary cause, bringing into existence the New Model Army. This was a regular force, paid and equipped in a businesslike fashion. Discipline, strongly colored by Puritan ideas of Godliness and sobriety, was strictly maintained. Morale, fed by religious sentiments, was high. This force was more than a match for the Cavaliers. By 1646 Charles's armies had been crushed and the king taken prisoner.

With victory in their grasp the Round-heads split into factions. On one side stood those committed to Presbyterianism and a retention of monarchy. On the other stood the dedicated advocates of religious independence, all of whom demanded an end of a state church. This faction, strong in the army, also advocated revolutionary political ideas such as more democratic elections, the abolition of monarchy, and the redistribution of property. Encouraged by this division, Charles made a new bid for power, posing as the champion of monarchy and Presbyterianism. The Independents, with Cromwell at their head, ended Charles's hope in a single battle in 1648. Convinced of the righteousness of his cause and backed by the victorious New Model Army, Cromwell acted swiftly to ensure the position of the victorious Independents. He forceably purged Parliament of all members not dedicated to his cause, creating the Rump Parliament as chief authority in the land. Early in 1649 a special court convicted Charles I of treason and executed him.

4. Experimentation in Government: Commonwealth and Protectorate (1649–60)

For eleven years after Charles I's death Cromwell's party sought to rule England without a king, experimenting desperately but unsuccessfully to establish a stable order. From the beginning the Cromwellians represented a minority and they never gained additional support. Their main strength was concentrated in the army, a fact that was destined to make many Englishmen suspicious.

The first experiment centered around establishing a republican form of government called the Commonwealth. The office of king and the House of Lords were abolished. A one-house Parliament was made the supreme authority. It was to be aided by a council of state made up of about forty men who were charged with conducting the daily affairs of government. With Cromwell as its leader the Commonwealth launched hopefully into the job of ruling an England distrustful of king-killers and religious radicals. The Commonwealth pursued intelligent policies. For instance, it sponsored a program of religious toleration. It also pursued a vigorous foreign policy. Cromwell led armies into both Ireland and Scotland and prevented these areas from slipping out of English hands. Steps were taken to revive the navy and to push England's commercial interests, especially against the Dutch. None of these policies, however, helped popularize the Commonwealth; resistance and criticism grew steadily. The Cromwellian faction never escaped the charge of being regicides, nor were their puritanical religious ideas acceptable to more than a small minority of Englishmen.

Cromwell blamed much of the trouble on the Rump Parliament, being convinced that the Parliamentary leaders were self-seekers. With characteristic vigor and self-righteousness he dissolved the Rump by force in 1653. The army and its officers were now completely in power. Cromwell tried appointing a Parliament to lead the Commonwealth. This hand-picked body (called Barebones Parliament in honor of Praise-God Barebones, the first name on the roll) failed to distinguish itself except by a series of extremely radical proposals and was likewise dissolved before the end of 1653.

Left in complete power, Cromwell and his friends then produced a written constitution entrusting power to a protector. The protector was to be advised by a council and guided by a one-house Parliament elected by property holders from districts of approximately equal population. Cromwell became the first protector late in 1653. When the new Parliament met in 1654 and began to criticize the protector, Cromwell dismissed it. Thereafter he assumed the role of virtual dictator. Although he called later parliaments, he seldom heeded their advice. To curb disorder, he imposed martial law on England, placing army officers in full authority in several areas of England. The rule of these puritanical soldiers was detested by most Englishmen, and so was the man responsible for their actions. Opinion began to

OLIVER CROMWELL, BY LELY. This portrait of the stern Puritan dictator suggests his strength of purpose and will. Modest and retiring by nature, Cromwell was forced by the pressure of events to assume constantly increasing authority, until he eventually became a dictator. (*The Bettmann Archive*)

run in favor of a restoration of monarchy. In 1657 a majority of the members of Parliament asked Cromwell to become king. Although he refused this honor, he did agree to changes in the constitution that made him protector for life. When he died in 1658, Cromwell had approached as nearly as possible to being king of England without having the formal title. The wheel had made almost a full circle since the day Cromwell and his soldiers thought that they had abolished monarchy by executing Charles I.

Perhaps no figure in England's history has caused more debate than Oliver Cromwell. He has been called everything from a religious bigot and bloody tyrant to a champion of democracy. No simple description will ever fit him. Unquestionably he was a man of great talent, especially capable in warfare and administration. He was driven by strong religious compulsions that made him feel that whatever he did was godly; he felt obligated to purify Englishmen of those things he considered sinful—gambling, drinking, swearing, ostentatious living, enjoying themselves on Sunday, and staying away from church services. Yet, a tolerant man by the standards of his day, he favored a religious settlement that would allow broad freedom to many groups. Although he frequently resorted to force as a means of solving his problems, he believed in parliamentary government and tried until his dying day to establish it. Certainly England has had few greater patriots. Seldom did Cromwell do anything for his personal gain; his life was lived for England. His failure was largely due to the fact that only a minority of Englishmen were willing to accept Puritanism and republicanism.

At Cromwell's death his son, Richard, became lord protector. This weak figure was soon swept aside by more powerful forces. By 1660 elements of Cromwell's army brought pressure to bear for restoration of the Stuarts as rulers of England. A new Parliament was elected and negotiations were opened with Charles Stuart, the son of Charles I. By May 1660 all parties were satisfied, and Charles appeared in London in triumph, greeted by a happy people tired of Puritanism and radicalism.

5. The Restoration (1660–88)

The Restoration of the Stuarts left unresolved the great questions that had been so bitterly fought over since 1603. Neither king nor Parliament had established its supremacy. Religious division had not been wiped out, nor had any principle of toleration been discovered. For twenty-eight years after 1660 these problems continued to disturb England. While Charles II steered the state toward absolutism and the religion of his choice, Parliament resisted, although not so effectively as under James I and Charles I.

When Charles II became king in 1660, he seemed genuinely interested in working with Parliament. Both the king and Parliament were eager for an end of radicalism. The

acts of the Commonwealth and the Protectorate governments were repealed but in a spirit of compromise and forgiveness. The king was provided with a fairly large, although not adequate, income. The Triennial Act was passed, assuring regular meetings of Parliament.

Only on the religious problem was there a lack of compromise. Probably the most significant legislation of the first year of Charles's reign was a series of laws, known as the Clarendon Code, imposing a new religious settlement. These laws re-established the Anglican Church and threatened to destroy the Independents and Presbyterians. The Act of Uniformity required all clergymen to abide by the Book of Common Prayer or to surrender their livings. The Corporation Act provided that all members of city governments worship in the Church of England. The Conventicle Act made religious meetings, except Anglican, illegal, and the Five Mile Act forbade all preachers who were not Anglicans to come within five miles of any city. The Clarendon Code raised immediate dissension within the ranks of the non-conformists, who were once more treated as criminals.

Moreover, the honeymoon between the king and Parliament was short-lived. A series of misfortunes befell England, Charles receiving the blame for most of them. Charles II became involved in a war with the Dutch, during which the Dutch fleet humiliated the English. In 1665 a plague struck England, and the next year a large part of London was destroyed by fire. Charles II's court became notorious for immorality, the king earning a reputation as its most profligate member. One member of Parliament, in an obvious reference to Charles's many illegitimate children, proposed that cradles be bought by the government in wholesale lots.

In the minds of some people England's misfortunes were divine retribution for royal immorality. Public wrath fell on Charles's chief minister, Clarendon, and Parliament forced him out of office. Parliament also grew stingier toward the king; whereupon

Charles turned to Louis XIV of France, who in an alliance of 1670 promised him a sizable subsidy, provided that Charles join France in a war on the Dutch and work for the restoration of Roman Catholicism in England. When, however, in 1672 Charles tried to set aside laws against Roman Catholics, Parliament was so outraged that it passed the Test Act (1673), excluding Roman Catholics from all public offices in England. And when Charles joined France in a war against the Dutch in 1672–74, Parliament again blocked him by refusing financial aid.

By the middle of his reign Charles seemed determined to end the deadlock between the crown and Parliament either by dispensing with Parliament altogether or by controlling it. He continued to rely on Louis XIV for money. He succeeded in building a court party devoted to monarchy and Anglicanism. The opposition scornfully dubbed the members of this party Tories (a term previously used to designate Irish bandits). An opposing party, committed to parliamentary supremacy and the tolerance of all Protestant groups, was also formed. Members of this party were called Whigs, after a term used to describe Scotch Presbyterians who murdered bishops. By skillful use of the Tories and with French money Charles managed to enjoy a great deal of freedom during his later years. Fear that he would use his power to restore Roman Catholicism, however, steadily increased, and his opponents pushed harder and harder for the Exclusion Act, which would have barred Charles's brother, James, from the throne. Charles kept the bill from passing, but his methods convinced the despairing Whigs that tyranny had returned to England.

Charles's successor, James II, inherited a strong position. However, he acted with such reckless abandon that his following soon melted away. His chief mistake was open avowal of Roman Catholicism. Early in his reign James was forced to call the army to crush a rebellion. When the danger had passed, he kept the army and began to appoint Roman Catholics as officers. The

Whigs, and even most Tories, would not accept this. In 1687 James issued the Declaration of Indulgence, relaxing the restrictions on all religious groups, Dissenters and Roman Catholics alike. Protestants interpreted this act as favorable to Roman Catholics. Finally, in 1688, a son was born to James by his Roman Catholic wife, assuring that his regime would be perpetuated by a Catholic successor.

This was the last straw. A group of prominent Tories and Whigs invited James's daughter, the Protestant Mary, and her husband, William of Orange, the rulers of the Netherlands, to accept England's throne. William, eager to ensure England's support against the French threat to his country, accepted. When he invaded England late in 1688, the great majority of the people rallied to his side, and James fled to France. For a second time the unhappy Stuarts had been forced off England's throne.

6. The Glorious Revolution

The flight of James II, unlike the death of Charles I, was not followed by a period of radical political experimentation. Instead, the Glorious Revolution was carried through without bloodshed and recrimination. A series of laws was passed that pacified England and established the basis for her future political development.

The major laws were enacted immediately after the accession of William and Mary. Parliament declared James deposed by virtue of abdicating his office. A new coronation oath was devised requiring William and Mary to swear to abide by decisions of Parliament as well as by the ancient laws of England. The Bill of Rights was passed in 1689. This charter spelled out in detail the laws to which the king must adhere. It laid down Parliament's authority to depose a king and choose a new one. It assured the members of Parliament the right of free speech, immunity from prosecution for statements made in debate, and freedom from royal intervention in elections. It declared illegal a whole series of acts: taxation without consent of Parliament, dispensing with laws, maintaining a standing army in peacetime, requiring excessive bail, depriving citizens of trial in the regular courts, interfering with jurors, and preventing people from petitioning the king. The Toleration Act was also enacted, allowing religious freedom to Puritans and Independents, although still keeping non-Protestants out of public office.

Accepting the crown on the basis of these laws and conditions, William and Mary acted with vigor to dispose of other sources of difficulty. In 1689–91 William led an army into Ireland, where James was attempting to stir up a rebellion that would put him back on the throne. William crushed the rebels and instituted a policy of depriving Irish Catholics of their land in favor of English landlords. Ireland was thus placed on a colonial status, to be exploited by England. Hard as this policy was for the Irish, it did deprive political rebels of a convenient base of operations against England.

William also conducted long negotiations to solve the problem of Scotland. These negotiations bore fruit after his death, when Parliament passed the Act of Union (1707), which joined the two kingdoms, gave Scotland a liberal number of seats in Parliament, and guaranteed her Presbyterian religious organization. The Act of Union created a political unit known thereafter as Great Britain.

Probably William's most significant act was to supply England with a new orientation in foreign affairs. A dedicated enemy of the schemes of Louis XIV to dominate Europe, William threw all of England's resources into the struggle against France. His action was decisive. Not only were Louis XIV's ambitious plans upset, but through these wars England became a great power and was well on the way to acquiring a great empire.

Still another significant issue remained to be settled—the succession problem. Mary died in 1694 and William in 1702, leaving the crown to Anne (1702–14), another daughter of James II. Even before William's

death it was apparent that Anne would have no heirs. To avoid the return of the Roman Catholic Stuarts, Parliament in 1701 passed the Act of Settlement. This law provided that none but Protestants would inherit the English crown. In line with this principle Parliament designated Sophia of the German state of Hanover, granddaughter of James I, and her heirs as successors to Anne. In spite of strong sentiment in favor of restoring the dynasty of James II, this act was honored in 1714, when George of Hanover became King George I of England.

7. The Emergence of the Cabinet System

The establishment of parliamentary supremacy in the wake of the Glorious Revolution left unsolved one more major political problem—that of the executive power. How would the daily affairs of government be conducted? Many were afraid to trust this task to the king, fearing that he would regain control over political life. Yet Parliament, composed chiefly of landowners and businessmen, was in no position to take up this burden. During the half century after 1688 a solution was found that permitted Parliament effectively to control the executive branch of the government while still assuring the skillful conduct of state business. The answer lay in the emergence of the cabinet.

English kings had long employed advisers to conduct governmental affairs and to shape policy. Up to 1688 these ministers had usually been chosen by the king and were responsible to him alone. After 1688 it became absolutely necessary for the king to gain parliamentary support for every phase of governmental policy. From William III's reign onward, therefore, royal ministers were increasingly chosen because of their influence in Parliament. Since Parliament tended to divide into parties that controlled large blocs of votes, it proved wisest for the king to seek out party leaders for posts as ministers and advisers.

After the accession of Anne this trend developed rapidly. Since Anne and the first Hanoverians, George I (1714–27) and George II (1727–60), were unfitted for the rigorous job of administering the state, the direction of the government and the formulation of policy fell into the hands of royal ministers who could get the approval of Parliament. This group of ministers slowly learned to accept mutual responsibility for the total operation of the government. This required that they all be members of the same party and stand together in Parliament. While their party held a majority in Parliament, they could enact their program; when they lost control over Parliament, they had to give way to a new cabinet that could control Parliament. One member of the cabinet, the prime minister, came to be recognized as the leader and spokesman of the whole group.

Anne relied heavily on the advice of John Churchill, duke of Marlborough, to conduct her government. However, a minister of the first two Georges, Robert Walpole, was the first real prime minister and the first to observe the principles of cabinet government. A Whig member of Parliament for many years, he learned well the potential power of a disciplined party. In 1721 he became George I's chief minister, primarily because of his power in Parliament, and virtually ran England until 1742. He surrounded himself with men who could control votes in Parliament and followed policies suitable to the interests of his party. A coarse, hard-drinking squire, Walpole was not above bribery and the shameless use of patronage to keep his party strong. His strength in Parliament made him the real ruler of England; even the king could not control or check his dominance. Walpole lost control of Parliament when he tried to keep England out of war with Spain, a policy that was not popu-

lar with most Englishmen. Having lost his control of Parliament, Walpole resigned as prime minister in 1742. However, the king had little choice but to appoint another prime minister who could command a majority vote in Parliament. The cabinet, under a prime minister, had taken over the executive branch of the government, exercising that power through a group of parliamentary leaders who devoted themselves to administration but who had to render account for their conduct of state affairs before Parliament.

The Glorious Revolution and the settlement that followed were a turning point in England's history. Two burning issues had been settled to the satisfaction of most Englishmen. Parliament, representing the landed and moneyed interests, replaced the king as supreme authority. Religious toleration was established for all Protestant sects, thus putting an end to religious uniformity. (Roman Catholics, Unitarians, Jews, and atheists were not given the right to worship freely or to exercise fully their rights as Englishmen.) Although much blood had been spilled deciding these issues, England emerged from her revolution with no deep scars. She had managed to hold her own in competition with other powers, especially France, which at the time enjoyed a more stable political system. In fact England had raised her prestige and power in world affairs during the seventeenth century and entered the eighteenth even stronger than she had been at the death of Elizabeth in 1603. With her political quarrels settled, however, she was able to increase her world power rapidly during the next two centuries. Her revolution against absolutism and her new constitutional monarchy were destined to serve as models for other nations ready to discard royal absolutism.

SUGGESTED READING

George Macaulay Trevelyan, *England Under the Stuarts*, rev. ed. (1946). A brilliantly written survey of the period of the English Revolution. The book contains delightful chapters on the social history of the seventeenth century and illuminating remarks about the leading personalities of the time.

T. B. Macaulay, *The History of England from the Accession of James the Second*. Many editions; the best is edited by C. H. Firth, 6 vols. (1913–15). This monumental study, originally published in 1849–61, is one of the great pieces of historical literature in the English language. It covers the period 1685–1702 in great detail. Its vivid style makes reading it a real pleasure. The author, strongly in favor of limited monarchy, is not always fair to the Stuarts.

C. Williams, *James I* (1953). A good biography that helps to clarify the issues that brought on the revolution in seventeenth-century England.

C. H. Firth, *Oliver Cromwell and the Rule of the Puritans in England*, 3rd ed. (1924). An excellent study of Cromwell's regime centering around the activities of Cromwell himself.

C. V. Wedgwood, *Oliver Cromwell* (1939). A brief biography presenting an excellent introduction to Cromwell and his age.

Arthur Bryant, *King Charles II* (1931). A sympathetic treatment of a ruler who has seldom been treated sympathetically by historians. This biography will help a reader to understand why the Restoration of the Stuarts in 1660 was popular at first and why the dynasty again lost favor.

George Macaulay Trevelyan, *The English Revolution, 1688–1689* (1939). A brilliant analysis of the nature and the significance of the stirring events of 1688–89 in England.

John Morley, *Walpole* (1889). A brief, readable biography of the colorful figure who was England's first prime minister.

Carl Stephenson and Frederick George Marcham, eds., *Sources of English Constitutional History* (1937). A reader will find included in this collection the fundamental charters of English liberty enacted during the revolutionary period of the seventeenth century. Every reader ought especially to read the Bill of Rights.

Samuel Pepys, *Diary*. Many editions; a good one was edited by G. Gregory Smith (1935). A fascinating picture of English life in the period of the Restoration emerges from this diary of an important literary figure who lived and wrote in London in the 1660's.

* John Locke, *Two Treatises of Government*. Many editions (a convenient one is available in a paperback edition by the Hafner Publishing Co.). These two short essays on political theory by a seventeenth-century Englishman provide the best source for an understanding of the political ideas that inspired the Glorious Revolution of 1688–89.

* John Milton, *Aeropagitica*. Many editions (a convenient one is edited by George H. Sabine in Crofts Classics). This essay on freedom of speech by the great seventeenth-century English poet will illustrate what at least some supporters of the English Revolution were fighting for.

Charles Howard McIlwain, ed., *The Political Works of James I* (1918). A few samples from this collection of James's political writings will illustrate the political theories that lay behind Stuart absolutism. The introduction by one of America's greatest scholars in the field of political theory is especially good.

CHAPTER 35

The Rise of Prussia and Russia

THE MOST significant political developments in Central and Eastern Europe during the seventeenth and eighteenth centuries were the rise of Prussia and Russia. At the opening of the seventeenth century the two chief powers in Central and Eastern Europe were the Ottoman and Hapsburg empires. Although the Moslem Ottoman Turks had been restrained by the Hapsburgs in the sixteenth century on both land and sea, they were about to renew their effort to conquer Christian Europe. The Austrian Hapsburgs, in addition to disputing the control of Southeastern Europe with the Turks, dominated the Holy Roman Empire, which included all of the German states. In Northeastern Europe, Sweden, Prussia, Poland, and Russia competed for hegemony, with the odds apparently favoring Sweden and Poland. By the end of the eighteenth century Prussia and Russia had emerged as great and growing powers, Poland had disappeared from the map, and Sweden and the Ottoman Empire were in decline. The Austrian Hapsburg Empire, though still a great power, was relatively static.

1. The Early Hohenzollerns

The history of Prussia is in large measure the history of the Hohenzollern family. This aggressive and prolific dynasty was first heard of in the tenth century. At that time the Hohenzollerns were obscure counts ruling over the castle of Zollern and a tiny bit of surrounding territory in southwest Germany just north of the Swiss border. In the twelfth century they became burgraves of Nuremberg, an important commercial city in Bavaria. Early in the fifteenth century the Holy Roman Emperor, looking for an able ruler for the mark of Brandenburg, a military province near the exposed northeastern border of the empire, chose the head of the house of Hohenzollern. Although its ruler was one of the seven electors of the Holy Roman Emperor, Brandenburg was a bleak and thinly populated little province for which nobody predicted a bright future. Yet around this nucleus the Hohenzollerns built the important state of Prussia, and later the German Empire—the world's most powerful and feared nation.

From the time the Hohenzollerns became margraves of Brandenburg early in the fifteenth century until they were finally overthrown at the end of World War I in 1918, they followed a threefold policy from which they never veered: militarism and territorial aggrandizement; paternal despotism; and centralized bureaucracy. No state in modern times has been so wedded to militarism as a cardinal feature of national life and national policy as that of the Hohenzollerns, and few modern states have been more autocratic in their government.

Early in the seventeenth century Brandenburg began to expand. In 1609 the Hohenzollerns inherited three little provinces in and near the Rhine Valley far to the west,

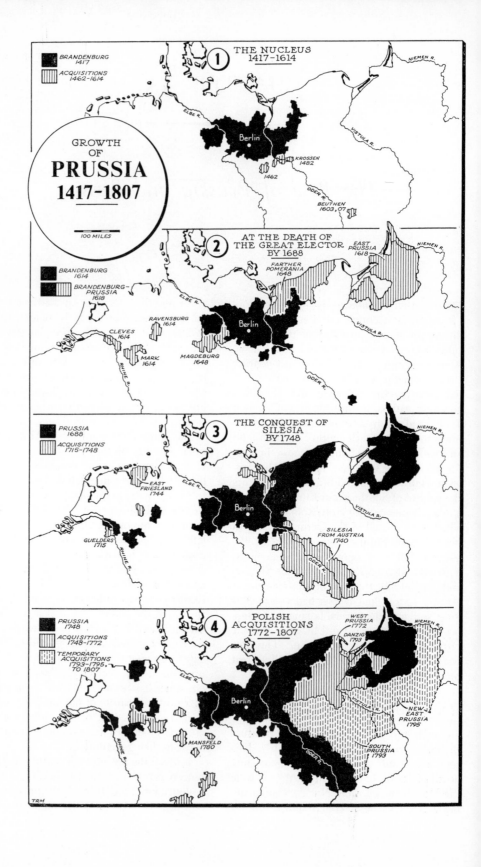

GROWTH
OF
PRUSSIA
1417-1807

100 MILES

① THE NUCLEUS 1417-1614

BRANDENBURG 1417
ACQUISITIONS 1462-1614

NIEMEN R.
ELBE R.
VISTULA R.
Berlin
KROSSEN 1482
1462
ODER R.
BEUTHEN 1603,07

② AT THE DEATH OF THE GREAT ELECTOR BY 1688

BRANDENBURG 1614
BRANDENBURG-PRUSSIA 1618

EAST PRUSSIA 1618
NIEMEN R.
FARTHER POMERANIA 1648
ELBE R.
Berlin
VISTULA R.
RAVENSBURG 1614
CLEVES 1614
MARK 1614
MAGDEBURG 1648
RHINE R.
ODER R.

③ THE CONQUEST OF SILESIA BY 1748

PRUSSIA 1688
ACQUISITIONS 1715-1748

NIEMEN R.
EAST FRIESLAND 1744
ELBE R.
Berlin
VISTULA R.
GUELDERS 1715
RHINE R.
SILESIA FROM AUSTRIA 1740
ODER R.

④ POLISH ACQUISITIONS 1772-1807

PRUSSIA 1748
ACQUISITIONS 1748-1772
TEMPORARY ACQUISITIONS 1793-1795 TO 1807

WEST PRUSSIA 1772
NIEMEN R.
DANZIG 1793
ELBE R.
Berlin
VISTULA R.
NEW EAST PRUSSIA 1795
MANSFELD 1780
RHINE R.
SOUTH PRUSSIA 1793
ODER R.

TRM

and nine years later they inherited East Prussia, a fief of Poland on the Baltic far to the east. In 1640 Frederick William, the Great Elector, one of the ablest of all the Hohenzollerns, became margrave and began filling in the territorial gaps. His first move was to take Brandenburg out of the Thirty Years' War, which had been devastating the Germanies for the past twenty-two years. While the other adversaries, France, Sweden, the Hapsburgs, and many of the small German states, exhausted themselves in eight more years of struggle, Brandenburg recouped her strength and resources. Re-entering the war shortly before its end, she was in a position to demand and get valuable territories. According to the terms of the Treaty of Westphalia (1648), Brandenburg received Eastern Pomerania, a sizable strip of territory that gave her valuable frontage on the Baltic, the large bishopric of Magdeburg, which straddled the Elbe, and several smaller bishoprics. Shortly afterward Frederick William gained the independence of East Prussia from Poland.

The Great Elector centralized and administered the governments of his scattered territories with energy and skill. He protected the native industries, improved communications, and aided agriculture. In a most intolerant age he followed a policy of religious toleration. When Louis XIV revoked the Edict of Nantes in 1685, Frederick William welcomed thousands of industrious Huguenots to Brandenburg. At the death of the Great Elector in 1688, Brandenburg was well on the road to becoming a great power.

The next Hohenzollern, Frederick I (1688–1713), acquired the title of king for the dynasty. The Hapsburg Holy Roman Emperor in 1701 granted Frederick the title in return for aid against Louis XIV in the War of the Spanish Succession. Frederick I chose Prussia rather than Brandenburg for the name of his kingdom, since Prussia was outside the Holy Roman Empire and a free sovereign state. Hence Brandenburg became Prussia.

From 1713 to 1740 Prussia was ruled by a vigorous militaristic autocrat, Frederick William I (since he was the first Frederick William to be king). Unquestioned absolutism, machinelike centralized bureaucratic administration, and above all militarism were the obsessions of this eccentric tyrant. He built the Prussian army into the most efficient and one of the largest fighting forces in Europe. And yet Frederick William was so efficient and miserly that he was also able to pass along to his talented son a well-filled treasury.

The talented son, the future Frederick the Great, was a "problem" child. An ardent lover of music, literature, and philosophy, young Frederick hated militarism and governmental details. He even attempted to flee the country to escape the stern discipline of his disgruntled father. Arrested, he was forced to undergo exceptionally rigorous training from the ground up, in the army and the government services. Eventually Frederick became enamored of both, and Frederick William I died happy, sure that the Hohenzollern state would pass into good hands.

2. The Emergence of Prussia as a Great Power Under Frederick the Great, 1740–86

In the same year that Frederick II became king of Prussia (1740) the beautiful and gracious young Maria Theresa became archduchess of the Austrian Hapsburg dominions. Maria Theresa's father, Emperor Charles VI, had spent much time in his last years attempting to safeguard his daughter's accession to the Hapsburg throne. He succeeded in obtaining the signatures of virtually every European sovereign, including the king of Prussia, to a document called the Pragmatic Sanction, which guaranteed the integrity of Maria Theresa's crown and territories. Two months after Charles VI died, however, Frederick II, without a declaration of war, marched his troops into and seized Silesia, one of the richest of the Hapsburg provinces. This Machiavellian act of the young Prussian king plunged most of the major European states into a series of

FREDERICUS.II

FREDERICK THE GREAT. A member of the great Hohenzollern family, this cynical ruler was Machiavellian in his outlook. By conquest and astute administration he raised Prussia to the rank of the great powers. (*The Bettmann Archive*)

bloody wars for the mastery of Central Europe. Bavaria, Saxony, France, and Spain rushed in to despoil Maria Theresa of her territories. Only Great Britain took the side of Austria. Great Britain was a bitter rival of France in India and North America, and she was also concerned for the Austrian Netherlands, with which she enjoyed a profitable trade, and for Hanover, whose ruling family now sat on the British throne.

The War of Austrian Succession lasted for eight years (1740–48). Maria Theresa successfully repelled the Bavarians, Saxons, French, and Spaniards, but she was unable to dislodge Frederick II from Silesia. Frederick, on his part, cynically deserted his allies. The Treaty of Aix-la-Chapelle in 1748 brought the hostilities to an end. Frederick retained Silesia, and Maria Theresa's husband, Francis of Lorraine, was recognized as Emperor of the Holy Roman Empire.

The only real gainer from the war was Frederick II. Silesia, a fertile province inhabited by more than a million German-speaking people, nearly doubled the population and resources of Prussia.

The Hapsburgs, however, had no intention of being thus despoiled of one of their fairest provinces by the upstart Hohenzollerns. The Hapsburgs, proud rulers over territories many times the size and population of Prussia and for centuries emperors of the Holy Roman Empire, of which Prussia was a member state, viewed the Hohenzollerns with condescension. Maria Theresa's able diplomat, Count Kaunitz, was soon at work lining up allies. Saxony, Sweden, Russia, and even France were won over. Spain, now ruled by the Bourbons, later followed France into the alliance. This time, however, Great Britain took the side of Prussia. She did this in order to be on the opposite side of her archenemy France, with whom she was already at war in India and North America, and to safeguard Hanover. This double shifting of alliances came to be called the Diplomatic Revolution. Since Great Britain was Prussia's only ally and since her aid was limited to subsidies and to tying down French forces overseas, the allies were certain that they would crush Frederick II. They were already dividing up his territories, leaving him only the little original Hohenzollern province of Brandenburg.

Frederick was not one to wait for his enemies to strike first. As soon as he became aware of their designs, he opened hostilities by overrunning Saxony. Thus began the Seven Years' War (1756–63), the bloodiest war in history up to that time. Frederick, with his slender resources, soon found himself at bay; the four greatest military powers on the continent of Europe were closing in on him from all directions. The Austrians advanced from the south, the Russians from the east, the Swedes from the north, and the French from the west. Hurling his disciplined but ever-dwindling army against first one and then another of his enemies, Frederick held them off for seven years. His lightning marches, tricky maneuvers, and indefatigable tenacity in the face of seemingly hopeless odds won for him the title, "the Great." But after six years the end appeared to be near. His treasury was empty, his manpower exhausted, much of his territory laid waste. The Russians even captured and burned his capital, Berlin. Then suddenly fortune changed. In 1762 the Russian Tsarina Elizabeth, one of his bitterest enemies, died and was succeeded by the weakling Peter III, who was an ardent admirer of Frederick II and who put Russia's forces at the disposal of Prussia. Although Peter III was soon murdered by a group of his own officers and court nobility, and Russia withdrew from the war, the remaining allies had no further stomach for the fight. The Peace of Hubertusburg in 1763 left things as they were at the beginning of the war, Prussia retaining the controversial Silesia. In the same year the Treaty of Paris brought to a close the colonial struggle between Great Britain and France in India and North America, leaving Great Britain master of both.

Having so narrowly escaped destruction, Frederick the Great spent the remaining twenty-three years of his life reconstructing his war-ravaged territories. His career as an enlightened despot will be surveyed in Chapter 38. Toiling long hours each day, he encouraged agriculture, subsidized and protected industry, and invited immigrants into his well-governed territories. In 1772 he joined Austria and Russia in the first partition of Poland. Frederick took West Prussia, thus joining East Prussia with the main body of the Prussian state. When Frederick II died in 1786, Prussia had been raised to the status of a great power, sharing equally with Austria the leadership of Central Europe. During his reign Prussia's size and population had more than doubled, and her military exploits pointed to a spectacular future.

3. Russia Before Peter the Great

While Prussia was becoming a great power in Central Europe, Russia was rising to prominence to the east. The first shaping of the Slavic tribes of Eastern Europe into what eventually became the Russian national state was begun by Viking invaders in the ninth century. These intrepid seamen moved out from their Scandinavian homes in all directions—across the Atlantic, into the Mediterranean, and up the rivers of what are now England, France, Germany, and Russia (the word *Russia* is apparently derived from the Swedish word for rower). Their most important commercial and political center in Eastern Europe was Kiev, which became Russia's first capital. Eventually, however, the Norse were swallowed up by the Slavic culture of their subjects.

In the tenth century Christianity was brought to Russia by missionaries from Constantinople. This is probably the most significant development in Russian history. Through the influence of the Greek Orthodox Church, whose headquarters were in Constantinople, Russia became a semi-oriental Byzantine civilization and was cut off from the Graeco-Roman and Roman Catholic culture common to the countries of Central and Western Europe. English, Spanish, Polish, and Swedish churchmen were constantly traveling to Rome, where they associated with churchmen from Italy, Hungary, France, and Germany. Russian churchmen, on the other hand, traveled to Constantinople, where they met only Greek, Serbian, Bulgarian, and Romanian churchmen of the Balkan Peninsula.

Second in importance only to Greek Orthodox Christianity in the infusion of oriental influence into Russian civilization was the Tartar conquest of the thirteenth century. Around the turn of the thirteenth century the Mongol conqueror Genghis Khan (1167–1227) had established a vast empire in Eastern Asia. Shortly after his death the Golden Horde, as the Mongol warriors were called, swept westward into Christian Europe. The thirteenth-century Europeans were no match for the oriental Tartars. Russia was easily overrun, and in 1241 a combined German and Polish army was defeated at Liegnitz in the heart of Central Europe. All Christian Europe appeared to be at the mercy of the yellow men. At that moment, however, the great khan back in Eastern Asia died, and the Tartar commander withdrew his forces to Russia and hastened back to Asia to seize his share of the spoils. The Golden Horde never resumed its triumphal surge into Western Christendom, but for two and a half centuries it inundated Russia. Although there was little mixing of blood between the Mongol Tartars and the Caucasian Russians, there was considerable mixing of cultures. When the Mongol tide finally receded near the end of the fifteenth century, a deposit of such characteristically oriental traits as backward-looking conservatism, fatalism, female seclusion, and absolutism in government had been added to the semi-oriental Byzantine cultural influence.

During the Tartar occupation the grand dukes of Muscovy managed to ingratiate themselves with their Mongol masters and build up their own influence and power. Moscow replaced Kiev as the political center of Russia. The first of the grand dukes of Muscovy to be generally recognized as tsar of Russia was Ivan III (1462–1505). In 1480 Ivan III defeated the rapidly declining Tartars and limited their power in Russia to the southeastern area. Ivan III greatly extended his sway both to the north and to the west by military conquest. A momentous event in Ivan III's reign was his marriage to Sophia Palaeologus, heiress to the now-defunct Byzantine (Eastern Roman) Empire. Ivan immediately declared himself successor to the Eastern Roman Caesars and adopted the title Tsar. When Ivan III (the Great) died, the foundations of a Russian national state had been laid.

Ivan IV (1533–84), the Terrible, in spite of his title added both to the authority of the Russian tsars and to the territories over which they ruled. He destroyed the remaining power of the Tartars in southeastern Russia and annexed most of their territory. The Ottoman Turks, however, seized the strategic Tartar territory north of the Black Sea. Although Ivan IV established trade relations with England by way of the White Sea and the Arctic Ocean, his efforts to gain a foothold on the Baltic were frustrated by Sweden and Poland. It was during Ivan IV's reign that Russia's conquest of Siberia was begun. Half a century later the Russian flag was planted on the shores of the Pacific.

The twenty-nine years following the death of Ivan IV were a time of troubles (1584–1613). Weak rulers and disputed successions resulted in such anarchy that the Poles were able to capture Moscow and hold it briefly. To end the political chaos, a group of leading nobles in 1613 chose Michael Romanov as tsar. The Romanov dynasty was to rule Russia until the Communist revolution of 1917. Throughout the seventeenth century Russia under the early Romanovs was slowly but gradually establishing commercial and cultural contacts with the West. Increasing numbers of traders, craftsmen, and adventurers from Central and Western Europe, particularly Germany, were coming into Russia to seek their fortunes. Thus the stage was set for Peter the Great at the end of the century to Westernize Russia and make her a first-rate European power.

4. Russia Under Peter the Great, 1689–1725

Peter I (1689–1725) [1] was a physical giant full of mental vitality and primitive animal instincts and emotions. At the age of seventeen he seized the reins of government from his malevolent elder sister, whom he confined along with his mother to a convent for the rest of their lives. For the next thirty-six years he devoted his boundless energy to the twofold policy of Westernizing Russia and of gaining windows to the West on the Baltic and Black seas.

During Peter's boisterous youth he had come in contact with foreign craftsmen in Moscow and had become enamored of Western technology, particularly shipbuild-

---

[1] In 1682 Peter I, at the age of ten, technically became joint ruler with his elder, idiotic brother, Ivan V. Until 1689, however, his rule was only nominal, and that date is usually considered to be the beginning of his reign.

PETER THE GREAT AT DEPTFORD DOCKYARD, FROM A PAINTING BY MACLISE. Preparatory to launching his program of Westernizing Russia, the young tsar made a tour of Western Europe. He studied Western techniques in Britain, the Dutch Netherlands, and Prussia. (*Courtesy, Royal Holloway College*)

ing. In 1697 the twenty-five-year-old tsar made a grand tour of Western Europe, seeking allies against the Turks and firsthand knowledge of Western ways. He failed to gain any allies, but he learned a great deal about Western customs and techniques, which he proceeded to introduce into Russia. In the Hohenzollern province of East Prussia, Peter studied one of the world's most efficient military organizations, in the Dutch Netherlands shipbuilding, in England shipbuilding, commerce, and finance.

On his way to Italy from Vienna he was suddenly called home by the revolt of his bodyguard. Slicing off hundreds of heads by his own hand, he crushed the revolt with a ruthlessness that cowed all potential troublemakers. To make his authority as absolute as that of the most autocratic Western European monarchs, he adopted their bureaucratic system in both central and local government. Western technicians were brought to Russia in large numbers, and new indus-

tries were subsidized and protected by mercantilist policies. Western social customs were introduced to the upper and middle classes of Russian society. Women were brought out of seclusion, and the long beards and flowing oriental robes of the men were cut off, Peter himself frequently wielding the shears. When the patriarch of the Russian Orthodox Church opposed the tsar's authority and some of his Westernizing policies, Peter abolished the patriarchate. He placed at the head of the church a Holy Synod composed of a committee of bishops and presided over by a lay procurator-general, all appointed by the tsar. Henceforth, the Orthodox Church was a powerful instrument of the Russian government. From first to last Peter the Great's chief concern was his military establishment. He built a navy and patterned his conscript army after that of Prussia. By the end of his reign Russia had one of the major fighting forces of Europe.

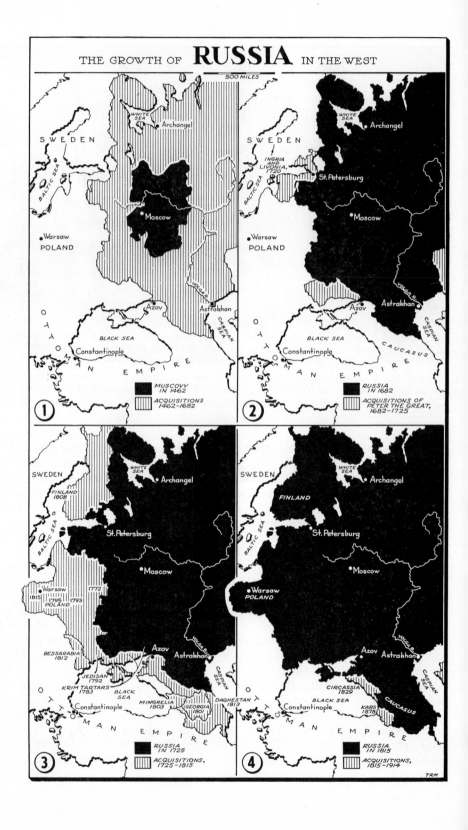

THE GROWTH OF **RUSSIA** IN THE WEST

Peter's efforts to gain windows to the West on the Black and Baltic seas were only partly successful. He did manage to seize Azov on the Black Sea from the Turks and hold it for fourteen years, but the Turks were still too strong for the Russians and blocked them off from the Black Sea for another half century. Against Sweden, who held the coveted shores of the Baltic Sea, Peter was more successful. In 1697 the fifteen-year-old Charles XII came to the throne of Sweden, which since the reign of Gustavus Adolphus in the early seventeenth century had been the greatest military power in Northern Europe. Hoping to take advantage of Charles XII's youth, Peter the Great formed an alliance with Denmark and Poland for the purpose of despoiling Sweden of valuable territories. Charles, however, proved to be a first-rate military genius. Not waiting for his enemies to ready their plans, he struck first at Denmark and forced her to sue for peace. Marching rapidly into Russia, he crushed a Russian army much larger than his own at Narva. Instead of pursuing the demoralized forces of Peter, however, he turned to Poland, defeated the Polish army, and placed a puppet king on the Polish throne. After spending seven years rearranging the affairs of Poland, Charles, known as the "Madman of the North," at last turned his attentions once more to Russia. But Peter had used the seven years of grace to rebuild his forces. He retreated before the advancing Swedes deep into the vast interior of Russia, scorching the earth behind him. In 1709 the forces of Charles XII, decimated by hunger and disease, were brought to bay and shattered at Poltava, in southern Russia. Charles escaped with a remnant of his army to Turkey, but the military strength of Sweden was spent. Nine years later Charles XII was killed fighting in Norway. By the Treaty of Nystad in 1721 Russia received the Swedish Baltic provinces of Livonia, Estonia, Ingria, and Karelia. On the Neva River near the Baltic Peter built a modern new capital, St. Petersburg, facing the West. At the death of Peter the Great in 1725 Russia was a great and growing power ready to play a major role in European affairs.

5. Russia Under Catherine the Great, 1762–96

Peter the Great was followed by a succession of weak or mediocre rulers who undid much of his work. After an interval of thirty-seven years Catherine the Great (1762–96) ascended to the Russian throne. Catherine was an obscure princess from one of the little German states. She had been married for political reasons to young Peter III, grandson of Peter the Great, while he was still heir to the Russian crown. After he became tsar, Peter III, a weakling, quickly alienated all classes of his subjects. The astute Catherine, meanwhile, was becoming a good Russian, popularizing herself with the people high and low. She was also reading widely from classical and French eighteenth-century authors. Less than a year after Peter III became tsar Catherine conspired with a group of aristocratic army officers, who murdered Peter and declared Catherine tsarina of Russia.

The Machiavellian tsarina prided herself on being an enlightened despot—fashionable in the late eighteenth century. That she was an intellectual is beyond question. She carried on a lively correspondence with Voltaire, D'Alembert, Frederick the Great, and other leading members of the eighteenth-century intelligentsia. She invited Diderot to St. Petersburg and became his friend and patron. She talked learnedly about freedom, education, and reform, and soon after her seizure of the throne she called a commission to study the question of reforms. All this made good salon talk, but none of it was translated into deeds. No one knew better than Catherine, as she admitted to a confidant, that an enlightened populace would endanger the position of all despots. The peasants, who constituted the great bulk of the Russian population and whose lot had been growing steadily worse since the days of Ivan the Terrible, were reduced to a position bordering on slavery.

Two peasant uprisings were put down in blood.

The chief significance of Catherine the Great in history lies in her aggressive foreign policy. Peter the Great had reached the Baltic by despoiling the Swedes. Catherine reached the Black Sea, the Balkan Peninsula, and the heart of Europe by defeating the Turks and destroying Poland. In two major wars between 1768 and 1792 Catherine defeated the Turks (something that Peter the Great had never been able to do) and seized all of their territory north of the Black Sea as far west as the Dniester River. Russia also gained a vague protectorate over the Christians in the Ottoman Empire, which gave her a standing opportunity to meddle in the internal affairs of the Turks. But Catherine fell short of her real goal, Constantinople. So certain was she of winning the old Byzantine capital on the Bosporus, which the Russian tsars had coveted since the days of Ivan III, that she named her second grandson Constantine. However, turning aside to join Prussia and Austria in the partitioning of the remainder of the Polish state, Catherine died before she could resume her drive on Constantinople. Already in 1772 Russia, Prussia, and Austria had seized strips of Poland. In 1793 Russia and Prussia enlarged their holdings, and in 1795 the three powers divided among themselves the remainder of the once-formidable Poland. Catherine's share, which was about two thirds of the total, brought Russia's western boundary deep into Central Europe. The second and third partitions of Poland and concern over the French Revolution, which began in 1789, absorbed Catherine's energies during the last years of her life. When she finally died in 1796, Russia was a nation ominous in size and power, and a major factor in European and world affairs.

6. The Disappearance of Poland and the Decline of Sweden and the Ottoman Empire

Poland, at the opening of the eighteenth century, was the third-largest country in Europe, exceeded in size only by Russia and Sweden. In the sixteenth and seventeenth centuries it had appeared that Poland would be one of the future major powers. At the beginning of the seventeenth century the Poles had taken advantage of Russia's time of troubles to capture Moscow. In the latter part of the century the Poles had saved Vienna from the Turks.

Actually, however, the Polish nation was far from sound. Sprawling over a large area between Russia and the German states, she enjoyed no natural boundaries either in the east or the west. The eastern half of her territory was inhabited by Russian-speaking people. Her northern provinces were peopled largely by Latvians, Lithuanians, and Germans. There were also many Germans in the west. Religious cleavages followed the language lines. The Poles themselves were militantly Roman Catholic under strong Jesuit influence. Some of the Russians were Orthodox and some were Uniates (orthodox Christians who recognized the headship of the Roman pope). The Latvians, Lithuanians, and Germans were mostly Lutherans. In the cities lived many Jews.

Moreover, there was no strong middle class to vitalize Poland's economy. In the late Middle Ages a rather flourishing overland commerce between the Black and the Baltic seas had flowed across Poland. But with the shifting of commercial routes and centers to the west in the early sixteenth century Poland's commerce had withered like that of Italy and the Germanies. Furthermore, the Polish nobility, jealous of its own power and fearful of an alliance between the bourgeoisie and the king, deliberately penalized commerce with severe restrictions. The great mass of the people were serfs, tilling the soil of the powerful nobility.

In the face of so many divisive forces, only a strong central government could have made Poland a stable national state. But here lay Poland's greatest weakness. The kingship was elective, and the great nobles who held the elective power saw to it that no strong king ever came to the throne to

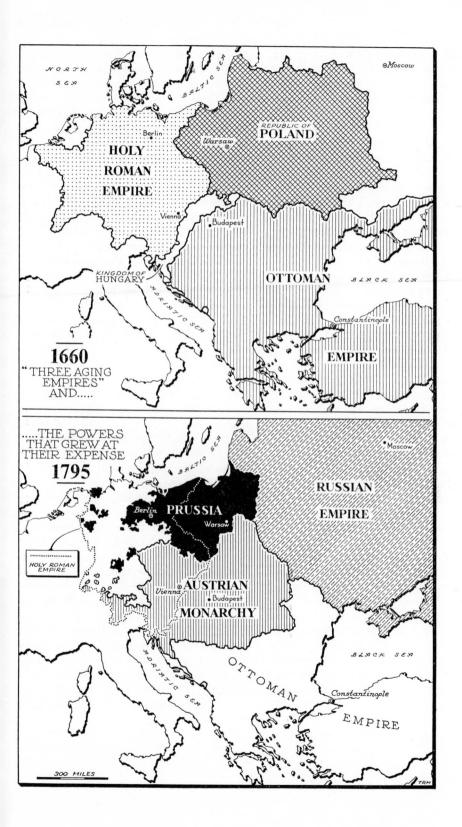

1660
"THREE AGING EMPIRES" AND.....

.....THE POWERS THAT GREW AT THEIR EXPENSE **1795**

threaten their own position. During the eighteenth century the kings were all foreigners or puppets of foreign powers. The legislative Diet was completely monopolized by the nobility. In order to safeguard each nobleman's rights unanimity was required for the passage of every measure. This meant that any nobleman could veto any proposed law (*liberum veto*). In addition, any nobleman could disband ("explode") the Diet and cancel all its acts. This system guaranteed virtual political anarchy. National spirit was practically nonexistent. The all-powerful nobles were far more concerned for their own private interests than for the well-being of the nation.

It would have been surprising had such a power vacuum as eighteenth-century Poland not invited the aggression of her ambitious neighbors. In 1772 Catherine the Great and Frederick the Great bargained to take slices of Polish territory. The somewhat less Machiavellian Maria Theresa of Austria, fearful of being outdistanced by Russia and Prussia, joined them, although her slice was beyond the Carpathian Mountains. Russia took a strip occupied by White Russians, and Prussia took West Prussia, joining up East Prussia with Brandenburg. This aggression stirred the Poles at long last to patriotic action. Sweeping reforms were passed, improving the condition of the peasants and the bourgeoisie and giving the king and the Diet the powers to act effectively. But it was too late. Russia and Prussia were determined to prevent the emergence of a vigorous Polish nation. In 1793 they marched in and seized additional slices of Poland. The Poles, under the leadership of Thaddeus Kosciusko, now flew to arms, although the arms were often only agricultural implements. They were no match for the professional armies of Russia, Prussia, and Austria, who in 1795 divided the remainder of Poland among themselves. Russia's share of Poland, about two thirds of the total, was inhabited largely by Russian-speaking people. Austria's share was inhabited by Roman Catholics, as was Austria itself. Prussia's share, however, except for part of West Prussia, was inhabited by people who were neither linguistically nor religiously akin to the Prussians and who proved to be a fruitful source for future trouble.

Poland was not the only victim in Eastern Europe of the rise of Prussia and Russia. Sweden and the Ottoman Empire declined, both relatively and actually. Sweden had become the dominant military power in Northern and Eastern Europe under Gustavus Adolphus in the early seventeenth century. At the opening of the eighteenth century she was second only to Russia in size among the nations of Europe, holding large areas east and south of the Baltic in addition to the homeland. However, her population and resources were too small to hold for long such far-flung territories, which were coveted by ambitious and growing Prussia and Russia. The youthful military genius Charles XII made a spectacular effort to hold them, but in the end he lost all of his trans-Baltic territories except Finland and dissipated Sweden's strength in so doing. Sweden has never been a major power since.

The Ottoman Turks, after reaching the gates of Vienna early in the sixteenth century and again late in the seventeenth century, weakened rapidly. The Treaty of Karlowitz in 1699 limited their power in Europe to the Balkan Peninsula and a strip of territory north of the Black Sea. Their two serious defeats at the hands of Catherine the Great marked the beginning of the crack-up of the Ottoman Empire. By the end of the eighteenth century the three dominant powers in Central and Eastern Europe were the relatively static Austrian Hapsburg Empire and the two rapidly rising military despotisms—Prussia and Russia.

———————◆•◆———————

SUGGESTED READING

* S. B. Fay, *The Rise of Brandenburg-Prussia to 1786* (Berkshire). A brief survey of the spectacular rise of Prussia to the death of Frederick the Great.

J. A. R. Marriott and C. G. Robertson, *The Evolution of Prussia* (1917). A useful survey of the rise of Prussia from the earliest Hohenzollerns to the beginning of World War I.

Ferdinand Schevill, *The Great Elector* (1947). A sound biography of the Hohenzollern statesman who laid the foundations for Prussia's later greatness.

R. R. Ergang, *The Potsdam Führer: Frederick William I of Prussia* (1941). A scholarly study of the typically militaristic Hohenzollern who was the father of Frederick the Great.

G. P. Gooch, *Frederick the Great, the Ruler, the Writer, the Man* (1947). A well-rounded biography of the brilliant soldier-philosopher king.

James F. Bright, *Maria Theresa* (1897). Still the standard biography of the beautiful and gracious Hapsburg empress who was unable to cope with her aggressive Hohenzollern rival, Frederick the Great.

Sidney Harcave, *Russia: A History* (1956). A readable and well-organized general history of Russia.

B. H. Sumner, *Peter the Great and the Emergence of Russia* (1950). A scholarly, brief, and well-written biography of the uncouth but statesmanlike tsar who made Russia a great power.

Kasimierz Walizewski, *The Romance of an Empress* (1894). Still probably the best biography of Catherine the Great. Combines excellent scholarship and good writing.

CHAPTER 36

Overseas Colonization
and Competition for Empire

Dᴜʀɪɴɢ the age of royal absolutism the European nations competed for overseas possessions and commerce no less than for control of Europe. England, France, and the Netherlands threw themselves vigorously into colonizing and commercial expansion in various quarters of the globe and created empires that surpassed those established by Spain and Portugal in the sixteenth century. And while Europe colonized, traded, and competed for world power more vigorously than ever, European civilization spread over a large area of the globe.

1. The English in North America

One of the areas attracting the English, French, and Dutch was the New World, where all three nations established thriving colonies during the seventeenth century. These nations directed their efforts toward North America, leaving Spain and Portugal in possession of their colonial empires south of the Rio Grande. The Northern European nations transplanted their ways of life across the Atlantic, pushed aside the native Indians, and quickly turned parts of North America into an annex of Europe.

England was unquestionably the most successful colonizer in North America. She had shown increasing interest in the New World throughout the sixteenth century but had been curbed by Spanish strength. That barrier was removed in 1588 with the destruction of the Spanish Armada and England soon capitalized on her opportunity. The first English colony was established at Jamestown, Virginia, in 1607 by a joint-stock company chartered by James I. After a period of great difficulty the Virginia colony took root and grew rapidly, attracting a large population and producing a good return economically. In the meantime a small group of Puritans had on their own authority planted a colony at Plymouth in 1620, drawing up their own "constitution" in the form of the Mayflower Compact and battling magnificently against the harsh environment. The Plymouth Colony was soon overshadowed by the colonization undertaken by another joint-stock company, the Massachusetts Bay Company, controlled largely by Puritans. In 1630 the company established a colony in Salem; soon thereafter Boston was established and became the headquarters of the company, which moved from England. A steady stream of emigrants moved to Massachusetts in the following years. Several new colonizing ventures were undertaken by the company from its American headquarters. In 1636 a group migrated to Connecticut, soon to be followed by others, most of whom resented the strong-handed tactics of the governors of the

Massachusetts Bay Company. In 1636 Roger Williams led a group to Rhode Island in hopes of escaping the religious dictates of the Puritan masters of Massachusetts, who liked Williams and his ideas on tolerance even less than he liked them. Both Connecticut and Rhode Island were eventually recognized as independent colonies. Other settlements were established in New Hampshire and Maine, although these did not become independent colonies.

Other colonies were established by proprietors, i.e., persons to whom the English king gave large grants of land. Maryland was established in 1632 through the efforts of Lord Baltimore, who tried to make his colony a refuge for Catholics. In 1633 eight English gentlemen were given proprietary rights over Carolina, and two centers of colonization were established shortly thereafter. In 1664 the English captured the Dutch colony of New Amsterdam, whereupon Charles II made his brother, the duke of York, its proprietor. Thus New York came into existence as an English colony. In 1681 William Penn received a grant from which grew the colony of Pennsylvania, where Penn hoped Quakers would find refuge. New Jersey and Delaware came into existence as offshoots of New York and Maryland. When in 1733 a colony was established in Georgia, England controlled the Atlantic seaboard from Maine to the Spanish colony in Florida.

The English were also active elsewhere in the Western Hemisphere. Profitable colonies were established in the West Indies, the chief ones being Barbados, Jamaica, and Bermuda. English explorers and traders penetrated into the Hudson Bay area and began to trade profitably with the Indians. Once established, the English colonies flourished everywhere in the New World. Population and wealth increased rapidly.

The new environment, the mixing of peoples, experimentation in government, different economic conditions, and numerous other factors combined to make it impossible for the colonists to recreate the English way of life on this "frontier." Eventually this was to cause England trouble, but for at least a century and a half England's colonial subjects remained loyal Englishmen, and her colonies supplied valuable wealth for the mother country.

2. The French and Dutch in North America

France was not so successful as England in colonizing North America. Her first American colony was established by Samuel de Champlain at Quebec on the St. Lawrence River in 1608, only a year after the founding of Jamestown. Although Champlain explored the whole St. Lawrence Valley to the Great Lakes, settlers were slow to come from France to live in Canada. Most of those who did leave France preferred to settle in the West Indies, where France had also established colonies. Not until the reign of Louis XIV did the French turn to a more vigorous policy. Colbert, Louis's economic minister, put all of New France under royal administration and sent the Comte de Frontenac off to the New World as governor. Frontenac exerted every effort to increase France's possessions. During the last quarter of the seventeenth century explorers and missionaries, such as La Salle, Joliet, and Marquette, explored the Mississippi Valley, allowing France to claim a huge territory, called Louisiana, which stretched from the Great Lakes to the Gulf of Mexico and included extensive lands on either side of the Mississippi. Territorially the French holdings in North America were much larger than those of the English.

Efforts to attract settlers to this rich territory were unsuccessful. Although the population grew after about 1675, still New France remained badly underpopulated. France closed her empire to non-Catholics, thus excluding the element that had been so important in populating England's colonies—the religiously dissatisfied. The French government, by making extensive grants to aristocrats, made it difficult for the lower classes to get land overseas. The excellent trading opportunities in the fur business attracted more attention than the less profitable pursuit of agriculture. French settlements were thus few and far between in the territory stretching from New Orleans to the mouth of the St. Lawrence. When England seized France's American empire in 1763, perhaps no more than eighty thousand people lived in New France, and most of these were in the St. Lawrence Valley.

Even this sparse population left its mark. The Roman Catholic Church was established firmly in New France. Missionaries were active converting the Indians. The French language was spoken everywhere. Larger communities, such as Quebec and New Orleans, imitated the ways of French society. Even to this day the influences of these early French colonists can be seen along the St. Lawrence Valley and in Louisiana.

The Dutch attempted to join the other powers in colonizing the North American wilds. In 1621 the Dutch West India Company was chartered to undertake colonization and commerce in the New World. In 1624 a colony was planted on Manhattan Island. Soon other Dutch communities were established in the Hudson Valley and on the Connecticut and Delaware rivers. The Dutch enjoyed only limited success, since Dutch interest and effort were concentrated chiefly on the more profitable East Indies. And in 1664 the English seized New Netherland during a war with the Dutch, ending Dutch colonization in North America.

3. European Penetration of the Far East

The nations that colonized North America in the seventeenth and eighteenth centuries—England, France, and the Netherlands—were equally aggressive in the Far East. Portugal had established her supremacy there in the sixteenth century, building a commercial empire based upon control of a few key ports in the Far East. Spain had sought to enter the Far East but had not progressed beyond the Philippines.

By 1600 Portugal had begun to lose her grip in the East. Conquered by Spain in 1580 and held in bondage for sixty years, she was unable to protect her empire in the East. The enterprising Dutch, who were successfully freeing themselves from Spanish control, were the chief beneficiaries. Early in the seventeenth century all the competing Dutch companies interested in Far Eastern trade were joined into a single Dutch East India Company, to which the Dutch government gave almost complete freedom of action. The company soon drove the Portuguese out of the Spice Islands, which became the center of the Dutch Empire. In 1641 Malacca on the Malay Peninsula was seized, giving the Dutch control of the seas around the East Indies. Ceylon and the Celebes were captured. The English tried to seize a share of this rich area but were driven out by the Dutch as early as 1623. To safeguard the sea route to the Indies, the Dutch established a colony at the Cape of Good Hope in South Africa. To watch its interest in the Indies, the Dutch East India Company established a governor-general in Java, who in turn set up several other governmental centers in the island empire. For years after this the Dutch continued to profit from their holdings in the Indies. The Dutch also made attempts to penetrate China and Japan, but both countries refused to deal with the Dutch and were too strong to permit entrance by force.

The English, although shut out of the East Indies by the Dutch, made rapid progress toward replacing the Portuguese in India. The English East India Company was chartered in 1600 and given a monopoly of English trade in the East. This company concentrated chiefly on India, slowly forcing the Portuguese to let English traders into that rich land. The company founded its own "factories" (trading posts) at key locations in India—Surat, Madras, Bombay, and Calcutta. For a long time the East India Company was content to exploit the trading opportunities available in these cities; the merchants interfered little with Indian affairs and as yet had little influence on Indian society.

Rather belatedly the French entered the

competition in the Far East. Again it took the farsighted Colbert to see what France was missing. He organized a French East India Company (1664), which soon established a French outpost at Pondicherry in India. From this center the French company soon built up a prosperous trade that returned large profits.

When one has seen how various European powers established trading depots in the seacoast cities of India and the East Indies, one knows almost the whole story of European penetration of the Far East during the seventeenth and eighteenth centuries. Except in the Philippines the existing patterns of life were barely disturbed by the arrival of the Europeans. In contrast with the New World most areas of the East were not rapidly Europeanized. Few Europeans went as colonists. An explanation for this contrast is not hard to discover. In the Far East the Europeans encountered ancient cultures, solidly founded and not inferior to that of Western Europe. A brief discussion of Indian civilization will illustrate why Europeans had to conduct themselves differently in the East than in the Americas and why European influences penetrated the Far East only slowly.

4. Indian Civilization

When the Europeans first began their penetration of India, that land was enjoying one of its rare moments of political unity. A branch of the Mongol horde of Tamerlane, known as the Moguls, had invaded India about 1500 and by the reign of Akbar (1562–1605) had conquered most of its petty states. Although this dynasty was Moslem, it managed to retain considerable authority in India until 1700. The secret of Mogul success lay in the tolerant attitude its emperors took toward the native Indian civilization. Such political unity, however, was an exception in Indian history. Since the beginnings of Indian civilization in the third millennium B.C., foreign invaders had repeatedly tried to unite the peninsula only to be defeated by the racial, linguistic, and geographical barriers that divided this vast and populous land. For long stretches of time Indian political life was dominated by numerous petty princes. Indian civilization did not possess a tradition of strong political organization; its strength lay elsewhere.

Indian society in the sixteenth and seventeen centuries gained its cohesion primarily from three interrelated and very ancient institutions—the village, the family, and the caste system. With the exception of a small minority of the population living in the coastal cities the great mass of the Indians lived in self-sufficient agricultural villages under the authority of the Brahmans (priests), whose role we will examine in a moment. Each village was made up of several families. Every family was a tightly knit unit, held together by blood ties, common ownership and exploitation of the land, and religion. Each village had its own government, amazingly democratic in its operation. The villages sometimes had to pay taxes to a faraway central authority, but seldom did they have much concern with the outside world.

Even more fundamental in the life of each Indian was the caste system. Its origins were ancient and are still poorly understood. Long before the beginning of the Christian era Indian society had been stratified into groups, each with its own customs, responsibilities, and rights. The system steadily became more complicated and more rigid. In ancient times there were four broad castes: the priests, the aristocratic warriors, the small landowners and artisans, and the laborers. The untouchables were those having no caste. As the centuries passed, numerous subgroups were created, and the rules regulating the conduct of each group became constantly more elaborate. By the time the Europeans became acquainted with Indian society there were hundreds of caste groups. Almost every occupational group in India constituted a special caste. Elaborate rules defining every detail of life within the caste and of relationships with other groups had been evolved. A member of a caste had his life clearly cut out for him from birth.

Education, marriage, occupation, manners, dress, and nearly everything else were clearly defined. Obviously this institution gave little freedom to the Indian, but just as obviously it provided him with a definite place in society and established a remarkably stable and unchanging social order.

The strength of the Indian caste system lay in the religious sanctions that stood behind it; every Indian accepted the system that bound him to his present lot because he believed that that system was the earthly embodiment of the divine order of the universe. More than anything else religion gave Indian civilization its distinctive qualities and made most Indians immune to Western influences.

The Indian religious system was already ancient when the Europeans first began settling in India. Several religious traditions, some dating back to the beginnings of Indian civilization, had merged to create the main body of Indian religious thought. By 500 B.C. a basic set of assumptions had been clearly formulated by religious and philosophical leaders and set down in a body of philosophical literature called the *Upanishads*. From the *Upanishads* later developed the chief religious systems of India (except Mohammedanism, which entered India from the outside). A brief description of the basic ideas contained in the *Upanishads* is the best starting place for an understanding of Indian religion.

The ancient Indian thinkers agreed that the universe is permeated by a spiritual force that creates and animates everything. This spiritual force is the only thing that is real. The world that man sees and experiences is merely an illusion, representing the spirit entrapped in material things. The destiny of spirits born to the flesh is to escape back to the perfect world of pure spirit.

At a certain phase of their path to perfection spirits are born into the material world. Once made flesh, spirits become excessively attached to earthly existence, piling up a record of activities not befitting a pure spirit. This record must be atoned for before a spirit achieves its ultimate perfection.

When death parts the spirit from its earthly prison, the soul carries its record with it. Therefore, the spirit must be reincarnated in some earthly form to continue its purification. The form that rebirth takes depends on the record of a spirit's previous activities; forces beyond man's control assign him to a status in this world and demand that he keep that status. Rebirth may occur many times, each time putting the spirit in a different shape and presenting it with new tests. Eventually the spirit will end its dependence on the material world and be freed from reincarnation. Toward that perfect state all things are destined.

Hinduism was by far the most significant religion that grew out of the concepts discussed above. The great spiritual force, which the philosophers said directed the universe, became gods. Most Hindus worship many gods, although three predominate: Brahma the Creator, Vishnu the Preserver, and Siva the Destroyer. No matter how many different gods are worshipped, the Hindu believes that they are all a part of a single spiritual order and thus in no sense competitive. To honor these gods, an elaborate set of rituals has developed over the centuries, chiefly under the guidance of the Brahmans or priests, who play a leading role in Indian society because they are necessary to approach the gods in the proper way. The Hindus take literally the idea that a part of the divine spirit dwells in every creature. This has led to the development of a complicated list of prohibitions against killing and eating animals, doing violence to other men, and mistreating one's own body. Since detachment from the world is a way of freeing the spirit, Hindus are strongly ascetic, often withdrawing from daily life for fasting, prayer, and chastisement of the flesh. All Hindus believe in reincarnation, contending that the caste system is the earthly form of this truth. Each caste is a kind of religious order representing a stage into which spirits are born on the path to perfection. It becomes every Hindu's religious duty to accept his caste and fulfill all the obligations attached to it. In the ascending structure of the caste system each grade represents a step nearer to spiritual perfection and liberation from the material world. The untouchable is the least pure of all humans and must suffer burdens equal to his impurity. The Brahman at the top of the caste system is nearest to perfection and is about to end the cycle of rebirth, a status that gives Brahmans the wisdom to control earthly society. The orthodox Hindu, therefore, accepts the established social system in India as a vital part of his religion and feels that to change it would be to tamper with the divine order.

Hinduism places a heavy emphasis on acceptance of one's lot and upon close observation of all the rituals and laws connected with one's earthly station. The good Hindu believes, worships, observes the law, and waits until repeated reincarnation delivers him. It is one of the most formalistic religions in the world.

However, the powerful stream of Indian religious life did not confine itself to that one channel. Buddhism, for example, illustrates how the basic set of beliefs which we have just noted could produce a different religion. Buddhism drew its original inspira-

THE TAJ MAHAL. Built in the seventeenth century by a ruler of the Moslem Mogul dynasty at Agra as a final resting place for himself and his consort, this beautiful building is one of the world's great architectural achievements. Although built in India and marked by Indian influences, the structure also shows strong Moslem influences, especially in the domes and slender towers. The building is made even more impressive by the splendid formal gardens in which it is set. (*United Press International Photo*)

tion from the teachings of Gautama Buddha (about 563–483 B.C.). Buddha, the son of a prince, was well educated in the philosophical ideas of the *Upanishads*. Rejecting his princely heritage to become a religious leader, Buddha preached a doctrine according to which men freed themselves from the suffering of this world by moral activity. He believed that all suffering was caused by the desire for things that did not befit human beings. To help men free themselves from such desires, Buddha laid down an enlightened moral code, called the Eightfold Path, which stressed love of others, good works, and rejection of sensual pleasures. By following this code Buddha felt that a man could help himself along the road to spiritual freedom. Buddha did not reject reincarnation; he taught merely that a morally strong man could speed up his own deliverance.

Buddha's teachings, originally an ethical protest against Hindu religious practices, were soon turned into a religion. His disciples, organizing themselves into monastic groups, turned Buddha into a god, began worshipping his statues, and devised rituals to give expression to his teachings. The new religion took deep roots in India and flourished for many centuries. Eventually it fell into decline and by 1500 virtually disappeared in India. In part this was due to the fact that several foreign invaders of India were converts to Buddhism, causing it to gain a reputation as a foreign religion. However, before it died in India, Buddhism had gained a foothold abroad, especially in China. In its new home it flourished and spread, until today it is one of the major religions of the world, practiced nearly everywhere in the Far East except India. Buddhism left its mark on India despite its disappearance there. Its moral earnestness, its explanation of suffering, and its denial of this world all became a part of the Indian religious tradition.

Indian religion accounted for many things about the civilization that the Europeans met in India in the early modern period. The Indians were inclined to accept this world passively, feeling that the individual's destiny lay elsewhere. Progress, competition for wealth, and the search for new things were not attractive to them. The good Indian took what life gave him reverently and humbly. Above all else he was not impressed by the Europeans. He was convinced that he had reflected as keenly and deeply as they about human problems and had arrived at answers superior to theirs. He could point to a remarkable art and literature to prove (to his own satisfaction, at least) the superiority of his way of life. Nothing the European could bring him would, in his mind, improve upon his institutions and ideas. He, therefore, refused to be affected by the advent of the Europeans. They, in turn, found that a few hundred soldiers and a few cannon could not shake the Indian's confidence in his village and family life, his caste system, and his religion. Only slowly and almost imperceptibly did the European way of life make any significant impression on the East.

5. The Struggle for Overseas Empire

In spite of nearly empty continents to occupy in the New World and rich trading opportunities to exploit in the highly civilized East, the aggressive European nations could not keep out of one another's way in their overseas expansion. In the sixteenth century the competition had begun with Dutch and English assaults on the Spanish and Portuguese empires. By the end of the seventeenth century the struggle for overseas empires had entered a critical phase, progressing rapidly toward a decision in the eighteenth.

This struggle did not arise because the world overseas had become too crowded with Europeans. As mercantilists the colonial and commercial powers of the eighteenth century believed that their wealth and self-sufficiency depended on absolute control of territories overseas and that they could strike a mortal blow at their European foes by depriving them of their colonies. Every European war was, therefore, extended overseas, and every major settlement of a European war included a redistribution of overseas possessions.

The Dutch were the first to engage in serious competition with other European powers. As we have previously noted, they began to dismember the Portuguese Empire in the Far East in the sixteenth century. England soon followed the Dutch lead. Although her attacks on the Spanish Empire in the New World were not especially profitable, England did succeed in seizing most of Portugal's Indian holdings during the seventeenth century.

By the middle of the seventeenth century rivalry began to increase between the English and the Dutch. As early as 1651 England passed her first Navigation Act, providing that all goods coming to and from England and her overseas possessions would be carried in English ships. This struck a blow at Dutch commercial power, which concentrated on providing shipping services for other nations. It also encouraged the growth of the English navy, badly neglected by the first two Stuart kings. On three different occasions between 1651 and 1688 England engaged the Dutch in warfare. In general, these wars were not decisive. England did annex New Netherland in 1664 but gave the Dutch territory elsewhere. Probably the chief result of the wars was to add to the growing strength of the English navy. Eventually the English and the Dutch began to see that France was the chief danger to both. The result was an alliance in 1689, when William of Orange became king of England. By that time the Netherlands no longer was the major sea power in Europe. The Dutch were content to keep their already-established holdings, letting the other nations compete for the rest of the world.

The Dutch and the English had real cause for alarm. Louis XIV threw France wholeheartedly into the competition for overseas possessions in Canada, Louisiana, the West Indies, and India—all areas near to England's centers of operation. From 1689 until 1763 England and France fought each other regularly in Europe, and each en-

gagement had its repercussions abroad.

Several times during the War of the League of Augsburg (1689–97) the English and the French engaged forces in North America, where the war was called King William's War. Neither in Europe nor in America was the action decisive, and no changes were made in the holdings of either combatant. England had more success during the War of the Spanish Succession (1701–13). In North America, where the struggle was called Queen Anne's War, England captured Arcadia (Nova Scotia) and received recognition of her claims to Newfoundland and Hudson Bay. From France's ally, Spain, she received Gibraltar and Minorca, assuring her entrance into the Mediterranean. Spain also granted to England the right to supply Spain's colonies with slaves (the *asiento*) and the privilege of sending one ship a year to the Spanish colonies in America. These concessions ended Spain's long effort to close her empire to outsiders and gave England the advantage over other nations in exploiting Spanish overseas holdings.

From 1713 to 1740 England and France remained at peace. During this calm neither nation was idle in overseas matters. France, realizing the weakness of her position, was especially active in North America. She tried to protect her holdings from English sea power by building a strong fort at Louisburg at the mouth of the St. Lawrence. She also began constructing a series of forts designed to keep the English colonists pinned to the Atlantic seaboard. England concentrated her efforts on widening the commercial breech she had made in Spain's empire in 1713. A new European war in 1740, the War of the Austrian Succession, led to a sharp conflict between England and France in America (King George's War) and in India. At the end of the war in 1748 each power restored its spoils to the other, England giving up Louisburg and France restoring Madras.

An eight-year truce ensued in Europe, each side preparing desperately for the struggle that everyone knew would soon reopen.

In North America, France went back to her policy of building a barrier against the westward expansion of the English colonies. Already the colonists were pushing across the Appalachians into the Ohio Valley, claiming the territory as part of their original grants from the English crown. The inevitable clash came in 1755, when the British tried to stop the French from occupying Fort Duquesne at the present site of Pittsburgh. The issue was clearly joined; one power must destroy the other in America.

In India a no less dramatic struggle was shaping. France had entered the scene later than England but had made steady progress up to 1740. Growing English sea power made France's position precarious. To offset this disadvantage, the French governor of Pondicherry, François Dupleix, decided to take advantage of the internal chaos in India resulting from the decline of Mogul authority. In return for concessions favorable to France he supplied troops and made promises to whatever political faction in India gave him the best advantage. The policy netted France a claim to most of southern India. Dupleix soon found his match in a lowly clerk of the British East India Company named Robert Clive, who began to fight fire with fire. Spending money liberally and making even greater promises to the Indians, Clive built a counteralliance of Indian princes and wrung generous concessions from them for his company. Soon an undeclared war was on in India. Dupleix was recalled to France in 1754, chiefly because his company did not trust his high-handed methods. A showdown opened in 1756 when an Indian prince attacked the British garrison in Calcutta. Having captured the garrison, the prince put 146 Englishmen into a tiny cell; by the next morning 123 were dead in this "Black Hole" of Calcutta. Clive decided to avenge this atrocity.

Thus, at the opening of the Seven Years' War (French and Indian War in America) in 1756 France and England were pitted against each other on three continents. We have previously examined the course of that war in Europe (see chap. 35). England, led by William Pitt, threw her chief efforts into the naval and colonial war and won a smashing victory. In North America the French held their own until 1757. The superior British forces, supported by the navy, overpowered the French outposts one by one. The decisive blow fell in 1759 when the British captured Quebec, opening all Canada to the British. British naval units captured the chief French holdings in the West Indies. In India, Robert Clive gave the British as great a victory as Quebec. Using his military resources brilliantly and gaining invaluable help from the navy, he smashed France's Indian allies and captured her trading centers. When Pondicherry fell in 1761, France was ruined in India. Perhaps even more important, Clive had added large territories to England's sphere of influence by conquering several native Indian states.

The Seven Years' War ended in 1763 with the Treaty of Paris. France surrendered Canada and all Louisiana east of the Mississippi (except New Orleans) to England. Spain, who had been an ally of France, ceded Florida to England. By a special treaty France compensated Spain for this loss by giving her the rest of Louisiana (west of the Mississippi). All of the French possessions in the West Indies except Guadeloupe and Martinique also fell to England. France's empire in India likewise went to Britain. The French were permitted to enjoy trading privileges in India, but Britain controlled the chief centers of trade, ending any hope of a French recovery of power there.

The Treaty of Paris closed an era in European expansion. Although the Dutch and the Spanish still had extensive holdings abroad, Great Britain had fought her way to supremacy in colonial and commercial affairs. She could now turn to the exploitation of her empire.

Since Columbus's voyage the Europeans had wrought an important change around the world. Energetic colonizers had planted European civilization on the soil of the New

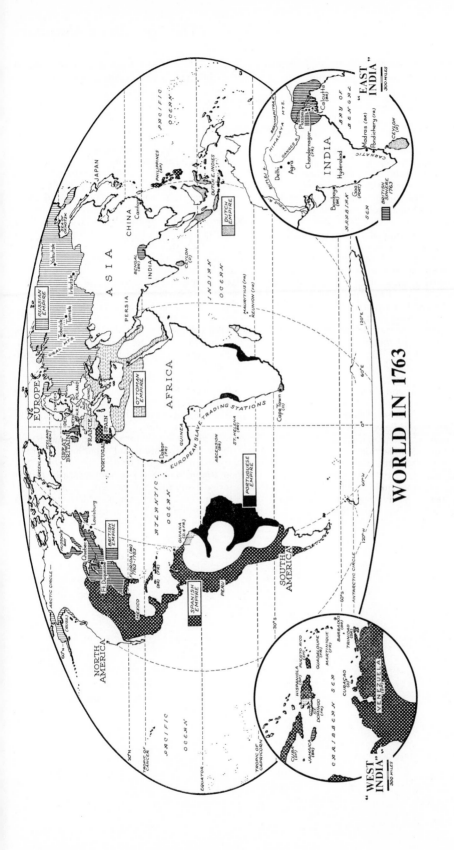

WORLD IN 1763

World. Enterprising merchants had begun to tap the wealth of a considerable part of the East. European history never again ceased to have a world-wide scope.

————— •◦• —————

SUGGESTED READING

Walter L. Dorn, *Competition for Empire, 1740–1763* (1940). An excellent study of the imperial conflicts during the critical years in the middle of the eighteenth century, emphasizing the causes of this conflict and the relationship between the internal policies of various European states and their overseas rivalry.

Herbert Eugene Bolton and Thomas Maitland Marshall, *The Colonization of North America, 1492–1783* (1936). A thorough study of the colonizing efforts of the European nations in North America, presenting a clear picture of their methods and of their competition.

Francis Parkman, *Montcalm and Wolfe*, 2 vols. (1905). An exciting treatment by a masterful historian of the conflict between England and France for North America during the years 1745–63.

Henry Dodwell, *Dupleix and Clive: The Beginning of Empire* (1920). A study of the clash between Britain and France for control of India.

W. B. Willcox, *Star of Empire: A Study of Britain as a World Power, 1485–1945* (1950). A well-written interpretation of British imperialism and its impact on world history.

Kenneth Scott Latourette. *A Short History of the Far East*, 3rd ed. (1957). An interesting introduction to the vast subject of Far Eastern history, written by an historian who has a sound knowledge of the history of that area.

W. H. Moreland and Atul Chandra Chatterjee, *A Short History of India*, 4th ed. (1957). A well-written survey of Indian history from its beginnings to the present with a proper balance between political, economic, and social developments and cultural history.

Kenneth Scott Latourette, *The Chinese: Their History and Culture*, 3rd rev. ed. (1946). A brief but stimulating treatment of Chinese history and culture by a well-known authority on Chinese history.

René Grousset, *The Civilizations of the East*, 4 vols. (1931–34). This major work by a renowned scholar provides the best introduction to the vast subject of Far Eastern cultural life. The volumes on India (Vol. II) and on China (Vol. III) are especially recommended. The work is improved by its excellent illustrations.

Sir Charles Eliot, *Hinduism and Buddhism: An Historical Study*, 3 vols. (1954). This long work, covering the two chief religions of the East in great detail, offers the most satisfactory introduction. Many shorter works are easier to read but usually help little in getting to the roots of Hinduism and Buddhism or their evolution through history.

Paul Radin, *The Story of the American Indian* rev. ed. (1934). An excellent introduction to the history of the American Indians and to their cultural achievements.

CHAPTER 37

———◆▶———

Literature, the Arts, and Religion

THE SPIRIT of royal absolutism, with its exaltation of kings, princes, and attendant nobility, and also its concern for order and form, was reflected in the literature, the arts, and certain religious movements of the seventeenth and eighteenth centuries. The prevailing styles were classicism in literature and music; baroque, in painting and architecture. Pietistic religious movements passively accepted royal absolutism as a form of government. Absolutism had its direct apologists in the field of political theory.

1. The Philosophy of Absolutism

In our twentieth-century concern for popular government we sometimes forget the service performed in early modern times by the royal monarchs. It was they who suppressed feudal turbulence, established law and order, and molded the first national states. Some were incompetent and some were predatory. However, the tragic example of Poland and the Holy Roman Empire, where the monarchs were dominated by the nobility and the local princes, would seem to indicate that in the first three centuries of the modern era, the absolutist kings generally served a useful, and possibly necessary, function. Their role was appreciated and defended by many of their subjects. We have already encountered Bishop Bossuet's eloquent defense of Louis XIV's claims to be God's duly ordained vicegerent on earth (see p. 390), and James I's espousal of di-

vine-right monarchy (see p. 399). The seventeenth-century philosopher Thomas Hobbes, dismayed by the civil strife then raging in England (the Puritan Revolution), decided that only absolute government could maintain law and order. In his *Leviathan* (1651) Hobbes theorized that basically selfish men for their own protection contracted with a prince to rule them; but, once having made the compact, they could not revoke it.[1] To be effective, the prince must be all-powerful, controlling even the religion of his subjects. The great Dutch political theorist Hugo Grotius argued not only for absolute governmental authority within the state but also for absolute sovereignty and equality of all states, large and small. His chief work, *The Law of War and Peace* (1625), was one of the earliest and probably the most influential of all treatises on international law. It was the outgrowth of Grotius's experiences during the revolt of the Netherlands against Spain and of his observation of some of the horrors of the Thirty Years' War in Germany. Both Hobbes and Grotius believed royal absolutism to be in accordance with the natural law.

2. The Golden Age of French Literature

The reign of Louis XIV (1643–1715), which marked the apogee of royal absolut-

---

[1] While proffering the social-contract theory of government Hobbes did not believe that it actually occurred as a historical event.

ism in France and indeed in all Europe, was also the golden age of French literature. The elegance, the sense of order, and the formalism of the court of the Grand Monarch were all reflected in the literature of the period, sometimes called the Augustan or the classical period of French literature. It was in the field of the drama that the French writers attained their greatest success. Corneille wrote elegant tragedies, of which *The Cid* and *Polyeucte* are among the best known, in the style of and often on the same subjects as the ancient Greek tragedies. The struggles of man against himself and against the universe furnish the dramatic conflicts. Corneille's craftsmanship and style are handsomely polished, though often exalted and exaggerated.

Even more exquisitely polished were the perfectly rhymed and metered couplets of Racine's tragedies. *Andromaque* relates the tragic story of Hector's wife after the death of her husband at the hands of Achilles and the ensuing fall of Troy. *Phèdre* is about the wife of the legendary Greek king Theseus who falls in love with her stepson. This story had also been the subject of plays by Euripides, Sophocles, and Seneca. As with the Greek and Roman dramatists abnormal love was a favorite theme with the French playwrights of the seventeenth century. Racine, an ardent Jansenist, turned later in life to religious subjects. *Esther* and *Athalie* are biblical plays of serene beauty.

One of the greatest of all the French dramatists was Molière. In his charming and profound comedies—such as *Tartuffe, Le Misanthrope,* and *Les Femmes Savantes* (*The Learned Ladies*)—Molière devastatingly portrays and satirizes all the fraudulent types that afflict human society: egotists, pedants, social climbers, false priests, and quack physicians. The tragic conflicts and the personality types of Corneille, Racine, and Molière are universal and eternal.

Other major French writers of the age of Louis XIV were Blaise Pascal, who took time out from his scientific and mathematical studies to write the marvelously styled *Provincial Letters* against the Jesuits and

his deeply reflective *Pensées* (*Thoughts*); Madame de Sévigné, who wrote 2200 *Letters* to her daughter, each a lengthy work of art; and the Duke de Saint-Simon, who spent the latter part of his life writing forty volumes of *Memoirs*. Madame de Sévigné and the Duke de Saint-Simon, both of whom were eyewitnesses of the court of Louis XIV, constitute two of the most important sources we have for the history and the life of those glamorous times.

The chief common denominator of all these writers is their emphasis upon and mastery of elegant and graceful form. In this they reflect the spirit of royal absolutism at its height. However, the form is valued not merely for its own sake, but as an artistic clothing for subtle and critical thought. It is little wonder that French literature in the late seventeenth century overshadowed that of all other countries of Europe, much as did French military and political influence. The lucid and graceful French language became the fashionable language of most of the royal courts and courtiers on the European continent.

French literature in the eighteenth century continued for the most part in the classical vein. Voltaire wrote dramas and poems carefully tailored to the dictates of classical formalism. His prose works exalted logic and the classical ideals of Greece and Rome. Only Rousseau among the major eighteenth-century French writers departed from the classical spirit to anticipate the romanticism of a later era. Voltaire and Rousseau, however, are much more important for the philosophic content of their works than for their literary artistry, and will be more fully examined in the following chapter, "The Intellectual Revolution."

3. The English Classical Writers

Next to France, England produced the most important literature in the seventeenth and early eighteenth centuries, and like the French the English authors generally wrote in the classical vein. The giant of English letters in the mid-seventeenth century was John Milton. This learned Puritan was steeped in the literature of ancient Greece and Rome. His exquisite lyrics *L'Allegro* and *Il Penseroso* and incomparable elegy, *Lycidas,* are thickly strewn with references to classical mythology. The conscientious Milton contributed much of his great talent and energy to public affairs. During the Puritan Revolution he went blind working as pamphleteer for the Puritan cause and as secretary for Oliver Cromwell. The chief literary product of this period of his life is *Areopagitica,* probably the noblest defense of freedom of the press ever penned. Milton's masterpiece is *Paradise Lost,* written in his blindness after the restoration of the Stuart kings had ruined his public career. *Paradise Lost* is an exalted poem of epic proportions based on the Genesis account of the rebellion of Satan against God and the temptation and fall of man. This most ambitious of themes is treated in stately blank verse of formal elegance. Even in this deeply religious work, holy writ is interwoven with classical pagan myth.

The two greatest poets to succeed Milton were John Dryden in the late seventeenth century and Alexander Pope in the early eighteenth century. Both were satirists, both displayed a massive knowledge of Greek and Roman lore, and both wrote chiefly in the formal rhymed couplets typical of the classical period. In the precision of their form, as in the sharpness of their satire, their appeal was to reason rather than to emotion. In these respects they resemble the great French classicist Voltaire, whom they preceded by a few decades.

The eighteenth century in English literature was primarily an age of prose. Following the great upheavals of the seventeenth century, the Puritan and Glorious revolutions, it was a time of political and religious bitterness and bickering. In pungent and incisive prose Jonathan Swift, in his *Gulliver's Travels* and political essays, and Richard Sheridan in his numerous dramas, pilloried the fops, pedants, bigots, and frauds of the day, much as Molière had done a century earlier across the channel. It was in the

eighteenth century that the English novel was born. Samuel Richardson, in *Clarissa Harlowe,* and Henry Fielding, in *Tom Jones,* used this medium to analyze human personality, emotions, and psychology, just as Corneille and Racine had used the poetic drama in France for the same purpose.

In the eighteenth century several writers —Robert Burns in Great Britain, Rousseau in France, Schiller and Goethe in Germany —anticipated romanticism (see pp. 550–5). But the prevailing spirit in eighteenth as in seventeenth century literature was classical. Precision, formalism, and ofttimes elegance marked the style. Pagan Greece and Rome furnished the models. The appeal was generally to reason. The royal monarchs and their courts had little to fear from this literature, even from the poetic and dramatic works of Voltaire. They could derive comfort from its formal order and laugh with the rest of the world at its satire, which was aimed at mankind in general rather than at ruling regimes.

4. Baroque Painting and Architecture

If the literature of the seventeenth and eighteenth centuries did not offend the absolutist kings and their aristocratic courtiers, the visual arts of the period usually glorified them. The dominant style of painting and architecture was the baroque, which was an elaboration of the classical style of the Renaissance. The baroque style was originally a product of the Counter Reformation and reflected the resurgence of the revitalized Roman Catholic Church led by the militant Jesuits. Later its massive and ornamental elegance reflected the wealth and power of the absolutist monarchs and their courts, then at the peak of their affluence.

The most popular of the baroque painters of the early seventeenth century was the Flemish Peter Paul Rubens. After studying the work of the Italian high Renaissance masters, Rubens returned to Antwerp and painted more than two thousand pictures, many of them huge in size. He operated what amounted to a painting factory, em-

CHRIST AT GETHSEMANE, BY EL GRECO. Baroque art was originally a product of the Roman Catholic Reformation, and this painting by the great Spanish baroque artist reveals the religious intensity engendered by the Catholic revival. El Greco deliberately distorted to attain a powerful effect. His work assumed great influence on nineteenth- and twentieth-century painting, despite the fact that he was regarded as insane by his contemporaries. (*Toledo Museum of Art, Gift of Edward Drummond Libbey, 1946*)

ploying dozens of artists who painted in the details designed and sketched by the master. Rubens, a devout Roman Catholic, first painted religious subjects. His sculpturesque and sensational *Descent from the Cross* undoubtedly reveals the influence of Michelangelo. His later subjects were pagan mythology, court life, and especially nude voluptuous women—all painted in the most brilliant and sensuous colors. All of these subjects appear in his most ambitious work —twenty-three colossal scenes (mostly imaginary) from the life of Marie de Médicis, widow of King Henry IV of France. Seldom, if ever, has a dull and colorless woman been more glamorized in paint.

Spain boasted two of the greatest seventeenth-century baroque painters: El Greco and Velásquez. El Greco, whose real name was Domenikos Theotokopoulos, was a native of the Greek island of Crete (hence "The Greek"). After studying the Italian Renaissance masters he settled down in Toledo and developed a style of his own, usually called mannerism or expressionism. By deliberate distortion and exaggeration he achieved sensational effect. *View of Toledo, St. Jerome in His Study,* and *Christ at Gethsemane* illustrate his genius. El Greco's favorite subject was the Roman Catholic Church, reinvigorated by the Counter Reformation. Considered to be a madman by his contemporaries, he is now regarded as the forerunner, if not the founder, of several schools of nineteenth- and twentieth-century painting. Velásquez was a painter of great versatility. Although much of his earlier work was of a religious nature, he also painted genre subjects (depicting the life of the common people) and, later, portraits. He is considered one of the greatest of portrait painters. As official court painter he exalted and glorified the Spanish royalty and ruling classes at a time when they had really passed their peak in world affairs. Velásquez was one of the chief pioneers of modern art; it was from him that the late nineteenth-century impressionists and realists received much of their inspiration.

France's chief contribution to baroque painting was Nicolas Poussin, who spent most of his life in Italy studying the Renaissance masters. Although his biblical and mythological scenes are much more serene and subtle than the works of Rubens and El Greco, they are more vibrant and pulsating than the Italian Renaissance paintings that inspired them. They must, therefore, be classified as baroque in style. Some critics think that Poussin's magnificent landscapes have never been surpassed.

In eighteenth-century Great Britain Reynolds, Gainsborough, Romney, and Lawrence (who lived and painted well into the nineteenth century) vied with each other for commissions to paint the portraits of royalty and aristocracy. The result was plumes, jewels, buckles, silks, brocades, and laces in dripping profusion. This flattering of the royalty and aristocracy, however, did not go unchallenged. Hogarth in Great Britain and Goya in Spain in the eighteenth and early nineteenth centuries pitilessly satirized the excesses and abuses of aristocratic society.

THE HON. MRS. GRAHAM, BY GAINSBOROUGH. Outside the Dutch Netherlands baroque painters vied with each other in flattering the royalty and aristocracy. It was against such aristocratic arrogance and inordinate display as here portrayed by Gainsborough that the philosophers of the Enlightenment and the French Revolution vented their wrath. (*Courtesy of the Board of Trustees for the National Galleries of Scotland*)

Their brushes matched the pens of Swift and Sheridan.

Only in the Dutch Netherlands did the age of the baroque fail to reflect the ascendancy of royalty. Here in the busy ports and market places commerce was king, and the great Dutch painters of the seventeenth century, notably Frans Hals and Rembrandt van Rijn, portrayed the bourgeoisie and the common people. Hals was one of the first great realistic genre painters. Rembrandt is universally recognized as one of the greatest artistic geniuses of all time. One of his favorite subjects was portraits of the Dutch bourgeoisie. He was not a popularizer, however, and he suffered many personal hardships rather than compromise the sincerity of his art. The tragic toll of these hardships upon him is strikingly revealed in a series of magnificent self-portraits. As a portrayer of character he has never been surpassed, perhaps not even equaled. His mastery of light and shade (chiaroscuro) seemed to illumine the very souls of his subjects. *Syndics of the Cloth Guild, Night Watch,* and *Anatomy Lesson of Dr. Tulp* are among his most powerful portrait studies. These three paintings also vividly depict the commerical prosperity, the festive urban life, and the growing interest in natural science, respectively, in the seventeenth-century Dutch Nether-

SYNDICS OF THE CLOTH GUILD, BY REMBRANDT. In the seventeenth-century Dutch Netherlands, commerce was king. Under the leadership of men like these, the tiny Dutch Netherlands attained a first-rank position in the world of science, philosophy, and trade. Rembrandt, one of the greatest portrait painters of all time, was probably also the greatest of the baroque painters. (*Courtesy, Rijksmuseum, Amsterdam*)

lands. Rembrandt's glowing idealization of people and landscapes anticipates the age of romanticism of the early nineteenth century.

Baroque architecture, like baroque painting, was an elaboration and ornamentation of the classical style of the Renaissance, and a product of the Roman Catholic Reformation. In the late sixteenth, seventeenth, and eighteenth centuries Jesuit churches sprang up all over the Roman Catholic world. The most important and one of the best examples of the baroque style is the Jesuit parent church, Il Gesù, in Rome. Also, like baroque painting, baroque architecture was later used to represent the gaudy splendor of the seventeenth- and eighteenth-century absolute monarchs and their courts.

Towering over all other monuments of baroque architecture, much as did St. Peter's over all other Renaissance structures, was the Versailles palace of Louis XIV. The exterior of Versailles is designed in long, horizontal classic lines. The interior is lavishly decorated with richly colored marbles, mosaics, inlaid woods, gilt, silver, silk, velvet, and brocade. Lebrun painted many of the ceilings. The salons and halls are lighted with ceiling-to-floor windows and mirrors and crystal chandeliers holding thousands of candles. The palace is surrounded by hundreds of acres of groves, walks, pools, terraces, fountains, statues, flowers, and clipped shrubs—all laid out in formal geometric patterns.

So dazzling was this symbol of royal absolutism that most European monarchs attempted to copy it. The most successful attempt was Maria Theresa's Schönbrunn Palace in Vienna. As late as the mid-nineteenth century, mad King Ludwig of Bavaria was building three palaces in the style of Versailles. One, Herrenchiemsee, is a remarkable duplication.

Two other notable examples of baroque architecture, seen by thousands of tourists in Paris, are the Hôtel des Invalides (Old Soldiers' Home) with its magnificent dome, and the Luxembourg Palace and Gardens. In England Sir Christopher Wren was the greatest architect of the baroque period. The great fire that destroyed most of the heart of London in 1666 provided Wren with an opportunity to build numerous baroque structures. His masterpiece is St. Paul's Cathedral, with its lofty dome and columns.

In the eighteenth century architecture tended to become more feminine and less massive, relying heavily upon multiple curves and lacy shell-like ornamentation. This style is usually referred to as rococo. One of the best examples of rococo is Frederick the Great's Sans Souci Palace at Potsdam. The rococo style, like the baroque, represented an age of aristocratic affluence.

THE PALACE OF VERSAILLES IN FRANCE. This chateau, built by Louis XIV in the late seventeenth century, is the greatest of all the monuments of baroque architecture. The palace is so huge that no single view can show the whole structure and also the elaborate detail. This view shows one wing of the palace and a bit of the hundreds of acres of formal gardens and parks that surround it. (*Ewing Galloway*)

5. The Great Age of Classical Music

The classical spirit pervaded the music of the seventeenth and eighteenth centuries as it did the literature and the visual arts; and, like the literature and the visual arts, seventeenth- and eighteenth-century music was an outgrowth of Renaissance developments.[2] The piano and the violin family of instruments, whose forebears appeared in the sixteenth century, developed rapidly in the seventeenth. In the late seventeenth and early eighteenth centuries the Italian families, Amati, Guarneri, and Stradivari, fashioned the greatest violins ever made. The seventeenth century was also marked by the rise of the opera. Alessandro Scarlatti in Italy, Lully in France, and Purcell in England popularized this grandiose combination of music and drama. The eighteenth was the great century of classical music— the age of Bach, Handel, Haydn, Mozart, and Beethoven.

Johann Sebastian Bach (1685–1750) was a member of a German family long distinguished in music. Noted in his own lifetime chiefly as an organist, he composed a vast array of great music for organ, harpsichord and clavichord (forerunner of the piano), orchestra, and chorus, much of which has been lost. Most of Bach's compositions were religiously inspired, and he holds the same position in Protestant music that the sixteenth-century Palestrina does in music of the Roman Catholic Church. Bach was not widely appreciated in his own day. It was not until Felix Mendelssohn in the nineteenth century "discovered" him that he became widely known. Today Bach is considered one of the greatest creative geniuses of all time—comparable to Leonardo da Vinci, Shakespeare, and Cervantes.

George Frederick Handel (1685–1759) was born in central Germany in the same year as Bach and not many miles distant. He studied Italian opera in Germany and Italy,

[2] Some music historians designate the music of the seventeenth and early eighteenth centuries, including that of Bach and Handel, as baroque, which was a forerunner of the classical.

writing forty-three operas himself. He became court musician of the elector of Hanover, and when the elector became King George I of England, Handel followed him there. Handel wrote an enormous quantity of music, both instrumental and vocal. All of it is marked by dignity, formal elegance, and melodious harmony—fitting for and appreciated in an age of royal splendor. His best-known work is the majestic oratorio *The Messiah*, heard every Christmas season.

Franz Joseph Haydn (1732–1809), unlike Handel, was primarily interested in instrumental music; he was the chief originator of the symphony. During his long career in Vienna, which he helped to make the music capital of the world, he wrote more than a hundred symphonies in addition to scores of compositions of other forms of music, particularly chamber music. It was in his hands that orchestral music really came into its own. All of his work is in the formal, classical style. As a friend of the younger Mozart, Haydn probably learned more than he taught.

Wolfgang Amadeus Mozart (1756–91) is regarded by many students as the greatest musical genius of all time. Born in Salzburg, he spent most of his adult life in Vienna. Mozart began composing at the age of five (possibly four) and gave public concerts on the harpsichord at the age of six. At twelve he wrote an opera. Before his untimely death at the age of thirty-five he wrote more than six hundred compositions in all the known musical forms. Symphonies, chamber music, and piano sonatas and concertos were his favorite forms. His best known operas are *The Marriage of Figaro*, *Don Giovanni*, and *The Magic Flute*. In the masterful hands of Mozart the classical style reached the peak of its perfection. Never was music so clear, melodic, precise, and logical. However, Mozart's material rewards in this world were few. Although the courts of many kings, princes, and aristocrats were graced by his marvelous music, whose spirit accorded with the formalism and authoritative orderliness of an age of absolutism, his opulent patrons gave him little money or honor. Even their servants looked down on him, and he was buried in a pauper's grave. But thousands of music-loving pilgrims have visited his birthplace in Salzburg since.

Upon the stage set by Bach, Handel, Haydn, and Mozart emerged the biggest figure in the history of music, Ludwig van Beethoven (1770–1827). Beethoven's dynamic genius overflowed the bounds of any calamity that could befall a musical genius —deafness. Although Beethoven studied under Haydn, the greatest influence in his life was Mozart, to whose work his earlier compositions bear a marked resemblance. To the classical style, however, the mature Beethoven added spontaneous and sometimes noisy emotion, thereby becoming the founder of the romantic style of a later gen-

BEETHOVEN WALKING IN THE VIENNA WOODS, FROM A PAINTING BY JULIUS SCHMIDT. Beethoven's genius overflowed the bounds of any school or style of music. He is considered today both as the last of the classical and the first of the romantic composers. He continued to compose during the last years of his life, although he had become totally deaf. A temperamental man with a stormy disposition, he is portrayed here as intensely serious. (*The Bettmann Archive*)

school or style. However, his training, his earlier work, and his fundamental style and form were classical. Beethoven, like Michelangelo, lived a tempestuous, trouble-filled life. He was born in Bonn in the German Rhineland of Flemish ancestry (hence the "van"). High strung, poor, unsocial, and frustratedly ambitious, he went to Vienna, the music capital of the world. In addition to personal and social maladjustment there came to him in his early prime the greatest eration. Beethoven lived through the upheavals of the French Revolution, Napoleon, and the surge of nationalism that overthrew the Napoleonic dictatorship. His keen interest in these dramatic events are revealed in his music (see p. 556). Beethoven was too much the perfectionist to write voluminously. However, his nine symphonies, chamber music, and numerous piano sonatas and concertos constitute the greatest and best-loved music in history.

6. Pietism in Religion

In a later chapter we shall study the critics of royal absolutism. First, however, we should take cognizance of the quietists, or religious pietists, who passively accepted royal political authority.

We have already observed the Jansenist movement within the Roman Catholic Church in France in the seventeenth century (see pp. 392–3). Although the Jansenists were by no means oblivious to the political and social issues of the day and actually participated in the Fronde uprising against Mazarin's tyranny, they were fundamentally a Puritanical pietistic group, seeking communion with God through prayer, meditation, and mild asceticism. Early in the eighteenth century Louis XIV, under the influence of the Jesuits, outlawed the Jansenists and destroyed their buildings. At the same time the pope declared them to be heretics. However, the spirit of Jansenism continued.

In Germany Philipp Spener (1635–1705) and Count Zinzendorf (1700–60) became leaders of pietist movements of considerable dimensions. Spener, a Lutheran pastor, recoiled from the formal officiousness that his church had fallen into after the heated religious strife of the sixteenth and early seventeenth centuries. He minimized dogma and external forms in favor of inner piety and holy living. His largely Lutheran following included some of the leading intellects of Germany. Count Zinzendorf, a well-to-do Saxon nobleman, undertook to restore the Bohemian Brethren, the persecuted and scattered followers of the early fifteenth-century reformer John Huss. He called his group the Moravian Brethren. The Moravians, too, shunned intricate dogma and formal ritual. They set up model communities based upon brotherly love, frugal living, hard work, and inner piety. Count Zinzendorf migrated to America and founded Moravian communities at Bethlehem and other Pennsylvania towns. Later many Moravian "Pennsylvania Dutch" Germans migrated southward along the Appalachian piedmont as far as Georgia, planting settlements, such as Winston-Salem in North Carolina, along the way.

In Lutheran Sweden, Emanuel Swedenborg (1688–1772), a distinguished scientist, inventor, and public servant, founded a movement somewhat like the Moravian Brethren, based upon his visions, which he took to be direct revelations of God. Swedenborg wrote several learned theological works stressing inner and outward piety and individual communion with God. His followers, who called themselves the Church of the New Jerusalem, also came in considerable numbers to America.

England, however, was the seat of the most widespread and influential pietistic movements of the seventeenth and eighteenth centuries. The first was the Society of Friends, or the Quakers, as they were generally called, founded by George Fox (1624–91). Fox, a man of great energy and stubborn independence, detested formalism in religion as well as in society and government. He believed that true Christianity is an individual matter—a matter of plain, pious living and of private communion with God under the guidance of divine "inner light." Opposed to war, to rank, and to intolerance, the Quakers refused military service, the use of titles, and the taking of oaths. In these respects the Quakers were different from most of the other pietists. They were considered dangerous to the established order and were severely persecuted. Probably the most prominent of the early Quakers was William Penn, a wealthy aristocrat, who in 1682 founded Pennsylvania as a refuge for members of his persecuted sect. Pennsylvania and the Quakers both prospered.

A more moderate and much more popular pietist movement was Methodism. The prime mover in Methodism was John Wesley (1703–91). While studying for the Anglican ministry at Oxford, John Wesley and a little band of his fellow students became disillusioned at the coldness and spiritual emptiness that had fallen upon the Anglican Church following the exciting religious controversies of the seventeenth century. They also deplored its subservience to the government and to the aristocracy. Wesley's little group began holding prayer meetings and visiting the poor and the sick. Their lives were such examples of piety and moderate regularity that their fellow students branded them "Methodists" in derision. After leaving Oxford, John Wesley and his brother, Charles, spent two years in the newly founded American colony of Georgia, trying unsuccessfully to convert the Indians. However, in Georgia they came in contact with some German pietists and became converted to a more fervent, evangelical type of Christianity. This they took with them back to England. When the Anglican churches closed their doors to John Wesley, he preached emotional sermons to huge throngs in the streets and fields. A tireless and dynamic soul stirrer, he rode horseback from one end of England to the other until well into his eighties. Charles Wesley wrote more than 6,500 hymns. George Whitefield, the most eloquent of all the early Methodists, electrified tens of thousands in England and America and converted many to pietistic Christianity. The real founder of Methodism in the American colonies was Francis Asbury (1745–1816) who duplicated in many respects the work of John Wesley in England. The Methodists played a prominent part in the two "Great Awakenings" in America—the first in the 1730's and 40's and the second at the opening of the nineteenth century. In both England and America the Methodists grew rapidly in numbers, mostly among the middle and lower classes.

The various pietist groups, unlike the eighteenth-century philosophers of the Enlightenment, were definitely not political revolutionaries. They were intensely interested in social reform—in education, health and sanitation, temperance, penal reform, and abolition of the slave trade. But they hoped to achieve these reforms by private charity rather than political action. They tended to accommodate themselves to absolute monarchy in the belief that spiritual and social conditions could be improved within that framework of government. John Wesley, for instance, though intensely interested in social reform in the American colonies, did not sympathize with their struggle for independence. It was not the pietists, but their contemporary rationalistic philosophers of the Enlightenment, who brought on the revolutionary era that toppled the thrones of many absolute monarchs and chastised or frightened the rest.

SUGGESTED READING

C. H. C. Wright, *French Classicism* (1920). A standard treatment of French literature in the "golden" age of Louis XIV.

Brander Matthews, *Molière* (1926). A good biography of probably the greatest of the French classical dramatists.

* Henry Fielding, *Tom Jones* (Modern Library). A lengthy novel revealing both the classical style of the early English novelists and English society in the eighteenth century.

Carl J. Friedrich, *The Age of the Baroque, 1610–1660* (1952). Has several good chapters on baroque art and literature and undertakes to relate the baroque spirit to the political and economic history of Europe during the first half of the seventeenth century.

Paul H. Lang, *Music in Western Civilization* (1941). Interprets the music of the various eras in the light of the history and culture of the times.

John M. Burk, *The Life and Works of Beethoven* (1943). A good biography of probably the greatest figure in the history of music, who composed in both the classical and the romantic vein.

Francis J. McConnell, *John Wesley* (1939). A scholarly but popularly written biography of the great eighteenth-century pietist, by a bishop in the Methodist Church.

Jacob Rosenberg, *Rembrandt*, 2 vols. (1948). The best biography of the greatest of the baroque painters.

SECTION 9

The Era of the French Revolution,

1776–1830

T he late eighteenth century was an era of revolution in the Western world—both in America and in Europe. The American Revolution, and the French Revolution, culminating in the exploits of Napoleon, had a strong impact on much of the rest of the world. These upheavals were preceded and in part induced by an intellectual movement known as the Enlightenment. This, in turn, was in large measure a product of the rise of natural science.

The late eighteenth-century revolutionary leaders in America and France were inspired to a considerable extent by the example of the English people, who a century earlier, it will be recalled, had cut off the head of one tyrant and overthrown another (see Chapter 34). They were inspired to an even greater degree, however, by the philosophers of the Enlightenment, in whose image they were striving to make over the world.

The related sequence of events in this revolutionary era was therefore: 1. The rise of natural science; 2. The intellectual revolution; 3. The American Revolution; 4. The French Revolution; 5. The era of Napoleon.

After the overthrow of Napoleon the forces of reaction attempted to unmake many of the revolutionary changes, but their success was only limited and temporary.

CHAPTER 38

The Intellectual Revolution

THE SO-CALLED intellectual revolution of the eighteenth century marked the triumph of a philosophy of materialistic rationalism and empiricism known as the Enlightenment. This philosophy was based largely upon a scientific attitude brought on by the rise of natural science. The story of the Intellectual Revolution, therefore, begins with the rise of natural science.

1. The Pioneer Science: Astronomy

The first branch of modern natural science to attract systematic attention was astronomy, and the founder of modern astronomy was Nicholaus Copernicus (1473–1543). Copernicus, whose real name was Koppernik, was a German-speaking Pole. Like so many other Northern European scholars in the fifteenth century he crossed the Alps to study in an Italian Renaissance university. It was from his Italian teachers that he received the ideas that led to his revolutionary concept of the structure of the universe. After returning to Poland he spent the rest of his life in an attempt to prove that the sun, not the earth, was the center of the solar system and that the earth and all the other planets revolved around the sun while rotating on their own axes. Although this idea had been held by a number of Greek astronomers of the third and second centuries before Christ, it had never gained wide acceptance. For at least thirteen hundred years the Western world had accepted the conclusions of the Hellenistic astronomer Claudius Ptolemy (second century A.D.). The Ptolemaic system, which placed the earth at the center of the universe, satisfied the senses and seemed to agree with certain statements in the Bible. The medieval Christian theologians, therefore, had come to regard the Ptolemaic system as the Christian view of the physical universe.

Copernicus was quite aware that his startling conclusions would arouse both the ridicule of laymen and the ire of churchmen. It was only near the end of his life that he could be persuaded to publish his views, and the first copy of his book, *Concerning the Movements of Heavenly Bodies*, reached him on the day of his death. Roman Catholic and Protestant leaders alike denounced the Copernican system as illogical, unbiblical, and unsettling to the Christian faith.

However, the new idea could not be suppressed. Nearly a century after Copernicus a German astronomer, Kepler, with the benefit of additional data, showed convincingly that Copernicus was fundamentally right. However, the mathematical laws governing the movements of heavenly bodies, which Kepler discovered, were not quite what Copernicus had believed them to be: the planets revolve around the sun in elliptical rather than circular orbits. Shortly thereafter Galileo (1564–1642), one of the truly great heroes of science and the first to use

ISAAC NEWTON, BY KNELLER. This portrait suggests Newton's youthful vigor and keenness. He was still in his twenties when he made some of his greatest discoveries, including integral calculus and the law of universal attraction. (*The Bettmann Archive*)

the telescope in astronomical observation, won over most contemporary scientists to the Copernican theory. Nonetheless, Galileo suffered much persecution from the clerical authorities.

The uphill trail blazed by Copernicus, Kepler, and Galileo was continued on to its lofty peak by Sir Isaac Newton (1642–1727). Newton was a frail boy, the son of an English small farmer. As a student at Cambridge University he was distinguished enough in mathematics to be chosen to stay on as professor after his graduation. Shortly after graduation, while still in his early twenties, Newton came forth with some of the most tremendous discoveries in the history of science, or indeed of the human intellect. He is probably best known for the law of universal attraction, or gravitation. The concept matured and was refined in Newton's mind over a period of years. As it finally appeared in his *Principia* (*The*

Mathematical Principles of Natural Knowledge), the law is stated with marvelous simplicity and precision: "Every particle of matter in the universe attracts every other particle with a force varying inversely as the square of the distance between them and directly proportional to the product of their masses." The modest Newton was so overcome by the grandeur of this law that he was unable to complete the confirming calculations, a task that he turned over to a trusted assistant. The secret of the entire physical universe appeared at last to have been solved. Two centuries were to elapse before Albert Einstein would raise grave doubts about the truth of Newton's theory.

Newton, in addition to his teaching and his prodigious scientific achievements, found time to perform public service. He became a member of Parliament and served for many years as active director of the royal mint. Knighted by Queen Anne, he was one of the few scientists before the nineteenth century to receive prominent public recognition in his own lifetime.

2. Other Sciences

Astronomy was only the first of many fields of modern natural science that came into being as Western man shifted the center of his interest from spiritual and moral matters to material things. In the seventeenth and eighteenth centuries such a galaxy of great names and discoveries appeared in the various branches of natural science that we can mention here only a few of the most significant.

In the sixteenth century Vesalius, a Fleming living in Italy, wrote the first comprehensive textbook on the structure of the human body to be based on careful observation. Because he dissected many human bodies in order to make his observations, he ran into serious opposition from clerical authorities. In disgust he gave up his scientific studies and became the personal physician of Emperor Charles V. In the seventeenth century William Harvey, an Englishman who also studied in Italy, discovered the major secrets of the circulatory system, thus making it possible for surgeons to operate on the human body with somewhat less fatal consequences than had previously been the case. Vesalius and Harvey are regarded as the founders of the science of anatomy.

The founding fathers of biological science were Linnaeus, the Swedish botanist, and Buffon, the French zoologist, both of whom lived in the eighteenth century. Since the varieties of plant and animal life are so enormous, one of the major problems in this field of knowledge is that of classification and nomenclature. Linnaeus worked out a system of names for the various species in both the plant and animal kingdoms that is still in use. He also worked out a system of classification of plant life that is partly used by botanists today. Buffon also did work in classifying the animal kingdom and wrote a vast natural history in forty-four volumes.

An Irish nobleman, Robert Boyle (seventeenth century), laid the foundations for the modern physical sciences by attacking many false assumptions inherited from the ancients and by beginning the systematic search for the basic physical elements. He discovered the law of gases, which still bears his name. Following Boyle's lead, Lavoisier in France (eighteenth century), discovered twenty-three of the basic elements. He also discovered the secrets of combustion and formulated the law of the conservation of matter. Lavoisier is generally considered to be the father of modern chemistry. He was beheaded by the terrorists during the French Revolution on a false political charge. Probably the most important developments in the founding of modern physics were the discoveries connected with electricity. A number of men, including Benjamin Franklin, contributed bits of knowledge concerning electricity, but it was the Italian physicist Volta (1745–1827) who first harnessed electricity by inventing the storage battery. The versatile Newton discovered the basic secrets of light and founded the science of optics. He also made important contributions to hydrostatics and hydrodynamics and formulated the three laws of

motion (which had been conceived earlier by Galileo). James Hutton, a Scottish farmer in quest of better agricultural techniques, made observations that led him to the conclusion that the earth's surface has been undergoing gradual changes over aeons of time. His *Theory of the Earth*, which appeared toward the end of the eighteenth century, is the first systematic treatise on geology.

3. The Tools of Science

Meanwhile, the tools necessary for the ever more rapid progress of natural science were being invented. The language in which science is expressed is mathematics. In the early seventeenth century a Scotsman, Sir John Napier, invented logarithms, by which the process of multiplying and dividing huge numbers can be greatly simplified. Shortly afterward the system was applied to the slide rule. About the same time, René Descartes, a Frenchman, adopted the symbols now used in algebra, and devised analytic geometry, a method of combining and interchanging algebra and geometry. In the latter part of the seventeenth century, sometimes called the century of genius, Newton and the German Wilhelm Leibnitz working independently, invented calculus, upon which many of the most intricate processes of advanced science and engineering are dependent.

During the seventeenth and eighteenth centuries some of the most basic instruments of science were invented. Both the telescope and the microscope were products of the Dutch Netherlands. However, it was Galileo who first used the telescope in systematic astronomical observations. Leeuwenhoek, a Dutchman, was the chief pioneer in the use of the microscope. He discovered bacteria two hundred years before Pasteur learned how to combat them; he also observed the cellular structure of plant and animal tissue, the structure of the blood, and its circulation through the capillary system. Another Dutchman, Huygens, invented the pendulum clock, making possible for the first time in history the precise measurement of small intervals of time. A German, Fahrenheit, greatly improved the thermometer and adopted the scale that bears his name. These are only a few of the most important instruments of science invented in the seventeenth and eighteenth centuries.

It is interesting that the universities played little or no part in this great drama. Nearly all of them were controlled by the churches, either Roman Catholic or Protestant. They looked askance at science. Scientific academies, however, played a significant role in the advancement of science. The earliest and most important of these were the Royal Society in England, chartered in 1662 by Charles II, and the Académie des Sciences in France, founded by Colbert four years later. These organizations and others patterned after them furnished laboratories, granted subsidies, brought scientists together to exchange ideas, published their findings, and encouraged scientific achievement generally.

4. The Enlightenment

The discovery of so many marvelous new truths concerning the physical universe could hardly have failed to have a strong impact upon man's thinking. Men began to speculate about the broader meaning of these new facts and concepts. The philosophical movement that was eventually formulated on the basis of the discoveries in natural science is called the Enlightenment. Among the various thinkers who contributed to the philosophy of the Enlightenment, three of the most influential were René Descartes, John Locke, and Voltaire, although only Voltaire may be properly considered a member of the movement.

Descartes (1596–1650), in addition to his pioneering in mathematics, was one of the first to ponder and write on scientific theory and methodology. His *Discourse on Method* was a landmark in the rise of the scientific spirit. It is an eloquent defense of the value of abstract reasoning. He would question all authority no matter how venerable—be it Aristotle or the Bible. "These are my books," said Descartes, pointing to a basket of rabbits about to be dissected. From a few simple and self-evident truths he would derive further truths by a process of deductive reasoning. "I think; therefore I am," he believed to be a safe starting point. Descartes believed that the whole material universe can be understood in terms of extension and motion. "Give me extension and motion," said Descartes, "and I will create the universe." Only mind and spirit were exempt from the principles of extension and motion. Though either commonplace or outworn and discarded today, the basic ideas of Cartesian philosophy were revolutionary in the seventeenth century. By challenging all established authority, by accepting as truth only what could be known by reason, and by assuming a purely mechanical universe, Descartes clashed head on with the prevailing Christian concepts of divine revelation and divine Providence.

John Locke (1632–1704) went a step further. This rugged English thinker would not exempt even the mind from the mechanical laws of the material universe. In his *Essay Concerning Human Understanding* Locke pictured the human brain at birth as a blank sheet of paper on which nothing would ever be written except by sense perception and reason. This concept ruled out innate ideas as well as revelation. Thus the mechanization of the whole universe was complete. Locke was the first behavioristic psychologist. Although Descartes's rationalism (pursuit of truth through reason) and Locke's empiricism (pursuit of knowledge through observation and experience) were by no means the same, they were one in rejecting divine revelation and authority. Both contributed heavily to the philosophy of the Enlightenment.

Of all the leading figures of the Enlightenment, Voltaire (1694–1778) was the most influential. It was his skillful pen that popularized the deep and original ideas of

Locke. Voltaire, the son of a Paris lawyer, became the idol of the French intelligentsia while still in his early twenties. His versatile mind was sparkling, his wit keen and sharp. A born skeptic and critic, he soon ran afoul the authorities of church and state. First he was imprisoned in the Bastille; later he was exiled to England. There he encountered the ideas of Locke and Newton and came to admire English parliamentary government and tolerance. Slipping back into France, he was hidden for a time and protected by a rich lady who became his mistress. Voltaire's facile mind and pen were never idle. He wrote poetry, drama, history, essays, letters, and scientific treatises—ninety volumes in all. The special target of his cynical wit was Christianity. Few men in history have dominated their age intellectually as Voltaire dominated the eighteenth century.

Whatever their literary form, the writings of Voltaire and his followers were filled with the philosophy of materialistic rationalism, commonly known as the Enlightenment.[1] The major principles of this philosophy are:

EMPIRICAL KNOWLEDGE

All we know and all we can ever know is what we learn through our senses and interpret with our reason. There are no such things as innate ideas or revealed truth.

MECHANISTIC UNIVERSE

The whole universe and everything in it, including man, are governed by a few simple and unchangeable laws. Anyone who thinks he can change one of these laws—can by praying, for instance, bring down the rain on his parched crops and perchance on his neighbor's unroofed house—is a dupe of his own egotism.

[1] For convenience we are using the term "materialistic rationalism" to include both rationalism and empiricism, both of which relied upon human intelligence and wisdom rather than divine revelation and authority, and were primarily interested in secular rather than sacred matters.

GOODNESS OF MAN

Man is naturally rational and good, but the peddlers of mystic religions have distorted his thinking and given him guilt complexes by preaching false doctrines of original sin and divine moral laws. Rid man's mind of this rubbish, and he can and will build for himself a perfect society.

GOODNESS OF NATURE

Nature is good and beautiful in its simplicity. Man has corrupted it with his complex political, social, and religious restrictions. A move back to nature would be a move toward wholesome vigor and freedom.

DEISM

This wonderful mechanism called the universe could not have come into being by

BUST OF VOLTAIRE, BY HOUDON. Voltaire played much the same role in the intellectual world of the eighteenth century as did Erasmus in the sixteenth. However, Erasmus possessed a genial wit, whereas Voltaire's was sharp and bitter. He regarded the Christian religion as the chief obstacle to intellectual and social progress. (*The Bettmann Archive*)

accident. Some infinite Divine Being must have created it and set it going. However, the finite mind of man cannot comprehend the infinite. Therefore, God is unknowable. Furthermore, God, having set His perfect mechanical laws in motion, will never tamper with them nor interfere in the affairs of man. He is impersonal.

In the eighteenth century these ideas came to be generally accepted by the intelligentsia throughout the Western world. A host of French philosophers joined Voltaire in contributing to Diderot's *Encyclopedia*. This gigantic work undertook to explore the whole world of knowledge. It did not stop with exploring, however, but interlarded and flavored the articles with the rationalistic and empiricist views of the writers.

Somewhat different from the other philosophers of the Enlightenment, though second only to Voltaire in influence on eighteenth-century thought, was Jean Jacques Rousseau (1712–78). One of the most original thinkers and charming writers of all time, Rousseau crusaded for a return to nature—beautiful, pure, simple nature. The message struck home to a society weary of arbitrary and often corrupt governmental bureaucracy and an oppressively artificial and elaborate code of social etiquette. Rousseau was lionized. Great ladies, including the Queen of France, began playing milkmaid. In his novel *La Nouvelle Héloïse*, Rousseau extolled the beauties of free love and uninhibited emotion. In *Émile* he expounded the "natural" way of rearing and educating children. He would let children do what they like and teach them "practical" knowledge. Although Rousseau agreed with his fellow philosophers of the Enlightenment on deism, the mechanistic universe, and the goodness of man and nature, he differed sharply with them on the matter of reason. Rousseau placed his faith in emotion, feeling, and intuition, rather than in cold reason. In this he was a forerunner of the romantic spirit and expounded its principles nearly a century before the movement reached its peak.

5. Conflict Between the Philosophers of the Enlightenment and the Christian Theologians

It is readily apparent that the beliefs of the Enlightenment were diametrically opposed to the doctrines of the Christian churches—Roman Catholic, Protestant, and Orthodox alike. In contrast to the unknowable, impersonal God of the deists the Christian theologians taught that God took on human form and revealed Himself to the finite mind of man in the personality of Jesus Christ. Furthermore, they maintained that God is interested in each one of His special creatures—that not a sparrow falls but what He sees and is concerned. To the empirical knowledge of the materialistic rationalists the Christian theologians would add divine truth revealed by God, either through Christ, the Bible, and the Church or directly, as in the case of the saints, the prophets, and sometimes even ordinary Christians. The Christian theologians would make the mechanistic universe subject to a miracle-working, prayer-answering Creator. They argued that, if God could create the laws of the material universe, He certainly could change them or set them aside if He so desired. The Christian theologians regarded the concept of the goodness of man as erroneous. They taught instead that man is a fallen creature, that all inherit Adam's original sin, that man must be "born again" of the spirit in order to attain eternal life. Some of the Christian theologians argued that the philosophy of the Enlightenment was itself a religion—based on faith. Since it has never been demonstrated that man is naturally good or that if freed from the influence of mystic religion he can and will build for himself an earthly paradise, these things must be taken on faith—faith that in others the philosophers were so quick to scorn.

Unfortunately the eighteenth-century battle for the minds of men was not limited to honorable debate. Both sides resorted to the tactics of smear and persecution. It is difficult, if not impossible, to determine which side struck the first low blow. The philosophers, ofttimes on the flimsiest of scientific evidence and with little knowledge of the Christian religion, would ridicule the miraculous and mystic teachings of the Bible and the churches. Pleading for tolerance, they proved themselves most intolerant of Christian doctrines they did not accept or understand. Voltaire devoted much time and space to pointing out scientific errors in the Bible. "*Écrasez l'infâme*" (Crush the infamous thing!) was his life motto. The "infamous thing" was, of course, Christianity. The Christian theologians, on the other hand, found it much easier to denounce the materialistic rationalists than to answer their arguments. In countries like France and Italy, where the churchmen were strongly entrenched in government, they did not hesitate to persecute the philosophers of the Enlightenment, censor their writings, or even to interrupt the work of scientists. The churchmen were often so ignorant and so corrupt that they laid themselves wide open to the attacks of their enemies. In that kind of struggle, of course, the churchmen were doomed to fail.

The materialistic rationalists won, and the French Revolution was in large measure an attempt to translate their ideas into practical institutions. It was not until the late nineteenth century that Christian theologians began to realize the true strength of their religion, to concentrate on spiritual and moral issues, and to rally their forces for a comeback (see Chapter 47).[2]

6. Political and Economic Aspects of the Enlightenment

The philosophers of the Enlightenment devoted a good deal of thought to matters of government. If man is by nature a rational

[2] The pietists, of course, concentrated on spiritual and moral issues. For the most part, however, they made their impact upon the lower classes rather than the intelligentsia, who were the chief protagonists in the debates over the philosophy of the Enlightenment. And only in England did the pietists gain a mass following even among the lower classes.

and good creature, then surely, if given the opportunity, he can quickly devise for himself efficient and benevolent political institutions. Corrupt tyrannies were no longer tolerable. Of the numerous "enlightened" thinkers in the field of political science three stand out above the others in influence. They are Locke, Montesquieu, and Rousseau. Locke's most eloquent plea was for the natural rights of man, which are life, liberty, and property. He theorizes, in his *Two Treatises of Civil Government*, that to safeguard these rights man voluntarily contracted to surrender a certain amount of his sovereignty to government. The powers of the government, however, whether it be monarchial or popular, are strictly limited. No government may violate the individual's right to life, liberty, and property. If it does, the people who set it up can and should overthrow it. These ideas were fundamental in the thinking of the makers of both the French and the American Revolution. Jefferson wrote many of Locke's ideas into the Declaration of Independence, frequently using his exact words. They likewise appear in the American Constitution and in numerous French declarations of liberty.

Baron de Montesquieu (1689-1755) was less a theorizer than a keen student of history and shrewd analyst of political systems. His masterpiece is *The Spirit of the Laws*. Although a great admirer of the English government after the Glorious Revolution, Montesquieu came to the conclusion that different types of government are best suited to various conditions. For instance, absolute monarchy is best for countries of vast area, limited monarchy for countries of moderate size like France, and republics for small states like Venice or Switzerland. Not only did he approve of Locke's doctrine of limited sovereignty, but he specified how it can best be secured—by a separation of powers and a system of checks and balances. The executive, the legislative, and the judicial functions of government should be carefully assigned to separate and equal branches, each checking the other. Herein probably lies Montesquieu's greatest practical contribution to the science of government. It was written into the American Constitution intact.

The real father of the theory of modern democracy was not Locke or Montesquieu, both of whom distrusted rule by the masses, but Rousseau. This morbid, erratic genius based the conclusions in his *Social Contract* and in his *Second Discourse* upon pure imagination. Man in his state of noble savagery was free, equal, and happy. It was only when some men began marking off plots of ground saying "this is mine" that inequality began. In order to restore their lost freedom and happiness men entered into a compact, each with all the others, surrendering their individual liberty to the whole. Since sovereignty is indivisible, the general will is all powerful. Members of the majority are free because they are in harmony with the general will. The minority are free only to join the majority. Here is democracy with a vengeance. Rousseau's influence on the leaders of the second and more radical phase of the French Revolution was great. But since it is only a short step from this kind of unrestrained democratic government to state-worshipping dictatorship, the influence of Rousseau is also clearly seen in the fascist and communist systems of the twentieth century.

Some of the eighteenth-century planners of the better life through reason turned their thoughts to economics. Since the late fifteenth century mercantilism had been the dominant economic theory and practice in Western Europe. This system of regulated nationalistic economy reached its peak in the seventeenth century. Only the Dutch Netherlands held out for free trade. But if, according to the fundamental assumptions of the Enlightenment, the universe is run by a few simple mechanical laws, why should there not be a similar natural order in the field of economics? A group of French physiocrats, led by Quesnay, personal physician to Louis XV, began to teach that economics has its own set of natural laws, that the most basic of these laws is that of supply and demand, and that these laws operate best when commerce is freed from governmental regulation. This doctrine came to be known as that of *laissez faire* (or free trade and enterprise).

The chief formalizer of the theory of *laissez faire* was Adam Smith, a Scottish professor of philosophy who associated with the physiocrats while sojourning in France. His *The Wealth of Nations*, published in 1776, has remained the bible of *laissez-faire* economics ever since. The ideas of the French physiocrats and Adam Smith strongly influenced the leaders of the American and French revolutions.

7. The Enlightened Despots

The philosophy of the Enlightenment was by no means a monopoly of the intelligentsia. By the middle of the eighteenth century it had become a fad. Sizable numbers of the nobility prided themselves on being followers of Voltaire (probably in most cases without realizing the practical implications of his philosophy). And nearly every country on the European continent was ruled by an "enlightened despot."

The most sensational of the enlightened despots was Frederick the Great of Prussia (1740–86). Frederick had from boyhood been an enthusiast for music, poetry, and philosophy. At the end of the Seven Years' War (1756–63), the second of his two bloody wars of aggression, he settled down as a model philosopher-king and attempted to apply the laws of reason to statecraft. Frederick was an avid reader of the French philosophers. He even invited Voltaire to visit him at Potsdam, but Prussia was not big enough to hold two such egos at once. The two prima donnas soon quarreled and parted. The philosopher-king, who was, of course, a deist, made much of religious toleration. However, he continued to penalize the Jews and never ceased to ridicule Christians of all denominations. He was a strong advocate of public education, although he spent only pennies for it as against dollars for the army. The centralized Prussian bureaucracy became the most efficient government in Europe in the hands of this able and energetic benevolent despot. True to the prevailing thought of the Enlightenment, however, he had no faith in popular self-government. Nor did he make a move to free the serfs or to end the feudal system in Prussia. Probably the most lasting of Frederick's contributions to Prussia were his codification of the law and improvements in the administration of justice. In the field of economy Frederick was a mercantilist, although he did share the physiocrats' appreciation of the importance of agriculture. Prussia's economy prospered increasingly during the last two decades of his reign. All in all, Prussia under Frederick the Great seemed to vindicate the contention of the philosophers of the Enlightenment that the rule of reason will quickly and painlessly usher in the good life.

The most sincere of all the enlightened despots was Joseph II of Austria (1780–90). However, he lacked the practical sagacity of Frederick the Great. His well-meaning but ill-conceived efforts to centralize the administration of the far-flung Hapsburg territories, to replace the numerous languages of his subjects with German, to secularize the strongly entrenched Roman Catholic Church, and to free the serfs in a society still based upon feudalism—all backfired.

More successful were the enlightened despots of Sweden, Tuscany, Sardinia, Spain, and Portugal. Even in Russia the bloody and immoral tyrant Catherine "the Great" talked and played at enlightened despotism. The deeds, of course, were lacking. Significantly France alone of the great powers on the continent failed to produce an enlightened ruler. Upon attaining the French throne in 1774 the well-meaning Louis XVI appointed the physiocrat Turgot as minister of finances. Turgot, a friend of Voltaire, initiated a program of sweeping reforms that might have forestalled the French Revolution. However, within two years time the powerfully entrenched vested interests persuaded the weak-willed king to dismiss him.

Although enlightened despotism achieved enough spectacular successes to gladden the hearts of some of the philosophers of the Enlightenment, the system soon exhibited two fundamental weaknesses. One was the egotism of the ambitious monarchs, which kept Europe in a state of almost constant war. The second was the uncertainty of hereditary succession. In every case the benevolent despots were succeeded by despots less benevolent, if not outright malevolent or degenerate. In any case the people had no choice. Europe's feudal society was not to be thus easily and painlessly reformed.

SUGGESTED READING

W. C. Dampier, A *History of Science and Its Relations with Philosophy and Religion* (1946). Probably the best single volume on this important subject. Readable and meaningful.

* E. A. Burtt, *The Metaphysical Foundations of Modern Science* (Anchor). A perceptive analysis of the philosophical implications of the rise of natural science from Copernicus to Newton. Particularly good chapters on the impact of Newton on philosophy and religion.

* Frank E. Manuel, *The Age of Reason* (Cornell). A brief, judicious survey of this controversial subject.

Carl Becker, *The Heavenly City of the Eighteenth Century Philosophers* (1932). This provocative little book captures the spirit of the Enlightenment. Becker shows that the rationalistic and empirical concepts of the eighteenth-century philosophers were taken on faith, much as those of Christianity or any other religion.

Montesquieu, *Persian and Chinese Letters* (1901). Originally published in 1721. Probably the best approach to Montesquieu's critical mind. He subtly ridicules the absolutist political systems of the seventeenth and eighteenth centuries.

N. L. Torrey, *The Spirit of Voltaire* (1938). A

competent analysis of one of the most in-fluential thinkers of modern times.

Voltaire, *Letters on the English* (Harvard Classics, Vol. XXXIV [1910]). Of Voltaire's scores of works on nearly every conceivable subject this is probably the best one to read to get at the general philosophy of the "intellectual dictator of the 18th century." The reader will find Voltaire a charming and stimulating writer.

* Rousseau, *Social Contract* (Hafner). Books by Rousseau are ever so much more rewarding than books about Rousseau. Few if any think-ers have influenced a wider variety of nineteenth- and twentieth-century movements. The *Social Contract* is probably his most important single work.

Rousseau, *Émile* (many editions). One of the most important books in the history of education. It has had even more influence on pedagogy in the twentieth century than in the eighteenth and the nineteenth centuries. The reader will find it difficult to cast off the spell of the "mad genius."

* Geoffrey Bruun, *The Enlightened Despots* (Berkshire). An excellent brief account.

CHAPTER 39

The American Revolution

THE POLITICAL and social ideas of the Enlightenment received their first test and their first application in a somewhat unexpected quarter—the British colonies in America. The American Revolution was a highly significant step in a series of events that altered the political structure of the Western European world by striking down the absolutist concepts of government that had prevailed since about 1500. The bold experiments of the Americans in justifying their rebellion and in shaping new political institutions served as an inspiration and a model for other nations. Placed in its proper setting, the American Revolution was one of the major events in modern world history.

1. American Colonial Society

The American Revolution was a complex movement. Behind all its complexity lay one fundamental fact. During the century and a half prior to 1776 American society had become different and separate from British and European societies. America was in the process of becoming independent long before 1776; the Revolution was the culmination of this process.

To the American of 1776 probably the most obvious sign of living in a world apart from Europe was the bustling economy that had been created in America's wilderness. This was an accomplishment that had to be attributed to hard work and ingenuity on the part of the colonists; no one in Great Britain could claim the credit.

The backbone of the colonial economy was the diversified agricultural system. The small, independently owned farms of New England and the middle colonies were complemented by the great plantations of certain areas of the South with their slave gangs. Between them they produced a large variety of crops: grain, tobacco, rice, indigo, vegetables, fruit, and many others. This system not only fed the rapidly growing population of the colonies but also supplied a surplus for export. Off to the west lay vast areas of land yet unexploited, creating an economic opportunity unknown in Europe.

The Americans had by no means neglected commerce and industry. Colonial merchants, especially in New England and the middle colonies, did a thriving business within America. They also reached across the seas to Great Britain, to the West Indies, and to the continent of Europe. The bulk of the overseas trade was in colonial raw materials, such as tobacco and lumber, which were shipped to Britain and Europe in exchange for manufactured goods and slaves. However, by 1776 the colonists were producing manufactured goods in spite of British protest. Numerous fortunes were made in New England by producing rum from West Indian molasses. A thriving shipbuilding industry also existed. Of course the colonists were not self-sufficient in 1776, but neither were they absolutely dependent on Great Britain and Europe. American entrepreneurs were intent on protecting and expanding their own interests. Already most

PIONEER FAMILY DEFENDING ITS LOG CABIN, FROM A PRINT BY WEGNER. Many of the hardy early American settlers and later frontiersmen lived in daily terror of Indian attacks. (*The Bettmann Archive*)

Americans were economically comfortable and confident that the future was bright, provided that they were free to pursue their own economic ends.

America's population—about 2,500,000 in 1776—was organized in a class structure outwardly similar to that of Great Britain. An aristocracy of rich merchants and planters, which dominated economic life, politics, religion, and manners, was conscious of its position and sought to retain it. A large, enterprising group of independent farmers, shopkeepers, artisans, and professional men was ranked below the aristocrats. There were some day laborers, tenant farmers, and indentured servants, who were condemned to the lower rank of society. And there were the Negro slaves. This class structure was not nearly so inflexible as that of Europe. Almost none of Europe's aristocracy

emigrated to America; the family trees of most of the aristocratic colonial families would not stand close examination. American aristocracy was based on wealth rather than on blood. It was possible for an enterprising and lucky man of the lower classes to attain aristocratic rank by amassing a fortune. The frontier also offered an escape to men of humble origin who resented aristocratic dictation. Colonial conditions thus loosened the bonds of aristocratic society and supplied a large measure of freedom for men of lesser rank and means.

Probably the sharpest differences between the new and old worlds were in political life. Although each American colony had its own government, a common pattern had developed by 1776. Each colony had a governor who represented the authority of the British crown and who was usually chosen by the crown. In theory the governor had extensive powers to direct colonial affairs and to curb colonial freedom. Each colony (except Pennsylvania) had a two-house legislature. The lower house was elected by property owners, while the upper house was usually appointed by the British king or by the governor. The powers of the colonial legislatures were never clearly defined, but in general they were extensive in local colonial affairs and in taxation. The governors had nearly absolute powers of veto over these bodies, but since they were at the mercy of the legislatures for salaries and funds, they were not usually in a position to exercise these powers. The colonists had a system of courts patterned after British courts and enjoyed the rights of Englishmen as incorporated in English common law.

In actual operation colonial governments grew accustomed to a wide range of freedom, and the colonists increasingly felt that it was their right to decide their own political fate. Prior to 1776 the colonists would have admitted that the British government had a superior authority over them, yet when it came to specific issues they would have argued that their own governments must have a voice in making decisions. The feeling was emerging that the colonial governments carried a weight equal to that of the British government. One hundred and fifty years of experience in self-government had created a breech wider than the Atlantic between Great Britain and her colonies.

Colonial religious life was unique. In spite of the fact that the colonies paid taxes to support churches that were often intolerant and dictatorial, there was still greater religious freedom in the colonies than in most of Europe. Puritanism flourished more vigorously in colonial New England than in Europe. Alongside such established religions as Puritanism and Anglicanism there was room for Presbyterians, Quakers, Lutherans, Dutch Reformed, Roman Catholics, and Jews. And during the Great Awakening in the eighteenth century a number of evangelical religions such as Methodism took root.

Prior to 1776 the colonists distinguished themselves least in cultural activities. The Americans did establish colleges and lower schools in an attempt to prepare men for careers in colonial society. Newspapers appeared in many areas. The rudiments of a distinctly American architectural style emerged. But little was produced in literature and art that is worthy of note; and in the final analysis colonial cultural life was still tied to Europe. Perhaps the most astounding development in colonial America was the ability of the colonists to keep abreast of Europe's chief cultural movements. Neither the sea barrier nor language nor the rigorous life in the colonies stopped Americans from absorbing the ideas of the Enlightenment and the implications of the new science.

Although there were by 1776 wide differences between American and British society, these differences did not spell revolution. Most Americans were still Englishmen and still closely attached to a European tradition. Their economic ideas, their political system, their religion, and their social concepts were fundamentally European, adapted to fit a new environment but not magically transformed into something new. Their revolt was inspired by the conviction that Britain was violating the very tradition that the colonists had inherited from her. The Revolution was not a case of the Americans repudiating Europe; it was more nearly a case of the Americans seeking to put into practice some of Europe's most prized and most advanced concepts in order to fulfill the promise of the society they had planted and nourished in America.

2. The Quarrel with Great Britain

Nowhere was there less understanding of the ferment in colonial society than in eighteenth-century Great Britain. Britain was a complacent nation, ruled by a narrow aristocracy that had forgotten its own seventeenth-century struggle for political reform. British interest in overseas colonies was primarily economic. In true mercantilist fashion the ruling class was convinced that British prosperity and power depended upon the exploitation of colonial resources. Little thought was given to the human factors involved in colonial relationships. Great Britain's policy toward her colonies was set forth in a series of Navigation Acts, which required that certain items produced in the colonies be sold only in Great Britain, that colonists purchase manufactured goods only in Britain, and that all shipping be carried in British or colonial ships. Britain's goal was to create a closed, self-sufficient economic system. She did not conspire to pillage the colonies for her benefit; she merely insisted that her interests have priority over colonial interests.

For many years Britain was extremely lax in administering her colonial policy. There was no effective agency for treating colonial problems, and the governors Britain sent to enforce her regulations got little backing from the mother country. It took the Seven Years' War to spur her into a program of reform intended to correct years of neglect. Her major concerns after 1763 lay with colonial defense, her war debt, and close economic regulation of the colonists who had long been guilty of disregarding the navigation laws. Great Britain was especially displeased with the Americans, who during the Seven Years' War had refused to raise troops and money, trafficked with the enemy, and openly defied British officials engaged in saving the colonies from the French.

The strife between Great Britain and the colonists began in the decade between 1763 and 1773. Britain enacted the Grenville (1764–65) and the Townshend (1767) acts, which consisted of a series of measures aimed at raising money and tightening colonial administration. She closed the trans-Allegheny territory to further settlement, laid taxes on numerous imports into the colonies and on business documents (the Stamp Tax), and took steps to give British businesses preferential treatment over colonial businesses. Of all these measures the most detestable to the colonists were the

Stamp Tax and the Tea Tax (a tax imposed on imported tea by the Townshend Acts). The colonists fought back with boycotts, fiery speeches, violence, and protest meetings such as the Stamp Act Congress. They claimed that they were Englishmen who were being taxed without representation in Parliament. In the face of colonial resistance Britain repealed some of these measures, but she persisted in her general policy of tightening control over the colonies. By 1768 she had sent troops to America and empowered her officials to seize American property in ways that violated British law. Slowly Americans began to question British authority on much wider grounds than taxation. Many colonists became convinced that Great Britain intended to deprive them of all traditional English liberties while stealing their wealth through taxation.

After 1773 the incessant quarreling hastened toward a crisis. Angered by the conduct of the Boston "Indians," who destroyed a cargo of tea belonging to the British East India Company, the British enacted the "Intolerable Acts." This piece of legislation closed the port of Boston, placed Massachusetts under the control of a military commander, quartered troops in Boston homes, and threatened those suspected of a major crime with transportation to Britain for trial in the English courts. As if this were not serious enough, the British passed the Quebec Act, which provided for joining all the territory north of the Ohio River and west of the Alleghenies to the province of Quebec, establishing a non-representative royal administration for this province, and granting toleration to the French Catholics. More than ever the Americans were convinced that Britain considered them second-class citizens.

The handful of radicals, the chief of whom was Samuel Adams, who had long been proclaiming the worst now gained numerous recruits. The First Continental Congress, meeting in 1774 to discuss the troubled situation, manifested the new spirit by adopting a bold statement that proclaimed the Intolerable Acts illegal and stated that

Parliament had violated man's natural rights. The increasing reference to "natural rights" in the arguments of the colonists was momentous. It signified that many colonists believed in a natural law superior to English law and in a right, perhaps even an obligation, to revolt if the English violated the natural law.

But Great Britain was through with concessions to the colonists. Even a new boycott of her goods by the colonists failed to dissuade her from teaching her troublesome children a lesson. Britain and the colonies slowly drifted into war. Hostilities opened in April 1775 with skirmishes at Lexington and Concord. In May 1775 the Second Continental Congress, led by men ready to declare independence, took steps to organize the war that had already started and put George Washington in command of the American armies.

Colonial opinion lagged behind the leaders, but once the shooting started it rapidly caught up. The rising cry was for independence. The most potent statement to that effect was delivered by Thomas Paine in his pamphlet, *Common Sense*, which appeared early in 1776. His stirring assault on monarchy and its evils and his scathing denunciation of British greed fired many Americans to take the final step.

Popular sentiment in favor of independence finally made itself felt in 1776 when various colonies instructed their delegations to the Second Continental Congress to break with Britain. On July 4, 1776, Congress issued the Declaration of Independence, the work of Thomas Jefferson, one of the radical leaders. Its magnificent preamble, leaning heavily on the political philosophy of John Locke and the European disciples of the Enlightenment, stated in strong words the doctrines of natural rights and government by contract. The British government had violated these rights and thus had no claim on the allegiance of its subjects, who were entitled to form a new contract to ensure their rights. The Declaration of Independence elevated the struggle at hand above a petty rebellion against legally constituted authority. It made America's struggle that of all "enlightened" men. Not only did it clarify the issues of 1776, but it inspired later generations to strike for liberty in the names of rights so fundamental that they were beyond the authority of any government.

3. The American Revolution

Only a few words can be devoted to the heroic struggle of the Americans for the cause to which they had pledged their lives, fortunes, and sacred honor. Their task seemed hopeless against mighty Britain, whose advantage, however, was offset by poor leadership, distance, and commitments elsewhere. The chief problem of the Americans was overcoming disunity. Many loyalists, or Tories, did not approve of the war against Great Britain. The patriots often disagreed about the course that the new nation should take. These divisions were almost miraculously set aside long enough to press the cause of independence to a successful conclusion.

When the war opened in 1775, the British were unprepared and had to withdraw from Boston to gather their resources, an event the Americans interpreted as a victory. Pushing their initial advantage, the Americans undertook an unsuccessful campaign against Canada in late 1775. By July 1776, Britain was ready to attack, seizing New York as a base of operations. The following months marked the darkest hours of the revolutionary cause. Washington's pitifully small army, poorly fed and armed, was hounded through New Jersey and Delaware; only the caution of the British commander, General Howe, saved it from destruction. Washington did manage to strike blows at Trenton and Princeton at the year's end, but these victories were valuable only in keeping up American morale.

The turning point came in 1777, when the British attempted to split the colonies by capturing the Hudson Valley. Their strategy consisted of driving down from Canada and up from New York. General John Bur-

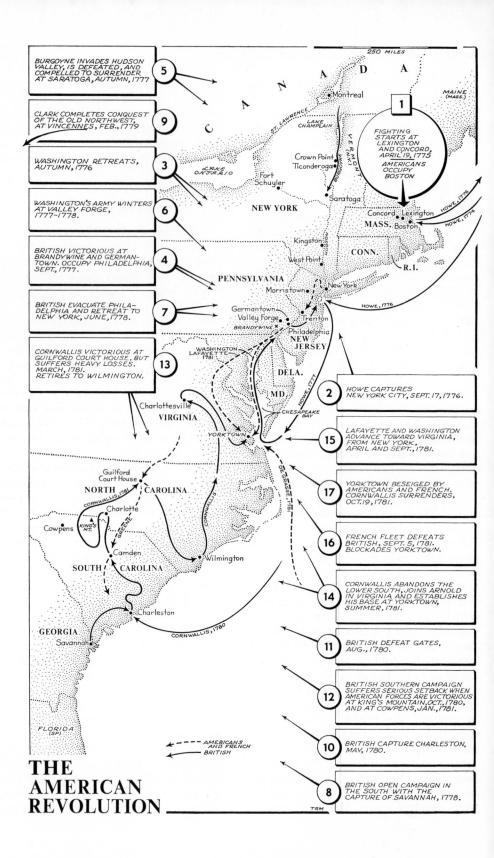

THE AMERICAN REVOLUTION

5 — BURGOYNE INVADES HUDSON VALLEY, IS DEFEATED, AND COMPELLED TO SURRENDER AT SARATOGA, AUTUMN, 1777.

9 — CLARK COMPLETES CONQUEST OF THE OLD NORTHWEST, AT VINCENNES, FEB., 1779.

3 — WASHINGTON RETREATS, AUTUMN, 1776.

6 — WASHINGTON'S ARMY WINTERS AT VALLEY FORGE, 1777–1778.

4 — BRITISH VICTORIOUS AT BRANDYWINE AND GERMANTOWN. OCCUPY PHILADELPHIA, SEPT, 1777.

7 — BRITISH EVACUATE PHILADELPHIA AND RETREAT TO NEW YORK, JUNE, 1778.

13 — CORNWALLIS VICTORIOUS AT GUILFORD COURT HOUSE, BUT SUFFERS HEAVY LOSSES. MARCH, 1781. RETIRES TO WILMINGTON.

1 — FIGHTING STARTS AT LEXINGTON AND CONCORD, APRIL 19, 1775. AMERICANS OCCUPY BOSTON.

2 — HOWE CAPTURES NEW YORK CITY, SEPT. 17, 1776.

15 — LAFAYETTE AND WASHINGTON ADVANCE TOWARD VIRGINIA, FROM NEW YORK, APRIL AND SEPT., 1781.

17 — YORKTOWN BESEIGED BY AMERICANS AND FRENCH. CORNWALLIS SURRENDERS, OCT. 19, 1781.

16 — FRENCH FLEET DEFEATS BRITISH, SEPT. 5, 1781. BLOCKADES YORKTOWN.

14 — CORNWALLIS ABANDONS THE LOWER SOUTH, JOINS ARNOLD IN VIRGINIA AND ESTABLISHES HIS BASE AT YORKTOWN, SUMMER, 1781.

11 — BRITISH DEFEAT GATES, AUG., 1780.

12 — BRITISH SOUTHERN CAMPAIGN SUFFERS SERIOUS SETBACK WHEN AMERICAN FORCES ARE VICTORIOUS AT KING'S MOUNTAIN, OCT., 1780, AND AT COWPENS, JAN., 1781.

10 — BRITISH CAPTURE CHARLESTON, MAY, 1780.

8 — BRITISH OPEN CAMPAIGN IN THE SOUTH WITH THE CAPTURE OF SAVANNAH, 1778.

250 MILES

- - - - AMERICANS AND FRENCH
——— BRITISH

TRM

goyne led the British armies from Canada. Under constant attack from the Americans, his progress was anything but spectacular. No help came from the south. Howe occupied himself in the useless capture of Philadelphia. While he enjoyed that victory, Burgoyne's effort turned into a disaster. Finally in October 1777, he surrendered at Saratoga.

American spirits rose rapidly as a result of this victory. Its chief effect was to swing the French to the American cause. France, moved by a desire to see Great Britain defeated and by a genuine sympathy for America's cause, had unofficially been offering help to the colonists since 1775. However, she had not committed herself fully, fearing that the Americans would either patch up their quarrel with the British or would be defeated, leaving France in a war from which nothing could be won. The victory at Saratoga convinced France that America had a chance for victory. In 1778 a formal alliance was agreed upon, and France began to supply needed money, ships, and troops. In the wake of Saratoga and the French commitment other European powers showed increasing friendliness toward America and hostility toward Britain. Spain and the Dutch eventually declared war on Britain. The British now had a world war on their hands; the pressure on America was considerably relieved.

After 1777 fighting in America was spread over a wide area. The British withdrew from Philadelphia and concentrated large forces in New York. Washington's army was chiefly engaged in watching these forces. The British threw their offensive effort into a campaign in the South, trying in 1780–81 to capture the Carolinas and Virginia. This campaign ended in a disastrous defeat at Yorktown, Virginia, in October 1781, Americans and French both sharing in the victory. This was the last major battle of the war, although hostilities officially continued until 1783. By 1781 Britain was anxious to end a war that threatened her position all around the world.

Peace negotiations were conducted in Paris. The American delegation, led by Benjamin Franklin, was sent with instructions to follow French leadership and to make no separate treaty with Britain. However, France, eager to deliver Britain a few more blows, was in no hurry to conclude the war. Moreover, she had hopes of reannexing the territories in North America that she had given up in 1763, since the new American nation as yet had no legal claim to these lands. Having detected the French intentions, the American delegates disregarded their instructions and began making a separate peace with the British. By the terms of the Treaty of Paris, 1783, Britain recognized America's independence and ceded to her all territories east of the Mississippi from the Great Lakes to Spanish Florida. The Americans agreed to honor all debts owed Britain and to make restoration to the Tories who had suffered during the war. France agreed to these terms, not wishing to carry on the struggle alone. The new American nation had won a magnificent victory to start its career.

4. Revolution and the Democratization of American Society

The American Revolution involved more than a successful war against Great Britain. Some Americans had drawn back in horror in 1775–76 at the prospect of dissolving the existing social and political order and building a new one. However, once the decision for independence was taken, there was no turning back. As the war progressed, moves were made to construct new institutions for America. In the years following 1776 the Americans showed a genius for combining traditional patterns of life with radical new ideas. Their revolution did not uproot the old social order completely in the name of any radical doctrine. Yet it did incorporate into the new order some of the most advanced ideas of the Enlightenment.

The first important efforts at reconstruction were made on the level of the states (as the colonies were called after July 4, 1776). New state governments, based on

British principles of government and on colonial political experience, were created in all of the colonies. The framers of these governments sought to create a political order that would protect men's liberties without falling into tyranny. Nearly every state drew up a written constitution carefully defining the structure and functions of the government. Elaborate bills of rights, stressing traditional English liberties, were included in the constitutions. Since sovereignty rested with the people, elections were provided for all officials. Two-house legislatures were established, the lower houses being controlled by property-holding voters and the upper houses being selected by the lower chambers. Legislatures were armed with extensive powers to control and check executive officials, who were universally suspected of being the chief instigators of tyranny. Independent judiciaries were almost universally adopted. The whole philosophy of separation of powers was thereby incorporated into the new state governments, signifying a strong conviction that the powers of government must be limited by constitutional safeguards. Taken as a whole, the state constitutions framed between 1776 and 1780 inaugurated a degree of popular control over government unknown in the contemporary world, although none of them was completely democratic.

The Revolution affected changes in other areas of life as significant as those altering the political structure. Several states took steps to disestablish state-supported churches, to institute religious toleration, and in general to separate political and religious life. Many states passed new land laws that tended to make it easier to gain ownership of property. Especially significant was the abolition of primogeniture, which required that the eldest son receive all of his father's land. Slavery was abolished in some Northern states, in part at least because this institution seemed out of place in a society dedicated to the principles of the Declaration of Independence. All of these liberalizing movements pointed toward greater freedom in the future.

Quite accidentally the Revolution had an important leveling effect in terms of the distribution of wealth. An inflation, caused by the efforts of the Americans to pay for the war with paper money, wiped out fortunes, aided debtors, and allowed new fortunes to be built. Many established merchants suffered heavy losses from the disturbance of foreign trade, but new opportunities in trade and industry emerged once America was free from the British commercial system. Small farmers flourished during the war, bolstered by easy money and high prices. Under these varied pressures the pre-Revolutionary social order did not survive intact. Again a greater degree of equality and freedom emerged to characterize life in the new nation.

5. Launching a New Nation

Even more challenging to the Americans was the problem of creating a central government for the new nation. Almost all Americans were conscious of the need to bind the states together into a single nation; no one seriously entertained the idea of thirteen separate nations to replace the authority of Great Britain. The vital issue was the form that the new government should take.

The first attempt at forming a national government was the work of the same radical group that had framed the Declaration of Independence. These men had a deep distrust for strong government over which the populace had no control. On the basis of this conviction they shaped the Articles of Confederation in 1777 and secured its acceptance by all the states by 1781. A national congress was created and given considerable powers to conduct foreign affairs, declare war, issue money, raise armies, fix weights and measures, and borrow money. The executive branch of the government was entrusted to a committee of thirteen, selected by congress. However, congress lacked the essential powers to tax and to regulate commerce, and on most vital issues its decisions had to be submitted to the states for final approval. The Articles of Confederation thus established a loose union of thirteen nearly independent states headed by a central government that could not compel them to do anything but could only encourage them to co-operate.

The Articles of Confederation survived until 1789. The central government made some decisions of lasting importance, such as provisions for the use of the public lands west of the Alleghenies. On the whole, however, the government was weak and indecisive. Little was done to curb the aggressive policies of Britain and Spain to the west. The grievous economic problems of the new nation were unresolved. The states, free to pursue their individual policies in economic affairs, often worked at cross-purposes. Some of them seriously threatened property rights, but the most frightening action of the states was their issuance of nearly worthless paper money that inflated prices, benefited the debtors, and nearly wiped out the fortunes of the wealthy.

In the face of the mounting evidence of the inadequacies of the confederation there was a rising sentiment for a strong central government. Many grew certain that too little government was as bad as too much. This new feeling finally led in May 1787 to the summoning of a convention to consider revising the Articles of Confederation. The men present were chiefly men of wealth and position, not a little disturbed by some of the radical moves being taken in the states they represented. This fact has sometimes led to the conclusion that the American constitution was framed by men bent on creating an instrument to safeguard the interests of the privileged few. Although there may be some truth in this position, delegates were also patriots interested in safeguarding all Americans and men with firm convictions, drawn chiefly from the philosophy of the Enlightenment, about what governments ought to be.

The convention immediately decided to scrap the Articles of Confederation and to write a new constitution. Once this task was undertaken, the delegates found themselves in broad agreement on many vital matters. They agreed that a written constitution enumerating the powers of the central government was necessary, that there must be popular control over the central government, and that every government must have built-in checks, necessitating the separation of powers of the various branches. No one believed that the states should be stripped of all power, yet all were convinced that the central government must have certain powers to deal independently with matters affecting national interests.

Working from these premises, the delegates quickly arrived at a basic framework for a new government. A two-house legislature, a president, and a national judiciary were to be established. Each branch was provided with specific functions, and an elaborate system of internal checks was provided to prevent any branch from exercising too much power. The powers of the national government as a whole in certain specific areas were enumerated, while all other matters were reserved to the states. The federal government was given clearly stated authority to coerce the states in those matters over which it had jurisdiction, and, to assure a degree of flexibility, provisions were made for amending the constitution.

In spite of broad agreement there were a few crucial points over which the delegates long debated. One centered around finding a way to safeguard the interests of the small states against the large. This issue was settled by providing that seats in the House of Representatives would be apportioned according to population (with slaves counting three fifths as much as freemen), while the Senate would be made up of two senators from each state whatever its size. Another problem was the method of choosing the president. Many wanted a strong executive but were fearful of allowing the populace to select him. It was finally agreed that the president would be chosen for four years by a special electoral college, the members of which were to be chosen by the states. Once these difficulties were ironed out the convention's work was done.

The new document was handed over to the states for ratification with the provision that when nine states approved the new government would go into effect. The constitution aroused stormy discussion within the states. However, one by one they fell into line. On June 21, 1788, the ninth state, New Hampshire, approved the constitution, and the new government was officially in existence. Within a month the crucial states of Virginia and New York accepted the constitution, assuring that it would be put into actual operation. Rhode Island held out until May 1790. Several states added a condition to their acceptance of the constitution, asking that a bill of rights, guaranteeing fundamental liberties, be added. This condition was filled shortly after the government began its operation by the addition of the first ten amendments to the constitution (1791).

The new government began operation in 1789 with George Washington as president. Congress was controlled by the Federalists, a group that had supported the constitution during the ratification struggle and that favored strong central government. During the next decade the federal system proved its worth. A federal court system was created. A cabinet emerged to assist the president in his executive duties. When taxes were levied and collected, the federal government was able to establish its credit and to put the government on a sound financial basis. The government steered its way safely through the stormy international waters disturbed by the French Revolution. Prosperity returned to America, easing the new government's burdens considerably. The Federalist leaders showed extreme skill.

In spite of their accomplishments, however, many Americans grew tired of the Federalists, who seldom hid the fact that they intended to use the government to protect property and wealth and that they hoped to increase the central government's power in order better to promote the interests of the wealthy. Those who were opposed to the Federalists began to rally around Thomas Jefferson, the Virginia aristocrat who did not subscribe to all the ideals of his class. A second party, the Republicans (not to be confused with the present Republican party, founded in 1854), took shape under Jefferson's leadership. The emergence of political parties added an element to the new government that the constitution makers had not foreseen. In 1800 Jefferson was elected president and the Federalists were routed. This election was probably the final proof of the workability of the new government, since it demonstrated that the American voters controlled the government and that they did not have to rebel to make their voices heard. If the founding fathers thought that they had created a government to serve the interests of a few (which they probably did not), they were disabused of that idea by Jefferson's victory in 1800.

Between 1775 and 1800 the Americans had put on an impressive display for the world. They had asserted their rights against tyranny by force of arms, demonstrating that no government was sacred once it began to oppress men. They had then proceeded in a rational fashion to establish thirteen state governments and a national government that were capable of action yet were restricted from abusing the inalienable rights of men. Furthermore, an ingenious federal system was worked out whereby state and national governments coexisted. These governments proved sensitive to popular control and made the exercise of popular sovereignty a fact. Everywhere liberal, enlightened men saw their dreams becoming a reality in America. Here was inspiration and guidance for those who might like to overhaul society elsewhere. The revolutionary era was launched in practice as well as in theory.

SUGGESTED READING

Curtis P. Nettels, *The Roots of American Civilization: A History of American Colonial Life* (1938). A well-written and thorough examination of American society in the colonial period, bringing out the development of factors that set America apart from England.

* Edmund S. Morgan, *The Birth of the Republic, 1763–89* (University of Chicago Press paperback). A short narrative account of the American Revolution that succeeds in packing a tremendous amount of information into a brief span. The book is especially good in introducing the reader to the major problems of interpretation in connection with the Revolution.

Charles M. Andrews, *The Colonial Background of the American Revolution*, rev. ed. (1931). A clearly presented study of conditions in the colonies and of British policy toward the colonies in the era prior to the Revolution.

John C. Miller, *Origins of the American Revolution* (1943). The most complete and thorough treatment of the many forces that contributed to the outbreak of the American Revolution.

* John C. Wahlke, ed., *The Causes of the American Revolution* (Amherst series). A collection of brief statements by some of the leading American historians on the causes of the American Revolution. This book must be used with care, however, since each author tends to state his case in the strongest possible fashion.

John Richard Alden, *The American Revolution, 1775–1783* (1954). A recent narrative account of the developments in America from 1775 to 1783; this book will provide a reader with a clear, balanced account of major events.

Willard M. Wallace, *Appeal to Arms: A Military History of the American Revolution* (1951). An interesting description of the major military campaigns of the American Revolution.

* Carl Becker, *The Declaration of Independence: A Study in the History of Political Ideas* (Vintage). Published in a hardback edition in 1942. A brilliant analysis of the Declaration of Independence in terms of the political ideals that inspired it.

Max Farrand, *The Framing of the Constitution of the United States* (1913). An excellent description of the proceedings of the Constitutional Convention and of the issues that divided its members.

C. G. Bowers, *Jefferson and Hamilton* (1925); and *Jefferson in Power* (1936). These books present in an exciting manner a clear picture of the problems connected with the launching of the new nation after the adoption of the Constitution. The discussion centers around the personalities of Jefferson and Hamilton, with Jefferson being given a much more sympathetic treatment.

* *Federalist Papers* (numerous editions; a convenient selection of essays from the complete work has been made by Ralph H. Gabriel and published in a paperback edition by the Liberal Arts Press). These essays by James Madison, Alexander Hamilton, and John Jay in support of the new Constitution supply the best introduction to the issues involved.

CHAPTER 40

The French Revolution, 1789–99

Dᴜʀɪɴɢ the long reign of Louis XV (1715–74) French prestige declined steadily from the lofty heights it had reached under Louis XIV. Louis XV was a vain, lazy, selfish, and cynical man who lavished more time and money on his mistresses, Madame de Pompadour and Madame du Barry, than on affairs of state. His participation in the War of Austrian Succession and the Seven Years' War resulted only in disgraceful defeats and the loss of France's empire in India and North America to Great Britain. His successor inherited an unbalanced budget and a discontented populace. Young Louis XVI (1774–92), though well-meaning, reasonably intelligent, and of good moral character, was not the man to restore the prestige of the throne. He was awkward, shy, and weak-willed when the situation called for decision. His reign was marked by one of the greatest and most far-reaching upheavals in the history of Western civilization—the French Revolution.

1. The Last Days of the Old Regime in France

France at the succession of Louis XVI, though somewhat weakened, was not in dire distress. With the possible exception of Great Britain she was still the richest and most influential nation in the world. During the reign of Louis XV, in spite of France's defeats and the loss of most of her empire, her commerce and prosperity had steadily increased. By 1774 only Great Britain, among the major powers, had a higher standard of living than France.

Discontent arose, however, from the maldistribution of wealth and privilege. Since the end of the reign of Louis XIV the nobility had made a comeback in high government office at the expense of the bourgeoisie, reversing a trend that dated from the fifteenth century. These offices, many of them useless, carried handsome salaries and pensions. Furthermore, the nobility was exempt from virtually all direct taxation. Socially, the nobles looked down on the ambitious bankers, lawyers, and merchants. The city proletariat was another group that failed to share in the rising prosperity, for wages had not risen nearly so fast as the cost of living.

The peasants, who constituted approximately nine tenths of the total population, were on the whole discontented. Although serfdom was rapidly disappearing, the peasants still owed many feudal dues and obligations—even most of those who owned their own land. Upon their backs fell the bulk of the direct taxes. They themselves could not hunt or fish, but the aristocracy hunted in their fields and the game ate their crops. They were compelled to keep up the public roads with their own unpaid labor. Most of the peasants were *métayers*, or share croppers, who, in addition to giving up half of their crops to the landlord for rent, paid many other feudal dues such as fees for the use of the lord's mill, bake oven, wine press, and breeding stock. Although the French peasants were better off than those of any other major country on the continent of Europe, their very well-being made them more ambitious to rid themselves of the remaining vestiges of feudalism.

Government was arbitrary. The king's decree was law. The Estates-General, the French counterpart of the British Parliament, had not met for nearly two centuries. Justice was capricious and corrupt. There were 237 different codes of law to confuse the litigants. There were no juries as in Great Britain. The king could arrest and imprison at will (although Louis XV and Louis XVI seldom did). The judges of the thirteen superior courts, called *parlements*, purchased their titles. Torture still prevailed. The Roman Catholic Church, possessing many of the privileges of government, was rich, powerful, intolerant of other religions, and highly aristocratic in its organization. This arbitrary system, which had been taken for normal in earlier days, seemed intolerable to the readers of Voltaire and Rousseau.

The breakdown of the old regime in France occurred in the field of finance. Louis XVI inherited a large and constantly growing national debt. It was not excessive for a rich nation like France; Great Britain and the Netherlands had higher per-capita debts. But, together with the exemption of the nobility and the clergy from direct taxation and extravagant expenditures by the government and the court, it spelled eventual bankruptcy. Furthermore, the corrupt system of tax collection, which made use of profiteering tax farmers (private contractors), allowed much of the revenue to be diverted from the treasury.

Upon assuming the throne Louis XVI appointed the physiocrat Turgot, a friend of Voltaire, as minister of finances. Turgot initiated a series of sweeping reforms that would have cleaned up the financial mess and alleviated much of the social discontent. However, the vested interests brought about his dismissal at the end of two years. A succession of ministers then tried all kinds of palliatives such as borrowing, pump-priming expenditures, better bookkeeping, but to no avail. By 1786 the debt was 3,000,000,000 livres,[1] and the annual deficit had reached 125,000,000. Even the aristocracy became alarmed and demanded reforms. In a desperate effort to save the old regime, Louis XVI called the Assembly of Notables in 1787 in an attempt to persuade them to consent to be taxed. When they refused, Louis had no alternative but to call the Estates-General —an act that precipitated the French Revolution.

2. The Triumph of the Third Estate

Throughout the winter of 1788–89 elections were being held for members of the Estates-General. All France was agog with excitement. Voltaire and Rousseau had done their work; it was generally believed that man could construct an earthly paradise if given a chance.

Since the Estates-General had not met for a hundred and seventy-five years, no one quite knew the procedure. Hundreds of pamphlets on the subject appeared, accompanied by widespread debate. By tradition each of the three estates, the clergy, the nobility, and the commoners, elected their own representatives. All males who had reached the age of twenty-five and paid taxes were permitted to vote. Since the Third Estate, including the bourgeoisie, the peasantry, and the proletariat, comprised more than nine tenths of the total population, it was given as many seats as the other two combined. This large representation for the Third Estate was not especially significant at the time, since by tradition the three estates sat separately and each group had one vote.

By April 1789, the delegates began to arrive at Versailles. Good will prevailed. Violent revolution was far from anyone's mind.

[1] The livre was technically worth about twenty cents, but its purchasing power in the eighteenth century was much greater than that of the mid-twentieth-century American dollar.

The delegates came armed with *cahiers*, the lists of grievances which had been called for by the king. Of the six hundred representatives of the Third Estate only twenty were peasants. The rest, except for a handful of liberal clergy and nobles, were bourgeois. Nearly all of the members of the Third Estate, as well as many members of the two privileged estates, were fully acquainted with the philosophy of Locke, Montesquieu, and Voltaire. Rousseau was a little too radical for these moderate men.

The first formal session was held on May 5. Immediately a sharp debate began over the method of voting. The two privileged estates demanded that, according to custom, the three estates meet separately and vote by order, that is, each estate cast one vote. This would mean that all attacks on privilege and inequality would be defeated by a vote of two to one. The Third Estate, already becoming disillusioned by the snobbish attitude of the royal court and of some of the members of the first two estates, demanded that the voting be by head. The three estates would meet jointly, each individual member casting one vote. This would mean that all measures for fundamental reform would pass, for, not only did the Third Estate have as many members as the other two combined, but a certain number of liberal clergy and noblemen sympathized with the common people and the cause of reform. Both sides realized that the outcome of this issue would be decisive.

On June 17, after six weeks of fruitless haggling, the Third Estate, now joined by several liberal members of the First and Second estates, declared itself the National Assembly of France and invited the other two estates to join it in the enactment of legislation. Three days later, on June 20, when the members of the Third Estate arrived at their meeting hall, they found it locked and guarded by royal troops. Adjourning to a nearby building used as an indoor tennis court, they took the "Tennis Court Oath," vowing never to disband until France had a constitution. It was the Third Estate's first act of defiance. On June 23 the king called the three estates into a royal session, at which he commanded them once and for all to meet separately and vote by order. The king, his ministers, and members of the first two estates filed out, but the Third Estate defiantly remained seated. When the Marquis de Dreux-Brézé returned to remind them of the king's orders, Mirabeau, a liberal nobleman elected by the Third Estate, jumped to his feet and shouted in his thundering voice, "Go and tell those who sent you that we are here by the will of the people and will not leave this place except at the point of the bayonet!" When the startled courtier repeated these words to his master, Louis XVI, with characteristic weakness, replied, "They mean to stay. Well damn it, let them stay." A few days later he reversed himself and ordered the three estates to meet jointly and vote by head.

The Third Estate had thus won the first round. However, alarming news soon began to arrive that the king was calling the professional troops of the frontier garrison to Versailles. It appeared that he was at last preparing to use force. At this critical juncture the Paris proletariat countered the threat of force with force. On July 14, a riotous Parisian mob marched on and destroyed the Bastille, a gloomy old fortress prison in the workingmen's quarter that symbolized the arbitrary tyranny of the old regime. July 14 has long been celebrated as the French national holiday. This show of force stayed the king's hand.

Throughout the remainder of July and August the spirit of violence spread from Paris to the rest of France, where it had been only desultory hitherto. Many nobles fled from France for their lives (the *émigrés*), and feudalism, for all practical purposes, came to an end. Since the peasants feared reprisals from the nobility and believed a widespread rumor that the nobles were raising brigand bands against the peasants, this period is known as the Great Fear. The legal end of feudalism came on August 4, when, during a hysterical night session of the National Assembly, one nobleman after another stood up and renounced

MIRABEAU ANSWERING THE MARQUIS DE DREUX-BRÉZÉ, FROM A PAINTING BY DELACROIX. Following the Royal Session, June 23, 1789, the Marquis de Dreux-Brézé, at the king's command, requested that the Third Estate withdraw and vote as a body. This would have allowed the First and Second Estates to outvote the Third. Count Mirabeau, speaking for the Third Estate, refused to leave. This bold act marked the beginning of the triumph of the Third Estate. (*Courtesy N.Y. Carlsberg Glyptotek, Copenhagen*)

STORMING OF THE BASTILLE. A former fortress turned into a prison, the Bastille was a symbol of arbitrary government of royal and aristocratic tyranny. Its destruction in 1789 by a Paris mob marked the beginning of large-scale mob violence in the French Revolution. The date of its destruction, July 14, has long been celebrated as the French national holiday. (*The Bettmann Archive*)

his feudal rights and privileges. After the excitement died down, the king once more began quietly to assemble troops around Versailles and Paris. In answer to this new threat of force a huge mob of Paris women on October 5 and 6 marched the eleven miles out to Versailles, surrounded the palace, and forced the king to accompany them to Paris, where he became a virtual prisoner of the Paris proletariat. As the carriage bearing the royal family rolled toward Paris, the surrounding mob shouted jubilantly, "We have the baker, the baker's wife, and the little cook boy! Now we shall have bread!" A few days later the National Assembly itself voted to move its sessions to Paris, where it came increasingly under the influence of the radical populace of the great city. The Third Estate had triumphed.

3. Making France an "Enlightened" Monarchy

The National Assembly could now at last settle down to the task of making France

over in the image of Voltaire and Montesquieu. During the next two years it passed a series of sweeping reforms that may be conveniently classified as follows:

JUDICIAL

An orderly system of lower and higher courts was established. Judges were to be elected for six-year terms. Torture was abolished. Juries in criminal cases were to be used for the first time in French history.

ECONOMIC

In accordance with the doctrine of *laissez faire*, guilds and trading associations were abolished. All occupations were declared open to all classes. Feudal obligations, including labor on the public roads, had already come to an end on the night of August 4. Internal tolls and customs were abolished.

FINANCIAL

The complex and unequal taxes, direct and indirect, were swept away. They were replaced by a tax on land and a tax on the profits of trade and industry. Both were uniform, and no one was exempt. Tax farming was, at long last, abolished. Expenditures were henceforth authorized only by the national legislature. To meet the pressing financial needs of the government, the National Assembly issued paper money called *assignats* to the value of 400,000,000 livres. To back up this paper money, the property of the Roman Catholic Church valued at approximately that amount was confiscated.

RELIGIOUS

The seizure of church property was the first step toward the nationalization of the Church. Monasticism was abolished. The secular clergy was to be elected by the people (including non-Roman Catholics) and their salaries paid by the state. The bishops were reduced in number, wealth, and power.

They were no longer to be invested by the pope. These measures were incorporated in the Civil Constitution of the Clergy, to which all the members of the clergy were required to take an oath of allegiance in order to perform their functions and draw their salaries. The pope, whose control over the organization and the clergy of the French church would have been broken, declared the Civil Constitution of the Clergy to be founded upon heretical principles and ordered the clergy to refuse to take the oath of allegiance. A majority of the clergy, including nearly all of the bishops, followed the pope's command. The defection of the "non-juring clergy" and of thousands of their devoted parishioners was the first serious split in the ranks of the revolutionists.

POLITICAL

One of the first constructive acts of the National Assembly was to draw up the Declaration of the Rights of Man. This document, which followed the English Bill of Rights by an even hundred years and preceded the American Bill of Rights by two years, was replete with the phrases of the philosophers of the Enlightenment. Life, liberty, and property were declared to be the natural rights of man. The declaration also provided for freedom of religion, speech, press, and assembly, together with the right to resist oppression and the right to freedom from arbitrary arrest and imprisonment.

The central government was patterned after the ideas of Montesquieu. Judicial, legislative, and executive powers were separated. Lawmaking was given to the single-chamber Legislative Assembly of 745 members elected for two-year terms. Voting, however, was limited to males at least twenty-five years of age who paid taxes equivalent to three days' wages. It is estimated that some four million adult males ("active" citizens) could meet these qualifications and that some three million remained "passive" citizens. Actually to sit in the Legislative Assembly required the payment of taxes equivalent to fifty days' wages.

Only about 50,000 Frenchmen could meet this qualification, and the weight of power fell to the bourgeoisie. The king was granted a suspensive veto over all but financial and constitutional measures, but three successive legislatures could pass a bill over the king's veto. The conduct of foreign relations was left in the hands of the king, but he could not declare war or make treaties without the consent of the Legislative Assembly. The king's expenditures were limited to a sum voted by the legislative body. France was greatly decentralized. For purposes of local government and administration the country was divided into eighty-three departments, each of which was administered by a small elected assembly.

In October 1791, the National Assembly declared its work to be completed and gave way to the Legislative Assembly, which had recently been elected under the new constitution. Had Voltaire and Montesquieu been alive, they would have had every right to say, "I told you so." Within a brief span of two years and with very little bloodshed, France had been made over. The monarchy had been limited and "enlightened." The Roman Catholic Church had been subordinated to the state. Individual rights and liberties had been defined and established. But Rousseau would have been unhappy. Actual majority rule had not been completely achieved.

4. Foreign War and the Failure of the Moderate Regime

The new government so optimistically launched was expected to last forever. Actually it lasted less than a year. Although the Legislative Assembly, elected under the restricted suffrage provisions of the new constitution, was made up largely of moderate men, it probably represented the wishes and the interests of the great majority of the French people. The chief gainers in the French Revolution thus far had been the bourgeoisie and the peasants. The bourgeoisie had gained political control over the country and social equality with the nobility.

Most of the peasants, who constituted the bulk of the French population, could now vote, and all of them were at last free from feudal obligations. To the numerous peasant landowners who owned their land before the Revolution were now added many others who had seized the lands of émigré nobles or had purchased confiscated Church lands. These two numerous classes were satisfied and wished to see the Revolution stop where it was, lest they lose their sacred property and their political dominance.

However, there were other groups that were quite dissatisfied. The royal family, the aristocracy, most of the clergy, and the army officers yearned for the restoration of their privileges. On the other hand, the city proletariat and some of the poorest peasants wished to see the Revolution continued on to more radical ground. They had gained little except theoretical rights and legal equality. Owning no property, they could not vote. Yet they had supplied the force that had saved the Third Estate and made the moderate reforms possible. Leadership for these disgruntled groups was found among the intelligentsia who were disciples of Rousseau. These intellectual radicals would be satisfied with nothing less than perfect democracy and complete equality.

The radical groups, although a definite minority of the French people, were well organized and ably led. In the Legislative Assembly itself the most liberal or radical group was the Girondins, so-called because their leaders came from the vicinity of Bordeaux in the department of Gironde. Outside the Assembly numerous clubs, of which the Jacobin Club became the most influential, were formed to debate and plan political matters. Although the Jacobins were and remained predominantly intellectual bourgeoisie and were moderate at first, they gradually became the most radical group in France. Three Jacobin leaders came to tower over all others. Jean Paul Marat, Swiss by birth, was an inordinately ambitious and frustrated physician and scientist turned popular journalist. His was the gift of rabble-rousing journalism. He incessantly de- manded the beheading of all those leaders who opposed the further extension of the Revolution. Georges Jacques Danton, a former lawyer in the king's council, was a thundering orator of great energy and ability. Maximilien de Robespierre, eventually to become dictator, was also a lawyer and former judge. This eloquent and sincere man was a fanatical disciple of Rousseau, bent upon the establishment of perfect democracy and equality. He also favored the total eradication of Christianity.

Events soon played into the hands of the radicals. The kings of Austria and Prussia, fearful of the spread of revolutionary ideas to their own lands and egged on by the French émigrés, began to make threatening moves and to issue meddlesome warnings to the French revolutionaries. In France the reactionaries believed that a successful war would enhance the prestige and power of the throne and that a defeat would result in the restoration of the old regime. Most of the radicals believed that war would expose the inefficiency and disloyalty of the king and bring about his downfall. When, therefore, in April 1792 Louis XVI appeared before the Legislative Assembly to request a declaration of war against Austria and Prussia, only seven votes were cast in the negative. Thus lightly was begun a war that was to last twenty-three years and affect most of the Western world.

The French armies, leaderless since nearly all of the high-ranking officers were members of the nobility and had either fled or been deposed, were badly defeated. As the Austrian and Prussian armies advanced toward Paris, panic seized the capital city. The king, who had already forfeited his popularity when he attempted to flee the country in June 1791, was now rightly suspected of being in treasonable communication with the enemy. On August 10, 1792, a huge Paris mob advanced on the king's palace. The royal family fled for its life to the Legislative Assembly, and not a minute too soon. The interior of the palace was wrecked, and several hundred of the Swiss guard were slain. The Legislative Assembly suspended

Louis XVI and called elections for a national convention to draw up a new constitution to take the place of the one that had just failed.

5. The Triumph of the Radicals and the Reign of Terror

The elections to the constitutional convention took place in an atmosphere of panic and violence. During the interim between the overthrow of the limited monarchy and the meeting of the convention, Danton assumed the emergency leadership of the nation. Feverishly he superintended the gathering of recruits and rushed them to the front. As the recruits were preparing to leave Paris, rumors spread that their wives and children would be murdered by the reactionary clergy and nobles. Violent elements began murdering members of the non-juring clergy and reactionary nobles who were being held in the prisons of Paris. During the first three weeks of September 1792, more than a thousand such victims were massacred. In the elections to the National Convention, held amid this hysteria and violence, the radicals won a sweeping victory. Most of the conservative elements prudently stayed away from the polls.

In the Legislative Assembly the Girondins had been the leftist group.[2] In the National Convention they found themselves on the extreme right. The new left was made up of the Jacobin followers of Marat, Danton, and Robespierre, mostly from the city of Paris. They came to be called the Mountain, since they occupied the highest seats in the convention hall. This radical convention, elected for the purpose of drawing up a new constitution, was to rule France for the next three years (1792–95)—the most exciting years of the Revolution.

The first act of the National Convention was to declare France a republic. Their next move was to dispose of the king. After a fair

[2] The present political connotation of the terms "right" and "left" derives from this period. In the Legislative Assembly the conservatives sat quite by chance on the speaker's right, the liberals and radicals on his left.

trial he was found unquestionably guilty of treasonable communication with the enemy and sent to the guillotine—an instrument adopted by the revolutionists for the more scientific and humane beheading of the condemned. The execution of Louis XVI, accompanied by proclamations of world revolution by the evangelical Jacobins, sent a shudder of horror through the royal courts of Europe. Furthermore, the hastily recruited French revolutionary armies, which had checked the Austrians and Prussians at Valmy in September 1792 had taken the offensive and overrun the Austrian Netherlands.

Austria and Prussia were now joined by Great Britain, the Dutch Netherlands, Spain, Portugal, Sardinia, and Naples in a great coalition bent upon the destruction of the French Revolution and the restoration of the old regime. The French armies were unable to stand up to such an array of armed might. But the defeats and invasions were not the worst disasters to confront the revolutionary government. The ignorant peasants of the Vendée region in western France, who had been stirred up by the non-juring clergy, rebelled against the radical government. The rebellion spread until some sixty of the eighty-three departments were affected. Major provincial cities such as Bordeaux, Lyons, and Marseilles were in revolt. Toulon, the chief French naval base on the Mediterranean, invited in the British fleet. Inside the Convention itself many of the moderate Girondins were sympathetic with the rebels.

Faced with what seemed to be inevitable disaster to their radical cause and indeed to the Revolution itself, the leaders of the Mountain decided on drastic action. Since the Paris Commune, as the city government was called, was already controlled completely by the Jacobins, the Mountain leaders conspired with it to incite a mob. On June 2, 1793, the National Convention, now dominated by the left wing and surrounded by a howling Paris mob, voted the expulsion and arrest of twenty-nine Girondin leaders. Having thus silenced all opposition within the convention, Robespierre, Danton, and their followers inaugurated a reign of terror. (Marat was assassinated in July.) Their goals were to unite France and to save and extend the Revolution.

For streamlined efficiency the National Convention delegated unlimited powers to a Committee of Public Safety, composed of twelve men working in secret. This all-powerful committee came under the dominance of Robespierre. At its beck and call was the Committee of General Security, a national police force. A Revolutionary Tribunal was set up to try, condemn, and execute suspects without the usual legal procedure and as quickly as possible. Agents of the Committee of Public Safety, called representatives on mission, carried the Terror to every nook and cranny of France. Although tens of thousands of persons, possibly half a million, were imprisoned during the Reign of Terror, only some 16,000 are believed to have been executed. The drastic policy was remarkably successful. The disaffected elements were quickly silenced, and the rebellions quelled. The defense of the republic was entrusted to Lazare Carnot. A *levée en masse* was ordered. All men, women, and children were called to the colors. The able-bodied young men were rapidly trained and rushed to the front. Everyone else contributed his bit to the war effort on the home front. This common activity for defense of country produced a high state of morale— the first mass national patriotism in history. Able new officers were found. The armies of the coalition were defeated on every front and hurled back beyond the frontiers.

6. Robespierre's Utopia of Rousseau

While Robespierre and his associates were saving the Revolution, they were also busy extending it to more radical ground. A fanatical disciple of Rousseau, Robespierre was determined to make France a deistic, semi-socialistic utopia where perfect liberty, equality, and fraternity would reign supreme. During the emergency of 1793 a maximum price was placed upon the necessities of life for the protection of the consumer, particularly the city proletariat. Efforts were made to force people to accept the badly inflated *assignats* at their face value. The lands of the *émigrés* were confiscated and sold in two- or three-acre farms to the peasants. Since these farms could be paid for over a long period of time, almost every French peasant could now become a landowner and most of them did. France has remained a nation of peasant proprietors ever since. The metric system was adopted; the Louvre Palace was turned into an art gallery; the national library and the national archives were founded; a law (never implemented) provided for a comprehensive national system of public education. The Rousseau type of democracy became popular in society. Women adopted the flowing robes and hair styles of ancient Greece. Silk knee breeches, the symbol of aristocracy, gave way to trousers. Rich and poor alike took pride in being *sans culottes* (without knee breeches). Titles of all kinds were discarded for Citizen and Citizeness.

One of Robespierre's greatest ambitions was to replace Christianity in France with the deistic religion of the Enlightenment. A group of his followers, mistaking him to be an atheist, set up in Notre Dame an actress of questionable morals as goddess of reason. Robespierre, however, was planning the establishment of the worship of the Supreme Being in the fashion of Rousseau. In an elaborate ceremony Robespierre, wearing a sky-blue suit and carrying a bouquet of red roses, led a procession across Paris to the scene of the festivities. Thus was inaugurated the "Republic of Virtue." Thousands of Christian churches were closed. Even the calendar was dechristianized by eliminating Sundays. The months were made equal and named after the seasons. The year I was dated from September 22, 1792, the date of the declaration of the republic.

Meanwhile, discontent with Robespierre and his policies was steadily increasing. The defeat of the invading armies of the coalition and the suppression of the internal rebellion removed the justification for the Terror, yet the Terror was intensified. When Danton counseled moderation, Robespierre sent even him and his most prominent followers to the guillotine. No one, not even the members of the National Convention, felt safe any longer. Finally, in July 1794, the convention found the courage and the leadership to overthrow Robespierre and send him to his own guillotine.

7. Reaction and the Rise of Napoleon

Since Robespierre was overthrown on July 27, which was 9 Thermidor by the revolutionary calendar, the reaction that followed is known as the Thermidorian Reaction. The propertied bourgeoisie, who quickly gained control of things, had been frightened and angered by the socialistic measures of Robespierre's regime. All such measures still in force were repealed. The Terror was brought to an end, and the chief terrorists executed. Armed bands of bourgeois hirelings went around for some time beating or killing Jacobins. In 1795 the National Convention finally got around to the task for which it had been elected three years earlier: the drawing up of a new constitution. The constitution reflected the conservative reaction. Only property owners could vote for members of the legislative bodies. Members of the Council of Elders, 250 in number, had to be forty years of age

and married. Members of the Council of Five Hundred had to be thirty years of age. Executive functions were placed in the hands of five directors, who were chosen for five-year terms by the two legislative councils. The directors must be forty years of age and married. In October 1795, the National Convention turned over its powers to the Directory, the name that was given to the new government.

The most significant development of the period of the Directory, 1795–99, was the rise to power of Napoleon Bonaparte. The directors, though men of reasonable competence, were unable to restore peace and social tranquillity. Though peace had already been made with Spain and Prussia, war with Great Britain, Austria, and Sardinia dragged on. Government finances were chaotic, and brigandage was rife. More and more people longed for a strong man who could bring peace abroad and order at home. Napoleon proved to be the man. The story of his rise to power will be told in the next chapter. When in November 1799 Napoleon overthrew the Directory and made himself dictator, the French Revolution had run full cycle from absolute Bourbon monarchy to absolute Napoleonic dictatorship. France had failed by popular democratic processes to establish the utopia promised by Voltaire, Montesquieu, and Rousseau. She would now try to achieve it by the dictatorship of a genius.

SUGGESTED READING

E. J. Lowell, *The Eve of the French Revolution* (1892). A brilliant description and analysis of all phases of French society before the Revolution and of the ideas of the reformer-philosophers. A masterpiece of historical writing.

* Alexis de Tocqueville, *The Old Regime and the Revolution* (Anchor). A penetrating analysis by one of France's most astute historians. De Tocqueville was the first to observe that the Revolution was not the result of widespread misery.

* Georges Lefebvre, *The Coming of the French Revolution* (Vintage). A brief but perceptive

analysis of the causes of the great revolution, incorporating the results of the latest and best scholarship.

Louis Madelin, *The French Revolution* (1928). Probably the best single-volume account of the Revolution. Combines deep scholarship with literary and dramatic skill.

* Leo Gershoy, *The Era of the French Revolution* (Anvil). A brief but scholarly survey by one of America's leading scholars on the French Revolution.

E. L. Higgins, *The French Revolution as Told by Contemporaries* (1938). The story is skillfully woven together with eyewitness accounts.

A good introduction to the use of original historical sources.

Madame de Campan, *Memoirs*, 2 vols. (1917). Originally published in 1822. Madame de Campan was for many years lady in waiting to Marie Antoinette. Her well-written memoirs are an important source for the character and personality of Marie Antoinette and Louis XVI, and also for the early part of the Revolution.

Crane Brinton, *The Jacobins* (1930). A scholarly monograph showing that the Jacobins, who dominated the radical and bloody phase of the French Revolution, were of the bourgeoisie and intelligentsia, not of the rabble.

J. M. Thompson, *Robespierre and the French Revolution* (1953). A brief and readable study of the chief leader of the bloody second phase of the Revolution. Sympathetic to Robespierre.

Anatole France, *The Gods Are Athirst* (published with the complete works, 31 vols., 1908–28). One of the best novels based on the French Revolution. Skillfully captures the spirit of the Revolution.

CHAPTER 41

The Era of Napoleon, 1799–1815

No INDIVIDUAL in modern times has enjoyed a more meteoric career than Napoleon Bonaparte, the modern counterpart of Alexander the Great and Julius Caesar. He was essentially a product of the Enlightenment and the French Revolution. His mission was to consolidate the Revolution in France and to spread its "enlightened" concepts and many of its institutions to most of the rest of Europe.

1. Napoleon's Rise to Power

Napoleon was born on the French island of Corsica in 1769. Corsicans speak Italian, and Napoleon never learned to speak French without an accent. At the age of nine he was sent to a military school in France. Here he was made fun of by his schoolmates because of his foreign accent and his small size. Already suffering from megalomania, he withdrew into himself, studied history, geography, and mathematics, and dreamed of future greatness. At sixteen he received his commission as second lieutenant of artillery. During several years of boring garrison duty he stuffed his photographic mind full of history, the classics, and the philosophy of the Enlightenment, particularly that of Rousseau. Had it not been for the French Revolution, his humble, foreign birth would probably have made it impossible for him to achieve much of anything.

Napoleon's first big chance came in 1793 at the siege of Toulon, France's Mediter-

ranean naval base, which had gone over to the side of the British. Since most of the regular army officers were nobles and had fled the country or been deposed, the young Napoleon was given an opportunity to try his plan for the recapture of the base. His plan worked brilliantly, and he attracted the attention of some important people, including General Paul Barras, who was to become one of the five directors. These contacts paid off two years later on 13 Vendémiaire (October 5, 1795). When the National Convention completed the constitution setting up the government of the Directory, the members of the Convention, fearful of losing power after so much bloodshed, decreed that two thirds of the members of the new legislative bodies must be chosen from among themselves. This decree angered a great many disgruntled people who, for one reason or another, wished to see an entirely new government come in. Royalist leaders seized the opportunity to arouse a huge Paris mob against the Convention. In the emergency the Convention appointed General Barras to defend it. Barras, in turn, called upon Napoleon, whose prowess with artillery he had observed at Toulon. Although the details of the fracas are uncertain, it would appear that Napoleon masterminded the defense of the Convention. (Barras and Napoleon in their memoirs both claim the leading role and belittle the part played by the other.) An artillery expert with no love for the French people, the ambitious Corsican had long before decided that the way to handle a mob was to let it have a "whiff of grapeshot." A few such whiffs from his skillfully placed artillery dispersed the mob, and Napoleon became the hero of the Convention.

The day of 13 Vendémiaire put Napoleon's star in the ascendancy. Although he was now only twenty-six, he demanded and got the command of the Army of the Interior. However, as an astute student of history, he realized that glamour and power could be won only in the field. Therefore, he requested and received command of the Army of Italy—the French army still fighting the Austrians and Sardinians in northern Italy. Napoleon's dynamism and skill quickly galvanized into fighting efficiency the lethargic French forces, who defeated the Austrians and Sardinians and forced them to sue for peace. Nor was the young general any less skilled in diplomacy and propaganda than in military strategy. He personally negotiated a favorable peace with Austria (a function that really belonged to the newly created French Directory) and sent back glowing reports of his exploits.

Soon the name Napoleon Bonaparte was on everyone's lips. The Directory, grappling with the unheroic problems left by the preceding revolutionary bodies, was concerned for its own existence. Fearing the presence of a popular and ambitious young general in France, it was only too glad to accede to Bonaparte's request to lead an expedition to Egypt as a means of striking at the British Empire. Napoleon's chief purposes in going to Egypt were personal and psychological. He sensed that the time was not yet ripe to overthrow the government, that exploits far away in the mystic East would greatly enhance his reputation, and that during his absence from France crises would arise enabling him to play the role of the returning savior. He was right. His victories in Egypt were of no military importance, but they did add to his personal glamour. (Scholars whom he took along discovered the Rosetta Stone, which unlocked the secrets of the ancient Egyptian language and history.)

Meanwhile, Great Britain persuaded Austria and Russia to join her in a second coalition against France. This was what Napoleon was looking for. His fleet having been destroyed by the British squadron under Lord Nelson, Napoleon deserted his army in Egypt and slipped back to France with a few chosen followers. France was electrified. With perfect timing General Bonaparte conspired with various members of the government and with the additional support of armed forces under his command overthrew the Directory, setting himself up as dictator. This *coup d'état* occurred on 18 Brumaire (November 9, 1799). Napoleon was only thirty years of age.

2. The Consulate—Peace and Reform, 1799–1804

Having seized absolute power by conspiracy and force, Napoleon drew up a constitution to conceal his dictatorship under the cloak of parliamentary forms. He gave himself the title of First Consul with the power to appoint key civilian and military personnel, declare war and make treaties, command the military forces, and initiate all legislation through a hand-picked council of state. Two other consuls without any significant powers served as camouflage. A self-perpetuating senate selected a tribunate of one hundred members and a legislative body of three hundred members from a list of candidates elected by all adult French males. The Tribunate discussed proposed legislation drawn up by the Council of State, and the Legislative Body voted on it without discussion. Thus the voters were led to believe that they were participating in the government, whereas in reality their voice was but faintly heard. Local government was again brought under the strict control of the central government by means of a system of powerful agents of the national government called prefects.

The First Consul's initial project was to restore law and order at home and peace abroad. The Directory had never been able to suppress brigandage. Life and property were not safe. Napoleon sent out military detachments that quickly put an end to lawlessness and restored the authority of the government, much to the satisfaction of the law-abiding citizens. He lost no time in making a treaty (1800) with the United States, bringing to an end a two-year undeclared naval war that had grown out of French seizures of American vessels and the pro-British and anti-French policies of John Adams's administration. Slipping over the Alps with a French army, the First Consul crushed the Austrian army in northern Italy in the battle of Marengo, knocking Austria out of the Second Coalition. Tsar Paul of Russia was cajoled with flattery and promises into making peace. Even Great Britain was persuaded to sign the Peace of Amiens in 1802, which, however, was to last little more than a year.

The young dictator next proceeded to create by enlightened despotism the permanent institutions that the revolutionary leaders had been unable to establish by the processes of popular government. Of all Napoleon's reforms the one of which he was the most proud was his Civil Code. The National Convention had set up a commission of lawyers to reduce to order the 237 different legal codes in use in France, but this commission had been unable to bring its work to fruition. Shortly after seizing power Napoleon appointed his own commission of legal experts to draw up a uniform code. When his experts proved unequal to the task, Napoleon threw himself into the project. The result was the Code Napoleon, which has been adopted by most of the nations that have since come into existence throughout the world. Later codes set in order criminal and commercial law. These achievements won for Napoleon the title "The Second Justinian."

The First Consul proved himself to be an astute financier. The numerous government notes, bonds, and obligations, all depreciated, were called in and uniformly refunded. Efficient agents of the central government fairly assessed and collected the taxes. Strict economy in expenditures made it possible to balance the French budget for the first time since the early days of Colbert. Napoleon capped France's financial structure with the Bank of France, a semi-national bank privately owned but regulated by the state. The bank handled government funds and was given certain monopolistic privileges such as the issuing of paper money. The bank established branches all over France and grew so strong that it later became a powerful influence on the government itself. During the great world depression of the 1930's it was able to remain on the gold standard longer than either the United States Treasury or the Bank of England. French business, however, never quite trusted Napoleon; it always felt uneasy as to what the dictator's next arbitrary move might be.

Napoleon was keenly aware of the importance of religion. "Always treat the pope," he counseled his diplomats, "as if he had 200,000 men." He himself was a Voltairian deist and a cynical moral relativist, believing that God was "always on the side with the most cannon." One of his first steps was to make peace with the pope and end the ten-year struggle between the French revolutionary governments and the Roman Catholic Church. After arduous negotiations the First Consul and the pope signed the Concordat of 1801, which was to govern the relations between the French state and the Roman Catholic Church until the beginning of the twentieth century. The Roman Catholic religion was declared to be the religion of the majority of French people. The state was to appoint the bishops, but only the pope could invest them in their offices. The bishops were to appoint and discipline the lower clergy, thus restoring the traditional episcopal principle of the Roman Church. The salaries of the clergy were to be paid by the state, and the clergy were to take an oath of allegiance to the state. The pope, in turn, accepted the permanent loss of church property seized by the National Assembly. Once the pope's signature was on the document, Napoleon, in his characteristic manner, violated its spirit by adding obnoxious "organic articles" that further subordinated the church to the state. According to these articles, the state was to pay the salaries of Protestant as well as Roman Catholic clergy, and all clergy were placed under the "police powers" of the state. Nevertheless, the Concordat was a remarkable achievement in a most difficult field.

Napoleon was also interested in pedagogy. All French schools were brought under the control of a national board of education called the University of France. His most significant and original contribution to education was the lycée, an institution that combined what in the United States would be the last two years of high school with the first two years of college. In addition, professional and technical schools were established. Napoleon had a low opinion of female education and of feminine mentality in general. Actually, he was chiefly interested in educational institutions as agencies of propaganda for the molding of loyal and efficient soldiers and citizens. However, the educational institutions created by Napoleon have served France well.

Napoleon's one outstanding failure during the period of the Consulate was his effort to restore France's lost empire in North America. He successfully pressured the weak Spanish government into returning the vast Louisiana territory to France. His plans to secure the approaches to Louisiana, however, miscarried when yellow fever and native resistance wrought havoc with a costly French expedition to San Domingo. Realizing that war with Great Britain was about to be renewed and that he could not hold Louisiana, he offered to sell it to the United States. President Jefferson eagerly accepted the offer, paying some $16,000,000 for what is now a third of the United States.

With the exception of the overseas imperial venture the first five years of Napoleon's dictatorship were spectacularly successful. The dictatorship itself was mild. Law and order at home and peace abroad had been attained. Financial stability, equal and efficient justice, religious tranquillity, and the foundations of an effective educational system had all been achieved. Public morale

was high. In 1804, as in 1791, the worshippers of Voltaire's materialistic rationalism must have felt vindicated. The benevolent genius on horseback seemed to have ushered in the utopia of human reason that the National Assembly appeared to have achieved a little more than a decade earlier. However, 1804 like 1791 was only a prelude to an era of war, violence, disillusionment, and reaction. Napoleon was not satisfied with his accomplishments. He yearned for more glory. In 1804 he crowned himself emperor of the French and sought further fields to conquer.

3. The Empire—War and Conquest

Great Britain, France's most inveterate foe, had become increasingly alarmed at Napoleon's growing strength. The French dictator had not only continued to build up his military forces but had taken advantage of the Peace of Amiens to further his commercial and imperial schemes at Great Britain's expense. Before the end of 1803 the British government declared war and the next year joined with Austria and Russia to form a third coalition against France. This was what Napoleon expected and wanted. He soon appeared at the English Channel opposite Great Britain at the head of a force sufficient to conquer the British Isles, if only the twenty-four-mile water barrier could be crossed. In the channel, however, lay the world's mightiest fleet, commanded by the greatest of all Britain's admirals, Lord Nelson. Napoleon was unable to lure Nelson away from the channel or to figure out any way to get past him. Meanwhile, he was watching the movements of the Austrians and Russians and readying his own army. When the time was ripe, he suddenly marched his army eastward, surrounded an exposed Austrian army at Ulm in southwest Germany, and forced it to surrender. But the day after Ulm, Lord Nelson sighted the combined French and Spanish fleets off Cape Trafalgar on the southwest point of Portugal and annihilated them (October 21, 1805). Although Nelson was killed early in the battle, his victory saved Great

Britain from the menace of a Napoleonic invasion and limited the scope of the French emperor's conquests to the continent of Europe. Trafalgar was one of the most decisive battles of all time.

On land, however, Napoleon seemed invincible. Moving his army eastward from Ulm, he met and crushed the oncoming combined forces of Austria and Russia at Austerlitz. Austria immediately sued for peace, and the demoralized Russians retreated toward their home country. At this juncture Prussia declared war on Napoleon. However, the time was inopportune, and the Prussian army, which, under Frederick the Great, had held most of Europe at bay, was no match for Napoleon. At Jena and Auerstedt Napoleon overwhelmed and virtually destroyed the Prussian force (1806). Two weeks later the French emperor was in Berlin. Hearing that the Russian troops were re-forming in Poland, Napoleon moved eastward to meet them. After being held to a draw by the Russians in a blinding snowstorm at Eylau, he defeated them decisively in the great battle of Friedland (1807). Tsar Alexander I now sued for peace. Although the Treaty of Tilsit (July 1807) was technically between equals, it actually left Napoleon master of the European continent with Alexander I a junior partner. Russia was given a free hand to deal with Turkey in Eastern Europe but was not permitted to take Constantinople, the prize that the Russians most desired. In return for a free hand in Eastern Europe Alexander promised to join Napoleon against Great Britain, and also to force Sweden to do so. Tilsit recognized the changes that Napoleon had already made in Central and Western Europe and left him free to make any others he wished.

Between 1806 and 1808 Napoleon remade the map of Europe. The puppet duchy of Warsaw was created out of part of Prussia's (and later, part of Austria's) Polish territory. Prussia's territory west of the Elbe was made a part of the kingdom of Westphalia, over which Napoleon's youngest brother, Jerome, was made king. Prussia

was thus virtually halved in size. The Holy Roman Empire was at long last abolished and its hundreds of little principalities greatly consolidated. A strip of German territory along the North Sea was annexed outright to France. The rest of German territory west of the Elbe was brought into the Confederation of the Rhine, with Napoleon as protector. Napoleon's younger brother, Louis, was made king of Holland, but when Louis began to favor the interests of his Dutch subjects over those of the French Empire, Napoleon deposed him and annexed his territory to France. The whole Italian Peninsula was brought under French dominance. Northwestern Italy down to and including Rome was annexed outright. Marshal Murat and Napoleon's sister Caroline were made king and queen of Naples. The northeastern third of the peninsula was made into the kingdom of Italy, with Napoleon as king and his stepson, Eugene, as viceroy. The coastal areas along the northeastern Adriatic Sea were detached from Austria and annexed to France. In 1808 Napoleon overthrew the weak Spanish royal house and made his elder brother, Joseph, king of Spain. Shortly before, the Portuguese royal family had fled to Brazil at the approach of a conquering French army.

Thus, by 1808, all Europe except the British Isles was under French control or French influence. No other conqueror has so dominated Europe. In all those territories under direct French control Napoleon's "enlightened" institutions and administrative efficiency were introduced. The rest of Europe, impressed with the effectiveness of the French revolutionary ideas and institutions, adopted many of them voluntarily. And yet this mighty Napoleonic empire was to last less than five years. By 1812 its downfall was at hand.

4. Decline and Fall of the Empire

A number of factors contributed to the decline and fall of the Napoleonic empire. One of the most obvious was British sea power. Because of it Great Britain alone of the European powers was able to withstand

200 MILES

St. Petersburg

RUSSIAN

Riga

COURLAND

Tilsit Kovno Vitebsk Borodino Moscow

Königsberg

Vilna Smolensk

Warsaw Brest-Litovsk

EMPIRE

NAPOLEON'S
RUSSIAN CAMPAIGN
JUNE TO DECEMBER
1812

SCOTLAND

NORTH SEA

Edinburgh

GREAT
BRITAIN

K. OF
HOLLAND

ENGLAND

Amsterdam

London

Plymouth

Dover

ENGLISH CHANNEL

Boulogne

Brussels

CHANNEL IS.
(BR)

Cherbourg

Amiens

Paris

Versailles

Valmy

Fontainebleau

EUROPE
1810

FRENCH
EMPIRE

GRAND
EMPIRE

ALLIED WITH
NAPOLEON

Nantes

Orléans

FRENCH

O C E A N

Rochefort

EMPIRE

Lyons

Bordeaux

Avignon

Coruña

Toulouse

CAPE
FINISTERRE

Marseilles

GALICIA

Burgos

Saragossa

Oporto

Barcelona

Almeida

Ciudad
Rodrigo

PORTUGAL

Talavera

Madrid

Lisbon

Ocaña

SPAIN

Elvas

BALEARIC IS.

MINORCA

Albuera

Valencia

IVIZA

MAJORCA

Baylen

Seville

ANDALUSIA

Cadiz

M E D

TRAFALGAR

GIBRALTAR
(BR)

Algiers

Tangier

ALGERIA
(TURK.)

MOROCCO

TRM

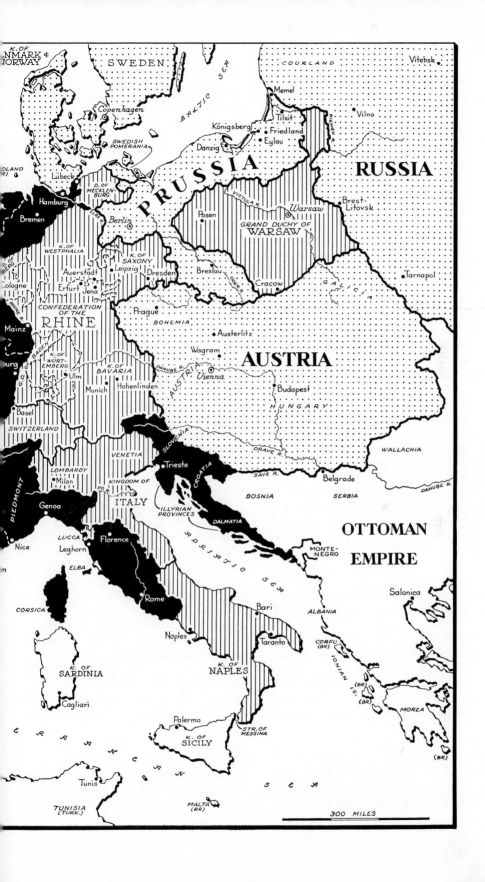

the Napoleonic military onslaught. After Trafalgar dashed Napoleon's hopes of invading the British Isles, he sought the destruction of "perfidious Albion" by economic pressure. In order to wreck the economy of the "nation of shopkeepers" he attempted to blockade the entire continent of Europe against British shipping. All British goods were confiscated. French privateers were set upon British merchant ships. These measures, known as "the Continental System," did cause Great Britain grave distress. However, with her control of the sea she was able to apply a more effective counterblockade against the Napoleon-dominated continent. She was able even to hold her own in the War of 1812 with the United States, which attempted to resist the British maritime restrictions. Since Europe was almost entirely dependent upon Great Britain for manufactured goods and tropical products, the Continental System created ever-increasing resentment against Napoleon's rule.

Another factor that undermined the Napoleonic empire was the rise of national spirit among the subjected peoples. The mass spirit of intense patriotism or nationalism, which had its origin in France during the *levée en masse* of 1793, spread to the rest of Europe in the wake of Napoleon's conquering armies. The first people to rebel openly against the French yoke were the proud Spaniards. Hardly had Napoleon's brother Joseph been planted upon the Spanish throne when his unwilling subjects rose up and chased him out of Madrid. The superior French armies, even when led by the emperor himself, were ineffective against the hit-and-run guerrilla tactics invented by the Spaniards. The British government, observing Napoleon's predicament in Spain, sent an army under Arthur Wellesley, the future duke of Wellington, to exploit the situation. Spain became a running abscess that drained away much of Napoleon's military strength. Meanwhile, Prussia, after the humiliation of Jena, had begun a rejuvenation under the leadership of Baron vom Stein. Partly in secret and partly in the open the Prussians modernized their institutions

and prepared for the day of liberation. In 1809 Austria declared war on Napoleon in a premature effort to free herself from subservience to the French Emperor. Although Austria was once more defeated, the heroic valor with which her armies fought served notice of the rising spirit of national pride and resistance. Napoleon could no longer enjoy the advantage of fighting with soldiers fired with the heady wine of nationalism against lethargic professional armies.

A third factor in the decline of the French colossus was Napoleon himself. He began to slow down—to lose his magic touch. Symptoms of the stomach cancer from which he is believed eventually to have died began to appear. As his enemies one after another adopted his winning tactics, he failed to come up with better ones.

The beginning of the end was a disastrous campaign against Russia in 1812. When Alexander I wearied of the hardships of the Continental System and opened his ports to the British, Napoleon, against the advice of his closest associates, decided to conquer Russia. Amassing an army of 600,000, the mightiest army ever assembled up to that time, he plunged into the vastness of Russia. Many of his troops, however, were unwilling conscripts from the puppet states. The Russian army retreated into the interior of the huge country, following a scorched-earth policy and drawing Napoleon ever farther from his base of supplies. Finally, after a bloody battle outside the gates of Moscow, Napoleon's hosts entered the city. However, Alexander I refused to make peace. A fire destroyed Moscow, leaving the invaders without shelter in the face of approaching winter. Napoleon began his retreat too late. The Russian winter caught his forces burdened down with loot. Tens of thousands froze or starved. Russian Cossacks, riding out of the blizzards, cut down or captured other thousands. Of the 600,000 men who marched into Russia, only some 20,000 escaped.

Napoleon dashed back to France to raise fresh conscripts, but the flower of French manhood was gone. One nation after an-

ON THE ROAD FROM WATERLOO TO PARIS, FROM A PAINTING BY STONE. On the road to Paris and exile after his final defeat at Waterloo, Napoleon stopped to rest at this humble peasant's cottage. The peasant's empty sleeve marks him as one of the tens of thousands of French veterans of the Napoleonic wars. It is impossible to know whether the great dreamer Napoleon saw in the flames past glories or vanquished hopes; perhaps both. (*Guildhall Art Gallery, London*)

other rose up to join the Russians in a war of liberation. At Leipzig in central Germany, in October 1813, Napoleon was at last decisively defeated. The next year the allies entered Paris and exiled Napoleon to the island of Elba, off the coast of Italy. When the allies began to squabble over the peace settlement, Napoleon escaped back to France and raised another army, but he was finally defeated by the duke of Wellington at Waterloo in Belgium, June 1815. This time he was imprisoned on the island of St. Helena in the South Atlantic, where he died six years later.

5. Napoleon's Impact on Latin America —Revolution and Independence

One vast area outside Europe upon which the impact of Napoleon was strong and im-

mediate was Latin America. During the eighteenth century discontent with colonial rule had been steadily mounting in the Spanish and Portuguese colonial empires in North and South America. As in the case of the thirteen English colonies in North America the resentment was directed primarily against the economic and political restrictions of the mother countries. As the native-born "Creoles" had come to outnumber the Spanish- and Portuguese-born settlers, the ties of loyalty to the mother countries had become more and more tenuous. The liberal writings of the French and British philosophers of the Enlightenment were smuggled into Latin America and made their converts, particularly among young intellectuals. These liberal Latin American intellectuals could not help being impressed by the successful revolt of the English colonies to the north and the setting up of a liberal New World republic. The French Revolution had an even more profound influence on them. When, therefore, Napoleon overthrew Ferdinand VII of Spain and placed his own brother, Joseph Bonaparte, on the Spanish throne, the sentiments of loyalty on the part of the colonies for the mother country, which were already weak, quickly became quite confused.

By 1810 the colonies were in open revolt. As with the English colonists three decades earlier the cause of the Latin American revolutionists seemed hopeless. In addition to the regular Spanish troops, they had to struggle against most of the wealthy Spanish settlers and the local Roman Catholic hierarchy. Eventually, however, two brilliant young leaders, Simón Bolívar and José San Martín, emerged to overcome the seemingly impossible obstacles and to lead the South American revolutionists to success. By 1822 the independence of Spanish South America was won. In the same year the issue was decided in Spain's Central American colonies and in Mexico, which then included the southwest quarter of what is now the United States. In all the former Spanish colonies, republics were established, although a long period of troubled apprenticeship preceded the establishment of reasonably stable popular governments. As a matter of fact, real stability appears still to be quite some time in the future.

In the huge Portuguese colony of Brazil the independence movement was delayed by the flight of the Portuguese royal family to Brazil in 1807. However, the return of the king to Portugal six years after Napoleon's fall and the efforts of the Portuguese government to reimpose the colonial status on Brazil quickly fanned the embers of revolt into flame. In 1822 the Portuguese king's son, Pedro, whom he had left behind as regent, yielded to native pressure and declared himself king of independent Brazil. In all of independent Latin America the Code Napoleon was adopted as the basis of civil law, and the impact of the Enlightenment on the political institutions was clearly visible.

6. Significance of the French Revolution and Napoleon

The French Revolution and its Napoleonic sequel had a profound effect upon the course of history. Like Pandora when she lifted the lid of her fateful box they let loose forces and ideas that have influenced and ofttimes shaken the world ever since, especially the revolutionary ideals of *Liberty, Equality, Fraternity.* Originally conceived in the eighteenth century by the philosophers of the Enlightenment, they were born materially in the American and French revolutions, and developed and spread by Napoleon.

Liberty, of course, has been one of the chief quests of the human race from its beginning to the present and has never at any time been perfectly attained. In the era of the French Revolution the ideal of liberty meant freedom from arbitrary authority—political, religious, economic, or social. It meant freedom of speech, press, conscience, assembly, person, and profession, and the sacredness of property. During the moderate first phase of the French Revolution a great deal of progress toward these goals was made. In the tumultuous and bloody second phase a good deal was lost. Under Napoleon's dictatorship there was no political liberty. However, he claimed that the efficiency, prosperity, and honor of his regime more than made up for the lack of popular government, for which, he believed, the world was not yet ready.

Equality meant essentially equality under the law and equality of opportunity for gain and advancement. It was only during the brief dictatorship of Robespierre that the absolute equality of all citizens became a cult. Its impracticability was soon evident. Napoleon's law codes were a great boon to the more moderate and practical kind of equality.

Fraternity manifested itself in the mass movements (sometimes violent) for reform, in the comradeship in the conscripted armies, and above all in the new popular and dynamic spirit of nationalism. These forces, released by the American and French revolutions, spread first to the rest of Europe, then to Latin America, and eventually to the rest of the world. They have played a dominant role in the nineteenth- and twentieth-century world.

———————●●———————

SUGGESTED READING

F. M. Kircheisen, *Napoleon* (1932). Probably the best single-volume biography of Napoleon. This is an English translation and abridgment of the nine-volume German biography by the greatest scholar of the Napoleonic era.

Albert Guérard, *Napoleon I* (1956). A brief and readable account by an able interpreter of French history.

R. M. Johnston, *The Corsican* (1910). This is a life of Napoleon skillfully put together from Napoleon's own words, drawn from many sources.

Geoffrey Bruun, *Europe and the French Imperium* (1938). A scholarly history of Europe during the Napoleonic era, 1799–1815. Probably the best single volume on the subject.

A. T. Mahan, *The Influence of Sea Power on the French Revolution and the Empire,* 2 vols. (1919). One of the most influential history books ever written. Excellent history and very readable. Mahan, an admiral in the United States Navy, maintains that in major wars sea power is decisive.

* Leo Tolstoy, *War and Peace* (Bantam). A lengthy novel about Napoleon's invasion of Russia, based upon excellent historical research.

Philip Guedalla, *The Duke* (1931). A popularly written biography of the duke of Wellington, conqueror of Napoleon.

Hildegarde Angell, *Simón Bolívar, South American Emancipator* (1930). A sound and readable biography of the chief hero of South American independence.

CHAPTER 42

---◆◆◆---

Aftermath: Restoration and Reaction

THE OVERTHROW of Napoleon in 1815 brought to an end, in Europe at least, the heroic and tumultuous epoch that had begun in 1789 with the meeting of the Estates-General. The intervening twenty-six years had been filled with great expectation, experimentation, turmoil, and war. Now mass disillusionment and weariness prevailed. The European royalty and aristocracy, at long last triumphant over revolutionary France, were determined to put an end not only to the Mirabeaus, Robespierres, and Napoleons, but also to the ideas of Voltaire and Rousseau. To achieve this goal, to redraw the mutilated map of Europe, and to set the clock back as far as was practically possible, the leaders of the victorious powers gathered at the Austrian capital of Vienna in the autumn of 1814. Thither also flocked representatives of every state in Europe, hundreds of dispossessed princes, agents of every conceivable interest, and adventurers.

1. The Congress of Vienna (1814–15)

The Congress of Vienna, which never actually met in formal session, was dominated by the big four victors over Napoleon. Great Britain was represented by her able foreign minister, Lord Castlereagh. Prussia's mediocre king, Frederick William III, headed his own delegation, as did Russia's tsar, the young dreamer, Alexander I. Austria's emperor, Francis I, played host to the assembled great. However, the real brains of the

Austrian delegation, and, indeed, the dominating spirit in the whole congress, was the Austrian chancellor, Prince Clemens von Metternich. As a guiding principle upon which to base their decisions the conferees decided upon "legitimacy." This meant that in redistributing various territories attention would be paid, not to the desires or interests of the people concerned, but to the legal claims of the former and future sovereigns. Many of the decisions formalized at Vienna had already been made by the big-four powers shortly before and after Napoleon's overthrow in April 1814.

Thanks in no small measure to the presence of the wily diplomat Talleyrand, France, the cause of all the turmoil, got off very lightly. Prussia would have severely punished and weakened France, but her three major colleagues were fearful of upsetting the balance of power. Already saddled with the restored Bourbons, France was merely reduced to the boundaries she had possessed before her annexations during the wars of the Revolution and Napoleon. The Congress of Vienna had imposed no indemnity upon France. However, because of Napoleon's return from Elba in the midst of the congress and his hundred-day fling that ended at Waterloo, the four great powers compelled France to cede the Saar Basin to Prussia, to pay an indemnity of $140,-000,000, and to return the art treasures stolen by Napoleon from the various galleries of Europe. To contain France within her frontiers and to ward off French aggression,

Prussia was given a sizable block of territory along the Rhine, Austrian Netherlands (Belgium) was annexed to the Dutch Netherlands, and Piedmont was enlarged by the annexation of the city-state of Genoa.

To safeguard her empire, Great Britain sought a balance of power on the continent and the acquisition of certain strategic territories. Becasue of her complete mastery over the seas she could have helped herself to any of the colonial possessions of France or the Napoleonic puppet states she desired. However, she limited herself to Helgoland in the North Sea, Malta, and the Ionian Islands in the Mediterranean, several small French and Spanish territories in the West Indies and the Indian Ocean, and the Dutch colonies of Ceylon off the tip of India, the Cape of Good Hope, and part of Dutch Guiana in South America.

Prussia, in addition to her valuable gains in the Rhineland, annexed Westphalia and Swedish Pomerania. In return for a portion of her Polish territory, including the city of Warsaw, which she ceded to Russia, she annexed two fifths of Saxony. These changes considerably strengthened and consolidated Prussia's territories and made her more homogeneously German and Western. However, her Rhineland territory was not contiguous to her main body—a situation that invited further aggression.

Russia received Finland from Sweden. Sweden got Norway from Denmark in return. Russia's acquisition of most of Prussia's Polish territory made the great majority of the Polish-speaking people subjects of Russia and brought Russia farther into the heart of Central Europe.

Austria, in exchange for the Belgian Netherlands, took the two rich Italian provinces of Lombardy and Venetia. Austrian princes were placed on the thrones of three other Italian states: Modena, Parma, and Tuscany. This pre-eminence in Italy, together with the presidency over the German Confederation, made Austria the dominant power in Central Europe. Her mastery over Italy and Germany was made possible by their political division and weakness. The Italian Peninsula was left divided into eight separate states with no political ties with each other. In the words of Metternich, Italy was "only a geographical expression."

The Holy Roman Empire, which Napoleon had destroyed, was not restored, but in its place was erected the equally weak and ineffective German Confederation. Napoleon's consolidation of the more than three hundred German states down to thirty-nine was allowed to stand, bringing the German people that much more political unity. However, Metternich saw to it that the government of the German Confederation was powerless and under the permanent presidency of Austria. Nevertheless, as future developments were to demonstrate, the overall settlement consolidated and strengthened the position of Prussia in relation to that of Austria.

Thus were the peoples and territories of Europe moved about by the great powers at Vienna like pawns on a chessboard, in complete disregard for the wishes of the people or for the spirit of nationalism that was now an increasingly virile force.

2. The Concert of Europe—First Rifts in the Metternich System

Metternich, having surveyed his work and seen "that it was good," set about to create machinery for perpetuating it. Conveniently at hand was the Holy Allicance, conceived by Alexander I to establish and safeguard the principles of the Christian religion. Russia (Orthodox), Austria (Roman Catholic), and Prussia (Protestant), representing the three major branches of Christendom, were to form the nucleus of the alliance. All the Christian states of Europe were invited to join. Only Great Britain and the Papal States did not. Metternich considered the Holy Alliance a "sonorous nothing," but saw in it an opportunity for influencing the tsar. Intended by Alexander I as a bulwark of Christianity, the Holy Alliance became under Metternich's influence a symbol of reaction and repression.

Much more potent as an agency for perpetuating the Vienna settlements was the

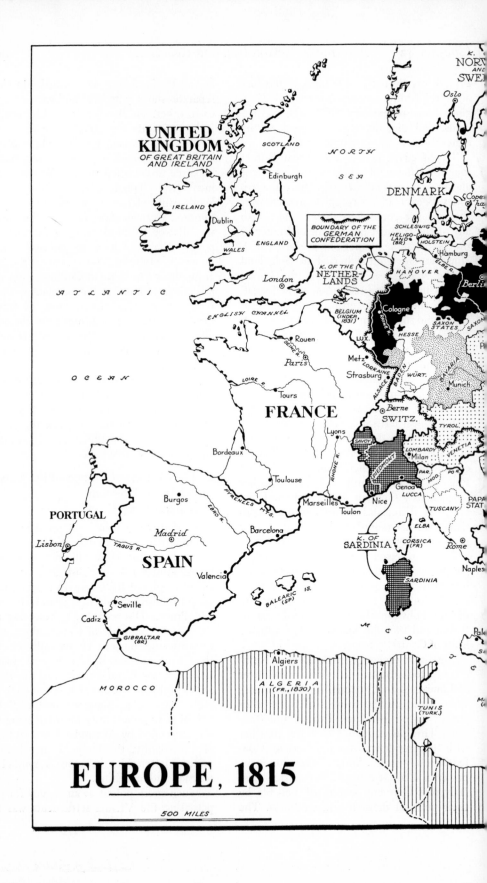

EUROPE, 1815

500 MILES

Quadruple Alliance. This was a military alliance of Austria, Russia, Prussia, and Great Britain created in November 1815, for the purpose of guaranteeing for twenty years the territorial boundaries established by the Vienna settlement. Metternich was determined to make of the alliance an international military police force that would spy out and suppress liberal or national movements wherever found. It was arranged that the four member powers should hold periodic congresses to carry out the purposes of the alliance.

The first congress was held at Aix-la-Chapelle in northwest Germany in 1818. The purpose was to arrange the withdrawal of occupation forces from French soil, France having completed the payment of her indemnity. Since France had demonstrated her good behavior under the restored Bourbon king, Louis XVIII, she was not only freed of occupying forces but was admitted to the Quadruple Alliance, which thereupon became the Quintuple Alliance. Congresses at Troppau in 1820 and at Laibach in 1821, both on Austrian soil, concerned themselves with an insurrection that had broken out in Naples against the tyrannical Bourbon king, Ferdinand I. An Austrian army was authorized to put down the insurrection and reestablish the hated Ferdinand I upon his throne. The Neapolitan liberal volunteers, no match for the Austrian regulars, were soon defeated, and their leaders executed, imprisoned, or exiled. What turned out to be the last of the congresses met in 1822 at Verona, in Austria's Italian province of Venetia, to deal with a liberal revolt in Spain against Ferdinand VII. This reactionary Bourbon tyrant, who had spent his seven years of captivity in France doing fancywork, had been restored to his throne upon the defeat of Napoleon. With the sanction of the Congress of Verona a French army crossed the Pyrenees and easily put down the rebellion.

The bloody vengeance that Ferdinand took upon the liberal rebels revolted the French soldiers who had restored him. Great Britain, however, was the first of the alliance powers to repudiate the Metternich system. At the Troppau congress, she clearly indicated her opposition to interfering in the internal affairs of other states. When the Verona congress decided, over her protest, upon intervention in Spain, Britain's representative withdrew from the congress, thereby starting the breakup of the concert of Europe.

The Metternich system soon received further blows, some from unexpected quarters. At the Congress of Verona, the like-minded Austrians, Russians, and Prussians had been alarmed, not only by the rebellion in the Spanish homeland, but also by the revolt of Spain's New World colonies. The brilliant success of the thirteen English colonies was a bad enough example for the European liberals. It must not be repeated in Latin America. When the corrupt government of Ferdinand VII proved incapable of putting down the revolt, Alexander I, with Metternich's blessing, proposed to send a Russian fleet to help coerce the colonies. Great Britain, however, enjoyed a lucrative trade with the rebellious colonies and did not wish to see them restored to Spanish dominion and commercial monopoly. Her foreign minister, Canning, who had succeeded Castlereagh in 1822, proposed to the government of the United States that Great Britain and the United States issue a joint statement against interference by the "Holy Alliance" in the affairs of the Western Hemisphere. To President Monroe and to his confidants, ex-Presidents Madison and Jefferson, this seemed a good idea. However, Secretary of State John Quincy Adams foresaw that the time might come when the United States would wish to invoke such a policy alone, perhaps even against Great Britain. The British would support the policy of the United States anyway because of their own self-interest. Adams convinced Monroe that the United States should proclaim the policy alone. When, therefore, the president in his message to Congress, in December 1823, announced what has come to be called the Monroe Doctrine, it was the Adams rather than the Canning version.

Monroe stated simply that the United States would regard any interference on the part of European powers in the affairs of the Western Hemisphere as an "unfriendly act." The United States was at the time, of course, a new and relatively weak nation, but Canning's immediate support of the American policy killed any further thought of "Holy Alliance" intervention in the New World, for Great Britain was the unchallenged mistress of the seas. The Monroe Doctrine was, however, more than a blow to Metternichism in Europe. It guaranteed the independence of Latin America and marked the beginning of active participation by the United States in affairs beyond her own immediate shores.

The next successful blow at repressive tyranny was struck by the Greeks against their Moslem Turkish overlords. The Greek revolt of 1821–29 is an excellent example of the influence of the past in world affairs. The Greeks had been treated no worse by their Turkish masters than the rest of the Christian European subjects of the Sultan —the Serbs, the Bulgarians, or the Romanians. However, the Greeks had the memory of a glorious past, which the others did not have, to spur them on to heroism. But the valiant efforts of the Greeks were not sufficient to resist the power of the whole Ottoman Empire. By 1827 they were on the point of being hopelessly crushed.

Meanwhile, the sympathies of the great powers were being aroused for the courageous Christian Greeks, who were being cruelly massacred by the Moslem Turks. Russia, Great Britain, and France in particular displayed a growing concern over the events in Greece. Russia's Orthodox Christian religion was the same as that of the Greeks. Furthermore, the Russians had long desired Constantinople, which controlled the strategic and commercial outlet to the Mediterranean. Great Britain was concerned over the possibility of Russia's dominance in the Near East. In addition, the ruling classes in Great Britain and France were steeped in the classical culture of ancient Greece. Lord Byron, the most popular literary figure in

Europe, lost his life fighting as a volunteer for Greece.

In 1827 these three powers, over Metternich's protest, intervened in the Greek revolt and defeated the Turks on land and sea. The Treaty of Adrianople in 1829 granted independence to most of the Greeks on the home peninsula and local autonomy to the Serbs and Romanians. The successful revolt of the Greeks was a victory for the resurging revolutionary principles of liberalism and nationalism that the reactionaries led by Metternich were struggling to suppress. The intervention of Russia, Great Britain, and France demolished the already-battered concert of Europe. The Treaty of Adrianople also hastened the crack-up of the once-potent Ottoman Empire.

The year 1830 was a bad one for Metternich. Successful revolutions in France and Belgium undid two of the settlements at Vienna. News of the revolution in France (which will be described in the next section) set off the revolt in Brussels. The union forced upon Belgium and the Netherlands at Vienna had never been a happy one, and Belgian discontent with Dutch rule had been mounting for fifteen years. In addition to differences in language the Belgians were Roman Catholic, whereas the Dutch were Calvinist. The Belgian economy was based on industry, the Dutch on commerce. Belgium, more populous than the Netherlands, was not given her fair share of representation in the government. When the halfhearted efforts of the Dutch failed to suppress the revolt, Austria and Russia threatened to intervene in the interests of legitimacy and tranquillity. However, they were deterred by British and French support of Belgian independence. By 1830, then, Metternich's international system of reaction and repression was definitely breached. In that year even France, the reactionaries' greatest concern, threw off the Bourbon yoke that the Congress of Vienna had imposed upon her.

3. The Bourbon Restoration in France

When the victorious armies of the coalition powers entered France and deposed

Napoleon in the spring of 1814, they brought "in their baggage" the members of the royal Bourbon family who had fled the Revolution. In their wake trooped the *émigré* nobility. A younger brother of the guillotined Louis XVI was placed on the throne as Louis XVIII. (The son of Louis XVI, who had died in prison in 1795, without having ruled, was considered to be Louis XVII.) The "restored" Bourbon king was now fifty-nine years of age and too fat and gouty to walk unassisted. He had traveled much and unwillingly during the long, lean years of his exile. When Napoleon returned from Elba in 1815, Louis XVIII had to flee once more. After Waterloo he returned to his throne, which he considered "the most comfortable of armchairs," determined to do nothing that might force him to leave it again.

Upon assuming the throne Louis XVIII issued a charter, or constitution, that retained Napoleon's administrative and legal system, and civil and religious liberty. Lawmaking was placed in the hands of a two-chambered legislature. The upper house was made hereditary, and the lower elected by a highly restricted electorate. Only those who paid direct annual taxes of 300 francs ($60) could vote; this limited the suffrage to about 100,000 out of a total population of nearly 30,000,000. The lower house could be prorogued or dissolved by the king. Since the king also appointed and controlled his own ministers and the host of civilian and military officials, carried on foreign relations, controlled the military forces, and enforced the laws, his power was only slightly limited by the charter.

Louis XVIII set out to use his powers with moderation in order that tranquillity might be restored. There were no wholesale punishments of revolutionary leaders. The peasant and bourgeois purchasers of church and noble lands were not dispossessed. However, most of the returned émigrés were of a different spirit. They came back from their unhappy exile angry and vengeful, demanding their old privileges and indemnification for their lands. Their leader was the king's

younger brother, the Comte d'Artois—a typical Bourbon who had "never learned anything and never forgotten anything." The reactionaries controlled both houses of the national legislature, since even in the lower elected house suffrage restrictions limited the voters to the aristocracy and the *nouveaux riches*. Louis XVIII found it increasingly difficult to hold these fire-eating reactionaries in check. Shortly before he died in 1824, he warned his incorrigible brother of the danger to the Bourbon dynasty if he did not adopt a more moderate attitude.

However, Charles X, as the Comte d'Artois now styled himself, was beyond moderation. He quickly aroused the animosity against his regime to an explosive pitch. The Napoleonic generals who had brought so much glory to France were immediately retired from duty. An indemnity was voted the émigrés for their confiscated lands, the money to be raised by reducing the interest on government bonds from 5 per cent to 3 per cent. This angered the upper bourgeoisie, who were bondholders. The peasants were alarmed by a proposed establishment of primogeniture, which seemed to endanger the principle of equality and the security of land titles. The Jesuits were brought back to France, and favors were bestowed upon the Roman Catholic Church. Opposition mounted rapidly. By 1827 Charles X had lost his majority in both houses of the national legislature. Totally blind to the political realities of the day, he twice dissolved the lower chamber and attempted to force the election of a friendly majority by censoring the press and using official pressure on the electorate. The hostile majorities only increased in number.

Finally in July 1830 the fatuous Bourbon decided to end the parliamentary regime and rule as a dictator. In a set of ordinances he dissolved the newly elected chamber, called for new elections, restricted the suffrage so drastically that only about 25,000 very rich citizens could vote, and abolished completely the freedom of the press. These tyrannical measures set off an uprising in Paris. The Paris proletariat erected barri-

cades in the streets that the disaffected rank
and file of the army were "unable" to break.
After three days of desultory fighting the in-
surgents had the upper hand, and the last
Bourbon king of France was on his way to
exile in England. A group of moderate opposition members of the lower chamber now
set themselves up as a provisional government and named a new king: Louis Philippe, head of the house of Orléans and a
cousin of the departed Bourbon. Louis Philippe, a well-known moderate liberal and
friend of the middle class, was accepted by
the great majority of the people of France.
The French people in July 1830, therefore,
showed Metternich and the rest of the
world that the spirit of the French Revolution was not dead, but for fifteen years had
been only dormant.

4. Restoration and Repression in the Germanies

In Central and Eastern Europe, particularly in the Germanies, Italy, and Russia,
the Metternich system was more secure.
The Germanies in 1815 consisted of thirty-
seven little states and two large ones—
Prussia and Austria. In all of them the influence of Metternich reigned supreme. At
the Congress of Vienna the Austrian prime
minister had seen to it that the Germanies
were reconstructed in such a way that German nationalism and liberalism would be
thwarted. The German Confederation was
an improvement over the old Holy Roman
Empire, which Napoleon had destroyed,
only in that Napoleon's consolidation of the
more than three hundred states down to
thirty-nine was allowed to stand. The
boundaries remained the same. The Diet
was only a gathering and debating place for
the representatives of the thirty-nine states.
The Confederation had no treasury and no
army at its command. There was not even a
flag to symbolize its German national character. Reactionary Austria enjoyed a permanent presidency over it.

The German nationalism and liberalism
that existed in 1815 centered primarily in
the little states, some of whose rulers defied
Metternich by granting liberal constitutions.
The national and liberal activities here were
largely the work of university students and
professors, who shortly after 1815 began to
form *Burschenschaften,* or brotherhoods, for
the purpose of promoting German nationalism, liberalism, and the Christian religion.
In 1817 in commemoration of the three
hundredth anniversary of Luther's publication of his momentous ninety-five theses, the
Burschenschaften staged a giant festival at
Wartburg, where Luther had hidden out
and begun his Bible translation. Although
the festivities were primarily religious in
character, enough enthusiasm for German
nationalism and liberalism was displayed to
fill Metternich with anxiety. The murder
two years later of a reactionary propagandist
by a fanatical student gave Metternich his
opportunity to strike. Calling together the
princes of the leading German states at
Carlsbad, he joined them in drawing up a
set of harsh decrees designed to crush the
embryonic national and liberal movements.
The *Burschenschaften* were outlawed. Strict
censorship was established. Classrooms and
libraries were supervised. Liberal students
and professors were terrorized by spies and
police. The Carlsbad Decrees succeeded in
suppressing for a number of years this first
outcropping of the revolutionary spirit in
Germany since the overthrow of Napoleon.
The spirit, however, was not really suppressed; it was merely driven underground.

In Prussia the militaristic, paternalistic,
despotic Hohenzollerns reigned. Behind
them stood the equally reactionary landed
aristocracy, the Junkers. In fact these sword-
bearing, monocled Junkers, who ruled feu-
dal-fashion over their peasants, officered the
Prussian army, and filled the key posts in
the civil service and administration, constituted the dominant factor in Prussian history in the nineteenth century. These military lords hated, not only liberalism in any
form, but also German nationalism. They
did not wish to see virile, martial Prussia
contaminated by association with the states
that were now infected with the French dis-

ease of liberalism. The *Burschenschaften* made only slight headway in Prussia and were quickly stamped out. It was only in the economic field that German unity received any encouragement from Prussia. Because her territory was separated into two non-contiguous segments, Prussia in 1819 began making commercial treaties with her little German neighbors, providing for the free flow of trade among them. By 1834 nearly all of the states of the German Confederation except Austria had joined the Prussian-sponsored *Zollverein* (customs union). Though it was not so intended, the *Zollverein* proved to be a forerunner of German political unity under Prussian leadership.

As was to be expected, Metternichism reached its height in Austria. The spirit of the French Revolution and Napoleon, with the one exception of nationalism, had hardly touched the Hapsburg state and its feudal society. In addition to the natural conservatism of the Hapsburgs and their chief minister Austria had a language problem that caused her rulers to fear liberalism and its companion nationalism like the plague. Austria proper is German-speaking, but during the sixteenth, seventeenth, and eighteenth centuries the Hapsburgs had annexed territories inhabited by Hungarian (Magyar), Czech, Slovak, Ruthenian, Polish, Romanian, Serb, Croat, and Slovene language groups. In 1815 two Italian-speaking provinces were added. Before 1789 these various language groups remained quiet under their feudal lords, the Hapsburg dynasty, and the Roman Catholic Church. However, with the mass nationalism, based largely on language, that followed in the wake of the French Revolution, these groups began to stir with national consciousness. Metternich saw clearly that if this new force were not suppressed the Hapsburg state would fall apart. Furthermore, nationalism unchecked would cause Austria to lose her dominance over Germany and Italy. The various German and Italian states would be drawn together into powerful national states from which Austria would be excluded, for, although Austria proper was German-speak-

ing, the fact that most of her subjects were non-German-speaking disqualified her from membership in a German nation. When these facts are considered, it is not surprising that Austria in 1815 was the most reactionary state in Europe save Russia. In the Hapsburg provinces Metternich's police and spies were everywhere. Permission to enter or to leave the country was made very difficult, lest dangerous ideas be brought in from the West. Classrooms, libraries, bookstores, and organizations of all kinds were supervised with suspicion. Censorship covered even music (in the country of Mozart and Beethoven) for fear that musical notes would be used as a cryptic code for conveying revolutionary ideas. On the surface these policies appeared for some time to succeed. Nevertheless, events would soon prove that even in the land of Metternich the liberal and national seeds blown in from France had found fertile soil.

5. Restoration and Repression in Italy

Austria's domination over Italy was even more complete than over Germany. Lombardy and Venetia were annexed outright. Modena, Parma, and Tuscany were under Austrian princes. The Papal States and Naples were under Austria's protection and guidance in both domestic and foreign affairs. In all these states the deposed aristocracy and clericals trooped back, full of hatred for French institutions and for the Italian liberals who had co-operated with Napoleon. Nearly all of the Italian intelligentsia were soon in prison or in exile. In the Papal States the Inquisition and Index were restored, and such Napoleonic innovations as street lighting were done away with. Of all the Italian states only Piedmont in the extreme northwest was free of direct Austrian control, but even here the restored heads of the house of Savoy were so reactionary as to fill Metternich with joy.

In considering Italy to be "safe," however, Metternich failed to reckon with the influence of history. Italy had had a glorious past. As the seat of the Roman Empire, it had ruled the Western world for many centuries. During the ten medieval centuries all roads still led to Rome, which was then the head of Western Christendom. In the fourteenth and fifteenth centuries Italy held the economic and cultural leadership of the West. Venice was queen of the seas and Florence was the center of the banking world. Both were fabulously rich in money and in culture.

The extraordinary brilliance of Venice, Florence, Milan, Rome, Pisa, Siena, Ravenna, and many other Italian city-states in the Renaissance period tended to develop a local rather than a national pride. This local state patriotism was in large measure responsible for Italy's division, weakness, and decay in early modern times. However, the French Revolution and Napoleon brought to Italy a new kind of nationalism and reawakened memories of past exploits. Very soon after 1815 Italian liberals began to form secret societies, called *Carbonari* (charcoal burners), which met at night around charcoal fires to plot freedom from Austrian and local tyranny and to plan for national unification. In the early thirties a romantic young intellectual, Giuseppe Mazzini, organized the Young Italy society, which was dedicated to the task of achieving a free, united, and liberal Italian nation. Although the first uprisings inspired by the Carbonari and Young Italy were crushed by Austrian arms, the Italian national movement was to gain momentum until its ends were achieved.

6. Reaction and Repression in Russia

Even primitive, autocratic, semi-Asiatic Russia had not escaped the influence of the French Revolution and Napoleon. She had joined in the second, third, fourth, and fifth coalitions against France, had been invaded and ravaged as far as Moscow in 1812, and had played a major role in the wars of liberation against Napoleon in 1813–14. Meanwhile, her young tsar, Alexander I, and many of his aristocratic young army officers had picked up romantic and liberal

ideas from the West. However, Russia was not yet ripe for Western liberalism. She was a vast agricultural nation with a feudal social structure and a very small urban bourgeoisie to serve as a liberal base. The Orthodox Christian Church, dominated by an upper clergy drawn from the aristocracy, was a handy governmental agency for controlling the masses. The unstable Alexander I fell under the influence of Metternich and of his own reactionary boyar magnates and soon repented of his liberalism. He sought atonement for his sins by volunteering to stamp out liberal movements in Naples, Spain, and Latin America. He did, however, remain a romantic idealist as long as he lived.

There was no trace of romanticism, however, in Nicholas I, Alexander's younger brother, who succeeded him in 1825. Nicholas was a handsome, dignified, austere autocrat whose military career wedded him to the concepts of stern discipline and unquestioned authority. A quixotic revolt by a group of young liberal officers on the occasion of his ascension to the throne and a full-scale revolt against Russian tyranny by his Polish subjects in 1830 further embittered him against liberalism in any form. Both revolts were crushed with an iron hand. For thirty years (1825–55) Nicholas I was to stand as the perfect symbol of absolute reaction and the armed guardian of the Metternich system. Russia, of all the great powers of Europe, was the least affected by the spirit of the French Revolution. When at the end of the nineteenth century she did begin to yield to liberal and revolutionary forces, it was with disorder and violence.

In Western and Central Europe, however, it was obvious by 1830 that the liberal and national forces created or released by the Intellectual and the French revolutions and spread by Napoleon were not dead, but only temporarily repressed. Greece, Belgium, and most of Spain's New World colonies had gained their freedom. The restored French Bourbons had been overthrown. In Great Britain the Reform Bill of 1832 opened a new liberal era (see pp. 519–

20). The fifteen years of restoration, reaction, and repression that followed the overthrow of Napoleon proved, therefore, to be only a brief interlude. By 1830 the revolutionary forces of liberalism and nationalism were once more on the march.

———— •◆• ————

SUGGESTED READING

Harold Nicolson, *The Congress of Vienna, a Study in Allied Unity 1812–1822* (1946). A readable account of the Congress and of the Concert of Europe, which it attempted to establish.

Crane Brinton, *The Lives of Talleyrand* (1936). A lively account of the wily French diplomat who figured prominently in the French Revolution, the era of Napoleon, and the Congress of Vienna.

Metternich, *Memoirs*, 5 vols. (1880–82). Good reading for the student who becomes interested in the personality who to a considerable degree dominated Europe from 1814 to 1848.

William Miller, *The Ottoman Empire and Its Successors, 1801–1927* (1928). Gives an account of the Greek struggle for independence.

Dexter Perkins, *Hands Off: A History of the Monroe Doctrine* (1927). A popular account by America's foremost authority on the subject of the first successful blow to the Metternich system.

Frederick Artz, *Reaction and Revolution, 1814–1832* (1950). A scholarly history of the eighteen years following the overthrow of Napoleon.

* A. J. May, *The Age of Metternich, 1814–1848* (Berkshire). A brief and lucid survey of the period.

J. C. Legge, *Rhyme and Revolution in Germany: A Study in German History, Life, Literature, and Character, 1813–1850* (1918). A well-written volume on an important subject about which very little is available in English.

SECTION 10

The Industrial Revolution—

First Phase:

The Dominance of the Middle Class,

1830–1870

W hile the French Revolution was releasing upon the world the explosive forces of liberalism and nationalism, the Industrial Revolution was introducing to the Western world new techniques of working and living. Indeed, most of world history in the nineteenth and twentieth centuries has centered around these three forces—liberalism of various hues, nationalism first moderate and then malignant, and industrialism with its manifold facets and problems. And if we broaden our concept of the Industrial Revolution to include the onrush of science, with which it was closely associated, we may venture to give it first place among all the forces that have influenced the history of the last two centuries. Beginning in Great Britain near the end of the eighteenth century, the Industrial Revolution spread first to Belgium and France, then to the United States, and eventually to most of the rest of the world. Everywhere it changed the pattern of life drastically.

The industrial bourgeoisie, who owned and benefited from the new power machines, quickly rose to a position of great wealth and power, justifying their good fortune with theories of laissez-faire economics. The proletariat, on the other hand, unable to compete with the machines, were greatly distressed. This distress eventually led the masses to organize, take up new theories of economics, and demand and get an increased share in government and in society. From approximately 1830 to 1870 the bourgeoisie was generally in control in the industrialized countries. From 1870 to 1914 the masses were moving toward the top. Meanwhile, science and technology were reshaping life and thought.

Without, therefore, minimizing such dynamic forces as liberalism and nationalism, what better title can be given the history of the nineteenth century than "The Industrial Revolution—First Phase: The Dominance of the Middle Class, 1830–70; Second Phase: The Emergence of the Masses, 1870–1914?" In the following section, which deals with the first phase, we shall see the bourgeoisie, with its machines and its own brand of liberalism, come to power in Great Britain, the United States, and France, and struggle for control in Central Europe. We shall see moderate nationalism, which in this period was closely associated with liberalism, on the march in Europe and in America, creating new nations such as Italy and Germany and energizing the old ones. Meanwhile, the spirit of romanticism prevailed in philosophy, literature, and the arts.

CHAPTER 43

The Industrial Revolution

THE Industrial Revolution had its beginning in Great Britain, which possessed an abundance of coal and iron, a large colonial empire to supply raw materials and markets, the world's largest merchant marine and navy to protect it, a stable government dominated by the capitalistic classes, an ample labor supply, and a great accumulation of liquid capital amassed from her lucrative commerce.

1. The Coming of the Machine

The textile industry was the first to become mechanized. In 1733 John Kay invented the flying shuttle, which doubled the speed of weaving cloth. In 1764 James Hargreaves, a humble English carpenter, hit upon the idea of hitching eight spindles to his wife's (Jenny) spinning wheel, instead of one. The result was the spinning jenny. The number of spindles was soon multiplied. Five years later Richard Arkwright, a barber, patented the water frame, a system of rollers driven by water power which spun a much finer and firmer thread than the jenny. In 1779 Samuel Crompton, combining the principles of the spinning Jenny and the water frame, produced the hybrid spinning mule—a great improvement over both. In 1785 an Anglican clergyman, Edmund Cartwright, invented the power loom.

The mechanization of both spinning and weaving greatly increased the demand for cotton. The meeting of this demand was made possible by a young American, Eli Whitney, who in 1793 invented the cotton gin. Removing the lint from the seeds by hand was a tedious process; one man could separate only five or six pounds a day. Cotton was therefore grown only in small patches. Whitney's gin not only made possible an adequate supply of cotton for Britain's mills but also in so doing brought into existence the huge cotton plantations, worked by Negro slaves, in the American South.

Meanwhile, a new source of power was found to help water drive the new machines. In 1769 James Watt, a University of Glasgow repairman-mechanic, invented the first steam engine that could be used to drive machinery. The power that could be generated by the steam engine was almost unlimited. Constant improvements in the making of iron and the mining of coal led to the production of still-better machines and guaranteed a sufficient supply of fuel to drive them.

Man now had the capacity to produce a practically boundless supply of goods. The enormous significance of these and other inventions for the future could not, of course, be seen at the time they were made. And today we have become so accustomed to them it is easy to forget their importance. However, the fact is that the inventors of these basic machines and processes were responsible for the coming of a new era. It is true that most of the principles and some of the processes were known in ancient and medieval times, but it was men like Hargreaves and Watt, aided by the favorable political and social setting (and by earlier experimenters), who developed the practical working machines. Most of these inventors were humble amateurs, who endured discouragement, scorn, and sometimes bankruptcy and persecution. One of the few exceptions was Richard Arkwright, who rose from barbering to wealth and knighthood. The intimate stories of these men and their inventions are filled with romance.

2. The Revolution in Transportation and Communications

An integral and necessary part of the Industrial Revolution was the improvement of transportation and communications. Otherwise sufficient quantities of raw materials to feed the hungry machines and adequate markets to absorb the finished products would not have been available. The last decades of the eighteenth century and the first decades of the nineteenth century were a time of road and canal building in Great Britain, France, and the United States. Roads had long been good in France, but in Great Britain and of course in the sprawling, young United States they were notoriously poor. Around the turn of the century Thomas Telford and John McAdam in Great Britain pioneered in the construction of well-drained and surfaced roads. In America Albert Gallatin inspired the construction of the Cumberland Road, or Old National Pike, which, begun in 1811, reached from Baltimore to Illinois by 1850. In Great Britain canals were particularly useful in the transportation of coal. However, the most important canal constructed in this period was the Erie, completed in 1825. The Erie Canal opened up the Great Lakes region to lucrative world communications and assured the primacy of New York City as America's chief port and metropolis.

Nevertheless, the real revolution in transportation came with the application of Watt's steam engine to locomotion. In 1807 Robert Fulton, capitalizing on the failures and partial successes of others, steamed his *Clermont* the hundred and fifty miles up the Hudson from New York to Albany in thirty-two hours. Twelve years later the *Savannah* crossed the Atlantic in twenty-nine days, using part steam and part sail. This was by no means record time, but in 1838, when the *Great Western* crossed the Atlantic in fifteen days entirely by steam, the last doubts as to the practicability of the steamship were dispelled.

Meanwhile, George Stephenson in Great Britain was developing the first successful locomotive. In 1825 he made his first convincing demonstration by hauling a train of thirty-four cars twenty-five miles at twelve miles an hour. Five years later his *Rocket* was pulling cars at the rate of twenty-nine miles an hour. The horse was on the way out.

The middle decades of the nineteenth century were a period of great railroad building in Northwestern Europe and the United States. Construction of the Baltimore and Ohio was begun in 1828, and two years later a few miles were opened for traffic. In 1852 Chicago, soon to become the world's leading railroad center, was reached by the New York Central system. By 1869 the Union Pacific had connected the Atlantic with the Pacific. All the while speed and efficiency were rapidly increasing.

Communications were developing faster yet. Until 1844 communications were no speedier than transportation except for a special courier service by horse or a crude system of signaling by semaphore. In that year, however, Samuel F. B. Morse sent a message by wire forty miles from Baltimore to Washington. The telegraph, transmitting messages instantaneously from one end of any length of wire to the other, caught on rapidly. In 1866 a telegraph cable was laid across the Atlantic, enabling news to travel from New York to London as quickly as from New York to Brooklyn. Ten years later Alexander Graham Bell, an American born in Scotland, invented the telephone, and shortly before the end of the century wireless telegraphy had begun.

It is difficult for us today to realize to

what degree or how quickly these inventions in the field of transportation and communications shrank the world. Julius Caesar could move his armies as rapidly as George Washington or Napoleon (actually a little more rapidly, thanks to the Roman roads), and Plato could gather news as quickly as Jefferson. Now, in the nineteenth century, far-off places suddenly became near, and strange peoples remained strange only to the primitive, the dull, or the lazy. More and more people, first the rich and then the poor, began to travel and to move their domiciles. The first important effect of the revolution in transportation and communications was to accelerate the Industrial Revolution by greatly facilitating the large-scale mobilization of capital, raw materials, and markets.

3. The Factory System

Another basic aspect of the Industrial Revolution was the rise of the factory system. Before the coming of the power machines goods were produced either by the non-capitalistic craft guilds or under the domestic, or "putting out," system. It is true that some factories, notably the woolen-manufacturing establishments in Florence, came into existence as early as the fourteenth century when commerce and capitalism were reviving, but they were usually on a small scale and exceptions to the general rule. Under the domestic system entrepreneur capitalists would purchase the raw materials and distribute them to numerous craftsmen who would spin, weave, sew, cut, carve, or mold the products by hand in their own cottages. The entrepreneur would then collect the finished products, pay the craftsmen by piece for their work, and market the wares. The workers under this system enjoyed the advantages of doing as much or as little work as they wished without supervision. They usually carried on farming operations in addition to their craftwork. On the other hand, since they were scattered throughout the countryside, they were unable to bring any group pressure to bear upon the employers or to achieve any uniformity of wage.

The smarter and more aggressive entrepreneur could easily cheat them, and wages were at rock bottom. The capitalists, too, were limited by this system. The operations were necessarily on a small scale, much time was lost distributing the raw materials from cottage to cottage and collecting the finished products, and uniformity of quality was virtually impossible to attain.

The coming of the power machines made the domestic system of manufacturing not only antiquated but practically impossible. The handcraftsmen discovered that it was impossible to compete with the machines, and since they were unable to buy them, they had to go wherever the machines were located. Thus factories, housing both the machines and the workers, came into existence. Crowded around the factories, hastily and cheaply built living quarters for the workers and their families soon appeared. This was the origin of the modern mill town and industrial city. The rise of the factory system eventually completed the process, begun six or seven hundred years earlier with the revival of commerce, of changing civilization in the industrialized areas from rural to urban.

4. The Agricultural Revolution

During this same period agriculture also was undergoing revolutionary changes in Western Europe and northern America. In the early eighteenth century Charles (Turnip) Townshend, grandfather of the author of the Townshend Acts, which helped to precipitate the American Revolution, began mixing diplomacy and statecraft with agriculture. He demonstrated that increased yields could be obtained through crop rotation and the use of root crops like turnips and clover. His contemporary and compatriot, Jethro Tull, invented the seed drill, which made it possible to plant seed in rows and thereby insure better fertilization and cultivation of the soil. Later in the eighteenth century another Englishman, Robert Bakewell, greatly improved the existing types of sheep and cattle by artificial breeding. These new methods were popularized in the late eighteenth century, largely through the efforts of Arthur Young in Britain and the French physiocrats. The mechanization of agriculture first began with the reaper, which the American inventor Cyrus McCormick patented in 1834. These improvements in agriculture, particularly the introduction of farming machinery, accelerated the enclosure movement in Great Britain, which had been going on since the sixteenth century. The increased efficiency achieved by the application of the new methods and the consolidation and enclosure of scattered strips and farms meant that larger harvests could now be produced by fewer laborers. The result in the most advanced of the industrialized countries was a surplus of farm laborers, who drifted off to the cities to seek jobs in the new factories. The industrial and the agricultural revolutions thus interacted upon each other while they produced an ever-increasing abundance of material goods for the eventual benefit of mankind.

5. The Triumph of the Bourgeoisie and the Distress of the Proletariat

With the exception of a relatively few capitalists and well-to-do consumers, the benefits of the Industrial Revolution were not immediate. The first to profit from the mechanization of industry were the owners of the new machines, the industrial bourgeoisie. Ever since the revival of commerce and capitalism in the eleventh and twelfth centuries, the capitalistic middle class had been gaining ground at the expense of the landed aristocracy. It had been a long, slow process with occasional setbacks. In the fifteenth and sixteenth centuries the middle class had formed an alliance with the national monarchs against the feudal lords. In the seventeenth and eighteenth centuries, first in England and then in America and France, the middle class had turned on the king and sharply curtailed his power.

Nonetheless, at the opening of the nineteenth century, the aristocracy in Great Britain and France were still powerful, and

everywhere else, except in the United States, they were dominant. But the coming of the power machines gave the industrial middle class such a monopoly over the fabrication and transportation of goods in the industrialized countries that they were able now to establish their supremacy over the upper and lower classes alike. Driving the handcraftsmen out of business and hiring them on their own terms, the industrial bourgeoisie amassed fortunes vaster than those of the merchant princes before them. With such wealth at their command they gained control not only over their nations' economies but over government and society as well.

The triumph of the industrial bourgeoisie did not, of course, occur overnight, nor did it occur simultaneously in all countries. It followed the course of the Industrial Revolution—coming first in Great Britain, next in Belgium and France, a little later in the United States, then in Germany, and near the end of the nineteenth century in Central and Eastern Europe, and Japan. By the middle of the twentieth century it was reaching most of the rest of the world. After 1870, when the Industrial Revolution had had its full impact in Germany and was beginning to reach the rest of the world, the masses were on the move and the heyday of bourgeois, *laissez-faire* economics had passed its peak. In those areas, therefore, the industrial bourgeoisie never gained complete mastery.

In Great Britain, Belgium, and France the years approximately from 1830 to 1870 represent an era of industrial middle-class dominance. In the United States, where the growth of industry was a little slower, the industrial bourgeoisie did not gain control until the Civil War (1861–65) and was not seriously challenged until the turn of the century. The next few chapters will deal primarily with the policies, struggles, and achievements of the industrial middle class in these countries.

By the same measure that the bourgeoisie gained in the first phase of the Industrial Revolution the proletariat lost. Men have never been equal since the beginning of organized society. The strong, the clever, the aggressive, and the fortunate have always enjoyed an advantage over their weaker, meeker, or less fortunate fellow men. Nevertheless, before the coming of the power machines, when workingmen lived by the strength of their muscles, there was a modicum of equality. One man's muscles are not too much stronger than another's. The willing worker, with reasonable luck, could hew out some kind of living in competition with his neighbors. No man, however, could compete with steam-driven machines that could do the work of hundreds of men.

The defeated craftsmen and the surplus or dispossessed agricultural workers had no recourse but to flock to the factories to seek employment tending the machines. The rapid increase in population, which had been going on since the middle of the eighteenth century, also swelled the ranks of the industrial proletariat. The owners, under these circumstances, were able to state their own terms. Wages were bid down to the barest subsistence level—sometimes fifty cents for a week of seven eighteen-hour days. Since women and children could tend many of the machines as efficiently as men and could be hired more cheaply, men were often replaced by their wives and children. Contracts were made with orphanages for the employment of the children. Little tots too small to dress themselves were marched off before daybreak to work all day in the factories. If they fell behind the pace, they were beaten. Sometimes they were chained to their machines. Crying could be heard at all times in the factories, particularly toward the end of the day. The factories and mines were dark, dirty, and dangerous. The dwellings of the workers were likely to be hovels clustered around smoky, noisy mills or mine entrances. The workers were frequently compelled to spend the pittance they did receive at company stores, paying monopoly prices arbitrarily set by the owners.

Work lost its dignity. The dull, monotonous, robot-like repetition of a single operation on an assembly line brought the worker

CHILD LABOR. This woodcut, dated 1853, portrays the supervisor of an English cotton factory whipping a young boy. Incidents similar to this were typical of the first phase of the Industrial Revolution. Such conditions set some economic philosophers, the democratic liberals, speculating on ways and means of controlling capitalism and making it serve all classes of people. Other thinkers, most notably Karl Marx, decided that the capitalistic system in the industrial ages was such an unmitigated evil that it would have to be destroyed. (*The Bettmann Archive*)

none of the satisfaction and pride of skilled craftsmanship. It is true that even in the most highly mechanized industrial systems there was still a considerable amount of skilled craftsmanship left, but even that became tainted with the connotation of the mill. This loss cannot be repaid with any amount of wage increases. Numerous investigations have shown that factory workers are more interested in personal and social dignity and recognition than in wages, hours, and working conditions.

During the first phase of the Industrial Revolution there was, of course, virtually no opportunity for the workers or their children to get an education. The picture of the mid-nineteenth century industrial proletariat is one of the most dismal in recorded his-

WENTWORTH STREET, WHITECHAPEL, BY GUS-
TAVE DORÉ. This woodcut portrays the squalor
of an early nineteenth-century English industrial
slum. The first phase of the Industrial Revolution
brought great wealth to many members of the
middle class, but equally great distress to the industrial working class. (*The Bettmann Archive*)

tory. Western man, after struggling toward
freedom against various forms of tyranny
for some six thousand years, was now threatened with a new kind of slavery—slavery to
the machine and the machine owner. And
yet it is interesting to observe that those who
worked in the mills and mines at their
worst were seldom willing to go back to agricultural life.

One of the industrial proletarian's first
reactions was violence. Throughout the winter of 1811–12, when the pressure of the
Napoleonic war and blockade against British commerce was added to the maladjustments of the Industrial Revolution, a wave
of personal violence and machine smashing
swept throughout Great Britain (the Lud-
dite riots). This type of reaction to the machine, of course, had no future. Parliament,
composed entirely of members of the property-holding classes, quickly made sabotage

a capital offense and suppressed violence
with a heavy hand. Several dozens of of-
fenders were hanged. Sporadic outbreaks of
violence, however, continued for several
years. This story was repeated in other countries as the Industrial Revolution spread. In
the United States in the middle decades of
the nineteenth century violence broke out
among the Irish immigrants working in the
anthracite coal mines of eastern Pennsylvania. The exploited miners formed secret
terror societies called Molly Maguires. For
a number of years they intimidated, even
murdered, unpopular bosses and unco-opera-
tive non-members. They were eventually
ferreted out by civil authorities and ruthlessly suppressed.

More peaceful efforts of the industrial
proletariat to bring group pressure upon
their employers by organizing unions also
at first met with defeat. In 1799 and 1800
the British Parliament passed Combination
Laws, which outlawed all labor combinations organized for the purpose of securing
better wages, hours, or working conditions.
The French and Belgian governments did
likewise. In the United States the owners
themselves organized for the purpose of
breaking up labor unions. Private detectives
and police were set upon labor leaders, who
were beaten, fired, and black-listed. It was
not until the latter part of the nineteenth
century that labor unions were able to make
any significant headway. Therefore, during
the first phase of the Industrial Revolution
as power machines belched and crunched
and ground out ever more and more goods
for those able to buy them, and great fortunes for their owners, they blighted the
lives of tens of thousands of workers, rob-
bing them of the dignity of their labor, and
threatening them with a new kind of slavery.

6. New Economic Theories—Classical, Liberal, and Utopian

CLASSICAL THEORY

It was inevitable that the Industrial Revolution should set men thinking about economics. The industrial bourgeoisie, seeking

intellectual support and justification for its good fortune, found perfectly suitable the doctrine of *laissez-faire*, which had been developed during the Enlightenment of the eighteenth century. This doctrine had been best stated by the Scottish philosopher Adam Smith in his classic *Wealth of Nations* (1776). The essence of Smith's theory is that economics, like the physical world, has its own natural laws. The most basic of the laws in economics are those of supply and demand. When left to operate alone, these laws will keep the economy in balance and in the long run work to the benefit of all. If the sanctity of property and contracts is respected, competition and free enterprise will provide incentive and keep prices down. Government regulations and collective bargaining only impede the workings of the natural laws of economics and destroy incentive. Government, therefore, should limit its activities in the economic field to the enforcement of order and of contracts, public education and health, national defense, and in rare instances the encouragement of necessary industries that private enterprise does not find profitable. Here was a theory readymade for the machine owners at a stage in the game when they held all the trump cards. Later, when competition became more severe and complex, the machine owners were to demand and receive a great deal of government protection. But in Great Britain in the early nineteenth century all that the industrial bourgeoisie needed was an opportunity to exploit its advantage. Little wonder that the *Wealth of Nations* became its bible.

A strong boost was given to *laissez-faire* thinking by a young Anglican clergyman, Thomas Malthus, who in 1798 published his *Essay on Population*. Malthus argued that, since population increases by a geometric ratio whereas food supply increases only by an arithmetic ratio, it is a basic natural law that population will outstrip the food supply. This alleged law has two important implications. One is that nothing can be done to improve the lot of the masses. If their condition is temporarily bet-

tered, they will immediately produce children in such numbers that the food supply will be outstripped and starvation will threaten all. Only poverty and privation hold them in check. The second implication is that the rich are not to blame for the misery of the poor; the poor are themselves responsible because of their incontinence. These ideas were so soothing to so many of the book-buying upper classes that Malthus quickly attained fame and wealth.

David Ricardo supplied further ammunition for the free-enterprise economists. Making a fortune in stock-market speculation, Ricardo purchased a seat in Parliament and spent the rest of his life thinking and writing on economics. In his chief work, *The Principles of Political Economy* (1817), he propounded the law of rent and the iron law of wages. Rent is determined by the difference in productivity of land. Take off all restrictions and subsidies and the poorest land goes out of cultivation, reducing the rent on the more productive lands proportionately. He argued for this idea so forcefully that it played an important part in the repeal of England's corn laws, which had maintained the price of grain at an artificially high level. More important in economic thinking was Ricardo's iron law of wages, according to which the natural wage is the subsistence level and the market wage tends to conform to it. Raise the market wage and the workers will multiply so rapidly that soon the law of supply and demand will bring the market wage down below the subsistence level. Then the workers will die off from malnutrition and disease and slow down their reproduction rate. Eventually they will become so scarce as to be able to bid the market wage up above the natural wage. Always, though, the pull is toward the subsistence level. This again was music in the ears of the industrial capitalists.

Probably the ultimate in *laissez-faire* thinking was reached by the sociologist Herbert Spencer. In his *Social Statics* (1851) Spencer likened competition in human society to the struggle for survival and the survival of the fittest in the animal kingdom.

Although *Social Statics* antedated Darwin's *Origin of Species* by eight years, in his later writings Spencer made abundant use of Darwin's work, applying the evolutionary principles to economics and to human society in general. It seems hard, said Spencer, that the weak and the inefficient should lose out and perish. "Nevertheless, when regarded not separately, but in connection with the interests of universal humanity, these harsh fatalities are seen to be full of the highest beneficence—the same beneficence which brings to early graves the children of diseased parents, and singles out the low-spirited, the intemperate, and the debilitated as the victims of an epidemic." Christian sentimentality and humanitarianism by protecting the weak and the unfortunate would destroy wholesome competition and eventually produce a degenerate society. Here was rugged individualism at its most rugged.

These thinkers (with the exception of Spencer) came to be called the classical economists, since they were the first to grapple philosophically with the economic problems of the Industrial Revolution. Their general attitude and assumptions were well expressed by the British utilitarian philosopher Jeremy Bentham, as early as 1789, in his *Principles of Morals and Legislation.* Bentham was an eighteenth-century materialistic rationalist who lived on until 1832, bridging the eighteenth and nineteenth centuries with his life and thought. The utilitarians believed that the useful is the good and that the chief purpose of government and society is to achieve "the greatest good to the greatest number." But since every individual is the best judge of his own best interests, the surest way to achieve general happiness is to allow each individual to follow his own enlightened self-interest. Individualism, then, is the best safeguard of the general welfare.

LIBERAL THEORY

The early-nineteenth-century classical economists who advocated free enterprise and individualism called themselves liberals.

However, a new type of liberal, more like the liberal of the twentieth century, soon appeared. The new type of economic liberal, while adhering to the sanctity of private property and to a large measure of individualism, believed that the Industrial Revolution had brought about the need for certain restrictions on both. In fact Bentham himself came to see the necessity for the state to protect the common weal against overly aggressive individuals. One of the first of the new type of liberal economists was the Swiss historian and philosopher Simonde de Sismondi. In his *New Principles of Political Economy* (1819) Sismondi challenged Bentham's fundamental assumption that the self-interests of the individuals promote the best interests of the common weal. He believed that power machines were interfering with the operation of Adam Smith's laws by glutting certain markets, oppressing labor, and creating monopolies. The true wealth of a nation, Sismondi believed, lay in the equitable distribution of goods and benefits among its citizenry. Therefore, he favored laws that would restrict the amassing of monopolistic fortunes, and divide great estates. He also advocated practices such as profit sharing and long-term job contracts that would give protection and security to the workers.

The German economist Friedrich List would subordinate economics to nationalism. In order to develop a well-rounded national life a nation should protect and encourage its manufacturing industry by a system of protective tariffs. List differed from the earlier mercantilists, however, in that he believed that free trade should be permitted for everything except manufactures. Forced to flee from Germany because of his liberal views (which seem quite mild today), he came to the United States. His chief work, *The National System of Political Economy,* was published in 1841. Long before that, in 1792, during Washington's first administration, Alexander Hamilton, without philosophizing very much about it, had secured the adoption of a protective tariff in the United States.

Probably the most influential of all the new type of economic liberals was John Stuart Mill (1806–73). Mill, a child prodigy, was brought up to be a good Benthamite. However, he was too sensitive and humanitarian to remain in the hard materialistic camp of the utilitarians. Moreover, living a generation after Smith, Malthus, Ricardo, and Bentham, he was able to see some of the evil effects of the Industrial Revolution. Although Mill in no wise rejected private property, capitalism, and free enterprise, he believed that in the machine age restrictions must be instituted by the state for the protection of the poor. Although production is bound by the iron laws of supply and demand, the distribution of goods is not. Public utilities such as railroads and gas and waterworks are natural monopolies and should be owned by the state. The state should provide free compulsory education for all and regulate child labor. He favored income and inheritance taxes as economic equalizers. Mill's chief work on economics, *Principles of Political Economy,* was published in 1848. In his later years he considered himself a socialist but would hardly be so regarded today. His are the views of many twentieth-century liberals.

UTOPIAN SOCIALISM

During the first phase of the Industrial Revolution the economies of the industrialized countries belonged to the bourgeoisie in thought as well as in deed. The theories of the classical economists enjoyed complete ascendancy. Even such an advanced liberal thinker as John Stuart Mill believed resolutely in private property and the capitalistic system. The hard-pressed proletariat, though increasingly disconcerted, was hardly capable of formulating new economic theories. However, the miserable plight of the industrial workers soon inspired a number of intellectuals to question the fundamentals of the existing system, such as private property and private enterprise for profit. Since the ideas of these intellectuals were only speculative dreams and offered no practical

course of action for the immediate present, their advocates came to be called utopian socialists. One of the first utopian socialists was the French nobleman Henri de Saint-Simon (1760–1825). He and his followers believed that society should be reorganized on a "Christian" basis, that all should work, and that the inheritance of private property should be abolished. His ideal society would be run according to the formula "from each according to his capacity, to each according to his deserts." Saint-Simon would reward the superior artists, scientists, engineers, and businessmen according to their merits. However, he laid down no plan of action for achieving his ideal society.

Charles Fourier (1772–1837), a Frenchman of middle-class origin, would do away with economic competition, the source of so much evil. Production, both agricultural and industrial, would be carried on by voluntary co-operatives, whose members would pool their resources and live in communal apartment houses. Distribution of goods and profits would be based upon the formula: workers, five twelfths; capitalists, four twelfths; management, three twelfths. Fourier's elaborate plans included many quixotic ideas and some others that have found their way into practice.

A step forward in socialistic thinking was taken by Louis Blanc (1811–82), another middle-class Frenchman. Louis Blanc would abolish the evils of selfish competitive capitalism by setting up a system of social workshops. The government would lend money to voluntary workingmen's co-operatives, which would establish and run the workshops. Distribution of the proceeds would be according to the formula, "from each according to his capacity, to each according to his needs." This was the formula later adopted by Karl Marx.

A different kind of utopian was Robert Owen (1771–1858). Born in Wales, Owen quickly made an industrial fortune in Manchester and bought large cotton mills in New Lanark, Scotland. In partnership with Jeremy Bentham, he set out early in the nineteenth century to make New Lanark a model socialist utopia. Wages were raised, hours shortened, working conditions improved, child labor abolished, educational and recreational facilities provided, sickness and old-age insurance established. Owen spent the rest of his life and fortune drawing plans for and setting up model socialistic communities. Several were set up in America, notably New Harmony, Indiana. All failed; nor was Owen's benevolent example followed by other industrialists. Obviously, mankind, after thousands of years of competing for private gain, was not yet ready suddenly to start living and working for the common weal.

The utopian socialists were all strongly influenced by the materialistic rationalism of the eighteenth-century Enlightenment. All were vigorously opposed to existing organized religion, although Saint-Simon believed that his ideal society should be dominated by a new social Christianity—a brand of Christianity that had never yet been tried. None of the utopian socialists had any real influence on their own times. They did, however, start a trend of economic thought that was to become influential later.

It was not until the second phase of the Industrial Revolution (1870–1914), when the masses began to stir and to move, that a virile type of socialism would arise. This later socialism would be a state socialism for the most part and would bear the stamp of Karl Marx. Meanwhile, the industrial bourgeoisie established its control over the economy, the government, and society in the industrialized countries—a control that until 1870 was not seriously challenged.

SUGGESTED READING

Herbert Heaton, *Economic History of Europe* (1948). One of the best general economic histories of Europe. Good chapters on the Industrial Revolution.

John Clapham, *The Economic Development of France and Germany, 1815–1914* (1936). Standard work on the subject.

Abbott Usher, *A History of Mechanical Inventions* (1929). Probably the best single volume on this subject.

L. C. A. Knowles, *Industrial and Commercial Revolutions in Great Britain during the Nineteenth Century* (1926). Somewhat technical but contains many useful facts and figures.

J. L. and B. Hammond, *The Black Age* (1947). A popularly written account of the misery of the industrial proletariat during the first phase of the Industrial Revolution.

* Adam Smith, *The Wealth of Nations* (Modern Library). The classic statement of *laissez-faire* economics, which dominated nineteenth-century liberal economic thought.

* T. R. Malthus, *An Essay on the Principles of Population as It Affects the Future Improvement of Society*, 2 vols. (Everyman's Library). First published in 1798. One of the most influential treatises on economic theory ever written.

H. W. Laidler, *History of Socialistic Thought* (1927). Good chapters on the early (utopian) socialists.

Robert Owen, *The Life of Robert Owen, by Himself* (1920). Originally published in 1857–58. Autobiography of one of the early philanthropic industrialists, who was considered to be a socialist in the nineteenth century but who would hardly be so considered today.

CHAPTER 44

———◆———

Triumph of Bourgeois Liberalism

LIBERALISM is a very difficult term to define. It is of various hues, and from time to time changes its complexion. In general, the term *liberalism* implies a belief in a wider distribution of this world's goods and privileges. During the first three quarters of the nineteenth century liberalism was closely associated with the middle classes, particularly the industrial bourgeoisie. It was usually strong in those areas where the Industrial Revolution was advanced, and weak where the Industrial Revolution was retarded. In addition to the industrial and commercial bourgeoisie (both great and small) intellectuals and professional people were likely to be liberal. The voice of the industrial proletariat, which after 1870 would be demanding a more radical kind of liberalism, was as yet scarcely heard. The chief wellsprings of this early liberalism were the philosophy of the Enlightenment and the English, American, and French revolutions.

1. General Nature of Nineteenth-Century Liberalism

The middle-class liberals of the nineteenth century prior to 1870 believed in popular government limited by a restricted suffrage and by constitutional guarantees of the rights of the individual. The role of the government should be that of a policeman, enforcing laws and contracts. Government should interfere in economic life as little as possible, leaving that realm to private enterprise. The nineteenth-century liberals were also anti-clerical, that is, they opposed the interference in government by organized religion. Sometimes, reflecting the influence of the Enlightenment, they were not only anti-clerical but anti-religious. Until 1870 the liberals were usually nationalists, since nationalism at that time was primarily concerned with freeing peoples from alien rule and uniting them under one flag. The chief opponents of the nineteenth-century liberals were the vested interests of an earlier day— the aristocracy, the clergy, the military— seeking to retain their favored positions. The peasantry (a term and status applicable in Europe but not in the United States) was still generally conservative, strongly influenced by the clergy and sometimes by the aristocracy, and not very active in politics.

After 1870 the nature of liberalism was to change. The industrial bourgeoisie, having acquired wealth and power, had by now become a vested interest itself and was hostile to further political and social changes. Its members joined, for the most part, the ranks of the conservatives. Their place in the liberal ranks was taken by the bulk of the industrial proletariat, which was at last becoming politically active. The new liberals (now chiefly the lower middle classes, the intelligentsia, and the proletariat) began to advocate a greatly increased amount of government interference in economic affairs in behalf of the masses. They also adopted a somewhat different attitude toward nationalism. After 1870 nationalism in the West, having in large measure attained its goals of achieving free and united national states, tended to become aggressive and militaristic. This type of nationalism posed a threat to the liberal democracy of the lower middle classes and the proletariat, now the chief liberal groups. After 1870, therefore, liberalism tended to be internationalist, although in times of international crisis and war nationalism continued to rally the loyalty of all classes.

The period from 1830 to 1870, then, was a time of triumph for bourgeois liberalism in Great Britain, the United States, and France, the first major countries to become industrialized. In Central Europe, where the Industrial Revolution was more retarded, this period marked middle-class liberalism's rise but not its triumph. In Eastern Europe the Industrial Revolution and bourgeois liberalism did not appear until after 1870.

2. Political and Social Reform in Great Britain, 1832–67

In Great Britain, the cradle of the Industrial Revolution, the industrial bourgeoisie began to bid for power soon after the Napoleonic wars came to an end. Although Great Britain had been since the thirteenth century the home of the rule of law and of representative government, her government in 1815 was far from democratic. The suffrage was so severely restricted by property qualifications that only about 5 per cent of the adult males could vote. Furthermore, the industrial cities of the north, which had grown up since the last distribution of seats in Parliament, were not represented at all. Both houses of Parliament were, therefore, monopolized by the landed aristocracy. It must be remembered, however, that the cleavage between the middle class and the aristocracy was not so sharp in Great Britain as on the continent. The law of primogeniture in Great Britain granted the eldest son the entire landed estate and permitted him alone to assume the title. The younger sons sought careers in the church,

in the military, or in business. This brought about much intermingling between the upper and the middle classes. The long-sustained prosperity of British commerce had produced a merchant class wealthy enough to purchase respectability, lands, and sometimes titles. The aristocracy frequently invested in commercial enterprises and later in industry. Before 1830 the two great political parties, the Whigs and the Tories, were hardly more than two rival groups of noble families. These facts help to explain why the great political and social struggles in nineteenth-century Britain, though sometimes bitter, lacked the violence of those on the continent.

A period of economic depression and unrest in Great Britain followed the ending of the Napoleonic wars in 1815. For twenty-two years, with only one brief interruption, Britain had been engaged in a desperate struggle with France—economic as well as military. Meanwhile, her industrial expansion had gone on apace. The war's end found British warehouses piled high with unsalable goods. Thousands of returning veterans found no jobs. Strikes and riots, which had begun during Napoleon's blockade, increased. The conservative Tory party, which had seen the country through the war, was strongly entrenched in power. Both the Tories and the slightly more liberal Whigs were still badly frightened by the specter of French revolutionary Jacobinism. The government, therefore, took strong measures. The writs of habeas corpus were suspended. The climax came in 1819, when troops fired upon a proletarian throng that had assembled outside Manchester to listen to reform speeches. A number were killed and several scores injured in this "Peterloo Massacre."

Within a few years, however, as the postwar crisis of depression and unrest eased, the Tory government yielded slightly to the pressure for reform. We have already seen how Foreign Secretary Canning by 1822 had deserted Metternich's reactionary concert of Europe and aided independence movements in Latin America and Greece.

During the 1820's the navigation laws were somewhat relaxed and the tariff slightly lowered. The Combination Laws were partially repealed, permitting laborers to organize unions, though not to strike. The civil disabilities against non-conforming Protestants and Roman Catholics were removed, permitting them to participate in political life on an equal basis with Anglicans. These measures, however, welcome as they were, did not get at the fundamental issue: broadening popular participation in the government. The pressure for suffrage reform continued to mount, particularly from the industrial bourgeoisie, which was gaining rapidly in wealth. Finally in 1831 the Whigs, long out of power, made common cause with the bourgeois liberals and drove the Tory government from office.

The new prime minister, Earl Grey, immediately introduced and forced through Parliament the Reform Bill of 1832. This bill redistributed the seats in the House of Commons, taking away many from the "rotten boroughs" (once-important towns that had dwindled in population or even disappeared entirely) and giving them to the industrial cities of the north. The suffrage was extended to all those who owned or rented property with an annual value of £10 ($50). It is estimated that the number of voters was thereby increased from approximately 450,000 to 650,000 out of a total population of some 16,500,000. The great majority of the newly enfranchised were members of the urban middle class. Although on the surface the Reform Bill of 1832 appears rather innocuous, it represents a great turning point in British history. The long era of dominance of the landed aristocracy had ended and that of the industrial bourgeoisie had begun. The supremacy of the House of Commons over the House of Lords, which had opposed the Reform Bill, was established. A new period of political and social reform had opened.

Both political parties recognized the new era. The Whig party, dominated by the industrial bourgeoisie but containing a right wing of liberal aristocrats and a left wing of intellectual radicals, changed its name to Liberal party—liberal of course in the pre-1870 sense. For the next half century the Liberals were dominant, under the leadership of such personalities as Lords Grey, Russell, and Palmerston, and eventually William E. Gladstone. The Tory party was still predominantly the party of the landed aristocracy, but it contained some bourgeois elements, and its more liberal wing, led first by Sir Robert Peel and later by Benjamin Disraeli, was now in the ascendancy. The somewhat discredited name "Tory" was changed to Conservative.

Both parties, conscious of the rising importance of public opinion, supported a series of reforms. In 1833 slavery was abolished in the British Empire with compensation for the owners. This achievement was made much easier by the fact that there were no slaves in Britain itself. The Municipal Corporations Act applied the principles of the Reform Bill of 1832 to local government. The barbarous penal code was reformed, reducing the number of capital offenses to three and generally softening the punishment of criminals. The penny post increased the circulation of mail and literature. Parliament granted small but gradually increasing subsidies to the schools, most of which were run by the Anglican Church. Between 1833 and 1847 Parliament passed a series of laws that prohibited the employment in textile mills of children under nine and limited the hours of older children and of women to ten hours a day. The employment of women and children in underground mines was prohibited. In 1846 the Corn Laws (the import tariff on grain) were repealed, greatly reducing the price of bread.

It must be remembered that these reforms were not the work of the masses but of the bourgeois liberals in conjunction with a liberal minority of the aristocracy and a few intellectual radicals. The only reform movement initiated by the proletariat in this period of bourgeois domination came to naught. This was the Chartist movement. The hard-pressed industrial proletariat, keenly aware that it had been by-passed by the Reform Bill of 1832 and that it was not sharing in the unprecedented national prosperity, was dissatisfied with the reforms of the bourgeois liberals. In 1838 proletarian leaders drew up a People's Charter, which demanded (1) universal manhood suffrage, (2) the secret ballot, (3) removal of property qualifications for members of Parliament, (4) pay for members of Parliament, (5) annual elections, and (6) equal electoral districts. The charter was twice presented to Parliament and twice summarily rejected. In 1848, when much of the European continent was ablaze with revolution, the Chartists planned a monster petition and demonstration in London. The frightened government prepared to use force. However, only a few mild disorders followed the third rejection, and the movement came to an end. Nevertheless, the Chartist movement left its influence. Before many decades had passed, all of the demands in the charter had been enacted into law except that for annual elections. The most immediate result was to make both political parties aware of the growing influence of the proletariat and of the advisability of winning its favor.

This awareness increased as the numbers and the restlessness of the proletariat increased. During the 1860's William E. Gladstone, a more advanced type of liberal, rose to the leadership of the Liberal party. In 1866 he introduced a reform bill that would have enfranchised large numbers of the proletariat. Although the bill was defeated and the Liberal ministry was forced to resign, the narrowness of the defeat plus the agitation of the workingmen, which now reached ominous proportions, convinced the rising young leader of the Conservatives, Benjamin Disraeli, that the reform was inevitable. The shrewd Disraeli decided to seize credit for the inevitable. The result was the Reform Bill of 1867, which, as amended by the Liberals, gave the franchise to the great majority of the urban proletariat. The Reform Bill of 1867, which doubled the electorate, marked the beginning of a new era in British history. Henceforth, the industrial bourgeoisie would have to share power with the industrial proletariat. Liberalism now took on a new and more radical meaning. It is a tribute to British moderation and to Britain's long tradition of the rule of law that such a revolutionary change should have taken place with so little violence.

3. Jeffersonian and Jacksonian Democracy in the United States

The march of liberal democracy in the United States did not follow the European pattern. In America there was never any entrenched aristocracy that had to be overcome as in Europe. The European immigrants who peopled the United States were almost entirely from the middle and lower ranks of society. They were determined to prevent the rise in America of a class system such as the one from which they had fled. The rough frontier situation in America aided them in their efforts. In the primitive American forests and prairies blood and title counted for little; muscle and energy counted for much. These factors, in addition to the British heritage of the rule of law, which most of the early settlers brought with them, and to the able leadership, which they developed within their own ranks, sent democracy in America racing on ahead of that in Europe. Nor was American democracy so closely associated with or dependent upon the Industrial Revolution as in Europe. Although the first factory was set up in America by Samuel Slater in Rhode Island, as early as 1791, the growth of machine industry was at first quite slow. French and British blockades during the Napoleonic wars and the War of 1812 with Britain cut the United States off from British manufactures and caused much American commercial capital to be diverted to manufacturing. Nevertheless, it was not until after the Civil War (1861–65) that industrialism in the United States became so advanced that the industrial bourgeoisie was able to gain dominance in politics and society.

The advance of democracy in the young American republic received a great boost with the election of Thomas Jefferson as president in 1800. The coming to power of this democratic theorist—the chief author of the Declaration of Independence—ended an era of aristocratic ascendancy under Presidents Washington and Adams. Although the rich and the wellborn raised a cry of anguish at the triumph of Jefferson, he was really a moderate man. It was not so much his radical acts as president but his democratic attitudes and principles that made his administration significant. The third president was a scholarly philosopher of liberty and democracy, not a rabble rouser. The toiling masses never felt comfortable around the elegant Virginian.

The first real man of the people to take the helm of the young republic was Andrew Jackson. A rawboned dueler, Indian fighter, and militia commander, Jackson rose from poverty to leadership on the Tennessee frontier. He emerged as the hero of the War of 1812. Without formal education Old Hickory possessed natural qualities of leadership and a flair for vote-getting. His election to the presidency in 1828 is often referred to as a revolution. However, the revolution of 1828, like that of 1800, was not so much a matter of deeds as of attitudes and spirit. The people's champion did attack and destroy the greatest concentration of private capital in the country, the national bank. He also tackled and crushed such formidable political giants of a more conservative nature as John C. Calhoun and Henry Clay. But there were no radical measures. In the Jacksonian era democracy was advancing as new states without property qualifications for voting were rapidly being admitted to the Union and as the older states were eliminating property qualifications from their voting requirements. However, the property requirement had never been a serious limitation to democracy in America, since land was so plentiful and cheap that almost everybody was a property owner. The revolution of 1828 was a revolution only in the sense that for the first

time a man came to the White House whom the common people could consider one of their own number. Henceforth, if undemocratic men or causes should triumph in the United States, it would not be because of the system but because free men would fail to take the time and trouble to inform themselves of the issues and to go to the polls to vote.

Industrialization never constituted the threat to the laboring man in the United States that it did in Europe. Although here and there one could find mill and mine conditions in America that rivaled those in Europe, there was too much free land in nineteenth-century America to permit the machine owners to exploit the workers too much for too long. Therefore, when the industrial bourgeoisie gained the political ascendancy in the late 1860's as a result of the Civil War and the rapid growth of industry, it was able to establish the bourgeois liberalism of the European variety in only a limited way and for only a few decades.

The real blight on democracy in the United States was the existence of Negro slavery in the Southern states. This curse not only cast a shadow over the whole American scene but threatened the life of the nation itself. However, this story belongs to the next chapter.

4. The Bourgeois Monarchy and the Revolution of 1848 in France

The rise of liberalism on the continent of Europe was much more turbulent than in Great Britain and the United States. Here industrialization occurred later than in Great Britain, and the forces of privilege and reaction were more strongly entrenched than in the United States.

The Industrial Revolution came to France during the reign of Louis Philippe, 1830–48. This member of the house of Orléans had been placed on the throne by the Parisian middle classes after the tyrannical Charles X, the last of the Bourbons, had been overthrown in the Revolution of 1830. Louis Philippe, recognizing that a new era of middle-class dominance had come to France, catered to this class. He assumed the role of the "Citizen King," casting aside the trappings of royalty and donning those of the Parisian bourgeoisie. His eighteen-year reign came to be called the bourgeois monarchy. His twofold policy, from which he never veered, was order and prosperity at home and peace abroad. One of his first acts was to lower the tax-paying require-ments for voting from 300 francs ($60) to 200 francs ($40) per year. This raised the electorate from approximately 100,000 to 250,000 in a nation of some 32,000,000 people and placed political control firmly in the hands of the middle class. Louis Phi-lippe's chief minister during the last eight years of his reign was François Guizot, one of the most eminent historians and teachers France has ever produced. Guizot was en-tirely to the liking of Louis Philippe in his domestic and foreign policies. He was a thoroughgoing liberal of the pre-1870 bour-geois variety. He believed in government by the property-owning classes, particularly the bourgeoisie. He, therefore, opposed any fur-ther extension of the suffrage, even to mem-bers of the intelligentsia like himself. Meanwhile, France continued to prosper, as the government pursued its policy of or-der and peace and encouragement to grow-ing industry.

Underneath, however, things were not going so smoothly as appeared on the sur-face. The national prosperity was not shared by the industrial proletariat, suffer-ing the usual hardships, insecurity, and maladjustments that always accompanied the advent of industrialization. Slums mushroomed in Paris and the industrial cities of the northeast. The distressed pro-letariat clamored for the right to vote and the right to organize unions, but got nei-ther. The growing discontent centered around the first minister. Guizot, a Prot-estant, was busily establishing a system of secular education in a Roman Catholic country. Even the policy of peace was be-coming tiresome to a people used to na-tional glamour and heroics. By 1847 the

mounting discontent began to express itself in a series of reform banquets, at which ora-tors demanded parliamentary and electoral reforms. Still almost no one anticipated a revolution.

The climax came in February 1848, when the government prohibited the holding of a banquet of ominous proportions. Street brawling broke out in Paris. Louis Philippe attempted to quiet the mob by dismissing the hated Guizot, but the appeasement failed. A shot fired during a brawl between a mob and the troops guarding the residence of Guizot unnerved the troops, who fired a murderous volley into the mob and set off a full-scale insurrection. Barricades flew up all over Paris, and when the disaffected na-tional guardsmen began going over to the rebels, Louis Philippe followed Guizot into exile in England.

The Paris proletariat had triumphed, but only for a fleeting moment. A group of bourgeois liberals hastily set up a provi-sional government in which the only prom-inent radical member was the socialist Louis Blanc. The provisional government immediately called for the election by uni-versal manhood suffrage of an assembly to draw up a new constitution. Under the pressure of the Paris proletariat the provi-sional government admitted the working-men to the national guard, thereby arming them, and set up emergency-relief national workshops. The workshops, however, were a parody on those outlined by Louis Blanc, who cried that they were deliberately planned so as to assure their failure. Work-ers of all kinds were paid forty cents a day to work on hastily arranged projects, and when more workers enrolled than could be used, the surplus workers were paid thirty cents a day to remain idle. Loafers and un-employed of all kinds, of course, rushed in by tens of thousands to receive the thirty cents. The resulting demoralization of la-bor and cost to the taxpayers thoroughly frightened all property owners, the peasants as well as the bourgeoisie. The elections held in April 1848 resulted in an over-whelming victory for the conservative republicans and limited monarchists—thanks to the conservatism of the landowning peasants, who constituted the great majority of the French population. The socialists were crushed. Even in Paris, their only real stronghold, they won a mere handful of seats.

One of the first acts of the newly elected constitutional assembly was to abolish the national workshops. The workers were told either to join the army or to go look for work in the provinces. The desperate Paris proletariat flew to arms and the barricades. "Better to die from bullets than from starvation!" For three days all-out war raged in the streets of Paris between the proletariat, armed with national-guard rifles, and the regular army of the conservative constitutional assembly, using artillery in addition to small arms. When the last barricade had been beaten down, several thousand, mostly workingmen, had been killed. More thousands were sent overseas to French colonial prisons. Louis Blanc fled to Great Britain. The bloody "June Days" widened the cleavage between radical urban Paris and conservative rural France—a cleavage that has long complicated France's public life.

The inexperienced constitutional assembly hurriedly drew up a constitution establishing the Second French Republic. (The First French Republic had been declared by the revolutionists in 1792 and had been overthrown by Napoleon in 1804.) Legislative power was given to a single-chamber legislature elected by universal manhood suffrage. All executive and administrative powers were placed in the hands of a president, also elected by universal manhood suffrage. The April elections had shown that in nineteenth-century France, with her millions of conservative landowning peasants, private property need not fear universal manhood suffrage. No system of checks and balances between the two branches of government was provided. The first presidential election, in December 1848, resulted in a sweeping victory for Louis Napoleon Bonaparte, nephew of Napoleon Bonaparte, as president. It took this ambitious adventurer only three years to destroy the weak constitution and to establish himself as dictator. As dictator, however, and later as emperor Louis Napoleon would carefully nurture the interests of the property-owning bourgeoisie and peasantry.

The Revolution of 1848 in France was the first violent reaction of the industrial proletariat against bourgeois liberalism. The proletariat was too small as yet to make any headway outside of Paris. The revolution shattered against the solid mass of landowning peasantry allied with the propertied bourgeoisie. Its bloody suppression left a heritage of proletarian bitterness that would cloud the future of France.

5. The Revolution of 1848 in Central Europe

The February explosion in Paris set Central Europe aflame with revolt. However, the Revolution of 1848 in Central Europe was quite different from that in France. The Revolution of 1848 in France was a revolt of the Paris industrial proletariat led by intellectual radicals against the bourgeois liberalism that had been dominant since 1830. The Revolution of 1848 in Central Europe was a rising of the intelligentsia and the middle classes with a little support from the proletariat against the aristocracy and royalty. In 1848 the Industrial Revolution was just coming to Central Europe; the industrial bourgeoisie and proletariat were both few and weak. Their role in the liberal movement was secondary to that of the intelligentsia—chiefly university professors, students, and journalists. Furthermore, in 1848 the cause of liberalism in Central Europe was mixed up with that of nationalism. The two forces frequently conflicted with each other, nationalism proving to be the more virile of the two. Both causes failed for the time being, and the story of their failure can be told here only in brief and general terms.

The most crucial center of revolution was Vienna. This beautiful metropolis was the seat of the Hapsburg government, which not only ruled over the various language groups of the Austrian Empire but dominated both the German Confederation and Italy. When early in March 1848 news of the events in Paris arrived in Vienna, the long-repressed university-student liberals began rioting in the streets and clamoring for an end to the Metternich system. As the uprising gained in momentum, Metternich was forced to flee for his life. The Hapsburg emperor, Ferdinand I, hastily abolished the repressive laws and promised constitutional representative government. However, he too was soon forced to flee his own capital. Meanwhile the Magyars in Hungary, under the leadership of the eloquent Louis Kossuth, set up a liberal autonomous Hungary. The Czechs did the same in Bohemia and called for a Pan-Slavic congress to meet at Prague. In Austria's Italian provinces of Lombardy and Venetia the rebellious populace drove the Austrian garrisons into defensive fortresses and declared their independence. Most of the other Italian states adopted liberal constitutions and prepared to dispatch troops to the aid of Lombardy and Venetia. By June 1848, it appeared that the Hapsburg Empire would become liberalized, fall apart along national (language group) lines, or both.

In Berlin, the capital of Prussia, the news from Paris and Vienna set the liberals demonstrating in the streets. The well-meaning but vacillating Hohenzollern king, Frederick William IV, promised a liberal constitution and support for German national unity. As in Paris an unauthorized volley into the mob set off bloody street fighting, which the king ended by making further concessions to the liberals. Hohenzollern Prussia, like Hapsburg Austria, appeared for the moment to be on the road to liberal popular government.

Meanwhile, in the rest of the German states, a group of self-appointed liberals called for a popularly elected assembly to meet at Frankfurt for the purpose of constructing a liberal and united German nation. This was a task so formidable that no one then or since has been able to accom-

plish it.[1] The drawing up of a code of individual rights and liberties for a people who had never known any was itself a time-consuming undertaking. The two questions confronting the Frankfurt Assembly were whether the German-speaking portions of the multilingual Hapsburg Empire should be included in the projected German nation, and who should head the new nation. Tied in with the Austrian question was that of religion. With Austria (and Bohemia, which was alleged to be predominantly German) the Roman Catholics would predominate, and without Austria and Bohemia the Protestants. For eleven precious months these knotty problems were debated. Eventually Austria virtually excluded herself by refusing to consider coming into the new German nation without her non-German provinces. By a narrow margin it was decided to offer the emperorship to the king of Prussia. But now it was too late. The situation in Vienna and Berlin had drastically changed.

In Austria the inexperience and weakness of the liberals and the rivalries and conflicts among the various language groups played into the hands of the Hapsburgs. Skillfully playing off one language group against another, the Austrian rulers beat down the liberal and national revolts one after the other. In Hungary they had the help of the reactionary Nicholas I of Russia, whose army crushed the rebels. In Italy a united effort of the various states failed to materialize. Only the kingdom of Sardinia sent significant aid to Lombardy and Venetia. Austrian arms easily prevailed. Everywhere in Italy except in the kingdom of Sardinia liberalism and nationalism were crushed.

In Prussia, too, the liberals were weak and inexperienced. The unstable Frederick William IV, after his first uncertainty,

[1] The Weimar Republic, 1919–33, was liberal but was virtually forced upon Germany by the victorious World War I Allies, who refused to make peace with the Hohenzollern Empire, and it lasted little more than a decade. (See Chapters 54 and 56.)

gradually fell under the influence of his militaristic and reactionary Junker advisers. Further stiffened by the news from Vienna that the Hapsburgs had regained their autocratic position, he spurned the German crown offered him by the Frankfurt Assembly and replaced the constitution drawn up by Prussian liberals with one that was a travesty of liberalism. The Hohenzollerns' rejection of the crown of a united liberal Germany blasted the hopes of the Frankfurt Assembly. When a few of the most determined attempted to continue their efforts, they were dispersed by Prussian troops. Many of the discouraged German liberals fled to America and became known as the Forty-eighters. Some of them, like Carl Schurz, played a distinguished role in liberal causes. The failure of the liberals to unite Germany in 1848 may be explained in large measure by the weakness of the industrial bourgeoisie and proletariat, which were as yet few in number. When the Industrial Revolution did make its influence seriously felt in Central Europe after mid-century, nationalism rather than liberalism would be its chief beneficiary.

6. Emancipation in Russia

Russia remained untouched by the Industrial Revolution and bourgeois liberalism in the period 1830–70, when these two forces were triumphing in Western Europe and emerging in Central Europe. Her few liberal reforms at this time came at the hands of the benevolent tsar, Alexander II (1855–81). Most noteworthy of his acts was the emancipation of the serfs, who constituted a majority of Russia's population. This was done in 1861—one year before President Lincoln issued his Emancipation Proclamation in the United States. The serfs did not get their lands free. The land was given over to collective groups called mirs, and the ex-serfs were compelled to pay the government redemption dues for a period of forty-nine years. Since they received only the poorest lands, their economic condition was really worse than before. Alexander decreed some legal and administrative reforms, but for the most part these became dead letters in the hands of hostile administrators. In the absence of political and social liberalization such as that which could be seen in Western Europe, Russia's intelligentsia tended to become defeatist and violent. The resulting nihilism and terrorism were direct antecedents to Russia's twentieth-century upheavals.

The first phase of the Industrial Revolution, 1830–70, then, was marked by the continued advance of democracy in the United States, the triumph of bourgeois liberalism in Great Britain and France, and the beginnings of moderate liberalism in Central Europe. Eastern Europe and the rest of the world were not yet directly affected by industrialization or the bourgeois liberalism that always followed in its wake.

----●◆●----

SUGGESTED READING

E. L. Woodward, *The Age of Reform, 1815–1870* (1938). A scholarly and somewhat detailed account of this important period in British history.

* John Stuart Mill, *Utilitarianism, Liberty, and Representative Government* (Everyman's Library). Probably the strongest contemporary statement of mid-nineteenth-century liberalism.

W. P. Hall, *Mr. Gladstone* (1931). A well-written biography of Great Britain's chief nineteenth-century liberal leader.

* Charles Dickens, *David Copperfield* (Modern Library, college edition). Immortal novel depicting English mid-nineteenth-century bourgeois society.

Claude Bowers, *Jefferson and Hamilton, the Struggle for Democracy in America* (1925). The liberal Jefferson is the hero of this dramatically written history.

A. M. Schlesinger, Jr., *The Age of Jackson* (1945). This book combines sound scholarship with fine writing. It portrays the triumph of common-man democracy in the United States.

D. W. Brogan, *The French Nation, from Na-*

poleon to Pétain, 1814–1946 (1957). A lively account by one of the best-informed historians of modern France.

Albert Guérard, *French Civilization in the Nineteenth Century* (1914). A thoughtful and gracefully written brief analysis.

Alexis de Tocqueville, *Recollections* (1896). Memoirs of one of France's most perceptive nineteenth-century intellects.

Arnold Whitridge, *Men in Crisis, the Revolutions of 1848* (1949). An interesting study of the 1848 struggle for liberalism in France and Central Europe, centered around the leading personalities in the upheaval.

Heinrich von Treitschke, *History of Germany in the 19th Century,* 7 vols. (1919). A monumental study of German history in the nineteenth century to 1848, by an ardent Prussian nationalist. The ambitious student will find this challenging and surprisingly readable.

CHAPTER 45

The Development of Nationalism in France and the United States

ONE of the most dynamic forces in the world of the nineteenth and twentieth centuries is nationalism. The variety of nationalism that we have known in the last century and a half was born in the French Revolution and nurtured by the Industrial Revolution. Until around 1870 it was relatively moderate and closely associated with liberalism. Since 1870 it has tended to become malignant and aggressive, ofttimes at war with liberalism. Before 1870 it was limited for the most part to Europe and America. Since 1870 it has spread to Asia and Africa without losing in any wise its vigor in the West.

1. The Nature of Nationalism

Nationalism may be defined as a feeling of loyalty to one's country. What are the essential factors that contribute to this feeling? What makes a German a German or a Pole a Pole even when there is no German or Polish national state?

By far the most important factor is language. Language is so basic to a people's culture that it is often mistaken for race. For instance one sometimes hears of the various races of the Austrian Empire, and the language groups there themselves often considered themselves racial groups, although it is impossible to establish anything

more than a cultural identity based largely on language. Language brings people together in understanding and separates them from those they cannot understand. Probably second in importance is a historical tradition of unity. The Belgians with their two languages and the Swiss with their three languages and two religions illustrate the importance of this factor. Religion can be a powerful factor, too, though not so important as language. The German Empire with its common language came and held together in spite of a serious religious cleavage, and the Austrian Empire fell apart along language lines in spite of a common religion and a long tradition of unity under the Hapsburgs. (In the long run, of course, religion may prove to be a more enduring force in history than nationalism itself.) Territorial compactness and natural boundaries are frequently contributing factors in nationalism.

The first group loyalty was probably to family, tribe, and clan, and to the territory occupied by them; then to language dialect groups. Loyalty to one's own kin and close associates and to the scenes of one's childhood is a natural thing. Loyalty to a large group or area like France or the United States requires conscious education. In Europe in the thirteenth, fourteenth, and fifteenth centuries the kings of France, England, Spain, and Portugal, aided by the rising middle class and by the ascendancy of one dialect over the others, created by conquest and consolidation the first four national states. Until the French Revolution, however, national loyalty was chiefly centered upon the ruling monarch or dynasty and was limited for the most part to the educated upper classes who participated in the government of the nation. The French Revolution gave birth to a new and more virile kind of nationalism. The establishment of equal rights and popular representative government, together with the abolition of old provincial boundary lines, brought the masses of people into direct partnership with the national government. Universal conscription into the revolutionary armies, which were raised first to save France from the invaders and later to spread abroad the blessings of the French Revolution, gave the people a sense of fraternity in a righteous cause—a crusade. Nationalism became a religion. Such mass dynamism made the revolutionary and Napoleonic armies irresistible. Nationalism soon spread to the other peoples of Europe. Since the French Revolution nationalism has been an ever-expanding force, increasing in scope as more and more people become aware of and participate in national affairs, and increasing in power as science and technology provide the national patriots with the tools to achieve their nationalistic purposes.

2. The Second Empire of Napoleon III: Years of Success, 1852–59

Nationalism was both used and advanced by Napoleon III of France, the most influential figure in world affairs from 1848 to 1870. Louis Napoleon Bonaparte was the nephew of Napoleon Bonaparte. His father was Louis Bonaparte, younger brother of Napoleon and king of Holland. His mother was Hortense, daughter of Napoleon's first wife, Josephine Beauharnais. After the overthrow of his father and his uncle young Louis Napoleon lived in Switzerland, Germany, and Italy, a political exile from France. Very early

he developed ideas of grandeur, particularly after the death of Napoleon's only son in 1832 left him the head of the Bonaparte Dynasty. On two occasions, in 1836 and again in 1840, the ambitious young adventurer attempted revolutions against the government of Louis Philippe. Both attempts were ludicrous failures. After the second attempt he was placed in prison, where he spent six years writing propaganda tracts. In 1846 he escaped to Britain. The Revolution of 1848 presented the tireless schemer with his great opportunity. Using his illustrious name with consummate skill and appealing to all classes of Frenchmen, he was overwhelmingly elected president of the Second French Republic. For the next twenty-two years Louis Napoleon was to dominate the world stage. The first eleven of those twenty-two years were years of spectacular success. Everything "the man of destiny" touched seemed to turn to gold. Then he lost his magic touch. The last eleven years of his life were years of decline, culminating in disaster for himself and for France.

No sooner had Louis Napoleon taken the oath as president, swearing to uphold and defend the constitution of the republic, than he started working to destroy it and make himself emperor. A gifted politician, he managed to take credit for all popular measures and to push the blame for all unpopular acts of government onto the reactionary and leaderless legislative body. By judicious appointments and dismissals he soon filled all key military and civilian administrative offices with his own supporters. A master showman, he posed as a friend of the urban and rural masses. The bourgeoisie liked his stand for law and order. He made a particularly firm alliance with the Roman Catholic Church by sending French troops to restore the pope to his throne, from which he had been driven by the Italian revolutionists of 1848, and by helping the Church regain control of French education. After three years of careful preparation Louis Napoleon seized dictatorial powers for himself in an almost bloodless *coup d'état* on December 2, 1851. The few courageous liberals such as Adolph Thiers and Victor Hugo, who attempted to save the republic, were quietly arrested and deported. Exactly one year later the French president had himself crowned Emperor Napoleon III. (Napoleon Bonaparte's son, who died in 1832 without having ruled, was declared to be Napoleon II.) It would appear that a great majority of the French people approved the deed.

Napoleon III considered himself heir to the spirit of Napoleon Bonaparte, who, he claimed, was a true child of the French Revolution. The new Napoleon believed in government by a powerful tribune (himself) based upon the popular will. This tribune would rise above all parties and rally all factions in a vigorous and benevolent program. Napoleon III was a supreme nationalist, seeking at all times to enhance the prestige of the French nation at home and abroad. The government of the Second Empire was actually a veiled dictatorship. All power, civilian and military, judicial and legislative, as well as executive, resided in the emperor. The veil was a legislative body elected by universal manhood suffrage. By manipulating the electoral machinery, by official pressure, and by a system of official candidates Napoleon III was able to control the elections. The legislative body had no control over the ministry. It could not even initiate legislation, this function being performed by the Council of State, appointed by the emperor. On occasion the emperor would seek the "advice" of the people by means of a plebescite. In many ways Napoleon III was the first dictator of the kind we have come to know in the twentieth century.

The second Napoleon was an economic liberal in the pre-1870 sense. He encouraged and dramatized the rapid expansion of the Industrial Revolution in France. Two giant investment banking corporations, the Crédit Mobilier and the Crédit Foncier, mobilized huge sums of capital that were poured into industry, railroads, and real estate. The Bank of France was expanded until each of the country's eighty-six departments (three in Algeria) had at least one branch. The emperor's free-trade policies culminated in the Cobden Treaty with Great Britain, 1860, which lowered the tariff on British manufactures in return for lower British rates on French products, of which wine was the most important. This was the heyday of the French industrial and financial bourgeoisie, which amassed great fortunes, sometimes, as in other countries, by means that would not bear inspection.

The urban proletariat was not overlooked by the benevolent dictator. Hospitals, nurseries, and homes for the aged were built. Although prices were rising steadily with the general prosperity, the price of bread for the wage earners was kept low by government subsidies. A system of voluntary social insurance was instituted for workingmen. Co-operatives were encouraged, and labor unions with limited rights to strike were partially legalized for the first time. The peasants were aided by free trade, more and better roads, railroads, canals, the draining of swamps, and the study and practice of scientific breeding. The landowning farmers liked the law and order and sacredness of private property.

All classes, except the liberal republicans, loved the return of court glamour. Banquets, parades, balls, and spectacles kindled memories of a glorious Gallic past—of Louis XIV and the first Napoleon. Under the guidance of Baron Haussmann, Paris was rebuilt into the world's most beautiful city. In Napoleon III's reign its population increased from approximately one million to two million. At the center of the court of the Second Empire was the glamorous Empress Eugénie. When Louis Napoleon usurped the French throne, his prospects were held in such low esteem that no royal family in Europe would furnish him a wife. In 1853 he married the Spanish Eugénie de Montijo, of noble but not royal rank. Although she was never popular with the French people, the world of fashion and royalty was soon deferring to her. Paris has remained the world's style capital ever since. In 1855 thousands of Europe's great, including

NAPOLEON III AND EMPRESS EUGÉNIE. From 1848 to 1870 Napoleon III was the most influential man in the world. Enigmatic and sphinx-like, his true character and motives are still debated. As he grew older and his health failed he came more and more under the influence of his glamorous Spanish wife, the Empress Eugénie, who strongly favored the war with Prussia in 1870 which proved disastrous to the Second Empire and to France. (*The Bettmann Archive*)

Queen Victoria, attended Napoleon's Paris Exposition to view the marvels of the Second Empire.

The peak of France's revived national prestige was reached during the Crimean War, 1854–56. Like his uncle the second Napoleon was not satisfied with spectacular domestic achievements. He yearned for farther fields to conquer. His opportunity came when Tsar Nicholas I of Russia attempted to dismember the Ottoman Empire, "the sick man of Europe," and to achieve Rus-

sia's historic goal: Constantinople and access to the world through the Turkish Straits. France did not relish the prospect of an ambitious new rival in the Mediterranean. (Great Britain, with her vast holdings and interests in the Near and Far East, was even more sensitive to this threat than was France.) A second source of Franco-Russian conflict arose when the tsar, as the great champion of Orthodox Christianity, attempted to gain a protectorate over all Christians in the Ottoman Empire and over the Christian holy places in the Turkish province of Palestine. France had been since the Crusades the leading champion of Roman Catholic interests in the Near East, including the Christian shrines in the Holy Land. And Napoleon III's strongest ally in France was the Roman Church. The Crimean War is sometimes spoken of as a purely useless and trivial war. In a sense all wars are useless, but in Russia's quest for an outlet through Constantinople, the rivalry of the great powers for control of the strategic Middle East, and the conflict between Orthodox and Roman Catholic Christianity we have three of the most stubborn and enduring issues in history—issues that are still with us. A fourth issue was personal and national. Nicholas I alone of the European monarchs had refused to recognize the French usurper as an equal.

In 1853 the Russian army and navy suddenly attacked the Turks. Early the next year Great Britain and France sent their naval and military forces into the Black Sea and laid siege to Russia's naval base, Sebastopol, on the Crimean Peninsula. Sardinia came into the war to gain the friendship of France and Great Britain. Austria maintained a hostile, and Prussia a friendly, neutrality toward Russia. The war was fought with gross inefficiency on both sides. The only real hero was the British nurse Florence Nightingale, whose efforts helped to inspire the creation of the International Red Cross eight years later (1864). Nicholas I died in 1855, humiliated by the knowledge that his creaking military machine was going to fail. The Peace of Paris in 1856 prohibited Russia's naval forces on the Black Sea and maintained the integrity of the Ottoman Empire. The autonomy of Serbia and the Romanian provinces of Moldavia and Wallachia under the suzerainty of Turkey was guaranteed by the great powers. The Roman Catholics were left in control of their shrines in the Holy Land. Great Britain at long last agreed to neutral rights on the high seas. The chief immediate beneficiary of the Crimean War was Napoleon III. His troops had fought better than the Russians or the British. He played host to the peace conference, which, of course, he made a colorful spectacle. French national patriotism was now at fever pitch and French prestige abroad at its highest point since the days of the Sun King, Louis XIV. Nationalism itself received a real boost as other peoples observed its success in France.

3. The Second Empire of Napoleon III: Years of Failure, 1859–70

By 1859 the second Napoleon had obtained, not only the loyalty of the great majority of his own people, but also a clear hegemony in the affairs of the European continent. France was prosperous and powerful. Then things began to go wrong. The emperor seemed to lose his magic touch. Suffering from a painful physical ailment (diagnosed as a stone in the bladder), he aged prematurely. The dynamic force of nationalism, which he understood and used so well in France, he greatly underestimated abroad. In his efforts to control the Italian and German national movements he failed dismally—in the latter case fatally.

The first serious blunder of Napoleon III came in 1859, when he made war on Austria in behalf of Italian freedom. (The details of this war belong to the following chapter.) The defeat of Austria set off a frenzy of Italian nationalism that threatened to dispossess all the rulers of the local states of Italy, including the pope. This alarmed and angered the French Roman Catholics, who blamed Napoleon. But when the French emperor deserted the Sardinians in the midst of the campaign, with the agreed-upon job only half done, he further alienated the French liberals, who were already unsympathetic to him.

The booming prosperity subsided after 1860. The Cobden Treaty, signed in that year, flooded France with cheap British manufactured goods with which the less advanced French industries could not compete. The French textile industry also suffered heavily as a result of the American Civil War, which cut off its cotton supply. Both the industrial bourgeoisie and proletariat were hard hit. Overexpansion and speculation began to take their toll.

One of Napoleon's most grandiose projects, one that brought much woe to France then and later, was the restoration of an overseas empire. The French have been conspicuously inept at colonial imperialism. For one thing the French people have always shown a marked disinclination to leave *la belle France* and make their homes elsewhere. The few who have gone to the French colonies have usually gone, not as colonists, but as governors, adventurers, and exploiters. And more often than not they have been royally hated by the natives. During the Second Empire the conquest and annexation of Algeria, begun by Louis Philippe, was completed. French influence was extended in Syria, Senegal, and China. The seizure of Indo-China was begun. Numerous islands in the Southwest Pacific were acquired. These aggrandizements, though adding to the national ego and prestige, brought France little immediate profit and much trouble.

By far the most ambitious of Napoleon's imperial schemes and the most momentous failure was the attempted conquest and annexation of Mexico. In 1855 the corrupt Mexican dictator, Santa Anna, backed by the military, the big landowners, and the Roman Catholic Church, was overthrown by the democratic liberals under the leadership of the gifted native Indian, Benito Juárez. The Juárez regime instituted sweeping reforms in behalf of individual civil liberties. It attacked all special privilege, particularly the privileges of the Roman Catholic Church, whose vast lands were confiscated. And as an emergency measure it suspended for two years the payment of interest on foreign debts.

This last measure presented Napoleon III with his opportunity. Joining with the other two chief creditors, Great Britain and Spain, he seized several Mexican ports in 1862, ostensibly to collect the debts. As soon as the British and the Spaniards saw that Napoleon had more ambitious plans in mind, they withdrew. The French armies then marched on to Mexico City, drove the Juárez government into the hinterland, and set up a Hapsburg prince, Maximilian, as puppet emperor for France. The government of the United States protested vigorously in the name of the Monroe Doctrine, but, embroiled in its own Civil War, it could only protest. As soon as the Civil War ended early in 1865 the American government dispatched victorious Union troops to the Mexican border. Napoleon III, now hard pressed at home, agreed to withdraw his troops. No sooner had the last French soldiers left Mexico City in 1867 than the Juárez forces captured and shot the well-meaning puppet, Emperor Maximilian. The Mexican fiasco greatly added to the growing unpopularity of Napoleon III with the French people.

More serious was the fact that the Mexican venture tied Napoleon's hands while events of grave consequence to France were occurring across the Rhine. The story of Bismarck's creation of the mighty German Empire will be told in the following chapter. Here it is necessary to relate only that Napoleon completely misjudged the situation, was repeatedly outsmarted by Bismarck, and when he attempted to retard the rapid growth of Prussia and to offset it by annexing Luxemburg, Belgium, and the left bank of the Rhine, he was helpless in the face of Prussian military power, since the best part of his own armies was in Mexico.

The distracted emperor attempted to al-

lay the mounting discontent of the liberals. Beginning in 1859, he made one concession after another to liberal parliamentary government until by 1870 the Second Empire was on paper, at least, a limited constitutional monarchy similar to that of Great Britain. But 1870 was too late. The showdown with Bismarck's rapidly forming German nation was at hand. The sick and discouraged Napoleon III blundered into a war with Germany for which his armies were woefully unprepared (see p. 548). He was defeated and captured, and his government was overthrown.

4. The Rapid Expansion of the United States

Between 1800 and 1870 the United States was the most rapidly growing nation in the world, both in area and in population. The purchase of the Louisiana Territory by Thomas Jefferson from Napoleon in 1803 for some $16,000,000 doubled the original area of the United States. In 1819 Florida was purchased from Spain for $5,000,000 (after two little chunks of west Florida had been seized in 1810 and 1813). Texas, which was even bigger then than now, was annexed in 1845. The next year the Oregon Country, including the present states of Oregon, Washington, and Idaho, was annexed after the settlement of a long-standing dispute with Great Britain. The annexation of Texas resulted in a war with Mexico, 1846–48. After a quick and easy victory the United States took a huge block of Mexican territory, comprising the present states of California, Arizona, New Mexico, Nevada, Utah, and parts of Colorado and Wyoming. This territory was enlarged to the south in 1853 by the Gadsden Purchase from Mexico ($10,000,000). These additions within a period of fifty years more than trebled the original territory of the young American nation.

Meanwhile, the growth in population was keeping pace with the increase in area. Between 1800 and 1870 the population of the United States increased from approximately

5,000,000 to 40,000,000. Added to the high rate of natural increase was an ever-increasing tide of immigration from Europe. After 1840 the largest immigrant groups were the Irish, most of whom settled in the cities of the Northeast, and the Germans, most of whom pushed on to the fertile lands of the Middle West. The absorption and Americanization of these millions of conflicting national groups are one of the miracles of nineteenth-century nationalism.

The War of 1812 with Great Britain, sometimes called the Second War for Independence, resulted in an upsurge of American national spirit. A new crop of nationally minded statesmen arose, the ablest of whom were Henry Clay, John C. Calhoun, and Daniel Webster. Even more dramatic was Andrew Jackson, a symbol of the rugged American frontier. The Western frontier itself was one of the greatest of the nationalizing influences. To it came people from all the seaboard states and from abroad who looked to the national government rather than to the states for protection, for roads and canals, and for land titles. Chief Justice John Marshall and Justice Joseph Story handed down from the Supreme Court bench opinion after opinion establishing the authority of the national government over the states.

It was in this period also that American culture began to free itself from strictly European influences. The American Indian began to be idealized by Henry Wadsworth Longfellow and James Fenimore Cooper. Washington Irving's pen made the legends of American colonial days enchanting. Gilbert Stuart and Charles Wilson Peale glamorized the portraits of American heroes. Probably the greatest nationalist influence of all was the little red schoolhouse, where rich and poor, German and Pole mingled and learned the American version of civilization and world affairs.

5. The Struggle Over Slavery

Over the world's most democratic and rapidly growing nation, however, hung a dark cloud that grew more menacing until it produced a destructive and well-nigh-fatal storm. This cloud was the growing national cleavage over the existence in the Southern states of Negro slavery. Slavery was totally incompatible with American ideals and traditions. By the beginning of the nineteenth century slavery had been banished from European society, although serfdom remained in the Hapsburg territories until 1848 and in Russia until 1861.

The first boatload of Negroes was brought to Virginia in 1619, one year before the Pilgrims landed at Plymouth Rock. Because of the tremendous amount of labor required to clear the American wilderness the African slave trade flourished throughout the colonial period. By the time of the American Revolution, Negro slaves constituted approximately one fifth of the total population of the thirteen colonies. Slavery was recognized and protected by the national constitution. Because of the climate and the diversified economy, however, slavery was proving to be unprofitable in the Northern states, and between 1777 and 1804 all of the states north of Maryland passed emancipation laws. South of the Mason and Dixon line (the boundary between Maryland and Pennsylvania), where agriculture reigned supreme, slavery continued to be profitable and prevalent. By 1789 most Americans, in the South as well as in the North, detested slavery. After the Revolution scores of antislavery societies were founded, the great majority of them in the South. It appeared that slavery in America was on its way to an early and peaceful end.

Some unforeseen developments, however, changed the attitude of the South toward emancipation, and a sharp line was drawn between the North and the South over the slavery issue. The first of these developments was Whitney's invention of the cotton gin in 1793. This machine made the raising of cotton so profitable that soon large cotton plantations worked by Negro slaves grew up throughout the South. The American South became the chief supplier of Britain's textile mills. Whereas in 1793 cotton exports from the United States were a mere trickle, by 1800 they had risen to over 30,000 five-hundred-pound bales valued at some $5,000,000. By 1859 they had risen to some 4,500,000 bales valued at over $200,000,000 —well over half the total value of American exports. At the same time the Negro population increased from some 700,000 in 1790 to nearly 4,000,000 in 1860, nearly all of it slave and all of the slaves in the South. By the mid-nineteenth century the Negro slaves outnumbered the whites in South Carolina and Mississippi, and in the rest of the deep South slaves were about equal in number to the whites. By 1830 the Southern economy had become so wedded to cotton and to Negro slavery that the Southern anti-slavery movement faltered and the defense of slavery was gaining momentum. Even more important than economic considerations in the development of pro-slavery sentiment in the South was the social problem. The Southern whites did not believe that they could absorb into their society or even live alongside so many free Negroes. Opposition to emancipation was even stronger among the poor whites than among the slaveowners.

This serious North-South cleavage over slavery was greatly aggravated in 1831 by the appearance in the North of a violent abolition movement under the leadership of William Lloyd Garrison and by an alarming slave insurrection in Virginia under the leadership of a Negro preacher, Nat Turner. By coincidence both of these events occurred in the same year. As Garrison's abolition movement gained momentum in the North, not without widespread opposition there, the South became increasingly frightened and angry. Every conceivable argument —from the Bible, history, Plato, Shakespeare, and the Constitution—was advanced to justify slavery. John C. Calhoun, the South's leading statesman and former extreme American nationalist, assumed the leadership of the Southern defense.

The showdown came over the extension of slavery to the Western territories. The population of the Northern states, with their growing industry, was rapidly outstripping that of the South. The immigrants pouring in from Europe avoided the slavery-ridden South almost to a man. The vast and fertile Northwest was filling up much more rapidly than the more limited Southwest; and whether the settlers in the Northwest came from the North or from Europe, they were determined to have none of slavery. As the Northwestern territories clamored for statehood, the Southerners took alarm. Already they were hopelessly outnumbered in the House of Representatives, whose membership is based upon population. Their only security in the national government lay in the Senate, where each state has two members. The Southerners did everything in their power to slow down the settlement of the West and insisted that the admission of every free state must be accompanied by the admission of a slave state in order that equality in the Senate be maintained. Henry Clay managed to stall off an open break by his Missouri Compromise in 1820 and by his compromise of 1850. But both measures were only makeshifts. Time and tide were on the side of the North. Geography, population, the growth of industrialization, and the march of liberalism in the Western world were irresistible. By 1852 the statesmen of moderation, Clay, Calhoun, and Webster, were dead, and younger and more uncompromising men came to power on both sides. In 1854 the Republican party was founded as a strictly Northern party committed to the restriction and ultimate extinction of slavery. In 1860, with Abraham Lincoln as its candidate, it won a sweeping victory over the Democrats, now split between North and South over the question of slavery. Lincoln's assurance that he would never molest slavery where it already existed but would only oppose its further extension offered little comfort for the South. The violent abolitionists were growing stronger in the North every day. The strictly Northern Republican party was now in power. What guarantee would the South have, once it lost its last stronghold, of equality in the Senate? Who would succeed Lincoln?

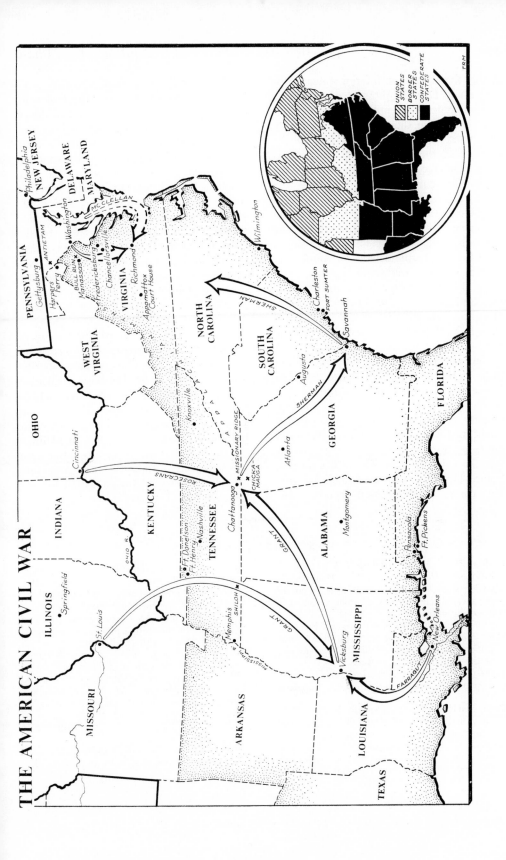

THE AMERICAN CIVIL WAR

Rather than accept an inferior status in the nation and face the prospect of eventually having some four million Negro slaves forcibly freed in their midst, eleven Southern states, constituting about half of the territory of the Union and a third of its population, seceded and set up their own independent government.

When it became clear that the Southern Confederacy meant to make the separation permanent, Lincoln proceeded to restore the Union by military force. The North had an overwhelming preponderance in population, wealth, industry, transportation, and naval power. But the South enjoyed brilliant military leadership and the further advantage of fighting on its own soil for what it belived to be the survival of its white civilization.

The war lasted four bloody years. For three of the four years it looked as if the Union could not be restored. Indeed, but for the genius, the character, and the personality of Lincoln it is possible that it might not have been restored. But after numerous discordant elements in the North were brought together, Great Britain and France tactfully neutralized, and the winning commanders and strategy found, the Southern armies were finally crushed.

Slavery was abolished and the Union restored, never to be seriously threatened again. However, the war left a legacy of sectional bitterness that was greatly deepened by the harsh policy of reconstruction followed by the victorious North. The conciliatory Lincoln was assassinated just five days after the war ended. The radical Republican congressional leaders, who now gained control of the government, treated the defeated and devastated South as a conquered province, forcing upon it twelve years of military occupation, political and economic exploitation, and Negro supremacy. In time, however, these wounds too healed over, but not entirely.

The victory of the North in the American Civil War was another great victory for nationalism. It was also a victory for the pre-1870 variety of liberalism, since it brought into power the Northern industrial bourgeoisie, who upon the death of Lincoln gained control of the now dominant Republican party. Thus in the United States, as in France, moderate nationalism and bourgeois liberalism joined hands during the first phase of the Industrial Revolution.

SUGGESTED READING

Carlton J. H. Hayes, *Historical Evolution of Modern Nationalism* (1931). A thought-provoking and gracefully written study of one of the most dynamic forces of modern times, by a leading authority on the subject.

Albert Guérard, *Napoleon III* (1943). Probably the best biography of the colorful French emperor who was the dominating personality of the mid-nineteenth century.

Philip Guedalla, *The Second Empire* (1922). A popularly written biography of Napoleon III.

Cecil Blanche Woodham-Smith, *Reason Why* (1954). A vivid and dramatic account and analysis of the Crimean War, centering on the charge of the Light Brigade. Combining good history with good writing, this is one of the few first-rate books on a war that seemed insignificant but that involved some of the most enduring problems in modern history. Mrs. Woodham-Smith has also written an excellent biography of Florence Nightingale.

Bernard De Voto, *Across the Wide Missouri* (1947). Dramatizes in a popular vein in westward expansion of the United States.

William E. Dodd, *The Cotton Kingdom* (1919). A little gem. A brilliant picture of life and thought in the American slave states.

George Fort Milton, *The Eve of Conflict* (1934). A readable and scholarly story of the issues and events leading to the American Civil War. The writer is a great admirer of Stephen A. Douglas.

Benjamin Thomas, *Lincoln* (1953). Probably the best single-volume biography of Lincoln. Lucidly written.

CHAPTER 46

The Triumph of Nationalism
in Italy and Germany

THE FAILURE of the Revolution of 1848 in Central Europe and the harsh repression that followed appeared to dash the hopes of liberalism and nationalism in both Italy and Germany. The forces of nationalism, however, were only stung to greater energy. Within a surprisingly short time after the disappointments of 1848 both the Italian and the German people were moving rapidly toward national unity.

1. Cavour Plans Italian Unity

Before 1848 three different plans for uniting Italy into a sovereign state had been proposed; each had its own following. One plan was to make Italy a liberal democratic republic. This was the plan of Giuseppe Mazzini, an inspiring speaker and writer but not a very practical organizer or man of action. His movement was called Young Italy. The second plan was to form an Italian confederacy under the leadership of the pope. The third plan was to make Italy a limited monarchy under the leadership of the house of Savoy, the ruling dynasty in the kingdom of Sardinia. During the Revolution of 1848 the first two plans were discredited. Mazzini's chaotic Roman Republic, which he set up after the rebellious populace had driven out the pope, outraged the Roman Catholic world and was over-thrown by a French army of Louis Napoleon. After this experience the pope bitterly opposed the unification of Italy, fearing that it would mean the loss of his political control over the Papal States.

On the other hand, the heroic role played by the kingdom of Sardinia in battling the Austrians against hopeless odds won for the house of Savoy the devotion and confidence of most Italian nationalists. However, the powerful Austrians were still in Lombardy and Venetia, the unsympathetic pope was still in the Papal States, and the rest of the Italian states were weak and divided. Despite the new prestige of Sardinia, therefore, the task of uniting Italy required the work of a genius. The genius soon appeared. He was Camillo Benso, Count di Cavour (1810–61).

Cavour was a member of a well-to-do noble family of Piedmont in the kingdom of Sardinia. (The kingdom of Sardinia was composed of Piedmont, the large island of Sardinia, and the little French-speaking provinces of Savoy and Nice.) Young Cavour showed such liberal tendencies that he was soon in trouble with both military and civilian authorities. Resigning his commission in the army, he traveled widely in Great Britain and France, where he developed great admiration for liberal constitutional monarchy. Back in Piedmont, Cavour proved himself to be an able businessman. He turned his ancestral estates into models of scientific agriculture and organized successful railroad and steamship companies and chemical and fertilizer factories. Shortly before the Revolution of 1848 he founded a newspaper *Il Risorgimento* (*The Resurrection*), which never ceased to preach Italian unity even through the discouragements of defeat. In 1850 the tireless Italian patriot was made minister of commerce and agriculture, and two years later prime minister of Sardinia.

CAVOUR. Count Camillo di Cavour, chief creator of the Italian nation, did not look impressive. A contemporary described him as a plump man with ill-fitting glasses and a myopic stare. Nor was he a good speaker; "I cannot make a speech," he once said, "but I can make Italy." And indeed, he was one of the most brilliant diplomats of all time. (*The Bettmann Archive*)

From the moment Cavour became prime minister in 1852 he devoted all of his prodigious energy to the seemingly impossible task of driving Austria out of Italy and creating a liberal Italian national monarchy. For seven years he strove to make Sardinia a model state that the others would be proud to follow. Though often sorely vexed by selfish political factions and tempted to use dictatorial methods, he carefully respected the liberal constitution that had been drawn up in 1848. On the economic front he applied his own private business efficiency to the economy of the state. Cavour was particularly interested in building railroads that ran through the various Italian states, believing that economic unity would facilitate political unity. The budget was balanced. Although taxes were high, the taxpayers were prosperous and confident that the tax money was being put to good use. The religious problem was a difficult one for Cavour. The numerous and powerful Roman Catholic clergy in Sardinia strongly opposed his liberal reforms and his plans for uniting Italy. Cavour, a nominal Roman Catholic, believed in "a free church in a free state." Special legal privileges for the clergy were abolished. The Jesuits were banished from Sardinia. Most of the monastic establishments were abolished and their properties confiscated. The remaining church property was made subject to taxation. Cavour, of course, could not have survived the clerical storm that followed had he not been sustained, as he was in all his measures, by his sovereign, King Victor Emmanuel II. Finally, the great minister built an efficient and, considering the size of the country, a large army.

Cavour saw clearly that little Sardinia, a state of less than five million people, could never defeat Austria alone. It must be done in alliance with a great power. Since Napoleon III's Second Empire was the only great power that might be interested, Cavour sent the efficient Sardinian army into the Crimean War in the hopes of winning French sympathy. The plan worked, and at the Paris Peace Conference in 1856 he was given an opportunity to state impressively to the world Italy's case against Austria. Also of help was Orsini, a fanatical Italian patriot, who attempted to assassinate Napoleon III in 1858. At his trial Orsini declared that other such attempts would be made in the future unless Napoleon helped Italy become united. The romantic French emperor, himself of Italian stock, was impressed. A few months later Napoleon met the Sardinian prime minister at Plombières, a French watering place, and there Cavour persuaded him to fight Austria. Sardinia would provoke Austria into a declaration of war; France would come in and help Sardinia drive the Austrians out of Lombardy and Venetia, which would then be annexed to the kingdom of Sardinia. In payment Sardinia would cede the two little French-speaking provinces of Savoy and Nice to France. Cavour left Plombières satisfied that his life's ambition was about to be accomplished.

2. The Making of the Italian Nation

When everything was in readiness in April 1859, Cavour easily provoked unsuspecting Austria into a declaration of war. To Austria's surprise French armies poured across the Alps to fight alongside the Sardinians. In the two bloody battles of Magenta and Solferino the Austrians were defeated and driven out of Lombardy. But, to the dismay of Cavour, Napoleon suddenly made a separate peace with Austria (the Agreement of Villafranca) on condition that Sardinia receive Lombardy but not Venetia. Napoleon appears to have been motivated by the surprising bloodiness of the battles, the threatening attitude of Prussia, who mobilized troops in the Rhineland, and the anger of the French Roman Catholics, who feared that the wild outburst of nationalism all over Italy following the victories over Austria threatened the independence of the Papal States.

Cavour, his hopes apparently dashed with victory within grasp, lost his poise for the only time in his life. He wanted to carry on the war alone to certain defeat but was restrained by King Victor Emmanuel. He

resigned but was soon recalled to his high post to direct the complex and fast-moving events. News of Magenta and Solferino set all Italy agog with nationalistic fervor. Early in 1860, under Cavour's behind-the-scenes direction, Tuscany, Modena, Parma, and Romagna (the northernmost of the Papal States) joined the kingdom of Sardinia, bringing together all of northern Italy except Venetia. However, with Austria in Venetia and French troops protecting the pope in central Italy, it looked as if the unification movement must now come to a halt.

At this juncture the rawboned Giuseppe Garibaldi, the most colorful of all the makers of the Italian nation, performed a daring exploit. With a thousand civilian warriors dressed in red shirts and slouch hats he sailed aboard two little ships from Piedmont. His goal was the conquest of the kingdom of the Two Sicilies, the largest and most populous of the Italian states, with a regular army of 100,000 men and a sizable navy. Cavour officially condemned the seemingly foolhardy expedition of the thousand but secretly aided it. Garibaldi's exploits read like a fairy story. He conquered the large island of Sicily, including Palermo, once the largest city in Europe, crossed the Strait of Messina, and entered triumphantly into Naples. The opposing troops, of course, had little heart for their cause and deserted to Garibaldi by the thousands after his first victories. Moving northward in the direction of Rome, Garibaldi defeated the last Neapolitan forces.

Fearful that the daring but undiplomatic Garibaldi would march on Rome and bring down the armies of Roman Catholic Europe and therefore ruin upon the rapidly forming Italian nation, Cavour made the last and most difficult great decision of his life. He sent the Sardinian army southward and seized all of the pope's remaining territory except the Patrimony of St. Peter (Rome and the territory immediately surrounding it). When Victor Emmanuel at the head of his army approached the forces of Gari-

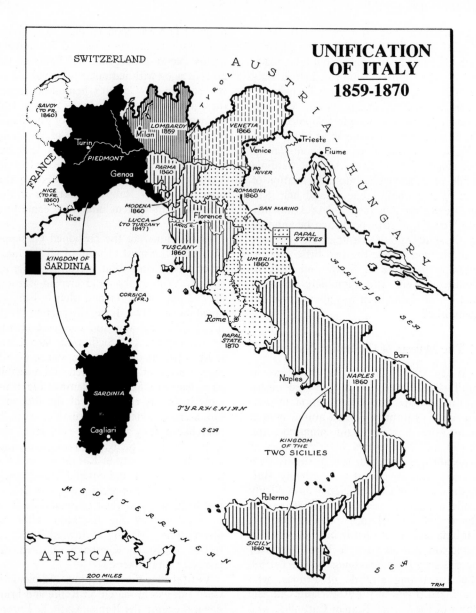

baldi, the gallant warrior and patriot submitted to his king and retired to the rocky
island of Caprera. The kingdom of Italy
was formally declared in March 1861, with
Victor Emmanuel II as king and the liberal
Sardinian Constitution of 1848 as the national charter. The red, white, and green
Sardinian flag now flew over all of Italy from
the Alps to Sicily except Venetia and Rome.
Those two provinces were not joined to the

Italian state until 1866 and 1870 respec-
tively, when, as we shall soon see, first
Austria and then France were defeated by
Prussia.

Cavour did not live to enjoy the fruits of
his labors. Less than three months after the
birth of his beloved Italian nation he was
dead, exhausted by his prodigious efforts
and achievements. Paunchy, with ill-fitting
glasses and a myopic stare, he was anything

but impressive in appearance. Neither was he an orator. "I cannot make a speech," he once truthfully said, "but I can make Italy." He was one of the greatest masters of diplomacy and statecraft of all time. The new nation was a monument to his genius and to the spirit of liberal nationalism.

3. The Hohenzollerns Assume the Leadership of a German National Movement

During the decade of the 1850's, after their defeats in 1848–49 both liberalism and nationalism began to make rapid headway in the Germanies. It was then that industrialization began to come more rapidly to the German states. In Prussia the rise of an industrial bourgeoisie and an industrial proletariat, both classes imbued with liberalism (of different hues) and nationalism, challenged for the first time the dominance of the Junker aristocracy, who abhorred liberalism (of all hues) and whose national loyalty was limited strictly to Prussia. It was also in the decade of the 1850's that the "Prussian School" of historians, Droysen, Sybel, and Treitschke, began to write their ponderous histories setting forth the German version of history. They were strongly influenced by the philosophy of Hegel (1770–1831), who had preached eloquently a version of history based on national cultures. Every epoch is characterized by a dominant spirit, said Hegel. The modern era belongs to the German spirit of liberty through disciplined order. Hegel, in turn, was undoubtedly influenced in part by the earlier German philosopher Herder (1744–1803). This was the beginning of the German master-race concept. The flowering of this superior German national culture required the political unity of the German people.

However, the experiences of 1848–49 had demonstrated that, without the support of Prussia and her autocratic rulers, the Hohenzollerns, a German national movement could not succeed. The conversion of the Hohenzollerns and the Prussian Junkers to German nationalism was facilitated by the

"Humiliation of Olmütz" in 1850. Shortly after the vacillating Frederick William IV had spurned the German national crown offered him by the Frankfurt Assembly in the spring of 1849, he attempted to reorganize the German Confederation under Prussian leadership. The Hapsburg government of Austria, now completely recovered from its embarrassments of 1848–49, mobilized its superior army and ordered him to cease. At the town of Olmütz in Austrian territory he abjectly yielded. After this the Hohenzollerns and more and more of the proud Junkers sought an opportunity to avenge the national insult to Prussia and replace Austria as leader of the Germanies.

In 1858 the unstable mind of Frederick William IV gave way, and his younger brother, who three years later became King William I, assumed the headship of the Prussian government as regent. Unlike his romantic and idealistic brother, William I was a typical Hohenzollern militarist. His first move was to rejuvenate and greatly strengthen the Prussian military machine. As minister of war he appointed an able organizer, Albrecht von Roon; and, as chief of staff, Helmuth von Moltke, one of the greatest strategists and tacticians of modern times. But their plans to make the Prussian army the most powerful military force in the world required large sums of money. The liberals, now strong in the Prussian Landtag, began to take alarm. Might not this all-powerful military machine be used to suppress liberalism? The liberals hoped that by holding up the military budget they might bargain for a stronger role for Parliament in the Prussian government. After several years of haggling the liberals in 1862 finally defeated the military budget. Liberalism and nationalism had come into head-on collision. William I, unskilled in and unsympathetic with parliamentary government, threatened to resign. As a last resort, on the advice of Roon and Moltke, he called to the chancellorship the one man who could and would force through the military program, Otto Eduard Leopold, Prince von Bismarck.

4. Bismarck Welds the North German Confederation

The man thus called to the head of the Prussian government at this critical time was to remain there for the next twenty-eight years. He stamped his iron will and his domineering personality, not only on Prussia and Germany, but also to a considerable degree on the rest of Europe and the world. Bismarck was a typical Prussian Junker. A blond giant with boundless energy, he was a firm believer in militarism and autocratic government. He had been a dueling, drinking university student, too restless for the academic life. Administrative work in the Prussian government had also failed

OTTO VON BISMARCK, FROM AN ENGRAVING BY WOODVILLE. Bismarck, who unified Germany, had little faith in democratic processes for achieving the purposes of state. He trusted rather "blood and iron." He is pictured here during one of his fist-pounding appearances in the German Reichstag. Even as an elderly man, the "Iron Chancellor" lost none of his overbearing forcefulness. And the German Empire bore in large measure the stamp of his personality and ideals. (*The Bettmann Archive*)

to challenge him. Back on his ancestral estates he was a hard-riding, hard-drinking country squire, lording it over his peasants and his neighbors. He detested liberalism in any form. He also detested German nationalism, which until 1849 was closely associated with liberalism. His loyalty was to Prussia alone. The other German states he considered weak and effeminate, unfit for union with manly, militaristic, autocratic Prussia. He had deplored Frederick William IV's temporizing with the liberals in 1848 and was pleased at his humiliation at the hands of reactionary Austria. Bismarck's views on liberalism never changed as long as he lived. However, his attitude toward German nationalism underwent a sudden and complete reversal when, as Prussia's delegate to the Diet of the German Confederation at Frankfurt, he saw at firsthand how Austria dominated Prussia. He became an ardent German nationalist—an enthusiast, not for a union of German states, but for a Prussianized Germany from which Austria would be banished. As ambassador to Russia and to France he gained valuable experiences for the key role he was to play in Germany.

Upon assuming the chancellorship of Prussia in 1862, Bismarck, with the backing of the king and the army, defied the liberal opposition in the Landtag, violated the constitution without hesitation, and collected illegally the funds necessary for the military program. "Not by speeches and minority resolutions," said Bismarck, "are the great questions of the time decided—that was the mistake of 1848 and 1849—but by blood and iron." He came to be known as the Iron Chancellor. Thus was Prussian liberalism crushed. Bismarck declared that a few glorious victories won on foreign soil would turn the Prussian liberals into fervent German nationalists. This prediction soon came true. The new army created by Bismarck, Roon, and Moltke was the most scientifically efficient military machine that had ever been devised. Behind it was a state and a people long conditioned mentally and physically to military discipline. The Junker

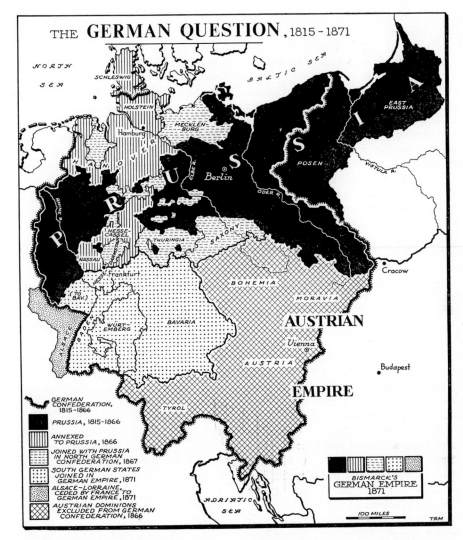

THE **GERMAN QUESTION**, 1815-1871

NORTH SEA

BALTIC SEA

SCHLESWIG

HOLSTEIN

MECKLEN-BURG

Hamburg

EAST PRUSSIA

P R U S S I A

HANOVER

ELBE R.

Berlin

POSEN

VISTULA R.

ODER R.

RHINE R.

HESSE-CASSEL

NASSAU

THURINGIA

SAXONY

Cracow

Frankfurt

(TO BAV.)

BADEN

WURT-EMBERG

BAVARIA

BOHEMIA

MORAVIA

AUSTRIAN

Vienna

AUSTRIA

Budapest

EMPIRE

TYROL

GERMAN CONFEDERATION, 1815-1866

PRUSSIA, 1815-1866

ANNEXED TO PRUSSIA, 1866

JOINED WITH PRUSSIA IN NORTH GERMAN CONFEDERATION, 1867

SOUTH GERMAN STATES JOINED IN GERMAN EMPIRE, 1871

ALSACE-LORRAINE, CEDED BY FRANCE TO GERMAN EMPIRE, 1871

AUSTRIAN DOMINIONS EXCLUDED FROM GERMAN CONFEDERATION, 1866

ADRIATIC SEA

BISMARCK'S GERMAN EMPIRE 1871

100 MILES

TRM

officers were used to command; the tow-headed privates and non-coms, mostly from the peasantry, were accustomed to obey. The latest and best equipment was provided. The whole machine worked with clocklike precision under the direction of a general staff. The subordinate officers were well versed in tactics and strategy and could be trusted to use their own judgment in local situations. The privates were well trained to fight in scattered, loose-order formations that made poor targets for the enemy. For the next three quarters of a century this army was first the envy of, then the model

for, the military machines of the other great world powers.

Bismarck lost little time in putting his new military machine to work. An opportunity soon presented itself in the form of a dispute with Denmark over the long-standing and most complex Schleswig-Holstein question. Schleswig and Holstein were two little provinces lying between Prussia and Denmark. Their population was partly German-speaking and partly Danish-speaking. Since 1815 they had been ruled by the king of Denmark, though they had not been incorporated into Denmark. In 1863 the Danish king suddenly annexed the two duchies outright. Bismarck, seeing an opportunity to test the Prussian army, to annex some territory, and also to embroil Austria, declared war on Denmark (1864). Since Holstein was a member of the German Confederation, Austria dared not hold back lest the leadership of the Confederation pass to Prussia. The string of Danish fortresses across the narrow peninsula, expected to block any invader for two years, was carried by the Prussian army in two weeks. Denmark sued for peace. Bismarck made the peace settlement as complicated as possible. By the terms of the Convention of Gastein, which he persuaded Austria to agree to, Schleswig and Holstein were to be ruled jointly by Prussia and Austria. Schleswig, however, was to be occupied by Prussia; Holstein by Austria. This unworkable arrangement Bismarck soon used to stir up trouble with Austria.

Confident now that the Prussian army was all that he had hoped and expected, Bismarck devoted the two years following the Danish War to feverish preparations for war with Austria. His first task was to obtain the support or the neutrality of the other three continental powers, Italy, Russia, and France. Prussia had been the first great power to recognize the new kingdom of Italy. Now promising her Venetia, Bismarck drew her into an alliance against Austria. It was always a cardinal principle of Bismarck to maintain friendly relations with Russia (at Prussia's back door). When Russia's Polish subjects revolted once more in 1863, Prussia alone of the great powers supported Russia. Of course Prussia had several million Polish subjects of her own to worry about. Bismarck neutralized Napoleon III by personal persuasion and deception. Visiting the French emperor at Biarritz, he dangled all sorts of vague possibilities before him, such as the annexation by France of Belgium and Luxemburg. Napoleon completely misjudged the military power of Prussia. He believed either that Austria would win the coming war or that an exhausting stalemate would enable France to

arbitrate the peace to her own advantage. Bismarck encouraged him in these misconceptions. By the spring of 1866, with everything in readiness, Bismarck created by threats and maneuvers a state of alarm in Austria. Finally, the Austrian government, realizing that it would require Austria twice as long as Prussia to mobilize her forces and fearing a sudden knockout blow, mobilized her army. Pretending that this was an act of war, Bismarck sent the Prussian army into Holstein, from which the Austrian forces were compelled to flee. Austria thereupon declared war.

In the Austro-Prussian War most of the little German states supported Austria. Their military forces, however, were quickly crushed beneath the Prussian steam roller. The world was astounded by the rapidity and ease with which Moltke's armies overwhelmed Austria, a nation of twice the size and population of Prussia and long the dominant power in Central Europe. The war is sometimes called the Seven Weeks' War. The issue was really decided in less than three weeks. Quickly taking the offensive, the Prussians soon brought the Austrians to bay in northern Bohemia. The Battle of Königgrätz (or Sadowa, as it is sometimes called) was one of the most decisive battles in history. The Austrians fought bravely, but, standing in close formation, they were mowed down by the Prussian infantry, which lay on the ground and fired from behind rocks and trees. The Prussians' breech-loading needle guns fired six times to the Austrian muzzle-loaders' once. As the Prussians marched rapidly toward Vienna, the Hapsburg government sued for peace. William I, Roon, and Moltke, their blood flaming with victory, wanted to crush and mutilate Austria, but Bismarck was looking into the future. He saw that Austria was now harmless to Prussia and would make a valuable ally or at least friend in Prussia's future wars. Restraining his king and his generals, he made the terms of the Treaty of Prague extremely lenient. Austria was to pay Prussia a very small indemnity and to accept the rearrangement of Germany by Prussia. She was also forced to cede Venetia to Italy as Italy's reward for fighting on the side of Prussia.

Following the victory over Austria, Bismarck reorganized Germany. Hanover, Nassau, Frankfurt, and Hesse-Cassel were annexed to Prussia outright, bridging the gap between Rhenish Prussia and the main body. The remaining twenty states north of the Main River were bound to Prussia in a North German Confederation. The Confederation was completely dominated by Prussia, which alone constituted four fifths of its area and population. Prussia's king and prime minister were made president and chancellor of the Confederation. Bismarck drafted the constitution for the North German Confederation. Its government was, of course, fundamentally autocratic. The chief administrative officer was the chancellor (Bismarck), who was responsible only to the King of Prussia as president, who appointed and dismissed him. The legislative body was composed of the Bundesrat, whose members were really ambassadors of the twenty-one state governments, and the Reichstag, whose members were elected by universal manhood suffrage. All new laws required the approval of both bodies. The Bundesrat was the more influential of the two. The Reichstag had no control over the chancellor and his cabinet as in Great Britain, and little control over the budget and the army and navy. If the Reichstag failed to vote a new budget, the old one automatically continued in force. This undemocratic constitution later became the constitution of the German Empire. Meanwhile, the former liberals in the Prussian Landtag, caught up in the nationalistic fervor following the victory over Austria, repented of their sins of having opposed Bismarck and voted him exoneration for having violated the constitution. The four predominantly Roman Catholic states south of the Main River (Bavaria, Württemberg, Baden, and part of Hesse-Darmstadt) were left out of the North German Confederation at the insistence of Napoleon III and because Bismarck preferred to have them come in later

by their own choice. He would not have long to wait.

5. The Franco-German War and the Creation of the German Empire

From the time Bismarck became a German nationalist he anticipated that France would have to be defeated before the German nation could emerge full grown. France, he reasoned, long the dominant power on the European continent, would not stand idle while a potentially more powerful rival grew up overnight across the Rhine. Napoleon III had been badly deceived as to the outcome of the Austro-Prussian War. Too late he realized his error and attempted to safeguard French security. He demanded that the four predominantly Roman Catholic German states south of the Main River be left out of the new German nation and that France receive some German territory west of the Rhine to offset Prussia's sudden expansion. As we have seen, the first proposal suited Bismarck's purposes; he was certain that he could get the south German states at a convenient time later. But he stood adamant against the cession of any German territory to France. He pointed out to Napoleon the hard truth that, whereas the victorious Prussian army was nearby ready for action, the best part of the French army was in Mexico. Both powers began to prepare for a showdown that appeared to be inevitable and not too far in the future. The Prussian army was refitted and enlarged, and the forces of the other twenty states in the North German Confederation integrated with it. Mistakes revealed in the Austrian war were noted and corrected. Napoleon III, for his part, recalled his army from Mexico and made efforts to renovate and enlarge the French military machine. These efforts, however, were crippled and delayed by the liberals in the Chamber of Deputies, who feared that Napoleon would use the strengthened army to crush the reviving French liberalism. Only a watered-down army-improvement bill was passed.

By 1870 Bismarck was eager for a military

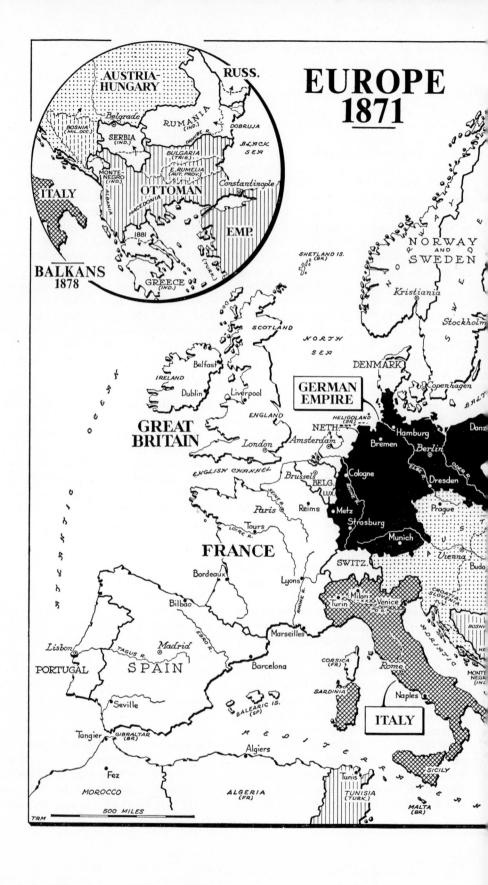

EUROPE
1871

BALKANS 1878 (inset)

- AUSTRIA-HUNGARY
- RUSS.
- Belgrade
- RUMANIA (IND.)
- DOBRUJA
- BOSNIA (MIL. OCC.)
- SERBIA (IND.)
- BLACK SEA
- BULGARIA (TRIB.)
- E. RUMELIA (AUT. PROV.)
- MONTE-NEGRO (IND.)
- ALBANIA
- OTTOMAN
- MACEDONIA
- Constantinople
- ITALY
- EMP.
- 1881
- GREECE (IND.)
- (TURK.)

SHETLAND IS. (BR)

NORWAY AND SWEDEN

Kristiania

Stockholm

SCOTLAND

NORTH SEA

DENMARK

Copenhagen

BALT

GERMAN EMPIRE

HELIGOLAND (BR)

IRELAND

Belfast

Dublin

Liverpool

ENGLAND

NETH.

Amsterdam

Hamburg

Bremen

Berlin

Danz

GREAT BRITAIN

London

ENGLISH CHANNEL

Brussels

BELG.

Cologne

Dresden

LUX.

Prague

Paris

Reims

Metz

Strasburg

Munich

Vienna

Buda

Tours

FRANCE

SWITZ.

CROATIA SLOVENIA

Bordeaux

Lyons

Milan

Turin

Venice

Bilbao

BOSNI

HE

MONTE NEGRO (IN

Marseilles

CORSICA (FR)

Rome

Lisbon

Madrid

PORTUGAL

SPAIN

Barcelona

SARDINIA

Naples

ITALY

Seville

BALEARIC IS. (SP)

Tangier

GIBRALTAR (BR)

MEDITERRANEAN

Algiers

SICILY

Fez

MOROCCO

ALGERIA (FR)

Tunis

TUNISIA (TURK.)

MALTA (BR)

500 MILES

TRM

ARCTIC OCEAN

NORTH CAPE

LAPPLAND

WHITE SEA

Archangel

FINLAND

Helsingfors

LAKE LADOGA

St. Petersburg

VOLGA R.

RUSSIAN

Riga

Moscow

Orenburg

URAL R.

Vilna

EMPIRE

PRUSSIA

Warsaw

POLAND

Kiev

VISTULA R.

AUSTRIA-HUNGARY

Odessa

DNIESTER R.

PRUTH R.

BESSARABIA

Rostov

DON R.

VOLGA R.

Astrakhan

CASPIAN SEA

HUNGARY

RUMANIA (TRIB.)

DANUBE R.

DOBRUJA

SEA OF AZOV

CRIMEA

CAUCASIA

Baku

SERBIA (TRIB.)

OTTOMAN

BULGARIA

BLACK SEA

Sevastopol

Sinope

Tabriz

Constantinople

EMPIRE

PERSIA

MACEDONIA

DARDA-NELLES

AEGEAN SEA

Smyrna

TIGRIS R.

Athens

GREECE (IND.)

EUPHRATES R.

MESOPOTAMIA

SYRIA

Bagdad

CRETE (TURK.)

CYPRUS (BR.)

SEA

ARABIA

BALKANS 1914

AUSTRIA-HUNGARY

RUSS.

Belgrade

BOSNIA (ANNEXED 1908)

Sarajevo

SERBIA

RUMANIA

DANUBE R.

1913

BLACK SEA

BULGARIA

MONTE NEGRO

E. RUMELIA 1885

1913

Constant-inople

ITALY

ALBANIA (IND.)

1913

1913

1913

OTTOMAN EMP.

GREECE

showdown with France. The army of the North German Confederation was at its peak. William I was getting old, and his more liberal son, the future Frederick III, had little use for Bismarck. The French army reforms, on the other hand, were just beginning and would not be completed until 1873. Bismarck's opportunity came when the Spanish crown was offered to a Hohenzollern prince. Bismarck persuaded the reluctant prince to accept the Spanish offer. The French immediately took alarm at the prospect of being surrounded by Hohenzollerns. Heavy French pressure was exerted on Prussia to which both the prince and King William I yielded. However, the excited French ministers were still not satisfied. Foreign Minister Duc de Gramont ordered the French ambassador to demand assurance from the Prussian king that a Hohenzollern would never sit on the throne of Spain. To this unreasonable demand William I politely refused to give assent. William I wired to Bismarck in Berlin a detailed account of this interview, which took place at Ems. Bismarck saw an opportunity to provoke the French into war. Cleverly editing the Ems dispatch so as to make it appear that the French ambassador and the Prussian king had insulted each other, he published it to the world. The French government, walking into Bismarck's trap, declared war.

The prevailing world military opinion was that this time Prussia had overreached herself and that Bismarck's work would be undone. But, as in the case of the Austro-Prussian War, the military might of Prussia was grossly underestimated. That of France was overestimated. The sordid character that underlay the surface glamour of Napoleon III's long dictatorship was quickly revealed. The usurper had surrounded himself with conspirators and adventurers like himself. Graft and corruption had robbed the army of its vital necessities. Confusion reigned everywhere. Men could not find their units; horses were without saddles, guns without ammunition. The French were able to mobilize only 300,000 troops to face the 800,-

000 fully trained and equipped veterans and reservists of Moltke. The four predominantly Roman Catholic South German states, far from joining Roman Catholic France as Napoleon III had hoped, threw in their lot with Protestant, German-speaking Prussia as Bismarck had anticipated.

The issue of the war was decided in a matter of weeks. With scientific precision Moltke's superior hosts moved into France. The French fought heroically but were overwhelmed. One French army was surrounded at the fortress city of Metz, where it surrendered three months later. Another French army under Marshall MacMahon and Emperor Napoleon III was surrounded at Sedan and surrendered on September 2. When this news reached Paris two days later, the liberals overthrew the government of the Second Empire and declared the Third French Republic. Within a matter of weeks Paris was surrounded by the Germans. For five months the great city held out; starvation forced it to surrender on January 28, 1871.

Bismarck forced upon stricken and helpless France a treaty designed to cripple her beyond recovery. The Treaty of Frankfurt required France to pay an indemnity of 5,000,000,000 francs ($1,000,000,000) in gold. German troops would remain on French soil until this amount was paid in full (which Bismarck mistakenly hoped and expected would take a long time). The provinces of Alsace and most of Lorraine were ceded to Germany. Although most of the inhabitants of these two border provinces speak a German dialect, their religion is Roman Catholic, and they had long been associated with France, to which they were unquestionably loyal. And since these provinces contained much of France's vital iron reserves, the seizure of Alsace and Lorraine long poisoned Franco-German relations.

On January 18, 1871, while the big German guns were still battering Paris, the heads of the twenty-five German states at war with France met on Bismarck's call at Versailles (behind the German lines) and in the Hall of Mirrors proclaimed William I emperor of the German Empire. The illiberal constitution that Bismarck had drafted for the North German Confederation became the constitution of the German Empire. Bismarck, of course, became its chancellor, and, unlike Cavour, he lived to rule over his creation for the next twenty years. The German Empire had now replaced France as the dominant power on the European continent and the chief rival of Great Britain for world hegemony.

The venturesome career of the totalitarian, glory-seeking Second Empire of Napoleon III and to a greater extent the rise of Bismarck's militaristic Prussianized German Empire marked the transition from moderate to malignant nationalism. After 1870 nationalism in the Western world would be less a matter of freeing language groups from alien rule and uniting them under one flag (although some of that still remained) than a matter of military aggrandizement on the part of language groups already free and united. This kind of nationalism was a dangerous foe, rather than a friend of liberalism.

———————◆•◆———————

SUGGESTED READING

W. R. Thayer, *The Life and Times of Cavour,* 2 vols. (1911). A truly great biography of the chief maker of the Italian nation.

G. M. Trevelyan, *Garibaldi and the Thousand* (1909). A masterpiece of historical writing. The dramatic story seems almost too fabulous to be true.

G. M. Trevelyan, *Garibaldi and the Making of Italy* (1911). In this volume the great British historian carries to completion the story of the exploits of Garibaldi and his heroic contributions to the making of Italy.

K. S. Pinson, *Modern Germany, Its History and Civilization* (1954). A useful survey with good chapters on the national unification movement.

Erich Eyck, *Bismarck and the German Empire* (1950). Probably the best single-volume biography of Bismarck in English. An abridgment and translation of the author's three-volume biography in German.

R. H. Lord, *The Origins of the War of 1870* (1924). A scholarly study of a highly controversial subject with repercussions continuing to the present time.

A. J. P. Taylor, *The Hapsburg Monarchy, 1809–1918* (1948). A brief and lively treatment of this complex subject.

R. W. Seton-Watson, *German, Slav, and Magyar* (1946). A study of the nationality complex of Southeastern Europe by the leading British expert on the subject.

CHAPTER 47

Romanticism in Philosophy, Literature, and the Arts

Schools of thought and art do not fall neatly into chronological patterns. Nevertheless, the student of history is frequently able to observe a prevailing vogue that characterizes the culture of a given era. Thus, although romanticism arose in the eighteenth century, the prevailing style in that century was still undoubtedly classical. Similarly, although classicism has continued on through the nineteenth century and into the present day, romanticism was unquestionably the dominant spirit in the first three quarters of the nineteenth century.

1. The Nature of Romanticism

The romantic spirit had many facets. Essentially, however, romanticism was a reaction against the rationalism and formalism of the classic spirit. Whereas classicism extolled reason and perfection of form, romanticism appealed to the emotions, to feeling, and to freedom and spontaneity of expression. Whereas the classicist was interested in the natural order and the laws of man and the universe, the romanticist loved to sing of woods and rills and lakes and lovers' lanes and daffodils and to dream of faraway or imaginary times and places.

Romanticism was associated with and was in large measure a product of the French Revolution and Napoleon. Many classicists had been interested in peacefully reforming society in accordance with the natural law. They did not anticipate the violent upheaval that came, although many of the radical revolutionary leaders and Napoleon believed themselves to be in the tradition of classical Greece and Rome. It was the romanticists, breaking sharply with past forms and traditions and with bold abandon trying the new, who reflected the revolutionary spirit. This does not mean that all romanticists were political radicals, or even liberals. Some, like Shelley and Heine, were. Others, like Edmund Burke and Sir Walter Scott, were conservatives representing a reaction against the excesses of the Revolution.

Nationalism was another facet of romanticism. Whether liberal or conservative, the romanticist was likely to be an ardent nationalist of the moderate pre-1870 type. The great romantic poet Lord Byron lost his life fighting for Greek national independence against the Turks. The romantic dreamer and orator Mazzini was called the soul of Italian nationalism. He spent most of his adult life in exile because of his labors for a free and united Italy. Herder, as early as the eighteenth century, had pleaded eloquently for a German national culture. The fraternity and the freedom so common to the national movements before 1870, no less than pride in real or imagined national achievements, gave outlet to the emotions of the romanticist.

Romanticism also represented in the main a reaction against the cold deism of the eighteenth century and a return to mystic religion. With the exception of the Reformation of the sixteenth century this was the first reversal in the general trend toward secularism, which began as early as the fourteenth, or possibly the thirteenth, century. The Roman Catholic Church had received hard blows in France at the hands of the Voltairian rationalists and the French Revolutionists, but after 1815 it made a strong comeback both in official status and in popularity. To a generation weary of war and violent change the church seemed a rock of stability. In Great Britain the Methodist movement, which had begun in the middle of the eighteenth century, grew rapidly. In the United States much of the anti-slavery movement sprang from moral and religious sources. The revival of religion as part of the romanticism of the early nineteenth century brought about a renewed interest in the Middle Ages. The classicists, almost without exception, had drawn their inspiration from pagan Greece and Rome. Now the Knights of the Round Table and Siegfried and Brunhild came back in style once more. No more perfect example of the romantic spirit can be cited than the novels and verse of Sir Walter Scott, whose subject matter was primarily medieval. Gothic architecture enjoyed a revival. The "Dark Ages" were transformed into the "Age of Faith."

Romanticism was a godsend to the societies of the industrialized countries during the first phase of the Industrial Revolution. Its optimism, its moral and religious idealism, and its nationalism constituted a ready-made justification of life for the prosperous industrial bourgeoisie. For the hard-pressed industrial proletariat, in as much as they were able to partake of such cultural luxuries, it provided escapism and spiritual food. If the factory workers dully tending their machines had had nothing but the mechanical universe and the impersonal deistic God of the classicists to sustain them, their lives would have been bleak indeed. Now at least they could dream and hope.

2. The Philosophy of Idealism

Any discussion of romantic thought must, almost of necessity, begin with Rousseau (1712–78), even though this disorderly French genius lived during the heyday of rationalistic classicism and almost a century before romanticism came into full flower. Rousseau, like most of his fellow philosophers of the Enlightenment such as Voltaire, Diderot, Montesquieu, was a deist, believing in the mechanical universe of natural laws. However, he differed sharply with them over the place of reason. Far from believing that man can know only what is perceived through his five senses and interpreted by reason, Rousseau placed his main reliance in feeling, instinct, and emotions. He also anticipated the romantic movement in his inordinate love of nature. He would stretch himself out on the ground, dig his fingers and toes into the dirt, kiss the earth, and weep for joy. This mad genius was a true romanticist in his revolt against the rules of formal society. Free love, undisciplined childhood and education, the noble savage—all were features of Rousseau's romantic revolt. His influence on later generations has been enormous.

It seems a far cry from the rough genius of Rousseau to the exquisitely ordered mansions of thought of Immanuel Kant (1724–1804), but the German philosopher was admittedly indebted to Rousseau. Kant, who was partly of Scottish ancestry, was a native of Königsberg in East Prussia. A frail and insignificant-looking little man who never traveled more than fifty miles from the place of his birth, he slowly developed into one of the most powerful and influential thinkers of modern times. He was often in difficulty with the Prussian government because of his liberal and unorthodox views. Kant started out as a scientist and always respected the methods of natural science. He was also steeped in the philosophy of the Enlightenment. However, he was not satisfied with the conclusions of the eighteenth-century materialistic rationalists. Eventually he thought on beyond them. Kant came to believe that there are in reality two worlds, not one—the physical realm and the spiritual realm, or the realm of ultimate reality. The first he called the realm of phenomena; the second the realm of noumena. In the physical realm of phenomena the approach to truth of Descartes, Locke, and Voltaire—sense perception and reason —suffices. However, in the spiritual realm of noumena, these methods fail. Ultimate spiritual truth may be attained only by faith, conviction, and feeling. Truths in the realm of the noumena, such as the existence of God or the immortality of the soul or the existence of good and evil, cannot be proved by reason. And yet we are justified in believing them because they reinforce our moral sense of right and wrong. His principal work, *Critique of Pure Reason*, was a metaphysical answer of the highest intellectual order to the philosophers of the Enlightenment. These ideas came to be called the philosophy of idealism. Kant and his early nineteenth-century followers represented a sharp reversal in the philosophical trend toward rationalism and materialism, which in a sense began in the thirteenth century with the efforts of Albertus Magnus and Thomas Aquinas to rationalize Christian doctrines.

The most influential of Kant's disciples was George William Hegel (1770–1831). Hegel's chief interest was the philosophy of history. Like his master he rejected the mechanistic unmoral universe of the Enlightenment. He believed, rather, that a benevolent but impersonal God created and runs the universe, making human society better by a process of purposeful evolution. This is achieved by a dialectical system of thesis, antithesis, and synthesis. Any given system or civilization (thesis) is challenged by its opposite (antithesis). From the struggle emerges a new system containing the best elements of both (synthesis). This synthesis then becomes a new thesis, which

when it has served its purpose is challenged by a new antithesis, and so on. Hegel believed that every historical epoch is dominated by a *zeitgeist* (spirit of the time). The zeitgeist of the nineteenth century was German civilization, whose greatest contribution was freedom through disciplined order. Hegel exalted the state. Only in and through the state can the inividual find meaning and be free. Hegel's influence on romanticism and on the early nineteenth century in general was probably greater than that of any other thinker. It can readily be seen that he also provided inspiration for some of the "isms" of the twentieth century, such as fascism and communism.

3. Romantic Literature

The spirit of romanticism can be made to come alive in no better way than by a study of the British romantic poets. A number of British writers began to break with the classic tradition during the course of the eighteenth century, while classicism was still in flower. The best known and probably the most illustrative of these writers was Robert Burns (1759–96). Born in a humble clay cottage, the Scottish poet lived a carefree life, as undisciplined as if he had been reared in accordance with Rousseau's *Émile*. Burns idealized the things of simple nature and the rustic rural life with which he was intimately acquainted. In spontaneous verse written in his native Scottish dialect, he wrote an ode to a field mouse, "Wee, sleekit, cow'rin', tim'rous beastie," which he had turned up with his plow. In *The Cotter's Saturday Night* we are given a charming and sympathetic firsthand picture of village life among the poor of Scotland. "Auld Lang Syne" is sung with nostalgia every New Year's Eve by millions throughout the English-speaking world. *John Anderson My Jo* could never have been written by Racine or Alexander Pope.

The romantic spirit, early reflected in the spontaneous, emotional, back-to-nature poetry of Robert Burns, reached maturity with William Wordsworth (1770–1850) and

Samuel Taylor Coleridge (1772–1834). The two were warm friends. Both were closely associated with the beautiful lake country of northwest England, Wordsworth by birth and Coleridge by adoption. They took a trip to Germany together, where they fell under the influence of Kant. Both were ardent, humanitarian social reformers. The two gifted poets collaborated on *Lyrical Ballads*, which appeared in 1798. *Lyrical Ballads* contains some of the best work of both men, such as Wordsworth's *Tintern Abbey* and Coleridge's *Ancient Mariner*. Both men were masters of versification and poetic expression. They were also lovers and mature students of nature, and both of them, particularly Wordsworth, were keenly aware of the brooding, mystical presence of the divine. Wordsworth's *Intimations of Immortality* is sublime in its spiritual depth and insight. In their ardent love of nature, their introspective concern for the individual, their preoccupation with the spiritual rather than the material, and their greater attention to substance than to form, Wordsworth and Coleridge broke distinctly with the spirit of classicism.

Once the vogue of romanticism was dignified and popularized in Great Britain by Wordsworth and Coleridge, a host of romantic writers burst forth into song. A younger trio of poetic geniuses of the highest order, Byron, Shelley, and Keats (all of whom lived briefly and died between the years 1788 and 1824), are known and loved wherever the English language is truly understood. All three gave spontaneous and unrestrained vent to their emotions. Byron and Shelley combined an exquisite aesthetic sense with irrepressible revolutionary zeal, defying the forms and customs of society. Keats was a gentler soul, who after a lifelong quest for the beautiful died at the age of twenty-six.

Meanwhile, Sir Walter Scott in novel and verse was devoting his longer life (1771–1832) to glorifying the Middle Ages and his native Scotland. Scott, unlike Byron and Shelley but like Wordsworth and Coleridge and most of the other romantic writers, was

conservative in his attitude toward public affairs.

The last of the British romanticists were Alfred Lord Tennyson (1809–92) and Robert Browning (1812–1889), who lived on and wrote well into the Victorian era. The young Tennyson's ardent nationalism, exaltation of the Middle Ages in *Idylls of the King*, interest in religion, and essential conservatism were all typically romantic. Browning, deeper and more subtle in thought though less lyrical than Tennyson, paralleled him in many ways.

Across the Atlantic, Longfellow, Cooper, and Irving, as we have seen, were founding an American national literature. In their subject matter, their style, and their attitudes they reflected the European romantic spirit. In fact Irving divided his time and his interests between Europe and America. Many other American writers in the early nineteenth century wrote in the romantic vein. We can mention here only a few of the most illustrative. Ralph Waldo Emerson (1803–82) was considered a religious radical and skeptic in his day. He gave up his Puritan pastorate (by then Unitarian) at Boston's Old North Church because of his heterodoxy. However, in his essays and poems it was the romantic philosophy of Kantian idealism, not the rationalism of the Enlightenment, that he introduced into America. Edgar Allan Poe (1809–49), short-story writer, literary critic, and romantic poet of a high order, was in a sense an American Shelley, though less ethereal and more morbid. Henry David Thoreau (1817–62) took Rousseau's back-to-nature idea more seriously than did its author. Rousseau, for all his passion for nature, would never have withdrawn from society for two years to live by Walden Pond in introspective solitude. Emerson, Poe, and Thoreau were all individualists to the point of being mild social revolutionaries. Thoreau preached civil disobedience and allowed himself to be put in jail rather than pay taxes for what he considered to be unworthy causes. The sensitive Poe, enduring oblivion and poverty, turned to drink and an early grave. Emerson weathered a storm of hostility from organized religion and society for his non-conformist views. All three were beautiful and romantic dreamers.

Romanticism came to German literature in the latter half of the eighteenth century, partly under the influence of the early British romanticists and partly as a result of the conscious effort of the Germans, led by Herder, to free themselves from bondage to French classical culture. Foremost among all German writers is Johann Wolfgang Goethe (1749–1832). Like Shakespeare, Leonardo da Vinci, and Beethoven, Goethe is a genius of such proportions that he overreaches any single cultural school or movement. However, in so far as it is possible to classify him he belongs more nearly to the romantic tradition than to any other, both in time and in spirit. His prodigious energies were devoted essentially to a lifelong (eighty-three years) search for the secrets of happiness and wisdom. His encyclopedic mind delved fruitfully into literature, philosophy, science, and public affairs. His novels, lyrics, essays, scientific and philosophical treatises, and dramas fill a hundred and thirty-two volumes. No writer except Shakespeare has had so many of his lyrics set to music. Goethe's masterpiece is *Faust*, a philosophical drama written in exquisite verse. It is about a medieval scholar who, dissatisfied with the fruits of knowledge, sells his soul to the devil in return for earthly pleasure and wisdom. Goethe explores the height and depth of human experience and aspiration. Faust was sixty years in the making. In his medieval interests, his fresh emotional spontaneity, his love of nature and of individual personality, and his courageous, robust, pioneering spirit Goethe was a romanticist.

Goethe's friend and protégé, Friedrich Schiller (1759–1805), was more popular in his own day than the master himself. Schiller drew heavily upon the Middle Ages and upon nationalism (when national aspirations were associated with freedom) for his dramas, histories, and lyrics. *William Tell*, a drama based upon the Swiss struggle for freedom from Hapsburg tyranny, is probably Schiller's best-known and most representative work. Neither Goethe nor Schiller can be considered a German nationalist in the narrow sense; both were universal in their interests and their appeal.

Heinrich Heine (1797–1856) was considered to be Goethe's successor as a writer of German lyrics, though not of Goethe's stature. Most of Heine's voluminous writing was in the field of romantic lyrical poetry. One of his most representative works was an ode to the Silesian weavers who rose up against the hardships caused by the Industrial Revolution, which was just coming to Germany, and were shot down by Prussian troops. Because of the hostility of the various German governments in the age of Metternich to his radical political ideas, Heine exiled himself from Germany. The last twenty-five years of his life were spent in Paris. Many of his later lyrics show a touch of the light gaiety of the French.

One would expect France, the home of Rousseau, the French Revolution, and irrepressible individualists, to be the seat of a flourishing literary romanticism. While this was true in a way, France produced only one romantic writer (Victor Hugo) of the stature of Wordsworth or Shelley. (Goethes, of course, come along only every two or three centuries or so.) Neither did French romanticism attain the glories of French classicism of the seventeenth and eighteenth centuries. François René Chateaubriand (1768–1848), a disillusioned nobleman who began writing during the reign of Napoleon I, was one of the first writers of influence to react against the rationalism of the Enlightenment. His *Genius of Christianity* is a return to mystic religion. He also dreamed and wrote of glorified Indians in faraway tropical America. Honoré de Balzac (1799–1850), the greatest of French novelists, set out to imitate Scott. However, he soon changed his setting from the Middle Ages to contemporary France of the early nineteenth century, becoming one of the first to write about the new industrial bourgeoisie. In forty-seven novels, called collectively *The*

Human Comedy, he attempted to depict the whole gamut of human nature. Some two thousand characters, many drawn with shrewd insight, parade before us. He foreshadows the realism of a later era. Alexander Dumas the elder (1802–70) has continued to delight young and old alike with his romantic and melodramatic *The Three Musketeers* and *The Count of Monte Cristo*, painting the haunting afterglow of medieval chivalry. Victor Hugo (1802–85) in his long and tumultuous life wrote a vast quantity of exquisite lyrics, dramas, essays, and fiction —all in the romantic tradition. His *Hunchback of Notre Dame* is medieval in setting. In *Les Misérables*, sometimes called the greatest of novels, he immortalizes and idealizes the masses of underprivileged mankind, preaching redemption and purification, not by planned social reform, but through suffering. We probably should not leave the subject of French romanticism without mentioning Jules Michelet (1798–1874), romantic French historian. In his *History of France* in seventeen volumes he tells the thrilling story of France's long and glorious achievements, usually with skillful historical craftsmanship and always with matchless grace.

The first great figure in Russian literature was the romantic poet Alexander Pushkin (1799–1837). The chief inspiration for his great lyrics, dramas, histories, novels, essays, and tales came from French and British writers, particularly Byron. Because of his revolutionary radicalism (of the French variety), he was for a while exiled by the Russian government to the Caucasus. Later he became a Russian nationalist, taking many of his themes from Russian history. His tragic drama *Boris Godunov* (patterned after Shakespeare) is considered to be his masterpiece. Probably Russia's greatest contribution to romantic literature was the work of two or the world's greatest novelists—Ivan Sergyeevich Turgenev (1818–83) and Feodor Dostoevski (1821–81). Both were ardent Russian nationalists, but their real love and loyalty were for the Russian common people, particularly the peasants. Because of their radicalism both were arrested. Dosto-

evski was exiled to Siberia for five years. Turgenev, after three years of imprisonment, spent the rest of his life abroad, mostly in Paris. In his masterpiece, *Fathers and Children*, Turgenev grapples powerfully with the problems of the older conservative Russian generation versus the younger generation, modern, sophisticated, and radical. Dostoevski's two greatest novels are *Crime and Punishment* and *The Brothers Karamazov*. In them he delves psychologically and mystically into the problems of evil and purification through suffering. He was deeply religious, but not in any formal or orthodox sense.

4. The Romantic Spirit in the Arts

Words fail miserably to convey the messages and the meanings expressed in the visual and musical arts. This is particularly true of art whose appeal is primarily to the emotions. (As in a card game one peek is worth several finesses.) Brevity, then, will be the soul of our treatment of romantic art.

The leading painters glorified nature, religion, and nationalism. John Constable (1776–1837) in Great Britain, Camille Corot (1796–1875) in France, and George Inness the elder (1825–94) in the United States painted dreamy, misty landscapes beautiful enough to have illustrated the moods of Wordsworth or Thoreau. Their idealizations of rural life would have delighted Rousseau and Burns. J. M. W. Turner (1775–1851) in England caught the romantic mood in his eerie impressions of seascapes and mythological subjects. Jean François Millet (1814–75) idealized both the French rural life (*The Sower* and *The Gleaners*) and mystic religion (*The Angelus*). His compatriot, Eugène Delacroix (1799–1863) depicted on canvas Byron's *The Prisoner of Chillon*. On great murals in the Louvre, the library of the Chamber of Deputies, and the Hôtel de Ville he portrayed glorious scenes from the national history of France.

The romantic movement was less pronounced in the field of architecture. Its chief

THE ANGELUS, BY MILLET. The spirit of romanticism that dominated the art and literature of Western Europe during the first half of the nineteenth century was in considerable measure a reaction against the formalism, rationalism, and deism of the eighteenth century. Romanticism was marked by a religious revival and also by admiration for the simple, rural life, which Millet effectively captures in this famous painting. (*Archives Photographiques, Paris*)

manifestation was a revived interest in Gothic style. The French, after several centuries of apathy if not scorn for anything associated with medievalism, suddenly showed a renewed interest in their magnificent Gothic monuments. It is significant that the houses of Parliament constructed in the early nineteenth century, when England was rapidly becoming industrialized, were built in the Gothic style.

The romantic spirit was caught and expressed by a host of great musicians. First and foremost was Beethoven (1770–1827), who was not only one of the greatest of classic composers but also the first of the romanticists. His earlier work was in the spirit of his idol, Mozart. In maturity his originality overflowed the bounds of classic forms, becoming freer, more individual and emotional. Beethoven lived through the upheavals of the French Revolution and Napoleon, and his keen interest in these dramatic events is reflected in his music. His Symphony No. 3 ("Eroica") was dedicated to Napoleon, whom Beethoven at first regarded as the embodiment of the democratic ideals of the French Revolution. His fifth and seventh symphonies were inspired by the German nationalistic upsurge, which helped to overthrow the French tyrant. Karl Maria von Weber (1786–1826), Franz Schubert (1797–1828), Felix Mendelssohn

(1809–47), and Robert Schumann (1810–56) carried on in the spirit of the great Beethoven. These gifted and youthful Germans expressed in their melodic music the same spontaneous and emotional spirit that their contemporaries Byron, Shelley, and Keats were expressing in English verse. A German by adoption was the colorful Hungarian-born Franz Liszt (1811–86). Liszt is believed to be probably the greatest concert pianist of all time. His glamorous personality and sensational, emotional compositions greatly popularized romantic music. Although Liszt was an international figure, his Hungarian folk music was characteristic of the growing national sentiment of the time.

THE HOUSES OF PARLIAMENT, LONDON. Accompanying the revival of interest in religion during the first half of the nineteenth century was a renewed interest in medieval ideals and artistic forms. The Houses of Parliament, which were built at this time, are examples of the Gothic style. (*Courtesy, British Travel Association*)

He befriended the youthful Richard Wagner, who later married one of Liszt's illegitimate daughters.

The romantic spirit is nowhere better illustrated than in the work of the Polish-French pianist-composer, Frédéric Chopin (1810–49). Chopin could express his sweet sorrows in dripping, lilting nocturnes, his sunny gaiety in bright waltzes and mazurkas, his national patriotism in stirring polonaises, or his deeper, dramatic moods in more formal ballades and concertos—all with equal skill and all in the romantic tradition. Meanwhile, other notable Frenchmen were writing romantic symphonies and operas. Gounod's *Faust* is an operatic version of Goethe's great theme. The haunting melodies of Bizet's (1838–75) *Carmen*, for example, are known wherever music is loved. The greatest Italian romantic composer was Giuseppe Verdi (1813–1901). His *La Traviata*, *Il Trovatore*, and *Rigoletto* are richly tuneful and spontaneous. Verdi was Italy's national cultural hero during the long, uphill fight for freedom and unity. His *Aïda* is Wagnerian in nature.

Richard Wagner (1813–83) brought to a dramatic close the romantic era in music, which Beethoven so brilliantly opened. Wagner's tempestuous life, like his music, illustrates and marks the transition from the romantic, moderately liberal and nationalistic early nineteenth century to the more violent, cynical, and materialistic spirit of the late nineteenth and early twentieth centuries. In his youth Wagner was a radical, and was exiled from Saxony in 1849 for his revolutionary, liberal, and national activities. Later he became an extreme German nationalist—even a German "master racist" of the type that has brought so much violence to the twentieth-century world. His operas, though containing some of the world's greatest music, are largely grandiloquent, strident, and extremely nationalistic. *Tannhäuser*, *The Meistersingers*, *Siegfried*, *Götterdämmerung*, *Lohengrin*, and *The Ring of the Nibelungs* not only added to the world's store of fine music but provided the Nazis with much thrill and comfort.

Since man is always a complex, emotional, and religious creature and only sometimes rational, the romanticists played a significant role in the eternal quest for an understanding of the mystery and beauty of life.

SUGGESTED READING

* *Philosophers Speak for Themselves: Berkeley, Hume, and Kant*, eds. T. V. Smith and Marjorie Grene (Phoenix). A handy approach to Kant.

Georg M. Brandes, *Main Currents in Nineteenth-Century Literature*, 6 vols. (1901–5). A classic work on the subject by a brilliant Danish scholar.

Wordsworth and Coleridge, *Lyrical Ballads* (complete poetical works of William Wordsworth, 1903). Probably the best single approach to the spirit of romanticism.

* Sir Walter Scott, *Ivanhoe* (Pocket Book). A famous novel in the romantic vein, glamorizing the medieval age of chivalry.

Hervey Allen, *Israfel: The Life and Times of Edgar Allen Poe* (1949). A good approach to American romanticism through one of its truest representatives.

Victor Hugo, *Les Misérables* (many editions). Called by some the world's greatest novel.

* Feodor Dostoevski, *Crime and Punishment* (Avon). One of the world's great novels exemplifying both the spirit of romanticism and the later spirit of psychological realism.

* Ivan Turgenev, *Fathers and Sons* (Rinehart). This Russian masterpiece depicts the conflict between the older (romantic) generation and the younger (realist) generation in nineteenth-century Russia.

Maurice Raynal, *The Nineteenth Century: Goya to Gauguin* (1951). A beautifully illustrated history of nineteenth-century painting.

Hugo Leichtentritt, *Music, History, and Ideas* (1938). A helpful study. Makes the music of the period of romanticism meaningful in the light of its historical setting.

SECTION II

The Industrial Revolution—

Second Phase:

The Emergence of the Masses,

1870–1914

T he Industrial Revolution, which in the years 1830–70 was still in its youth and limited primarily to Western Europe and the United States, grew to burly manhood between 1870 and 1914 and penetrated Eastern Europe and Asia. In its earlier phase it had brought the industrial bourgeoisie to power in the industrialized countries and had facilitated the growth of liberalism and nationalism. In its second phase, which is sometimes called the Second Industrial Revolution, it caused a stirring of the masses, the first widespread rumblings of violent social upheaval, and international and intercontinental clashes. The intelligentsia became obsessed with the wonders of science; the masses with the marvels of technology. Old values were called to question. The period 1870–1914 opened with great promise and ended with the greatest holocaust in history up to that time.

CHAPTER 48

The Onrush of Technology and Science

THE PERIOD 1870–1914 was a time of technological and scientific advancement such as the world had never known. Since the seventeenth century interest in technology and science had been steadily growing in Western Europe. By the late nineteenth century discovery and invention begat discovery and invention in geometric ratio. Industry mushroomed, pouring forth an ever-increasing volume of comforts of life. Transportation and communications were speeded up, making easier the development of huge and far-flung corporate empires. Scientists seemed to be on the verge of banishing the last mysteries of the physical universe.

One might assume that theory (science) would precede practice (technology). And today, as technology grows more and more complex, this is largely the case. In the past, however, the opposite has been true more often than not. Man was using the wheel long before he understood the mathematics of the circle. We shall, therefore, begin this chapter by discussing the growth of technology.

1. The Rapid Growth and Spread of Industry

The first phase of the Industrial Revolution (before 1870) has often been called the age of iron; the second phase (since 1870) the age of steel. Certainly steel has been the chief sinew of industry and trans-portation since the last quarter of the nineteenth century. Until the mid-nineteenth century steel was hard to make and very expensive. The discovery of the Bessemer process (1856) and the Thomas–Gilchrist process (1878) of removing impurities from molten iron greatly speeded up and cheapened the production of steel. In 1870 the total annual steel production in the entire world was approximately 1,000,000 tons, of which about half was produced by Great Britain, a fourth by Germany, and an eighth by the United States. By 1914 the world's annual production had increased more than fiftyfold; the United States was producing approximately half of the total, Germany a fourth, and Great Britain an eighth. Coal production followed somewhat the same pattern, with Great Britain dropping from first to second place behind the United States. Out of this steel were made tools and machines that constantly increased in numbers and efficiency. By 1914 in the industrialized countries these increasingly automatic machines fabricated most of the metal, textile, leather, and wood products and produced and processed much of the food.

The power to drive the steel machines was increasing in like proportion. In 1914 probably nine tenths of the world's industrial power was still provided by the steam engine, which had been vastly improved since the Watt-Boulton model had made its appearance. Other and more efficient power generators, however, were rapidly coming to the fore. Between 1831 and 1882 the dynamo for generating electricity was developed by a number of inventors, the most important of whom were Michael Faraday (British), the Siemens brothers (Germans), and Thomas A. Edison (American). In 1888 the electric motor was invented by Nikola Tesla, a naturalized American born in Croatia. The first practical internal-combustion engine was invented by Gottlieb Daimler (German) in 1883. Four years later he put it to work in the first automobile. In 1892 the Diesel engine, efficiently burning cheap crude oil, was invented by Rudolf Diesel (German). The invention of these two oil-burning engines gave birth to the vast oil industry. Sir Charles Parsons (British) patented the steam turbine in 1884. The turbine proved to be so efficient that it was soon used to drive the largest ships, and eventually to generate most of the world's electric power.

In the last decades of the nineteenth century pure science was playing an increasingly vital role in industry, and both science and industry were being applied to agriculture. Physics contributed most heavily to the rapidly growing electrical industry. Chemistry made possible such important industries as synthetic dyes, wood pulp, paper, plastics, synthetic fibers, photography, and motion pictures. The electrical and chemical industries were most highly developed in Germany. The mechanization of agriculture made its first big advances in the great grain-growing areas of the United States, Canada, and Australia, although Western Europe was also steadily increasing its agricultural yields through the use of farm machinery and scientific farming techniques.

The Industrial Revolution also spread geographically in this period. In 1870 Great Britain produced more industrial goods than the rest of the world combined. Besides Great Britain, only Belgium and France were well developed industrially. In the United States and Germany the Industrial Revolution was just beginning to make headway. Between 1870 and 1914 the

United States and Germany made tremendous industrial strides and surpassed Great Britain. By 1914 the Industrial Revolution had penetrated Central and Eastern Europe, Japan, Canada, Australia, and New Zealand; even India had a small textile industry. However, it was still in Western Europe and the United States that most of the world's industry was to be found, and the greatest part of Asia, Africa, and Latin America was still unindustrialized.

2. The Speeding Up of Transport

Between 1870 and 1914 a large part of humanity became mobile. Whereas before 1870 relatively few people in the world had ever seen more of the world than could be seen on a single day's journey by foot or on horseback, by 1914 millions of people were traveling considerable distances, often by rapid conveyance. Even in places like China, Turkey, and Brazil railroads chugged along, hauling people for distances and at speeds unknown before.

This was the greatest era of railroad building in history. There had been a rather lively building of railroads before 1870 in Western Europe and the United States. However, between 1870 and 1914 the world's mileage more than quintupled. In fact there has been relatively little railroad building since. The increase in speed and efficiency was proportionate to the increase in mileage.

At the same time the steamship was making comparable progress. It had stiff competition from the sailing ship until near the end of the nineteenth century. Steel hulls of great size, turbine engines, and screw propellers, however, were too much for the beautiful sails. The opening of the Suez Canal in 1869 and the Panama Canal in 1914, together with the increase in the size and speed of ships, brought the world and its peoples, commodities, and markets much closer together. Events would soon prove, however, that the world's peoples had not yet learned to live together.

During the last three decades of the nineteenth century the humble bicycle became a common and important means of locomotion, especially in Europe. Millions of people found this a cheap and pleasant means of stepping up their speed and radius; many depended upon it to get to and from their work. But the bicycle was not fast enough for the industrial age. When Gottlieb Daimler attached his little combustion engine to a wagon in 1887, the automobile was born. The automobile quickly captured the imagination of daring and skillful pioneers. Daimler sold his patent to a French company, and until the end of the century the French led the field in automobile development and production. Leadership passed to America with the founding of the Ford Motor Company in 1902. Henry Ford, who started out as a bicycle mechanic, was the father of two momentous ideas that revolutionized not only the automobile industry but industry in general. The first was that

high wages and cheap products would create markets and profits hitherto undreamed of while permitting the common man to share in the fruits of technology and science. The second was the assembly-line method of mass production. (Eli Whitney had introduced the idea of interchangeable parts a century earlier.) The rapid growth of the automobile not only made the masses much more mobile but created vast new industrial empires in oil, rubber, and concrete. Its social and psychological effects are still fluid and unfathomed.

Another invention of this period was the airplane. The first successful heavier-than-air flying machine was flown by Wilbur and Orville Wright in 1903 over the sand dunes at Kitty Hawk, North Carolina. By 1914 aviation was still in its infancy. However, the use of airplanes in World War I, largely for reconnaissance but also for fighting and

ASSEMBLY LINE OF THE FORD PLANT, DEARBORN, MICHIGAN. At the turn of the twentieth century Henry Ford raised wages and introduced the assembly line method of mass production, to create home markets of a size unknown by nineteenth–century imperialists. Ford also brought the fruits of the Industrial Revolution within the grasp of the masses. (*Courtesy of the Ford Motor Company*)

bombing, suggested a tremendous future for aviation.

It goes almost without saying that the new technology of steel and power and speed created a myriad of machines and gadgets to satisfy the material wants of those who could afford to buy them. But it also created restlessness among those who could not.

3. The Growth of Corporate Business and Monopoly

At the same time that industry was growing by leaps and bounds, individual companies were growing larger and combining to form monopolistic mergers or trusts. Such undertakings as railroads, shipping lines, and iron and steel mills were too large for all but a very few individuals to finance. As a rule, therefore, enterprises of this scope were carried on by joint-stock companies. Entrepreneur capitalists would raise the necessary capital outlay by organizing a corporation and selling stock in it to other capitalists. The actual operation of the larger industries would be carried on by hired managers, while the owners of the great industries were far removed from the day-to-day operations. The managers, who hired and fired and supervised the workmen, were working for the absentee owners, and their jobs depended on the amount of profit they could show. They were under constant pressure to pay the workers as little as possible and get from them as much work as possible. The capitalistic owners, often as not banks or insurance companies, rarely came in contact with the workers and their problems. This is what is meant by the term "soulless corporations."

The giant corporations were equally "soulless" in dealing with each other. In this rugged era of unrestrained competition the big and strong frequently destroyed the small and weak. The premium was on size and strength. The result was combines, mergers, and monopolistic trusts. The organizer of the first monopolistic trust was John D. Rockefeller. Rockefeller began refining oil during the Civil War and in 1870 organized the Standard Oil Company in Ohio. By shrewd efficiency and ruthless competition he gained control over so much of the oil-refining business in Ohio and western Pennsylvania that he was able to bargain with the railroads for a lower rate than they charged his competitors. With this advantage he was able either to drive most of his competitors out of business or force them to sell out to him on his own terms. In 1882 he organized his thirty-nine affiliated companies into the Standard Oil Trust, so-called because the member companies surrendered their stock to nine trustees who made the policies and distributed the profits. This trust dominated the oil business of the entire United States. It could crush smaller competing companies by price cutting. It could fix prices and set wages. It could influence state and national legislation. It could produce more and better oil. It could produce cheaper oil—if it chose. And it could compete with foreign nations more advantageously than numerous little companies.

The spectacular success of Rockefeller's Standard Oil Trust soon made it the model for many others, particularly in the United States, in Germany, in Japan, and to a lesser extent in Great Britain. The German monopolistic combinations such as the giant I. G. Farben Industries (chemicals and dyes) were called cartels. They received government encouragement and support, particularly in their operations abroad. In Japan three quarters of the nation's industry fell under the control of five families.

Although the United States began restricting some of the predatory practices of the trusts in 1890, all the industrialized countries encouraged the investment of capital in corporations by passing laws that limited the liability of stockholders to the amount of money invested (hence the "Ltd." usually seen after the name of a British corporation or combine). By 1914 most of the world's rapidly growing industry was controlled by a few great corporations and trusts. Although their stockholders were numbered by the thousands, they were really controlled by a relatively few banks and wealthy individuals. And between the owners of these corporations and the myriads of workers in them there lay a great gulf.

4. The Onrush of Natural Science: Physical and Biological

Theoretical or "pure" science advanced hand in hand with technology and applied science. The greatest advances in the field of the physical sciences in the nineteenth and early twentieth centuries had to do with discovering the nature of matter, energy, and electricity. John Dalton (1766–1844), a gifted British scientist and teacher of humble origin, started a fruitful line of inquiry by reviving the theory that all matter is composed of atoms. The atomic theory had been introduced by the ancient Greeks, and others had speculated about it from time to time. Dalton got on what turned out to be the right trail when he came to the conclusion that what distinguishes the various chemical elements is the weight of the atoms of which each element is composed. Building on Dalton's theories, the Russian chemist Dimitri Mendeléev (1834–1907) worked out around 1870 a periodic chart showing the atomic weight of all the known elements and indicating by gaps in the chart that others remained to be discovered. Both Dalton and Mendeléev thought that the atom was an indivisible solid. However, in the 1890's, the British physicist Joseph Thomson (1856–1940) and the Dutch physicist Hendrik Lorentz (1853–1928) independently discovered that atoms are composed of still smaller particles, which Lorentz named electrons. Also in the 1890's the German physicist Wilhelm von Röntgen (1845–1923) discovered X-rays, and the French physicist Pierre Curie (1859–1906) and his Polish wife discovered radium and more about radioactivity.

These were marvelous discoveries, and many scientists assumed that the fundamental secrets concerning the nature of matter had finally been learned. However, this was far from being the case. Thomson's theories were further developed early in the twentieth century by another British physicist, Sir Ernest Rutherford (1871–1937). Rutherford conceived of each atom as a miniature solar system, the nucleus being the sun and the electrons the planets. Furthermore—and this was most shocking—Thomson and Rutherford suggested that the neutrons and electrons might not be matter at all but merely positive and negative charges of electricity. Thus matter was threatening to become electricity.

Meanwhile, Albert Einstein (1879–1955), a German physicist who later fled to America—one of the greatest scientific geniuses of all time—was assailing all the time-honored concepts, not only about the stability of matter, but also about time, space, and motion. The amazing Einstein

ALBERT EINSTEIN. This German mathematician and physicist was one of the greatest scientific geniuses of the twentieth century. His theories helped to undermine beliefs long held to be fact, thereby opening broad vistas for future scientific achievements. Like many other liberal intellectuals Einstein fled the tyranny of Nazi Germany and settled in the United States. (*United Press International Photo*)

came up with a formula equating mass and energy: $E = mc^2$ (E = energy in ergs; m = mass in grams; c = the speed of light in centimeters per second). According to this startling formula, the atomic energy in a lump of coal is some three billion times as great as the energy obtained by burning the coal—a truth that was proved several decades later with the development of the atomic bomb. In 1905 Einstein proposed his theory of relativity, which made time, space, and motion relative to each other and to the observer, not the absolutes they had always been conceived to be. These are only a few of the most basic achievements in the physical sciences in the period 1870–1914. Little wonder that the intellectual world was fascinated and obsessed by them.

However, in the nineteenth century the intellectual world was even more interested in and influenced by developments in the biological sciences. Evolution, like the atomic theory, had been suggested by the ancient Greeks and from time to time afterward. With the revival of scientific interests and attitudes in the seventeenth and eighteenth centuries the thoughts of a number of men turned to the problem of the origin of the present world and its phenomena. By the mid-nineteenth century the concept of a slow and gradual development of the earth's crust and its inhabitants was not at all uncommon among intellectuals. The time was ripe for a first-rate scientist to supply the evidence. The man who did so was Charles Darwin (1809–82), the Einstein of the biological sciences.

Darwin was of a distinguished British family. The study of medicine at Edinburgh and theology at Cambridge failed to challenge him. The world of plants and, to a somewhat lesser extent, animals was his first love—or, rather, his consuming passion. In spite of frail health he turned his prodigious energy and powers of observation and reflection to the amassing of biological knowledge. Gradually he developed his concept of evolution. Of great influence on his thinking was Malthus's *Essay on Population*, which described the struggle of human be-

ings for food and survival, and Sir Charles Lyell's *Principles of Geology* (1830–33), which was the first really scientific treatise on geology. Lyell demonstrated by the study of fossils the likelihood of a gradual evolution of the earth's crust and of plant and animal forms over eons of time. Darwin published *The Origin of Species* in 1859. In this historic work he described with an impressive array of factual data, convincing reasoning, and lucid prose the long, slow evolution of present plant and animal species from simpler forms through a process of natural selection. In the struggle for survival in nature's jungle the fittest survived. Those specimens that possessed the more useful characteristics—for instance the horse with the longer legs—survived to produce more offspring and to transmit their superior qualities both inherited and acquired to future generations.[1] Twelve years later (1871) in his *Descent of Man*, he undertook to show how man himself evolved from more primitive species by the process. Although Darwin's work leaves many fundamental questions unanswered and his belief in the transmission of acquired traits has been pretty well discredited by the German scientist August Weismann and the Austrian monk Gregor Mendel, his main thesis quickly gained general acceptance in the scientific world.

Few books in history have had so much influence as *The Origin of Species*. (The religious storm it created will be discussed in the following chapter.) The industrial bourgeoisie seized upon Darwin's theory as an explanation and a justification of its own success. Rulers and dominant groups everywhere derived comfort from it, while the underdogs were inspired to struggle all the harder to survive. Philosophers, notably Her-

[1] The chief apostle of the transmission of acquired characteristics was the French naturalist Jean Baptiste de Lamarck (1744–1829). Darwin was unhappy with this theory but he did not have sufficient knowledge of the laws of genetics to be able to refute it. The theory was generally accepted in Darwin's time. Darwin did relegate it to a secondary position in his evolutionary hypothesis, however.

bert Spencer, undertook to broaden the principle of evolution to make it the key to all truth. Meanwhile, Darwin's brilliant work not only popularized but significantly contributed to the advancement of the biological sciences.

5. The Development of Medical Science

Medical science lagged far behind the physical and biological sciences at the opening of the nineteenth century. The seventeenth- and eighteenth-century scientists had made great progress in discovering the secrets of the stars, of the elements, and of plants and animals, but where the ailments of the human body were concerned they were still holding to theories of the Greek physician Galen, of the second century A.D. The medical profession was a lowly one. George Washington was bled to death in 1799 by a physician who was following the standard practices of the time.

Much groundwork had been laid, however, for medical progress. In the sixteenth century Vesalius made great advances in the study of human anatomy. In the seventeenth century Harvey discovered the circulatory system, while Leeuwenhoek and Malpighi were using the newly invented microscope to explore the structure of human tissue and to discover the existence of microbes. By the late eighteenth century the British scientist Edward Jenner was successfully inoculating against smallpox, though he did not understand the secret of its success. During the 1840's anesthesia was discovered and used successfully. However, the whole field of germ diseases and infections was still a mystery.

The secrets of bacteria, their nature and their control, began to be discovered first by the French chemist Louis Pasteur (1822–95). During the 1860's Pasteur, after indefatigable and imaginative research, discovered that fermentation is caused by bacteria that move through the air and can be destroyed by boiling (or by pasteurization). Later he discovered that many diseases of men and animals also are caused by bacteria

and that some of them can be prevented by vaccination. His spectacular services to French agriculture and to mankind made him the most honored man in France. Robert Koch (1843–1910), a humble country doctor in Eastern Germany, hearing of Pasteur's first discoveries, picked up the trail and discovered the germs causing anthrax (a deadly disease of cattle), tuberculosis, sleeping sickness, and many other diseases. He became a professor at the University of Berlin and was awarded the Nobel prize. Also building on Pasteur's foundations was the renowned British surgeon Joseph Lister (1827–1912), who applied the new knowledge of bacteria to the use of antisepsis and eventually asepsis in surgery. His amazing success in controlling infection opened a new era in surgery, and Lister was raised to the peerage by the British government. The honors bestowed upon Pasteur, Koch, and Lister, in contrast to the persecutions suffered by so many of the sixteenth- and seventeenth-century scientists, are striking evidence of the triumph of science and the scientific spirit in the nineteenth century. In the last decades of that century the governments of the European and Europeanized countries began to recognize that health is a public matter by passing health and sanitation laws.

6. The Rise of Social Science

The spectacular successes of the natural sciences, both pure and applied, in the nineteenth century encouraged scholars to attempt to apply the techniques and principles of natural science to the study of man and society. The result was the birth of two new sciences, psychology and sociology, both of which soon became popular. The functioning of man's mind has, of course, long been a matter of great interest to man. During the vogue of materialistic and mechanistic concepts of the universe in the eighteenth and again in the late nineteenth centuries, the tendency was to make the human brain mechanical in its operations. This mechanistic approach to psychology came to be called behaviorism. John Locke (1632–1704) had laid the foundations for behavioristic psychology by maintaining that man's mind operates mechanically, as does Newton's universe. Locke believed that the human brain at birth is a blank sheet of paper on which nothing would ever be written except by the perceptions of the five senses as interpreted by reason. The first behaviorist to bring psychology into the laboratory was Wilhelm Wundt (1832–1920). In his famous laboratory at Leipzig he and his enthusiastic students tested human reactions and tried all sorts of carefully controlled and measured experiments on cats and dogs, assuming that the findings were applicable to human beings.

The Russian scientist Ivan Pavlov (1849–1936), pursuing Wundt's line of attack, excited the intellectual world with the discovery of the conditioned reflex. Pavlov showed meat to a hungry dog and the dog's mouth watered. Then Pavlov rang a bell while showing the meat. Eventually the dog's mouth watered when only the bell was rung. The immediate and fascinating implication was that many of our human responses are purely mechanical reflexes produced by stimuli of which we are often unaware. This was a big step toward the concept of the mechanization of the mind and body of man. The Italian Cesare Lombroso (1836–1909) argued that criminals are born with mental and physical aberrations and are therefore not morally responsible for their acts. The Frenchman Alfred Binet (1857–1911) devised tests for measuring intelligence, a procedure that soon became the vogue.

The greatest stir of all in the rapidly growing field of psychology was created by the Austrian scientist Sigmund Freud (1856–1939). Freud believed that much neurosis and abnormality are the result of suppressed and frustrated drives of early life, particularly the sex drive—frustrations that then fester in the subconscious. He came to the conclusion that the correct therapy for such neurosis was to bring to the consciousness of the sufferer the facts and circumstances of the original frustration. Freud achieved some remarkable cures, thus founding psychoanalysis, which eventually became a fad. His influence on the development of modern psychiatry has been great. The implications of Freud's theories had a profound effect upon pedagogy in the twentieth century, especially in the United States. Many parents and teachers refused to discipline children for fear of frustrating them and giving them Freudian complexes.

It was not psychology, however, but sociology that in the nineteenth century claimed the title, "queen of the social sciences." This new study was founded and named by Auguste Comte (1798–1857), a somewhat eccentric Frenchman of great energy and imagination. The history of mankind, said Comte, may be divided into three epochs. The first was religious, when mystical or supernatural explanations were assigned to all phenomena. The second was metaphysical, when general laws and abstract principles were taken as explanatory principles. The third, which man was on the point of entering, was the specific or positive, when the truth would be discovered by the scientific gathering of factual data. Comte had utter scorn for the first, and little respect for the second, epochs. He believed that man and society are as susceptible to scientific investigation as minerals, plants, and the lower animals. His religion was the worship of humanity, and he had great faith in the future of mankind. These ideas are called positivism. Comte's followers, eager and numerous, placed great faith in statistics. They amassed vast arrays of statistical data on every conceivable social problem. They tended to scorn supernatural religion of all kinds, morals and ideals, chronological history, and individual biography.

Second only to Comte in importance in the founding and promotion of sociology was the indefatigable and seemingly indestructible little Englishman Herbert Spencer (1820–1903). Spencer shared Comte's scorn for mystical religion and denied that morals should be based upon religion. He also shared Comte's faith in the progress of man. In his seven-volume *System of Synthetic Philosophy* Spencer undertook to synthesize all human and social phenomena into one grand evolutionary system.

Man's natural interest in himself and in human society, together with the scientific spirit of the times, guaranteed for the social sciences great popularity. Anthropologists and archaeologists dug feverishly into man's physical and cultural past. Political scientists and economists tended to forsake theory for the statistical and "practical." Strenuous efforts were made to make history a social science. Leopold von Ranke (1795–1886) strove to make history coldly scientific and morally neutral. History, he insisted, should be based upon an exhaustive accumulation and analysis of documentary evidence. Ranke's historical attitude and methodology were imported from Germany into the United States. They became the standard in both countries. Efforts were also made to make history topical and statistical rather than chronological and to focus upon social trends and forces rather than individuals. During the late nineteenth and early twentieth centuries this approach was very popular, particularly in Germany and the United States.

To a visitor from Mars it must have appeared that the Western world in 1914 was on the brink of Utopia. Better and better machines, driven by greater and greater power, were turning out more and more goods and labor-saving devices every day. Natural scientists appeared to be solving the last mysteries of the material universe. Medical scientists appeared to be banishing pain and disease from the earth. Social scientists were amassing voluminous knowledge about man's mind and his social relationships. The cult of progress enjoyed wide popularity. Political liberalism was on the march. And yet we now know that the half-century which followed turned out to be the bloodiest period in the history of the world, more fear- and hate-ridden than any previous era.

SUGGESTED READING

Carlton J. H. Hayes, *A Generation of Materialism, 1871–1900* (1941). This excellent volume combines a wealth of factual information with thoughtful analysis and a graceful writing style.

Abbott Usher, *A History of Mechanical Inventions* (1929). An excellent book for the student with a flair for things mechanical, and a useful book for all students of the nineteenth and twentieth centuries.

W. C. Dampier, *A History of Science and Its Relation with Philosophy and Religion* (1946). Probably the best volume on this important subject.

* Charles Darwin, *The Origin of Species and the Descent of Man* (Modern Library). Many students will be surprised to find these books (two books in one volume), two of the most influential and controversial ever written, lucid and fascinating.

Eve Curie, *Madame Curie: A Biography* (1937). A romantic true story of one of the discoverers of radioactivity, by her daughter.

Arthur Compton, *Atomic Quest* (1956). A lucid account of the making and the use of the first atomic bombs, by one of the chief scientists responsible for the achievement. It is non-technical and goes into the human and spiritual implications of atomic fission.

Sigmund Freud, *An Outline of Psychoanalysis* (1949). A good introduction to one of the most influential scientists and thinkers of the late nineteenth and early twentieth centuries.

Ida M. Tarbell, *History of the Standard Oil Company*, 2 vols. (1904). An exposé of the history and practices of John D. Rockefeller's pioneer monopoly trust. Written in a journalistic style, this book did much to arouse public opinion and to inspire congressional anti-monopoly legislation.

CHAPTER 49

The Challenge to Christianity

WHATEVER one's religious faith may be —Christian, Judaistic, Buddhist, or rationalistic; orthodox or skeptic; evangelistic or apathetic—he can hardly deny the tremendous influence of religion in history. In the Middle East empires rise and fall, conquerors come and go, but Islam remains, setting the pattern of ideals and thought and to a considerable degree the life of the people. The same is true of Hinduism in India and Confucianism in China. In Western civilization the great religious base, the great commonality, is Christianity, with its roots of Judaistic ethics and monotheism. Before the nineteenth century Christianity had withstood many assaults: the Arian heresy in its formative years; conflict between pope and emperor, conflict between the Western and the Eastern churches, and various heresies in the middle ages; the Great Schism in the fourteenth and fifteenth centuries; the Protestant Revolt in the sixteenth century; and the rationalistic assault in the eighteenth century. In the latter part of the nineteenth century, however, the Christian religion was to undergo a challenge more serious and fundamental than any of these.

1. The Various Forces and Influences Opposed to Mystic Religion in the Period 1870–1914

Of the various factors and developments during the second phase of the Industrial Revolution (1870–1914) that were hostile to mystic or supernatural religion, undoubtedly the most direct and challenging was the rapid growth of science and the scientific spirit. However, there were others that will become clearer in the following chapters but should be considered briefly here.

The phenomenal growth of technology and industry, which we have already examined, was in many ways inimical to religious faith and practices. In the industrialized areas it began to appear that the power machines would soon supply all of man's material needs and banish grinding toil from the earth. Preoccupation with creature comforts and pleasure gadgets undreamed of a few years earlier now tended to overshadow interest in the sacred and spiritual things of this world and the next. Dazzling speed did not seem to be conducive to meditation and devotion. The Industrial Revolution also brought about a mass migration of people, from farm to city and from country to country, tearing them loose from their old social patterns and institutions of which the church had long been one of the chief. Members of the flocks became separated from their pastors. And in the growing industrial cities, with their movement and relative excitement, many of the newcomers seemed no longer to need the church for their social life and entertainment.

The liberal and radical political movements of the late nineteenth century were for the most part anti-clerical and often anti-religious. The established churches in Europe, particularly the Roman Catholic Church, had long been allied with the conservative aristocracy and royalty. Liberals, when they came to power, usually proceeded to attack the powers, the privileges, and the property of the established church. France is a good example. After the revolutionary era had ended with the overthrow of Napoleon, the Roman Catholic Church made a comeback. It allied itself with the Bourbon regime and with Napoleon III's Second Empire, and opposed liberal movements, including the setting up of the Third French Republic. The liberal leaders of the Third French Republic immediately adopted anti-clerical policies. During the 1880's the Ferry Laws loosened the hold of the Church on education by setting up a rival and favored system of public secular schools, from which the teaching of religion was banned. In 1901 the Associations Law virtually destroyed the Church's schools by outlawing the Roman Catholic teaching orders, or associations. In 1905 church and state were completely separated. In all the industrialized countries in this period public secular education made great strides, usually under the sponsorship of liberal parties. Marxist socialism, which began to make headway between 1870 and 1914, was militantly materialistic and atheistic.

A third factor inimical to supernatural religion during the second phase of the Industrial Revolution was the growth of *malignant nationalism*, which afflicted all of the great industrialized powers. Nationalism became itself a religion and drew the allegiance of millions away from their traditional faiths. International Roman Catholicism and international Judaism were particularly hard hit. Between 1872 and 1878 Bismarck waged an unrelenting *Kulturkampf* (battle for civilization) against the Roman Catholic Church in Germany. (See p. 594) Bismarck regarded as intolerable the allegiance of millions of German citizens to a non-German pope and the formation of a Roman Catholic political party in Germany. The anti-semitism that raised its ugly head

in many countries at this time may be attributed in part to the resentment against the international character of Judaism and also to racism, which is an extreme form of malignant nationalism. In France a Jewish army captain, Alfred Dreyfus, was "framed" and sent to Devil's Island. He became the center of a political storm that threatened to tear the Third Republic apart. Bloody pogroms in Russia drove tens of thousands of Russian and Polish Jews to America. Many Jews themselves after centuries of dispersion became nationalistic and started a movement (Zionism) to set up a Jewish national state in Palestine. Although Bismarck lost his battle against the Roman Catholics in Germany, manifestations of extreme nationalism, such as these, generally represented serious setbacks to supernatural religion either from direct assault or from transfer of allegiance.

2. The Conflict Between Natural Science and Christianity

With the exception of the evolutionary hypothesis the challenge to Christianity by natural science was more indirect than direct. The marvelous achievements of the scientists caused many to place great faith in man and in his ability to do for himself whatever needed to be done. The scientific attitude ran counter to the traditional attitude of religious faith. The discovery of more and more of the secrets of the material world made it possible to attribute to natural causes many phenomena that previously had been attributed to divine intervention. Disease germs, for instance, now appeared to be doing things that had long been ascribed to God. In fact there appeared to many at the end of the nineteenth century to be less and less place and need for God. Many people who thought that way would change their minds after two disastrous world wars and the threat of a third (atomic) war, but in the meantime the tide was definitely scientific and materialistic.

The greatest issues between natural science and religion to be raised in the nineteenth century grew out of Darwin's evolutionary hypothesis. The publication of *The Origin of Species* in 1859 created an immediate religious storm. The proposal of a long, gradual, and seemingly mechanistic evolution of all present species from simpler forms appeared to contradict the account of divine creation given in the first chapter of Genesis. If Darwin should prove to be right and Genesis wrong, what faith could be put in the divine inspiration and the reliability of the rest of the Bible, upon which so much of Christianity depends? The whole process of evolution as suggested by Darwin appeared to leave God out of the affairs of the universe entirely. Any doubt concerning Darwin's place for man in his evolutionary hypothesis was removed twelve years later, when he published *The Descent of Man*. Man, like all other living things, evolved from more primitive species. This appeared to refute, not only the biblical account of man's creation, but also God's purpose, according to the Bible, of creating man in His own image as a temple of the Holy Spirit. On this new evidence, in the view of many, man seemed to be just another animal, albeit the highest.

Churchmen throughout Christendom raged against Darwin and his hypothesis. His character and his motives were assailed. His thesis was attacked and ridiculed. Some of the criticism was sound. There is still no empirical evidence for the existence of many of the hypothesized evolutionary stages. A good bit of the theorizing done by Darwin and his contemporaries has since been generally repudiated by most biologists. And although there is abundant evidence of evolution within a given species, neither Darwin nor anyone else has ever demonstrated the evolution of one species out of another—the origin of a species. However, most of the criticism of the churchmen sprang from ignorance, fear, and habits of thought growing out of the uses and abuses of unquestioned authority. Efforts were made, sometimes successful, to suppress the reading of Darwin's books and the teaching of the evolutionary hypothesis in the schools.

Darwin himself, a gentle and modest scholar of the highest order but not a controversialist, refrained for the most part from attacking the churchmen. He merely defended his thesis when he considered it to be incorrectly or unfairly attacked. However, he was not lacking in doughty champions able and willing to assail the forces of religion with the religious forces' own techniques. Thomas Huxley (1825–95), a biologist, surgeon in the British navy, and president of the Royal Society, popularized Darwin's work in dozens of vigorous and lucid books and pamphlets and heaped withering scorn upon the churchmen. He called himself "Darwin's bulldog." Herbert Spencer was carried away with Darwin's thesis and built a system of philosophy around the idea of evolution. Spencer considered evolution the key to all truth and all progress. He was vitriolic in his denunciations of the ideals and practices of the Christian religion, which he regarded as the major enemy of both truth and progress. Ernst Haeckel (1834–1919), a prolific German scientist and popularizer, made great and sometimes ridiculous claims for evolution and for science. He claimed that scientists would very soon be solving all the remaining mysteries of life and even creating life. The conflict between the evolutionists and the Christian churchmen that raged in Western Europe in the last four decades of the nineteenth century did not reach its climax in the United States until the 1920's. We shall examine its outcome presently.

3. The Assault of Social Science on Christianity

The assault of social science upon Christianity was very much more direct and severe than that of natural science. Social science deals specifically with man and society, as does religion. It was inevitable that two approaches to the same subject from diametrically opposite points of view should come into head-on collision. Also, social science is much less exact than natural science, and social scientists are more given to generalizing and philosophizing on complex subjects with less precise data.

Anthropologists dug into man's distant past to unearth the primitive origins of his culture, of which religion is always an important part. Nearly all of them concluded that religion is based upon primitive superstition. In 1890 Sir James Frazer (1854–1941) brought out *The Golden Bough*, a vast and fascinating history of early myths, superstitions, and cults, from which he believed that present-day religions, including Christianity, are derived. For instance, he shows that it was customary among many primitive tribes to eat their grain god and drink their wine god, hoping thereby to partake of their strength. *The Golden Bough* went through edition after edition, each bigger than the one preceding, until it reached twelve volumes. It is still a good seller in abridged form.

The behavioristic psychologists attempted to mechanize man's mind and his emotions, including religious faith (or "ecstasy," as they sometimes called it). They had man creating God in man's own image in order to have a big brother to lean on in time of need. Some of them saw God as man's creation as a ready answer to the unanswerable.

The historians, who in the period 1870–1914 attempted to make history a social science, assigned natural, usually economic, causes to all religious developments and institutions. The famed German historian of religion Adolf von Harnack (1851–1930) believed Christianity to be an outgrowth of Greek philosophy. Historians of the warfare between science and religion in this period nearly always made science the hero and religion the villain.

It was the sociologists, however, who of all the social scientists in the period 1870–1914 were the most persistently and pointedly hostile to religion. Supernatural religion had no place whatever in Comte's positivism, humanity itself being the object of worship. Through volume after volume of Herbert Spencer's sociological writings ran a vein of hostility to mystic religion in general and to Christianity in particular. Mechanical evolu-

tion became, for Spencer, the key to all social progress. Even morals evolved. Religious faith retarded social progress and obscured our vision of the evolutionary social process.

4. The Higher Criticism

Finally, the scientific spirit of the second phase of the Industrial Revolution brought forth a number of biblical scholars, who subjected the Bible to searching scrutiny and analysis—some for the purpose of establishing its exact meaning, and others for the purpose of detecting error or fraud. This type of scholarship is called "higher criticism."

The first prominent nineteenth-century "higher critic" of the Bible was David Strauss (1808–74), a Lutheran theologian at the University of Tübingen in Germany. After long years of laborious work Strauss brought out a *Life of Jesus* in four volumes, which stripped Christ of his divinity and undertook to explain in purely natural terms the miracles and prophecies recorded in the New Testament. Strauss asserted that the New Testament was a very unreliable document, that the authorship of the four Gospels could not be proved, and that the four accounts of the life of Jesus were contradictory.

Much more popular and influential was the charming one-volume *La Vie de Jésus* by Ernest Renan (1823–92), a French scholar and a Roman Catholic. Renan pictured Christ in solely human and natural terms. Christ was the gentlest, wisest, best, and most charming creature who ever lived. We should all worship him and follow his example. But he was man, not God. Renan attributed Christ's belief in his own divinity to hallucinations. But it was these psychological aberrations that gave him his power and drive and much of his appeal. Renan's *Life of Jesus* was greeted with immediate and continuing enthusiasm by the intellectual world of the late nineteenth and early twentieth centuries. Here at last seemed to be the solution to the most stubborn mystery of all—the answer that the materialistic "scientific" philosophers had long been looking for. It was the rationalization and the humanization of the most influential figure of all time, who proclaimed himself to be God and who attracted the greatest following in history, the intellectual elite no less than the unlettered masses. The work of Strauss and Renan and the numerous other "higher critics" appeared to many to bring religion within the compass of onrushing science.

5. The Christian Response

The reaction of Christianity to the various nineteenth-century challenges and assaults may be classified under three broad headings: (1) uncompromising rejection, (2) surrender to the challenges and assaults, (3) moderate compromise, or accommodation of the fundamentals of the faith to proved new truth and new conditions. On the whole the Roman Catholics were able to meet the challenge more quickly and easily than the Protestants. This is because the Roman Catholics were more centralized and authoritative in their organization than the Protestants and were less dependent upon the Bible (now under attack) for doctrinal authority. The Roman Catholic Church could achieve by papal decree and clerical discipline what the various Protestant denominations, with their less authoritative and sometimes democratic procedures, required years to accomplish. The Eastern Orthodox Christians were not much affected by the nineteenth-century challenges, since they were located mostly in Russia and the Balkan Peninsula, where science and technology arrived only in the last decade of the century, and then very slowly.

The first reaction of Christianity to the new challenges was angry rejection of the new ideas and forces. In 1864 Pope Pius IX (1846–78) issued a *Syllabus of Errors*, errors that Roman Catholics were to avoid. These errors, eighty in all, included separation of church and state, civil marriage, secular education, freedom of speech and press, reli-

gious toleration, liberty of conscience, Freemasonry, liberalism, and materialism. This list was strengthened and brought up to date by Pius X (1903–14), who issued another *Syllabus* in 1907 specifically condemning all those Christians who would compromise their doctrines. In 1870 Pius IX called the Vatican council (the first general council since that at Trent in the sixteenth century), which pronounced the doctrine of papal infallibility. According to this doctrine, the pope, when speaking *ex cathedra* (that is, officially *from the chair* of St. Peter) on a matter of faith or morals, is not subject to error. This was the most authoritarian position that the Church and the pope had ever taken, and it came at a time when the intellectual, political, and religious trends in the world seemed to be in the opposite direction. (The pope has used this power only once, as of 1959.) In the late nineteenth and early twentieth centuries the Roman Catholic hierarchy excommunicated numerous members and several priests who had compromised the official doctrines of the Church. By 1914 discipline appeared to have been fairly well restored.

The Protestants had no such disciplinary means and weapons at their disposal. Their difficulties in this respect are illustrated by the failure of the Anglican hierarchy in Great Britain to discipline certain heterodox clergymen. The cases were appealed to the highest secular court; the established Anglican Church, which is subordinate to the British government, was overruled. In Germany, Kaiser Wilhelm II (1888–1918) freely interfered in the affairs of the official Lutheran Church in behalf of compromise (modernist) doctrines. In general, fundamentalism in the Protestant churches was a local or individual matter. However, fundamentalist sects were by no means rare. They interpreted the Bible, including the first chapter of Genesis, literally, and denounced all scientific beliefs that did not accord with it. As science and technology rushed on, the fundamentalist position became harder and harder to maintain.

The second reaction of Christianity to the

nineteenth-century challenges and assaults was surrender to them. Many Christians, Roman Catholics and Protestants alike, lost their faith, left their church, and became atheists or agnostics. But many more who lost the traditional faith remained in their church and attempted to change its doctrines. They granted the claims of science and the "higher criticism," and they sympathized with the materialism, liberalism, and extreme nationalism of the day. They continued to go to church, to sing the hymns, to say the prayers, and to recite the creeds, but they did not believe what they sang, said, and recited. They would reject the supernatural and deny the divinity of Christ. They would make the Bible a book of good literature and high ethical ideals; Christ, a great social reformer; and the church, an instrument for the promotion of good will, wholesome fellowship, racial tolerance, temperance, charity, patriotism, and so on. These Christians came to be called modernists. The Roman Catholic Church, as we have seen, declared officially against modernism in 1907, and by 1914 it appeared either to have suppressed the modernists in its ranks or driven them under cover. In the various Protestant churches modernism competed with fundamentalism, both extreme and moderate, and by 1914 modernism tended to gain the upper hand. In the United States modernism in the Protestant churches did not reach its peak until the 1920's and 1930's.

The third reaction of Christianity, the one that appears to prevail today, was moderate compromise: a cheerful acceptance of proved scientific facts and reasonable deductions therefrom together with attempts to harmonize the findings of science with the fundamentals of the Christian faith. This involved the interpretation figuratively of certain passages in the Bible, particularly in the first chapter of Genesis, and the admission of a few errors in various versions of the Bible. On the other hand, it was soon found that many of the anti-Christian claims of the scientists and higher critics had been hasty and ill-founded.

Many of the higher critics of this period were anything but scientifically objective, setting out deliberately to debunk the Bible. And the anti-Christian scientists were, for the most part, not first-rate scholars like Darwin, but second-raters—popularizers and publicists, who knew as little about the Christian religion as the militant fundamentalists knew about science. When first-rate men of good will on both sides moved in on the problem, it was discovered that little, if any, conflict existed between the proved facts and principles of science and the fundamental doctrines of the Christian faith. Of course, many questions remain unanswered in the minds of honest men on both sides. A second feature of this harmonizing Christian reaction was an increased awareness of the responsibility of the Christian churches to participate actively in the social and political problems of the day.

The Roman Catholics were the first to reach this middle position. From 1878 to 1903 the Roman Church was headed by the ablest pope of modern times, Leo XIII. This elderly, frail, and scholarly man was elected pope at one of the most critical times in the Church's history. It was not thought that he would live long, and he was expected only to hold the rival factions together during his few remaining years, after which a strong pope would be elected. Instead, he lived for twenty-five more years and proved himself to be a brilliant and vigorous theologian, administrator, and statesman. Leo XIII quickly removed any doubts concerning the willingness of the Roman Catholic Church to compromise its historic doctrines. He proclaimed Thomas Aquinas the official Roman Catholic theologian and philosopher and established numerous centers of higher learning for the study and propagation of St. Thomas's theology and philosophy. He invited all Protestants and Eastern Orthodox Christians to accept papal supremacy, Roman Catholic doctrines and practices, and to return to the Roman fold. He demanded a privileged status for the Roman Catholic

Church in all states, independent of the secular government when in a minority and superior to the secular government when in a majority. On the other hand, Leo XIII welcomed new scientific beliefs on condition that they be proved, opened the Vatican's archives to research scholars, and brought a number of first-rate physicists and the latest scientific equipment to the Vatican observatory. As to the evolution controversy Leo XIII and his successors gradually took the postition that natural science was not the province of the Church and that the Church, therefore, would not make official pronouncements on it; that the evolutionary concept was not in itself repugnant to the doctrines of the Church; that evolution could be taught in the Church's schools as a possible hypothesis, and, when and if satisfactorily proved, it could be taught as fact; that the first chapter of Genesis should be taken figuratively; and that within these premises belief in evolution was a private and individual matter.

Leo XIII also faced up squarely and boldly to the economic and social challenges of the second phase of the Industrial Revolution. In 1891, in the most famous of all his encyclicals, *Rerum Novarum* (new things), he denounced materialism and Marxian socialism and proclaimed the sanctity of private property. He did, however, declare limits to the use of private property. Labor must not be treated as a commodity; workers must be paid a fair living wage and protected against too long hours, injury, and disease. Leo XIII advocated a wider distribution of property, labor unions for collective bargaining, and farming co-operatives. Roman Catholic labor unions were soon organized to challenge the socialist-dominated unions.

Protestantism groped its way slowly, and often painfully, toward a position similar in general to that of Leo XIII. However, Protestantism never claimed so exalted a place for the church within the state, nor was it ever so firm in its stand on capital and labor.

Early in the twentieth century a number of developments strengthened the hands of the theologians. The discovery, by Rutherford and Einstein, that the atom is really composed of particles of electricity or energy and Einstein's theory of relativity undermined belief in the stability of matter and confidence in materialism. Natural scientists were no longer so sure of themselves. Many things in the material world, long regarded as certain, suddenly became less certain. The two world wars, the great depression, and the violence of fascist and communist dictatorships raised grave doubts concerning some of the optimistic tenets of the social scientists and the modernists.

Shortly after the close of World War I the brilliant Swiss Protestant theologian and philosopher Karl Barth (1886–) began to beckon the disillusioned Western Christian world to return to an enlightened fundamentalism. The time had come, said Barth, for the Christian churches to concern themselves less with social and political problems, which he called the worship of and reliance upon man, and to concern themselves more with the worship of God and reliance upon divine Providence. A neo-Calvinist, Barth believes that God still rules the universe and that the Scriptures are His word to man. Barth's fundamentalism differs from the earlier fundamentalism in that it is propounded in the full light of recent science and philosophy and with an impressive display of intellectualism. Probably Barth's most illustrious follower is Reinhold Niebuhr (1892–) in the United States. However, Niebuhr believes that the Christian churches should be actively engaged both in the worship of God and in humanitarian political and social endeavors.

As to evolution, the eminent French scientist Lecomte du Noüy expressed the views of many intellectual Christians, both Protestant and Roman Catholic, in his *Human Destiny* (1947). Noüy argued impressively that evolution could not have occurred by blind chance, that it must have been divinely guided. The millions of years that God took to create man did not trouble Noüy. Just as a day is long for an insect that has a life span of one day, but short to man, so time that seems long to man would be short to a timeless being like God. Lecomte du Noüy believed that with the appearance of man evolution ceased to be physical, so far as man was concerned, and became spiritual, Christ being the perfect summation. This is a far cry from the fulminations of Huxley and the early fundamentalists. By the time of World War II (1939–45) the trend in Protestantism appeared to be definitely toward a moderate and somewhat intellectualized fundamentalism.

Protestantism, like Roman Catholicism under Leo XIII, assumed a more direct and organized interest in social problems. Some Protestants, like the Anglican clergyman, novelist, and historian Charles Kingsley (1819–75), became so outraged at the lot of the industrial proletariat that they advocated Christian socialism. Another Anglican clergyman, William Booth (1829–1912), founded the Salvation Army, which concentrated on rescue mission work in the industrial slums. The Young Men's Christian Association specialized in wholesome recreation for underprivileged youth; the Quakers, in charities.

Although Eastern Orthodox Christianity was not so seriously challenged in the period 1870–1914 as were Roman Catholic and Protestant Christianity in the more materially advanced West, Orthodox Russia produced one of the foremost Christian social reformers of the time—Count Leo Tolstoi (1828–1910). This wealthy and aristocratic but sensitive literary artist became greatly disturbed by the condition of the wretched poor in Russia's cities. In his book *What Shall We Do Then?* Tolstoi advocates Christian socialism, which he believed to be taught in the four Gospels. The rich should share their goods with the poor and also the physical toil of the poor. Tolstoi practiced his own preaching. Divesting himself of his great wealth, he lived the life of a common laborer and still found time and inspiration to continue his writing.

Judaism was affected by the various challenges of the second phase of the Industrial Revolution in much the same way as Christianity. Many Jews drifted away from their religious beliefs and practices entirely. Many others became Reformed Jews (modernists). Those who remained true to the old religion were called Orthodox Jews. It was not until the mid-twentieth century that Mohammedan, Hindu, Buddhist, and Confucianist lands began seriously to feel the impact of technology, science, political liberalism and radicalism, and malignant na-

DR. ALBERT SCHWEITZER WITH ONE OF HIS PATIENTS. During the period 1870–1914, when Christianity was on the defensive at home, it was more vigorous than ever in its foreign missionary activity. By 1914 more than forty million people outside Western Christendom professed the Christian faith. One of the most prominent of the Christian missionaries is the French Protestant Dr. Albert Schweitzer, eminent scholar, musician, and physician, who in 1913 at the age of thirty-eight chose to devote the rest of his life to medical missionary work in the jungles of French Equatorial Africa. (*United Press International Photo*)

tionalism. The responses of those religions are not yet clear.

It is an interesting fact that Christianity, so beset on its home grounds by challenges, assaults, and internal divisions during the period 1870–1914, was never more zealous in sending out missionaries to propagate the faith abroad. Roman Catholic, Protestant, and Eastern Orthodox missionaries vied with each other in converting the heathen in Asia and Africa. Probably the most renowned Christian missionary of the early twentieth century is the French Protestant Albert Schweitzer (1875–   ). An eminent philosopher, historian, musician, and surgeon, Schweitzer in 1913 went into the jungles of French Equatorial Africa to spend the rest of his life ministering to the medical needs of the primitive tribesmen and teach-ing them the Christian message by the example of his life.

By 1914 more than forty million people outside Western Christendom professed the Christian faith. However, since the Christian missionaries also brought Western technology, science, and liberal political ideas to Asia and Africa and since they were often associated in the minds of the native peoples with Western imperialism and exploitation, the over-all influence of Christianity on the two largest continents is extremely complex and obscure. The scope and intensity of this Christian foreign-missionary activity, however, is striking evidence of Christianity's continued vitality in the West, although that vitality was not so clear then as it has become since. In 1914 Christianity in the West was still on the defensive.

SUGGESTED READING

Thomas Huxley, *Lay Sermons* (1870). Eloquent and ofttimes vitriolic defense of Darwinism against the Christian theologians.

Sir James Frazer, *The Golden Bough* (1948). An abridgment of the original twelve-volume work, which first appeared 1890–1915. An attempt to prove that Christianity evolved from primitive myths and superstitions. A fascinating collection of religious myths.

* Ernest Renan, *Life of Jesus* (Modern Library). A psychological study of Christ, attempting to demonstrate that, although he was the most charming personality in history, he was really a man suffering from hallucinations that he was God. This attractively written book has had an enormous influence and has had numerous twentieth-century best-seller emulators.

Carlton J. H. Hayes, *A Generation of Materialism, 1871–1900* (1941). A brilliant analysis of the various late-nineteenth-century challenges to and assaults on Christianity, and of Christianity's responses to them. It is particularly good on the Roman Catholic response.

* Lecomte du Noüy, *Human Destiny* (Mentor).

This brilliant and challenging book by an eminent French scientist gives a lucid explanation of the evolutionary process and attempts to demonstrate that it could not have happened by blind chance.

William Hordern, *Layman's Guide to Protestant Theology* (1955). More than lives up to its title. An excellent antidote to the naïve assumption that anyone who is not a Catholic is a Protestant, or that Christianity consists of positive thinking and helping old ladies across the street. Written with clarity and vigor for the serious layman.

K. S. Latourette, *A History of the Expansion of Christianity*, 7 vols. (1929 ff.) Vols. V and VI; *The Great Century, 1800–1914* (1941). Deals with the nineteenth century, when Christianity, severely challenged in the West, made its greatest conquests abroad.

Arnold Toynbee, *An Historian's Approach to Religion* (1956). A brilliant work by one of the most learned and provocative of all historians. Much of the material is drawn from his ten-volume *A Study of History*.

CHAPTER 50

The Movement of the Masses[1]

THE FIRST phase of the Industrial Revolution brought the industrial bourgeoisie to power in the industrialized countries. The industrial proletariat was too small, too impoverished, and too bewildered to make its influence strongly felt. It is true that it had stirred on occasion, as in 1830 and 1848, but it had been suppressed with relative ease. During the second phase of the Industrial Revolution, however, not only the industrial proletariat, its numbers greatly augmented by the rapid growth of industry, but the masses in general began to assert themselves. In wider and wider areas they demanded and obtained the ballot and education. They organized and greatly increased their bargaining power. Politicians, journalists, manufacturers, salesmen, social theorists, and artists began to seek their support and to cater to their tastes. The industrial bourgeoisie still had the upper hand, but now it was being seriously challenged.

1. The Growth of Population and the Great Migrations

Prior to the Industrial Revolution the population of Europe was largely rural, relatively stable in size, and immobile. During the course of the nineteenth century it changed drastically in all three respects. The

[1] For much of the material in this chapter the authors are gratefully indebted to Carlton J. H. Hayes, A Generation of Materialism, 1871–1900 (New York: Harper & Brothers, 1941).

total population of Europe, which had begun to increase moderately but definitely in the sixteenth century, and markedly in the eighteenth century, is believed to have more than doubled during the nineteenth century. At the same time there was a great movement of people from country to city and from Europe to overseas areas, chiefly the United States. These changes were at their peak between 1870 and 1914. For a time it was believed that the world's birth rate had suddenly jumped. It would now appear that this was not true and that in Europe at least the birth rate actually declined after 1870. The revolutionary advances in medicine brought the death rate sharply down; technology and science greatly increased the production and distribution of food, enabling the European world to sustain a larger and healthier population. The movement to the city was brought about by the opportunities in industry and commerce, the growing attractiveness of cities, and the application of mechanization and science to agriculture, which now required fewer workers to produce greater yields. Urban population exceeded the rural in England by 1850, in Germany by 1914, and in the United States by 1920. It is estimated that in the period 1870–1914 more than a hundred million Europeans moved from the country to the city. By 1914 Western civilization was definitely urban.

The overseas migration of Europeans be-

WELCOME TO THE LAND OF FREEDOM. A variety of emotions is displayed on the faces of these immigrants as they pass the Statue of Liberty in New York harbor on their way to a new life. During the second phase of the Industrial Revolution, 1870–1914, more than thirty million Europeans migrated from their homelands to settle overseas, most of them in the United States. This movement of the masses dwarfed all migrations of peoples during earlier times. (*The Bettmann Archive*)

tween 1870 and 1914 was phenomenal. Ever since the first settlements in the New World in the early sixteenth century there had been a sizable trickle of Europeans to the Americas. This trickle had become a flowing stream in the early and mid-nineteenth century. During the second phase of the Industrial Revolution (1870–1914) it swelled into a rushing torrent. In this brief span of forty-four years more than 30,000,000 Europeans left their homelands and migrated to the New World or the British self-governing dominions. The great bulk of them came to the United States. Never in history had there been such a movement of peoples. The great folk migrations of ancient and medieval times were puny by comparison. These mass migrations were made possible, of course, by the improvements in transportation—railroads and steamships. In addi-

tion to the migrations many more people were now traveling for pleasure. With the coming of the automobile at the turn of the century so much of mankind took to wheels that tourism eventually became one of the world's biggest businesses. The masses were truly on the move, but not just physically, they were on the move politically, socially, and economically as well.

2. The March of Democracy in the United States and Great Britain

The period 1830–70 was marked in most of the Western world by the increasing vogue of liberal, constitutional, and limited government under the domination of the bourgeoisie. The period 1870–1914 was characterized by a surge toward democracy—government of, by, and for the masses. The most democratic nations in the world in 1870 were the United States, Great Britain, France, and Switzerland.

In the United States practically all white males had gained the ballot by the end of the Jacksonian era in 1837. In 1870 the Fifteenth Amendment granted the recently freed Negroes political equality with the whites, although most of them were illegally denied the ballot in the Southern states. Between 1890 and 1914 eleven Western states gave the ballot to women, and in 1920 the Nineteenth Amendment granted women equal political rights with men. But universal suffrage does not in itself guarantee real democracy. From the death of Lincoln in 1865 until the accession of Theodore Roosevelt in 1901 the government and the economy of the country were dominated by big-business interests that controlled the dominant "Old Guard" wing of the Republican party. Although this was a period of enormous over-all economic development, wealth was very unequally distributed. Western and Southern farmers clamored for public regulation of the railroads, upon which they were dependent. Small business, labor, and the consumer demanded protection against the monopolistic practices and prices of the great trusts, which were protected by a prohibitively high tariff. Millions deplored the city slums, the corrupt spoils system in the civil service, and the squandering of natural resources by private interests.

The first great political leader to rally the discontented to a crusade for reform was William Jennings Bryan (1860–1925). Although the silver-tongued Democrat electrified the masses with his eloquence and made three tries for the presidency, he failed to break the grip of the Republican Old Guard. The second reform crusader to appear on the American political scene was the liberal "progressive" Republican Theodore Roosevelt (1858–1919), who adopted much of Bryan's philosophy and program. (With the appearance of Bryan and Theodore Roosevelt the term *liberal* took on the post-1870 meaning in America,

as we shall soon see.) No public figure had ever so caught the imagination of the American people as the youthful, swashbuckling, "roughrider," hero of the Spanish-American War, Teddy Roosevelt. Stepping up from the vice-presidency in 1901 upon the assassination of President McKinley, "T.R.," as he was popularly known, immediately launched a vigorous program of reform. The Interstate Commerce Act of 1887 and the Sherman Anti-Trust Act of 1890, which had lain dormant, were activated. Organized labor was given support in its unequal fight with organized capital. Pure food and drug acts restricted the corporations and safeguarded the public health. The merit system was extended in the federal civil service. Some two million acres of forests were nationalized, and irrigation dams were built.

When Roosevelt's hand-picked successor, William Howard Taft, joined hands with the reactionary Republicans, "T.R." ran against him in 1912 with the support of the Progressive Republicans. The split in the Republican ranks gave the Democrats, under the leadership of Woodrow Wilson (1856–1924), their first clear-cut victory since the Civil War. In fact many of the Old Guard are believed to have voted for Wilson, whom they did not know, in preference to the "terrible Teddy," whom they did know. Wilson, however, proved to be more liberal than Roosevelt. With the Democrats in control of both houses of Congress, Wilson's administration sharply lowered the tariff, passed the Clayton Anti-Trust Act, gave further encouragement to organized labor, and set up the Federal Reserve Banking System, that removed control of the nation's financial policies from the hands of private financial interests on Wall Street and placed them in the hands of the federal government. In 1914 the United States was still at the front of the world procession toward democracy. Woman suffrage was granted in 1920. After that date the biggest flaw remaining in American democracy was the refusal of the Southern states to allow the Negroes to exercise their constitutional right to vote.

Politically if not socially Great Britain, the mother of parliamentary government, kept pace with the United States in the march toward liberal democracy. Britain still had her royalty (though her sovereign was now a figurehead), her lords and ladies, an established Church, and a people most respectful of law and tradition. However, the Reform Bill of 1867 had enfranchised the bulk of the industrial proletariat, and William E. Gladstone's Reform Bill of 1884 enfranchised most of the rural males. After 1884 virtually every male householder or renter in Great Britain could vote. Woman suffrage came in 1918. The Parliamentary Reform Act of 1911 stripped the House of Lords of most of its former power and made the popularly elected House of Commons supreme. Yet until the end of the nineteenth century both the Conservative and Liberal parties were controlled by the aristocracy and the wealthy bourgeoisie. Although both parties were fairly benevolent toward the working classes, the large and discontented industrial proletariat wanted its fair share in the government. Between 1881 and 1906 it turned to a program of moderate Socialism, and with the aid of a number of intellectual radicals, notably George Bernard Shaw, H. G. Wells, and Sidney and Beatrice Webb, formed the Labor party.

In 1906 the rejuvenated Liberal party came to power under the actual, if not official, leadership of the fiery young Welshman David Lloyd George, who also had the backing of the Labor party. Between 1906 and 1911 Lloyd George put through Parliament a revolutionary program of accident, sickness, old-age, and unemployment insurance. To meet the enormous cost to the government, he introduced and forced through the reluctant House of Lords his famous budget of 1909, which shifted the "heaviest burden [of taxation] to the broadest backs." A steeply graduated income tax and high taxes on unearned increment, inheritances, idle parks of the landed aristocracy, and mining royalties struck heavily at the rich. By 1914 Great Britain was well

on the road to social and economic as well as political democracy.

Between 1867 and 1909 she granted self-governing dominion status to Canada, Australia, New Zealand, and the Union of South Africa. In 1914 she at long last even granted self-government to Ireland, although the outbreak of World War I in that year delayed its implementation until 1922.

3. Democratic Advances on the Continent of Europe

During the second phase of the Industrial Revolution liberal democracy was much less secure in France than in the United States and Great Britain. With the crash of the Second Empire of Napoleon III in the Franco-German War of 1870–71, the Third French Republic was proclaimed. The first elections, however, held in February 1871, after the surrender of Paris, resulted in a sweeping victory for the monarchists. This somewhat surprising result may be explained by the fact that the republican leaders wanted to continue the unpopular and hopeless war with Germany. The city of Paris, made up largely of the liberal bourgeoisie and the radical proletariat, was unwilling to submit to the domination of conservative rural France. It declared its independence from the rest of France and set up its own city government, or commune. Two months (April–May 1871) of fighting, culminating in a week of all-out warfare in the streets of Paris, were required for the rest of the French nation to subdue the Paris Commune. Some ten thousand persons, mostly Parisians, were killed. This tragedy further frightened the conservatives.

However, the royalist majority was split into a Bourbon faction and an Orléanist faction, neither of which was willing to yield to the other. Taking advantage of this split in the ranks of the monarchists, the liberal minority succeeded in 1875 in drawing up and putting into effect a republican constitution. The constitution provided for a Chamber of Deputies elected by universal manhood suffrage, a Senate elected by a complicated indirect method, and a rather powerless president to be elected by the two legislative bodies. Most of the executive functions of the republic were to be carried on by a cabinet of ministers dependent upon the Chamber of Deputies. It was not until four years later, however, that the liberal republicans under the leadership of the eloquent Léon Gambetta gained actual control of the republic.

But the Third French Republic, so furtively born, was still not safe. Powerful groups were hostile to it. The chief of these were the various factions of monarchists (Bourbons, Orléanists, and Bonapartists), the professional military, the Roman Catholic hierarchy, and large numbers of peasants who were strongly influenced by the clergy. In the late 1880's these factions rallied around a handsome man on horseback, General Boulanger, who became so popular that he might have overthrown the republic had he been bolder and more skillful or had the republican leaders been less courageous. As it turned out, when he was summoned to answer charges of treason against the republic, he fled and committed suicide. In the 1890's these anti-republican forces rallied again around a group of army conspirators who framed the Jewish captain, Alfred Dreyfus, and sent him to prison on Devil's Island. This time the enemies of the republic were aided by rising malignant nationalsim and anti-semitism. It required five years for the republicans, inspired by the novelist, Émile Zola, to get Dreyfus acquitted and the anti-republican army officers who had framed him punished. The Dreyfus case strengthened the republic and discredited its enemies.

Democratic government did not work so smoothly in France as in the United States and Great Britain. The Voltairian tradition of extreme individualism, the animosity between clericalist and anti-clericalist, the sharp cleavage between radical urban Paris and conservative rural France, lingering provincial loyalty, and a historic suspicion of strong government and high taxes—all

contributed to the formation of a multiplicity of political parties. This meant that the cabinet was forced to rely on the support of a precarious combination of parties (a bloc) in order to carry on the executive functions of the government. In France the Chamber of Deputies could overthrow a cabinet without having to risk an immediate national election as in Great Britain. As a result, there was a rapid turnover of French ministries. During the forty-three years from 1871 to 1914 no fewer than fifty ministries attempted to govern France. However, as cabinets rose and fell, the actual details of administration were carried on with relatively little interruption by a stable civil service, firmly built in the tradition of Richelieu and Napoleon. Unfortunately this low-paid but securely intrenched army of civil servants has often been haughty and self-seeking.

As the twentieth century opened, democratic government in France appeared to be firmly established and increasingly responsive to the will of the masses. Factory laws were giving the workers increased protection. Between 1905 and 1910 a limited program of unemployment, old-age, accident, and sickness insurance was inaugurated. This program of social legislation, however, was only a modest beginning and the French masses, becoming more politically conscious and active, expressed their discontent in strikes and increased votes for the socialist party.

Mountainous little Switzerland is a shining example of what democratic government can do. Surrounded by dangerous political enemies, split into three language groups (German, French, and Italian) and two major religions (Calvinist and Roman Catholic), she has nonetheless enjoyed peace and political stability ever since the overthrow of Napoleon in 1815. In 1848 she set up the Swiss Federal Republic, with authority neatly balanced between the central government and the twenty-two cantons, and universal manhood suffrage—the first permanent universal manhood suffrage in the world. Under this democratic government the Swiss have been prosperous and progressive.

The peoples in the little countries of Northern Europe also witnessed the triumph of democratic government during this period. Belgium adopted universal manhood suffrage in 1893. Here the weighted vote was established, men of wealth and education getting two or three additional votes. The Dutch Netherlands extended the suffrage in 1887 and again in 1896; in 1917 manhood suffrage was made universal. Norway adopted universal manhood suffrage in 1898, Sweden in 1909, and Denmark in 1914. In 1907 Norway became the first European country to grant the vote to women. In these five nations the traditional respect for government and the relatively high degree of literacy made democracy a vigorous reality.

In Spain and Austria universal manhood suffrage was granted in 1907, in Italy in 1912, and in all the Balkan states except Serbia by 1914. In these areas, however, the illiteracy, poverty, and political inexperience of the people combined with a traditional suspicion of all government to make democracy a flimsy and unstable thing. In Austria the clashes among the various language groups further hamstrung the functioning of democracy. In Hungary no progress toward democracy was made at all.

Even in authoritarian and disciplined Germany and autocratic Russia the increasing clamor of the people for active participation in the government was heard. In order to lessen the appeal of the Socialists to the German workingman Bismarck, in the decade of the 1880's, inaugurated a program of social insurance. (See pp. 594–5.) In the German elections of 1912 the Social Democratic (workingmen's) party polled four and one half million votes and became the largest party in the Reichstag. Universal manhood suffrage had existed since the setting up of the empire in 1871, but the popularly elected Reichstag, although its approval was required for all new laws, lacked the prestige and power of the lower houses in the United States, Great Britain,

and France. Nor was the cabinet responsible to it, as in Great Britain and France. In Russia the liberals, taking advantage of Russia's defeat in the Russo-Japanese War of 1904–5, forced Tsar Nicholas II (1894–1917) to set up a representative Duma, although it, too, had no real control over the tsar's government. However, in both Germany and Russia between 1870 and 1914, authoritarian government and malignant nationalism were much stronger forces than was liberal democracy. Therefore, their history will be examined in the following chapter.

Also conspicuously lagging in the march toward democracy in the Western world during the second phase of the Industrial Revolution was Latin America. Most of this vast area is made up of lofty mountains, arid wastes, or steaming jungle, and the Industrial Revolution had made little headway there. Its masses were poverty-stricken and illiterate. Although its twenty governments were all republics in form (Brazil after 1891 and Cuba after 1900), they were really dictatorships of strong and often violent men.

4. Popular Education and Journalism

If democratic government was to function effectively, the electorate had to be literate and reasonably well informed, for a democratic government cannot rise and remain very long above the level of the voters who sustain it. Fortunately for democracy, therefore, the second phase of the Industrial Revolution was also a period of great advances in popular education in the industrialized areas. Contributing to this development were urbanization, improvements in transportation, the increase in wealth, and the growing confidence and ambition of the masses.

In 1870 northern Germany and Scandinavia were the only places where practically everyone could read and write. In the United States most of the states had free public elementary schools, but a fifth of the total population was still illiterate (a figure so high because it included the large Negro ex-slave population in the South). In Great Britain a third of the people were still illiterate, in France and Belgium a half, in Spain and Italy three fourths, in Russia and the Balkans nine tenths, and in Latin America all except a very few. Between 1868 and 1881 national systems of free public education were established in Austria-Hungary, Great Britain, the German Empire, Switzerland, Italy, the Netherlands, Belgium, and France. (In Scandinavia and most states in the United States free public education already existed.) Attendance was made compulsory in Scandinavia, most states in the United States, Germany, Switzerland, France, Great Britain, Italy, and Austria-Hungary, although in Italy and Austria-Hungary enforcement was very lax. For the most part the systems were as yet limited to elementary schools. Nevertheless by 1914 illiteracy had practically ceased to exist in Scandinavia, Germany, Great Britain, and the Netherlands. The illiteracy rate was less than 10 per cent in the United States, Canada, France, and Belgium. In Italy it had been reduced to 25 per cent, in Spain, Russia, and the Balkans to a little more than 50 per cent. In Latin America, Argentina and Chile had made noteworthy inroads on the mass illiteracy. Literacy, of course, is only the first step toward education. The enormous and difficult task of really educating the masses remained.

Hardly less potent than public education as an influence on the minds of the restless masses was popular journalism. Popular journalism was impossible before mass literacy provided a market for its wares. In 1870 newspapers were relatively few, small, and expensive, and written for a limited educated clientele. The London *Times*, probably the world's most influential newspaper, had a daily circulation of some fifty thousand. However, the second phase of the Industrial Revolution—with its improved machinery, transportation, and communications; the growth of liberalism, which stood for freedom of the press; and above all the growing literacy of the masses—brought forth a new kind of newspaper, cheap, sensational, and popular in its appeal. One of the pioneer popular journalists was Joseph Pulitzer (1847–1911), a Hungarian immigrant to the United States. Pulitzer founded the St. Louis *Post Dispatch* and bought and built up the New York *World* until it became the country's biggest newspaper. With screaming headlines, flag-waving patriotism, easy catchy style, sensational news, popular causes and features, and, above all, comics, he made a fortune and became a great influence in politics. His comic strip *The Yellow Kid* was so popular and sought after by other newspapers that it gave the name "yellow journalism" to the new type of publication. In the 1890's William Randolph Hearst built a great newspaper empire patterned after Pulitzer's. In Great Britain Alfred Harmsworth founded the halfpenny popular *Daily Mail*, made a fortune, became Lord Northcliffe, and bought the London *Times* itself. Before the end of the century five newspapers—two in London, two in Paris, and one in Berlin—had a daily circulation of more than a million each. *Le Petit Journal* in Paris had a circulation of more than two and a quarter million. This type of newspaper not only catered to the masses but also became a powerful molder of public opinion. Hearst boasted, with a modicum of truth, that he manufactured the Spanish-American War. Since the popular newspapers made their money chiefly from advertising rather than from sales, they came increasingly to reflect the viewpoints of their chief advertisers, the great corporations. The big newspapers were themselves, of course, big business. Although they catered to the masses, they did not always represent their interests.

5. Labor Unions and Co-operatives

One of the most important manifestations of the movement of the masses in the second phase of the Industrial Revolution was the formation of labor unions and various types of co-operatives. Democratic legislation, public education, and popular journalism were, for the most part, things done *for* the masses, not *by* them. Labor unions and co-operatives, however, represented direct action by the masses themselves. Wherever industrialization occurred, distressed laborers almost immediately attempted to protect themselves by banding together. However, until around 1870, inexperience, poverty, hostile government, and unfavorable public opinion caused most of their efforts to fail. Anti-labor union laws were not fully repealed in Great Britain until 1871. In France they were not fully repealed until 1884. In Germany, Bismarck persecuted labor unions until his dismissal in 1890. During the 1870's and early 1880's the union movement in Europe was limited chiefly to skilled workmen, organized by crafts, who were moderate in their aims and methods.

In the late 1880's unionization spread rapidly to unskilled workmen, cut across craft lines, and adopted socialistic programs (often Marxist) and more violent methods. In Great Britain the labor unions formed the national Trade Union Congress in 1868, and later they became identified with the Labor party, which was founded between 1881 and 1906. In Germany the individual unions formed in 1890 a national organization that was frankly Marxist. In France in 1895 the various unions banded together in the giant C.G.T. (Confédération Générale du Travail—General Confederation of Labor) with an extreme Marxist (syndicalist) program. In the United States the unionization of labor was retarded by the abundance of free land (until the 1890's), to which distressed laborers could flee, and by a strong influx of cheap labor from Europe. It was not until 1886 that Samuel Gompers, an immigrant from Great Britain, organized the American Federation of Labor, the first successful national labor organization in America. The A.F. of L. was a federation of craft unions of skilled workers. It was non-political in its aims and relatively moderate in its methods, and it grew rapidly. By 1914 in the industrialized countries the industrial proletariat was suf-

ficiently large in numbers and organized (though only a minority was as yet unionized) to make itself a power to be reckoned with, both in the factories and mines and at the polls.

Meanwhile, a much bigger portion of the masses was participating in the milder co-operatives of various types, reversing a five-hundred-year trend away from medieval collectivism toward individualistic and competitive capitalism. In 1914 in Great Britain membership in co-operative retail stores, fraternal insurance (friendly) societies, and credit associations is estimated to have been some fourteen million, the great bulk of whom were wage earners. These organizations also provided much-needed social fellowship for the proletariat. In the 1880's Denmark became the home of the agricultural co-operative movement. By 1914 nearly all of Denmark's agricultural commodities were co-operatively produced and marketed, and the movement had spread to most of Northern Europe, to Italy, and to the United States.

6. Marxian Socialism

The most radical movement of the masses during the second phase of the Industrial Revolution was Marxian socialism. Strictly speaking, Marxism was not really a movement of the masses, but rather a movement for the masses begun and carried on by small groups, usually intellectuals. Nevertheless, its influence on the masses between 1870 and 1914 was significant, and since 1914 it has been an enormous factor in world history. It was a product and a compound of various nineteenth-century forces —industrialism, materialism, science, Hegelian philosophy, Darwinian concepts, and the momentary confusion and decline of Christianity. Nor should the influence of the eighteenth-century Enlightenment and the French Revolution on Marxism be overlooked. Its founder, Karl Marx (1818–83), was a brilliant Prussian Jew who, having attained his Ph.D. in philosophy and history, was denied an academic position. Exiled from Prussia and later from France because of his radical ideas, he spent the last thirty-four years of his life in London. Marx collaborated with his friend Friedrich Engels, intellectual son of a wealthy German manufacturer, in writing the *Communist Manifesto* (1848) and *Das Kapital*, the first volume of which appeared in 1867. These two works present the chief fundamentals of the Marxist philosophy, which in the twentieth century is known as communism. Although Marx's ideas continually evolved and frequently contradict themselves, the salient points of his philosophy are as follows:

ECONOMIC INTERPRETATION OF HISTORY

The good things of life are material. "Religion is the opiate of the people," an ideological veil behind which the "haves" achieve their selfish purposes. The dominant characteristic of an historical epoch is its prevailing system of production, which determines every phase of human culture.

CLASS STRUGGLE

"The history of all hitherto existing society is the history of class struggles"; in ancient times freeman versus slave; in medieval times landlord versus serf; in modern times capital versus labor. The bourgeoisie, having overcome the aristocracy, will in time be displaced by the proletariat.

SURPLUS VALUE

The one fundamental law of capitalist economy is the law of surplus value. The worker, who is paid only a subsistence wage, creates, by his work, value in excess of his wage. This excess value is the source of profit for the capitalist.

INEVITABILITY OF COMMUNISM

The working of the law of surplus value makes it impossible for wages ever to catch up with prices. If wages should be raised, the profit differential working in an accumu-

lative manner will raise even higher the price of the commodity that the worker has to buy back from the capitalist. The capitalists will become richer and fewer; the workers will become poorer and more numerous. Furthermore, the capitalistic system is characterized by alternating periods of prosperity and depression and wars resulting from the rivalries of economic imperialism. Under capitalism, then, the law of surplus value plus boom, bust, and war will finally produce such misery that someday, in a time of depression or war, the workingmen will stage a giant revolution, destroy the capitalistic system, and set up a classless society. Meanwhile, the proletariat must fan the flames of class hatred, sabotage capitalistic governments, and work constantly for their final destruction.

INTERNATIONALISM

Workers in all countries have more in common with each other than they have with the capitalists of their own country. They should unite and obliterate national boundary lines in their struggle against the common enemy—the bourgeoisie.

After Marx's death his followers, though splitting up into sects, tended to regard him as a religious prophet. Indeed Marx appears to have regarded himself somewhat as a prophet, dealing in dogmatic absolutes and in grandiose and stirring, though often vague, phraseology. The most important figure to arise among Marx's orthodox followers was the Russian intellectual Nikolai Lenin (1870–1924). Lenin, a much more effective organizer and leader than Marx, advocated a more positive and violent type of revolutionary activity carried on by a small, highly trained, and constantly purged group of dedicated men. Lenin's greatest influence came after 1914 (see Chapter 55). The chief development in Marxism, from the death of Marx in 1883 to 1914, was a moderate revisionism, led by the German socialist Eduard Bernstein. The revisionists became tired of working and waiting for the total collapse of capitalism. Things were not going as Marx had predicted. The rich were not becoming fewer nor the poor poorer. The condition of the workingmen was steadily improving. Bernstein advocated co-operation with the capitalistic classes to obtain all the practical benefits possible for labor here and now and a gradual approach to socialism.

In Germany, where socialism had its greatest success before 1914, the Social Democratic party adopted in practice, if not in theory, this more moderate type of Marxism during the 1890's. By 1914 it was able to poll some four and a half million votes and had become the largest party in Germany. The French Socialists were more radical and violent than the Germans. In 1905 the orthodox and revisionist wings of the French Socialists joined to form the United Socialist party under the leadership of the scholar-

orator Jean Jaurès. By 1914 they numbered a million and a half voters and had 101 seats in the Chamber of Deputies. Contrary to the expectations of Marx, socialism in Great Britain was weak and mild. Among the earliest British Socialists were George Bernard Shaw, H. G. Wells, and Sidney and Beatrice Webb. These intellectual radicals formed the Fabian Society, which was committed to moderation and gradualism. The Labor party, founded between 1881 and 1906 was also mild and grew slowly before 1914. Neither the Fabian Society nor the Labor party could be called Marxist, although both were influenced by Marx. In the United States, too, the socialist movement was relatively weak and (in retrospect) mild. The first prominent American Socialist, Eugene V. Debs, did manage to poll nearly a million votes in 1912 and again in 1920. In 1920 he conducted his

MARX, ENGELS, LENIN, AND STALIN, BY VASILOV. One of the major responses to the economic and social maladjustments and the rapidly changing intellectual and spiritual values in the nineteenth century was the doctrine of Karl Marx. Today this doctrine is known as Communism, and these men have been its chief prophets. (*Sovfoto*)

campaign from a jail cell, where he had been placed because of his opposition to America's participation in World War I.

Marxism probably set back the rise of the masses by many decades. It frightened the propertied classes, intensified class hatred, and played into the hands of demagogues and dictators at a time when the masses were beginning to gain a greater voice in government, educational advantages, and a larger share of this world's goods and privileges.

———•◦•———

SUGGESTED READING

Carlton J. H. Hayes, *A Generation of Materialism, 1871–1900* (1941). This provocatively written volume contains a wealth of information on the late-nineteenth-century migrations; liberal, co-operative, and socialistic movements; and popular education and journalism.

H. P. Fairchild, *Immigration, a World Movement and Its American Significance* (1933). A good approach to this subject.

* Henry Pringle, *Theodore Roosevelt* (Harvest Books). A sound biography of this dynamic leader, written in a journalistic vein.

Arthur Link, *Woodrow Wilson: The New Freedom* (1956). The second volume of Link's projected eight-volume biography of Wilson. This volume treats of Wilson's great liberal reform program, 1913–17.

Thomas Jones, *Lloyd George* (1951). A good biography of the fiery British reformer.

D. W. Brogan, *France under the Republic* (1940). The best volume in English on the Third French Republic. Brilliantly written.

Thomas Kirkup, *History of Socialism*, 5th rev. ed. by E. R. Pease (1920). Still probably the best brief introduction to the subject.

* Karl Marx and Friedrich Engels, *Communist Manifesto* (Gateway). This pamphlet, which can be read in an hour or so, is the best approach to the fundamental philosophy of the father of communism.

CHAPTER 51

Malignant Nationalism: Militarism

Between 1870 and 1914 much of the enthusiasm and energy of the masses was channeled into the rapidly swelling stream of national patriotic fervor. From its birth during the French Revolution until 1870 mass nationalism had been for the most part relatively mild, constructive, and often defensive. It was usually associated with liberalism and concerned with the achievement of national freedom and unity. After 1870 it became more aggressive and militaristic. Politicians and journalists used it to manipulate the mind of the masses. Generals used it to invigorate their armies, now armed with the instruments of technology and science. It became (in its totality including militarism, wars, and imperialism) the world's biggest business. Although the new nationalism was a strong and important force in Great Britain, France, and the United States during the second phase of the Industrial Revolution, it was somewhat overshadowed in those countries by the growth of political and economic democracy. In Germany, Russia, and Southeastern Europe just the reverse was true. There democracy, though making some progress, was smothered by malignant nationalism.

1. General Nature of the New Nationalism

The chief model and inspiration for the new nationalism was Bismarck's Prussia. At a time when the whole Western world seemed to be moving toward liberalism and democracy Bismarck had crushed liberal opposition at home with blood and iron. He also defeated Austria, who had overshadowed Prussia in the Germanies, and then France, long the foremost military power on the continent of Europe and a nation with a liberal tradition. The autocratic, militaristic German Empire, which he welded together, was the world's most powerful and seemingly most efficient nation. These Prussian exploits appeared to bear out the evolutionary teachings of Darwin and Spencer with respect to the survival of the fittest. Most of the Prussian liberals who had first opposed Bismarck now repented and sought and received forgiveness. The rest of the world was dazzled and awed by the Prussianized German Empire. Philosophers began to develop new theories to fit the new facts.

Probably the two most influential thinkers in the development of the new nationalistic concepts were George William Hegel (1770–1831) and Friedrich Nietzsche (1844–1900). We have already seen (see p. 541) how Hegel influenced the Prussian school of historians and the formation of the German Empire through his belief that individual freedom depends upon ordered discipline under a strong state and that the *zeitgeist* (spirit of the time) of the nineteenth century was the spirit of German civilization. However, Hegel, a disciple of

Kant, considered himself a liberal and an idealist and undoubtedly would have disapproved of the excesses to which later Germans went in his name. Nietzsche, on the other hand, though neither a nationalist nor a racist, had no use for liberalism and exerted an even more powerful influence upon German nationalists. Nietzsche frankly discarded all liberalism and idealism and considered the Christian religion fit only for slaves. He preached naked force, unbridled self-assertive egotism, the will to power, and the doctrine of the superman. This philosophy was declared to be realism, and its application in statecraft *realpolitik*. Most German historians after 1870 quickly shifted from Hegel's moderation to Nietzsche's extremism. Heinrich von Treitschke, the most influential German historian of the time, proclaimed that Germany's victory over France demonstrated the superiority of military autocracy over liberalism. Only strong states ought to exist. Dissident minorities, individualism, and parliamentary inefficiency must not be tolerated.

The new nationalism was by no means limited to Germany. The French historian Hippolyte Taine blamed France's defeat in 1870 on the corrupting influence of liberalism born in the French Revolution and bred during the nineteenth century. He would take France back to her good old rugged days of the old regime. In Great Britain, Thomas Carlyle in thunderous prose exalted heroes and hero worship, specifically the Prussian variety. Rudyard Kipling, in rhyme if not poetry, sang of the glorious British Empire and the "white man's burden" of ruling and civilizing backward peoples. Slavophilism, the cult of the superiority of Slavic culture and Slavic peoples, became popular in Russia. In the United States the new nationalism was symbolized by rough-riding Teddy Roosevelt and his "big stick" diplomacy. Roosevelt was an admirer of the virile German Empire.

The most extreme feature of the new militant nationalism was racism. People of every nation began to think and talk of themselves as a distinct and superior breed.

Language was more than ever confused with race. Thus one spoke of the various "races" in the Austro-Hungarian Empire. By far the most popular and serious of all the racial cults was the Aryan myth. The term *Aryan*, which was originally a linguistic term referring to the ancient Persians (Iranians) and later to all peoples speaking Indo-European languages, was now applied to the Germanic- or Teutonic-speaking peoples or to the Nordic (tall blond) type of Northern Europeans. After Germany's spectacular military triumphs and economic developments under Bismarck the term *Aryan* came to be applied more specifically to Germans and to the energetic, aggressive, military qualities they were supposed to possess. Oddly enough, the two chief formulators of the Aryan myth were a Frenchman, Comte de Gobineau, and the renegade Englishman Houston Stewart Chamberlain, who deserted his homeland and became a German citizen. Their ideas, however, were taken much more seriously in Germany than in France or Great Britain. Richard Wagner became a leading racist, repenting of his earlier liberalism to write violent propaganda tracts and to compose grandiose operas stridently extolling the virtues of the early Nordic (German) supermen—Siegfried and the Nibelungs.

The chief immediate victims of the new nationalism were various linguistic minority groups, particularly in Germany, Russia, and Hungary, who were subjected to heavy pressure to give up their native languages and become good Germans, Russians, or Hungarians. The Jews, though hardly a linguistic group, were especially hard hit. In Germany an anti-Semitic party founded in 1887 polled 285,000 votes eleven years later. In Russia during the 1880's the Jews were subjected to such persecutions, including bloody pogroms, that more than a quarter million of them fled, mostly to the United States, in spite of strenuous efforts to prevent their leaving. Another bitter and dangerous fruit of the new nationalism was a series of "pan" movements, particularly pan-Germanism and pan-Slavism. These were moves to bring all German-speaking people under the German flag and all Slavic-speaking people under the Russian flag. If implemented, these programs were certain to lead to wars on a continental if not global scale. In fact militarism was one of the cardinal features of the new nationalism. After 1870 every nation in Europe except Great Britain undertook to copy the German military system, including universal conscription. Great Britain poured a proportionate amount of faith, effort, and money into her navy. Generals and admirals became ever more popular and influential, and Europe became an armed camp.

2. The German Empire Under Bismarck and Kaiser Wilhelm II

The center of this new and militant type of nationalism and in many ways its cause was the German Empire. The blood-and-iron method in which it was created by Bismarck and the Prussian military, its autocratic constitution, and its strong-handed leadership, first by the Iron Chancellor and then by Kaiser Wilhelm II, guaranteed that the German Empire would be an enlarged Prussia—a military autocracy. The German Empire possessed the world's most powerful army, a large, energetic, and disciplined population, a rapidly growing industrial machine, and a fervent and restless national spirit. At first it excited the awe and envy, but eventually the fear and hatred, of much of the rest of the world. Bismarck ruled over his creation as Chancellor for almost twenty years.

Bismarck's first concern after the defeat of France and the declaration of the empire in 1870–71 was to complete the consolidation and the nationalization of the German states and people. The law codes, the currencies, and the military forces of the twenty-five lesser states were brought into conformity with those of Prussia. Banking and railroads were brought under the control of the national government. The empire's spawning industry was protected against British competition by a high tariff.

The French in Alsace-Lorraine, the Danes in Schleswig, and the more than three million Poles in the eastern districts were subjected to severe pressure to give up their language and traditions and to become good Germans. However, Bismarck learned that loyalty was one thing that could not be achieved by force.

Two groups in Germany excited Bismarck's suspicion and wrath: the Roman Catholics (the Black International) and the Socialists (the Red International). Any German who had a foreign loyalty was intolerable to the imperious Junker. From 1872 to 1878 Bismarck waged unrelenting warfare against the Roman Catholics, which he termed the *Kulturkampf* (battle for civilization). The Jesuits were expelled, civil marriage was made compulsory, and all education, including that of Roman Catholic priests, was brought under state control and largely secularized. When the Roman Catholic clergy and most of the laity, that constituted approximately one third of the total German population, resisted and rallied to the pope, hundreds of priests and six bishops were arrested. However, it was all to no avail. The Roman Catholic Center party in the Reichstag became stronger, and by 1878 Bismarck needed its support for what he considered to be a struggle of greater importance—that against the Socialists. In 1878 upon the accession of a more conciliatory pope, Leo XIII, Bismarck "went to Canossa" and had the most severe of the anti-Catholic legislation repealed.

In the same year he began a twelve-year crusade against the internationally minded Socialists. He outlawed their publications, their organizations, and their meetings, and set the brutal German police force upon them. But he only drove them underground. Throughout the decade of the 1880's Bismarck sought to undercut the Socialists' appeal to the workingman by pioneering the first system of social insurance in history. Accident, sickness, and old-age insurance was provided for the industrial proletariat, the funds being raised by compulsory contributions from the workers, the employees, and the state. These laws antedated similar legislation in Great Britain and France by twenty years. Although Bismarck's motives were not benevolent or humanitarian and the payments were mere pittances, his measures represented a momentous new departure in the history of labor relations.

Bismarck's foreign policy after 1871 was one of security and retrenchment. He knew that France would be unforgiving and revengeful, forever seeking an opportunity to regain Alsace and Lorraine. Of France alone he had little fear. But of France in league with other powers, particularly Russia and Great Britain, he had great fear. Therefore, his consistent policy was to maintain a close military alliance with Austria-Hungary and cordial relations with Russia and Great Britain. He carefully nurtured British friendship by refraining from naval and imperial rivalry. It is true that Bismarck eventually yielded to the German expansionists and annexed some large chunks of worthless territory in Africa and some islands in the Southwest Pacific, but Britain apparently did not want them. In 1873 Bismarck formed the Three Emperors' League among Germany, Austria-Hungary, and Russia. When the interests of Austria-Hungary and Russia proved to be incompatible, this league was replaced in 1879–82 by the Triple Alliance among Germany, Austria-Hungary, and Italy, a separate "reinsurance treaty" of friendship and neutrality being made with Russia. Of course Bismarck did not depend wholly upon diplomacy, and throughout this period the German military machine was made ever more powerful.

Bismarck's policies provided security for Germany but only insecurity for France and later other nations. As the industry and wealth of the German Empire came to match and complement the strength of her army, the rest of the world became increasingly uneasy. To make matters worse, the imperious chancellor bullied France and manufactured war scares whenever the military budget was being voted on by the Reichstag. The bitter fruit from these seeds would be harvested later.

Kaiser Wilhelm I died in 1888 in his ninety-first year. After the ninety-nine-day reign of his dying son, Frederick III, his grandson, Wilhelm II, became Kaiser. Wilhelm II (1888–1918) was twenty-nine years of age when he ascended the throne of the most powerful nation in the world. He had been brought up in the army, which was his first love. Egotistical and bombastic by nature, he disliked both his father and his mother, the daughter of Queen Victoria. It may be that a withered left arm gave him a sense of inferiority for which he was attempting to compensate. He was a dabbler in theology, history, and the arts, and gave advice and instructions freely to the leading figures in those fields. He was also an eloquent and willing speaker. Soon after ascending the throne he announced, "Everyone who is against me, I shall crush!" In a speech to some young inductees into the army he stated, "In the presence of the socialist agitation it may happen—though God forfend—that I shall order you to shoot down your relations, brothers, yes even parents—but you must obey my commands without murmuring." Nevertheless, Wilhelm II possessed considerable charm and had his generous and humanitarian moments.

The young Kaiser's personality and policies soon clashed with those of Bismarck. In 1890, just two years after he became emperor, Wilhelm II dismissed Bismarck as chancellor. The immediate cause was disagreement over the control of the ministry and the repeal of the anti-Socialist laws, which Bismarck wished to be continued. The real reason, however, was that there was simply not room enough in Germany for two such prima donnas.

Bismarck's foreign policy was quickly reversed. The reinsurance treaty with Russia was immediately allowed to lapse, as the Kaiser assumed a keen interest in extending German hegemony over the Balkans and the Ottoman Empire, areas that the Russians considered to be vital to their own interests and ambitions. In 1894 Russia formed an alliance with France, the very thing that Bismarck had worked so hard to prevent. Wilhelm II also soon alienated Great Britain. His extension of German influence in the Near East, particularly his Berlin-to-Bagdad railroad project (see pp. 609–10), threatened an area in which Great Britain had many vital interests and through which ran her "life line" to India and the Far East. In China, too, German interests began to rival those of the British.

ister of marine. His purpose was to create a German navy equivalent to the army built by Roon and Moltke a generation earlier. He projected, and the Reichstag voted, an enormous naval building program, which was steadily increased until in 1908 it called for twenty-eight new battleships of the biggest and latest design. The purpose of this program, which was freely and officially admitted, was to give Germany a battle fleet

THE KAISER, HINDENBURG, AND LUDENDORFF IN CONFERENCE. During the second phase of the Industrial Revolution, nationalism became malignant and militaristic. Most awesome of the military powers was the German Empire, whose armies came close to conquering all of Europe in World War I. Here Kaiser Wilhelm II (*center*) confers with his two top World War I generals. (*The Bettmann Archive*)

It was the Kaiser's naval policy, however, that alarmed the British the most. Wilhelm was an ardent and lifelong navalist. "The waves beat powerfully at our national gates," he cried, "and call us as a great nation to maintain our place in the world. . . ." Germany's "place in the sun" was a favorite phrase of the Hohenzollern emperor. In 1896 Admiral von Tirpitz was made min-

so great that "a war against the mightiest naval power would endanger the supremacy of that power." Great Britain, whose food supply as well as her empire depended upon naval supremacy, took utmost alarm. Failing in her efforts to reach an understanding with the Kaiser's government, she launched a huge and almost ruinous naval building program of her own. In 1904 she joined France, and in 1907 Russia, in the Triple Entente, which was in reality a defensive military alliance. The interests and policies of Great Britain, France, and Russia had long been so discordant that nothing less than the maximum alarm could have brought them together. Thus in seventeen years the Kaiser had undone Bismarck's diplomacy and brought about the "encirclement" of the Fatherland by three of the world's greatest powers.

Germany's economic exploits under Bismarck and the Kaiser were no less phenomenal than those in the military realm. In 1870 Great Britain was the world's leading power in manufacturing and commerce; Germany counted for little in either. By 1914 Germany was a clear second to Great Britain in industry and commerce; in many areas, such as the production of steel and machinery, she had far outstripped Great Britain. In the up-and-coming chemical and electrical industries and in scientific agriculture and forestry Germany was far in advance of all other nations. She was also ahead of all other nations in the application of science to industry and in industrial and scientific research. By 1914 her merchant marine had captured the lion's share of the lucrative transatlantic passenger traffic. The Hamburg-American and the North German Lloyd lines (in which the Hohenzollerns were said to be heavily invested) were the biggest steamship companies in the world. At a time when other industrial nations, particularly the United States, were beginning to restrict the giant monopolistic trusts, the German imperial government was encouraging and subsidizing its cartels in order that they might compete more effectively against foreign companies. More and more of the world's market was captured by German business. "Made in Germany" became a familiar mark from the Andean plateau to the Congo jungles. Germany's population, keeping pace with her economy, increased from 41,000,000 in 1870 to 65,000,000 in 1914. Meanwhile, her heavy emigration (which had reached a peak in the 1880's of some 250,000 a year, most of it to the

United States) dwindled to a mere trickle. In 1914 the number of German emigrants was less than the number of workers coming into Germany from neighboring countries. Only the United States was keeping pace with Germany in over-all economic advancement.

The industrialization of Germany, although accompanied by the growth of a large and prosperous bourgeoisie and a numerous proletariat, did not produce a tide of liberalism as it did in the other Western industrialized nations. The capitalistic classes, imbued with militaristic nationalism after 1866, allied themselves with the autocratic government. Only the Social Democratic party (workingmen) and the small and weak Progressive party (intellectuals, professional and small businessmen) advocated responsible democratic government. But even the Social Democratic party, by 1914 the largest party in the empire, was inundated by the flood of militant nationalism that welled up during the international crises that preceded World War I.

Germany's spectacular achievements between 1870 and 1914 excited the awe and admiration of the rest of the world. However, her continuingly autocratic government in a world where democratic liberalism was on the march, her overweening military power and rapidly growing naval strength, her venture into imperialism, her inordinate nationalism, and her irresponsible, egotistical monarch aroused increasing fear and resentment abroad. Germany's militarism and aggressive nationalism had the effect of intensifying the same forces in the other great powers of Europe.

3. Russia Under Alexander III and Nicholas II

Another great power whose malignant nationalism helped to strangle liberalism during the second phase of the Industrial Revolution was the empire of the Russian tsars. A strong wave of dissatisfaction arose during the later years of the long rule of

Alexander II (1855–81). The ex-serfs were cruelly disappointed by the fruits of emancipation (decreed in 1861). In many ways their economic condition was worse than before. Another revolt of Russia's Polish subjects in 1863 made Alexander II more reactionary. His failure to follow through with more sweeping democratic reforms after the emancipation of the serfs disappointed the liberals, who were mostly intellectual young aristocrats. In despair over the possibility of reforming the huge, sprawling, semi-oriental, Russian Empire by orderly methods, these young intellectuals became radical and negativist. They set out to destroy Russia's society, government, and church in order to build a new and modern Russia from the ground up. They called their movement nihilism (nothingness). When their efforts were spurned by the illiterate masses, whom they were seeking to uplift, a more violent wing of the nihilists turned to terror and assassination to achieve their ends. Numerous bureaucrats and police officials were slain by terrorists, and Tsar Alexander II himself was killed by a nihilist bomb just as he was preparing to liberalize the government.

The new tsar, Alexander III (1881–94), was a harsh, reactionary autocrat. Blaming his father's death on softness, he set out to exterminate all liberalism in Russia. The stern and ruthless Plehve was made head of the secret police, whose agents were soon everywhere. Thousands of liberal suspects were arrested. Some were shot or exiled to Siberia. In his sweeping reactionary program of "Russification," Alexander III relied heavily upon his former tutor Pobedonostsev, whom he made procurator-general of the Holy Synod. As an antidote to Western liberalism Pobedonostsev invoked the most extreme form of Russian nationalism, Slavophilism (love of Slavic culture). According to this cult, the Slavic "races" had a culture of their own, which was different from and superior to that of the West. The salient features of this culture were autocratic government under an omnipotent tsar, a feudalistic agrarian society, and the Orthodox Church. Since Russia was the greatest Slavic

power, it was her mission to keep the culture pure and to serve as a model for the lesser Slavic nations and peoples. The censored press, the closely supervised schools, and, above all, the clergy of the Orthodox Church became potent agencies for the propagation of the cult. The great novelist Feodor Dostoevski was an important proponent of this Russian counterpart to Germany's Aryan myth. Non-Orthodox religions were persecuted. Language minority groups—the Poles, the Baltic peoples, the Finns, and even the Ukranians—were forced to use the Russian language. We have already observed the treatment of the Jews, for whom the harshest persecution was reserved. Associated with Slavophilism was pan-Slavism, the belief that all the other Slavic-speaking groups (Poles, Czechs, Slovaks, Ruthenians, Serbs, Croats, Slovenes, and Bulgarians) should be brought either under direct Russian control or into federation with Russia. This would result in the dismemberment of the German, Austro-Hungarian, and Ottoman empires, all of which contained Slavic minority groups.

Alexander III was succeeded by Nicholas II (1894–1917), a well-meaning but weak man who was strongly influenced by his neurotic German wife and eventually by the mystic charlatan monk Rasputin. Although Nicholas attempted to continue the policies of his father, he was unable to make them work. During the decade of the 1890's the Industrial Revolution finally reached Russia, resulting in the appearance of an industrial bourgeoisie and an industrial proletariat. Liberalism and radicalism reappeared among these new classes, and now there was no strong-handed Alexander III to check them. Of the various liberal and radical parties that emerged the one of greatest significance for the future was the Social Democratic party. This was a Marxist party whose leadership was made up almost entirely of intellectual radicals whose chief concern was for the industrial proletariat. In 1903 the Social Democrats split into a moderate, gradualist wing called the Mensheviks (minority) and a violent revolutionary wing called the Bolsheviks (majority). The Bolsheviks were led by the brilliant and dynamic Nikolai Lenin, who was living in exile in Switzerland.

Taking advantage of the embarrassment of the tsar's government because of Russia's defeat by Japan in 1904–5 (see p. 608), the various liberal and radical groups clamored for reform. In July 1904 the hated Plehve, head of the secret police, was assassinated. In January 1905, some fifteen hundred peaceful demonstrators were shot down in front of the Royal Palace in St. Petersburg by the tsar's guard. This bloody event, known as Red Sunday, fanned the flames of discontent. In October 1905, a general strike, in which the Bolshevik Leon Trotsky played a prominent role, completely paralyzed the country for ten days. Nicholas II, yielding at last, issued a manifesto that promised civil liberties and a popularly elected Duma. However, before the Duma could be elected, the return of the Russian troops from the Far East and a huge loan from Russia's ally, France, strengthened the hand of the tsar. During the next two years he and his advisers succeeded in reducing the Duma to an undemocratically elected body that had no real control over the government. Nevertheless, a break had been made in Russia's autocratic system, and it appeared that the voice of the people was beginning to be heard.

However, as in Germany between 1905 and 1914, a series of international crises engulfed the rising liberalism in a torrent of malignant nationalism, militarism, and war. The eventual winners in Russia were not the liberals but the hardy Bolsheviks.

4. National Movements in Southeast Europe

While nationalism between 1870 and 1914 was crushing minority language groups in the German and the Russian empires, it was pulling the Austrian and the Ottoman empires apart along language lines. After Austria's defeat by Prussia in 1866 the dominant German minority in Austria felt obliged to take into partnership the aggressive and restless Magyars of Hungary. The *Ausgleich* (compromise) of 1867 set up the Dual Monarchy of Austria-Hungary. Each country had its own separate parliament. But the two were united under a common ruler, the head of the house of Hapsburg; common ministries of war, finance, and foreign affairs; and joint delegations from the two parliaments whose duty was to co-ordinate policies wherever possible. This arrangement was essentially an alliance between the Germans of Austria and the Magyars of Hungary against the Slavic, Romanian, and Italian language groups, which constituted a majority of the total population of the Dual Monarchy. In effect, the Germans said to the Magyars: "You take care of your minorities [mostly Slavs] and we will take care of ours."

Austria followed a relatively moderate policy in dealing with her subject language groups. Cultural autonomy was granted, and the suffrage was gradually extended until in 1907 all adult males were given the vote. However, the subject peoples were more interested in nationalism than in democracy. The various language groups resurrected traditions of a glorious cultural and political past—much of it pure fantasy. The prosperous Czechs of Bohemia were particularly adamant. The problem was confounded by the fact that many of the language groups had kinsmen outside the Dual Monarchy whom they wished to join and who deliberately stirred up their disloyalty. Such groups were the Italians, the Poles, the Ruthenians (Ukranians), the Serbs, and the Romanians. Parliamentary sessions in Austria frequently degenerated into screaming, inkstand-throwing melees among the various language groups. Hungary made no pretense of conciliation. The Magyar aristocracy ruled over their Slovak, Romanian, Serb, and Croat minorities with an iron hand and refused participation in the government to their own Magyar masses. The nationalist discontent in Hungary was even greater than it was in Austria; the Croats and Serbs, desirous of joining their inde-

UNITS OF THE BRITISH FLEET, 1918. During the period 1870–1914, the British navy was supreme on the seas, as was the German army on land. Britain's sea power enabled her to control an empire that included one fourth of all the territory and people of the world. (*United Press International Photo*)

pendent Serb kinsmen in the formation of a Yugo (Southern) Slav state, were particularly troublesome. When explosive nationalism finally blew Austria-Hungary apart in 1914–18, much of the world was drawn into the conflict.

The Balkan portion of the Ottoman Empire between 1870 and 1914 was a hornets' nest of militant nationalism. The hatred of the Christian Balkan language groups for their Moslem Turkish masters was exceeded only by their hatred for each other. The once-potent Ottoman Empire crumbled throughout the course of the nineteenth century, and one Balkan language group after another, now aflame with national pride and ambition, emerged as independent nations. Meanwhile, all the great powers of Europe became involved in the strategic and troubled area of the Near East. Russia, Austria-Hungary, Great Britain, France, Germany, and Italy had important imperial, economic, and military interests in the Balkans. In addition, Russia

and Austria-Hungary had serious nationalistic interests there. Russia considered herself as the big brother and protector of the Slavic-speaking Serbs and Bulgarians. Austria-Hungary's large Romanian and Yugoslav populations desired union with their free kinsmen in Romania and Serbia. Between 1829 and 1913 first the Greeks, then the Serbs, Romanians, and Bulgarians, and finally the Albanians gained their independence from the Ottoman Empire. In each case a major crisis occurred among the great powers. These Balkan crises became progressively more severe and finally culminated in World War I.

5. The New Nationalism in Great Britain, France, and the United States

Malignant nationalism appears to beget malignant nationalism. Great Britain, long the unchallenged mistress of the seas and of the world's commerce and markets, did not relish the appearance of a dangerous rival.

In the face of Germany's swift rise to power and prestige the British took renewed pride in their dominant navy and in their empire, which contained one fourth of all the earth's territory and people. Most well-to-do Britishers thought themselves to be so superior to the other peoples of Europe that they became the most unpopular of all travelers on the continent. To some observers it appeared that Great Britain was as big a bully on the seas and overseas as Germany was on the continent of Europe.

French pride was only intensified by France's defeat at the hands of Germany in 1870–71. The statue dedicated to the city of Strasbourg in the Place de la Concorde in Paris was draped in perpetual mourning as a constant reminder of the day of revenge. France greatly speeded up her overseas empire building and increased the size of her armed forces until they were larger in proportion to her population than those of the German Empire. She sought and found military allies. When a general strike in 1910 threatened the nation's military security and war preparations, Aristide Briand, himself a radical and former socialist, did not hesitate to use the armed forces to break it up.

The United States was the slowest of the great powers to catch the new spirit. She had an ocean between herself and the militant nationalism of Europe, and she was still busy exploiting the richest of the continents and absorbing and Americanizing the millions of European immigrants pouring through her gates. Nevertheless, Theodore Roosevelt's "big stick" policy in dealing with the little neighbors to the south, particularly his seizing Panama from a friendly neighbor and afterward boasting of it, smacked of the power politics of Europe. The European powers could see no justification for the claims of the United States to sovereignty over the whole Western Hemisphere. In Latin America the big Yankee to the north was the most unpopular nation in the world.

When the first shots of World War I sounded in 1914, all groups, including the internationalist socialists (except for a mere handful), rallied to the flags and trumpets of their respective nations. Many promising liberal and democratic movements came to an end, some of them permanently. Aggressive nationalism proved to be a stronger force during the second phase of the Industrial Revolution than liberalism or democracy.

SUGGESTED READING

Jacques Barzun, *Race, a Study in Modern Superstition* (1937). A thoughtful study of an aspect of the question of nationalism about which much nonsense is believed and written.

Carlton J. H. Hayes, *Essays on Nationalism* (1926). Probably the best survey of this important and often elusive subject.

W. H. Dawson, *The German Empire, 1867–1914*, 2 vols. (1919). Probably the best general history in English.

Erich Eyck, *Bismarck and the German Empire* (1950). Probably the best single-volume biography of Bismarck in English. Approximately half of the volume is devoted to the period 1871–90.

S. C. Hammer, *William the Second* (1917). A good, brief sketch, based largely on the Kaiser's speeches and other contemporary documents.

L. L. Snyder, *From Bismarck to Hitler: The Background of Modern German Nationalism* (1935). A study of the malignant German nationalism that has had a great impact upon the twentieth-century world.

Sidney Harcave, *Russia: A History* (1956). A concise and well-organized general history of Russia.

* M. M. Karpovich, *Imperial Russia, 1801–1917* (Berkshire). An excellent brief account.

H. Seton-Watson, *The Decline of Imperial Russia, 1855–1914* (1953). A scholarly and readable study of the rise of liberalism and radicalism in late-nineteenth- and early-twentieth-century Russia and the gradual weakening of the tsarist aristocracy.

Oscar Jásze, *The Dissolution of the Habsburg Monarchy* (1929). The story of the tearing apart of the Austro-Hungarian Empire by the various national language groups.

Hans Kohn, *Nationalism and Imperialism in the Hither East* (1932). A competent study of seething nationalism in this critical and strategic area.

CHAPTER 52

European Imperialism in Asia and Africa

IMPERIALISM went hand in hand with the new aggressive type of nationalism. During the second phase of the Industrial Revolution, European power and influence were extended to those portions of the globe which had not previously been affected: the Near, Middle, and Far East, the remaining coastal regions and the whole vast interior of Africa, and even the frozen wastes of Antarctica. This new wave of European imperialism was accompanied by increasingly severe friction between the European imperialists and the "native" peoples, and rivalry among the European imperial powers themselves.

1. A New Burst of European Expansion

We have already seen that from the fifteenth to the eighteenth centuries the national monarchies of Europe discovered and conquered most of the Western Hemisphere, the west coast of Africa, and Southern Asia. Then from 1763 until 1870 there came a lull in expansion; Europe was busy with revolution and counterrevolution, industrialization, and nation building. The period 1870–1914, however, witnessed a new burst of European expansion that brought practically all of the remaining portions of the earth's surface under European influence or domination.

One of the chief impulses behind the new thrust was undoubtedly economic. The rapid expansion of industry in Europe and the United States demanded greater markets, new sources for raw materials, and investment outlets for surplus capital. Until Henry Ford demonstrated in the 1920's that low prices and high wages would develop an almost limitless home market, it was generally assumed that the exploitation of home and foreign markets by high prices and low wages was the only way in which industry could succeed. This idea resulted in the acquisition of more and more technologically backward areas by the industrial powers. Furthermore, science and technology gave the industrialized nations such a military advantage that the conquest and control of the unindustrialized areas was relatively easy.

Probably an even greater impulse to the new imperialism was the new nationalism. Much of the territory seized by the great powers between 1870 and 1914 had no economic value whatever; some, in fact, was an economic liability. However, it flattered the national ego to see its colors spread over the map. It also provided military and naval bases and manpower for the hungry military machines, that were an integral part of militant nationalism. In Europe the conservative parties based upon the landed aristocracy were even more imperialistic than the liberal parties based upon industrial and commercial interests. Many of the imperial governors, generals, and admirals came from the conservative aristocracy. National egotism also gave the citizens of the great Western powers a sense of mission; they were bringing the blessings of civilization to backward peoples. Rudyard Kipling expressed the genuine belief of many Westerners when he sang in rhyme of the "white man's burden" to hold in tutelage and to civilize the "lesser breeds" of the earth. The heady wine of nationalism gave the Westerners during the second phase of the Industrial Revolution the same advantage over the Asians and Africans that the French Revolutionists and Napoleon had enjoyed over the rest of continental Europe. It was an advantage that would not last.

Another motivating factor in the new imperialism was the evangelizing zeal of the Christian religion. Christianity has always followed its founder's command, "Go ye into all the world and preach the gospel to every creature," and it has been the most aggressive of all religions. At the very time that it was wavering under attack in its homelands in the West it was carrying on foreign missionary activity of unprecedented scope and intensity. And it was gaining millions of converts in Asia and Africa. Much of the work of the Christian missionaries was undone by their association in the minds of the natives with economic and nationalistic imperialistic exploiters; but how much it is impossible to say.

2. The Exploitation and Awakening of China

One of the most important scenes of European imperialism during the second phase of the Industrial Revolution was China. This huge and populous country was the seat of the oldest continuous civilization in the world. For some five thousand years China had been a vast melting pot, absorbing invading peoples and cultures and welding them into a tough but resilient civilization. The military conquerors were always themselves swallowed up or conquered by Chinese culture. By far the greatest influence in molding Chinese civilization was Confucianism. Confucius lived five hundred years before Christ. He was reared in

poverty, the son of a youthful mother and an aged father. A prodigy both in scholarship and personality, he attracted a body of devoted disciples who wrote down his sayings. Eventually he rose to high political office but resigned in protest against the immorality of his ruler.

The teachings of Confucius really belong to the realm of philosophy rather than religion. The flavor of his life and thought is much more closely akin to that of Socrates, who lived in Greece only a hundred years after Confucius, than to that of the mystic religious leaders such as Christ, Buddha, or Mohammed. Confucius was only vaguely concerned with the Deity, who, he assumed, governs the universe and is on the side of righteousness. On the other hand, he was very much concerned with and very optimistic about man and his ability through reason to build the good life here on earth. Wisdom, reason, patience, tolerance, and gentleness were the virtues taught by Confucius. These could be developed by the ruling classes and transmitted to the masses by example and persuasion. Confucius was history-minded and held in high esteem the lessons that can be learned from the experiences of the past. He also emphasized family loyalty and filial piety.

Needless to say, the practice of Confucianism, as in all religions, fell far short of the ideal. The use of force was never absent from Chinese government or society. Respect for the past and for family was corrupted into backward-looking ultraconservatism, and an elaborate ritual was built around ancestor worship. Nevertheless, the teachings of Confucius served as a standard that, like Christianity in the West, was at least tacitly accepted by the great majority. The scholar was exalted, not the soldier as in the West. In fact in no other civilization has the scholar been so revered. For centuries examinations for the civil service, which was the chief avenue for advancement, were based largely upon the Confucian classics. This guaranteed that the best minds and the ruling classes of China would be steeped in Confucianism.

IMPERIALISM IN ASIA, 1840-191[4]

St. Petersburg •Archangel

Moscow

RUSSIAN

Samara •Tobolsk

EUROPE
ASIA

Toms[k]

Omsk   TRANS-SIBERIAN

OB. R.

Constant-
inople

BLACK
SEA

**OTTOMAN
EMP.**

Astrakhan

CASPIAN
SEA

1846

ARAL
SEA

1873

LAKE
BALKHASH

1854

SUEZ
CANAL

Cairo
EGYPT   •Jerusalem   •Mosul   Baku
1873

Bagdad

1881
1884
Merv

1864   •Tashkent   1860-65
1876

Teheran

TURKESTAN

SINKIANG

RUSSIAN   SPHERE 1907

•Basra

PERSIA

BOKHARA
1868

1885

1895

•Kashgar

20°N

•Mecca

JERSIAN SPHERE
1907

PERSIAN GULF

BRITISH SPHERE 1907

RED SEA

ARABIA

OMAN

Karachi

AFGHAN-
ISTAN

Kabul•

KASHMIR
1846

PUNJAB

BALUCH-
ISTAN
1883

INDUS

MAL

NEPAL

TIB

BRAHMAPUTRA R.

YEMEN

Aden
(BR.,1839)

60°E

Diu
(PORT.)

Bombay•

•Delhi

GANGES R.

INDIA   •Calcutta

BRITISH

Goa
(PORT.)

•Hyderabad

•Yanaon (FR)

BAY
BENG

•Madras

Pondicherry (FR)
Karikal (FR)

AND
(B

CEYLON

EQUATOR

INDIA

JEHOL

MANCHURIA

Mukden•

GREAT
WALL

Kinchow

•Peking

LIAOTUNG
PEN.

Tientsin•

•Taku

GULF
OF
CHILI

Dairen
Port Arthur

(LEASE TO {RUSSIA, 1898
JAPAN, 1905})

KOREA

CHIHLI

GRAND CANAL

Chifu•

Wei-hai-wei
(BR., 1898)

Tsinan•

SHANTUNG

Kiaochow
(GER.,1898)

•Tsingtao

YELLOW

S
E
A

CRITICAL AREA
1895-1905

150 MILES

1000 MILES

TRM

Considering themselves superior to all other peoples, the Chinese gradually went into isolation. A great wall (never completed) was constructed along the borders in an effort to retain the old and keep out the new. They received numerous European traders and Christian missionaries in the sixteenth and seventeenth centuries, but closed their doors rather tightly thereafter. As science, technology, and dynamic capitalism and nationalism developed in the West, China fell far behind in strength and energy. By the nineteenth century her medieval society, under the corrupt and declining Manchu dynasty, constituted a power vacuum that tempted exploitation by the West. The first Europeans to force them-

selves upon the Chinese were the British. Going to war in 1839, when the Chinese officials interfered with their sale of opium in China, the British, with their modern weapons, easily defeated the Chinese, who were still using medieval arms. By the terms of the Treaty of Nanking (1842) the Chinese ceded Hong Kong to the British, opened many of their ports to foreign trade free of restricting tariffs, and granted the foreigners extraterritorial rights, such as trial by their own courts, on Chinese soil. This was the first of a series of unequal treaties and the signal for all the great Western powers to rush into China and seize what they could. In the ensuing scramble it was the rivalry among the great powers them-

"Freighters" on the Burma Road, 1914. The use of these Chinese coolies as beasts of burden illustrates the exploitation of the Asian and African masses by their own native rulers and by Western imperialist powers. Such exploitation led in the twentieth century to upheavals that shook the whole world. (*United Press International Photo*)

selves rather than Chinese resistance that saved China from complete loss of independence.

The British got the lion's share. In addition to Hong Kong and concessions in the Canton area of the southeast they gained a virtual trading monopoly in the Yangtze Valley, which was the richest and most populous part of China. They also gained footholds in the capital city of Peking and its port city of Tientsin in the north, in the Shantung Peninsula, and in Manchuria. They gained dominion over Tibet. In the 1880's they annexed Burma, which owed a tenuous allegiance to China. The French took Southeast China and the large Hainan Island as their sphere. In the 1880's they completed the detachment of Indo-China from Chinese sovereignty. The Russians took Manchuria as their sphere, annexed a large strip of China's northeast coast, including the port of Vladivostok, and became active in Korea. The Germans carved out for themselves most of the strategically located Shantung Peninsula and built a powerful naval base at Kiaochow. In 1894 the rejuvenated and modernized Japanese went to war with China. They easily defeated her and not only took away Formosa and Korea but forced China to pay a huge indemnity. Even the United States got into the act. The United States had launched upon an imperialist program in the Far East in 1898 by seizing the Philippine Islands and Guam from Spain. Now, fearful for her growing trade with China, she attempted to gain a sphere of influence in Fukien Province and demanded an Open Door policy in China with equal trading opportunities for all. Little if anything came of either of these projects, however.

Meanwhile, Chinese nationalism was being aroused by the Western and Japanese aggressions against the "Celestial Empire." The first overt reaction was the Taiping Rebellion of 1853 against the corrupt and conniving Manchu dynasty. The reforming rebels were finally put down eleven years later by Manchu armies, organized by an American military adventurer, Frederick Ward, and led by a British general, Charles (Chinese) Gordon. In 1899 a serious uprising against the foreign exploiters, known as the Boxer Rebellion, took place. Thousands of Chinese Christians and several scores of foreigners were slain. This, too, was put down by the Chinese officials with the aid of British, French, German, Russian, Italian, Japanese, and American troops. The rebels were severely punished, and China was forced to pay the foreign governments a large indemnity.

Meanwhile, a more far-reaching revolutionary movement aimed not only at freeing China from foreign exploitation but also at modernizing and democratizing her society and government was being organized by Dr. Sun Yat-sen (1866–1925). Sun Yat-sen, the son of a Chinese coolie, studied in

DR. SUN YAT-SEN. One of the most important figures in the movement to free the Asian and African masses from native and Western exploitation was Dr. Sun Yat-sen, leader of the Chinese Revolution of 1911. The "three principles of the people" which Sun Yat-sen formulated were national independence, democracy, and social justice. (*United Press International Photo*)

a British mission school in Hawaii, became a Christian, and later graduated from the British medical school at Hong Kong. Eloquent and dynamic, he organized his followers into the Kuomintang party, which was committed to a three-point program: (1) national independence, (2) democratic government, (3) social justice. In 1911 the Kuomintang launched a revolution against the Manchu dynasty, declared a republic, and elected Sun Yat-sen as provisional president. The revolution swept all Southern China. The following year the Manchu governing officials, attempting to save themselves, set aside the six-year-old puppet emperor, declared a republic, and elected as provisional president an ambitious, self-seeking war lord, General Yuan. The foreign powers supported the Yuan government, and the idealistic Sun Yat-sen, in behalf of national unity, yielded to General Yuan. However, the two were incompatible, and the union lasted only nine years. When World War I opened a new era in 1914, China was torn with revolution and division—convulsions that would rock the world in the decades to follow. Western imperialism in China was soon to backfire with a vengeance.

3. The Emergence of Japan

Japan's reaction to Western intrusion was quite different from that of China. The Japanese people inhabit four large islands and some three thousand little ones stretching along the eastern coast of Asia for a distance of about two thousand miles. Their culture had spilled over from the Chinese mainland. However, Buddhism and emperor-worshipping Shintoism, rather than Confucianism, were the two chief religions. Like China, Japan had admitted the sixteenth- and seventeenth-century European traders and Christian missionaries but after a few years had thrown them out and closed her doors. At mid-nineteenth century the Japanese were living in isolation. Their stage of technical knowledge and their feudal society ruled over by military chieftains were quite similar to those of Europe five hundred years earlier.

In 1853, eleven years after the Treaty of Nanking opened up China, an American navy commodore, Matthew C. Perry, steamed into Tokyo Bay and so overawed the Japanese that they opened their ports to shipwrecked American sailors and to American trade. The alert Japanese were much impressed by the technological superiority of the Americans. In 1868, just fifteen years later, a group of forward-looking young Japanese overthrew the existing government and began reorganizing the Japanese government and society along modern Western lines. Taking what they considered to be the best from the various Western nations, they patterned their public education system after that of the United States, their legal system after the French, and their navy after the British. However, it was Bismarck's Germany that impressed the Japanese the most. They built a military machine and an authoritarian government on the model of the German Empire.

In an incredibly short time Japan became a modern, industrialized, military, and, on the surface at least, a Westernized power. In 1894, as we have already observed, she attacked China, defeated her with ease, and forced her to pay a large indemnity and to give up Korea (which Japan annexed in 1910) and the large island of Formosa. In 1902 Great Britain became the first Western power to treat an oriental nation as an equal by entering into a military alliance with Japan. Thus strengthened and reassured, Japan attacked Russia in 1904 and, to everyone's surprise, defeated her on land and at sea. As her reward she took the southern half of Sakhalin Island and Russia's railroad and port concessions in southern Manchuria, thereby becoming the dominant power in that large and valuable section of China. By 1914 Japan was a first-rate Europeanized power—industrialized, militaristic, imperialistic, and filled with malignant nationalism. Two vital ingredients of European civilization, however, Christianity and liberalism, were still lacking.

4. Competition for the Strategic Near and Middle East

The term *Near East* usually refers to the area at the eastern end of the Mediterranean: Egypt, the old Ottoman Empire, and the Balkan Peninsula. In the period 1870–1914 the term *Middle East* usually meant the area of the Persian Gulf, the territory northwest of India, and sometimes Tibet. (By the middle of the twentieth century the term *Middle East* was generally used to designate the whole area from and including Egypt and Turkey to the western borders of India.) Before the development of its oil resources after World War I this area (with the exception of the Balkan Peninsula) was relatively barren, poor, and sparsely settled. It was inhabited chiefly by Moslems who were hostile to Europeans. The main importance of the area, therefore, was strategic. It is the land bridge between the world's two largest land masses—the continents of Eurasia and Africa. The opening in 1869 of the Suez Canal, which shortened the sailing distance between Western Europe and the Far East by five thousand miles, doubled the strategic value of the Near and Middle East. Indeed Suez quickly became probably the most vital single commercial and military focal point in the world.

The Suez Canal was built by a French company between 1859 and 1869. However, in 1875 Great Britain, taking advantage of the Egyptian government's financial distress, purchased the khedive's controlling portion of the canal stock. Seven years later, to quell an anti-European insurrection, the British occupied Egypt with their military forces. The French acquiesced in the establishment of Britain's control over Egypt and the Suez Canal in return for British support of French dominance in Morocco.

Serious competition for the British in the Near East soon came from an unexpected source. Wilhelm II, upon becoming Kaiser of the German Empire in 1888, immediately began to show a keen interest in the Ottoman Empire. Sultan Abdul Hamid II (1876–1909) was such a cruel slaughterer of his Christian subjects that he was called in the Western world "Abdul the Damned." However, Wilhelm II in 1889 paid Abdul Hamid a visit in Constantinople and declared himself to be the friend and benefactor not only of the Turks but of all the Moslems. Friendship was followed by economic concessions and German investments in the Ottoman Empire. A second visit by the Kaiser in 1899 led to a concession to Germany to build a railroad from the Bosporus to the Persian Gulf. This, with its European connection, was the famous Berlin-to-Bagdad railroad. The British took alarm. The Bagdad Railroad, with a fortified terminus on the Persian Gulf, would undercut Britain's longer water route to the East and threaten India, Britain's richest prize. A projected branch running down through Syria and Palestine to Hedjaz would menace the Suez Canal itself.

Russia was equally concerned. Since the days of Ivan III in the fifteenth century one of Russia's major ambitions has been to gain a warm water outlet to the world through the Turkish Straits at Constantinople. As a matter of fact, since the tenth century Russia has looked to Constantinople as the seat and legitimate capital of her Orthodox religion and Byzantine culture. As we have seen, the decay of the Ottoman Empire in the nineteenth century encouraged Russia to try for Constantinople, and only the intervention of Great Britain and France in the Crimean War (1854–56) prevented her from attaining her goal. Again in 1877–78 Russia defeated Turkey and threatened to dominate the whole Balkan Peninsula. This time Great Britain and Austria-Hungary forced Russia to submit to a general settlement by the European powers. At the Congress of Berlin, 1878, Russian ambitions in the Near East were once more thwarted. Bismarck's support of Austria-Hungary and Great Britain at the Congress of Berlin marked the beginning of German-Russian estrangement. Russia's defeat by Japan in 1904–5 caused her to intensify her pressure toward the Middle and Near East. Her southward expansion from Siberia so menaced India that Great Britain in the late nineteenth century and the beginning of the twentieth extended the northwest Indian frontier to the Khyber Pass and crossed over the Himalayas to checkmate Russian influence in Tibet, Afghanistan, and Persia.

The new German threat in the Near and Middle East, however, caused the British and the Russians to settle their long-standing differences. In 1907 they neutralized Tibet and Afghanistan and divided Persia into three spheres of influence—a Russian sphere in the north, a British sphere in the south, and an "independent" sphere in the center. Great Britain, Russia, and France, now diplomatic allies, prevented the sale of Bagdad Railroad bonds in their respective countries in an effort to embarrass the financing of the costly undertaking. Germany went right ahead, however, with the extension of her influence in the Balkans and the Ottoman Empire. In 1913 Germany even dispatched a military mission to Constantinople to reorganize and instruct the Turkish army. The Ottoman Empire's friendship and eventual alliance with Germany was undoubtedly motivated by her greater fear of Russia. By 1914 the area of the Near and Middle East was a giant powder keg with fuses leading to St. Petersburg, Berlin, and London.

5. The Scramble for Africa

At the opening of the nineteenth century Africa was not the seat of hoary civilizations, as was Asia. The brilliant ancient civilizations of Egypt, Carthage, and Rome all lay in ruins. The Moslem religion still existed throughout North Africa, but the once-vigorous Moslem civilization was now squalid and tribal except for a few rich potentates. The Portuguese, Spanish, British, and French had trading posts along the gold, ivory, and slave coast on the west. The Dutch and Portuguese had posts and settlements around the southern cape. But most of the huge continent still lay dark, mysterious, and untroubled. By 1870 the African scene had still not changed very much. During the middle decades of the nineteenth century the interior was explored for the first time, notably by David Livingston, a Scottish missionary, and Henry Morton Stanley, a British journalist. The French had conquered Algeria and made it a part of France, and had pushed up the Senegal River in the west. The British had taken the Cape Colony from the Dutch by the Treaty of Vienna in 1815, and the Dutch settlers had trekked northward into the interior. After 1870, however, the scene changed drastically. The explorers' tales of strange wild animals and primitive peoples, of jungles, ivory, and gold, excited the imagination of Western European adventurers, machine owners, and evangelical Christians. The new burst of industrialism and nationalism supplied much of the impetus.

After 1870 there took place such a mad scramble for Africa among the great, and not so great, powers of Western Europe that by 1914 the only independent areas left were Ethiopia in the east and Liberia in the west. Ethiopia, with French aid, had repulsed an invading Italian army, and Liberia was sponsored by the United States as a hoped-for receptacle of liberated Negro slaves. The rest of the huge continent had been seized by France, Great Britain, Germany, Portugal, Belgium, Italy, and Spain (listed in the approximate order of size of territory held). (See map p. 611.) The treatment of the primitive natives was very similar to that accorded the New World Indians in the sixteenth and seventeenth centuries.

The looting of so much territory did not occur, of course, without serious international incidents and crises. One such incident occurred at Fashoda in the Sudan in 1898. A French expedition under General Marchand, bent on establishing an all-French axis across Africa from west to east, arrived at Fashoda and hoisted the French flag. The British, however, claimed the Sudan as an appendage of Egypt. Furthermore, they were interested in a Cape to Cairo railroad running through all-British territory even though they were already

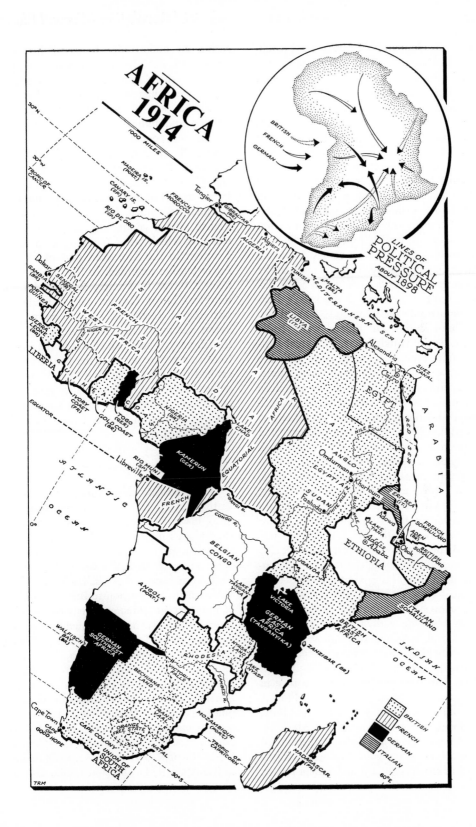

AFRICA
1914

1000 MILES

LINES OF
POLITICAL
PRESSURE
ABOUT 1898

BRITISH
FRENCH
GERMAN

30°N

30°W

TROPIC OF
CANCER

MADEIRA IS.
(PORT.)

CANARY IS.
(SP.)

RIO DE ORO
(SP.)

FRENCH
MOROCCO

Tangier
GIBRALTAR (BR.)

Algiers
ALGERIA

TUNISIA

MALTA
(BR.)

MEDITERRANEAN SEA

Alexandria
SUEZ
CANAL

Dakar
GAMBIA (BR.)
PORT.
GUINEA

SENEGAL
FRENCH WEST AFRICA
NIGER R.
S A H A R A   D E S E R T
AFRICA

LIBYA
(IT.)

EGYPT

SIERRA
LEONE
(BR.)

LIBERIA

GUINEA
IVORY
COAST
(FR.)
GOLD COAST
(BR.)
TOGO
(GER.)

NIGERIA
(BR.)
LAKE
CHAD

Cairo

NILE RIVER

RED SEA

ARABIA

EQUATOR

KAMERUN
(GER.)

EQUATORIAL

RIO MUNI
(SP.)
Libreville

FRENCH

UBANGI R.

CONGO R.

Anglo-
Omdurman
EGYPTIAN
Khartoum
SUDAN
Fashoda
WHITE NILE
BLUE NILE

ERITREA

Adowa
FRENCH
SOMALILAND
ADEN
(BR.)
Obok
BRITISH
SOMALILAND

Addis
Abeba
ETHIOPIA

0°

ATLANTIC
OCEAN

BELGIAN
CONGO

ANGOLA
(PORT.)

LAKE
TANGANYIKA
UGANDA

LAKE
TAYA

ITALIAN
SOMALILAND

LAKE
VICTORIA

GERMAN
EAST
AFRICA
(TANGANYIKA)

BRITISH
EAST
AFRICA

INDIAN
OCEAN

GERMAN
SOUTHWEST
AFRICA

WALFISCH
BAY
(BR.)

RHODESIA
NYASA LAND
LAKE
NYASA

VICTORIA
FALLS
BECHUANA-
LAND
ZAMBEZI R.
TRANS-
VAAL

ZANZIBAR (BR.)

Cape Town
CAPE OF
GOOD HOPE

CAPE COLONY
ORANGE
FREE STATE
NATAL

MOZAMBIQUE
(PORT.)

MADAGASCAR
(FR.)

TROPIC OF
CAPRICORN

60°E

UNION OF
SOUTH
AFRICA

30°S

BRITISH
FRENCH
GERMAN
ITALIAN

TRM

blocked by German East Africa. Lord Kitchener, therefore, hurried down from the north with a superior British force and compelled the French to withdraw.

In South Africa the British fought a major war with the Dutch settlers (1899–1902). When British settlers began to move into Cape Colony after the Congress of Vienna had ceded it to Great Britain in 1815, the Calvinist Dutch Boers (farmers) who had settled there in the seventeenth century and wished to live the biblical patriarchal life, trekked northward far into the interior. Eventually the British recognized the independence of the two Boer states, Transvaal and Orange Free State. When, however, the richest gold mines in the world were discovered in the Transvaal in the 1880's, British immigrants (Uitlanders) flooded in. The unwelcome Uitlanders were badly treated by the Dutch Boers. The great British empire builder, Cecil Rhodes, with the support of powerful interests back home, was determined to brush aside the two little Boer republics. When the able Boer president, Paul Kruger, saw the British intent, he opened hostilities. What the world expected to be an easy victory for the British took three years of all-out military effort, involving severe casualties and enormous costs. Britain's treatment of the defeated Boers, however, was lenient. They were taken into partnership in the Union of South Africa; and their war hero, General Botha, was elected the Union's first president. During the course of the struggle, a telegram of congratulation from the German Kaiser to President Kruger and the British seizure of a German ship attempting to violate the British blockade caused great tension between Great Britain and Germany. Only the superiority of the British navy, as the Kaiser admitted, prevented him from going to war.

The British navy also proved decisive in two crises over Morocco. In 1905 France, with the approval of Great Britain, Italy, and Spain, began the conquest of Morocco. She claimed that it was necessary because of continual raids by wild Moroccan tribesmen on French Algeria. The German Kaiser,

seeing an opportunity to assert his own power and possibly to break up the Triple Entente, which France, Great Britain, and Russia were then forming, appeared at the Moroccan port of Tangier on a German warship and indicated his support of Moroccan independence. Great tension followed. At an international conference at Algeciras, France, supported by her own ally, Great Britain, and by Germany's ally, Italy, won a limited control over Morocco. Disorder continued, however, and in 1911 France sent a conquering army into Morocco, at which point Germany dispatched a cruiser to the Moroccan port of Agadir. Again tension mounted. In the face of Germany's threat to France, Britain's foreign minister, Lloyd George, talked loudly of war. Again Germany backed down. Between Germany and Morocco stood the British navy. These two efforts of the Kaiser to drive a wedge between the Entente powers had the effect of driving them closer together. Moreover, his own ally, Italy, had proved uncertain. These two crises growing out of imperialism hastened the coming of World War I.

6. The British Empire

Of all the European overseas empires the British was by far the most successful. Indeed, it was the dazzling size and wealth of the British Empire that helped to excite the other European powers to greater imperialistic activity. By 1914 the British Empire included one fourth of all the land and people of the earth. In addition to Britain's spheres of influence in China and her African territories, which we have just mentioned, the empire included four great self-governing dominions: Canada, Australia, New Zealand, and the Union of South Africa. It also included British Honduras in Central America; British Guiana in South America; numerous islands in the West Indies; strategic steppingstones along her Mediterranean–Red Sea life line such as Gilbraltar, Malta, Cyprus, and Aden; scores of islands in the Atlantic, Pacific, and Indian Oceans;

Malaya; Ceylon; parts of New Guinea and Borneo; and, above all, India. Nor should we forget the English-speaking United States—Britain's prodigal son who made good and who would return more than once in time of need to rescue the mother country.

Great Britain's commerce with her empire was enormous. In 1914 her foreign investments, most of which were in the empire, totaled twenty billion dollars—one fourth of the total wealth of the homeland. (By comparison, France had nine billions invested abroad, Germany six. The United States was a debtor nation.) The empire, furthermore, provided lucrative and oft-times glamorous careers for thousands of British governors, army and navy officers, diplomats, and civil servants of every description.

In the latter part of the nineteenth century Great Britain adopted the policy of granting self-government to the English-speaking portions of her empire. Canada, which had gained self-government in 1849, was granted dominion status in 1867. With dominion status the only remaining effective bond was allegiance to the British crown. The British governor general was only a figurehead like the king at home. Australia was made a self-governing dominion in 1900, New Zealand in 1907, and the Union of South Africa in 1909. The policy was successful. All the dominions rallied to the mother country in both world wars.

Great Britain's richest imperial prize was India. India's more than three hundred million inhabitants accounted for at least three fourths of the total population of the whole empire. India was nearly twenty times as large as Great Britain and more than seven times as populous. She was the mother country's best customer and supplied many minerals and raw materials. Until 1858 In-

dia was governed by the British East India Company, a private joint-stock company. However, the great Sepoy Mutiny of 1857, the first large-scale uprising of the Indians against British rule, caused the British government to take over the government of India from the company. Between 1858 and 1914 Great Britain spent millions of dollars in India on railroads, industries, education, and public health. The enormous growth of India's population, which more than doubled during the period, is testimony to the improvement in the conditions of life under British rule. However, the British took out of India more than they brought in, and they showed no inclination to grant self-government. Indian dissatisfaction with British rule mounted steadily. In the late nineteenth century nationalism, which had provided so much aggressive energy for Europe, was coming to Asia—to India as well as to Japan and China. In 1885 the All Indian Congress party was formed for the purpose of achieving Indian independence. By 1914 it was becoming obvious that India would not remain a placid and profitable colony much longer.

The European world's technology, its dynamic capitalism, and above all its aggressive nationalism had enabled it between 1870 and 1914 to subject most of the rest of the world to its control. The tail wagged the dog. By 1914 the European world had come to look upon this as a normal and permanent thing. Near the end of the nineteenth century and early in the twentieth century, however, those same forces were coming to Asia and Africa as they had come to Japan a bit earlier. Asia and Africa would soon begin to free themselves from European domination, but not without struggles that would shake the twentieth-century world.

SUGGESTED READING

P. T. Moon, *Imperialism and World Politics* (1936). Probably the best general survey on the subject.

E. M. Winslow, *The Pattern of Imperialism: A Study in Theories of Power* (1948). Attempts to demonstrate that imperialism is more political than economic in motivation.

J. A. Hobson, *Imperialism: A Study* (1902). A famous attack on imperialism.

* D. E. Owen, *Imperialism and Nationalism in the Far East* (Berkshire). A good brief survey.

K. S. Latourette, *The Development of China* (1946). A lucid history by a scholar well versed in the subject.

K. S. Latourette, *The History of Japan* (1947). A sound account written in a vigorous, readable style.

E. M. Earle, *Turkey, the Great Powers, and the Bagdad Railway* (1923). A scholarly and well-written account of the early-nineteenth-century rivalries of the great powers in the strategic Near East.

C. W. de Kiewiet, *A History of South Africa: Social and Economic* (1946). The story of a glamorous and strife-ridden area of the world. Combines careful scholarship with lucid and dramatic writing.

Basil Williams, *Cecil Rhodes* (1921). Probably the best biography of the great British empire builder.

H. T. Priestly, *France Overseas* (1939). A factual and detailed account of France's large and troublesome colonial empire.

M. E. Townsend, *The Rise and Fall of Germany's Colonial Empire, 1884–1918* (1930). A detailed and lucid treatment of Germany's disturbing thrust into imperial competition.

G. E. Elton, *Imperial Commonwealth* (1946). A lively defense of the British Empire and Commonwealth.

CHAPTER 53

Philosophy, Literature, and the Arts

THE MATERIALISM of science and technology, the cynicism that accompanied the challenged and wavering religious and moral values, and the restlessness of the masses are reflected in the thought and art of the second phase of the Industrial Revolution, 1870–1914. There was no sudden or drastic breaking away from the spirit of idealism and romanticism that prevailed in the thought and art of the bourgeois-dominated first phase of the Industrial Revolution, 1830–70. Both idealism and romanticism continued on into the second phase, 1870–1914, and beyond. Indeed, there were so many divergent trends and schools of thought and art during the second phase of the Industrial Revolution that the term *eclectic* is sometimes used to characterize the culture of that period. Nevertheless, we may detect certain trends that stand out as significant. It is doubly important that we detect these trends, for many of them that developed in this period have carried on past the mid-twentieth century.

1. The General Nature of Thought and Art During the Second Phase of the Industrial Revolution, 1870–1914

The prevailing idealism and optimism that characterized the thought of the early nineteenth century tended after 1870 to give way to materialism, pragmatism, and pessimism—in spite of material advancements never before dreamed of. During the Second Phase of the Industrial Revolution literature was characterized by realism of various types. The arts tended first toward impressionism and then toward more open revolt against the standards of the past. In music, however, there was a much stronger carry-over of traditional styles and values than in the rest of the arts.

The chief influences behind the new trends were undoubtedly the intellectual and sociological problems created by science and technology. Darwinism, the new psychology, and the discontent of the industrial proletariat run through the literature and art of the period like a refrain. Darwinism appeared to many to make man an animal, a brute, struggling for survival in a heartless, competitive world governed by blind chance. This was a sharp break with the romantic idealists, who saw man as a child of God, and the world as a thing of beauty governed by a benevolent Divine Being.

The new psychology made man's mind as well as his body mechanical and animal-like. Furthermore, it discovered in the dark subconscious recesses of the mind selfish and brutish desires. These disenchanting concepts represented a radical departure, not only from those of the romantic idealists of the early nineteenth century, but also from the ideas of the eighteenth-century philosophers of the Enlightenment, who believed in the essential goodness of nature and the perfectibility of man. The rapid development of technology during the so-called Second Industrial Revolution made the proletariat so numerous and so restless that it could no longer be ignored, either by the bourgeois capitalists or by the writers and artists. The smug all's-right-with-the-world attitude that the writers and painters expressed in the bourgeois-dominated early and mid-nineteenth century now gave way to sordidly realistic writing and painting about the slums and the uprooted.

Finally Einstein's relativity theory and the startling ideas of the physicists with respect to the stability of the atom, that is, of matter itself, which came toward the end of this period, heightened the wave of cynicism, disillusionment, and revolt. Nor did the Christian religion, then wavering under heavy assault, give out the guiding light that it had long provided in the Western world. It should be noted, however, that the pessimism that tended to prevail among the thinkers and artists of the second phase of the Industrial Revolution did not always reflect the attitude of the masses, who were at last on the move toward a greater share of this world's material goods and privileges.

2. The Philosophy of Disenchantment

Although the Darwinian concept of evolution by natural selection made some of the philosophers of the late nineteenth century, such as Thomas Huxley, Herbert Spencer, and Ernst Haeckel, extremely optimistic about man and society evolving ever onward and upward, it had the opposite effect on others. A forerunner of the pessimistic type of materialism that was to have so much influence on the twentieth century was Arthur Schopenhauer (1788–1860). In *The World as Will and Idea*, published in 1818, forty-one years before *The Origin of Species*, this German thinker set forth the idea that one force governs and motivates the whole world of animate life, and that force is will—the will to survive. The world, therefore, is a cruel and heartless place full of struggling and competing creatures, a place where the strong and fierce devour the weak and gentle. The only possible happiness to be found in it is by ascetic denial and withdrawal. They suffer least who participate least in the hard, competitive world.

This line of thinking (at least a variation of it) was carried to its ultimate by an admirer of Schopenhauer, Friedrich Nietzsche (1844–1900). Nietzsche was a disillusioned German theological student turned philosopher. A pain- and nerve-racked genius, he finally went completely insane. Two of his most influential works are *Thus Spake Zarathustra* and *Beyond Good and Evil*. Like Schopenhauer he believed that the greatest force in the animate world is will. However, this will is not only to survive but, in the strong at least, to achieve power. "The will to power" was Nietzsche's key phrase. If a superior society were to emerge, it would have to come about through the efforts of strong and gifted individuals who would rise to power because of their superior strength, will, and intelligence. Anything that contributes to power is good, be it brute strength, will, boldness, cunning, or intelligence. Whatever leads to weakness is bad, be it gentleness, modesty, generosity, or compassion. The two greatest enemies of the good society are democracy and Christianity. Democracy is the rule of the mediocre masses, cattle. But it was against Christianity that Nietzsche hurled his sharpest invectives; he believed Christianity to be the greatest curse of Western civilization: a slave religion that extolls the vices of slavery such as meekness, compassion, sacrifice, and charity to compensate for actual weakness. Needless to say, Nietzsche was not very popular with the late-nineteenth-century masses, who were obsessed with the marvels and promises of science and technology. However, his influence upon the twentieth century was great. Malignant nationalism, militarism, and fascism drew heavily from his fertile mind and facile pen.

Another twentieth-century cult that drew heavily from Nietzsche was existentialism. The best-known exponent of this philosophy, which enjoys great popularity with the mid-twentieth-century intelligentsia, particularly in France and Germany, is Jean-Paul Sartre (1905–   ). Sartre defines his doctrine as an attempt to draw out all the logical implications of a consistent atheism. He rejects all absolute moral laws or values. Man is a finite but free creature responsible only to himself in a universe devoid of purpose. This sophisticated and often vague cult not only reflects the influence of the late-nineteenth-century philosophers of disenchantment but also represents a revolt against such absolutes as Christianity and twentieth-century Marxism and fascism.

Less pessimistic and violent than Schopenhauer's and Nietzsche's cult of the will but equally as materialistic was the philosophy of pragmatism. The chief founder of this school of thought, which has been so potent and widespread in the twentieth century, was William James (1842–1910), a German-trained professor of psychology and philosophy at Harvard University. Pragmatism reflected the uncertainties aroused by atomic physicists around the turn of the century. James rejected all absolutes of logic and religion. Truth is a relative thing dependent upon the individual and the circumstances. A thing is true if it works and is useful. We cannot know ultimate religious or moral truths, for instance, but if a particular religious faith gives an individual confidence and peace of mind, then it is practical and therefore true for him. Thus spiritual, moral, and human values become as relative in the minds of William James and the pragmatists as the physical world in the mind of Albert Einstein.

One of James's most influential disciples was John Dewey (1859–1952), a professor of philosophy at Columbia University. Dewey introduced the principle of pragmatism into the classroom. If, for instance, experimentation proved that children found modeling a bust of Julius Caesar more interesting than learning Latin grammar, as indeed many did, much of the latter was discarded in favor of the former. Or if statistical studies showed that woodwork or typing was more often used in later life than algebra, then places were found for these useful skills, if necessary, at the expense of algebra. Everyone must be educated both for practical living and for citizenship. Dewey's pragmatism did much to enliven and democratize mass education in an age when the masses were moving to the fore. Unfortunately, in the hands of some of his more extreme disciples and imagined disciples who possessed more enthusiasm than wisdom, thousands of twentieth-century classrooms became amusement centers for unrestrained children, large and small. It was in these classrooms that the philosophy of disenchantment—of relativism, cynicism, materialism, pragmatism—was likely to be disseminated by word and example to the masses.

3. Realistic Literature

Much of the literature of the second phase of the Industrial Revolution, like the philosophy, reflected the materialism, the cynicism, and the pessimism of the age. However, there was a strong carry-over of romanticism beyond 1870 and into the twentieth century. The romantic poets Victor Hugo, Robert Browning, and Alfred Tennyson lived on until 1885, 1889, and 1892 respectively. Although Browning was a rugged and analytical realist when probing the depths of human psychology and emotions, he tended at times to be an idealist and an optimist, believing that "God's in his heaven, all's right with the world." And although in 1850 the young Tennyson in his *In Memoriam* revealed a religious skepticism bold for the time, in 1889—well into a cynical age—he hoped to see his "Pilot face to face" when he had "crossed the bar." Nevertheless, the prevailing and most significant trend in literature in the period 1870–1914 was realism. It was expressed most generally in the novel and drama rather than poetry. Realism tended to depict the seamy, sordid side of human nature and society. It villainized the smug, *nouveau riche* industrial bourgeoisie and its religious and moral hypocrisy without idealizing the uprooted and distressed proletariat.

France took the lead in realistic literature. Balzac (see pp. 554–5), who died in 1850, though essentially a romantic novelist, had foreshadowed realism. In his forty-seven novels and two thousand characters he subjected the dominant middle class to increasingly exact and severe scrutiny. The first French novelist to catch the full flavor of realism was Gustave Flaubert (1821–80). His *Madame Bovary* related the illicit sex life of the wife of a small-town French physician in such full and unblushing detail that it scandalized a public not yet accustomed to such unrestrained "realism." *Madame Bovary* became a model to other novelists. Émile Zola (1840–1902), though interested like Flaubert in individual personality, was more concerned with social problems, particularly those created by industrialization. Zola was a bold and radical republican who, it will be remembered, bearded the French military lion and played a prominent role in finally securing justice for Dreyfus. In twenty penetrating but sometimes tedious novels he depicted and analyzed the problems of a changing society. His sympathy was with the industrial proletariat, but he suffered no illusions as to the natural goodness of man, including the distressed lower classes. The greatest and most influential of the French realistic novelists was Anatole France (1844–1924), whose real name was Jacques Thibault. Anatole France was essentially an Epicurean. With a light touch he satirized the bourgeois society and the Christian religion and morals of the second phase of the Industrial Revolution. The volume and the influence of his lucid writings were enormous. Three of his best-known novels are *Penguin Island, The Garden of Epicurus*, and *The Revolt of the Angels*. In later life he took an active part as a Socialist in the struggle to improve the status of the lower classes.

Charles Dickens (1812–70) in Great Britain, like Balzac in France, combined romanticism and realism. In his sentimentality, his moralizing, his optimism, and his spontaneous gush of words he was a romantic. In his zeal for social reform, his pilloring

of bourgeois arrogance and corrupt bourgeois institutions, and his graphic and often sordid detailing of the life of the urban proletariat, he was the first of the British realists. In *David Copperfield, Oliver Twist, The Pickwick Papers* a galaxy of characters of the middle and lower walks of life in industrial Britain parade realistically before us. Thomas Hardy (1840–1928), unlike Dickens, had a completely pessimistic view of the universe. His vivid characters—ordinary English countryside folks—struggle Darwin-like against fate, environment, and their own frail natures without any help from God or Hardy. *The Return of the Native, The Mayor of Casterbridge*, and *Tess of the D'Urbervilles* are some of the best examples in any language of the realistic novel. H. G. Wells (1866–1946) placed his faith in materialistic science, technology, and social reform. He fascinated a science-obsessed age with novels that made a world of scientific marvels and supermen seem real and at hand. High on Wells's list of outworn institutions that must be discarded before a scientific and socialistic utopia could be created was supernatural religion. Probably the greatest of all the British realists was George Bernard Shaw (1856–1950). Of Irish birth, the indefatigable and seemingly indestructible Shaw early crossed over to London, where he long remained the gadfly of bourgeois society. In scores of urbane and sophisticated novels, essays, and plays, he charmingly but caustically taunted Christianity, capitalism, and democracy. Shaw was a cynic, a Socialist, and a stark materialist. He was the epitome of late-nineteenth-century and early-twentieth-century realism.

In the United States the era of the realistic novel began with the jarring writing of Theodore Dreiser (1871–1945). Dreiser was a member of a large German immigrant family who moved about in poverty from place to place in the Middle West, the Roman Catholic father trying unsuccessfully to keep the restless children in line. Dreiser's novels depicted in hard, rough detail the life and the philosophy of the disenchanted and uprooted proletariat, living in a materialistic, industrial world of changing values. His first novel *Sister Carrie*, which appeared in 1900, was an American industrial version of *Madame Bovary* told with raw unrestraint. To escape poverty, Carrie became the mistress of a succession of men. The progressive degeneration of the characters constitutes the theme of the novel. Editors were so shocked at the frank and open presentation of lurid details that Dreiser had great difficulty getting the book published. The success of *Sister Carrie* was immediate, and other novels in a like vein followed. His masterpiece was *An American Tragedy*, published twenty-five years later. It was not only Dreiser's narrative that startled the generation of the early twentieth century, but his philosophy as well. He pictured an amoral world of materialistic science and technology where human animals struggle for survival, motivated by unedifying Freudian drives.

Dreiser's brand of realism, or naturalism, as the more extreme form of realism is sometimes called, became the dominant trend in American fiction as the century progressed. In the disillusioned decade of the nineteen twenties H. L. Mencken (1880–1956) laughed hoarsely to scorn all Christian values. He held in derision both the hypocritical and "Puritanical" bourgeoisie and the stupid, vulgar masses. Sinclair Lewis (1885–1951) continued in the same vein, but with a lighter touch. Babbitt, Elmer Gantry, and Arrowsmith, deflated heroes in Sinclair Lewis's novels by those titles, became stereotypes of typical Americans in the minds of tens of thousands of untypical American readers of books. William Faulkner (1897–), with much greater artistry, sophistication, and sympathy, carried realism probably to its ultimate. In *Sanctuary* he tears away the veil woven by civilization to conceal the perverted and animal-like natures of ordinary people. In *A Fable* he exposes the conspiratorial greed with which the leaders organize society and enforce conformity to it.

One of the most influential of the realists was the Norwegian playwright Henrik Ibsen (1828–1906). A frustrated artist embittered by youthful poverty, Ibsen ridiculed bourgeois society in his popular dramas. In what is probably his best-known play, *A Doll's House*, one of his heroines revolts against the "doll's house" that her stodgy, hypocritical, middle-class husband created for her. In *An Enemy of the People*, Ibsen reveals the fickleness of the masses and their unfitness for democratic government. *Ghosts* deals with the social and personal problems of syphilis. Ibsen had a wide international following. He was the chief inspiration for the youthful George Bernard Shaw. In Germany, Gerhart Hauptmann (1862–1946) dramatized the dislocation of the proletariat during the early stages of the Industrial Revolution. In Russia, Dostoevski and Turgenev (see p. 555) combined realism with romanticism in much the same manner as did Balzac in France and Dickens in Great Britain. Leo Tolstoi (1828–1910) was more of a realist and dedicated his life and writing almost exclusively to social reform. His masterpiece, *War and Peace*, is a stirring plea for pacifism. Later he sought to combine Christianity with socialism, giving up his great inherited wealth to set a good example. Anton Chekhov (1860–1904) wrote polished but realistic and pessimistic plays about Russian peasant life. Maxim Gorky (1868–1936), up from the proletarian ranks, analyzed the social problems of the Russian masses in his dramas and novels. He was a revolutionary and later a Communist.

It is a far cry from Dickens to Faulkner, or from Tolstoi to Mencken, and yet realistic literature, with all its differing varieties, had many things in common. It reflected almost invariably the social dislocation brought about by the Industrial Revolution, particularly in its more advanced second phase. It reflected the materialism of an age of science and technology. It displayed over and over again the influence of Darwin and of Freud. It was increasingly concerned with the disillusionment and cynicism brought about by changing religious and moral values. This last factor is probably the most fundamental and significant of them all.

ON THE TERRACE, BY RENOIR. The first painters to reflect the rapidly changing values of the middle and late nineteenth century were the impressionists, represented here by Renoir. They put to use recent scientific discoveries concerning light and color. Sunlit parks, shimmering lakes and rivers, and subtle, sophisticated portraits delighted them. Omitting much detail, they painted suggestive shapes, forms, and colors, leaving the rest to the imagination. (*Courtesy of The Art Institute of Chicago, Mr. and Mrs. L. L. Coburn Memorial Collection*)

4. Impressionistic and Modern Painting and Sculpture

France, the birthplace of realistic literature, was also the chief seat of the impressionistic and modern painting and sculpture that predominated during the second phase of the Industrial Revolution. Impressionism was a mild and sophisticated revolt against the artistic standards that had prevailed since the late fifteenth century. It reflected the intellectual challenge to traditional values and institutions that arose with the startling advances of science in the late nineteenth century. It took its chief inspiration from the seventeenth-century Spanish painters Velásquez and El Greco, from Japanese art, which was rediscovered after 1853, and from new scientific knowledge concerning the nature of color and light. Impressionistic painting was informal, unposed, and random-angled. It sought to convey by studied casualness the impression of a view one gets at a glance. The chief founder of the impressionistic style of painting was the Frenchman Édouard Manet (1832–83). Among his more illustrious disciples were Claude Monet (1840–1926) and Auguste Renoir (1841–1919) in France, and James McNeill Whistler (1834–1903), an Ameri-

STARRY NIGHT, BY VAN GOGH. Near the end of the nineteenth century and early in the twentieth century modernist painters such as Cézanne, Gauguin, and Van Gogh went far beyond the impressionists in breaking with long-established traditions. Van Gogh's stars are here painted in yellow swirls against a sombre purple sky. The tree in the foreground suggests an ominous, leaping flame. Considered mad by most of his contemporaries, Van Gogh is now generally regarded as one of the great artistic geniuses. (*The Museum of Modern Art, New York. Acquired through the Lillie P. Bliss Bequest*)

can expatriate in Europe. These artists painted sunlit parks and landscapes, shimmering lakes and rivers, and subtle, sophisticated portraits. They omitted much detail, painting in only suggestive shapes, forms, and colors as first impressions, and leaving the rest to the imagination. Their work was sensuous, decorative, and mildly iconoclastic.

The breach that the impressionists made with the long-established traditions was

Gogh (1853–90) broke openly with every artistic standard of the past. Gauguin was not interested in painting the literal document of his subject, but only what the subject meant to him. He painted patterns formed in his mind by objects rather than the objects themselves, using the most violent reds, yellows, and greens. He finally went primitive, deserting Western civilization for the South Sea islands. Gauguin's friend, Van Gogh, would squeeze out paint

NIGHT FISHING AT ANTIBES, BY PICASSO. The revolt against long-established standards and traditions in art, begun by the impressionists, was probably carried to its ultimate in the twentieth century by Pablo Picasso. The great distortion and disjointedness of this modernist painting reflects the social and political unrest of a technically advanced age. It was painted in 1939, the year of the beginning of the second world holocaust. (*The Museum of Modern Art, New York. Mrs. Simon Guggenheim Fund*)

greatly widened near the end of the nineteenth century and early in the twentieth by more radical modern painters. The new trend was led by Paul Cézanne (1839–1906), a lifelong friend of Émile Zola. Cézanne distorted freely in order to achieve a more powerful effect, and applied thick paint to attain the appearance of solidity and roundness. Going far beyond Cézanne, the gifted but eccentric Frenchman Paul Gauguin (1848–1903) and Dutchman Vincent van

directly from the tube on to the canvas to achieve weird but striking effects. Like Gauguin, Van Gogh was an expressionist, freely distorting the images of nature to make them express his own feelings. Cézanne, Gauguin, and Van Gogh were the forerunners of many iconoclastic schools, such as cubism and futurism, that marked twentieth-century painting.

Two of the most influential of the revolutionary modern painters were the Frenchman Henri Matisse (1869–1954) and the Spanish-born (French by adoption) Pablo Picasso (1881–   ), both of whom received their chief inspiration from Cézanne. In some of their work they carried distortion to great extremes. Matisse became enamored with primitive culture. Picasso's figures during one phase of his long career became geometric (hence cubism) and disjointed. He occasionally gave up color entirely for black and white.

It is characteristic of an age of intellectual revolt and crumbling values (the Hellenistic period was such an age) that the artists turn inward. During the second phase of the Industrial Revolution painting became highly individualistic. The artists tended to paint such personal objects as fruit, still life, and mandolins. Furthermore, they turned to figures on the periphery of a disintegrating society, such as prostitutes, solitary drinkers, blind beggars, and circus performers. The figures were separate, not joined. This disjointedness and the symbols of science, machinery, and speed, which were so prominent in this painting, surely represented an age of intellectual revolt against traditional values, of materialistic science and technology, and of mass movement. Unfortunately much of this painting was so technical and highly specialized that it could be appreciated only by a relatively few, at a time when the many were coming to the fore seeking enlightenment.

The rapid growth of cities and of wealth during the second phase of the Industrial Revolution was responsible for the production of a large quantity of sculpture to decorate the new public buildings, squares, and parks. Most of it was patterned after the styles of the past, either classical or baroque, more often the latter. Probably the two sculptors of the period who most truly reflected the spirit of their own time and of future trends were Constantin Meunier (1831–1905) in Belgium and Auguste Rodin (1840–1917) in France. Meunier was the first great sculptor to recognize the importance of the industrial proletariat. Among his rugged and realistic statues are

The Hammersmith, The Puddler, The Mine Girl, and *The Old Mine Horse.* Rodin introduced impressionism into sculpture. His most famous statue, *The Thinker,* illus-

THE THINKER, BY RODIN. This impressionistic masterpiece suggests the Darwinian concept of the emergence of man from a lower form, an idea that played a very prominent role in man's thinking during the second phase of the Industrial Revolution, and later. (*Courtesy of The Metropolitan Museum of Art*)

trates not only impressionistic art but also the Darwinian concept of man's emergence from a lower form. Rodin was the forerunner of much of the modern, abstract, and symbolistic sculpture of the twentieth century.

5. Functional Architecture

The architecture of the period 1870–1914, like the sculpture, combined the old with the new. The prevailing style in the numerous and increasingly large public buildings continued to be classical, or baroque. Gothic architecture, which enjoyed a revival in the early part of the nineteenth century, was now limited primarily to university buildings and to churches. Even Byzantine, Moorish, and oriental models appeared here and there throughout the West as the world was brought closer together by rapid communications.

The first great architect to develop a style appropriate to an age of steel, science, and speed was the American Louis Henry Sullivan (1856–1924). Sullivan pointed out that "Form follows function." That is to say, the style of buildings is determined by their intended use and by the materials used in their construction. This has always been true; Greek, Roman, Gothic buildings served utilitarian purposes, both secular and religious. Furthermore, the columns, posts and lintels, arches, vaults, and heavy walls that characterized these styles were the only known means of supporting massive or lofty structures. But in an age of structural steel

this was no longer true. The architectural devices of the past had lost their utility, were purely decorative. And in fast-moving, crowded, and growing New York and Chicago what sense did horizontal Greek or Moorish lines make? Sullivan designed the steel-supported skyscraper.

But Sullivan and his followers were not satisfied with the principle "Form follows function." They decided that function is the sole purpose of architecture. The application of this principle came to be known as "functional architecture." Structural steel, reinforced concrete, and glass brick made it possible for the functional architects to achieve unbroken horizontal lines impossible to the Greeks, and towering heights combined with gracefulness and light that the medieval Gothic builders never dreamed of. Furthermore, the spirit of intellectual revolt against the standards and values of the past gave the architects a

THE ROBIE HOUSE, DESIGNED BY FRANK LLOYD WRIGHT. Form has always followed function in architecture, but to the functional architects such as Louis Sullivan and Frank Lloyd Wright, function was the main purpose of architecture. In 1909 Wright designed the Robie House in Chicago for the broad sunlit expanses of the American prairie. Overhanging cantilevers, unbroken horizontal lines, and spacious interiors were features of designs by the functional architects. (*Courtesy of Frank Lloyd Wright and The Museum of Modern Art*)

freedom to experiment never before enjoyed. Finally, unprecedented wealth and technological advances provided them with the means to execute their ideas. Some of the massive utilitarian structures of this and later periods, such as a number of the railway stations, some of the American skyscrapers like the Philadelphia Savings Fund Society Building and the United Nations Building, and the Firth of Forth, Brooklyn, Golden Gate, and Straits of Mackinac bridges are creditable monuments to an age of materialism.

Sullivan's most illustrious student and one of the most influential figures in the development of functional architecture was Frank Lloyd Wright (1869–1959) in the United States. Wright made brilliant use of the cantilever (projecting member supported at only one end) to achieve striking horizontal lines and an unobstructed spaciousness appropriate on the American prairie. These effects were made possible by the tensile strength of steel. Wright combined artistic skill with a Shavian scorn for traditional values and institutions.

6. Music Old and New

Of all the arts music showed the least responsiveness to the materialistic and scientific spirit of the second phase of the Industrial Revolution. Some of the greatest romantic composers of the first phase lived well on into the second. Wagner lived until 1883, Verdi until 1901. Their ranks were joined in the late nineteenth century by such great romanticists as Camille Saint-Saëns (1835–1925) in France and Peter Tschaikovsky (1840–93) in Russia. Nor was there any lessening in the spirit of nationalism in music, which was such an important ingredient of romanticism. We have already seen (Chapters 47 and 51) how Wagner's nationalism became more militant after 1870. Tschaikovsky combined Russian nationalism with his romanticism. More strictly nationalist in their themes and folk tunes were the Russian Nicholas Rimsky-Korsakov (1844–1908); the Czech

Anton Dvořák (1841–1904); the Norwegian Edvard Grieg (1843–1907); and the Finn Jean Sibelius (1865–1957). Not only romanticism but also classicism was carried over into the late nineteenth century by the great German composer Johannes Brahms (1833–97). Spending the last thirty-five years of his life in the Hapsburg capital of Vienna, Brahms became an ardent Hungarian nationalist without giving up loyalty to his native Germany. Probably more than any other musician Brahms resembles Beethoven in style. Like Beethoven he combined the classical spirit with the romantic.

The most important innovator in music in the period 1870–1914 was the French composer Claude Debussy (1862–1918). Debussy was the father of impressionistic music. Experimenting with subtle and sophisticated dissonances, he was to music what Manet and Renoir were to painting. Following Dubussy's lead were such modern composers as Maurice Ravel (1875–1938) in France, and Igor Stravinsky (1882–) Sergei Prokofiev (1891–1953), and Dimitri Shostakovich (1906–) in Russia. Stravinsky, with his more violent and impetuous dissonances, bears somewhat the same relationship to Debussy as does Picasso to Renoir in painting. America's most significant contribution to music in an age of noisy technology and stirring masses was probably jazz, a development in which George Gershwin (1898–1937) played an important part. The radical, dissonant, and often noisy music of the followers of Debussy surely reflected the spirit of an age of materialistic technology and science, of cynical disenchantment, and of intellectual revolt against traditional values. We must not forget, however, that in any typical concert in the Western world in 1914 or in 1950 Mozart, Beethoven, and Schubert would still predominate over Debussy and Stravinsky. The new grew up alongside but did not replace the old.

Meanwhile, looming ever larger in the materialistic, cynical, restless mind of the West from 1870 to 1914 was the spirit of nationalism. The malignancy that characterized the nationalism of this period was ominous, now that the aggressive nations were peopled by the "animal masses" of Darwin and Freud—animal masses whose claws and teeth were made ever so much sharper by science and technology. In 1914 Western man appeared to be on the threshold of a materialistic utopia, free from disease, grinding toil, and want. And yet the haunting pessimism of the time proved to be warranted.

—◆•◆—

SUGGESTED READING

* The Philosophy of Nietzsche (Modern Library). Includes Thus Spake Zarathustra, Nietzsche's most renowned work. The best way to get at the ideas of this thinker, who believed that Christianity is the greatest softening and corrupting influence in Western civilization, is to read some of his vigorous writing. Nietzsche was the father of much twentieth-century fascist thought.

John Dewey, Democracy and Education (1916). A major work by the philosopher who introduced the idea of pragmatism into American education. By the mid-twentieth century his influence was global.

* Henrik Ibsen, Ghosts; An Enemy of the People; A Doll's House; The Master Builder (Modern Library). Four of the best-known plays by the great Norwegian pioneer of realistic drama.

Émile Zola, The Fat and the Thin (1908). One of Zola's realistic novels. The setting is Paris's famous produce market, Les Halles. The fat are the prosperous, well-adjusted conformists; the thin are the lean and hungry non-conformists.

Anatole France, The Revolt of the Angels (1923). A typically urbane and cynical novel by the great French realist. A fantasy written with sophisticated artistry.

* Thomas Hardy, The Return of the Native (Pocket Books). One of the best of Hardy's numerous realistic novels. It reflects the pessimism and disenchantment that characterized much of the literature and philosophy of the late nineteenth and early twentieth century.

Theodore Dreiser, An American Tragedy (memorial edition, with an introduction by H. L. Mencken [1946]). Greatest novel of the founder of American realism. It makes man an animal, and life a stark jungle. A picture of America's cynical twenties and thirties.

Sinclair Lewis, Babbitt (1922). A typical novel by the popular American realist.

William Faulkner, A Fable (1954). A powerful allegory written with the usual Faulknerian artistry on the theme of conformity and nonconformity to organized society.

W. H. Wright, Modern Painting (1930). A good general survey.

M. Raynal, The Nineteenth Century: Goya to Gauguin (1951). An excellent treatment, beautifully illustrated.

Curt Sachs, Our Musical Heritage (1948). A meaningful history of music, for the layman.

SECTION 12

———◆———

The Era of the Two World Wars,

1914–59

T he twentieth century opened with great promise. Natural science appeared to be solving the last mysteries of the physical world. Technology seemed to be banishing want and grinding toil from the face of the earth. The masses were on the move, gaining ever more freedom and a larger share of this world's goods and privileges. Few would have dreamed that the next half century would be the bloodiest and most violent five decades in all history. During the course of those five decades two global wars shattered much of the world. Violent communist and fascist dictatorships stalked among the ruins, challenging the dazed and seemingly paralyzed forces of liberal democracy. Western empires in Asia and Africa crumbled as Asians and Africans adopted Western technology and imbibed the heady wine of nationalism. For those who survived, the first half of the twentieth century was a challenging time to live.

CHAPTER 54

---◆---

World War I, 1914–18

THE FIRST blow that rocked the twentieth-century world was World War I. To most of mankind, busy with its daily tasks, it seemed to be a sudden and unforeseen disaster. To statesmen and informed students of world affairs it was the snapping of long-developing tensions.

1. Origins of the War

World War I began as a showdown between two hostile alliances of European powers: the Triple Alliance, composed of Germany, Austria-Hungary, and Italy; and the Triple Entente, composed of Great Britain, France, and Russia. This system of alliances was begun by Bismarck shortly after his defeat of France and the creation of the German Empire in 1870–71. In 1873, as a safeguard against a revengeful France, or indeed against any hostile combination against Germany, Bismarck formed the Three Emperors' League, composed of Germany, Austria-Hungary, and Russia. When the interests and ambitions of Austria-Hungary and Russia proved to be incompatible, Bismarck replaced Russia with Italy (1879–82) to form the Triple Alliance. However, so long as he remained at the head of the German government, he carefully nurtured cordial relations with Russia and also with Great Britain. This policy left France isolated and subject to repeated German bullying.

Bismarck's diplomatic work was quickly undone by Kaiser Wilhelm II, who ascended the German imperial throne in 1888 and dismissed Bismarck two years later. Wilhelm II immediately dropped the friendship pact with Russia and began to antagonize Great Britain by his grandiose schemes in the Near and Far East and by his huge naval building program. France was now able to form an alliance with Russia (1894) and an entente (understanding) with Great Britain (1904). In 1907 the Triple Entente was formed after Great Britain and Russia had settled their long-standing differences in Asia. Only an intense fear of Germany could have reconciled the deep-seated and divergent interests that had long existed among these three powers.

Suspicion, hatred, and fear between the two power combinations mounted steadily. A ruinous armaments race ensued; the powers of the Triple Entente strove desperately to overcome Germany's long lead in land forces, while Germany sought to erase Great Britain's naval advantage. Rivalries and conflicts among the various members of the two alliances cropped up all over the world, threatening to embroil all the other members. In 1905–6 and again in 1911 two such clashes occurred in Morocco between France and Germany (see p. 612). Two occurred in the Balkans between Russia and Austria-Hungary. In 1908 Austria-Hungary suddenly annexed two provinces, Bosnia and Herzegovina, which were inhabited by Serbs and Croats. Serbia had planned to annex these territories, peopled by her own linguistic kinsmen. She appealed to her big Slavic brother, Russia. Russia threatened Austria-Hungary, whereupon Germany rattled her mighty sword and forced Russia to back down. A second Balkan crisis occurred in 1912–13. The various Balkan states defeated Turkey and then fought among themselves over the spoils. Victorious Serbia threatened to expand. Austria-Hungary not only thwarted Serbia's expansion to the Adriatic Sea but threatened to annihilate her. Again Serbia appealed to Russia and again Germany forced Russia to back down. Each of these crises brought the world close to war, increased international tension, and speeded up preparations for a final showdown.

It was in the Balkans that the fatal explosion finally occurred. Here the interests of Russia and Austria-Hungary clashed head-on. The Serbs, Bulgarians, Romanians, and Greeks were religious (Orthodox) and cultural (Byzantine) kinsmen of the Russians. The Serbs and Bulgarians were also linguistic (Slavic) kinsmen of the Russians. Moreover, the Balkan Peninsula was of great economic and strategic interest to Russia. Since the days of Ivan III in the fifteenth century Russia had sought control of the Bosporus and Dardanelles (the Turkish Straits) as a water outlet to the West. Austria-Hungary's interests in the Balkans were, perhaps, even more vital than those of Russia. The Dual Monarchy's chief interest in the area grew out of the polyglot nature of its empire. It was composed of numerous language groups, some of which, particularly the Serbs, Croats, Slovenes, and Romanians, had linguistic kinsmen in the Balkans.

As the Ottoman Empire in the Balkan Peninsula disintegrated in the nineteenth and early twentieth centuries, the various Balkan language groups emerged as independent nations. These free peoples constituted a strong attraction for the members of their language groups in Austria-Hungary, who wished to break loose and join them. This was particularly true of Serbia, which attracted the Hapsburgs's

Yugoslav subjects (the Serbs, Croats, and Slovenes). But if the Hapsburgs' Yugoslavs should join Serbia, Austria-Hungary's other language minorities—Italians, Czechs, Slovaks, Poles, Romanians, and Ruthenians —would also demand their freedom from Austrian and Hungarian rule and the Dual Monarchy would fall apart. Austria-Hungary, therefore, felt that she must control the Balkan Peninsula in self-defense. It was also the only direction in which she could expand, particularly after her exclusion from Germany in 1866. And the militancy that characterized the nationalism after 1870 caused all nations to feel that they must expand.

Overlying the clashing interests of Russia and Austria-Hungary in the Balkans were those of Germany and Great Britain. Germany felt that she must maintain the integrity of the Dual Monarchy, which was her only effective and reliable ally. Then, too, her own ambitions in the Balkans and the Near and Middle East were great. One of Kaiser Wilhelm II's chief imperial projects was the Berlin-to-Bagdad railway (see pp. 609–10), which would make German power dominant in the Ottoman Empire if not the whole Near and Middle East. This scheme gravely menaced Great Britain's own imperial life line running through Suez as well as her immediate interests in the Near and Middle East. Germany's project also threatened to blight permanently Russia's hopes of gaining an outlet through the Turkish Straits and to cut Russia off strategically from her allies. France and Italy also had interests in the Balkans and in the Near and Middle East, but their primary concern was their commitments to their respective allies.

When, therefore, a third crisis occurred in the Balkans in the summer of 1914, all the great powers of Europe were automatically involved. The two Moroccan crises, the two Balkan crises, and the feverish armaments race had brought the tension in Europe to the breaking point. All that was needed was an incident.

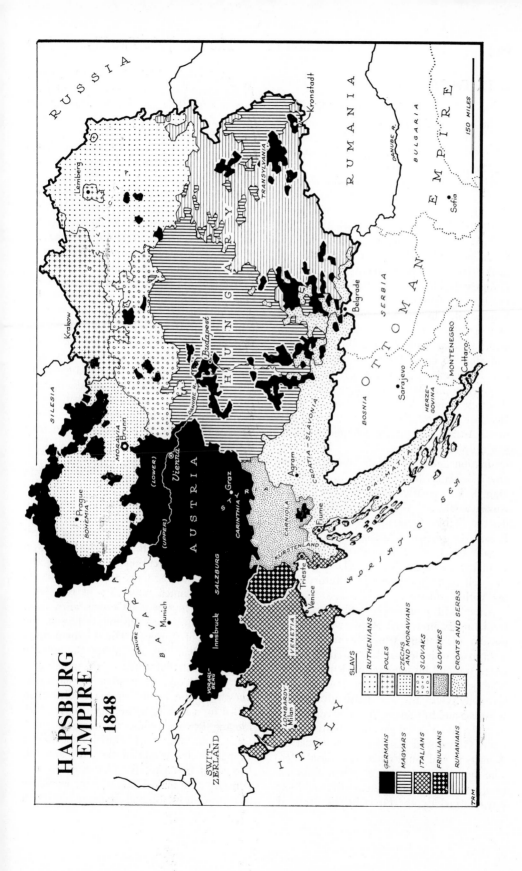

HAPSBURG EMPIRE 1848

RUSSIA

RUMANIA

OTTOMAN EMPIRE

BULGARIA

Sofia

Kronstadt

TRANSYLVANIA

Lemberg

Krakow

H U N G A R Y

Budapest

Belgrade

SERBIA

Brünn

MORAVIA

DANUBE R.

Vienna

(LOWER)

Prague

BOHEMIA

SILESIA

AUSTRIA

(UPPER)

Graz

CARINTHIA

CARNIOLA

CROATIA-SLAVONIA

Agram

BOSNIA

HERZE-GOVINA

Sarajevo

MONTENEGRO

Cattaro

DALMATIA

ADRIATIC SEA

Fiume

KÜSTENLAND

Trieste

Venice

VENETIA

SALZBURG

Innsbruck

VORARL-BERG

Munich

B A V A R I A

DANUBE R.

SWIT-ZERLAND

ITALY

LOMBARDY

Milan

150 MILES

SLAVS

GERMANS	RUTHENIANS
MAGYARS	POLES
ITALIANS	CZECHS AND MORAVIANS
FRIULIANS	SLOVAKS
RUMANIANS	SLOVENES
	CROATS AND SERBS

T.R.M.

2. The Fatal Explosion

The incident was the shooting at Sarajevo of the Austrian Archduke Francis Ferdinand by a Serb on June 28, 1914. The assassination was a deliberate plot involving numerous Serbian army officers. Francis Ferdinand, heir to the Austro-Hungarian throne, was singled out because the Serbs feared that his liberal policy toward the Yugoslavs in Austria-Hungary would allay their discontent, thereby lessening their desire to break away and join Serbia. After the assassination the government of Austria-Hungary decided to crush Serbia and establish her own dominance in the Balkans once and for all. This would require the backing of Germany, for clearly Russia would not stand aside and allow her Serbian kinsmen and allies to be so treated or her own national interests to be violated. At a fateful conference in Berlin ten days after the shooting Kaiser Wilhelm II gave Austria-Hungary Germany's "blank check." He urged Austria-Hungary to act quickly while world opinion was still outraged by the assassination and promised to support her in any emergency. This promise by the German Kaiser greatly intensified the crisis. Russia would not allow Austria-Hungary to destroy Serbia; Germany would not allow Russia to defeat Austria-Hungary; and France and Great Britain would not allow Germany to defeat Russia, whose support they felt to be indispensable in future dealings with Germany.

Armed with Germany's blank check, Austria-Hungary presented Serbia with an impossible ultimatum. When Serbia failed to yield to all of its terms, Austria-Hungary declared war and invaded Serbia. Russia mobilized her forces against Austria-Hungary and Germany. Germany sent harsh ultimatums to Russia and to France. When Russia failed to reply and France gave an unsatisfactory reply, Germany declared war on Russia on August 1, and on France two days later. The next day, August 4, when German troops violated Belgian neutrality on their way to attack France, Great Britain declared war on Germany. Thus, by August 4, 1914, all the great powers of Europe except Italy were at war. Italy claimed that she was not obligated to aid her allies, Germany and Austria-Hungary, since they were the aggressors. The following year, she entered the war on the side of the Entente powers. To the side of Germany and Austria-Hungary came Turkey and Bulgaria; these were referred to as the Central Powers. To the side of the Entente powers, who came to be called the Allies, eventually came much of the rest of the world—some thirty-two nations in all. This was truly a world war.

In following the tragic events just related one can hardly fail to be impressed by the great role played by the spirit of malignant nationalism. It was aggressive nationalism that destroyed much of the spiritual unity of Western Christendom, that motivated much of the revived imperial competition, that energized the massive armies, that refused to yield or compromise in times of crisis, that made international law impossible, and produced international anarchy instead.

3. Germany's Near Triumph

In a long-drawn-out war the advantage would appear to lie with the Allies in view of their superior manpower and resources and their control of the seas. However, Germany had no intention of permitting the conflict to become long, and few world observers saw much possibility of the Allies preventing the superior German army from winning a quick and crushing victory on the mainland of Europe. The German high command had long anticipated the military situation that confronted it in August 1914, and had developed a plan of operation known as the Schlieffen plan. This plan called for a holding action against the slow-moving Russians while the main German forces concentrated on a quick knockout of France, which possessed the only army in the world that gave the Germans any real concern. The main German blow would be a surprise thrust through Belgium, despite a

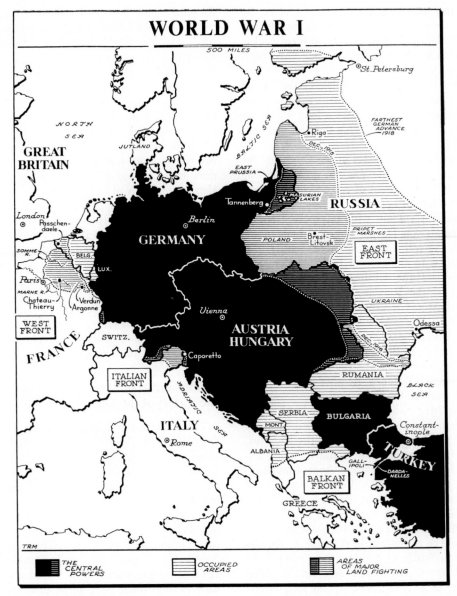

WORLD WAR I

500 MILES

GREAT BRITAIN

NORTH SEA

JUTLAND

BALTIC SEA

St. Petersburg

Riga

FARTHEST
GERMAN
ADVANCE
1918

DEC. 1915

EAST PRUSSIA

London

Passchen-
daele

SOMME R.

BELG.

Paris

LUX.

MARNE R.

Chateau-
Thierry

Verdun
Argonne

WEST
FRONT

FRANCE

SWITZ.

GERMANY

Berlin

Tannenberg

MASURIAN
LAKES

POLAND

Brest-
Litovsk

RUSSIA

PRIPET
MARSHES

EAST
FRONT

UKRAINE

DEC. 1916

Odessa

Vienna

AUSTRIA
HUNGARY

Caporetto

ITALIAN
FRONT

ADRIATIC SEA

ITALY

Rome

SERBIA

MONT.

ALBANIA

RUMANIA

BLACK
SEA

BULGARIA

Constant-
inople

GALL-
IPOLI

TURKEY

DARDA-
NELLES

BALKAN
FRONT

GREECE

TRM

| ■ THE CENTRAL POWERS | ☰ OCCUPIED AREAS | ☰ AREAS OF MAJOR LAND FIGHTING |

treaty of neutrality signed by all the great powers, including Germany. Pouring through Belgium, the German army would capture Paris and destroy the French armies in the field. It was calculated that no more than six weeks would be required to crush France. Then the Germans would concentrate on and destroy Russia with relative ease. Great Britain, her allies gone, would sue for peace.

The Schlieffen plan came near succeeding. Unexpected Belgian resistance held up the Germans long enough for the French to redeploy their forces to the north and for the British to throw their small army across the channel. Nevertheless, the seemingly irresistible German juggernaut crunched ahead; by the first week in September it was outside Paris ahead of schedule. At this juncture the desperate French and British armies turned on the Germans and in the bloody seven-day Battle of the Marne not only defeated them but drove them back a few miles. Both sides extended their lines from the Swiss border to the North Sea and entrenched. The First Battle of the Marne was one of the decisive battles in history, for it forced on the Germans a long war of attrition that made possible their ultimate defeat.

An important factor in the Germans' defeat at the Marne was the detachment at the critical moment of 100,000 of their best troops for use against the Russians, who had invaded Germany with unexpected speed. Generals von Hindenburg and Ludendorff, with several divisions, were hastily dispatched to the eastern front. Under their command the reinforced German armies trapped the Russians at Tannenberg and administered a crushing defeat that sent them reeling back into Russia. Meanwhile, the British navy swept the Germans from the surface of the seas and set up a blockade of Germany. However, the Germans quickly discovered Britain's Achilles' heel with a new weapon: the submarine.

In 1915 the Germans staged a holding operation in the west while they delivered a series of hammer blows upon the Russians, driving deep into Russia and inflicting immense casualties. A major Anglo-French effort to come to the aid of the hard-pressed Russians by breaking through the Dardanelles was beaten back by sea and by land with heavy losses. In 1916 Germany returned to the assault in the west. In the six-month Battle of Verdun the French held back the Germans but were virtually bled white in so doing. The equally long Battle of the Somme between the British and the Germans was even bloodier. Like Verdun it ended in a stalemate. In the Battle of Jutland, the biggest naval battle in history up to that time, the British fleet thwarted the effort of the German fleet to break the blockade, but suffered serious losses.

By 1917 Germany and her allies, though beginning to show signs of strain, appeared to be close to victory. French morale

dropped at the front and behind the lines; numerous units of the battered army mutinied. The Germans launched an unlimited submarine campaign against Great Britain that soon brought her near starvation. The combined German and Austro-Hungarian forces administered a crushing defeat to Italy. In November 1917, Russia, suffering unbearable hardships at the front and behind the lines, succumbed to the Communist Revolution and soon thereafter withdrew from the war. (The story of the Russian Revolution will be told in the following chapter.) And although the harsh terms forced upon helpless Russia by the Germans in the Treaty of Brest-Litovsk strengthened the resolve of the remaining Allies to fight to the finish, the Germans were now able for the first time in the war to concentrate their full strength on the weary French and British. The prospects for the Allies seemed dim. It was at this critical juncture that the United States entered the war and bolstered up the sagging Allied cause.

4. The Entry of the United States and the Victory of the Allies

When the war had begun in 1914, President Woodrow Wilson had admonished the American people to remain neutral in thought as well as in deed. However, from the beginning the great majority of public opinion in the United States, as indeed in the entire world, regarded Germany and her allies as the aggressors. As Germany came nearer and nearer to victory, most Americans, Republicans and Democrats alike, came increasingly to fear that a German victory would be a world calamity in which the United States would be an eventual victim. To the holders of this view it would be clearly in the self-interest of the United States to help prevent the fall of France and Great Britain rather than to have to face up someday to a victorious Germany alone. But eventually the German government gave the United States little choice. Early in the war the Germans violated American neutrality by using their embassy in Washington as a nest for spies and saboteurs against American industry and transportation. This was to prevent the selling of munitions to Great Britain and France. Early in 1917 the German government, anticipating war with the United States, offered Texas, New Mexico, and Arizona to Mexico as a reward for attacking the United States. Apparently California was to be offered to Japan. The Zimmerman Note, making this offer, was intercepted by British intelligence and turned over to the United States. For some strange reason the German government admitted its authenticity.

The sinking of American ships by German submarines, however, provided the immediate impetus for America's entry into the war. When the Germans first began large-scale sinkings of merchant and passenger ships in 1915, President Wilson had protested so vigorously that the Germans finally agreed to desist. Great Britain and France, it is true, had seized some American ships attempting to evade the blockade of Germany, but no lives had been lost and damages had been paid. Early in 1917 the German high command decided to launch an unlimited submarine campaign against enemy and neutral shipping alike. The German leaders fully expected that this course would bring the United States into the war, but they believed that Great Britain and France would be crushed before any appreciable American weight could be brought to bear in Europe. Upon the announcement of this policy the American government immediately broke off diplomatic relations with Germany. After several American ships had been sunk, President Wilson, on April 6, asked Congress to declare war, not on the German people, but on the German imperial government. The vote for war—82 to 6 in the Senate and 373 to 50 in the House of Representatives—probably reflected the opinion of the American people.

Although a full year elapsed before American troops were able to play an important role at the front, the boost in Allied morale was immediate and the Americans lost no time supplying financial, material, and naval aid. And although the total sacrifice and contribution of the United States to Allied victory were relatively small as compared to those of France and Great Britain, America's role, coming as it did when both sides were approaching exhaustion, was probably decisive. At the beginning of 1918 the race was between Germany and the United States. Germany transferred troops from the Russian front to overwhelm Great Britain and France before large numbers of American troops could arrive, while the United States strove to raise, train, and transport to France sufficient forces to stem the German tide. Again the advantage appeared to lie with Germany.

In March 1918, Field Marshal Ludendorff, now in personal command of the German armies, launched the first of a series of massive blows on the western front designed to end the war. The British and French were driven back with heavy losses. In desperation they at long last agreed to a unified command under France's Marshal Ferdinand Foch. The Americans, under General John J. Pershing, also accepted his command. By the middle of June, Ludendorff had launched four great drives, and the Allied lines had been battered so thin that, when the climactic fifth drive began along the Marne River in mid-July 1918, Ludendorff wired the Kaiser: "If the attack succeeds, the war will be over and we will have won it." When Foch heard the opening German barrage, he wired his government: "If the present German attack succeeds, the war is over and we have lost it." The Germans were stopped by a narrow margin. Foch, now receiving a swelling stream of fresh American troops and armaments, immediately ordered a counterattack. In the Allied counterattack the tank, developed by the foresight of young Winston Churchill, first lord of the British Admiralty, proved to be the decisive weapon. German strength and morale waned rapidly, and Ludendorff soon realized that the war was lost.

The first of the Central Powers to go out

AMERICAN HOWITZER PLATOON ADVANCING ON AN ENTRENCHED GERMAN POSITION, 1918. World War I smashed the world of the nineteenth century and ushered in an era of global violence. The entry of the United States into the war when both sides were nearing exhaustion helped prevent a German victory. (*United Press International Photo*)

of the war was Bulgaria, which at the end of September 1918, surrendered to French, British, and Serbian forces operating from the Greek port of Salonika. A month later Turkey surrendered to British imperial forces in the Near East. Austria-Hungary, her various language groups in revolt, surrendered on November 3 to Italian, British, and French forces driving in from Italy. The following day, a full-fledged mutiny, which had been brewing for several days broke out in the German navy and quickly spread throughout Germany. On November 11, the German commanders, their armies hopelessly beaten and in full retreat from France and Belgium, accepted Foch's armistice terms, which amounted to outright surrender.

5. The Peace Settlement

The Allied statesmen who gathered in Paris in January 1919, to try to make a lasting peace, were confronted with a formidable task. Much of the world had been shattered by a war of unprecedented scope and destructiveness. Nine million men had been killed in battle. A much larger number had died of diseases traceable to the war. Twenty-one million had been wounded. The financial and material losses were incalculable. No Western power was solvent. (Even the United States, the most fortunate of the Western powers, was saddled with a huge national debt that she has never been able to reduce significantly.) The German, Austro-Hungarian, Ottoman, and Russian empires had collapsed. The British and French empires were seriously weakened. A tenth of the richest part of France had been laid waste. Hate and disillusionment poisoned the atmosphere.

Although all thirty-two of the victorious Allies were represented at the Paris Peace Conference, the great decisions were really made by the leaders of the Big Three: France, Great Britain, and the United States. The French delegation was headed by Premier Georges Clemenceau, the aged but virile "Tiger of France." As host to the conference and head of the nation that had done the most to defeat Germany and that had suffered the most, he expected to dominate the decisions. Leading the British delegation was the eloquent and fiery "Little Welsh Attorney," Prime Minister David Lloyd George. As spokesman for the British Empire, which comprised one fourth of all the land and people in the world, he also expected to dominate the conference. At the head of the American delegation was President Woodrow Wilson. A fundamental and bitter clash immediately developed between Clemenceau, who wanted a hard peace that would mutilate Germany and make her harmless in the future, and Wilson, who wanted a "just" peace free of vindictiveness of any kind. Specifically Clemenceau demanded the detachment from Germany of all her territory west of the Rhine and its annexation to or control by France. Only by this means, he believed, could the power balance be tipped in favor of France and French security safeguarded against another German assault. Wilson would not tolerate another "Alsace-Lorraine in reverse." In the end he proved to be more eloquent and stubborn than Clemenceau, and to his side eventually came Lloyd George. Great Britain needed the trade of a recovered Germany and did not wish to see France become too dominant on the continent. The Treaty of Versailles with Germany reflected Wilson's ideas in fundamental principles though not in every detail.

Six months of hard work and bitter wrangling were required to draw up the Treaty of Versailles. Its most important terms were, in brief, as follows. Germany and her allies were forced to accept full responsibility for the war. Germany was compelled to give up all her overseas colonies and concessions. Alsace and Lorraine were returned to France. Three tiny districts were ceded

WOODROW WILSON. President Wilson played a prominent—possibly dominant—role in the Paris Peace Conference of 1919. He was the chief architect of the League of Nations, in which he placed his hopes for world peace. Although the United States refused to join, and the League failed to prevent World War II, it served as a model for the United Nations. (*Underwood and Underwood News Photos*)

to Belgium, and the Danish-speaking portion of Schleswig was returned to Denmark. The Polish-speaking areas of Eastern Germany, most of which had been seized by Prussia in the eighteenth century, were ceded to the resurrected Polish state. With one exception, wherever doubt existed as to the wishes of the people in the affected areas, plebiscites were held to determine

EUROPE
1923

AREAS LOST BY
GERMANY

AREAS LOST BY
RUSSIA

AREAS LOST BY
OTTOMAN EMPIRE

ARCTIC

Nar

ICELAND
(DEN.)

Reykjavik

FAEROE IS.
(DEN.)

NORWAY

SWEDE

Oslo

Stock

SCAPA
FLOW

NORTH
SEA

Edinburgh

ULSTER

IRISH
FREE
STATE

Dublin

GREAT
BRITAIN

DENMARK

GERMAN
WEIMAR REPU

ATLANTIC

Liverpool

London

Amsterdam

NETH.

Hamburg

Bremen

Berlin

Dan

POLISH
CORRIDOR

ENGLISH CHANNEL

Brussels

BELG.

RUHR

Cologne

Weimar

Dresden

OCEAN

Paris

LUX.

Prague

Tesche

Metz

SAAR

Frankfurt

CZEC

Versailles

Strasburg

Stuttgart

Munich

DANUBE

Vienna

FRANCE

Geneva

SWITZ

AUSTRIA

Bud

Bordeaux

Locarno

Trent

PORTUGAL

Bilbao

Marseilles

Trieste

Fiume

Florence

Zara
(IT.)

YU

Lisbon

Madrid

SPAIN

Barcelona

CORSICA
(FR)

ITALY

Rome

ADRIATIC SEA

Seville

BALEARIC IS.
(SP.)

SARDINIA
(IT.)

Naples

Cadiz

Tangier

GIBRALTAR
(BR)

SP. MOROCCO

Algiers

MEDITE

SICILY

MOROCCO
(FR.)

ALGERIA
(FR.)

TUNISIA
(FR.)

MALTA
(BR.)

TRM

500 MILES

their desires. The exception was the Polish Corridor, which was cut along the Vistula River to give Poland an outlet to the sea. Although this territory had been seized from Poland by Frederick the Great and approximately half its population was still Polish-speaking, its cession to Poland severed East Prussia from the main body of Germany and gave Hitler his excuse for beginning World War II. Germany's army was cut down from the most powerful military machine in history to 100,000 officers and men, who were to be long-term volunteers to prevent a rapid turnover of trained personnel. Her navy was reduced from the world's second greatest to six small battleships, six cruisers, and a larger number of auxiliary vessels. She was permitted no submarines, no military aviation, no poison gas (which she had introduced during the war), and no offensive weapons such as tanks and heavy artillery. Germany's Rhineland was to be permanently demilitarized, and her munitions industries were made subject to Allied inspection. Her general staff was to be dismantled and her top war leaders tried for violations of the rules and customs of war and, if found guilty, punished. (The Kaiser fled to the Netherlands just before Germany collapsed, and the Netherlands refused to give him up.) Germany was prohibited from making economic reprisals against her neighbors and her former enemies. Finally, Germany was held liable for an indemnity that in 1921 was set by an Allied reparations commission at approximately $33,000,000,000. Wilson and Lloyd George believed these terms to be just. Clemenceau considered them to be suicidally lenient. They were based, of course, on the assumption that Germany was the guilty aggressor.

The treaties with Germany's allies were more severe than the Treaty of Versailles. This was because the principle followed in territorial rearrangements was freedom or union of all national language groups, and Germany was more homogeneous linguistically than were her allies. The polyglot Austro-Hungarian Empire was split up along language lines. The Czechs and Slovaks were formed into the new state of Czechoslovakia, which unfortunately also included German and other minorities. The Poles were joined to Poland, the Romanians to Romania, the Italians to Italy, and the Serbes, Croats, and Slovenes to Serbia, which now became Yugoslavia. Thus the Dual Monarchy was cut down from a nation of 50,000,000, second in area only to Russia among the nations of Europe, to an Austria of 6,500,000 German-speaking Austrians and a Hungary of 8,000,000 Magyars. Austria was forbidden to unite with Germany. Bulgaria lost her territory along the Aegean Sea to Greece and became one of the smallest Balkan states. Turkey was shorn of her far-flung non-Turkish territories. The new Turkey included only the Anatolian plateau in Asia and the city of Constantinople and its immediate hinterland in Europe. The boundary lines, in spite of the painstaking care of Wilson and scores of experts in drawing them, left many language minority groups to breed future conflicts.

6. The League of Nations

Wilson, quite aware of the impossibility of making perfect treaties, placed his chief hopes for peace in an association of nations that would settle peaceably the tensions and conflicts that were certain to arise in the future. Fearful that, if left to future negotiations, the forming of such an association might be shunted aside or put off indefinitely, he insisted that its framework be incorporated in the treaty with Germany. The first twenty-six articles of the Treaty of Versailles constitute the covenant of the League of Nations. Aware also that the United States and some of the other great powers were not yet willing to surrender their absolute sovereignty to a world government, Wilson felt it necessary to settle for a league that lacked the power to compel the major nations to obey its decisions. He hoped and believed that the United States and the other great powers could be persuaded to join such a league and that it would become a steppingstone to eventual world government.

The central body in the League of Nations, which served as a general clearing house and forum for discussion, was the General Assembly. All members of the League were represented in the General Assembly and all members had one vote, large and small alike. In addition to serving as a discussion forum the General Assembly supervised the work of numerous specialized agencies and participated in the choosing of members of all the other bodies in the League. The nearest thing the League had to an executive organ was the Council. This was made up of five permanent members and six non-permanent members, chosen for three-year terms on a staggered basis by the General Assembly. The five permanent members were to be the United States, Great Britain, France, Italy, and Japan. The Council was empowered to make decisions and recommendations relative to the prevention of war. Its decisions required unanimity, which meant that all the permanent members possessed a permanent veto over its work. Carrying on the day-to-day business of the League, such as recording and publishing all treaties, was the Secretariat, headed by a Secretary-General. Closely associated with the League was the Permanent Court of International Justice, with headquarters at The Hague in the Netherlands. The World Court, as it was generally called, was to settle international legal, but not political, disputes.

The League of Nations had no military forces at its command. Its only teeth, so to speak, were Article X and Article XVI. Article X stated that every member undertook to guarantee the territorial integrity of every other member. This meant that in case one member was attacked, all the other members were morally obligated to come to its aid. However, there was no way to compel them to do so. Article XVI stated that, if a nation went to war in violation of a decision of the League, all the members of the League were to boycott the aggressor. This weapon (economic sanctions) could have been a potent deterrent if faithfully applied. In the last analysis, however, the success of the League of Nations depended primarily upon its support by the Big Three victorious democracies—the United States, Great Britain, and France.

The refusal of the United States to join the League (see pp. 663–4) was a body blow. Great Britain and France immediately lost faith in it and began to pursue their traditional nationalistic aims. Nevertheless, for twelve years the League achieved some noteworthy accomplishments. Sixty-two nations joined it. Germany was admitted in 1926, and the Soviet Union in 1934. The League supervised the carrying out of many of the terms of the treaties, aided tens of thousands of war refugees, gave financial aid to insolvent nations, settled numerous international disputes, and promoted international understanding and good will and humanitarian measures. However, in no case did it undertake to discipline a great power, and many observers feared the outcome of such a test. The test came in 1931, when Japan invaded Manchuria. The League's failure to pass it marked the beginning of its end and of the return to war.

————— •◆• —————

SUGGESTED READING

R. J. Sontag, *European Diplomatic History, 1871–1932* (1933). A scholarly and readable survey.

E. Brandenburg, *From Bismarck to the World War* (1927). A history of the foreign policy of the German Empire preceding World War I. The author, a German, attempts with considerable success to present an objective picture of the origins of World War I, but from the German point of view.

B. E. Schmitt, *Triple Alliance and Triple Entente* (1934). Well-documented history of the formation of the two systems of alliances that led up to World War I. Well written.

S. B. Fay, *The Origins of the World War*, 2 vols. (1928). A scholarly and lucid study of

the background of World War I. Favorable
to Germany.

B. E. Schmitt, *The Coming of the War, 1914,*
2 vols. (1930). A detailed documentary analysis of the chain of events immediately preceding and leading to World War I. The student
will find this scholarly work surprisingly readable.

C. R. M. F. Cruttwell, *History of the Great
War, 1914–1918* (1934). Probably the best
single volume on World War I.

Jules Romains, *Verdun* (1939). A novel about
the great battle of World War I, based upon
excellent historical research.

Charles Seymour, *American Diplomacy during
the World War* (1942). An excellent account
of the circumstances of America's entry into
World War I, by a leading authority on the
subject.

Stephen Bonsal, *Unfinished Business* (1944).
An eyewitness account of the Paris Peace Conference of 1919 by Colonel House's private
interperter. Written in a journalistic style.

P. Birdsall, *Versailles Twenty Years After*
(1941). A perspicacious analysis of the controversial Treaty of Versailles, written with the
benefit of twenty years of hindsight. Probably
the best single volume on the subject.

CHAPTER 55

The Triumph of Communism in Russia

ONE of the most important and ominous of the immediate fruits of World War I was the triumph of communism in Russia. In the postwar years, when the statesmen of the Western democracies were attempting to restore the shattered world of 1914, the Russian Communist leaders were striving to destroy the existing Western civilization, based upon Christianity, liberalism, and capitalism, and to create an entirely new world based upon the blueprints of Marx and Lenin. In Russia they appear in large measure to have succeeded. Their plans for world revolution, however, fell far short of their mark. The final results of their efforts, both in Russia and in the world at large, cannot yet, of course, be known.

1. The Bolshevik Revolution of 1917

The violent Russian upheaval of 1917 was the result of maladjustments and discontent that had been long developing. Russia, except for a handful of intelligentsia, had been virtually by-passed by the great liberalizing movements, such as the Renaissance and the Intellectual and French revolutions, which had influenced Western Europe. The Industrial Revolution, which brought in its wake bourgeois liberalism and proletarian radicalism, reached Russia only in the 1890's. While Western and parts of Central Europe and the United States were becoming industrialized and increasingly liberal-

ized, Russia remained a land of primitive and illiterate peasants, feudal aristocracy, and tsarist autocracy. Many of the frustrated Russian intelligentsia in the latter half of the nineteenth century turned to terroristic nihilism and then to Marxism (see pp. 598-9). The violent wing of the Russian Marxist party, the Bolsheviks, boycotted the abortive liberal revolution of 1905-6, seeking instead the total destruction of Russia's capitalistic society. The Bolshevik leaders were hunted down by the state police and shot, imprisoned, or exiled. Those who escaped bided their time, many of them abroad, plotting the eventual overthrow of the tsar's government.

The Bolsheviks' opportunity came in 1917. During the first three years of World War I Russia suffered staggering losses at the hands of the superior German armies. Behind the lines the suffering of the civilian population, much of which could be attributed to the corrupt bureaucracy of the tsar, was acute. By 1917 many Russians felt that they had suffered enough. In March of that year a mild revolution in Petrograd [1] overthrew the government of the well-meaning but incompetent Nicholas II and set up a moderate bourgeois regime, in which Alexander Kerensky came to be the leading fig-

[1] At the beginning of World War I the Russians changed the name of St. Petersburg, which was a German name, to Petrograd, its Russian form. When Lenin died in 1924, it was changed to Leningrad.

ure. The Kerensky regime attempted to liberalize the Russian government and to continue the war against Germany in co-operation with the Allies. Both tasks appeared to be beyond the capacity of the inexperienced new government. At the battle front morale was low; weapons and munitions were nearly spent. Spreading anarchy harassed the home front.

In order to increase the chaos and remove Russia from the war the German government, in April 1917, transported the top Bolshevik leader, Nikolai Lenin, from his place of exile in Switzerland to the Russian border. This brilliant and dynamic leader quickly organized the radical forces against the moderate government. A clever phrasemaker, Lenin knew how to appeal to all the disaffected elements. "Peace to the army, land to the peasants, ownership of the factories to the workers!" To Lenin's side in Petrograd flocked the other Bolshevik leaders whom the Kerensky regime, in a conciliatory effort, had released from their various prisons and exiles: Leon Trotsky, Joseph Stalin, and the rest. In November 1917, the Bolsheviks, under Lenin's skillful direction and perfect timing, overthrew the moderate Kerensky government and set up a Communist dictatorship.

2. Early Communist Experiments and their Failure

In order to free himself for the enormous task of refashioning Russian society Lenin immediately opened peace negotiations with the Germans. (The Russian troops were deserting in droves to grab lands and jobs in the new utopia.) The Germans, realizing Russia's helplessness, demanded the harshest of terms. Lenin attempted to stall them off, but when the Germans threatened to march on Petrograd and Moscow, he was forced to sign the Treaty of Brest-Litovsk (March 1918). Russia lost Finland, Estonia, Latvia, Lithuania, the Ukraine, Bessarabia, her Polish provinces, and some of her Trans-Caucasian territory. These lands contained one third of Russia's European population,

three fourths of her iron, and nine tenths of her coal. In addition she was compelled to pay a heavy indemnity.

But these hard terms were not the end, or the worst, of Lenin's woes. Two years of bitter civil war followed the peace with Germany. The aristocracy, including most of the higher army officers, faced with extermination, flew to arms against the Bolshevik regime. These "white" forces were aided by various other disaffected groups and by French, British, Polish, Japanese, and a few American troops. It was with the greatest of difficulty that the "red" armies, hastily organized by Trotsky, finally liquidated the "whites." In doing so the Bolsheviks regained the Ukraine. However, a large additional strip of territory was lost to Poland, thanks largely to French armed intervention on the side of the Poles.

In the midst of these disasters Lenin's Bolshevik regime undertook to create out of the wreckage of the Russian Empire a pilot Marxist state. (For Marxist theory and Lenin's amendments to it, see pp. 588-9.) In place of the tsarist hierarchy a pyramid of people's councils, or soviets, dominated by handfuls of Communist-party members was set up. Capitalism (including even the use of money) was abolished. All industry and commerce were placed under the management of committees of workers responsible to Communist-party commissars. The land, far from being distributed to the peasants, as they had been led to believe, was nationalized and turned over to the management of local peasant committees, who distributed it to individual peasants to be worked with their own labor. All crop surpluses were expropriated by the state.

Russia's war-torn economy was soon in shambles. The workers did not know how to run factories and trains, nor did they know how to distribute the goods. When the peasants saw that their surpluses would be seized by the government, they refused to raise more than they needed for themselves. By 1921 some thirty million Russians were threatened with starvation, and in spite of considerable foreign relief, particularly from the United States, many hundreds of thousands did starve. Lenin, a realist, saw the necessity for retreat. In 1921 he launched the NEP (New Economic Policy), which was a temporary compromise with capitalism. In order to provide incentive, industries employing fewer than twenty workers were permitted to operate under private ownership. These little industrial capitalists were called "nepmen." Enterprising peasants, called kulaks, were permitted to own and rent land and hire laborers. Money and credit were restored. This small-scale capitalistic activity was closely supervised and regulated by the state. However, the NEP provided enough incentive to pull the Russian economy out of its chaotic stagnation. In 1923 just as the new policy was beginning to function, Lenin suffered a paralytic stroke; he died the following year.

3. Stalin and the Five-Year Plans

Lenin's death precipitated a power struggle among his chief associates. The world assumed that his successor would be Leon Trotsky, who had been the chief organizer of the Red Army and had planned its victory over the Whites. A brilliant and eloquent Communist theorist, Trotsky was an apostle of world revolution, and such an uncompromising Communist that he opposed the NEP. At the time of Lenin's death he was the commisar of foreign affairs. Trotsky and the world, however, underestimated Joseph Stalin, executive secretary of the Communist party. This unobtrusive and taciturn little man was an unscrupulous behind-the-scenes operator. Stalin was the son of poverty-stricken ex-serfs. Expelled from an Orthodox seminary because of his Marxist views and activities, this hard and cynical youth became a professional revolutionist and terrorist. (Stalin is a pseudonym meaning steel.) He was repeatedly arrested and imprisoned and repeatedly escaped. World War I found him in a Siberian prison. Taking advantage of the amnesty granted to all political prisoners by the Kerensky regime in 1917, Stalin hastened to Petrograd, where

he became a devoted and undeviating associate of Lenin. He played a prominent role in the civil war against the Whites and became executive secretary of the Communist party. In this key position he made himself master of the all-important party machinery. In his last will and testament Lenin declared that Stalin was "too hard, too cruel" to be fit for the headship of the government. Nevertheless, the astute Stalin soon maneuvered himself into absolute dictatorship over Russia. Conspiring with one prominent group of Bolsheviks after another and playing off one faction against another, Stalin crushed Trotsky, had him expelled from the party, and exiled him from Russia. In 1940 Trotsky was murdered in Mexico, presumably by an agent of Stalin. Eventually Stalin executed all of his top Bolshevik associates and rivals. By 1928 his dictatorship over Russia was complete.

In that year Stalin launched the first of a series of five-year plans that his planning commissions had been preparing for several years. The five-year plans were units of planned economy with certain specific goals or objectives to be achieved every five years. They marked the end of the NEP, which had served its purpose of pulling the Communist economy through its first major crises. The objectives of the first five-year plan were: (1) the elimination of the last remnants of capitalism, (2) the industrialization of the Soviet Union, (3) the collectivization and mechanization of agriculture, and (4) national defense.

Achievement of the first goal meant the liquidation of the nepmen and the kulaks. When tens of thousands of the independent peasant proprietor kulaks resisted collectivization, Stalin ruthlessly exterminated them. The consolidation of their farms into mechanized collectives and the organization of giant state farms went on apace. The state farms were huge outlays up to 300,000 acres in size run by Communist-party managers and hired laborers. Every effort was made to mechanize them. Vast tracts of land in southeast Russia and Siberia were brought under cultivation for the first time. The collective farms were of various types, the most common of which was the artel, which the kulaks were first encouraged and later forced to join. In this type of collective independent farmers surrendered their lands and horses but retained their houses, gardens, cattle, pigs, and chickens for their own private use. The artel was run by elected managers who were instructed and supervised by party officials. Elimination of the tiny individual tracts, each one of which had been surrounded by ditches or hedgerows, made mechanization possible. From the harvest of a collective was set aside a certain amount for taxes, insurance, improvements, and feed. A large part had to be sold to the state at a fixed price. The rest was distributed to the peasant members in proportion to the amount of their original contribution to the collective in land and horses and to the amount and quality of their work. The mechanization of Russia's primitive agriculture required the construction of huge quantities of tractors and farm machinery.

Since the Industrial Revolution was still in its infancy in Russia in 1928, industrialization meant building from the ground up and concentration on producer goods. Western engineers and technicians were lured to Russia with high salaries. Capital was obtained by exporting scarce supplies of wheat, often at ruinously low prices. At the cost of much privation enormous strides were made. Steel mills, power plants, foundries, mines, refineries, and railroads were built all over the Soviet Union. At Dnepropetrovsk on the Dnieper River the world's largest dam and hydroelectric power plant were constructed. At the end of 1932 it was announced that all the goals of the first five-year plan had been reached several months ahead of time.

The second five-year plan, which was launched immediately, called for a greater production of consumer goods: the gadgets and comforts of life that are usually referred to as the standard of living. These were the things the Russian masses had never had and were now striving for. But hardly had the second five-year plan begun when Hitler came to power in Germany with a program calling for the conquest and enslavement of Russia. Stalin immediately shifted the chief emphasis from production of consumer goods to production of weapons of defense —and not a minute too soon. Russia escaped from total conquest by Nazi Germany by a hairsbreadth (see pp. 676–82).

The economic achievements of Communist Russia have been beyond doubt phenomenal. When the Bolsheviks took over in 1917, Russia was a defeated, war-torn, primitive, agricultural country. Twenty-four years later, when the Germans invaded her in 1941, she was the fourth-greatest industrial power in the world; in a number of categories she had surpassed both Great Britain and Germany and was second only to the United States. She could never have withstood the German assault had this not been true. Russia's agriculture was no longer primitive but largely mechanized. By the mid-1930's new crop records were established almost every year. Food rationing was abandoned. Most of these achievements had been made since 1928. They were made, of course, at the cost of total loss of individual freedom (although there had never been much freedom in Russia under the tsars), the liquidation of tens of thousands who sought to retain some measure of freedom, and the privation and forced labor of the rest.

4. The Soviet Political System

The Bolsheviks, on coming to power, broke up the Russian Empire into eleven socialist republics: Russia proper and ten other language or dialect areas. In 1939–40 five more were added from territories seized by Russia at the outbreak of World War II. Thus the Soviet Union is in theory a union of sixteen autonomous republics. (U.S.S.R. stands for Union of Soviet Socialist Republics.) Actually, however, Russia itself constitutes at least four fifths of the total area and population, and the so-called Union is in reality a monolithic police state.

The Soviet system of government as originally set up consisted of a pyramid of elected councils (the word *soviet* means council)—village, district, county, and provincial—culminating in the Union Congress of Soviets, which met once every two years and chose executive and administrative boards. Voting was by show of hands in mass meetings. The urban vote was given more than double the weight of the rural vote, since Bolshevism's chief concern was the industrial proletariat. In 1936 Stalin promulgated a new constitution, which appeared to be more democratic. Voting was to be by secret ballot, the differential between the urban and the rural vote was abolished, and the members of the various soviets in the pyramid were to be elected directly by the local districts. The member republics in the Union were allegedly granted complete autonomy.

When one examines the actual functioning of the soviet system, however, it quickly becomes apparent that the new constitution, like the old, is entirely farcical as far as democracy is concerned. Only the Communist party is permitted to engage in organized political activity. It names the official candidates, makes all political policies and platforms, and conducts all election promotion and propaganda. Opposition to the party's official candidates and program is considered to be disloyal and is ferreted out and crushed by the state police, both secret and regular. The all-powerful Communist party is organized on an authoritarian basis. The Politburo,[1] of eleven men sitting behind closed doors and responsible only to themselves, makes all decisions, which are transmitted without question down through the party chain of command to the local cells. Blind and unquestioning obedience to superiors is demanded of all party members. Party members are carefully selected and trained. On Lenin's insistence the total number has been kept relatively small, never more than seven million out of a total population of nearly two hundred million. Those of questionable loyalty or zeal are

[1] The name of the Politburo was changed to Presidium after World War II.

constantly purged. During the late 1930's a series of purges liquidated hundreds of party members, including a number of the top military and civilian officials in the Soviet Union. Thus constitutions, elections, and elected governmental bodies in Communist Russia are a sham. There is no democracy and no political or civil liberty. The Soviet Union is a dictatorship and a police state.

5. Soviet Education, Arts, and Religion

In 1917 more than 60 per cent of the Russian people were illiterate. It was Lenin's belief that a Communist state requires an educated populace in order to succeed. Nearly all of the top Bolsheviks themselves were educated men—in fact they would be considered members of the intelligentsia in almost any time or place. Little could be done in the educational field in the first turbulent years of the Communist regime, but education received major attention in Stalin's five-year plans. In 1928 the Communists launched the vastest program of free compulsory secular education in history. The program covered all levels—elementary, secondary, and higher—for both young and adults. It included a comprehensive system of technical and on-the-job training. Science and engineering were particularly stressed. By the middle of the twentieth century Soviet universities and institutes were graduating more than twice as many engineers as were those of the United States, the most materially advanced and mechanics-conscious capitalistic country. All Soviet engineers were receiving five years of training instead of the four usual in the United States. Of course Soviet education was interlarded with Communist propaganda, but it was far from being limited to propaganda. In 1941 Stalin announced that illiteracy had been banished from Russia. The quality of Soviet education is difficult to assess. It is certain that much of it was crude and makeshift and that the truth was often deliberately distorted. On the other hand, Western assumptions that Soviet science and engineering were too shoddy to produce tanks that would run and planes that would fly, not to speak of nuclear fission, proved to be dangerous miscalculations. Another facet of Soviet education was emphasis upon physical education. The results of this emphasis became apparent in international athletic competition. They would undoubtedly become more apparent in case of another major war.

Nor were advanced scholarship and the arts neglected in the Soviet Union. The world's most extensive program of scholarships, prizes, and institutes was inaugurated for the purpose of encouraging and subsidizing superior talent. Soviet musicians, architects, painters, and aesthetic dancers more than held their own in international competition. American visitors to the Soviet Union were repeatedly surprised at the great interest of the people in the arts and in classical literature. Yet even the arts ran afoul the Communist police state. All liberal, bourgeois, or capitalistic literature (which was most of it) was heavily censored. In 1958 Boris Pasternak was officially rebuked for his novel *Doctor Zhivago*, which portrays the Communist revolution in an unfavorable light. Under pressure he declined the Nobel prize for literature. Such world-renowned composers as Prokofiev and Shostakovich occasionally fell into official disfavor because of their modern "bourgeois" music. When some powerful commissar decided that the Mendelian law of genetics, which is generally accepted in the world of science, ran counter to the party line, Soviet geneticists were forced to disclaim it. Such incidents lead one to wonder how long the arts and pure science can flourish in a police state.

Of all the facets of communism and of its clash with Western Christian civilization probably the most fundamental is religion. The weakening of Christianity in the late nineteenth century, in the face of onrushing science, technology, and malignant nationalism, was undoubtedly a major factor in the rise of Marxist materialism. Marx and Lenin both were keenly aware of the impor-

tance of religion. They considered religion "the opiate of the people"—a concoction of the "haves" to quiet the "have nots" lest they demand and seize their share of this world's goods. But communism is itself a religion. Stark materialism and class hatred are its basic doctrines. Marx and Lenin are its major prophets, and their writings are its scriptures. The religious policy of the Bolsheviks, upon gaining power in Russia, was quite similar to that of the French Revolutionists in 1789–94. All church property was confiscated. The churches themselves were turned into museums or clubs of various kinds, although they were sometimes leased to religious congregations for purposes of worship. No religious instruction whatever was permitted in the schools, which were all public and secular. The churches were forbidden to give organized religious instruction and even to maintain seminaries for the training of their own clergy. On the other hand, the schools were flooded with Communist propaganda. An oath of atheism is required for membership in the Communist party. Physical attacks on the clergy and the faithful occurred from time to time, and of course active participation in religious activities was certain to blight a young Russian's career under the Communist regime.

The Communist leaders have always claimed that their harsh treatment of the churches was necessitated by the active opposition of the churches to the Communist government. They claim that when they first came to power they granted religious freedom for the first time in Russian history, but that the churches immediately used this freedom to advocate the overthrow of the very government that granted it. They further claim that churches have always been the tools and agents of capitalistic governments and interests. Whatever truth there may be in these claims, it would appear that religion has remained a great problem and danger to the Soviet regime. Mankind is inherently religious, and churches have nearly always thrived under persecution. Religious groups with international connections, such as the Roman Catholics, Lutherans, and Jews, have attracted sympathy abroad and projected the religious problem into Russia's foreign affairs.

6. Soviet Foreign Policy

It is Soviet foreign policy that is of greatest concern to the rest of the world. Were the Soviet Union an isolated island, the rest of the world might look upon it as an interesting and perhaps exotic experiment and wish it well. But, far from being an isolated island, it is very much in and of the world to which it has always loomed as an ominous threat. It occupies one sixth of the land surface of the earth, including the strategic heartland of the world's greatest land mass. It has huge physical resources. Its population of some two hundred million is rapidly increasing. The Marxist ideology, as modified by Lenin, is activist and violent. What is the foreign policy of the Soviet Union? The rest of the world wants, indeed demands, to know. Is it world conquest, world revolution, or both? These questions are as difficult as they are pressing, partly because of the secretiveness and callous duplicity of the Soviet police state and partly because of the hysteria that has so often accompanied the quest for the answers.

When the Bolsheviks first took over in 1917, they confidently expected most of the capitalistic governments in the war-weary world to collapse soon and follow Russia along the path of communism. To encourage them to do so and to avoid fulfillment of the harsh terms of the Treaty of Brest-Litovsk, the Communist leaders began an active campaign of revolutionary infiltration and subversion abroad, particularly in Germany. Although some headway was made in Germany, Bavaria falling under Communist control for a brief time, the only country to go Communist was Hungary, where Béla Kun set up a Communist dictatorship that lasted six months. To guide and aid the Communist parties in other countries in the common cause of world revolution, the Bolsheviks set up the Comintern (Communist International) with headquarters in Moscow.

The Western capitalistic powers were as antagonistic to the Soviet Union as was the Soviet Union to them. Thinking that the Bolshevik regime would soon collapse, France, Great Britain, Japan, and the United States landed troops on Russian soil in 1918 and aided the counterrevolutionary White forces. France helped the Poles to seize a large strip of Russian-speaking territory. Great Britain and France organized the anti-Soviet regimes in the countries of Eastern Europe bordering the Soviet Union into a *cordon sanitaire* (health or quarantine belt). For several years no Western power would recognize the Bolshevik regime. The Soviet Union was refused admission to the League of Nations until 1934, eight years after Germany had been admitted and one year after she had withdrawn under the guidance of Hitler. Even then the Western powers steadfastly refused to co-operate with the Soviet Union in any collective action against the rising Fascist menace.

Nonetheless, the failure of the Communist movements abroad and of the Bolshevik's early efforts to communize Russia overnight caused the Soviet leaders to adopt a more conciliatory attitude toward the capitalistic powers. The NEP needed foreign commerce and foreign capital in order to function. However, as long as Lenin lived, his inveterate hatred of capitalism kept the spirit of conciliation at a minimum. As noted previously, after his death in 1924 a momentous struggle for top place ensued between Trotsky and Stalin. Trotsky, an uncompromising apostle of pure communism and of world revolution, opposed the NEP and all accommodation to the capitalistic world. Stalin, on the other hand, was a practical realist and compromiser. He lacked the world view of the learned and philosophical Trotsky. His prime interest was in making the Communist regime a going concern in the Soviet Union; in Marxist terminology he advocated "communism in one country." No sooner had Stalin begun to gain the ascendancy over Trotsky than he offered trade concessions to trade-hungry capitalistic powers in return for recognition of the Soviet regime. Great Britain and France yielded to these inducements in 1924. (Germany had recognized the Soviet Union in 1922 in order to frighten her Allied conquerors.) Following the lead of Great Britain and France, one capitalistic state after another recognized the Soviet Union. The United States, which held off until 1933, was the last one to do so.

The five-year plans, which began in 1928, required much Western capital and technical assistance, and by that time Stalin's triumph over Trotsky was complete. Therefore, the next ten years represented the high tide of Soviet tractability toward the capitalistic Western democracies. Stalin showed little or no interest in the Comintern, which was allowed to languish. His

foreign minister, Maxim Litvinov, became a respected and even popular figure in Geneva, Paris, London, and Washington. Of course the Soviet Union's fear of the growing Nazi German menace after 1931 was a significant factor in her conciliatory attitude toward the capitalistic democracies. It was impossible to know whether Stalin was sincere or whether he was merely using the capitalistic democracies until the Soviet Union was strong enough to go it alone and possibly turn against them. At any rate, the honeymoon ended in 1938 with the Munich crisis (see pp. 670–1). From that time Stalin was apparently convinced that real co-operation with the Western democracies was impossible. The co-operation forced upon the Soviet Union and most of the capitalistic world by the common Axis assailants during World War II lasted only until victory was assured.

SUGGESTED READING

* G. Vernadsky, *The Russian Revolution, 1917–1931* (Berkshire). A brief account by a leading scholar in the field.

Crane Brinton, *The Anatomy of Revolution* (1952). An interesting comparison of the Russian, French, American, and English revolutions.

J. A. White, *The Siberian Intervention* (1950). The story of the American and Japanese intervention in Asiatic Russia at the end of World War I—an affair little known in America.

David Shub, *Lenin* (1948). Probably the best biography of the chief founder of Soviet communism.

Isaac Deutscher, *Stalin: A Political Biography* (1949). Not only an excellent biography of

the Soviet dictator but a good history of the whole communist movement in Russia.

Harry Schwartz, *Russia's Soviet Economy* (1954). Written by a New York *Times* reporter and economics specialist after spending many years in the Soviet Union.

Louis Fischer, *The Soviets in World Affairs* (1951). A readable analysis by an astute observer of Soviet and world affairs.

Edward Crankshaw, *Russia and the Russians* (1948). A provocative attempt to explain why the Russians act and think as they do. Written in a journalistic style by a British journalist-historian who spent several years in the Soviet Union during World War II.

CHAPTER 56

The Triumph of Fascism in Italy, Germany, and Japan

A FRUIT of World War I more bitter and poisonous even than communism was fascism. We cannot yet know which of these violently anti-liberal forces will prove to have the more enduring vigor. But there is no question that fascism constituted the more immediate threat to liberal democracy. It was fascism that broke down the peace settlement and brought on World War II. Mussolini set up the first Fascist dictatorship in Italy. However, it was Fascist Germany and Japan that became the most virulent threat to the liberal world.

1. Mussolini Creates the First Fascist State

Italy emerged from World War I battered and humiliated. Although she was one of the victorious Allies, her armies had made a poor showing and she had achieved few of the grandiose ambitions for which she had entered the war. In the Paris peace settlements she had been awarded the adjacent Italian-speaking areas of Austria-Hungary, but had been denied further acquisitions east of the Adriatic and the Turkish and German provinces in Asia and Africa, some of which she ardently desired. These frustrations were severe blows to Italian national pride, which had been born during the unification movement of the nineteenth century

and heightened during the war. Italy's weak economy emerged from the war acutely maladjusted. The national debt was huge and the treasury empty. The inflated currency, together with a shortage of goods, raised prices ruinously. Hundreds of thousands of demobilized veterans could find no jobs. In the summer of 1919 widespread disorders broke out. Veterans began seizing and squatting on idle, and sometimes on cultivated, lands. Sit-down strikes developed in the factories. During the winter of 1920–21 several hundred factories were seized by the workers. Bolshevik agents arrived from Russia to exploit the distress. The Italian government, torn by factions, seemed too weak to prevent the disorder and protect private property. Although the strife diminished and the Communist threat waned before the end of 1921, the landlords and the factory owners were thoroughly frightened. Many of them, and indeed many small business and professional men, longed for vigorous leadership and a strong government. The vigorous leader who stepped forward was Benito Mussolini. The strong government was his Fascist dictatorship.

Mussolini was a dynamic organizer and leader. The son of a humble blacksmith, he became first a teacher and later a radical journalist and agitator. Before World War I he was a pacifistic socialist, but during the war he became a violent nationalist. After the war he began organizing unemployed veterans into a political-action group with a socialistic and extremely nationalistic program. During the labor disturbances of 1919–21 Mussolini stood aside until it became apparent that the radical workingmen's cause would lose, then he threw his support to the capitalists and the landlords. Crying that he was saving Italy from communism and waving the flag of nationalism, Mussolini organized his veterans into terror squads of black-shirted "Fascisti," who beat up the leaderless radical workingmen and their liberal supporters. He thereby gained the support of the frightened capitalists and landed aristocracy. By 1922 Mussolini's Fascist party was strong enough to "march on Rome" and seize control of the faction-paralyzed government. Appointed premier by the weak and distraught King Victor Emmanuel III, Mussolini quickly turned his premiership into a dictatorship. All opposition was silenced. Only the Fascist party (like the Communist party in the Soviet Union) could engage in organized political activity. The press and the schools were turned into Fascist propaganda agencies. The secret police were everywhere. Eventually the Chamber of Deputies itself was replaced by Mussolini's hand-picked Fascist political and economic councils.

Italy's economic life was strictly regimented, but in such a way as to favor the capitalistic classes. Private property and profits were carefully protected. All labor unions were abolished except those controlled by the Fascist party. Strikes and lockouts were forbidden. Wages, working conditions, and labor-management disputes were settled by compulsory arbitration under Fascist party direction. An elaborate system of planned economy was set up for the purpose of modernizing, co-ordinating, and increasing Italy's production of both industrial and agricultural goods. The very complicated economic and political machinery that Mussolini created for these purposes was called the corporate state. Under the whip and drive of Mussolini remarka-

ble increases in production were achieved. Trains began to run on time, the budget was balanced, and the currency was stabilized. But taxes were the highest in the world, and labor's share in the fruits of increased production was small.

Fascism, however, was primarily political in character, not economic. The essence of its ideology was nationalism—malignant nationalism run wild. Mussolini understood the dynamic energizing quality of this kind of nationalism. His writings and speeches rang with such masculine words as "will," "discipline," "sacrifice," "decision," and "conquest." "The goal," he cried, "is always —Empire! To build a city, to found a colony, to establish an empire, these are the prodigies of the human spirit. . . . We must resolutely abandon the whole liberal phraseology and way of thinking. . . . Discipline. Discipline at home in order that we may present the granite block of a single national will. . . . War alone brings up to the highest tension all human energy and puts the stamp of nobility upon the people who have the courage to meet it." The Fascists adopted the trappings and symbols of ancient Rome. The word "fascism" itself comes from the word "fasces," meaning a bundle of rods surrounding an ax borne by Roman magistrates as a symbol of authority. Here we have the arrogant militaristic nationalism of the late nineteenth century, including the supermen and master race of Carlyle, Wagner, and Nietzsche, come to full flower.

Fascism, of course, clashed head-on with Christianity both in spirit and in deeds. In fact every fundamental principle in Fascist philosophy has its opposite in Christian doctrine: love thy neighbor—hate and conquer thy neighbor; blessed are the meek—blessed are the strong-willed and arrogant; blessed are the peacemakers—blessed are the warmakers. One quite possible explanation for the rise of materialistic and cynical fascism and communism is the weakening of Christianity in the late nineteenth and early twentieth centuries. Nevertheless, Mussolini realized the advantage of coming to terms with the powerful Roman Catholic Church and made a treaty with the pope in 1929. The pope recognized Mussolini's regime. (Since the pope had been despoiled of his territories, 1860–70, he had refused to recognize the Italian government.) In return Mussolini paid him $39,000,000 in cash and $52,-000,000 in 5-per-cent government bonds from a hard-pressed national treasury and allowed the teaching of religion by Roman Catholic clergy in the public schools. This seeming accord, however, was uneasy and quarrelsome from the start.

The building of a powerful army and navy and the recovery of Italy's national prestige were always uppermost in Mussolini's thoughts. Fascist Italy's militarism, self-assertiveness, and expansive ambitions played an important part in the breakdown of the peace settlement and the return to war. Before we examine these activities, however, we must trace the rise and triumph of fascism in Germany and Japan, both of which were more powerful and dangerous to the rest of the world than was Italy.

2. Germany Refuses to Accept the Peace Settlement

Germany emerged from World War I defeated, humiliated, and angry. As late as July 1918, she had seemed to be invincible —on the threshold of victory. Four months later she had been forced to surrender, hopelessly beaten. Then, she was compelled to sign a dictated peace treaty, the terms of which she considered unjust. Furthermore, she was virtually forced to submit to a democratic government by Woodrow Wilson, who refused to negotiate with the Hohenzollern regime. The Weimar Republic (so-called from the birthplace of Goethe and Schiller, where its constitution was drawn up), which the Germans set up in 1919, was, on paper, a model of liberal democracy. However, it was lacking in historical precedent and in genuine popular support. The German people, never before having had a democratic government, were inexperienced in its practices. Even worse, the Weimar

Republic was set up under foreign pressure and signed the hated Treaty of Versailles. That it was able to function for ten years with reasonable effectiveness was due more to necessity than to inherent strength.

Germany violated many of the disarmament clauses of the Treaty of Versailles from the start. Old military units and organizations continued to function under assumed names. Many weapons were hidden away, and many war plants were not dismantled. The 100,000-man army permitted her became the world's best-trained officer corps and could be quickly expanded into a powerful army. Forbidden weapons such as tanks and artillery were perfected and tested on Russian and Swedish soil. Denied any military aviation, Germany became the world's leading nation in civil aviation. Her airfields, aircraft factories, and trained pilots and technicians could, of course, be easily converted to military purposes. When the British, in accordance with the treaty, tried to take possession of the German battle fleet interned at Scapa Flow in the British Isles, the German sailors scuttled their ships. Swift and powerful pocket battleships within the 10,000-ton treaty limit were constructed to serve as commerce raiders in the next war. Two prominent German leaders, Walter Rathenau and Matthias Erzberger, who were accused of advocating conciliation with the Western democracies, were assassinated by members of the professional military. The assassins were widely acclaimed as national heroes. When the German people went to the polls for the first time in 1925 to elect a president, their choice was their top military hero, Field Marshal Paul von Hindenburg. Most Germans were obviously looking to the day of revenge.

The first overt clash between recalcitrant Germany and the former Allies occurred over reparations. In 1921 the reparations commission that had been established at the Paris Peace Conference set Germany's reparations bill at approximately $33,000,000,-000, to be paid over a long period of time. Although the Germans had been compelled by the Treaty of Versailles to accept in advance liability for whatever figure was set, they received the announcement of this amount with indignation. German governmental and financial leaders boasted both in public and in private that they would never pay it. The Weimar Republic refused to tax heavily the wealth of the great industrialists, and much of their wealth was permitted to leave the country. Germany defaulted on the very first annual payment. To the exasperated French, who were taxing themselves to the bone, trying desperately to repair the ravages of the war, this was the last straw. Early in 1923 French, Belgian, and Italian troops occupied the Ruhr Valley, Germany's richest industrial area. The Germans fought back sullenly with passive resistance. The French countered by trying to stir up a secession movement from Germany in the Rhineland. Bloodshed between the occupying troops and the civilian population was frequent. Although the occupying forces were unable to collect any reparations, Germany's economy was paralyzed and wild inflation swept the country. Thus more seeds of bitterness were sown.

After eight months of struggle the German leaders realized the futility of resistance. In August 1923, Gustav Stresemann came to the head of the German government and offered conciliation. An international commission headed by Charles G. Dawes of the United States drew up a plan for the withdrawal of the occupying forces, for an international loan to Germany, and for the orderly payment of Germany's reparations installments. Her economy quickly recovered. From 1924 to 1929 Germany was the most prosperous nation in Europe and made her reparations payments as scheduled. In 1929 another international commission headed by Owen D. Young, an American financier, reduced Germany's total liability from $33,000,000,000 to the equivalent of a cash payment of $9,000,000,000. However, the world depression struck Germany in that year, and after 1931 no further payments were made.

Meanwhile, under Stresemann's leadership Germany sought a *rapprochement* with her former enemies. In 1925 she signed the Treaty of Locarno with France, Great Britain, Italy, and Belgium, guaranteeing Germany's existing frontiers with France and Belgium. In 1926 Germany was admitted to the League of Nations, and Stresemann was elected president of the Council. This apparent good will, however, was deceptive. The old German militarism and nationalism, made more malignant by the sting of defeat, were still strong. The spirit of sullen hatred and revenge toward the former Allies filled the hearts of many Germans. Even Stresemann, we now know from his memoirs, was merely biding his time until Germany was strong enough to reassert herself. He was constantly deceiving the Western democracies and playing one off against the other. However, a far more sinister force was at work in postwar Germany, capitalizing on the economic and social maladjustment and the frustrated militarism and nationalism. This force was national socialism, organized and led by Adolph Hitler.

3. The Rise of Hitler and National Socialism

Adolph Hitler was the neurotic and maladjusted son of a petty Austrian customs official and a young, sensitive, unhappily married mother. As a child he already suffered delusions of grandeur. Of an artistic temperament, he went off to Vienna at an early age to seek an artist's career. Denied admission to the art academies for lack of training and too proud to work with his muscles, he lived for years in poverty and squalor. He fed his ego with German masterrace theories and filled his heart with hatred of the Jews. At the outbreak of World War I Hitler was in Munich, Germany, a house painter. The ardent young German nationalist threw himself eagerly into the war, which he considered to be a righteous crusade for the beloved fatherland. Attaining the rank of corporal, he got his first taste for command. When the war ended, he was in a hospital, a victim of poison gas. This is believed to account for the strange, hoarse resonance in his voice that unnerved the listener. After the war Hitler frequented beer cellars, haranguing demobilized and unemployed troops and organizing them into violent political-action groups. He soon discovered his magnetic powers of leadership. The disgruntled and the disenchanted, particularly the frustrated young intellectuals and demobilized lesser army officers, began attaching themselves to Hitler in increasing numbers. He organized them into the National Socialist (Nazi) party. Among his most important early followers were Hermann Goering, who became second in command; Rudolph Hess, who became head of the party; and Paul Joseph Goebbels, who became the chief Nazi propagandist. As early as 1923 Hitler, in league with the popular war hero Field Marshal Ludendorff, made his first grab for power. It was premature, however, and Hitler was jailed for nearly a year. While in jail he wrote *Mein Kampf* (*My Struggle*), which became the Nazi bible and blueprint.

National socialism, as outlined in *Mein Kampf*, was the German brand of fascism. In fact the Nazis were heavily indebted to Mussolini for both ideology and methodology. At the center of its basic philosophy is the German master-race concept. The old Nordic myth of Gobineau and Chamberlain was revived. The terms "German," "Nordic," and "Aryan" were used interchangeably without regard to scientific fact. It was held that the Germans, the only pure representatives of the tall, blond Nordic "race," are superior to and destined to conquer and rule all other peoples. Militarism, indomitable will, pride, aggressiveness, and brute strength were held to be virtues; gentleness, peacefulness, tolerance, pity, and modesty, vices.

As a specific program of action, national socialism was primarily concerned with foreign affairs. It called for repudiation of the Treaty of Versailles; all-out rearmament; the recovery of all territories, including colonies, lost at the end of World War I; and the annexation of all neighboring German-speaking territories such as Austria, the Netherlands, and most of Switzerland. Then the master race must have *Lebensraum* (living space). This was to be obtained by driving to the east (*Drang nach Osten*), particularly by conquering and enslaving the Soviet Union. There can be little question that in the Nazi mind world conquest was the ultimate goal.

The domestic program was vague and contradictory. Trusts and department stores were to be nationalized. Unearned income was to be abolished. Communism was to be destroyed, and labor unions rigidly controlled. Finally, persecution of the Jews was always part and parcel of the Nazi program. Persecution was later changed to extermination.

The capitalistic classes never took the socialistic aspects of Hitler's program seriously. As in Italy, they looked to the Fascists to provide strong government, protect property, and control the working classes. Hitler also copied many of Mussolini's techniques. The rank and file of Nazi party members, wearing brown shirts, were organized along military lines as storm troopers. They marched, sang, intimidated, and beat up the opposition. An elite corps of black-shirted "SS" troops supervised and policed the brown shirts. Pagan symbolism was adopted —appropriately since Nazism represented the antithesis of everything that Christianity stands for. All party members swore unquestioning and undying allegiance to Hitler.

4. The Triumph of Hitler

At first national socialism grew slowly but steadily. From 1925 to 1929, when Germany under Stresemann's leadership was the most prosperous nation in Europe and was being wooed by her former enemies, Nazi party membership grew from 27,000 to 178,000. After the great depression of 1929, which struck Germany along with the rest of the capitalistic world, the Nazis gained rapidly. In the parliamentary elections of 1930 they obtained several million votes and increased their seats in the Reichstag from 12 to 107. They were now strong enough to disrupt the orderly functioning of parliamentary government, and President Hindenburg resorted to ruling by presidential decree. In the presidential election of 1932 Hitler ran as the Nazi candidate. The moderate and liberal parties, which in 1925 had feared and opposed Hindenburg, now persuaded him to run again as the only man who could stop Hitler. (Hindenburg was now eighty-five years old.) Hitler got enough votes to force a runoff election against the popular and venerable idol. In the runoff election Hindenburg was elected, but Hitler received 13,400,000 votes. In parliamentary elections a few months later the Nazis obtained 230 out of 648 seats in the Reichstag, the largest number ever held by any party under the Weimar Republic. Hindenburg now offered to make Hitler vice-chancellor, but Hitler, sensing complete dictatorship in the offing, refused. In November 1932, after still another parliamentary election resulted in a gain for the Communists, Hindenburg offered Hitler the headship of a coalition government, but Hitler again refused.

Meanwhile, the Nazis, under Hitler's instructions, paralyzed Germany's economic and political life with violence. When the chaos threatened to play into the hands of the Communists, Hindenburg, in January 1933, offered and Hitler accepted the chancellorship. Franz von Papen, head of the militaristic Nationalist party, was made vice-chancellor. It was the great industrialists who finally gave the Nazis the necessary support to come to power. Hitler, determined to have nothing less than complete dictatorship, immediately called for parliamentary elections, to be held on March 5. Now in official control of the state police and the agencies of information and propaganda in addition to their own highly disciplined party machinery, the Nazis made full use of the intervening five weeks to frighten and confuse the people. Like the Fascists in Italy they exaggerated and exploited the Communist threat. Five days before the elections they set fire to the Reichstag building and blamed the Communists. The elections themselves, however, were by secret ballot and relatively free. The Communists polled 4,800,000 votes, the Center (Roman Catholic) party 5,500,000, the Social Democrats (workers and small business and professional men's party) 7,800,000, the Nazis 17,000,000, and von Papen's Nationalists 3,000,000. The Nazi and the Nationalist vote combined gave Hitler 52 per cent of the seats in the Reichstag. A few days later Hitler, wearing his Nazi party uniform, appeared before the newly elected Reichstag, from which the Communists were excluded, and demanded dictatorial powers for four years. They were granted with only ninety-four opposing (Social Democratic) votes. Long before the four years had expired the moderate parties had been destroyed, and the Nazi dictatorship was total.

5. Nazi Germany

The Reichstag, having voted Hitler dictatorial powers, adjourned, to meet henceforth only on the call of the *Führer* (leader) for the purpose of voting approval of his acts. Hitler disbanded all the political parties except the National Socialist party. All administration and local government were placed in the hands of Nazi officials. Freedom of speech, press, and assembly was abolished. An elaborate and all-powerful secret police, the Gestapo, was established under the direction of the heartless Heinrich Himmler to spy out and destroy opposition to the Nazis. Concentration camps with their torture and gas chambers soon held thousands of victims. Hitler's most intense hatred was vented upon the Jews, who were subjected to every conceivable humiliation. As fast as their services could be dispensed with, they were driven out of public and professional life. Eventually the Nazis embarked upon a program to exterminate all the Jews under their control. It is estimated that by the end of World War II the Nazis had murdered 6,000,000 Jews out of a world total of 15,000,000.

The control and molding of thought always held high priority in Nazi activities.

NAZI TROOPS PARADE IN BERLIN. During the 1930's, while the democratic world was tormented by economic depression and paralyzed by indecision, Germany's military might grew rapidly under the guidance of Adolf Hitler. Here German troops parade through Berlin in a display of Nazi strength and militarism. At the extreme left of the picture, Hitler salutes his troops. (*United Press International Photo*)

Indeed, this appears to be an absolute necessity for any totalitarian dictatorship. Under the direction of Dr. Paul Joseph Goebbels, minister of propaganda, the German press and radio spewed forth a constant stream of false or distorted information. To read or listen to anything else was made a crime. An incessant hate campaign was waged against the liberal democratic world. The schools were, of course, Nazified. Only Nazi party members could be school administrators. Unsympathetic teachers were dismissed and punished. Members of Nazi youth organizations were set to spy on their teachers and parents. Textbooks were rewritten to conform to German master-race theories. The burning of liberal books, sometimes even those of Germany's greatest literary figures, such as Goethe and Schiller, became a national fad. The Nazi minister of education admitted that the sole function of education was the creation of Nazis. Hitler wrote in *Mein Kampf* that the German youth's ". . . entire education and development has to be directed at giving him the conviction of being absolutely superior to the others . . . the belief in the invincibility of his entire nationality." The arts were Nazified, only party members or sympathizers being permitted to publish, exhibit, or perform publicly.

Since national socialism was essentially an anti-Christian religion, the Nazis realized the necessity of controlling the Christian churches. The Lutheran Church, which was the official state church and included more than half the German people in its membership, was easily brought under Nazi domination. Nazi officials de-Christianized the German Lutheran Church and turned it into a powerful Nazi propaganda agency. The few Lutheran pastors, like Martin Niemöller, who resisted were thrown into concentration camps. The smaller Protestant denominations met the same fate. Hitler found it much more difficult to deal with the Roman Catholic Church, whose higher authority lay outside Germany. Although he soon signed a concordat with the pope, the terms proved to be unworkable. Roman Catholic clergy, churches, and schools were subjected to constantly increasing pressures, indignities, and physical abuse.

The Nazis rejuvenated and regimented Germany's economic life. The property and the profits of the capitalistic classes were given special consideration. Labor unions were brought under Nazi control, and a system of enforced arbitration of disputes between labor and management was set up along the lines that Mussolini had established in Italy. Strikes and lockouts were forbidden. The entire German economy was forced into the over-all pattern and policies of the Nazi government. The vast rearmament program gave employment to millions. Super-highways, airfields, hospitals, and apartment houses were built all over Germany. The most intricate financial trickery was resorted to, but the Nazis expected eventually to finance their huge undertakings out of the spoils of victorious war.

All other activities of Nazi Germany were subordinated to the prime purpose of making a military comeback. Shortly after assuming power Hitler took Germany out of the League of Nations and out of the disarmament conference that was in progress in Geneva. Rearmament was pushed as rapidly as possible, and in 1935 Hitler openly repudiated the disarmament clauses of the Treaty of Versailles. In 1934 the Nazis made their first attempt to seize Austria but succeeded only in assassinating Austria's Chancellor Dollfuss. In 1936 Hitler remilitarized the Rhineland and sent decisive aid to General Franco's fascist rebels in Spain. The following year he made an alliance with the two other fascist powers, Italy and Japan. This Berlin-Rome-Tokyo Axis was aimed specifically at the Soviet Union. In reality it was an aggressive alliance against the non-fascist world. Before tracing the fascist aggressions that plunged the world into World War II, however, we must examine briefly the triumph of fascism in the third member of the Axis—Japan.

6. The Triumph of Fascism in Japan

We have already observed (see p. 608) Japan's remarkable modernization and emergence as a great power between 1853 and 1914. She participated in World War I on the side of the Allies and received Germany's island possessions in the Pacific north of the equator as her reward. At the Washington Naval Conference in 1922 she gained a 5:5:3 naval ratio to the United States and Great Britain. That is, for every five capital ships of the United States Great Britain would have five and Japan three. This represented a significant gain for Japan. Of greater importance, Japan gained a military monopoly in East Asia and the Western Pacific when Great Britain agreed not to fortify anything east of Singapore and the United States agreed not to fortify anything west of Pearl Harbor. Japan in the early 1920's stood at the crossroads. She could use her great energies and skills either to develop her own institutions and raise her standard of living or to become a predatory military state. She could hardly stand still. On her three thousand islands, with a total area no greater than that of the state of California, lived a rapidly increasing population of 60,000,000. Only 14 per cent of Japanese land is arable and she possesses very few natural resources. Her quickly built industries had overexpanded during the wartime prosperity. The postwar deflation and sharp competition from her former allies brought severe economic stresses.

Three divergent groups competed for the leadership of postwar Japan. The dominant group was made up of the great industrialists. Seventy-five per cent of Japan's industry and capital was concentrated in the hands of five great families, called the *Zaibatsu*. This handful of industrial giants had such a strangle hold on Japanese economy that it was also able to control the highly restricted government. The Zaibatsu, enjoying such an economic and political monopoly, wished to see no fundamental change in Japanese society and advocated the peaceful, economic penetration of Asia.

The liberals constituted the second group. This group, with university professors and students providing much of the leadership, set out to broaden the suffrage, which was restricted to the well-to-do, to permit the unionization of labor for collective bargaining, and to diminish the power of the military. Because of the political inexperience and the long tradition of passive submission to authority on the part of the Japanese masses these were difficult undertakings. They were made more difficult by the activities of a small group of Communists directed from Moscow, who confused liberal reform movements and tainted them with the suspicion of treason. Nevertheless, encouraging progress toward liberal democracy was made. In 1925 the suffrage was broadened. Soon afterward two liberal political parties appeared. The military budget was reduced. The prestige of the professional military declined to such an extent that many officers ceased wearing their uniforms in public.

The professional military, however, was determined to strengthen and exploit its own traditional power. In the late 1920's a group of restless and ambitious young army officers began to accuse the top brass of softness and plotted to seize control of both the armed forces and the government. When a coup planned for early 1931 was exposed and blocked, the military conspirators decided on a bold move to throw the country into such hysteria and confusion that they could seize power. In October 1931 the Japanese army stationed in Manchuria made an unauthorized attack on the Chinese forces and began the conquest of all Manchuria. The next year, 1932, Japanese forces attacked Shanghai, the chief port of China. Once fighting began with huge and potentially dangerous China, war fever and patriotic hysteria swept over Japan, just as the army plotters had foreseen. They now assassinated the premier of Japan and numerous other governmental and civilian leaders, cowing the rest into submission. The military Fascist masters of Japan immediately turned to the destruction of the liberals. Liberal university professors were accused of disloyalty and silenced, dismissed, or imprisoned. As in Italy and Germany the schools and the press and radio were made organs of fascist propaganda. All democratic processes of government and civil rights were destroyed. The military and the state police were given unlimited authority. The Zaibatsu were corrupted and won over with lush military contracts.

Meanwhile, the Japanese armies overran all of Manchuria, which was created into the puppet state of Manchukuo. When the League of Nations declared Japan an aggressor and ordered her to withdraw from Manchuria, she defied the League and instead withdrew from that organization. In 1937 Japan joined the Berlin-Rome-Tokyo Axis. In the same year she began an all-out assault on China proper. By 1937, therefore, the fascist powers were on the march. The democratic powers, on the other hand, whose very existence was imperiled, stood as if paralyzed.

SUGGESTED READING

H. W. Schneider, *Making the Fascist State* (1929). A good study of the origin of fascism and the sources of its ideology.

William Ebenstein, *Fascist Italy* (1939). A sound account of the pioneer Fascist state.

J. W. Wheeler-Bennett, *Nemesis of Power* (1954). A scholarly and well-written study of the German professional military and its part in the rise, triumph, and aggressions of German fascism.

Konrad Heiden, *Der Führer: Hitler's Rise to Power* (1935). Probably the best biography of Hitler for the period up to the establishment of his dictatorship. Analytical and lucid. Written by an eyewitness of many of the events.

Adolf Hitler, *Mein Kampf* (1939). Hitler's own life story and philosophy. Written in the exalted, hysterical vein of a mad genius.

The Goebbels Diaries, 1942–43, tr. and ed. by L. P. Lochner (1948). The revealing and self-incriminating diary of the diabolical dwarf who was Hitler's minister of propaganda.

William L. Shirer, *Berlin Diary* (1941). One of the best pictures of Nazi Germany just before and during the first years of World War II. Written with charm and great insight by a reporter for the Columbia Broadcasting Company.

C. Yanaga, *Japan since Perry* (1949). A factual account written in a crisp style. Good chapters on the rise to power and the aggressions of Japanese fascism.

CHAPTER 57

Paralysis of the Democratic West

THE FRUITS of World War I in the democratic West were economic instability,
political and social unrest, and intellectual
disillusionment. These weaknesses paralyzed
the Western democracies at a time when
Christian, liberal civilization was being seriously challenged by communism and fascism. The efforts of the distraught and dis-
united democratic powers to appease the fascist aggressors culminated in World War II.

1. Isolationism, Boom, and Bust in the United States

The United States emerged from World
War I the world's richest and most influential nation. Although her entry into the
war at its most critical phase was probably
decisive in determining the outcome, she
suffered far less war damage than any of the
other major participants. President Wilson
assumed the leading role in the making
of the peace settlements and in the creation
of the League of Nations. The rest of the
world looked to the United States to play
the leading role in supporting the League
and maintaining the peace.

When President Wilson returned from
Paris in the summer of 1919 and sought to
persuade his country to join the League of
Nations, he found his political enemies in
power. Acceptance by the United States of
the League's covenant, which was incorporated into the Treaty of Versailles, required
the ratification of the United States Senate

by a two-thirds vote. By virtue of a Republican majority of one in the Senate the chair-
manship of the Foreign Relations Committee, through which the treaty must first pass,
was held by Wilson's bitterest personal enemy, Henry Cabot Lodge. Lodge was determined to destroy Wilson's handiwork. Indeed, before the exact nature of the League
was known and while Wilson was consulting
Republican opinion concerning the League,
Lodge obtained the signatures of thirty-nine
senators, more than enough votes to defeat
the treaty, to a round robin agreeing to vote
against whatever proposal Wilson brought
back from Paris. Since it appeared that possibly a majority of the American people favored the League in 1919, Lodge decided to
defeat the treaty by a flank attack. He therefore attached fourteen amendments that
Wilson could not ask the other members of
the League to accept. (Some of these deliberately offended Great Britain, and some
of them demanded a privileged position for
the United States.) As a matter of fact, had
Wilson accepted the obnoxious amendments, Lodge probably would have found
other means of defeating the treaty. Wilson
set out on a speaking tour to rally American
public opinion to the treaty, but suffered a
paralytic stroke in the midst of the campaign. As Wilson was unable thereafter to
lead the fight for the treaty and was unwilling to give the leadership to others, Lodge
easily defeated ratification in the Senate.

Since the American people were never

given an opportunity to vote on the League, it is impossible to know what their verdict would have been. Such national organizations as the Federal Council of Churches, the American Bar Association, the American Federation of Labor, and the American Bankers Association declared themselves in favor of the League. Also, some of the Republican elder statesmen such as Elihu Root, Charles Evans Hughes, and ex-presi-

AMERICAN DEPRESSION BREADLINE. These jobless and homeless men wait in line for a free Thanksgiving (1936) dinner as guests of New York City. Scenes such as this help to explain the paralysis of the democratic West in the face of the growing fascist menace. During the 1930's, the depression-ridden Western democracies were so harassed by their own domestic problems that they were reluctant to assume the added burden of restraining the fascist powers. (*United Press International Photo*)

dent William Howard Taft worked for America's entrance into the League. The League was not an issue in the presidential election of 1920. However, the victor, Warren G. Harding, announced that the League was now a dead issue. And during the cynical and disillusioned decade of the 1920's American public opinion became overwhelmingly isolationist. When, therefore, during the international crises of the 1930's the harassed British and French governments sought the support of the United States against the fascist aggressors, they sought in vain.

The decade following the First World War was a period of unprecedented prosperity in the United States. The all-out war effort brought about a great expansion of American industry and unleashed huge quantities of money and credit. Prices and wages soared. In 1914 the United States had been a debtor nation. She emerged from the war a creditor to most of Europe to the amount of ten billion dollars, a figure that doubled during the next ten years. Her chief economic competitors came out of the war battered and shaken. Between 1919 and 1929 American production, profits, and purchasing power reached heights never before attained anywhere in the world. However, it was an uneven and unsound prosperity. Agriculture was depressed with surplus commodities and low prices, which meant low purchasing power for great stretches of the South and the Middle West. Nor did wages climb as rapidly as profits and prices in the industrial Northeast. These facts, plus increasing automation, meant growing unemployment and industrial surpluses. Labor unions declined in membership and bargaining power. Foreign markets were killed off by a policy of higher and higher tariffs designed to protect American industry from foreign competition. The government's philosophy of non-interference with free enterprise (except with tariffs) permitted unlimited speculation in the soaring stock market, often with other people's money and with unrestrained use of credit.

The stock market crashed in October

1929. Values tumbled. Thousands of banks and businesses failed. Millions were thrown out of work. The economic depression spread over the entire capitalistic world. For four years the Hoover administration, confident of the essential soundness of *laissez-faire* economy, refused to permit large-scale government relief measures, hoping and expecting that the natural economic laws would soon bring back prosperity. But the depression only deepened.

In the presidential election of 1932 the Democratic candidate, Franklin D. Roosevelt, defeated Hoover by some seven million votes, ending twelve years of Republican rule. The Roosevelt administration immediately launched a series of sweeping economic and social reforms that came to be called the New Deal. The New Deal was not a radical, new departure, but rather a further advance along the line charted by Theodore Roosevelt's Progressivism and Woodrow Wilson's New Freedom. First of all, emergency measures were taken to relieve the suffering of the twelve million unemployed and their families. The chief of these was the setting up of the huge Public Works Administration, which undertook to avoid the humiliation of the dole by providing useful work of at least some dignity. The Wagner Act strengthened the position of the labor unions by guaranteeing the right of collective bargaining. Old-age and unemployment insurance was inaugurated. For the desperate farmers measures were passed that granted debt relief, commodity loans, price supports, and payments for acreage reduction. Deflation was checked by a devaluation of the dollar. Investments and deposits were protected by strict government supervision. Steps were taken to conserve the nation's natural resources against wasteful private exploitation. Gradually mass confidence was restored and the nation's economy began to prosper again, though far below the boom proportions of the roaring twenties. However, many members of the business community believed that the New Deal discouraged free enterprise and incentive. They thought that the New Deal was making the

United States over into a socialistic "welfare state" and argued that the depression eventually would have ended of its own accord through the working of the natural laws of *laissez-faire* economics. The depression appears to have had no appreciable effect upon the prevailing mood of isolationism in the United States.

2. The Harassed British Empire

Great Britain emerged from World War I a victor. Her greatest prewar military and economic rival was defeated and apparently eliminated. The British Empire still included one fourth of all the land and people on the globe, but her economy, her empire, and her world position were shaken beyond recovery. Britain's far-flung possessions in Asia and Africa were beginning to stir restlessly, as the spirit of nationalism, which long had provided the European world with so much of its expansive energy, spread eastward. Great Britain found it advisable to grant freedom to her self-governing dominions, hoping to retain their loyalty. The Statute of Westminster in 1931 gave complete independence and equality with the mother country to Canada, Australia, New Zealand, the Union of South Africa, Newfoundland, and the Irish Free State (free since 1922). These former colonies had been free in reality ever since they had gained dominion status (1867–1922). Now the only remaining legal tie was loyalty to the common British crown. The British Empire was thus transformed into the British Empire and Commonwealth. Although the dominions remained loyal (with the exception of Ireland, which severed all relations in 1939), Great Britain could no longer count upon them with certainty to support her in her world policies with their manpower and resources, nor could she count upon her restless colonies. Furthermore, Britain was now clearly second to the United States as an industrial and financial power. (It would require many years, however, for British statesmen to readjust their thinking to the reality of their country's reduced position.)

At home postwar Britain was harassed with acute economic problems. Her national debt had quintupled during the war. She owed the United States more than four billion dollars. German submarines had taken a toll of nine million tons of her ships with their cargoes. Her exports met sharply increased competition in the world markets, particularly from the United States. Rising protective tariffs all over the world hindered her commerce. Her mines and industrial plants were antiquated and in disrepair. Returning servicemen found few jobs. Unemployment hovered around three million, a figure that came to be accepted as normal. Government support for the unemployed, sick, aged, and destitute proved to be the most staggering of all of Britain's financial problems.

These chronic economic ills were reflected in Great Britain's troubled postwar politics. In 1922 the Conservatives broke up Lloyd George's wartime coalition government of Liberals and Conservatives and won the ensuing parliamentary elections. Under first Bonar Law and then Stanley Baldwin they sought to restore classic nineteenth-century capitalism by means of rigid retrenchment of government spending, particularly for social services. This policy was so hard on the distressed masses that in 1924 a Labor-Liberal coalition headed by the Labor-party leader, Ramsay MacDonald, ousted the Conservatives. The Labor party was now stronger than the Liberal party, and as times grew harder and feelings more bitter, the once-great Liberal party was virtually crushed between the more extreme parties —Labor on the left and Conservative on the right. MacDonald's ministry lasted less than a year. Dependent upon the Liberals for his majority, he was forced to follow a moderate course. When he recognized the Soviet Union and made a commercial treaty with her, the Conservatives were able to capitalize on public suspicion and drive him from power. From 1925 to 1929 the Conservatives wrestled with rising discontent, strikes, and the steady growth of the Labor party. In 1929

a victory of the Labor party, supported by the much-dwindled Liberals, again brought Ramsay MacDonald to the head of the government. His moderation in the face of the deepening economic depression, however, caused the majority of his Labor followers to repudiate him two years later. MacDonald, therefore, in 1931 formed a National coalition of right-wing Laborites, Liberals, and Conservatives to deal with the mounting domestic and foreign crises. This National coalition, which was really dominated by the Conservatives, ruled Great Britain until the end of World War II. Before the outbreak of World War II, it was on the whole ineffective in dealing with both the economic and social maladjustments at home and the menacing fascist aggressions abroad. The Conservative prime ministers Stanley Baldwin and Neville Chamberlain, who followed Ramsay MacDonald as head of the National government in 1935 and 1937 respectively, appeared still to be living in the nineteenth century.

3. Frustrated France

Although France enjoyed the advantage of being more self-sufficient economically than Great Britain, she had suffered more grievous wounds in World War I than had her island neighbor. Most of the fighting had taken place on her soil. A tenth—the most productive tenth—of her area had been devastated. The retreating Germans had deliberately laid waste much of what had not been destroyed in battle. Orchards were chopped down, and mines were wrecked, many beyond repair. Even more tragic was the loss of life. France, with the lowest birth rate of any major nation in the world, suffered by far the heaviest casualties per capita of any of the combatants. Out of a population of less than forty million, she suffered 1,385,000 battle deaths and 1,700,-000 wounded. These casualties were suffered largely by France's most productive male age groups. The civilian death rate from direct and indirect causes had also been high.

France had fewer people in 1918 than in 1914 even after the return of Alsace and Lorraine.

The postwar French economy was confronted with a staggering job of reconstruction and an equally staggering war debt. In addition to her domestic debt France owed the United States and Great Britain approximately four billion dollars each. To meet these obligations and to finance the reconstruction, the French government counted on German reparations, but, as we have already seen (pp. 655–6), practically none was forthcoming. Inflation became a chronic headache. A more basic and long-range problem was French industry, which was rapidly falling behind its competitors. The highly individualistic French had not gone in for large-scale corporate industry, as had the Americans, British, and Germans. The little French family industries could not compete with the mass production of American, British, and German corporations. A like situation prevailed in French agriculture, most of which was carried on on thousands of little family farms too tiny to use machinery profitably. Industrial and agricultural production per worker was lower in France than in any other major Western nation.

Considering the serious plight of France's postwar economy and the habitual disorderliness with which her multiparty democracy traditionally functioned (see p. 585), one is impressed by the remarkable stability of the French government during the decade of the 1920's. From 1919 to 1924 a Right bloc of conservative parties was in power. It followed an anti-labor, pro-business policy. It also favored the Roman Catholic Church and pressed hard for collection of German reparations. Meanwhile, discontent among the laboring classes was mounting. In 1924, the year of MacDonald's first Labor ministry in Great Britain, the parties of the Left under the leadership of Édouard Herriot were victorious. Like MacDonald, Herriot pursued a pro-labor policy, advocating an increase in social service, and soft money.

He was also conciliatory toward Russia and Germany. But, also like MacDonald, he lasted less than a year. From 1926 to 1929 a strong right of center National bloc under the leadership of Raymond Poincaré was in power. Poincaré checked the inflation by rigid retrenchment. Upon his retirement in 1929, however, the increasing pressure of discontent threw the country into political turmoil. No leader or political combination seemed to be capable of dealing with the economic crisis brought on by the world depression, the growing menace of fascism, or the unrest in the French colonies. Ministry followed ministry in rapid succession. Scandals and riots occurred, and fascist groups appeared. In 1936 the Popular Front, consisting of left-wing parties under the leadership of the mild Socialist Léon Blum, came to power. The Blum ministry obtained a forty-hour week and annual two weeks' vacations with pay for the workers. It also nationalized the Bank of France and the great munitions industries. This was too much for the powerful propertied interests, who drove Blum from office the following year. The Right parties who regained control, however, were unable to agree upon firm policies, domestic or foreign.

Thus France, like Great Britain, in the face of resurgent Nazi Germany, swashbuckling Mussolini, and militaristic Japan, could summon no strength or unity. The propertied classes were unwilling to share their wealth or privileges or to change their nineteenth-century practices. They feared and hated Léon Blum more than they feared Hitler. The working classes felt that they had little to work or fight for. The army was basking in past glory. Seeking to maintain the *status quo*, the French were defense-minded. They constructed the Maginot Line, fortifications along the German border, and formed defensive alliances with Poland, Czechoslovakia, Yugoslavia, and Romania. These alliances were no stronger than the faith those small countries had in France's ability to defend them, which by the late 1930's was very little.

4. The Breakdown of the League of Nations

The only international agency that existed for the maintenance of the peace was the League of Nations, which after the defection of the United States was largely dependent upon Great Britain and France for support against aggression. For twelve years the League supervised the implementation of the peace treaties, administered relief to tens of thousands of war victims, promoted international good will, and settled numerous international disputes. None of these settlements, however, involved the disciplining of a major power, and thoughtful observers dreaded the time when the League would be called upon to do so.

The first major power to challenge the League was Japan. It will be recalled (see p. 661) that in 1931 the Japanese militarists began the conquest of Manchuria, partly to create a war fever preparatory to setting up a fascist dictatorship in Japan and partly as the first step in a vast program of military aggression. China, the legal owner of Manchuria and a member of the League of Nations, appealed to the League for protection. The League appointed a commission headed by Britain's earl of Lytton to make an on-the-spot investigation. The Lytton Commission reported that Japan was guilty of aggression, having violated her solemn obligations both as a League member and as a signatory of the Kellogg-Briand Pact of Paris (1928), which outlawed war as an instrument of national policy. The Commission made no recommendations for League action, however, since such action would be largely dependent upon Great Britain and France for enforcement and since developments indicated that these two democracies were not willing to risk the use of force.

The British and French governments realized the seriousness and significance of this first major challenge to the League and to the peace of the world. Soon after the beginning of Japan's aggression they sought the support of the United States in a vigorous move to stop Japan through the agency of the League. Secretary of State Henry L. Stimson, fully aware of the significance of the crisis, wholeheartedly approved of joint measures by the three democracies. However, President Hoover, reflecting the isolationist sentiment of American public opinion, would not consent to the use of force, the threat of force, or even economic pressure by the United States. Stimson could offer the British and the French only words of disapproval of Japan's acts. The British and French governments, harassed by their own domestic economic and political problems and the rising menace of fascism in Europe, could not bring themselves to act alone. The League, without their backing, did nothing. It had failed its first major test and was on the way out as a potent force for peace. Japan's successful defiance of the League of Nations convinced Mussolini and Hitler that they could safely launch aggressions of their own.

The deathblow to the League was struck by Mussolini. Late in 1934 the Italian fascist dictator attacked Ethiopia, a large primitive country in East Africa. This was designed to be the first step in the restoration of the ancient Roman Empire. Ethiopia was a member of the League and appealed to the League for protection. Great Britain, concerned for her vital interests in the Near and Middle East and for her life line to the Far East, now became greatly agitated. Under the leadership of Great Britain and France the League declared Mussolini to be the aggressor and invoked economic sanctions (Article XVI) against him. A list of commodities that League members were not to sell Mussolini was drawn up. However, the list did not include petroleum, and it soon became apparent that this was the article upon which the success of his aggression depended. The League prepared to add oil to the boycott list. But it quickly became apparent that, to be effective, the embargo would require the co-operation of the United States. American exports of oil to Mussolini had trebled since the beginning of his campaign against Ethiopia. When the British and French governments requested the co-operation of the United States in withholding excess oil from Mussolini, Secretary of State Cordell Hull and President Roosevelt were sympathetic. Roosevelt requested the American oil companies to refrain voluntarily from selling Mussolini oil in excess of the normal peacetime amount. The oil companies, however, refused to comply. Roosevelt then asked Congress to pass legislation restricting the excess sales. A battle royal ensued between the president and the oil companies for the support of Congress. The oil companies won. The press and public opinion were overwhelmingly isolationist, and Congress, in denying Roosevelt's request, reflected that view. Mussolini got his oil. Britain and France, unwilling to resort to the only other means of stopping him, a shooting war, gave up the League struggle. Mussolini conquered Ethiopia. The League of Nations, for all practical purposes, was dead.

5. Appeasement of the Fascist Aggressors

The most serious consequence of the demise of the League of Nations was the unleashing of Nazi Germany. Since the triumph of the Nazis in 1933 Germany had been feverishly preparing for a military comeback. In March 1936, Hitler ordered his armed forces into the Rhineland, which, according to the Treaty of Versailles, was to be permanently demilitarized. France, recognizing this move as the gravest threat and challenge to herself, called loudly to Great Britain for support. The British offered none. The French fretted and fumed but in the end did nothing. Hitler had won his gamble. It was France's last opportunity to save herself by striking down Hitler. Shortly afterward Nazi Germany had become too strong. The French capitalistic classes, including many army officers, were apparently more concerned about Léon Blum's approaching premiership than about the threat of Nazi Germany.

Fascism's next triumph was in Spain. Modern liberal and industrial civilization had by-passed Spain. Until 1931 she was dominated by the landed aristocracy, a few rich capitalists, aristocratic army officers, and the Roman Catholic Church. The mass of the people were poverty-stricken, illiterate, and landless peasants. Since the turn of the century, however, and particularly since 1918, the pressure of discontent had been rising. In 1931 the dictatorial king yielded to this pressure and granted an election. The forces of liberal reform won such a sweeping victory that the king fled the country. The liberals then proceeded to make over the Spanish nation. They drew up a democratic constitution, granted labor the right to unionize, began a sweeping program of public education, started to modernize the army by placing promotions on a merit basis, granted religious freedom, secularized the property of the Roman Catholic Church, and planned to break up the great estates into peasant-owned farms. There was, of course, much confusion, and many people were inspired by false hopes. After two years the conservative propertied interests, with the vigorous support of the pope, won the elections by a narrow margin and began to undo the reforms. Early in 1936, however, the liberals again won a clear-cut victory and resumed their drastic reform program. The privileged classes were now desperate. In July 1936, under the leadership of General Francisco Franco, they launched an armed rebellion against the liberal government. Although the Rebels enjoyed the advantage of professional military leadership, the regular army, and most of the country's wealth, they were unable to make headway against the Loyalists, who enjoyed the support of the majority of the rank and file of the people.

The Spanish Civil War soon became a battlefield in the world struggle of fascism, liberalism, and communism. Hitler and Mussolini, seeing in it an opportunity to advance the cause of fascism, gain a like-minded ally and a strategic military position, and test and rehearse their new weapons and units, sent abundant arms and troops to aid Franco. The Loyalists appealed to the democracies for aid but received none.

A few volunteers from the democracies fought as individuals in the Loyalist cause. The only nation that supported the Loyalists was the Soviet Union. But the amount of aid she could send to the Loyalists was quite small and probably did more harm than good since it tainted the Loyalist cause with the suspicion of communism. After three years of terrific slaughter Franco and his German and Italian allies beat down the last organized Loyalist resistance. A typical fascist dictatorship was established over Spain. Liberalism was shattered. The Communist cause in Spain, on the other hand, was somewhat strengthened. At the beginning of the civil war the Communists constituted only a small minority on the Loyalist side. Not a single member of the Loyalist cabinet was a Communist. However, thanks to limited support from the Soviet Union and to the Communists' skill at underground activity, they fared much better in defeat than did the liberals. The world prestige of fascist Germany and Italy rose while that of the democracies declined further.

The year, 1937, was the year of decision—the point of no return on the road to war. As noted previously, in that year the three great fascist powers formed the Berlin-Rome-Tokyo Axis, which was aimed specifically at the Soviet Union but was in reality an alliance of fascist aggressors against the rest of the world. In that year the military strength of the Axis powers—their war plants running day and night—forged ahead of that of the rest of the world. They were now out of hand. In that year the Nazis blueprinted their timetable of conquests, and Japan began her all-out assault on China.

Early in 1938 the Nazis' timetable began to function. In March they overran Austria without opposition, annexing the six and a half million Austrians to the German *Reich* (Empire). Great Britain and France denounced this open aggression and violation of the Treaty of Versailles but did nothing.

Almost immediately Hitler turned his big propaganda guns on his next victim, Czech-oslovakia. In constructing this little country out of Austro-Hungarian territory at the end of World War I the Allied peacemakers had left three and a half million German-speaking people on the Czech side of the border. Although these Sudeten Germans had never been a part of Germany and were separated from Germany by the high Sudeten Mountain wall, Hitler now claimed them. His main consideration in attacking Czechoslovakia was military. The little Czech republic was allied with France and Russia, and in the coming war that Hitler was planning against those two countries Czechoslovakia could be a threat to the German flank. The "Bohemian bastion" has long been a vital strategic position in Central Europe. Furthermore, the Czech defenses were patterned after those of the French. Possession of them would give the Germans a blueprint of the Maginot Line.

As early as May 1938, Hitler threatened Czechoslovakia. The Czechs, however, surprised him by rushing to their defenses. Hitler spent the next four months arousing his people to readiness for war and softening up the democracies by keeping them in a constant state of tension and alarm. This psychological warfare culminated in a giant Nazi rally at Nuremberg in mid-September. There Hitler screamed to his frenzied followers that if the Sudeten areas were not surrendered to him by October 1 he would march. With France and the Soviet Union standing firm in their alliance with Czechoslovakia, the world anxiously awaited the beginning of a major conflict that was likely to become World War II.

At this juncture Prime Minister Neville Chamberlain took it upon himself to fly to Hitler's lair at Berchtesgaden and plead for a compromise. The upshot was a conference at Munich on September 28, 1938. The participants were Hitler, Mussolini, Chamberlain, and Premier Édouard Daladier of France. Chamberlain persuaded Daladier to yield to Hitler's demands for the Sudeten areas of Czechoslovakia. Czechoslovakia and the Soviet Union, France's allies, were not consulted. This was one of Hitlers greatest

THE MUNICH CONFEREES, SEPTEMBER 1938. From left to right are Neville Chamberlain of Great Britain, Edouard Daladier of France, Adolf Hitler of Germany, Benito Mussolini of Italy, and Mussolini's aide and son-in-law, Count Ciano. At the Munich Conference, Chamberlain and Daladier yielded to Hitler's threats, deserted Czechoslovakia, and alienated the Soviet Union, which was allied with France. (*United Press International Photo*)

triumphs. By enticing Great Britain and France to leave France's allies, Czechoslovakia and the Soviet Union, in the lurch Hitler had driven a wedge between the Soviet Union and the Western democracies. The Soviet leaders never trusted the Western democracies again. Neither did many of the other countries of the world that were watching to see where their greatest safety lay. The Munich "sellout" represented the lowest ebb to which the cause of liberal democracy in the world had ever sunk.

6. The Return to War

Although the four participating powers at Munich had agreed to become joint protec-tors of what remained of Czechoslovakia, in March 1939, Hitler overran without warning the remainder of the stricken little republic. This crass act of betrayal opened the eyes even of Neville Chamberlain to the fact that fascism could not be appeased. There was no limit to its perfidious ambition. When, therefore, immediately following the rape of Czechoslovakia Hitler threatened Poland, Great Britain and France decided to draw a line. In April 1939, they made a guarantee to Poland that they would come to her aid if she were attacked and resisted the attack. The fat was now in the fire. Hitler, however, was not deterred. He was demanding among other things the return to Germany of the Polish Corridor, which separated East Prussia from the rest of Germany, and the city of Danzig, which was governed by the League of Nations. By now, however, it was apparent to all that specific Nazi demands were merely excuses for unlimited aggression. Throughout the summer of 1939 the Germans made feverish preparations for war and kept up a drumfire of vilification of Poland and the democracies. Meanwhile, both sides were bidding for the support of the Soviet Union.

On August 23, 1939 the world was stunned by the signing of a ten-year peace pact by Hitler and Stalin. In return for the Soviet Union's neutrality while Germany conquered Poland Hitler gave Stalin a free hand to reannex the territories in Eastern Europe, including eastern Poland, that Russia had lost at the end of World War I.

With the Soviet Union safely neutralized Hitler readied the attack on Poland as quickly as possible. At the last moment the British government instructed its ambassador in Berlin to ask Hitler what concessions by Poland he would accept to refrain from war. Hitler informed the British ambassador that he was not interested in concessions, that his army and his people were ready and eager for war and that he could not disappoint them now. The wires between Warsaw and Berlin were cut, lest the Poles make a last-minute peaceable surrender to Hitler's demands. At dawn on September 1 the Germans launched an all-out attack on Poland by land, sea, and air. Two days later Great Britain and France declared war on Germany, Hitler having ignored their ultimatum to desist. World War II had begun.

SUGGESTED READING

* Frederick L. Allen, *Only Yesterday* (Bantam). A vivid account of the roaring twenties in America, written in a journalistic style.
* Robert E. Sherwood, *Roosevelt and Hopkins*, 2 vols. (Bantam). This is a brilliantly written account of the Roosevelt administration by one of America's foremost literary figures and a writer of Roosevelt's speeches. It covers both the New Deal and World War II. Sherwood presents much colorful behind-the-scenes detail.

Robert Graves and Alan Hodge, *The Long Week-End: A Social History of Great Britain, 1918–1939* (1941). A vivid social history of Great Britain between the two world wars. Penetrating observations written in a witty journalistic style.
* E. J. Knapton, *France since Versailles* (Berkshire). A brief survey of French history since the end of World War I.
* Herbert Luethy, *France against Herself* (Meridian). An analysis of the various factors that

account for the paralysis of France since the end of World War I. Luethy is a Swiss journalist who spent ten years in France making this study.

Léon Blum, *For All Mankind* (1946). A lucidly written little book by a French pre-World War II Socialist premier, written in a German prison. Although the book exudes good will and forgiveness, Blum blames France's collapse chiefly on the selfish bourgeoisie, who placed their own entrenched interests above those of the nation.

Claude G. Bowers, *My Mission to Spain* (1954). The story of the triumph of fascism in Spain by America's ambassador to Spain during the Spanish Civil War.

Winston Churchill, *The Gathering Storm* (1948). The first volume of Churchill's magnificent six-volume history of World War II. This volume traces with authority and insight, and in matchless prose, the coming and the first eight months of the war.

CHAPTER 58

World War II, 1939–45

To much of the disillusioned and paralyzed democratic world the outbreak of World War II seemed the beginning of the end of liberal Western civilization, that had been so long developing. What instruments of destruction science and technology had developed since World War I nobody knew. The Nazis boasted that the German airforce was capable of destroying all the cities of the non-fascist world. For two years these dire fears and threats appeared to be justified. The seemingly invincible German and Japanese military machines swept on to victory after victory.

1. Two Years of Axis Triumph

The mechanized might of Nazi Germany overwhelmed Poland in a matter of days. Striking without official warning at dawn, September 1, 1939, the German air force caught the Polish air force on its various airfields and destroyed it on the ground. Thereafter the German *Luftwaffe*, by ravaging Polish cities and communications centers and harassing troop movements, prevented the complete mobilization of the Polish army. Meanwhile, Nazi tanks and infantry poured into Poland from the north, west, and south. Within two weeks' time Warsaw was surrounded and being pounded to rubble by German artillery. At this juncture the forces of the Soviet Union, in accordance with the August 23 pact with Hitler, moved into eastern Poland and occu-

pied the Russian-speaking areas seized from her after World War I (see p. 646). From the beginning of the invasion the Poles, fighting courageously but hopelessly, cried for help from France and Great Britain. The French and the British mobilized their armies along the German West Wall fortifications, and the British fleet blockaded Germany by sea. But that was all. At the time no fighter planes had the range to fly from French or British bases to Poland and back, and the French and British understandably did not wish to provoke the lightning by bombing German cities. Western military leaders, basing their views on the experiences of World War I, believed it to be suicidal to attack elaborate fortifications. They believed that sooner or later Hitler would be forced to attack the French Maginot Line and would be destroyed. This thinking was little consolation to the Poles. Warsaw surrendered on September 27, less than a month after the fighting began.

The Soviet Union, in accordance with her agreement with Hitler, proceeded to reannex the remaining territories in Eastern Europe that she had lost at the end of World War I. Shortly after Poland surrendered, the Soviet Union demanded military bases in Estonia, Latvia, and Lithuania. The three little Baltic republics appealed to Hitler but were told to comply. The following spring they were absorbed politically into the Soviet Union. In October 1939, the Soviet Union demanded three strategic little strips of Finnish territory: the Karelian Isthmus, which put the Finnish border within artillery range of the great city of Leningrad; a strip of territory near the Russian Arctic port of Murmansk; and the naval base of Hangö, which guarded the sea approaches to Leningrad. On Hangö the Soviets wanted a thirty-year lease; the other territories were to be ceded outright. When the Finnish government refused, the Soviet Union attacked Finland and took these territories by force. In June 1940, while Hitler was busy in Western Europe, the Soviet Union demanded and procured from Romania the return of Bessarabia. With Bessarabia she also took the little province of northern Bukovina, which she had never previously owned.

Early in April 1940, the Germans suddenly overran Denmark and Norway. The British fleet, attempting to intercept the invasion of Norway, was beaten off with heavy losses by the German air force. Denmark and Norway provided the Nazis with important food, timber, and mineral resources, sea and air bases, and a safe route for vital iron ore coming from Sweden.

On May 10, 1940, the German armies assaulted Luxemburg, the Netherlands, Belgium, and France in the mightiest onslaught in history up to that time. Luxemburg offered no resistance. The Netherlands fought heroically but was overwhelmed in six days. Belgium lasted nineteen days, but when she fell, the French and British armies in Belgium fell with her. Trusting to the Maginot Line to hold along the German border, the British army and a large part of the French army moved into Belgium to support the hard-pressed Belgian forces. In a surprise move through the Ardennes forest powerful German mechanized forces on May 14 smashed through the French defenses at Sedan and drove quickly to the English Channel, cutting off the Belgian, British, and French armies in Belgium. Although some 300,000 British and a few French troops escaped by sea from Dunkirk, all of the Belgian troops, the bulk of the French troops together with their weapons and sup-

plies, and the British weapons and supplies were captured. Only five more days of fighting, June 5–10, were required for the Germans to crush the remaining organized French resistance and turn the French retreat into a disorderly rout. On June 10 Paris was declared an open city. On that day Mussolini, thinking it safe, declared war on France and Great Britain. On June 16 Marshal Philippe Pétain replaced Paul Reynaud as premier of France and the following day dispatched a surrender team to Hitler. On June 25 the "fighting" ceased. The collapse of the French military machine after five days of fighting was the most colossal military debacle in history. It was the one military machine in the world thought to be able to stand up to the Nazis. Hitler forced upon the helpless French a harsh treaty. The northern half of France and all the Atlantic costal area were placed under German occupation. The unoccupied portion was compelled to disarm and co-operate with Germany. Some two million French prisoners were held as hostages to French good behavior. In unoccupied France, Marshal Pétain and Pierre Laval set up a semi-fascist regime, with headquarters at Vichy, and undertook to co-operate with Hitler.

The collapse of France left Great Britain to face the Axis fury alone (except for the Chinese Nationalist forces still holding out against the Japanese in the Chinese interior). Hitler now demanded that she surrender or suffer annihilation. Her situation was desperate. Nearly all of her land armaments had been lost at Dunkirk. Against the nearly one hundred and fifty battle-tried Nazi divisions she had only one fully-equipped division. And although Great Britain did have the English Channel and the world's greatest navy, the fighting around Norway had demonstrated that navies could no longer control narrow waters dominated by a hostile air force. Britain's chief weapon of defense was her relatively small but efficient air force. Not the least of her assets was Winston Churchill, who on May 10, 1940, had at last replaced Neville Chamberlain

as prime minister. The dynamic and eloquent Churchill dified Hitler. "We shall
fight on the beaches, in the fields, in the
streets, in the hills. We shall never surrender."

Throughout the month of July 1940, Nazi
invasion forces gathered along the French
coast opposite Britain, twenty-four miles
away. To make the crossing, however, absolute control of the air over the channel was
required. Early in August, therefore, swarms
of German bombers and fighter escorts flew
over the channel, seeking to destroy the British air force and its landing fields. In the
ensuing air battles the British pilots in their
swift Spitfires and heavily armed and ma-
neuverable Hurricanes knocked down German planes at the ratio of two to one. Nevertheless, by the end of August the British air
forces were facing annihilation by sheer
weight of numbers. At this critical juncture
the Nazis suddenly shifted to massive day-
light attacks on London, the world's largest
city. The destruction and the suffering were
immense, but the toll of German planes
taken by the British fighters was so great
that early in October the Nazis shifted to
less effective night attacks. Although the

LONDON STREET AFTER A GERMAN AIR RAID, JANUARY 1941. During the first three years of
World War II the superior German air force wrecked scores of cities in enemy countries, leaving
wreckage such as this in London in their wake. Hitler's failure to conquer Great Britain in the
Battle of Britain, August 1940 to July 1941, was his first serious setback. (*United Press International Photo*)

destructive air raids on Great Britain's cities, together with even more menacing submarine attacks on British shipping, continued until the end of the war, the immediate threat of invasion had now passed and the Battle of Britain had been won.

While the Battle of Britain was at its height, Mussolini set in operation his grandiose schemes for conquering an empire. Upon entering the war in June 1940, he had closed the Mediterranean to British shipping. In September his armies moved on Egypt and the Suez Canal from Libya to the west and from Ethiopia to the south. In October his armies attacked Greece from Albania. To meet this threat, Churchill made one of the most daring and farsighted military moves in history. Believing Suez to be the most strategic spot in the world in a global war, he sent half of Britain's scarce supply of tanks and artillery around Africa to Egypt while the Nazis stood poised across the channel for the invasion of Great Britain. Mussolini's forces met disaster everywhere. The Greeks defeated them and drove them back into Albania. A squadron of British torpedo planes delivered a lethal blow to the Italian fleet at its Taranto base. During the winter of 1940–41 the fascist armies moving on Egypt were completely destroyed by light mobile British forces. Mussolini's bubble had burst with a feeble plop. Henceforth he was hardly more than a prisoner of the German forces that were sent to save him.

When in October 1940, it became evident that Great Britain could not be invaded that year, Hitler ordered his planners to complete blueprints for the earliest possible invasion of the Soviet Union. The conquest of the Soviet Union had always been uppermost in Hitler's thoughts, but he had hoped first to dispose of the French and British threat to his rear. The plans, which were quickly perfected, called for an assault date not later than May 15, 1941. But first the Balkan flank was to be secured. Hungary and Romania joined the Axis Alliance in November 1940, Bulgaria in March 1941. Immediately Nazi forces poured into those

countries. Yugoslavia and Greece, however, refused to yield to Hitler's threats, and the Germans attacked them in April 1941. Yugoslavia was overrun in eleven days, Greece in three weeks. British forces that Churchill had dispatched to Greece were driven out of the peninsula and also off the island of Crete. Suez now appeared to be doomed. It was open to attack through the Balkans to the north; to the west was Erwin Rommel's Afrika Korps, which Hitler had sent down through Italy; pro-Nazi movements had broken out in Iraq, Iran, and French Syria. At this juncture, however, Hitler hurled his legions against the Soviet Union, giving the British a breathing spell to recoup their strength in the Near and Middle East.

On June 22, 1941, the Germans launched against the Soviet Union the most massive assault in history. They were joined by the Hungarians, the Romanians, and the Finns. There were one hundred sixty divisions in all. (Eventually the figure rose to two hundred fifty.) And although Stalin was able to throw an equal number of divisions against the invaders, his troops were not so well trained or equipped. Hitler instructed his troops to treat the Russians as barbarians. He expected to crush Soviet resistance in six weeks. The top British and American military leaders were of the same opinion. The Russians fought with unexpected skill and determination, but the Nazi war machine crunched ever forward until by December 1 it was within sight of Moscow. Leningrad was surrounded, and Rostov, the gateway to the Caucasus oil fields, was captured. The richest and most productive part of the Soviet Union was in German hands. The Russians had suffered such staggering casualties that Hitler announced that the Soviet Union was destroyed and would never rise again. The Japanese war lords, taking him at his word and thinking the golden hour had struck, attacked the United States on December 7, 1941. By that time, however, the arctic winter and Soviet counterattacks had forced the Germans to retreat. The Soviet Union was still alive, and the United States was now in the war.

2. The Entry of the United States into the War

The entry of the United States into the war—the one thing that might conceivably turn the tide—was not a sudden but a gradual involvement. We have already observed the refusal of the American people to co-operate with the League of Nations in checking Japan in 1931 and fascist Italy in 1935. To make assurance doubly sure, an isolationist Congress in 1935, '36, and '37 passed a series of neutrality laws limiting the powers of the president to carry out his constitutional functions of conducting the nation's foreign relations. At the same time Congress steadfastly refused to increase the nation's military budget in the face of the rising fascist menace. During the Munich and Polish crises President Roosevelt pleaded with Hitler and Mussolini not to plunge the world into war, but the fascist dictators scorned his pleas, realizing that his hands were tied. The outbreak of the war in Europe caused hardly a ripple in the isolationist sentiment of the American public and of Congress. The French army and Maginot Line and the British navy were believed by most of the isolationists to be capable of containing the Nazis.

But suddenly in May–June 1940, the picture totally changed. The French army and Maginot Line ceased to exist, and the British navy was in grave danger. Much of it would be used up in the defense of Britain in case of invasion. The American people, now seized with consternation, cried for drastic action. Roosevelt promptly came forward with a three-point program: (1) all-out rearmament, (2) bipartisanship in foreign affairs, (3) all aid to those fighting the Axis (which at the moment meant Great Britain) short of war. There was no opposition to the first proposal, and Congress quickly voted seventeen and a half billion dollars for defense. Although there were a few partisan murmurings, Roosevelt activated the second proposal by appointing two prominent internationalist Republicans, Henry L. Stimson and Frank Knox, as secretary of war and secretary of the navy, respectively. Over the aid-to-Britain proposal, however, powerful opposition arose. This opposition was led largely by stalwart Republican isolationists such as Senator Robert Taft, Colonel R. R. McCormick (publisher of the Chicago *Tribune*), and Charles A. Lindbergh, although a few Democratic isolationists such as Senator Burton K. Wheeler of Montana also participated.

The victory of Wendell Willkie, an internationalist Republican, over Robert Taft for the Republican presidential nomination in July 1940 made it easier for Roosevelt to implement his aid-to-Britain proposal. He immediately dispatched a quantity of World War I arms and ammunition to Britain, and in September 1940, he exchanged fifty World War I destroyers for eight British air and naval bases in the Western Hemisphere. These weapons played an important role in the Battle of Britain. By the end of the year, however, Churchill informed Roosevelt that Britain was nearing exhaustion. Thereupon Roosevelt proposed and in March 1941, Congress passed the Lend Lease Act, which authorized the President to sell, lend, lease, or give any commodity to any nation whose defense he deemed necessary for the safety of the United States. Congress also voted a first installment of seven billion dollars to finance the measure.

The British navy, stretched thin over the world's sea lanes, however, was unable to guard Britain's Lend Lease ships from German submarines. It soon became apparent that if the Lend Lease billions were to achieve their purpose, the ships carrying the goods would have to be convoyed by the American navy. The sinking of an American ship in the South Atlantic by a German submarine led the American government in June and July 1941, to close all Axis consulates and freeze all Axis assets in the United States and begin convoying Lend Lease goods as far as Iceland. Meanwhile, Lend Lease was extended to the Soviet Union when that country was attacked by Germany. In October 1941, two American destroyers on the Iceland convoying run were torpedoed by German submarines with a loss of one hundred and twenty-six American lives. Roosevelt stated that "the shooting war has started. And history has recorded who fired the first shot."

In August 1941, Roosevelt and Churchill had met at sea and drawn up the Atlantic Charter: a joint statement of ideals and war purposes. In it appeared such pregnant phrases as: ". . . Their countries seek no aggrandisement, territorial or other . . . They respect the right of all peoples to choose the form of government under which they will live . . . After the final destruction of the Nazi tyranny . . . the establishment of a wider and permanent system of general security . . ." The Soviet Union subscribed to the Atlantic Charter shortly afterward. Thus, by October 1941, the United States was engaged in a shooting—but not yet official—war with Germany and was in a virtual alliance with Great Britain, one of the belligerents. The American people's eyes were on the Atlantic, where at any moment some new German act of aggression might make war official and total.

It was not in the Atlantic, however, but in the Pacific that the history-changing blow was struck; and not by Germany, but by Japan. Early in 1939 the Japanese, having conquered all the populous coastal areas of China and having driven Chiang Kai-shek's forces far into the bleak Chinese interior, turned southward toward the territories of Southeast Asia and the Southwest Pacific. These territories, rich in rubber, tin, rice, copra, and oil, belonged (with the exception of independent Thailand) to France, the Netherlands, Great Britain, and the United States. Since the French, Dutch, and British had their hands full in Europe with the growing Nazi menace, President Roosevelt transferred the American fleet from the Atlantic to Pearl Harbor in Hawaii as a deterrent to further Japanese aggression. He also gave the Japanese the required six months' notice of the termination of the commercial treaty of 1911. These moves appear to have given the Japanese war lords pause.

In 1940, however, after Hitler's conquest of France and the Netherlands and threatened conquest of Great Britain the Japanese became much bolder. They took advantage of France's helplessness to occupy northern French Indo-China and threatened the Dutch East Indies. The Roosevelt administration, seeking to restrain the Axis with all pressure short of war, now embargoed the shipment of all commodities to Japan except petroleum, and made a loan of seventy-five million dollars to Chiang Kai-shek. Oil was left out of the embargo for fear the Japanese would strike immediately the oil-rich Dutch East Indies. Again the Japanese halted. But in the following year, 1941, when the Germans overran the Balkans and launched what promised to be a lethal attack on the Soviet Union, the Japanese leaders decided that the day of Axis world triumph was at hand. In July 1941, therefore, they greatly stepped up their war preparations, poured troops into southern Indo-China for an obvious assault on the Dutch and British East Indies, and launched an all-out hate campaign against the United States in the army-controlled press.

The Roosevelt administration, deciding that further conciliation was virtually hopeless, froze all Japanese assets in the United States, which had the effect of embargoing oil. On November 25 the Japanese fleet was ordered to sail for its attack position. The next day the United States, having intercepted and decoded the order, made a final conciliatory offer, which the Japanese government spurned. Roosevelt, realizing that an attack was in motion but not knowing where, sent to Emperor Hirohito a last personal plea, which was intercepted by Japanese army officials. Early Sunday morning on December 7, 1941, a large squadron of Japanese bombers and torpedo planes took off from carriers that had sneaked to a position north of Hawaii and caught by surprise the American fleet anchored in Pearl Harbor. With little loss to themselves, the Japanese planes knocked out eight battleships, three cruisers, and three destroyers. At the same time they destroyed the American air force in Hawaii on the ground. Later in the day Japan declared the existence of a state of war with the United States. The next day, December 8, the United States Congress declared war on Japan. Three days later, December 11, Germany and Italy, making good their promise to Japan, declared war on the United States. The next day, December 12, the United States replied in kind.

3. Climax and Turning Point of the War, June–August 1942

The entry of the United States, with her enormous resources and industrial potential, changed the whole complexion of the war. It made possible the turning of the tide. However, many months would be required to mobilize America's resources, and the Axis was determined to win the victory before American mobilization could be achieved. To bring about Allied solidarity, Churchill hastened to Washington, where on January 1, 1942, he and Roosevelt launched the United Nations Alliance. Twenty-six nations, of which the United States, Great Britain, and the Soviet Union were the Big Three, promised to give their all to the common effort, to make no separate peace, and to abide by the principles of the Atlantic Charter. By the end of the war the number of member nations had risen to forty-seven.

The now global war was fought in three major theaters: (1) Russia, (2) the Mediterranean and Western Europe, and (3) the Pacific. The Axis powers made their climactic bid for victory on all three fronts between June and August 1942. The biggest front in terms of numbers of men, weapons, and casualties involved was that in Russia. The Germans, after having been stopped in December 1941, by the Russian winter and counterattacks, resumed their forward thrust in June 1942, this time in the southern sector. Refreshed and re-equipped, they seemed irresistible. By August they had reached the outskirts of Stalingrad on the Volga. Stalin now ordered a do-or-die stand. For six months the battle of Stalingrad raged. In January 1943 the Russians closed a pincer

behind the Germans in Stalingrad and captured 300,000 of them. This was the turning point. The Germans began a slow but general retreat.

The critical battle on the Mediterranean and Western European front was fought in Egypt. General Rommel's tough Afrika Korps in its first drive on Suez in 1941 had been stopped and pushed back into Libya by the British. Now in June 1942, Rommel, greatly strengthened, struck the British desert forces a shattering blow and chased them in near rout to El Alamein, only sixty-five miles from Alexandria. Suez seemed doomed, and the British fleet prepared to evacuate the Mediterranean before it could be bottled up. Churchill rushed to the scene and put in a team of winning commanders: Sir Harold Alexander in over-all command and Sir Bernard Montgomery as field commander. In August, Rommel assaulted the British positions at El Alamein and was stopped. A race to build up men and supplies ensued; the British, with massive aid from the United States, won. Late in October 1942, Montgomery's superior Eighth Army attacked Rommel's forces and after a desperate battle drove them back across the desert in defeat. Suez and the Middle East were now saved from the Axis, and for the first time Great Britain and the United States were in a position to assume the offensive.

The war in the Pacific was predominantly naval in character. Three days after Pearl Harbor, Japanese carrier-based torpedo planes struck the British Asiatic fleet a crippling blow in the Gulf of Siam. Now, with unchallenged mastery of the Pacific the Japanese were able to conquer with relative ease a vast area in the Southwest Pacific and Southeast Asia in the space of a few months. The American islands of Wake, Guam, and the Philippines; British Hong Kong and Malaya; and the Dutch East Indies were overrun. The great British bastion, Singapore, fell on February 15, 1942. Burma was conquered in March. In May a strong Japanese fleet was turned back by the American fleet in the Battle of the Coral Sea,

northeast of Australia. However, the main Japanese fleet was preparing a major thrust at Hawaii, which could have been taken easily immediately after Pearl Harbor. The United States navy, which was in possession of the Japanese code, massed for an all-out battle. Early in June 1942, just as the Stalingrad and El Alamein campaigns were beginning, the two fleets came within carrier-plane range of each other off Midway Island, a thousand miles west of Hawaii. The climactic Battle of Midway was fought at long range entirely by aircraft and submarines. American planes sank all four of the Japanese carriers, while the Japanese were able to destroy only one of three American carriers. Pounded from the air and without air cover, the Japanese commander ordered a retreat, never to become so bold again. In August 1942, the Americans assumed the offensive by attacking Guadalcanal in the Solomon Islands northeast of Australia. With the advantage of hindsight we can now see that the tide was turning on all three fronts by August 1942.

4. Victory on the Russian Front

Although the greatest crises had passed by the end of 1942, two and a half more years of bloody fighting were required to subdue the Axis. In fact the defeat of the Axis could not have been achieved at all without a high degree of co-operation among the Big Three allies. President Roosevelt, with his winsome personality, played an important part in maintaining mutual confidence and co-operation among the chief Allied powers, which were so divergent in their ideologies and specific interests. The chief planners of the co-ordinated global strategy were Churchill for Great Britain, Stalin for the Soviet Union, and Army Chief of Staff George Catlett Marshall for the United States.

The Battle of Russia was the greatest and most destructive battle in history. Some nine million men (five hundred divisions) were engaged. For two and a half years after Stalingrad the Germans were slowly beaten

back, doggedly contesting every foot of ground. At last, in April of 1945, the Russians entered Berlin. Along the fifteen hundred miles between Stalingrad and Berlin lay the wreckage of the greater part of Hitler's war machine, the most powerful engine of destruction the world had ever seen. But the richest and most productive part of the Soviet Union lay devastated. Fifteen million Russians had been killed.

5. Victory on the Mediterranean and Western European Front

Early in November 1942, just as the Germans were beginning to retreat from El Alamein, a combined Anglo-American force under the command of General Dwight D. Eisenhower landed in French North Africa. By February 1943, the converging forces of Eisenhower and Montgomery cornered the Afrika Korps in Tunisia, where it surrendered in May. Rommel himself, on Hitler's orders, had flown back to Germany. In July 1943, Eisenhower's troops, now including those of Montgomery, conquered the island of Sicily. Early in September the Anglo-Americans invaded the southern tip of Italy. Mussolini was overthrown by his own military leaders, and Italy surrendered. However, the peninsula was held by strong German forces. By December 1943, the Allies had reached Cassino Pass, about seventy-five miles south of Rome. At this point the major objectives in the Mediterranean area had been achieved, and Eisenhower, along with most of his forces, was transferred to Great Britain to command the main Anglo-American thrust across the channel.

This thrust came on June 6, 1944. Thanks in large measure to complete Allied mastery of the skies, successful landings were made on the Normandy coast. After a rapid build-up the Anglo-Americans broke out of the beach head and before the end of the year cleared practically all of France of the enemy. Germany, meanwhile, was being pulverized from the air. Early in 1945 the American and British forces, now joined by French units, broke through the German

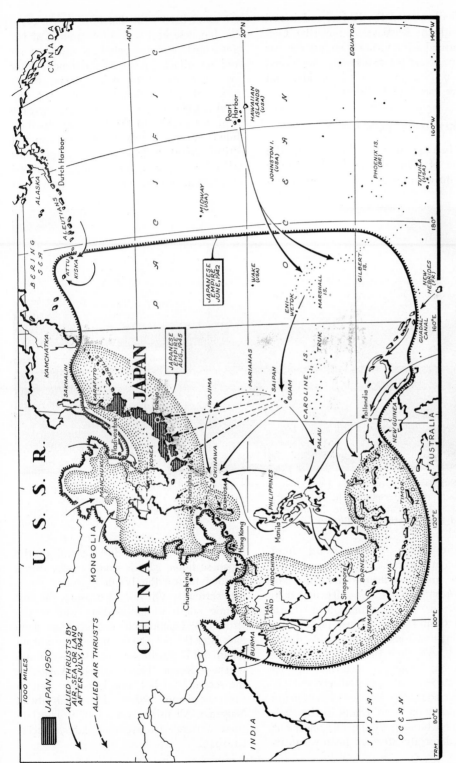

THE ALLIED OFFENSIVES IN THE PACIFIC

West Wall, crossed the Rhine, and joined hands with the Russians on the Elbe. Germany surrendered on May 8, ending the war in Europe. Near the end Hitler and several other top Nazis committed suicide, and Mussolini was shot by Italian partisans.

6. Victory on the Pacific Front

Early in 1943 American forces under the command of General Douglas MacArthur began with a strong naval escort an island-

est naval battle, the Battle of Leyte Gulf, the Japanese fleet was annihilated. Cut off, uncovered, and subjected to ceaseless air and sea attacks, Japan was doomed. After Germany surrendered in May 1945, American, British, and Russian troops that had been engaged in the European theater were deployed rapidly to the Far East. In mid-July the atomic bomb, which American and British scientists had been developing for several years, was successfully completed and tested. In order to avoid the heavy and

First Submarine Atom Bomb Explosion, Bikini, July 1946. A cruiser and a battleship may be seen in the waterspout. The first atomic bomb dropped on Hiroshima, August 6, 1945, ushered in a new era of warfare. Man now had within his grasp the power of self-destruction. (*United Press International Photo*)

hopping campaign northwestward from their base in Australia. At the same time the main American fleet under the command of Admiral Chester Nimitz, now definitely superior to the Japanese fleet, thrust westward from Hawaii toward Japan, capturing the numerous Japanese-held islands in its path. Although the islands, many of them covered by jungles, were bloodily defended, success was achieved everywhere. In October 1944, the American forces made a bold landing on Leyte Island in the Philippines. This brought the Japanese fleet out for a last desperate effort. In history's great-

useless casualties that a direct assault on the Japanese home islands would cause, it was decided to use the bomb to shock Japan into surrender. On August 6, 1945, the first atomic bomb to be used in warfare destroyed the Japanese city of Hiroshima. Two days later the Soviet Union declared war on Japan and began to overrun Manchuria and northern Korea. The next day, August 9, the second and last atomic bomb then in existence demolished the industrial city of Nagasaki. All this was too much. The Japanese surrendered five days later, August 14, 1945.

World War II had ended. Twenty-two million people had been killed, and thirty-four million had been wounded. Property and moral losses were beyond calculation. Among the casualties was President Roosevelt, who died on April 12, 1945, only a few months before he could have seen the fruition of his prodigious efforts to bring about the defeat of the Axis and the destruction of fascism.

SUGGESTED READING

Winston Churchill, *The Second World War,* 6 vols. (1948–53). The best history of World War II that probably ever will be written. Many readers will be surprised to find themselves completing the six volumes.

Fletcher Pratt, *War for the World* (1950). A sound brief survey.

Pertinax, *The Gravediggers of France* (1944). An analysis of the French collapse in 1940 by a shrewd French journalist. Pertinax, whose real name is André Géraud, places the blame on Premiers Daladier and Reynaud and Generals Gamelin and Pétain.

* Robert E. Sherwood, *Roosevelt and Hopkins,* 2 vols. (Bantam). An excellent behind-the-scenes account of America's wartime president and his chief adviser and assistant, by one of the writers of Roosevelt's speeches and a close friend of Harry Hopkins. Brilliantly written.

H. L. Stimson and McGeorge Bundy, *On Active Service in Peace and War* (1947). Ably written autobiography of America's secretary of war during World War II.

The War Reports of General of the Army George C. Marshall, General of the Army H. H. Arnold, Fleet Admiral Ernest J. King (1947). The official accounts of America's part in the military operations in World War II by America's Army, Air Force, and Navy chiefs of staff. Marshall's second report is particularly lucid and pithy. It outlines and explains America's military operations in both the European and the Pacific theaters.

Dwight D. Eisenhower, *Crusade in Europe* (1948). A popularly written account of the Anglo-American military operations in the European theater by the commander of the forces of the Western Allies.

S. E. Morison, *History of United States Naval Operations in World War II,* 12 vols. (1947–58), to be 14 vols. when completed. Detailed official account, extremely well written and illustrated.

H. R. Trevor-Roper, *The Last Days of Hitler* (1947). A scholarly study of the dramatic end of the chief villain of the World War II era.

Arthur Compton, *Atomic Quest* (1956). A popularly written story of the making and the dropping of the atomic bombs that shocked Japan into surrender. Written by one of the top scientists who brought the bomb into existence.

CHAPTER 59

The Cold War in Europe, 1945–59

I N 1945 the leaders of the victorious nations were once again confronted with
the problem of restoring a shattered world
and making a lasting peace. Now that atomic
weapons were here, peace had become a
matter of utmost necessity. To act as a
watchdog over the peace the world's leaders,
as in 1919, set up an international organization: this time, the United Nations Organization. However, from the beginning, the
work of the UNO was seriously hampered by
hostility between the United States and the
Soviet Union. This hostility, which came to
be called the "Cold War," pervaded and
poisoned every area of postwar international
relations.

1. The United Nations Organization

The chief father of the United Nations
Organization was Franklin Roosevelt. Determined to avoid two major mistakes that
Wilson had made in creating the League of
Nations, Roosevelt (1) saw to it that the
UNO was born before the war ended and the
postwar squabbling among the Allies began,
and (2) gave leading roles in the creation of
the UNO to several important Republicans,
of whom Senator Arthur Vandenberg of
Michigan was the most influential, so that it
should not become a political party issue.
The principles and details of the UNO Charter were threshed out at a number of high-
level conferences held during the course of
the war. The formal launching of the organ-

ization took place at a conference in San
Francisco in April 1945, a few days after
Roosevelt died and less than a month before
Germany surrendered.

In structure and procedure the UNO
bears a close resemblance to the League of
Nations. The General Assembly, in which
each member state has one vote, serves as a
general clearinghouse and supervisor over
the work of all other UNO bodies and agencies. It meets regularly once each year and
may be called on other occasions by the Secretary-General. Any matter that endangers
the world's peace may be brought to its attention at any time. The UNO body that
was given special guardianship over the
peace is the Security Council. It is composed
of five permanent and six non-permanent
members. The five permanent members are
the United States, the Soviet Union, Great
Britain, France, and China. The six non-
permanent members are elected by the General Assembly for two-year terms, three
retiring each year. The Security Council remains in permanent session and has under
its direction the Military Staff Committee,
to which the various nations are supposed to
make available certain earmarked armed
forces. Also under the Security Council is
the Atomic Energy Control Committee.
Because of the chronic hostility between the
Soviet Union and the United States, however, these two committees have never been
able to function effectively.

The fundamental character of the Secu-

UNITED NATIONS BUILDINGS, NEW YORK. John D. Rockefeller, Jr., donated the site in the heart of New York City on which the United Nations headquarters buildings were constructed. The rectangular skyscraper houses the Secretariat offices, the General Assembly meets in the domed building, and the low, foreground building holds the council chambers and conference rooms. These buildings are good examples of modern functional architecture. (*Courtesy of The United Nations*)

rity Council and, indeed, of the whole UNO is really determined by the voting procedure in the Security Council. Any action involving the use of force or the threat of force requires seven votes, including those of all five permanent members. This means that each of the five permanent members of the Security Council has a perpetual veto over forceful actions of the UNO and cannot be acted against by that body. This crippling veto was incorporated into the charter because the Big Three sponsoring powers—the United States, the Soviet Union, and Great Britain—all were unwilling to submit to the UNO's authority. The Soviet Union, finding herself in a constant minority, used the veto to block action to which she was opposed more than seventy-five times during the first ten years of the UNO's existence.

The Social and Economic Council supervises the work of a number of specialized agencies such as the International Labor Organization (ILO), the United Nations Educational, Scientific, and Cultural Organization (UNESCO), the World Bank, and the International Monetary Fund. The Trusteeship Council is designed to supervise the rule of peoples held under control or trusteeship by other nations. The International Court of Justice decides international legal disputes. The day-to-day detailed work of the UNO is done by the Secretariat, composed of some three thousand full-time professional employees presided over by the Secretary-General, who is elected by the Security Council and the General Assembly. This important post was held first by Trygvie Lie of Norway and then by Dag Hammarskjold of Sweden, both very able men. As a permanent headquarters, the UNO chose a site in New York City donated by John D. Rockefeller, Jr.

The United Nations has done an enormous amount of work in the economic, cultural, and humanitarian fields, most of which has failed to make the headlines. It has stopped wars between Israel and the Arab states, India and Pakistan, and the Netherlands and Indonesia. Its biggest accomplishments to date have been the stop-

ping of a major conflict in Korea (see pp. 709–12) and a dangerous war in Egypt (see pp. 719–20). In both cases the support of the United States contributed heavily to the UNO's success. Its biggest failure to date has been its inability to ease the tension between the Soviet Union and the United States. This tension threatens to undo the achievements of the UNO and engulf the world in atomic war.

2. The Yalta Agreements

Soviet-American postwar disagreements first began over the Yalta Agreements. Indeed, the disagreements began even before the fighting in Europe had ended. In February 1945, Roosevelt, Churchill, and Stalin, with their top military and civilian advisers, came together at Yalta in southern Russia for the purpose of co-ordinating the last Allied blows against the Axis and laying the groundwork for postwar co-operation. The conference marked the culmination of wartime good will and co-operation among the Big Three allied powers. At the time of the conference victory was in sight, barring unforeseen disasters. However, victory was not so near or so certain that it could be guaranteed without the continued co-operation of the Big Three. The Soviet armies were approaching the Oder River, which at one point runs only forty miles from Berlin. But the German West Wall fortifications and the Rhine, Weser, and Elbe rivers still lay between Berlin and the American, British, and French forces. Had Stalin become offended at Yalta, for instance, and permitted Hitler to transfer the two thirds of his forces that were facing the Russians to the western front behind the West Wall and the Rhine, a bloody prospect would have confronted the Western Allies. In the Far East the Japanese fleet had been annihilated, and Japan was being subjected to incessant bombardment from the air and the sea. However, she still had large and well-equipped armies on the home islands and in China, Manchuria, and Korea. American military authorities estimated that it would

YALTA CONFEREES. At the Yalta Conference, February 1945, Churchill, Roosevelt, and Stalin, representing the Big Three Allied Powers, made a series of agreements concerning the major postwar problems. At the time of the conference, victory over the Axis was in sight. (*Acme Photo*)

cost the United States and Great Britain a million casualties to dispose of these forces without the participation of the Soviet Union. Churchill estimated two million casualties. The atomic bomb was not yet in existence.

The questions of military strategy were harmoniously worked out by the three military staffs present. The four chief areas of discussion among Roosevelt, Churchill, and Stalin were (1) the UNO Charter, (2) Germany, (3) Eastern Europe, and (4) the Far East. Agreements were quickly reached on questions concerning the UNO Charter, the veto being the chief one. The three conferees also found themselves in close agreement concerning Germany. They agreed on stern measures, including complete denazification with severe punishment for the top

Nazis, total demilitarization, the division of the country into four occupation zones, and a long period of occupation by the Allies. Further details were left to a later conference following Germany's surrender. The only point of serious disagreement concerning Germany was the amount of reparations to be paid. Roosevelt and Churchill thought Stalin's demand for ten billion dollars' worth somewhat excessive. This, too, was left for later agreement.

A sharp cleavage developed over the areas of Eastern Europe that had just been liberated from German control by the Soviet armies. Stalin announced that the territories he had recovered in 1939–40 (eastern Poland, Lithuania, Latvia, Estonia, strips of Finland, and Bessarabia) were really Russian territories that had been taken from

Russia by force at the end of World War I and that under no condition would they be the subject of discussion. Roosevelt and Churchill did not formally concede these points, but they did not make an issue of them. They were primarily concerned over the fate of Poland west of the Curzon Line, Hungary, Yugoslavia, Bulgaria, and Romania—all of which were behind the Soviet lines. (For some reason the Soviets never overran and occupied Finland, which was a defeated enemy country.)

Roosevelt and Churchill insisted that in accordance with the principles of the Atlantic Charter, to which the Soviet Union had subscribed, these countries must be given complete independence. Stalin argued that these countries had been the doors through which Russia had been invaded in both world wars and that they were vital to the Soviet Union's security. He pointed out that Romania, Hungary, and Finland had attacked Russia as Hitler's allies, that Bulgaria had co-operated with Hitler as his ally, and that the Soviets' military lines to Germany and Austria ran through Poland, Romania, and Hungary. Therefore, he asserted, the Soviet Union's security demanded that she maintain a measure of control over these countries. Roosevelt and Churchill were adamant and somehow persuaded Stalin to yield to their position. The official protocol signed at Yalta by Roosevelt, Churchill, and Stalin called for free and unfettered elections as soon as possible for these liberated peoples of Eastern Europe, with all non-fascist parties participating. Such elections were almost certain to result in democratic, anti-Communist, and anti-Russian victories.

In regard to the Far East, Roosevelt was guided by the advice of the top American military authorities. It was their purpose to bring the Soviet Union into the Japanese war as soon as possible, thereby saving, it was believed, a million and possibly two million American and British casualties. As payment for the Soviet Union's entry into the Japanese war not later than three months after Germany's surrender, Roose-

velt offered Stalin the return of the southern half of Sakhalin Island and the railroad and port facilities in Manchuria that Japan had taken from Russia in 1905. (Generalissimo Chiang Kai-shek readily agreed to the Manchurian concessions.) Also, the Soviet Union was to regain the Kurile Islands, which Japan had obtained from Russia in 1875. Korea was to be given her independence. However, the United States was to conquer the Japanese in Korea south of the thirty-eighth parallel, and the Soviets were to liberate the portion of Korea lying north of the thirty-eighth parallel. Stalin agreed to these terms, and the Yalta Conference ended with warm cordiality. Within two weeks after the conference adjourned, however, disputes arose over the agreements, and the United States and the Soviet Union have been in conflict over them ever since.

3. The Soviet-American Controversy over Eastern Europe

It was over Eastern Europe that Soviet-American accord first broke down. On February 24, 1945, exactly two weeks after the Yalta Conference adjourned, the American and British representatives on the Allied Council in Bucharest began to press for the democratization of the Romanian government, which was a puppet of the Soviet occupying forces. Whereupon the Soviet deputy foreign minister arrived from Moscow and browbeat the Romanian government into setting up an all-Communist regime. The Soviet government then announced that the Romanian question was settled. This, of course, was a crass violation of both the spirit and the letter of the Yalta Agreements. A week later the American ambassador to Moscow, Averell Harriman, reported to President Roosevelt that Soviet Foreign Minister Molotov was refusing to proceed with the implementation of the Yalta Agreements in regard to Poland. Whether Stalin had deliberately deceived Roosevelt and Churchill at Yalta or whether he had changed his mind after returning to Moscow is not certain. It was now clear, however, that the Soviet Union was determined to keep a tight control over the areas of Eastern Europe that its armies had liberated from the Germans. These Soviet violations of their solemn agreements were a source of great disappointment and worry to Roosevelt, who was rapidly approaching his grave. He counseled patience and firmness in dealing with the Soviet Union. There was really nothing else to be done at the time, since the war with Germany and Japan was still in progress and the areas in Eastern Europe in question were behind the Soviet lines.

President Truman, who succeeded Roosevelt on April 12, 1945, was in favor of a much tougher policy toward the Soviet Union. At a Big Three conference at Potsdam in July 1945, shortly after Germany had surrendered, arrangements were made for a council of foreign ministers to draw up peace treaties with Germany's former satellites: Finland, Hungary, Romania, Bulgaria, and Italy. For sixteen months Secretary of State James F. Byrnes haggled with Molotov over the treaties. Finally, in December 1946, agreements were reached. Finland and Romania formally renounced the territories they had lost to the Soviet Union in 1940. The Soviet Union was awarded as reparations $300,000,000 each from Finland and Romania, $200,000,000 from Hungary, and $100,000,000 from Italy. Of greater importance were a guarantee to the peoples of the five defeated states of "the enjoyment of human rights and the fundamental freedoms" and the promise of the Soviet Union to withdraw her occupying forces from Romania, Hungary, and Bulgaria within ninety days after the formal signing of the treaties. The formal signing took place in Paris on February 10, 1947. Long before the expiration of the ninety days, however, Soviet-American relations had drastically worsened.

Secretary of State Byrnes resigned as soon as he had affixed his signature to the treaties, and was replaced by General George Catlett Marshall, America's forceful wartime army chief of staff. Under Marshall the State Department quickly took on the crisp vigor of a War Department. Both Truman and Marshall believed that in view of the Soviet Union's sullen unco-operativeness since the end of the war the time had come for the United States to adopt a get-tough-with Russia policy. The immediate occasion for the inauguration of the new policy was the situation in Greece and Turkey, both of which were under severe Soviet pressure: Greece, from communism within; Turkey, from direct Soviet military threats. In January 1947, the British government, which had been supporting both Greece and Turkey with troops and money since the end of the war, announced that after March 31 it would be unable to continue to do so. On March 12, 1947, President Truman appeared before Congress and requested authorization to send American military and civilian personnel into Greece and Turkey. "I believe," he said, "that it must be the policy of the United States to support free peoples who are resisting attempted subjugation by armed minorities or by outside pressures." He asked for $400,000,000 to implement the new program and warned that this was only a starter. Congress greeted this announcement with a standing ovation. The new policy, which was soon called the Truman Doctrine, meant that the United States would draw a military ring around the Soviet Union and its satellites from Manchuria to Norway. It was the policy of military containment. All real diplomatic negotiations between the United States and the Soviet Union, of course, ceased immediately. The Soviet Union made no further pretense of withdrawing from the areas of Eastern Europe occupied by her troops; instead she tightened the iron curtain that she had drawn around them.

In June 1947, Secretary of State Marshall supplemented the Truman Doctrine with the Marshall Plan. This was an offer of comprehensive economic aid to all European countries (except fascist Spain) who would order their economies, stabilize their currencies, and co-operate with each other in bringing about general economic recov-

PRESIDENT HARRY S. TRUMAN AND GENERAL GEORGE C. MARSHALL. President Truman, who succeeded Franklin D. Roosevelt in April 1945, adopted a "get tough with Russia" policy. On March 12, 1947, he formulated the Truman Doctrine, which was the policy of military containment of the Soviet Union. To implement this policy Truman appointed as Secretary of State America's forceful World War II Army Chief of Staff, General George C. Marshall, who sponsored the Marshall Plan for economic assistance. (*United Press International Photo*)

ery. All the countries of Europe except the Soviet Union and her satellites hastened to accept Marshall's terms and American aid. The Soviet Union regarded the Marshall Plan as a scheme of the United States to shore up Europe's and her own tottering capitalism, to lure away the Soviet satellites, and to make the European countries economic satellites of the United States. She therefore forbade the countries of Eastern Europe under her control or influence to participate. Congress voted $5,300,000,000 as the first of four installments totaling some $17,000,000,000 for Marshall Plan aid. The later installments were trimmed somewhat.

In the fall of 1947 the Soviet Union be-

gan a series of vigorous moves to counter the Truman Doctrine and the Marshall Plan. In September 1947, she set up the Communist Information Bureau, or Cominform, the better to co-ordinate policies of the Soviet Union, Poland, Hungary, Romania, Bulgaria, Albania, Yugoslavia, and Czechoslovakia. This was in reality a restoration of the old Comintern, which was the Communist International working for world revolution. The following year the Cominform was supplemented by the Council for Economic Mutual Assistance. This was a Soviet Marshall Plan of her own. At the same time the Soviet Union severely tightened her grip on her satellites. The local Communist parties were rigorously purged of moderates and national patriots. In Hungary a parliamentary agrarian regime was replaced by a Communist dictatorship, and Roman Catholic Cardinal Mindszenty was imprisoned for life for alleged treason against the Communist regime.

One tragic victim of the stepping-up of the Cold War was Czechoslovakia. This little republic, lying geographically between the two armed camps, had tried to remain on friendly terms with both sides. In February 1948, a Soviet-inspired and supported Communist coup overthrew the enlightened liberal regime of President Eduard Beneš and drew Czechoslovakia behind the iron curtain. Soviet efforts to tighten the reins on Yugoslavia, however, backfired. In March 1948 Communist dictator Marshal Tito severed his ties with Moscow and established relations with the capitalistic West.

After the death of Stalin in 1953 the Soviet government, under the leadership of Nikita Khrushchev, head of the Communist party, made overtures to the United States to end the Cold War. At the same time it relaxed somewhat its iron grip on the satellites. Long-suppressed discontent in the satellites immediately manifested itself, particularly in Poland and Hungary. In October 1956, the Polish people elected a native Polish Communist regime to replace the Soviet-oriented one. At the same time a massive anti-Communist nationalist revolt broke out in Hungary, only to be bloodily suppressed by the Soviet army. Tens of thousands of Hungarians were killed and imprisoned. At least two hundred thousand fled the country, many of them to the United States. The day of liberation was not yet, but the action of the suppressed peoples indicated that it must come eventually.

4. The Soviet-American Struggle over Germany

The biggest prize over which the Soviet Union and the United States struggled in the years after World War II was Germany.

The Soviet Union, fearing above everything else a revived and rearmed Germany, was determined to keep her permanently weak and as much as possible under Soviet domination. The United States, on the other hand, having little fear of Germany and seeing in her a valuable potential ally against the Soviet Union, soon set out to restore and rearm her. Fear of a rearmed Germany in alliance with the United States undoubtedly greatly strengthened the Soviet Union's determination to keep Eastern Europe under Soviet control.

The policies and principles to be followed in the government of Germany were agreed upon by the United States, the Soviet Union, and Great Britain at a conference held in Potsdam outside Berlin, in July 1945, shortly after Germany had surrendered. Truman, Stalin, and Clement Attlee, whose Labor party had just defeated Churchill's Conservatives, represented the Big Three. The cordiality that had prevailed at Yalta five months earlier had vanished; suspicion and self-interest reigned instead. On most issues Truman and Attlee lined up against Stalin.

The Potsdam Agreements tentatively set the eastern boundary of Germany, pending a formal treaty settlement, at the line of the Oder and Neisse rivers (see map p. 696). The portion of Germany lying east of this line, containing some six million Germans, was awarded tentatively to Poland except for the port city of Königsberg in East Prussia and its immediate hinterland, which were awarded to the Soviet Union. The rest of Germany was divided into four occupation zones: American, Russian, British, and French. Berlin, which was in the Russian zone, was divided into four sectors and made the headquarters of a four-power coordinating commission. The four occupying powers were to remove from their zones as reparations war plants and peacetime industrial plants in excess of Germany's peacetime needs. Although no total amounts were agreed upon, the Soviet Union assumed as final the ten-billion-dollar figure that was tentatively agreed upon for her at Yalta.

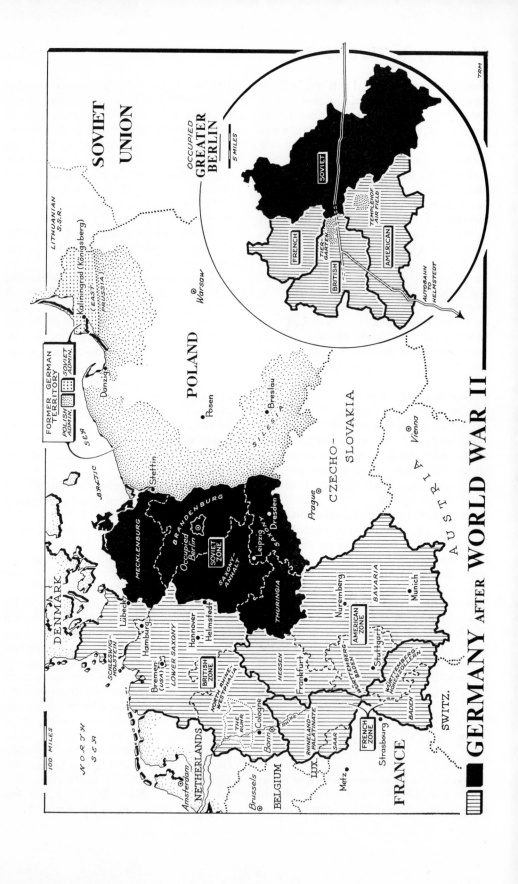

GERMANY AFTER WORLD WAR II

Since the Soviet Union's zone was primarily agricultural, it was agreed at Potsdam that she should have in addition to removals from her own zone 25 per cent of the reparations removed from the three western zones. The principles agreed upon as the joint policy to be followed in the governing of Germany were the five D's: demilitarization, deindustrialization, denazification, democratization, and decentralization.

In the implementation of the Potsdam Agreements in governing the four zones sharp cleavages soon developed among the occupying powers, particularly between the United States and the Soviet Union. The only major question over which there was substantial agreement was that of punishment of the top Nazis. A court consisting of judges and prosecuting attorneys from the four occupying powers was set up at Nuremberg for the purpose. After lengthy public trials twelve of the leading Nazis were condemned to death by hanging, three to life imprisonment, four to prison terms of ten to twenty years. But there the four-power unity ceased. The Soviet Union was determined upon a long, hard occupation of Germany. She dropped an iron curtain in front of her zone, proceeded to communize its government and economy, and enforced the five D's (except for democratization) to the letter. The United States, on the other hand, pursued from the first a much more lenient policy. The commander of the American zone during the first four years was General Lucius D. Clay. Clay was a great admirer of the German professional military officers and refused to punish them. He was also a believer in free enterprise and big business and soon took steps to restore Germany's private industry. The problem of denazification he soon turned over to the Germans themselves.

The British Labor government adopted a German policy somewhat more moderate than that of the Soviet Union, but more severe than that of the United States. The British authorities believed that socialization of German industry would be an adequate safeguard against remilitarization and

aggression. The French agreed with the harsh policy of the Soviet Union, as indeed did virtually all of Europe. Since, however, the French and the British economies had been wrecked by the war and they were heavily dependent upon the United States, France and Britain were eventually persuaded to support the American policy.

The Soviets from the beginning complained bitterly of the softness of the Americans toward demilitarization, denazification, and deindustrialization. Clay, in turn, denounced the Soviets for refusal to co-ordinate the economy of their zone with that of the western zones, and early in 1946 he stopped further deliveries of reparations to the Soviet Union from the American zone. After the inauguration of the Truman Doctrine and the Marshall Plan in the spring of 1947 relations between the United States and the Soviet Union in Germany worsened rapidly. In August 1947 Clay announced a sharp stepping-up of the economy of the American and British zones, which had been merged the previous year. This raised the level far above that prescribed by the Potsdam Agreements and was made possible only by Marshall Plan aid. In December 1947 Secretary of State Marshall, reflecting the new get-tough-with-Russia policy, walked out of the London Conference of Foreign Ministers, thereby breaking up the four-power arrangement for governing Germany. Shortly afterward the French, sensing an open East-West break, reluctantly took the side of the United States and merged their zone with the American and British zones.

In March 1948 Clay announced the projected creation of an independent west German state. To the Soviet leaders this was the last straw. They attempted to dissuade the Western powers from going ahead with the project by blockading the three Western zones of Berlin in the hope of starving them out. For eleven months, June 1948 to May 1949, the Soviets stopped all land traffic across their zone from the West to Berlin. The Western powers defeated the blockade by means of a giant air lift. However, the

EUROPE
1959

AREAS OF GERMANY PLACED
UNDER SOVIET AND POLISH
ADMINISTRATION, 1945

500 MILES

T.R.MILLER

POPULATION
DENSITY

*PERSONS
PER SQUARE MILE*

UNDER 5
5-100
101-250
OVER 250

tension was great. Clay himself urged direct military action against the Soviet Union's blockading forces.

Meanwhile, the United States proceeded undeterred in the setting up of the German Federal Republic, which began to function in September 1949. It was a liberal democratic government similar to the Weimar Republic. The Christian Democratic party, a slightly right-of-center party with Roman Catholic leanings, won the first election, and its leader, the elderly and pro-Western Dr. Konrad Adenauer, became the first chancellor. The Western powers replaced their military governors with civilian commissioners and relaxed their control over Germany. One month later (October 1949) the Soviet Union set up the German Democratic Republic in its zone. It was a Communist Soviet puppet state. The United States and the Soviet Union feverishly set about to rearm Western and Eastern Germany, respectively. However, a fearful France delayed the rearmament of Western Germany until 1955. Severe labor riots against the Communist dictatorship in Eastern Germany in 1953 demonstrated that the Soviet Union could hardly depend on her East German satellite in a showdown. Meanwhile, Western Germany's industrial economy recovered by leaps and bounds. By 1957 she had regained her former industrial supremacy in Western Europe. In 1959 the United States made preparations to arm Western Germany with nuclear weapons. Once more the Soviet Union threatened to blockade Berlin and demanded a summit conference on the German question.

5. The Atlantic Community

The postwar distress in Western Europe, coupled with the threat of communism and of Soviet aggrandisement, prompted the Western European democracies to draw closer together. As the tempo of the Cold War between the United States and the Soviet Union increased, the United States undertook to organize the Atlantic community of nations into a formal alliance. The

military effectiveness of the alliance, however, was uncertain because of the war-torn condition of the major European members.

In Great Britain the Labor party swept to victory in elections held in July 1945, just as the war was coming to an end. Clement Attlee succeeded Churchill as prime minister. The problems confronting Britain and the Labor government were indeed formidable. More than half of Great Britain's merchant marine had been sunk; a third of her buildings had been destroyed or damaged; her foreign investments had been liquidated and used up; she owed the United States eighteen and a half billion dollars; her empire was crumbling. To distribute the burden fairly, the Labor government strictly rationed the short supplies, raised taxes on the rich, and lowered taxes on the poor. It nationalized (1) the Bank of England, (2) the coal mines and the electrical and gas industries, (3) inland transportation, and (4) the steel industry. Altogether some 20 per cent of Britain's economy was socialized. A vast program of social security, public education, public housing, and national health insurance was launched. Steps were taken to bring an end to British imperialism. The six years of Labor rule were years of austerity for the middle and upper classes. However, the general morale of the people was high, and Britain made a more rapid recovery than any other war-ravaged country. By 1948 her production and exports were higher than before the war, and the masses of the people were enjoying more security, services, and material goods than ever before. In 1951 Churchill and the Conservatives returned to power. With the exception of denationalizing the steel industry they tampered little with the socialistic program at home. They did attempt to retard the liquidation of the empire and adopted a more self-assertive foreign policy. However, Great Britain was now far outdistanced as a world power by the United States and the Soviet Union.

France emerged from the war not only ravaged but, unlike Britain, defeated and demoralized. General Charles de Gaulle returned to France in 1944 with the American and British liberators, who gave official recognition to the government he set up in Paris. However, the first postwar elections, held in October 1945, resulted in a sweeping victory for the parties of the left with which the authoritarian De Gaulle could not co-operate. He therefore went into tem-

American Cold War. The Communists, constituting about one fourth of the electorate, deserted the leftist coalition and supported the Soviet Union. The United States gave strong support to the capitalistic classes and exerted heavy pressure on the Fourth Republic to take the American side in the Cold War. The result was a slight swing to

CHARLES DE GAULLE. After leading the Free French movement during World War II and assuming the leadership of France after the Germans were driven out, General de Gaulle retired to private life in 1946 when he was unable to persuade the French people to strengthen the executive position in the government. After the French army in Algeria revolted against the French government in May 1958, De Gaulle was recalled by popular acclaim and given an overwhelming mandate to rewrite the constitution. With dispatch he set up the Fifth French Republic and was elected its first president. (*United Press International Photo*)

porary retirement. The leftist coalition, suspicious of authority, drew up a constitution very similar to that of the Third Republic, with its weak executive. The Fourth Republic, like the Third, was plagued by a multiplicity of parties. In 1947, just as the leftist coalition was preparing to launch a socialistic reform program similar to that of the British Labor government, France became enmeshed in the sharply intensified Soviet-

the right in French politics and the adherence of a reluctant, frustrated, and divided France to the American Cold War camp.

Although the Fourth French Republic experienced a strong, if uneven, economic recovery, it was unable to cope with the problem of the disintegrating French Empire. After suffering several humiliating defeats, France in 1954 granted independence to

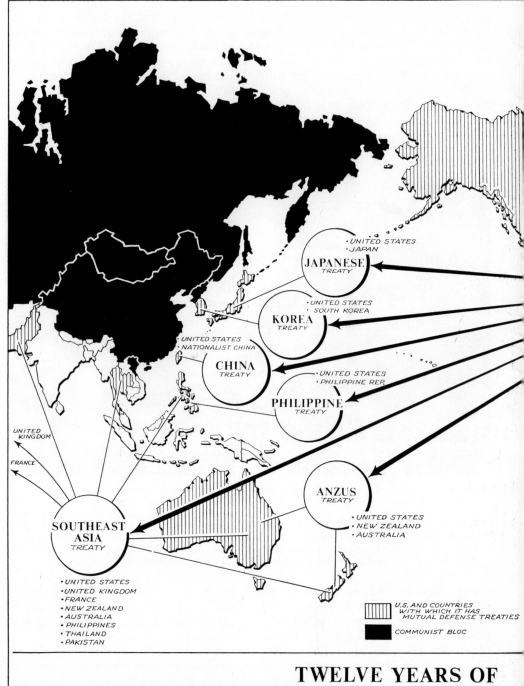

· UNITED STATES
· JAPAN

JAPANESE
TREATY

· UNITED STATES
· SOUTH KOREA

KOREA
TREATY

· UNITED STATES
· NATIONALIST CHINA

CHINA
TREATY

· UNITED STATES
· PHILIPPINE REP.

PHILIPPINE
TREATY

UNITED
KINGDOM

FRANCE

ANZUS
TREATY

· UNITED STATES
· NEW ZEALAND
· AUSTRALIA

**SOUTHEAST
ASIA**
TREATY

· UNITED STATES
· UNITED KINGDOM
· FRANCE
· NEW ZEALAND
· AUSTRALIA
· PHILIPPINES
· THAILAND
· PAKISTAN

U.S. AND COUNTRIES
WITH WHICH IT HAS
MUTUAL DEFENSE TREATIES

COMMUNIST BLOC

TWELVE YEARS OF

TRM

- UNITED STATES
- CANADA
- ICELAND
- NORWAY
- UNITED KINGDOM
- NETHERLANDS
- DENMARK
- BELGIUM
- LUXEMBOURG
- PORTUGAL
- FRANCE
- ITALY
- GREECE
- TURKEY
- WEST GERMANY

NORTH ATLANTIC *TREATY*

RIO *TREATY*

- UNITED STATES
- MEXICO
- CUBA
- HAITI
- DOMINICAN REP.
- HONDURAS
- GUATEMALA
- EL SALVADOR
- NICARAGUA
- COSTA RICA
- PANAMA
- COLOMBIA
- VENEZUELA
- ECUADOR
- PERU
- BRAZIL
- BOLIVIA
- PARAGUAY
- CHILE
- ARGENTINA
- URUGUAY

U.S. CONTAINMENT

Indo China (Viet Nam). Two years later she granted independence to Morocco and Tunisia. Her inability to solve the Algerian problem, however (see p. 722), led to the mutiny of the French army in Algeria in May 1958, which brought about the fall of the government and the recall of Charles de Gaulle by popular demand. De Gaulle drew up a new constitution which greatly strengthened the executive branch of the government. In December 1958 De Gaulle was elected first president of the Fifth French Republic by an overwhelming majority. He immediately granted independence to all the French colonies except Algeria, for which he projected a long-range program of economic and social reform. De Gaulle was probably the only man in France who could re-establish civilian control over the mutinous army. He undertook to strengthen France's capitalistic economy by means of an austerity program and to raise French prestige by demanding an equal voice with the United States and Great Britain in the formulation of Western policy. In the Cold War, De Gaulle definitely aligned the Fifth French Republic on the side of the West. And he contributed to Western unity by cultivating friendly relations with the German Federal Republic.

The story of postwar Italy is quite similar to that of France, except that she was much poorer, that the corrupting hand of fascism had lain upon her for eighteen years longer, and that her Communists were more numerous. By 1948 she too seemed to be definitely in the camp of the United States.

Of the Western powers only the United States emerged from the war virtually unscathed materially. The war had forced billions of dollars into circulation, ended the long depression, and destroyed much of her foreign competition. Under President Truman's Democratic administration (1945–53) and President Eisenhower's Republican administration (1953–) she enjoyed an economic prosperity such as no other nation in history had ever before experienced.

Many Americans, however, feared that such an island of lush prosperity in the midst of an impoverished world could not last. They believed it to be to the vital interest of the United States to shore up the shaky capitalism in Western Europe and to promote a closer economic and military unity of the Atlantic community of nations. For these purposes the American Congress appropriated many billions of dollars to implement the Marshall Plan.

In 1950 France's Foreign Minister Robert Schuman astonished the world by offering to pool French coal and steel with that of Germany and other Western European nations. Under his leadership the European Coal and Steel Community was set up in 1951 to pool the coal and steel industries of France, Western Germany, Italy, Belgium, the Netherlands, and Luxemburg. In 1949 under Winston Churchill's leadership the Council of Europe was established with headquarters at Strasbourg. This was designed as a step toward the political integration of Great Britain, France, Italy, Ireland, Belgium, the Netherlands, Luxemburg, Denmark, Norway, and Sweden. In 1951 the German Federal Republic was admitted. The most comprehensive move yet made to organize an Atlantic Community of nations was taken in 1949 under American leadership with the formation of the North Atlantic Treaty Organization (NATO). This was a defensive military pact signed by the United States, Canada, Great Britain, France, Italy, Portugal, Belgium, the Netherlands, Luxemburg, Denmark, Norway, and Iceland. Greece and Turkey were admitted in 1951, and Western Germany in 1955. According to the terms of the pact, all the members are committed to come to the military aid of any member that is attacked. Thus by 1959 the threat of the Soviet Union and of international communism appeared to be doing for the Western nations what they had seemed never to be able to do for themselves: to place the first restraints on unbridled nationalism.

———•——

SUGGESTED READING

E. R. Stettinius, Jr., *Roosevelt and the Russians: The Yalta Conference* (1949). An eyewitness account of the Yalta Conference by the American secretary of state.

S. S. Fenichall and P. Andrews, *United Nations* (1952). An excellent brief survey of the history, structure, and achievements of the UN.

Harry E. Truman, *Memoirs*, 2 vols. (1955). The fresh and salty memoirs of the belligerent man who inherited the enormous postwar problems left by Franklin Roosevelt. Unlike Roosevelt, Truman was always "tough" with the Russians.

W. Bedell Smith, *My Three Years in Moscow* (1950). The story of the developing Cold War between the Soviet Union and the United States, by Eisenhower's wartime chief of staff, who was also America's ambassador to the Soviet Union during the three critical years 1946–49.

John Gunther, *Behind the Curtain* (1948). Journalistic account of Gunther's travels through Russia's satellite countries east of the iron curtain during the early days of the Cold War. As usual, Gunther managed to interview the key figures in the various countries.

Lucius D. Clay, *Decision in Germany* (1950). The story of Soviet-American postwar conflict over Germany, by the commander of the American zone during the first four years of military occupation.

Francis Williams, *Socialist Britain* (1949). A lucid and sympathetic account of the Labor party regime in Great Britain, 1945–49. A former adviser of Prime Minister Attlee, Williams is intimately acquainted with the inner workings of the Labor party and its program.

Charles de Gaulle, *War Memoirs*: Vol. I, *The Call to Honor 1940–1942*; Vol. II, *Unity 1942–1944* (1955–59). These memoirs of General de Gaulle give a vivid insight into the personality and the policies of one of France's most important postwar figures.

* Herbert Luethy, *France against Herself* (Meridian). This brilliant analysis of the various complexes that have paralyzed France since 1918 presents a detailed and clear picture of postwar France, 1945–55.

CHAPTER 60

---◆►---

The Emergence of Asia and Its
Challenge to the West

Asia was an important area of conflict in the Cold War between the United States and the Soviet Union. However, it is a serious mistake to think of mid-twentieth-century Asia as a mere pawn in the Soviet-American world struggle. The vast and populous Asian continent was at last astir and out of the control of either the United States or the Soviet Union. Japan, in the latter part of the nineteenth century, had been the first Asian country to adopt Western technology and aggressive nationalism and the first to become a great power. In the twentieth century the rest of Asia began to move in the same direction. The movement was sharply accelerated by the two world wars. After World War II Asia became a real challenge to the West.

1. Japan Between East and West

Japan emerged from World War II defeated on sea and land, the shocked victim of history's first two atomic bombs used for military purposes. Since the United States had played by far the major role in the defeat of Japan, she refused to share the occupation and government of the Japanese islands with her former allies. President Truman appointed General Douglas MacArthur Supreme Commander of the Allied

Powers (SCAP) in Japan and gave him absolute authority. To advise MacArthur, the Allied Council, composed of representatives from the United States, the Soviet Union, Great Britain, and China, was set up in Tokyo. To formulate policy, the Far Eastern Commission was set up in Washington, composed of representatives from the eleven nations most interested in Far Eastern affairs. However, the final decision, either to accept or to ignore the advice of these two bodies, lay with MacArthur. When the Soviet Union, which had used seventy divisions in crushing the Japanese forces in Manchuria and North Korea and was a next-door neighbor to Japan, realized that she was going to be denied a real part in the control of Japan, she refused for four months to participate in the advisory commissions. MacArthur's only directives came from the United States government, which shortly after the Japanese surrender drew up a four-point policy for postwar Japan: (1) Japan was to be limited to the four "home" islands and some small ones in the immediate vicinity. (2) Japan was to be completely demilitarized. (3) Civil, political, and religious rights and liberties for the Japanese people were to be encouraged. (4) Japan's economy was to be developed for her peacetime needs.

For a year and a half General MacArthur ruled Japan with a firm but liberal and benevolent hand. He was fortunate to have at his side the submissive Emperor Hirohito, who urged his people to obey the American commander. A democratic constitution similar to that of Great Britain was drawn up and put into effect. In the first elections under the new constitution the Social Democrats, who were somewhat similar to the British Laborites, won the largest number of seats in the national legislature. Japanese laborers were permitted to form unions for the first time, and they did so with a relish. The five great families who monopolized three fourths of Japan's industry and finance disbanded their monopolistic combinations under pressure from MacArthur. Demilitarization was carried on apace, including the trial and execution or imprisonment of a number of top war leaders. Of greatest significance was MacArthur's land-reform program. The great mass of Japanese farmers were poverty-stricken landless share croppers, giving up from 50 to 70 per cent of their yield to absentee landlords. Laws sponsored by MacArthur forced the landlords to sell to the government all land in excess of seven and a half acres (more in less fertile areas). The government, in turn, sold the land in plots of seven and a half acres to the tenant farmers, who were given thirty years to pay for them. By the end of 1946 Japan appeared to be well on the way to liberal democracy.

Early in 1947 when the Soviet-American Cold War was being stepped up in intensity, General MacArthur suddenly reversed his liberal policy in Japan. He first cracked down on the newly formed labor unions. Industrial decentralization ceased, and land redistribution slowed down. The reactionary former militarists and imperialists, sensing the changed atmosphere, quickly reasserted themselves. They insisted that a remilitarized Japan was a necessary link in the containment chain that the United States was forging around the Soviet Union. By 1949 the conservative parties were firmly in control of the Japanese government once more. On the other hand, a number of left-wing liberals in cynical disillusionment began turning to communism.

In 1951 President Truman commissioned John Foster Dulles, a prominent Republican lawyer and businessman, to draw up a formal treaty with Japan. The terms granted the United States military bases in Japan and a protectorate over the Ryukyu Islands (including Okinawa) and Japan's former mandated islands in the Pacific. Japan was to pay no indemnity, and was to be free to rearm and to make her own alliances. Although forty-six nations signed the treaty, India, Burma, the Soviet Union, and the Soviet satellites refused. China was not permitted to sign. The Soviet Union complained bitterly that Japan's closest neighbors, the Soviet Union and China, were allowed no part in the making of the treaty and accused the United States of sowing the seeds of future wars by rearming Japan. The Soviet Union's own aggressive acts in nearby Korea (see pp. 709–12) had done much to influence America's Japanese policy. By 1951 Japan was clearly a military and economic protégé of the United States. Economically, at least, her situation gave cause for grave concern. On the relatively barren Japanese islands, smaller in area than California, lived more than eighty million people. Japan's heavy industry had few sources for raw materials, and most of her natural market, the East Asiatic mainland, was under hostile Communist control. The United States, Japan's sponsor and benefactor, was strictly opposed to trading with the Soviet and Asiatic Communists.

2. The Rise of Communist China

By the mid-twentieth century the center of power and influence in Asia was passing from Japan to China. Here, a massive upheaval involving one fourth of the world's population was taking place. Sun Yat-sen, after launching his mighty revolution against both China's foreign exploiters and her own reactionary and conniving government (see pp. 607–8), died in 1925, in the very hour

POPULATION
DENSITY

PERSONS
PER SQUARE MILE

☐ UNDER 5
▨ 5-100
▨ 101-250
■ OVER 250

SPITZBERGEN
(NOR.)

ARCTIC

FRANZ JOSEF
LAND
(USSR)

NORWAY

BARENTS
SEA

SWEDEN

NOVAYA
ZEMLYA

FINLAND

KARA
SEA

Archangel

Vorkuta

Igarka

SOVIET

Moscow

Kuibyshev

Sverdlovsk

Omsk

Tomsk

Istanbul

BLACK
SEA

Ankara

TURKEY

Batum

Astrakhan

Karaganda

Urumchi

CYPRUS

SUEZ CANAL

LEBANON

SYRIA
(UNITED ARAB
REPUBLIC)

ISRAEL

Cairo

CASPIAN
SEA

Baku

ARAL
SEA

LAKE
BALKHASH

EGYPT
(UNITED ARAB
REPUBLIC)

JORDAN

Bagdad

Teheran

Bukhara

Tashkent

SINKIANG

IRAQ

Basra

IRAN

AFGHAN-
ISTAN

Kabul

JAMMU
AND
KASHMIR

TIBET

Lhasa

KUWAIT

SUDAN

Mecca

SAUDI

BAHREIN

QATAR

PAKISTAN

INDUS R.

NEPAL

BHUTAN

PERSIAN GULF

ARABIA

Riyadh

Karachi

New
Delhi

GANGES R.

RED SEA

ERITREA

YEMEN

OMAN

INDIA

Calcutta

EAST
PAK.

FR.
SOMALILAND

ADEN PROT.
(BR.)

Bombay

Djibouti

Aden

SOCOTRA
(BR.)

ARABIAN

SEA

Goa
(PORT.)

Hyderabad

ETHIOPIA

BR.
SOMALILAND

LACCADIVE IS.
(INDIA)

Madras

Pondichéry

BAY OF

SOMALIA

EQUATOR

INDIAN

MALDIVE IS.
(BR.)

Colombo

CEYLON

BENGAL

ASIA, 1959

OCEAN

1000 MILES

T.R.MILLER

of success. His place at the head of the revolutionary Chinese government was taken by his young and vigorous supporter, General Chiang Kai-shek. Chiang Kai-shek, a professional soldier, was much more interested in making China a powerful and independent nation than in liberalizing her government and society. Under him the revolutionary Kuomintang party, then dominant in China, swung definitely to the right. When the Chinese Nationalist armies were defeated by the Japanese in 1937-38 and driven deep into the interior, Chiang Kai-shek and the Kuomintang party were cut off from the chief bases of their liberal support, which were the great coastal cities. Heavily dependent then upon the war lords and landlords of the interior, they swung still further to the right. The long years of relative inactivity at Chungking (1939-45) had a demoralizing effect not only upon Chiang Kai-shek's military forces but upon the Kuomintang-party leaders themselves.

Meanwhile, a rival movement very different in nature and purpose from Chiang Kai-shek's Kuomintang was making rapid headway in China. This movement was communism. During the 1920's, when China's hoary Confucian civilization was crumbling faster than Sun Yat-sen's Western Christian liberalism could replace it, another Western influence moved into the vacuum: Marxist materialism. The hostility that the Western democracies showed to Sun Yat-sen's revolutionary liberal movement greatly encouraged the Chinese Communists. In 1927 the Communists found an able leader in the scholarly and shrewd Mao Tse-tung. This plain-living man of humble origin had risen to leadership by sheer force of intellect, personality, and energy. Chiang Kai-shek exerted every effort to crush the Chinese Communists—much more, in fact, than to drive out the Japanese invader. During the years 1939-45, when the Kuomintang forces were inactive in Chungking and getting further and further out of touch with the Chinese masses, Mao Tse-tung's Communists were waging incessant guerrilla warfare against the Japanese and gaining a greater following among the Chinese people.

Following the surrender of Japan in Au-

THE OLD AND THE NEW IN CHINA. Mao Tse-tung is shown with two Tibetan Buddhist lamas. Materialistic, atheistic Communism inevitably clashed with China's ancient religions. Upon coming to power in China in 1949 Mao Tse-tung promised to respect the Buddhist religion in Tibet. However, by 1959 he had so violated his promise that the Dalai Lama, head of the Buddhist faith in Tibet, fled to India for his life. (*United Press International Photo*)

gust 1945, a bitter struggle for the control of China ensued between Chiang Kai-shek's Kuomintang forces, now known as the Chinese Nationalists, and the Chinese Communists. In this struggle the United States supported the Nationalists. The American army and navy transported Chiang Kai-shek's forces hither and yon to vital areas and seized and held strategic places until Nationalist forces could arrive. Furthermore, Chiang Kai-shek was supplied with American money and weapons. However, the Communists won the support of ever-increasing numbers of the Chinese people. Tens of thousands of people in the populous coastal areas who had endured the Japanese invaders for eight years were outraged when Kuomintang landlords and politicians, having sat the war out in Chungking, returned demanding back rent and back taxes. Morale in the long-inactive and graft-ridden Nationalist armies was low, while that in the Communist armies, toughened by the continuous fighting against the Japanese, was high.

It was in Manchuria that the tide first turned in favor of the Communists. When the Russians, who had overrun Japanese-held Manchuria in the last days of the war, withdrew early in 1946, the United States army and navy rushed Chinese Nationalist forces in by sea and air, while the Chinese Communists moved in on foot. The Communists, using Japanese weapons that had been left behind by the Russians and American weapons and munitions that were surrendered by the low-spirited Nationalists, began to gain the upper hand in 1947. By the end of 1948 the last Nationalist forces had been driven out of Manchuria, and their morale had dropped to the point approaching demoralization. During 1949 the victorious Communists swept over the entire Chinese mainland. Chiang Kai-shek with a remnant of his Nationalist forces, mostly officers, fled to the island of Formosa, where after June 1950, they were protected by the United States navy. In 1949 Mao Tse-tung proclaimed the People's Republic of China and the following year formed an alliance with the Soviet Union. With Soviet aid he began the enormous task of industrializing and communizing the world's most populous nation.

American support of Chiang Kai-shek greatly angered the Chinese Communists. In 1950 they entered the Korean War (see the following section) against the forces of the United Nations, which were mostly American. After the Korean War, friction between Red China and the United States continued unabated.

In 1958 Mao Tse-tung launched a program of communizing Chinese society more comprehensive than anything that was ever undertaken in the Soviet Union. The Chinese people were organized into completely regimented communes. Even the family, the most sacred feature of the Confucian tradition, was broken up. China's large and rapidly growing population was set to building irrigation dams and ditches, steel mills, factories, railroads, schools, and hospitals. Never in history had a revolution so vast been undertaken.

3. The Korean War

The bitter left-right conflict among the Asiatic peoples and the global Cold War struggle between the United States and the Soviet Union merged in Korea to produce a shooting war of major proportions. In August 1945, in accordance with the Yalta agreements, the forces of the Soviet Union overran Japanese-held Korea north of the thirty-eighth parallel, and the American forces did the same in Korea south of the thirty-eighth parallel. These moves were supposed to be for the purpose of setting up a free and united Korean nation. However, the Soviet Union immediately proceeded to set up in North Korea a Communist dictatorship. The land was distributed to the peasants, and the industry was nationalized. In South Korea the United States authorities sponsored a right-wing government under the leadership of the aged and reactionary Korean patriot Syngman Rhee. Late in 1948 the Soviet forces withdrew from North Korea, leaving behind an energetic Communist regime well armed with the latest Soviet weapons. Six months later the American forces withdrew from South Korea, leaving behind the Syngman Rhee landlord regime armed mostly with the weapons that had been captured from the Japanese. Both the North and South Korean governments talked loudly of conquering each other.

On June 25 (June 24, American time), 1950, North Korea suddenly attacked South Korea. The high-spirited and well-armed North Korean Communists easily defeated the low-spirited and poorly armed South Koreans. The armies of Syngman Rhee, made up largely of disgruntled landless tenant farmers, melted away. The Truman administration quickly decided that the Communist aggression in Korea was the Soviet Union's first move to conquer the world by military force and that there must not be another Munich. Secretary of State Dean Acheson persuaded the United Nations to take drastic action. Taking advantage of the absence of the Soviet Union's representative, the Security Council called upon all the members of the United Nations to furnish military forces to repel the North Korean aggression and asked President Truman to name the commander of the United Nations forces. Truman named MacArthur. Truman also announced that he had already ordered American forces into the Korean War, that the American navy would protect Chiang Kai-shek's Chinese Nationalists on Formosa against the Chinese Communists, and that American aid to the French fighting the native Communists in Indo-China would be greatly increased.

A race ensued between the North Korean Communists, sweeping over South Korea, and the United Nations forces, mostly Americans, who were building up a defense perimeter around Korea's southernmost port of Pusan. When the North Koreans came up against this perimeter, they were unable to break through. By mid-September 1950, the United Nations forces under MacArthur's command pouring in through Pusan were strong enough to assume the offensive. The breakout from the defense perimeter

was accompanied by an amphibious landing behind the Communist lines. The North Korean forces were shattered and driven out of South Korea in less than three weeks' time. MacArthur was now authorized by the United Nations General Assembly (the Soviet representative having returned to the Security Council with his veto) to conquer North Korea. By late November 1950, MacArthur's forces were approaching the Yalu River, which forms the Korean-Chinese border. At this point large Chinese Communist forces crossed over the Yalu, placing themselves between the United Nations forces and the Chinese border. On November 24 MacArthur ordered an attack on the Chinese Communists. The Chinese Communists severely defeated MacArthur's forces and drove them in headlong retreat back down the peninsula. Eventually—January–March 1951—the battle line became stabilized along the thirty-eighth parallel, where the war had started. The Communists could advance no farther, and MacArthur's forces could make no appreciable headway against the Chinese and North Korean Communists.

MacArthur cried loudly for all available American military forces and for the blockade and bombing of Red China. However, the military authorities in Washington, now headed by George Catlett Marshall, who was made secretary of defense upon the outbreak of the Korean War, refused the request. They feared involvement in all-out war with the Soviet Union, which hitherto had limited its aid to the North Korean and Chinese Communists to the selling of weapons. The American military authorities in Washington were also opposed to stripping the home front and the critical Western European and Middle Eastern danger areas of defenses. Since the Communist aggression in Korea had been checked, Washington wished to see the Korean War simmer down with a minimum of further casualties. When MacArthur persisted in public criticism of the American government's policies and disobeyed the orders of his superiors to cease making policy pronouncements, he

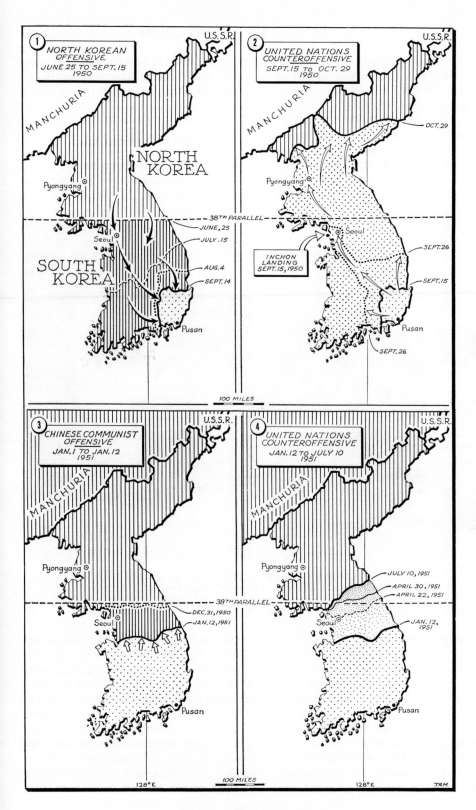

THE KOREAN WAR

was replaced in April 1951, by General Matthew Ridgway, both as commander of the United Nations forces in Korea and as supreme commander in Japan.

In June 1951, the Soviet Union proposed the beginning of peace negotiations in Korea. Both sides readily agreed. However, two years of haggling, accompanied by intermittent fighting at the front, ensued before an armistice was finally signed in July 1953. To-

nificance is the fact that a revolutionary new Asiatic power, Red China, had fought the greatest Western power, the United States, to a standstill.

4. The Revolt of Southern Asia

Practically all of Southern Asia, it will be recalled (see Chapters 36 and 52), came under the domination of the British, the

Korean War Damage. The upheaval of the Asiatic masses against their own rulers and against Western imperialism, and the global "cold war" conflict in Korea, 1950–53, combined to produce tens of thousands of victims such as these. Here Koreans are pictured removing the rubble in Seoul after their capital had been won by United Nations forces. (*Acme Photo*)

tal casualties—dead, wounded, captured, and missing—were approximately a million and a half on each side, of which some 145,-000 were Americans and 900,000 Chinese Communists. Most of the rest were Koreans. The battle line ended just about where it had started. However, the first Communist military aggression had been checked with severe punishment. The United Nations Organization had functioned effectively and increased its prestige. Probably of equal significance is the fact that a revolutionary new

Dutch, and the French during the seventeenth, eighteenth, and nineteenth centuries. Those three Western imperialist powers brought to Southern Asia many of the blessings of Western civilization: advanced technology, public education and sanitation, administrative efficiency, and Christianity. Those things, however, failed to reach the great majority of the people, and there can be little doubt that the Europeans took out of their Asiatic colonies more than they brought in. The British, the Dutch, and the French amassed great fortunes out of the exploitation of the teeming millions of technologically backward Asiatic peoples.

During the second half of the nineteenth century the spirit of nationalism began to arise in Southern Asia, just as it did in Japan and China. By the end of World War I all Southern Asia was smoldering with the spirit of national independence. Shortly after the close of World War II many of the smoldering embers burst into flame. Only the British were farsighted enough to anticipate the conflagration and grant independence peaceably to most of their Asiatic colonies. (The British may have been influenced to a certain extent by the freeing of the Philippine Islands by the United States. The Philippines, which the United States had taken from Spain in 1899, had never proved profitable. Indeed, Philippine sugar and pineapples competed seriously with American sugar and pineapples grown in Hawaii. Philippine independence, voted by Congress in 1934, became a reality in 1946.)

By far the biggest and most populous Southern Asiatic country is India. It was Great Britain's richest colonial prize. When one considers the number of British pounds invested in India, the size of Britain's commerce with India, and the thousands of British careers connected with the Indian service, it is not difficult to understand Britain's reluctance to give up such a prize. Moreover, India's importance to Great Britain increased, rather than diminished, as a result of the shattering blows of the two world wars to Britain's economy. However, the rising tide of Indian nationalism could not be stemmed.

The Indian National Congress party, founded in 1885, constantly gained influence in its campaign for Indian independence. After World War I, Mohandas K. Gandhi (1869–1948), one of the most dynamic personalities of the twentieth century, assumed the leadership of the Congress party. This middle-class Hindu, educated in Great Britain, was a master of the psychology of the Indian masses. His chief tactics were passive resistance and civil disobedience. The British were unable to cope with him. The gentle little white-robed Mahatma (Great Spirit), whether sitting at his spinning wheel, subsisting on goat's milk, or fasting in a British prison, was a beloved symbol of national independence, not only to India's millions but also to millions of other Asiatic and African colonials.

Indian nationalism reached its peak during World War II, but Churchill would not hear of Indian independence. "I did not become His Majesty's first minister," said the doughty warrior "in order to preside over the liquidation of the British Empire." The British Labor party, however, upon coming to power in 1945 immediately announced its determination to grant Indian independence. In 1947 the Hindu portion of India, containing some 336,000,000 people, became the Dominion of India. In the same year the Moslem portions, with a population of more than 70,000,000, became the Dominion of Pakistan. Dominion status meant complete independence with voluntary membership in the British Commonwealth of Nations.

Religious and national strife soon broke out between Hindu India and Moslem Pakistan. Gandhi tried to quell the strife, but he was assassinated in 1948 by a fanatical Hindu nationalist. Thus the "Great Spirit" himself became another victim of malignant nationalism. Open war between the two states finally began in 1948 over possession of the disputed state of Kashmir, which is inhabited by both Moslems and Hindus. Although the United Nations was able to stop the war, it has not yet succeeded in settling the dispute.

Even before the aged Gandhi's death the leadership of the Congress party had passed to one of his most devoted followers, Jawaharlal Nehru. This handsome, wealthy, British-educated Hindu of the highest (Brahman) caste became the first prime minister of the independent Union of India. The problems confronting him were staggering. Most of India's teeming millions were poverty-stricken and illiterate, and it was to

GANDHI AND NEHRU. Mahatma Gandhi, subsisting on goat's milk and sitting at his spinning wheel, became the beloved symbol of India's struggle for independence from Great Britain. Gandhi is shown here with Jawaharlal Nehru (*left*), who became leader of the Indian masses after Gandhi's assassination in 1948 by a fanatical Hindu nationalist. Nehru had become the first prime minister of the independent Union of India the previous year. (*United Press International Photo*)

such depressed people that communism was making its strongest appeal. Nehru inaugurated a liberal and mildly socialistic program somewhat similar to that of the British Labor government. Not the least of his problems was avoiding embroilment in the Soviet-American Cold War. India's proximity to both the Soviet Union and Red China made this danger acute.

In 1948 the British Labor government granted complete independence to Burma and dominion status to Ceylon. Burma immediately launched a liberal reform pro-

gram even more vigorous than that of India. Malaya was granted independence in 1957, leaving only Hong Kong as a reminder of an era of British imperialism in Asia.

The Dutch East Indies were even more important to the Netherlands than was India to Great Britain. These islands, stretching three thousand miles from Sumatra to New Guinea and containing more than seventy million people, are rich in rubber, rice, copra, oil, tin, coffee, sugar, quinine, pepper, and spices. The spirit of nationalism, which arose in the islands in the nineteenth century, came to a head during World War II, when the conquering Japanese promised the inhabitants independence after the war. Immediately after the surrender of Japan in 1945 an able native nationalist leader, Achmed Soekarno, proclaimed the independent Republic of Indonesia. The Dutch, returning to the islands after the departure of the Japanese, fiercely resisted this independence movement. Violating a truce that was arranged by the United Nations and greatly aided by Marshall Plan money from the United States, the Dutch defeated the Indonesians and captured the nationalist leaders, including Soekarno. Early in 1949 India's Nehru called a conference of leaders from nineteen Far Eastern states, who strongly condemned the Dutch actions and demanded the independence of Indonesia. When the United States, working through the United Nations, supported this policy, the Dutch yielded. By the end of 1949 they had granted independence to the Republic of Indonesia on a basis similar to that of the British dominions. Soekarno became its first president.

Of all the European colonial regimes in Asia that of the French in Indo-China was probably the most predatory and the most hated. As in Indonesia the rising tide of nationalism reached a peak in Indo-China during World War II, when the country was overrun by the Japanese. As ultimate defeat became obvious, Japan promised the Indo-Chinese their independence. Immediately after the surrender of Japan in August 1945 the Indo-Chinese nationalists, under the leadership of Ho Chi Minh, a Russian-trained Communist, proclaimed the independent "democratic" Republic of Viet Nam. The returning French imperialists were fiercely resisted by the native Communist nationalists. Heavy fighting ensued, in which the French were aided by American Marshall Plan money. When the North Korean Communists began their aggression against South Korea in June 1950, the United States greatly increased her aid to the French in Indo-China. Meanwhile, Ho Chi Minh began to receive aid from the Chi-

nese Communists after they had overrun China in 1949. Thus a costly and dangerous war raged in Viet Nam. The majority of the Viet Namese people apparently preferred the Communists to the French imperialists, and the forces of Ho Chi Minh won victory after victory in spite of massive American aid to the French. In 1954 the French government of Premier Mendès-France agreed to a humiliating armistice with Ho Chi Minh and ceded the northern half of Viet Nam to the Communists. Although South Viet Nam technically remained a part of the French Union, French influence there quickly vanished. South Viet Nam turned from France to the United States for aid and protection.

Seeking a broader base for defense against Communist aggression in Asia, Secretary of State John Foster Dulles in 1954 engineered the Manila Pact. This was a mutual agreement of the United States, Great Britain, France, the Philippines, Thailand, Pakistan, Australia, and New Zealand to resist further Communist aggression in Southeast Asia. India, Burma, and Indonesia significantly abstained from signing the pact. America's policy of military containment of communism was obviously less successful in Asia than in Europe, a major reason undoubtedly being that communism in Asia was associated with the upsurge of popular nationalism against Western imperialism.

5. The Embattled Middle East

One of the most explosive areas in the mid-twentieth-century world was the Middle East, that area between and including Egypt and Pakistan, where East meets West. (The tendency in mid-twentieth-century usage is to include in the term "Middle East" much of the area that was formerly designated as "Near East.") In global terms it is probably the most strategic area in the world. It forms the bridge between the world's two greatest land masses, Eurasia and Africa; and through it pass the chief communication lines between the East and the West. The Middle East is the heart of

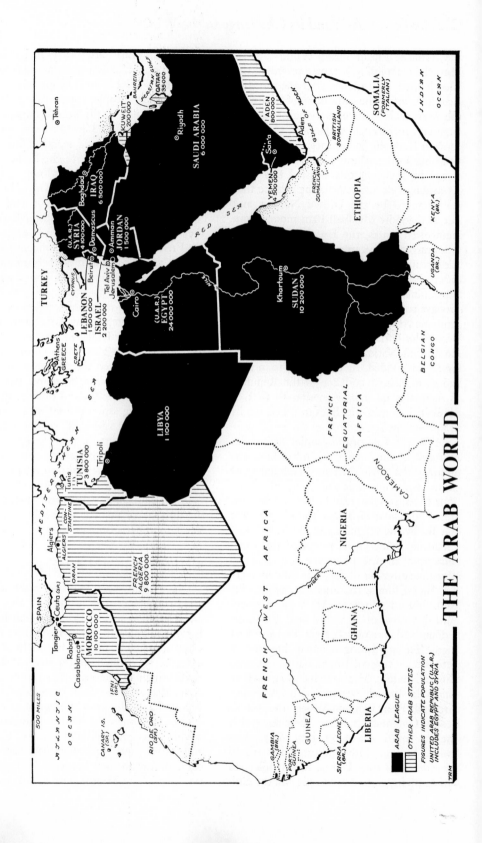

THE ARAB WORLD

FIGURES INDICATE POPULATION
UNITED ARAB REPUBLIC (U.A.R.)
INCLUDES EGYPT AND SYRIA

ARAB LEAGUE
OTHER ARAB STATES

the Moslem world, which stretches from Morocco to Pakistan and contains more than 300,000,000 followers of the Prophet. It is also the heart of the tumultuous Arab world, the Moslem and the Arab worlds being in large measure, but not entirely, coterminous. Moreover, it was discovered in the twentieth century that the area contains more than half of the world's known oil reserves. At mid-twentieth century the Middle East, the most fought-over area in history, was one of the most sensitive spots in the Soviet-American Cold War.

During the early twentieth century, while the great European powers competed for control of the Middle East, Arab nationalism was rising. This nationalism was vented first against the British, who were the dominant power in that area. Before World War I Great Britain controlled Egypt, including the Suez Canal, Cyprus, and a sphere of influence in Persia. After the war she took Palestine, Trans-Jordan, and Iraq as mandates under the League of Nations. However, as anti-British hostility mounted, Great Britain began to relax her control. In 1922 Egypt was granted self-government, although British troops remained in the country and Great Britain retained control of the Suez Canal. By the end of World War II only Cyprus, Palestine, and the Suez Canal remained in Britain's possession, and the British were bidding strongly for Arab friendship. However, continued British possession of the Suez Canal and the admission of tens of thousands of Jews to Palestine under the Balfour Declaration of 1917 proved to be effective barriers to Anglo-Arab accord.

Palestine was the ancient home of the Jews. However, in A.D. 70 they were dispersed by the government of the Roman Empire. In the seventh century the Moslem Arabs conquered Palestine and lived there until the twentieth century—thirteen hundred years. In the late nineteenth century the Zionist movement began. This was a movement to restore Palestine as a national home for the Jews. During the anti-Semitic persecutions of the Hitler era thousands of European Jewish refugees, many of them wealthy, poured into Palestine, buying up the land and dispossessing the Arabs. Eventually nearly a million Arabs were dispossessed and driven out of Palestine. The whole Arab and Moslem world became incensed. Great Britain gradually came to favor the Arabs over the Jews, probably because of the Arabs' oil and their strategic location. With Great Britain's blessings Egypt, Syria, Lebanon, Trans-Jordan, Iraq, Saudi-Arabia, and Yemen formed in 1945 the Arab League, embracing some forty-five million people.

In 1948 the British Labor government turned Palestine over to the United Nations. The Jews immediately proclaimed the State of Israel and accepted the boundary lines that the United Nations had drawn to divide Palestine between the Jews and the Arabs. The Arab League, to which the arrangement was entirely unsatisfactory, began hostilities with a view to exterminating the Jewish state. Tiny Israel, however, well armed and well financed, was more than a match for the Arabs. After a year of fighting the United Nations succeeded in bringing about a truce. But Arab nationalism was now thoroughly aroused, and border raids recurred as the Arabs armed for a revival of the struggle. Israel, in the meantime, receiving financial aid from Jews abroad, prospered, built modern cities, introduced irrigation and scientific agriculture, and became a vigorous, democratic, co-operative Western society in the midst of a feudalistic and largely primitive Moslem Arab world.

Meanwhile, Great Britain continued to be a prime target of rampaging Arab nationalism. In 1951 the Iranian government nationalized the properties of the Anglo-Iranian Oil Company, including the largest refinery in the world. (In 1932 Persia changed its name to Iran.) Long months of serious tension followed, during which both Britain and Iran suffered from the cessation of operations of the refinery. Eventually, with the aid of the United States and the United Nations a compromise was reached, and operations were resumed.

Two Views of Israel. The establishment of the modern and essentially Western state of Israel as a national home for the Jews in the midst of the feudal Moslem Arab world created one of the most troublesome tension spots of the mid-twentieth century. The rising spirit of Arab nationalism, as well as the entire Moslem world, became inflamed when nearly a million native Arabs were dispossessed of their homes upon the creation of the Jewish state. These views show the Negev Desert (*above*), which comprises most of the southern portion of Israel, and the modern city of Tel Aviv (*below*). (*United Press International Photo, above; Screen Traveler, from Gendreau, below*)

However, it was Suez that proved to be the most critical issue. In 1952 a military coup led by extreme Egyptian nationalists overthrew the corrupt government of Egypt's King Farouk. Soon the fiery nationalist agitator, Gamel Abdel Nasser, emerged as dictator of Egypt. Nasser set out to make himself the leader of the whole Arab world and to inflame it against the West. Shades of Tarik, Saladin, and Suleiman appeared. Nasser's first targets were Israel and the Suez Canal Zone. Egyptian raids against Israel were stepped up, and preparations for a war of extermination were openly made. Threatening demands and gestures against the Canal Zone resulted in the British withdrawal in 1954. In 1955 Nasser nationalized the Suez Canal in violation of a solemn treaty between Egypt and Great Britain. The Soviet Union, seeing an opportunity to advance her interests in the Middle East by befriending the Arabs, sold arms to Nasser.

In November 1956, Israel and Great Britain suddenly attacked Egypt. They were joined by France, which was incensed at Nasser's encouragement and support of France's rebellious Arab subjects in Algeria, Morocco, and Tunisia. The Israelis made rapid headway against the Egyptians, while the British and the French bombed Egyptian airfields and made landings in the Canal Zone. Nasser hastened to block the canal with sunken ships. Within a few days the Soviet Union threatened to enter the war on the side of Egypt. At this critical juncture the United States announced that she would fight if the Soviet Union intervened, and brought heavy pressure on the British, French, and Israelis to cease hostilities. They had no alternative but to comply, and the United Nations supervised their withdrawal. Once again militant nationalism— this time Arab nationalism in the Middle East—had threatened to plunge the world

KHRUSHCHEV AND NASSER. In 1954 General Gamal Abdel Nasser became president and virtual dictator of Egypt and assumed leadership of the Arab nationalists. He sought financial and technical aid from both the United States and the Soviet Union and cleverly played one against the other. Here he is shown at a meeting with Soviet Premier Nikita Khrushchev in the Kremlin, May 1958. (*United Press International Photo*)

WESTERN DEFENSE SYSTEM (W.D.S.)
COLONIES OF W.D.S. NATIONS
NATIONS HOST TO W.D.S. AIR BASES
NEUTRAL AND UNCOMMITTED NATIO
COMMUNIST BLOC

TRM

into war. It was aided and abetted, of course, by religious hatred, cultural friction, communism, and oil.

In 1958 the ferment in the Middle East again involved the great powers. The conservative government of Iraq was overthrown by leftist nationalist elements, and King Faisal was murdered. The United States and Great Britain, fearing a Soviet-inspired Communist upheaval throughout the Middle East, rushed troops into Lebanon and Jordan, respectively. Although the Communist

threat proved to be exaggerated and the American and British troops were withdrawn after a few months, the episode demonstrated that the continuing unrest in the Middle East constituted a serious danger to world peace.

6. The Awakening of Africa

By the mid-twentieth century large areas of Africa, the last of the continents to rise against Western imperialism, were also astir. Great Britain's troubles in Africa were by no means limited to Egypt. In one African colony after another the primitive Negroes caught the spirit of nationalism and turned in resentment against their white masters. Native terror bands, notably the Mau Mau in Kenya, made British life and property increasingly unsafe. In 1957 Great Britain granted dominion status, which is equivalent to complete independence, to her Gold Coast colony, which became the Republic of Ghana. This was undoubtedly the first step in the eventual freeing of her remaining African colonies. In the British Dominion of South Africa race relations took a decided turn for the worse in 1948, when the white minority, alarmed at the growing unrest of the native Negro majority, took severe repressive measures.

The end of World War II found France's huge North African empire seething with unrest. Its population, largely Moslem, was agitated by the rampaging Arab nationalism in the Middle East. France's greatly diminished position in Europe and the world and her unstable economy made her reluctant to give up her North African empire, in which she had a large investment. Nevertheless, as the unrest flared into open rebellion and one halfway measure after another failed, France, in 1956, granted independence to Morocco and Tunisia. The problem of independence or autonomy for Algeria was much more complex because of the presence there of a million and a quarter French settlers who feared reprisals from the eight million Moslem Algerians. Moreover, Algeria had been made an integral part of the

French nation in the nineteenth century. Increasing bloodshed in Algeria during the 1950's played a prominent role in the fall of numerous French cabinets. And since the bloodshed tended to inflame the whole Moslem world against the West, France's Algerian problem complicated her relations with her allies, particularly the United States.

In 1954 the smoldering Algerian discontent with French rule burst into open revolt—a revolt that the regular French army was unable to quell. In May 1958 the harassed French army in Algeria, fearful that the government of the Fourth Republic was preparing to grant Algerian independence, mutinied and threatened to set up a military dictatorship in France. This emergency brought about the fall of the Fourth French Republic and the recall of Charles de Gaulle. De Gaulle, after setting up the Fifth French Republic with its strong executive, undertook to restore the authority of the government over the army and to placate both the French and the Algerians in Algeria by means of a long-range program of economic and social improvements. It was a formidable task. To many, it appeared to be a hopeless one. Meanwhile, De Gaulle granted independence to all the other French colonies, most of which were in Africa, and invited them to form a voluntary union with France. All but one, French Guinea, did so.

At mid-twentieth century, then, the expansion of the European world, which began in the fifteenth century, had after five hundred years been very definitely reversed. The East now challenged the West.

SUGGESTED READING

Owen Lattimore, *The Situation in Asia* (1949). A hard-hitting and perceptive little book. Quite critical of the Western powers, including the United States, for supporting the relics of colonialism. Overly optimistic about the possibility of co-operating with Communist regimes.

K. S. Latourette, *The American Record in the Far East, 1945–1951* (1952). A sound and

readable survey by a well-informed scholar of the Far East.

William O. Douglas, *North from Malaya* (1953). A perceptive and charmingly written description and analysis of the postwar Far East, by the much-traveled associate justice of the U.S. Supreme Court.

Robert Payne, *Mao Tse-tung: Ruler of Red China* (1950). A vivid and somewhat sympathetic biography of the Communist leader who commands one fourth of the world's population.

* Mohandas K. Gandhi, *Autobiography: The Story of My Experiments with Truth* (Beacon). The life story and philosophy of one of the most influential personalities of the twentieth century.

* Jawaharlal Nehru, *Toward Freedom* (Beacon). Autobiography of the successor to Gandhi as the leader of India's millions and one of the key figures of the mid-twentieth century.

Chester Bowles, *Ambassador's Report* (1954). An enlightening and entertaining account of India's efforts under Nehru to steer an independent and progressive course. Bowles was United States ambassador to India, 1951–53.

William O. Douglas, *Strange Lands and Friendly People* (1951). A vivid firsthand account of the strategic Middle East and its peoples, customs, and aspirations. Justice Douglas penetrated remote and primitive areas and became intimately acquainted with the people.

Arnold J. Toynbee, *A Study of History*, abridged by D. C. Somervell (abridgment of Vols. I–VI, 1947; abridgment of Vols. VII–X, 1957). The most prodigious effort ever made to synthesize and make a meaningful pattern of all human history. The student who reads D. C. Somervell's excellent abridgments of Toynbee's monumental work will be challenged and stimulated.

Index

PRINTER'S NOTE

This book is set in Linotype ELECTRA. *This face cannot be classified as either "modern" or "old-style." It is not based on any historical model, nor does it echo any particular period or style. It avoids the extreme contrast between "thick" and "thin" elements that marks most "modern" faces, and attempts to give a feeling of fluidity, power, and speed.*

The book was composed, printed, and bound by Kingsport Press, Inc., Kingsport, Tennessee. Paper manufactured by S. D. Warren Company, Boston, Massachusetts.